D1135998

Collins
FRENCH
DICTIONARY
POCKET EDITION

Published by Collins
An imprint of HarperCollins Publishers
Westerhill Road
Bishopbriggs
Glasgow G64 2QT

Eighth Edition 2017

10 9 8 7 6 5 4 3 2 1

© HarperCollins Publishers 1998, 2001, 2002, 2007, 2010, 2013, 2017

ISBN 978-0-00-818362-2

Collins® is a registered trademark of HarperCollins Publishers Limited

collinsdictionary.com

Typeset by Davidson Publishing Solutions, Glasgow

Printed in Italy by Grafica Veneta S.p.A.

The contents of this publication are believed correct at the time of printing. Nevertheless, the Publisher can accept no responsibility for errors or omissions, changes in the detail given or for any expense or loss thereby caused.

HarperCollins does not warrant that any website mentioned in this title will be provided uninterrupted, that any website will be error free, that defects will be corrected, or that the website or the server that makes it available are free of viruses or bugs. For full terms and conditions please refer to the site terms provided on the website.

A catalogue record for this book is available from the British Library.

If you would like to comment on any aspect of this book, please contact us at the given address or online.
E-mail: dictionaries@harpercollins.co.uk
 facebook.com/collinsdictionary
 @collinsdict

Acknowledgements

We would like to thank those authors and publishers who kindly gave permission for copyright material to be used in the Collins Corpus. We would also like to thank Times Newspapers Ltd for providing valuable data.

HarperCollins
PUBLISHERS
Since 1817

TABLE DES MATIÈRES

CONTENTS

EDITOR
Maree Airlie

CONTRIBUTORS
Jean-François Allan
Cécile Aubinière-Robb
Katya Browne
Sabine Citron
Laurence Larroche
Wendy Lee
Cordelia Lilly
Catherine Love

FOR THE PUBLISHER
Gerry Breslin
Helen Newstead
Sheena Shanks

Based on the first edition
of the Collins Gem French
Dictionary under the direction
of Pierre-Henri Cousin.

INTRODUCTION

Nous sommes très heureux que vous ayez choisi ce dictionnaire Collins et espérons que vous aimerez l'utiliser et que vous en tirerez profit au lycée, à la maison, en vacances ou au travail.

Cette introduction a pour but de vous donner quelques conseils sur la façon d'utiliser au mieux votre dictionnaire, en vous référant non seulement à son importante nomenclature mais aussi aux informations contenues dans chaque entrée. Ceci vous aidera à lire et à comprendre, mais aussi à communiquer et à vous exprimer en anglais contemporain.

Au début du dictionnaire, vous trouverez la liste des abréviations utilisées dans le texte et celle de la transcription des sons par des symboles phonétiques. Vous y trouverez également la liste des verbes irréguliers en anglais, suivis d'une section finale sur les nombres et sur les expressions de temps.

COMMENT UTILISER VOTRE DICTIONNAIRE

Ce dictionnaire offre une richesse d'informations et utilise diverses formes et tailles de caractères, symboles, abréviations, parenthèses et crochets. Les conventions et symboles utilisés sont expliqués dans les sections qui suivent.

ENTRÉES

Les mots que vous cherchez dans le dictionnaire – les entrées – sont classés par ordre alphabétique. Ils sont imprimés en couleur pour pouvoir être repérés rapidement. Les entrées figurant en haut de page indiquent le premier (sur la page de gauche) et le dernier mot (sur la page de droite) des deux pages en question.

Des informations sur l'usage ou sur la forme de certaines entrées sont données entre parenthèses, après la transcription phonétique. Ces indications apparaissent sous forme abrégée et en italiques (par ex. (*fam*), (*Comm*)).

Pour plus de facilité, les mots de la même famille sont regroupés sous la même entrée (**ronger**, **rongeur** ; **accept**, **acceptance**) et apparaissent également en couleur.

Les expressions courantes dans lesquelles apparaît l'entrée sont indiquées par des caractères romains gras différents (par exemple **retard** [...] **avoir du ~**).

TRANSCRIPTION PHONÉTIQUE
La transcription phonétique de chaque entrée (indiquant sa prononciation) est présentée entre crochets immédiatement après l'entrée (par ex. **fumer** [fyme] ; **knee** [niː]). La liste des symboles phonétiques figure aux pages xii et xiii.

TRADUCTIONS
Les traductions des entrées apparaissent en caractères ordinaires ; lorsque plusieurs sens ou usages coexistent, ces traductions sont séparées par un point-virgule. Vous trouverez des synonymes de l'entrée en italique entre parenthèses avant les traductions (par ex. **poser** (*installer: moquette, carrelage*)) ou des mots qui fournissent le contexte dans lequel l'entrée est susceptible d'être utilisée (par ex. **poser** (*question*)).

MOTS-CLÉS
Une importance particulière est accordée à certains mots français et anglais qui sont considérés comme des « mots-clés » dans chacune des langues. Cela peut être dû à leur utilisation très fréquente ou au fait qu'ils ont divers types d'usage (par ex. **vouloir**, **plus** ; **get**, **that**). L'utilisation de triangles et de chiffres aide à distinguer différentes catégories grammaticales et différents sens. D'autres renseignements utiles apparaissent en italique et entre parenthèses dans la langue de l'utilisateur.

Les catégories grammaticales sont données sous forme abrégée et en italique après la transcription phonétique (par ex. *vt, adv, conj*). Les genres des noms français sont indiqués de la manière suivante : *nm* pour un nom masculin et *nf* pour un nom féminin. Le féminin et le pluriel irréguliers de certains noms sont également indiqués (par ex. **directeur, -trice** ; **cheval, -aux**).

Le masculin et le féminin des adjectifs sont indiqués lorsque ces deux formes sont différentes (par ex. **noir, e**). Lorsque l'adjectif a un féminin ou un pluriel irrégulier, ces formes sont clairement indiquées (par ex. **net, nette**). Les pluriels irréguliers des noms et les formes irrégulières des verbes anglais sont indiqués entre parenthèses, avant la catégorie grammaticale (par ex. **man** (*pl* **men**) *n* ; **give** (*pt* **gave**; *pp* **given**) *vt*).

INTRODUCTION

We are delighted that you have chosen this Collins French dictionary and hope you will enjoy and benefit from using it at school, at home, on holiday or at work.

This introduction gives you a few tips on how to get the most out of your dictionary – not simply from its comprehensive wordlist but also from the information provided in each entry. This will help you to read and understand modern French, as well as communicate and express yourself in the language.

This dictionary begins by listing the abbreviations used in the text and illustrating the sounds shown by the phonetic symbols. You will also find French verb tables, followed by a final section on numbers and time expressions.

USING YOUR COLLINS DICTIONARY

A wealth of information is presented in the dictionary, using various typefaces, sizes of type, symbols, abbreviations and brackets. The various conventions and symbols used are explained in the following sections.

HEADWORDS

The words you look up in a dictionary – 'headwords' – are listed alphabetically. They are printed in **colour** for rapid identification. The headwords appearing at the top of each page indicate the first (if it appears on a left-hand page) and last word (if it appears on a right-hand page) dealt with on the page in question.

Information about the usage or form of certain headwords is given in brackets after the phonetic spelling. This usually appears in abbreviated form and in italics (e.g. (*inf*), (*Comm*)).

Where appropriate, words related to headwords are grouped in the same entry (**ronger**, **rongeur**; **accept**, **acceptance**) and are also in colour.

Common expressions in which the headword appears are shown in a bold roman type (e.g. **inquire** [...] **to ~ about**).

PHONETIC SPELLINGS

The phonetic spelling of each headword (indicating its pronunciation) is given in square brackets immediately after the headword (e.g. **fumer** [fyme]; **knee** [niː]). A list of these symbols is given on pages xii and xiii.

TRANSLATIONS

Headword translations are given in ordinary type and, where more than one meaning or usage exists, these are separated by a semi-colon. You will often find other words in italics in brackets before the translations. These offer suggested contexts in which the headword might appear (e.g. **rough** (*voice*) [...] (*plan*)) or provide synonyms (e.g. **rough** (*manner: coarse*)). The gender of the translation also appears in italics immediately following the key element of the translation.

KEYWORDS

Special status is given to certain French and English words which are considered as 'key' words in each language. They may, for example, occur very frequently or have several types of usage (e.g. **vouloir**, **plus**; **get**, **that**). A combination of triangles and numbers helps you to distinguish different parts of speech and different meanings. Further helpful information is provided in brackets and italics.

GRAMMATICAL INFORMATION

Parts of speech are given in abbreviated form in italics after the phonetic spellings of headwords (e.g. *vt*, *adv*, *conj*). Genders of French nouns are indicated as follows: *nm* for a masculine noun and *nf* for a feminine noun. Feminine and irregular plural forms of nouns are also shown (**directeur, -trice**; **cheval, -aux**).

Adjectives are given in both masculine and feminine forms where these forms are different (e.g. **noir, e**). Clear information is provided where adjectives have an irregular feminine or plural form (e.g. **net, nette**).

ABRÉVIATIONS

ABBREVIATIONS

abréviation	*ab(b)r*	abbreviation
adjectif, locution adjectivale	*adj*	adjective, adjectival phrase
administration	*Admin*	administration
adverbe, locution adverbiale	*adv*	adverb, adverbial phrase
agriculture	*Agr*	agriculture
anatomie	*Anat*	anatomy
architecture	*Archit*	architecture
article défini	*art déf*	definite article
article indéfini	*art indéf*	indefinite article
automobile	*Aut(o)*	automobiles
aviation, voyages aériens	*Aviat*	flying, air travel
biologie	*Bio(l)*	biology
botanique	*Bot*	botany
anglais britannique	*BRIT*	British English
chimie	*Chem*	chemistry
commerce, finance, banque	*Comm*	commerce, finance, banking
informatique	*Comput*	computing
conjonction	*conj*	conjunction
construction	*Constr*	building
nom utilisé comme adjectif	*cpd*	compound element
cuisine	*Culin*	cookery
article défini	*def art*	definite article
économie	*Écon, Econ*	economics
électricité, électronique	*Élec, Elec*	electricity, electronics
en particulier	*esp*	especially
exclamation, interjection	*excl*	exclamation, interjection
féminin	*f*	feminine
langue familière (! emploi vulgaire)	*fam(!)*	colloquial usage (! particularly offensive)
emploi figuré	*fig*	figurative use
(verbe anglais) dont la particule est inséparable	*fus*	(phrasal verb) where the particle is inseparable
généralement	*gén, gen*	generally
géographie, géologie	*Géo, Geo*	geography, geology
géométrie	*Géom, Geom*	geometry
article indéfini	*indef art*	indefinite article
langue familière (! emploi vulgaire)	*inf(!)*	colloquial usage (! particularly offensive)
infinitif	*infin*	infinitive
informatique	*Inform*	computing
invariable	*inv*	invariable
irrégulier	*irreg*	irregular
domaine juridique	*Jur*	law

ABRÉVIATIONS

ABBREVIATIONS

grammaire, linguistique	*Ling*	grammar, linguistics
masculin	*m*	masculine
mathématiques, algèbre	*Math*	mathematics, calculus
médecine	*Méd, Med*	medical term, medicine
masculin ou féminin	*m/f*	masculine or feminine
domaine militaire, armée	*Mil*	military matters
musique	*Mus*	music
nom	*n*	noun
navigation, nautisme	*Navig, Naut*	sailing, navigation
nom ou adjectif numéral	*num*	numeral noun or adjective
	o.s.	oneself
péjoratif	*péj, pej*	derogatory, pejorative
photographie	*Phot(o)*	photography
physiologie	*Physiol*	physiology
pluriel	*pl*	plural
politique	*Pol*	politics
participe passé	*pp*	past participle
préposition	*prép, prep*	preposition
pronom	*pron*	pronoun
psychologie, psychiatrie	*Psych*	psychology, psychiatry
temps du passé	*pt*	past tense
quelque chose	*qch*	
quelqu'un	*qn*	
religion, domaine ecclésiastique	*Rel*	religion
	sb	somebody
enseignement, système scolaire et universitaire	*Scol*	schooling, schools and universities
singulier	*sg*	singular
	sth	something
subjonctif	*sub*	subjunctive
sujet (grammatical)	*subj*	(grammatical) subject
techniques, technologie	*Tech*	technical term, technology
télécommunications	*Tél, Tel*	telecommunications
télévision	*TV*	television
typographie	*Typ(o)*	typography, printing
anglais des États-Unis	*US*	American English
verbe (auxiliaire)	*vb (aux)*	(auxiliary) verb
verbe intransitif	*vi*	intransitive verb
verbe transitif	*vt*	transitive verb
zoologie	*Zool*	zoology
marque déposée	®	registered trademark
indique une équivalence culturelle	≈	indicates a cultural equivalent

TRANSCRIPTION PHONÉTIQUE

CONSONNES		CONSONANTS
NB. **p, b, t, d, k, g** sont suivis d'une aspiration en anglais.		NB. **p, b, t, d, k, g** are not aspirated in French.
pou**p**ée	p	**p**up**p**y
bom**b**e	b	**b**a**b**y
ten**t**e **th**ermal	t	**t**en**t**
din**d**e	d	**d**a**dd**y
co**q** **qu**i **k**épi	k	**c**ork **k**iss **ch**ord
ga**g**e ba**gu**e	g	**g**a**g** **gu**ess
sale **c**e na**ti**on	s	**s**o ri**c**e ki**ss**
zéro ro**s**e	z	cou**s**in buz**z**
ta**ch**e **ch**at	ʃ	**sh**eep **s**ugar
gilet **j**uge	ʒ	plea**s**ure bei**g**e
	tʃ	**ch**ur**ch**
	dʒ	**j**u**dg**e **g**eneral
fer **ph**are	f	**f**arm ra**ff**le
ver**v**eine	v	**v**ery re**v**el
	θ	**th**in ma**th**s
	ð	**th**at o**th**er
lent sa**l**e	l	**l**ittle ba**ll**
rare **r**ent**r**er	R	
	r	**r**at **r**are
ma**m**an fe**mm**e	m	**m**u**mm**y co**mb**
non bo**nn**e	n	**n**o ra**n**
a**gn**eau vi**gn**e	ɲ	
	ŋ	si**ng**ing ba**n**k
	h	**h**at re**h**earse
yeux pa**ill**e p**i**ed	j	**y**et
n**ou**er **ou**i	w	**w**all **w**ail
h**ui**le l**u**i	ɥ	
	x	lo**ch**
DIVERS	r	**MISCELLANEOUS**
pour l'anglais : le r final se prononce en liaison devant une voyelle		in English transcription: final r can be pronounced before a vowel
pour l'anglais : précède la syllabe accentuée	'	in French wordlist: no liaison before aspirate **h** and **y**

En règle générale, la prononciation est donnée entre crochets après chaque entrée. Toutefois, du côté anglais-français et dans le cas des expressions composées de deux ou plusieurs mots non réunis par un trait d'union et faisant l'objet d'une entrée séparée, la prononciation doit être cherchée sous chacun des mots constitutifs de l'expression en question.

PHONETIC TRANSCRIPTION

VOYELLES

NB. La mise en équivalence de certains sons n'indique qu'une ressemblance approximative.

VOWELS

NB. The pairing of some vowel sounds only indicates approximate equivalence.

ici vie lyrique	i i:	heel bead
	ɪ	hit pity
jouer été	e	
lait jouet merci	ɛ	set tent
plat amour	a æ	bat apple
bas pâte	ɑ ɑ:	after car calm
	ʌ	fun cousin
le premier	ə	over above
beurre peur	œ	
peu deux	ø ə:	urgent fern work
or homme	ɔ	wash pot
mot eau gauche	o ɔ:	born cork
genou roue	u	full hook
	u:	boom shoe
rue urne	y	

DIPHTONGUES

DIPHTHONGS

	ɪə	beer tier
	ɛə	tear fair there
	eɪ	date plaice day
	aɪ	life buy cry
	au	owl foul now
	əu	low no
	ɔɪ	boil boy oily
	uə	poor tour

NASALES

NASAL VOWELS

matin plein	ɛ̃
brun	œ̃
sang an dans	ɑ̃
non pont	ɔ̃

In general, we give the pronunciation of each entry in square brackets after the word in question. However, on the English-French side, where the entry is composed of two or more unhyphenated words, each of which is given elsewhere in this dictionary, you will find the pronunciation of each word in its alphabetical position.

FRENCH VERB FORMS

a Present participle **b** Past participle **c** Present **d** Imperfect **e** Future
f Conditional **g** Present subjunctive

1 **ARRIVER a** arrivant **b** arrivé
c arrive, arrives, arrive, arrivons,
arrivez, arrivent **d** arrivais
e arriverai **f** arriverais **g** arrive

2 **FINIR a** finissant **b** fini **c** finis, finis,
finit, finissons, finissez, finissent
d finissais **e** finirai **f** finirais
g finisse

3 **PLACER a** plaçant **b** placé **c** place,
places, place, plaçons, placez,
placent **d** plaçais, plaçais, plaçait,
placions, placiez, plaçaient
e placerai, placeras, placera,
placerons, placerez, placeront
f placerais, placerais, placerait,
placerions, placeriez, placeraient
g place

3 **BOUGER a** bougeant **b** bougé
c bouge, bougeons **d** bougeais,
bougions **e** bougerai **f** bougerais
g bouge

4 **appeler a** appelant **b** appelé
c appelle, appelons **d** appelais
e appellerai **f** appellerais **g** appelle

4 **jeter a** jetant **b** jeté **c** jette, jetons
d jetais **e** jetterai **f** jetterais **g** jette

5 **geler a** gelant **b** gelé **c** gèle, gelons
d gelais **e** gèlerai **f** gèlerais **g** gèle

6 **CÉDER a** cédant **b** cédé **c** cède,
cèdes, cède, cédons, cédez,
cèdent **d** cédais, cédais, cédait,
cédions, cédiez, cédaient
e céderai, céderas, cédera,
céderons, céderez, céderont
f céderais, céderais, céderait,
céderions, céderiez, céderaient
g cède

7 **épier a** épiant **b** épié **c** épie, épions
d épiais **e** épierai **f** épierais **g** épie

8 **noyer a** noyant **b** noyé **c** noie,
noyons **d** noyais **e** noierai
f noierais **g** noie

9 **ALLER a** allant **b** allé **c** vais, vas,
va, allons, allez, vont **d** allais
e irai **f** irais **g** aille

10 **HAÏR a** haïssant **b** haï **c** hais,
hais, hait, haïssons, haïssez,
haïssent **d** haïssais, haïssais,
haïssait, haïssions, haïssiez,
haïssaient **e** haïrai, haïras, haïra,
haïrons, haïrez, haïront **f** haïrais,
haïrais, haïrait, haïrions, haïriez,
haïraient **g** haïsse

11 **courir a** courant **b** couru **c** cours,
courons **d** courais **e** courrai
g coure

12 **cueillir a** cueillant **b** cueilli
c cueille, cueillons **d** cueillais
e cueillerai **g** cueille

13 **assaillir – a** assaillant **b** assailli
c assaille, assaillons **d** assaillais
e assaillirai **g** assaille

14 **servir a** servant **b** servi **c** sers,
servons **d** servais **g** serve

15 **bouillir a** bouillant **b** bouilli
c bous, bouillons **d** bouillais
g bouille

16 **partir a** partant **b** parti **c** pars,
partons **d** partais **g** parte

17 **fuir a** fuyant **b** fui **c** fuis, fuyons,

fuient **d** fuyais **g** fuie
18 couvrir a couvrant **b** couvert
c couvre, couvrons **d** couvrais
g couvre
19 mourir a mourant **b** mort
c meurs, mourons, meurent
d mourais **e** mourrai **g** meure
20 vêtir a vêtant **b** vêtu **c** vêts,
vêtons **d** vêtais **e** vêtirai **g** vête
21 acquérir a acquérant **b** acquis
c acquiers, acquérons,
acquièrent **d** acquérais
e acquerrai **g** acquière
22 venir a venant **b** venu **c** viens,
venons, viennent **d** venais
e viendrai **g** vienne
23 pleuvoir a pleuvant **b** plu **c** pleut,
pleuvent **d** pleuvait **e** pleuvra
g pleuve
24 prévoir *like* voir **e** prévoirai
25 pourvoir a pourvoyant **b** pourvu
c pourvois, pourvoyons,
pourvoient **d** pourvoyais
g pourvoie
26 asseoir a asseyant **b** assis
c assieds, asseyons, asseyez,
asseyent **d** asseyais **e** assiérai
g asseye
27 MOUVOIR a mouvant **b** mû
c meus, meus, meut, mouvons,
mouvez, meuvent **d** mouvais
e mouvrai **f** mouvrais **g** meuve,
meuves, meuve, mouvions,
mouviez, meuvent
28 RECEVOIR a recevant **b** reçu
c reçois, reçois, reçoit, recevons,
recevez, reçoivent **d** recevais
e recevrai **f** recevrais **g** reçoive
29 valoir a valant **b** valu **c** vaux,

vaut, valons **d** valais **e** vaudrai
g vaille
30 voir a voyant **b** vu **c** vois, voyons,
voient **d** voyais **e** verrai **g** voie
31 vouloir a voulant **b** voulu **c** veux,
veut, voulons, veulent **d** voulais
e voudrai **g** veuille ; *impératif*
veuillez !
32 savoir a sachant **b** su **c** sais,
savons, savent **d** savais **e** saurai
g sache *impératif* sache ! sachons !
sachez !
33 pouvoir a pouvant **b** pu **c** peux,
peut, pouvons, peuvent
d pouvais **e** pourrai **g** puisse
34 AVOIR a ayant **b** eu **c** ai, as, a,
avons, avez, ont **d** avais **e** aurai
f aurais **g** aie, aies, ait, ayons,
ayez, aient
35 conclure a concluant **b** conclu
c conclus, concluons **d** concluais
g conclue
36 rire a riant **b** ri **c** ris, rions **d** riais
g rie
37 dire a disant **b** dit **c** dis, disons,
dites, disent **d** disais **g** dise
38 nuire a nuisant **b** nui **c** nuis,
nuisons **d** nuisais **e** nuirai **f** nuirais
g nuise
39 écrire a écrivant **b** écrit **c** écris,
écrivons **d** écrivais **g** écrive
40 suivre a suivant **b** suivi **c** suis,
suivons **d** suivais **g** suive
41 RENDRE a rendant **b** rendu
c rends, rends, rend, rendons,
rendez, rendent **d** rendais
e rendrai **f** rendrais **g** rende
42 vaincre a vainquant **b** vaincu
c vaincs, vainc, vainquons

d vainquais g vainque

43 **lire a** lisant **b** lu **c** lis, lisons
d lisais g lise

44 **croire a** croyant **b** cru **c** crois,
croyons, croient **d** croyais **g** croie

45 **CLORE a** closant **b** clos **c** clos,
clos, clôt, closent **e** clorai, cloras,
clora, clorons, clorez, cloront
f clorais, clorais, clorait, clorions,
cloriez, cloraient

46 **vivre a** vivant **b** vécu **c** vis, vivons
d vivais g vive

47 **MOUDRE a** moulant **b** moulu
c mouds, mouds, moud,
moulons, moulez, moulent
d moulais, moulais, moulait,
moulions, mouliez, moulaient
e moudrai, moudras, moudra,
moudrons, moudrez, moudront
f moudrais, moudrais, moudrait,
moudrions, moudriez,
moudraient **g** moule

48 **coudre a** cousant **b** cousu
c couds, cousons, cousez,
cousent **d** cousais **g** couse

49 **joindre a** joignant **b** joint **c** joins,
joignons **d** joignais **g** joigne

50 **TRAIRE a** trayant **b** trait **c** trais,
trais, trait, trayons, trayez,
traient **d** trayais, trayais, trayait,
trayions, trayiez, trayaient
e trairai, trairas, traira, trairons,
trairez, trairont **f** trairais,
trairais, trairait, trairions,
trairiez, trairaient **g** traie

51 **ABSOUDRE a** absolvant
b absous **c** absous, absous,

absout, absolvons, absolvez,
absolvent **d** absolvais, absolvais,
absolvait, absolvions, absolviez,
absolvaient **e** absoudrai,
absoudras, absoudra,
absoudrons, absoudrez,
absoudront **f** absoudrais,
absoudrais, absoudrait,
absoudrions, absoudriez,
absoudraient **g** absolve

52 **craindre a** craignant **b** craint
c crains, craignons **d** craignais
g craigne

53 **boire a** buvant **b** bu **c** bois,
buvons, boivent **d** buvais **g** boive

54 **plaire a** plaisant **b** plu **c** plais,
plaît, plaisons **d** plaisais **g** plaise

55 **croître a** croissant **b** crû **c** croîs,
croissons **d** croissais **g** croisse

56 **mettre a** mettant **b** mis **c** mets,
mettons **d** mettais **g** mette

57 **connaître a** connaissant
b connu **c** connais, connaît,
connaissons **d** connaissais
g connaisse

58 **prendre a** prenant **b** pris
c prends, prenons, prennent
d prenais **g** prenne

59 **naître a** naissant **b** né **c** nais,
naît, naissons **d** naissais **g** naisse

60 **FAIRE a** faisant **b** fait **c** fais, fais,
fait, faisons, faites, font **d** faisais
e ferai **f** ferais **g** fasse

61 **ÊTRE a** étant **b** été **c** suis, es,
est, sommes, êtes, sont **d** étais
e serai **f** serais **g** sois, sois, soit,
soyons, soyez, soient

VERBES IRRÉGULIERS ANGLAIS

PRÉSENT	PASSÉ	PARTICIPE	PRÉSENT	PASSÉ	PARTICIPE
arise	arose	arisen	fall	fell	fallen
awake	awoke	awoken	feed	fed	fed
be	was, were	been	feel	felt	felt
(am, is,			fight	fought	fought
are; being)			find	found	found
bear	bore	born(e)	flee	fled	fled
beat	beat	beaten	fling	flung	flung
become	became	become	fly	flew	flown
begin	began	begun	forbid	forbad(e)	forbidden
bend	bent	bent	forecast	forecast	forecast
bet	bet,	bet,	forget	forgot	forgotten
	betted	betted	forgive	forgave	forgiven
bid (at auction,	bid	bid	forsake	forsook	forsaken
cards)			freeze	froze	frozen
bid (say)	bade	bidden	get	got	got,
bind	bound	bound			(us) gotten
bite	bit	bitten	give	gave	given
bleed	bled	bled	go (goes)	went	gone
blow	blew	blown	grind	ground	ground
break	broke	broken	grow	grew	grown
breed	bred	bred	hang	hung	hung
bring	brought	brought	hang (execute)	hanged	hanged
build	built	built	have	had	had
burn	burnt,	burnt,	hear	heard	heard
	burned	burned	hide	hid	hidden
burst	burst	burst	hit	hit	hit
buy	bought	bought	hold	held	held
can	could	(been able)	hurt	hurt	hurt
cast	cast	cast	keep	kept	kept
catch	caught	caught	kneel	knelt,	knelt,
choose	chose	chosen		kneeled	kneeled
cling	clung	clung	know	knew	known
come	came	come	lay	laid	laid
cost	cost	cost	lead	led	led
cost (work	costed	costed	lean	leant,	leant,
out price of)				leaned	leaned
creep	crept	crept	leap	leapt,	leapt,
cut	cut	cut		leaped	leaped
deal	dealt	dealt	learn	learnt,	learnt,
dig	dug	dug		learned	learned
do (does)	did	done	leave	left	left
draw	drew	drawn	lend	lent	lent
dream	dreamed,	dreamed,	let	let	let
	dreamt	dreamt	lie (lying)	lay	lain
drink	drank	drunk	light	lit,	lit,
drive	drove	driven		lighted	lighted
dwell	dwelt	dwelt	lose	lost	lost
eat	ate	eaten	make	made	made

PRÉSENT	PASSÉ	PARTICIPE	PRÉSENT	PASSÉ	PARTICIPE
may	might	–	speed	sped,	sped,
mean	meant	meant		speeded	speeded
meet	met	met	spell	spelt,	spelt,
mistake	mistook	mistaken		spelled	spelled
mow	mowed	mown,	spend	spent	spent
		mowed	spill	spilt,	spilt,
must	(had to)	(had to)		spilled	spilled
pay	paid	paid	spin	spun	spun
put	put	put	spit	spat	spat
quit	quit,	quit,	spoil	spoiled,	spoiled,
	quitted	quitted		spoilt	spoilt
read	read	read	spread	spread	spread
rid	rid	rid	spring	sprang	sprung
ride	rode	ridden	stand	stood	stood
ring	rang	rung	steal	stole	stolen
rise	rose	risen	stick	stuck	stuck
run	ran	run	sting	stung	stung
saw	sawed	sawed,	stink	stank	stunk
		sawn	stride	strode	stridden
say	said	said	strike	struck	struck
see	saw	seen	strive	strove	striven
seek	sought	sought	swear	swore	sworn
sell	sold	sold	sweep	swept	swept
send	sent	sent	swell	swelled	swollen,
set	set	set			swelled
sew	sewed	sewn	swim	swam	swum
shake	shook	shaken	swing	swung	swung
shear	sheared	shorn,	take	took	taken
		sheared	teach	taught	taught
shed	shed	shed	tear	tore	torn
shine	shone	shone	tell	told	told
shoot	shot	shot	think	thought	thought
show	showed	shown	throw	threw	thrown
shrink	shrank	shrunk	thrust	thrust	thrust
shut	shut	shut	tread	trod	trodden
sing	sang	sung	wake	woke,	woken,
sink	sank	sunk		waked	waked
sit	sat	sat	wear	wore	worn
slay	slew	slain	weave	wove	woven
sleep	slept	slept	weave (wind)	weaved	weaved
slide	slid	slid	wed	wedded,	wedded,
sling	slung	slung		wed	wed
slit	slit	slit	weep	wept	wept
smell	smelt,	smelt,	win	won	won
	smelled	smelled	wind	wound	wound
sow	sowed	sown,	wring	wrung	wrung
		sowed	write	wrote	written
speak	spoke	spoken			

LES NOMBRES

un (une)	1	one
deux	2	two
trois	3	three
quatre	4	four
cinq	5	five
six	6	six
sept	7	seven
huit	8	eight
neuf	9	nine
dix	10	ten
onze	11	eleven
douze	12	twelve
treize	13	thirteen
quatorze	14	fourteen
quinze	15	fifteen
seize	16	sixteen
dix-sept	17	seventeen
dix-huit	18	eighteen
dix-neuf	19	nineteen
vingt	20	twenty
vingt et un (une)	21	twenty-one
vingt-deux	22	twenty-two
trente	30	thirty
quarante	40	forty
cinquante	50	fifty
soixante	60	sixty
soixante-dix	70	seventy
soixante-et-onze	71	seventy-one
soixante-douze	72	seventy-two
quatre-vingts	80	eighty
quatre-vingt-un (-une)	81	eighty-one
quatre-vingt-dix	90	ninety
cent	100	a hundred, one hundred
cent un (une)	101	a hundred and one
deux cents	200	two hundred
deux cent un (une)	201	two hundred and one
quatre cents	400	four hundred
mille	1000	a thousand
cinq mille	5000	five thousand
un million	1000000	a million

LES NOMBRES

premier (première), 1er (1ère)
deuxième, 2e or 2ème
troisième, 3e or 3ème
quatrième, 4e or 4ème
cinquième, 5e or 5ème
sixième, 6e or 6ème
septième
huitième
neuvième
dixième
onzième
douzième
treizième
quartorzième
quinzième
seizième
dix-septième
dix-huitième
dix-neuvième
vingtième
vingt-et-unième
vingt-deuxième
trentième
centième
cent-unième
millième

LES FRACTIONS ETC.
un demi
un tiers
un quart
un cinquième
zéro virgule cinq, 0,5
trois virgule quatre, 3,4
dix pour cent
cent pour cent

EXEMPLES
elle habite au septième (étage)
il habite au sept
au chapitre/à la page sept
il est arrivé (le) septième

NUMBERS

first, 1st
second, 2nd
third, 3rd
fourth, 4th
fifth, 5th
sixth, 6th
seventh
eighth
ninth
tenth
eleventh
twelfth
thirteenth
fourteenth
fifteenth
sixteenth
seventeenth
eighteenth
nineteenth
twentieth
twenty-first
twenty-second
thirtieth
hundredth
hundred-and-first
thousandth

FRACTIONS ETC.
a half
a third
a quarter
a fifth
(nought) point five, 0.5
three point four, 3.4
ten per cent
a hundred per cent

EXAMPLES
she lives on the 7th floor
he lives at number 7
chapter/page 7
he came in 7th

L'HEURE

quelle heure est-il ?

il est …

minuit	
une heure (du matin)	
une heure cinq	
une heure dix	
une heure et quart	
une heure vingt-cinq	
une heure et demie, une heure trente	
deux heures moins vingt-cinq, une heure trente-cinq	
deux heures moins vingt, une heure quarante	
deux heures moins le quart, une heure quarante-cinq	
deux heures moins dix, une heure cinquante	
midi	
deux heures (de l'après-midi), quatorze heures	
sept heures (du soir), dix-neuf heures	

à quelle heure ?

à minuit
à sept heures

dans vingt minutes
il y a un quart d'heure

THE TIME

what time is it?

_it's_ ou _it is …_

midnight, twelve p.m.
one o'clock (in the morning), one (a.m.)

five past one
ten past one
a quarter past one, one fifteen

twenty-five past one, one twenty-five
half-past one, one thirty
twenty-five to two, one thirty-five
twenty to two, one forty

a quarter to two, one forty-five
ten to two, one fifty

twelve o'clock, midday, noon

two o'clock (in the afternoon), two (p.m.)
seven o'clock (in the evening), seven (p.m.)

(at) what time?

at midnight
at seven o'clock

in twenty minutes
fifteen minutes ago

a

a [a] *vb voir* **avoir**

○ **MOT-CLÉ**

à [a] (*à + le* = **au**, *à + les* = **aux**) *prép* **1** (*endroit, situation*) at, in; **être à Paris/au Portugal** to be in Paris/Portugal; **être à la maison/à l'école** to be at home/at school; **à la campagne** in the country; **c'est à 10 m/km/à 20 minutes (d'ici)** it's 10 m/km/20 minutes away

2 (*direction*) to; **aller à Paris/au Portugal** to go to Paris/Portugal; **aller à la maison/à l'école** to go home/to school; **à la campagne** to the country

3 (*temps*): **à 3 heures/minuit** at 3 o'clock/midnight; **au printemps** in the spring; **au mois de juin** in June; **à Noël/Pâques** at Christmas/Easter; **à demain/la semaine prochaine!** see you tomorrow/next week!

4 (*attribution, appartenance*) to; **le livre est à Paul/à lui/à nous** this book is Paul's/his/ours; **donner qch à qn** to give sth to sb; **un ami à moi** a friend of mine

5 (*moyen*) with; **se chauffer au gaz** to have gas heating; **à bicyclette** on a *ou* by bicycle; **à pied** on foot; **à la main/machine** by hand/machine

6 (*provenance*) from; **boire à la bouteille** to drink from the bottle

7 (*caractérisation, manière*): **l'homme aux yeux bleus** the man with the blue eyes; **à la russe** the Russian way

8 (*but, destination*): **tasse à café** coffee cup; **maison à vendre** house for sale; **je n'ai rien à lire** I don't have anything to read; **à bien réfléchir ...** thinking about it ..., on reflection ...

9 (*rapport, évaluation, distribution*): **100 km/unités à l'heure** 100 km/units per *ou* an hour; **payé à l'heure** paid by the hour; **cinq à six** five to six

10 (*conséquence, résultat*): **à ce qu'il prétend** according to him; **à leur grande surprise** much to their surprise; **à nous trois nous n'avons pas su le faire** we couldn't do it even between the three of us; **ils sont arrivés à quatre** four of them arrived (together)

abaisser [abese] /1/ *vt* to lower, bring down; (*manette*) to pull down; **s'abaisser** *vi* to go down; (*fig*) to demean o.s.

abandon [abɑ̃dɔ̃] *nm* abandoning; giving up; withdrawal; **être à l'~** to be in a state of neglect; **laisser à l'~** to abandon

abandonner [abɑ̃dɔne] /1/ *vt* (*personne*) to leave, abandon, desert; (*projet, activité*) to abandon, give up; (*Sport*) to retire *ou* withdraw from; (*céder*) to surrender; **s'~ à** (*paresse, plaisirs*) to give o.s. up to

abat-jour [abaʒuR] *nm inv* lampshade

abats [aba] *nmpl (de bœuf, porc)* offal
sg; *(de volaille)* giblets
abattement [abatmɑ̃] *nm*: **~ fiscal**
≈ tax allowance
abattoir [abatwaʀ] *nm*
slaughterhouse
abattre [abatʀ] /41/ *vt (arbre)* to
cut down, fell; *(mur, maison)* to pull
down; *(avion, personne)* to shoot
down; *(animal)* to shoot, kill; *(fig)* to
wear out, tire out; to demoralize;
s'abattre *vi* to crash down; **ne pas
se laisser ~** to keep one's spirits up,
not to let things get one down; **s'~
sur** to beat down on; *(coups, injures)*
to rain down on; **~ du travail** *ou*
de la besogne to get through a lot
of work
abbaye [abei] *nf* abbey
abbé [abe] *nm* priest; *(d'abbaye)* abbot
abcès [apsɛ] *nm* abscess
abdiquer [abdike] /1/ *vi* to abdicate
abdominal, e, -aux
[abdɔminal, -o] *adj* abdominal;
abdominaux *nmpl*: **faire des
abdominaux** to do sit-ups
abeille [abɛj] *nf* bee
aberrant, e [abeʀɑ̃, -ɑ̃t] *adj* absurd
aberration [abeʀasjɔ̃] *nf*
aberration
abîme [abim] *nm* abyss, gulf
abîmer [abime] /1/ *vt* to spoil,
damage; **s'abîmer** *vi* to get spoilt *ou*
damaged
aboiement [abwamɑ̃] *nm* bark,
barking *no pl*
abolir [abɔliʀ] /2/ *vt* to abolish
abominable [abɔminabl] *adj*
abominable
abondance [abɔ̃dɑ̃s] *nf* abundance
abondant, e [abɔ̃dɑ̃, -ɑ̃t] *adj*
plentiful, abundant, copious;
abonder /1/ *vi* to abound, be
plentiful; **abonder dans le sens de
qn** to concur with sb
abonné, e [abɔne] *nm/f* subscriber;
season ticket holder
abonnement [abɔnmɑ̃] *nm*

subscription; *(pour transports en
commun, concerts)* season ticket
abonner [abɔne] /1/ *vt*: **s'abonner
à** to subscribe to, take out a
subscription to ; **s'~ aux tweets de
qn sur Twitter** to follow sb on Twitter
abord [abɔʀ] *nm*: **abords** *nmpl*
(environs) surroundings; **d'~** first; **au
premier ~** at first sight, initially
abordable [abɔʀdabl] *adj (personne)*
approachable; *(prix)* reasonable
aborder [abɔʀde] /1/ *vi* to land ▷ *vt*
(sujet, difficulté) to tackle; *(personne)* to
approach; *(rivage etc)* to reach
aboutir [abutiʀ] /2/ *vi (négociations
etc)* to succeed; **~ à/dans/sur** to
end up at/in/on; **n'~ à rien** to come
to nothing
aboyer [abwaje] /8/ *vi* to bark
abréger [abʀeʒe] /3, 6/ *vt* to shorten
abreuver [abʀœve] /1/: **s'abreuver**
vi to drink; **abreuvoir** *nm* watering
place
abréviation [abʀevjasjɔ̃] *nf*
abbreviation
abri [abʀi] *nm* shelter; **être à l'~**
to be under cover; **se mettre à l'~**
to shelter; **à l'~ de** sheltered from;
(danger) safe from
abricot [abʀiko] *nm* apricot
abriter [abʀite] /1/ *vt* to shelter;
s'abriter *vi* to shelter, take cover
abrupt, e [abʀypt] *adj* sheer, steep;
(ton) abrupt
abruti, e [abʀyti] *adj* stunned,
dazed ▷ *nm/f (fam)* idiot; **~ de travail**
overworked
absence [apsɑ̃s] *nf* absence; *(Méd)*
blackout; **en l'~ de** in the absence of;
avoir des ~s to have mental blanks
absent, e [apsɑ̃, -ɑ̃t] *adj* absent
▷ *nm/f* absentee; **absenter** /1/:
s'absenter *vi* to take time off work;
(sortir) to leave, go out
absolu, e [apsɔly] *adj* absolute;
absolument *adv* absolutely
absorbant, e [apsɔʀbɑ̃, -ɑ̃t] *adj*
absorbent

absorber [apsɔʀbe] /1/ *vt* to absorb; (*gén, Méd*: *manger, boire*) to take

abstenir [apstəniʀ] /22/: **s'abstenir** *vi*: **s'~ de qch/de faire** to refrain from sth/from doing

abstrait, e [apstʀɛ, -ɛt] *adj* abstract

absurde [apsyʀd] *adj* absurd

abus [aby] *nm* abuse; **~ de confiance** breach of trust; **il y a de l'~!** (*fam*) that's a bit much!; **abuser** /1/ *vi* to go too far, overstep the mark; **s'abuser** *vi* (*se méprendre*) to be mistaken; **abuser de** (*violer, duper*) to take advantage of; **abusif, -ive** *adj* exorbitant; (*punition*) excessive

académie [akademi] *nf* academy; (*Scol: circonscription*) ≈ regional education authority; *see note* **"Académie française"**

○ **ACADÉMIE FRANÇAISE**

The *Académie française* was founded by Cardinal Richelieu in 1635, during the reign of Louis XIII. It is made up of forty elected scholars and writers who are known as 'les Quarante' or 'les Immortels'. One of the *Académie's* functions is to keep an eye on the development of the French language, and its recommendations are frequently the subject of lively public debate. It has produced several editions of its famous dictionary and also awards various literary prizes.

acajou [akaʒu] *nm* mahogany

acariâtre [akaʀjɑtʀ] *adj* cantankerous

accablant, e [akɑblɑ̃, -ɑ̃t] *adj* (*chaleur*) oppressive; (*témoignage, preuve*) overwhelming

accabler [akɑble] /1/ *vt* to overwhelm, overcome; **~ qn d'injures** to heap *ou* shower abuse on sb; **~ qn de travail** to overwork sb

accalmie [akalmi] *nf* lull

accaparer [akapaʀe] /1/ *vt* to monopolize; (*travail etc*) to take up (all) the time *ou* attention of

accéder [aksede] /6/: **~ à** *vt* (*lieu*) to reach; (*accorder: requête*) to grant, accede to

accélérateur [akseleʀatœʀ] *nm* accelerator

accélérer [akseleʀe] /6/ *vt* to speed up ▷ *vi* to accelerate

accent [aksɑ̃] *nm* accent; (*Phonétique, fig*) stress; **mettre l'~ sur** (*fig*) to stress; **~ aigu/grave/circonflexe** acute/grave/circumflex accent; **accentuer** /1/ *vt* (*Ling*) to accent; (*fig*) to accentuate, emphasize; **s'accentuer** *vi* to become more marked *ou* pronounced

acceptation [aksɛptasjɔ̃] *nf* acceptance

accepter [aksɛpte] /1/ *vt* to accept; **~ de faire** to agree to do

accès [aksɛ] *nm* (*à un lieu*) access; (*Méd: de toux*) fit; (: *de fièvre*) bout; **d'~ facile/malaisé** easily/not easily accessible; **facile d'~** easy to get to; **~ de colère** fit of anger; **accessible** *adj* accessible; (*livre, sujet*): **accessible à qn** within the reach of sb

accessoire [akseswaʀ] *adj* secondary; (*frais*) incidental ▷ *nm* accessory; (*Théât*) prop

accident [aksidɑ̃] *nm* accident; **par ~** by chance; **~ de la route** road accident; **accidenté, e** *adj* damaged *ou* injured (in an accident); (*relief, terrain*) uneven; hilly; **accidentel, le** *adj* accidental

acclamer [aklame] /1/ *vt* to cheer, acclaim

acclimater [aklimate] /1/: **s'acclimater** *vi* to become acclimatized

accolade [akɔlad] *nf* (*amicale*) embrace; (*signe*) brace

accommoder [akɔmɔde] /1/ *vt* (*Culin*) to prepare; **s'accommoder**

de to put up with; (se contenter de) to make do with

accompagnateur, -trice [akɔ̃paɲatœʀ, -tʀis] nm/f (Mus) accompanist; (de voyage) guide; (de voyage organisé) courier

accompagner [akɔ̃paɲe] /1/ vt to accompany, be ou go ou come with; (Mus) to accompany

accompli, e [akɔ̃pli] adj accomplished

accomplir [akɔ̃pliʀ] /2/ vt (tâche, projet) to carry out; (souhait) to fulfil; **s'accomplir** vi to be fulfilled

accord [akɔʀ] nm agreement; (entre des styles, tons etc) harmony; (Mus) chord; **se mettre d'~** to come to an agreement (with each other); **être d'~** to agree; **d'~!** OK!

accordéon [akɔʀdeɔ̃] nm (Mus) accordion

accorder [akɔʀde] /1/ vt (faveur, délai) to grant; **~ de l'importance/de la valeur à qch** to attach importance/value to sth; (harmoniser) to match; (Mus) to tune

accoster [akɔste] /1/ vt (Navig) to draw alongside ▷ vi to berth

accouchement [akuʃmɑ̃] nm delivery, (child)birth; labour

accoucher [akuʃe] /1/ vi to give birth, have a baby; **~ d'un garçon** to give birth to a boy

accouder [akude] /1/: **s'accouder** vi: **s'~ à/contre/sur** to rest one's elbows on/against/on; **accoudoir** nm armrest

accoupler [akuple] /1/ vt to couple; (pour la reproduction) to mate; **s'accoupler** vi to mate

accourir [akuʀiʀ] /11/ vi to rush ou run up

accoutumance [akutymɑ̃s] nf (gén) adaptation; (Méd) addiction

accoutumé, e [akutyme] adj (habituel) customary, usual

accoutumer [akutyme] /1/ vt: **s'accoutumer à** to get accustomed ou used to

accroc [akʀo] nm (déchirure) tear; (fig) hitch, snag

accrochage [akʀɔʃaʒ] nm (Auto) (minor) collision; (dispute) clash, brush

accrocher [akʀɔʃe] /1/ vt (suspendre) to hang; (fig) to catch, attract; **s'accrocher** (se disputer) to have a clash ou brush; **~ qch à** (suspendre) to hang sth (up) on; (attacher: remorque) to hitch sth (up) to; (déchirer) to catch sth (on); **il a accroché ma voiture** he bumped into my car; **s'~ à** (rester pris à) to catch on; (agripper, fig) to hang on ou cling to

accroissement [akʀwasmɑ̃] nm increase

accroître [akʀwatʀ] /55/ vt: **s'accroître** vi to increase

accroupir [akʀupiʀ] /2/: **s'accroupir** vi to squat, crouch (down)

accru, e [akʀy] pp de **accroître**

accueil [akœj] nm welcome; **comité/centre d'~** reception committee/centre; **accueillir** /12/ vt to welcome; (aller chercher) to meet, collect

accumuler [akymyle] /1/ vt to accumulate, amass; **s'accumuler** vi to accumulate; to pile up

accusation [akyzasjɔ̃] nf (gén) accusation; (Jur) charge; (partie): **l'~** the prosecution

accusé, e [akyze] nm/f accused; (prévenu(e)) defendant ▷ nm: **~ de réception** acknowledgement of receipt

accuser [akyze] /1/ vt to accuse; (fig) to emphasize, bring out; (: montrer) to show; **~ qn de** to accuse sb of; (Jur) to charge sb with; **~ réception de** to acknowledge receipt of

acéré, e [aseʀe] adj sharp

acharné, e [aʃaʀne] adj (lutte, adversaire) fierce, bitter; (travail) relentless

acharner [aʃaʀne] /1/: **s'acharner** vi: **s'~ sur** to go at fiercely; **s'~ contre**

to set o.s. against; (*malchance*) to hound; **s'~ à faire** to try doggedly to do; to persist in doing

achat [aʃa] *nm* purchase; **faire l'~ de** to buy; **faire des ~s** to do some shopping

acheter [aʃte] /5/ *vt* to buy, purchase; (*soudoyer*) to buy; **~ qch à** (*marchand*) to buy ou purchase sth from; (*ami etc: offrir*) to buy sth for; **acheteur, -euse** *nm/f* buyer; shopper; (*Comm*) buyer

achever [aʃ(ə)ve] /5/ *vt* to complete, finish; (*blessé*) to finish off; **s'achever** *vi* to end

acide [asid] *adj* sour, sharp; (*Chimie*) acid(ic) ▷ *nm* acid; **acidulé, e** *adj* slightly acid; **bonbons acidulés** acid drops

acier [asje] *nm* steel; **aciérie** *nf* steelworks *sg*

acné [akne] *nf* acne

acompte [akɔ̃t] *nm* deposit

à-côté [akote] *nm* side-issue; (*argent*) extra

à-coup [aku] *nm:* **par ~s** by fits and starts

acoustique [akustik] *nf* (*d'une salle*) acoustics *pl*

acquéreur [akerœr] *nm* buyer, purchaser

acquérir [akerir] /21/ *vt* to acquire

acquis, e [aki, -iz] *pp de* **acquérir** ▷ *nm* (accumulated) experience; **son aide nous est ~e** we can count on ou be sure of his help

acquitter [akite] /1/ *vt* (*Jur*) to acquit; (*facture*) to pay, settle; **s'~ de** to discharge; (*promesse, tâche*) to fulfil

âcre [ɑkr] *adj* acrid, pungent

acrobate [akrɔbat] *nm/f* acrobat; **acrobatie** *nf* acrobatics *sg*

acte [akt] *nm* act, action; (*Théât*) act; **prendre ~ de** to note, take note of; **faire ~ de présence** to put in an appearance; **faire ~ de candidature** to submit an application; **~ de**

mariage/naissance marriage/birth certificate

acteur [aktœr] *nm* actor

actif, -ive [aktif, -iv] *adj* active ▷ *nm* (*Comm*) assets *pl*; (*fig*): **avoir à son ~** to have to one's credit; **population active** working population

action [aksjɔ̃] *nf* (*gén*) action; (*Comm*) share; **une bonne/mauvaise ~** a good/an unkind deed; **actionnaire** *nm/f* shareholder; **actionner** /1/ *vt* (*mécanisme*) to activate; (*machine*) to operate

activer [aktive] /1/ *vt* to speed up; **s'activer** *vi* to bustle about; (*se hâter*) to hurry up

activité [aktivite] *nf* activity; **en ~** (*volcan*) active; (*fonctionnaire*) in active life

actrice [aktris] *nf* actress

actualité [aktɥalite] *nf* (*d'un problème*) topicality; (*événements*): **l'~** current events; **les ~s** (*Ciné, TV*) the news; **d'~** topical

actuel, le [aktɥɛl] *adj* (*présent*) present; (*d'actualité*) topical; **à l'heure ~le** at this moment in time; **actuellement** [aktɥɛlmɑ̃] *adv* at present, at the present time

> Attention à ne pas traduire *actuellement* par *actually*.

acuponcture [akypɔ̃ktyr] *nf* acupuncture

adaptateur, -trice [adaptatœr, -tris] *nm/f* adapter

adapter [adapte] /1/ *vt* to adapt; **s'~ (à)** (*personne*) to adapt (to); **~ qch à** (*approprier*) to adapt sth to (fit); **~ qch sur/dans/à** (*fixer*) to fit sth on/into/to

addition [adisjɔ̃] *nf* addition; (*au café*) bill; **additionner** /1/ *vt* to add (up)

adepte [adɛpt] *nm/f* follower

adéquat, e [adekwa(t), -at] *adj* appropriate, suitable

adhérent, e [aderɑ̃, -ɑ̃t] *nm/f* member

adhérer [adeʀe] /6/: **~ à** (coller) to adhere ou stick to; (se rallier à: parti, club) to join; **adhésif, -ive** adj adhesive, sticky; **ruban adhésif** sticky ou adhesive tape

adieu, x [adjø] excl goodbye ▷ nm farewell

adjectif [adʒɛktif] nm adjective

adjoint, e [adʒwɛ̃, -wɛ̃t] nm/f assistant; **~ au maire** deputy mayor; **directeur ~** assistant manager

admettre [admɛtʀ] /56/ vt (visiteur) to admit; (candidat: Scol) to pass; (tolérer) to allow, accept; (reconnaître) to admit, acknowledge

administrateur, -trice [administʀatœʀ, -tʀis] nm/f (Comm) director; (Admin) administrator

administration [administʀasjɔ̃] nf administration; **l'A~** ≈ the Civil Service

administrer [administʀe] /1/ vt (firme) to manage, run; (biens, remède, sacrement etc) to administer

admirable [admiʀabl] adj admirable, wonderful

admirateur, -trice [admiʀatœʀ, -tʀis] nm/f admirer

admiration [admiʀasjɔ̃] nf admiration

admirer [admiʀe] /1/ vt to admire

admis, e [admi, -iz] pp de **admettre**

admissible [admisibl] adj (candidat) eligible; (comportement) admissible, acceptable

ADN sigle m (= acide désoxyribonucléique) DNA

ado [ado] (fam) nm/f teen

adolescence [adɔlesɑ̃s] nf adolescence

adolescent, e [adɔlesɑ̃, -ɑ̃t] nm/f adolescent, teenager

adopter [adɔpte] /1/ vt to adopt; **adoptif, -ive** adj (parents) adoptive; (fils, patrie) adopted

adorable [adɔʀabl] adj adorable

adorer [adɔʀe] /1/ vt to adore; (Rel) to worship

adosser [adose] /1/ vt: **~ qch à** ou **contre** to stand sth against; **s'~ à** ou **contre** to lean with one's back against

adoucir [adusiʀ] /2/ vt (goût, température) to make milder; (avec du sucre) to sweeten; (peau, voix, eau) to soften; **s'adoucir** vi (caractère) to mellow

adresse [adʀɛs] nf skill, dexterity; (domicile) address; **~ électronique** email address

adresser [adʀese] /1/ vt (lettre: expédier) to send; (: écrire l'adresse sur) to address; (injure, compliments) to address; **s'adresser à** (parler à) to speak to, address; (s'informer auprès de) to go and see (: bureau) to enquire at; (livre, conseil) to be aimed at; **~ la parole à qn** to speak to ou address sb

adroit, e [adʀwa, -wat] adj skilled

ADSL sigle m (= asymmetric digital subscriber line) ADSL, broadband

adulte [adylt] nm/f adult, grown-up ▷ adj (personne, attitude) adult, grown-up; (chien, arbre) fully-grown, mature

adverbe [advɛʀb] nm adverb

adversaire [advɛʀsɛʀ] nm/f (Sport, gén) opponent, adversary

aération [aeʀasjɔ̃] nf airing; (circulation de l'air) ventilation

aérer [aeʀe] /6/ vt to air; (fig) to lighten

aérien, ne [aeʀjɛ̃, -ɛn] adj (Aviat) air cpd, aerial; (câble, métro) overhead; (fig) light; **compagnie ~ne** airline (company)

aéro: aérobic nf aerobics sg; **aérogare** nf airport (buildings); (en ville) air terminal; **aéroglisseur** nm hovercraft; **aérophagie** nf (Méd) wind, aerophagia (Méd); **aéroport** nm airport; **aérosol** nm aerosol

affaiblir [afeblir] /2/: **s'affaiblir** vi to weaken

affaire [afɛʀ] nf (problème, question) matter; (criminelle, judiciaire) case; (scandaleuse etc) affair; (entreprise) business; (*marché, transaction*) (business) deal, (piece of) business *no pl*; (*occasion intéressante*) good deal; **affaires** *nfpl* affairs; (*activité commerciale*) business *sg*; (*effets personnels*) things, belongings; **~s de sport** sports gear; **tirer qn/se tirer d'~** to get sb/o.s. out of trouble; **ceci fera l'~** this will do (nicely); **avoir ~ à** (*en contact*) to be dealing with; **ce sont mes ~s** (*cela me concerne*) that's my business; **occupe-toi de tes ~s!** mind your own business!; **les ~s étrangères** (*Pol*) foreign affairs; **affairer** /1/: **s'affairer** *vi* to busy o.s., bustle about

affamé, e [afame] *adj* starving

affecter [afɛkte] /1/ *vt* to affect; **~ qch à** to allocate *ou* allot sth to; **~ qn à** to appoint sb to; (*diplomate*) to post sb to

affectif, -ive [afɛktif, -iv] *adj* emotional

affection [afɛksjɔ̃] *nf* affection; (*mal*) ailment; **affectionner** /1/ *vt* to be fond of; **affectueux, -euse** *adj* affectionate

affichage [afiʃaʒ] *nm* billposting; (*électronique*) display; **"~ interdit"** "stick no bills"; **à cristaux liquides** liquid crystal display, LCD

affiche [afiʃ] *nf* poster; (*officielle*) (public) notice; (*Théât*) bill; **être à l'~** to be on

afficher [afiʃe] /1/ *vt* (*affiche*) to put up; (*réunion*) to put up a notice about; (*électroniquement*) to display; (*fig*) to exhibit, display; **s'afficher** *vi* (*péj*) to flaunt o.s.; (*électroniquement*) to be displayed; **"défense d'~"** "no bill posters"

affilée [afile]: **d'~** *adv* at a stretch

affirmatif, -ive [afiʀmatif, -iv] *adj* affirmative

affirmer [afiʀme] /1/ *vt* to assert

affligé, e [afliʒe] *adj* distressed, grieved; **~ de** (*maladie, tare*) afflicted with

affliger [afliʒe] /3/ *vt* (*peiner*) to distress, grieve

affluence [aflyɑ̃s] *nf* crowds *pl*; **heures d'~** rush hour *sg*; **jours d'~** busiest days

affluent [aflyɑ̃] *nm* tributary

affolement [afɔlmɑ̃] *nm* panic

affoler [afɔle] /1/ *vt* to throw into a panic; **s'affoler** *vi* to panic

affranchir [afʀɑ̃ʃiʀ] /2/ *vt* to put a stamp *ou* stamps on; (*à la machine*) to frank (*BRIT*), meter (*US*); (*fig*) to free, liberate; **affranchissement** *nm* postage

affreux, -euse [afʀø, -øz] *adj* dreadful, awful

affront [afʀɔ̃] *nm* affront; **affrontement** *nm* clash, confrontation

affronter [afʀɔ̃te] /1/ *vt* to confront, face

affût [afy] *nm*: **à l'~ (de)** (*gibier*) lying in wait (for); (*fig*) on the look-out (for)

Afghanistan [afganistɑ̃] *nm*: **l'~** Afghanistan

afin [afɛ̃]: **~ que** *conj* so that, in order that; **~ de faire** in order to do, so as to do

africain, e [afʀikɛ̃, -ɛn] *adj* African ▷ *nm/f*: **A~, e** African

Afrique [afʀik] *nf*: **l'~** Africa; **l'~ australe/du Nord/du Sud** southern/North/South Africa

agacer [agase] /3/ *vt* to irritate

âge [aʒ] *nm* age; **quel ~ as-tu?** how old are you?; **prendre de l'~** to be getting on (in years); **le troisième ~** (*personnes âgées*) senior citizens; (*période*) retirement; **âgé, e** *adj* old, elderly; **âgé de 10 ans** 10 years old

agence [aʒɑ̃s] *nf* agency, office; (*succursale*) branch; **~ immobilière** estate agent's (office) (*BRIT*), real estate office (*US*); **~ de voyages** travel agency

agenda [aʒɛ̃da] *nm* diary; **~ électronique** PDA

Attention à ne pas traduire *agenda* par le mot anglais *agenda*.

agenouiller [aʒ(ə)nuje] /1/: **s'agenouiller** vi to kneel (down)

agent, e [aʒɑ̃, -ɑ̃t] nm/f (aussi: **~(e) de police**) policeman (policewoman); (Admin) official, officer; **~ immobilier** estate agent (BRIT), realtor (US)

agglomération [aglɔmeʀasjɔ̃] nf town; (Auto) built-up area; **l'~ parisienne** the urban area of Paris

aggraver [agʀave] /1/: **s'aggraver** vi to worsen

agile [aʒil] adj agile, nimble

agir [aʒiʀ] /2/ vi to act; **il s'agit de** it's a matter ou question of; (ça traite de) it is about; **il s'agit de faire** we (ou you etc) must do; **de quoi s'agit-il?** what is it about?

agitation [aʒitasjɔ̃] nf (hustle and) bustle; (trouble) agitation, excitement; (politique) unrest, agitation

agité, e [aʒite] adj fidgety, restless; (troublé) agitated, perturbed; (mer) rough

agiter [aʒite] /1/ vt (bouteille, chiffon) to shake; (bras, mains) to wave; (préoccuper, exciter) to trouble

agneau, x [aɲo] nm lamb

agonie [agɔni] nf mortal agony, death pangs pl; (fig) death throes pl

agrafe [agʀaf] nf (de vêtement) hook, fastener; (de bureau) staple; **agrafer** /1/ vt to fasten; to staple; **agrafeuse** [agʀaføz] nf stapler

agrandir [agʀɑ̃diʀ] /2/ vt to extend; **s'agrandir** vi (ville, famille) to grow, expand; (trou, écart) to get bigger; **agrandissement** nm (photographie) enlargement

agréable [agʀeabl] adj pleasant, nice

agréé, e [agʀee] adj: **concessionnaire ~** registered dealer

agréer [agʀee] /1/ vt (requête) to accept; **~ à** to please, suit; **veuillez ~, Monsieur/Madame,**

mes salutations distinguées (personne nommée) yours sincerely; (personne non nommée) yours faithfully

agrégation [agʀegasjɔ̃] nf highest teaching diploma in France; **agrégé, e** nm/f holder of the agrégation

agrément [agʀemɑ̃] nm (accord) consent, approval; (attraits) charm, attractiveness; (plaisir) pleasure

agresser [agʀese] /1/ vt to attack; **agresseur** nm aggressor, attacker; (Pol, Mil) aggressor; **agressif, -ive** adj aggressive

agricole [agʀikɔl] adj agricultural; **agriculteur, -trice** nm/f farmer; **agriculture** nf agriculture; farming

agripper [agʀipe] /1/ vt to grab, clutch; **s'~ à** to cling (on) to, clutch, grip

agroalimentaire [agʀɔalimɑ̃tɛʀ] nm farm-produce industry

agrumes [agʀym] nmpl citrus fruit(s)

aguets [agɛ]: **aux ~** adv; **être aux ~** to be on the look-out

ai [ɛ] vb voir **avoir**

aide [ɛd] nm/f assistant ▷ nf assistance, help; (secours financier) aid; **à l'~ de** with the help ou aid of; **appeler (qn) à l'~** to call for help (from sb); **~ judiciaire** legal aid; **~ ménagère** nf ≈ home help (BRIT) ou helper (US); **aide-mémoire** nm inv memoranda pages pl; (key facts) handbook

aider [ede] /1/ vt to help; **~ à qch** to help (towards) sth; **~ qn à faire qch** to help sb to do sth; **s'~ de** (se servir de) to use, make use of

aide-soignant, e [ɛdswaɲɑ̃, -ɑ̃t] nm/f auxiliary nurse

aie etc [ɛ] vb voir **avoir**

aïe [aj] excl ouch!

aigle [ɛgl] nm eagle

aigre [ɛgʀ] adj sour, sharp; (fig) sharp, cutting; **aigre-doux, -douce** adj (sauce) sweet and sour; **aigreur** nf sourness; sharpness

aigu, ë [egy] *adj* (*objet, arête*) sharp; (*son, voix*) high-pitched, shrill; (*note*) high(-pitched)

aiguille [eguij] *nf* needle; (*de montre*) hand; **~ à tricoter** knitting needle

aiguiser [egize] /1/ *vt* to sharpen; (*fig*) to stimulate (: *sens*) to excite

ail [aj] *nm* garlic

aile [ɛl] *nf* wing; **aileron** *nm* (*de requin*) fin; **ailier** *nm* winger

aille *etc* [aj] *vb voir* **aller**

ailleurs [ajœʀ] *adv* elsewhere, somewhere else; **partout/nulle part ~** everywhere/nowhere else; **d'~** (*du reste*) moreover, besides; **par ~** (*d'autre part*) moreover, furthermore

aimable [ɛmabl] *adj* kind, nice

aimant [ɛmã] *nm* magnet

aimer [eme] /1/ *vt* to love; (*d'amitié, affection, par goût*) to like; **j'aimerais ...** (*souhait*) I would like ...; **j'aime faire du ski** I like skiing; **je t'aime** I love you; **bien ~ qn/qch** to like sb/sth; **j'aime mieux Paul (que Pierre)** I prefer Paul (to Pierre); **j'aimerais autant** *ou* **mieux y aller maintenant** I'd sooner *ou* rather go now

aine [ɛn] *nf* groin

aîné, e [ene] *adj* elder, older; (*le plus âgé*) eldest, oldest ▷ *nm/f* oldest child *ou* one, oldest boy *ou* son/girl *ou* daughter

ainsi [ɛ̃si] *adv* (*de cette façon*) like this, in this way, thus; (*ce faisant*) thus ▷ *conj* thus, so; **~ que** (*comme*) (just) as; (*et aussi*) as well as; **pour ~ dire** so to speak; **et ~ de suite** and so on (and so forth)

air [ɛʀ] *nm* air; (*mélodie*) tune; (*expression*) look, air; **paroles/menaces en l'~** empty words/threats; **prendre l'~** to get some (fresh) air; **avoir l'~** (*sembler*) to look, appear; **avoir l'~ triste** to look *ou* seem sad; **avoir l'~ de qch** to look like sth; **avoir l'~ de faire** to look as though one is doing

airbag [ɛʀbag] *nm* airbag

aisance [ɛzɑ̃s] *nf* ease; (*richesse*) affluence

aise [ɛz] *nf* comfort; **être à l'~** *ou* **à son ~** to be comfortable; (*pas embarrassé*) to be at ease; (*financièrement*) to be comfortably off; **se mettre à l'~** to make o.s. comfortable; **être mal à l'~** *ou* **à son ~** to be uncomfortable; (*gêné*) to be ill at ease; **en faire à son ~** to do as one likes; **aisé, e** *adj* easy; (*assez riche*) well-to-do, well-off

aisselle [ɛsɛl] *nf* armpit

ait [ɛ] *vb voir* **avoir**

ajonc [aʒɔ̃] *nm* gorse *no pl*

ajourner [aʒuʀne] /1/ *vt* (*réunion*) to adjourn; (*décision*) to defer, postpone

ajouter [aʒute] /1/ *vt* to add

alarme [alaʀm] *nf* alarm; **donner l'~** to give *ou* raise the alarm; **alarmer** /1/ *vt* to alarm; **s'alarmer** *vi* to become alarmed

Albanie [albani] *nf*: **l'~** Albania

album [albɔm] *nm* album

alcool [alkɔl] *nm*: **l'~** alcohol; **un ~** a spirit, a brandy; **bière sans ~** non-alcoholic *ou* alcohol-free beer; **~ à brûler** methylated spirits (BRIT), wood alcohol (US); **~ à 90°** surgical spirit; **alcoolique** *adj, nm/f* alcoholic; **alcoolisé, e** *adj* alcoholic; **une boisson non alcoolisée** a soft drink; **alcoolisme** *nm* alcoholism; **alco(o)test®** *nm* Breathalyser® ; (*test*) breath-test

aléatoire [aleatwaʀ] *adj* uncertain; (*Inform, Statistique*) random

alentour [alɑ̃tuʀ] *adv* around (about); **alentours** *nmpl* surroundings; **aux ~s de** in the vicinity *ou* neighbourhood of, around about; (*temps*) around about

alerte [alɛʀt] *adj* agile, nimble; (*style*) brisk, lively ▷ *nf* alert; warning; **~ à la bombe** bomb scare; **alerter** /1/ *vt* to alert

algèbre [alʒɛbʀ] *nf* algebra

Alger [alʒe] n Algiers

Algérie [alʒeʀi] nf: **l'~** Algeria; **algérien, ne** adj Algerian ▷ nm/f: **Algérien, ne** Algerian

algue [alg] nf seaweed no pl; (Bot) alga

alibi [alibi] nm alibi

aligner [aliɲe] /1/ vt to align, line up; (idées, chiffres) to string together; (adapter): **~ qch sur** to bring sth into alignment with; **s'aligner** (soldats etc) to line up; **s'~ sur** (Pol) to align o.s. with

aliment [alimã] nm food; **alimentation** nf (en eau etc, de moteur) supplying; (commerce) food trade; (régime) diet; (Inform) feed; **alimentation (générale)** (general) grocer's; **alimenter** /1/ vt to feed; (Tech): **alimenter (en)** to supply (with), feed (with); (fig) to sustain, keep going

allaiter [alete] /1/ vt to (breast-)feed, nurse; (animal) to suckle

allécher [aleʃe] /6/ vt: **~ qn** to make sb's mouth water; to tempt sb, entice sb

allée [ale] nf (de jardin) path; (en ville) avenue, drive; **~s et venues** comings and goings

allégé, e [aleʒe] adj (yaourt etc) low-fat

alléger [aleʒe] /6, 3/ vt (voiture) to make lighter; (chargement) to lighten; (souffrance) to alleviate, soothe

Allemagne [almaɲ] nf: **l'~** Germany; **allemand, e** adj German ▷ nm (Ling) German ▷ nm/f: **Allemand, e** German

aller [ale] /9/ nm (trajet) outward journey; (billet) single (BRIT) ou one-way ticket ▷ vi (gén) to go; **~ simple** (billet) single (BRIT) ou one-way ticket; **~ (et) retour (AR)** return trip ou journey (BRIT), round trip (US); (billet) return (BRIT) ou round-trip (US) ticket; **~ à** (convenir) to suit; (forme, pointure etc) to fit;

~ avec (couleurs, style etc) to go (well) with; **je vais le faire/me fâcher** I'm going to do it/to get angry; **~ voir/ chercher qn** to go and see/look for sb; **comment allez-vous?** how are you?; **comment ça va?** how are you?; (affaires etc) how are things?; **il va bien/mal** he's well/ not well, he's fine/ill; **ça va bien/mal** (affaires etc) it's going well/not going well; **~ mieux** to be better; **allez!** come on!; **allons!** come now!

allergie [alɛʀʒi] nf allergy

allergique [alɛʀʒik] adj: **~ à** allergic to

alliance [aljɑ̃s] nf (Mil, Pol) alliance; (bague) wedding ring

allier [alje] /7/ vt (Pol, gén) to ally; (fig) to combine; **s'allier** to become allies; (éléments, caractéristiques) to combine

allô [alo] excl hullo, hallo

allocation [alɔkasjɔ̃] nf allowance; **~ (de) chômage** unemployment benefit; **~s familiales** ≈ child benefit

allonger [alɔ̃ʒe] /3/ vt to lengthen, make longer; (étendre: bras, jambe) to stretch (out); **s'allonger** vi to get longer; (se coucher) to lie down, stretch out; **~ le pas** to hasten one's step(s)

allumage [alymaʒ] nm (Auto) ignition

allume-cigare [alymsigaʀ] nm inv cigar lighter

allumer [alyme] /1/ vt (lampe, phare, radio) to put ou switch on; (pièce) to put ou switch the light(s) on in; (feu, bougie, cigare, pipe, gaz) to light; **s'allumer** vi (lumière, lampe) to come ou go on

allumette [alymɛt] nf match

allure [alyʀ] nf (vitesse) speed; (: à pied) pace; (démarche) walk; (aspect, air) look; **avoir de l'~** to have style; **à toute ~** at full speed

allusion [a(l)lyzjɔ̃] nf allusion; (sous-entendu) hint; **faire ~ à** to allude ou refer to; to hint at

○ **MOT-CLÉ**

alors [alɔʀ] *adv* **1** (*à ce moment-là*) then, at that time; **il habitait alors à Paris** he lived in Paris at that time **2** (*par conséquent*) then; **tu as fini? alors je m'en vais** have you finished? I'm going then

3: et alors? so (what?)

▶ *conj*: **alors que** (*au moment où*) when, as; **il est arrivé alors que je partais** he arrived as I was leaving; (*tandis que*) whereas, while; **alors que son frère travaillait dur, lui se reposait** while his brother was working hard, HE would rest; (*bien que*) even though; **il a été puni alors qu'il n'a rien fait** he was punished, even though he had done nothing

alourdir [aluʀdiʀ] /2/ *vt* to weigh down, make heavy
Alpes [alp] *nfpl*: **les ~** the Alps
alphabet [alfabɛ] *nm* alphabet; (*livre*) ABC (book)
alpinisme [alpinism] *nm* mountaineering, climbing
Alsace [alzas] *nf* Alsace; **alsacien, ne** *adj* Alsatian ▷ *nm/f*: **Alsacien, ne** Alsatian
altermondialisme [altɛʀmɔ̃djalism] *nm* anti-globalism; **altermondialiste** *adj*, *nm/f* anti-globalist
alternatif, -ive [altɛʀnatif, -iv] *adj* alternating ▷ *nf* alternative; **alternative** *nf* (*choix*) alternative; **alterner** /1/ *vt* to alternate
altitude [altityd] *nf* altitude, height
alto [alto] *nm* (*instrument*) viola
aluminium [alyminjɔm] *nm* aluminium (BRIT), aluminum (US)
amabilité [amabilite] *nf* kindness
amaigrissant, e [amegʀisɑ̃, -ɑ̃t] *adj*: **régime ~** slimming (BRIT) ou weight-reduction (US) diet
amande [amɑ̃d] *nf* (*de l'amandier*) almond; **amandier** *nm* almond (tree)

amant [amɑ̃] *nm* lover
amas [ama] *nm* heap, pile; **amasser** /1/ *vt* to amass
amateur [amatœʀ] *nm* amateur; **en ~** (*péj*) amateurishly; **~ de musique/ sport** *etc* music/sport *etc* lover
ambassade [ɑ̃basad] *nf* embassy; **l'~ de France** the French Embassy; **ambassadeur, -drice** *nm/f* ambassador/ambassadress
ambiance [ɑ̃bjɑ̃s] *nf* atmosphere; **il y a de l'~** everyone's having a good time
ambigu, ë [ɑ̃bigy] *adj* ambiguous
ambitieux, -euse [ɑ̃bisjø, -jøz] *adj* ambitious
ambition [ɑ̃bisjɔ̃] *nf* ambition
ambulance [ɑ̃bylɑ̃s] *nf* ambulance; **ambulancier, -ière** *nm/f* ambulanceman/woman (BRIT), paramedic (US)
âme [ɑm] *nf* soul; **~ sœur** kindred spirit
amélioration [ameljɔʀasjɔ̃] *nf* improvement
améliorer [ameljɔʀe] /1/ *vt* to improve; **s'améliorer** *vi* to improve, get better
aménager [amenaʒe] /3/ *vt* (*agencer*) to fit out; (: *terrain*) to lay out; (: *quartier, territoire*) to develop; (*installer*) to fix up, put in; **ferme aménagée** converted farmhouse
amende [amɑ̃d] *nf* fine; **faire ~ honorable** to make amends
amener [am(ə)ne] /5/ *vt* to bring; (*causer*) to bring about; **s'amener** *vi* (*fam*) to show up, turn up; **~ qn à qch/à faire** to lead sb to sth/to do
amer, amère [amɛʀ] *adj* bitter
américain, e [ameʀikɛ̃, -ɛn] *adj* American ▷ *nm/f*: **A~, e** American
Amérique [ameʀik] *nf* America; **l'~ centrale** Central America; **l'~ latine** Latin America; **l'~ du Nord** North America; **l'~ du Sud** South America
amertume [amɛʀtym] *nf* bitterness

ameublement [amœbləmã] *nm*
furnishing; (*meubles*) furniture
ami, e [ami] *nm/f* friend; (*amant/
maîtresse*) boyfriend/girlfriend ▷ *adj*:
pays/groupe ~ friendly country/
group; **petit ~/petite ~e** boyfriend/
girlfriend
amiable [amjabl] : **à l'~** *adv* (*Jur*) out
of court; (*gén*) amicably
amiante [amjãt] *nm* asbestos
amical, e, -aux [amikal, -o] *adj*
friendly; **amicalement** *adv* in a
friendly way; (*formule épistolaire*)
regards
amincir [amẽsiR] /2/ *vt*: **~ qn**
to make sb thinner *ou* slimmer;
(*vêtement*) to make sb look slimmer
amincissant, e [amẽsisã, -ãt] *adj*
slimming; **régime ~** diet; **crème ~e**
slimming cream
amiral, -aux [amiral, -o] *nm*
admiral
amitié [amitje] *nf* friendship;
prendre en ~ to take a liking to;
faire *ou* **présenter ses ~s à qn** to
send sb one's best wishes; **~s** (*formule
épistolaire*) (with) best wishes
amonceler [amõs(ə)le] /4/ *vt* to pile
ou heap up; **s'amonceler** to pile *ou*
heap up; (*fig*) to accumulate
amont [amõ]: **en ~** *adv* upstream
amorce [amɔRs] *nf* (*sur un hameçon*)
bait; (*explosif*) cap; (*tube*) primer;
(: *contenu*) priming; (*fig: début*)
beginning(s), start
amortir [amɔRtiR] /2/ *vt* (*atténuer:
choc*) to absorb, cushion; (: *bruit,
douleur*) to deaden; (*Comm: dette*)
to pay off; **~ un abonnement** to
make a season ticket pay (for itself);
amortisseur *nm* shock absorber
amour [amuR] *nm* love; **faire l'~** to
make love; **amoureux, -euse** *adj*
(*regard, tempérament*) amorous; (*vie,
problèmes*) love *cpd*; (*personne*): **être
amoureux (de qn)** to be in love
(with sb) ▷ *nmpl* courting couple(s);
amour-propre *nm* self-esteem, pride

ampère [ãpɛR] *nm* amp(ere)
amphithéâtre [ãfiteɑtR] *nm*
amphitheatre; (*d'université*) lecture
hall *ou* theatre
ample [ãpl] *adj* (*vêtement*) roomy,
ample; (*gestes, mouvement*) broad;
(*ressources*) ample; **amplement**
adv: **amplement suffisant** more
than enough; **ampleur** *nf* (*de dégâts,
problème*) extent
amplificateur [ãplifikatœR] *nm*
amplifier
amplifier [ãplifje] /7/ *vt* (*fig*) to
expand, increase
ampoule [ãpul] *nf* (*électrique*) bulb;
(*de médicament*) phial; (*aux mains,
pieds*) blister
amusant, e [amyzã, -ãt] *adj*
(*divertissant, spirituel*) entertaining,
amusing; (*comique*) funny, amusing
amuse-gueule [amyzgœl] *nm inv*
appetizer, snack
amusement [amyzmã] *nm* (*voir
amusé*) amusement; (*jeu etc*) pastime,
diversion
amuser [amyze] /1/ *vt* (*divertir*) to
entertain, amuse; (*égayer, faire rire*) to
amuse; **s'amuser** *vi* (*jouer*) to amuse
o.s.; (*se divertir*) to enjoy o.s., have
fun; (*fig*) to mess around
amygdale [amidal] *nf* tonsil
an [ã] *nm* year; **être âgé de** *ou* **avoir
3 ans** to be 3 (years old); **le jour de
l'an, le premier de l'an, le nouvel
an** New Year's Day
analphabète [analfabɛt] *nm/f*
illiterate
analyse [analiz] *nf* analysis; (*Méd*)
test; **analyser** /1/ *vt* to analyse;
(*Méd*) to test
ananas [anana(s)] *nm* pineapple
anatomie [anatɔmi] *nf* anatomy
ancêtre [ãsɛtR] *nm/f* ancestor
anchois [ãʃwa] *nm* anchovy
ancien, ne [ãsjẽ, -jɛn] *adj* old; (*de
jadis, de l'antiquité*) ancient; (*précédent,
ex-*) former, old; (*par l'expérience*)
senior ▷ *nm/f* (*dans une tribu etc*) elder;

ancienneté nf (Admin) (length of) service; (privilèges obtenus) seniority

ancre [ãkʀ] nf anchor; **jeter/lever l'~** to cast/weigh anchor; **ancrer** /1/ vt (Constr: câble etc) to anchor; (fig) to fix firmly

Andorre [ãdɔʀ] nf Andorra

andouille [ãduj] nf (Culin) sausage made of chitterlings; (fam) clot, nit

âne [ɑn] nm donkey, ass; (péj) dunce

anéantir [aneãtiʀ] /2/ vt to annihilate, wipe out; (fig) to obliterate, destroy

anémie [anemi] nf anaemia; **anémique** adj anaemic

anesthésie [anɛstezi] nf anaesthesia; **~ générale/locale** general/local anaesthetic; **faire une ~ locale à qn** to give sb a local anaesthetic

ange [ãʒ] nm angel; **être aux ~s** to be over the moon

angine [ãʒin] nf throat infection; **~ de poitrine** angina (pectoris)

anglais, e [ãglɛ, -ɛz] adj English ▷ nm (Ling) English ▷ nm/f: **A~, e** Englishman/woman; **les A~** the English; **filer à l'~e** to take French leave

angle [ãgl] nm angle; (coin) corner

Angleterre [ãglətɛʀ] nf: **l'~** England

anglo... [ãglɔ] préfixe Anglo-, anglo(-); **anglophone** adj English-speaking

angoisse [ãgwas] nf: **l'~** anguish no pl; **angoissé, e** adj (personne) distressed

anguille [ãgij] nf eel

animal, e, -aux [animal, -o] adj, nm animal

animateur, -trice [animatœʀ, -tʀis] nm/f (de télévision) host; (de groupe) leader, organizer

animation [animasjõ] nf (voir animé) busyness; liveliness; (Ciné: technique) animation

animé, e [anime] adj (rue, lieu) busy, lively; (conversation, réunion) lively, animated

animer [anime] /1/ vt (ville, soirée) to liven up; (mettre en mouvement) to drive

anis [ani(s)] nm (Culin) aniseed; (Bot) anise

ankyloser [ãkiloze] /1/: **s'ankyloser** vi to get stiff

anneau, x [ano] nm (de rideau, bague) ring; (de chaîne) link

année [ane] nf year

annexe [anɛks] adj (problème) related; (document) appended; (salle) adjoining ▷ nf (bâtiment) annex(e); (jointe à une lettre, un dossier) enclosure

anniversaire [anivɛʀsɛʀ] nm birthday; (d'un événement, bâtiment) anniversary

annonce [anõs] nf announcement; (signe, indice) sign; (aussi: **~ publicitaire**) advertisement; **les petites ~s** the small ou classified ads

annoncer [anõse] /3/ vt to announce; (être le signe de) to herald; **s'annoncer bien/difficile** to look promising/difficult

annuaire [anɥɛʀ] nm yearbook, annual; **~ téléphonique** (telephone) directory, phone book

annuel, le [anɥɛl] adj annual, yearly

annulation [anylasjõ] nf cancellation

annuler [anyle] /1/ vt (rendez-vous, voyage) to cancel, call off; (jugement) to quash (BRIT), repeal (US); (Math, Physique) to cancel out

anonymat [anɔnima] nm anonymity; **garder l'~** to remain anonymous

anonyme [anɔnim] adj anonymous; (fig) impersonal

anorak [anɔʀak] nm anorak

anorexie [anɔʀɛksi] nf anorexia

anormal, e, -aux [anɔʀmal, -o] adj abnormal

ANPE sigle f (= Agence nationale pour l'emploi) national employment agency (functions include job creation)

antarctique [ɑ̃taʀktik] *adj* Antarctic
▷ *nm*: **l'A~** the Antarctic
antenne [ɑ̃tɛn] *nf* (*de radio, télévision*)
aerial; (*d'insecte*) antenna, feeler;
(*poste avancé*) outpost; (*petite
succursale*) sub-branch; (*de branche*) **passer
à/avoir l'~** to go/be on the air;
~ parabolique satellite dish
antérieur, e [ɑ̃teʀjœʀ] *adj* (*d'avant*)
previous, earlier; (*de devant*) front
anti... [ɑ̃ti] *préfixe* anti...;
antialcoolique *adj* anti-alcohol;
antibiotique *nm* antibiotic;
antibrouillard *adj*: **phare
antibrouillard** fog lamp
anticipation [ɑ̃tisipasjɔ̃] *nf*: **livre/
film d'~** science fiction book/film
anticipé, e [ɑ̃tisipe] *adj*: **avec mes
remerciements ~s** thanking you in
advance *ou* anticipation
anticiper [ɑ̃tisipe] /1/ *vt* (*événement,
coup*) to anticipate, foresee
anti: anticorps *nm* antibody;
antidote *nm* antidote; **antigel** *nm*
antifreeze; **antihistaminique** *nm*
antihistamine
antillais, e [ɑ̃tije, -ɛz] *adj* West
Indian, Caribbean ▷ *nm/f*: **A~, e** West
Indian, Caribbean
Antilles [ɑ̃tij] *nfpl*: **les ~** the West
Indies; **les Grandes/Petites ~** the
Greater/Lesser Antilles
antilope [ɑ̃tilɔp] *nf* antelope
anti: antimite(s) *adj, nm*: **(produit)
antimite(s)** mothproofer, moth
repellent; **antimondialisation** *nf*
anti-globalization; **antipathique**
adj unpleasant, disagreeable;
antipelliculaire *adj* anti-dandruff
antiquaire [ɑ̃tikɛʀ] *nm/f* antique
dealer
antique [ɑ̃tik] *adj* antique; (*très
vieux*) ancient, antiquated; **antiquité**
nf (*objet*) antique; **l'Antiquité**
Antiquity; **magasin/marchand
d'antiquités** antique shop/dealer
anti: antirabique *adj* rabies *cpd*;
antirouille *adj inv* anti-rust *cpd*;

antisémite *adj* anti-Semitic;
antiseptique *adj, nm* antiseptic;
antivirus *nm* (*Inform*) antivirus
(program); **antivol** *adj, nm*:
(dispositif) antivol antitheft device
anxieux, -euse [ɑ̃ksjø, -jøz] *adj*
anxious, worried
AOC *sigle f* (= *Appellation d'origine
contrôlée*) guarantee of quality of wine
août [u(t)] *nm* August
apaiser [apeze] /1/ *vt* (*colère*) to calm;
(*douleur*) to soothe; (*personne*) to calm
(down), pacify; **s'apaiser** *vi* (*tempête,
bruit*) to die down, subside; (*personne*)
to calm down
apercevoir [apɛʀsəvwaʀ] /28/ *vt* to
see; **s'apercevoir de** *vt* to notice; **s'~
que** to notice that
aperçu [apɛʀsy] *nm* (*vue d'ensemble*)
general survey
apéritif, -ive [apeʀitif, -iv] *adj*
which stimulates the appetite ▷ *nm*
(*boisson*) aperitif; (*réunion*) (pre-lunch
ou -dinner) drinks *pl*
à-peu-près [apøpʀɛ] *nm inv* (*péj*)
vague approximation
apeuré, e [apœʀe] *adj* frightened,
scared
aphte [aft] *nm* mouth ulcer
apitoyer [apitwaje] /8/ *vt* to move
to pity; **s'~ (sur qn/qch)** to feel pity
ou compassion (for sb/over sth)
aplatir [aplatiʀ] /2/ *vt* to flatten;
s'aplatir *vi* to become flatter; (*écrasé*)
to be flattened
aplomb [aplɔ̃] *nm* (*équilibre*) balance,
equilibrium; (*fig*) self-assurance
nerve; **d'~** steady
apostrophe [apɔstʀɔf] *nf* (*signe*)
apostrophe
apparaître [apaʀɛtʀ] /57/ *vi* to
appear
appareil [apaʀɛj] *nm* (*outil, machine*)
piece of apparatus, device; (*électrique
etc*) appliance; (*avion*) (aero)plane,
aircraft *inv*; (*téléphonique*) telephone;
(*dentier*) brace (BRIT), braces (US); **qui
est à l'~?** who's speaking?; **dans le**

plus simple ~ in one's birthday suit; **~ (photo)** camera; **~ numérique** digital camera; **appareiller** /1/ vi (Navig) to cast off, get under way ▷ vt (assortir) to match up

apparemment [aparamã] adv apparently

apparence [aparãs] nf appearance; **en ~** apparently

apparent, e [aparã, -ãt] adj visible; (évident) obvious; (superficiel) apparent

apparenté, e [aparãte] adj: **~ à** related to; (fig) similar to

apparition [aparisjõ] nf appearance; (surnaturelle) apparition

appartement [apartəmã] nm flat (BRIT), apartment (US)

appartenir [apartənir] /22/: **~ à** vt to belong to; **il lui appartient de** it is up to him to

apparu, e [apary] pp de **apparaître**

appât [apɑ] nm (Pêche) bait; (fig) lure, bait

appel [apɛl] nm call; (nominal) roll call (: Scol) register; (Mil: recrutement) call-up; **faire ~ à** (invoquer) to appeal to; (avoir recours à) to call on; (nécessiter) to call for, require; **faire ou interjeter ~** (Jur) to appeal; **faire l'~** to call the roll; (Scol) to call the register; **sans ~** (fig) final, irrevocable; **~ d'offres** (Comm) invitation to tender; **faire un ~ de phares** to flash one's headlights; **~ (téléphonique)** (tele)phone call

appelé [ap(ə)le] nm (Mil) conscript

appeler [ap(ə)le] /4/ vt to call; (faire venir: médecin etc) to call, send for; **s'appeler** vi: **elle s'appelle Gabrielle** her name is Gabrielle, she's called Gabrielle; **comment vous appelez-vous?** what's your name?; **comment ça s'appelle?** what is it ou that called?

appendicite [apãdisit] nf appendicitis

appesantir [apəzãtir] /2/: **s'appesantir** vi to grow heavier; **s'~ sur** (fig) to dwell at length on

appétissant, e [apetisã, -ãt] adj appetizing, mouth-watering

appétit [apeti] nm appetite; **bon ~!** enjoy your meal!

applaudir [aplodir] /2/ vt to applaud ▷ vi to applaud, clap; **applaudissements** nmpl applause sg, clapping sg

appli [apli] nf app

application [aplikasjõ] nf application

appliquer [aplike] /1/ vt to apply; (loi) to enforce; **s'appliquer** vi (élève etc) to apply o.s.; **s'~ à** to apply to

appoint [apwẽ] nm (extra) contribution ou help; **avoir/faire l'~** to have/give the right change ou money; **chauffage d'~** extra heating

apporter [aporte] /1/ vt to bring

appréciable [apresjabl] adj appreciable

apprécier [apresje] /7/ vt to appreciate; (évaluer) to estimate, assess

appréhender [apreãde] /1/ vt (craindre) to dread; (arrêter) to apprehend

apprendre [aprãdr] /58/ vt to learn; (événement, résultats) to learn of, hear of; **~ qch à qn** (informer) to tell sb (of) sth; (enseigner) to teach sb sth; **~ à faire qch** to learn to do sth; **~ à qn à faire qch** to teach sb to do sth; **apprenti, e** nm/f apprentice; **apprentissage** nm learning; (Comm, Scol: période) apprenticeship

apprêter [aprete] /1/: **s'apprêter** vi: **s'~ à qch/à faire qch** to prepare for sth/for doing sth

appris, e [apri, -iz] pp de **apprendre**

apprivoiser [aprivwaze] /1/ vt to tame

approbation [aprobasjõ] nf approval

approcher [aprɔʃe] /1/ vi to approach, come near ▷ vt to approach; (rapprocher): **~ qch (de qch)** to bring ou put ou move sth near (to sth); **s'approcher de** to approach, go *ou* come *ou* move near to; **~ de** (*lieu, but*) to draw near to; (*quantité, moment*) to approach

approfondir [apʁɔfɔ̃diʁ] /2/ *vt* to deepen; (*question*) to go further into

approprié, e [apʁɔpʁije] *adj*: **~ (à)** appropriate (to), suited (to)

approprier [apʁɔpʁije] /7/: **s'approprier** *vt* to appropriate, take over; **s'~ en** to stock up with

approuver [apʁuve] /1/ *vt* to agree with; (*trouver louable*) to approve of

approvisionner [apʁɔvizjɔne] /1/ *vt* to supply; (*compte bancaire*) to pay funds into; **s'~ en** to stock up with

approximatif, -ive [apʁɔksimatif, -iv] *adj* approximate, rough; (*imprécis*) vague

appt *abr* = **appartement**

appui [apɥi] *nm* support; **prendre ~ sur** to lean on; (*objet*) to rest on; **l'~ de la fenêtre** the windowsill, the window ledge

appuyer [apɥije] /8/ *vt* (*poser, soutenir: personne, demande*) to support, back (up) ▷ *vi*: **~ sur** (*bouton*) to press, push; (*mot, détail*) to stress, emphasize; **s'appuyer sur** *vt* to lean on; (*compter sur*) to rely on; **~ qch sur/contre/à** to lean *ou* rest sth on/ against/on; **~ sur le frein** to brake, to apply the brakes

après [apʁɛ] *prép* after ▷ *adv* afterwards; **deux heures ~** two hours later; **~ qu'il est parti/avoir fait** after he left/having done; **courir ~ qn** to run after sb; **crier ~ qn** to shout at sb; **être toujours ~ qn** (*critiquer etc*) to be always on at sb; **~ quoi** after which; **d'~** (*selon*) according to; **~ coup** after the event, afterwards; **~ tout** (*au fond*) after all; **et (puis) ~?** so what?; **après-demain** *adv* the day after tomorrow; **après-midi** [apʁɛmidi] *nm ou f inv* afternoon; **après-rasage** *nm inv* after-shave; **après-shampooing**

nm inv conditioner; **après-ski** *nm inv* snow boot

après-soleil [apʁɛsɔlɛj] *adj inv* after-sun *cpd* ▷ *nm* after-sun cream *ou* lotion

apte [apt] *adj*: **~ à qch/faire qch** capable of sth/doing sth; **~ (au service)** (*Mil*) fit (for service)

aquarelle [akwaʁɛl] *nf* watercolour

aquarium [akwaʁjɔm] *nm* aquarium

arabe [aʁab] *adj* Arabic; (*désert, cheval*) Arabian; (*nation, peuple*) Arab ▷ *nm* (*Ling*) Arabic ▷ *nm/f*: **A~** Arab

Arabie [aʁabi] *nf*: **l'~ Saoudite** *ou* **Séoudite** Saudi Arabia

arachide [aʁaʃid] *nf* groundnut (plant); (*graine*) peanut, groundnut

araignée [aʁeɲe] *nf* spider

arbitraire [aʁbitʁɛʁ] *adj* arbitrary

arbitre [aʁbitʁ] *nm* (*Sport*) referee (: *Tennis, Cricket*) umpire; (*fig*) arbiter, judge; (*Jur*) arbitrator; **arbitrer** /1/ *vt* to referee; to umpire; to arbitrate

arbre [aʁbʁ] *nm* tree; (*Tech*) shaft

arbuste [aʁbyst] *nm* small shrub

arc [aʁk] *nm* (*arme*) bow; (*Géom*) arc; (*Archit*) arch; **en ~ de cercle** semi-circular

arcade [aʁkad] *nf* arch(way); **~s** arcade *sg*, arches

arc-en-ciel [aʁkɑ̃sjɛl] *nm* rainbow

arche [aʁʃ] *nf* arch; **~ de Noé** Noah's Ark

archéologie [aʁkeɔlɔʒi] *nf* arch(a)eology; **archéologue** *nm/f* arch(a)eologist

archet [aʁʃɛ] *nm* bow

archipel [aʁʃipɛl] *nm* archipelago

architecte [aʁʃitɛkt] *nm* architect

architecture [aʁʃitɛktyʁ] *nf* architecture

archives [aʁʃiv] *nfpl* (*collection*) archives

arctique [aʁktik] *adj* Arctic ▷ *nm*: **l'A~** the Arctic

ardent, e [aʁdɑ̃, -ɑ̃t] *adj* (*soleil*) blazing; (*amour*) ardent, passionate; (*prière*) fervent

ardoise [aʀdwaz] nf slate

ardu, e [aʀdy] adj (travail) arduous; (problème) difficult

arène [aʀɛn] nf arena; **arènes** nfpl bull-ring sg

arête [aʀɛt] nf (de poisson) bone; (d'une montagne) ridge

argent [aʀʒɑ̃] nm (métal) silver; (monnaie) money; **~ de poche** pocket money; **~ liquide** ready money, (ready) cash; **argenterie** nf silverware

argentin, e [aʀʒɑ̃tɛ̃, -in] adj Argentinian ▷ nm/f: **A~, e** Argentinian

Argentine [aʀʒɑ̃tin] nf: **l'~** Argentina

argentique [aʀʒɑ̃tik] adj (appareil photo) film cpd

argile [aʀʒil] nf clay

argot [aʀgo] nm slang; **argotique** adj slang cpd; (très familier) slangy

argument [aʀgymɑ̃] nm argument

argumenter [aʀgymɑ̃te] /1/ vi to argue

aride [aʀid] adj arid

aristocratie [aʀistɔkʀasi] nf aristocracy; **aristocratique** adj aristocratic

arithmétique [aʀitmetik] adj arithmetic(al) ▷ nf arithmetic

arme [aʀm] nf weapon; **armes** nfpl weapons, arms; (blason) (coat of) arms; **~ à feu** firearm; **~s de destruction massive** weapons of mass destruction

armée [aʀme] nf army; **~ de l'air** Air Force; **~ de terre** Army

armer [aʀme] /1/ vt to arm; (arme à feu) to cock; (appareil photo) to wind on; **s'armer** vi: **s'~ de** to arm o.s. with; **~ qch de** to reinforce sth with

armistice [aʀmistis] nm armistice; **l'A~** ≈ Remembrance (BRIT) ou Veterans (US) Day

armoire [aʀmwaʀ] nf (tall) cupboard; (penderie) wardrobe (BRIT), closet (US)

armure [aʀmyʀ] nf armour no pl, suit of armour; **armurier** nm gunsmith

arnaque [aʀnak] (fam) nf swindling; **c'est de l'~** it's daylight robbery; **arnaquer** /1/ (fam) vt to do (fam)

arobase [aʀobaz] nf (Inform) 'at' symbol; **"paul ~ société point fr"** "paul at société dot fr"

aromates [aʀɔmat] nmpl seasoning sg, herbs (and spices)

aromathérapie [aʀɔmateʀapi] nf aromatherapy

aromatisé, e [aʀɔmatize] adj flavoured

arôme [aʀom] nm aroma

arracher [aʀaʃe] /1/ vt to pull out; (page etc) to tear off, tear out; (légume, herbe, souche) to pull up; (bras etc) to tear off; **s'arracher** vt (article très recherché) to fight over; **~ qch à qn** to snatch sth from sb; (fig) to wring sth out of sb

arrangement [aʀɑ̃ʒmɑ̃] nm arrangement

arranger [aʀɑ̃ʒe] /3/ vt to arrange; (réparer) to fix, put right; (régler) to settle, sort out; (convenir à) to suit, be convenient for; **cela m'arrange** that suits me (fine); **s'arranger** vi (se mettre d'accord) to come to an agreement ou arrangement; **je vais m'~** I'll manage; **ça va s'~** it'll sort itself out

arrestation [aʀɛstasjɔ̃] nf arrest

arrêt [aʀɛ] nm stopping; (de bus etc) stop; (Jur) judgment, decision; **être à l'~** to be stopped; **rester** ou **tomber en ~ devant** to stop short in front of; **sans ~** non-stop; (fréquemment) continually; **~ de travail** stoppage (of work)

arrêter [aʀete] /1/ vt to stop; (chauffage etc) to turn off, switch off; (fixer: date etc) to appoint, decide on; (criminel, suspect) to arrest; **s'arrêter** vi to stop; **~ de faire** to stop doing

arrhes [aʀ] nfpl deposit sg

arrière [aʀjɛʀ] nm back; (Sport) fullback ▷ adj inv: **siège/roue**

~ back ou rear seat/wheel; **à l'~**
behind, at the back; **en ~** behind;
(*regarder*) back, behind; (*tomber*,
aller) backwards; **arrière-goût** nm
aftertaste; **arrière-grand-mère** nf
great-grandmother; **arrière-grand-
père** nm great-grandfather; **arrière-
pays** nm inv hinterland; **arrière-
pensée** nf ulterior motive; (*doute*)
mental reservation; **arrière-plan**
nm background; **à l'arrière-plan** in
the background; **arrière-saison** nf
late autumn

arrimer [aʀime] /1/ vt (*cargaison*) to
stow; (*fixer*) to secure

arrivage [aʀivaʒ] nm consignment

arrivée [aʀive] nf arrival; (*ligne
d'arrivée*) finish

arriver [aʀive] /1/ vi to arrive;
(*survenir*) to happen, occur; **il arrive
à Paris à 8 h** he gets to ou arrives in
Paris at 8; **~ à** (*atteindre*) to reach; **~ à
(faire) qch** to manage (to do) sth;
en ~ à faire ... to end up doing ...; **il
arrive que ...** it happens that ...; **il
lui arrive de faire ...** he sometimes
does ...

arrobase [aʀɔbaz] nf (*Inform*) 'at'
symbol

arrogance [aʀɔgãs] nf arrogance

arrogant, e [aʀɔgã, -ãt] adj arrogant

arrondissement [aʀɔdismã] nm
(*Admin*) ≈ district

arroser [aʀoze] /1/ vt to water;
(*victoire etc*) to celebrate (over a
drink); (*Culin*) to baste; **arrosoir** nm
watering can

arsenal, -aux [aʀsənal, -o] nm
(*Navig*) naval dockyard; (*Mil*) arsenal;
(*fig*) gear, paraphernalia

art [aʀ] nm art

artère [aʀtɛʀ] nf (*Anat*) artery; (*rue*)
main road

arthrite [aʀtʀit] nf arthritis

artichaut [aʀtiʃo] nm artichoke

article [aʀtikl] nm article; (*Comm*)
item, article; **à l'~ de la mort** at the
point of death

articulation [aʀtikylasjɔ̃] nf
articulation; (*Anat*) joint

articuler [aʀtikyle] /1/ vt to
articulate

artificiel, le [aʀtifisjɛl] adj artificial

artisan [aʀtizã] nm artisan, (self-
employed) craftsman; **artisanal, e,
-aux** [aʀtizanal, -o] adj of ou made
by craftsmen; (*péj*) cottage industry
cpd; **de fabrication artisanale**
home-made; **artisanat** [aʀtizana]
nm arts and crafts pl

artiste [aʀtist] nm/f artist; (*Théât*,
Mus) performer; (*de variétés*)
entertainer; **artistique** adj artistic

as vb [a]; voir **avoir** ▷ nm [ɑs] ace

ascenseur [asãsœʀ] nm lift (*BRIT*),
elevator (*US*)

ascension [asãsjɔ̃] nf ascent; (*de
montagne*) climb; **l'A~** (*Rel*) the
Ascension

○ **L'ASCENSION**

○
○ The *fête de l'Ascension* is a public
○ holiday in France. It always falls on
○ a Thursday, usually in May. Many
○ French people take the following
○ Friday off work too and enjoy a long
○ weekend.

asiatique [azjatik] adj Asian, Asiatic
▷ nm/f: **A~** Asian

Asie [azi] nf: **l'~** Asia

asile [azil] nm (*refuge*) refuge,
sanctuary; **droit d'~** (*Pol*) (political)
asylum

aspect [aspɛ] nm appearance, look;
(*fig*) aspect, side; **à l'~ de** at the
sight of

asperge [aspɛʀʒ] nf asparagus no pl

asperger [aspɛʀʒe] /3/ vt to spray,
sprinkle

asphalte [asfalt] nm asphalt

asphyxier [asfiksje] /7/ vt to
suffocate, asphyxiate; (*fig*) to stifle

aspirateur [aspiʀatœʀ] nm vacuum
cleaner; **passer l'~** to vacuum

aspirer [aspiʀe] /1/ vt (air) to inhale; (liquide) to suck (up); (appareil) to suck ou draw up; ~ **à** to aspire to

aspirine [aspiʀin] nf aspirin

assagir [asaʒiʀ] /2/ vt, **s'assagir** vi to quieten down, settle down

assaillir [asajiʀ] /13/ vt to assail, attack

assaisonnement [asɛzɔnmɑ̃] nm seasoning

assaisonner [asɛzɔne] /1/ vt to season

assassin [asasɛ̃] nm murderer; assassin; **assassiner** /1/ vt to murder; (Pol) to assassinate

assaut [aso] nm assault, attack; **prendre d'~** to (take by) storm, assault; **donner l'~ (à)** to attack

assécher [aseʃe] /6/ vt to drain

assemblage [asɑ̃blaʒ] nm (action) assembling; **un ~ de** (fig) a collection of

assemblée [asɑ̃ble] nf (réunion) meeting; (public, assistance) gathering; (Pol) assembly; **l'A~ nationale (AN)** the (French) National Assembly

assembler [asɑ̃ble] /1/ vt (joindre, monter) to assemble, put together; (amasser) to gather (together), collect (together); **s'assembler** vi to gather

asseoir [aswaʀ] /26/ vt (malade, bébé) to sit up; (personne debout) to sit down; (autorité, réputation) to establish; **s'asseoir** vi to sit (o.s.) down

assez [ase] adv (suffisamment) enough, sufficiently; (passablement) rather, quite, fairly; ~ **de pain/ livres** enough ou sufficient bread/ books; **vous en avez ~?** have you got enough?; **j'en ai ~!** I've had enough!

assidu, e [asidy] adj assiduous, painstaking; (régulier) regular

assied etc [asje] vb voir **asseoir**

assiérai etc [asjeʀe] vb voir **asseoir**

assiette [asjɛt] nf plate; (contenu) plate(ful); **il n'est pas dans son ~** he's not feeling quite himself; ~ **à dessert** dessert ou side plate; ~ **anglaise** assorted cold meats; ~ **creuse** (soup) dish, soup plate; ~ **plate** (dinner) plate

assimiler [asimile] /1/ vt to assimilate, absorb; (comparer): ~ **qch/qn à** to liken ou compare sth/ sb to; **s'assimiler** (s'intégrer) to be assimilated ou absorbed

assis, e [asi, -iz] pp de **asseoir** ▷ adj sitting (down), seated

assistance [asistɑ̃s] nf (public) audience; (aide) assistance; **enfant de l'A~ (publique)** child in care

assistant, e [asistɑ̃, -ɑ̃t] nm/f assistant; (d'université) probationary lecturer; ~**e sociale** social worker

assisté, e [asiste] adj (Auto) power-assisted; ~ **par ordinateur** computer-assisted; **direction ~e** power steering

assister [asiste] /1/ vt to assist; ~ **à** (scène, événement) to witness; (conférence) to attend, be (present) at; (spectacle, match) to be at, see

association [asɔsjasjɔ̃] nf association

associé, e [asɔsje] nm/f associate; (Comm) partner

associer [asɔsje] /7/ vt to associate; ~ **qn à** (profits) to give sb a share of; (affaire) to make sb a partner in; (joie, triomphe) to include sb in; ~ **qch à** (joindre, allier) to combine sth with; **s'associer** vi to join together; **s'~ à** (couleurs, qualités) to be combined with; (opinions, joie de qn) to share in; **s'~ à** ou **avec qn pour faire** to join (forces) ou join together with sb to do

assoiffé, e [aswafe] adj thirsty

assommer [asɔme] /1/ vt (étourdir, abrutir) to knock out, stun

Assomption [asɔ̃psjɔ̃] nf: **l'~** the Assumption

L'ASSOMPTION

The *fête de l'Assomption*, more commonly known as "le 15 août" is a national holiday in France. Traditionally, large numbers of holidaymakers leave home on 15 August, frequently causing chaos on the roads.

assorti, e [asɔʀti] *adj* matched, matching; **fromages/légumes** **~s** assorted cheeses/vegetables; **~ à** matching; **assortiment** *nm* assortment, selection

assortir [asɔʀtiʀ] /2/ *vt* to match; **~ qch à** to match sth with; **~ qch de** to accompany sth with

assouplir [asupliʀ] /2/ *vt* to make supple; (*fig*) to relax; **assouplissant** *nm* (fabric) softener

assumer [asyme] /1/ *vt* (*fonction, emploi*) to assume, take on

assurance [asyʀɑ̃s] *nf* (*certitude*) assurance; (*confiance en soi*) (self-) confidence; (*contrat*) insurance (policy); (*secteur commercial*) insurance; **~ au tiers** third party insurance; **~ maladie (AM)** health insurance; **~ tous risques** (*Auto*) comprehensive insurance; **~s sociales (AS)** ≈ National Insurance (*BRIT*), ≈ Social Security (*US*); **assurance-vie** *nf* life assurance *ou* insurance

assuré, e [asyʀe] *adj* (*réussite, échec, victoire etc*) certain, sure; (*démarche, voix*) assured; (*pas*) steady ▷ *nm/f* insured (person); **assurément** *adv* assuredly, most certainly

assurer [asyʀe] /1/ *vt* (*Comm*) to insure; (*victoire etc*) to ensure; (*frontières, pouvoir*) to make secure; (*service, garde*) to provide, operate; **s'assurer (contre)** (*Comm*) to insure o.s. (against); **~ à qn que** to assure sb that; **~ qn de** to assure sb of; **s'~ de/ que** (*vérifier*) to make sure of/that; **s'~ (de)** (*aide de qn*) to secure

asthmatique [asmatik] *adj, nm/f* asthmatic

asthme [asm] *nm* asthma

asticot [astiko] *nm* maggot

astre [astʀ] *nm* star

astrologie [astʀɔlɔʒi] *nf* astrology

astronaute [astʀonot] *nm/f* astronaut

astronomie [astʀɔnɔmi] *nf* astronomy

astuce [astys] *nf* shrewdness, astuteness; (*truc*) trick, clever way; **astucieux, -euse** *adj* clever

atelier [atəlje] *nm* workshop; (*de peintre*) studio

athée [ate] *adj* atheistic ▷ *nm/f* atheist

Athènes [atɛn] *n* Athens

athlète [atlɛt] *nm/f* (*Sport*) athlete; **athlétisme** *nm* athletics *sg*

atlantique [atlɑ̃tik] *adj* Atlantic ▷ *nm*: **l'(océan) A~** the Atlantic (Ocean)

atlas [atlɑs] *nm* atlas

atmosphère [atmɔsfɛʀ] *nf* atmosphere

atome [atom] *nm* atom; **atomique** *adj* atomic; nuclear

atomiseur [atɔmizœʀ] *nm* atomizer

atout [atu] *nm* trump; (*fig*) asset

atroce [atʀos] *adj* atrocious

attachant, e [ataʃɑ̃, -ɑ̃t] *adj* engaging, likeable

attache [ataʃ] *nf* clip, fastener; (*fig*) tie

attacher [ataʃe] /1/ *vt* to tie up; (*étiquette*) to attach, tie on; (*ceinture*) to fasten; (*souliers*) to do up ▷ *vi* (*poêle, riz*) to stick; **s'~ à** (*par affection*) to become attached to; **~ qch à** to tie *ou* fasten *ou* attach sth to

attaque [atak] *nf* attack; (*cérébrale*) stroke; (*d'épilepsie*) fit

attaquer [atake] /1/ *vt* to attack; (*en justice*) to sue ▷ *vi* to attack; **s'attaquer à** *vt* (*personne*) to attack; (*épidémie, misère*) to tackle

attarder [ataʀde] /1/: **s'attarder** *vi* to linger

atteindre [atɛ̃dʀ] /49/ vt to reach; (blesser) to hit; (émouvoir) to affect; **atteint, e** adj (Méd): **être atteint de** to be suffering from ▷ nf attack; **hors d'atteinte** out of reach; **porter atteinte à** to strike a blow at

attendant [atɑ̃dɑ̃]: **en ~** adv meanwhile, in the meantime

attendre [atɑ̃dʀ] /41/ vt to wait for; (être destiné ou réservé à) to await, be in store for ▷ vi to wait; **s'~ à (ce que)** to expect (that); **attendez-moi, s'il vous plaît** wait for me, please; **~ un enfant** to be expecting a baby; **~ de faire/d'être** to wait until one does/is; **attendez qu'il vienne** wait until he comes; **~ qch de** to expect sth of;

    Attention à ne pas traduire
    attendre par to attend.

attendrir [atɑ̃dʀiʀ] /2/ vt to move (to pity); (viande) to tenderize

attendu, e [atɑ̃dy] adj (événement) long-awaited; (prévu) expected; **~ que** considering that, since

attentat [atɑ̃ta] nm assassination attempt; **~ à la pudeur** indecent assault no pl; **~ suicide** suicide bombing

attente [atɑ̃t] nf wait; (espérance) expectation

attenter [atɑ̃te] /1/: **~ à** vt (liberté) to violate; **~ à la vie de qn** to make an attempt on sb's life

attentif, -ive [atɑ̃tif, -iv] adj (auditeur) attentive; (travail) careful; **~ à** paying attention to

attention [atɑ̃sjɔ̃] nf attention; (prévenance) attention, thoughtfulness no pl; **à l'~ de** for the attention of; **faire ~ (à)** to be careful (of); **faire ~ (à ce) que** to be ou make sure that; **~!** careful!, watch out!; **~ à la voiture!** watch out for that car!; **attentionné, e** [atɑ̃sjɔne] adj thoughtful, considerate

atténuer [atenɥe] /1/ vt (douleur) to alleviate, ease; (couleurs) to soften;

s'atténuer vi to ease; (violence etc) to abate

atterrir [ateʀiʀ] /2/ vi to land; **atterrissage** nm landing

attestation nf certificate

attirant, e [atiʀɑ̃, -ɑ̃t] adj attractive, appealing

attirer [atiʀe] /1/ vt to attract; (appâter) to lure, entice; **~ qn dans un coin/vers soi** to draw sb into a corner/towards one; **~ l'attention de qn** to attract sb's attention; **~ l'attention de qn sur qch** to draw sb's attention to sth; **s'~ des ennuis** to bring trouble upon o.s., get into trouble

attitude [atityd] nf attitude; (position du corps) bearing

attraction [atʀaksjɔ̃] nf attraction; (de cabaret, cirque) number

attrait [atʀɛ] nm appeal, attraction

attraper [atʀape] /1/ vt to catch; (habitude, amende) to get, pick up; (fam: duper) to con; **se faire ~** (fam) to be told off

attrayant, e [atʀɛjɑ̃, -ɑ̃t] adj attractive

attribuer [atʀibɥe] /1/ vt (prix) to award; (rôle, tâche) to allocate, assign; (imputer): **~ qch à** to attribute sth to; **s'attribuer** vt (s'approprier) to claim for o.s.

attrister [atʀiste] /1/ vt to sadden

attroupement [atʀupmɑ̃] nm crowd

attrouper [atʀupe] /1/: **s'attrouper** vi to gather

au [o] prép voir **à**

aubaine [obɛn] nf godsend

aube [ob] nf dawn, daybreak; **à l'~** at dawn ou daybreak

aubépine [obepin] nf hawthorn

auberge [obɛʀʒ] nf inn; **~ de jeunesse** youth hostel

aubergine [obɛʀʒin] nf aubergine

aucun, e [okœ̃, -yn] adj, pron no; (positif) any ▷ pron none; (positif) any(one); **sans ~ doute** without any doubt; **plus qu'~ autre** more than any other; **il le fera mieux qu'~ de nous** he'll do it better than any of us; **~ des deux** neither of the two; **~ d'entre eux** none of them

audace [odas] *nf* daring, boldness; (*péj*) audacity; **audacieux, -euse** *adj* daring, bold

au-delà [od(ə)la] *adv* beyond ▷ *nm*: **l'~** the hereafter; **~ de** beyond

au-dessous [odsu] *adv* underneath; below; **~ de** under(neath), below; (*limite, somme etc*) below, under; (*dignité, condition*) below

au-dessus [odsy] *adv* above; **~ de** above

au-devant [od(ə)vã]: **~ de** *prép*: **aller ~ de** (*personne, danger*) to go (out) and meet; (*souhaits de qn*) to anticipate

audience [odjãs] *nf* audience; (*Jur: séance*) hearing

audio-visuel, le [odjovizɥɛl] *adj* audio-visual

audition [odisjɔ̃] *nf* (*ouïe, écoute*) hearing; (*Jur: de témoins*) examination; (*Mus, Théât: épreuve*) audition

auditoire [oditwaʀ] *nm* audience

augmentation [ogmɑ̃tasjɔ̃] *nf* increase; **~ (de salaire)** rise (in salary) (*BRIT*), (pay) raise (*US*)

augmenter [ogmɑ̃te] /1/ *vt* to increase; (*salaire, prix*) to increase, raise, put up; (*employé*) to increase the salary of ▷ *vi* to increase

augure [ogyʀ] *nm*: **de bon/mauvais ~** of good/ill omen

aujourd'hui [oʒuʀdɥi] *adv* today

aumône [omon] *nf* alms *sg* (*pl inv*); **aumônier** *nm* chaplain

auparavant [opaʀavã] *adv* before(hand)

auprès [opʀɛ]: **~ de** *prép* next to, close to; (*recourir, s'adresser*) to; (*en comparaison de*) compared with

auquel [okɛl] *pron voir* **lequel**

aurai *etc* [ɔʀe] *vb voir* **avoir**

aurons *etc* [oʀɔ̃] *vb voir* **avoir**

aurore [ɔʀɔʀ] *nf* dawn, daybreak

ausculter [ɔskylte] /1/ *vt* to sound

aussi [osi] *adv* (*également*) also, too; (*de comparaison*) as ▷ *conj* therefore, consequently; **~ fort que** as strong as; **moi ~** me too

aussitôt [osito] *adv* straight away, immediately; **~ que** as soon as

austère [ɔstɛʀ] *adj* austere

austral, e [ɔstʀal] *adj* southern

Australie [ɔstʀali] *nf*: **l'~** Australia; **australien, ne** *adj* Australian ▷ *nm/f*: **Australien, ne** Australian

autant [otã] *adv* so much; **je ne savais pas que tu la détestais ~** I didn't know you hated her so much; (*comparatif*): **~ (que)** as much (as); (*nombre*) as many (as); **~ (de)** so much (*ou* many); as much (*ou* many); **~ partir** we (*ou* you *etc*) may as well leave; **~ dire que ...** one might as well say that ...; **pour ~** for all that; **d'~ plus/mieux (que)** all the more/the better (since)

autel [otɛl] *nm* altar

auteur [otœʀ] *nm* author

authentique [otɑ̃tik] *adj* authentic, genuine

auto [oto] *nf* car; **autobiographie** *nf* autobiography; **autobronzant** *nm* self-tanning cream (*or lotion etc*); **autobus** *nm* bus; **autocar** *nm* coach

autochtone [ɔtɔktɔn] *nm/f* native

auto: autocollant, e *adj* self-adhesive; (*enveloppe*) self-seal ▷ *nm* sticker; **autocuiseur** *nm* pressure cooker; **autodéfense** *nf* self-defence; **autodidacte** *nm/f* self-taught person; **auto-école** *nf* driving school; **autographe** *nm* autograph

automate [ɔtɔmat] *nm* (*machine*) (automatic) machine

automatique [ɔtɔmatik] *adj* automatic ▷ *nm*: **l'~** ≈ direct dialling

automne [ɔtɔn] *nm* autumn (*BRIT*), fall (*US*)

automobile [ɔtɔmɔbil] *adj* motor *cpd* ▷ *nf* (motor) car; **automobiliste** *nm/f* motorist

automutiler [otomytile] /1/: **s'automutiler** *vt* to self-harm
autonome [ɔtɔnɔm] *adj* autonomous; **autonomie** *nf* autonomy; (*Pol*) self-government
autopsie [ɔtɔpsi] *nf* post-mortem (examination), autopsy
autoradio [otoʀadjo] *nf* car radio
autorisation [ɔtɔʀizasjɔ̃] *nf* authorization; (*papiers*) permit
autorisé, e [ɔtɔʀize] *adj* (*opinion, sources*) authoritative
autoriser [ɔtɔʀize] /1/ *vt* to give permission for, authorize; (*fig*) to allow (of)
autoritaire [ɔtɔʀitɛʀ] *adj* authoritarian
autorité [ɔtɔʀite] *nf* authority; **faire ~** to be authoritative
autoroute [otoʀut] *nf* motorway (*BRIT*), expressway (*US*); **~ de l'information** (*Inform*) information superhighway

auto-stop [otostɔp] *nm*: **faire de l'~** to hitch-hike; **prendre qn en ~** to give sb a lift; **auto-stoppeur, -euse** *nm/f* hitch-hiker
autour [otuʀ] *adv* around; **~ de** around; **tout ~** all around

 MOT-CLÉ

autre [otʀ] *adj* **1** (*différent*) other, different; **je préférerais un**

autre verre I'd prefer another *ou* a different glass
2 (*supplémentaire*) other; **je voudrais un autre verre d'eau** I'd like another glass of water
3: **autre chose** something else; **autre part** somewhere else; **d'autre part** on the other hand
▸ *pron*: **un autre** another (one); **nous/vous autres** us/you; **d'autres** others; **l'autre** the other (one); **les autres** the others; (*autrui*) others; **l'un et l'autre** both of them; **se détester l'un l'autre/les uns les autres** to hate each other *ou* one another; **d'une semaine/minute à l'autre** from one week/minute *ou* moment to the next; (*incessamment*) any week/minute *ou* moment now; **entre autres** (*personnes*) among others; (*choses*) among other things

autrefois [otʀəfwa] *adv* in the past
autrement [otʀəmɑ̃] *adv* differently; (*d'une manière différente*) in another way; (*sinon*) otherwise; **~ dit** in other words
Autriche [otʀiʃ] *nf*: **l'~** Austria; **autrichien, ne** *adj* Austrian ▸ *nm/f*: **Autrichien, ne** Austrian
autruche [otʀyʃ] *nf* ostrich
aux [o] *prép voir* **à**
auxiliaire [ɔksiljɛʀ] *adj, nm/f* auxiliary
auxquels, auxquelles [okɛl] *pron voir* **lequel**
avalanche [avalɑ̃ʃ] *nf* avalanche
avaler [avale] /1/ *vt* to swallow
avance [avɑ̃s] *nf* (*de troupes etc*) advance; (*progrès*) progress; (*d'argent*) advance; (*opposé à retard*) lead; **avances** *nfpl* (*amoureuses*) advances; **(être) en ~** (to be) early; (*sur un programme*) (to be) ahead of schedule; **d'~, à l'~** in advance
avancé, e [avɑ̃se] *adj* advanced; (*travail etc*) well on, well under way

avancement [avɑ̃smɑ̃] nm
(professionnel) promotion

avancer [avɑ̃se] /3/ vi to move
forward, advance; (projet, travail) to
make progress; (montre, réveil) to be
fast to gain ▷ vt to move forward,
advance; (argent) to advance; (montre,
pendule) to put forward; **s'avancer**
vi to move forward, advance; (fig) to
commit o.s.

avant [avɑ̃] prép before ▷ adj inv:
siège/roue ~ front seat/wheel
▷ nm (d'un véhicule, bâtiment) front;
(Sport: joueur) forward; **~ qu'il
parte/de partir** before he leaves/
leaving; **~ tout** (surtout) above all;
à l'~ (dans un véhicule) in (the) front;
en ~ (se pencher, tomber) forward(s);
partir en ~ to go on ahead; **en ~ de**
in front of

avantage [avɑ̃taʒ] nm advantage;
~s sociaux fringe benefits;
avantager /3/ vt (favoriser) to favour;
(embellir) to flatter; **avantageux,
-euse** adj (prix) attractive

avant- avant-bras nm inv forearm;
avant-coureur adj inv: **signe
avant-coureur** advance indication
ou sign; **avant-dernier, -ière** adj,
nm/f next to last, last but one;
avant-goût nm foretaste; **avant-
hier** adv the day before yesterday;
avant-première nf (de film) preview;
avant-veille nf: **l'avant-veille** two
days before

avare [avaʀ] adj miserly, avaricious
▷ nm/f miser; **~ de compliments**
stingy ou sparing with one's
compliments

avec [avɛk] prép with; (à l'égard de)
to(wards), with; **et ~ ça?** (dans un
magasin) anything ou something else?

avenir [avniʀ] nm: **l'~** the future; **à
l'~** in future; **carrière/politicien
d'~** career/politician with prospects
ou a future

aventure [avɑ̃tyʀ] nf: **l'~** adventure;
une ~ (amoureuse) an affair;

aventureux, -euse adj adventurous,
venturesome; (projet) risky, chancy

avenue [avny] nf avenue

avérer [aveʀe] /6/: **s'avérer** vr:
s'~ faux/coûteux to prove (to be)
wrong/expensive

averse [avɛʀs] nf shower

averti, e [avɛʀti] adj (well-)
informed

avertir [avɛʀtiʀ] /2/ vt: **~ qn (de
qch/que)** to warn sb (of sth/that);
(renseigner) to inform sb (of sth/
that); **avertissement** nm warning;
avertisseur nm horn, siren

aveu, x [avø] nm confession

aveugle [avœgl] adj blind ▷ nm/f
blind person

aviation [avjasjɔ̃] nf aviation; (sport,
métier de pilote) flying; (Mil) air force

avide [avid] adj eager; (péj) greedy,
grasping

avion [avjɔ̃] nm (aero)plane (BRIT),
(air)plane (US); **aller (quelque part)
en ~** to go (somewhere) by plane, fly
(somewhere); **par ~** by airmail; **~ à
réaction** jet (plane)

aviron [aviʀɔ̃] nm oar; (sport): **l'~**
rowing

avis [avi] nm opinion; (notification)
notice; **à mon ~** in my opinion;
changer d'~ to change one's mind;
jusqu'à nouvel ~ until further notice

aviser [avize] /1/ vt (informer): **~ qn
de/que** to advise ou inform ou notify
sb of/that ▷ vi to think about things,
assess the situation; **nous aviserons
sur place** we'll work something out
once we're there; **s'~ de qch/que**
to become suddenly aware of sth/
that; **s'~ de faire** to take it into one's
head to do

avocat, e [avɔka, -at] nm/f (Jur)
≈ barrister (BRIT), lawyer ▷ nm
(Culin) avocado (pear); **l'~ de la
défense/partie civile** the counsel
for the defence/plaintiff; **~ général**
assistant public prosecutor

avoine [avwan] nf oats pl

MOT-CLÉ

avoir [avwaʀ] /34/ vt **1** (posséder)
to have; **elle a deux enfants/une
belle maison** she has (got) two
children/a lovely house; **il a les yeux
bleus** he has (got) blue eyes; **vous
avez du sel?** do you have any salt?;
avoir du courage/de la patience to
be brave/patient
2 (éprouver): **avoir de la peine** to be
ou feel sad; voir aussi **faim, peur**
3 (âge, dimensions) to be; **il a 3 ans** he
is 3 (years old); **le mur a 3 mètres de
haut** the wall is 3 metres high
4 (fam: duper) to do, have; **on vous a
eu!** you've been done ou had!; (fait une
plaisanterie) we ou they had you there
5: **en avoir contre qn** to have a
grudge against sb; **en avoir assez**
to be fed up; **j'en ai pour une demi-
heure** it'll take me half an hour
6 (obtenir, attraper) to get; **j'ai réussi
à avoir mon train** I managed to
get ou catch my train; **j'ai réussi à
avoir le renseignement qu'il me
fallait** I managed to get (hold of) the
information I needed
▶ vb aux **1** to have; **avoir mangé/
dormi** to have eaten/slept
2 (avoir +à +infinitif): **avoir à faire
qch** to have to do sth; **vous n'avez
qu'à lui demander** you only have
to ask him
▶ vb impers **1**: **il y a** (+ singulier)
there is; (+ pluriel) there are; **il y
avait du café/des gâteaux** there
was coffee/there were cakes; **qu'y
a-t-il?, qu'est-ce qu'il y a?** what's
the matter?, what is it?; **il doit y
avoir une explication** there must
be an explanation; **il n'y a qu'à ...**
we (ou you etc) will just have to ...; **il
ne peut y en avoir qu'un** there can
only be one
2: **il y a** (temporel): **il y a 10 ans**
10 years ago; **il y a 10 ans/
longtemps que je le connais** I've

known him for 10 years/a long time;
il y a 10 ans qu'il est arrivé it's 10
years since he arrived
▶ nm assets pl, resources pl; (Comm)
credit

avortement [avɔʀtəmɑ̃] nm
abortion
avouer [avwe] /1/ vt (crime, défaut)
to confess (to); **~ avoir fait/que** to
admit ou confess to having done/that
avril [avʀil] nm April
axe [aks] nm axis (pl axes); (de roue etc)
axle; (fig) main line; **~ routier** trunk
road (BRIT), main road, highway (US)
ayons etc [ɛjɔ̃] vb voir **avoir**

bâbord [babɔʀ] *nm*: **à** *ou* **par ~** to port, on the port side

baby-foot [babifut] *nm inv* table football

baby-sitting [babisitiŋ] *nm* baby-sitting; **faire du ~** to baby-sit

bac [bak] *nm* (*récipient*) tub

baccalauréat [bakalɔʀea] *nm* ≈ high school diploma

bâcler [bakle] /1/ *vt* to botch (up)

baffe [baf] *nf* (*fam*) slap, clout

bafouiller [bafuje] /1/ *vi, vt* to stammer

bagage [bagaʒ] *nm*: **~s** luggage *sg*; (*connaissances*) background, knowledge; **~s à main** hand-luggage

bagarre [bagaʀ] *nf* fight, brawl; **bagarrer** /1/: **se bagarrer** *vi* to (have a) fight

bagnole [baɲɔl] *nf* (*fam*) car

bague [bag] *nf* ring; **~ de fiançailles** engagement ring

baguette [bagɛt] *nf* stick; (*cuisine chinoise*) chopstick; (*de chef d'orchestre*) baton; (*pain*) stick of (French) bread; **~ magique** magic wand

baie [bɛ] *nf* (*Géo*) bay; (*fruit*) berry; **~ (vitrée)** picture window

baignade [bɛɲad] *nf* bathing; **"~ interdite"** "no bathing"

baigner [beɲe] /1/ *vt* (*bébé*) to bath; **se baigner** *vi* to go swimming *ou* bathing; **baignoire** *nf* bath(tub)

bail (*pl* **baux**) [baj, bo] *nm* lease

bâiller [baje] /1/ *vi* to yawn; (*être ouvert*) to gape

bain [bɛ̃] *nm* bath; **prendre un ~** to have a bath; **se mettre dans le ~** (*fig*) to get into (the way of) it *ou* things; **~ de bouche** mouthwash; **~ moussant** bubble bath; **~ de soleil; prendre un ~ de soleil** to sunbathe; **bain-marie** *nm*: **faire chauffer au bain-marie** (*boîte etc*) to immerse in boiling water

baiser [beze] /1/ *nm* kiss ▷ *vt* (*main, front*) to kiss; (*fam!*) to screw (*!*)

baisse [bɛs] *nf* fall, drop; **en ~** falling

baisser [bese] /1/ *vt* to lower; (*radio, chauffage*) to turn down ▷ *vi* to fall, drop, go down; (*vue, santé*) to fail, dwindle; **se baisser** *vi* to bend down

bal [bal] *nm* dance; (*grande soirée*) ball; **~ costumé/masqué** fancy-dress/masked ball

balade [balad] (*fam*) *nf* (*à pied*) walk, stroll; (*en voiture*) drive; **balader** /1/ (*fam*): **se balader** *vi* to go for a walk *ou* stroll; to go for a drive; **baladeur** [baladœʀ] *nm* personal stereo, Walkman®

balai [balɛ] *nm* broom, brush

balance [balɑ̃s] *nf* scales *pl*; (*signe*): **la B~** Libra; **~ commerciale** balance of trade

balancer [balɑ̃se] /3/ *vt* to swing; (*lancer*) to fling, chuck; (*renvoyer, jeter*) to chuck out; **se balancer** *vi* to swing; to rock; **se ~ de qch** (*fam*) not to give a toss about sth; **balançoire** nf swing; (sur pivot) seesaw

balayer [baleje] /8/ vt (feuilles etc) to sweep up, brush up; (pièce, cour) to sweep; (chasser) to sweep away ou aside; (radar) to scan; **balayeur, -euse** [balejœʀ, -øz] nm/f road sweeper ▷ nf (engin) road sweeper

balbutier [balbysje] /7/ vi, vt to stammer

balcon [balkɔ̃] nm balcony; (Théât) dress circle

Bâle [bɑl] n Basle ou Basel

Baléares [baleaʀ] nfpl: **les ~** the Balearic Islands, the Balearics

baleine [balɛn] nf whale

balise [baliz] nf (Navig) beacon, (marker) buoy; (Aviat) runway light, beacon; (Auto, Ski) sign, marker; **baliser** /1/ vt to mark out (with beacons ou lights etc)

balle [bal] nf (de fusil) bullet; (de sport) ball; (fam: franc) franc

ballerine [bal(ə)ʀin] nf (danseuse) ballet dancer; (chaussure) pump, ballet shoe

ballet [balɛ] nm ballet

ballon [balɔ̃] nm (de sport) ball; (jouet, Aviat) balloon; **~ de football** football; **~ d'oxygène** oxygen bottle

balnéaire [balneɛʀ] adj seaside cpd; **station ~** seaside resort

balustrade [balystʀad] nf railings pl, handrail

bambin [bɑ̃bɛ̃] nm little child

bambou [bɑ̃bu] nm bamboo

banal, e [banal] adj banal, commonplace; (péj) trite; **banalité** nf banality

banane [banan] nf banana; (sac) waist-bag, bum-bag

banc [bɑ̃] nm seat, bench; (de poissons) shoal; **~ d'essai** (fig) testing ground

bancaire [bɑ̃kɛʀ] adj banking; (chèque, carte) bank cpd

bancal, e [bɑ̃kal] adj wobbly

bandage [bɑ̃daʒ] nm bandage

bande [bɑ̃d] nf (de tissu etc) strip; (Méd) bandage; (motif, dessin) stripe; (groupe) band; (péj): **une ~ de** a bunch ou crowd of; **faire ~ à part** to keep to o.s.; **~ dessinée (BD)** comic strip; **~ magnétique** magnetic tape; **~ sonore** sound track

bande-annonce [bɑ̃danɔ̃s] nf trailer

bandeau, x [bɑ̃do] nm headband; (sur les yeux) blindfold

bander [bɑ̃de] /1/ vt (blessure) to bandage; **~ les yeux à qn** to blindfold sb

bandit [bɑ̃di] nm bandit

bandoulière [bɑ̃duljɛʀ] nf: **en ~** (slung ou worn) across the shoulder

Bangladesh [bɑ̃gladɛʃ] nm: **le ~** Bangladesh

banlieue [bɑ̃ljø] nf suburbs pl; **quartiers de ~** suburban areas; **trains de ~** commuter trains

bannir [baniʀ] /2/ vt to banish

banque [bɑ̃k] nf bank; (activités) banking; **~ de données** data bank

banquet [bɑ̃kɛ] nm dinner; (d'apparat) banquet

banquette [bɑ̃kɛt] nf seat

banquier [bɑ̃kje] nm banker

banquise [bɑ̃kiz] nf ice field

baptême [batɛm] nm christening; baptism; **~ de l'air** first flight

baptiser [batize] /1/ vt to christen; to baptize

bar [baʀ] nm bar

baraque [baʀak] nf shed; (fam) house; **~ foraine** fairground stand; **baraqué, e** (fam) adj well-built, hefty

barbant, e [baʀbɑ̃, -ɑ̃t] adj (fam) deadly (boring)

barbare [baʀbaʀ] adj barbaric

barbe [baʀb] nf beard; **(au nez et) à la ~ de qn** (fig) under sb's very nose; **la ~!** (fam) damn it!; **quelle ~!** (fam) what a drag ou bore!; **~ à papa** candy-floss (BRIT), cotton candy (US)

barbelé [baʀbəle] adj, nm: **(fil de fer) ~** barbed wire no pl

barbiturique [baʀbityʀik] *nm*
barbiturate

barbouiller [baʀbuje] /1/ *vt* to daub;
avoir l'estomac barbouillé to feel
queasy *ou* sick

barbu, e [baʀby] *adj* bearded

barder [baʀde] /1/ *vi* (*fam*): **ça va ~**
sparks will fly

barème [baʀɛm] *nm* (*Scol*) scale;
(*liste*) table

baril [baʀi(l)] *nm* barrel; (*de poudre*)
keg

bariolé, e [baʀjɔle] *adj* many-
coloured, rainbow-coloured

baromètre [baʀɔmɛtʀ] *nm* barometer

baron [baʀɔ̃] *nm* baron

baronne [baʀɔn] *nf* baroness

baroque [baʀɔk] *adj* (*Art*) baroque;
(*fig*) weird

barque [baʀk] *nf* small boat

barquette [baʀkɛt] *nf* small boat-
shaped tart; (*récipient: en aluminium*)
tub; (: *en bois*) basket; (*pour repas*)
tray; (*pour fruits*) punnet

barrage [baʀaʒ] *nm* dam; (*sur route*)
roadblock, barricade

barre [baʀ] *nf* (*de fer etc*) rod; (*Navig*)
helm; (*écrite*) line, stroke

barreau, x [baʀo] *nm* bar; (*Jur*): **le
~** the Bar

barrer [baʀe] /1/ *vt* (*route etc*) to
block; (*mot*) to cross out; (*chèque*)
to cross (*BRIT*); (*Navig*) to steer; **se
barrer** *vi* (*fam*) to clear off

barrette [baʀɛt] *nf* (*pour cheveux*)
(hair) slide (*BRIT*) *ou* clip (*US*)

barricader [baʀikade] /1/: **se
barricader** *vi*: **se ~ chez soi** to
lock o.s. in

barrière [baʀjɛʀ] *nf* fence; (*obstacle*)
barrier; (*porte*) gate

barrique [baʀik] *nf* barrel, cask

bar-tabac [baʀtaba] *nm* bar (*which
sells tobacco and stamps*)

bas, basse [bɑ, bɑs] *adj* low ▷ *nm*
(*vêtement*) stocking; (*partie inférieure*):
le ~ de the lower part *ou* foot *ou*
bottom of ▷ *adv* low; (*parler*) softly;

au ~ mot at the lowest estimate;
enfant en ~ âge young child; **en
~** down below; (*d'une liste, d'un mur
etc*) at (*ou* to) the bottom; (*dans une
maison*) downstairs; **en ~ de** at the
bottom of; **à ~ la dictature!** down
with dictatorship!

bas-côté [bakote] *nm* (*de route*) verge
(*BRIT*), shoulder (*US*)

basculer [baskyle] /1/ *vi* to fall over,
topple (over); (*benne*) to tip up ▷ *vt*
(*contenu*) to tip out; (*benne*) tip up

base [bɑz] *nf* base; (*fondement,
principe*) basis (*pl* bases); **la ~** (*Pol*) the
rank and file; **de ~** basic; **à ~ de café
etc** coffee *etc* -based; **~ de données**
database; **baser** /1/ *vt*: **baser qch
sur** to base sth on; **se baser sur**
(*données, preuves*) to base one's
argument on

bas-fond [bafɔ̃] *nm* (*Navig*) shallow;
bas-fonds *nmpl* (*fig*) dregs

basilic [bazilik] *nm* (*Culin*) basil

basket [baskɛt] *nm* basketball

baskets [baskɛt] *nfpl* trainers (*BRIT*),
sneakers (*US*)

basque [bask] *adj* Basque ▷ *nm/f*: **B~**
Basque; **le Pays ~** the Basque country

basse [bɑs] *adj voir* **bas** ▷ *nf* (*Mus*)
bass; **basse-cour** *nf* farmyard

bassin [basɛ̃] *nm* (*pièce d'eau*) pond,
pool; (*de fontaine, Géo*) basin; (*Anat*)
pelvis; (*portuaire*) dock

bassine [basin] *nf* basin; (*contenu*)
bowl, bowlful

basson [bɑsɔ̃] *nm* bassoon

bat [ba] *vb voir* **battre**

bataille [bataj] *nf* battle; (*rixe*) fight;
elle avait les cheveux en ~ her hair
was a mess

bateau, x [bato] *nm* boat; ship;
bateau-mouche *nm* (*passenger*)
pleasure boat (*on the Seine*)

bâti, e [bɑti] *adj* (*terrain*) developed;
bien ~ well-built

bâtiment [bɑtimɑ̃] *nm* building;
(*Navig*) ship, vessel; (*industrie*): **le ~**
the building trade

bâtir [bɑtiʀ] /2/ vt to build
bâtisse [bɑtis] nf building
bâton [bɑtɔ̃] nm stick; **parler à ~s rompus** to chat about this and that
bats [ba] vb voir **battre**
battement [batmɑ̃] nm (de cœur) beat; (intervalle) interval (between classes, trains etc); **10 minutes de ~** 10 minutes to spare
batterie [batʀi] nf (Mil, Élec) battery; (Mus) drums pl, drum kit; **~ de cuisine** kitchen utensils pl; (casseroles etc) pots and pans pl
batteur [batœʀ] nm (Mus) drummer; (appareil) whisk
battre [batʀ] /41/ vt to beat; (blé) to thresh; (cartes) to shuffle; (passer au peigne fin) to scour ▷ vi (cœur) to beat; (volets etc) to bang, rattle; **se battre** vi to fight; **~ la mesure** to beat time; **~ son plein** to be at its height, be going full swing; **~ des mains** to clap one's hands
baume [bom] nm balm
bavard, e [bavaʀ, -aʀd] adj (very) talkative; gossipy; **bavarder** /1/ vi to chatter; (indiscrètement) to gossip; (révéler un secret) to blab
baver [bave] /1/ vi to dribble; (chien) to slobber, slaver; **en ~** (fam) to have a hard time (of it)
bavoir [bavwaʀ] nm bib
bavure [bavyʀ] nf smudge; (fig) hitch; (policière etc) blunder
bazar [bazaʀ] nm general store; (fam) jumble; **bazarder** /1/ vt (fam) to chuck out
BCBG sigle adj (= bon chic bon genre) smart and trendy, ≈ preppy
BD sigle f = **bande dessinée**
bd abr = **boulevard**
béant, e [beɑ̃, -ɑ̃t] adj gaping
beau (bel), belle, beaux [bo, bɛl] adj beautiful, lovely; (homme) handsome ▷ adv: **il fait ~** the weather's fine ▷ nm: **un ~ jour** one (fine) day; **de plus belle** more than ever, even more; **bel et bien** well

and truly; **le plus ~ c'est que ...** the best of it is that ...; **on a ~ essayer** however hard ou no matter how hard we try; **faire le ~** (chien) to sit up and beg

 MOT-CLÉ

beaucoup [boku] adv **1** a lot; **il boit beaucoup** he drinks a lot; **il ne boit pas beaucoup** he doesn't drink much ou a lot
2 (suivi de plus, trop etc) much, a lot; **il est beaucoup plus grand** he is much ou a lot ou far taller; **c'est beaucoup plus cher** it's a lot ou much more expensive; **il a beaucoup plus de temps que moi** he has much ou a lot more time than me; **il y a beaucoup plus de touristes ici** there are a lot ou many more tourists here; **beaucoup trop vite** much too fast; **il fume beaucoup trop** he smokes far too much
3: **beaucoup de** (nombre) many, a lot of; (quantité) a lot of; **beaucoup d'étudiants/de touristes** a lot of ou many students/tourists; **beaucoup de courage** a lot of courage; **il n'a pas beaucoup d'argent** he hasn't got much ou a lot of money
4: **de beaucoup** by far

beau: beau-fils nm son-in-law; (remariage) stepson; **beau-frère** nm brother-in-law; **beau-père** nm father-in-law; (remariage) stepfather
beauté [bote] nf beauty; **de toute ~** beautiful; **finir qch en ~** to complete sth brilliantly
beaux-arts [bozaʀ] nmpl fine arts
beaux-parents [boparɑ̃] nmpl wife's/husband's family, in-laws
bébé [bebe] nm baby
bec [bɛk] nm beak, bill; (de cafetière etc) spout; (de casserole etc) lip; (fam) mouth; **~ de gaz** (street) gaslamp

bêche [bɛʃ] nf spade; **bêcher** /1/ vt to dig

bedaine [bədɛn] nf paunch

bedonnant, e [bədɔnɑ̃, -ɑ̃t] adj potbellied

bée [be] adj: **bouche ~** gaping

bégayer [begeje] /8/ vt, vi to stammer

beige [bɛʒ] adj beige

beignet [bɛɲɛ] nm fritter

bel [bɛl] adj m voir **beau**

bêler [bele] /1/ vi to bleat

belette [bəlɛt] nf weasel

belge [bɛlʒ] adj Belgian ▷ nm/f: **B~** Belgian

Belgique [bɛlʒik] nf: **la ~** Belgium

bélier [belje] nm ram; (signe): **le B~** Aries

belle [bɛl] adj voir **beau** ▷ nf (Sport): **la ~** the decider; **belle-fille** nf daughter-in-law; (remariage) stepdaughter; **belle-mère** nf mother-in-law; (remariage) stepmother; **belle-sœur** nf sister-in-law

belvédère [bɛlvedɛʀ] nm panoramic viewpoint (or small building there)

bémol [bemɔl] nm (Mus) flat

bénédiction [benediksjɔ̃] nf blessing

bénéfice [benefis] nm (Comm) profit; (avantage) benefit; **bénéficier** /7/ vi: **bénéficier de** to enjoy; (profiter) to benefit by ou from; **bénéfique** adj beneficial

Benelux [benelyks] nm: **le ~** Benelux, the Benelux countries

bénévole [benevɔl] adj voluntary, unpaid

bénin, -igne [benɛ̃, -iɲ] adj minor, mild; (tumeur) benign

bénir [beniʀ] /2/ vt to bless; **bénit, e** adj consecrated; **eau bénite** holy water

benne [bɛn] nf skip; (de téléphérique) (cable) car; **~ à ordures** (amovible) skip

béquille [bekij] nf crutch; (de bicyclette) stand

berceau, x [bɛʀso] nm cradle, crib

bercer [bɛʀse] /3/ vt to rock, cradle; (musique etc) to lull; **~ qn de** (promesses etc) to delude sb with; **berceuse** nf lullaby

béret [beʀɛ] nm (aussi: **~ basque**) beret

berge [bɛʀʒ] nf bank

berger, -ère [bɛʀʒe, -ɛʀ] nm/f shepherd/shepherdess; **~ allemand** alsatian (dog) (BRIT), German shepherd (dog) (US)

Berlin [bɛʀlɛ̃] n Berlin

Bermudes [bɛʀmyd] nfpl: **les (îles) ~** Bermuda

Berne [bɛʀn] n Bern

berner [bɛʀne] /1/ vt to fool

besogne [bəzɔɲ] nf work no pl, job

besoin [bəzwɛ̃] nm need; (pauvreté): **le ~** need, want; **faire ses ~s** to relieve o.s.; **avoir ~ de qch/faire qch** to need sth/to do sth; **au ~** if need be; **être dans le ~** to be in need ou want

bestiole [bɛstjɔl] nf (tiny) creature

bétail [betaj] nm livestock, cattle pl

bête [bɛt] nf animal; (bestiole) insect, creature ▷ adj stupid, silly; **chercher la petite ~** to nit-pick; **~ noire** pet hate; **~ sauvage** wild beast

bêtise [betiz] nf stupidity; (action, remarque) stupid thing (to say ou do)

béton [betɔ̃] nm concrete; **(en) ~** (fig: alibi, argument) cast iron; **~ armé** reinforced concrete

betterave [bɛtʀav] nf beetroot (BRIT), beet (US); **~ sucrière** sugar beet

Beur [bœʀ] nm/f see note **"Beur"**

> ● **BEUR**
> ●
> ● *Beur* is a term used to refer to a
> ● person born in France of North
> ● African immigrant parents. It is
> ● not racist and is often used by the
> ● media, anti-racist groups and
> ● second-generation North Africans
> ● themselves. The word itself comes
> ● from back slang or 'verlan'.

beurre [bœʀ] *nm* butter; **beurrer** /1/ *vt* to butter; **beurrier** *nm* butter dish

biais [bjɛ] *nm* (*moyen*) device, expedient; (*aspect*) angle; **en ~, de ~** (*obliquement*) at an angle; **par le ~ de** by means of

bibelot [biblo] *nm* trinket, curio

biberon [bibʀɔ̃] *nm* (feeding) bottle; **nourrir au ~** to bottle-feed

bible [bibl] *nf* bible

bibliobus [biblijobys] *nm* mobile library van

bibliothécaire *nm/f* librarian

bibliothèque *nf* library; (*meuble*) bookcase

bic® [bik] *nm* Biro®

bicarbonate [bikaʀbɔnat] *nm*: **~ (de soude)** bicarbonate of soda

biceps [bisɛps] *nm* biceps

biche [biʃ] *nf* doe

bicolore [bikɔlɔʀ] *adj* two-coloured

bicoque [bikɔk] *nf* (*péj*) shack

bicyclette [bisiklɛt] *nf* bicycle

bidet [bidɛ] *nm* bidet

bidon [bidɔ̃] *nm* can ▷ *adj inv* (*fam*) phoney

bidonville [bidɔ̃vil] *nm* shanty town

bidule [bidyl] *nm* (*fam*) thingamajig

MOT-CLÉ

bien [bjɛ̃] *nm* **1** (*avantage, profit*): **faire du bien à qn** to do sb good; **dire du bien de** to speak well of; **c'est pour son bien** it's for his own good
2 (*possession, patrimoine*) possession, property; **son bien le plus précieux** his most treasured possession; **avoir du bien** to have property; **biens (de consommation** *etc*) (consumer *etc*) goods
3 (*moral*): **le bien** good; **distinguer le bien du mal** to tell good from evil
▷ *adv* **1** (*de façon satisfaisante*) well; **elle travaille/mange bien** she works/eats well; **croyant bien faire, je/il ...** thinking I/he was doing the right thing, I/he ...; **tiens-toi bien!** (*assieds-toi correctement*)

sit up straight!; (*debout*) stand up straight!; (*sois sage*) behave yourself!; (*prépare-toi*) wait for it!
2 (*valeur intensive*) quite; **bien jeune** quite young; **bien assez** quite enough; **bien mieux** (very) much better; **bien du temps/des gens** quite a time/a number of people; **j'espère bien y aller** I do hope to go; **je veux bien le faire** (*concession*) I'm quite willing to do it; **il faut bien le faire** it has to be done; **cela fait bien deux ans que je ne l'ai pas vu** I haven't seen him for at least *ou* a good two years; **Paul est bien venu, n'est-ce pas?** Paul HAS come, hasn't he?; **où peut-il bien être passé?** where on earth can he have got to?
▷ *excl* right!, OK!, fine!; **(c'est) bien fait!** it serves you (*ou* him *etc*) right!; **bien sûr!** certainly!
▷ *adj inv* **1** (*en bonne forme, à l'aise*): **je me sens bien** I feel fine; **je ne me sens pas bien** I don't feel well; **on est bien dans ce fauteuil** this chair is very comfortable
2 (*joli, beau*) good-looking; **tu es bien dans cette robe** you look good in that dress
3 (*satisfaisant*) good; **elle est bien, cette maison/secrétaire** it's a good house/she's a good secretary; **c'est très bien (comme ça)** it's fine (like that); **c'est bien?** is that all right?
4 (*moralement*) right; (: *personne*) good, nice; (*respectable*) respectable; **ce n'est pas bien de ...** it's not right to ...; **elle est bien, cette femme** she's a nice woman, she's a good sort; **des gens bien** respectable people
5 (*en bons termes*): **être bien avec qn** to be on good terms with sb; **bien-aimé, e** *adj, nm/f* beloved; **bien-être** *nm* well-being; **bienfaisance** *nf* charity; **bienfait** *nm* act of generosity, benefaction; (*de la science etc*) benefit; **bienfaiteur, -trice**

nm/f benefactor/benefactress;
bien-fondé *nm* soundness; **bien que**
conj although

bientôt [bjɛ̃to] *adv* soon; **à ~** see
you soon
bienveillant, e [bjɛ̃vεjɑ̃, -ɑ̃t] *adj*
kindly
bienvenu, e [bjɛ̃vny] *adj* welcome
▷ *nf*: **souhaiter la ~e à** to welcome;
~e à welcome to
bière [bjεR] *nf* (*boisson*) beer; (*cercueil*)
bier; **~ blonde** lager; **~ brune** brown
ale (*BRIT*), dark beer (*US*); **~ (à la)
pression** draught beer
bifteck [biftεk] *nm* steak
bigoudi [bigudi] *nm* curler
bijou, x [biʒu] *nm* jewel; **bijouterie**
nf jeweller's (shop); **bijoutier, -ière**
nm/f jeweller
bikini [bikini] *nm* bikini
bilan [bilɑ̃] *nm* (*Comm*) balance
sheet(s); (*fig*) (net) outcome (: *de
victimes*) toll; **faire le ~ de** to assess;
to review; **déposer son ~** to file a
bankruptcy statement; **~ de santé**
check-up
bile [bil] *nf* bile; **se faire de la ~** (*fam*)
to worry o.s. sick
bilieux, -euse [biljø, -øz] *adj* bilious;
(*fig: colérique*) testy
bilingue [bilɛ̃g] *adj* bilingual
billard [bijaR] *nm* billiards *sg*; (*table*)
billiard table
bille [bij] *nf* ball; (*du jeu de billes*)
marble
billet [bijε] *nm* (*aussi*: **~ de banque**)
(bank)note; (*de cinéma, de bus
etc*) ticket; (*courte lettre*) note;
~ électronique e-ticket; **billetterie**
nf ticket office; (*distributeur*) ticket
dispenser; (*Banque*) cash dispenser
billion [biljɔ̃] *nm* billion (*BRIT*),
trillion (*US*)
bimensuel, le [bimɑ̃sɥεl] *adj*
bimonthly
bio [bjo] *adj* organic
bio... [bjɔ] *préfixe* bio...;

biocarburant [bjokaRbyRɑ̃] *nm*
biofuel; **biochimie** *nf* biochemistry;
biodiesel *nm* biodiesel; **biogazole** *nm*
biodiesel; **biographie** *nf* biography;
biologie *nf* biology; **biologique** *adj*
biological; **biométrie** *nf* biometrics;
biotechnologie *nf* biotechnology;
bioterrorisme *nm* bioterrorism
bipolaire [bipɔlεR] *adj* bipolar
Birmanie [biRmani] *nf* Burma
bis¹, e [bi, biz] *adj* (*couleur*) greyish
brown ▷ *nf* (*baiser*) kiss; (*vent*) North
wind; **faire une** *ou* **la ~e à qn** to kiss
sb; **grosses ~es (de)** (*sur lettre*) love
and kisses (from)
bis² [bis] *adv*: **12 ~** 12a *ou* A ▷ *excl*,
nm encore
biscotte [biskɔt] *nf* toasted bread
(*sold in packets*)
biscuit [biskɥi] *nm* biscuit (*BRIT*),
cookie (*US*)
bise [biz] *nf voir* **bis²**
bisexuel, le [bisεksɥεl] *adj* bisexual
bisou [bizu] *nm* (*fam*) kiss
bissextile [bisεkstil] *adj*: **année ~**
leap year
bistro(t) [bistRo] *nm* bistro, café
bitume [bitym] *nm* asphalt
bizarre [bizaR] *adj* strange, odd
blague [blag] *nf* (*propos*) joke; (*farce*)
trick; **sans ~!** no kidding!; **blaguer**
/1/ *vi* to joke
blaireau, x [blεRo] *nm* (*Zool*) badger;
(*brosse*) shaving brush
blâme [blɑm] *nm* blame; (*sanction*)
reprimand; **blâmer** /1/ *vt* to blame
blanc, blanche [blɑ̃, blɑ̃ʃ] *adj* white;
(*non imprimé*) blank ▷ *nm/f* white,
white man/woman ▷ *nm* (*couleur*)
white; (*espace non écrit*) blank; (*aussi*:
~ d'œuf) (egg-)white; (*aussi*: **~ de
poulet**) breast, white meat; (*aussi*:
vin ~) white wine ▷ *nf* (*Mus*) minim
(*BRIT*), half-note (*US*); **chèque
en ~** blank cheque; **à ~** (*chauffer*)
white-hot; (*tirer, charger*) with blanks;
~ cassé off-white; **blancheur** *nf*
whiteness

blanchir [blãʃiʀ] /2/ vt (gén) to whiten; (linge) to launder; (Culin) to blanch; (fig: disculper) to clear ▷ vi (cheveux) to go white; **blanchisserie** nf laundry

blason [blazɔ̃] nm coat of arms

blasphème [blasfɛm] nm blasphemy

blazer [blazɛʀ] nm blazer

blé [ble] nm wheat

bled [blɛd] nm (péj) hole

blême [blɛm] adj pale

blessé, e [blese] adj injured ▷ nm/f injured person, casualty

blesser [blese] /1/ vt to injure; (délibérément) to wound; (offenser) to hurt; **se blesser** to injure o.s.; **se ~ au pied** etc to injure one's foot etc; **blessure** nf (accidentelle) injury; (intentionnelle) wound

bleu, e [blø] adj blue; (bifteck) very rare ▷ nm (couleur) blue; (contusion) bruise; (vêtement: aussi: **~s**) overalls pl; **fromage ~** blue cheese; **~ marine/nuit/roi** navy/midnight/royal blue; **bleuet** nm cornflower

bloc [blɔk] nm (de pierre etc) block; (de papier à lettres) pad; (ensemble) group, block; **serré à ~** tightened right down; **en ~** as a whole; **~ opératoire** operating ou theatre block; **blocage** nm (des prix) freezing; (Psych) hang-up; **bloc-notes** nm note pad

blog [blɔg] nm blog; **blogosphère** nf blogosphere; **bloguer** /1/ vi to blog

blond, e [blɔ̃, -ɔ̃d] adj fair; blond; (sable, blés) golden

bloquer [blɔke] /1/ vt (passage) to block; (pièce mobile) to jam; (crédits, compte) to freeze

blottir [blɔtiʀ] /2/: **se blottir** vi to huddle up

blouse [bluz] nf overall

blouson [bluzɔ̃] nm blouson (jacket); **~ noir** (fig) ≈ rocker

bluff [blœf] nm bluff

bobine [bɔbin] nf reel; (Élec) coil

bobo [bobo] sigle m/f (= bourgeois bohème) boho

bocal, -aux [bɔkal, -o] nm jar

bock [bɔk] nm glass of beer

bœuf (pl **bœufs**) [bœf, bø] nm ox; (Culin) beef

bof [bɔf] excl (fam: indifférence) don't care!; (pas terrible) nothing special

bohémien, ne [bɔemjɛ̃, -ɛn] nm/f gipsy

boire [bwaʀ] /53/ vt to drink; (s'imprégner de) to soak up; **~ un coup** to have a drink

bois [bwa] nm wood; **de ~, en ~** wooden; **boisé, e** adj woody, wooded

boisson [bwasɔ̃] nf drink

boîte [bwat] nf box; (fam: entreprise) firm; **aliments en ~** canned ou tinned (BRIT) foods; **~ à gants** glove compartment; **~ à ordures** dustbin (BRIT), trash can (US); **~ aux lettres** letter box; **~ d'allumettes** box of matches; (vide) matchbox; **~ de conserves** can ou tin (BRIT) (of food); **~ de nuit** night club; **~ de vitesses** gear box; **~ postale (BP)** PO box; **~ vocale** voice mail

boiter [bwate] /1/ vi to limp; (fig: raisonnement) to be shaky

boîtier [bwatje] nm case

boive etc [bwav] vb voir **boire**

bol [bɔl] nm bowl; **un ~ d'air** a breath of fresh air; **en avoir ras le ~** (fam) to have had a bellyful; **avoir du ~** (fam) to be lucky

bombarder [bɔ̃baʀde] /1/ vt to bomb; **~ qn de** (cailloux, lettres) to bombard sb with

bombe [bɔ̃b] nf bomb; (atomiseur) (aerosol) spray

MOT-CLÉ

bon, bonne [bɔ̃, bɔn] adj **1** (agréable, satisfaisant) good; **un bon repas/restaurant** a good meal/restaurant; **être bon en maths** to be good at maths

2 (*charitable*): **être bon (envers)** to be good (to)

3 (*correct*) right; **le bon numéro/moment** the right number/moment

4 (*souhaits*): **bon anniversaire!** happy birthday!; **bon courage!** good luck!; **bon séjour!** enjoy your stay!; **bon voyage!** have a good trip!; **bonne année!** happy New Year!; **bonne chance!** good luck!; **bonne fête!** happy holiday!; **bonne nuit!** good night!

5 (*approprié*): **bon à/pour** fit to/for; **à quoi bon (...)?** what's the point *ou* use (of ...)?

6: **bon enfant** *adj inv* accommodating, easy-going; **bonne femme** (*péj*) woman; **de bonne heure** early; **bon marché** cheap; **bon mot** witticism; **bon sens** common sense; **bon vivant** jovial chap; **bonnes œuvres** charitable works, charities

▶ *nm* **1** (*billet*) voucher; (*aussi*: **bon cadeau**) gift voucher; **bon d'essence** petrol coupon; **bon du Trésor** Treasury bond

2: **avoir du bon** to have its good points; **pour de bon** for good

▶ *adv*: **il fait bon** it's *ou* the weather is fine; **sentir bon** to smell good; **tenir bon** to stand firm

▶ *excl* good!; **ah bon?** really?; **bon, je reste** right, I'll stay; *voir aussi* **bonne**

bonbon [bɔ̃bɔ̃] *nm* (boiled) sweet
bond [bɔ̃] *nm* (leap; **faire un ~** to leap in the air
bondé, e [bɔ̃de] *adj* packed (full)
bondir [bɔ̃diʀ] /2/ *vi* to leap
bonheur [bɔnœʀ] *nm* happiness; **porter ~ (à qn)** to bring (sb) luck; **au petit ~** haphazardly; **par ~** fortunately
bonhomme [bɔnɔm] (*pl* **bonshommes**) *nm* fellow; **~ de neige** snowman

bonjour [bɔ̃ʒuʀ] *excl, nm* hello; (*selon l'heure*) good morning (*ou* afternoon); **c'est simple comme ~!** it's easy as pie!
bonne [bɔn] *adj f voir* **bon** ▷ *nf* (*domestique*) maid
bonnet [bɔnɛ] *nm* hat; (*de soutien-gorge*) cup; **~ de bain** bathing cap
bonsoir [bɔ̃swaʀ] *excl* good evening
bonté [bɔ̃te] *nf* kindness *no pl*
bonus [bɔnys] *nm* (Assurances) no-claims bonus; (*de DVD*) extras *pl*
bord [bɔʀ] *nm* (*de table, verre, falaise*) edge; (*de rivière, lac*) bank; (*de route*) side; **(monter) à ~** (to go) on board; **jeter par-dessus ~** to throw overboard; **le commandant de ~/ les hommes du ~** the ship's master/ crew; **au ~ de la mer/route** at the seaside/roadside; **être au ~ des larmes** to be on the verge of tears
bordeaux [bɔʀdo] *nm* Bordeaux ▷ *adj inv* maroon
bordel [bɔʀdɛl] *nm* brothel; (*fam!*) bloody (BRIT) *ou* goddamn (US) mess (!)
border [bɔʀde] /1/ *vt* (*être le long de*) to line, border; (*qn dans son lit*) to tuck up; **~ qch de** (*garnir*) to trim sth with
bordure [bɔʀdyʀ] *nf* border; **en ~ de** on the edge of
borne [bɔʀn] *nf* boundary stone; (*aussi*: **~ kilométrique**) kilometre-marker, ≈ milestone; **bornes** *nfpl* (*fig*) limits; **dépasser les ~s** to go too far
borné, e [bɔʀne] *adj* (*personne*) narrow-minded
borner [bɔʀne] /1/ *vt*: **se ~ à faire** (*se contenter de*) to content o.s. with doing; (*se limiter à*) to limit o.s. to doing
bosniaque [bɔznjak] *adj* Bosnian ▷ *nm/f*: **B~** Bosnian
Bosnie-Herzégovine [bɔsniɛʀzegɔvin] *nf* Bosnia-Herzegovina
bosquet [bɔskɛ] *nm* grove

bosse [bɔs] nf (de terrain etc) bump; (enflure) lump; (du bossu, du chameau) hump; **avoir la ~ des maths** etc (fam) to have a gift for maths etc; **il a roulé sa ~** (fam) he's been around

bosser [bɔse] /1/ vi (fam) to work; (: dur) to slave (away)

bossu, e [bɔsy] nm/f hunchback

botanique [bɔtanik] nf botany ▷ adj botanic(al)

botte [bɔt] nf (soulier) (high) boot; (gerbe): **~ de paille** bundle of straw; **~ de radis/d'asperges** bunch of radishes/asparagus; **~s de caoutchouc** wellington boots

bottine [bɔtin] nf ankle boot

bouc [buk] nm goat; (barbe) goatee; **~ émissaire** scapegoat

boucan [bukā] nm din, racket

bouche [buʃ] nf mouth; **faire du ~ à - à qn** to give sb the kiss of life (BRIT), give sb mouth-to-mouth resuscitation; **rester ~ bée** to stand open-mouthed; **~ d'égout** manhole; **~ d'incendie** fire hydrant; **~ de métro** métro entrance

bouché, e [buʃe] adj (flacon etc) stoppered; (temps, ciel) overcast; (péj: personne) thick; **avoir le nez ~** to have a blocked(-up) nose; **c'est un secteur ~** there's no future in that area; **l'évier est ~** the sink's blocked

bouchée [buʃe] nf mouthful; **~s à la reine** chicken vol-au-vents

boucher [buʃe] /1/ nm butcher ▷ vt (pour colmater) to stop up; (trou) to fill up; (obstruer) to block (up); **se boucher** vi (tuyau etc) to block up, get blocked up; **j'ai le nez bouché** my nose is blocked; **se ~ le nez** to hold one's nose

bouchère [buʃɛr] nf butcher

boucherie nf butcher's (shop); (fig) slaughter

bouchon [buʃɔ̃] nm (en liège) cork; (autre matière) stopper; (de tube) top; (fig: embouteillage) holdup; (Pêche) float

boucle [bukl] nf (forme, figure) loop; (objet) buckle; **~ (de cheveux)** curl; **~ d'oreille** earring

bouclé, e [bukle] adj (cheveux) curly

boucler [bukle] /1/ vt (fermer: ceinture etc) to fasten; (terminer) to finish off; (enfermer) to shut away; (quartier) to seal off ▷ vi to curl

bouder [bude] /1/ vi to sulk ▷ vt (personne) to refuse to have anything to do with

boudin [budɛ̃] nm: **~ (noir)** black pudding; **~ blanc** white pudding

boue [bu] nf mud

bouée [bwe] nf buoy; **~ (de sauvetage)** lifebuoy

boueux, -euse [bwø, -øz] adj muddy

bouffe [buf] nf (fam) grub, food

bouffée [bufe] nf (de cigarette) puff; **une ~ d'air pur** a breath of fresh air; **~ de chaleur** hot flush (BRIT) ou flash (US)

bouffer [bufe] /1/ vi (fam) to eat

bouffi, e [bufi] adj swollen

bouger [buʒe] /3/ vi to move; (dent etc) to be loose; (s'activer) to get moving ▷ vt to move; **les prix/les couleurs n'ont pas bougé** prices/ colours haven't changed

bougie [buʒi] nf candle; (Auto) spark(ing) plug

bouillabaisse [bujabɛs] nf type of fish soup

bouillant, e [bujā, -āt] adj (qui bout) boiling; (très chaud) boiling (hot)

bouillie [buji] nf (de bébé) cereal; **en ~** (fig) crushed

bouillir [bujir] /15/ vi to boil ▷ vt to boil; **~ de colère** etc to seethe with anger etc

bouilloire [bujwar] nf kettle

bouillon [bujɔ̃] nm (Culin) stock no pl; **bouillonner** /1/ vi to bubble; (fig: idées) to bubble up

bouillotte [bujɔt] nf hot-water bottle

boulanger, -ère [bulāʒe, -ɛr] nm/f baker; **boulangerie** nf bakery

boule [bul] nf (gén) ball; (de pétanque) bowl; **~ de neige** snowball
boulette [bulɛt] nf (de viande) meatball
boulevard [bulvaʀ] nm boulevard
bouleversement [bulvɛʀsəmã] nm upheaval
bouleverser [bulvɛʀse] /1/ vt (émouvoir) to overwhelm; (causer du chagrin à) to distress; (pays, vie) to disrupt; (papiers, objets) to turn upside down
boulimie [bulimi] nf bulimia
boulimique [bulimik] adj bulimic
boulon [bulɔ̃] nm bolt
boulot¹ [bulo] nm (fam: travail) work
boulot², te [bulo, -ɔt] adj plump, tubby
boum [bum] nm bang ▷ nf (fam) party
bouquet [bukɛ] nm (de fleurs) bunch (of flowers), bouquet; (de persil etc) bunch; **c'est le ~!** that's the last straw!
bouquin [bukɛ̃] nm (fam) book; **bouquiner** /1/ vi (fam) to read
bourdon [buʀdɔ̃] nm bumblebee
bourg [buʀ] nm small market town (ou village)
bourgeois, e [buʀʒwa, -waz] adj ≈ (upper) middle class; **bourgeoisie** nf ≈ upper middle classes pl
bourgeon [buʀʒɔ̃] nm bud
Bourgogne [buʀgɔɲ] nf: **la ~** Burgundy ▷ nm: **b~** Burgundy (wine)
bourguignon, ne [buʀgiɲɔ̃, -ɔn] adj of ou from Burgundy, Burgundian
bourrasque [buʀask] nf squall
bourratif, -ive [buʀatif, -iv] (fam) adj filling, stodgy
bourré, e [buʀe] adj (rempli): **~ de** crammed full of; (fam: ivre) pickled, plastered
bourrer [buʀe] /1/ vt (pipe) to fill; (poêle) to pack; (valise) to cram (full)
bourru, e [buʀy] adj surly, gruff
bourse [buʀs] nf (subvention) grant; (porte-monnaie) purse; **la B~** the Stock Exchange

bous [bu] vb voir **bouillir**
bousculade [buskylad] nf (hâte) rush; (poussée) crush; **bousculer** /1/ vt (heurter) to knock into; (fig) to push, rush
boussole [busɔl] nf compass
bout [bu] vb voir **bouillir** ▷ nm bit; (d'un bâton etc) tip; (d'une ficelle, table, rue, période) end; **au ~ de** at the end of, after; **pousser qn à ~** to push sb to the limit (of his patience); **venir à ~ de** to manage to finish (off) ou overcome; **à ~ portant** at point-blank range
bouteille [butɛj] nf bottle; (de gaz butane) cylinder
boutique [butik] nf shop
bouton [butɔ̃] nm button; (Bot) bud; (sur la peau) spot; **boutonner** /1/ vt to button up; **boutonnière** nf buttonhole; **bouton-pression** nm press stud
bovin, e [bɔvɛ̃, -in] adj bovine ▷ nm: **~s** cattle pl
bowling [boliŋ] nm (tenpin) bowling; (salle) bowling alley
boxe [bɔks] nf boxing
BP sigle f = **boîte postale**
bracelet [bʀaslɛ] nm bracelet
braconnier [bʀakɔnje] nm poacher
brader [bʀade] /1/ vt to sell off; **braderie** nf cut-price (BRIT) ou cut-rate (US) stall
braguette [bʀagɛt] nf fly, flies pl (BRIT), zipper (US)
braise [bʀɛz] nf embers pl
brancard [bʀãkaʀ] nm (civière) stretcher; **brancardier** nm stretcher-bearer
branche [bʀãʃ] nf branch
branché, e [bʀãʃe] adj (fam) trendy
brancher [bʀãʃe] /1/ vt to connect (up); (en mettant la prise) to plug in
brandir [bʀãdiʀ] /2/ vt to brandish
braquer [bʀake] /1/ vi (Auto) to turn (the wheel) ▷ vt (revolver etc): **~ qch sur** to aim sth at, point sth at; (mettre en colère): **~ qn** to antagonize sb

bras [bʀɑ] *nm* arm; **~ dessus ~ dessous** arm in arm; **se retrouver avec qch sur les ~** (*fam*) to be landed with sth; **~ droit** (*fig*) right hand man
brassard [bʀasaʀ] *nm* armband
brasse [bʀas] *nf* (*nage*) breast-stroke; **~ papillon** butterfly(-stroke)
brassée [bʀase] *nf* armful
brasser [bʀase] /1/ *vt* to mix; **~ l'argent/les affaires** to handle a lot of money/ business
brasserie [bʀasʀi] *nf* (*restaurant*) bar (*selling food*); (*usine*) brewery
brave [bʀav] *adj* (*courageux*) brave; (*bon, gentil*) good, kind
braver [bʀave] /1/ *vt* to defy
bravo [bʀavo] *excl* bravo! ▷ *nm* cheer
bravoure [bʀavuʀ] *nf* bravery
break [bʀɛk] *nm* (*Auto*) estate car
brebis [bʀəbi] *nf* ewe; **~ galeuse** black sheep
bredouiller [bʀəduje] /1/ *vi, vt* to mumble, stammer
bref, brève [bʀɛf, bʀɛv] *adj* short, brief ▷ *adv* in short; **d'un ton ~** sharply, curtly; **en ~** in short, in brief
Brésil [bʀezil] *nm*: **le ~** Brazil
Bretagne [bʀətaɲ] *nf*: **la ~** Brittany
bretelle [bʀətɛl] *nf* (*de vêtement*) strap; (*d'autoroute*) slip road (BRIT), entrance *ou* exit ramp (US); **bretelles** *nfpl* (*pour pantalon*) braces (BRIT), suspenders (US)
breton, ne [bʀətɔ̃, -ɔn] *adj* Breton ▷ *nm/f*: **B~, ne** Breton
brève [bʀɛv] *adj f voir* **bref**
brevet [bʀəvɛ] *nm* diploma, certificate; **~ (des collèges)** *school certificate, taken at approx. 16 years*; **~ (d'invention)** patent; **breveté, e** *adj* patented
bricolage [bʀikɔlaʒ] *nm*: **le ~** do-it-yourself (jobs)
bricoler [bʀikɔle] /1/ *vi* (*en amateur*) to do DIY jobs; (*passe-temps*) to potter about ▷ *vt* (*réparer*) to fix up; **bricoleur, -euse** *nm/f* handyman/ woman, DIY enthusiast

bridge [bʀidʒ] *nm* (*Cartes*) bridge
brièvement [bʀijɛvmɑ̃] *adv* briefly
brigade [bʀigad] *nf* (*Police*) squad; (*Mil*) brigade; **brigadier** *nm* ≈ sergeant
brillamment [bʀijamɑ̃] *adv* brilliantly
brillant, e [bʀijɑ̃, -ɑ̃t] *adj* (*remarquable*) bright; (*luisant*) shiny, shining
briller [bʀije] /1/ *vi* to shine
brin [bʀɛ̃] *nm* (*de laine, ficelle etc*) strand; (*fig*): **un ~ de** a bit of
brindille [bʀɛ̃dij] *nf* twig
brioche [bʀijɔʃ] *nf* brioche (bun); (*fam: ventre*) paunch
brique [bʀik] *nf* brick; (*de lait*) carton
briquet [bʀikɛ] *nm* (*cigarette*) lighter
brise [bʀiz] *nf* breeze
briser [bʀize] /1/ *vt* to break; **se briser** *vi* to break
britannique [bʀitanik] *adj* British ▷ *nm/f*: **B~** Briton, British person; **les B~s** the British
brocante [bʀɔkɑ̃t] *nf* (*objets*) secondhand goods *pl*, junk; **brocanteur, -euse** *nm/f* junk shop owner; junk dealer
broche [bʀɔʃ] *nf* brooch; (*Culin*) spit; (*Méd*) pin; **à la ~** spit-roasted
broché, e [bʀɔʃe] *adj* (*livre*) paper-backed
brochet [bʀɔʃɛ] *nm* pike *inv*
brochette [bʀɔʃɛt] *nf* (*ustensile*) skewer; (*plat*) kebab
brochure [bʀɔʃyʀ] *nf* pamphlet, brochure, booklet
broder [bʀɔde] /1/ *vt* to embroider ▷ *vi*: **~ (sur des faits** *ou* **une histoire)** to embroider the facts; **broderie** *nf* embroidery
bronches [bʀɔ̃ʃ] *nfpl* bronchial tubes; **bronchite** *nf* bronchitis
bronze [bʀɔ̃z] *nm* bronze
bronzer [bʀɔ̃ze] /1/ *vi* to get a tan; **se bronzer** to sunbathe
brosse [bʀɔs] *nf* brush; **coiffé en ~** with a crewcut; **~ à cheveux**

hairbrush; **~ à dents** toothbrush; **~ à habits** clothesbrush; **brosser** /1/ vt (nettoyer) to brush; (fig: tableau etc) to paint; **se brosser les dents** to brush one's teeth

brouette [bʀuɛt] nf wheelbarrow

brouillard [bʀujaʀ] nm fog

brouiller [bʀuje] /1/ vt (œufs, message) to scramble; (idées) to mix up; (rendre trouble) to cloud; (désunir: amis) to set at odds; **se brouiller** vi (ciel, vue) to cloud over; **se ~ (avec)** to fall out (with)

brouillon, ne [bʀujɔ̃, -ɔn] adj (sans soin) untidy; (qui manque d'organisation) disorganized ▷ nm (first) draft; **(papier) ~** rough paper

broussailles [bʀusaj] nfpl undergrowth sg; **broussailleux, -euse** adj bushy

brousse [bʀus] nf: **la ~** the bush

brouter [bʀute] /1/ vi to graze

brugnon [bʀyɲɔ̃] nm nectarine

bruiner [bʀɥine] /1/ vb impers: **il bruine** it's drizzling, there's a drizzle

bruit [bʀɥi] nm: **un ~** a noise, a sound; (fig: rumeur) a rumour; **le ~** noise; **sans ~** without a sound, noiselessly; **~ de fond** background noise

brûlant, e [bʀylɑ̃, -ɑ̃t] adj burning (hot); (liquide) boiling (hot)

brûlé, e [bʀyle] adj (fig: démasqué) blown ▷ nm: **odeur de ~** smell of burning

brûler [bʀyle] /1/ vt to burn; (eau bouillante) to scald; (consommer: électricité, essence) to use; (: feu rouge, signal) to go through (without stopping) ▷ vi to burn; **se brûler** to burn o.s.; (s'ébouillanter) to scald o.s.; **tu brûles** (jeu) you're getting warm ou hot

brûlure [bʀylyʀ] nf (lésion) burn; **~s d'estomac** heartburn sg

brume [bʀym] nf mist

brumeux, -euse [bʀymø, -øz] adj misty

brun, e [bʀœ̃, -yn] adj (gén, bière) brown; (cheveux, personne, tabac) dark; **elle est ~e** she's got dark hair

brunch [bʀœntʃ] nm brunch

brushing [bʀœʃiŋ] nm blow-dry

brusque [bʀysk] adj abrupt

brut, e [bʀyt] adj (diamant) uncut; (soie, minéral) raw; (Comm) gross; **(pétrole) ~** crude (oil)

brutal, e, -aux [bʀytal, -o] adj brutal

Bruxelles [bʀysɛl] n Brussels

bruyamment [bʀɥijamɑ̃] adv noisily

bruyant, e [bʀɥijɑ̃, -ɑ̃t] adj noisy

bruyère [bʀyjɛʀ] nf heather

BTS sigle m (= Brevet de technicien supérieur) vocational training certificate taken at end of two-year higher education course

bu, e [by] pp de **boire**

buccal, e, -aux [bykal, -o] adj: **par voie ~e** orally

bûche [byʃ] nf log; **prendre une ~** (fig) to come a cropper (BRIT), fall flat on one's face; **~ de Noël** Yule log

bûcher [byʃe] /1/ nm (funéraire) pyre; (supplice) stake ▷ vi (fam) to swot , slave (away) ▷ vt to swot up , slave away at

budget [bydʒɛ] nm budget

buée [bɥe] nf (sur une vitre) mist

buffet [byfɛ] nm (meuble) sideboard; (de réception) buffet; **~ (de gare)** (station) buffet, snack bar

buis [bɥi] nm box tree; (bois) box(wood)

buisson [bɥisɔ̃] nm bush

bulbe [bylb] nm (Bot, Anat) bulb

Bulgarie [bylgaʀi] nf: **la ~** Bulgaria

bulle [byl] nf bubble

bulletin [byltɛ̃] nm (communiqué, journal) bulletin; (Scol) report; **~ d'informations** news bulletin; **~ (de vote)** ballot paper; **~ météorologique** weather report

bureau, x [byʀo] nm (meuble) desk; (pièce, service) office; (Inform) desktop; **~ de change** (foreign) exchange office *ou* bureau; **~ de poste** post office; **~ de tabac** tobacconist's (shop); **bureaucratie** [byʀɔkʀasi] *nf* bureaucracy

bus¹ *vb* [by] *voir* **boire**

bus² *nm* [bys] (*véhicule*) bus

buste [byst] *nm* (*Anat*) chest (: *de femme*) bust

but [by] *vb voir* **boire** ▷ *nm* (*cible*) target; (*fig*) goal, aim; (*Football etc*) goal; **de ~ en blanc** point-blank; **avoir pour ~ de faire** to aim to do; **dans le ~ de** with the intention of

butane [bytan] *nm* butane; (*domestique*) calor gas® (BRIT), butane

butiner [bytine] /1/ *vi* (*abeilles*) to gather nectar

buvais *etc* [byvɛ] *vb voir* **boire**

buvard [byvaʀ] *nm* blotter

buvette [byvɛt] *nf* bar

c' [s] *pron voir* **ce**

ça [sa] *pron* (*pour désigner*) this (: *plus loin*) that; (*comme sujet indéfini*) it; **ça m'étonne que** it surprises me that; **ça va?** how are you?; how are things?; (*d'accord?*) OK?, all right?; **où ça?** where's that?; **pourquoi ça?** why's that?; **qui ça?** who's that?; **ça alors!** (*désapprobation*) well!, really!; **c'est ça** that's right; **ça y est** that's it

cabane [kaban] *nf* hut, cabin

cabaret [kabaʀɛ] *nm* night club

cabillaud [kabijo] *nm* cod *inv*

cabine [kabin] *nf* (*de bateau*) cabin; (*de piscine etc*) cubicle; (*de camion, train*) cab; (*d'avion*) cockpit; **~ d'essayage** fitting room; **~ (téléphonique)** call *ou* (tele) phone box

cabinet [kabinɛ] *nm* (*petite pièce*) closet; (*de médecin*) surgery (BRIT), office (US); (*de notaire etc*) office (: *clientèle*) practice; (*Pol*) cabinet;

cabinets nmpl (w.-c.) toilet sg; **~ de toilette** toilet

câble [kɑbl] nm cable; **le ~** (TV) cable television, cablevision (US)

cacahuète [kakaɥɛt] nf peanut

cacao [kakao] nm cocoa

cache [kaʃ] nm mask, card (for masking)

cache-cache [kaʃkaʃ] nm: **jouer à ~** to play hide-and-seek

cachemire [kaʃmiʀ] nm cashmere

cacher [kaʃe] /1/ vt to hide, conceal; **~ qch à qn** to hide ou conceal sth from sb; **se cacher** vi (volontairement) to hide; (être caché) to be hidden ou concealed

cachet [kaʃɛ] nm (comprimé) tablet; (de la poste) postmark; (rétribution) fee; (fig) style, character

cachette [kaʃɛt] nf hiding place; **en ~** on the sly, secretly

cactus [kaktys] nm cactus

cadavre [kadɑvʀ] nm corpse, (dead) body

Caddie® [kadi] nm (supermarket) trolley (BRIT), (grocery) cart (US)

cadeau, x [kado] nm present, gift; **faire un ~ à qn** to give sb a present ou gift; **faire ~ de qch à qn** to make a present of sth to sb, give sb sth as a present

cadenas [kadnɑ] nm padlock

cadet, te [kadɛ, -ɛt] adj younger; (le plus jeune) youngest ▷ nm/f youngest child ou one

cadran [kadʀɑ̃] nm dial; **~ solaire** sundial

cadre [kɑdʀ] nm frame; (environnement) surroundings pl ▷ nm/f (Admin) managerial employee, executive; **dans le ~ de** (fig) within the framework ou context of

cafard [kafaʀ] nm cockroach; **avoir le ~** to be down in the dumps

café [kafe] nm coffee; (bistro) café ▷ adj inv coffee cpd; **~ au lait** white coffee; **~ noir** black coffee; **café-tabac** nm tobacconist's or newsagent's also serving coffee and spirits; **cafétéria** [kafeteʀja] nf cafeteria; **cafetière** nf (pot) coffee-pot

cage [kaʒ] nf cage; **~ d'escalier** (stair) well; **~ thoracique** rib cage

cageot [kaʒo] nm crate

cagoule [kagul] nf (passe-montagne) balaclava

cahier [kaje] nm notebook; **~ de brouillons** rough book, jotter; **~ d'exercices** exercise book

caille [kaj] nf quail

caillou, x [kaju] nm (little) stone; **cailloux, -euse** adj stony

Caire [kɛʀ] nm: **le ~** Cairo

caisse [kɛs] nf box; (où l'on met la recette) till; (où l'on paye) cash desk (BRIT), checkout counter; (: au supermarché) checkout; (de banque) cashier's desk; **~ enregistreuse** cash register; **~ d'épargne (CE)** savings bank; **~ de retraite** pension fund; **caissier, -ière** nm/f cashier

cake [kɛk] nm fruit cake

calandre [kalɑ̃dʀ] nf radiator grill

calcaire [kalkɛʀ] nm limestone ▷ adj (eau) hard; (Géo) limestone cpd

calcul [kalkyl] nm calculation; **le ~** (Scol) arithmetic; **~ (biliaire)** (gall) stone; **calculateur** nm, **calculatrice** nf calculator; **calculer** /1/ vt to calculate, work out; **calculette** nf (pocket) calculator

cale [kal] nf (de bateau) hold; (en bois) wedge

calé, e [kale] adj (fam) clever, bright

caleçon [kalsɔ̃] nm (d'homme) boxer shorts; (de femme) leggings

calendrier [kalɑ̃dʀije] nm calendar; (fig) timetable

calepin [kalpɛ̃] nm notebook

caler [kale] /1/ vt to wedge ▷ vi (moteur, véhicule) to stall

calibre [kalibʀ] nm calibre

câlin, e [kɑlɛ̃, -in] adj cuddly, cuddlesome; (regard, voix) tender

calmant [kalmɑ̃] nm tranquillizer, sedative; (contre la douleur) painkiller

calme [kalm] *adj* calm, quiet ▷ *nm* calm(ness), quietness; **sans perdre son ~** without losing one's cool *ou* calmness; **calmer** /1/ *vt* to calm (down); (*douleur, inquiétude*) to ease, soothe; **se calmer** *vi* to calm down

calorie [kalɔri] *nf* calorie

camarade [kamarad] *nm/f* friend, pal; (*Pol*) comrade

Cambodge [kãbɔdʒ] *nm*: **le ~** Cambodia

cambriolage [kãbrijɔlaʒ] *nm* burglary; **cambrioler** /1/ *vt* to burgle (*BRIT*), burglarize (*US*); **cambrioleur, -euse** *nm/f* burglar

camelote [kamlɔt] (*fam*) *nf* rubbish, trash, junk

caméra [kamera] *nf* (*Ciné, TV*) camera; (*d'amateur*) cine-camera

Cameroun [kamrun] *nm*: **le ~** Cameroon

caméscope® [kameskɔp] *nm* camcorder

camion [kamjõ] *nm* lorry (*BRIT*), truck; **~ de dépannage** breakdown (*BRIT*) *ou* tow (*US*) truck; **camionnette** *nf* (small) van; **camionneur** *nm* (*entrepreneur*) haulage contractor (*BRIT*), trucker (*US*); (*chauffeur*) lorry (*BRIT*) *ou* truck driver

camomille [kamɔmij] *nf* camomile; (*boisson*) camomile tea

camp [kã] *nm* camp; (*fig*) side

campagnard, e [kãpaɲar, -ard] *adj* country *cpd*

campagne [kãpaɲ] *nf* country, countryside; (*Mil, Pol, Comm*) campaign; **à la ~** in/to the country

camper [kãpe] /1/ *vi* to camp ▷ *vt* to sketch; **se ~ devant** to plant o.s. in front of; **campeur, -euse** *nm/f* camper

camping [kãpiɲ] *nm* camping; **(terrain de) ~** campsite, camping site; **faire du ~** to go camping; **camping-car** *nm* camper, motorhome (*US*); **camping-gaz®** *nm inv* camp(ing) stove

Canada [kanada] *nm*: **le ~** Canada; **canadien, ne** *adj* Canadian ▷ *nm/f*: **Canadien, ne** Canadian ▷ *nf* (*veste*) fur-lined jacket

canal, -aux [kanal, -o] *nm* canal; (*naturel, TV*) channel; **canalisation** *nf* (*tuyau*) pipe

canapé [kanape] *nm* settee, sofa

canard [kanar] *nm* duck; (*fam: journal*) rag

cancer [kãser] *nm* cancer; (*signe*): **le C~** Cancer

cancre [kãkr] *nm* dunce

candidat, e [kãdida, -at] *nm/f* candidate; (*à un poste*) applicant, candidate; **candidature** *nf* (*Pol*) candidature; (*à poste*) application; **poser sa candidature à un poste** to apply for a job

cane [kan] *nf* (female) duck

canette [kanɛt] *nf* (*de bière*) (flip-top) bottle

canevas [kanva] *nm* (*Couture*) canvas (for tapestry work)

caniche [kaniʃ] *nm* poodle

canicule [kanikyl] *nf* scorching heat

canif [kanif] *nm* penknife, pocket knife

canne [kan] *nf* (walking) stick; **~ à pêche** fishing rod; **~ à sucre** sugar cane

cannelle [kanɛl] *nf* cinnamon

canoë [kanɔe] *nm* canoe; (*sport*) canoeing; **~ (kayak)** kayak

canot [kano] *nm* ding(h)y; **~ pneumatique** rubber *ou* inflatable ding(h)y; **~ de sauvetage** lifeboat

cantatrice [kãtatris] *nf* (opera) singer

cantine [kãtin] *nf* canteen

canton [kãtõ] *nm* district (*consisting of several communes*); (*en Suisse*) canton

caoutchouc [kautʃu] *nm* rubber; **~ mousse** foam rubber; **en ~** rubber *cpd*

CAP *sigle m* (= *Certificat d'aptitude professionnelle*) vocational training certificate taken at secondary school

cap [kap] nm (Géo) cape; (promontoire) headland; (fig: tournant) watershed; (Navig): **changer de ~** to change course; **mettre le ~ sur** to head for
capable [kapabl] adj able, capable; **~ de qch/faire** capable of sth/doing
capacité [kapasite] nf ability; (Jur, Inform, d'un récipient) capacity
cape [kap] nf cape, cloak; **rire sous ~** to laugh up one's sleeve
CAPES [kapɛs] sigle m (= Certificat d'aptitude au professorat de l'enseignement du second degré) secondary teaching diploma
capitaine [kapitɛn] nm captain
capital, e, -aux [kapital, -o] adj (œuvre) major; (question, rôle) fundamental ⊳ nm capital; (fig) stock ⊳ nf (ville) capital; (lettre) capital (letter); **d'une importance ~e** of capital importance; **capitaux** nmpl (fonds) capital sg; **~ (social)** authorized capital; **~ d'exploitation** working capital; **capitalisme** nm capitalism; **capitaliste** adj, nm/f capitalist
caporal, -aux [kapɔral, -o] nm lance corporal
capot [kapo] nm (Auto) bonnet (BRIT), hood (US)
câpre [kɑpr] nf caper
caprice [kapris] nm whim, caprice; **faire des ~s** to be temperamental; **capricieux, -euse** adj (fantasque) capricious; whimsical; (enfant) temperamental
Capricorne [kaprikɔrn] nm: **le ~** Capricorn
capsule [kapsyl] nf (de bouteille) cap; cap; (Bot etc, spatiale) capsule
capter [kapte] /1/ vt (ondes radio) to pick up; (fig) to win, capture
captivant, e [kaptivɑ̃, -ɑ̃t] adj captivating
capture [kaptyr] nf (action) capture; **~ d'écran** (Inform) screenshot
capturer [kaptyre] /1/ vt to capture
capuche [kapyʃ] nf hood

capuchon [kapyʃɔ̃] nm hood; (de stylo) cap, top
car [kar] nm coach (BRIT), bus ⊳ conj because, for
carabine [karabin] nf rifle
caractère [karaktɛr] nm (gén) character; **en ~s gras** in bold type; **en petits ~s** in small print; **en ~s d'imprimerie** in block capitals; **avoir bon/mauvais ~** to be good-/ill-natured ou tempered
caractériser [karakterize] /1/ vt to characterize; **se ~ par** to be characterized ou distinguished by
caractéristique [karakteristik] adj, nf characteristic
carafe [karaf] nf decanter; (pour eau, vin ordinaire) carafe
caraïbe [karaib] adj Caribbean; **les Caraïbes** nfpl the Caribbean (Islands)
carambolage [karɑ̃bɔlaʒ] nm multiple crash, pileup
caramel [karamɛl] nm (bonbon) caramel, toffee; (substance) caramel
caravane [karavan] nf caravan; **caravaning** nm caravanning
carbone [karbɔn] nm carbon; (double) carbon (copy)
carbonique [karbɔnik] adj: **gaz ~** carbon dioxide; **neige ~** dry ice
carbonisé, e [karbɔnize] adj charred
carburant [karbyrɑ̃] nm (motor) fuel
carburateur [karbyratœr] nm carburettor
cardiaque [kardjak] adj cardiac, heart cpd ⊳ nm/f heart patient; **être ~** to have a heart condition
cardigan [kardigɑ̃] nm cardigan
cardiologue [kardjɔlɔg] nm/f cardiologist, heart specialist
Carême [karɛm] nm: **le ~** Lent
carence [karɑ̃s] nf (manque) deficiency
caresse [karɛs] nf caress
caresser [karese] /1/ vt to caress; (animal) to stroke

cargaison [kaʀɡɛzɔ̃] nf cargo, freight

cargo [kaʀɡo] nm freighter

caricature [kaʀikatyʀ] nf caricature

carie [kaʀi] nf: **la ~ (dentaire)** tooth decay; **une ~** a bad tooth

carnaval [kaʀnaval] nm carnival

carnet [kaʀnɛ] nm (calepin) notebook; (de tickets, timbres etc) book; **~ de chèques** cheque book

carotte [kaʀɔt] nf carrot

carré, e [kaʀe] adj square; (fig: franc) straightforward ▷ nm (Math) square; **kilomètre ~** square kilometre

carreau, x [kaʀo] nm (en faïence etc) (floor) tile; (au mur) (wall) tile; (de fenêtre) (window) pane; (motif) check, square; (Cartes: couleur) diamonds pl; **tissu à ~x** checked fabric

carrefour [kaʀfuʀ] nm crossroads sg

carrelage [kaʀlaʒ] nm (sol) (tiled) floor

carrelet [kaʀlɛ] nm (poisson) plaice

carrément [kaʀemɑ̃] adv (franchement) straight out, bluntly; (sans détours, sans hésiter) straight; (intensif) completely; **c'est ~ impossible** it's completely impossible

carrière [kaʀjɛʀ] nf (de roches) quarry; (métier) career; **militaire de ~** professional soldier

carrosserie [kaʀɔsʀi] nf body, bodywork no pl (BRIT)

carrure [kaʀyʀ] nf build; (fig) calibre

cartable [kaʀtabl] nm satchel, (school)bag

carte [kaʀt] nf (de géographie) map; (marine, du ciel) chart; (de fichier, d'abonnement etc, à jouer) card; (au restaurant) menu; (aussi: **~ postale**) (post)card; (aussi: **~ de visite**) (visiting) card; **avoir/donner ~ blanche** to have/give carte blanche ou a free hand; **à la ~** (au restaurant) à la carte; **~ à puce** smartcard; **~ bancaire** cash card; **C~ Bleue®** debit card; **~ de crédit** credit card; **~ de fidélité** loyalty card; **~ d'identité** identity card; **la**

~ grise (Auto) ≈ the (car) registration document; **~ mémoire** (d'appareil photo numérique) memory card; **~ routière** road map; **~ de séjour** residence permit; **~ SIM** SIM card; **~ téléphonique** phonecard

carter [kaʀtɛʀ] nm sump

carton [kaʀtɔ̃] nm (matériau) cardboard; (boîte) (cardboard) box; **faire un ~** to score a hit; **~ (à dessin)** portfolio

cartouche [kaʀtuʃ] nf cartridge; (de cigarettes) carton

cas [kɑ] nm case; **ne faire aucun ~ de** to take no notice of; **en aucun ~** on no account; **au ~ où** in case; **en ~ de** in case of, in the event of; **en ~ de besoin** if need be; **en tout ~** in any case, at any rate

cascade [kaskad] nf waterfall, cascade

case [kɑz] nf (hutte) hut; (compartiment) compartment; (sur un formulaire, de mots croisés) box

caser [kɑze] /1/ (fam) vt (mettre) to put; (loger) to put up; **se caser** vi (se marier) to settle down; (trouver un emploi) to find a (steady) job

caserne [kazɛʀn] nf barracks

casier [kazje] nm (case) compartment; (pour courrier) pigeonhole (: à clef) locker; **~ judiciaire** police record

casino [kazino] nm casino

casque [kask] nm helmet; (chez le coiffeur) (hair-)dryer; (pour audition) (head-)phones pl, headset

casquette [kaskɛt] nf cap

casse-croûte nm inv snack

casse-noisettes, casse-noix nm inv nutcrackers pl

casse-pieds nm/f inv (fam): **il est ~, c'est un ~** he's a pain (in the neck)

casser [kɑse] /1/ vt, vt (Jur) to quash; **se casser** vi, vt to break; **~ les pieds à qn** (fam: irriter) to get on sb's nerves; **se ~ la tête** (fam) to go to a lot of trouble

casserole [kasʀɔl] nf saucepan

casse-tête [kɑstɛt] nm inv
(difficultés) headache (fig)
cassette [kasɛt] nf (bande
magnétique) cassette; (coffret) casket
cassis [kasis] nm blackcurrant
cassoulet [kasulɛ] nm sausage and
bean hotpot
catalogue [katalɔg] nm catalogue
catalytique [katalitik] adj: **pot ~**
catalytic converter
catastrophe [katastʀɔf] nf
catastrophe, disaster
catéchisme [kateʃism] nm catechism
catégorie [kategɔʀi] nf category;
  catégorique adj categorical
cathédrale [katedʀal] nf cathedral
catholique [katɔlik] adj, nm/f
  (Roman) Catholic; **pas très ~** a bit
  shady ou fishy
cauchemar [koʃmaʀ] nm nightmare
cause [koz] nf cause; (Jur) lawsuit,
  case; **à ~ de** because of, owing to;
  pour ~ de on account of; **(et) pour ~**
  and for (a very) good reason; **être en
  ~** (intérêts) to be at stake; **remettre
  en ~** to challenge; **causer** /1/ vt to
  cause ▷ vi to chat, talk
caution [kosjɔ̃] nf guarantee, security;
  (Jur) bail (bond); (fig) backing, support;
  libéré sous ~ released on bail
cavalier, -ière [kavalje, -jɛʀ] adj
  (désinvolte) offhand ▷ nm/f rider; (au
  bal) partner ▷ nm (Échecs) knight
cave [kav] nf cellar
caverne [kavɛʀn] nf cave
CD sigle m (= compact disc) CD
CDD sigle m (= contrat à durée
  déterminée) fixed-term contract
CDI sigle m (= centre de documentation et
  d'information) school library; (= contrat
  à durée indéterminée) permanent ou
  open-ended contract
CD-ROM [sedeʀɔm] nm inv CD-Rom

MOT-CLÉ

ce, cette [sə, sɛt] (devant nm **cet**
+ voyelle ou h aspiré; pl **ces**) adj dém

(proximité) this; these pl; (non-
proximité) that; those pl; **cette
maison(-ci/là)** this/that house;
cette nuit (qui vient) tonight; (passée)
last night
▷ pron **1**: **c'est** it's, it is; **c'est un
peintre** he's ou he is a painter; **ce
sont des peintres** they're ou they
are painters; **c'est le facteur** etc (à
la porte) it's the postman etc; **qui est-
ce?** who is it?; (en désignant) who is
he/she?; **qu'est-ce?** what is it?; **c'est
toi qui lui as parlé** it was you who
spoke to him
2: **c'est ça** (correct) that's right
3: **ce qui, ce que** what; **ce qui me
plaît, c'est sa franchise** what I
like about him ou her is his ou her
frankness; **il est bête, ce qui me
chagrine** he's stupid, which saddens
me; **tout ce qui bouge** everything
that ou which moves; **tout ce que
je sais** all I know; **ce dont j'ai parlé**
what I talked about; **ce que c'est
grand!** it's so big!; voir aussi **c'est-à-
dire; -ci; est-ce que; n'est-ce pas**

ceci [səsi] pron this
céder [sede] /6/ vt to give up ▷ vi
  (pont, barrage) to give way; (personne)
  to give in; **~ à** to yield to, to give in to
cédérom [sedeʀɔm] nm CD-ROM
CEDEX [sedɛks] sigle m (= courrier
  d'entreprise à distribution exceptionnelle)
  accelerated postal service for bulk users
cédille [sedij] nf cedilla
ceinture [sɛ̃tyʀ] nf belt; (taille) waist;
  ~ de sécurité safety ou seat belt
cela [s(ə)la] pron that; (comme sujet
  indéfini) it; **~ m'étonne que** it
  surprises me that; **quand/où ~?**
  when/where (was that)?
célèbre [selɛbʀ] adj famous;
  célébrer /6/ vt to celebrate
céleri [sɛlʀi] nm: **~(-rave)** celeriac;
  ~ (en branche) celery
célibataire [selibatɛʀ] adj single,
  unmarried ▷ nm/f bachelor/

unmarried *ou* single woman; **mère ~** single *ou* unmarried mother

celle, celles [sɛl] *pron voir* **celui**

cellule [selyl] *nf* (*gén*) cell; **~ souche** stem cell

cellulite [selylit] *nf* cellulite

⊙ **MOT-CLÉ**

celui, celle (*mpl* **ceux**, *fpl* **celles**) [səlɥi, sɛl] *pron* 1 : **celui-ci/là, celle-ci/là** this one/that one; **ceux-ci, celles-ci** these (ones); **ceux-là, celles-là** those (ones); **celui de mon frère** my brother's; **celui du salon/ du dessous** the one in (*ou* from) the lounge/below

2 (+ *relatif*): **celui qui bouge** the one which *ou* that moves; (*personne*) the one who moves; **celui que je vois** the one (which *ou* that) I see; (*personne*) the one (whom) I see; **celui dont je parle** the one I'm talking about

3 (*valeur indéfinie*): **celui qui veut** whoever wants

cendre [sɑ̃dʀ] *nf* ash; **~s** (*d'un défunt*) ashes; **sous la ~** (*Culin*) in (the) embers; **cendrier** *nm* ashtray

censé, e [sɑ̃se] *adj*: **être ~ faire** to be supposed to do

censeur [sɑ̃sœʀ] *nm* (*Scol*) deputy head (*BRIT*), vice-principal (*US*)

censure [sɑ̃syʀ] *nf* censorship; **censurer** /1/ *vt* (*Ciné, Presse*) to censor; (*Pol*) to censure

cent [sɑ̃] *num* a hundred, one hundred ▷ *nm* (*US, Canada, partie de l'euro etc*) cent; **centaine** *nf*: **une centaine (de)** about a hundred, a hundred or so; **des centaines (de)** hundreds (of); **centenaire** *adj* hundred-year-old ▷ *nm* (*anniversaire*) centenary; (*monnaie*) cent; **centième** *num* hundredth; **centigrade** *nm* centigrade; **centilitre** *nm* centilitre ; **centime** *nm* centime; **centime**

d'euro euro cent; **centimètre** *nm* centimetre ; (*ruban*) tape measure, measuring tape

central, e, -aux [sɑ̃tʀal, -o] *adj* central ▷ *nm*: **~ (téléphonique)** (telephone) exchange ▷ *nf* power station; **~e électrique/nucléaire** electric/nuclear power station

centre [sɑ̃tʀ] *nm* centre ; **~ commercial/sportif/culturel** shopping/sports/arts centre; **~ d'appels** call centre; **centre-ville** *nm* town centre (*BRIT*) *ou* center (*US*)

cèpe [sɛp] *nm* (edible) boletus

cependant [s(ə)pɑ̃dɑ̃] *adv* however, nevertheless

céramique [seʀamik] *nf* ceramics *sg*

cercle [sɛʀkl] *nm* circle; **~ vicieux** vicious circle

cercueil [sɛʀkœj] *nm* coffin

céréale [seʀeal] *nf* cereal

cérémonie [seʀemɔni] *nf* ceremony; **sans ~** (*inviter, manger*) informally

cerf [sɛʀ] *nm* stag

cerf-volant [sɛʀvɔlɑ̃] *nm* kite

cerise [səʀiz] *nf* cherry; **cerisier** *nm* cherry (tree)

cerner [sɛʀne] /1/ *vt* (*Mil etc*) to surround; (*fig: problème*) to delimit, define

certain, e [sɛʀtɛ̃, -ɛn] *adj* certain; **~ (de/que)** certain *ou* sure (of/ that); **d'un ~ âge** past one's prime, not so young; **un ~ temps** (quite) some time; **sûr et ~** absolutely certain; **un ~ Georges** someone called Georges; **~s** *pron* some; **certainement** *adv* (*probablement*) most probably *ou* likely; (*bien sûr*) certainly, of course

certes [sɛʀt] *adv* (*sans doute*) admittedly; (*bien sûr*) of course; indeed (yes)

certificat [sɛʀtifika] *nm* certificate

certifier [sɛʀtifje] /7/ *vt*: **~ qch à qn** to guarantee sth to sb

certitude [sɛʀtityd] *nf* certainty

cerveau, x [sɛʀvo] *nm* brain

cervelas [sɛʀvəla] *nm* saveloy

cervelle [sɛʀvɛl] *nf* (*Anat*) brain; (*Culin*) brain(s)

CES *sigle m* (= *Collège d'enseignement secondaire*) ≈ (junior) secondary school

ces [se] *adj dém voir* **ce**

cesse [sɛs]: **sans ~** *adv* (*tout le temps*) continually, constantly; (*sans interruption*) continuously; **il n'avait de ~ que** he would not rest until; **cesser** /1/ *vt* to stop ▷ *vi* to stop, cease; **cesser de faire** to stop doing; **cessez-le-feu** *nm inv* ceasefire

c'est-à-dire [sɛtadiʀ] *adv* that is (to say)

cet [sɛt] *adj dém voir* **ce**

ceux [sø] *pron voir* **celui**

chacun, e [ʃakœ̃, -yn] *pron* each; (*indéfini*) everyone, everybody

chagrin, e [ʃagʀɛ̃, -in] *adj* morose ▷ *nm* grief, sorrow; **avoir du ~** to be grieved *ou* sorrowful

chahut [ʃay] *nm* uproar; **chahuter** /1/ *vt* to rag, bait ▷ *vi* to make an uproar

chaîne [ʃɛn] *nf* chain; (*Radio, TV: stations*) channel; **travail à la ~** production line work; **réactions en ~** chain reactions; **~ (haute-fidélité** *ou* **hi-fi)** hi-fi system; **~ (de montagnes)** (mountain) range

chair [ʃɛʀ] *nf* flesh; **avoir la ~ de poule** to have goose pimples *ou* goose flesh; **bien en ~** plump, well-padded; **en ~ et en os** in the flesh; **~ à saucisse** sausage meat

chaise [ʃɛz] *nf* chair; **~ longue** deckchair

châle [ʃal] *nm* shawl

chaleur [ʃalœʀ] *nf* heat; (*fig: d'accueil*) warmth; **chaleureux, -euse** *adj* warm

chamailler [ʃamaje] /1/: **se chamailler** *vi* to squabble, bicker

chambre [ʃɑ̃bʀ] *nf* bedroom; (*Pol*) chamber; (*Comm*) chamber; **faire ~ à part** to sleep in separate rooms; **~ à un lit/deux lits** single/twin-bedded room; **~ à air** (*de pneu*) (inner) tube; **~ d'amis** spare *ou* guest room; **~ à**

coucher bedroom; **~ d'hôte** ≈ bed and breakfast (*in private home*); **~ meublée** bedsit(ter) (*BRIT*), furnished room; **~ noire** (*Photo*) dark room

chameau, x [ʃamo] *nm* camel

chamois [ʃamwa] *nm* chamois

champ [ʃɑ̃] *nm* field; **~ de bataille** battlefield; **~ de courses** racecourse

champagne [ʃɑ̃paɲ] *nm* champagne

champignon [ʃɑ̃piɲɔ̃] *nm* mushroom; (*terme générique*) fungus; **~ de couche** *ou* **de Paris** button mushroom

champion, ne [ʃɑ̃pjɔ̃, -ɔn] *adj, nm/f* champion; **championnat** *nm* championship

chance [ʃɑ̃s] *nf*: **la ~** luck; **chances** *nfpl* (*probabilités*) chances; **avoir de la ~** to be lucky; **il a des ~s de gagner** he has a chance of winning; **bonne ~!** good luck!

change [ʃɑ̃ʒ] *nm* (*Comm*) exchange

changement [ʃɑ̃ʒmɑ̃] *nm* change; **~ climatique** climate change; **~ de vitesse** gears *pl*; (*action*) gear change

changer [ʃɑ̃ʒe] /3/ *vt* (*modifier*) to change, alter; (*remplacer, Comm*) to change ▷ *vi* to change, alter; **se changer** *vi* to change (o.s.); **~ de** (*remplacer: adresse, nom, voiture etc*) to change one's; **~ de train** to change trains; **~ d'avis**, **~ d'idée** to change one's mind; **~ de vitesse** to change gear; **~ qn/qch de place** to move sb/sth to another place

chanson [ʃɑ̃sɔ̃] *nf* song

chant [ʃɑ̃] *nm* song; (*art vocal*) singing; (*d'église*) hymn

chantage [ʃɑ̃taʒ] *nm* blackmail; **faire du ~** to use blackmail

chanter [ʃɑ̃te] /1/ *vt, vi* to sing; **si cela lui chante** (*fam*) if he feels like it *ou* fancies it; **chanteur, -euse** *nm/f* singer

chantier [ʃɑ̃tje] *nm* (building) site; (*sur une route*) roadworks *pl*; **mettre en ~** to start work on; **~ naval** shipyard

chantilly [ʃɑ̃tiji] nf voir **crème**

chantonner [ʃɑ̃tɔne] /1/ vi, vt to sing to oneself, hum

chapeau, x [ʃapo] nm hat; **~!** well done!

chapelle [ʃapɛl] nf chapel

chapitre [ʃapitʀ] nm chapter

chaque [ʃak] adj each, every; (indéfini) every

char [ʃaʀ] nm: **~ (d'assaut)** tank; **~ à voile** sand yacht

charbon [ʃaʀbɔ̃] nm coal; **~ de bois** charcoal

charcuterie [ʃaʀkytʀi] nf (magasin) pork butcher's shop and delicatessen; (produits) cooked pork meats pl; **charcutier, -ière** nm/f pork butcher

chardon [ʃaʀdɔ̃] nm thistle

charge [ʃaʀʒ] nf (fardeau) load; (Élec, Mil, Jur) charge; (rôle, mission) responsibility; **charges** nfpl (du loyer) service charges; **à la ~ de** (dépendant de) dependent upon; (aux frais de) chargeable to; **prendre en ~** to take charge of; (véhicule) to take on; (dépenses) to take care of; **~s sociales** social security contributions

chargement [ʃaʀʒəmɑ̃] nm (objets) load

charger [ʃaʀʒe] /3/ vt (voiture, fusil, caméra) to load; (batterie) to charge ▷ vi (Mil etc) to charge; **se ~ de** to see to, take care of

chargeur [ʃaʀʒœʀ] nm (de batterie) charger

chariot [ʃaʀjo] nm trolley; (charrette) waggon

charité [ʃaʀite] nf charity; **faire la ~ à** to give (something) to

charmant, e [ʃaʀmɑ̃, -ɑ̃t] adj charming

charme [ʃaʀm] nm charm; **charmer** /1/ vt to charm

charpente [ʃaʀpɑ̃t] nf frame(work); **charpentier** nm carpenter

charrette [ʃaʀɛt] nf cart

charter [tʃaʀtœʀ] nm (vol) charter flight

chasse [ʃas] nf hunting; (au fusil) shooting; (poursuite) chase; (aussi: **~ d'eau**) flush; **prendre en ~** to give chase to; **tirer la ~ (d'eau)** to flush the toilet, pull the chain; **~ à courre** hunting; **chasse-neige** nm inv snowplough (BRIT), snowplow (US); **chasser** /1/ vt to hunt; (expulser) to chase away ou out, drive away ou out; **chasseur, -euse** nm/f hunter ▷ nm (avion) fighter

chat¹ [ʃa] nm cat

chat² [tʃat] nm (Internet: salon) chat room; (: conversation) chat

châtaigne [ʃatɛɲ] nf chestnut

châtain [ʃatɛ̃] adj inv chestnut (brown); (personne) chestnut-haired

château, x [ʃato] nm (forteresse) castle; (résidence royale) palace; (manoir) mansion; **~ d'eau** water tower; **~ fort** stronghold, fortified castle

châtiment [ʃatimɑ̃] nm punishment

chaton [ʃatɔ̃] nm (Zool) kitten

chatouiller [ʃatuje] /1/ vt to tickle; **chatouilleux, -euse** [ʃatujø, -øz] adj ticklish; (fig) touchy, over-sensitive

chatte [ʃat] nf (she-)cat

chatter [tʃate] /1/ vi (Internet) to chat

chaud, e [ʃo, -od] adj (gén) warm; (très chaud) hot ▷ nm: **il fait ~** it's warm; it's hot; **avoir ~** to be warm; to be hot; **ça me tient ~** it keeps me warm; **rester au ~** to stay in the warm

chaudière [ʃodjɛʀ] nf boiler

chauffage [ʃofaʒ] nm heating; **~ central** central heating

chauffe-eau [ʃofo] nm inv water heater

chauffer [ʃofe] /1/ vt to heat ▷ vi to heat up, warm up; (trop chauffer: moteur) to overheat; **se chauffer** vi (au soleil) to warm o.s.

chauffeur [ʃofœʀ] nm driver; (privé) chauffeur

chaumière [ʃomjɛʀ] nf (thatched) cottage

chaussée [ʃose] nf road(way)

chausser [ʃose] /1/ vt (bottes, skis) to put on; (enfant) to put shoes on; **~ du 38/42** to take size 38/42

chaussette [ʃosɛt] nf sock

chausson [ʃosɔ̃] nm slipper; (de bébé) bootee; **~ (aux pommes)** (apple) turnover

chaussure [ʃosyr] nf shoe; **~s basses** flat shoes; **~s montantes** ankle boots; **~s de ski** ski boots

chauve [ʃov] adj bald; **chauve-souris** nf bat

chauvin, e [ʃovɛ̃, -in] adj chauvinistic

chaux [ʃo] nf lime; **blanchi à la ~** whitewashed

chef [ʃɛf] nm head, leader; (de cuisine) chef; **général/commandant en ~** general-/commander-in-chief; **~ d'accusation** charge; **~ d'entreprise** company head; **~ d'état** head of state; **~ de famille** head of the family; **~ de file** (de parti etc) leader; **~ de gare** station master; **~ d'orchestre** conductor; **chef-d'œuvre** nm masterpiece; **chef-lieu** nm county town

chelou, e [ʃəlu] (fam) adj sketchy, dodgy

chemin [ʃəmɛ̃] nm path; (itinéraire, direction, trajet) way; **en ~** on the way; **~ de fer** railway (BRIT), railroad (US)

cheminée [ʃəmine] nf chimney; (à l'intérieur) chimney piece, fireplace; (de bateau) funnel

chemise [ʃəmiz] nf shirt; (dossier) folder; **~ de nuit** nightdress

chemisier [ʃəmizje] nm blouse

chêne [ʃɛn] nm oak (tree); (bois) oak

chenil [ʃənil] nm kennels pl

chenille [ʃənij] nf (Zool) caterpillar

chèque [ʃɛk] nm cheque (BRIT), check (US); **faire/toucher un ~** to write/cash a cheque; **par ~** by cheque; **~ barré/sans provision** crossed (BRIT)/bad cheque; **~ de voyage** traveller's cheque; **chéquier** [ʃekje] nm cheque book

cher, -ère [ʃɛr] adj (aimé) dear; (coûteux) expensive, dear ▷ adv: **cela coûte ~** it's expensive

chercher [ʃɛrʃe] /1/ vt to look for; (gloire etc) to seek; **aller ~** to go for, go and fetch; **~ à faire** to try to do; **chercheur, -euse** nm/f researcher

chéri, e [ʃeri] adj beloved, dear; **(mon) ~** darling

cheval, -aux [ʃəval, -o] nm horse; (Auto): **~ (vapeur)** horsepower no pl; **faire du ~** to ride; **à ~** on horseback; **à ~ sur** astride; (fig) overlapping; **~ de course** race horse

chevalier [ʃəvalje] nm knight

chevaux [ʃəvo] nmpl voir **cheval**

chevet [ʃəvɛ] nm: **au ~ de qn** at sb's bedside; **lampe de ~** bedside lamp

cheveu, x [ʃəvø] nm hair ▷ nmpl (chevelure) hair sg; **avoir les ~x courts/en brosse** to have short hair/a crew cut

cheville [ʃəvij] nf (Anat) ankle; (de bois) peg; (pour enfoncer une vis) plug

chèvre [ʃɛvr] nf (she-)goat

chèvrefeuille [ʃɛvrəfœj] nm honeysuckle

chevreuil [ʃəvrœj] nm roe deer inv; (Culin) venison

 MOT-CLÉ

chez [ʃe] prép **1** (à la demeure de) at; (: direction) to; **chez qn** at/to sb's house ou place; **je suis chez moi** I'm at home; **je rentre chez moi** I'm going home; **allons chez Nathalie** let's go to Nathalie's

2 (+profession) at; (: direction) to; **chez le boulanger/dentiste** at ou to the baker's/dentist's

3 (dans le caractère, l'œuvre de) in; **chez ce poète** in this poet's work; **c'est ce que je préfère chez lui** that's what I like best about him

chic [ʃik] adj inv chic, smart; (généreux) nice, decent ▷ nm stylishness; **avoir**

le ~ de ou **pour** to have the knack of ou for; **~!** great!

chicorée [ʃikɔʀe] nf (café) chicory; (salade) endive

chien [ʃjɛ̃] nm dog; (de pistolet) hammer; **~ d'aveugle** guide dog; **~ de garde** guard dog

chienne [ʃjɛn] nf (she-)dog, bitch

chiffon [ʃifɔ̃] nm (piece of) rag; **chiffonner** /1/ vt to crumple; (tracasser) to concern

chiffre [ʃifʀ] nm (représentant un nombre) figure; numeral; (montant, total) total, sum; **en ~s ronds** in round figures; **~ d'affaires (CA)** turnover; **chiffrer** /1/ vt (dépense) to put a figure to, assess; (message) to (en)code, cipher ▷ vi: **chiffrer à, se chiffrer à** to add up to

chignon [ʃiɲɔ̃] nm chignon, bun

Chili [ʃili] nm: **le ~** Chile; **chilien, ne** adj Chilean ▷ nm/f: **Chilien, ne** Chilean

chimie [ʃimi] nf chemistry; **chimiothérapie** [ʃimjoteʀapi] nf chemotherapy; **chimique** adj chemical; **produits chimiques** chemicals

chimpanzé [ʃɛ̃pɑ̃ze] nm chimpanzee

Chine [ʃin] nf: **la ~** China; **chinois, e** adj Chinese ▷ nm (Ling) Chinese ▷ nm/f: **Chinois, e** Chinese

chiot [ʃjo] nm pup(py)

chips [ʃips] nfpl crisps (BRIT), (potato) chips (US)

chirurgie [ʃiʀyʀʒi] nf surgery; **~ esthétique** cosmetic ou plastic surgery; **chirurgien, ne** nm/f surgeon

chlore [klɔʀ] nm chlorine

choc [ʃɔk] nm (heurt) impact; shock; (collision) crash; (moral) shock; (affrontement) clash

chocolat [ʃɔkɔla] nm chocolate; **~ au lait** milk chocolate

chœur [kœʀ] nm (chorale) choir; (Opéra, Théât) chorus; **en ~** in chorus

choisir [ʃwaziʀ] /2/ vt to choose, select

choix [ʃwa] nm choice; selection; **avoir le ~** to have the choice; **de premier ~** (Comm) class ou grade one; **de ~** choice cpd, selected; **au ~** as you wish ou prefer

chômage [ʃomaʒ] nm unemployment; **mettre au ~** to make redundant, put out of work; **être au ~** to be unemployed ou out of work; **chômeur, -euse** nm/f unemployed person

chope [ʃɔp] nf tankard

choquer [ʃɔke] /1/ vt (offenser) to shock; (commotionner) to shake (up)

chorale [kɔʀal] nf choir

chose [ʃoz] nf thing; **c'est peu de ~** it's nothing much

chou, x [ʃu] nm cabbage; **mon petit ~** (my) sweetheart; **~ à la crème** cream bun (made of choux pastry); **~ de Bruxelles** Brussels sprout; **choucroute** nf sauerkraut

chouette [ʃwɛt] nf owl ▷ adj (fam) great, smashing

chou-fleur [ʃuflœʀ] nm cauliflower

chrétien, ne [kʀetjɛ̃, -ɛn] adj, nm/f Christian

Christ [kʀist] nm: **le ~** Christ; **christianisme** nm Christianity

chronique [kʀɔnik] adj chronic ▷ nf (de journal) column, page; (historique) chronicle; (Radio, TV): **la ~ sportive/théâtrale** the sports/ theatre review

chronologique [kʀɔnɔlɔʒik] adj chronological

chronomètre [kʀɔnɔmɛtʀ] nm stopwatch; **chronométrer** /6/ vt to time

chrysanthème [kʀizɑ̃tɛm] nm chrysanthemum

CHRYSANTHÈME

Chrysanthemums are strongly associated with funerals in France, and therefore should not be given as gifts.

chuchotement [ʃyʃɔtmɑ̃] nm
whisper
chuchoter [ʃyʃɔte] /1/ vt, vi to
whisper
chut excl [ʃyt] sh!
chute [ʃyt] nf fall; (déchet) scrap;
faire une ~ (de 10 m) to fall (10 m);
~s de pluie/neige rain/snowfalls;
~ (d'eau) waterfall; **~ libre** free fall
Chypre [ʃipʀ] nm/f Cyprus
-ci [si] adv voir **par** ▷ adj dém: **ce
garçon~/-là** this/that boy; **ces
femmes~/-là** these/those women
cible [sibl] nf target
cicatrice [sikatʀis] nf scar;
cicatriser /1/ vt to heal
ci-contre [sikɔ̃tʀ] adv opposite
ci-dessous [sidəsu] adv below
ci-dessus [sidəsy] adv above
cidre [sidʀ] nm cider
Cie abr (= compagnie) Co
ciel [sjɛl] nm sky; (Rel) heaven
cieux [sjø] nmpl voir **ciel**
cigale [sigal] nf cicada
cigare [sigaʀ] nm cigar
cigarette [sigaʀɛt] nf cigarette;
~ électronique e-cigarette
ci-inclus, e [siɛ̃kly, -yz] adj, adv
enclosed
ci-joint, e [siʒwɛ̃, -ɛ̃t] adj, adv
enclosed
cil [sil] nm (eye)lash
cime [sim] nf top; (montagne) peak
ciment [simɑ̃] nm cement
cimetière [simtjɛʀ] nm cemetery;
(d'église) churchyard
cinéaste [sineast] nm/f film-maker
cinéma [sinema] nm cinema
cinq [sɛ̃k] num five; **cinquantaine**
nf: **une cinquantaine (de)** about
fifty; **avoir la cinquantaine** (âge) to
be around fifty; **cinquante** num fifty;
cinquantenaire adj, nm/f fifty-year-
old; **cinquième** num fifth ▷ nf (Scol)
year 8 (BRIT), seventh grade (US)
cintre [sɛ̃tʀ] nm coat-hanger
cintré, e [sɛ̃tʀe] adj (chemise) fitted
cirage [siʀaʒ] nm (shoe) polish

circonflexe [siʀkɔ̃flɛks] adj: **accent
~** circumflex accent
circonstance [siʀkɔ̃stɑ̃s] nf
circumstance; (occasion) occasion;
~s atténuantes mitigating
circumstances
circuit [siʀkɥi] nm (trajet) tour,
(round) trip; (Élec, Tech) circuit
circulaire [siʀkylɛʀ] adj, nf circular
circulation [siʀkylasjɔ̃] nf
circulation; (Auto): **la ~** (the) traffic
circuler [siʀkyle] /1/ vi (véhicules)
to drive (along); (passants) to walk
along; (train etc) to run; (sang, devises)
to circulate; **faire ~** (nouvelle) to
spread (about), circulate; (badauds)
to move on
cire [siʀ] nf wax; **ciré** nm oilskin; **cirer**
[siʀe] /1/ vt to wax, polish
cirque [siʀk] nm circus; (fig) chaos,
bedlam; **quel ~!** what a carry-on!
ciseau, x [sizo] nm: **~ (à bois)** chisel
▷ nmpl (paire de ciseaux) (pair of) scissors
citadin, e [sitadɛ̃, -in] nm/f city dweller
citation [sitasjɔ̃] nf (d'auteur)
quotation; (Jur) summons sg
cité [site] nf town; (plus grande)
city; **~ universitaire** students'
residences pl
citer [site] /1/ vt (un auteur) to quote
(from); (nommer) to name; (Jur) to
summon
citoyen, ne [sitwajɛ̃, -ɛn] nm/f
citizen
citron [sitʀɔ̃] nm lemon; **~ pressé**
(fresh) lemon juice; **~ vert** lime;
citronnade nf still lemonade
citrouille [sitʀuj] nf pumpkin
civet [sive] nm: **~ de lapin** rabbit stew
civière [sivjɛʀ] nf stretcher
civil, e [sivil] adj (Jur, Admin, poli) civil;
(non militaire) civilian; **en ~** in civilian
clothes; **dans le ~** in civilian life
civilisation [sivilizasjɔ̃] nf
civilization
clair, e [klɛʀ] adj light; (chambre)
light, bright; (eau, son, fig) clear ▷ adv:
voir ~ to see clearly ▷ nm: **mettre au ~**

(*notes etc*) to tidy up; **tirer qch au ~** to clear sth up, clarify sth; **~ de lune** moonlight; **clairement** *adv* clearly

clairière [klɛRjɛR] *nf* clearing

clandestin, e [klɑ̃dɛstɛ̃, -in] *adj* clandestine, covert; (*Pol*) underground, clandestine; (*travailleur, immigration*) illegal; **passager ~** stowaway

claque [klak] *nf* (*gifle*) slap; **claquer** /1/ *vi* (*porte*) to bang, slam; (*fam: mourir*) to snuff it ▷ *vt* (*porte*) to slam, bang; (*doigts*) to snap; (*fam: dépenser*) to blow; **elle claquait des dents** her teeth were chattering; **être claqué** (*fam*) to be dead tired; **se claquer un muscle** to pull *ou* strain a muscle; **claquettes** *nfpl* tap-dancing *sg*; (*chaussures*) flip-flops

clarinette [klaRinɛt] *nf* clarinet

classe [klɑs] *nf* class; (*Scol: local*) class(room); (: *leçon*) class; (: *élèves*) class; **aller en ~** to go to school; **classement** *nm* (*rang: Scol*) place; (: *Sport*) placing; (*liste: Scol*) class list (in order of merit); (: *Sport*) placings *pl*

classer [klɑse] /1/ *vt* (*idées, livres*) to classify; (*papiers*) to file; (*candidat, concurrent*) to grade; (*Jur: affaire*) to close; **se ~ premier/dernier** to come first/last; (*Sport*) to finish first/last; **classeur** *nm* (*cahier*) file

classique [klasik] *adj* (*sobre, coupe etc*) classic(al), classical; (*habituel*) standard, classic

clavicule [klavikyl] *nf* collarbone

clavier [klavje] *nm* keyboard; (*de portable*) keypad

clé [kle] *nf* key; (*Mus*) clef; (*de mécanicien*) spanner (*BRIT*), wrench (*US*); **prix ~s en main** (*d'une voiture*) on-the-road price; ; **~ de contact** ignition key; **~ USB** USB key

clergé [klɛRʒe] *nm* clergy

clic [klik] *nm* (*Inform*) click

cliché [kliʃe] *nm* (*fig*) cliché; (*Photo*) negative; print; (*Typo*) (printing) plate; (*Ling*) cliché

client, e [klijɑ̃, -ɑ̃t] *nm/f* (*acheteur*) customer, client; (*d'hôtel*) guest, patron; (*du docteur*) patient; (*de l'avocat*) client; **clientèle** *nf* (*du magasin*) customers *pl*, clientèle; (*du docteur, de l'avocat*) practice

cligner [kliɲe] /1/ *vi*: **~ des yeux** to blink (one's eyes); **~ de l'œil** to wink; **clignotant** *nm* (*Auto*) indicator; **clignoter** /1/ *vi* (*étoiles etc*) to twinkle; (*lumière*) to flicker

climat [klima] *nm* climate

climatisation [klimatizasjɔ̃] *nf* air conditioning; **climatisé, e** *adj* air-conditioned

clin d'œil [klɛ̃dœj] *nm* wink; **en un ~** in a flash

clinique [klinik] *nf* (private) clinic

clip [klip] *nm* (*pince*) clip; (*boucle d'oreille*) clip-on; **(vidéo) ~** pop (*ou* promotional) video

cliquer [klike] /1/ *vi* (*Inform*) to click; **~ deux fois** to double-click ▷ *vt* to click; **~ sur** to click on

clochard, e [klɔʃaR, -aRd] *nm/f* tramp

cloche [klɔʃ] *nf* (*d'église*) bell; (*fam*) clot; **clocher** /1/ *nm* church tower; (*en pointe*) steeple ▷ *vi* (*fam*) to be *ou* go wrong; **de clocher** (*péj*) parochial

cloison [klwazɔ̃] *nf* partition (wall)

clonage [klɔnaʒ] *nm* cloning

cloner [klɔne] /1/ *vt* to clone

cloque [klɔk] *nf* blister

clore [klɔR] /45/ *vt* to close

clôture [klotyR] *nf* closure; (*barrière*) enclosure

clou [klu] *nm* nail; **clous** *nmpl* = **passage clouté**; **pneus à ~s** studded tyres; **le ~ du spectacle** the highlight of the show; **~ de girofle** clove

clown [klun] *nm* clown

club [klœb] *nm* club

CNRS *sigle m* (= *Centre national de la recherche scientifique*) ≈ SERC (*BRIT*), ≈ NSF (*US*)

coaguler [kɔagyle] /1/ vi, vt, **se coaguler** vi (sang) to coagulate

cobaye [kɔbaj] nm guinea-pig

coca [kɔka] nm Coke®

cocaïne [kɔkain] nf cocaine

coccinelle [kɔksinɛl] nf ladybird (BRIT), ladybug (US)

cocher [kɔʃe] /1/ vt to tick off

cochon, ne [kɔʃɔ̃, -ɔn] nm pig ▷ adj (fam) dirty, smutty; **~ d'Inde** guinea-pig; **cochonnerie** nf (fam: saleté) filth; (marchandises) rubbish, trash

cocktail [kɔktɛl] nm cocktail; (réception) cocktail party

cocorico [kɔkɔriko] excl, nm cock-a-doodle-do

cocotte [kɔkɔt] nf (en fonte) casserole; **ma ~** (fam) sweetie (pie); **~ (minute)**® pressure cooker

code [kɔd] nm code ▷ adj: **phares ~s** dipped lights; **se mettre en ~(s)** to dip (BRIT) ou dim (US) one's (head) lights; **~ à barres** bar code; **~ civil** Common Law; **~ pénal** penal code; **~ postal** (numéro) postcode (BRIT), zip code (US); **~ de la route** highway code; **~ secret** cipher

cœur [kœr] nm heart; (Cartes: couleur) hearts pl; (: carte) heart; **avoir bon ~** to be kind-hearted; **avoir mal au ~** to feel sick; **par ~** by heart; **de bon ~** willingly; **cela lui tient à ~** that's (very) close to his heart

coffre [kɔfr] nm (meuble) chest; (d'auto) boot (BRIT), trunk (US); **coffre-fort** nm safe; **coffret** nm casket

cognac [kɔɲak] nm brandy, cognac

cogner [kɔɲe] /1/ vi to knock; **se ~ contre** to knock ou bump into; **se ~ la tête** to bang one's head

cohérent, e [kɔerɑ̃, -ɑ̃t] adj coherent, consistent

coiffé, e [kwafe] adj: **bien/mal ~** with tidy/untidy hair; **~ d'un béret** wearing a beret

coiffer [kwafe] /1/ vt (fig: surmonter) to cover, top; **~ qn** to do sb's hair; **se**

coiffer vi to do one's hair; **coiffeur, -euse** nm/f hairdresser ▷ nf (table) dressing table; **coiffure** nf (cheveux) hairstyle, hairdo; (art): **la coiffure** hairdressing

coin [kwɛ̃] nm corner; (pour coincer) wedge; **l'épicerie du ~** the local grocer; **dans le ~** (aux alentours) in the area, around about; (habiter) locally; **je ne suis pas du ~** I'm not from here; **au ~ du feu** by the fireside; **regard en ~** side(ways) glance

coincé, e [kwɛ̃se] adj stuck, jammed; (fig: inhibé) inhibited, with hang-ups

coïncidence [kɔɛ̃sidɑ̃s] nf coincidence

coing [kwɛ̃] nm quince

col [kɔl] nm (de chemise) collar; (encolure, cou) neck; (de montagne) pass; **~ roulé** polo-neck; **~ de l'utérus** cervix

colère [kɔlɛr] nf anger; **une ~** a fit of anger; **être en ~ (contre qn)** to be angry (with sb); **mettre qn en ~** to make sb angry; **se mettre en ~ contre qn** to get angry with sb; **se mettre en ~** to get angry; **coléreux, -euse, colérique** adj quick-tempered, irascible

colin [kɔlɛ̃] nm hake

colique [kɔlik] nf diarrhoea

colis [kɔli] nm parcel

collaborer [kɔ(l)labɔre] /1/ vi to collaborate; **~ à** to collaborate on; (revue) to contribute to

collant, e [kɔlɑ̃, -ɑ̃t] adj sticky; (robe etc) clinging, skintight; (péj) clinging ▷ nm (bas) tights pl; (de danseur) leotard

colle [kɔl] nf glue; (à papiers peints) (wallpaper) paste; (devinette) teaser, riddle; (Scol: fam) detention

collecte [kɔlɛkt] nf collection; **collectif, -ive** adj collective; (visite, billet etc) group cpd

collection [kɔlɛksjɔ̃] nf collection; (Édition) series; **collectionner** /1/ vt (tableaux, timbres) to

collect; **collectionneur, -euse**
[kɔlɛksjɔnœʀ, -øz] nm/f collector
collectivité [kɔlɛktivite] nf group;
les ~s locales local authorities
collège [kɔlɛʒ] nm (école) (secondary)
school; (assemblée) body; **collégien,
ne** nm/f secondary school pupil
(BRIT), high school student (US)
collègue [kɔ(l)lɛg] nm/f colleague
coller [kɔle] /1/ vt (papier, timbre)
to stick (on); (affiche) to stick up;
(enveloppe) to stick down; (morceaux)
to stick ou glue together; (Inform) to
paste; (fam: mettre, fourrer) to stick,
shove; (Scol: fam) to keep in ▷ vi
(être collant) to be sticky; (adhérer) to
stick; **~ à** to stick to; **être collé à un
examen** (fam) to fail an exam
collier [kɔlje] nm (bijou) necklace; (de
chien, Tech) collar
colline [kɔlin] nf hill
collision [kɔlizjɔ̃] nf collision, crash;
entrer en ~ (avec) to collide (with)
collyre [kɔliʀ] nm eye lotion
colombe [kɔlɔ̃b] nf dove
Colombie [kɔlɔ̃bi] nf: **la ~** Colombia
colonie [kɔlɔni] nf colony; **~ (de
vacances)** holiday camp (for children)
colonne [kɔlɔn] nf column; **se
mettre en ~ par deux/quatre** to
get into twos/fours; **~ (vertébrale)**
spine, spinal column
colorant [kɔlɔʀɑ̃] nm colouring
colorer [kɔlɔʀe] /1/ vt to colour
colorier [kɔlɔʀje] /7/ vt to colour (in)
coloris [kɔlɔʀi] nm colour, shade
colza [kɔlza] nm rape(seed)
coma [kɔma] nm coma; **être dans le
~** to be in a coma
combat [kɔ̃ba] nm fight; fighting
no pl; **~ de boxe** boxing match;
combattant nm: **ancien
combattant** war veteran;
combattre /41/ vt to fight; (épidémie,
ignorance) to combat, fight against
combien [kɔ̃bjɛ̃] adv (quantité) how
much; (nombre) how many; **~ de**
how much; (nombre) how many;

~ de temps how long; **~ coûte/
pèse ceci?** how much does this cost/
weigh?; **on est le ~ aujourd'hui?**
(fam) what's the date today?
combinaison [kɔ̃binɛzɔ̃] nf
combination; (astuce) scheme; (de
femme) slip; (de plongée) wetsuit; (bleu
de travail) boilersuit (BRIT), coveralls
pl (US)
combiné [kɔ̃bine] nm (aussi:
~ téléphonique) receiver
comble [kɔ̃bl] adj (salle) packed
(full) ▷ nm (du bonheur, plaisir) height;
combles nmpl (Constr) attic sg, loft sg;
c'est le ~! that beats everything!
combler [kɔ̃ble] /1/ vt (trou) to fill in;
(besoin, lacune) to fill; (déficit) to make
good; (satisfaire) fulfil
comédie [kɔmedi] nf comedy; (fig)
playacting no pl; **faire une ~** (fig) to
make a fuss; **~ musicale** musical;
comédien, ne nm/f actor/actress
comestible [kɔmɛstibl] adj edible
comique [kɔmik] adj (drôle) comical;
(Théât) comic ▷ nm (artiste) comic,
comedian
commandant [kɔmɑ̃dɑ̃] nm (gén)
commander, commandant; (Navig)
captain
commande [kɔmɑ̃d] nf (Comm)
order; **commandes** nfpl (Aviat etc)
controls; **sur ~** to order; **commander**
/1/ vt (Comm) to order; (diriger,
ordonner) to command; **commander
à qn de faire** to command ou order
sb to do

 MOT-CLÉ

comme [kɔm] prép **1** (comparaison)
like; **tout comme son père** just like
his father; **fort comme un bœuf** as
strong as an ox; **joli comme tout**
ever so pretty
2 (manière) like; **faites-le comme ça**
do it like this, do it this way; **comme
ci, comme ça** so-so, middling
3 (en tant que) as a; **donner comme**

prix to give as a prize; **travailler comme secrétaire** to work as a secretary

4: **comme il faut** adv properly

▶ conj **1** (ainsi que) as; **elle écrit comme elle parle** she writes as she talks; **comme si** as if

2 (au moment où, alors que) as; **il est parti comme j'arrivais** he left as I arrived

3 (parce que, puisque) as; **comme il était en retard, il ...** as he was late, he ...

▶ adv: **comme il est fort/c'est bon!** he's so strong/it's so good!

commencement [kɔmɑ̃smɑ̃] nm beginning, start

commencer [kɔmɑ̃se] /3/ vt, vi to begin, start; **~ à** ou **de faire** to begin ou start doing

comment [kɔmɑ̃] adv how; **~?** (que dites-vous) (I beg your) pardon?; **et ~!** and how!

commentaire [kɔmɑ̃tɛʀ] nm comment; remark; **~ (de texte)** commentary

commerçant, e [kɔmɛʀsɑ̃, -ɑ̃t] nm/f shopkeeper, trader

commerce [kɔmɛʀs] nm (activité) trade, commerce; (boutique) business; **~ électronique** e-commerce; **~ équitable** fair trade; **commercial, e, -aux** adj commercial, trading; (péj) commercial; **commercialiser** /1/ vt to market

commettre [kɔmɛtʀ] /56/ vt to commit

commissaire [kɔmisɛʀ] nm (de police) ≈ (police) superintendent; **~ aux comptes** (Admin) auditor; **commissariat** nm police station

commission [kɔmisjɔ̃] nf (comité, pourcentage) commission; (message) message; (course) errand; **commissions** nfpl (achats) shopping sg

commode [kɔmɔd] adj (pratique) convenient, handy; (facile) easy; (personne): **pas ~** awkward (to deal with) ▷ nf chest of drawers

commun, e [kɔmœ̃, -yn] adj common; (pièce) communal, shared; (réunion, effort) joint ▷ nf (Admin) commune, ≈ district (: urbaine) ≈ borough; **communs** nmpl (bâtiments) outbuildings; **cela sort du ~** it's out of the ordinary; **le ~ des mortels** the common run of people; **en ~** (faire) jointly; **mettre en ~** to pool, share; **d'un ~ accord** of one accord

communauté [kɔmynote] nf community

commune [kɔmyn] adj f, nf voir **commun**

communication [kɔmynikasjɔ̃] nf communication

communier [kɔmynje] /7/ vi (Rel) to receive communion

communion [kɔmynjɔ̃] nf communion

communiquer [kɔmynike] /1/ vt (nouvelle, dossier) to pass on, convey; (peur etc) to communicate ▷ vi to communicate; **se ~ à** (se propager) to spread to

communisme [kɔmynism] nm communism; **communiste** adj, nm/f communist

commutateur [kɔmytatœʀ] nm (Élec) (change-over) switch, commutator

compact, e [kɔ̃pakt] adj (dense) dense; (appareil) compact

compagne [kɔ̃paɲ] nf companion

compagnie [kɔ̃paɲi] nf (firme, Mil) company; **tenir ~ à qn** to keep sb company; **fausser ~ à qn** to give sb the slip, slip ou sneak away from sb; **~ aérienne** airline (company)

compagnon [kɔ̃paɲɔ̃] nm companion

comparable [kɔ̃paʀabl] adj: **~ (à)** comparable (to)

comparaison [kɔ̃parɛzɔ̃] nf comparison

comparer [kɔ̃pare] /1/ vt to compare; **~ qch/qn à** ou **et** (pour choisir) to compare sth/sb with ou and; (pour établir une similitude) to compare sth/sb to ou and

compartiment [kɔ̃partimɑ̃] nm compartment

compas [kɔ̃pa] nm (Géom) (pair of) compasses pl; (Navig) compass

compatible [kɔ̃patibl] adj compatible

compatriote [kɔ̃patrijɔt] nm/f compatriot

compensation [kɔ̃pɑ̃sasjɔ̃] nf compensation

compenser [kɔ̃pɑ̃se] /1/ vt to compensate for, make up for

compétence [kɔ̃petɑ̃s] nf competence

compétent, e [kɔ̃petɑ̃, -ɑ̃t] adj (apte) competent, capable

compétition [kɔ̃petisjɔ̃] nf (gén) competition; (Sport: épreuve) event; **la ~ automobile** motor racing

complément [kɔ̃plemɑ̃] nm complement; (reste) remainder; **~ d'information** (Admin) supplementary ou further information; **complémentaire** adj complementary; (additionnel) supplementary

complet, -ète [kɔ̃plɛ, -ɛt] adj complete; (plein: hôtel etc) full ▷ nm (aussi: **~-veston**) suit; **pain ~** wholemeal bread; **complètement** adv completely; **compléter** /6/ vt (porter à la quantité voulue) to complete; (augmenter: connaissances, études) to complement, supplement; (: garde-robe) to add to

complexe [kɔ̃plɛks] adj complex ▷ nm: **~ hospitalier/industriel** hospital/industrial complex; **complexé, e** adj mixed-up, hung-up

complication [kɔ̃plikasjɔ̃] nf complexity, intricacy; (difficulté, ennui) complication; **complications** nfpl (Méd) complications

complice [kɔ̃plis] nm accomplice

compliment [kɔ̃plimɑ̃] nm (louange) compliment; **compliments** nmpl (félicitations) congratulations

compliqué, e [kɔ̃plike] adj complicated, complex; (personne) complicated

comportement [kɔ̃pɔrtəmɑ̃] nm behaviour

comporter [kɔ̃pɔrte] /1/ vt (consister en) to consist of, comprise; (être équipé de) to have; **se comporter** vi to behave

composer [kɔ̃poze] /1/ vt (musique, texte) to compose; (mélange, équipe) to make up; (faire partie de) to make up, form ▷ vi (transiger) to come to terms; **se ~ de** to be composed of, be made up of; **~ un numéro** (au téléphone) to dial a number; **compositeur, -trice** nm/f (Mus) composer; **composition** nf composition; (Scol) test

composter [kɔ̃pɔste] /1/ vt (billet) to punch

- **COMPOSTER**
-
- In France you have to punch your
- ticket on the platform to validate it
- before getting onto the train.

compote [kɔ̃pɔt] nf stewed fruit no pl; **~ de pommes** stewed apples

compréhensible [kɔ̃preɑ̃sibl] adj comprehensible; (attitude) understandable

compréhensif, -ive [kɔ̃preɑ̃sif, -iv] adj understanding

▌ Attention à ne pas traduire compréhensif par comprehensive.

comprendre [kɔ̃prɑ̃dr] /58/ vt to understand; (se composer de) to comprise, consist of

compresse [kɔ̃prɛs] nf compress

comprimé [kɔ̃prime] nm tablet

compris, e [kɔ̃pʀi, -iz] *pp de*
comprendre ▷ *adj (inclus)* included;
~ entre *(situé)* contained between;
**la maison ~e/non ~e, y/non ~ la
maison** including/excluding the
house; **100 euros tout ~** 100 euros
all inclusive *ou* all-in

comptabilité [kɔ̃tabilite] *nf*
(activité, technique) accounting,
accountancy; accounts *pl*, books
pl; *(service)* accounts office *ou*
department

comptable [kɔ̃tabl] *nm/f*
accountant

comptant [kɔ̃tɑ̃] *adv*: **payer ~** to pay
cash; **acheter ~** to buy for cash

compte [kɔ̃t] *nm* count; *(total,
montant)* count, (right) number;
(bancaire, facture) account; **comptes**
nmpl accounts, books; *(fig)*
explanation *sg*; **en fin de ~** all things
considered; **s'en tirer à bon ~** to get
off lightly; **pour le ~ de** on behalf
of; **pour son propre ~** for one's own
benefit; **travailler à son ~** to work
for oneself; **régler un ~** *(s'acquitter de
qch)* to settle an account; *(se venger)* to
get one's own back; **rendre des ~s à
qn** *(fig)* to be answerable to sb; **tenir
~ de qch** to take sth into account;
~ courant (CC) current account;
~ à rebours countdown; **~ rendu**
account, report; *(de film, livre)* review;
voir aussi **rendre**; **compte-gouttes**
nm inv dropper

compter [kɔ̃te] /1/ *vt* to count;
(facturer) to charge for; *(avoir à son
actif, comporter)* to have; *(prévoir)*
to allow, reckon on; *(penser, espérer)*:
~ réussir/revenir to expect to
succeed/return ▷ *vi* to count; *(être
économe)* to economize; *(figurer)*:
~ parmi to be *ou* rank among; **~ sur**
to count (up)on; **~ avec qch/qn** to
reckon with *ou* take account of sth/
sb; **sans ~ que** besides which

compteur [kɔ̃tœʀ] *nm* meter; **~ de
vitesse** speedometer

comptine [kɔ̃tin] *nf* nursery rhyme

comptoir [kɔ̃twaʀ] *nm (de magasin)*
counter; *(de café)* counter, bar

con, ne [kɔ̃, kɔn] *adj (fam!)* bloody
(BRIT!) *ou* damned stupid

concentrer [kɔ̃sɑ̃tʀe] /1/ *vt* to
concentrate; **se concentrer** *vi* to
concentrate

concerner [kɔ̃sɛʀne] /1/ *vt* to
concern; **en ce qui me concerne** as
far as I am concerned

concert [kɔ̃sɛʀ] *nm* concert; **de ~**
(décider) unanimously

concessionnaire [kɔ̃sesjɔnɛʀ]
nm/f agent, dealer

concevoir [kɔ̃s(ə)vwaʀ] /28/ *vt (idée,
projet)* to conceive (of); *(comprendre)*
to understand; *(enfant)* to conceive;
maison bien/mal conçue well-/
badly-designed *ou* -planned house

concierge [kɔ̃sjɛʀʒ] *nm/f* caretaker

concis, e [kɔ̃si, -iz] *adj* concise

conclure [kɔ̃klyʀ] /35/ *vt* to
conclude; **conclusion** *nf* conclusion

conçois [kɔ̃swa] *vb voir* **concevoir**

concombre [kɔ̃kɔ̃bʀ] *nm* cucumber

concours [kɔ̃kuʀ] *nm* competition;
(Scol) competitive examination;
(assistance) aid, help; **~ de
circonstances** combination of
circumstances; **~ hippique** horse
show; *voir* **'hors-concours**

concret, -ète [kɔ̃kʀɛ, -ɛt] *adj*
concrete

conçu, e [kɔ̃sy] *pp de* **concevoir**

concubinage [kɔ̃kybinaʒ] *nm (Jur)*
cohabitation

concurrence [kɔ̃kyʀɑ̃s] *nf*
competition; **jusqu'à ~ de** up to;
faire ~ à to be in competition with

concurrent, e [kɔ̃kyʀɑ̃, -ɑ̃t] *nm/f*
(Sport, Écon etc) competitor; *(Scol)*
candidate

condamner [kɔ̃dane] /1/ *vt (blâmer)*
to condemn; *(Jur)* to sentence; *(porte,
ouverture)* to fill in, block up; **~ qn à
deux ans de prison** to sentence sb to
two years' imprisonment

condensation [kɔ̃dɑ̃sasjɔ̃] *nf* condensation

condition [kɔ̃disjɔ̃] *nf* condition; **conditions** *nfpl* (*tarif, prix*) terms; (*circonstances*) conditions; **sans ~** unconditionally; **à ~ de** *ou* **que** provided that; **conditionnel, le** *nm* conditional (tense)

conditionnement [kɔ̃disjɔnmɑ̃] *nm* (*emballage*) packaging

condoléances [kɔ̃dɔleɑ̃s] *nfpl* condolences

conducteur, -trice [kɔ̃dyktœr, -tris] *nm/f* driver ▷ *nm* (*Élec etc*) conductor

conduire [kɔ̃dɥir] /38/ *vt* to drive; (*délégation, troupeau*) to lead; **se conduire** *vi* to behave; **~ vers/à** to lead towards/to; **~ qn quelque part** to take sb somewhere; to drive sb somewhere

conduite [kɔ̃dɥit] *nf* (*comportement*) behaviour; (*d'eau, de gaz*) pipe; **sous la ~ de** led by

confection [kɔ̃fɛksjɔ̃] *nf* (*fabrication*) making; (*Couture*): **la ~** the clothing industry

conférence [kɔ̃ferɑ̃s] *nf* (*exposé*) lecture; (*pourparlers*) conference; **~ de presse** press conference

confesser [kɔ̃fese] /1/ *vt* to confess; **confession** *nf* confession; (*culte: catholique etc*) denomination

confetti [kɔ̃feti] *nm* confetti *no pl*

confiance [kɔ̃fjɑ̃s] *nf* (*en l'honnêteté de qn*) confidence, trust; (*en la valeur de qch*) faith; **avoir ~ en** to have confidence *ou* faith in, trust; **faire ~ à** to trust; **mettre qn en ~** to win sb's trust; **~ en soi** self-confidence; *voir* **question**

confiant, e [kɔ̃fjɑ̃, -ɑ̃t] *adj* confident; trusting

confidence [kɔ̃fidɑ̃s] *nf* confidence; **confidentiel, le** *adj* confidential

confier [kɔ̃fje] /7/ *vt*: **~ à qn** (*objet en dépôt, travail etc*) to entrust to sb; (*secret, pensée*) to confide to sb; **se ~ à qn** to confide in sb

confirmation [kɔ̃firmasjɔ̃] *nf* confirmation

confirmer [kɔ̃firme] /1/ *vt* to confirm

confiserie [kɔ̃fizri] *nf* (*magasin*) confectioner's *ou* sweet shop; **confiseries** *nfpl* (*bonbons*) confectionery *sg*

confisquer [kɔ̃fiske] /1/ *vt* to confiscate

confit, e [kɔ̃fi, -it] *adj*: **fruits ~s** crystallized fruits ▷ *nm*: **~ d'oie** potted goose

confiture [kɔ̃fityr] *nf* jam

conflit [kɔ̃fli] *nm* conflict

confondre [kɔ̃fɔ̃dr] /41/ *vt* (*jumeaux, faits*) to confuse, mix up; (*témoin, menteur*) to confound; **se confondre** *vi* to merge; **se ~ en excuses** to offer profuse apologies

conforme [kɔ̃fɔrm] *adj*: **~ à** (*en accord avec: loi, règle*) in accordance with; **conformément** *adv*: **conformément à** in accordance with; **conformer** /1/ *vt*: **se conformer à** to conform to

confort [kɔ̃fɔr] *nm* comfort; **tout ~** (*Comm*) with all mod cons (BRIT) *ou* modern conveniences; **confortable** *adj* comfortable

confronter [kɔ̃frɔ̃te] /1/ *vt* to confront

confus, e [kɔ̃fy, -yz] *adj* (*vague*) confused; (*embarrassé*) embarrassed; **confusion** *nf* (*voir confus*) confusion; embarrassment; (*voir confondre*) confusion; mixing up

congé [kɔ̃ʒe] *nm* (*vacances*) holiday; **en ~** on holiday; **semaine/jour de ~** week/day off; **prendre ~ de qn** to take one's leave of sb; **donner son ~ à** to hand *ou* give in one's notice to; **~ de maladie** sick leave; **~ de maternité** maternity leave; **~s payés** paid holiday *ou* leave

congédier [kɔ̃ʒedje] /7/ *vt* to dismiss

congélateur [kɔ̃ʒelatœr] *nm* freezer

congeler [kɔ̃ʒ(ə)le] /5/ vt to freeze; **les produits congelés** frozen foods; **se congeler** vi to freeze

congestion [kɔ̃ʒɛstjɔ̃] nf congestion

Congo [kɔ̃go] nm: **le ~** the Congo

congrès [kɔ̃grɛ] nm congress

conifère [kɔnifɛr] nm conifer

conjoint, e [kɔ̃ʒwɛ̃, -wɛ̃t] adj joint ▷ nm/f spouse

conjonctivite [kɔ̃ʒɔ̃ktivit] nf conjunctivitis

conjoncture [kɔ̃ʒɔ̃ktyr] nf circumstances pl; **la ~ (économique)** the economic climate ou situation

conjugaison [kɔ̃ʒygɛzɔ̃] nf (Ling) conjugation

connaissance [kɔnɛsɑ̃s] nf (savoir) knowledge no pl; (personne connue) acquaintance; **être sans ~** to be unconscious; **perdre/reprendre ~** to lose/regain consciousness; **à ma/sa ~** to (the best of) my/his knowledge; **faire ~ avec qn** ou **la ~ de qn** to meet sb

connaisseur, -euse [kɔnɛsœr, -øz] nm/f connoisseur

connaître [kɔnɛtr] /57/ vt to know; (éprouver) to experience; (avoir: succès) to have; to enjoy; **~ de nom/vue** to know by name/sight; **ils se sont connus à Genève** they (first) met in Geneva; **s'y ~ en qch** to know about sth

connecter [kɔnɛkte] /1/ vt to connect; **se ~ à Internet** to log onto the Internet

connerie [kɔnri] nf (fam) (bloody) stupid (BRIT) ou damn-fool (US) thing to do ou say

connexion [kɔnɛksjɔ̃] nf connection

connu, e [kɔny] adj (célèbre) well-known

conquérir [kɔ̃kerir] /21/ vt to conquer; **conquête** nf conquest

consacrer [kɔ̃sakre] /1/ vt (Rel) to consecrate; **~ qch à** (employer) to devote ou dedicate sth to; **se ~ à**

qch/faire to dedicate ou devote o.s. to sth/to doing

conscience [kɔ̃sjɑ̃s] nf conscience; **avoir/prendre ~ de** to be/become aware of; **perdre/reprendre ~** to lose/regain consciousness; **avoir bonne/mauvaise ~** to have a clear/guilty conscience; **consciencieux, -euse** adj conscientious; **conscient, e** adj conscious

consécutif, -ive [kɔ̃sekytif, -iv] adj consecutive; **~ à** following upon

conseil [kɔ̃sɛj] nm (avis) piece of advice; (assemblée) council; **donner un ~** ou **des ~s à qn** to give sb (a piece of) advice; **prendre ~ (auprès de qn)** to take advice (from sb); **~ d'administration (CA)** board (of directors); **~ général** regional council; **le ~ des ministres** ≈ the Cabinet; **~ municipal (CM)** town council

conseiller¹ [kɔ̃seje] vt (personne) to advise; (méthode, action) to recommend, advise; **~ à qn de faire qch** to advise sb to do sth

conseiller², -ière [kɔ̃seje, -ɛr] nm/f adviser; **~ d'orientation** (Scol) careers adviser (BRIT), (school) counselor (US)

consentement [kɔ̃sɑ̃tmɑ̃] nm consent

consentir [kɔ̃sɑ̃tir] /16/ vt: **~ (à qch/faire)** to agree ou consent (to sth/to doing)

conséquence [kɔ̃sekɑ̃s] nf consequence; **en ~** (donc) consequently; (de façon appropriée) accordingly; **conséquent, e** adj logical, rational; (fam: important) substantial; **par conséquent** consequently

conservateur, -trice [kɔ̃sɛrvatœr, -tris] nm/f (Pol) conservative; (de musée) curator ▷ nm (pour aliments) preservative

conservatoire [kɔ̃sɛrvatwar] nm academy

conserve [kɔ̃sɛʀv] nf (gén pl) canned ou tinned (BRIT) food; **en ~** canned, tinned (BRIT)

conserver [kɔ̃sɛʀve] /1/ vt (faculté) to retain, keep; (amis, livres) to keep; (préserver, Culin) to preserve

considérable [kɔ̃sideʀabl] adj considerable, significant, extensive

considération [kɔ̃sideʀasjɔ̃] nf consideration; (estime) esteem

considérer [kɔ̃sideʀe] /6/ vt to consider; **~ qch comme** to regard sth as

consigne [kɔ̃siɲ] nf (de gare) left luggage (office) (BRIT), checkroom (US); (ordre, instruction) instructions pl; **~ automatique** left-luggage locker

consister [kɔ̃siste] /1/ vi: **~ en/ dans/à faire** to consist of/in/ in doing

consoler [kɔ̃sɔle] /1/ vt to console

consommateur, -trice [kɔ̃sɔmatœʀ, -tʀis] nm/f (Écon) consumer; (dans un café) customer

consommation [kɔ̃sɔmasjɔ̃] nf (Écon) consumption; (boisson) drink; **de ~** (biens, société) consumer cpd

consommer [kɔ̃sɔme] /1/ vt (personne) to eat ou drink, consume; (voiture, usine, poêle) to use, consume; (Jur: mariage) to consummate ▷ vi (dans un café) to (have a) drink

consonne [kɔ̃sɔn] nf consonant

constamment [kɔ̃stamɑ̃] adv constantly

constant, e [kɔ̃stɑ̃, -ɑ̃t] adj constant; (personne) steadfast

constat [kɔ̃sta] nm (de police) report; **~ (à l'amiable)** (jointly agreed) statement for insurance purposes; **~ d'échec** acknowledgement of failure

constatation [kɔ̃statasjɔ̃] nf (remarque) observation

constater [kɔ̃state] /1/ vt (remarquer) to note; (Admin, Jur: attester) to certify

consterner [kɔ̃stɛʀne] /1/ vt to dismay

constipé, e [kɔ̃stipe] adj constipated

constitué, e [kɔ̃stitɥe] adj: **~ de** made up ou composed of

constituer [kɔ̃stitɥe] /1/ vt (comité, équipe) to set up; (dossier, collection) to put together; (éléments, parties: composer) to make up, constitute; (: représenter, être) to constitute; **se ~ prisonnier** to give o.s. up

constructeur [kɔ̃stʀyktœʀ] nm/f manufacturer, builder

constructif, -ive [kɔ̃stʀyktif, -iv] adj constructive

construction [kɔ̃stʀyksjɔ̃] nf construction, building

construire [kɔ̃stʀɥiʀ] /38/ vt to build, construct

consul [kɔ̃syl] nm consul; **consulat** nm consulate

consultant, e adj, nm consultant

consultation [kɔ̃syltasjɔ̃] nf consultation; **heures de ~** (Méd) surgery (BRIT) ou office (US) hours

consulter [kɔ̃sylte] /1/ vt to consult ▷ vi (médecin) to hold surgery (BRIT), be in (the office) (US)

contact [kɔ̃takt] nm contact; **au ~ de** (air, peau) on contact with; (gens) through contact with; **mettre/ couper le ~** (Auto) to switch on/off the ignition; **entrer en ~** to come into contact with; **prendre ~ avec** to get in touch ou contact with; **contacter** /1/ vt to contact, get in touch with

contagieux, -euse [kɔ̃taʒjø, -øz] adj infectious; (par le contact) contagious

contaminer [kɔ̃tamine] /1/ vt to contaminate

conte [kɔ̃t] nm tale; **~ de fées** fairy tale

contempler [kɔ̃tɑ̃ple] /1/ vt to contemplate, gaze at

contemporain, e [kɔ̃tɑ̃pɔʀɛ̃, -ɛn] adj, nm/f contemporary

contenir [kɔ̃t(ə)niʀ] /22/ vt to contain; (avoir une capacité de) to hold

content, e [kɔ̃tɑ̃, -ɑ̃t] *adj* pleased, glad; **~ de** pleased with; **contenter** /1/ *vt* to satisfy, please; **se contenter de** to content o.s. with

contenu, e [kɔ̃t(ə)ny] *nm* (*d'un bol*) contents *pl*; (*d'un texte*) content

conter [kɔ̃te] /1/ *vt* to recount, relate

conteste [kɔ̃tɛst]: **sans ~** *adv* unquestionably, indisputably; **contester** /1/ *vt* to question ▷ *vi* (*Pol, gén*) to rebel (against established authority)

contexte [kɔ̃tɛkst] *nm* context

continent [kɔ̃tinɑ̃] *nm* continent

continu, e [kɔ̃tiny] *adj* continuous; **faire la journée ~e** to work without taking a full lunch break; **(courant) ~** direct current, DC

continuel, le [kɔ̃tinɥɛl] *adj* (*qui se répète*) constant, continual; (*continu*) continuous

continuer [kɔ̃tinɥe] /1/ *vt* (*travail, voyage etc*) to continue (with), carry on (with), go on with; (*prolonger: alignement, rue*) to continue ▷ *vi* (*pluie, vie, bruit*) to continue, go on; **~ à** *ou* **de faire** to go on *ou* continue doing

contourner [kɔ̃turne] /1/ *vt* to bypass, walk *ou* drive round; (*difficulté*) to get round

contraceptif, -ive [kɔ̃trasɛptif, -iv] *adj, nm* contraceptive; **contraception** *nf* contraception

contracté, e [kɔ̃trakte] *adj* tense

contracter [kɔ̃trakte] /1/ *vt* (*muscle etc*) to tense, contract; (*maladie, dette, obligation*) to contract; (*assurance*) to take out; **se contracter** *vi* (*métal, muscles*) to contract

contractuel, le [kɔ̃traktɥɛl] *nm/f* (*agent*) traffic warden

contradiction [kɔ̃tradiksjɔ̃] *nf* contradiction; **contradictoire** *adj* contradictory, conflicting

contraignant, e [kɔ̃trɛɲɑ̃, -ɑ̃t] *adj* restricting

contraindre [kɔ̃trɛ̃dr] /52/ *vt*: **~ qn à faire** to force *ou* compel sb to do

contraint, e *pp de* **contraindre** ▷ *nf* constraint

contraire [kɔ̃trɛr] *adj, nm* opposite; **~ à** contrary to; **au ~** on the contrary

contrarier [kɔ̃trarje] /7/ *vt* (*personne*) to annoy; (*projets*) to thwart, frustrate; **contrariété** [kɔ̃trarjete] *nf* annoyance

contraste [kɔ̃trast] *nm* contrast

contrat [kɔ̃tra] *nm* contract

contravention [kɔ̃travɑ̃sjɔ̃] *nf* parking ticket

contre [kɔ̃tr] *prép* against; (*en échange*) (in exchange) for; **par ~** on the other hand

contrebande [kɔ̃trəbɑ̃d] *nf* (*trafic*) contraband, smuggling; (*marchandise*) contraband, smuggled goods *pl*; **faire la ~ de** to smuggle

contrebas [kɔ̃trəba]: **en ~** *adv* (down) below

contrebasse [kɔ̃trəbas] *nf* (double) bass

contre: contrecoup *nm* repercussions *pl*; **contredire** /37/ *vt* (*personne*) to contradict; (*témoignage, assertion, faits*) to refute

contrefaçon [kɔ̃trəfasɔ̃] *nf* forgery

contre: contre-indication (*pl* **contre-indications**) *nf* (*Méd*) contra-indication; **"contre-indication en cas d'eczéma"** "should not be used by people with eczema"; **contre-indiqué, e** *adj* (*Méd*) contraindicated; (*déconseillé*) unadvisable, ill-advised

contremaître [kɔ̃trəmɛtr] *nm* foreman

contre-plaqué [kɔ̃trəplake] *nm* plywood

contresens [kɔ̃trəsɑ̃s] *nm* (*erreur*) misinterpretation; (*mauvaise traduction*) mistranslation; **à ~** the wrong way

contretemps [kɔ̃trətɑ̃] *nm* hitch; **à ~** (*fig*) at an inopportune moment

contribuer [kɔ̃tribɥe] /1/: **~ à** *vt* to contribute towards; **contribution** *nf* contribution;

mettre à contribution to call upon; **contributions directes/indirectes** direct/indirect taxation

contrôle [kɔ̃tʀol] nm checking no pl, check; monitoring; (test) test, examination: **perdre le ~ de son véhicule** to lose control of one's vehicle; **~ continu** (Scol) continuous assessment; **~ d'identité** identity check

contrôler [kɔ̃tʀole] /1/ vt (vérifier) to check; (surveiller: opérations) to supervise; (: prix) to monitor, control; (maîtriser, Comm: firme) to control; **contrôleur, -euse** nm/f (de train) (ticket) inspector; (de bus) (bus) conductor/tress

controversé, e [kɔ̃tʀɔvɛʀse] adj (personnage, question) controversial

contusion [kɔ̃tyzjɔ̃] nf bruise, contusion

convaincre [kɔ̃vɛ̃kʀ] /42/ vt: **~ qn (de qch)** to convince sb (of sth); **~ qn (de faire)** to persuade sb (to do)

convalescence [kɔ̃valesɑ̃s] nf convalescence

convenable [kɔ̃vnabl] adj suitable; (assez bon) decent

convenir [kɔ̃vniʀ] /22/ vi to be suitable; **~ à** to suit; **~ de** (bien-fondé de qch) to admit (to), acknowledge; (date, somme etc) to agree upon; **~ que** (admettre) to admit that; **~ de faire qch** to agree to do sth

convention [kɔ̃vɑ̃sjɔ̃] nf convention; **conventions** nfpl (convenances) convention sg; **~ collective** (Écon) collective agreement; **conventionné, e** adj (Admin) applying charges laid down by the state

convenu, e [kɔ̃vny] pp de **convenir** ▷ adj agreed

conversation [kɔ̃vɛʀsasjɔ̃] nf conversation

convertir [kɔ̃vɛʀtiʀ] /2/ vt: **~ qn (à)** to convert sb (to); **~ qch en** to convert sth into; **se ~ (à)** to be converted (to)

conviction [kɔ̃viksjɔ̃] nf conviction

convienne etc [kɔ̃vjɛn] vb voir **convenir**

convivial, e [kɔ̃vivjal] adj (Inform) user-friendly

convocation [kɔ̃vɔkasjɔ̃] nf (document) notification to attend; (Jur) summons sg

convoquer [kɔ̃vɔke] /1/ vt (assemblée) to convene; (subordonné, témoin) to summon; (candidat) to ask to attend

coopération [kɔɔpeʀasjɔ̃] nf cooperation; (Admin): **la C~** ≈ Voluntary Service Overseas (BRIT) ou the Peace Corps (US: done as alternative to military service)

coopérer [kɔɔpeʀe] /6/ vi: **~ (à)** to co-operate (in)

coordonné, e [kɔɔʀdɔne] adj coordinated; **coordonnées** nfpl (détails personnels) address, phone number, schedule etc

coordonner [kɔɔʀdɔne] /1/ vt to coordinate

copain, copine nm/f pal; (petit ami) boyfriend; (petite amie) girlfriend

copie [kɔpi] nf copy; (Scol) script, paper; **copier** /7/ vt, vi to copy; **copier coller** (Inform) copy and paste; **copier sur** to copy from; **copieur** nm (photo)copier

copieux, -euse [kɔpjø, -øz] adj copious

copine [kɔpin] nf voir **copain**

coq [kɔk] nm cockerel

coque [kɔk] nf (de noix, mollusque) shell; (de bateau) hull; **à la ~** (Culin) (soft-)boiled

coquelicot [kɔkliko] nm poppy

coqueluche [kɔklyʃ] nf whooping-cough

coquet, te [kɔkɛ, -ɛt] adj appearance-conscious; (logement) smart, charming

coquetier [kɔk(ə)tje] nm egg-cup

coquillage [kɔkijaʒ] nm (mollusque) shellfish inv; (coquille) shell

coquille [kɔkij] *nf* shell; (*Typo*) misprint; **~ St Jacques** scallop

coquin, e [kɔkɛ̃, -in] *adj* mischievous, roguish; (*polisson*) naughty

cor [kɔʀ] *nm* (*Mus*) horn; (*Méd*): **~ (au pied)** corn

corail, -aux [kɔʀaj, -o] *nm* coral *no pl*

Coran [kɔʀɑ̃] *nm*: **le ~** the Koran

corbeau, x [kɔʀbo] *nm* crow

corbeille [kɔʀbɛj] *nf* basket; (*Inform*) recycle bin; **~ à papier** waste paper basket *ou* bin

corde [kɔʀd] *nf* rope; (*de violon, raquette, d'arc*) string; **usé jusqu'à la ~** threadbare; **~ à linge** washing *ou* clothes line; **~ à sauter** skipping rope; **~s vocales** vocal cords

cordée [kɔʀde] *nf* (*d'alpinistes*) rope, roped party

cordialement [kɔʀdjalmɑ̃] *adv* (*formule épistolaire*) (kind) regards

cordon [kɔʀdɔ̃] *nm* cord, string; **~ sanitaire/de police** sanitary/ police cordon; **~ ombilical** umbilical cord

cordonnerie [kɔʀdɔnʀi] *nf* shoe repairer's *ou* mender's (shop); **cordonnier** *nm* shoe repairer *ou* mender

Corée [kɔʀe] *nf*: **la ~ du Sud/du Nord** South/North Korea

coriace [kɔʀjas] *adj* tough

corne [kɔʀn] *nf* horn; (*de cerf*) antler

cornée [kɔʀne] *nf* cornea

corneille [kɔʀnɛj] *nf* crow

cornemuse [kɔʀnəmyz] *nf* bagpipes *pl*

cornet [kɔʀnɛ] *nm* (paper) cone; (*de glace*) cornet, cone

corniche [kɔʀniʃ] *nf* (*route*) coast road

cornichon [kɔʀniʃɔ̃] *nm* gherkin

Cornouailles [kɔʀnwaj] *fpl* Cornwall

corporel, le [kɔʀpɔʀɛl] *adj* bodily; (*punition*) corporal

corps [kɔʀ] *nm* body; **à ~ perdu** headlong; **prendre ~** to take shape; **le ~ électoral** the electorate; **le ~ enseignant** the teaching profession

correct, e [kɔʀɛkt] *adj* correct; **correcteur, -trice** *nm/f* (*Scol*) examiner; **correction** *nf* (*voir corriger*) correction; (*voir correct*) correctness; (*coups*) thrashing

correspondance [kɔʀɛspɔ̃dɑ̃s] *nf* correspondence; (*de train, d'avion*) connection; **cours par ~** correspondence course; **vente par ~** mail-order business

correspondant, e [kɔʀɛspɔ̃dɑ̃, -ɑ̃t] *nm/f* correspondent; (*Tél*) person phoning (*ou* being phoned)

correspondre [kɔʀɛspɔ̃dʀ] /41/ *vi* to correspond, tally; **~ à** to correspond to; **~ avec qn** to correspond with sb

corrida [kɔʀida] *nf* bullfight

corridor [kɔʀidɔʀ] *nm* corridor

corrigé [kɔʀiʒe] *nm* (*Scol: d'exercice*) correct version

corriger [kɔʀiʒe] /3/ *vt* (*devoir*) to correct; (*punir*) to thrash; **~ qn de** (*défaut*) to cure sb of

corrompre [kɔʀɔ̃pʀ] /41/ *vt* to corrupt; (*acheter: témoin etc*) to bribe

corruption [kɔʀypsjɔ̃] *nf* corruption; (*de témoins*) bribery

corse [kɔʀs] *adj* Corsican ▷ *nm/f*: **C~** Corsican ▷ *nf*: **la C~** Corsica

corsé, e [kɔʀse] *adj* (*café etc*) full-flavoured (*BRIT*) *ou* -flavored (*US*); (*sauce*) spicy; (*problème*) tough

cortège [kɔʀtɛʒ] *nm* procession

cortisone [kɔʀtizɔn] *nf* cortisone

corvée [kɔʀve] *nf* chore, drudgery *no pl*

cosmétique [kɔsmetik] *nm* beauty care product

cosmopolite [kɔsmɔpɔlit] *adj* cosmopolitan

costaud, e [kɔsto, -od] *adj* strong, sturdy

costume [kɔstym] *nm* (*d'homme*) suit; (*de théâtre*) costume; **costumé, e** *adj* dressed up

cote [kɔt] *nf* (*en Bourse etc*) quotation; **~ d'alerte** danger *ou* flood level; **~ de popularité** popularity rating

côte [kot] *nf* (*rivage*) coast(line); (*pente*) hill; (*Anat*) rib; (*d'un tricot, tissu*) rib, ribbing *no pl*; **~ à ~** side by side; **la C~ (d'Azur)** the (French) Riviera

côté [kote] *nm* (*gén*) side; (*direction*) way, direction; **de chaque ~ (de)** on each side of; **de tous les ~s** from all directions; **de quel ~ est-il parti?** which way *ou* in which direction did he go?; **de ce/de l'autre ~** this/the other way; **du ~ de** (*provenance*) from; (*direction*) towards; **du ~ de Lyon** (*proximité*) near Lyons; **de ~** (*regarder*) sideways; **mettre de ~** to put aside, put on one side; **mettre de l'argent de ~** to save some money; **à ~** (*right*) nearby; (*voisins*) next door; **à ~ de** beside; next to; (*fig*) in comparison to; **être aux ~s de** to be by the side of

Côte d'Ivoire [kotdivwar] *nf*: **la ~** Côte d'Ivoire, the Ivory Coast

côtelette [kotlɛt] *nf* chop

côtier, -ière [kotje, -jɛr] *adj* coastal

cotisation [kotizasjɔ̃] *nf* subscription, dues *pl*; (*pour une pension*) contributions *pl*

cotiser [kotize] /1/ *vi*: **~ (à)** to pay contributions (to); **se cotiser** *vi* to club together

coton [kotɔ̃] *nm* cotton; **~ hydrophile** cotton wool (BRIT), absorbent cotton (US)

Coton-Tige® *nm* cotton bud

cou [ku] *nm* neck

couchant [kuʃɑ̃] *adj*: **soleil ~** setting sun

couche [kuʃ] *nf* layer; (*de peinture, vernis*) coat; (*de bébé*) nappy (BRIT), diaper (US); **~s sociales** social levels *ou* strata

couché, e [kuʃe] *adj* lying down; (*au lit*) in bed

coucher [kuʃe] /1/ *vt* (*personne*) to put to bed (: *loger*) to put up; (*objet*) to lay on its side ▷ *vi* to sleep; **~ avec qn** to sleep with sb; **se coucher** *vi* (*pour dormir*) to go to bed; (*pour se reposer*) to lie down; (*soleil*) to set; **~ de soleil** sunset

couchette [kuʃɛt] *nf* couchette; (*pour voyageur, sur bateau*) berth

coucou [kuku] *nm* cuckoo

coude [kud] *nm* (*Anat*) elbow; (*de tuyau, de la route*) bend; **~ à ~** shoulder to shoulder, side by side

coudre [kudr] /48/ *vt* (*bouton*) to sew on ▷ *vi* to sew

couette [kwɛt] *nf* duvet; **couettes** *nfpl* (*cheveux*) bunches

couffin [kufɛ̃] *nm* Moses basket

couler [kule] /1/ *vi* to flow, run; (*fuir: stylo, récipient*) to leak; (: *nez*) to run; (*sombrer: bateau*) to sink ▷ *vt* (*cloche, sculpture*) to cast; (*bateau*) to sink; (*faire échouer: personne*) to bring down, ruin

couleur [kulœr] *nf* colour (BRIT), color (US); (*Cartes*) suit; **en ~s** (*film*) in colo(u)r; **télévision en ~s** colo(u)r television; **de ~** (*homme, femme: vieilli*) colo(u)red

couleuvre [kulœvr] *nf* grass snake

coulisse [kulis] *nf* (*Tech*) runner; **coulisses** *nfpl* (*Théât*) wings; (*fig*): **dans les ~s** behind the scenes

couloir [kulwar] *nm* corridor, passage; (*d'avion*) aisle; (*de bus*) gangway; **~ aérien** air corridor *ou* lane; **~ de navigation** shipping lane

coup [ku] *nm* (*heurt, choc*) knock; (*affectif*) blow, shock; (*agressif*) blow; (*avec arme à feu*) shot; (*de l'horloge*) stroke; (*Sport: golf*) stroke; (: *tennis*) shot; (*fam: fois*) time; **~ de coude/genou** nudge (with the elbow)/with the knee; **donner un ~ de balai** to give the floor a sweep; **être dans le/hors du ~** to be/not to be in on it; (*à la page*) to be hip *ou* trendy; **du ~** as a result; **d'un seul ~** (*subitement*) suddenly; (*à la fois*) at one go; **du premier ~** first time *ou* go; **du même ~** at the same time; **à ~ sûr** definitely, without fail; **après ~** afterwards; **~ sur ~** in quick succession; **sur le ~**

outright; **sous le ~ de** (*surprise etc*) under the influence of; **à tous les ~s** every time; **tenir le ~** to hold out; **~ de chance** stroke of luck; **~ de couteau** stab (of a knife); **~ d'envoi** kick-off; **~ d'essai** first attempt; **~ d'état** coup d'état; **~ de feu** shot; **~ de filet** (*Police*) haul; **~ de foudre** (*fig*) love at first sight; **~ franc** free kick; **~ de frein** (sharp) braking *no pl*; **~ de grâce** coup de grâce; **~ de main: donner un ~ de main à qn** to give sb a (helping) hand; **~ d'œil** glance; **~ de pied** kick; **~ de poing** punch; **~ de soleil** sunburn *no pl*; **~ de sonnette** ring of the bell; **~ de téléphone** phone call; **~ de tête** (*fig*) (sudden) impulse; **~ de théâtre** (*fig*) dramatic turn of events; **~ de tonnerre** clap of thunder; **~ de vent** gust of wind; **en ~ de vent** (*rapidement*) in a tearing hurry

coupable [kupabl] *adj* guilty ▷ *nm/f* (*gén*) culprit; (*Jur*) guilty party

coupe [kup] *nf* (*verre*) goblet; (*à fruits*) dish; (*Sport*) cup; (*de cheveux, de vêtement*) cut; (*graphique, plan*) (cross) section

couper [kupe] /1/ *vt* to cut; (*retrancher*) to cut (out); (*route, courant*) to cut off; (*appétit*) to take away; (*vin, cidre: à table*) to dilute (with water) ▷ *vi* to cut; (*prendre un raccourci*) to take a short-cut; **se couper** *vi* (*se blesser*) to cut o.s.; **~ la parole à qn** to cut sb short; **nous avons été coupés** we've been cut off

couple [kupl] *nm* couple

couplet [kuplɛ] *nm* verse

coupole [kupɔl] *nf* dome

coupon [kupɔ̃] *nm* (*ticket*) coupon; (*de tissu*) remnant

coupure [kupyʀ] *nf* cut; (*billet de banque*) note; (*de journal*) cutting; **~ de courant** power cut

cour [kuʀ] *nf* (*de ferme, jardin*) (court) yard; (*d'immeuble*) back yard; (*Jur,* *royale*) court; **faire la ~ à qn** to court sb; **~ d'assises** court of assizes; **~ de récréation** playground

courage [kuʀaʒ] *nm* courage, bravery; **courageux, -euse** *adj* brave, courageous

couramment [kuʀamɑ̃] *adv* commonly; (*parler*) fluently

courant, e [kuʀɑ̃, -ɑ̃t] *adj* (*fréquent*) common; (*Comm, gén: normal*) standard; (*en cours*) current ▷ *nm* current; (*fig*) movement; (: *d'opinion*) trend; **être au ~ (de)** (*fait, nouvelle*) to know (about); **mettre qn au ~ (de)** to tell sb (about); (*nouveau travail etc*) to teach sb the basics (of); **se tenir au ~ (de)** (*techniques etc*) to keep o.s. up-to-date (on); **dans le ~ de** (*pendant*) in the course of; **le 10 ~** (*Comm*) the 10th inst.; **~ d'air** draught; **~ électrique** (electric) current, power

courbature [kuʀbatyʀ] *nf* ache

courbe [kuʀb] *adj* curved ▷ *nf* curve

coureur, -euse [kuʀœʀ, -øz] *nm/f* (*Sport*) runner (*ou* driver); (*péj*) womanizer/manhunter

courge [kuʀʒ] *nf* (*Culin*) marrow; **courgette** *nf* courgette (BRIT), zucchini (US)

courir [kuʀiʀ] /11/ *vi* to run ▷ *vt* (*Sport: épreuve*) to compete in; (: *risque*) to run; (: *danger*) to face; **~ les cafés/bals** to do the rounds of the cafés/ dances; **le bruit court que** the rumour is going round that

couronne [kuʀɔn] *nf* crown; (*de fleurs*) wreath, circlet

courons [kuʀɔ̃] *vb voir* **courir**

courriel [kuʀjɛl] *nm* email

courrier [kuʀje] *nm* mail, post; (*lettres à écrire*) letters *pl*; **est-ce que j'ai du ~?** are there any letters for me?; **~ électronique** email

▮ Attention à ne pas traduire *courrier* par le mot anglais *courier*.

courroie [kuʀwa] *nf* strap; (*Tech*) belt

courrons *etc* [kuʀɔ̃] *vb voir* **courir**

cours [kuʀ] nm (leçon) class
(: particulier) lesson; (série de leçons)
course; (écoulement) flow; (Comm:
de devises) rate; (: de denrées) price;
donner libre ~ à to give free
expression to; **avoir ~** (Scol) to have a
class ou lecture; **en ~** (année) current;
(travaux) in progress; **en ~ de route**
on the way; **au ~ de** in the course of,
during; **le ~ du change** the exchange
rate; **~ d'eau** waterway; **~ du soir**
night school

course [kuʀs] nf running; (Sport:
épreuve) race; (d'un taxi, autocar)
journey, trip; (petite mission) errand;
courses nfpl (achats) shopping sg;
faire les ou **ses ~s** to go shopping

court, e [kuʀ, kuʀt] adj short ▷ adv
short ▷ nm: **~ (de tennis)** (tennis)
court; **à ~ de** short of; **prendre qn
de ~** to catch sb unawares; **court-
circuit** nm short-circuit

courtoisie [kuʀtwazi] nf courtesy

couru, e [kuʀy] pp de **courir**

cousais etc [kuzɛ] vb voir **coudre**

couscous [kuskus] nm couscous

cousin, e [kuzɛ̃, -in] nm/f cousin

coussin [kusɛ̃] nm cushion

cousu, e [kuzy] pp de **coudre**

coût [ku] nm cost; **le ~ de la vie** the
cost of living

couteau, x [kuto] nm knife

coûter [kute] /1/ vt to cost ▷ vi
to cost; **~ cher** to be expensive;
combien ça coûte? how much is it?,
what does it cost?; **coûte que coûte**
at all costs; **coûteux, -euse** adj
costly, expensive

coutume [kutym] nf custom

couture [kutyʀ] nf sewing;
(profession) dress-making; (points)
seam; **couturier** nm fashion
designer; **couturière** nf dressmaker

couvent [kuvɑ̃] nm (de sœurs)
convent; (de frères) monastery

couver [kuve] /1/ vt to hatch;
(maladie) to be sickening for ▷ vi (feu)
to smoulder; (révolte) to be brewing

couvercle [kuvɛʀkl] nm lid; (de
bombe aérosol etc, qui se visse) cap, top

couvert, e [kuvɛʀ, -ɛʀt] pp de
couvrir ▷ adj (ciel) overcast ▷ nm
place setting; (place à table) place;
couverts nmpl (ustensiles) cutlery sg;
~ de covered with ou in; **mettre le ~**
to lay the table

couverture [kuvɛʀtyʀ] nf blanket;
(de livre, fig, Assurances) cover; (Presse)
coverage

couvre-lit [kuvʀəli] nm bedspread

couvrir [kuvʀiʀ] /18/ vt to cover;
se couvrir vi (ciel) to cloud over;
(s'habiller) to cover up; (se coiffer) to
put on one's hat

cow-boy [koboj] nm cowboy

crabe [kʀɑb] nm crab

cracher [kʀaʃe] /1/ vi to spit ▷ vt
to spit out

crachin [kʀaʃɛ̃] nm drizzle

craie [kʀɛ] nf chalk

craindre [kʀɛ̃dʀ] /52/ vt to fear, be
afraid of; (être sensible à: chaleur, froid)
to be easily damaged by

crainte [kʀɛ̃t] nf fear; **de ~ de/
que** for fear of/that; **craintif, -ive**
adj timid

crampe [kʀɑ̃p] nf cramp; **j'ai une ~ à
la jambe** I've got cramp in my leg

cramponner [kʀɑ̃pɔne] /1/: **se
cramponner** vi: **se ~ (à)** to hang ou
cling on (to)

cran [kʀɑ̃] nm (entaille) notch; (de
courroie) hole; (courage) guts pl

crâne [kʀɑn] nm skull

crapaud [kʀapo] nm toad

craquement [kʀakmɑ̃] nm crack,
snap; (du plancher) creak, creaking
no pl

craquer [kʀake] /1/ vi (bois, plancher)
to creak; (fil, branche) to snap;
(couture) to come apart; (fig: accusé)
to break down, fall apart ▷ vt: **~ une
allumette** to strike a match; **j'ai
craqué** (fam) I couldn't resist it

crasse [kʀas] nf grime, filth;
crasseux, -euse adj filthy

cravache [kʀavaʃ] nf (riding) crop
cravate [kʀavat] nf tie
crawl [kʀol] nm crawl; **dos ~é**
backstroke
crayon [kʀɛjɔ̃] nm pencil; **~ à bille**
ball-point pen; **~ de couleur** crayon;
crayon-feutre (pl **crayons-feutres**)
nm felt(-tip) pen
création [kʀeasjɔ̃] nf creation
crèche [kʀɛʃ] nf (de Noël) crib;
(garderie) crèche, day nursery
crédit [kʀedi] nm (gén) credit; **crédits**
nmpl funds; **acheter à ~** to buy on
credit ou on easy terms; **faire ~ à**
qn to give sb credit; **créditer** /1/ vt:
créditer un compte (de) to credit an
account (with)
créer [kʀee] /1/ vt to create
crémaillère [kʀemajɛʀ] nf: **pendre**
la ~ to have a house-warming party
crème [kʀɛm] nf cream; (entremets)
cream dessert ▷ adj inv cream; **un**
(café) ~ = a white coffee; **~ anglaise**
(egg) custard; **~ chantilly** whipped
cream; **~ à raser** shaving cream;
~ solaire sun cream
créneau, x [kʀeno] nm (de
fortification) crenel(le); (fig, aussi
Comm) gap, slot; (Auto): **faire un ~** to
reverse into a parking space (between
cars alongside the kerb)
crêpe [kʀɛp] nf (galette) pancake
▷ nm (tissu) crêpe; **crêperie** nf
pancake shop ou restaurant
crépuscule [kʀepyskyl] nm twilight,
dusk
cresson [kʀesɔ̃] nm watercress
creuser [kʀøze] /1/ vt (trou, tunnel)
to dig; (sol) to dig a hole in; (fig) to go
(deeply) into; **ça creuse** that gives
you a real appetite; **se ~ (la cervelle)**
to rack one's brains
creux, -euse [kʀø, -øz] adj hollow
▷ nm hollow; **heures creuses**
slack periods; (électricité, téléphone)
off-peak periods; **avoir un ~** (fam)
to be hungry
crevaison [kʀəvɛzɔ̃] nf puncture

crevé, e [kʀəve] adj (fam: fatigué)
shattered, (BRIT) exhausted
crever [kʀəve] /5/ vt (tambour,
ballon) to burst ▷ vi (pneu) to burst;
(automobiliste) to have a puncture
(BRIT) ou a flat (tire) (US); (fam) to die
crevette [kʀəvɛt] nf: **~ (rose)**
prawn; **~ grise** shrimp
cri [kʀi] nm cry, shout; (d'animal:
spécifique) cry, call; **c'est le dernier ~**
(fig) it's the latest fashion
criard, e [kʀijaʀ, -aʀd] adj (couleur)
garish, loud; (voix) yelling
cric [kʀik] nm (Auto) jack
crier [kʀije] /7/ vi (pour appeler) to
shout, cry (out); (de peur, de douleur
etc) to scream, yell ▷ vt (ordre, injure)
to shout (out), yell (out)
crime [kʀim] nm crime; (meurtre)
murder; **criminel, le** nm/f criminal;
murderer
crin [kʀɛ̃] nm (de cheval) hair no pl
crinière [kʀinjɛʀ] nf mane
crique [kʀik] nf creek, inlet
criquet [kʀikɛ] nm grasshopper
crise [kʀiz] nf crisis (pl crises); (Méd)
attack (: d'épilepsie) fit; **~ cardiaque**
heart attack; **avoir une ~ de foie** to
have really bad indigestion; **piquer**
une ~ de nerfs to go hysterical
cristal, -aux [kʀistal, -o] nm crystal
critère [kʀitɛʀ] nm criterion (pl criteria)
critiquable [kʀitikabl] adj open
to criticism
critique [kʀitik] adj critical ▷ nm/f
(de théâtre, musique) critic ▷ nf
criticism; (Théât etc article) review
critiquer [kʀitike] /1/ vt (dénigrer)
to criticize; (évaluer, juger) to assess,
examine (critically)
croate [kʀɔat] adj Croatian ▷ nm
(Ling) Croat, Croatian ▷ nm/f: **C~**
Croat, Croatian
Croatie [kʀɔasi] nf: **la ~** Croatia
crochet [kʀɔʃɛ] nm hook; (détour)
detour; (Tricot: aiguille) crochet hook;
(: technique) crochet; **vivre aux ~s de**
qn to live ou sponge off sb

crocodile [kʀɔkɔdil] nm crocodile
croire [kʀwaʀ] /44/ vt to believe; **se ~ fort** to think one is strong; **~ que** to believe ou think that; **~ à, ~ en** to believe in
croisade [kʀwazad] nf crusade
croisement [kʀwazmã] nm (carrefour) crossroads sg; (Bio) crossing (: résultat) crossbreed
croiser [kʀwaze] /1/ vt (personne, voiture) to pass; (route) to cross, cut across; (Bio) to cross; **se croiser** vi (personnes, véhicules) to pass each other; (routes) to cross; (regards) to meet; **se ~ les bras** (fig) to fold one's arms, to twiddle one's thumbs
croisière [kʀwazjɛʀ] nf cruise
croissance [kʀwasãs] nf growth
croissant, e [kʀwasã, -ãt] adj growing ▷ nm (à manger) croissant; (motif) crescent
croître [kʀwatʀ] /55/ vi to grow
croix [kʀwa] nf cross; **la C~ Rouge** the Red Cross
croque-madame [kʀɔkmadam] nm inv toasted cheese sandwich with a fried egg on top
croque-monsieur [kʀɔkməsjø] nm inv toasted ham and cheese sandwich
croquer [kʀɔke] /1/ vt (manger) to crunch (: fruit) to munch; (dessiner) to sketch; **chocolat à ~** plain dessert chocolate
croquis [kʀɔki] nm sketch
crotte [kʀɔt] nf droppings pl; **crottin** [kʀɔtɛ̃] nm dung, manure; (fromage) (small round) cheese (made of goat's milk)
croustillant, e [kʀustijã, -ãt] adj crisp
croûte [kʀut] nf crust; (du fromage) rind; (Méd) scab; **en ~** (Culin) in pastry
croûton [kʀutɔ̃] nm (Culin) crouton; (bout du pain) crust, heel
croyant, e [kʀwajã, -ãt] nm/f believer
CRS sigle fpl (= Compagnies républicaines de sécurité) state security police force ▷ sigle m member of the CRS

cru, e [kʀy] pp de **croire** ▷ adj (non cuit) raw; (lumière, couleur) harsh; (paroles, langage) crude ▷ nm (vignoble) vineyard; (vin) wine; **un grand ~** a great vintage; **jambon ~** Parma ham
crû [kʀy] pp de **croître**
cruauté [kʀyote] nf cruelty
cruche [kʀyʃ] nf pitcher, (earthenware) jug
crucifix [kʀysifi] nm crucifix
crudité [kʀydite] nf crudeness no pl; **crudités** nfpl (Culin) selection of raw vegetables
crue [kʀy] nf (inondation) flood; voir aussi **cru**
cruel, le [kʀyɛl] adj cruel
crus, crûs etc [kʀy] vb voir **croire**; **croître**
crustacés [kʀystase] nmpl shellfish
Cuba [kyba] nm Cuba; **cubain, e** adj Cuban ▷ nm/f: **Cubain, e** Cuban
cube [kyb] nm cube; (jouet) brick; **mètre ~** cubic metre; **2 au ~ = 8** 2 cubed is 8
cueillette [kœjɛt] nf picking; (quantité) crop, harvest
cueillir [kœjiʀ] /12/ vt (fruits, fleurs) to pick, gather; (fig) to catch
cuiller, cuillère [kɥijɛʀ] nf spoon; **~ à café** coffee spoon; (Culin) ≈ teaspoonful; **~ à soupe** soup spoon; (Culin) ≈ tablespoonful; **cuillerée** nf spoonful
cuir [kɥiʀ] nm leather; (avant tannage) hide; **~ chevelu** scalp
cuire [kɥiʀ] /38/ vt: (aliments) to cook; (au four) to bake ▷ vi to cook; **bien cuit** (viande) well done; **trop cuit** overdone
cuisine [kɥizin] nf (pièce) kitchen; (art culinaire) cookery, cooking; (nourriture) cooking, food; **faire la ~** to cook; **cuisiné, e** adj: **plat cuisiné** ready-made meal ou dish; **cuisiner** /1/ vt to cook; (fam) to grill ▷ vi to cook; **cuisinier, -ière** nm/f cook ▷ nf (poêle) cooker
cuisse [kɥis] nf thigh; (Culin) leg

cuisson [kɥisɔ̃] nf cooking

cuit, e [kɥi, -it] pp de **cuire**

cuivre [kɥivR] nm copper; **les ~s** (Mus) the brass

cul [ky] nm (fam!) arse (!)

culminant, e [kylminɑ̃, -ɑ̃t] adj: **point ~** highest point

culot [kylo] (fam) nm (effronterie) cheek

culotte [kylɔt] nf (de femme) panties pl, knickers pl (BRIT)

culte [kylt] nm (religion) religion; (hommage, vénération) worship; (protestant) service

cultivateur, -trice [kyltivatœR, -tRis] nm/f farmer

cultivé, e [kyltive] adj (personne) cultured, cultivated

cultiver [kyltive] /1/ vt to cultivate; (légumes) to grow, cultivate

culture [kyltyR] nf cultivation; (connaissances etc) culture; **les ~s intensives** intensive farming; **~ OGM** GM crop; **~ physique** physical training; **culturel, le** adj cultural

cumin [kymɛ̃] nm cumin

cure [kyR] nf (Méd) course of treatment; **~ d'amaigrissement** slimming course; **~ de repos** rest cure

curé [kyRe] nm parish priest

cure-dent [kyRdɑ̃] nm toothpick

curieux, -euse [kyRjø, -øz] adj (étrange) strange, curious; (indiscret) curious, inquisitive ▷ nmpl (badauds) onlookers; **curiosité** nf curiosity; (site) unusual feature ou sight

curriculum vitae [kyRikylɔmvite] nm inv curriculum vitae

curseur [kyRsœR] nm (Inform) cursor; (de règle) slide; (de fermeture-éclair) slider

cutané, e [kytane] adj skin cpd

cuve [kyv] nf vat; (à mazout etc) tank

cuvée [kyve] nf vintage

cuvette [kyvɛt] nf (récipient) bowl, basin; (Géo) basin

CV sigle m (Auto); = **cheval (vapeur)**; (Admin) = **curriculum vitae**

cybercafé [sibɛRkafe] nm Internet café

cyberespace [sibɛRɛspas] nm cyberspace

cybernaute [sibɛRnot] nm/f Internet user

cyclable [siklabl] adj: **piste ~** cycle track

cycle [sikl] nm cycle; **cyclisme** [siklism] nm cycling; **cycliste** [siklist] nm/f cyclist ▷ adj cycle cpd; **coureur cycliste** racing cyclist

cyclomoteur [siklomɔtœR] nm moped

cyclone [siklon] nm hurricane

cygne [siɲ] nm swan

cylindre [silɛ̃dR] nm cylinder; **cylindrée** nf (Auto) (cubic) capacity; **une (voiture de) grosse cylindrée** a big-engined car

cymbale [sɛ̃bal] nf cymbal

cynique [sinik] adj cynical

cystite [sistit] nf cystitis

d

d' prép, art voir **de**

dactylo [daktilo] nf (aussi: **~graphe**) typist; (aussi: **~graphie**) typing

dada [dada] nm hobby-horse

daim [dɛ̃] nm (fallow) deer inv; (cuir suédé) suede

daltonien, ne [daltɔnjɛ̃, -ɛn] adj colour-blind

dame [dam] nf lady; (Cartes, Échecs) queen; **dames** nfpl (jeu) draughts sg (BRIT), checkers sg (US)

Danemark [danmark] nm: **le ~** Denmark

danger [dɑ̃ʒe] nm danger; **mettre en ~** (personne) to put in danger; (projet, carrière) to jeopardize; **être en ~** (personne) to be in danger; **être en ~ de mort** to be in peril of one's life; **être hors de ~** to be out of danger; **dangereux, -euse** adj dangerous

danois, e [danwa, -waz] adj Danish ▷ nm (Ling) Danish ▷ nm/f: **D~, e** Dane

dans [dɑ̃] prép **1** (position) in; (: à l'intérieur de) inside; **c'est dans le tiroir/le salon** it's in the drawer/lounge; **dans la boîte** in ou inside the box; **marcher dans la ville/la rue** to walk about the town/along the street; **je l'ai lu dans le journal** I read it in the newspaper

2 (direction) into; **elle a couru dans le salon** she ran into the lounge; **monter dans une voiture/le bus** to get into a car/on to the bus

3 (provenance) out of, from; **je l'ai pris dans le tiroir/salon** I took it out of ou from the drawer/lounge; **boire dans un verre** to drink out of ou from a glass

4 (temps) in; **dans deux mois** in two months, in two months' time

5 (approximation) about; **dans les 20 euros** about 20 euros

danse [dɑ̃s] nf: **la ~** dancing; (classique) (ballet) dancing; **une ~** a dance; **danser** /1/ vi, vt to dance; **danseur, -euse** nm/f ballet dancer; (au bal etc) dancer (: cavalier) partner

date [dat] nf date; **de longue ~** longstanding; **~ de naissance** date of birth; **~ limite** deadline; **dater** /1/ vt, vi to date; **dater de** to date from; **à dater de** (as) from

datte [dat] nf date

dauphin [dofɛ̃] nm (Zool) dolphin

davantage [davɑ̃taʒ] adv more; (plus longtemps) longer; **~ de** more

MOT-CLÉ

de, d' [də, d] (de + le = **du**, de + les = **des**) prép **1** (appartenance) of; **le toit de la maison** the roof of the house; **la voiture d'Elisabeth/de mes parents** Elisabeth's/my parents' car

2 (provenance) from; **il vient de Londres** he comes from London; **elle**

est sortie du cinéma she came out of the cinema

3 (*moyen*) with; **je l'ai fait de mes propres mains** I did it with my own two hands

4 (*caractérisation, mesure*): **un mur de brique/bureau d'acajou** a brick wall/mahogany desk; **un billet de 10 euros** a 10 euro note; **une pièce de 2 m de large** *ou* **large de 2 m** a room 2 m wide, a 2m-wide room; **un bébé de 10 mois** a 10-month-old baby; **12 mois de crédit/travail** 12 months' credit/work; **elle est payée 20 euros de l'heure** she's paid 20 euros an hour *ou* per hour; **augmenter de 10 euros** to increase by 10 euros

5 (*rapport*) from; **de quatre à six** from four to six

6 (*cause*): **mourir de faim** to die of hunger; **rouge de colère** red with fury

7 (*vb + de + infin*) to; **il m'a dit de rester** he told me to stay

▶ *art* **1** (*phrases affirmatives*) some (*souvent omis*); **du vin, de l'eau, des pommes** (some) wine, (some) water, (some) apples; **des enfants sont venus** some children came; **pendant des mois** for months

2 (*phrases interrogatives et négatives*) any; **a-t-il du vin?** has he got any wine?; **il n'a pas de pommes/d'enfants** he hasn't (got) any apples/children, he has no apples/children

dé [de] *nm* (*à jouer*) die *ou* dice; (*aussi*: **dé à coudre**) thimble

déballer [debale] /1/ *vt* to unpack

débarcadère [debaʀkadɛʀ] *nm* wharf

débardeur [debaʀdœʀ] *nm* (*pour femme*) vest top; (*pour homme*) sleeveless top

débarquer [debaʀke] /1/ *vt* to unload, land ▷ *vi* to disembark; (*fig*) to turn up

débarras [debaʀɑ] *nm* (*pièce*) lumber room; (*placard*) junk cupboard; **bon ~!** good riddance!; **débarrasser** /1/ *vt*

to clear ▷ *vi* (*enlever le couvert*) to clear away; **se débarrasser de** *vt* to get rid of; **débarrasser qn de** (*vêtements, paquets*) to relieve sb of

débat [deba] *nm* discussion, debate; **débattre** /41/ *vt* to discuss, debate; **se débattre** *vi* to struggle

débit [debi] *nm* (*d'un liquide, fleuve*) (rate of) flow; (*d'un magasin*) turnover (of goods); (*élocution*) delivery; (*bancaire*) debit; **~ de boissons** drinking establishment; **~ de tabac** tobacconist's (shop)

déblayer [debleje] /8/ *vt* to clear

débloquer [debloke] /1/ *vt* (*frein, fonds*) to release; (*prix, crédits*) to free ▷ *vi* (*fam*) to talk rubbish

déboîter [debwate] /1/ *vt* (*Auto*) to pull out; **se ~ le genou** *etc* to dislocate one's knee *etc*

débordé, e [debɔʀde] *adj*: **être ~ de** (*travail, demandes*) to be snowed under with

déborder [debɔʀde] /1/ *vi* to overflow; (*lait etc*) to boil over; **~ (de) qch** (*dépasser*) to extend beyond sth; **~ de** (*joie, zèle*) to be brimming over with *ou* bursting with

débouché [debuʃe] *nm* (*pour vendre*) outlet; (*perspective d'emploi*) opening

déboucher [debuʃe] /1/ *vt* (*évier, tuyau etc*) to unblock; (*bouteille*) to uncork ▷ *vi*: **~ de** to emerge from; **~ sur** (*études*) to lead on to

debout [dəbu] *adv*: **être ~** (*personne*) to be standing, stand; (*levé, éveillé*) to be up (and about); **se mettre ~** to get up (on one's feet); **se tenir ~** to stand; **~!** stand up!; (*du lit*) get up!; **cette histoire ne tient pas ~** this story doesn't hold water

déboutonner [debutɔne] /1/ *vt* to undo, unbutton

débraillé, e [debʀaje] *adj* slovenly, untidy

débrancher [debʀɑ̃ʃe] /1/ *vt* (*appareil électrique*) to unplug; (*téléphone, courant électrique*) to disconnect

débrayage [debʀɛjaʒ] nm (Auto) clutch; **débrayer** /8/ vi (Auto) to declutch; (cesser le travail) to stop work

débris [debʀi] nm fragment ▷ nmpl: **des ~ de verre** bits of glass

débrouillard, e [debʀujaʀ, -aʀd] adj smart, resourceful

débrouiller [debʀuje] /1/ vt to disentangle, untangle; **se débrouiller** vi to manage; **débrouillez-vous** you'll have to sort things out yourself

début [deby] nm beginning, start; **débuts** nmpl (de carrière) début sg; **~ juin** in early June; **débutant, e** nm/f beginner, novice; **débuter** /1/ vi to begin, start; (faire ses débuts) to start out

décaféiné, e [dekafeine] adj decaffeinated

décalage [dekalaʒ] nm gap; **~ horaire** time difference (between time zones), time-lag

décaler [dekale] /1/ vt to shift forward ou back

décapotable [dekapɔtabl] adj convertible

décapsuleur [dekapsylœʀ] nm bottle-opener

décédé, e [desede] adj deceased

décéder [desede] /6/ vi to die

décembre [desɑ̃bʀ] nm December

décennie [deseni] nf decade

décent, e [desɑ̃, -ɑ̃t] adj decent

déception [desɛpsjɔ̃] nf disappointment

décès [desɛ] nm death

décevoir [des(ə)vwaʀ] /28/ vt to disappoint

décharge [deʃaʀʒ] nf (dépôt d'ordures) rubbish tip ou dump; (électrique) electrical discharge; **décharger** /3/ vt (marchandise, véhicule) to unload; (faire feu) to discharge, fire; **décharger qn de** (responsabilité) to relieve sb of, release sb from

déchausser [deʃose] /1/ vt (skis) to take off; **se déchausser** vi to take

off one's shoes; (dent) to come ou work loose

déchet [deʃɛ] nm (de bois, tissu etc) scrap; **déchets** nmpl (ordures) refuse sg, rubbish sg; **~s nucléaires** nuclear waste

déchiffrer [deʃifʀe] /1/ vt to decipher

déchirant, e [deʃiʀɑ̃, -ɑ̃t] adj heart-rending

déchirement [deʃiʀmɑ̃] nm (chagrin) wrench, heartbreak; (gén pl: conflit) rift, split

déchirer [deʃiʀe] /1/ vt to tear; (mettre en morceaux) to tear up; (arracher) to tear out; (fig) to tear apart; **se déchirer** vi to tear, rip; **se ~ un muscle/tendon** to tear a muscle/ tendon

déchirure [deʃiʀyʀ] nf (accroc) tear, rip; **~ musculaire** torn muscle

décidé, e [deside] adj (personne, air) determined; **c'est ~** it's decided; **décidément** adv really

décider [deside] /1/ vt: **~ qch** to decide on sth; **~ de faire/que** to decide to do/that; **~ qn (à faire qch)** to persuade ou induce sb (to do sth); **se ~ à faire** to decide ou make up one's mind to do; **se ~ pour qch** to decide on ou in favour of sth

décimal, e, -aux [desimal, -o] adj decimal

décimètre [desimɛtʀ] nm decimetre

décisif, -ive [desizif, -iv] adj decisive

décision [desizjɔ̃] nf decision

déclaration [deklaʀasjɔ̃] nf declaration; (discours: Pol etc) statement; **~ (d'impôts)** ≈ tax return; **~ de revenus** statement of income; **faire une ~ de vol** to report a theft

déclarer [deklaʀe] /1/ vt to declare; (décès, naissance) to register; **se déclarer** vi (feu, maladie) to break out

déclencher [deklɑ̃ʃe] /1/ vt (mécanisme etc) to release; (sonnerie) to set off; (attaque, grève) to launch; (provoquer) to trigger off; **se déclencher** vi (sonnerie) to go off

décliner [dekline] /1/ *vi* to decline
▷ *vt* (*invitation*) to decline; (*nom,
adresse*) to state

décoiffer [dekwafe] /1/ *vt*: **~ qn**
to mess up sb's hair; **je suis toute
décoiffée** my hair is in a real mess

déçois *etc* [deswa] *vb voir* **décevoir**

décollage [dekɔlaʒ] *nm* (*Aviat, Écon*)
takeoff

décoller [dekɔle] /1/ *vt* to unstick ▷ *vi*
(*avion*) to take off; **se décoller** *vi* to
come unstuck

décolleté, e [dekɔlte] *adj* low-cut
▷ *nm* low neck(line); (*plongeant*)
cleavage

décolorer [dekɔlɔʀe] /1/: **se
décolorer** *vi* to fade; **se faire ~ les
cheveux** to have one's hair bleached

décommander [dekɔmɑ̃de] /1/
vt to cancel; **se décommander** *vi*
to cancel

déconcerter [dekɔ̃sɛʀte] /1/ *vt* to
disconcert, confound

décongeler [dekɔ̃ʒ(ə)le] /5/ *vt* to
thaw (out)

déconner [dekɔne] /1/ *vi* (*fam!*)
to talk (a load of) rubbish (BRIT) *ou*
garbage (US)

déconseiller [dekɔ̃seje] /1/ *vt*: **~ qch
(à qn)** to advise (sb) against sth;
c'est déconseillé it's not advised *ou*
advisable

décontracté, e [dekɔ̃tʀakte] *adj*
relaxed, laid-back (*fam*)

décontracter [dekɔ̃tʀakte] /1/: **se
décontracter** *vi* to relax

décor [dekɔʀ] *nm* décor; (*paysage*)
scenery; **décorateur, -trice** *nm/f*
(*interior*) decorator; **décoration**
nf decoration; **décorer** /1/ *vt* to
decorate

décortiquer [dekɔʀtike] /1/ *vt* to
shell; (*fig: texte*) to dissect

découdre /48/: **se découdre** *vi* to
come unstitched

découper [dekupe] /1/ *vt* (*papier,
tissu etc*) to cut up; (*volaille, viande*) to
carve; (*manche, article*) to cut out

décourager [dekuʀaʒe] /3/ *vt* to
discourage; **se décourager** *vi* to lose
heart, become discouraged

décousu, e [dekuzy] *adj* unstitched;
(*fig*) disjointed, disconnected

découvert, e [dekuvɛʀ, -ɛʀt] *adj*
(*tête*) bare, uncovered; (*lieu*) open,
exposed ▷ *nm* (*bancaire*) overdraft
▷ *nf* discovery; **faire la ~e de** to
discover

découvrir [dekuvʀiʀ] /18/ *vt* to
discover; (*enlever ce qui couvre ou
protège*) to uncover; (*montrer, dévoiler*)
to reveal; **se découvrir** *vi* (*chapeau*)
to take off one's hat; (*se déshabiller*) to
take something off; (*ciel*) to clear

décrire [dekʀiʀ] /39/ *vt* to describe

décrocher [dekʀɔʃe] /1/ *vt* (*dépendre*)
to take down; (*téléphone*) to take
off the hook; (: *pour répondre*): **~ (le
téléphone)** to pick up *ou* lift the
receiver; (*fig: contrat etc*) to get, land
▷ *vi* (*fam: abandonner*) to drop out;
(: *cesser d'écouter*) to switch off

déçu, e [desy] *pp de* **décevoir**

dédaigner [dedeɲe] /1/ *vt* to
despise, scorn; (*négliger*) to disregard,
spurn; **dédaigneux, -euse** *adj*
scornful, disdainful; **dédain** *nm*
scorn, disdain

dedans [dədɑ̃] *adv* inside; (*pas en
plein air*) indoors, inside ▷ *nm* inside;
au ~ inside

dédicacer [dedikase] /3/ *vt*: **~ (à qn)**
to sign (for sb), autograph (for sb)

dédier [dedje] /7/ *vt*: **~ à** to dedicate
to

dédommagement [dedɔmaʒmɑ̃]
nm compensation

dédommager [dedɔmaʒe] /3/ *vt*:
~ qn (de) to compensate sb (for)

dédouaner [dedwane] /1/ *vt* to clear
through customs

déduire [deduiʀ] /38/ *vt*: **~ qch (de)**
(*ôter*) to deduct sth (from); (*conclure*)
to deduce *ou* infer sth (from)

défaillance [defajɑ̃s] *nf* (*syncope*)
blackout; (*fatigue*) (sudden) weakness

no pl; (*technique*) fault, failure;
~ cardiaque heart failure

défaire [defɛʀ] /60/ *vt* (*installation*, *échafaudage*) to take down, dismantle; (*paquet etc, nœud*, *vêtement*) to undo; **se défaire** *vi* to come undone; **se ~ de** to get rid of

défait, e [defɛ, -ɛt] *adj* (*visage*) haggard, ravaged ▷ *nf* defeat

défaut [defo] *nm* (*moral*) fault, failing; defect; (*d'étoffe, métal*) fault, flaw; (*manque, carence*) **~ de** shortage of; **prendre qn en ~** to catch sb out; **faire ~** (*manquer*) to be lacking; **à ~ de** for lack *ou* want of

défavorable [defavɔʀabl] *adj* unfavourable (BRIT), unfavorable (US)

défavoriser [defavɔʀize] /1/ *vt* to put at a disadvantage

défectueux, -euse [defɛktɥø, -øz] *adj* faulty, defective

défendre [defɑ̃dʀ] /41/ *vt* to defend; (*interdire*) to forbid; **se défendre** *vi* to defend o.s.; **~ à qn qch/de faire** to forbid sb sth/to do; **il se défend** (*fig*) he can hold his own; **se ~ de/ contre** (*se protéger*) to protect o.s. from/against; **se ~ de** (*se garder de*) to refrain from

défense [defɑ̃s] *nf* defence; (*d'éléphant etc*) tusk; **ministre de la ~** Minister of Defence (BRIT), Defence Secretary; **"~ de fumer/cracher"** "no smoking/spitting"

défi [defi] *nm* challenge; **lancer un ~ à qn** to challenge sb; **sur un ton de ~** defiantly

déficit [defisit] *nm* (*Comm*) deficit

défier [defje] /7/ *vt* (*provoquer*) to challenge; (*fig*) to defy; **~ qn de faire** to challenge *ou* defy sb to do

défigurer [defigyʀe] /1/ *vt* to disfigure

défilé [defile] *nm* (*Géo*) (narrow) gorge *ou* pass; (*soldats*) parade; (*manifestants*) procession, march

défiler [defile] /1/ *vi* (*troupes*) to march past; (*sportifs*) to parade;

(*manifestants*) to march; (*visiteurs*) to pour, stream; **faire ~ un document** (*Inform*) to scroll a document; **se défiler** *vi*: **il s'est défilé** (*fam*) he wriggled out of it

définir [definiʀ] /2/ *vt* to define

définitif, -ive [definitif, -iv] *adj* (*final*) final, definitive; (*pour longtemps*) permanent, definitive; (*sans appel*) definite ▷ *nf*: **en définitive** eventually; (*somme toute*) when all is said and done; **définitivement** *adv* permanently

déformer [defɔʀme] /1/ *vt* to put out of shape; (*pensée, fait*) to distort; **se déformer** *vi* to lose its shape

défouler [defule] /1/: **se défouler** *vi* to unwind, let off steam

défunt, e [defœ̃, -œ̃t] *adj*: **son ~ père** his late father ▷ *nm/f* deceased

dégagé, e [degaʒe] *adj* (*route, ciel*) clear; **sur un ton ~** casually

dégager [degaʒe] /3/ *vt* (*exhaler*) to give off; (*délivrer*) to free, extricate; (*désencombrer*) to clear; (*isoler, mettre en valeur*) to bring out; **se dégager** *vi* (*passage, ciel*) to clear; **~ qn de** (*engagement, parole etc*) to release *ou* free sb from

dégâts [degɑ] *nmpl* damage *sg*; **faire des ~** to damage

dégel [deʒɛl] *nm* thaw; **dégeler** /5/ *vt* to thaw (out)

dégivrer [deʒivʀe] /1/ *vt* (*frigo*) to defrost; (*vitres*) to de-ice

dégonflé, e [degɔ̃fle] *adj* (*pneu*) flat

dégonfler [degɔ̃fle] /1/ *vt* (*pneu, ballon*) to let down, deflate; **se dégonfler** *vi* (*fam*) to chicken out

dégouliner [deguline] /1/ *vi* to trickle, drip

dégourdi, e [deguʀdi] *adj* smart, resourceful

dégourdir [deguʀdiʀ] /2/ *vt*: **se ~ (les jambes)** to stretch one's legs

dégoût [degu] *nm* disgust, distaste; **dégoûtant, e** *adj* disgusting; **dégoûté, e** *adj* disgusted; **dégoûté**

de sick of; **dégoûter** /1/ *vt* to disgust; **dégoûter qn de qch** to put sb off sth

dégrader [degrade] /1/ *vt* (*Mil: officier*) to degrade; (*abîmer*) to damage, deface; **se dégrader** *vi* (*relations, situation*) to deteriorate

degré [dəgʀe] *nm* degree

dégressif, -ive [degʀesif, -iv] *adj* on a decreasing scale

dégringoler [degʀɛ̃gɔle] /1/ *vi* to tumble (down)

déguisement [degizmɑ̃] *nm* (*pour s'amuser*) fancy dress

déguiser [degize] /1/: **se déguiser (en)** *vi* (*se costumer*) to dress up (as); (*pour tromper*) to disguise o.s. (as)

dégustation [degystasjɔ̃] *nf* (*de fromages etc*) sampling; **~ de vin(s)** wine-tasting

déguster [degyste] /1/ *vt* (*vins*) to taste; (*fromages etc*) to sample; (*savourer*) to enjoy

dehors [dəɔʀ] *adv* outside; (*en plein air*) outdoors ▷ *nm* outside ▷ *nmpl* (*apparences*) appearances; **mettre** ou **jeter ~** to throw out; **au ~** outside; **au ~ de** outside; **en ~ de** apart from

déjà [deʒa] *adv* already; (*auparavant*) before, already

déjeuner [deʒœne] /1/ *vi* to (have) lunch; (*le matin*) to have breakfast ▷ *nm* lunch

delà [dəla] *adv*: **en ~ (de), au ~ (de)** beyond

délacer [delase] /3/ *vt* (*chaussures*) to undo, unlace

délai [delɛ] *nm* (*attente*) waiting period; (*sursis*) extension (of time); (*temps accordé*) time limit; **sans ~** without delay; **dans les ~s** within the time limit

délaisser [delese] /1/ *vt* to abandon, desert

délasser [delɑse] /1/ *vt* to relax; **se délasser** *vi* to relax

délavé, e [delave] *adj* faded

délayer [deleje] /8/ *vt* (*Culin*) to mix (with water *etc*); (*peinture*) to thin down

delco® [dɛlko] *nm* (*Auto*) distributor

délégué, e [delege] *nm/f* representative

déléguer [delege] /6/ *vt* to delegate

délibéré, e [delibeʀe] *adj* (*conscient*) deliberate

délicat, e [delika, -at] *adj* delicate; (*plein de tact*) tactful; (*attentionné*) thoughtful; **délicatement** *adv* delicately; (*avec douceur*) gently

délice [delis] *nm* delight

délicieux, -euse [delisjø, -øz] *adj* (*au goût*) delicious; (*sensation, impression*) delightful

délimiter [delimite] /1/ *vt* (*terrain*) to delimit, demarcate

délinquant, e [delɛ̃kɑ̃, -ɑ̃t] *adj, nm/f* delinquent

délirer [deliʀe] /1/ *vi* to be delirious; **tu délires!** (*fam*) you're crazy!

délit [deli] *nm* (*criminal*) offence

délivrer [delivʀe] /1/ *vt* (*prisonnier*) to (set) free, release; (*passeport, certificat*) to issue

deltaplane® [dɛltaplan] *nm* hang-glider

déluge [delyʒ] *nm* (*biblique*) Flood; (*grosse pluie*) downpour

demain [d(ə)mɛ̃] *adv* tomorrow; **~ matin/soir** tomorrow morning/ evening

demande [d(ə)mɑ̃d] *nf* (*requête*) request; (*revendication*) demand; (*formulaire*) application; (*Écon*): **la ~** demand; **"~s d'emploi"** "situations wanted"

demandé, e [d(ə)mɑ̃de] *adj* (*article etc*): **très ~** (very) much in demand

demander [d(ə)mɑ̃de] /1/ *vt* to ask for; (*date, heure, chemin*) to ask; (*requérir, nécessiter*) to require, demand; **~ qch à qn** to ask sb for sth; **~ à qn de faire** to ask sb to do; **se ~ si/pourquoi** *etc* to wonder if/why *etc*; **je ne demande pas mieux** I'm asking nothing more; **demandeur, -euse** *nm/f*: **demandeur d'asile**

asylum-seeker; **demandeur d'emploi** job-seeker

démangeaison [demãʒɛzɔ̃] nf itching; **avoir des ~s** to be itching

démanger [demãʒe] /3/ vi to itch

démaquillant [demakijã] nm make-up remover

démaquiller [demakije] /1/ vt: **se démaquiller** to remove one's make-up

démarche [demarʃ] nf (allure) gait, walk; (intervention) step; (fig: intellectuelle) thought processes pl; **faire les ~s nécessaires (pour obtenir qch)** to take the necessary steps (to obtain sth)

démarrage [demaraʒ] nm start

démarrer [demare] /1/ vi (conducteur) to start (up); (véhicule) to move off; (travaux, affaire) to get moving; **démarreur** nm (Auto) starter

démêlant, e [demelã, -ãt] adj: **crème ~e** (hair) conditioner ▷ nm conditioner

démêler [demele] /1/ vt to untangle; **démêlés** nmpl problems

déménagement [demenaʒmã] nm move; **entreprise/camion de ~** removal (BRIT) ou moving (US) firm/van

déménager [demenaʒe] /3/ vt (meubles) to (re)move ▷ vi to move (house); **déménageur** nm removal man

démerder [demɛrde] /1/: **se démerder** vi (fam!) to bloody well manage for o.s.

démettre [demɛtr] /56/ vt: **~ qn de** (fonction, poste) to dismiss sb from; **se ~ l'épaule** etc to dislocate one's shoulder etc

demeurer [d(ə)mœre] /1/ vi (habiter) to live; (rester) to remain

demi, e [dəmi] adj half; **et ~: trois heures/bouteilles et ~es** three and a half hours/bottles ▷ nm (bière: = 0.25 litre) ≈ half-pint; **il est 2 heures et ~e** it's half past 2; **il est midi et ~** it's

half past 12; **à ~** half-; **à la ~e** (heure) on the half-hour; **demi-douzaine** nf half-dozen, half a dozen; **demi-finale** nf semifinal; **demi-frère** nm half-brother; **demi-heure** nf: **une demi-heure** a half-hour, half an hour; **demi-journée** nf half-day, half a day; **demi-litre** nm half-litre (BRIT), half-liter (US), half a litre ou liter; **demi-livre** nf half-pound, half a pound; **demi-pension** nf half-board; **demi-pensionnaire** nm/f: **être demi-pensionnaire** to take school lunches

démis, e adj (épaule etc) dislocated

demi-sœur [dəmisœr] nf half-sister

démission [demisjɔ̃] nf resignation; **donner sa ~** to give ou hand in one's notice; **démissionner** /1/ vi to resign

demi-tarif [dəmitarif] nm half-price; (Transports) half-fare; **voyager à ~** to travel half-fare

demi-tour [dəmitur] nm about-turn; **faire ~** to turn (and go) back

démocratie [demɔkrasi] nf democracy; **démocratique** adj democratic

démodé, e [demɔde] adj old-fashioned

demoiselle [d(ə)mwazɛl] nf (jeune fille) young lady; (célibataire) single lady, maiden lady; **~ d'honneur** bridesmaid

démolir [demɔlir] /2/ vt to demolish

démon [demɔ̃] nm (enfant turbulent) devil, demon; **le D~** the Devil

démonstration [demɔ̃strasjɔ̃] nf demonstration

démonter [demɔ̃te] /1/ vt (machine etc) to take down, dismantle; **se démonter** vi (meuble) to be dismantled, be taken to pieces; (personne) to lose countenance

démontrer [demɔ̃tre] /1/ vt to demonstrate

démouler [demule] /1/ vt to turn out

démuni, e [demyni] adj (sans argent) impoverished; **~ de** without

dénicher [deniʃe] /1/ vt (fam: objet) to unearth; (: restaurant etc) to discover

dénier [denje] /7/ vt to deny

dénivellation [denivelasjɔ̃] nf (pente) ramp

dénombrer [denɔ̃bʀe] /1/ vt to count

dénomination [denɔminasjɔ̃] nf designation, appellation

dénoncer [denɔ̃se] /3/ vt to denounce; **se dénoncer** to give o.s. up, come forward

dénouement [denumɑ̃] nm outcome

dénouer [denwe] /1/ vt to unknot, undo

denrée [dɑ̃ʀe] nf (aussi: **~ alimentaire**) food(stuff)

dense [dɑ̃s] adj dense; **densité** nf density

dent [dɑ̃] nf tooth; **~ de lait/sagesse** milk/wisdom tooth; **dentaire** adj dental; **cabinet dentaire** dental surgery

dentelle [dɑ̃tɛl] nf lace no pl

dentier [dɑ̃tje] nm denture

dentifrice [dɑ̃tifʀis] nm: **(pâte) ~** toothpaste

dentiste nm/f dentist

dentition [dɑ̃tisjɔ̃] nf teeth pl

dénué, e [denɥe] adj: **~ de** devoid of

déodorant [deɔdɔʀɑ̃] nm deodorant

déontologie [deɔ̃tɔlɔʒi] nf (professional) code of practice

dépannage [depanaʒ] nm: **service/ camion de ~** (Auto) breakdown service/truck

dépanner [depane] /1/ vt (voiture, télévision) to fix, repair; (fig) to bail out, help out; **dépanneuse** nf breakdown lorry (BRIT), tow truck (US)

dépareillé, e [depaʀeje] adj (collection, service) incomplete; (gant, volume, objet) odd

départ [depaʀ] nm departure; (Sport) start; **au ~** at the start; **la veille de son ~** the day before he leaves/left

département [depaʀtəmɑ̃] nm department

○ **DÉPARTEMENTS**
○
○
○ France is divided into 96
○ administrative units called
○ départements. These local
○ government divisions are headed
○ by a state-appointed 'préfet',
○ and administered by an elected
○ 'Conseil général'. Départements are
○ usually named after prominent
○ geographical features such as
○ rivers or mountain ranges.

dépassé, e [depase] adj superseded, outmoded; (fig) out of one's depth

dépasser [depase] /1/ vt (véhicule, concurrent) to overtake; (endroit) to pass, go past; (somme, limite) to exceed; (fig: en beauté etc) to surpass, outshine ▷ vi (jupon) to show; **se dépasser** to excel o.s.

dépaysé, e [depeize] adj disoriented

dépaysement [depeizmɑ̃] nm change of scenery

dépêcher [depeʃe] /1/: **se dépêcher** vi to hurry

dépendance [depɑ̃dɑ̃s] nf dependence no pl; (bâtiment) outbuilding

dépendre [depɑ̃dʀ] /41/ vt: **~ de** vt to depend on, to be dependent on; **ça dépend** it depends

dépens [depɑ̃] nmpl: **aux ~ de** at the expense of

dépense [depɑ̃s] nf spending no pl, expense, expenditure no pl; **dépenser** /1/ vt to spend; (fig) to expend, use up; **se dépenser** vi to exert o.s.

dépeupler [depœple] /1/: **se dépeupler** vi to become depopulated

dépilatoire [depilatwaʀ] adj: **crème ~** hair-removing ou depilatory cream

dépister [depiste] /1/ vt to detect; (voleur) to track down

dépit [depi] *nm* vexation, frustration; **en ~ de** in spite of; **en ~ du bon sens** contrary to all good sense; **dépité, e** *adj* vexed, frustrated

déplacé, e [deplase] *adj* (*propos*) out of place, uncalled-for

déplacement [deplasmã] *nm* (*voyage*) trip, travelling *no pl*; **en ~** away (on a trip)

déplacer [deplase] /3/ *vt* (*table, voiture*) to move, shift; **se déplacer** *vi* to move; (*voyager*) to travel; **se ~ une vertèbre** to slip a disc

déplaire [deplɛʀ] /54/ *vi*: **ceci me déplaît** I don't like this, I dislike this; **se ~ quelque part** to dislike it *ou* be unhappy somewhere; **déplaisant, e** *adj* disagreeable

dépliant [deplijã] *nm* leaflet

déplier [deplije] /7/ *vt* to unfold

déposer [depoze] /1/ *vt* (*gén: mettre, poser*) to lay down, put down; (*à la banque, à la consigne*) to deposit; (*passager*) to drop (off), set down; (*roi*) to depose; (*marque*) to register; (*plainte*) to lodge; **se déposer** *vi* to settle; **dépositaire** *nm/f* (*Comm*) agent; **déposition** *nf* statement

dépôt [depo] *nm* (*à la banque, sédiment*) deposit; (*entrepôt, réserve*) warehouse, store

dépourvu, e [depuʀvy] *adj*: **~ de** lacking in, without; **prendre qn au ~** to catch sb unawares

dépression *nf* depression; **~ (nerveuse)** (nervous) breakdown

déprimant, e [depʀimã, -ãt] *adj* depressing

déprimer [depʀime] /1/ *vt* to depress

MOT-CLÉ

depuis [dəpɥi] *prép* **1** (*point de départ dans le temps*) since; **il habite Paris depuis 1983/l'an dernier** he has been living in Paris since 1983/last year; **depuis quand?** since when?;

depuis quand le connaissez-vous? how long have you known him?
2 (*temps écoulé*) for; **il habite Paris depuis cinq ans** he has been living in Paris for five years; **je le connais depuis trois ans** I've known him for three years
3 (*lieu*): **il a plu depuis Metz** it's been raining since Metz; **elle a téléphoné depuis Valence** she rang from Valence
4 (*quantité, rang*) from; **depuis les plus petits jusqu'aux plus grands** from the youngest to the oldest
▶ *adv* (*temps*) since (then); **je ne lui ai pas parlé depuis** I haven't spoken to him since (then); **depuis que** *conj* (ever) since; **depuis qu'il m'a dit ça** (ever) since he said that to me

député, e [depyte] *nm/f* (*Pol*) ≈ Member of Parliament (BRIT), ≈ Congressman/woman (US)

dérangement [deʀãʒmã] *nm* (*gêne, déplacement*) trouble; (*gastrique etc*) disorder; **en ~** (*téléphone*) out of order

déranger [deʀãʒe] /3/ *vt* (*personne*) to trouble, bother; (*projets*) to disrupt, upset; (*objets, vêtements*) to disarrange; **se déranger**; *vi*: **surtout ne vous dérangez pas pour moi** please don't put yourself out on my account; **est-ce que cela vous dérange si ...?** do you mind if ...?

déraper [deʀape] /1/ *vi* (*voiture*) to skid; (*personne, semelles, couteau*) to slip

dérégler [deʀegle] /6/ *vt* (*mécanisme*) to put out of order; (*estomac*) to upset

dérisoire [deʀizwaʀ] *adj* derisory

dérive [deʀiv] *nf*: **aller à la ~** (*Navig, fig*) to drift

dérivé, e [deʀive] *nm* (*Tech*) by-product

dermatologue [dɛʀmatɔlɔg] *nm/f* dermatologist

dernier, -ière [dɛʀnje, -jɛʀ] *adj* last; (*le plus récent: gén avant n*) latest,

d

last; **lundi/le mois ~** last Monday/month; **le ~ cri** the last word (in fashion); **en ~** last; **ce ~, cette dernière** the latter; **dernièrement** adv recently

dérogation [deʀɔgasjɔ̃] nf (special) dispensation

dérouiller [deʀuje] /1/ vt: **se ~ les jambes** to stretch one's legs (fig)

déroulement [deʀulmɑ̃] nm (d'une opération etc) progress

dérouler [deʀule] /1/ vt (ficelle) to unwind; **se dérouler** vi (avoir lieu) to take place; (se passer) to go; **tout s'est déroulé comme prévu** everything went as planned

dérouter [deʀute] /1/ vt (avion, train) to reroute, divert; (étonner) to disconcert, throw (out)

derrière [dɛʀjɛʀ] adv, prép behind ▷ nm (d'une maison) back; (postérieur) behind, bottom; **les pattes de ~** the back legs, the hind legs; **par ~** from behind; (fig) behind one's back

des [de] art voir **de**

dès [dɛ] prép from; **~ que** as soon as; **~ son retour** as soon as he was (ou is) back

désaccord [dezakɔʀ] nm disagreement

désagréable [dezagʀeabl] adj unpleasant

désagrément [dezagʀemɑ̃] nm annoyance, trouble no pl

désaltérer [dezalteʀe] /6/ vt: **se désaltérer** to quench: one's thirst

désapprobateur, -trice [dezapʀɔbatœʀ, -tʀis] adj disapproving

désapprouver [dezapʀuve] /1/ vt to disapprove of

désarmant, e [dezaʀmɑ̃, -ɑ̃t] adj disarming

désastre [dezastʀ] nm disaster; **désastreux, -euse** adj disastrous

désavantage [dezavɑ̃taʒ] nm disadvantage; **désavantager** /3/ vt to put at a disadvantage

descendre [desɑ̃dʀ] /41/ vt (escalier, montagne) to go (ou come) down; (valise, paquet) to take ou get down; (étagère etc) to lower; (fam: abattre) to shoot down ▷ vi to go (ou come) down; (passager: s'arrêter) to get out, alight; **~ à pied/en voiture** to walk/drive down; **~ de** (famille) to be descended from; **~ du train** to get out of ou off the train; **~ d'un arbre** to climb down from a tree; **~ de cheval** to dismount; **~ à l'hôtel** to stay at a hotel

descente [desɑ̃t] nf descent, going down; (chemin) way down; (Ski) downhill (race); **au milieu de la ~** halfway down; **~ de lit** bedside rug; **~ (de police)** (police) raid

description [dɛskʀipsjɔ̃] nf description

déséquilibre [dezekilibʀ] nm (position): **être en ~** to be unsteady; (fig: des forces, du budget) imbalance

désert, e [dezɛʀ, -ɛʀt] adj deserted ▷ nm desert; **désertique** adj desert cpd

désespéré, e [dezɛspeʀe] adj desperate

désespérer [dezɛspeʀe] /6/ vi: **~ de** to despair of; **désespoir** nm despair; **en désespoir de cause** in desperation

déshabiller [dezabije] /1/ vt to undress; **se déshabiller** vi to undress (o.s.)

déshydraté, e [dezidʀate] adj dehydrated

désigner [dezine] /1/ vt (montrer) to point out, indicate; (dénommer) to denote; (candidat etc) to name

désinfectant, e [dezɛ̃fɛktɑ̃, -ɑ̃t] adj, nm disinfectant

désinfecter [dezɛ̃fɛkte] /1/ vt to disinfect

désintéressé, e [dezɛ̃teʀese] adj disinterested, unselfish

désintéresser [dezɛ̃teʀese] /1/ vt: **se désintéresser (de)** to lose interest (in)

désintoxication [dezɛ̃tɔksikasjɔ̃] *nf*: **faire une cure de ~** to have *ou* undergo treatment for alcoholism (*ou* drug addiction)

désinvolte [dezɛ̃vɔlt] *adj* casual, off-hand

désir [deziʀ] *nm* wish; (*fort, sensuel*) desire; **désirer** /1/ *vt* to want, wish for; (*sexuellement*) to desire; **je désire ...** (*formule de politesse*) I would like ...

désister [deziste] /1/: **se désister** *vi* to stand down, withdraw

désobéir [dezɔbeiʀ] /2/ *vi*: **~ (à qn/qch)** to disobey (sb/sth); **désobéissant, e** *adj* disobedient

désodorisant [dezɔdɔʀizɑ̃] *nm* air freshener, deodorizer

désolé, e [dezɔle] *adj* (*paysage*) desolate; **je suis ~** I'm sorry

désordonné, e [dezɔʀdɔne] *adj* untidy

désordre [dezɔʀdʀ] *nm* disorder(liness), untidiness; (*anarchie*) disorder; **en ~** in a mess, untidy

désormais [dezɔʀmɛ] *adv* from now on

desquels, desquelles [dekɛl] *voir* **lequel**

dessécher [deseʃe] /6/: **se dessécher** *vi* to dry out

desserrer [deseʀe] /1/ *vt* to loosen; (*frein*) to release

dessert [desɛʀ] *nm* dessert, pudding

desservir [desɛʀviʀ] /14/ *vt* (*ville, quartier*) to serve; (*débarrasser*): **~ (la table)** to clear the table

dessin [desɛ̃] *nm* (*œuvre, art*) drawing; (*motif*) pattern, design; **~ animé** cartoon (film); **~ humoristique** cartoon; **dessinateur, -trice** *nm/f* drawer; (*de bandes dessinées*) cartoonist; (*industriel*) draughtsman (BRIT), draftsman (US); **dessiner** /1/ *vt* to draw; (*concevoir*) to design; **se dessiner** *vi* (*forme*) to be outlined; (*fig: solution*) to emerge

dessous [d(ə)su] *adv* underneath, beneath ▷ *nm* underside; **les voisins du ~** the downstairs neighbours ▷ *nmpl* (*sous-vêtements*) underwear *sg*; **en ~** underneath; below; **par ~** underneath; below; **avoir le ~** to get the worst of it; **dessous-de-plat** *nm inv* tablemat

dessus [d(ə)sy] *adv* on top; (*collé, écrit*) on it ▷ *nm* top; **les voisins/l'appartement du ~** the upstairs neighbours/flat; **en ~** above; **par ~** *adv* over it; *prép* over; **au-~** above; **avoir/prendre le ~** to have/ get the upper hand; **sens ~ dessous** upside down; **dessus-de-lit** *nm inv* bedspread

destin [destɛ̃] *nm* fate; (*avenir*) destiny

destinataire [destinatɛʀ] *nm/f* (*Postes*) addressee; (*d'un colis*) consignee

destination [destinasjɔ̃] *nf* (*lieu*) destination; (*usage*) purpose; **à ~ de** bound for; travelling to

destiner [destine] /1/ *vt*: **~ qch à qn** (*envisager de donner*) to intend sb to have sth; (*adresser*) to intend sth for sb; **se ~ à l'enseignement** to intend to become a teacher; **être destiné à** (*usage*) to be intended *ou* meant for

détachant [detaʃɑ̃] *nm* stain remover

détacher [detaʃe] /1/ *vt* (*enlever*) to detach, remove; (*délier*) to untie; (*Admin*): **~ qn (auprès de *ou* à)** to post sb (to); **se détacher** *vi* (*se séparer*) to come off; (*page*) to come out; (*se défaire*) to come undone; **se ~ sur** to stand out against; **se ~ de** (*se désintéresser*) to grow away from

détail [detaj] *nm* detail; (*Comm*): **le ~** retail; **au ~** (*Comm*) retail; **en ~** in detail; **détaillant, e** *nm/f* retailer; **détaillé, e** *adj* (*récit, plan, explications*) detailed; (*facture*) itemized; **détailler** /1/ *vt* (*expliquer*) to explain in detail

détecter [detɛkte] /1/ *vt* to detect

détective [detɛktiv] *nm* detective; **~ (privé)** private detective *ou* investigator

déteindre [detɛ̃dʀ] /52/ vi to fade; (au lavage) to run; **~ sur** (vêtement) to run into; (fig) to rub off on

détendre [detɑ̃dʀ] /41/ vt (personne, atmosphère, corps, esprit) to relax; **se détendre** vi (ressort) to lose its tension; (personne) to relax

détenir [det(ə)niʀ] /22/ vt (fortune, objet, secret) to be in possession of; (prisonnier) to detain; (record) to hold; **~ le pouvoir** to be in power

détente [detɑ̃t] nf relaxation

détention [detɑ̃sjɔ̃] nf (de fortune, objet, secret) possession; (captivité) detention; **~ préventive** (pre-trial) custody

détenu, e [det(ə)ny] pp de **détenir** ▷ nm/f prisoner

détergent [detɛʀʒɑ̃] nm detergent

détériorer [deteʀjɔʀe] /1/ vt to damage; **se détériorer** vi to deteriorate

déterminé, e [detɛʀmine] adj (résolu) determined; (précis) specific, definite

déterminer [detɛʀmine] /1/ vt (fixer) to determine; **~ qn à faire** to decide sb to do; **se ~ à faire** to make up one's mind to do

détester [detɛste] /1/ vt to hate, detest

détour [detuʀ] nm detour; (tournant) bend, curve; **ça vaut le ~** it's worth the trip; **sans ~** (fig) plainly

détourné, e [detuʀne] adj (sentier, chemin, moyen) roundabout

détourner [detuʀne] /1/ vt to divert; (par la force) to hijack; (yeux, tête) to turn away; (de l'argent) to embezzle; **se détourner** vi to turn away

détraquer [detʀake] /1/ vt to put out of order; (estomac) to upset; **se détraquer** vi to go wrong

détriment [detʀimɑ̃] nm: **au ~ de** to the detriment of

détroit [detʀwa] nm strait

détruire [detʀɥiʀ] /38/ vt to destroy

dette [dɛt] nf debt

DEUG [døg] sigle m = **Diplôme d'études universitaires générales**

- **DEUG**
-
- French students sit their DEUG
- ('diplôme d'études universitaires
- générales') after two years at
- university. They can then choose to
- leave university altogether, or go
- on to study for their 'licence'. The
- certificate specifies the student's
- major subject and may be awarded
- with distinction.

deuil [dœj] nm (perte) bereavement; (période) mourning; **prendre le/être en ~** to go into/be in mourning

deux [dø] num two; **les ~** both; **ses ~ mains** both his hands, his two hands; **~ fois** twice; **deuxième** num second; **deuxièmement** adv secondly; **deux-pièces** nm inv (tailleur) two-piece (suit); (de bain) two-piece (swimsuit); (appartement) two-roomed flat (BRIT) ou apartment (US); **deux-points** nm inv colon sg; **deux-roues** nm inv two-wheeled vehicle

devais etc [dəvɛ] vb voir **devoir**

dévaluation [devalɥasjɔ̃] nf devaluation

devancer [d(ə)vɑ̃se] /3/ vt to get ahead of; (arriver avant) to arrive before; (prévenir) to anticipate

devant [d(ə)vɑ̃] adv in front; (à distance: en avant) ahead ▷ prép in front of; (en avant) ahead of; (avec mouvement: passer) past; (fig) before, in front of (: vu) in view of ▷ nm front; **prendre les ~s** to make the first move; **les pattes de ~** the front legs, the forelegs; **par ~** (boutonner) at the front; (entrer) in the front way; **aller au-~ de qn** to go out to meet sb; **aller au-~ de** (désirs de qn) to anticipate

devanture [d(ə)vɑ̃tyʀ] nf (étalage) display; (vitrine) (shop) window

développement [dev(ə)lɔpmɑ̃] nm development; **pays en voie de ~** developing countries; **~ durable** sustainable development

développer [dev(ə)lɔpe] /1/ vt to develop; **se développer** vi to develop

devenir [dəv(ə)niʀ] /22/ vi to become; **que sont-ils devenus?** what has become of them?

devez [dəve] vb voir **devoir**

déviation [devjasjɔ̃] nf (Auto) diversion (BRIT), detour (US)

devienne etc [dəvjɛn] vb voir **devenir**

deviner [d(ə)vine] /1/ vt to guess; (apercevoir) to distinguish; **devinette** nf riddle

devis [d(ə)vi] nm estimate, quotation

devise [dəviz] nf (formule) motto, watchword; **devises** nfpl (argent) currency sg

dévisser [devise] /1/ vt to unscrew, undo; **se dévisser** vi to come unscrewed

devoir [d(ə)vwaʀ] /28/ nm duty; (Scol) homework no pl (: en classe) exercise ▷ vt (argent, respect); **~ qch (à qn)** to owe (sb) sth; **combien est-ce que je vous dois?** how much do I owe you?; **il doit le faire** (obligation) he has to do it, he must do it; **cela devait arriver un jour** it was bound to happen; **il doit partir demain** (intention) he is due to leave tomorrow; **il doit être tard** (probabilité) it must be late

dévorer [devɔʀe] /1/ vt to devour; (feu, soucis) to consume; **~ qn/qch des yeux** ou **du regard** (convoitise) to eye sb/sth greedily

dévoué, e [devwe] adj devoted

dévouer [devwe] /1/: **se dévouer** vi (se sacrifier): **se ~ (pour)** to sacrifice o.s. (for); (se consacrer): **se ~ à** to devote ou dedicate o.s. to

devrai etc [dəvʀe] vb voir **devoir**

dézipper [dezipe] /1/ vt to unzip

diabète [djabɛt] nm diabetes sg; **diabétique** nm/f diabetic

diable [djabl] nm devil

diabolo [djabɔlo] nm (boisson) lemonade and fruit cordial

diagnostic [djagnɔstik] nm diagnosis sg; **diagnostiquer** /1/ vt to diagnose

diagonal, e, -aux [djagɔnal, -o] adj, nf diagonal; **en ~e** diagonally

diagramme [djagʀam] nm chart, graph

dialecte [djalɛkt] nm dialect

dialogue [djalɔg] nm dialogue

diamant [djamɑ̃] nm diamond

diamètre [djamɛtʀ] nm diameter

diapo [djapo], **diapositive** [djapozitiv] nf transparency, slide

diarrhée [djaʀe] nf diarrhoea

dictateur [diktatœʀ] nm dictator; **dictature** [diktatyʀ] nf dictatorship

dictée [dikte] nf dictation

dicter [dikte] /1/ vt to dictate

dictionnaire [diksjɔnɛʀ] nm dictionary

dièse [djɛz] nm sharp

diesel [djezɛl] nm, adj inv diesel

diète [djɛt] nf (jeûne) starvation diet; (régime) diet; **diététique** adj: **magasin diététique** health food shop (BRIT) ou store (US)

dieu, x [djø] nm god; **D~** God; **mon D~!** good heavens!

différemment [difeʀamɑ̃] adv differently

différence [difeʀɑ̃s] nf difference; **à la ~ de** unlike; **différencier** /7/ vt to differentiate

différent, e [difeʀɑ̃, -ɑ̃t] adj (dissemblable) different; **~ de** different from; **~s objets** different ou various objects

différer [difeʀe] /6/ vt to postpone, put off ▷ vi: **~ (de)** to differ (from)

difficile [difisil] adj difficult; (exigeant) hard to please; **difficilement** adv with difficulty

difficulté [difikylte] nf difficulty; **en ~** (bateau, alpiniste) in trouble ou difficulties

diffuser [difyze] /1/ vt (chaleur, bruit, lumière) to diffuse; (émission, musique) to broadcast; (nouvelle, idée) to circulate; (Comm) to distribute

digérer [diʒeʀe] /6/ vt to digest; (fig: accepter) to stomach, put up with; **digestif, -ive** nm (after-dinner) liqueur; **digestion** nf digestion

digne [diɲ] adj dignified; **~ de** worthy of; **~ de foi** trustworthy; **dignité** nf dignity

digue [dig] nf dike, dyke

dilemme [dilɛm] nm dilemma

diligence [diliʒɑ̃s] nf stagecoach

diluer [dilɥe] /1/ vt to dilute

dimanche [dimɑ̃ʃ] nm Sunday

dimension [dimɑ̃sjɔ̃] nf (grandeur) size; (dimensions) dimensions

diminuer [diminɥe] /1/ vt to reduce, decrease; (ardeur etc) to lessen; (dénigrer) to belittle ▷ vi to decrease, diminish; **diminutif** nm (surnom) pet name

dinde [dɛ̃d] nf turkey

dindon [dɛ̃dɔ̃] nm turkey

dîner [dine] /1/ nm dinner ▷ vi to have dinner

dingue [dɛ̃g] adj (fam) crazy

dinosaure [dinɔzɔʀ] nm dinosaur

diplomate [diplɔmat] adj diplomatic ▷ nm diplomat; (fig) diplomatist; **diplomatie** nf diplomacy

diplôme [diplom] nm diploma certificate; **avoir des ~s** to have qualifications; **diplômé, e** adj qualified

dire [diʀ] /37/ vt to say; (secret, mensonge) to tell; **se dire** (à soi-même) to say to oneself ▷ nm: **au ~ de** according to; **~ qch à qn** to tell sb sth; **~ à qn qu'il fasse** ou **de faire** to tell sb to do; **on dirait que** they say that; **on dirait que** it looks (ou sounds etc) as though; **que dites-vous de** (penser) what do you think of; **si cela lui dit** if he fancies it; **dis donc!**, **dites donc!** (pour attirer l'attention)

hey!; (au fait) by the way; **ceci** ou **cela dit** that being said; **ça ne se dit pas** (impoli) you shouldn't say that; (pas en usage) you don't say that

direct, e [diʀɛkt] adj direct ▷ nm: **en ~** (émission) live; **directement** adv directly

directeur, -trice [diʀɛktœʀ, -tʀis] nm/f (d'entreprise) director; (de service) manager/eress; (d'école) head(teacher) (BRIT), principal (US)

direction [diʀɛksjɔ̃] nf (d'entreprise) management; (Auto) steering; (sens) direction; **"toutes ~s"** "all routes"

dirent [diʀ] vb voir **dire**

dirigeant, e [diʀiʒɑ̃, -ɑ̃t] adj (classes) ruling ▷ nm/f (d'un parti etc) leader

diriger [diʀiʒe] /3/ vt (entreprise) to manage, run; (véhicule) to steer; (orchestre) to conduct; (recherches, travaux) to supervise; (arme): **~ sur** to point ou level ou aim at; **se diriger** vi (s'orienter) to find one's way; **~ son regard sur** to look in the direction of; **se ~ vers** ou **sur** to make ou head for

dis [di] vb voir **dire**

discerner [disɛʀne] /1/ vt to discern, make out

discipline [disiplin] nf discipline; **discipliner** /1/ vt to discipline

discontinu, e [diskɔ̃tiny] adj intermittent

discontinuer [diskɔ̃tinɥe] /1/ vi: **sans ~** without stopping, without a break

discothèque [diskɔtɛk] nf (boîte de nuit) disco(thèque)

discours [diskuʀ] nm speech

discret, -ète [diskʀɛ, -ɛt] adj discreet; (fig: musique, style, maquillage) unobtrusive; **discrétion** nf discretion; **à discrétion** as much as one wants

discrimination nf discrimination; **sans ~** indiscriminately

discussion [diskysjɔ̃] nf discussion

discutable [diskytabl] adj debatable

discuter [diskyte] /1/ vt (contester) to question, dispute; (débattre: prix) to discuss ▷ vi to talk; (protester) to argue; **~ de** to discuss

dise etc [diz] vb voir **dire**

disjoncteur [disʒɔ̃ktœʀ] nm (Élec) circuit breaker

disloquer [disloke] /1/: **se disloquer** vi (parti, empire) to break up; (meuble) to come apart; **se ~ l'épaule** to dislocate one's shoulder

disons etc [dizɔ̃] vb voir **dire**

disparaître [disparɛtr] /57/ vi to disappear; (se perdre: traditions etc) to die out; (personne: mourir) to die; **faire ~** (objet, tache, trace) to remove; (personne, douleur) to get rid of

disparition [disparisjɔ̃] nf disappearance; **espèce en voie de ~** endangered species

disparu, e [dispary] nm/f missing person; **être porté ~** to be reported missing

dispensaire [dispãsɛʀ] nm community clinic

dispenser [dispãse] /1/ vt: **~ qn de** to exempt sb from

disperser [dispɛʀse] /1/ vt to scatter; **se disperser** vi to scatter

disponible [disponibl] adj available

disposé, e [dispoze] adj: **bien/mal ~** (humeur) in a good/bad mood; **~ à** (prêt à) willing ou prepared to

disposer [dispoze] /1/ vt to arrange ▷ vi: **vous pouvez ~** you may leave; **~ de** to have (at one's disposal); **se ~ à faire** to prepare to do, be about to do

dispositif [dispozitif] nm device; (fig) system, plan of action

disposition [dispozisjɔ̃] nf (arrangement) arrangement, layout; (humeur) mood; **prendre ses ~s** to make arrangements; **avoir des ~s pour la musique** etc to have a special aptitude for music etc; **à la ~ de qn** at sb's disposal; **je suis à votre ~** I am at your service

disproportionné, e [disproporsjone] adj disproportionate, out of all proportion

dispute [dispyt] nf quarrel, argument; **disputer** /1/ vt (match) to play; (combat) to fight; **se disputer** vi to quarrel

disqualifier [diskalifje] /7/ vt to disqualify

disque [disk] nm (Mus) record; (forme, pièce) disc; (Sport) discus; **~ compact** compact disc; **~ dur** hard disk; **disquette** nf floppy (disk), diskette

dissertation [disɛʀtasjɔ̃] nf (Scol) essay

dissimuler [disimyle] /1/ vt to conceal

dissipé, e [disipe] adj (indiscipliné) unruly

dissolvant [disɔlvã] nm nail polish remover

dissuader [disɥade] /1/ vt: **~ qn de faire/de qch** to dissuade sb from doing/from sth

distance [distãs] nf distance; (fig: écart) gap; **à ~** at ou from a distance; **distancer** /3/ vt to outdistance

distant, e [distã, -ãt] adj (réservé) distant; **~ de** (lieu) far away ou a long way from

distillerie [distilʀi] nf distillery

distinct, e [distɛ̃(kt), distɛ̃kt] adj distinct; **distinctement** [distɛ̃ktəmã] adv distinctly; **distinctif, -ive** adj distinctive

distingué, e [distɛ̃ge] adj distinguished

distinguer [distɛ̃ge] /1/ vt to distinguish; **se distinguer** vi: **se ~ (de)** to distinguish o.s. ou be distinguished (from)

distraction [distraksjɔ̃] nf (manque d'attention) absent-mindedness; (passe-temps) distraction, entertainment

distraire [distrɛʀ] /50/ vt (déranger) to distract; (divertir) to entertain, divert; **se distraire** vi to amuse ou enjoy o.s.; **distrait, e** [distʀɛ, -ɛt] *pp de* **distraire** ▷ *adj* absent-minded

distrayant, e [distʀɛjɑ̃, -ɑ̃t] *adj* entertaining

distribuer [distʀibɥe] /1/ *vt* to distribute; to hand out; (*Cartes*) to deal (out); (*courrier*) to deliver; **distributeur** *nm* (*Auto, Comm*) distributor; (*automatique*) (vending) machine; **distributeur de billets** cash dispenser

dit, e [di, dit] *pp de* **dire** ▷ *adj* (*fixé*): **le jour ~** the arranged day; (*surnommé*): **X, ~ Pierrot** X, known as *ou* called Pierrot

dites [dit] *vb voir* **dire**

divan [divɑ̃] *nm* divan

divers, e [divɛʀ, -ɛʀs] *adj* (*varié*) diverse, varied; (*différent*) different, various; **~es personnes** various *ou* several people

diversité [divɛʀsite] *nf* diversity, variety

divertir [divɛʀtiʀ] /2/: **se divertir** *vi* to amuse *ou* enjoy o.s.; **divertissement** *nm* entertainment

diviser [divize] /1/ *vt* to divide; **division** *nf* division

divorce [divɔʀs] *nm* divorce; **divorcé, e** *nm/f* divorcee; **divorcer** /3/ *vi* to get a divorce, get divorced; **divorcer de** *ou* **d'avec qn** to divorce sb

divulguer [divylge] /1/ *vt* to disclose

dix [di, dis, diz] *num* ten; **dix-huit** *num* eighteen; **dix-huitième** *num* eighteenth; **dixième** *num* tenth; **dix-neuf** *num* nineteen; **dix-neuvième** *num* nineteenth; **dix-sept** *num* seventeen; **dix-septième** *num* seventeenth

dizaine [dizɛn] *nf*: **une ~ (de)** about ten, ten or so

do [do] *nm* (*note*) C; (*en chantant la gamme*) do(h)

docile [dɔsil] *adj* docile

dock [dɔk] *nm* dock; **docker** *nm* docker

docteur, e [dɔktœʀ] *nm/f* doctor; **doctorat** *nm*: **doctorat (d'Université)** ≈ doctorate

doctrine [dɔktʀin] *nf* doctrine

document [dɔkymɑ̃] *nm* document; **documentaire** *adj, nm* documentary; **documentation** *nf* documentation, literature; **documenter** /1/ *vt*: **se documenter (sur)** to gather information *ou* material (on *ou* about)

dodo [dodo] *nm*: **aller faire ~** to go to beddy-byes

dogue [dɔg] *nm* mastiff

doigt [dwa] *nm* finger; **à deux ~s de** within an ace (BRIT) *ou* an inch of; **un ~ de lait/whisky** a drop of milk/ whisky; **~ de pied** toe

doit *etc* [dwa] *vb voir* **devoir**

dollar [dɔlaʀ] *nm* dollar

domaine [dɔmɛn] *nm* estate, property; (*fig*) domain, field

domestique [dɔmɛstik] *adj* domestic ▷ *nm/f* servant, domestic

domicile [dɔmisil] *nm* home, place of residence; **à ~** at home; **livrer à ~** to deliver; **domicilié, e** *adj*: **être domicilié à** to have one's home in *ou* at

dominant, e [dɔminɑ̃, -ɑ̃t] *adj* (*opinion*) predominant

dominer [dɔmine] /1/ *vt* to dominate; (*sujet*) to master; (*surpasser*) to outclass, surpass; (*surplomber*) to tower above, dominate ▷ *vi* to be in the dominant position; **se dominer** *vi* to control o.s.

domino [dɔmino] *nm* domino; **dominos** *nmpl* (*jeu*) dominoes *sg*

dommage [dɔmaʒ] *nm*: **~s** (*dégâts, pertes*) damage *no pl*; **c'est ~ de faire/que** it's a shame *ou* pity to do/ that; **quel ~!, c'est ~!** what a pity *ou* shame!

dompter [dɔ̃(p)te] /1/ *vt* to tame; **dompteur, -euse** *nm/f* trainer

DOM-ROM [dɔmʀɔm] *sigle m(pl)* (= *Département(s) et Régions/*

Territoire(s) d'outre-mer) French overseas departments and regions

don [dɔ̃] *nm* gift; *(charité)* donation; **avoir des ~s pour** to have a gift *ou* talent for; **elle a le ~ de m'énerver** she's got a knack of getting on my nerves

donc [dɔ̃k] *conj* therefore, so; *(après une digression)* so, then

dongle [dɔ̃gl] *nm* dongle

donné, e [dɔne] *adj (convenu: lieu, heure)* given; *(pas cher)* very cheap; **données** *nfpl* data; **c'est ~** it's a gift; **étant ~ que ...** given that ...

donner [dɔne] /1/ *vt* to give; *(vieux habits etc)* to give away; *(spectacle)* to put on; **~ qch à qn** to give sb sth, give sth to sb; **~ sur** *(fenêtre, chambre)* to look (out) onto; **ça donne soif/faim** it makes you (feel) thirsty/hungry; **se ~ à fond (à son travail)** to give one's all (to one's work); **se ~ du mal** *ou* **de la peine (pour faire qch)** to go to a lot of trouble (to do sth); **s'en ~ à cœur joie** *(fam)* to have a great time (of it)

 MOT-CLÉ

dont [dɔ̃] *pron relatif* **1** *(appartenance: objets)* whose, of which; *(: êtres animés)* whose; **la maison dont le toit est rouge** the house the roof of which is red, the house whose roof is red; **l'homme dont je connais la sœur** the man whose sister I know **2** *(parmi lesquel(le)s)*: **deux livres, dont l'un est ...** two books, one of which is ...; **il y avait plusieurs personnes, dont Gabrielle** there were several people, among them Gabrielle; **10 blessés, dont 2 grièvement** 10 injured, 2 of them seriously

3 *(complément d'adjectif, de verbe)*: **le fils dont il est si fier** the son he's so proud of; **le pays dont il est originaire** the country he's from; **ce**

dont je parle what I'm talking about; **la façon dont il l'a fait** the way (in which) he did it

dopage [dɔpaʒ] *nm (Sport)* drug use; *(de cheval)* doping

doré, e [dɔʀe] *adj* golden; *(avec dorure)* gilt, gilded

dorénavant [dɔʀenavɑ̃] *adv* henceforth

dorer [dɔʀe] /1/ *vt* to gild; **(faire) ~** *(Culin)* to brown

dorloter [dɔʀlɔte] /1/ *vt* to pamper

dormir [dɔʀmiʀ] /16/ *vi* to sleep; *(être endormi)* to be asleep

dortoir [dɔʀtwaʀ] *nm* dormitory

dos [do] *nm* back; *(de livre)* spine; **"voir au ~"** "see over"; **de ~** from the back

dosage [dozaʒ] *nm* mixture

dose [doz] *nf* dose; **doser** /1/ *vt* to measure out; **il faut savoir doser ses efforts** you have to be able to pace yourself

dossier [dosje] *nm (renseignements, fichier)* file; *(de chaise)* back; *(Presse)* feature; *(Inform)* folder; **un ~ scolaire** a school report

douane [dwan] *nf* customs *pl*; **douanier, -ière** *adj* customs *cpd* ▷ *nm* customs officer

double [dubl] *adj, adv* double ▷ *nm* *(autre exemplaire)* duplicate, copy; *(sosie)* double; *(Tennis)* doubles *sg*; *(2 fois plus)*: **le ~ (de)** twice as much *(ou* many) (as); **en ~ (exemplaire)** in duplicate; **faire ~ emploi** to be redundant; **double-cliquer** /1/ *vi* *(Inform)* to double-click

doubler [duble] /1/ *vt (multiplier par 2)* to double; *(vêtement)* to line; *(dépasser)* to overtake, pass; *(film)* to dub; *(acteur)* to stand in for ▷ *vi* to double

doublure [dublyʀ] *nf* lining; *(Ciné)* stand-in

douce [dus] *adj f voir* **doux**; **douceâtre** *adj* sickly sweet;

doucement adv gently; (lentement) slowly; **douceur** nf softness; (de climat) mildness; (de quelqu'un) gentleness

douche [duʃ] nf shower; **prendre une ~** to have ou take a shower; **doucher** /1/: **se doucher** vi to have ou take a shower

doué, e [dwe] adj gifted, talented; **être ~ pour** to have a gift for

douille [duj] nf (Élec) socket

douillet, te [dujɛ, -ɛt] adj cosy; (péj: à la douleur) soft

douleur [dulœʀ] nf pain; (chagrin) grief, distress; **douloureux, -euse** adj painful

doute [dut] nm doubt; **sans ~** no doubt; (probablement) probably; **sans nul** ou **aucun ~** without a(ny) doubt; **douter** /1/ vt to doubt; **douter de** (allié, sincérité de qn) to have (one's) doubts about, doubt; (résultat, réussite) to be doubtful of; **douter que** to doubt whether ou if; **se douter de qch/que** to suspect sth/that; **je m'en doutais** I thought as much; **douteux, -euse** adj (incertain) doubtful; (péj) dubious-looking

Douvres [duvʀ] n Dover

doux, douce [du, dus] adj soft; (sucré, agréable) sweet; (peu fort: moutarde etc, clément: climat) mild; (pas brusque) gentle

douzaine [duzɛn] nf (12) dozen; (environ 12) **une ~ (de)** a dozen or so

douze [duz] num twelve; **douzième** num twelfth

dragée [dʀaʒe] nf sugared almond

draguer [dʀage] /1/ vt (rivière) to dredge; (fam) to try and pick up

dramatique [dʀamatik] adj dramatic; (tragique) tragic ▷ nf (TV) (television) drama

drame [dʀam] nm drama

drap [dʀa] nm (de lit) sheet; (tissu) woollen fabric

drapeau, x [dʀapo] nm flag

drap-housse [dʀaus] nm fitted sheet

dresser [dʀese] /1/ vt (mettre vertical, monter) to put up, erect; (liste, bilan, contrat) to draw up; (animal) to train; **se dresser** vi (falaise, obstacle) to stand; (personne) to draw o.s. up; **~ l'oreille** to prick up one's ears; **~ qn contre qn d'autre** to set sb against sb else

drogue [dʀɔg] nf drug; **la ~** drugs pl; **drogué, e** nm/f drug addict; **droguer** /1/ vt (victime) to drug; **se droguer** vi (aux stupéfiants) to take drugs; (péj: de médicaments) to dose o.s. up; **droguerie** nf ≈ hardware shop (BRIT) ou store (US); **droguiste** nm ≈ keeper (ou owner) of a hardware shop ou store

droit, e [dʀwa, dʀwat] adj (non courbe) straight; (vertical) upright, straight; (fig: loyal, franc) upright, straight(forward); (opposé à gauche) right, right-hand ▷ adv straight ▷ nm (prérogative) right; (taxe) duty, tax; (: d'inscription) fee; (lois, branche) **le ~** law ▷ nf (Pol) right (wing); **avoir le ~ de** to be allowed to; **avoir ~ à** to be entitled to; **être dans son ~** to be within one's rights; **à ~e** on the right; (direction) (to the) right; **~s d'auteur** royalties; **~s d'inscription** enrolment ou registration fees; **droitier, -ière** adj right-handed

drôle [dʀol] adj (amusant) funny, amusing; (bizarre) funny, peculiar; **un ~ de ...** (bizarre) a strange ou funny ...; (intensif) an incredible ..., a terrific ...

dromadaire [dʀɔmadɛʀ] nm dromedary

du [dy] art voir **de**

dû, due [dy] pp de **devoir** ▷ adj (somme) owing, owed; (causé par): **dû à** due to ▷ nm due

dune [dyn] nf dune

duplex [dyplɛks] nm (appartement) split-level apartment, duplex

duquel [dykɛl] voir **lequel**

dur, e [dyʀ] *adj* (*pierre, siège, travail, problème*) hard; (*lumière, voix, climat*) harsh; (*sévère*) hard, harsh; (*cruel*) hard(-hearted); (*porte, col*) stiff; (*viande*) tough ▷ *adv* hard ▷ *nm* (*fam: meneur*) tough nut; **~ d'oreille** hard of hearing

durant [dyʀɑ̃] *prép* (*au cours de*) during; (*pendant*) for; **des mois ~** for months

durcir [dyʀsiʀ] /2/ *vt, vi* to harden; **se durcir** *vi* to harden

durée [dyʀe] *nf* length; (*d'une pile etc*) life; **de courte ~** (*séjour, répit*) brief

durement [dyʀmɑ̃] *adv* harshly

durer [dyʀe] /1/ *vi* to last

dureté [dyʀte] *nf* hardness; harshness; stiffness; toughness

durit® [dyʀit] *nf* (*car radiator*) hose

duvet [dyvɛ] *nm* down

DVD *sigle m* (= *digital versatile disc*) DVD

dynamique [dinamik] *adj* dynamic; **dynamisme** *nm* dynamism

dynamo [dinamo] *nf* dynamo

dyslexie [dislɛksi] *nf* dyslexia, word blindness

eau, x [o] *nf* water ▷ *nfpl* (*Méd*) waters; **prendre l'~** to leak, let in water; **tomber à l'~** (*fig*) to fall through; **~ de Cologne** eau de Cologne; **~ courante** running water; **~ douce** fresh water; **~ gazeuse** sparkling (mineral) water; **~ de Javel** bleach; **~ minérale** mineral water; **~ plate** still water; **~ salée** salt water; **~ de toilette** toilet water; **eau-de-vie** *nf* brandy

ébène [ebɛn] *nf* ebony; **ébéniste** [ebenist] *nm* cabinetmaker

éblouir [ebluiʀ] /2/ *vt* to dazzle

éboueur [ebwœʀ] *nm* dustman (BRIT), garbage man (US)

ébouillanter [ebujɑ̃te] /1/ *vt* to scald; (*Culin*) to blanch

éboulement [ebulmɑ̃] *nm* rock fall

ébranler [ebʀɑ̃le] /1/ *vt* to shake; (*rendre instable*) to weaken; **s'ébranler** *vi* (*partir*) to move off

ébullition [ebylisjɔ̃] *nf* boiling point; **en ~** boiling

écaille [ekɑj] *nf* (*de poisson*) scale; (*matière*) tortoiseshell; **écailler** /1/ *vt* (*poisson*) to scale; **s'écailler** *vi* to flake *ou* peel (off)

écart [ekaʀ] *nm* gap; **à l'~** out of the way; **à l'~ de** away from; **faire un ~** (*voiture*) to swerve

écarté, e [ekaʀte] *adj* (*lieu*) out-of-the-way, remote; (*ouvert*): **les jambes ~es** legs apart; **les bras ~s** arms outstretched

écarter [ekaʀte] /1/ *vt* (*séparer*) to move apart, separate; (*éloigner*) to push back, move away; (*ouvrir: bras, jambes*) to spread, open; (*: rideau*) to draw (back); (*éliminer: candidat, possibilité*) to dismiss; **s'écarter** *vi* to part; (*personne*) to move away; **s'~ de** to wander from

échafaudage [eʃafodaʒ] *nm* scaffolding

échalote [eʃalɔt] *nf* shallot

échange [eʃɑ̃ʒ] *nm* exchange; **en ~ de** in exchange *ou* return for; **échanger** /3/ *vt*: **échanger qch (contre)** to exchange sth (for)

échantillon [eʃɑ̃tijɔ̃] *nm* sample

échapper [eʃape] /1/: **~ à** *vt* (*gardien*) to escape (from); (*punition, péril*) to escape; **~ à qn** (*détail, sens*) to escape sb; (*objet qu'on tient*) to slip out of sb's hands; **laisser ~** (*cri etc*) to let out; **l'~ belle** to have a narrow escape

écharde [eʃaʀd] *nf* splinter (of wood)

écharpe [eʃaʀp] *nf* scarf; **avoir le bras en ~** to have one's arm in a sling

échauffer [eʃofe] /1/ *vt* (*métal, moteur*) to overheat; **s'échauffer** *vi* (*Sport*) to warm up; (*discussion*) to become heated

échéance [eʃeɑ̃s] *nf* (*d'un paiement: date*) settlement date; (*fig*) deadline; **à brève/longue ~** in the short/long term

échéant [eʃeɑ̃]: **le cas ~** *adv* if the case arises

échec [eʃɛk] *nm* failure; (*Échecs*): **~ et mat/au roi** checkmate/check;

échecs *nmpl* (*jeu*) chess *sg*; **tenir en ~** to hold in check

échelle [eʃɛl] *nf* ladder; (*fig, d'une carte*) scale

échelon [eʃ(ə)lɔ̃] *nm* (*d'échelle*) rung; (*Admin*) grade; **échelonner** /1/ *vt* to space out, spread out

échiquier [eʃikje] *nm* chessboard

écho [eko] *nm* echo; **échographie** *nf*: **passer une échographie** to have a scan

échouer [eʃwe] /1/ *vi* to fail; **s'échouer** *vi* to run aground

éclabousser [eklabuse] /1/ *vt* to splash

éclair [eklɛʀ] *nm* (*d'orage*) flash of lightning, lightning *no pl*; (*gâteau*) éclair

éclairage [eklɛʀaʒ] *nm* lighting

éclaircie [eklɛʀsi] *nf* bright *ou* sunny interval

éclaircir [eklɛʀsiʀ] /2/ *vt* to lighten; (*fig: mystère*) to clear up; (*point*) to clarify; **s'éclaircir** *vi* (*ciel*) to brighten up; **s'~ la voix** to clear one's throat; **éclaircissement** *nm* clarification

éclairer [eklɛʀe] /1/ *vt* (*lieu*) to light (up); (*personne: avec une lampe de poche etc*) to light the way for; (*fig: rendre compréhensible*) to shed light on ▷ *vi*: **~ mal/bien** to give a poor/good light; **s'~ à la bougie/l'électricité** to use candlelight/have electric lighting

éclat [ekla] *nm* (*de bombe, de verre*) fragment; (*du soleil, d'une couleur etc*) brightness, brilliance; (*d'une cérémonie*) splendour; (*scandale*): **faire un ~** to cause a commotion; **~ de rire** burst *ou* roar of laughter; **~ de voix** shout

éclatant, e [eklatɑ̃, -ɑ̃t] *adj* brilliant

éclater [eklate] /1/ *vi* (*pneu*) to burst; (*bombe*) to explode; (*guerre, épidémie*) to break out; (*groupe, parti*) to break up; **~ de rire/en sanglots** to burst out laughing/sobbing

écluse [eklyz] *nf* lock

écœurant, e [ekœʀɑ̃, -ɑ̃t] *adj* sickening; (*gâteau etc*) sickly

écœurer [ekœʀe] vt: **~ qn** (nourriture) to make sb feel sick; (fig: conduite, personne) to disgust sb

école [ekɔl] nf school; **aller à l'~** to go to school; **~ maternelle** nursery school; **~ primaire** primary (BRIT) ou grade (US) school; **~ secondaire** secondary (BRIT) ou high (US) school; **écolier, -ière** nm/f schoolboy/girl

écologie [ekɔlɔʒi] nf ecology; **écologique** adj environment-friendly; **écologiste** nm/f ecologist

économe [ekɔnɔm] adj thrifty ▷ nm/f (de lycée etc) bursar (BRIT), treasurer (US)

économie [ekɔnɔmi] nf economy; (gain: d'argent, de temps etc) saving; (science) economics sg; **économies** nfpl (pécule) savings; **économique** adj (avantageux) economical; (Écon) economic; **économiser** /1/ vt, vi to save

écorce [ekɔʀs] nf bark; (de fruit) peel

écorcher [ekɔʀʃe] /1/ vt: **s'~ le genou** etc to scrape ou graze one's knee etc; **écorchure** nf graze

écossais, e [ekɔsɛ, -ɛz] adj Scottish ▷ nm/f: **É~, e** Scot

Écosse [ekɔs] nf: **l'~** Scotland

écotaxe [ekɔtaks] nf green tax

écouter [ekute] /1/ vt to listen to; **s'écouter** vi (malade) to be a bit of a hypochondriac; **si je m'écoutais** if I followed my instincts; **écouteur** nm (Tél) receiver; **écouteurs** nmpl (casque) headphones, headset sg

écran [ekʀɑ̃] nm screen; **le petit ~** television; **~ tactile** touchscreen; **~ total** sunblock

écrasant, e [ekʀazɑ̃, -ɑ̃t] adj overwhelming

écraser [ekʀaze] /1/ vt to crush; (piéton) to run over; **s'~ (au sol)** vi to crash; **s'~ contre** to crash into

écrémé, e [ekʀeme] adj (lait) skimmed

écrevisse [ekʀəvis] nf crayfish inv

écrire [ekʀiʀ] /39/ vt, vi to write; **s'écrire** vi to write to one another;

ça s'écrit comment? how is it spelt?; **écrit** nm (examen) written paper; **par écrit** in writing

écriteau, x [ekʀito] nm notice, sign

écriture [ekʀityʀ] nf writing; **écritures** nfpl (Comm) accounts, books; **l'É~ (sainte), les É~s** the Scriptures

écrivain [ekʀivɛ̃] nm writer

écrou [ekʀu] nm nut

écrouler [ekʀule] /1/: **s'écrouler** vi to collapse

écru, e [ekʀy] adj off-white, écru

écume [ekym] nf foam

écureuil [ekyʀœj] nm squirrel

écurie [ekyʀi] nf stable

eczéma [ɛgzema] nm eczema

EDF sigle f (= Électricité de France) national electricity company

Édimbourg [edɛ̃buʀ] n Edinburgh

éditer [edite] /1/ vt (publier) to publish; (annoter) to edit; **éditeur, -trice** nm/f publisher; **édition** nf edition; **l'édition** publishing

édredon [edʀədɔ̃] nm eiderdown

éducateur, -trice [edykatœʀ, -tʀis] nm/f teacher; (en école spécialisée) instructor

éducatif, -ive [edykatif, -iv] adj educational

éducation [edykasjɔ̃] nf education; (familiale) upbringing; (manières) (good) manners pl

édulcorant [edylkɔʀɑ̃] nm sweetener

éduquer [edyke] /1/ vt to educate; (élever) to bring up

effacer [efase] /3/ vt to erase, rub out; **s'effacer** vi (inscription etc) to wear off; (pour laisser passer) to step aside

effarant, e [efaʀɑ̃, -ɑ̃t] adj alarming

effectif, -ive [efɛktif, -iv] adj real ▷ nm (Scol) total number of pupils; (Comm) manpower sg; **effectivement** adv (réellement) actually, really; (en effet) indeed

effectuer [efɛktɥe] /1/ vt (opération, mission) to carry out; (déplacement, trajet) to make

effervescent, e [efɛʀvesɑ̃, -ɑ̃t] *adj* effervescent

effet [efɛ] *nm* effect; (*impression*) impression; **effets** *nmpl* (*vêtements etc*) things; **faire ~** (*médicament*) to take effect; **faire de l'~** (*impressionner*) to make an impression; **faire bon/ mauvais ~ sur qn** to make a good/ bad impression on sb; **en ~** indeed; **~ de serre** greenhouse effect

efficace [efikas] *adj* (*personne*) efficient; (*action, médicament*) effective; **efficacité** *nf* efficiency; effectiveness

effondrer [efɔ̃dʀe] /1/: **s'effondrer** *vi* to collapse

efforcer [efɔʀse] /3/: **s'efforcer de** *vt*: **s'~ de faire** to try hard to do

effort [efɔʀ] *nm* effort

effrayant, e [efʀɛjɑ̃, -ɑ̃t] *adj* frightening

effrayer [efʀeje] /8/ *vt* to frighten, scare; **s'effrayer (de)** to be frightened *ou* scared (by)

effréné, e [efʀene] *adj* wild

effronté, e [efʀɔ̃te] *adj* insolent

effroyable [efʀwajabl] *adj* horrifying, appalling

égal, e, -aux [egal, -o] *adj* equal; (*constant: vitesse*) steady ▷ *nm/f* equal; **être ~ à** (*prix, nombre*) to be equal to; **ça m'est ~** it's all the same to me, I don't mind; **sans ~** matchless, unequalled; **d'~ à ~** as equals; **également** *adv* equally; (*aussi*) too, as well; **égaler** /1/ *vt* to equal; **égaliser** /1/ *vt* (*sol, salaires*) to level (out); (*chances*) to equalize ▷ *vi* (*Sport*) to equalize; **égalité** *nf* equality; **être à égalité (de points)** to be level

égard [egaʀ] *nm*: **égards** *nmpl* consideration *sg*; **à cet ~** in this respect; **par ~ pour** out of consideration for; **à l'~ de** towards

égarer [egaʀe] /1/ *vt* to mislay; **s'égarer** *vi* to get lost, lose one's way; (*objet*) to go astray

églefin [egləfɛ̃] *nm* haddock

église [egliz] *nf* church; **aller à l'~** to go to church

égoïsme [egɔism] *nm* selfishness; **égoïste** *adj* selfish

égout [egu] *nm* sewer

égoutter [egute] /1/ *vi* to drip; **s'égoutter** *vi* to drip; **égouttoir** *nm* draining board; (*mobile*) draining rack

égratignure [egʀatiɲyʀ] *nf* scratch

Égypte [eʒipt] *nf*: **l'~** Egypt; **égyptien, ne** *adj* Egyptian ▷ *nm/f*: **Égyptien, ne** Egyptian

eh [e] *excl* hey!; **eh bien** well

élaborer [elabɔʀe] /1/ *vt* to elaborate; (*projet, stratégie*) to work out; (*rapport*) to draft

élan [elɑ̃] *nm* (*Zool*) elk, moose; (*Sport*) run up; (*fig: de tendresse etc*) surge; **prendre son ~/de l'~** to take a run up/gather speed

élancer [elɑ̃se] /3/: **s'élancer** *vi* to dash, hurl o.s.

élargir [elaʀʒiʀ] /2/ *vt* to widen; **s'élargir** *vi* to widen; (*vêtement*) to stretch

élastique [elastik] *adj* elastic ▷ *nm* (*de bureau*) rubber band; (*pour la couture*) elastic *no pl*

élection [elɛksjɔ̃] *nf* election

électricien, ne [elɛktʀisjɛ̃, -ɛn] *nm/f* electrician

électricité [elɛktʀisite] *nf* electricity; **allumer/éteindre l'~** to put on/off the light

électrique [elɛktʀik] *adj* electric(al)

électrocuter [elɛktʀɔkyte] /1/ *vt* to electrocute

électroménager [elɛktʀɔmenaʒe] *adj*: **appareils ~s** domestic (electrical) appliances ▷ *nm*: **l'~** household appliances

électronique [elɛktʀɔnik] *adj* electronic ▷ *nf* electronics *sg*

élégance [elegɑ̃s] *nf* elegance

élégant, e [elegɑ̃, -ɑ̃t] *adj* elegant

élément [elemɑ̃] *nm* element; (*pièce*) component, part; **élémentaire** *adj* elementary

éléphant [elefɑ̃] *nm* elephant

élevage [el(ə)vaʒ] *nm* breeding; (*de bovins*) cattle breeding *ou* rearing; **truite d'~** farmed trout

élevé, e [el(ə)ve] *adj* high; **bien/mal ~** well-/ill-mannered

élève [elɛv] *nm/f* pupil

élever [el(ə)ve] /5/ *vt* (*enfant*) to bring up, raise; (*bétail, volaille*) to breed; (*hausser: taux, niveau*) to raise; (*édifier: monument*) to put up, erect; **s'élever** *vi* (*avion, alpiniste*) to go up; (*niveau, température, aussi*) to rise; **s'~ à** (*frais, dégâts*) to amount to, add up to; **s'~ contre** to rise up against; **~ la voix** to raise one's voice; **éleveur, -euse** *nm/f* stock breeder

éliminatoire [eliminatwaʀ] *nf* (*Sport*) heat

éliminer [elimine] /1/ *vt* to eliminate

élire [eliʀ] /43/ *vt* to elect

elle [ɛl] *pron* (*sujet*) she; (: *chose*) it; (*complément*) her; it; **~s** (*sujet*) they; (*complément*) them; **~-même** herself; itself; **~s-mêmes** themselves; *voir* **il**

éloigné, e [elwaɲe] *adj* distant, far-off; (*parent*) distant

éloigner [elwaɲe] /1/ *vt* (*échéance*) to put off, postpone; (*soupçons, danger*) to ward off; **~ qch (de)** to move *ou* take sth away (from); **s'éloigner (de)** (*personne*) to go away (from); (*véhicule*) to move away (from); (*affectivement*) to become estranged (from); **~ qn (de)** to take sb away *ou* remove sb (from)

élu, e [ely] *pp de* **élire** ▷ *nm/f* (*Pol*) elected representative

Élysée [elize] *nm*: **(le palais de) l'~** the Élysée palace

émail, -aux [emaj, -o] *nm* enamel

e-mail [imɛl] *nm* email; **envoyer qch par ~** to email sth

émanciper [emɑ̃sipe] /1/: **s'émanciper** *vi* (*fig*) to become emancipated *ou* liberated

emballage [ɑ̃balaʒ] *nm* (*papier*) wrapping; (*carton*) packaging

emballer [ɑ̃bale] /1/ *vt* to wrap (up); (*dans un carton*) to pack (up); (*fig: fam*) to thrill (to bits); **s'emballer** *vi* (*moteur*) to race; (*cheval*) to bolt; (*fig: personne*) to get carried away

embarcadère [ɑ̃baʀkadɛʀ] *nm* landing stage (BRIT), pier

embarquement [ɑ̃baʀkəmɑ̃] *nm* embarkation; (*de marchandises*) loading; (*de passagers*) boarding

embarquer [ɑ̃baʀke] /1/ *vt* (*personne*) to embark; (*marchandise*) to load; (*fam*) to cart off ▷ *vi* (*passager*) to board; **s'embarquer** *vi* to board; **s'~ dans** (*affaire, aventure*) to embark upon

embarras [ɑ̃baʀa] *nm* (*confusion*) embarrassment; **être dans l'~** to be in a predicament *ou* an awkward position; **vous n'avez que l'~ du choix** the only problem is choosing

embarrassant, e [ɑ̃baʀasɑ̃, -ɑ̃t] *adj* embarrassing

embarrasser [ɑ̃baʀase] /1/ *vt* (*encombrer*) to clutter (up); (*gêner*) to hinder, hamper; to put in an awkward position; **s'embarrasser de** to burden o.s. with

embaucher [ɑ̃boʃe] /1/ *vt* to take on, hire

embêtant, e [ɑ̃bɛtɑ̃, -ɑ̃t] *adj* annoying

embêter [ɑ̃bete] /1/ *vt* to bother; **s'embêter** *vi* (*s'ennuyer*) to be bored

emblée [ɑ̃ble]: **d'~** *adv* straightaway

embouchure [ɑ̃buʃyʀ] *nf* (*Géo*) mouth

embourber [ɑ̃buʀbe] /1/: **s'embourber** *vi* to get stuck in the mud

embouteillage [ɑ̃butɛjaʒ] *nm* traffic jam, (traffic) holdup (BRIT)

embranchement [ɑ̃bʀɑ̃ʃmɑ̃] *nm*
(*routier*) junction

embrasser [ɑ̃bʀase] /1/ *vt* to kiss;
(*sujet, période*) to embrace, encompass

embrayage [ɑ̃bʀejaʒ] *nm* clutch

embrouiller [ɑ̃bʀuje] /1/ *vt* (*fils*) to
tangle (up); (*fiches, idées, personne*) to
muddle up; **s'embrouiller** *vi* to get
in a muddle

embruns [ɑ̃bʀœ̃] *nmpl* sea spray *sg*

embué, e [ɑ̃bɥe] *adj* misted up

émeraude [em(ə)ʀod] *nf* emerald

émerger [emɛʀʒe] /3/ *vi* to emerge;
(*faire saillie, aussi fig*) to stand out

émeri [em(ə)ʀi] *nm*: **toile** *ou* **papier**
~ emery paper

émerveiller [emɛʀveje] /1/ *vt* to
fill with wonder; **s'émerveiller de**
to marvel at

émettre [emɛtʀ] /56/ *vt* (*son, lumière*)
to give out, emit; (*message etc: Radio*)
to transmit; (*billet, timbre, emprunt,
chèque*) to issue; (*hypothèse, avis*) to
voice, put forward ▷ *vi* to broadcast

émeus *etc* [emø] *vb voir* **émouvoir**

émeute [emøt] *nf* riot

émigrer [emigʀe] /1/ *vi* to emigrate

émincer [emɛ̃se] /3/ *vt* to slice thinly

émission [emisjɔ̃] *nf* (*voir
émettre*) emission; (*d'un message*)
transmission; (*de billet, timbre,
emprunt, chèque*) issue; (*Radio, TV*)
programme, broadcast

emmêler [ɑ̃mele] /1/ *vt* to tangle
(up); (*fig*) to muddle up; **s'emmêler** *vi*
to get into a tangle

emménager [ɑ̃menaʒe] /3/ *vi* to
move in; **~ dans** to move into

emmener [ɑ̃m(ə)ne] /5/ *vt* to take
(with one); (*comme otage, capture*) to
take away; **~ qn au cinéma** to take
sb to the cinema

emmerder [ɑ̃mɛʀde] /1/ (!) *vt* to
bug, bother; **s'emmerder** *vi* to be
bored stiff

émoticone [emɔtikɔn] *nm* smiley

émotif, -ive [emɔtif, -iv] *adj* emotional

émotion [emɔsjɔ̃] *nf* emotion

émouvoir [emuvwaʀ] /27/ *vt* to
move; **s'émouvoir** *vi* to be moved;
to be roused

empaqueter [ɑ̃pakte] /4/ *vt* to
pack up

emparer [ɑ̃paʀe] /1/: **s'emparer de**
vt (*objet*) to seize, grab; (*comme otage,
Mil*) to seize; (*peur etc*) to take hold of

empêchement [ɑ̃pɛʃmɑ̃] *nm*
(unexpected) obstacle, hitch

empêcher [ɑ̃peʃe] /1/ *vt* to prevent;
~ qn de faire to prevent *ou* stop sb
(from) doing; **il n'empêche que**
nevertheless; **il n'a pas pu s'~ de rire**
he couldn't help laughing

empereur [ɑ̃pʀœʀ] *nm* emperor

empiffrer [ɑ̃pifʀe] /1/: **s'empiffrer** *vi*
(*péj*) to stuff o.s.

empiler [ɑ̃pile] /1/ *vt* to pile (up)

empire [ɑ̃piʀ] *nm* empire; (*fig*)
influence

empirer [ɑ̃piʀe] /1/ *vi* to worsen,
deteriorate

emplacement [ɑ̃plasmɑ̃] *nm* site

emploi [ɑ̃plwa] *nm* use; (*poste*) job,
situation; (*Comm, Écon*) employment;
mode d'~ directions for use; **~ du
temps** timetable, schedule

employé, e [ɑ̃plwaje] *nm/f*
employee; **~ de bureau/banque**
office/bank employee *ou* clerk

employer [ɑ̃plwaje] /8/ *vt* to use;
(*ouvrier, main-d'œuvre*) to employ; **s'~
à qch/à faire** to apply *ou* devote o.s.
to sth/to doing; **employeur, -euse**
nm/f employer

empoigner [ɑ̃pwaɲe] /1/ *vt* to grab

empoisonner [ɑ̃pwazɔne] /1/ *vt* to
poison; (*empester: air, pièce*) to stink
out; (*fam*): **~ qn** to drive sb mad

emporter [ɑ̃pɔʀte] /1/ *vt* to take
(with one); (*en dérobant ou enlevant,
emmener: blessés, voyageurs*) to take
away; (*entraîner*) to carry away *ou*
along; (*rivière, vent*) to carry away;
s'emporter *vi* (*de colère*) to fly into a
rage; **l'~ (sur)** to get the upper hand
(of); **plats à ~** take-away meals

empreint, e [ɑ̃pʀɛ̃, -ɛ̃t] *adj*: **~ de** marked with ▷ *nf* (*de pied, main*) print; **~e (digitale)** fingerprint; **~e écologique** carbon footprint

empressé, e [ɑ̃pʀese] *adj* attentive

empresser [ɑ̃pʀese] /1/: **s'empresser** *vi*: **s'~ auprès de qn** to surround sb with attentions; **s'~ de faire** to hasten to do

emprisonner [ɑ̃pʀizɔne] /1/ *vt* to imprison

emprunt [ɑ̃pʀœ̃] *nm* loan (*from debtor's point of view*)

emprunter [ɑ̃pʀœ̃te] /1/ *vt* to borrow; (*itinéraire*) to take, follow

ému, e [emy] *pp de* **émouvoir** ▷ *adj* (*gratitude*) touched; (*compassion*) moved

○ **MOT-CLÉ**

en [ɑ̃] *prép* **1** (*endroit, pays*) in; (: *direction*) to; **habiter en France/ ville** to live in France/town; **aller en France/ville** to go to France/town
2 (*moment, temps*) in; **en été/juin** in summer/June; **en 3 jours/20 ans** in 3 days/20 years
3 (*moyen*) by; **en avion/taxi** by plane/taxi
4 (*composition*) made of; **c'est en verre/coton/laine** it's (made of) glass/cotton/wool; **un collier en argent** a silver necklace
5 (*description, état*): **une femme (habillée) en rouge** a woman (dressed) in red; **peindre qch en rouge** to paint sth red; **en T/étoile** T-/star-shaped; **en chemise/chaussettes** in one's shirt sleeves/socks; **en soldat** as a soldier; **cassé en plusieurs morceaux** broken into several pieces; **en réparation** being repaired, under repair; **en vacances** on holiday; **en deuil** in mourning; **le même en plus grand** the same but *ou* only bigger
6 (*avec gérondif*) while; on; **en dormant** while sleeping, as one

sleeps; **en sortant** on going out, as he *etc* went out; **sortir en courant** to run out
7: **en tant que** as; **je te parle en ami** I'm talking to you as a friend
▷ *pron* **1** (*indéfini*): **j'en ai/veux** I have/want some; **en as-tu?** have you got any?; **je n'en veux pas** I don't want any; **j'en ai deux** I've got two; **combien y en a-t-il?** how many (of them) are there?; **j'en ai assez** I've got enough (of it *ou* them); (*j'en ai marre*) I've had enough
2 (*provenance*) from there; **j'en viens** I've come from there
3 (*cause*): **il en est malade/perd le sommeil** he is ill/can't sleep because of it
4 (*complément de nom, d'adjectif, de verbe*): **j'en connais les dangers** I know its *ou* the dangers; **j'en suis fier/ai besoin** I am proud of it/need it

encadrer [ɑ̃kadʀe] /1/ *vt* (*tableau, image*) to frame; (*fig: entourer*) to surround; (*personnel, soldats etc*) to train

encaisser [ɑ̃kese] /1/ *vt* (*chèque*) to cash; (*argent*) to collect; (*fig: coup, défaite*) to take

en-cas [ɑ̃kɑ] *nm inv* snack

enceinte [ɑ̃sɛ̃t] *adj f*: **~ (de six mois)** (six months) pregnant ▷ *nf* (*mur*) wall; (*espace*) enclosure; **~ (acoustique)** speaker

encens [ɑ̃sɑ̃] *nm* incense

encercler [ɑ̃sɛʀkle] /1/ *vt* to surround

enchaîner [ɑ̃ʃene] /1/ *vt* to chain up; (*mouvements, séquences*) to link (together) ▷ *vi* to carry on

enchanté, e [ɑ̃ʃɑ̃te] *adj* (*ravi*) delighted; (*ensorcelé*) enchanted; **~ (de faire votre connaissance)** pleased to meet you

enchère [ɑ̃ʃɛʀ] *nf* bid; **mettre/ vendre aux ~s** to put up for (sale by)/ sell by auction

enclencher [ãklãʃe] /1/ vt (mécanisme) to engage; **s'enclencher** vi to engage

encombrant, e [ãkɔ̃bʀã, -ãt] adj cumbersome, bulky

encombrement [ãkɔ̃bʀəmã] nm: **être pris dans un ~** to be stuck in a traffic jam

encombrer [ãkɔ̃bʀe] /1/ vt to clutter (up); (gêner) to hamper; **s'encombrer de** (bagages etc) to load ou burden o.s. with

  MOT-CLÉ

encore [ãkɔʀ] adv 1 (continuation) still; **il y travaille encore** he's still working on it; **pas encore** not yet
2 (de nouveau) again; **j'irai encore demain** I'll go again tomorrow; **encore une fois** (once) again
3 (en plus) more; **encore un peu de viande?** a little more meat?; **encore deux jours** two more days
4 (intensif) even, still; **encore plus fort/mieux** even louder/better, louder/better still; **quoi encore?** what now?
5 (restriction) even so ou then, only; **encore pourrais-je le faire si …** even so, I might be able to do it if …; **si encore** if only

encourager [ãkuʀaʒe] /3/ vt to encourage; **~ qn à faire qch** to encourage sb to do sth

encourir [ãkuʀiʀ] /11/ vt to incur

encre [ãkʀ] nf ink; **~ de Chine** Indian ink

encyclopédie [ãsiklɔpedi] nf encyclopaedia

endetter [ãdete] /1/: **s'endetter** vi to get into debt

endive [ãdiv] nf chicory no pl

endormi, e [ãdɔʀmi] adj asleep

endormir [ãdɔʀmiʀ] /16/ vt to put to sleep; (chaleur etc) to send to sleep; (Méd: dent, nerf) to anaesthetize; (fig: soupçons) to allay; **s'endormir** vi to fall asleep, go to sleep

endroit [ãdʀwa] nm place; (opposé à l'envers) right side; **à l'~** (vêtement) the right way out; (objet posé) the right way round

endurance [ãdyʀãs] nf endurance

endurant, e [ãdyʀã, -ãt] adj tough, hardy

endurcir [ãdyʀsiʀ] /2/: **s'endurcir** vi (physiquement) to become tougher; (moralement) to become hardened

endurer [ãdyʀe] /1/ vt to endure, bear

énergétique [enɛʀʒetik] adj (aliment) energizing

énergie [enɛʀʒi] nf (Physique) energy; (Tech) power; (morale) vigour, spirit; **énergique** adj energetic; vigorous; (mesures) drastic, stringent

énervant, e [enɛʀvã, -ãt] adj irritating, annoying

énerver [enɛʀve] /1/ vt to irritate, annoy; **s'énerver** vi to get excited, get worked up

enfance [ãfãs] nf childhood

enfant [ãfã] nm/f child; **enfantin, e** adj childlike; (langage) children's cpd

enfer [ãfɛʀ] nm hell

enfermer [ãfɛʀme] /1/ vt to shut up; (à clef, interner) to lock up; **s'enfermer** to shut o.s. away

enfiler [ãfile] /1/ vt (vêtement) to slip on; (perles) to string; (aiguille) to thread; **~ un tee-shirt** to slip into a T-shirt

enfin [ãfɛ̃] adv at last; (en énumérant) lastly; (de restriction, résignation) still; (pour conclure) in a word; (somme toute) after all

enflammer [ãflame] /1/: **s'enflammer** vi to catch fire; (Méd) to become inflamed

enflé, e [ãfle] adj swollen

enfler [ãfle] /1/ vi to swell (up)

enfoncer [ãfɔ̃se] /3/ vt (clou) to drive in; (faire pénétrer): **~ qch dans** to push (ou drive) sth into; (forcer: porte) to break open; **s'enfoncer** vi to sink; **s'~ dans** to sink into; (forêt, ville) to disappear into

enfouir [ɑ̃fwiʀ] /2/ vt (dans le sol) to bury; (dans un tiroir etc) to tuck away

enfuir [ɑ̃fɥiʀ] /17/: **s'enfuir** vi to run away ou off

engagement [ɑ̃gaʒmɑ̃] nm commitment; **sans ~** without obligation

engager [ɑ̃gaʒe] /3/ vt (embaucher) to take on; (: artiste) to engage; (commencer) to start; (lier) to bind, commit; (impliquer, entraîner) to involve; (investir) to invest, lay out; (introduire, clé) to insert; (inciter) **~ qn à faire** to urge sb to do; **s'engager** vi (Mil) to enlist; (promettre) to commit o.s.; (débuter: conversation etc) to start (up); **s'~ à faire** to undertake to do; **s'~ dans** (rue, passage) to turn into; (fig: affaire, discussion) to enter into, embark on

engelures [ɑ̃ʒlyʀ] nfpl chilblains

engin [ɑ̃ʒɛ̃] nm machine; (outil) instrument; (Auto) vehicle; (Aviat) aircraft inv

Attention à ne pas traduire engin par le mot anglais engine.

engloutir [ɑ̃glutiʀ] /2/ vt to swallow up

engouement [ɑ̃gumɑ̃] nm (sudden) passion

engouffrer [ɑ̃gufʀe] /1/ vt to swallow up, devour; **s'engouffrer dans** to rush into

engourdir [ɑ̃guʀdiʀ] /2/ vt to numb; (fig) to dull, blunt; **s'engourdir** vi to go numb

engrais [ɑ̃gʀɛ] nm manure; **~ (chimique)** (chemical) fertilizer

engraisser [ɑ̃gʀese] /1/ vt to fatten (up)

engrenage [ɑ̃gʀənaʒ] nm gears pl, gearing; (fig) chain

engueuler [ɑ̃gœle] /1/ vt (fam) to bawl at ou out

enhardir [ɑ̃aʀdiʀ] /2/: **s'enhardir** vi to grow bolder

énigme [enigm] nf riddle

enivrer [ɑ̃nivʀe] /1/ vt: **s'enivrer** to get drunk

enjamber [ɑ̃ʒɑ̃be] /1/ vt to stride over

enjeu, x [ɑ̃ʒø] nm stakes pl

enjoué, e [ɑ̃ʒwe] adj playful

enlaidir [ɑ̃lediʀ] /2/ vt to make ugly ▷ vi to become ugly

enlèvement [ɑ̃lɛvmɑ̃] nm (rapt) abduction, kidnapping

enlever [ɑ̃l(ə)ve] /5/ vt (ôter: gén) to remove; (: vêtement, lunettes) to take off; (emporter: ordures etc) to collect; (kidnapper) to abduct, kidnap; (obtenir: prix, contrat) to win; (prendre) **~ qch à qn** to take sth (away) from sb

enliser [ɑ̃lize] /1/: **s'enliser** vi to sink, get stuck

enneigé, e [ɑ̃neʒe] adj snowy

ennemi, e [ɛnmi] adj hostile; (Mil) enemy cpd ▷ nm/f enemy

ennui [ɑ̃nɥi] nm (lassitude) boredom; (difficulté) trouble no pl; **avoir des ~s** to have problems; **ennuyer** /8/ vt to bother; (lasser) to bore; **s'ennuyer** vi to be bored; **si cela ne vous ennuie pas** if it's no trouble to you; **ennuyeux, -euse** adj boring, tedious; (agaçant) annoying

énorme [enɔʀm] adj enormous, huge; **énormément** adv enormously; **énormément de neige/gens** an enormous amount of snow/number of people

enquête [ɑ̃kɛt] nf (de journaliste, de police) investigation; (judiciaire, administrative) inquiry; (sondage d'opinion) survey; **enquêter** /1/ vi to investigate; **enquêter (sur)** to do a survey (on)

enragé, e [ɑ̃ʀaʒe] adj (Méd) rabid, with rabies; (fig) fanatical

enrageant, e [ɑ̃ʀaʒɑ̃, -ɑ̃t] adj infuriating

enrager [ɑ̃ʀaʒe] /3/ vi to be furious

enregistrement [ɑ̃ʀ(ə)ʒistʀəmɑ̃] nm recording; **~ des bagages** baggage check-in

enregistrer [ɑ̃R(ə)ʒistRe] /1/ vt (Mus) to record; (fig: mémoriser) to make a mental note of; (bagages: à l'aéroport) to check in

enrhumer [ɑ̃Ryme] /1/: **s'enrhumer** vi to catch a cold

enrichir [ɑ̃RiʃiR] /2/ vt to make rich(er); (fig) to enrich; **s'enrichir** vi to get rich(er)

enrouer [ɑ̃Rwe] /1/: **s'enrouer** vi to go hoarse

enrouler [ɑ̃Rule] /1/ vt (fil, corde) to wind (up); **s'enrouler** to coil up; **~ qch autour de** to wind sth (a)round

enseignant, e [ɑ̃sɛɲɑ̃, -ɑ̃t] nm/f teacher

enseignement [ɑ̃sɛɲ(ə)mɑ̃] nm teaching; (Admin) education

enseigner [ɑ̃seɲe] /1/ vt, vi to teach; **~ qch à qn/à qn que** to teach sb sth/sb that

ensemble [ɑ̃sɑ̃bl] adv together ⊳ nm (assemblage) set; (vêtements) outfit; (unité, harmonie) unity; **l'~ du/ de la** (totalité) the whole ou entire; **impression/idée d'~** overall ou general impression/idea; **dans l'~ (en gros)** on the whole

ensoleillé, e [ɑ̃sɔleje] adj sunny

ensuite [ɑ̃sɥit] adv then, next; (plus tard) afterwards, later

entamer [ɑ̃tame] /1/ vt (pain, bouteille) to start; (hostilités, pourparlers) to open

entasser [ɑ̃tase] /1/ vt (empiler) to pile up, heap up; **s'entasser** vi (s'amonceler) to pile up; **s'~ dans** to cram into

entendre [ɑ̃tɑ̃dR] /41/ vt to hear; (comprendre) to understand; (vouloir dire) to mean; **s'entendre** vi (sympathiser) to get on; (se mettre d'accord) to agree; **j'ai entendu dire que** I've heard (it said) that; **~ parler de** to hear of

entendu, e [ɑ̃tɑ̃dy] adj (réglé) agreed; (au courant: air) knowing; **(c'est) ~** all right, agreed; **bien ~** of course

entente [ɑ̃tɑ̃t] nf understanding; (accord, traité) agreement; **à double ~ (sens)** with a double meaning

enterrement [ɑ̃tɛRmɑ̃] nm (cérémonie) funeral, burial

enterrer [ɑ̃teRe] /1/ vt to bury

entêtant, e [ɑ̃tɛtɑ̃, -ɑ̃t] adj heady

en-tête [ɑ̃tɛt] nm heading; **papier à ~** headed notepaper

entêté, e [ɑ̃tete] adj stubborn

entêter [ɑ̃tete] /1/: **s'entêter** vi: **s'~ (à faire)** to persist (in doing)

enthousiasme [ɑ̃tuzjasm] nm enthusiasm; **enthousiasmer** /1/ vt to fill with enthusiasm; **s'enthousiasmer (pour qch)** to get enthusiastic (about sth); **enthousiaste** adj enthusiastic

entier, -ière [ɑ̃tje, -jɛR] adj whole; (total, complet: satisfaction etc) complete; (fig: caractère) unbending ⊳ nm (Math) whole; **en ~** totally; **lait ~** full-cream milk; **entièrement** adv entirely, wholly

entonnoir [ɑ̃tɔnwaR] nm funnel

entorse [ɑ̃tɔRs] nf (Méd) sprain; (fig): **~ à la loi/au règlement** infringement of the law/rule

entourage [ɑ̃tuRaʒ] nm circle; (famille) family (circle); (ce qui enclôt) surround

entourer [ɑ̃tuRe] /1/ vt to surround; (apporter son soutien à) to rally round; **~ de** to surround with; **s'entourer de** to surround o.s. with

entracte [ɑ̃tRakt] nm interval

entraide [ɑ̃tRɛd] nf mutual aid ou assistance

entrain [ɑ̃tRɛ̃] nm spirit; **avec ~** energetically; **faire qch sans ~** to do sth half-heartedly ou without enthusiasm

entraînement [ɑ̃tRɛnmɑ̃] nm training

entraîner [ɑ̃tRene] /1/ vt (charrier) to carry ou drag along; (Tech) to drive; (emmener: personne) to take (off); (mener à l'assaut, influencer) to lead;

(*Sport*) to train; (*impliquer*) to entail; **~ qn à faire** (*inciter*) to lead sb to do; **s'entraîner** *vi* (*Sport*) to train; **s'~ à qch/à faire** to train o.s. for sth/to do; **entraîneur** *nm/f* (*Sport*) coach, trainer ▷ *nm* (*Hippisme*) trainer

entre [ɑ̃tʀ] *prép* between; (*parmi*) among(st); **l'un d'~ eux** one of them/us; **~ autres (choses)** among other things; **ils se battent ~ eux** they are fighting among(st) themselves; **entrecôte** *nf* entrecôte *ou* rib steak

entrée [ɑ̃tʀe] *nf* entrance; (*accès: au cinéma etc*) admission; (*billet*) (admission) ticket; (*Culin*) first course

entre: entrefilet *nm* (*article*) paragraph, short report; **entremets** *nm* (cream) dessert

entrepôt [ɑ̃tʀəpo] *nm* warehouse

entreprendre [ɑ̃tʀəpʀɑ̃dʀ] /58/ *vt* (*se lancer dans*) to undertake; (*commencer*) to begin *ou* start (upon)

entrepreneur, -euse [ɑ̃tʀəpʀənœʀ, -øz] *nm/f:* **~ (en bâtiment)** (building) contractor

entrepris, e [ɑ̃tʀəpʀi, -iz] *pp de* **entreprendre** ▷ *nf* (*société*) firm, business; (*action*) undertaking, venture

entrer [ɑ̃tʀe] /1/ *vi* to go (*ou* come) in, enter ▷ *vt* (*Inform*) to input, enter; **~ dans** (*gén*) to enter; (*pièce*) to go (*ou* come) into, enter; (*club*) to join; (*heurter*) to run into; **(faire) ~ qch dans** to get sth into; **~ à l'hôpital** to go into hospital; **faire ~** (*visiteur*) to show in

entre-temps [ɑ̃tʀətɑ̃] *adv* meanwhile

entretenir [ɑ̃tʀət(ə)niʀ] /22/ *vt* to maintain; (*famille, maîtresse*) to support, keep; **~ qn (de)** to speak to sb (about)

entretien [ɑ̃tʀətjɛ̃] *nm* maintenance; (*discussion*) discussion, talk; (*pour un emploi*) interview

entrevoir [ɑ̃tʀəvwaʀ] /30/ *vt* (*à peine*) to make out; (*brièvement*) to catch a glimpse of

entrevu, e [ɑ̃tʀəvy] *pp de* **entrevoir** ▷ *nf* (*audience*) interview

entrouvert, e [ɑ̃tʀuvɛʀ, -ɛʀt] *adj* half-open

énumérer [enymeʀe] /6/ *vt* to list

envahir [ɑ̃vaiʀ] /2/ *vt* to invade; (*inquiétude, peur*) to come over; **envahissant, e** *adj* (*péj: personne*) intrusive

enveloppe [ɑ̃v(ə)lɔp] *nf* (*de lettre*) envelope; (*crédits*) budget; **envelopper** /1/ *vt* to wrap; (*fig*) to envelop, shroud

enverrai *etc* [ɑ̃veʀe] *vb voir* **envoyer**

envers [ɑ̃vɛʀ] *prép* towards, to ▷ *nm* other side; (*d'une étoffe*) wrong side; **à l'~** (*verticalement*) upside down; (*pull*) back to front; (*vêtement*) inside out

envie [ɑ̃vi] *nf* (*sentiment*) envy; (*souhait*) desire, wish; **avoir ~ de** to feel like; (*désir plus fort*) to want; **avoir ~ de faire** to feel like doing; to want to do; **avoir ~ que** to wish that; **cette glace me fait ~** I fancy some of that ice cream; **envier** /7/ *vt* to envy; **envieux, -euse** *adj* envious

environ [ɑ̃viʀɔ̃] *adv:* **~ 3 h/2 km** (around) about 3 o'clock/2 km; *voir aussi* **environs**

environnant, e [ɑ̃viʀɔnɑ̃, -ɑ̃t] *adj* surrounding

environnement [ɑ̃viʀɔnmɑ̃] *nm* environment

environs [ɑ̃viʀɔ̃] *nmpl* surroundings; **aux ~ de** around

envisager [ɑ̃vizaʒe] /3/ *vt* to contemplate; (*avoir en vue*) to envisage; **~ de faire** to consider doing

envoler [ɑ̃vɔle] /1/: **s'envoler** *vi* (*oiseau*) to fly away *ou* off; (*avion*) to take off; (*papier, feuille*) to blow away; (*fig*) to vanish (into thin air)

envoyé, e [ɑ̃vwaje] *nm/f* (*Pol*) envoy; (*Presse*) correspondent; **~ spécial** special correspondent

envoyer [ɑ̃vwaje] /8/ *vt* to send; (*lancer*) to hurl, throw; **~ chercher**

to send for; **~ promener qn** (*fam*) to
send sb packing

éolien, ne [eɔljɛ̃, -ɛn] *adj* wind ▷ *nf*
wind turbine

épagneul, e [epaɲœl] *nm/f* spaniel

épais, se [epɛ, -ɛs] *adj* thick;
épaisseur *nf* thickness

épanouir [epanwiʀ] /2/: **s'épanouir**
vi (*fleur*) to bloom, open out; (*visage*)
to light up; (*se développer*) to blossom
(out)

épargne [epaʀɲ] *nf* saving

épargner [epaʀɲe] /1/ *vt* to save; (*ne
pas tuer ou endommager*) to spare ▷ *vi*
to save; **~ qch à qn** to spare sb sth

éparpiller [epaʀpije] /1/ *vt* to
scatter; **s'éparpiller** *vi* to scatter; (*fig*)
to dissipate one's efforts

épatant, e [epatɑ̃, -ɑ̃t] *adj* (*fam*) super

épater [epate] /1/ *vt* (*fam*) to amaze;
(: *impressionner*) to impress

épaule [epol] *nf* shoulder

épave [epav] *nf* wreck

épée [epe] *nf* sword

épeler [ep(ə)le] /4/ *vt* to spell

éperon [epʀɔ̃] *nm* spur

épervier [epɛʀvje] *nm* sparrowhawk

épi [epi] *nm* (*de blé, d'orge*) ear; (*de
maïs*) cob

épice [epis] *nf* spice

épicé, e [epise] *adj* spicy

épicer [epise] /3/ *vt* to spice

épicerie [episʀi] *nf* grocer's
shop; (*denrées*) groceries *pl*; **~ fine**
delicatessen (shop); **épicier, -ière**
nm/f grocer

épidémie [epidemi] *nf* epidemic

épiderme [epidɛʀm] *nm* skin

épier [epje] /7/ *vt* to spy on, watch
closely

épilepsie [epilɛpsi] *nf* epilepsy

épiler [epile] /1/ *vt* (*jambes*) to remove
the hair from; (*sourcils*) to pluck

épinards [epinaʀ] *nmpl* spinach *sg*

épine [epin] *nf* thorn, prickle; (*d'oursin
etc*) spine

épingle [epɛ̃gl] *nf* pin; **~ de nourrice**
ou **de sûreté** *ou* **double** safety pin

épisode [epizɔd] *nm* episode; **film/
roman à ~s** serial; **épisodique** *adj*
occasional

épluche-légumes [eplyʃlegym] *nm
inv* potato peeler

éplucher [eplyʃe] /1/ *vt* (*fruit,
légumes*) to peel; (*comptes, dossier*)
to go over with a fine-tooth comb;
épluchures *nfpl* peelings

éponge [epɔ̃ʒ] *nf* sponge; **éponger**
/3/ *vt* (*liquide*) to mop *ou* sponge
up; (*surface*) to sponge; (*fig: déficit*)
to soak up

époque [epɔk] *nf* (*de l'histoire*) age,
era; (*de l'année, la vie*) time; **d'~**
(*meuble*) period *cpd*

épouse [epuz] *nf* wife; **épouser** /1/
vt to marry

épousseter [epuste] /4/ *vt* to dust

épouvantable [epuvɑ̃tabl] *adj*
appalling, dreadful

épouvantail [epuvɑ̃taj] *nm*
scarecrow

épouvante [epuvɑ̃t] *nf* terror; **film
d'~** horror film; **épouvanter** /1/ *vt*
to terrify

époux [epu] *nm* husband ▷ *nmpl*: **les
~** the (married) couple

épreuve [epʀœv] *nf* (*d'examen*) test;
(*malheur, difficulté*) trial, ordeal;
(*Photo*) print; (*Typo*) proof; (*Sport*)
event; **à toute ~** unfailing; **mettre à
l'~** to put to the test

éprouver [epʀuve] /1/ *vt* (*tester*) to
test; to afflict, distress; (*ressentir*) to
experience

EPS *sigle f* (= *Éducation physique et
sportive*) ≈ PE

épuisé, e [epɥize] *adj* exhausted;
(*livre*) out of print; **épuisement** *nm*
exhaustion

épuiser [epɥize] /1/ *vt* (*fatiguer*) to
exhaust, wear *ou* tire out; (*stock, sujet*)
to exhaust; **s'épuiser** *vi* to wear *ou*
tire o.s. out, exhaust o.s.

épuisette [epɥizɛt] *nf* shrimping net

équateur [ekwatœʀ] *nm* equator;
(la république de) l'É~ Ecuador

équation [ekwasjɔ̃] *nf* equation
équerre [ekeʀ] *nf* (*à dessin*) (set) square
équilibre [ekilibʀ] *nm* balance; **garder/perdre l'~** to keep/lose one's balance; **être en ~** to be balanced; **équilibré, e** *adj* well-balanced; **équilibrer** /1/ *vt* to balance; **s'équilibrer** *vi* to balance
équipage [ekipaʒ] *nm* crew
équipe [ekip] *nf* team; **travailler en ~** to work as a team
équipé, e [ekipe] *adj*: **bien/mal ~** well-/poorly-equipped
équipement [ekipmɑ̃] *nm* equipment
équiper [ekipe] /1/ *vt* to equip; **~ qn/qch de** to equip sb/sth with
équipier, -ière [ekipje, -jeʀ] *nm/f* team member
équitation [ekitasjɔ̃] *nf* (horse-) riding; **faire de l'~** to go (horse-)riding
équivalent, e [ekivalɑ̃, -ɑ̃t] *adj, nm* equivalent
équivaloir [ekivalwaʀ] /29/: **~ à** *vt* to be equivalent to
érable [eʀabl] *nm* maple
érafler [eʀafle] /1/ *vt* to scratch; **éraflure** *nf* scratch
ère [eʀ] *nf* era; **en l'an 1050 de notre ~** in the year 1050 A.D.
érection [eʀeksjɔ̃] *nf* erection
éroder [eʀɔde] /1/ *vt* to erode
érotique [eʀɔtik] *adj* erotic
errer [eʀe] /1/ *vi* to wander
erreur [eʀœʀ] *nf* mistake, error; **par ~** by mistake; **faire ~** to be mistaken
éruption [eʀypsjɔ̃] *nf* eruption; (*boutons*) rash
es [e] *vb voir* **être**
ès [es] *prép*: **licencié ès lettres/ sciences** ≈ Bachelor of Arts/Science
ESB *sigle f* (= *encéphalopathie spongiforme bovine*) BSE
escabeau, x [eskabo] *nm* (*tabouret*) stool; (*échelle*) stepladder
escalade [eskalad] *nf* climbing *no pl*; (*Pol etc*) escalation; **escalader** /1/ *vt* to climb

escale [eskal] *nf* (*Navig: durée*) call; (*: port*) port of call; (*Aviat*) stop(over); **faire ~ à** (*Navig*) to put in at; (*Aviat*) to stop over at; **vol sans ~** nonstop flight
escalier [eskalje] *nm* stairs *pl*; **dans l'~** *ou* **les ~s** on the stairs; **~ mécanique** *ou* **roulant** escalator
escapade [eskapad] *nf*: **faire une ~** to go on a jaunt; (*s'enfuir*) to run away *ou* off
escargot [eskaʀgo] *nm* snail
escarpé, e [eskaʀpe] *adj* steep
esclavage [esklavaʒ] *nm* slavery
esclave [esklav] *nm/f* slave
escompte [eskɔ̃t] *nm* discount
escrime [eskʀim] *nf* fencing
escroc [eskʀo] *nm* swindler, con-man; **escroquer** /1/ *vt*: **escroquer qn (de qch)/qch à qn** to swindle sb (out of sth)/sth out of sb; **escroquerie** [eskʀɔkʀi] *nf* swindle
espace [espas] *nm* space; **espacer** /3/ *vt* to space out; **s'espacer** *vi* (*visites etc*) to become less frequent
espadon [espadɔ̃] *nm* swordfish *inv*
espadrille [espadʀij] *nf* rope-soled sandal
Espagne [espaɲ] *nf*: **l'~** Spain; **espagnol, e** *adj* Spanish ▷ *nm* (*Ling*) Spanish ▷ *nm/f*: **Espagnol, e** Spaniard
espèce [espes] *nf* (*Bio, Bot, Zool*) species *inv*; (*gén: sorte*) sort, kind, type; (*péj*): **~ de maladroit/de brute!** you clumsy oaf/you brute!; **espèces** *nfpl* (*Comm*) cash *sg*; **payer en ~s** to pay (in) cash
espérance [espeʀɑ̃s] *nf* hope; **~ de vie** life expectancy
espérer [espeʀe] /6/ *vt* to hope for; **j'espère (bien)** I hope so; **~ que/ faire** to hope that/to do
espiègle [espjegl] *adj* mischievous
espion, ne [espjɔ̃, -ɔn] *nm/f* spy; **espionnage** *nm* espionage, spying; **espionner** /1/ *vt* to spy (up)on

espoir [ɛspwaʀ] nm hope; **dans l'~ de/que** in the hope of/that; **reprendre ~** not to lose hope

esprit [ɛspʀi] nm (pensée, intellect) mind; (humour, ironie) wit; (mentalité, d'une loi etc, fantôme etc) spirit; **faire de l'~** to try to be witty; **reprendre ses ~s** to come to; **perdre l'~** to lose one's mind

esquimau, de, x [ɛskimo, -od] adj Eskimo ▷ nm: **E~®** ice lolly (BRIT), popsicle (US) ▷ nm/f: **E~, de** Eskimo

essai [ɛsɛ] nm (tentative) attempt, try; (de produit) testing; (Rugby) try; (Littérature) essay; **à l'~** on a trial basis; **mettre à l'~** to put to the test

essaim [ɛsɛ̃] nm swarm

essayer [eseje] /8/ vt to try; (vêtement, chaussures) to try (on); (restaurant, méthode, voiture) to try (out) ▷ vi to try; **~ de faire** to try ou attempt to do

essence [esɑ̃s] nf (de voiture) petrol (BRIT), gas(oline) (US); (extrait de plante) essence; (espèce: d'arbre) species inv

essentiel, le [esɑ̃sjɛl] adj essential; **c'est l'~** (ce qui importe) that's the main thing; **l'~ de** the main part of

essieu, x [esjø] nm axle

essor [esɔʀ] nm (de l'économie etc) rapid expansion

essorer [esɔʀe] /1/ vt (en tordant) to wring (out); (par la force centrifuge) to spin-dry; **essoreuse** nf spin-dryer

essouffler [esufle] /1/: **s'essouffler** vi to get out of breath

essuie-glace [esɥiglas] nm windscreen (BRIT) ou windshield (US) wiper

essuyer [esɥije] /8/ vt to wipe; (fig: subir) to suffer; **s'essuyer** (après le bain) to dry o.s.; **~ la vaisselle** to dry up

est vb [ɛ] voir **être** ▷ nm [ɛst]: **l'~** the east ▷ adj inv [ɛst] east; (région) east(ern); **à l'~** in the east; (direction) to the east, east(wards); **à l'~ de** (to the) east of

est-ce que [ɛskə] adv: **~ c'est cher/c'était bon?** is it expensive/ was it good?; **quand est-ce qu'il part?** when does he leave?, when is he leaving?; voir aussi **que**

esthéticienne [ɛstetisjɛn] nf beautician

esthétique [ɛstetik] adj attractive

estimation [ɛstimasjɔ̃] nf valuation; (chiffre) estimate

estime [ɛstim] nf esteem, regard; **estimer** /1/ vt (respecter) to esteem; (expertiser: bijou) to value; (évaluer: coût etc) to assess, estimate; (penser): **estimer que/être** to consider that/o.s. to be

estival, e, -aux [ɛstival, -o] adj summer cpd

estivant, e [ɛstivɑ̃, -ɑ̃t] nm/f (summer) holiday-maker

estomac [ɛstɔma] nm stomach

estragon [ɛstʀagɔ̃] nm tarragon

estuaire [ɛstɥɛʀ] nm estuary

et [e] conj and; **et lui?** what about him?; **et alors?** so what?

étable [etabl] nf cowshed

établi, e [etabli] nm (work)bench

établir [etabliʀ] /2/ vt (papiers d'identité, facture) to make out; (liste, programme) to draw up; (gouvernement, artisan etc) to set up; (réputation, usage, fait, culpabilité, relations) to establish; **s'établir** vi to be established; **s'~ (à son compte)** to set up in business; **s'~ à/près de** to settle in/near

établissement [etablismɑ̃] nm (entreprise, institution) establishment; **~ scolaire** school, educational establishment

étage [etaʒ] nm (d'immeuble) storey, floor; **au 2ème ~** on the 2nd (BRIT) ou 3rd (US) floor; **à l'~** upstairs; **c'est à quel ~?** what floor is it on?

étagère [etaʒɛʀ] nf (rayon) shelf; (meuble) shelves pl

étai [etɛ] nm stay, prop

étain [etɛ̃] nm pewter no pl

étais etc [etɛ] vb voir **être**

étaler [etale] /1/ vt (carte, nappe) to spread (out); (peinture, liquide) to spread; (échelonner: paiements, dates, vacances) to spread, stagger; (marchandises) to display; (richesses, connaissances) to parade; **s'étaler** vi (liquide) to spread out; (fam) to fall flat on one's face; **s'~ sur** (paiements etc) to be spread over

étalon [etalɔ̃] nm (cheval) stallion

étanche [etɑ̃ʃ] adj (récipient) watertight; (montre, vêtement) waterproof

étang [etɑ̃] nm pond

étant [etɑ̃] vb voir **être**; **donné**

étape [etap] nf stage; (lieu d'arrivée) stopping place; (: Cyclisme) staging point

état [eta] nm (Pol, condition) state; **en bon/mauvais ~** in good/poor condition; **en ~ (de marche)** in (working) order; **remettre en ~** to repair; **hors d'~** out of order; **être en ~/hors d'~ de faire** to be in a state/in no fit state to do; **être dans tous ses ~s** to be in a state; **faire ~ de** (alléguer) to put forward; **l'É~** the State; **~ civil** civil status; **~ des lieux** inventory of fixtures; **États-Unis** nmpl: **les États-Unis (d'Amérique)** the United States (of America)

et cætera, et cetera, etc. [ɛtsetera] adv etc

été [ete] pp de **être** ▷ nm summer

éteindre [etɛ̃dʁ] /52/ vt (lampe, lumière, radio, chauffage) to turn ou switch off; (cigarette, incendie, bougie) to put out, extinguish; **s'éteindre** vi (feu, lumière) to go out; (mourir) to pass away; **éteint, e** adj (fig) lacklustre, dull; (volcan) extinct

étendre [etɑ̃dʁ] /41/ vt (pâte, liquide) to spread; (carte etc) to spread out; (lessive, linge) to hang up ou out; (bras, jambes) to stretch out; (fig: agrandir) to extend; **s'étendre** vi (augmenter, se propager) to spread; (terrain, forêt

etc): **s'~ jusqu'à/de ... à** to stretch as far as/from ... to; **s'~ sur** (se coucher) to lie down (on); (fig: expliquer) to elaborate ou enlarge (upon)

étendu, e [etɑ̃dy] adj extensive

éternel, le [etɛʁnɛl] adj eternal

éternité [etɛʁnite] nf eternity; **ça a duré une ~** it lasted for ages

éternuement [etɛʁnymɑ̃] nm sneeze

éternuer [etɛʁnɥe] /1/ vi to sneeze

êtes [ɛt(z)] vb voir **être**

Éthiopie [etjɔpi] nf: **l'~** Ethiopia

étiez [etje] vb voir **être**

étinceler [etɛ̃s(ə)le] /4/ vi to sparkle

étincelle [etɛ̃sɛl] nf spark

étiquette [etikɛt] nf label; (protocole): **l'~** etiquette

étirer [etiʁe] /1/ vt to stretch out; **s'étirer** vi (personne) to stretch; (convoi, route): **s'~ sur** to stretch out over

étoile [etwal] nf star; **à la belle ~** (out) in the open; **~ filante** shooting star; **~ de mer** starfish; **étoilé, e** adj starry

étonnant, e [etɔnɑ̃, -ɑ̃t] adj surprising

étonnement [etɔnmɑ̃] nm surprise, amazing

étonner [etɔne] /1/ vt to surprise, amaze; **s'étonner que/de** to be surprised that/at; **cela m'~ait (que)** (j'en doute) I'd be (very) surprised (if)

étouffer [etufe] /1/ vt to suffocate; (bruit) to muffle; (scandale) to hush up ▷ vi to suffocate; **s'étouffer** vi (en mangeant etc) to choke; **on étouffe** it's stifling

étourderie [etuʁdəʁi] nf (caractère) absent-mindedness no pl; (faute) thoughtless blunder

étourdi, e [etuʁdi] adj (distrait) scatterbrained, heedless

étourdir [etuʁdiʁ] /2/ vt (assommer) to stun, daze; (griser) to make dizzy ou giddy; **étourdissement** nm dizzy spell

étrange [etʀɑ̃ʒ] *adj* strange

étranger, -ère [etʀɑ̃ʒe, -ɛʀ] *adj*
foreign; (*pas de la famille, non familier*)
strange ▷ *nm/f* foreigner; stranger
▷ *nm*: **à l'~** abroad

étrangler [etʀɑ̃gle] /1/ *vt* to
strangle; **s'étrangler** *vi* (*en mangeant
etc*) to choke

 MOT-CLÉ

être [ɛtʀ] /61/ *nm* being; **être
humain** human being
▷ *vb copule* **1** (*état, description*) to
be; **il est instituteur** he is *ou* he's
a teacher; **vous êtes grand/
intelligent/fatigué** you are *ou* you're
tall/clever/tired
2 (+*à: appartenir*) to be; **le livre est
à Paul** the book is Paul's *ou* belongs
to Paul; **c'est à moi/eux** it is *ou* it's
mine/theirs
3 (+*de: provenance*): **il est de Paris** he
is from Paris; (: *appartenance*): **il est
des nôtres** he is one of us
4 (*date*): **nous sommes le 10 janvier**
it's the 10th of January (today)
▷ *vi* to be; **je ne serai pas ici demain**
I won't be here tomorrow
▷ *vb aux* **1** to have; to be; **être arrivé/
allé** to have arrived/gone; **il est
parti** he has left, he has gone
2 (*forme passive*) to be; **être fait par**
to be made by; **il a été promu** he has
been promoted
3 (+*à* +*inf, obligation, but*): **c'est à
réparer** it needs repairing; **c'est
à essayer** it should be tried; **il est
à espérer que ...** it is *ou* it's to be
hoped that ...
▷ *vb impers* **1**: **il est** (+ *adj*) it is; **il est
impossible de le faire** it's impossible
to do it
2: **il est** (*heure, date*): **il est 10 heures**
it is *ou* it's 10 o'clock
3 (*emphatique*): **c'est moi** it's me;
c'est à lui de le faire it's up to him
to do it

étrennes [etʀɛn] *nfpl* ≈ Christmas
box *sg*

étrier [etʀije] *nm* stirrup

étroit, e [etʀwa, -wat] *adj*
narrow; (*vêtement*) tight; (*fig: liens,
collaboration*) close; **à l'~** cramped;
~ d'esprit narrow-minded

étude [etyd] *nf* studying; (*ouvrage,
rapport*) study; (*Scol: salle de travail*)
study room; **études** *nfpl* (*Scol*)
studies; **être à l'~** (*projet etc*) to be
under consideration; **faire des ~s
(de droit/médecine)** to study (law/
medicine)

étudiant, e [etydjɑ̃, -ɑ̃t] *nm/f* student

étudier [etydje] /7/ *vt, vi* to study

étui [etɥi] *nm* case

eu, eue [y] *pp de* **avoir**

euh [ø] *excl* er

euro [øʀo] *nm* euro

Europe [øʀɔp] *nf*: **l'~** Europe;
européen, ne *adj* European ▷ *nm/f*:
Européen, ne European

eus *etc* [y] *vb voir* **avoir**

eux [ø] *pron* (*sujet*) they; (*objet*) them

évacuer [evakɥe] /1/ *vt* to evacuate

évader [evade] /1/: **s'évader** *vi* to
escape

évaluer [evalɥe] /1/ *vt* (*expertiser*)
to assess, evaluate; (*juger
approximativement*) to estimate

évangile [evɑ̃ʒil] *nm* gospel; **É~**
Gospel

évanouir [evanwiʀ] /2/: **s'évanouir**
vi to faint; (*disparaître*) to vanish,
disappear; **évanouissement** *nm*
(*syncope*) fainting fit

évaporer [evapɔʀe] /1/: **s'évaporer**
vi to evaporate

évasion [evazjɔ̃] *nf* escape

éveillé, e [eveje] *adj* awake; (*vif*)
alert, sharp; **éveiller** /1/ *vt* to (a)
waken; (*soupçons etc*) to arouse;
s'éveiller *vi* to (a)waken; (*fig*) to be
aroused

événement [evɛnmɑ̃] *nm* event

éventail [evɑ̃taj] *nm* fan; (*choix*)
range

éventualité [evãtyalite] *nf* eventuality; possibility; **dans l'~ de** in the event of

éventuel, le [evãtyɛl] *adj* possible

Attention à ne pas traduire *éventuel* par *eventual*.

éventuellement [evãtyɛlmã] *adv* possibly

Attention à ne pas traduire *éventuellement* par *eventually*.

évêque [evɛk] *nm* bishop

évidemment [evidamã] *adv* (*bien sûr*) of course; (*certainement*) obviously

évidence [evidãs] *nf* obviousness; (*fait*) obvious fact; **de toute ~** quite obviously *ou* evidently; **être en ~** to be clearly visible; **mettre en ~** (*fait*) to highlight; **évident, e** *adj* obvious, evident; **ce n'est pas évident** it's not as simple as all that

évier [evje] *nm* (kitchen) sink

éviter [evite] /1/ *vt* to avoid; **~ de faire/que qch ne se passe** to avoid doing/sth happening; **~ qch à qn** to spare sb sth

évoluer [evɔlɥe] /1/ *vi* (*enfant, maladie*) to develop; (*situation, moralement*) to evolve, develop; (*aller et venir*) to move about; **évolution** *nf* development; evolution

évoquer [evɔke] /1/ *vt* to call to mind, evoke; (*mentionner*) to mention

ex- [ɛks] *préfixe* ex-; **son ~mari** her ex-husband; **son ~femme** his ex-wife

exact, e [ɛgza(kt), ɛgzakt] *adj* exact; (*correct*) correct; (*ponctuel*) punctual; **l'heure ~e** the right *ou* exact time; **exactement** *adv* exactly

ex aequo [ɛgzeko] *adj* equally placed; **arriver ~** to finish neck and neck

exagéré, e [ɛgzaʒeʀe] *adj* (*prix etc*) excessive

exagérer [ɛgzaʒeʀe] /6/ *vt* to exaggerate ▷ *vi* (*abuser*) to go too far; (*déformer les faits*) to exaggerate

examen [ɛgzamɛ̃] *nm* examination; (*Scol*) exam, examination; **à l'~** under

consideration; **~ médical** (medical) examination; (*analyse*) test

examinateur, -trice [ɛgzaminatœʀ, -tʀis] *nm/f* examiner

examiner [ɛgzamine] /1/ *vt* to examine

exaspérant, e [ɛgzaspeʀã, -ãt] *adj* exasperating

exaspérer [ɛgzaspeʀe] /6/ *vt* to exasperate

exaucer [ɛgzose] /3/ *vt* (*vœu*) to grant

excéder [ɛksede] /6/ *vt* (*dépasser*) to exceed; (*agacer*) to exasperate

excellent, e [ɛksɛlã, -ãt] *adj* excellent

excentrique [ɛksãtʀik] *adj* eccentric

excepté, e [ɛksɛpte] *adj*, *prép*: **les élèves ~s, ~ les élèves** except for *ou* apart from the pupils

exception [ɛksɛpsjɔ̃] *nf* exception; **à l'~ de** except for, with the exception of; **d'~** (*mesure, loi*) special, exceptional; **exceptionnel, le** *adj* exceptional; **exceptionnellement** *adv* exceptionally

excès [ɛksɛ] *nm* surplus ▷ *nmpl* excesses; **faire des ~** to overindulge; **~ de vitesse** speeding *no pl*; **excessif, -ive** *adj* excessive

excitant, e [ɛksitã, -ãt] *adj* exciting ▷ *nm* stimulant; **excitation** *nf* (*état*) excitement

exciter [ɛksite] /1/ *vt* to excite; (*café etc*) to stimulate; **s'exciter** *vi* to get excited

exclamer [ɛksklame] /1/: **s'exclamer** *vi* to exclaim

exclu, e [ɛkskly] *adj*: **il est/n'est pas ~ que ...** it's out of the question/not impossible that ...

exclure [ɛksklyʀ] /35/ *vt* (*faire sortir*) to expel; (*ne pas compter*) to exclude, leave out; (*rendre impossible*) to exclude, rule out; **exclusif, -ive** *adj* exclusive; **exclusion** *nf* expulsion; **à l'exclusion de** with the exclusion *ou* exception of; **exclusivité** *nf* (*Comm*)

e

exclusive rights *pl*; **film passant en exclusivité à** film showing only at

excursion [ɛkskyʀsjɔ̃] *nf* (*en autocar*) excursion, trip; (*à pied*) walk, hike

excuse [ɛkskyz] *nf* excuse; **excuses** *nfpl* (*regret*) apology *sg*, apologies; **excuser** /1/ *vt* to excuse; **s'excuser (de)** to apologize (for); **"excusez-moi"** "I'm sorry"; (*pour attirer l'attention*) "excuse me"

exécuter [ɛgzekyte] /1/ *vt* (*prisonnier*) to execute; (*tâche etc*) to execute, carry out; (*Mus: jouer*) to perform, execute; **s'exécuter** *vi* to comply

exemplaire [ɛgzɑ̃plɛʀ] *nm* copy

exemple [ɛgzɑ̃pl] *nm* example; **par ~** for instance, for example; **donner l'~** to set an example

exercer [ɛgzɛʀse] /3/ *vt* (*pratiquer*) to exercise, practise; (*influence, contrôle, pression*) to exert; (*former*) to exercise, train; **s'exercer** *vi* (*médecin*) to be in practice; (*sportif, musicien*) to practise

exercice [ɛgzɛʀsis] *nm* exercise

exhiber [ɛgzibe] /1/ *vt* (*montrer: papiers, certificat*) to present, produce; (*péj*) to display, flaunt; **s'exhiber** *vi* to parade; (*exhibitionniste*) to expose o.s.; **exhibitionniste** *nm/f* exhibitionist

exigeant, e [ɛgziʒɑ̃, -ɑ̃t] *adj* demanding; (*péj*) hard to please

exiger [ɛgziʒe] /3/ *vt* to demand, require

exil [ɛgzil] *nm* exile; **exiler** /1/ *vt* to exile; **s'exiler** *vi* to go into exile

existence [ɛgzistɑ̃s] *nf* existence

exister [ɛgziste] /1/ *vi* to exist; **il existe un/des** there is a/are (some)

exorbitant, e [ɛgzɔʀbitɑ̃, -ɑ̃t] *adj* exorbitant

exotique [ɛgzɔtik] *adj* exotic; **yaourt aux fruits ~s** tropical fruit yoghurt

expédier [ɛkspedje] /7/ *vt* (*lettre, paquet*) to send; (*troupes, renfort*) to dispatch; (*péj: travail etc*) to dispose of, dispatch; **expéditeur, -trice** *nm/f* sender; **expédition** *nf* sending; (*scientifique, sportive, Mil*) expedition

expérience [ɛkspeʀjɑ̃s] *nf* (*de la vie, des choses*) experience; (*scientifique*) experiment

expérimenté, e [ɛkspeʀimɑ̃te] *adj* experienced

expérimenter [ɛkspeʀimɑ̃te] /1/ *vt* to test out, experiment with

expert, e [ɛkspɛʀ, -ɛʀt] *adj* ▷ *nm* expert; **~ en assurances** insurance valuer; **expert-comptable** *nm* ≈ chartered (*BRIT*) *ou* certified public (*US*) accountant

expirer [ɛkspiʀe] /1/ *vi* (*prendre fin, lit: mourir*) to expire; (*respirer*) to breathe out

explication [ɛksplikasjɔ̃] *nf* explanation; (*discussion*) discussion; (*dispute*) argument

explicite [ɛksplisit] *adj* explicit

expliquer [ɛksplike] /1/ *vt* to explain; **s'expliquer** to explain o.s.; **s'~ avec qn** (*discuter*) to explain o.s. to sb

exploit [ɛksplwa] *nm* exploit, feat; **exploitant** *nm/f*: **exploitant (agricole)** farmer; **exploitation** *nf* exploitation; (*d'une entreprise*) running;

exploitation agricole farming concern; **exploiter** /1/ *vt* (*personne, don*) to exploit; (*entreprise, ferme*) to run, operate; (*mine*) to exploit, work

explorer [ɛksplɔʀe] /1/ *vt* to explore

exploser [ɛksploze] /1/ *vi* to explode, blow up; (*engin explosif*) to go off; (*personne: de colère*) to explode; **explosif, -ive** *adj, nm* explosive; **explosion** *nf* explosion; **explosion de joie/colère** outburst of joy/rage

exportateur, -trice [ɛkspɔʀtatœʀ, -tʀis] *adj* export *cpd*, exporting ▷ *nm* exporter

exportation [ɛkspɔʀtasjɔ̃] *nf* (*action*) exportation; (*produit*) export

exporter [ɛkspɔʀte] /1/ *vt* to export

exposant [ɛkspozɑ̃] *nm* exhibitor

exposé, e [εkspoze] nm talk ▷ adj:
~ au sud facing south

exposer [εkspoze] /1/ vt
(marchandise) to display; (peinture) to
exhibit, show; (parler de) to explain,
set out; (mettre en danger, orienter,
Photo) to expose; **s'exposer à** (soleil,
danger) to expose o.s. to; **exposition**
nf (manifestation) exhibition; (Photo)
exposure

exprès¹ [εkspʀε] adv (délibérément)
on purpose; (spécialement) specially;
faire ~ de faire qch to do sth on
purpose

exprès², -esse [εkspʀεs] adj inv
(Postes: lettre, colis) express

express [εkspʀεs] adj, nm: **(café) ~**
espresso; **(train) ~** fast train

expressif, -ive [εkspʀesif, -iv] adj
expressive

expression [εkspʀesjɔ̃] nf
expression

exprimer [εkspʀime] /1/ vt
(sentiment, idée) to express; (jus,
liquide) to press out; **s'exprimer** vi
(personne) to express o.s.

expulser [εkspylse] /1/ vt to expel;
(locataire) to evict; (Football) to
send off

exquis, e [εkski, -iz] adj exquisite

extasier [εkstɑzje] /7/: **s'extasier** vi:
s'~ sur to go into raptures over

exténuer [εkstenɥe] /1/ vt to
exhaust

extérieur, e [εksteʀjœʀ] adj (porte,
mur etc) outer, outside; (commerce,
politique) foreign; (influences, pressions)
external; (apparent: calme, gaieté etc)
outer ▷ nm (d'une maison, d'un récipient
etc) outside, exterior; (apparence)
exterior; **à l'~** outside; (à l'étranger)
abroad

externat [εksteʀna] nm day school

externe [εksteʀn] adj external, outer
▷ nm/f (Méd) non-resident medical
student, extern (US); (Scol) day pupil

extincteur [εkstɛ̃ktœʀ] nm (fire)
extinguisher

extinction [εkstɛ̃ksjɔ̃] nf: **~ de voix**
loss of voice

extra [εkstʀa] adj inv first-rate; (fam)
fantastic ▷ nm inv extra help

extraire [εkstʀεʀ] /50/ vt to extract;
~ qch de to extract sth from; **extrait**
nm extract; **extrait de naissance**
birth certificate

extraordinaire [εkstʀaɔʀdinεʀ]
adj extraordinary; (Pol, Admin:
mesures etc) special

extravagant, e [εkstʀavagɑ̃, -ɑ̃t]
adj extravagant

extraverti, e [εkstʀavεʀti] adj
extrovert

extrême [εkstʀεm] adj, nm extreme;
d'un ~ à l'autre from one extreme
to another; **extrêmement** adv
extremely; **Extrême-Orient** nm:
l'Extrême-Orient the Far East

extrémité [εkstʀemite] nf
end; (situation) straits pl, plight;
(geste désespéré) extreme action;
extrémités nfpl (pieds et mains)
extremities

exubérant, e [εgzybeʀɑ̃, -ɑ̃t] adj
exuberant

e

f

F abr (= franc) fr.; (appartement): **un
F2/F3** a 2-/3-roomed flat (BRIT) ou
apartment (US)
fa [fa] nm inv (Mus) F; (en chantant la
gamme) fa
fabricant, e [fabʀikɑ̃, -ɑ̃t] nm/f
manufacturer
fabrication [fabʀikasjɔ̃] nf
manufacture
fabrique [fabʀik] nf factory;
fabriquer [fabʀike] /1/ vt to make;
(industriellement) to manufacture;
(fam): **qu'est-ce qu'il fabrique?**
what is he up to?
fac [fak] nf (fam: Scol) (= faculté) Uni
(BRIT fam), ≈ college (US)
façade [fasad] nf front, façade
face [fas] nf face; (fig: aspect) side ▷ adj:
le côté ~ heads; **en ~ de** opposite;
(fig) in front of; **de ~** face on; **~ à**
facing; (fig) faced with, in the face of;
faire ~ à to face; **~ à ~** adv facing each
other; **face-à-face** nm inv encounter

fâché, e [faʃe] adj angry; (désolé)
sorry
fâcher [faʃe] /1/ vt to anger; **se
fâcher** vi to get angry; **se ~ avec** (se
brouiller) to fall out with
facile [fasil] adj easy; (caractère)
easy-going; **facilement** adv easily;
facilité nf easiness; (disposition, don)
aptitude; **facilités** nfpl (possibilités)
facilities; (Comm) terms; **faciliter** /1/
vt to make easier
façon [fasɔ̃] nf (manière) way; (d'une
robe etc) making-up; cut; **façons**
nfpl (péj) fuss sg; **sans ~** adv without
fuss; **non merci, sans ~** no thanks,
honestly; **de ~ à** so as to; **de ~ à ce
que** so that; **de toute ~** anyway, in
any case
facteur, -trice [faktœʀ, -tʀis] nm/f
postman/woman (BRIT), mailman/
woman (US) ▷ nm (Math, gén: élément)
factor
facture [faktyʀ] nf (à payer: gén) bill;
(: Comm) invoice
facultatif, -ive [fakyltatif, -iv] adj
optional
faculté [fakylte] nf (intellectuelle,
d'université) faculty; (pouvoir,
possibilité) power
fade [fad] adj insipid
faible [fɛbl] adj weak; (voix, lumière,
vent) faint; (rendement, intensité,
revenu etc) low ▷ nm (pour quelqu'un)
weakness, soft spot; **faiblesse** nf
weakness; **faiblir** [feblir] /2/ vi
to weaken; (lumière) to dim; (vent)
to drop
faïence [fajɑ̃s] nf earthenware no pl
faillir [fajir] /2/ vi: **j'ai failli tomber/
lui dire** I almost ou nearly fell/
told him
faillite [fajit] nf bankruptcy; **faire ~**
to go bankrupt
faim [fɛ̃] nf hunger; **avoir ~** to be
hungry; **rester sur sa ~** (aussi fig) to
be left wanting more
fainéant, e [fɛneɑ̃, -ɑ̃t] nm/f idler,
loafer

○ **MOT-CLÉ**

faire [fɛʀ] /60/ *vt* **1** (*fabriquer, être l'auteur de*) to make; **faire du vin/ une offre/un film** to make wine/ an offer/a film; **faire du bruit** to make a noise

2 (*effectuer: travail, opération*) to do; **que faites-vous?** (*quel métier etc*) what do you do?; (*quelle activité: au moment de la question*) what are you doing?; **faire la lessive/le ménage** to do the washing/the housework

3 (*études*) to do; (*sport, musique*) to play; **faire du droit/du français** to do law/French; **faire du rugby/ piano** to play rugby/the piano

4 (*visiter*): **faire les magasins** to go shopping; **faire l'Europe** to tour *ou* do Europe

5 (*distance*): **faire du 50 (à l'heure)** to do 50 (km an hour); **nous avons fait 1000 km en 2 jours** we did *ou* covered 1000 km in 2 days

6 (*simuler*): **faire le malade/ l'ignorant** to act the invalid/the fool

7 (*transformer, avoir un effet sur*): **faire de qn un frustré/avocat** to make sb frustrated/a lawyer; **ça ne me fait rien** (*m'est égal*) I don't care *ou* mind; (*me laisse froid*) it has no effect on me; **ça ne fait rien** it doesn't matter; **faire que** (*impliquer*) to mean that

8 (*calculs, prix, mesures*): **deux et deux font quatre** two and two are *ou* make four; **ça fait 10 m/15 euros** it's 10 m/15 euros; **je vous le fais 10 euros** I'll let you have it for 10 euros; **je fais du 40** I take a size 40

9: **qu'a-t-il fait de sa valise/de sa sœur?** what has he done with his case/his sister?

10: **ne faire que: il ne fait que critiquer** (*sans cesse*) all he (ever) does is criticize; (*seulement*) he's only criticizing

11 (*dire*) to say; **vraiment? fit-il** really? he said

12 (*maladie*) to have; **faire du diabète/de la tension** to have diabetes *sg*/high blood pressure

▶ *vi* **1** (*agir, s'y prendre*) to act, do; **il faut faire vite** we (*ou* you *etc*) must act quickly; **comment a-t-il fait pour?** how did he manage to?; **faites comme chez vous** make yourself at home

2 (*paraître*) to look; **faire vieux/ démodé** to look old/old-fashioned; **ça fait bien** it looks good

3 (*remplaçant un autre verbe*) to do; **ne le casse pas comme je l'ai fait** don't break it as I did; **je peux le voir? — faites!** can I see it? — please do!

▶ *vb impers* **1**: **il fait beau** *etc* the weather is fine *etc*; *voir aussi* **froid; jour** *etc*

2 (*temps écoulé, durée*): **ça fait deux ans qu'il est parti** it's two years since he left; **ça fait deux ans qu'il y est** he's been there for two years

▶ *vb aux* **1**: **faire** (+*infinitif: action directe*) to make; **faire tomber/ bouger qch** to make sth fall/ move; **faire démarrer un moteur/ chauffer de l'eau** to start up an engine/heat some water; **cela fait dormir** it makes you sleep; **faire travailler les enfants** to make the children work *ou* get the children to work; **il m'a fait traverser la rue** he helped me to cross the road

2: **faire** (+*infinitif: indirectement, par un intermédiaire*): **faire réparer qch** to get *ou* have sth repaired; **faire punir les enfants** to have the children punished

se faire *vr* **1** (*vin, fromage*) to mature

2 (*être convenable*): **cela se fait beaucoup/ne se fait pas** it's done a lot/not done

3 (+*nom ou pron*): **se faire une jupe** to make o.s. a skirt; **se faire des amis** to make friends; **se faire du souci** to worry; **il ne s'en fait pas** he doesn't worry

4 (+adj: devenir): **se faire vieux** to be getting old; (: délibérément): **se faire beau** to do o.s. up

5: **se faire à** (s'habituer) to get used to; **je n'arrive pas à me faire à la nourriture/au climat** I can't get used to the food/climate

6 (: +infinitif): **se faire examiner la vue/opérer** to have one's eyes tested/have an operation; **se faire couper les cheveux** to get one's hair cut; **il va se faire tuer/punir** he's going to get himself killed/get (himself) punished; **il s'est fait aider** he got somebody to help him; **il s'est fait aider par Simon** he got Simon to help him; **se faire faire un vêtement** to get a garment made for o.s.

7 (impersonnel): **comment se fait-il/faisait-il que?** how is it/was it that?

faire-part [fɛrpar] nm inv announcement (of birth, marriage etc)

faisan, e [fəzɑ̃, -an] nm/f pheasant

faisons etc [fəzɔ̃] vb voir **faire**

fait¹ [fɛ] nm (événement) event, occurrence; (réalité, donnée) fact; **être au ~ (de)** to be informed (of); **au ~** (à propos) by the way; **en venir au ~** to get to the point; **du ~ de ceci/qu'il a menti** because of ou on account of this/his having lied; **de ce ~** for this reason; **en ~** in fact; **prendre qn sur le ~** to catch sb in the act; **~ divers** (short) news item

fait², e [fɛ, fɛt] adj (mûr: fromage, melon) ripe; **c'est bien ~ (pour lui ou eux** etc**)** it serves him (ou them etc) right

faites [fɛt] vb voir **faire**

falaise [falɛz] nf cliff

falloir [falwar] /29/ vb impers: **il faut faire les lits** we (ou you etc) have to ou must make the beds; **il faut que je fasse les lits** I have to ou must make the beds; **il a fallu qu'il parte** he had to leave; **il faudrait qu'elle rentre** she should come ou go back, she ought to come ou go back; **il faut faire attention** you have to be careful; **il me faudrait 100 euros** I would need 100 euros; **il vous faut tourner à gauche après l'église** you have to turn left past the church; **nous avons ce qu'il (nous) faut** we have what we need; **il ne fallait pas** you shouldn't have (done); **s'en falloir** vi: **il s'en est fallu de 10 euros/5 minutes** we (ou they etc) were 10 euros short/5 minutes late (ou early); **il s'en faut de beaucoup qu'il soit ...** he is far from being ...; **il s'en est fallu de peu que cela n'arrive** it very nearly happened; **comme il faut** adj proper; adv properly

famé, e [fame] adj: **mal ~** disreputable, of ill repute

fameux, -euse [famø, -øz] adj (illustre) famous; (bon: repas, plat etc) first-rate, first-class; (intensif): **un ~ problème** etc a real problem etc

familial, e, -aux [familjal, -o] adj family cpd

familiarité [familjarite] nf familiarity

familier, -ière [familje, -jɛr] adj (connu, impertinent) familiar; (atmosphère) informal, friendly; (Ling) informal, colloquial ▷ nm regular (visitor)

famille [famij] nf family; **il a de la ~ à Paris** he has relatives in Paris

famine [famin] nf famine

fana [fana] adj, nm/f (fam) = **fanatique**

fanatique [fanatik] adj: **~ (de)** fanatical (about) ▷ nm/f fanatic

faner [fane] /1/: **se faner** vi to fade

fanfare [fɑ̃far] nf (orchestre) brass band; (musique) fanfare

fantaisie [fɑ̃tezi] nf (spontanéité) fancy, imagination; (caprice) whim ▷ adj: **bijou (de) ~** (piece of) costume jewellery (BRIT) ou jewelry (US)

fantasme [fɑ̃tasm] nm fantasy
fantastique [fɑ̃tastik] adj fantastic
fantôme [fɑ̃tom] nm ghost, phantom
faon [fɑ̃] nm fawn (deer)
FAQ sigle f (= foire aux questions) FAQ pl
farce [faʀs] nf (viande) stuffing;
(blague) (practical) joke; (Théât) farce;
farcir /2/ vt (viande) to stuff
farder [faʀde] /1/: **se farder** vi to
make o.s. up
farine [faʀin] nf flour
farouche [faʀuʃ] adj shy, timid
fart [faʀt] nm (ski) wax
fascination [fasinasjɔ̃] nf
fascination
fasciner [fasine] /1/ vt to fascinate
fascisme [faʃism] nm fascism
fasse etc [fas] vb voir **faire**
fastidieux, -euse [fastidjø, -øz] adj
tedious, tiresome
fatal, e [fatal] adj fatal; (inévitable)
inevitable; **fatalité** nf (destin) fate;
(coïncidence) fateful coincidence
fatidique [fatidik] adj fateful
fatigant, e [fatigɑ̃, -ɑ̃t] adj tiring;
(agaçant) tiresome
fatigue [fatig] nf tiredness, fatigue;
fatigué, e adj tired; **fatiguer** /1/ vt
to tire, make tired; (fig: agacer) to
annoy ▷ vi (moteur) to labour, strain;
se fatiguer to get tired
fauché, e [foʃe] adj (fam) broke
faucher [foʃe] /1/ vt (herbe) to cut;
(champs, blés) to reap; (véhicule) to
mow down; (fam: voler) to pinch
faucon [fokɔ̃] nm falcon, hawk
faudra etc [fodʀa] vb voir **falloir**
faufiler [fofile] /1/: **se faufiler** vi: **se
~ dans** to edge one's way into; **se ~
parmi/entre** to thread one's way
among/between
faune [fon] nf (Zool) wildlife, fauna
fausse [fos] adj f voir **faux²**;
faussement adv (accuser) wrongly,
wrongfully; (croire) falsely
fausser [fose] /1/ vt (objet) to bend,
buckle; (fig) to distort; **~ compagnie
à qn** to give sb the slip

faut [fo] vb voir **falloir**
faute [fot] nf (erreur) mistake, error;
(péché, manquement) misdemeanour;
(Football etc) offence; (Tennis) fault;
c'est de sa/ma ~ it's his/my fault;
être en ~ to be in the wrong; **~ de**
(temps, argent) for ou through lack
of; **sans ~** without fail; **~ de frappe**
typing error; **~ professionnelle**
professional misconduct no pl
fauteuil [fotœj] nm armchair;
~ d'orchestre seat in the front
stalls (BRIT) ou the orchestra (US);
~ roulant wheelchair
fautif, -ive [fotif, -iv] adj (incorrect)
incorrect, inaccurate; (responsable)
at fault, in the wrong; **il se sentait ~**
he felt guilty
fauve [fov] nm wildcat ▷ adj (couleur)
fawn
faux¹ [fo] nf scythe
faux², fausse [fo, fos] adj (inexact)
wrong; (piano, voix) out of tune; (billet)
fake, forged; (sournois, postiche) false
▷ adv (Mus) out of tune ▷ nm (copie)
fake, forgery; **faire ~ bond à qn** to
let sb down; **~ frais** nm pl extras,
incidental expenses; **~ mouvement**
awkward movement; **faire un ~
pas** to trip; (fig) to make a faux pas;
~ témoignage (délit) perjury; **fausse
alerte** false alarm; **fausse couche**
miscarriage; **fausse note** wrong
note; **faux-filet** nm sirloin
faveur [favœʀ] nf favour;
traitement de ~ preferential
treatment; **en ~ de** in favo(u)r of
favorable [favoʀabl] adj favo(u)-
rable
favori, te [favoʀi, -it] adj, nm/f
favo(u)rite
favoriser [favoʀize] /1/ vt to favour
fax [faks] nm fax
fécond, e [fekɔ̃, -ɔ̃d] adj fertile;
féconder /1/ vt to fertilize
féculent [fekylɑ̃] nm starchy food
fédéral, e, -aux [fedeʀal, -o] adj
federal

fée [fe] *nf* fairy
feignant, e [fɛɲɑ̃, -ɑ̃t] *nm/f*
= **fainéant**
feindre [fɛ̃dʀ] /52/ *vt* to feign; **~ de
faire** to pretend to do
fêler [fele] /1/ *vt* to crack
félicitations [felisitasjɔ̃] *nfpl*
congratulations
féliciter [felisite] /1/ *vt*: **~ qn (de)** to
congratulate sb (on)
félin, e [felɛ̃, -in] *nm* (big) cat
femelle [fəmɛl] *adj, nf* female
féminin, e [feminɛ̃, -in] *adj*
feminine; (*sexe*) female; (*équipe,
vêtements etc*) women's ▷ *nm* (*Ling*)
feminine; **féministe** *adj* feminist
femme [fam] *nf* woman; (*épouse*)
wife; **~ de chambre** chambermaid;
~ au foyer housewife; **~ de ménage**
cleaning lady
fémur [femyʀ] *nm* femur, thighbone
fendre [fɑ̃dʀ] /41/ *vt* (*couper en deux*)
to split; (*fissurer*) to crack; (*traverser*)
to cut through; **se fendre** *vi* to crack
fenêtre [f(ə)nɛtʀ] *nf* window
fenouil [fənuj] *nm* fennel
fente [fɑ̃t] *nf* (*fissure*) crack; (*de boîte à
lettres etc*) slit
fer [fɛʀ] *nm* iron; **~ à cheval** horseshoe;
~ forgé wrought iron; **~ à friser**
curling tongs; **~ (à repasser)** iron
ferai *etc* [fəʀe] *vb voir* **faire**
fer-blanc [fɛʀblɑ̃] *nm* tin(plate)
férié, e [feʀje] *adj*: **jour ~** public
holiday
ferions *etc* [fəʀjɔ̃] *vb voir* **faire**
ferme [fɛʀm] *adj* firm ▷ *adv* (*travailler
etc*) hard ▷ *nf* (*exploitation*) farm;
(*maison*) farmhouse
fermé, e [fɛʀme] *adj* closed, shut;
(*gaz, eau etc*) off; (*fig: milieu*) exclusive
fermenter [fɛʀmɑ̃te] /1/ *vi* to ferment
fermer [fɛʀme] /1/ *vt* to close, shut;
(*cesser l'exploitation de*) to close down,
shut down; (*eau, lumière, électricité,
robinet*) to turn off; (*aéroport, route*)
to close ▷ *vi* to close, shut; (*magasin:
définitivement*) to close down, shut

down; **se fermer** *vi* to close, shut; **~
à clef** to lock
fermeté [fɛʀməte] *nf* firmness
fermeture [fɛʀmətyʀ] *nf* closing;
(*dispositif*) catch; **heure de ~** closing
time; **~ éclair**® *ou* **à glissière** zip
(fastener) (BRIT), zipper (US)
fermier, -ière [fɛʀmje, -jɛʀ] *nm/f*
farmer
féroce [feʀɔs] *adj* ferocious, fierce
ferons *etc* [fəʀɔ̃] *vb voir* **faire**
ferrer [feʀe] /1/ *vt* (*cheval*) to shoe
ferroviaire [feʀɔvjɛʀ] *adj* rail *cpd*,
railway *cpd* (BRIT), railroad *cpd* (US)
ferry(-boat) [feʀe(bot)] *nm* ferry
fertile [fɛʀtil] *adj* fertile; **~ en
incidents** eventful, packed with
incidents
fervent, e [fɛʀvɑ̃, -ɑ̃t] *adj* fervent
fesse [fɛs] *nf* buttock; **fessée** *nf*
spanking
festin [fɛstɛ̃] *nm* feast
festival [fɛstival] *nm* festival
festivités [fɛstivite] *nfpl* festivities
fêtard, e [fɛtaʀ, -aʀd] (*fam*) *nm/f* (*péj*)
high liver, merrymaker
fête [fɛt] *nf* (*religieuse*) feast; (*publique*)
holiday; (*réception*) party; (*kermesse*)
fête, fair; (*du nom*) feast day, name
day; **faire la ~** to live it up; **faire ~
à qn** to give sb a warm welcome;
les ~s (de fin d'année) the festive
season; **la salle/le comité des ~s**
the village hall/festival committee;
la ~ des Mères/Pères Mother's/
Father's Day; **~ foraine** (fun)fair; **la
~ de la musique**; *see note* **"fête de la
musique"**; **fêter** /1/ *vt* to celebrate;
(*personne*) to have a celebration for

○ **FÊTE DE LA MUSIQUE**
○
○ The *Fête de la Musique* is a music
○ festival which has taken place
○ every year since 1981. On 21 June
○ throughout France local musicians
○ perform free of charge in parks,
○ streets and squares.

feu, x [fø] *nm* (*gén*) fire; (*signal lumineux*) light; (*de cuisinière*) ring; **feux** *nmpl* (*Auto*) (traffic) lights; **au ~!** (*incendie*) fire!; **à ~ doux/vif** over a slow/brisk heat; **à petit ~** (*Culin*) over a gentle heat; (*fig*) slowly; **faire ~** to fire; **ne pas faire long ~** not to last long; **prendre ~** to catch fire; **mettre le ~ à** to set fire to; **faire du ~** to make a fire; **avez-vous du ~?** (*pour cigarette*) have you (got) a light?; **~ rouge/vert/orange** red/green/amber (BRIT) *ou* yellow (US) light; **~ arrière** rear light; **~ d'artifice** firework; (*spectacle*) fireworks *pl*; **~ de joie** bonfire; **~x de brouillard** fog lights *ou* lamps; **~x de croisement** dipped (BRIT) *ou* dimmed (US) headlights; **~x de position** sidelights; **~x de route** (*Auto*) headlights (on full (BRIT) *ou* high (US) beam)

feuillage [fœjaʒ] *nm* foliage, leaves *pl*

feuille [fœj] *nf* (*d'arbre*) leaf; **~ (de papier)** sheet (of paper); **~ de calcul** spreadsheet; **~ d'impôts** tax form; **~ de maladie** medical expenses claim form; **~ de paye** pay slip

feuillet [fœjɛ] *nm* leaf

feuilleté, e [fœjte] *adj*: **pâte ~** flaky pastry

feuilleter [fœjte] /4/ *vt* (*livre*) to leaf through

feuilleton [fœjtɔ̃] *nm* serial

feutre [føtʀ] *nm* felt; (*chapeau*) felt hat; (*stylo*) felt-tip(ped pen); **feutré, e** *adj* (*pas, voix, atmosphère*) muffled

fève [fɛv] *nf* broad bean

février [fevʀije] *nm* February

fiable [fjabl] *adj* reliable

fiançailles [fjɑ̃saj] *nfpl* engagement *sg*

fiancé, e [fjɑ̃se] *nm/f* fiancé (fiancée) ▷ *adj*: **être ~ (à)** to be engaged (to)

fibre [fibʀ] *nf* fibre; **~ de verre** fibreglass

ficeler [fis(ə)le] /4/ *vt* to tie up

ficelle [fisɛl] *nf* string *no pl*; (*morceau*) piece *ou* length of string

fiche [fiʃ] *nf* (*carte*) (index) card; (*formulaire*) form; (*Élec*) plug; **~ de paye** pay slip

ficher [fiʃe] *vt* (*dans un fichier*) to file; (: *Police*) to put on file; (*fam*: *faire*) to do; (: *donner*) to give; (: *mettre*) to stick *ou* shove; **fiche(-moi) le camp** (*fam*) clear off; **fiche-moi la paix** (*fam*) leave me alone; **se ~ de** (*fam*: *rire de*) to make fun of; (: *être indifférent à*) not to care about

fichier [fiʃje] *nm* file; **~ joint** (*Inform*) attachment

fichu, e [fiʃy] *pp de* **ficher** ▷ *adj* (*fam*: *fini, inutilisable*) bust, done for; (: *intensif*) wretched, darned ▷ *nm* (*foulard*) (head)scarf; **mal ~** feeling lousy

fictif, -ive [fiktif, -iv] *adj* fictitious

fiction [fiksjɔ̃] *nf* fiction; (*fait imaginé*) invention

fidèle [fidɛl] *adj*: **~ (à)** faithful (to) ▷ *nm/f* (*Rel*): **les ~s** (*à l'église*) the congregation; **fidélité** *nf* (*d'un conjoint*) fidelity, faithfulness; (*d'un ami, client*) loyalty

fier¹ [fje]: **se ~ à** *vt* to trust

fier², fière [fjɛʀ] *adj* proud; **~ de** proud of; **fierté** *nf* pride

fièvre [fjɛvʀ] *nf* fever; **avoir de la ~/39 de ~** to have a high temperature/a temperature of 39°C; **fiévreux, -euse** *adj* feverish

figer [fiʒe] /3/: **se figer** *vi* to congeal; (*personne*) to freeze

fignoler [fiɲɔle] /1/ *vt* to put the finishing touches to

figue [fig] *nf* fig; **figuier** *nm* fig tree

figurant, e [figyʀɑ̃, -ɑ̃t] *nm/f* (*Théât*) walk-on; (*Ciné*) extra

figure [figyʀ] *nf* (*visage*) face; (*image, tracé, forme, personnage*) figure; (*illustration*) picture, diagram

figuré, e [figyʀe] *adj* (*sens*) figurative

figurer [figyʀe] /1/ *vi* to appear ▷ *vt* to represent; **se ~ que** to imagine that

fil [fil] *nm* (*brin, fig: d'une histoire*) thread; (*d'un couteau*) edge; **au ~ des**

années with the passing of the years; **au ~ de l'eau** with the stream *ou* current; **coup de ~** (*fam*) phone call; **donner/recevoir un coup de ~** to make/get a phone call; **~ électrique** electric wire; **~ de fer** wire; **~ de fer barbelé** barbed wire

file [fil] *nf* line; (*Auto*) lane; **~ (d'attente)** queue (BRIT), line (US); **à la ~ (d'affilée)** in succession; **à la** *ou* **en ~ indienne** in single file

filer [file] /1/ *vt* (*tissu, toile, verre*) to spin; (*prendre en filature*) to shadow, tail; (*fam: donner*): **~ qch à qn** to slip sb sth ▷ *vi* (*bas, maille, liquide, pâte*) to run; (*aller vite*) to fly past *ou* by; (*fam: partir*) to make off; **~ doux** to behave o.s.

filet [file] *nm* net; (*Culin*) fillet; (*d'eau, de sang*) trickle; **~ (à provisions)** string bag

filial, e, -aux [filjal, -o] *adj* filial ▷ *nf* (*Comm*) subsidiary

filière [filjɛR] *nf* (*carrière*) path; **suivre la ~** to work one's way up (through the hierarchy)

fille [fij] *nf* girl; (*opposé à fils*) daughter; **vieille ~** old maid; **fillette** *nf* (little) girl

filleul, e [fijœl] *nm/f* godchild, godson (goddaughter)

film [film] *nm* (*pour photo*) (roll of) film; (*œuvre*) film, picture, movie

fils [fis] *nm* son; **~ à papa** (*péj*) daddy's boy

filtre [filtR] *nm* filter; **filtrer** /1/ *vt* to filter; (*fig: candidats, visiteurs*) to screen

fin¹ [fɛ̃] *nf* end; **fins** *nfpl* (*but*) ends; **~ mai** at the end of May; **prendre ~** to come to an end; **mettre ~ à** to put an end to; **à la ~** in the end, eventually; **en ~ de compte** in the end; **sans ~** endless

fin², e [fɛ̃, fin] *adj* (*papier, couche, fil*) thin; (*cheveux, poudre, pointe, visage*) fine; (*taille*) neat, slim; (*esprit, remarque*) subtle ▷ *adv* (*moudre, couper*) finely; **~ prêt/soûl** quite ready/drunk; **avoir la vue/l'ouïe ~e** to have keen eyesight/hearing; **or/linge/vin ~** fine gold/linen/wine; **~es herbes** mixed herbs

final, e [final] *adj*, *nf* final ▷ *nm* (*Mus*) finale; **quarts de ~e** quarter finals; **finalement** *adv* finally, in the end; (*après tout*) after all

finance [finãs] *nf* finance; **finances** *nfpl* (*situation financière*) finances; (*activités financières*) finance *sg*; **moyennant ~** for a fee *ou* consideration; **financer** /3/ *vt* to finance; **financier, -ière** *adj* financial

finesse [fines] *nf* thinness; (*raffinement*) fineness; (*subtilité*) subtlety

fini, e [fini] *adj* finished; (*Math*) finite ▷ *nm* (*d'un objet manufacturé*) finish

finir [finiR] /2/ *vt* to finish, end ▷ *vi* to finish, end; **~ de faire** to finish doing; (*cesser*) to stop doing; **~ par faire** to end *ou* finish up doing; **il finit par m'agacer** he's beginning to get on my nerves; **en ~ avec** to be *ou* have done with; **il va mal ~** he will come to a bad end

finition [finisjɔ̃] *nf* (*résultat*) finish

finlandais, e [fɛ̃lɑ̃dɛ, -ɛz] *adj* Finnish ▷ *nm/f*: **F~, e** Finn

Finlande [fɛ̃lɑ̃d] *nf*: **la ~** Finland

finnois, e [finwa, -waz] *adj* Finnish ▷ *nm* (*Ling*) Finnish

fioul [fjul] *nm* fuel oil

firme [firm] *nf* firm

fis [fi] *vb voir* **faire**

fisc [fisk] *nm* tax authorities *pl*; **fiscal, e, -aux** *adj* tax *cpd*, fiscal; **fiscalité** *nf* tax system

fissure [fisyR] *nf* crack; **fissurer** /1/ *vt* to crack; **se fissurer** *vi* to crack

fit [fi] *vb voir* **faire**

fixation [fiksasjɔ̃] *nf* (*attache*) fastening; (*Psych*) fixation

fixe [fiks] *adj* fixed; (*emploi*) steady, regular ▷ *nm* (*salaire*) basic salary; (*téléphone*) landline; **à heure ~** at a set time; **menu à prix ~** set menu

fixé, e [fikse] adj: **être ~ (sur)** (savoir à quoi s'en tenir) to have made up one's mind (about)

fixer [fikse] /1/ vt (attacher): **~ qch (à/sur)** to fix ou fasten sth (to/onto); (déterminer) to fix, set; (poser son regard sur) to stare at; **se fixer** (s'établir) to settle down; **se ~ sur** (attention) to focus on

flacon [flakɔ̃] nm bottle

flageolet [flaʒɔlɛ] nm (Culin) dwarf kidney bean

flagrant, e [flagʁɑ̃, -ɑ̃t] adj flagrant, blatant; **en ~ délit** in the act

flair [flɛʁ] nm sense of smell; (fig) intuition; **flairer** /1/ vt (humer) to sniff (at); (détecter) to scent

flamand, e [flamɑ̃, -ɑ̃d] adj Flemish ⊳ nm (Ling) Flemish ⊳ nm/f: **F~, e** Fleming

flamant [flamɑ̃] nm flamingo

flambant [flɑ̃bɑ̃] adv: **~ neuf** brand new

flambé, e [flɑ̃be] adj (Culin) flambé

flambée [flɑ̃be] nf blaze; **~ des prix** (sudden) shooting up of prices

flamber [flɑ̃be] /1/ vi to blaze (up)

flamboyer [flɑ̃bwaje] /8/ vi to blaze (up)

flamme [flɑm] nf flame; (fig) fire, fervour; **en ~s** on fire, ablaze

flan [flɑ̃] nm (Culin) custard tart ou pie

flanc [flɑ̃] nm side; (Mil) flank

flancher [flɑ̃ʃe] /1/ vi to fail, pack up

flanelle [flanɛl] nf flannel

flâner [flɑne] /1/ vi to stroll

flanquer [flɑ̃ke] /1/ vt to flank; (fam: mettre) to chuck, shove; **~ par terre/à la porte** (jeter) to fling to the ground/chuck out

flaque [flak] nf (d'eau) puddle; (d'huile, de sang etc) pool

flash [flaʃ] nm (pl **flashes**) nm (Photo) flash; **~ (d'information)** newsflash

flatter [flate] /1/ vt to flatter; **se ~ de qch** to pride o.s. on sth; **flatteur, -euse** adj flattering

flèche [flɛʃ] nf arrow; (de clocher) spire; **monter en ~** (fig) to soar, rocket; **partir en ~** to be off like a shot; **fléchette** nf dart

fléchir [fleʃiʁ] /2/: **se fléchir** vi to wither

fleur [flœʁ] nf flower; (d'un arbre) blossom; **être en ~** (arbre) to be in blossom; **tissu à ~s** flowered ou flowery fabric

fleuri, e [flœʁi] adj (jardin) in flower ou bloom; (style, tissu, papier) flowery; (teint) glowing

fleurir [flœʁiʁ] /2/ vi (rose) to flower; (arbre) to blossom; (fig) to flourish ⊳ vt (tombe) to put flowers on; (chambre) to decorate with flowers

fleuriste [flœʁist] nm/f florist

fleuve [flœv] nm river

flexible [flɛksibl] adj flexible

flic [flik] nm (fam: péj) cop

flipper [flipœʁ] nm pinball (machine)

flirter [flœʁte] /1/ vi to flirt

flocon [flɔkɔ̃] nm flake

flore [flɔʁ] nf flora

florissant, e [flɔʁisɑ̃, -ɑ̃t] adj (économie) flourishing

flot [flo] nm flood, stream; **flots** nmpl (de la mer) waves; **être à ~** (Navig) to be afloat; **entrer à ~s** to stream ou pour in

flottant, e [flɔtɑ̃, -ɑ̃t] adj (vêtement) loose(-fitting)

flotte [flɔt] nf (Navig) fleet; (fam: eau) water; (: pluie) rain

flotter [flɔte] /1/ vi to float; (nuage, odeur) to drift; (drapeau) to fly; (vêtements) to hang loose ⊳ vb impers (fam: pleuvoir): **il flotte** it's raining; **faire ~** to float; **flotteur** nm float

flou, e [flu] adj fuzzy, blurred; (fig) woolly (BRIT), vague

fluide [flɥid] adj fluid; (circulation etc) flowing freely ⊳ nm fluid

fluor [flyɔʁ] nm: **dentifrice au ~** fluoride toothpaste

fluorescent, e [flyɔʁesɑ̃, -ɑ̃t] adj fluorescent

f

flûte [flyt] nf (aussi: ~ **traversière**) flute; (verre) flute glass; (pain) (thin) baguette; ~! drat it!; ~ **(à bec)** recorder

flux [fly] nm incoming tide; (écoulement) flow; **le ~ et le re~** the ebb and flow

foc [fɔk] nm jib

foi [fwa] nf faith; **digne de ~** reliable; **être de bonne/mauvaise ~** to be in good faith/not to be in good faith

foie [fwa] nm liver; **crise de ~** stomach upset

foin [fwɛ̃] nm hay; **faire du ~** (fam) to kick up a row

foire [fwaʀ] nf fair; (fête foraine) (fun)fair; ~ **aux questions** (Internet) frequently asked questions; **faire la ~** to whoop it up; ~ **(exposition)** trade fair

fois [fwa] nf time; **une/deux ~** once/twice; **deux ~ deux** twice two; **une ~** (passé) once; (futur) sometime; **une (bonne) ~ pour toutes** once and for all; **une ~ que c'est fait** once it's done; **des ~** (parfois) sometimes; **à la ~** (ensemble) (all) at once

fol [fɔl] adj m voir **fou**

folie [fɔli] nf (d'une décision, d'un acte) madness, folly; (état) madness, insanity; **la ~ des grandeurs** delusions of grandeur; **faire des ~s** (en dépenses) to be extravagant

folklorique [fɔlklɔʀik] adj folk cpd; (fam) weird

folle [fɔl] adj f, nf voir **fou**; **follement** adv (très) madly, wildly

foncé, e [fɔ̃se] adj dark

foncer [fɔ̃se] /3/ vi to go darker; (fam: aller vite) to tear ou belt along; ~ **sur** to charge at

fonction [fɔ̃ksjɔ̃] nf function; (emploi, poste) post, position; **fonctions** nfpl (professionnelles) duties; **voiture de ~** company car; **en ~ de** (par rapport à) according to; **faire ~ de** to serve as; **la ~ publique** the state ou civil (BRIT) service; **fonctionnaire** nm/f

state employee ou official; (dans l'administration) ≈ civil servant; **fonctionner** /1/ vi to work, function

fond [fɔ̃] nm voir aussi **fonds**; (d'un récipient, trou) bottom; (d'une salle, scène) back; (d'un tableau, décor) background; (opposé à la forme) content; (Sport): **le ~** long distance (running); **au ~ de** at the bottom of; at the back of; **à ~** (connaître, soutenir) thoroughly; (appuyer, visser) right down ou home; **à ~ (de train)** (fam) full tilt; **dans le ~, au ~** (en somme) basically, really; **de ~ en comble** from top to bottom; ~ **de teint** foundation

fondamental, e, -aux [fɔ̃damɑ̃tal, -o] adj fundamental

fondant, e [fɔ̃dɑ̃, -ɑ̃t] adj (neige) melting; (poire) that melts in the mouth

fondation [fɔ̃dasjɔ̃] nf founding; (établissement) foundation; **fondations** nfpl (d'une maison) foundations

fondé, e [fɔ̃de] adj (accusation etc) well-founded; **être ~ à croire** to have grounds for believing ou good reason to believe

fondement [fɔ̃dmɑ̃] nm: **sans ~** (rumeur etc) groundless, unfounded

fonder [fɔ̃de] /1/ vt to found; (fig): ~ **qch sur** to base sth on; **se ~ sur** (personne) to base o.s. on

fonderie [fɔ̃dʀi] nf smelting works sg

fondre [fɔ̃dʀ] /41/ vt (aussi: **faire ~**) to melt; (dans l'eau) to dissolve; (fig: mélanger) to merge, blend ▷ vi (à la chaleur) to melt; to dissolve; (fig) to melt away; (se précipiter): ~ **sur** to swoop down on; ~ **en larmes** to dissolve into tears

fonds [fɔ̃] nm (Comm): ~ **(de commerce)** business ▷ nmpl (argent) funds

fondu, e [fɔ̃dy] adj (beurre, neige) melted; (métal) molten ▷ nf (Culin) fondue

font [fɔ̃] *vb voir* **faire**

fontaine [fɔ̃tɛn] *nf* fountain; (*source*) spring

fonte [fɔ̃t] *nf* melting; (*métal*) cast iron; **la ~ des neiges** the (spring) thaw

foot [fut], **football** [futbol] *nm* football, soccer; **footballeur, -euse** *nm/f* footballer, (BRIT), football *ou* soccer player

footing [futiŋ] *nm* jogging; **faire du ~** to go jogging

forain, e [fɔʀɛ̃, -ɛn] *adj* fairground *cpd* ▷ *nm* (*marchand*) stallholder; (*acteur etc*) fairground entertainer

forçat [fɔʀsa] *nm* convict

force [fɔʀs] *nf* strength, (*Physique, Mécanique*) force; **forces** *nfpl* (*physiques*) strength *sg*; (*Mil*) forces; **à ~ de faire** by dint of doing; **de ~** forcibly, by force; **dans la ~ de l'âge** in the prime of life; **les ~s de l'ordre** the police

forcé, e [fɔʀse] *adj* forced; **c'est ~!** it's inevitable!; **forcément** *adv* inevitably; **pas forcément** not necessarily

forcer [fɔʀse] /3/ *vt* to force; (*moteur, voix*) to strain ▷ *vi* (*Sport*) to overtax o.s.; **se ~ à faire qch** to force o.s. to do sth; **~ la dose/l'allure** to overdo it/increase the pace

forestier, -ière [fɔʀɛstje, -jɛʀ] *adj* forest *cpd*

forêt [fɔʀɛ] *nf* forest

forfait [fɔʀfɛ] *nm* (*Comm*) all-in deal *ou* price; **déclarer ~** to withdraw; **forfaitaire** *adj* inclusive

forge [fɔʀʒ] *nf* forge, smithy; **forgeron** *nm* (black)smith

formaliser [fɔʀmalize] /1/: **se formaliser** *vi*: **se ~ (de)** to take offence (at)

formalité [fɔʀmalite] *nf* formality; **simple ~** mere formality

format [fɔʀma] *nm* size; **formater** /1/ *vt* (*disque*) to format

formation [fɔʀmasjɔ̃] *nf* forming; training; **la ~ permanente** *ou*

continue continuing education; **la ~ professionnelle** vocational training

forme [fɔʀm] *nf* (*gén*) form; (*d'un objet*) shape, form; **formes** *nfpl* (*bonnes manières*) proprieties; (*d'une femme*) figure *sg*; **en ~ de poire** pear-shaped, in the shape of a pear; **être en (bonne ou pleine) ~** (*Sport etc*) to be on form; **en bonne et due ~** in due form

formel, le [fɔʀmɛl] *adj* (*preuve, décision*) definite, positive; **formellement** *adv* (*interdit*) strictly; (*absolument*) positively

former [fɔʀme] /1/ *vt* to form; (*éduquer*) to train; **se former** *vi* to form

formidable [fɔʀmidabl] *adj* tremendous

formulaire [fɔʀmylɛʀ] *nm* form

formule [fɔʀmyl] *nf* (*gén*) formula; (*expression*) phrase; **~ de politesse** polite phrase; (*en fin de lettre*) letter ending

fort, e [fɔʀ, fɔʀt] *adj* strong; (*intensité, rendement*) high, great; (*corpulent*) large; (*doué*) good; **être ~ (en)** to be good (at) ▷ *adv* (*serrer, frapper*) hard; (*sonner*) loud(ly); (*beaucoup*) greatly, very much; (*très*) very ▷ *nm* (*édifice*) fort; (*point fort*) strong point, forte; **~e tête** rebel; **forteresse** *nf* fortress

fortifiant [fɔʀtifjɑ̃] *nm* tonic

fortune [fɔʀtyn] *nf* fortune; **faire ~** to make one's fortune; **de ~** makeshift; **fortuné, e** *adj* wealthy

forum [fɔʀɔm] *nm* forum; **~ de discussion** (*Internet*) message board

fosse [fos] *nf* (*grand trou*) pit; (*tombe*) grave

fossé [fose] *nm* ditch; (*fig*) gulf, gap

fossette [fosɛt] *nf* dimple

fossile [fosil] *nm* fossil ▷ *adj* fossilized, fossil *cpd*

fou (fol), folle [fu, fɔl] *adj* mad; (*déréglé etc*) wild, erratic; (*fam: extrême, très grand*) terrific, tremendous ▷ *nm/f* madman/woman ▷ *nm* (*du* *roi*) jester; **être ~ de** to be mad *ou* crazy about; **avoir le ~ rire** to have the giggles

foudre [fudʀ] *nf*: **la ~** lightning

foudroyant, e [fudʀwajɑ̃, -ɑ̃t] *adj* (*progrès*) lightning *cpd*; (*succès*) stunning; (*maladie, poison*) violent

fouet [fwɛ] *nm* whip; (*Culin*) whisk; **de plein ~** *adv* (*se heurter*) head on; **fouetter** /1/ *vt* to whip; (*crème*) to whisk

fougère [fuʒɛʀ] *nf* fern

fougue [fug] *nf* ardour, spirit; **fougueux, -euse** *adj* fiery

fouille [fuj] *nf* search; **fouilles** *nfpl* (*archéologiques*) excavations; **fouiller** /1/ *vt* to search; (*creuser*) to dig ▷ *vi*: **fouiller dans/parmi** to rummage in/among; **fouillis** *nm* jumble, muddle

foulard [fulaʀ] *nm* scarf

foule [ful] *nf* crowd; **la ~** crowds *pl*; **une ~ de** masses of

foulée [fule] *nf* stride

fouler [fule] /1/ *vt* to press; (*sol*) to tread upon; **se ~ la cheville** to sprain one's ankle; **ne pas se ~** not to overexert o.s.; **il ne se foule pas** he doesn't put himself out; **foulure** *nf* sprain

four [fuʀ] *nm* oven; (*de potier*) kiln; (*Théât: échec*) flop

fourche [fuʀʃ] *nf* pitchfork

fourchette [fuʀʃɛt] *nf* fork; (*Statistique*) bracket, margin

fourgon [fuʀgɔ̃] *nm* van; (*Rail*) wag(g)on; **fourgonnette** *nf* (delivery) van

fourmi [fuʀmi] *nf* ant; **avoir des ~s dans les jambes/mains** to have pins and needles in one's legs/hands; **fourmilière** *nf* ant-hill; **fourmiller** /1/ *vi* to swarm

fourneau, x [fuʀno] *nm* stove

fourni, e [fuʀni] *adj* (*barbe, cheveux*) thick; (*magasin*): **bien ~ (en)** well stocked (with)

fournir [fuʀniʀ] /2/ *vt* to supply; (*preuve, exemple*) to provide, supply; (*effort*) to put in; **~ qch à qn** to

supply sth to sb, supply *ou* provide sb with sth; **fournisseur, -euse** *nm/f* supplier; **fournisseur d'accès à Internet** (Internet) service provider, ISP; **fourniture** *nf* supply(ing); **fournitures scolaires** school stationery

fourrage [fuʀaʒ] *nm* fodder

fourré, e [fuʀe] *adj* (*bonbon, chocolat*) filled; (*manteau, botte*) fur-lined ▷ *nm* thicket

fourrer [fuʀe] /1/ *vt* (*fam*) to stick, shove; **se ~ dans/sous** to get into/under

fourrière [fuʀjɛʀ] *nf* pound

fourrure [fuʀyʀ] *nf* fur; (*pelage*) coat

foutre [futʀ] *vt* (*fam!*) = **ficher**; **foutu, e** *adj* (*fam!*) = **fichu**

foyer [fwaje] *nm* (*de cheminée*) hearth; (*famille*) family; (*domicile*) home; (*local de réunion*) (social) club; (*résidence*) hostel; (*salon*) foyer; **lunettes à double ~** bi-focal glasses

fracassant, e [fʀakasɑ̃, -ɑ̃t] *adj* (*succès*) staggering

fraction [fʀaksjɔ̃] *nf* fraction

fracturation [fʀaktyʀasjɔ̃] *nf*: **~ hydraulique** fracking

fracture [fʀaktyʀ] *nf* fracture; **~ du crâne** fractured skull; **fracturer** /1/ *vt* (*coffre, serrure*) to break open; (*os, membre*) to fracture; **se fracturer le crâne** to fracture one's skull

fragile [fʀaʒil] *adj* fragile, delicate; (*fig*) frail; **fragilité** *nf* fragility

fragment [fʀagmɑ̃] *nm* (*d'un objet*) fragment, piece

fraîche [fʀɛʃ] *adj f voir* **frais**; **fraîcheur** *nf* coolness; (*d'un aliment*) freshness; *voir* **frais**; **fraîchir** /2/ *vi* to get cooler; (*vent*) to freshen

frais, fraîche [fʀɛ, fʀɛʃ] *adj* (*air, eau, accueil*) cool; (*petit pois, œufs, nouvelles, couleur, troupes*) fresh ▷ *adv* (*récemment*) newly, fresh(ly) ▷ *nm*: **mettre au ~** to put in a cool place; **prendre le ~** to take a breath of cool air ▷ *nmpl* (*débours*) expenses; (*Comm*) costs; **il fait ~** it's cool; **servir ~** serve chilled; **faire des ~** to go to a lot of expense; **~ généraux** overheads; **~ de scolarité** school fees (BRIT), tuition (US)

fraise [fʀɛz] nf strawberry; **~ des bois** wild strawberry

framboise [fʀɑ̃bwaz] nf raspberry

franc, franche [fʀɑ̃, fʀɑ̃ʃ] adj (personne) frank, straightforward; (visage) open; (net: refus, couleur) clear; (: coupure) clean; (intensif) downright ▷ nm franc

français, e [fʀɑ̃sɛ, -ɛz] adj French ▷ nm (Ling) French ▷ nm/f: **F~, e** Frenchman/woman

France [fʀɑ̃s] nf: **la ~** France; **~ 2, ~ 3** public-sector television channels

● **FRANCE TÉLÉVISION**
●
● France 2 and France 3 are public-
● sector television channels. France
● 2 is a national general interest and
● entertainment channel; France
● 3 provides regional news and
● information as well as programmes
● for the national network.

franche [fʀɑ̃ʃ] adj f voir **franc**;
franchement adv frankly; clearly; (nettement) definitely; (tout à fait) downright

franchir [fʀɑ̃ʃiʀ] /2/ vt (obstacle) to clear, get over; (seuil, ligne, rivière) to cross; (distance) to cover

franchise [fʀɑ̃ʃiz] nf frankness; (douanière) exemption; (Assurances) excess

franc-maçon [fʀɑ̃masɔ̃] nm Freemason

franco [fʀɑ̃ko] adv (Comm): **~ (de port)** postage paid

francophone [fʀɑ̃kɔfɔn] adj French-speaking

franc-parler [fʀɑ̃paʀle] nm inv outspokenness; **avoir son ~** to speak one's mind

frange [fʀɑ̃ʒ] nf fringe

frangipane [fʀɑ̃ʒipan] nf almond paste

frappant, e [fʀapɑ̃, -ɑ̃t] adj striking

frappé, e [fʀape] adj iced

frapper [fʀape] /1/ vt to hit, strike; (étonner) to strike; **~ dans ses mains** to clap one's hands; **frappé de stupeur** dumbfounded

fraternel, le [fʀatɛʀnɛl] adj brotherly, fraternal; **fraternité** nf brotherhood

fraude [fʀod] nf fraud; (Scol) cheating; **passer qch en ~** to smuggle sth in (ou out); **~ fiscale** tax evasion

frayeur [fʀejœʀ] nf fright

fredonner [fʀədɔne] /1/ vt to hum

freezer [fʀizœʀ] nm freezing compartment

frein [fʀɛ̃] nm brake; **mettre un ~ à** (fig) to put a brake on, check; **~ à main** handbrake; **freiner** /1/ vi to brake ▷ vt (progrès etc) to check

frêle [fʀɛl] adj frail, fragile

frelon [fʀəlɔ̃] nm hornet

frémir [fʀemiʀ] /2/ vi (de froid, de peur) to shudder; (de colère) to shake; (de joie, feuillage) to quiver

frêne [fʀɛn] nm ash (tree)

fréquemment [fʀekamɑ̃] adv frequently

fréquent, e [fʀekɑ̃, -ɑ̃t] adj frequent

fréquentation [fʀekɑ̃tasjɔ̃] nf frequenting; **fréquentations** nfpl (relations) company sg; **avoir de mauvaises ~s** to be in with the wrong crowd, keep bad company

fréquenté, e [fʀekɑ̃te] adj: **très ~** (very) busy; **mal ~** patronized by disreputable elements

fréquenter [fʀekɑ̃te] /1/ vt (lieu) to frequent; (personne) to see; **se fréquenter** to see a lot of each other

frère [fʀɛʀ] nm brother

fresque [fʀɛsk] nf (Art) fresco

fret [fʀɛ(t)] nm freight

friand, e [fʀijɑ̃, -ɑ̃d] *adj*: **~ de** very fond of ▷ *nm*: **~ au fromage** cheese puff

friandise [fʀijɑ̃diz] *nf* sweet

fric [fʀik] *nm* (*fam*) cash, bread

friche [fʀiʃ]: **en ~** *adj, adv* (lying) fallow

friction [fʀiksjɔ̃] *nf* (*massage*) rub, rub-down; (*Tech, fig*) friction

frigidaire® [fʀiʒidɛʀ] *nm* refrigerator

frigo [fʀigo] *nm* fridge

frigorifique [fʀigɔʀifik] *adj* refrigerating

frileux, -euse [fʀilø, -øz] *adj* sensitive to (the) cold

frimer [fʀime] /1/ *vi* (*fam*) to show off

fringale [fʀɛ̃gal] *nf* (*fam*): **avoir la ~** to be ravenous

fringues [fʀɛ̃g] *nfpl* (*fam*) clothes

fripé, e [fʀipe] *adj* crumpled

frire [fʀiʀ] *vt* to fry ▷ *vi* to fry

frisé, e [fʀize] *adj* (*cheveux*) curly; (*personne*) curly-haired

frisson [fʀisɔ̃] *nm* (*de froid*) shiver; (*de peur*) shudder; **frissonner** /1/ *vi* (*de fièvre, froid*) to shiver; (*d'horreur*) to shudder

frit, e [fʀi, fʀit] *pp de* **frire** ▷ *nf*: **(pommes) ~es** chips (BRIT), French fries; **friteuse** *nf* deep fryer, chip pan (BRIT); **friture** *nf* (*huile*) (deep) fat; (*plat*): **friture (de poissons)** fried fish

froid, e [fʀwa, fʀwad] *adj* ▷ *nm* cold; **il fait ~** it's cold; **avoir ~** to be cold; **prendre ~** to catch a chill *ou* cold; **être en ~ avec** to be on bad terms with; **froidement** *adv* (*accueillir*) coldly; (*décider*) coolly

froisser [fʀwase] /1/ *vt* to crumple (up), crease; (*fig*) to hurt, offend; **se froisser** *vi* to crumple, crease; (*personne*) to take offence (BRIT) *ou* offense (US); **se ~ un muscle** to strain a muscle

frôler [fʀole] /1/ *vt* to brush against; (*projectile*) to skim past; (*fig*) to come

very close to, come within a hair's breadth of

fromage [fʀɔmaʒ] *nm* cheese; **~ blanc** soft white cheese

froment [fʀɔmɑ̃] *nm* wheat

froncer [fʀɔ̃se] /3/ *vt* to gather; **~ les sourcils** to frown

front [fʀɔ̃] *nm* forehead, brow; (*Mil, Météorologie, Pol*) front; **de ~** (*se heurter*) head-on; (*rouler*) together (2 or 3 abreast); (*simultanément*) at once; **faire ~ à** to face up to

frontalier, -ière [fʀɔ̃talje, -jɛʀ] *adj* border *cpd*, frontier *cpd* ▷ **(travailleurs) ~s** commuters from across the border

frontière [fʀɔ̃tjɛʀ] *nf* frontier, border

frotter [fʀɔte] /1/ *vi* to rub, scrape ▷ *vt* to rub; (*pommes de terre, plancher*) to scrub; **~ une allumette** to strike a match

fruit [fʀɥi] *nm* fruit *no pl*; **~s de mer** seafood(s); **~s secs** dried fruit *sg*; **fruité, e** [fʀɥite] *adj* fruity; **fruitier, -ière** *adj*: **arbre fruitier** fruit tree

frustrer [fʀystʀe] /1/ *vt* to frustrate

fuel(-oil) [fjul(ɔjl)] *nm* fuel oil; (*pour chauffer*) heating oil

fugace [fygas] *adj* fleeting

fugitif, -ive [fyʒitif, -iv] *adj* (*lueur, amour*) fleeting ▷ *nm/f* fugitive

fugue [fyg] *nf*: **faire une ~** to run away, abscond

fuir [fɥiʀ] /17/ *vt* to flee from; (*éviter*) to shun ▷ *vi* to run away; (*gaz, robinet*) to leak

fuite [fɥit] *nf* flight; (*divulgation*) leak; **être en ~** to be on the run; **mettre en ~** to put to flight

fulgurant, e [fylgyʀɑ̃, -ɑ̃t] *adj* lightning *cpd*, dazzling

fumé, e [fyme] *adj* (*Culin*) smoked; (*verre*) tinted ▷ *nf* smoke

fumer [fyme] /1/ *vi* to smoke; (*liquide*) to steam ▷ *vt* to smoke

fûmes [fym] *vb voir* **être**

fumeur, -euse [fymœʀ, -øz] *nm/f* smoker

fumier [fymje] *nm* manure
funérailles [fyneʀɑj] *nfpl* funeral *sg*
fur [fyʀ]: **au ~ et à mesure** *adv* as one goes along; **au ~ et à mesure que** as
furet [fyʀɛ] *nm* ferret
fureter [fyʀ(ə)te] /5/ *vi* (*péj*) to nose about
fureur [fyʀœʀ] *nf* fury; **être en ~** to be infuriated; **faire ~** to be all the rage
furie [fyʀi] *nf* fury; (*femme*) shrew, vixen; **en ~** (*mer*) raging; **furieux, -euse** *adj* furious
furoncle [fyʀɔ̃kl] *nm* boil
furtif, -ive [fyʀtif, -iv] *adj* furtive
fus [fy] *vb voir* **être**
fusain [fyzɛ̃] *nm* (*Art*) charcoal
fuseau, x [fyzo] *nm* (*pantalon*) (ski-)pants *pl*; (*pour filer*) spindle; **~ horaire** time zone
fusée [fyze] *nf* rocket
fusible [fyzibl] *nm* (*Élec: fil*) fuse wire; (*: fiche*) fuse
fusil [fyzi] *nm* (*de guerre, à canon rayé*) rifle, gun; (*de chasse, à canon lisse*) shotgun, gun; **fusillade** *nf* gunfire *no pl*, shooting *no pl*; **fusiller** /1/ *vt* to shoot; **fusiller qn du regard** to look daggers at sb
fusionner [fyzjɔne] /1/ *vi* to merge
fût [fy] *vb voir* **être** ▷ *nm* (*tonneau*) barrel, cask
futé, e [fyte] *adj* crafty; **Bison ~**® TV and radio traffic monitoring service
futile [fytil] *adj* futile; (*frivole*) frivolous
futur, e [fytyʀ] *adj, nm* future
fuyard, e [fɥijaʀ, -aʀd] *nm/f* runaway

g

Gabon [gabɔ̃] *nm*: **le ~** Gabon
gâcher [gɑʃe] /1/ *vt* (*gâter*) to spoil; (*gaspiller*) to waste; **gâchis** *nm* waste *no pl*
gaffe [gaf] *nf* blunder; **faire ~** (*fam*) to watch out
gage [gaʒ] *nm* (*dans un jeu*) forfeit; (*fig: de fidélité*) token; **gages** *nmpl* (*salaire*) wages; **mettre en ~** to pawn
gagnant, e [gaɲɑ̃, -ɑ̃t] *adj*: **billet/ numéro ~** winning ticket/number ▷ *nm/f* winner
gagne-pain [gaɲpɛ̃] *nm inv* job
gagner [gaɲe] /1/ *vt* to win; (*somme d'argent, revenu*) to earn; (*aller vers, atteindre*) to reach; (*s'emparer de*) to overcome; (*envahir*) to spread to ▷ *vi* to win; (*fig*) to gain; **~ du temps/ de la place** to gain time/save space; **~ sa vie** to earn one's living
gai, e [ge] *adj* cheerful; (*un peu ivre*) merry; **gaiement** *adv* cheerfully;

gaieté nf cheerfulness; **de gaieté de cœur** with a light heart

gain [gɛ̃] nm (revenu) earnings pl; (bénéfice: gén pl) profits pl

gala [gala] nm official reception; **soirée de ~** gala evening

galant, e [galɑ̃, -ɑ̃t] adj (courtois) courteous, gentlemanly; (entreprenant) flirtatious, gallant; (scène, rendez-vous) romantic

galerie [galʀi] nf (Théât) circle; (de voiture) roof rack; (fig: spectateurs) audience; **~ marchande** shopping mall; **~ de peinture** (private) art gallery

galet [galɛ] nm pebble

galette [galɛt] nf flat pastry cake; **la ~ des Rois** cake traditionally eaten on Twelfth Night

○ **GALETTE DES ROIS**
○
○ A galette des Rois is a cake eaten
○ on Twelfth Night containing a
○ figurine. The person who finds it
○ is the king (or queen) and gets a
○ paper crown. They then choose
○ someone else to be their queen
○ (or king).

galipette [galipɛt] nf somersault

Galles [gal] nfpl: **le pays de ~** Wales; **gallois, e** adj Welsh ▷ nm (Ling) Welsh ▷ nm/f: **Gallois, e** Welshman(-woman)

galocher [galɔʃe] (fam) vt to French kiss

galon [galɔ̃] nm (Mil) stripe; (décoratif) piece of braid

galop [galo] nm gallop; **galoper** /1/ vi to gallop

gambader [gɑ̃bade] /1/ vi (animal, enfant) to leap about

gamin, e [gamɛ̃, -in] nm/f kid ▷ adj mischievous

gamme [gam] nf (Mus) scale; (fig) range

gang [gɑ̃g] nm (de criminels) gang

gant [gɑ̃] nm glove; **~ de toilette** (face) flannel (BRIT), face cloth

garage [gaʀaʒ] nm garage; **garagiste** nm/f garage owner; (mécanicien) garage mechanic

garantie [gaʀɑ̃ti] nf guarantee; **(bon de) ~** guarantee ou warranty slip

garantir [gaʀɑ̃tiʀ] /2/ vt to guarantee; **je vous garantis que** I can assure you that

garçon [gaʀsɔ̃] nm boy; (aussi: **~ de café**) waiter; **vieux ~** (célibataire) bachelor; **~ de courses** messenger

garde [gaʀd] nm (de prisonnier) guard; (de domaine etc) warden; (soldat, sentinelle) guardsman ▷ nf (de soldats) guard; **de ~** on duty; **monter la ~** to stand guard; **mettre en ~** to warn; **prendre ~ (à)** to be careful (of); **~ champêtre** nm rural policeman; **~ du corps** nm bodyguard; **~ à vue** nf (Jur) ≈ police custody; **garde-boue** nm inv mudguard; **garde-chasse** nm gamekeeper

garder [gaʀde] /1/ vt (conserver) to keep; (surveiller: enfants) to look after; (: immeuble, lieu, prisonnier) to guard; **se garder** vi (aliment: se conserver) to keep; **se ~ de faire** to be careful not to do; **~ le lit/la chambre** to stay in bed/indoors; **pêche/chasse gardée** private fishing/hunting (ground)

garderie [gaʀdəʀi] nf day nursery, crèche

garde-robe [gaʀdəʀɔb] nf wardrobe

gardien, ne [gaʀdjɛ̃, -ɛn] nm/f (garde) guard; (de prison) warder; (de domaine, réserve) warden; (de musée etc) attendant; (de phare, cimetière) keeper; (d'immeuble) caretaker; (fig) guardian; **~ de but** goalkeeper; **~ de nuit** night watchman; **~ de la paix** policeman

gare [gaʀ] nf (railway) station ▷ excl: **~ à ...** mind ...!; **~ à toi!** watch out!; **~ routière** bus station

garer [gaʀe] /1/ vt to park; **se garer** vi to park

garni, e [gaʀni] adj (plat) served with vegetables (and chips, pasta or rice)

garniture [garnityr] nf (Culin)
vegetables pl; **~ de frein** brake lining
gars [ga] nm guy
Gascogne [gaskɔɲ] nf: **la ~** Gascony;
le golfe de ~ the Bay of Biscay
gas-oil [gazɔjl] nm diesel oil
gaspiller [gaspije] /1/ vt to waste
gastronome [gastrɔnɔm] nm/f
gourmet; **gastronomique** adj
gastronomic
gâteau, x [gato] nm cake; **~ sec**
biscuit
gâter [gate] /1/ vt to spoil; **se gâter**
vi (dent, fruit) to go bad; (temps,
situation) to change for the worse
gâteux, -euse [gatø, -øz] adj senile
gauche [goʃ] adj left, left-hand;
(maladroit) awkward, clumsy ▷ nf
(Pol) left (wing); **le bras ~** the left
arm; **le côté ~** the left-hand side;
à ~ on the left; (direction) (to the)
left; **gaucher, -ère** adj left-handed;
gauchiste nm/f leftist
gaufre [gofr] nf waffle
gaufrette [gofrɛt] nf wafer
gaulois, e [golwa, -waz] adj Gallic
▷ nm/f: **G~, e** Gaul
gaz [gaz] nm inv gas; **ça sent le ~** I can
smell gas, there's a smell of gas
gaze [gaz] nf gauze
gazette [gazɛt] nf news sheet
gazeux, -euse [gazø, -øz] adj (eau)
sparkling; (boisson) fizzy
gazoduc [gazodyk] nm gas pipeline
gazon [gazɔ̃] nm (herbe) grass;
(pelouse) lawn
géant, e [ʒeɑ̃, -ɑ̃t] adj gigantic;
(Comm) giant-size ▷ nm/f giant
geindre [ʒɛ̃dr] /52/ vi to groan, moan
gel [ʒɛl] nm frost; **~ douche** shower
gel
gélatine [ʒelatin] nf gelatine
gelé, e [ʒəle] adj frozen ▷ nf jelly;
(gel) frost
geler [ʒ(ə)le] /5/ vt, vi to freeze; **il
gèle** it's freezing
gélule [ʒelyl] nf (Méd) capsule
Gémeaux [ʒemo] nmpl: **les ~** Gemini

gémir [ʒemir] /2/ vi to groan, moan
gênant, e [ʒenɑ̃, -ɑ̃t] adj (objet) in the
way; (histoire, personne) embarrassing
gencive [ʒɑ̃siv] nf gum
gendarme [ʒɑ̃darm] nm gendarme;
gendarmerie nf military police force in
countryside and small towns; their police
station or barracks
gendre [ʒɑ̃dr] nm son-in-law
gêné, e [ʒene] adj embarrassed
gêner [ʒene] /1/ vt (incommoder) to
bother; (encombrer) to be in the way
of; (embarrasser): **~ qn** to make sb feel
ill-at-ease; **se gêner** to put o.s. out;
ne vous gênez pas! don't mind me!
général, e, -aux [ʒeneral, -o] adj,
nm general; **en ~** usually, in general;
généralement adv generally;
généraliser /1/ vt, vi to generalize;
se généraliser vi to become
widespread; **généraliste** nm/f
general practitioner, GP
génération [ʒenerasjɔ̃] nf generation
généreux, -euse [ʒenerø, -øz] adj
generous
générique [ʒenerik] nm (Ciné, TV)
credits pl
générosité [ʒenerozite] nf
generosity
genêt [ʒ(ə)nɛ] nm (Bot) broom no pl
génétique [ʒenetik] adj genetic
Genève [ʒ(ə)nɛv] n Geneva
génial, e, -aux [ʒenjal, -o] adj of
genius; (fam: formidable) fantastic,
brilliant
génie [ʒeni] nm genius; (Mil): **le
~** ≈ the Engineers pl; **~ civil** civil
engineering
genièvre [ʒənjɛvr] nm juniper (tree)
génisse [ʒenis] nf heifer
génital, e, -aux [ʒenital, -o] adj
genital; **les parties ~es** the genitals
génois, e [ʒenwa, -waz] adj Genoese
▷ nf (gâteau) ≈ sponge cake
génome [ʒenom] nm genome
genou, x [ʒ(ə)nu] nm knee; **à ~x**
on one's knees; **se mettre à ~x** to
kneel down

g

genre [ʒɑ̃R] nm kind, type, sort; (Ling) gender; **avoir bon ~** to look a nice sort; **avoir mauvais ~** to be coarse-looking; **ce n'est pas son ~** it's not like him

gens [ʒɑ̃] nmpl (f in some phrases) people pl

gentil, le [ʒɑ̃ti, -ij] adj kind; (enfant: sage) good; (sympathique: endroit etc) nice; **gentillesse** nf kindness; **gentiment** adv kindly

géographie [ʒeɔgRafi] nf geography

géologie [ʒeɔlɔʒi] nf geology

géomètre [ʒeɔmɛtR] nm: **(arpenteur-)~** (land) surveyor

géométrie [ʒeɔmetRi] nf geometry; **géométrique** adj geometric

géranium [ʒeRanjɔm] nm geranium

gérant, e [ʒeRɑ̃, -ɑ̃t] nm/f manager/ manageress; **~ d'immeuble** managing agent

gerbe [ʒɛRb] nf (de fleurs, d'eau) spray; (de blé) sheaf

gercé, e [ʒɛRse] adj chapped

gerçure [ʒɛRsyR] nf crack

gérer [ʒeRe] /6/ vt to manage

germain, e [ʒɛRmɛ̃, -ɛn] adj: **cousin ~** first cousin

germe [ʒɛRm] nm germ; **germer** /1/ vi to sprout; (semence) to germinate

geste [ʒɛst] nm gesture

gestion [ʒɛstjɔ̃] nf management

Ghana [gana] nm: **le ~** Ghana

gibier [ʒibje] nm (animaux) game

gicler [ʒikle] /1/ vi to spurt, squirt

gifle [ʒifl] nf slap (in the face); **gifler** /1/ vt to slap (in the face)

gigantesque [ʒigɑ̃tɛsk] adj gigantic

gigot [ʒigo] nm leg (of mutton ou lamb)

gigoter [ʒigɔte] /1/ vi to wriggle (about)

gilet [ʒilɛ] nm waistcoat; (pull) cardigan; **~ de sauvetage** life jacket

gin [dʒin] nm gin; **~-tonic** gin and tonic

gingembre [ʒɛ̃ʒɑ̃bR] nm ginger

girafe [ʒiRaf] nf giraffe

giratoire [ʒiRatwaR] adj: **sens ~** roundabout

girofle [ʒiRɔfl] nm: **clou de ~** clove

girouette [ʒiRwɛt] nf weather vane ou cock

gitan, e [ʒitɑ̃, -an] nm/f gipsy

gîte [ʒit] nm (maison) home; (abri) shelter; **~ (rural)** (country) holiday cottage ou apartment, gîte (self-catering accommodation in the country)

givre [ʒivR] nm (hoar) frost; **givré, e** adj covered in frost; (fam: fou) nuts; **citron givré/orange givrée** lemon/ orange sorbet (served in fruit skin)

glace [glas] nf ice; (crème glacée) ice cream; (miroir) mirror; (de voiture) window

glacé, e [glase] adj (mains, vent, pluie) freezing; (lac) frozen; (boisson) iced

glacer [glase] /3/ vt to freeze; (gâteau) to ice; **~ qn** (intimider) to chill sb; (fig) to make sb's blood run cold

glacial, e [glasjal] adj icy

glacier [glasje] nm (Géo) glacier; (marchand) ice-cream maker

glacière [glasjɛR] nf icebox

glaçon [glasɔ̃] nm icicle; (pour boisson) ice cube

glaïeul [glajœl] nm gladiola

glaise [glɛz] nf clay

gland [glɑ̃] nm acorn; (décoration) tassel

glande [glɑ̃d] nf gland

glissade [glisad] nf (par jeu) slide; (chute) slip; **faire des ~s** to slide

glissant, e [glisɑ̃, -ɑ̃t] adj slippery

glissement [glismɑ̃] nm: **~ de terrain** landslide

glisser [glise] /1/ vi (avancer) to glide ou slide along; (coulisser, tomber) to slide; (déraper) to slip; (être glissant) to be slippery ▷ vt to slip; **se ~ dans/ entre** to slip into/between

global, e, -aux [glɔbal, -o] adj overall

globe [glɔb] nm globe

globule [glɔbyl] nm (du sang): **~ blanc/rouge** white/red corpuscle

gloire [glwaʀ] *nf* glory

glousser [gluse] /1/ *vi* to cluck; *(rire)* to chuckle

glouton, ne [glutɔ̃, -ɔn] *adj* gluttonous

gluant, e [glyɑ̃, -ɑ̃t] *adj* sticky, gummy

glucose [glykoz] *nm* glucose

glycine [glisin] *nf* wisteria

GO *sigle fpl (= grandes ondes)* LW

goal [gol] *nm* goalkeeper

gobelet [gɔblɛ] *nm (en métal)* tumbler; *(en plastique)* beaker; *(à dés)* cup

goéland [gɔelɑ̃] *nm* (sea)gull

goélette [gɔelɛt] *nf* schooner

goinfre [gwɛ̃fʀ] *nm* glutton

golf [gɔlf] *nm* golf; *(terrain)* golf course; **~ miniature** crazy *ou* miniature golf

golfe [gɔlf] *nm* gulf; *(petit)* bay

gomme [gɔm] *nf (à effacer)* rubber (BRIT), eraser; **gommer** /1/ *vt* to rub out (BRIT), erase

gonflé, e [gɔ̃fle] *adj* swollen; **il est ~** *(fam: courageux)* he's got some nerve; *(: impertinent)* he's got a nerve

gonfler [gɔ̃fle] /1/ *vt (pneu, ballon)* to inflate, blow up; *(nombre, importance)* to inflate ▷ *vi* to swell (up); *(Culin: pâte)* to rise

gonzesse [gɔ̃zɛs] *nf (fam)* chick, bird (BRIT)

googler [gugle] /1/ *vi* to google

gorge [gɔʀʒ] *nf (Anat)* throat; *(Géo)* gorge

gorgé, e [gɔʀʒe] *adj*: **~ de** filled with ▷ *nf (petite)* sip; *(grande)* gulp

gorille [gɔʀij] *nm* gorilla; *(fam)* bodyguard

gosse [gɔs] *nm/f* kid

goudron [gudʀɔ̃] *nm* tar; **goudronner** /1/ *vt* to tar(mac) (BRIT), asphalt (US)

gouffre [gufʀ] *nm* abyss, gulf

goulot [gulo] *nm* neck; **boire au ~** to drink from the bottle

goulu, e [guly] *adj* greedy

gourde [guʀd] *nf (récipient)* flask; *(fam) (clumsy)* clot *ou* oaf ▷ *adj* oafish

gourdin [guʀdɛ̃] *nm* club, bludgeon

gourmand, e [guʀmɑ̃, -ɑ̃d] *adj* greedy; **gourmandise** *nf* greed; *(bonbon)* sweet

gousse [gus] *nf*: **~ d'ail** clove of garlic

goût [gu] *nm* taste; **de bon ~** tasteful; **de mauvais ~** tasteless; **avoir bon/ mauvais ~** to taste nice/nasty; **prendre ~ à** to develop a taste *ou* a liking for

goûter [gute] /1/ *vt (essayer)* to taste; *(apprécier)* to enjoy ▷ *vi* to have (afternoon) tea ▷ *nm* (afternoon) tea; **je peux ~?** can I have a taste?

goutte [gut] *nf* drop; *(Méd)* gout; *(alcool)* nip (BRIT), drop (US); **tomber ~ à ~** to drip; **goutte-à-goutte** *nm inv (Méd)* drip

gouttière [gutjɛʀ] *nf* gutter

gouvernail [guvɛʀnaj] *nm* rudder; *(barre)* helm, tiller

gouvernement [guvɛʀnəmɑ̃] *nm* government

gouverner [guvɛʀne] /1/ *vt* to govern

grâce [gʀɑs] *nf (charme, Rel)* grace; *(faveur)* favour; *(Jur)* pardon; **faire ~ à qn de qch** to spare sb sth; **demander ~** to beg for mercy; **~ à** thanks to; **gracieux, -euse** *adj* graceful

grade [gʀad] *nm* rank; **monter en ~** to be promoted

gradin [gʀadɛ̃] *nm* tier; *(de stade)* step; **gradins** *nmpl (de stade)* terracing *no pl*

gradué, e [gʀadɥe] *adj*: **verre ~** measuring jug

graduel, le [gʀadɥɛl] *adj* gradual

graduer [gʀadɥe] /1/ *vt (effort etc)* to increase gradually; *(règle, verre)* to graduate

graffiti [gʀafiti] *nmpl* graffiti

grain [gʀɛ̃] *nm (gén)* grain; *(Navig)* squall; **~ de beauté** beauty spot; **~ de café** coffee bean; **~ de poivre** peppercorn

graine [gʀɛn] nf seed
graissage [gʀesaʒ] nm lubrication, greasing
graisse [gʀɛs] nf fat; (lubrifiant) grease; **graisser** /1/ vt to lubricate, grease; (tacher) to make greasy; **graisseux, -euse** adj greasy
grammaire [gʀamɛʀ] nf grammar
gramme [gʀam] nm gramme
grand, e [gʀɑ̃, gʀɑ̃d] adj (haut) tall; (gros, vaste, large) big, large; (long) long; (plus âgé) big; (adulte) grown-up; (important, brillant) great ▷ adv:
~ ouvert wide open; **au ~ air** in the open (air); **les ~s blessés/brûlés** the severely injured/burned; **~ ensemble** housing scheme; **~ magasin** department store; **~e personne** grown-up; **~e surface** hypermarket; **~es écoles** prestige university-level colleges with competitive entrance examinations; **~es lignes** (Rail) main lines; **~es vacances** summer holidays (BRIT) ou vacation (US); **grand-chose** nm/f inv: **pas grand-chose** not much; **Grande-Bretagne** nf: **la Grande-Bretagne** (Great) Britain; **grandeur** nf (dimension) size; **grandeur nature** life-size; **grandiose** adj imposing; **grandir** /2/ vi to grow; grow ▷ vt: **grandir qn** (vêtement, chaussure) to make sb look taller; **grand-mère** nf grandmother; **grand-peine**: **à grand-peine** adv with (great) difficulty; **grand-père** nm grandfather; **grands-parents** nmpl grandparents
grange [gʀɑ̃ʒ] nf barn
granit [gʀanit] nm granite
graphique [gʀafik] adj graphic ▷ nm graph
grappe [gʀap] nf cluster; **~ de raisin** bunch of grapes
gras, se [gʀɑ, gʀɑs] adj (viande, soupe) fatty; (personne) fat; (surface, main, cheveux) greasy; (plaisanterie) coarse; (Typo) bold ▷ nm (Culin) fat; **faire la ~se matinée** to have a lie-in

(BRIT), sleep late; **grassement** adv: **grassement payé** handsomely paid
gratifiant, e [gʀatifjɑ̃, -ɑ̃t] adj gratifying, rewarding
gratin [gʀatɛ̃] nm (Culin) cheese- (ou crumb-)topped dish (: croûte) topping; **tout le ~ parisien** all the best people of Paris; **gratiné** adj (Culin) au gratin
gratis [gʀatis] adv free
gratitude [gʀatityd] nf gratitude
gratte-ciel [gʀatsjɛl] nm inv skyscraper
gratter [gʀate] /1/ vt (frotter) to scrape; (avec un ongle) to scratch; (enlever: avec un outil) to scrape off; (: avec un ongle) to scratch off ▷ vi (irriter) to be scratchy; (démanger) to itch; **se gratter** to scratch o.s.
gratuit, e [gʀatɥi, -ɥit] adj (entrée) free; (fig) gratuitous
grave [gʀav] adj (maladie, accident) serious, bad; (sujet, problème) serious, grave; (personne, air) grave, solemn; (voix, son) deep, low-pitched; **gravement** adv seriously; (parler, regarder) gravely
graver [gʀave] /1/ vt (plaque, nom) to engrave; (CD, DVD) to burn
graveur [gʀavœʀ] nm engraver; **~ de CD/DVD** CD/DVD burner or writer
gravier [gʀavje] nm (loose) gravel no pl; **gravillons** nmpl gravel sg
gravir [gʀaviʀ] /2/ vt to climb (up)
gravité [gʀavite] nf (de maladie, d'accident) seriousness; (de sujet, problème) gravity
graviter [gʀavite] /1/ vi to revolve
gravure [gʀavyʀ] nf engraving; (reproduction) print
gré [gʀe] nm: **à son ~** to his liking; **contre le ~ de qn** against sb's will; **de son (plein) ~** of one's own free will; **de ~ ou de force** whether one likes it or not; **de bon ~** willingly; **bon ~ mal ~** like it or not; **savoir (bien) ~ à qn de qch** to be (most) grateful to sb for sth

grec, grecque [grɛk] adj Greek; (classique: vase etc) Grecian ▷ nm (Ling) Greek ▷ nm/f: **Grec, Grecque** Greek

Grèce [grɛs] nf: **la ~** Greece

greffe [grɛf] nf (Bot, Méd: de tissu) graft; (Méd: d'organe) transplant; **greffer** /1/ vt (Bot, Méd: tissu) to graft; (Méd: organe) to transplant

grêle [grɛl] adj (very) thin ▷ nf hail; **grêler** /1/ vb impers: **il grêle** it's hailing; **grêlon** nm hailstone

grelot [grəlo] nm little bell

grelotter [grəlɔte] /1/ vi to shiver

grenade [grənad] nf (explosive) grenade; (Bot) pomegranate; **grenadine** nf grenadine

grenier [grənje] nm attic; (de ferme) loft

grenouille [grənuj] nf frog

grès [grɛ] nm sandstone; (poterie) stoneware

grève [grɛv] nf (d'ouvriers) strike; (plage) shore; **se mettre en/faire ~** to go on/be on strike; **~ de la faim** hunger strike; **~ sauvage** wildcat strike

gréviste [grevist] nm/f striker

grièvement [grijɛvmã] adv seriously

griffe [grif] nf claw; (d'un couturier, parfumeur) label; **griffer** /1/ vt to scratch

grignoter [griɲɔte] /1/ vt (personne) to nibble at; (souris) to gnaw at ▷ vi to nibble

gril [gril] nm steak ou grill pan; **grillade** nf grill

grillage [grijaʒ] nm (treillis) wire netting; (clôture) wire fencing

grille [grij] nf (portail) (metal) gate; (clôture) railings pl; (d'égout) (metal) grate; grid

grille-pain [grijpɛ̃] nm inv toaster

griller [grije] /1/ vt (aussi: **faire ~**) (pain) to toast; (viande) to grill; (châtaignes) to roast; (fig: ampoule etc) to burn out; **~ un feu rouge** to jump the lights

grillon [grijɔ̃] nm cricket

grimace [grimas] nf grimace; (pour faire rire): **faire des ~s** to pull ou make faces

grimper [grɛ̃pe] /1/ vi, vt to climb

grincer [grɛ̃se] /3/ vi (porte, roue) to grate; (plancher) to creak; **~ des dents** to grind one's teeth

grincheux, -euse [grɛ̃ʃø, -øz] adj grumpy

grippe [grip] nf flu, influenza; **~ A** swine flu; **~ aviaire** bird flu; **grippé, e** adj: **être grippé** to have (the) flu

gris, e [gri, griz] adj grey; (ivre) tipsy

grisaille [grizaj] nf greyness, dullness

griser [grize] /1/ vt to intoxicate

grive [griv] nf thrush

Groenland [grɔɛnlãd] nm: **le ~** Greenland

grogner [grɔɲe] /1/ vi to growl; (fig) to grumble; **grognon, ne** adj grumpy

grommeler [grɔmle] /4/ vi to mutter to o.s.

gronder [grɔ̃de] /1/ vi to rumble; (fig: révolte) to be brewing ▷ vt to scold; **se faire ~** to get a telling-off

gros, se [gro, gros] adj big, large; (obèse) fat; (travaux, dégâts) extensive; (large) thick; (rhume, averse) heavy ▷ adv: **risquer/gagner ~** to risk/win a lot ▷ nm/f fat man/woman ▷ nm (Comm): **le ~** the wholesale business; **prix de ~** wholesale price; **par ~ temps/~se mer** in rough weather/ heavy seas; **le ~ de** the bulk of; **en ~** roughly; (Comm) wholesale; **~ lot** jackpot; **~ mot** swearword; **~ plan** (Photo) close-up; **~ sel** cooking salt; **~ titre** headline; **~se caisse** big drum

groseille [grozɛj] nf: **~ (rouge)/ (blanche)** red/white currant; **~ à maquereau** gooseberry

grosse [gros] adj f voir **gros**; **grossesse** nf pregnancy; **grosseur** nf size; (tumeur) lump

grossier, -ière [grosje, -jɛr] adj coarse; (insolent) rude; (dessin) rough; (*travail*) roughly done; (*imitation, instrument*) crude; (*évident: erreur*) gross; **grossièrement** *adv* (*vulgairement*) coarsely; (*sommairement*) roughly; crudely; (*en gros*) roughly; **grossièreté** *nf* rudeness; (*mot*): **dire des grossièretés** to use coarse language

grossir [gʀosiʀ] /2/ *vi* (*personne*) to put on weight ▷ *vt* (*exagérer*) to exaggerate; (*au microscope*) to magnify; (*vêtement*): **~ qn** to make sb look fatter

grossiste [gʀosist] *nm/f* wholesaler

grotesque [gʀotɛsk] *adj* (*extravagant*) grotesque; (*ridicule*) ludicrous

grotte [gʀot] *nf* cave

groupe [gʀup] *nm* group; **~ de parole** support group; **~ sanguin** blood group; **~ scolaire** school complex; **grouper** /1/ *vt* to group; **se grouper** *vi* to get together

grue [gʀy] *nf* crane

GSM [ʒeɛsɛm] *nm, adj* GSM

guenon [ɡənɔ̃] *nf* female monkey

guépard [ɡepaʀ] *nm* cheetah

guêpe [ɡɛp] *nf* wasp

guère [ɡɛʀ] *adv* (*avec adjectif, adverbe*): **ne ... ~** hardly; (*avec verbe: pas beaucoup*): **ne ... ~** (*tournure négative*) much; (*pas souvent*) hardly ever; (*tournure négative*) (very) long; **il n'y a ~ que/de** there's hardly anybody (*ou* anything) but/hardly any; **ce n'est ~ difficile** it's hardly difficult; **nous n'avons ~ de temps** we have hardly any time

guérilla [ɡeʀija] *nf* guerrilla warfare

guérillero [ɡeʀijeʀo] *nm* guerrilla

guérir [ɡeʀiʀ] /2/ *vt* (*personne, maladie*) to cure; (*membre, plaie*) to heal ▷ *vi* (*personne, malade*) to recover, be cured; (*maladie*) to be cured; (*plaie, chagrin, blessure*) to heal; **guérison** *nf* (*de maladie*) curing; (*de membre, plaie*) healing; (*de malade*) recovery; **guérisseur, -euse** *nm/f* healer

guerre [ɡɛʀ] *nf* war; **en ~** at war; **faire la ~ à** to wage war against; **~ civile/mondiale** civil/world war; **guerrier, -ière** *adj* warlike ▷ *nm/f* warrior

guet [ɡɛ] *nm*: **faire le ~** to be on the watch *ou* look-out; **guet-apens** [ɡɛtapɑ̃] *nm* ambush; **guetter** /1/ *vt* (*épier*) to watch (intently); (*attendre*) to watch (out) for; (*: pour surprendre*) to be lying in wait for

gueule [ɡœl] *nf* (*d'animal*) mouth; (*fam: visage*) mug; (*: bouche*) gob (!), mouth; **ta ~!** (*fam*) shut up!; **avoir la ~ de bois** (*fam*) to have a hangover, be hung over; **gueuler** /1/ *vi* to bawl

gui [ɡi] *nm* mistletoe

guichet [ɡiʃɛ] *nm* (*de bureau, banque*) counter; **les ~s** (*à la gare, au théâtre*) the ticket office

guide [ɡid] *nm* (*personne*) guide; (*livre*) guide(book) ▷ *nf* (*fille scout*) (girl) guide; **guider** /1/ *vt* to guide

guidon [ɡidɔ̃] *nm* handlebars *pl*

guignol [ɡiɲɔl] *nm* ≈ Punch and Judy show; (*fig*) clown

guillemets [ɡijmɛ] *nmpl*: **entre ~** in inverted commas *ou* quotation marks

guindé, e [ɡɛ̃de] *adj* (*personne, air*) stiff, starchy; (*style*) stilted

Guinée [ɡine] *nf*: **la (République de) ~** (the Republic of) Guinea

guirlande [ɡiʀlɑ̃d] *nf* (*fleurs*) garland; **~ de Noël** tinsel *no pl*

guise [ɡiz] *nf*: **à votre ~** as you wish *ou* please; **en ~ de** by way of

guitare [ɡitaʀ] *nf* guitar

Guyane [ɡɥijan] *nf*: **la ~ (française)** (French) Guiana

gym [ʒim] *nf* (*exercices*) gym; **gymnase** *nm* gym(nasium); **gymnaste** *nm/f* gymnast; **gymnastique** *nf* gymnastics *sg*; (*au réveil etc*) keep-fit exercises *pl*

gynécologie [ʒinekɔlɔʒi] *nf* gynaecology; **gynécologique** *adj* gynaecological; **gynécologue** *nm/f* gynaecologist

h

habile [abil] *adj* skilful; (*malin*) clever; **habileté** [abilte] *nf* skill, skilfulness; cleverness

habillé, e [abije] *adj* dressed; (*chic*) dressy

habiller [abije] /1/ *vt* to dress; (*fournir en vêtements*) to clothe; (*couvrir*) to cover; **s'habiller** *vi* to dress (o.s.); (*se déguiser, mettre des vêtements chic*) to dress up

habit [abi] *nm* outfit; **habits** *nmpl* (*vêtements*) clothes; **~ (de soirée)** evening dress; (*pour homme*) tails *pl*

habitant, e [abitɑ̃, -ɑ̃t] *nm/f* inhabitant; (*d'une maison*) occupant; **loger chez l'~** to stay with the locals

habitation [abitasjɔ̃] *nf* house; **~s à loyer modéré (HLM)** ≈ council flats

habiter [abite] /1/ *vt* to live in ▷ *vi:* **~ à/dans** to live in *ou* at/in

habitude [abityd] *nf* habit; **avoir l'~ de faire** to be in the habit of doing; (*expérience*) to be used to doing;

avoir l'~ **des enfants** to be used to children; **d'~** usually; **comme d'~** as usual

habitué, e [abitɥe] *nm/f (de maison)* regular visitor; (*client*) regular (customer)

habituel, le [abitɥɛl] *adj* usual

habituer [abitɥe] /1/ *vt:* **~ qn à** to get sb used to; **s'habituer à** to get used to

'hache ['aʃ] *nf* axe

'hacher ['aʃe] /1/ *vt (viande)* to mince ; (*persil*) to chop; **'hachis** *nm* mince *no pl;* **hachis Parmentier** ≈ shepherd's pie

'haie ['ɛ] *nf* hedge; (*Sport*) hurdle

'haillons ['ajɔ̃] *nmpl* rags

'haine ['ɛn] *nf* hatred

'haïr ['aiʀ] /10/ *vt* to detest, hate

'hâlé, e ['ɑle] *adj (sun)* tanned, sunburnt

haleine [alɛn] *nf* breath; **hors d'~** out of breath; **tenir en ~** (*attention*) to hold spellbound; (*en attente*) to keep in suspense; **de longue ~** long-term

'haleter ['alte] /5/ *vi* to pant

'hall ['ol] *nm* hall

'halle ['al] *nf (covered)* market; **'halles** *nfpl (d'une grande ville)* central food market *sg*

hallucination [alysinasjɔ̃] *nf* hallucination

'halte ['alt] *nf* stop, break; (*escale*) stopping place ▷ *excl* stop!; **faire ~** to stop

haltère [altɛʀ] *nm* dumbbell, barbell; **(poids et) ~s** (*activité*) weightlifting *sg;* **haltérophilie** *nf* weightlifting

'hamac ['amak] *nm* hammock

'hamburger ['ɑ̃burɡœʀ] *nm* hamburger

'hameau, x ['amo] *nm* hamlet

hameçon [amsɔ̃] *nm (fish)* hook

'hamster ['amstɛʀ] *nm* hamster

'hanche ['ɑ̃ʃ] *nf* hip

'hand-ball ['ɑ̃dbal] *nm* handball

'handicapé, e ['ɑ̃dikape] *adj*
disabled ▷ *nm/f* person with a
disability; **~ mental/physique**
person with learning difficulties/
a disability; **~ moteur** person with
a movement disorder

'hangar ['ɑ̃gaʀ] *nm* shed; (*Aviat*)
hangar

'hanneton ['antɔ̃] *nm* cockchafer

'hanter ['ɑ̃te] /1/ *vt* to haunt

'hantise ['ɑ̃tiz] *nf* obsessive fear

'harceler ['aʀsəle] /5/ *vt* to harass;
~ qn de questions to plague sb with
questions

'hardi, e ['aʀdi] *adj* bold, daring

'hareng ['aʀɑ̃] *nm* herring; **~ saur**
kipper, smoked herring

'hargne ['aʀɲ] *nf* aggressivity,
aggressiveness; **'hargneux, -euse**
adj aggressive

'haricot ['aʀiko] *nm* bean; **~ blanc/
rouge** haricot/kidney bean; **~ vert**
French (*BRIT*) *ou* green bean

harmonica [aʀmɔnika] *nm* mouth
organ

harmonie [aʀmɔni] *nf* harmony;
harmonieux, -euse *adj* harmonious;
(*couleurs, couple*) well-matched

'harpe ['aʀp] *nf* harp

'hasard ['azaʀ] *nm*: **le ~** chance, fate;
un ~ a coincidence; **au ~** (*sans but*)
aimlessly; (*à l'aveuglette*) at random;
par ~ by chance; **à tout ~** (*en espérant
trouver ce qu'on cherche*) on the off
chance; (*en cas de besoin*) just in case

'hâte ['ɑt] *nf* haste; **à la ~** hurriedly,
hastily; **en ~** posthaste, with all
possible speed; **avoir ~ de** to be
eager *ou* anxious to; **'hâter** /1/ *vt* to
hasten; **se 'hâter** to hurry; **'hâtif,
-ive** *adj* (*travail*) hurried; (*décision*)
hasty

'hausse ['os] *nf* rise, increase; **être en
~** to be going up; **'hausser** /1/ *vt* to
raise; **hausser les épaules** to shrug
(one's shoulders)

'haut, e ['o, 'ot] *adj* high; (*grand*) tall
▷ *adv* high ▷ *nm* top (part); **de 3 m de ~**
3 m high, 3 m in height; **en ~ lieu**
in high places; **à ~e voix, (tout) ~**
aloud, out loud; **des ~s et des bas**
ups and downs; **du ~ de** from the top
of; **de ~ en bas** from top to bottom;
plus ~ higher up, further up; (*dans un
texte*) above; (*parler*) louder; **en ~**
(*être/aller*) at (*ou* to) the top; (*dans une
maison*) upstairs; **en ~ de** at the top
of; **~ débit** broadband

'hautain, e ['otɛ̃, -ɛn] *adj* haughty

'hautbois ['obwa] *nm* oboe

'hauteur ['otœʀ] *nf* height; **à la ~
de** (*sur la même ligne*) level with; (*fig:
tâche, situation*) equal to; **à la ~** (*fig*)
up to it

'haut-parleur ['opaʀlœʀ] *nm* (loud)
speaker

Hawaï [awai] *n* Hawaii; **les îles ~** the
Hawaiian Islands

'Haye ['ɛ] *n*: **la '~** the Hague

hebdomadaire [ɛbdɔmadɛʀ] *adj*,
nm weekly

hébergement [ebɛʀʒəmɑ̃] *nm*
accommodation

héberger [ebɛʀʒe] /3/ *vt* (*touristes*) to
accommodate, lodge; (*amis*) to put
up; (*réfugiés*) to take in

hébergeur [ebɛʀʒœʀ] *nm* (*Internet*)
host

hébreu, x [ebʀø] *adj m, nm* Hebrew

Hébrides [ebʀid] *nf*: **les ~** the
Hebrides

hectare [ɛktaʀ] *nm* hectare

'hein ['ɛ̃] *excl* eh?

'hélas ['elas] *excl* alas! ▷ *adv*
unfortunately

'héler ['ele] /6/ *vt* to hail

hélice [elis] *nf* propeller

hélicoptère [elikɔptɛʀ] *nm*
helicopter

helvétique [ɛlvetik] *adj* Swiss

hématome [ematom] *nm*
haematoma

hémisphère [emisfɛʀ] *nm*: **~ nord/
sud** northern/southern hemisphere

hémorragie [emɔʀaʒi] *nf* bleeding
no pl, haemorrhage

hémorroïdes [emɔʀɔid] *nfpl* piles, haemorrhoids

'hennir ['eniʀ] /2/ *vi* to neigh, whinny

hépatite [epatit] *nf* hepatitis

herbe [ɛʀb] *nf* grass; (*Culin, Méd*) herb; **~s de Provence** mixed herbs; **en ~** unripe; (*fig*) budding; **herbicide** *nm* weed-killer; **herboriste** *nm/f* herbalist

héréditaire [eʀeditɛʀ] *adj* hereditary

'hérisson ['eʀisɔ̃] *nm* hedgehog

héritage [eʀitaʒ] *nm* inheritance; (*coutumes, système*) heritage; legacy

hériter [eʀite] /1/ *vi*: **~ de qch (de qn)** to inherit sth (from sb); **héritier, -ière** *nm/f* heir/heiress

hermétique [ɛʀmetik] *adj* airtight; (*à l'eau*) watertight; (*fig: écrivain, style*) abstruse; (: *visage*) impenetrable

hermine [ɛʀmin] *nf* ermine

'hernie ['ɛʀni] *nf* hernia

héroïne [eʀɔin] *nf* heroine; (*drogue*) heroin

héroïque [eʀɔik] *adj* heroic

'héron ['eʀɔ̃] *nm* heron

'héros ['eʀo] *nm* hero

hésitant, e [ezitɑ̃, -ɑ̃t] *adj* hesitant

hésitation [ezitasjɔ̃] *nf* hesitation

hésiter [ezite] /1/ *vi*: **~ (à faire)** to hesitate (to do)

hétérosexuel, le [eteʀɔsɛkɥɛl] *adj* heterosexual

'hêtre ['ɛtʀ] *nm* beech

heure [œʀ] *nf* hour; (*Scol*) period; (*moment, moment fixé*) time; **c'est l'~** it's time; **quelle ~ est-il?** what time is it?; **2 ~s (du matin)** 2 o'clock (in the morning); **être à l'~** to be on time; (*montre*) to be right; **mettre à l'~** to set right; **à toute ~** at any time; **24 ~s sur 24** round the clock, 24 hours a day; **à l'~ qu'il est** at this time (of day); (*fig*) now; **à l'~ actuelle** at the present time; **sur l'~** at once; **à une ~ avancée (de la nuit)** at a late hour (of the night); **de bonne ~** early; **~ de pointe** rush hour; (*téléphone*) peak period; **~s de bureau** office hours; **~s supplémentaires** overtime *sg*

heureusement [œʀøzmɑ̃] *adv* (*par bonheur*) fortunately, luckily

heureux, -euse [œʀø, -øz] *adj* happy; (*chanceux*) lucky, fortunate

'heurt ['œʀ] *nm* (*choc*) collision

'heurter ['œʀte] /1/ *vt* (*mur*) to strike, hit; (*personne*) to collide with

hexagone [ɛgzagɔn] *nm* hexagon; **l'H~** (*la France*) France (*because of its roughly hexagonal shape*)

hiberner [ibɛʀne] /1/ *vi* to hibernate

'hibou, x ['ibu] *nm* owl

'hideux, -euse ['idø, -øz] *adj* hideous

hier [jɛʀ] *adv* yesterday; **~ matin/ soir/midi** yesterday morning/ evening/lunchtime; **toute la journée d'~** all day yesterday; **toute la matinée d'~** all yesterday morning

'hiérarchie ['jeʀaʀʃi] *nf* hierarchy

hindou, e [ɛ̃du] *adj* Hindu ▷ *nm/f*: **H~, e** Hindu; (*Indien*) Indian

hippique [ipik] *adj* equestrian, horse *cpd*; **un club ~** a riding centre; **un concours ~** a horse show; **hippisme** [ipism] *nm* (horse-)riding

hippodrome [ipɔdʀom] *nm* racecourse

hippopotame [ipɔpɔtam] *nm* hippopotamus

hirondelle [iʀɔ̃dɛl] *nf* swallow

'hisser ['ise] /1/ *vt* to hoist, haul up

histoire [istwaʀ] *nf* (*science, événements*) history; (*anecdote, récit, mensonge*) story; (*affaire*) business *no pl*; (*chichis: gén pl*) fuss *no pl*; **histoires** *nfpl* (*ennuis*) trouble *sg*; **~ géo** humanities *pl*; **historique** *adj* historical; (*important*) historic ▷ *nm*: **faire l'historique de** to give the background to

'hit-parade ['itpaʀad] *nm*: **le ~** the charts

hiver [ivɛʀ] *nm* winter; **hivernal, e, -aux** *adj* winter *cpd*; (*comme en hiver*) wintry; **hiverner** /1/ *vi* to winter

h

HLM *sigle m* ou *f* (= *habitations à loyer modéré*) low-rent, state-owned housing; **un(e)** ~ ≈ a council flat (*ou* house)

'**hobby** [ɔbi] *nm* hobby

'**hocher** [ɔʃe] /1/ *vt*: ~ **la tête** to nod; (*signe négatif ou dubitatif*) to shake one's head

'**hockey** [ɔkɛ] *nm*: ~ (**sur glace/gazon**) (ice/field) hockey

'**hold-up** [ɔldœp] *nm inv* hold-up

'**hollandais, e** [ɔlɑ̃dɛ, -ɛz] *adj* Dutch ▷ *nm* (*Ling*) Dutch ▷ *nm/f*: **H~, e** Dutchman/woman

'**Hollande** [ɔlɑ̃d] *nf*: **la** ~ Holland

'**homard** [ɔmar] *nm* lobster

homéopathique [ɔmeɔpatik] *adj* homoeopathic

homicide [ɔmisid] *nm* murder; ~ **involontaire** manslaughter

hommage [ɔmaʒ] *nm* tribute; **rendre** ~ **à** to pay tribute to

homme [ɔm] *nm* man; ~ **d'affaires** businessman; ~ **d'État** statesman; ~ **de main** hired man; ~ **de paille** stooge; ~ **politique** politician; **l'~ de la rue** the man in the street

homogène *adj* homogeneous

homologue *nm/f* counterpart

homologué, e *adj* (*Sport*) ratified; (*tarif*) authorized

homonyme *nm* (*Ling*) homonym; (*d'une personne*) namesake

homoparental, e, -aux [ɔmɔparɑ̃tal, o] *adj* (*famille*) same-sex

homosexuel, le *adj* homosexual

'**Hong-Kong** [ɔ̃gkɔ̃g] *n* Hong Kong

'**Hongrie** [ɔ̃gri] *nf*: **la** ~ Hungary; '**hongrois, e** *adj* Hungarian ▷ *nm* (*Ling*) Hungarian ▷ *nm/f*: **Hongrois, e** Hungarian

honnête [ɔnɛt] *adj* (*intègre*) honest; (*juste, satisfaisant*) fair; **honnêtement** *adv* honestly; **honnêteté** *nf* honesty

honneur [ɔnœr] *nm* honour; (*mérite*): **l'~ lui revient** the credit is his; **en l'~ de** (*personne*) in honour of;

(*événement*) on the occasion of; **faire** ~ **à** (*engagements*) to honour; (*famille, professeur*) to be a credit to; (*fig: repas etc*) to do justice to

honorable [ɔnɔrabl] *adj* worthy, honourable; (*suffisant*) decent

honoraire [ɔnɔrɛr] *adj* honorary; **honoraires** *nmpl* fees; **professeur** ~ professor emeritus

honorer [ɔnɔre] /1/ *vt* to honour; (*estimer*) to hold in high regard; (*faire honneur à*) to do credit to

'**honte** [ɔ̃t] *nf* shame; **avoir** ~ **de** to be ashamed of; **faire** ~ **à qn** to make sb (feel) ashamed; '**honteux, -euse** *adj* ashamed; (*conduite, acte*) shameful, disgraceful

hôpital, -aux [ɔpital, -o] *nm* hospital; **où est l'~ le plus proche?** where is the nearest hospital?

'**hoquet** [ɔkɛ] *nm*: **avoir le** ~ to have (the) hiccups

horaire [ɔrɛr] *adj* hourly ▷ *nm* timetable, schedule; **horaires** *nmpl* (*heures de travail*) hours; ~ **flexible** *ou* **mobile** *ou* **à la carte** *ou* **souple** flex(i)time

horizon [ɔrizɔ̃] *nm* horizon

horizontal, e, -aux *adj* horizontal

horloge [ɔrlɔʒ] *nf* clock; **l'~ parlante** the speaking clock; **horloger, -ère** *nm/f* watchmaker; clockmaker

'**hormis** [ɔrmi] *prép* save

horoscope [ɔrɔskɔp] *nm* horoscope

horreur [ɔrœr] *nf* horror; **quelle** ~! how awful!; **avoir** ~ **de** to loathe *ou* detest; **horrible** *adj* horrible; **horrifier** /7/ *vt* to horrify

'**hors** [ɔr] *prép*: ~ **de** out of; ~ **pair** outstanding; ~ **de propos** inopportune; ~ **service (HS)**, ~ **d'usage** out of service; **être** ~ **de soi** to be beside o.s.; '**hors-bord** *nm inv* speedboat (with outboard motor); '**hors-d'œuvre** *nm inv* hors d'œuvre; '**hors-la-loi** *nm inv* outlaw; '**hors-taxe** *adj* duty-free

hortensia [ɔrtɑ̃sja] *nm* hydrangea

hospice [ɔspis] nm (de vieillards) home

hospitalier, -ière [ɔspitalje, -jɛʀ] adj (accueillant) hospitable; (Méd: service, centre) hospital cpd

hospitaliser [ɔspitalize] /1/ vt to take (ou send) to hospital, hospitalize

hospitalité [ɔspitalite] nf hospitality

hostie [ɔsti] nf host

hostile [ɔstil] adj hostile; **hostilité** nf hostility

hôte [ot] nm (maître de maison) host ▷ nm/f (invité) guest

hôtel [otɛl] nm hotel; **aller à l'~** to stay in a hotel; **~ (particulier)** (private) mansion; **~ de ville** town hall; see note **"hôtels"**; **hôtellerie** [otɛlʀi] nf hotel business

● **HÔTELS**
●
● There are six categories of hotel
● in France, from zero ('non classé')
● to four stars and luxury four
● stars ('quatre étoiles luxe'). Prices
● include VAT but not breakfast. In
● some towns, guests pay a small
● additional tourist tax, the 'taxe
● de séjour'.

hôtesse [otɛs] nf hostess; **~ de l'air** flight attendant

'**houblon** ['ublɔ̃] nm (Bot) hop; (pour la bière) hops pl

'**houille** ['uj] nf coal; **~ blanche** hydroelectric power

'**houle** ['ul] nf swell; '**houleux, -euse** adj stormy

'**hourra** ['uʀa] excl hurrah!

'**housse** ['us] nf cover

'**houx** ['u] nm holly

hovercraft [ovœʀkʀaft] nm hovercraft

'**hublot** ['yblo] nm porthole

'**huche** ['yʃ] nf: **huche à pain** bread bin

'**huer** ['ɥe] /1/ vt to boo

huile [ɥil] nf oil

huissier [ɥisje] nm usher; (Jur) ≈ bailiff

'**huit** ['ɥi(t)] num eight; **samedi en ~** a week on Saturday; **dans ~ jours** in a week('s time); '**huitaine** ['ɥitɛn] nf: **une huitaine de jours** a week or so; '**huitième** num eighth

huître [ɥitʀ] nf oyster

humain, e [ymɛ̃, -ɛn] adj human; (compatissant) humane ▷ nm human (being); **humanitaire** adj humanitarian; **humanité** nf humanity

humble [œ̃bl] adj humble

'**humer** ['yme] /1/ vt (parfum) to inhale; (pour sentir) to smell

humeur [ymœʀ] nf mood; **de bonne/mauvaise ~** in a good/ bad mood

humide [ymid] adj damp; (main, yeux) moist; (climat, chaleur) humid; (saison, route) wet

humilier [ymilje] /7/ vt to humiliate

humilité [ymilite] nf humility, humbleness

humoristique [ymɔʀistik] adj humorous

humour [ymuʀ] nm humour; **avoir de l'~** to have a sense of humour; **~ noir** sick humour

'**huppé, e** ['ype] adj (fam) posh

'**hurlement** ['yʀləmɑ̃] nm howling no pl, howl; yelling no pl

'**hurler** ['yʀle] /1/ vi to howl, yell

'**hutte** ['yt] nf hut

hydratant, e [idʀatɑ̃, -ɑ̃t] adj (crème) moisturizing

hydraulique [idʀolik] adj hydraulic

hydravion [idʀavjɔ̃] nm seaplane

hydrogène [idʀɔʒɛn] nm hydrogen

hydroglisseur [idʀɔglisœʀ] nm hydroplane

hyène [jɛn] nf hyena

hygiène [iʒjɛn] nf hygiene

hygiénique [iʒenik] adj hygienic

hymne [imn] nm hymn

hyperlien [ipɛʀljɛ̃] nm hyperlink

hypermarché [ipεrmarʃe] *nm*
hypermarket
hypermétrope [ipεrmetrɔp] *adj*
long-sighted
hypertension [ipεrtãsjõ] *nf* high
blood pressure
hypnose [ipnoz] *nf* hypnosis;
hypnotiser /1/ *vt* to hypnotize
hypocrisie [ipɔkrizi] *nf* hypocrisy;
hypocrite *adj* hypocritical
hypothèque [ipɔtεk] *nf* mortgage
hypothèse [ipɔtεz] *nf* hypothesis
hystérique [isterik] *adj* hysterical

iceberg [isbεrg] *nm* iceberg
ici [isi] *adv* here; **jusqu'~** as far as this;
(*temporel*) until now; **d'~ là** by then;
d'~ demain by tomorrow; in the
meantime; **d'~ peu** before long
icône [ikon] *nf* icon
idéal, e, -aux [ideal, -o] *adj* ideal
▷ *nm* ideal; **idéaliste** *adj* idealistic
▷ *nm/f* idealist
idée [ide] *nf* idea; **se faire des ~s** to
imagine things, get ideas into one's
head; **avoir dans l'~ que** to have an
idea that; **~s noires** black *ou* dark
thoughts; **~s reçues** accepted ideas
ou wisdom
identifier [idãtifje] /7/ *vt* to identify;
s'identifier *vi*: **s'~ avec** *ou* **à qn/qch**
(*héros etc*) to identify with sb/sth
identique [idãtik] *adj*: **~ (à)**
identical (to)
identité [idãtite] *nf* identity
idiot, e [idjo, idjɔt] *adj* idiotic
▷ *nm/f* idiot

idole [idɔl] nf idol

if [if] nm yew

ignoble [iɲɔbl] adj vile

ignorant, e [iɲɔʀɑ̃, -ɑ̃t] adj ignorant; **~ de** ignorant of, not aware of

ignorer [iɲɔʀe] /1/ vt not to know; (personne) to ignore

il [il] pron he; (animal, chose, en tournure impersonnelle) it; **il neige** it's snowing; **Pierre est-il arrivé?** has Pierre arrived?; **il a gagné** he won; voir aussi **avoir**

île [il] nf island; **l'~ Maurice** Mauritius; **les ~s anglo-normandes** the Channel Islands; **les ~s Britanniques** the British Isles

illégal, e, -aux [ilegal, -o] adj illegal

illimité, e [ilimite] adj unlimited

illisible [ilizibl] adj illegible; (roman) unreadable

illogique [ilɔʒik] adj illogical

illuminer [ilymine] /1/ vt to light up; (monument, rue: pour une fête) to illuminate; (: au moyen de projecteurs) floodlight

illusion [ilyzjɔ̃] nf illusion; **se faire des ~s** to delude o.s.; **faire ~** to delude ou fool people

illustration [ilystʀasjɔ̃] nf illustration

illustré, e [ilystʀe] adj illustrated ▷ nm comic

illustrer [ilystʀe] /1/ vt to illustrate; **s'illustrer** to become famous, win fame

ils [il] pron they

image [imaʒ] nf (gén) picture; (comparaison, ressemblance) image; **~ de marque** brand image; (d'une personne) (public) image; **imagé, e** adj (texte) full of imagery; (langage) colourful

imaginaire [imaʒinɛʀ] adj imaginary

imagination [imaʒinasjɔ̃] nf imagination; **avoir de l'~** to be imaginative

imaginer [imaʒine] /1/ vt to imagine; (inventer: expédient, mesure)

to devise, think up; **s'imaginer** vt (se figurer: scène etc) to imagine, picture; **s'~ que** to imagine that

imam [imam] nm imam

imbécile [ɛ̃besil] adj idiotic ▷ nm/f idiot

imbu, e [ɛ̃by] adj: **~ de** full of

imitateur, -trice [imitatœʀ, -tʀis] nm/f (gén) imitator; (Music-Hall) impersonator

imitation [imitasjɔ̃] nf imitation; (de personalité) impersonation

imiter [imite] /1/ vt to imitate; (contrefaire) to forge; (ressembler à) to look like

immangeable [ɛ̃mɑ̃ʒabl] adj inedible

immatriculation [imatʀikylasjɔ̃] nf registration

> **IMMATRICULATION**
>
> The last two numbers on vehicle
> licence plates used to show which
> 'département' of France the vehicle
> was registered in. For example,
> a car registered in Paris had the
> number 75 on its licence plates. In
> 2009, a new alphanumeric system
> was introduced, in which the
> 'département' number no longer
> features. Displaying this number
> to the right of the plate is now
> optional.

immatriculer [imatʀikyle] /1/ vt to register; **faire/se faire ~** to register

immédiat, e [imedja, -at] adj immediate ▷ nm: **dans l'~** for the time being; **immédiatement** adv immediately

immense [imɑ̃s] adj immense

immerger [imɛʀʒe] /3/ vt to immerse, submerge

immeuble [imœbl] nm building; **~ locatif** block of rented flats

immigration [imigʀasjɔ̃] nf immigration

immigré, e [imigʀe] *nm/f*
immigrant

imminent, e [iminɑ̃, -ɑ̃t] *adj*
imminent

immobile [imɔbil] *adj* still,
motionless

immobilier, -ière [imɔbilje,
-jɛʀ] *adj* property *cpd* ▷ *nm*: **l'~** the
property *ou* the real estate business

immobiliser [imɔbilize] /1/ *vt* (*gén*)
to immobilize; (*circulation, véhicule,
affaires*) to bring to a standstill;
s'immobiliser (*personne*) to stand
still; (*machine, véhicule*) to come to a
halt *ou* a standstill

immoral, e, -aux [imɔʀal, -o] *adj*
immoral

immortel, le [imɔʀtɛl] *adj* immortal

immunisé, e [im(m)ynize] *adj*: **~
contre** immune to

immunité [imynite] *nf* immunity

impact [ɛ̃pakt] *nm* impact

impair, e [ɛ̃pɛʀ] *adj* odd ▷ *nm* faux
pas, blunder

impardonnable [ɛ̃paʀdɔnabl] *adj*
unpardonable, unforgivable

imparfait, e [ɛ̃paʀfɛ, -ɛt] *adj*
imperfect

impartial, e, -aux [ɛ̃paʀsjal, -o] *adj*
impartial, unbiased

impasse [ɛ̃pɑs] *nf* dead-end, cul-de-
sac; (*fig*) deadlock

impassible [ɛ̃pasibl] *adj* impassive

impatience [ɛ̃pasjɑ̃s] *nf* impatience

impatient, e [ɛ̃pasjɑ̃, -ɑ̃t] *adj*
impatient; **impatienter** /1/:
s'impatienter *vi* to get impatient

impeccable [ɛ̃pekabl] *adj* faultless;
(*propre*) spotlessly clean; (*fam*)
smashing

impensable [ɛ̃pɑ̃sabl] *adj* (*événement
hypothétique*) unthinkable; (*événement
qui a eu lieu*) unbelievable

impératif, -ive [ɛ̃peʀatif, -iv] *adj*
imperative ▷ *nm* (*Ling*) imperative;
impératifs *nmpl* (*exigences: d'une
fonction, d'une charge*) requirements;
(*: de la mode*) demands

impératrice [ɛ̃peʀatʀis] *nf* empress

imperceptible [ɛ̃pɛʀsɛptibl] *adj*
imperceptible

impérial, e, -aux [ɛ̃peʀjal, -o] *adj*
imperial

impérieux, -euse [ɛ̃peʀjø, -øz] *adj*
(*caractère, ton*) imperious; (*obligation,
besoin*) pressing, urgent

impérissable [ɛ̃peʀisabl] *adj*
undying

imperméable [ɛ̃pɛʀmeabl] *adj*
waterproof; (*fig*): **~ à** impervious to
▷ *nm* raincoat

impertinent, e [ɛ̃pɛʀtinɑ̃, -ɑ̃t] *adj*
impertinent

impitoyable [ɛ̃pitwajabl] *adj*
pitiless, merciless

implanter [ɛ̃plɑ̃te] /1/: **s'implanter
dans** *vi* to be established in

impliquer [ɛ̃plike] /1/ *vt* to imply;
~ qn (dans) to implicate sb (in)

impoli, e [ɛ̃pɔli] *adj* impolite, rude

impopulaire [ɛ̃pɔpylɛʀ] *adj*
unpopular

importance [ɛ̃pɔʀtɑ̃s] *nf*
importance; (*de somme*) size; **sans ~**
unimportant

important, e [ɛ̃pɔʀtɑ̃, -ɑ̃t] *adj*
important; (*en quantité: somme,
retard*) considerable, sizeable;
(*: gamme, dégâts*) extensive; (*péj: airs,
ton*) self-important ▷ *nm*: **l'~** the
important thing

importateur, -trice [ɛ̃pɔʀtatœʀ,
-tʀis] *nm/f* importer

importation [ɛ̃pɔʀtasjɔ̃] *nf* (*produit*)
import

importer [ɛ̃pɔʀte] /1/ *vt* (*Comm*)
to import; (*maladies, plantes*) to
introduce ▷ *vi* (*être important*) to
matter; **il importe qu'il fasse** it is
important that he should do; **peu
m'importe** (*je n'ai pas de préférence*)
I don't mind; (*je m'en moque*) I don't
care; **peu importe (que)** it doesn't
matter (if); *voir aussi* **n'importe**

importun, e [ɛ̃pɔʀtœ̃, -yn] *adj*
irksome, importunate; (*arrivée, visite*)

inopportune, ill-timed ▷ *nm* intruder; **importuner** /1/ *vt* to bother

imposant, e [ɛ̃pozɑ̃, -ɑ̃t] *adj* imposing

imposer [ɛ̃poze] /1/ *vt* (*taxer*) to tax; **~ qch à qn** to impose sth on sb; **s'imposer** (*être nécessaire*) to be imperative; **en ~ à** to impress; **s'~ comme** to emerge as; **s'~ par** to win recognition through

impossible [ɛ̃pɔsibl] *adj* impossible; **il m'est ~ de le faire** it is impossible for me to do it, I can't possibly do it; **faire l'~ (pour que)** to do one's utmost (so that)

imposteur [ɛ̃pɔstœr] *nm* impostor

impôt [ɛ̃po] *nm* tax; **~ sur le chiffre d'affaires** corporation (BRIT) *ou* corporate (US) tax; **~ foncier** land tax; **~ sur le revenu** income tax; **~s locaux** rates, local taxes (US), ≈ council tax (BRIT)

impotent, e [ɛ̃pɔtɑ̃, -ɑ̃t] *adj* disabled

impraticable [ɛ̃pratikabl] *adj* (*projet*) impracticable, unworkable; (*piste*) impassable

imprécis, e [ɛ̃presi, -iz] *adj* imprecise

imprégner [ɛ̃preɲe] /6/ *vt*: **~ (de)** (*tissu, tampon*) to soak *ou* impregnate (with); (*lieu, air*) to fill (with); **s'imprégner de** (*fig*) to absorb

imprenable [ɛ̃prənabl] *adj* (*forteresse*) impregnable; **vue ~** unimpeded outlook

impression [ɛ̃presjɔ̃] *nf* impression; (*d'un ouvrage, tissu*) printing; **faire bonne/mauvaise ~** to make a good/bad impression; **impressionnant, e** *adj* (*imposant*) impressive; (*bouleversant*) upsetting; **impressionner** /1/ *vt* (*frapper*) to impress; (*troubler*) to upset

imprévisible [ɛ̃previzibl] *adj* unforeseeable

imprévu, e [ɛ̃prevy] *adj* unforeseen, unexpected ▷ *nm* (*incident*) unexpected incident; **des vacances pleines d'~** holidays full of surprises; **en cas d'~** if anything unexpected happens; **sauf ~** unless anything unexpected crops up

imprimante [ɛ̃primɑ̃t] *nf* printer; **~ à laser** laser printer

imprimé [ɛ̃prime] *nm* (*formulaire*) printed form; (*Postes*) printed matter *no pl*; (*tissu*) printed fabric; **un ~ à fleurs/pois** (*tissu*) a floral/polka-dot print

imprimer [ɛ̃prime] /1/ *vt* to print; (*publier*) to publish; **imprimerie** *nf* printing; (*établissement*) printing works *sg*; **imprimeur** *nm* printer

impropre [ɛ̃prɔpr] *adj* inappropriate; **~ à** unsuitable for

improviser [ɛ̃provize] /1/ *vt, vi* to improvize

improviste [ɛ̃provist]: **à l'~** *adv* unexpectedly, without warning

imprudence [ɛ̃prydɑ̃s] *nf* (*d'une personne, d'une action*) carelessness *no pl*; (*d'une remarque*) imprudence *no pl*; **commettre une ~** to do something foolish

imprudent, e [ɛ̃prydɑ̃, -ɑ̃t] *adj* (*conducteur, geste, action*) careless; (*remarque*) unwise, imprudent; (*projet*) foolhardy

impuissant, e [ɛ̃pɥisɑ̃, -ɑ̃t] *adj* helpless; (*sans effet*) ineffectual; (*sexuellement*) impotent

impulsif, -ive [ɛ̃pylsif, -iv] *adj* impulsive

impulsion [ɛ̃pylsjɔ̃] *nf* (*Élec, instinct*) impulse; (*élan, influence*) impetus

inabordable [inabɔrdabl] *adj* (*cher*) prohibitive

inacceptable [inaksɛptabl] *adj* unacceptable

inaccessible [inaksesibl] *adj* inaccessible; **~ à** impervious to

inachevé, e [inaʃve] *adj* unfinished

inactif, -ive [inaktif, -iv] *adj* inactive; (*remède*) ineffective; (*Bourse: marché*) slack

inadapté, e [inadapte] *adj (Psych)*
maladjusted; **~ à** not adapted to,
unsuited to

inadéquat, e [inadekwa, -wat] *adj*
inadequate

inadmissible [inadmisibl] *adj*
inadmissible

inadvertance [inadvɛrtɑ̃s]: **par ~**
adv inadvertently

inanimé, e [inanime] *adj (matière)*
inanimate; *(évanoui)* unconscious;
(sans vie) lifeless

inanition [inanisjɔ̃] *nf*: **tomber d'~**
to faint with hunger (and exhaustion)

inaperçu, e [inapɛrsy] *adj*: **passer
~** to go unnoticed

inapte [inapt] *adj*: **~ à** incapable of;
(Mil) unfit for

inattendu, e [inatɑ̃dy] *adj*
unexpected

inattentif, -ive [inatɑ̃tif, -iv] *adj*
inattentive; **~ à** *(dangers, détails)*
heedless of; **inattention** *nf*
inattention; **faute d'inattention**
careless mistake

inaugurer [inɔgyre] /1/ *vt*
(monument) to unveil; *(exposition,
usine)* to open; *(fig)* to inaugurate

inavouable [inavwabl] *adj*
(bénéfices) undisclosable; *(honteux)*
shameful

incalculable [ɛ̃kalkylabl] *adj*
incalculable

incapable [ɛ̃kapabl] *adj* incapable;
~ de faire incapable of doing;
(empêché) unable to do

incapacité [ɛ̃kapasite] *nf*
(incompétence) incapability;
(impossibilité) incapacity; **être dans
l'~ de faire** to be unable to do

incarcérer [ɛ̃karsere] /6/ *vt* to
incarcerate, imprison

incassable [ɛ̃kasabl] *adj* unbreakable

incendie [ɛ̃sɑ̃di] *nm* fire; **~ criminel**
arson *no pl*; **~ de forêt** forest fire;
incendier /7/ *vt (mettre le feu à)*
to set fire to, set alight; *(brûler
complètement)* to burn down

incertain, e [ɛ̃sɛrtɛ̃, -ɛn] *adj*
uncertain; *(temps)* unsettled;
(imprécis: contours) indistinct, blurred;
incertitude *nf* uncertainty

incessamment [ɛ̃sesamɑ̃] *adv*
very shortly

incident [ɛ̃sidɑ̃] *nm* incident; **~ de
parcours** minor hitch *ou* setback;
~ technique technical difficulties *pl*

incinérer [ɛ̃sinere] /6/ *vt (ordures)* to
incinerate; *(mort)* to cremate

incisif, -ive [ɛ̃sizif, -iv] *adj* incisive
▷ *nf* incisor

inciter [ɛ̃site] /1/ *vt*: **~ qn à (faire)
qch** to prompt *ou* encourage sb to
do sth; *(à la révolte etc)* to incite sb
to do sth

incivilité [ɛ̃sivilite] *nf (grossièreté)*
incivility; **incivilités** *nfpl* antisocial
behaviour *sg*

inclinable [ɛ̃klinabl] *adj*: **siège à
dossier ~** reclining seat

inclination [ɛ̃klinasjɔ̃] *nf (penchant)*
inclination

incliner [ɛ̃kline] /1/ *vt (bouteille)* to
tilt ▷ *vi*: **~ à qch/à faire** to incline
towards sth/doing; **s'incliner** *vi*
(route) to slope; **s'~ (devant)** to bow
(before)

inclure [ɛ̃klyr] /35/ *vt* to include;
(joindre à un envoi) to enclose

inclus, e [ɛ̃kly, -yz] *pp de* **inclure**
▷ *adj* included; *(joint à un envoi)*
enclosed; *(compris: frais, dépense)*
included; **jusqu'au 10 mars ~** until
10th March inclusive

incognito [ɛ̃kɔɲito] *adv* incognito
▷ *nm*: **garder l'~** to remain incognito

incohérent, e [ɛ̃kɔerɑ̃, -ɑ̃t] *adj*
(comportement) inconsistent; *(geste,
langage, texte)* incoherent

incollable [ɛ̃kɔlabl] *adj (riz)* that
does not stick; *(fam)*: **il est ~** he's got
all the answers

incolore [ɛ̃kɔlɔr] *adj* colourless

incommoder [ɛ̃kɔmɔde] /1/ *vt*:
~ qn *(chaleur, odeur)* to bother *ou*
inconvenience sb

incomparable [ε̃kɔ̃paʀabl] *adj*
incomparable

incompatible [ε̃kɔ̃patibl] *adj*
incompatible

incompétent, e [ε̃kɔ̃petã, -ãt] *adj*
incompetent

incomplet, -ète [ε̃kɔ̃plε, -εt] *adj*
incomplete

incompréhensible [ε̃kɔ̃pʀeãsibl]
adj incomprehensible

incompris, e [ε̃kɔ̃pʀi, -iz] *adj*
misunderstood

inconcevable [ε̃kɔ̃svabl] *adj*
inconceivable

inconfortable [ε̃kɔ̃fɔʀtabl] *adj*
uncomfortable

incongru, e [ε̃kɔ̃gʀy] *adj* unseemly

inconnu, e [ε̃kɔny] *adj* unknown
▷ *nm/f* stranger ▷ *nm*: **l'~** the
unknown ▷ *nf* unknown factor

inconsciemment [ε̃kɔ̃sjamã] *adv*
unconsciously

inconscient, e [ε̃kɔ̃sjã, -ãt] *adj*
unconscious; (*irréfléchi*) thoughtless,
reckless; (*sentiment*) subconscious
▷ *nm* (*Psych*): **l'~** the unconscious;
~ de unaware of

inconsidéré, e [ε̃kɔ̃sideʀe] *adj*
ill-considered

inconsistant, e [ε̃kɔ̃sistã, -ãt] *adj*
flimsy, weak

inconsolable [ε̃kɔ̃sɔlabl] *adj*
inconsolable

incontestable [ε̃kɔ̃tεstabl] *adj*
indisputable

incontinent, e [ε̃kɔ̃tinã, -ãt] *adj*
incontinent

incontournable [ε̃kɔ̃tuʀnabl] *adj*
unavoidable

incontrôlable [ε̃kɔ̃tʀolabl]
adj unverifiable; (*irrépressible*)
uncontrollable

inconvénient [ε̃kɔ̃venjã] *nm*
disadvantage, drawback; **si vous
n'y voyez pas d'~** if you have no
objections

incorporer [ε̃kɔʀpɔʀe] /1/ *vt*: **~ (à)**
to mix in (with); **~ (dans)** (*paragraphe
etc*) to incorporate (in); (*Mil: appeler*)
to recruit (into); **il a très bien su s'~
à notre groupe** he was very easily
incorporated into our group

incorrect, e [ε̃kɔʀεkt] *adj* (*impropre,
inconvenant*) improper; (*défectueux*)
faulty; (*inexact*) incorrect; (*impoli*)
impolite; (*déloyal*) underhand

incorrigible [ε̃kɔʀiʒibl] *adj*
incorrigible

incrédule [ε̃kʀedyl] *adj* incredulous;
(*Rel*) unbelieving

incroyable [ε̃kʀwajabl] *adj* incredible

incruster [ε̃kʀyste] /1/ *vt*:
s'incruster *vi* (*invité*) to take root;
~ qch dans/qch de (*Art*) to inlay sth
into/sth with

inculpé, e [ε̃kylpe] *nm/f* accused

inculper [ε̃kylpe] /1/ *vt*: **~ (de)** to
charge (with)

inculquer [ε̃kylke] /1/ *vt*: **~ qch à** to
inculcate sth in, instil sth into

Inde [ε̃d] *nf*: **l'~** India

indécent, e [ε̃desã, -ãt] *adj* indecent

indécis, e [ε̃desi, -iz] *adj* (*par nature*)
indecisive; (*perplexe*) undecided

indéfendable [ε̃defãdabl] *adj*
indefensible

indéfini, e [ε̃defini] *adj* (*imprécis,
incertain*) undefined; (*illimité, Ling*)
indefinite; **indéfiniment** *adv*
indefinitely; **indéfinissable** *adj*
indefinable

indélébile [ε̃delebil] *adj* indelible

indélicat, e [ε̃delika, -at] *adj* tactless

indemne [ε̃dεmn] *adj* unharmed;
indemniser /1/ *vt*: **indemniser qn
(de)** to compensate sb (for)

indemnité [ε̃dεmnite] *nf*
(*dédommagement*) compensation
no pl; (*allocation*) allowance; **~ de
licenciement** redundancy payment

indépendamment [ε̃depãdamã]
adv independently; **~ de** (*abstraction
faite de*) irrespective of; (*en plus de*)
over and above

indépendance [ε̃depãdãs] *nf*
independence

indépendant, e [ɛ̃depɑ̃dɑ̃, -ɑ̃t] *adj*
independent; **~ de** independent of;
travailleur ~ self-employed worker

indescriptible [ɛ̃dɛskʀiptibl] *adj*
indescribable

indésirable [ɛ̃deziʀabl] *adj*
undesirable

indestructible [ɛ̃dɛstʀyktibl] *adj*
indestructible

indéterminé, e [ɛ̃detɛʀmine] *adj*
(date, cause, nature) unspecified;
(forme, longueur, quantité)
indeterminate

index [ɛ̃dɛks] *nm (doigt)* index finger;
(d'un livre etc) index; **mettre à l'~** to
blacklist

indicateur [ɛ̃dikatœʀ] *nm (Police)*
informer; *(Tech)* gauge; indicator
▷ *adj*: **poteau ~** signpost; **~ des
chemins de fer** railway timetable;
~ de rues street directory

indicatif, -ive [ɛ̃dikatif, -iv] *adj*: **à
titre ~** for (your) information ▷ *nm*
(Ling) indicative; *(d'une émission)*
theme *ou* signature tune; *(Tél)* dialling
code (BRIT), area code (US); **quel est
l'~ de ...** what's the code for ...?

indication [ɛ̃dikasjɔ̃] *nf* indication;
(renseignement) information *no
pl*; **indications** *nfpl (directives)*
instructions

indice [ɛ̃dis] *nm (marque, signe)*
indication, sign; *(Police: lors d'une
enquête)* clue; *(Jur: présomption)*
piece of evidence; *(Science, Écon,
Tech)* index; **~ de protection** (sun
protection) factor

indicible [ɛ̃disibl] *adj* inexpressible

indien, ne [ɛ̃djɛ̃, -ɛn] *adj* Indian
▷ *nm/f*: **I~, ne** Indian

indifféremment [ɛ̃difeʀamɑ̃] *adv*
(sans distinction) equally

indifférence [ɛ̃difeʀɑ̃s] *nf* indifference

indifférent, e [ɛ̃difeʀɑ̃, -ɑ̃t] *adj*
(peu intéressé) indifferent; **ça m'est
~ (que ...)** it doesn't matter to me
(whether ...); **elle m'est ~e** I am
indifferent to her

indigène [ɛ̃diʒɛn] *adj* native,
indigenous; *(de la région)* local ▷ *nm/f*
native

indigeste [ɛ̃diʒɛst] *adj* indigestible

indigestion [ɛ̃diʒɛstjɔ̃] *nf*
indigestion *no pl*; **avoir une ~** to have
indigestion

indigne [ɛ̃diɲ] *adj*: **~ (de)** unworthy
(of)

indigner [ɛ̃diɲe] /1/ *vt*: **s'indigner
(de/contre)** to be (*ou* become)
indignant (at)

indiqué, e [ɛ̃dike] *adj (date, lieu)*
given; *(adéquat)* appropriate;
(conseillé) advisable

indiquer [ɛ̃dike] /1/ *vt*: **~ qch/qn
à qn** to point sth/sb out to sb; *(faire
connaître: médecin, lieu, restaurant)*
to tell sb of sth/sb; *(pendule, aiguille)*
to show; *(étiquette, plan)* to show,
indicate; *(renseigner sur)* to point
out, tell; *(déterminer: date, lieu)* to
give, state; *(dénoter)* to indicate,
point to; **pourriez-vous m'~ les
toilettes/l'heure?** could you direct
me to the toilets/tell me the time?

indiscipliné, e [ɛ̃disipline] *adj*
undisciplined

indiscret, -ète [ɛ̃diskʀɛ, -ɛt] *adj*
indiscreet

indiscutable [ɛ̃diskytabl] *adj*
indisputable

indispensable [ɛ̃dispɑ̃sabl] *adj*
indispensable, essential

indisposé, e [ɛ̃dispoze] *adj*
indisposed

indistinct, e [ɛ̃distɛ̃, -ɛ̃kt] *adj*
indistinct; **indistinctement** *adv*
(voir, prononcer) indistinctly; *(sans
distinction)* indiscriminately

individu [ɛ̃dividy] *nm* individual;
individuel, le *adj (gén)* individual;
(opinion, livret, contrôle, avantages)
personal; **chambre individuelle**
single room; **maison individuelle**
detached house; **propriété
individuelle** personal *ou* private
property

indolore [ɛ̃dɔlɔʀ] adj painless

Indonésie [ɛ̃dɔnezi] nf: **l'~** Indonesia

indu, e [ɛ̃dy] adj: **à une heure ~e** at some ungodly hour

indulgent, e [ɛ̃dylʒɑ̃, -ɑ̃t] adj (parent, regard) indulgent; (juge, examinateur) lenient

industrialisé, e [ɛ̃dystʀijalize] adj industrialized

industrie [ɛ̃dystʀi] nf industry; **industriel, le** adj industrial ▷ nm industrialist

inébranlable [inebʀɑ̃labl] adj (masse, colonne) solid; (personne, certitude, foi) unwavering

inédit, e [inedi, -it] adj (correspondance etc) (hitherto) unpublished; (spectacle, moyen) novel, original; (film) unreleased

inefficace [inefikas] adj (remède, moyen) ineffective; (machine, employé) inefficient

inégal, e, -aux [inegal, -o] adj unequal; (irrégulier) uneven; **inégalable** adj matchless; **inégalé, e** adj (record) unequalled; (beauté) unrivalled; **inégalité** nf inequality

inépuisable [inepɥizabl] adj inexhaustible

inerte [inɛʀt] adj (immobile) lifeless; (apathique) passive

inespéré, e [inɛspeʀe] adj unhoped-for, unexpected

inestimable [inɛstimabl] adj priceless; (fig: bienfait) invaluable

inévitable [inevitabl] adj unavoidable; (fatal, habituel) inevitable

inexact, e [inɛgzakt] adj inaccurate

inexcusable [inɛkskyzabl] adj unforgivable

inexplicable [inɛksplikabl] adj inexplicable

in extremis [inɛkstʀemis] adv at the last minute ▷ adj last-minute

infaillible [ɛ̃fajibl] adj infallible

infarctus [ɛ̃faʀktys] nm: **~ (du myocarde)** coronary (thrombosis)

infatigable [ɛ̃fatigabl] adj tireless

infect, e [ɛ̃fɛkt] adj revolting; (repas, vin) revolting, foul; (personne) obnoxious; (temps) foul

infecter [ɛ̃fɛkte] /1/ vt (atmosphère, eau) to contaminate; (Méd) to infect; **s'infecter** to become infected ou septic; **infection** nf infection; (puanteur) stench

inférieur, e [ɛ̃feʀjœʀ] adj lower; (en qualité, intelligence) inferior ▷ nm/f inferior; **~ à** (somme, quantité) less ou smaller than; (moins bon que) inferior to

infernal, e, -aux [ɛ̃fɛʀnal, -o] adj (insupportable: chaleur, rythme) infernal; (: enfant) horrid; (méchanceté, complot) diabolical

infidèle [ɛ̃fidɛl] adj unfaithful

infiltrer [ɛ̃filtʀe] /1/: **s'infiltrer** vi: **s'~ dans** to penetrate into; (liquide) to seep into; (fig: noyauter) to infiltrate

infime [ɛ̃fim] adj minute, tiny

infini, e [ɛ̃fini] adj infinite ▷ nm infinity; **à l'~** endlessly; **infiniment** adv infinitely; **infinité** nf: **une infinité de** an infinite number of

infinitif, -ive [ɛ̃finitif, -iv] nm infinitive

infirme [ɛ̃fiʀm] adj disabled ▷ nm/f person with a disability

infirmerie [ɛ̃fiʀməʀi] nf sick bay

infirmier, -ière [ɛ̃fiʀmje, -jɛʀ] nm/f nurse; **infirmière chef** sister

infirmité [ɛ̃fiʀmite] nf disability

inflammable [ɛ̃flamabl] adj (in) flammable

inflation [ɛ̃flasjɔ̃] nf inflation

influençable [ɛ̃flyɑ̃sabl] adj easily influenced

influence [ɛ̃flyɑ̃s] nf influence; **influencer** /3/ vt to influence; **influent, e** adj influential

informaticien, ne [ɛ̃fɔʀmatisjɛ̃, -ɛn] nm/f computer scientist

information [ɛ̃fɔʀmasjɔ̃] nf (renseignement) piece of information; (Presse, TV: nouvelle) item of news; (*diffusion de renseignements*, *Inform*) information; (*Jur*) inquiry, investigation; **informations** *nfpl* (TV) news *sg*

informatique [ɛ̃fɔʀmatik] *nf* (*technique*) data processing; (*science*) computer science ▷ *adj* computer *cpd*; **informatiser** /1/ *vt* to computerize

informer [ɛ̃fɔʀme] /1/ *vt*: ~ **qn (de)** to inform sb (of); **s'informer (sur)** to inform o.s. (about); **s'~ (de qch/ si)** to inquire *ou* find out (about sth/ whether *ou* if)

infos [ɛ̃fo] *nfpl* (= *informations*) news

infraction [ɛ̃fʀaksjɔ̃] *nf* offence; ~ **à** violation *ou* breach of; **être en ~** to be in breach of the law

infranchissable [ɛ̃fʀɑ̃ʃisabl] *adj* impassable; (*fig*) insuperable

infrarouge [ɛ̃fʀaʀuʒ] *adj* infrared

infrastructure [ɛ̃fʀastʀyktyʀ] *nf* (*Aviat*, *Mil*) ground installations *pl*; (*Écon*: *touristique etc*) facilities *pl*

infuser [ɛ̃fyze] /1/ *vt* (*thé*) to brew; (*tisane*) to infuse ▷ *vi* to brew; to infuse; **infusion** *nf* (*tisane*) herb tea

ingénier [ɛ̃ʒenje] /7/: **s'ingénier** *vi*: **s'~ à faire** to strive to do

ingénierie [ɛ̃ʒeniʀi] *nf* engineering

ingénieur [ɛ̃ʒenjœʀ] *nm* engineer; ~ **du son** sound engineer

ingénieux, -euse [ɛ̃ʒenjø, -øz] *adj* ingenious, clever

ingrat, e [ɛ̃gʀa, -at] *adj* (*personne*) ungrateful; (*travail, sujet*) thankless; (*visage*) unprepossessing

ingrédient [ɛ̃gʀedjɑ̃] *nm* ingredient

inhabité, e [inabite] *adj* uninhabited

inhabituel, le [inabityɛl] *adj* unusual

inhibition [inibisjɔ̃] *nf* inhibition

inhumain, e [inymɛ̃, -ɛn] *adj* inhuman

inimaginable [inimaʒinabl] *adj* unimaginable

ininterrompu, e [inɛ̃teʀɔ̃py] *adj* (*file, série*) unbroken; (*flot, vacarme*) uninterrupted, non-stop; (*effort*) unremitting, continuous; (*suite, ligne*) unbroken

initial, e, -aux [inisjal, -o] *adj* initial; **initiales** *nfpl* initials

initiation [inisjasjɔ̃] *nf*: ~ **à** introduction to

initiative [inisjativ] *nf* initiative

initier [inisje] /7/ *vt*: ~ **qn à** to initiate sb into; (*faire découvrir: art, jeu*) to introduce sb to

injecter [ɛ̃ʒɛkte] /1/ *vt* to inject; **injection** *nf* injection; **à injection** (*Auto*) fuel injection *cpd*

injure [ɛ̃ʒyʀ] *nf* insult, abuse *no pl*; **injurier** /7/ *vt* to insult, abuse; **injurieux, -euse** *adj* abusive, insulting

injuste [ɛ̃ʒyst] *adj* unjust, unfair; **injustice** [ɛ̃ʒystis] *nf* injustice

inlassable [ɛ̃lasabl] *adj* tireless

inné, e [ine] *adj* innate, inborn

innocent, e [inɔsɑ̃, -ɑ̃t] *adj* innocent; **innocenter** /1/ *vt* to clear, prove innocent

innombrable [inɔ̃bʀabl] *adj* innumerable

innover [inɔve] /1/ *vi*: ~ **en matière d'art** to break new ground in the field of art

inoccupé, e [inɔkype] *adj* unoccupied

inodore [inɔdɔʀ] *adj* (*gaz*) odourless; (*fleur*) scentless

inoffensif, -ive [inɔfɑ̃sif, -iv] *adj* harmless, innocuous

inondation [inɔ̃dasjɔ̃] *nf* flood

inonder [inɔ̃de] /1/ *vt* to flood; ~ **de** to flood *ou* swamp with

inopportun, e [inɔpɔʀtœ̃, -yn] *adj* ill-timed, untimely

inoubliable [inublijabl] *adj* unforgettable

inouï, e [inwi] *adj* unheard-of, extraordinary

inox [inɔks] *nm* stainless (steel)

inquiet, -ète [ɛ̃kjɛ, -ɛt] *adj* anxious; **inquiétant, e** *adj* worrying, disturbing; **inquiéter** /6/ vt to worry; **s'inquiéter** to worry; **s'inquiéter de** to worry about; (s'enquérir de) to inquire about; **inquiétude** nf anxiety

insaisissable [ɛ̃sezizabl] adj (fugitif, ennemi) elusive; (différence, nuance) imperceptible

insalubre [ɛ̃salybʀ] adj insalubrious

insatisfait, e [ɛ̃satisfɛ, -ɛt] adj (non comblé) unsatisfied; (mécontent) dissatisfied

inscription [ɛ̃skʀipsjɔ̃] nf inscription; (à une institution) enrolment

inscrire [ɛ̃skʀiʀ] /39/ vt (marquer: sur son calepin etc) to note ou write down; (: sur un mur, une affiche etc) to write; (: dans la pierre, le métal) to inscribe; (mettre: sur une liste, un budget etc) to put down; **~ qn à** (club, école etc) to enrol sb at; **s'inscrire** (pour une excursion etc) to put one's name down; **s'~ (à)** (club, parti) to join; (université) to register ou enrol (at); (examen, concours) to register ou enter (for)

insecte [ɛ̃sɛkt] nm insect; **insecticide** nm insecticide

insensé, e [ɛ̃sɑ̃se] adj mad

insensible [ɛ̃sɑ̃sibl] adj (nerf, membre) numb; (dur, indifférent) insensitive

inséparable [ɛ̃sepaʀabl] adj: **~ (de)** inseparable (from) ▷ nmpl: **~s** (oiseaux) lovebirds

insigne [ɛ̃siɲ] nm (d'un parti, club) badge ▷ adj distinguished; **insignes** nmpl (d'une fonction) insignia pl

insignifiant, e [ɛ̃siɲifjɑ̃, -ɑ̃t] adj insignificant; trivial

insinuer [ɛ̃sinɥe] /1/ vt to insinuate; **s'insinuer dans** (fig) to worm one's way into

insipide [ɛ̃sipid] adj insipid

insister [ɛ̃siste] /1/ vi to insist; (s'obstiner) to keep on; **~ sur** (détail, note) to stress

insolation [ɛ̃sɔlasjɔ̃] nf (Méd) sunstroke no pl

insolent, e [ɛ̃sɔlɑ̃, -ɑ̃t] adj insolent

insolite [ɛ̃sɔlit] adj strange, unusual

insomnie [ɛ̃sɔmni] nf insomnia no pl; **avoir des ~s** to sleep badly

insouciant, e [ɛ̃susjɑ̃, -ɑ̃t] adj carefree; **~ du danger** heedless of (the) danger

insoupçonnable [ɛ̃supsɔnabl] adj unsuspected; (personne) above suspicion

insoupçonné, e [ɛ̃supsɔne] adj unsuspected

insoutenable [ɛ̃sutnabl] adj (argument) untenable; (chaleur) unbearable

inspecter [ɛ̃spɛkte] /1/ vt to inspect; **inspecteur, -trice** nm/f inspector; **inspecteur d'Académie** (regional) director of education; **inspecteur des finances** ≈ tax inspector (BRIT), ≈ Internal Revenue Service agent (US); **inspecteur (de police)** (police) inspector; **inspection** nf inspection

inspirer [ɛ̃spiʀe] /1/ vt (gén) to inspire ▷ vi (aspirer) to breathe in; **s'inspirer de** to be inspired by

instable [ɛ̃stabl] adj (meuble, équilibre) unsteady; (population, temps) unsettled; (paix, régime, caractère) unstable

installation [ɛ̃stalasjɔ̃] nf (mise en place) installation; **installations** nfpl installations; (industrielles) plant sg; (de sport, dans un camping) facilities; **l'~ électrique** wiring

installer [ɛ̃stale] /1/ vt to put; (meuble) to put in; (rideau, étagère, tente) to put up; (appartement) to fit out; **s'installer** (s'établir: artisan, dentiste etc) to set o.s. up; (emménager) to settle in; (sur un siège, à un emplacement) to settle (down); (fig: maladie, grève) to take a firm hold ou grip; **s'~ à l'hôtel/chez qn** to move into a hotel/in with sb

instance [ɛ̃stɑ̃s] nf (Admin: autorité) authority; **affaire en ~** matter pending; **être en ~ de divorce** to be awaiting a divorce

instant [ɛ̃stɑ̃] nm moment, instant; **dans un ~** in a moment; **à l'~** this instant; **je l'ai vu à l'~** I've just this minute seen him, I saw him a moment ago; **pour l'~** for the moment, for the time being

instantané, e [ɛ̃stɑ̃tane] adj (lait, café) instant; (explosion, mort) instantaneous ▷ nm snapshot

instar [ɛ̃staʀ] : **à l'~ de** prép following the example of, like

instaurer [ɛ̃stɔʀe] /1/ vt to institute; (couvre-feu) to impose; **s'instaurer** vi (collaboration, paix etc) to be established; (doute) to set in

instinct [ɛ̃stɛ̃] nm instinct; **instinctivement** adv instinctively

instituer [ɛ̃stitɥe] /1/ vt to establish

institut [ɛ̃stity] nm institute; **~ de beauté** beauty salon; **I~ universitaire de technologie (IUT)** ≈ Institute of technology

instituteur, -trice [ɛ̃stitytœʀ, -tʀis] nm/f (primary (BRIT) ou grade (US) school) teacher

institution [ɛ̃stitysjɔ̃] nf institution; (collège) private school; **institutions** nfpl (structures politiques et sociales) institutions

instructif, -ive [ɛ̃stʀyktif, -iv] adj instructive

instruction [ɛ̃stʀyksjɔ̃] nf (enseignement, savoir) education; (Jur) (preliminary) investigation and hearing; **instructions** nfpl (mode d'emploi) instructions; **~ civique** civics sg

instruire [ɛ̃stʀɥiʀ] /38/ vt (élèves) to teach; (recrues) to train; (Jur: affaire) to conduct the investigation for; **s'instruire** to educate o.s.; **instruit, e** adj educated

instrument [ɛ̃stʀymɑ̃] nm instrument; **~ à cordes/vent** stringed/wind instrument; **~ de mesure** measuring instrument; **~ de musique** musical instrument; **~ de travail** (working) tool

insu [ɛ̃sy] nm: **à l'~ de qn** without sb knowing

insuffisant, e [ɛ̃syfizɑ̃, -ɑ̃t] adj (en quantité) insufficient; (en qualité) inadequate; (sur une copie) poor

insulaire [ɛ̃sylɛʀ] adj island cpd; (attitude) insular

insuline [ɛ̃sylin] nf insulin

insulte [ɛ̃sylt] nf insult; **insulter** /1/ vt to insult

insupportable [ɛ̃sypɔʀtabl] adj unbearable

insurmontable [ɛ̃syʀmɔ̃tabl] adj (difficulté) insuperable; (aversion) unconquerable

intact, e [ɛ̃takt] adj intact

intarissable [ɛ̃taʀisabl] adj inexhaustible

intégral, e, -aux [ɛ̃tegʀal, -o] adj complete; **texte ~** unabridged version; **bronzage ~** all-over suntan; **intégralement** adv in full; **intégralité** nf whole (ou full) amount; **dans son intégralité** in its entirety; **intégrant, e** adj: **faire partie intégrante de** to be an integral part of

intègre [ɛ̃tegʀ] adj upright

intégrer [ɛ̃tegʀe] /6/ : **s'intégrer** vr: **s'~ à** ou **dans** to become integrated into; **bien s'~** to fit in

intégrisme [ɛ̃tegʀism] nm fundamentalism

intellectuel, le [ɛ̃telɛktɥɛl] adj, nm/f intellectual; (péj) highbrow

intelligence [ɛ̃teliʒɑ̃s] nf intelligence; (compréhension): **l'~ de** the understanding of; (complicité): **regard d'~** glance of complicity; (accord): **vivre en bonne ~ avec qn** to be on good terms with sb

intelligent, e [ɛ̃teliʒɑ̃, -ɑ̃t] adj intelligent

intelligible [ɛ̃teliʒibl] adj intelligible

intempéries [ɛ̃tɑ̃peʀi] nfpl bad weather sg

intenable [ɛ̃tnabl] adj unbearable

intendant, e [ɛ̃tɑ̃dɑ̃, -ɑ̃t] nm/f (Mil) quartermaster; (Scol) bursar

intense [ɛ̃tɑ̃s] *adj* intense; **intensif, -ive** *adj* intensive; **cours intensif** crash course

intenter [ɛ̃tɑ̃te] /1/ *vt*: **~ un procès contre** *ou* **à qn** to start proceedings against sb

intention [ɛ̃tɑ̃sjɔ̃] *nf* intention; (*Jur*) intent; **avoir l'~ de faire** to intend to do; **à l'~ de** for; (*renseignement*) for the benefit *ou* information of; (*film, ouvrage*) aimed at; **à cette ~** with this aim in view; **intentionné, e** *adj*: **bien intentionné** well-meaning *ou* -intentioned; **mal intentionné** ill-intentioned

interactif, -ive [ɛ̃teʀaktif, -iv] *adj* (*aussi Inform*) interactive

intercepter [ɛ̃tɛʀsɛpte] /1/ *vt* to intercept; (*lumière, chaleur*) to cut off

interchangeable [ɛ̃tɛʀʃɑ̃ʒabl] *adj* interchangeable

interdiction [ɛ̃tɛʀdiksjɔ̃] *nf* ban; **~ de fumer** no smoking

interdire [ɛ̃tɛʀdiʀ] /37/ *vt* to forbid; (*Admin*) to ban, prohibit; (: *journal, livre*) to ban; **~ à qn de faire** to forbid sb to do; (*empêchement*) to prevent *ou* preclude sb from doing

interdit, e [ɛ̃tɛʀdi, -it] *pp de* **interdire** ▷ *adj* (*stupéfait*) taken aback; **film ~ aux moins de 18/12 ans** ≈ 18-/12A-rated film; **stationnement ~** no parking

intéressant, e [ɛ̃teʀesɑ̃, -ɑ̃t] *adj* interesting; (*avantageux*) attractive

intéressé, e [ɛ̃teʀese] *adj* (*parties*) involved, concerned; (*amitié, motifs*) self-interested

intéresser [ɛ̃teʀese] /1/ *vt* (*captiver*) to interest; (*toucher*) to be of interest *ou* concern to; (*Admin: concerner*) to affect, concern; **s'intéresser à** *vi* to take an interest in

intérêt [ɛ̃teʀe] *nm* interest; (*égoïsme*) self-interest; **tu as ~ à accepter** it's in your interest to accept; **tu as ~ à te dépêcher** you'd better hurry

intérieur, e [ɛ̃teʀjœʀ] *adj* (*mur, escalier, poche*) inside; (*commerce, politique*) domestic; (*cour, calme, vie*) inner; (*navigation*) inland ▷ *nm* (*d'une maison, d'un récipient etc*) inside; (*d'un pays, aussi décor, mobilier*) interior; **l'I~** (the Department of) the Interior, ≈ the Home Office (*BRIT*); **à l'~ (de)** inside; **intérieurement** *adv* inwardly

intérim [ɛ̃teʀim] *nm* interim period; **assurer l'~ (de)** to deputize (for); **président par ~** interim president; **faire de l'~** to temp

intérimaire [ɛ̃teʀimɛʀ] *adj* (*directeur, ministre*) acting; (*secrétaire, personnel*) temporary ▷ *nm/f* (*secrétaire etc*) temporary, temp (*BRIT*)

interlocuteur, -trice [ɛ̃tɛʀlɔkytœʀ, -tʀis] *nm/f* speaker; **son ~** the person he *ou* she was speaking to

intermédiaire [ɛ̃tɛʀmedjɛʀ] *adj* intermediate; (*solution*) temporary ▷ *nm/f* intermediary; (*Comm*) middleman; **sans ~** directly; **par l'~ de** through

interminable [ɛ̃tɛʀminabl] *adj* never-ending

intermittence [ɛ̃tɛʀmitɑ̃s] *nf*: **par ~** intermittently, sporadically

internat [ɛ̃tɛʀna] *nm* boarding school

international, e, -aux [ɛ̃tɛʀnasjɔnal, -o] *adj*, *nm/f* international

internaute [ɛ̃tɛʀnot] *nm/f* Internet user

interne [ɛ̃tɛʀn] *adj* internal ▷ *nm/f* (*Scol*) boarder; (*Méd*) houseman

Internet [ɛ̃tɛʀnɛt] *nm*: **l'~** the Internet

interpeller [ɛ̃tɛʀpele] /1/ *vt* (*appeler*) to call out to; (*apostropher*) to shout at; (*Police*) to take in for questioning; (*Pol*) to question; (*concerner*) to concern

interphone [ɛ̃tɛʀfɔn] *nm* intercom; (*d'immeuble*) entry phone

interposer [ɛ̃tɛʀpoze] /1/ vt;
s'interposer to intervene; **par
personnes interposées** through a
third party
interprète [ɛ̃tɛʀpʀɛt] nm/f
interpreter; (porte-parole) spokesman
interpréter [ɛ̃tɛʀpʀete] /6/ vt to
interpret; (jouer) to play; (chanter)
to sing
interrogatif, -ive [ɛ̃teʀɔgatif, -iv]
adj (Ling) interrogative
interrogation [ɛ̃teʀɔgasjɔ̃] nf
question; (Scol) (written ou oral) test
interrogatoire [ɛ̃teʀɔgatwaʀ] nm
(Police) questioning no pl; (Jur, aussi fig)
cross-examination
interroger [ɛ̃teʀɔʒe] /3/ vt to
question; (Inform) to search; (Scol)
to test
interrompre [ɛ̃teʀɔ̃pʀ] /41/ vt (gén)
to interrupt; (négociations) to break
off; (match) to stop; **s'interrompre** to
break off; **interrupteur** nm switch;
interruption nf interruption; (pause)
break; **sans interruption** without a
break; **interruption volontaire de
grossesse** abortion
intersection [ɛ̃tɛʀsɛksjɔ̃] nf
intersection
intervalle [ɛ̃tɛʀval] nm (espace)
space; (de temps) interval; **dans l'~** in
the meantime; **à deux jours d'~** two
days apart
intervenir [ɛ̃tɛʀvəniʀ] /22/ vi (gén)
to intervene; **~ auprès de/en faveur
de qn** to intervene with/on behalf
of sb; **intervention** nf intervention;
(discours) speech; **intervention
(chirurgicale)** operation
interview [ɛ̃tɛʀvju] nf interview
intestin, e [ɛ̃tɛstɛ̃, -in] adj internal
▷ nm intestine
intime [ɛ̃tim] adj intimate; (vie,
journal) private; (convictions) inmost;
(dîner, cérémonie) quiet ▷ nm/f close
friend; **un journal ~** a diary
intimider [ɛ̃timide] /1/ vt to
intimidate

intimité [ɛ̃timite] nf: **dans l'~** in
private; (sans formalités) with only a
few friends, quietly
intolérable [ɛ̃tɔleʀabl] adj
intolerable
intox [ɛ̃tɔks] (fam) nf brainwashing
intoxication [ɛ̃tɔksikasjɔ̃] nf: **~
alimentaire** food poisoning
intoxiquer [ɛ̃tɔksike] /1/ vt to
poison; (fig) to brainwash
intraitable [ɛ̃tʀɛtabl] adj inflexible,
uncompromising
intransigeant, e [ɛ̃tʀɑ̃ziʒɑ̃, -ɑ̃t] adj
intransigent
intrépide [ɛ̃tʀepid] adj dauntless
intrigue [ɛ̃tʀig] nf (scénario) plot;
intriguer /1/ vt to puzzle, intrigue
introduction [ɛ̃tʀɔdyksjɔ̃] nf
introduction
introduire [ɛ̃tʀɔdɥiʀ] /38/ vt to
introduce; (visiteur) to show in;
(aiguille, clef): **~ qch dans** to insert
ou introduce sth into; **s'introduire** vi
(techniques, usages) to be introduced;
s'~ dans to gain entry into; (dans un
groupe) to get o.s. accepted into
introuvable [ɛ̃tʀuvabl] adj
which cannot be found; (Comm)
unobtainable
intrus, e [ɛ̃tʀy, -yz] nm/f intruder
intuition [ɛ̃tɥisjɔ̃] nf intuition
inusable [inyzabl] adj hard-wearing
inutile [inytil] adj useless; (superflu)
unnecessary; **inutilement** adv
needlessly; **inutilisable** adj unusable
invalide [ɛ̃valid] adj disabled ▷ nm/f:
~ de guerre disabled ex-serviceman
invariable [ɛ̃vaʀjabl] adj invariable
invasion [ɛ̃vazjɔ̃] nf invasion
inventaire [ɛ̃vɑ̃tɛʀ] nm inventory;
(Comm: liste) stocklist; (: opération)
stocktaking no pl
inventer [ɛ̃vɑ̃te] /1/ vt to invent;
(subterfuge) to devise, invent;
(histoire, excuse) to make up, invent;
inventeur, -trice nm/f inventor;
inventif, -ive adj inventive;
invention nf invention

inverse [ɛ̃vɛʀs] *adj* opposite ▷ *nm*
inverse; **l'~** the opposite; **dans
l'ordre ~** in the reverse order; **dans le
sens ~ des aiguilles d'une montre**
anti-clockwise; **en sens ~** in (*ou* from)
the opposite direction; **inversement**
adv conversely; **inverser** /1/ *vt* to
reverse, invert; (*Élec*) to reverse

investir [ɛ̃vɛstiʀ] /2/ *vt* to invest;
~ qn de (*d'une fonction, d'un pouvoir*)
to vest *ou* invest sb with; **s'investir**
vi (*Psych*) to involve o.s.; **s'~ dans** to
put a lot into; **investissement** *nm*
investment

invisible [ɛ̃vizibl] *adj* invisible
invitation [ɛ̃vitasjɔ̃] *nf* invitation
invité, e [ɛ̃vite] *nm/f* guest
inviter [ɛ̃vite] /1/ *vt* to invite; **~ qn à
faire qch** to invite sb to do sth
invivable [ɛ̃vivabl] *adj* unbearable
involontaire [ɛ̃vɔlɔ̃tɛʀ] *adj*
(*mouvement*) involuntary; (*insulte*)
unintentional; (*complice*) unwitting
invoquer [ɛ̃vɔke] /1/ *vt* (*Dieu, muse*)
to call upon, invoke; (*prétexte*) to put
forward (as an excuse); (*loi, texte*)
to refer to
invraisemblable [ɛ̃vʀɛsɑ̃blabl] *adj*
(*fait, nouvelle*) unlikely, improbable;
(*bizarre*) incredible
iode [jɔd] *nm* iodine
irai *etc* [iʀe] *vb voir* **aller**
Irak [iʀak] *nm*: **l'~** Iraq *ou* Irak;
irakien, ne *adj* Iraqi ▷ *nm/f*: **Irakien,
ne** Iraqi
Iran [iʀɑ̃] *nm*: **l'~** Iran; **iranien, ne** *adj*
Iranian ▷ *nm/f*: **Iranien, ne** Iranian
irions *etc* [iʀjɔ̃] *vb voir* **aller**
iris [iʀis] *nm* iris
irlandais, e [iʀlɑ̃dɛ, -ɛz] *adj* Irish
▷ *nm/f*: **I~, e** Irishman/woman
Irlande [iʀlɑ̃d] *nf*: **l'~** Ireland; **la
République d'~** the Irish Republic;
~ du Nord Northern Ireland; **la mer
d'~** the Irish Sea
ironie [iʀɔni] *nf* irony; **ironique** *adj*
ironical; **ironiser** /1/ *vi* to be ironical
irons *etc* [iʀɔ̃] *vb voir* **aller**

irradier [iʀadje] /7/ *vt* to irradiate
irraisonné, e [iʀezɔne] *adj* irrational
irrationnel, le [iʀasjɔnɛl] *adj*
irrational
irréalisable [iʀealizabl] *adj*
unrealizable; (*projet*) impracticable
irrécupérable [iʀekypeʀabl] *adj*
beyond repair; (*personne*) beyond
redemption *ou* recall
irréel, le [iʀeɛl] *adj* unreal
irréfléchi, e [iʀefleʃi] *adj*
thoughtless
irrégularité [iʀegylaʀite] *nf*
irregularity; (*de travail, d'effort, de
qualité*) unevenness *no pl*
irrégulier, -ière [iʀegylje, -jɛʀ]
adj irregular; (*travail, effort, qualité*)
uneven; (*élève, athlète*) erratic
irrémédiable [iʀemedjabl] *adj*
irreparable
irremplaçable [iʀɑ̃plasabl] *adj*
irreplaceable
irréparable [iʀepaʀabl] *adj* beyond
repair; (*fig*) irreparable
irréprochable [iʀepʀɔʃabl] *adj*
irreproachable, beyond reproach;
(*tenue, toilette*) impeccable
irrésistible [iʀezistibl] *adj*
irresistible; (*preuve, logique*)
compelling; (*amusant*) hilarious
irrésolu, e [iʀezɔly] *adj* irresolute
irrespectueux, -euse [iʀɛspɛktɥø,
-øz] *adj* disrespectful
irresponsable [iʀɛspɔ̃sabl] *adj*
irresponsible
irriguer [iʀige] /1/ *vt* to irrigate
irritable [iʀitabl] *adj* irritable
irriter [iʀite] /1/ *vt* to irritate
irruption [iʀypsjɔ̃] *nf*: **faire ~ chez
qn** to burst in on sb
Islam [islam] *nm*: **l'~** Islam;
islamique *adj* Islamic; **islamophobie**
nf Islamophobia
Islande [islɑ̃d] *nf*: **l'~** Iceland
isolant, e [izɔlɑ̃, -ɑ̃t] *adj* insulating;
(*insonorisant*) soundproofing
isolation [izɔlasjɔ̃] *nf* insulation;
~ acoustique soundproofing

isolé, e [izɔle] *adj* isolated; *(contre le froid)* insulated

isoler [izɔle] /1/ *vt* to isolate; *(prisonnier)* to put in solitary confinement; *(ville)* to cut off, isolate; *(contre le froid)* to insulate; **s'isoler** *vi* to isolate o.s.

Israël [israɛl] *nm*: **l'~** Israel; **israélien, ne** *adj* Israeli ▷ *nm/f*: **Israélien, ne** Israeli; **israélite** *adj* Jewish ▷ *nm/f*: **Israélite** Jew/Jewess

issu, e [isy] *adj*: **~ de** *(né de)* descended from; *(résultant de)* stemming from ▷ *nf (ouverture, sortie)* exit; *(solution)* way out, solution; *(dénouement)* outcome; **à l'~e de** at the conclusion *ou* close of; **voie sans ~e** dead end; **~e de secours** emergency exit

Italie [itali] *nf*: **l'~** Italy; **italien, ne** *adj* Italian ▷ *nm (Ling)* Italian ▷ *nm/f*: **Italien, ne** Italian

italique [italik] *nm*: **en ~(s)** in italics

itinéraire [itineʀɛʀ] *nm* itinerary, route; **~ bis** alternative route

IUT *sigle m* = **Institut universitaire de technologie**

IVG *sigle f* (= *interruption volontaire de grossesse*) abortion

ivoire [ivwaʀ] *nm* ivory

ivre [ivʀ] *adj* drunk; **~ de** *(colère)* wild with; **ivrogne** *nm/f* drunkard

J

j' [ʒ] *pron voir* **je**

jacinthe [ʒasɛ̃t] *nf* hyacinth

jadis [ʒadis] *adv* formerly

jaillir [ʒajiʀ] /2/ *vi (liquide)* to spurt out; *(cris, réponses)* to burst out

jais [ʒɛ] *nm* jet; **(d'un noir) de ~** jet-black

jalousie [ʒaluzi] *nf* jealousy; *(store)* (venetian) blind

jaloux, -ouse [ʒalu, -uz] *adj* jealous; **être ~ de qn/qch** to be jealous of sb/sth

jamaïquain, e [ʒamaikɛ̃, -ɛn] *adj* Jamaican ▷ *nm/f*: **J~, e** Jamaican

Jamaïque [ʒamaik] *nf*: **la ~** Jamaica

jamais [ʒamɛ] *adv* never; *(sans négation)* ever; **ne ... ~** never; **si ~ ...** if ever ...; **je ne suis ~ allé en Espagne** I've never been to Spain

jambe [ʒɑ̃b] *nf* leg

jambon [ʒɑ̃bɔ̃] *nm* ham

jante [ʒɑ̃t] *nf (wheel)* rim

janvier [ʒɑ̃vje] *nm* January

Japon [ʒapɔ̃] nm: **le ~** Japan;
japonais, e adj Japanese ▷ nm (Ling)
Japanese ▷ nm/f: **Japonais, e** Japanese
jardin [ʒaʀdɛ̃] nm garden; **~
d'enfants** nursery school; **jardinage**
nm gardening; **jardiner** /1/ vi
to garden; **jardinier, -ière** nm/f
gardener ▷ nf (de fenêtre) window
box; **jardinière (de légumes)** (Culin)
mixed vegetables
jargon [ʒaʀɡɔ̃] nm (charabia)
gibberish; (publicitaire, scientifique
etc) jargon
jarret [ʒaʀɛ] nm back of knee; (Culin)
knuckle, shin
jauge [ʒoʒ] nf (instrument) gauge;
~ (de niveau) d'huile (Auto) dipstick
jaune [ʒon] adj, nm yellow ▷ adv
(fam): **rire ~** to laugh on the other
side of one's face; **~ d'œuf** (egg)
yolk; **jaunir** /2/ vi, vt to turn yellow;
jaunisse nf jaundice
Javel [ʒavɛl] nf voir **eau**
javelot [ʒavlo] nm javelin
J.-C. sigle m = **Jésus-Christ**
je, j' [ʒə, ʒ] pron I
jean [dʒin] nm jeans pl
Jésus-Christ [ʒezykʀi(st)] n Jesus
Christ; **600 avant/après ~** 600
B.C./A.D.
jet [ʒɛ] nm (lancer: action) throwing
no pl; (: résultat) throw; (jaillissement:
d'eaux) jet; (: de sang) spurt; **~ d'eau**
spray
jetable [ʒətabl] adj disposable
jetée [ʒəte] nf jetty; (grande) pier
jeter [ʒəte] /4/ vt (gén) to throw;
(se défaire de) to throw away ou out;
~ qch à qn to throw sth to sb; (de
façon agressive) to throw sth at sb;
~ un coup d'œil (à) to take a look
(at); **~ un sort à qn** to cast a spell on
sb; **se ~ sur** to throw o.s. onto; **se ~
dans** (fleuve) to flow into
jeton [ʒətɔ̃] nm (au jeu) counter
jette etc [ʒɛt] vb voir **jeter**
jeu, x [ʒø] nm (divertissement, Tech:
d'une pièce) play; (Tennis: partie,

Football etc: façon de jouer) game;
(Théât etc) acting; (série d'objets, jouet)
set; (Cartes) hand; (au casino): **le ~**
gambling; **en ~** at stake; **remettre
en ~** to throw in; **entrer/mettre en ~**
to come/bring into play; **~ de cartes**
pack of cards; **~ d'échecs** chess set;
~ de hasard game of chance; **~ de
mots** pun; **~ de société** board game;
~ télévisé television quiz; **~ vidéo**
video game
jeudi [ʒødi] nm Thursday
jeun [ʒœ̃]: **à ~** adv on an empty
stomach; **être à ~** to have eaten
nothing; **rester à ~** not to eat
anything
jeune [ʒœn] adj young; **les ~s** young
people; **~ fille** girl; **~ homme** young
man; **~s gens** young people
jeûne [ʒøn] nm fast
jeunesse [ʒœnɛs] nf youth; (aspect)
youthfulness
joaillier, -ière [ʒoaje, -jɛʀ] nm/f
jeweller
jogging [dʒɔɡiŋ] nm jogging;
(survêtement) tracksuit; **faire du ~**
to go jogging
joie [ʒwa] nf joy
joindre [ʒwɛ̃dʀ] /49/ vt to join;
(contacter) to contact, get in touch
with; **~ qch à** (à une lettre) to enclose
sth with; **~ un fichier à un mail**
(Inform) to attach a file to an email;
se ~ à qn to join sb; **se ~ à qch** to
join in sth
joint, e [ʒwɛ̃, -ɛ̃t] adj: **~ (à)** (lettre,
paquet) attached (to), enclosed
(with) ▷ nm joint; (ligne) join; **pièce
~e** (de lettre) enclosure; (de mail)
attachment; **~ de culasse** cylinder
head gasket
joli, e [ʒɔli] adj pretty, attractive; **une
~e somme/situation** a nice little
sum/situation; **c'est du ~!** (ironique)
that's very nice!; **tout ça, c'est bien
~ mais ...** that's all very well but ...
jonc [ʒɔ̃] nm (bul)rush
jonction [ʒɔ̃ksjɔ̃] nf junction

jongleur, -euse [ʒɔ̃glœʀ, -øz] nm/f
juggler

jonquille [ʒɔ̃kij] nf daffodil

Jordanie [ʒɔʀdani] nf: **la ~** Jordan

joue [ʒu] nf cheek

jouer [ʒwe] /1/ vt to play; (somme
d'argent, réputation) to stake, wager;
(simuler: sentiment) to affect, feign
▷ vi to play; (Théât, Ciné) to act; (au
casino) to gamble; (bois, porte: se
voiler) to warp; (clef, pièce: avoir du jeu)
to be loose; **~ sur** (miser) to gamble
on; **~ de** (Mus) to play; **~ à** (jeu, sport,
roulette) to play; **~ un tour à qn** to
play a trick on sb; **~ la comédie** to
put on an act; **~ serré** to play a close
game; **à toi/nous de ~** it's your/our
go ou turn; **bien joué!** well done!; **on
joue Hamlet au théâtre X** Hamlet is
on at the X theatre

jouet [ʒwɛ] nm toy; **être le ~ de**
(illusion etc) to be the victim of

joueur, -euse [ʒwœʀ, -øz] nm/f
player; **être beau/mauvais ~** to be a
good/bad loser

jouir [ʒwiʀ] /2/ vi (sexe: fam) to come
▷ vt: **~ de** to enjoy

jour [ʒuʀ] nm day; (opposé à la nuit)
day, daytime; (clarté) daylight; (fig:
aspect, ouverture) opening; **sous un ~
favorable/nouveau** in a favourable/
new light; **de ~** (crème, service) day cpd;
travailler de ~ to work during the
day; **voyager de ~** to travel by day; **au
~ le ~** from day to day; **de nos ~s** these
days; **du ~ au lendemain** overnight;
il fait ~ it's daylight; **au grand ~** (fig)
in the open; **mettre au ~** to disclose;
mettre à ~ to bring up to date;
donner le ~ à to give birth to; **voir le
~** to be born; **~ férié** public holiday; **le
~ J** D-day; **~ ouvrable** working day

journal, -aux [ʒuʀnal, -o] nm
(news)paper; (personnel) journal;
(intime) diary; **~ de bord** log; **~ parlé/
télévisé** radio/television news sg

journalier, -ière [ʒuʀnalje, -jɛʀ] adj
daily; (banal) everyday

journalisme [ʒuʀnalism] nm
journalism; **journaliste** nm/f
journalist

journée [ʒuʀne] nf day; **la ~
continue** the 9 to 5 working day
(with short lunch break)

joyau, x [ʒwajo] nm gem, jewel

joyeux, -euse [ʒwajø, -øz] adj joyful,
merry; **~ Noël!** Merry ou Happy
Christmas!; **~ anniversaire!** many
happy returns!

jubiler [ʒybile] /1/ vi to be jubilant,
exult

judas [ʒyda] nm (trou) spy-hole

judiciaire [ʒydisjɛʀ] adj judicial

judicieux, -euse [ʒydisjø, -øz] adj
judicious

judo [ʒydo] nm judo

juge [ʒyʒ] nm judge; **~ d'instruction**
examining (BRIT) ou committing
(US) magistrate; **~ de paix** justice
of the peace

jugé [ʒyʒe] nm: **au ~** adv by guesswork

jugement [ʒyʒmɑ̃] nm judgment;
(Jur: au pénal) sentence; (: au civil)
decision

juger [ʒyʒe] /3/ vt to judge;
(estimer) to consider; **~ qn/qch
satisfaisant** to consider sb/sth (to
be) satisfactory; **~ bon de faire** to
consider it a good idea to do

juif, -ive [ʒɥif, -iv] adj Jewish
▷ nm/f: **J~, -ive** Jewish man/woman
ou Jew

juillet [ʒɥijɛ] nm July

LE 14 JUILLET

- Le 14 juillet is a national holiday in
- France and commemorates the
- storming of the Bastille during the
- French Revolution. Throughout
- the country there are celebrations,
- which feature parades, music,
- dancing and firework displays. In
- Paris a military parade along the
- Champs-Élysées is attended by the
- President.

juin [ʒɥɛ̃] nm June
jumeau, -elle, x [ʒymo, -ɛl] adj, nm/f twin
jumeler [ʒymle] /4/ vt to twin
jumelle [ʒymɛl] adj f, nf voir **jumeau**
jument [ʒymɑ̃] nf mare
jungle [ʒɔ̃gl] nf jungle
jupe [ʒyp] nf skirt
jupon [ʒypɔ̃] nm waist slip ou petticoat
juré, e [ʒyʀe] nm/f juror ▷ adj: **ennemi ~** sworn ou avowed enemy
jurer [ʒyʀe] /1/ vt (obéissance etc) to swear, vow ▷ vi (dire des jurons) to swear, curse; (dissoner): **~ (avec)** to clash (with); **~ de faire/que** to swear ou vow to do/that; **~ de qch** (s'en porter garant) to swear to sth
juridique [ʒyʀidik] adj legal
juron [ʒyʀɔ̃] nm curse, swearword
jury [ʒyʀi] nm jury; (Art, Sport) panel of judges; (Scol) board (of examiners), jury
jus [ʒy] nm juice; (de viande) gravy, (meat) juice; **~ de fruits** fruit juice
jusque [ʒysk]: **jusqu'à** prép (endroit) as far as, (up) to; (moment) until, till; (limite) up to; **~ sur/dans** up to; (y compris) even on/in; **jusqu'à ce que** until; **jusqu'à présent** ou **maintenant** so far; **jusqu'où?** how far?
justaucorps [ʒystokɔʀ] nm inv leotard
juste [ʒyst] adj (équitable) just, fair; (légitime) just; (exact, vrai) right; (pertinent) apt; (étroit) tight; (insuffisant) on the short side ▷ adv right; (chanter) in tune; (seulement) just; **~ assez/au-dessus** just enough/above; **pouvoir tout ~ faire** to be only just able to do; **au ~** exactly; **le ~ milieu** the happy medium; **c'était ~** it was a close thing; **justement** adv justly; (précisément) just, precisely; **justesse** nf (précision) accuracy; (d'une remarque) aptness; (d'une opinion) soundness; **de justesse** only just

justice [ʒystis] nf (équité) fairness, justice; (Admin) justice; **rendre ~ à qn** to do sb justice
justificatif, -ive [ʒystifikatif, -iv] adj (document etc) supporting; **pièce justificative** written proof
justifier [ʒystifje] /7/ vt to justify; **~ de** to prove
juteux, -euse [ʒytø, -øz] adj juicy
juvénile [ʒyvenil] adj youthful

K [kɑ] *nm inv* K

kaki [kaki] *adj inv* khaki

kangourou [kɑ̃guʀu] *nm* kangaroo

karaté [kaʀate] *nm* karate

kascher [kaʃɛʀ] *adj inv* kosher

kayak [kajak] *nm* kayak; **faire du ~** to go kayaking

képi [kepi] *nm* kepi

kermesse [kɛʀmɛs] *nf* bazaar, (charity) fête; village fair

kidnapper [kidnape] /1/ *vt* to kidnap

kilo [kilo] *nm* kilo; **kilogramme** *nm* kilogramme; **kilométrage** *nm* number of kilometres travelled, ≈ mileage; **kilomètre** *nm* kilometre; **kilométrique** *adj* (*distance*) in kilometres

kinésithérapeute [kineziteʀapøt] *nm/f* physiotherapist

kiosque [kjɔsk] *nm* kiosk, stall

kir [kiʀ] *nm* kir (*white wine with blackcurrant liqueur*)

kit [kit] *nm* kit; **~ piéton** *ou* **mains libres** hands-free kit; **en ~** in kit form

kiwi [kiwi] *nm* kiwi

klaxon [klaksɔn] *nm* horn; **klaxonner** /1/ *vi, vt* to hoot (*BRIT*), honk (one's horn) (*US*)

km *abr* (= *kilomètre*) km

km/h *abr* (= *kilomètres/heure*) km/h, kph

K.-O. *adj inv* shattered, knackered

Kosovo [kɔsɔvo] *nm*: **le ~** Kosovo

Koweit, Kuweit [kɔwɛt] *nm*: **le ~** Kuwait

k-way® [kawɛ] *nm* (lightweight nylon) cagoule

kyste [kist] *nm* cyst

l' [l] *art déf voir* **le**

la [la] *art déf voir* **le** ▷ *nm (Mus)* A; *(en chantant la gamme)* la

là [la] *adv* there; *(ici)* here; *(dans le temps)* then; **elle n'est pas là** she isn't here; **c'est là que** this is where; **là où** where; **de là** *(fig)* hence; **par là** *(fig)* by that; *voir aussi* **-ci; celui; là-bas** *adv* there

labo [labo] *nm (= laboratoire)* lab

laboratoire [laboratwar] *nm* laboratory; **~ de langues/d'analyses** language-/(medical) analysis laboratory

laborieux, -euse [laborjø, -øz] *adj (tâche)* laborious

labourer /1/ *vt* to plough

labyrinthe [labiʀɛ̃t] *nm* labyrinth, maze

lac [lak] *nm* lake

lacet [lasɛ] *nm (de chaussure)* lace; *(de route)* sharp bend; *(piège)* snare

lâche [lɑʃ] *adj (poltron)* cowardly; *(desserré)* loose, slack ▷ *nm/f* coward

lâcher [lɑʃe] /1/ *vt* to let go of; *(ce qui tombe, abandonner)* to drop; *(oiseau, animal: libérer)* to release, set free; *(fig: mot, remarque)* to let slip, come out with ▷ *vi (freins)* to fail; **~ les amarres** *(Navig)* to cast off (the moorings); **~ prise** to let go

lacrymogène [lakrimɔʒɛn] *adj*: **grenade/gaz ~** tear gas grenade/tear gas

lacune [lakyn] *nf* gap

là-dedans [ladədɑ̃] *adv* inside (there), in it; *(fig)* in that

là-dessous [ladsu] *adv* underneath, under there; *(fig)* behind that

là-dessus [ladsy] *adv* on there; *(fig: sur ces mots)* at that point; *(: à ce sujet)* about that

ladite [ladit] *adj f voir* **ledit**

lagune [lagyn] *nf* lagoon

là-haut [lao] *adv* up there

laid, e [lɛ, lɛd] *adj* ugly; **laideur** *nf* ugliness *no pl*

lainage [lɛnaʒ] *nm (vêtement)* woollen garment; *(étoffe)* woollen material

laine [lɛn] *nf* wool

laïque [laik] *adj* lay, civil; *(Scol)* state *cpd (as opposed to private and Roman Catholic)* ▷ *nm/f* layman(-woman)

laisse [lɛs] *nf (de chien)* lead, leash; **tenir en ~** to keep on a lead *ou* leash

laisser [lese] /1/ *vt* to leave ▷ *vb aux*: **~ qn faire** to let sb do; **se ~ aller** to let o.s. go; **laisse-toi faire** let me *(ou* him) do it; **laisser-aller** *nm* carelessness, slovenliness; **laissez-passer** *nm inv* pass

lait [lɛ] *nm* milk; **frère/sœur de ~** foster brother/sister; **~ écrémé/entier/concentré/condensé** skimmed/full-fat/condensed/evaporated milk; **laitage** *nm* dairy product; **laiterie** *nf* dairy; **laitier, -ière** *adj* dairy *cpd* ▷ *nm/f* milkman (dairywoman)

laiton [lɛtɔ̃] *nm* brass

laitue [lety] *nf* lettuce

lambeau, x [lãbo] *nm* scrap; **en ~x** in tatters, tattered

lame [lam] *nf* blade; (*vague*) wave; (*lamelle*) strip; **~ de fond** ground swell *no pl*; **~ de rasoir** razor blade; **lamelle** *nf* small blade

lamentable [lamãtabl] *adj* appalling

lamenter [lamãte] /1/: **se lamenter** *vi*: **se ~ (sur)** to moan (over)

lampadaire [lãpadɛʀ] *nm* (*de salon*) standard lamp; (*dans la rue*) street lamp

lampe [lãp] *nf* lamp; (*Tech*) valve; **~ à pétrole** oil lamp; **~ à bronzer** sunlamp; **~ de poche** torch (BRIT), flashlight (US); **~ halogène** halogen lamp

lance [lãs] *nf* spear; **~ d'incendie** fire hose

lancée [lãse] *nf*: **être/continuer sur sa ~** to be under way/keep going

lancement [lãsmã] *nm* launching *no pl*

lance-pierres [lãspjɛʀ] *nm inv* catapult

lancer [lãse] /3/ *nm* (*Sport*) throwing *no pl*, throw ▷ *vt* to throw; (*émettre, projeter*) to throw out, send out; (*produit, fusée, bateau, artiste*) to launch; (*injure*) to hurl, fling; **se lancer** *vi* (*prendre de l'élan*) to build up speed; (*se précipiter*): **se ~ sur** *ou* **contre** to rush at; **~ du poids** putting the shot; **~ qch à qn** to throw sth to sb; (*de façon agressive*) to throw sth at sb; **~ un cri** *ou* **un appel** to shout *ou* call out; **se ~ dans** (*discussion*) to launch into; (*aventure*) to embark on

landau [lãdo] *nm* pram (BRIT), baby carriage (US)

lande [lãd] *nf* moor

langage [lãgaʒ] *nm* language

langouste [lãgust] *nf* crayfish *inv*; **langoustine** *nf* Dublin Bay prawn

langue [lãg] *nf* (*Anat, Culin*) tongue; (*Ling*) language; **tirer la ~ (à)** to stick out one's tongue (at); **de ~ française** French-speaking; **~ maternelle** native language, mother tongue; **~s vivantes** modern languages

langueur [lãgœʀ] *nf* languidness

languir [lãgiʀ] /2/ *vi* to languish; (*conversation*) to flag; **faire ~ qn** to keep sb waiting

lanière [lanjɛʀ] *nf* (*de fouet*) lash; (*de valise, bretelle*) strap

lanterne [lãtɛʀn] *nf* (*portable*) lantern; (*électrique*) light, lamp; (*de voiture*) (side)light

laper [lape] /1/ *vt* to lap up

lapidaire [lapidɛʀ] *adj* (*fig*) terse

lapin [lapɛ̃] *nm* rabbit; (*peau*) rabbitskin; (*fourrure*) cony; **poser un ~ à qn** to stand sb up

Laponie [laponi] *nf*: **la ~** Lapland

laps [laps] *nm*: **~ de temps** space of time, time *no pl*

laque [lak] *nf* (*vernis*) lacquer; (*pour cheveux*) hair spray

laquelle [lakɛl] *pron voir* **lequel**

larcin [laʀsɛ̃] *nm* theft

lard [laʀ] *nm* (*graisse*) fat; (*bacon*) (streaky) bacon

lardon [laʀdõ] *nm* piece of chopped bacon

large [laʀʒ] *adj* wide; broad; (*fig*) generous ▷ *adv*: **calculer/voir ~** to allow extra/think big ▷ *nm* (*largeur*): **5 m de ~** = 5 m wide *ou* in width; (*mer*): **le ~** the open sea; **au ~ de** off; **~ d'esprit** broad-minded; **largement** *adv* widely; (*de loin*) greatly; (*amplement, au minimum*) easily; (*donner etc*) generously; **c'est largement suffisant** that's ample; **largesse** *nf* generosity; **largesses** *nfpl* (*dons*) liberalities; **largeur** *nf* (*qu'on mesure*) width; (*impression visuelle*) wideness, width; (*d'esprit*) broadness

larguer [laʀge] /1/ *vt* to drop; **~ les amarres** to cast off (the moorings)

larme [laʀm] *nf* tear; (*fig*): **une ~ de** a drop of; **en ~s** in tears; **larmoyer** /8/ *vi* (*yeux*) to water; (*se plaindre*) to whimper

larvé, e [laRve] *adj (fig)* latent
laryngite [laRɛ̃ʒit] *nf* laryngitis
las, lasse [lɑ, lɑs] *adj* weary
laser [lazɛR] *nm*: **(rayon) ~** laser (beam); **chaîne** *ou* **platine ~** compact disc (player); **disque ~** compact disc
lasse [lɑs] *adj f voir* **las**
lasser [lɑse] /1/ *vt* to weary, tire
latéral, e, -aux [lateRal, -o] *adj* side *cpd*, lateral
latin, e [latɛ̃, -in] *adj* Latin ▷ *nm (Ling)* Latin ▷ *nm/f*: **L~, e** Latin
latitude [latityd] *nf* latitude
lauréat, e [lɔRea, -at] *nm/f* winner
laurier [lɔRje] *nm (Bot)* laurel; *(Culin)* bay leaves *pl*
lavable [lavabl] *adj* washable
lavabo [lavabo] *nm* washbasin; **lavabos** *nmpl* toilet *sg*
lavage [lavaʒ] *nm* washing *no pl*, wash; **~ de cerveau** brainwashing *no pl*
lavande [lavɑ̃d] *nf* lavender
lave [lav] *nf* lava *no pl*
lave-linge [lavlɛ̃ʒ] *nm inv* washing machine
laver [lave] /1/ *vt* to wash; *(tache)* to wash off; **se laver** *vi* to have a wash, wash; **se ~ les mains/dents** to wash one's hands/clean one's teeth; **~ la vaisselle/le linge** to wash the dishes/clothes; **~ qn de** *(accusation)* to clear sb of; **laverie** *nf*: **laverie (automatique)** Launderette® *(BRIT)*, Laundromat® *(US)*; **lavette** *nf* dish cloth; *(fam)* drip; **laveur, -euse** *nm/f* cleaner; **lave-vaisselle** *nm inv* dishwasher; **lavoir** *nm* wash house; *(évier)* sink
laxatif, -ive [laksatif, -iv] *adj, nm* laxative
layette [lɛjɛt] *nf* layette

MOT-CLÉ

le, la, l' [lə, la, l] *(pl* **les***) art déf* **1** the; **le livre/la pomme/l'arbre** the book/the apple/the tree; **les étudiants** the students
2 *(noms abstraits)*: **le courage/ l'amour/la jeunesse** courage/ love/youth
3 *(indiquant la possession)*: **se casser la jambe** *etc* to break one's leg *etc*; **levez la main** put your hand up; **avoir les yeux gris/le nez rouge** to have grey eyes/a red nose
4 *(temps)*: **le matin/soir** in the morning/evening; mornings/ evenings; **le jeudi** *etc (d'habitude)* on Thursdays *etc*; *(ce jeudi-là etc)* on (the) Thursday
5 *(distribution, évaluation)* a, an; **trois euros le mètre/kilo** three euros a *ou* per metre/kilo; **le tiers/quart de** a third/quarter of
▶ *pron* **1** *(personne: mâle)* him; *(: femelle)* her; *(: pluriel)* them; **je le/ la/les vois** I can see him/her/them
2 *(animal, chose: singulier)* it; *(: pluriel)* them; **je le (ou la) vois** I can see it; **je les vois** I can see them
3 *(remplaçant une phrase)*: **je ne le savais pas** I didn't know (about it); **il était riche et ne l'est plus** he was once rich but no longer is

lécher [leʃe] /6/ *vt* to lick; *(laper: lait, eau)* to lick *ou* lap up; **se ~ les doigts/lèvres** to lick one's fingers/ lips; **lèche-vitrines** *nm inv*: **faire du lèche-vitrines** to go window-shopping
leçon [ləsɔ̃] *nf* lesson; **faire la ~ à** *(fig)* to give a lecture to; **~s de conduite** driving lessons; **~s particulières** private lessons *ou* tuition *sg (BRIT)*
lecteur, -trice [lɛktœR, -tRis] *nm/f* reader; *(d'université)* (foreign language) assistant ▷ *nm (Tech)*: **~ de cassettes** cassette player; **~ de disquette(s)** disk drive; **~ de CD/DVD** CD/DVD player; **~ MP3** MP3 player
lecture [lɛktyR] *nf* reading

Attention à ne pas traduire *lecture* par le mot anglais *lecture*.

ledit, ladite [lədit, lɑdit] (*mpl* **lesdits**, *fpl* **lesdites**) *adj* the aforesaid

légal, e, -aux [legal, -o] *adj* legal; **légaliser** /1/ *vt* to legalize; **légalité** *nf* legality

légendaire [leʒãdɛʀ] *adj* legendary

légende [leʒãd] *nf* (*mythe*) legend; (*de carte, plan*) key; (*de dessin*) caption

léger, -ère [leʒe, -ɛʀ] *adj* light; (*bruit, retard*) slight; (*superficiel*) thoughtless; (*volage*) free and easy; **à la légère** (*parler, agir*) rashly, thoughtlessly; **légèrement** *adv* (*s'habiller, bouger*) lightly; **légèrement plus grand** slightly bigger; **manger légèrement** to eat a light meal; **légèreté** *nf* lightness; (*d'une remarque*) flippancy

législatif, -ive [leʒislatif, -iv] *adj* legislative; **législatives** *nfpl* general election *sg*

légitime [leʒitim] *adj* (*Jur*) lawful, legitimate; (*fig*) rightful, legitimate; **en état de ~ défense** in self-defence

legs [lɛg] *nm* legacy

léguer [lege] /6/ *vt*: **~ qch à qn** (*Jur*) to bequeath sth to sb

légume [legym] *nm* vegetable; **~s verts** green vegetables; **~s secs** pulses

lendemain [lãdmɛ̃] *nm*: **le ~ the** next *ou* following day; **le ~ matin/ soir** the next *ou* following morning/ evening; **le ~ de** the day after

lent, e [lã, lãt] *adj* slow; **lentement** *adv* slowly; **lenteur** *nf* slowness *no pl*

lentille [lãtij] *nf* (*Optique*) lens *sg*; (*Bot*) lentil; **~s de contact** contact lenses

léopard [leɔpaʀ] *nm* leopard

lèpre [lɛpʀ] *nf* leprosy

 MOT-CLÉ

lequel, laquelle [ləkɛl, lakɛl] (*mpl* **lesquels**, *fpl* **lesquelles**) (*à + lequel* = **auquel**, *de + lequel* = **duquel** *etc*) *pron* **1** (*interrogatif*) which, which one; **lequel des deux?** which one?
2 (*relatif: personne: sujet*) who; (*: objet, après préposition*) whom; (*: chose*) which
▶ *adj*: **auquel cas** in which case

les [le] *art déf, pron voir* **le**

lesbienne [lɛsbjɛn] *nf* lesbian

lesdits, lesdites [ledi, ledit] *adj pl voir* **ledit**

léser [leze] /6/ *vt* to wrong

lésiner [lezine] /1/ *vi*: **ne pas ~ sur les moyens** (*pour mariage etc*) to push the boat out

lésion [lezjɔ̃] *nf* lesion, damage *no pl*

lessive [lesiv] *nf* (*poudre*) washing powder; (*linge*) washing *no pl*, wash; **lessiver** /1/ *vt* to wash; (*fam: fatiguer*) to tire out, exhaust

lest [lɛst] *nm* ballast

leste [lɛst] *adj* sprightly, nimble

lettre [lɛtʀ] *nf* letter; **lettres** *nfpl* (*étude, culture*) literature *sg*; (*Scol*) arts (subjects); **à la ~** literally; **en toutes ~s** in full; **~ piégée** letter bomb

leucémie [løsemi] *nf* leukaemia

 MOT-CLÉ

leur [lœʀ] *adj poss* their; **leur maison** their house; **leurs amis** their friends
▶ *pron* **1** (*objet indirect*) (to) them; **je leur ai dit la vérité** I told them the truth; **je le leur ai donné** I gave it to them, I gave them it
2 (*possessif*): **le (la) leur, les leurs** theirs

levain [ləvɛ̃] *nm* leaven

levé, e [ləve] *adj*: **être ~** to be up; **levée** *nf* (*Postes*) collection

lever [ləve] /5/ *vt* (*vitre, bras etc*) to raise; (*soulever de terre, supprimer: interdiction, siège*) to lift; (*impôts, armée*) to levy ▷ *vi* to rise ▷ *nm*: **au ~** on getting up; **se lever** *vi* to get up; (*soleil*) to rise; (*jour*) to break;

(*brouillard*) to lift; **ça va se ~** (*temps*) it's going to clear up; **~ du jour** daybreak; **~ de soleil** sunrise

levier [ləvje] *nm* lever

lèvre [lɛvʀ] *nf* lip

lévrier [levʀije] *nm* greyhound

levure [ləvyʀ] *nf* yeast; **~ chimique** baking powder

lexique [lɛksik] *nm* vocabulary, lexicon; (*glossaire*) vocabulary

lézard [lezaʀ] *nm* lizard

lézarde [lezaʀd] *nf* crack

liaison [ljɛzɔ̃] *nf* (*rapport*) connection; (*Rail, Aviat etc*) link; (*amoureuse*) affair; (*Culin, Phonétique*) liaison; **entrer/être en ~ avec** to get/be in contact with

liane [ljan] *nf* creeper

liasse [ljas] *nf* wad, bundle

Liban [libã] *nm*: **le ~** (the) Lebanon

libeller [libele] /1/ *vt* (*chèque, mandat*): **~ (au nom de)** to make out (to); (*lettre*) to word

libellule [libelyl] *nf* dragonfly

libéral, e, -aux [libeʀal, -o] *adj, nm/f* liberal; **les professions ~es** liberal professions

libérer [libeʀe] /6/ *vt* (*délivrer*) to free, liberate (*Psych*) to liberate; (*relâcher: prisonnier*) to discharge, release; (*gaz, cran d'arrêt*) to release; **se libérer** *vi* (*de rendez-vous*) to get out of previous engagements

liberté [libɛʀte] *nf* freedom; (*loisir*) free time; **libertés** *nfpl* (*privautés*) liberties; **mettre/être en ~** to set/ be free; **en ~ provisoire/surveillée/ conditionnelle** on bail/probation/ parole

libraire [libʀɛʀ] *nm/f* bookseller

librairie [libʀɛʀi] *nf* bookshop

Attention à ne pas traduire *librairie* par library.

libre [libʀ] *adj* free; (*route*) clear; (*place etc*) free; (*ligne*) not engaged; (*Scol*) non-state; **~ de qch/de faire** free from sth/to do; **~ arbitre** free will; **libre-échange** *nm* free trade; **libre-service** *nm inv* self-service store

Libye [libi] *nf*: **la ~** Libya

licence [lisɑ̃s] *nf* (*permis*) permit; (*diplôme*) (first) degree; (*liberté*) liberty; **licencié, e** *nm/f* (*Scol*): **licencié ès lettres/en droit** ≈ Bachelor of Arts/Law

licenciement [lisɑ̃simɑ̃] *nm* redundancy

licencier [lisɑ̃sje] /7/ *vt* (*renvoyer*) to dismiss; (*débaucher*) to make redundant

licite [lisit] *adj* lawful

lie [li] *nf* dregs *pl*, sediment

lié, e [lje] *adj*: **très ~ avec** very friendly with *ou* close to

Liechtenstein [liʃtɛnʃtajn] *nm*: **le ~** Liechtenstein

liège [ljɛʒ] *nm* cork

lien [ljɛ̃] *nm* (*corde, fig: affectif, culturel*) bond; (*rapport*) link, connection; **~ de parenté** family tie; **~ hypertexte** hyperlink

lier [lje] /7/ *vt* (*attacher*) to tie up; (*joindre*) to link up; (*fig: unir, engager*) to bind; **~ conversation (avec)** to strike up a conversation (with); **~ connaissance avec** to get to know

lierre [ljɛʀ] *nm* ivy

lieu, x [ljø] *nm* place; **lieux** *nmpl* (*locaux*) premises; (*endroit: d'un accident etc*) scene *sg*; **arriver/être sur les ~x** to arrive/be on the scene; **en premier ~** in the first place; **en dernier ~** lastly; **avoir ~** to take place; **tenir ~ de** to serve as; **donner ~ à** to give rise to; **au ~ de** instead of; **~ commun** commonplace; **lieu-dit** (*pl* **lieux-dits**) *nm* locality

lieutenant [ljøtnɑ̃] *nm* lieutenant

lièvre [ljɛvʀ] *nm* hare

ligament [ligamɑ̃] *nm* ligament

ligne [liɲ] *nf* (*gén*) line; (*Transports: liaison*) service; (*: trajet*) route; (*silhouette*) figure; **garder la ~** to keep one's figure; **en ~** (*Inform*) online; **entrer en ~ de compte** to be taken into account; **~ fixe** (*Tél*) landline

ligné, e [liɲe] *adj*: **papier ~** ruled paper ▷ *nf* line, lineage
ligoter [ligɔte] /1/ *vt* to tie up
ligue [lig] *nf* league
lilas [lila] *nm* lilac
limace [limas] *nf* slug
limande [limɑ̃d] *nf* dab
lime [lim] *nf* file; **~ à ongles** nail file; **limer** /1/ *vt* to file
limitation [limitasjɔ̃] *nf*: **~ de vitesse** speed limit
limite [limit] *nf* (*de terrain*) boundary; (*partie ou point extrême*) limit; **à la ~** (*au pire*) if the worst comes (*ou* came) to the worst; **vitesse/charge ~** maximum speed/load; **cas ~** borderline case; **date ~** deadline; **date ~ de vente/consommation** sell-by/best-before date; **limiter** /1/ *vt* (*restreindre*) to limit, restrict; (*délimiter*) to border; **limitrophe** *adj* border *cpd*
limoger [limɔʒe] /3/ *vt* to dismiss
limon [limɔ̃] *nm* silt
limonade [limɔnad] *nf* lemonade
lin [lɛ̃] *nm* (*tissu, toile*) linen
linceul [lɛ̃sœl] *nm* shroud
linge [lɛ̃ʒ] *nm* (*serviettes etc*) linen; (*aussi*: **~ de corps**) underwear; (*lessive*) washing; **lingerie** *nf* lingerie, underwear
lingot [lɛ̃go] *nm* ingot
linguistique [lɛ̃ɡɥistik] *adj* linguistic ▷ *nf* linguistics *sg*
lion, ne [ljɔ̃, ljɔn] *nm/f* lion (lioness); (*signe*) **le L~** Leo; **lionceau, x** *nm* lion cub
liqueur [likœʀ] *nf* liqueur
liquidation [likidasjɔ̃] *nf* (*vente*) sale, liquidation; (*Comm*) clearance (sale)
liquide [likid] *adj* liquid ▷ *nm* liquid; (*Comm*): **en ~** in ready money *ou* cash; **je n'ai pas de ~** I haven't got any cash; **liquider** /1/ *vt* to liquidate; (*Comm: articles*) to clear, sell off
lire [liʀ] /43/ *nf* (*monnaie*) lira ▷ *vt*, *vi* to read

lis *vb* [li] *voir* **lire** ▷ *nm* [lis] = **lys**
Lisbonne [lizbɔn] *n* Lisbon
liseuse [lizøz] *nf* e-reader
lisible [lizibl] *adj* legible
lisière [lizjɛʀ] *nf* (*de forêt*) edge
lisons [lizɔ̃] *vb voir* **lire**
lisse [lis] *adj* smooth
lisseur [li:sœʀ] *nf* straighteners
liste [list] *nf* list; **faire la ~ de** to list; **~ électorale** electoral roll; **~ de mariage** wedding (present) list; **listing** *nm* (*Inform*) printout
lit [li] *nm* bed; **petit ~, ~ à une place** single bed; **grand ~, ~ à deux places** double bed; **faire son ~** to make one's bed; **aller/se mettre au ~** to go to/get into bed; **~ de camp** camp bed; **~ d'enfant** cot (BRIT), crib (US)
literie [litʀi] *nf* bedding, bedclothes *pl*
litige [litiʒ] *nm* dispute
litre [litʀ] *nm* litre
littéraire [literɛʀ] *adj* literary ▷ *nm/f* arts student; **elle est très ~** she's very literary
littéral, e, -aux [literal, -o] *adj* literal
littérature [literatyʀ] *nf* literature
littoral, e, -aux [litɔral, -o] *nm* coast
livide [livid] *adj* livid, pallid
livraison [livʀɛzɔ̃] *nf* delivery
livre [livʀ] *nm* book ▷ *nf* (*poids, monnaie*) pound; **~ numérique** e-book; **~ de poche** paperback
livré, e [livʀe] *adj*: **~ à soi-même** left to oneself *ou* one's own devices
livrer [livʀe] /1/ *vt* (*Comm*) to deliver; (*otage, coupable*) to hand over; (*secret, information*) to give away; **se ~ à** (*se rendre*) to give o.s. up to; (*faire: pratiques, actes*) to indulge in; (*enquête*) to carry out
livret [livʀɛ] *nm* booklet; (*d'opéra*) libretto; **~ de caisse d'épargne** (savings) bank-book; **~ de famille** (official) family record book; **~ scolaire** (school) report book

livreur, -euse [livʀœʀ, -øz] nm/f
delivery boy ou man/girl ou woman
local, e, -aux [lɔkal, -o] adj local
▷ nm (salle) premises pl ▷ nmpl
premises; **localité** nf locality
locataire [lɔkatɛʀ] nm/f tenant; (de
chambre) lodger
location [lɔkasjɔ̃] nf (par le locataire)
renting; (par le propriétaire) renting
out, letting; (bureau) booking office;
"~ de voitures" "car hire (BRIT) ou
rental (US)"; **habiter en ~** to live in
rented accommodation; **prendre
une ~ (pour les vacances)** to rent a
house etc (for the holidays)

■ Attention à ne pas traduire
location par le mot anglais location.

locomotive [lɔkɔmɔtiv] nf
locomotive, engine
locution [lɔkysjɔ̃] nf phrase
loge [lɔʒ] nf (Théât: d'artiste) dressing
room; (: de spectateurs) box; (de
concierge, franc-maçon) lodge
logement [lɔʒmɑ̃] nm flat (BRIT),
apartment (US); accommodation no
pl (BRIT), accommodations pl (US);
(Pol, Admin): **le ~** housing
loger [lɔʒe] /3/ vt to accommodate
▷ vi to live; **se loger** vr: **trouver à
se ~** to find accommodation; **se ~
dans** (balle, flèche) to lodge itself in;
être logé, nourri to have board and
lodging; **logeur, -euse** nm/f
landlord (landlady)
logiciel [lɔʒisjɛl] nm piece of
software
logique [lɔʒik] adj logical ▷ nf logic
logo [lɔgo] nm logo
loi [lwa] nf law; **faire la ~** to lay down
the law
loin [lwɛ̃] adv far; (dans le temps: futur)
a long way off; (: passé) a long time
ago; **plus** ~ further; **~ de** far from;
~ d'ici a long way from here; **au ~**
far off; **de ~** from a distance; (fig: de
beaucoup) by far
lointain, e [lwɛ̃tɛ̃, -ɛn] adj faraway,
distant; (dans le futur, passé) distant;

(cause, parent) remote, distant ▷ nm:
dans le ~ in the distance
loir [lwaʀ] nm dormouse
Loire [lwaʀ] nf: **la ~** the Loire
loisir [lwaziʀ] nm: **heures de ~**
spare time; **loisirs** nmpl (temps libre)
leisure sg; (activités) leisure activities;
avoir le ~ de faire to have the time
ou opportunity to do; **(tout) à ~**
at leisure
londonien, ne [lɔ̃dɔnjɛ̃, -ɛn] adj
London cpd, of London ▷ nm/f: **L~,
ne** Londoner
Londres [lɔ̃dʀ] n London
long, longue [lɔ̃, lɔ̃g] adj long ▷ adv:
en savoir ~ to know a great deal
▷ nm: **de 3 m de ~** 3 m long, 3 m in
length; **ne pas faire ~ feu** not to last
long; **(tout) le ~ de** (all) along; **tout
au ~ de** (année, vie) throughout; **de
~ en large** (marcher) to and fro, up
and down
longer [lɔ̃ʒe] /3/ vt to go (ou walk
ou drive) along(side); (mur, route)
to border
longiligne [lɔ̃ʒiliɲ] adj long-limbed
longitude [lɔ̃ʒityd] nf longitude
longtemps [lɔ̃tɑ̃] adv (for) a long
time, (for) long; **avant ~** before
long; **pour/pendant ~** for a long
time; **mettre ~ à faire** to take a long
time to do; **il en a pour ~** he'll be a
long time
longue [lɔ̃g] adj f voir long ▷ nf: **à
la ~** in the end; **longuement** adv
(longtemps) for a long time; (en détail)
at length
longueur [lɔ̃gœʀ] nf length;
longueurs nfpl (fig: d'un film etc)
tedious parts; **en ~** lengthwise; **tirer
en ~** to drag on; **à ~ de journée** all
day long
loquet [lɔkɛ] nm latch
lorgner [lɔʀɲe] /1/ vt to eye; (fig) to
have one's eye on
lors [lɔʀ]: **~ de** prép (au moment de)
at the time of; (pendant) during;
~ même que even though

lorsque [lɔʀsk] *conj* when, as
losange [lozɑ̃ʒ] *nm* diamond
lot [lo] *nm* (*part*) share; (*de loterie*) prize; (*fig: destin*) fate, lot; (*Comm, Inform*) batch; **le gros ~** the jackpot
loterie [lɔtʀi] *nf* lottery
lotion [losjɔ̃] *nf* lotion; **~ après rasage** after-shave (lotion)
lotissement [lɔtismɑ̃] *nm* housing development; (*parcelle*) (building) plot, lot
loto [lɔto] *nm* lotto
lotte [lɔt] *nf* monkfish
louange [lwɑ̃ʒ] *nf*: **à la ~ de** in praise of; **louanges** *nfpl* praise *sg*
loubar(d) [lubaʀ] *nm* (*fam*) lout
louche [luʃ] *adj* shady, fishy, dubious ▷ *nf* ladle; **loucher** /1/ *vi* to squint
louer [lwe] /1/ *vt* (*maison: propriétaire*) to let, rent (out); (*: locataire*) to rent; (*voiture etc: entreprise*) to hire out (BRIT), rent (out); (*: locataire*) to hire (BRIT), rent; (*réserver*) to book; (*faire l'éloge de*) to praise; **"à ~"** "to let" (BRIT), "for rent" (US)
loup [lu] *nm* wolf; **jeune ~** young go-getter
loupe [lup] *nf* magnifying glass; **à la ~** in minute detail
louper [lupe] /1/ *vt* (*fam: manquer*) to miss; (*examen*) to flunk
lourd, e [luʀ, luʀd] *adj* heavy; (*chaleur, temps*) sultry; **~ de** (*menaces*) charged with; (*conséquences*) fraught with; **lourdaud, e** *adj* clumsy; **lourdement** *adv* heavily
loutre [lutʀ] *nf* otter
louveteau, x [luvto] *nm* wolf-cub; (*scout*) cub (scout)
louvoyer [luvwaje] /8/ *vi* (*fig*) to hedge, evade the issue
loyal, e, -aux [lwajal, -o] *adj* (*fidèle*) loyal, faithful; (*fair-play*) fair; **loyauté** *nf* loyalty, faithfulness; fairness
loyer [lwaje] *nm* rent
lu, e [ly] *pp de* **lire**
lubie [lybi] *nf* whim, craze
lubrifiant [lybʀifjɑ̃] *nm* lubricant

lubrifier [lybʀifje] /7/ *vt* to lubricate
lubrique [lybʀik] *adj* lecherous
lucarne [lykaʀn] *nf* skylight
lucide [lysid] *adj* lucid; (*accidenté*) conscious
lucratif, -ive [lykʀatif, -iv] *adj* lucrative; profitable; **à but non ~** non profit-making
lueur [lɥœʀ] *nf* (*chatoyante*) glimmer *no pl*; (*pâle*) (faint) light; (*fig*) glimmer, gleam
luge [lyʒ] *nf* sledge (BRIT), sled (US)
lugubre [lygybʀ] *adj* gloomy; dismal

MOT-CLÉ

lui [lɥi] *pron* **1** (*objet indirect: mâle*) (to) him; (*: femelle*) (to) her; (*: chose, animal*) (to) it; **je lui ai parlé** I have spoken to him (*ou* to her); **il lui a offert un cadeau** he gave him (*ou* her) a present
2 (*après préposition, comparatif: personne*) him; (*: chose, animal*) it; **elle est contente de lui** she is pleased with him; **je la connais mieux que lui** I know her better than he does; I know her better than him; **cette voiture est à lui** this car belongs to him, this is HIS car; **c'est à lui de jouer** it's his turn *ou* go
3 (*sujet, forme emphatique*) he; **lui, il est à Paris** HE is in Paris; **c'est lui qui l'a fait** HE did it
4 (*objet, forme emphatique*) him; **c'est lui que j'attends** I'm waiting for HIM
5: **lui-même** himself; itself

luire [lɥiʀ] /38/ *vi* to shine; (*reflets chauds, cuivrés*) to glow
lumière [lymjɛʀ] *nf* light; **mettre en ~** (*fig*) to highlight; **~ du jour/soleil** day/sunlight
luminaire [lyminɛʀ] *nm* lamp, light
lumineux, -euse [lyminø, -øz] *adj* luminous; (*éclairé*) illuminated; (*ciel, journée, couleur*) bright; (*rayon etc*) of light, light *cpd*; (*fig: regard*) radiant

lunatique [lynatik] *adj* whimsical, temperamental

lundi [lœ̃di] *nm* Monday; **on est ~** it's Monday; **le(s) ~(s)** on Mondays; **à ~!** see you (on) Monday!; **~ de Pâques** Easter Monday

lune [lyn] *nf* moon; **~ de miel** honeymoon

lunette [lynɛt] *nf*: **~s** glasses, spectacles; (*protectrices*) goggles; **~ arrière** (*Auto*) rear window; **~s noires** dark glasses; **~s de soleil** sunglasses

lustre [lystʀ] *nm* (*de plafond*) chandelier; (*fig: éclat*) lustre; **lustrer** /1/ *vt*: **lustrer qch** to make sth shine

luth [lyt] *nm* lute

lutin [lytɛ̃] *nm* imp, goblin

lutte [lyt] *nf* (*conflit*) struggle; (*Sport*): **la ~** wrestling; **lutter** /1/ *vi* to fight, struggle

luxe [lyks] *nm* luxury; **de ~** luxury *cpd*

Luxembourg [lyksɑ̃buʀ] *nm*: **le ~** Luxembourg

luxer [lykse] /1/ *vt*: **se ~ l'épaule** to dislocate one's shoulder

luxueux, -euse [lyksɥø, -øz] *adj* luxurious

lycée [lise] *nm* (state) secondary (*BRIT*) *ou* high (*US*) school; **lycéen, ne** *nm/f* secondary school pupil

Lyon [ljɔ̃] *n* Lyons

lyophilisé, e [ljɔfilize] *adj* (*café*) freeze-dried

lyrique [liʀik] *adj* lyrical; (*Opéra*) lyric; **artiste ~** opera singer

lys [lis] *nm* lily

M *abr* = **Monsieur**

m' [m] *pron voir* **me**

ma [ma] *adj poss voir* **mon**

macaron [makaʀɔ̃] *nm* (*gâteau*) macaroon; (*insigne*) (round) badge

macaroni(s) [makaʀɔni] *nm* (*pl*) macaroni *sg*; **~ au gratin** macaroni cheese (*BRIT*), macaroni and cheese (*US*)

Macédoine [masedwan] *nf* Macedonia

macédoine [masedwan] *nf*: **~ de fruits** fruit salad; **~ de légumes** mixed vegetables *pl*

macérer [maseʀe] /6/ *vi, vt* to macerate; (*dans du vinaigre*) to pickle

mâcher [maʃe] /1/ *vt* to chew; **ne pas ~ ses mots** not to mince one's words

machin [maʃɛ̃] *nm* (*fam*) thingamajig; (*personne*): **M~(e)** what's-his(*ou* her)-name

machinal, e, -aux [maʃinal, -o] *adj*
mechanical, automatic
machination [maʃinasjɔ̃] *nf*
frame-up
machine [maʃin] *nf* machine;
(*locomotive*) engine; **~ à laver/
coudre/tricoter** washing/sewing/
knitting machine; **~ à sous** fruit
machine
mâchoire [maʃwaʀ] *nf* jaw
mâchonner [maʃɔne] /1/ *vt* to
chew (at)
maçon [masɔ̃] *nm* bricklayer;
(*constructeur*) builder; **maçonnerie**
nf (*murs*) brickwork; (: *de pierre*)
masonry, stonework
Madagascar [madagaskaʀ] *nf*
Madagascar
Madame [madam] (*pl* **Mesdames**)
nf: **~ X** Mrs X; **occupez-vous de
~/Monsieur/Mademoiselle**
please serve this lady/gentleman/
(young) lady; **bonjour ~/
Monsieur/Mademoiselle** good
morning; (*ton déférent*) good
morning Madam/Sir/Madam; (*le
nom est connu*) good morning Mrs
X/Mr X/Miss X; **~/Monsieur/
Mademoiselle!** (*pour appeler*)
excuse me!; **~/Monsieur/
Mademoiselle** (*sur lettre*) Dear
Madam/Sir/Madam; **chère ~/cher
Monsieur/chère Mademoiselle**
Dear Mrs X/Mr X/Miss X;
Mesdames Ladies; **mesdames,
mesdemoiselles, messieurs** ladies
and gentlemen
madeleine [madlɛn] *nf* madeleine,
≈ sponge finger cake
Mademoiselle [madmwazɛl] (*pl*
Mesdemoiselles) *nf* Miss; *voir aussi*
Madame
Madère [madɛʀ] *nf* Madeira ▷ *nm*:
madère Madeira (wine)
Madrid [madʀid] *n* Madrid
magasin [magazɛ̃] *nm* (*boutique*)
shop; (*entrepôt*) warehouse; **en ~**
(*Comm*) in stock

magazine [magazin] *nm* magazine
Maghreb [magʀɛb] *nm*: **le ~**
North(-West) Africa; **maghrébin,
e** *adj* North African ▷ *nm/f*:
Maghrébin, e North African
magicien, ne [maʒisjɛ̃, -ɛn] *nm/f*
magician
magie [maʒi] *nf* magic; **magique** *adj*
magic; (*fig*) magical
magistral, e, -aux [maʒistral, -o]
adj (*œuvre, adresse*) masterly; (*ton*)
authoritative; **cours ~** lecture
magistrat [maʒistra] *nm*
magistrate
magnétique [maɲetik] *adj*
magnetic
magnétophone [maɲetɔfɔn] *nm*
tape recorder; **~ à cassettes** cassette
recorder
magnétoscope [maɲetɔskɔp] *nm*:
~ (à cassette) video (recorder)
magnifique [maɲifik] *adj*
magnificent
magret [magʀɛ] *nm*: **~ de canard**
duck breast
mai [mɛ] *nm* May; *voir aussi* **juillet**

- commemorates the surrender of
- the German army to Eisenhower
- on 7 May, 1945. It is marked by
- parades of ex-servicemen and
- ex-servicewomen in most towns.
- The social upheavals of May and
- June 1968, with their student
- demonstrations, workers' strikes
- and general rioting, are usually
- referred to as 'les événements de
- mai 68'. De Gaulle's Government
- survived, but reforms in
- education and a move towards
- decentralization ensued.

maigre [mɛgʀ] adj (very) thin, skinny; (viande) lean; (fromage) low-fat; (végétation) thin, sparse; (fig) poor, meagre, skimpy; **jours ~s** days of abstinence, fish days; **maigreur** nf thinness; **maigrir** /2/ vi to get thinner, lose weight; **maigrir de 2 kilos** to lose 2 kilos

mail [mɛl] nm email

maille [maj] nf stitch; **~ à l'endroit/à l'envers** plain/purl stitch

maillet [majɛ] nm mallet

maillon [majɔ̃] nm link

maillot [majo] nm (aussi: **~ de corps**) vest; (de sportif) jersey; **~ de bain** swimming ou bathing (BRIT) costume, swimsuit; (d'homme) (swimming ou bathing (BRIT) trunks pl

main [mɛ̃] nf hand; **à la ~** (tenir, avoir) in one's hand; (faire, tricoter etc) by hand; **se donner la ~** to hold hands; **donner** ou **tendre la ~ à qn** to hold out one's hand to sb; **se serrer la ~** to shake hands; **serrer la ~ à qn** to shake hands with sb; **sous la ~** to ou at hand; **haut les ~s!** hands up!; **attaque à ~ armée** armed attack; **à remettre en ~s propres** to be delivered personally; **mettre la dernière ~ à** to put the finishing touches to; **se faire/perdre la ~** to get one's hand in/lose one's touch;

avoir qch bien en ~ to have got the hang of sth; **main-d'œuvre** nf manpower, labour; **mainmise** nf (fig): **avoir la mainmise sur** to have a grip ou stranglehold on

mains-libres [mɛ̃libʀ] adj inv (téléphone, kit) hands-free

maint, e [mɛ̃, mɛ̃t] adj many a; **~s** many; **à ~es reprises** time and (time) again

maintenant [mɛ̃tnɑ̃] adv now; (actuellement) nowadays

maintenir [mɛ̃tniʀ] /22/ vt (retenir, soutenir) to support; (contenir: foule etc) to keep in check; (conserver) to maintain; **se maintenir** vi (prix) to keep steady; (préjugé) to persist

maintien [mɛ̃tjɛ̃] nm maintaining; (attitude) bearing

maire [mɛʀ] nm mayor; **mairie** nf (bâtiment) town hall; (administration) town council

mais [mɛ] conj but; **~ non!** of course not!; **~ enfin** but after all; (indignation) look here!

maïs [mais] nm maize (BRIT), corn (US)

maison [mɛzɔ̃] nf house; (chez-soi) home; (Comm) firm ▷ adj inv (Culin) home-made; (Comm) in-house, own; **à la ~** at home; (direction) home; **~ close** brothel; **~ des jeunes** ≈ youth club; **~ mère** parent company; **~ de passe** = maison close; **~ de repos** convalescent home; **~ de retraite** old people's home; **~ de santé** psychiatric facility

maître, -esse [mɛtʀ, mɛtʀɛs] nm/f master (mistress); (Scol) teacher, schoolmaster/-mistress ▷ nm (peintre etc) master; (titre): **M~ (Mᵉ)** Maître (term of address for lawyers etc) ▷ adj (principal, essentiel) main; **être ~ de** (soi-même, situation) to be in control of; **une maîtresse femme** a forceful woman; **~ chanteur** blackmailer; **~/maîtresse d'école** schoolmaster/-mistress; **~ d'hôtel**

(*domestique*) butler; (*d'hôtel*) head waiter; **~ nageur** lifeguard; **maîtresse de maison** hostess; (*ménagère*) housewife

maîtrise [metʀiz] *nf* (*aussi:* **~ de soi**) self-control, self-possession; (*habileté*) skill, mastery; (*suprématie*) mastery, command; (*diplôme*) ≈ master's degree; **maîtriser** /1/ *vt* (*cheval, incendie*) to (bring under) control; (*sujet*) to master; (*émotion*) to control, master; **se maîtriser** to control o.s.

majestueux, -euse [maʒɛstɥø, -øz] *adj* majestic

majeur, e [maʒœʀ] *adj* (*important*) major; (*Jur*) of age ▷ *nm* (*doigt*) middle finger; **en ~e partie** for the most part; **la ~e partie de** most of

majorer [maʒɔʀe] /1/ *vt* to increase

majoritaire [maʒɔʀitɛʀ] *adj* majority *cpd*

majorité [maʒɔʀite] *nf* (*gén*) majority; (*parti*) party in power; **en ~** (*composé etc*) mainly; **avoir la ~** to have the majority

majuscule [maʒyskyl] *adj, nf*: **(lettre) ~** capital (letter)

mal (*pl* **maux**) [mal, mo] *nm* (*opposé au bien*) evil; (*tort, dommage*) harm; (*douleur physique*) pain, ache; (*maladie*) illness, sickness *no pl* ▷ *adv* badly ▷ *adj*: **être ~ (à l'aise)** to be uncomfortable; **être ~ avec qn** to be on bad terms with sb; **il a ~ compris** he misunderstood; **se sentir** *ou* **se trouver ~** to feel ill *ou* unwell; **dire/ penser du ~ de** to speak/think ill of; **avoir du ~ à faire qch** to have trouble doing sth; **se donner du ~ pour faire qch** to go to a lot of trouble to do sth; **ne voir aucun ~ à** to see no harm in, see nothing wrong in; **faire du ~ à qn** to hurt sb; **se faire ~** to hurt o.s.; **ça fait ~** it hurts; **j'ai ~ au dos** my back aches; **avoir ~ à la tête/à la gorge** to have a headache/a sore throat; **avoir ~ aux dents/à l'oreille** to have toothache/earache; **avoir le ~ du pays** to be homesick; **~ de mer** seasickness; **~ en point** in a bad state; *voir aussi* **cœur**

malade [malad] *adj* ill, sick; (*poitrine, jambe*) bad; (*plante*) diseased ▷ *nm/f* invalid, sick person; (*à l'hôpital etc*) patient; **tomber ~** to fall ill; **être ~ du cœur** to have heart trouble *ou* a bad heart; **~ mental** mentally ill person; **maladie** *nf* (*spécifique*) disease, illness; (*mauvaise santé*) illness, sickness; **maladif, -ive** *adj* sickly; (*curiosité, besoin*) pathological

maladresse [maladʀɛs] *nf* clumsiness *no pl*; (*gaffe*) blunder

maladroit, e [maladʀwa, -wat] *adj* clumsy

malaise [malɛz] *nm* (*Méd*) feeling of faintness; (*fig*) uneasiness, malaise; **avoir un ~** to feel faint *ou* dizzy

Malaisie [malɛzi] *nf*: **la ~** Malaysia

malaria [malaʀja] *nf* malaria

malaxer [malakse] /1/ *vt* (*pétrir*) to knead; (*mêler*) to mix

malbouffe [malbuf] *nf* (*fam*): **la ~** junk food

malchance [malʃɑ̃s] *nf* misfortune, ill luck *no pl*; **par ~** unfortunately; **malchanceux, -euse** *adj* unlucky

mâle [mɑl] *adj* (*Élec, Tech*) male; (*viril: voix, traits*) manly ▷ *nm* male

malédiction [malediksjɔ̃] *nf* curse

mal: malentendant, e *nm/f*: **les malentendants** the hard of hearing; **malentendu** *nm* misunderstanding; **il y a eu un malentendu** there's been a misunderstanding; **malfaçon** *nf* fault; **malfaisant, e** *adj* evil, harmful; **malfaiteur** *nm* lawbreaker, criminal; (*voleur*) burglar, thief; **malfamé, e** *adj* disreputable

malgache [malgaʃ] *adj* Malagasy, Madagascan ▷ *nm* (*Ling*) Malagasy ▷ *nm/f*: **M~** Malagasy, Madagascan

malgré [malgʀe] *prép* in spite of, despite; **~ tout** in spite of everything

malheur [malœʀ] *nm* (*situation*) adversity, misfortune; (*événement*) misfortune (: *plus fort*) disaster, tragedy; **faire un ~** to be a smash hit; **malheureusement** *adv* unfortunately; **malheureux, -euse** *adj* (*triste*) unhappy, miserable; (*infortuné, regrettable*) unfortunate; (*malchanceux*) unlucky; (*insignifiant*) wretched ▷ *nm/f* poor soul

malhonnête [malɔnɛt] *adj* dishonest; **malhonnêteté** *nf* dishonesty

malice [malis] *nf* mischievousness; (*méchanceté*) **par ~** out of malice *ou* spite; **sans ~** guileless; **malicieux, -euse** *adj* mischievous

⬛ Attention à ne pas traduire *malicieux* par *malicious*.

malin, -igne [malɛ̃, -iɲ] *adj* (*futé*) (*f gén* **maline**) smart, shrewd; (*Méd*) malignant

malingre [malɛ̃gʀ] *adj* puny

malle [mal] *nf* trunk; **mallette** *nf* (*small*) suitcase; (*pour documents*) attaché case

malmener [malmǝne] /5/ *vt* to manhandle; (*fig*) to give a rough ride to

malodorant, e [malɔdɔʀɑ̃, -ɑ̃t] *adj* foul-smelling

malpoli, e [malpɔli] *adj* impolite

malsain, e [malsɛ̃, -ɛn] *adj* unhealthy

malt [malt] *nm* malt

Malte [malt] *nf* Malta

maltraiter [maltʀete] /1/ *vt* to manhandle, ill-treat

malveillance [malvɛjɑ̃s] *nf* (*animosité*) ill will; (*intention de nuire*) malevolence

malversation [malvɛʀsasjɔ̃] *nf* embezzlement

maman [mamɑ̃] *nf* mum(my)

mamelle [mamɛl] *nf* teat

mamelon [mamlɔ̃] *nm* (*Anat*) nipple

mamie [mami] *nf* (*fam*) granny

mammifère [mamifɛʀ] *nm* mammal

mammouth [mamut] *nm* mammoth

manche [mɑ̃ʃ] *nf* (*de vêtement*) sleeve; (*d'un jeu, tournoi*) round; (*Géo*): **la M~** the (English) Channel ▷ *nm* (*d'outil, casserole*) handle; (*de pelle, pioche etc*) shaft; **à ~s courtes/ longues** short-/long-sleeved; **~ à balai** broomstick; (*Aviat, Inform*) joystick *nm inv*

manchette [mɑ̃ʃɛt] *nf* (*de chemise*) cuff; (*coup*) forearm blow; (*titre*) headline

manchot [mɑ̃ʃo] *nm* one-armed man; armless man; (*Zool*) penguin

mandarine [mɑ̃daʀin] *nf* mandarin (orange), tangerine

mandat [mɑ̃da] *nm* (*postal*) postal *ou* money order; (*d'un député etc*) mandate; (*procuration*) power of attorney, proxy; (*Police*) warrant; **~ d'arrêt** warrant for arrest; **~ de perquisition** search warrant; **mandataire** *nm/f* (*représentant, délégué*) representative; (*Jur*) proxy

manège [manɛʒ] *nm* riding school; (*à la foire*) roundabout (BRIT), merry-go-round; (*fig*) game, ploy

manette [manɛt] *nf* lever, tap; **~ de jeu** joystick

mangeable [mɑ̃ʒabl] *adj* edible, eatable

mangeoire [mɑ̃ʒwaʀ] *nf* trough, manger

manger [mɑ̃ʒe] /3/ *vt* to eat; (*ronger: rouille etc*) to eat into *ou* away ▷ *vi* to eat; **donner à ~ à** (*enfant*) to feed

mangue [mɑ̃g] *nf* mango

maniable [manjabl] *adj* (*outil*) handy; (*voiture, voilier*) easy to handle

maniaque [manjak] *adj* finicky, fussy ▷ *nm/f* (*méticuleux*) fusspot; (*fou*) maniac

manie [mani] *nf* mania; (*tic*) odd habit; **avoir la ~ de** to be obsessive about

manier [manje] /7/ *vt* to handle

maniéré, e [manjeʀe] *adj* affected

manière [manjɛʀ] nf (façon) way, manner; **manières** nfpl (attitude) manners; (chichis) fuss sg; **de ~ à** so as to; **de cette ~** in this way ou manner; **d'une ~ générale** generally speaking, as a general rule; **de toute ~** in any case; **d'une certaine ~** in a (certain) way

manifestant, e [manifɛstã, -ãt] nm/f demonstrator

manifestation [manifɛstasjɔ̃] nf (de joie, mécontentement) expression, demonstration; (symptôme) outward sign; (fête etc) event; (Pol) demonstration

manifeste [manifɛst] adj obvious, evident ▷ nm manifesto; **manifester** /1/ vt (volonté, intentions) to show, indicate; (joie, peur) to express, show ▷ vi to demonstrate; **se manifester** vi (émotion) to show ou express itself; (difficultés) to arise; (symptômes) to appear

manigancer [manigãse] /3/ vt to plot

manipulation [manipylasjɔ̃] nf handling; (Pol, génétique) manipulation

manipuler [manipyle] /1/ vt to handle; (fig) to manipulate

manivelle [manivɛl] nf crank

mannequin [mankɛ̃] nm (Couture) dummy; (Mode) model

manœuvre [manœvʀ] nf (gén) manoeuvre (BRIT), maneuver (US) ▷ nm labourer; **manœuvrer** /1/ vt to manoeuvre (BRIT), maneuver (US); (levier, machine) to operate ▷ vi to manoeuvre ou maneuver

manoir [manwaʀ] nm manor ou country house

manque [mãk] nm (insuffisance, vide) emptiness, gap; (Méd) withdrawal; **~ de** lack of; **être en état de ~** to suffer withdrawal symptoms

manqué [mãke] adj failed; **garçon ~** tomboy

manquer [mãke] /1/ vi (faire défaut) to be lacking; (être absent) to be missing; (échouer) to fail ▷ vt to miss ▷ vb impers: **il (nous) manque encore 10 euros** we are still 10 euros short; **il manque des pages (au livre)** there are some pages missing ou some pages are missing (from the book); **~ à qn** (absent etc): **il/cela me manque** I miss him/that; **~ à** (règles etc) to be in breach of, fail to observe; **~ de** to lack; **ne pas ~ de faire: je ne manquerai pas de le lui dire** I'll be sure to tell him; **il a manqué (de) se tuer** he very nearly got killed

mansarde [mãsaʀd] nf attic; **mansardé, e** adj: **chambre mansardée** attic room

manteau, x [mãto] nm coat

manucure [manykyʀ] nf manicurist

manuel, le [manɥɛl] adj manual ▷ nm (ouvrage) manual, handbook

manufacture [manyfaktyʀ] nf factory; **manufacturé, e** adj manufactured

manuscrit, e [manyskʀi, -it] adj handwritten ▷ nm manuscript

manutention [manytãsjɔ̃] nf (Comm) handling

mappemonde [mapmɔ̃d] nf (plane) map of the world; (sphère) globe

maquereau, x [makʀo] nm (Zool) mackerel inv; (fam) pimp

maquette [makɛt] nf (d'un décor, bâtiment, véhicule) (scale) model

maquillage [makijaʒ] nm making up; (produits) make-up

maquiller [makije] /1/ vt (personne, visage) to make up; (truquer: passeport, statistique) to fake; (: voiture volée) to do over (respray etc); **se maquiller** vi to make o.s. up

maquis [maki] nm (Géo) scrub; (Mil) maquis, underground fighting no pl

maraîcher, -ère [maʀeʃe, maʀɛʃɛʀ] adj: **cultures maraîchères** market gardening sg ▷ nm/f market gardener

marais [maʀɛ] nm marsh, swamp

marasme [maʀasm] nm stagnation, sluggishness

marathon [maʀatɔ̃] nm marathon

marbre [maʀbʀ] nm marble

marc [maʀ] nm (de raisin, pommes) marc

marchand, e [maʀʃɑ̃, -ɑ̃d] nm/f shopkeeper, tradesman/-woman; (au marché) stallholder; **~ de charbon/vins** coal/wine merchant ▷ adj: **prix/valeur ~(e)** market price/value; **~/e de fruits** fruiterer (BRIT), fruit seller (US); **~/e de journaux** newsagent; **~/e de légumes** greengrocer (BRIT), produce dealer (US); **~/e de poisson** fishmonger (BRIT), fish seller (US); **marchander** /1/ vi to bargain, haggle; **marchandise** nf goods pl, merchandise no pl

marche [maʀʃ] nf (d'escalier) step; (activité) walking; (promenade, trajet, allure) walk; (démarche) walk, gait; (Mil, Mus) march; (fonctionnement) running; (des événements) course; **dans le sens de la ~** (Rail) facing the engine; **en ~** (monter etc) while the vehicle is moving ou in motion; **mettre en ~** to start; **se mettre en ~** (personne) to get moving; (machine) to start; **être en état de ~** to be in working order; **~ arrière** reverse (gear); **faire ~ arrière** to reverse; (fig) to backtrack, back-pedal; **~ à suivre** (correct) procedure

marché [maʀʃe] nm market; (transaction) bargain, deal; **faire du ~ noir** to buy and sell on the black market; **~ aux puces** flea market

marcher [maʀʃe] /1/ vi to walk; (Mil) to march; (aller: voiture, train, affaires) to go; (prospérer) to go well; (fonctionner) to work, run; (fam: consentir) to go along, agree; (: croire naïvement) to be taken in; **faire ~ qn** (pour rire) to pull sb's leg; (pour tromper) to lead sb up the garden path; **marcheur, -euse** nm/f walker

mardi [maʀdi] nm Tuesday; **M~ gras** Shrove Tuesday

mare [maʀ] nf pond; (flaque) pool

marécage [maʀekaʒ] nm marsh, swamp; **marécageux, -euse** adj marshy

maréchal, -aux [maʀeʃal, -o] nm marshal

marée [maʀe] nf tide; (poissons) fresh (sea) fish; **~ haute/basse** high/low tide; **~ noire** oil slick

marelle [maʀɛl] nf: **(jouer à) la ~** (to play) hopscotch

margarine [maʀgaʀin] nf margarine

marge [maʀʒ] nf margin; **en ~ de** (fig) on the fringe of; **~ bénéficiaire** profit margin

marginal, e, -aux [maʀʒinal, -o] nm/f (original) eccentric; (déshérité) dropout

marguerite [maʀgəʀit] nf marguerite, (oxeye) daisy; (d'imprimante) daisy-wheel

mari [maʀi] nm husband

mariage [maʀjaʒ] nm marriage; (noce) wedding; **~ civil/religieux** registry office (BRIT) ou civil/church wedding

marié, e [maʀje] adj married ▷ nm/f (bride)groom/bride; **les ~s** the bride and groom; **les (jeunes) ~s** the newly-weds

marier [maʀje] /7/ vt to marry; (fig) to blend; **se ~ (avec)** to marry, get married (to)

marin, e [maʀɛ̃, -in] adj sea cpd, marine ▷ nm sailor ▷ nf navy; **~e marchande** merchant navy

marine [maʀin] adj f voir **marin** ▷ adj inv navy (blue) ▷ nm (Mil) marine

mariner [maʀine] /1/ vt to marinate

marionnette [maʀjɔnɛt] nf puppet

maritalement [maʀitalmɑ̃] adv: **vivre ~** to live together (as husband and wife)

maritime [maʀitim] adj sea cpd, maritime

mark [maʀk] nm mark

m

marmelade [maʀməlad] nf stewed fruit, compote; **~ d'oranges** (orange) marmalade

marmite [maʀmit] nf (cooking-) pot

marmonner [maʀmɔne] /1/ vt, vi to mumble, mutter

marmotter [maʀmɔte] /1/ vt to mumble

Maroc [maʀɔk] nm: **le ~** Morocco; **marocain, e** [maʀɔkɛ̃, -ɛn] adj Moroccan ▷ nm/f: **Marocain, e** Moroccan

maroquinerie [maʀɔkinʀi] nf (commerce) leather shop; (articles) fine leather goods pl

marquant, e [maʀkɑ̃, -ɑ̃t] adj outstanding

marque [maʀk] nf mark; (Comm: de nourriture) brand; (: de voiture, produits manufacturés) make; (: de disques) label; **de ~** high-class; (personnage, hôte) distinguished; **~ déposée** registered trademark; **~ de fabrique** trademark; **une grande ~ de vin** a well-known brand of wine

marquer [maʀke] /1/ vt to mark; (inscrire) to write down; (bétail) to brand; (Sport: but etc) to score; (: joueur) to mark; (accentuer: taille etc) to emphasize; (manifester: refus, intérêt) to show ▷ vi (événement, personnalité) to stand out, be outstanding; (Sport) to score; **~ les points** to keep the score

marqueterie [maʀkɛtʀi] nf inlaid work, marquetry

marquis, e [maʀki, -iz] nm/f marquis ou marquess (marchioness)

marraine [maʀɛn] nf godmother

marrant, e [maʀɑ̃, -ɑ̃t] adj (fam) funny

marre [maʀ] adv (fam): **en avoir ~ de** to be fed up with

marrer [maʀe] /1/: **se marrer** vi (fam) to have a (good) laugh

marron, ne [maʀɔ̃, -ɔn] nm (fruit) chestnut ▷ adj inv brown ▷ adj (péj) crooked; **~s glacés** marrons glacés; **marronnier** nm chestnut (tree)

mars [maʀs] nm March

Marseille [maʀsɛj] n Marseilles

marteau, x [maʀto] nm hammer; **être ~** (fam) to be nuts; **marteau-piqueur** nm pneumatic drill

marteler [maʀtəle] /5/ vt to hammer

martien, ne [maʀsjɛ̃, -ɛn] adj Martian, of ou from Mars

martyr, e [maʀtiʀ] nm/f martyr ▷ adj martyred; **enfants ~s** battered children; **martyre** nm martyrdom; (fig: sens affaibli) agony, torture; **martyriser** /1/ vt (Rel) to martyr; (fig) to bully (: enfant) to batter

marxiste [maʀksist] adj, nm/f Marxist

mascara [maskaʀa] nm mascara

masculin, e [maskylɛ̃, -in] adj masculine; (sexe, population) male; (équipe, vêtements) men's; (viril) manly ▷ nm masculine

masochiste [mazɔʃist] adj masochistic

masque [mask] nm mask; **~ de beauté** face pack; **~ de plongée** diving mask; **masquer** /1/ vt (cacher: porte, goût) to hide, conceal; (dissimuler: vérité, projet) to mask, obscure

massacre [masakʀ] nm massacre, slaughter; **massacrer** /1/ vt to massacre, slaughter; (texte etc) to murder

massage [masaʒ] nm massage

masse [mas] nf mass; (Élec) earth; (maillet) sledgehammer; **une ~ de** (fam) masses ou loads of; **la ~** (péj) the masses ou loads of; the masses pl: **en ~** (adv: en bloc) in bulk; (en foule) en masse; adj: exécutions, production) mass cpd

masser [mase] /1/ vt (assembler: gens) to gather; (pétrir) to massage; **se masser** vi (foule) to gather; **masseur, -euse** nm/f masseur(-euse)

massif, -ive [masif, -iv] adj (porte) solid, massive; (visage) heavy, large;

(*bois*, *or*) solid; (*dose*) massive; (*déportations etc*) mass cpd ▷ nm (*montagneux*) massif; (*de fleurs*) clump, bank; **le M~ Central** the Massif Central

massue [masy] nf club, bludgeon

mastic [mastik] nm (*pour vitres*) putty; (*pour fentes*) filler

mastiquer [mastike] /1/ vt (*aliment*) to chew, masticate

mat, e [mat] adj (*couleur, métal*) mat(t); (*bruit, son*) dull ▷ adj inv (*Échecs*): **être ~** to be checkmate

mât [mɑ] nm (*Navig*) mast; (*poteau*) pole, post

match [matʃ] nm match; **faire ~ nul** to draw; **~ aller** first leg; **~ retour** second leg, return match

matelas [matla] nm mattress; **~ pneumatique** air bed ou mattress

matelot [matlo] nm sailor, seaman

mater [mate] /1/ vt (*personne*) to bring to heel, subdue; (*révolte*) to put down

matérialiser [materjalize] /1/: **se matérialiser** vi to materialize

matérialiste [materjalist] adj materialistic

matériau, x [materjo] nm material; **matériaux** nmpl material(s)

matériel, le [materjɛl] adj material ▷ nm equipment no pl; (*de camping etc*) gear no pl; (*Inform*) hardware

maternel, le [matɛrnɛl] adj (*amour, geste*) motherly, maternal; (*grand-père, oncle*) maternal ▷ nf (*aussi*: **école maternelle**) (state) nursery school

maternité [matɛrnite] nf (*établissement*) maternity hospital; (*état de mère*) motherhood, maternity; (*grossesse*) pregnancy; **congé de ~** maternity leave

mathématique [matematik] adj mathematical; **mathématiques** nfpl mathematics sg

maths [mat] nfpl maths

matière [matjɛr] nf matter; (*Comm, Tech*) material; matter no pl; (*fig: d'un*

livre etc) subject matter, material; (*Scol*) subject; **en ~ de** as regards; **~s grasses** fat (content) sg; **~s premières** raw materials

Matignon [matiɲɔ̃] nm: **(l'hôtel) ~** the French Prime Minister's residence

matin [matɛ̃] nm, adv morning; **le ~** (*pendant le matin*) in the morning; **demain/hier/dimanche ~** tomorrow/yesterday/Sunday morning; **tous les ~s** every morning; **du ~ au soir** from morning till night; **une heure du ~** one o'clock in the morning; **de grand** ou **bon ~** early in the morning; **matinal, e, -aux** [matinal, -o] adj (*toilette, gymnastique*) morning cpd; **être matinal** (*personne*) to be up early; (*habituellement*) to be an early riser; **matinée** nf morning; (*spectacle*) matinée

matou [matu] nm tom(cat)

matraque [matrak] nf (*de policier*) truncheon (BRIT), billy (US)

matricule [matrikyl] nm (*Mil*) regimental number; (*Admin*) reference number

matrimonial, e, -aux [matrimɔnjal, -o] adj marital, marriage cpd

maudit, e [modi, -it] adj (*fam: satané*) blasted, confounded

maugréer [mogree] /1/ vi to grumble

maussade [mosad] adj sullen; (*ciel, temps*) gloomy

mauvais, e [mɔvɛ, -ɛz] adj bad; (*méchant, malveillant*) malicious, spiteful; (*faux*): **le ~ numéro** the wrong number ▷ adv: **il fait ~** the weather is bad; **sentir ~** to have a nasty smell, smell bad ou nasty; **la mer est ~e** the sea is rough; **~e plaisanterie** nasty trick; **~ joueur** bad loser; **~e herbe** weed; **~e langue** gossip, scandalmonger (BRIT)

mauve [mov] adj mauve

maux [mo] nmpl voir **mal**

m

maximum [maksimɔm] *adj, nm*
maximum; **au ~** (*le plus possible*) as
much as one can; (*tout au plus*) at the
(very) most *ou* maximum; **faire le ~**
to do one's level best

mayonnaise [majɔnɛz] *nf*
mayonnaise

mazout [mazut] *nm* (*fuel*) oil

me, m' [mə, m] *pron* (*direct: téléphoner,
attendre etc*) me; (*indirect: parler, donner
etc*) (to) me; (*réfléchi*) myself

mec [mɛk] *nm* (*fam*) guy, bloke (BRIT)

mécanicien, ne [mekanisjɛ̃,
-ɛn] *nm/f* mechanic; (*Rail*) (train *ou*
engine) driver

mécanique [mekanik] *adj*
mechanical ▷ *nf* (*science*) mechanics
sg; (*mécanisme*) mechanism; **ennui ~**
engine trouble *no pl*

mécanisme [mekanism] *nm*
mechanism

méchamment [meʃamɑ̃] *adv*
nastily, maliciously; spitefully

méchanceté [meʃɑ̃ste] *nf* nastiness,
maliciousness; **dire des ~s à qn** to
say spiteful things to sb

méchant, e [meʃɑ̃, -ɑ̃t] *adj* nasty,
malicious, spiteful; (*enfant: pas sage*)
naughty; (*animal*) vicious

mèche [mɛʃ] *nf* (*de lampe, bougie*)
wick; (*d'un explosif*) fuse; (*de cheveux*)
lock; **se faire faire des ~s** to have
highlights put in one's hair; **de ~ avec**
in league with

méchoui [meʃwi] *nm* whole sheep
barbecue

méconnaissable [mekɔnɛsabl] *adj*
unrecognizable

méconnaître [mekɔnɛtr] /57/
vt (*ignorer*) to be unaware of;
(*mésestimer*) to misjudge

mécontent, e [mekɔ̃tɑ̃, -ɑ̃t]
adj: **~ (de)** discontented *ou*
dissatisfied *ou* displeased
(with); (*contrarié*) annoyed
(at); **mécontentement** *nm*
dissatisfaction, discontent,
displeasure; (*irritation*) annoyance

Mecque [mɛk] *nf*: **la ~** Mecca

médaille [medaj] *nf* medal

médaillon [medajɔ̃] *nm* (*bijou*) locket

médecin [medsɛ̃] *nm* doctor

médecine [medsin] *nf* medicine

média [medja] *nmpl*: **les ~** the
media; **médiatique** *adj* media *cpd*

médical, e, -aux [medikal, -o] *adj*
medical; **passer une visite ~e** to
have a medical

médicament [medikamɑ̃] *nm*
medicine, drug

médiéval, e, -aux [medjeval, -o]
adj medieval

médiocre [medjɔkr] *adj* mediocre,
poor

méditer [medite] /1/ *vi* to meditate

Méditerranée [mediterane]
nf: **la (mer) ~** the Mediterranean
(Sea); **méditerranéen, ne**
adj Mediterranean ▷ *nm/f*:
Méditerranéen, ne Mediterranean

méduse [medyz] *nf* jellyfish

méfait [mefɛ] *nm* (*faute*)
misdemeanour, wrongdoing;
méfaits *nmpl* (*ravages*) ravages,
damage *sg*

méfiance [mefjɑ̃s] *nf* mistrust,
distrust

méfiant, e [mefjɑ̃, -ɑ̃t] *adj*
mistrustful, distrustful

méfier [mefje] /7/: **se méfier** *vi* to be
wary; (*faire attention*) to be careful; **se
~ de** to mistrust, distrust, be wary of

méga-octet [megaɔktɛ] *nm*
megabyte

mégarde [megard] *nf*: **par ~**
(*accidentellement*) accidentally; (*par
erreur*) by mistake

mégère [meʒɛr] *nf* shrew

mégot [mego] *nm* cigarette end
ou butt

meilleur, e [mɛjœr] *adj, adv* better
▷ *nm*: **le ~** the best; **le ~ des deux** the
better of the two; **il fait ~ qu'hier**
it's better weather than yesterday;
~ marché cheaper

mél [mɛl] *nm* email

mélancolie [melɑ̃kɔli] nf
melancholy, gloom; **mélancolique**
adj melancholy

mélange [melɑ̃ʒ] nm mixture;
mélanger /3/ vt to mix; (vins,
couleurs) to blend; (mettre en désordre,
confondre) to mix up, muddle (up)

mêlée [mele] nf mêlée, scramble;
(Rugby) scrum(mage)

mêler [mele] /1/ vt (substances, odeurs,
races) to mix; (embrouiller) to muddle
(up), mix up; **se ~** vi to mix; **se ~
à** (personne) to join; (s'associer à) to mix
with; **se ~ de** (personne) to meddle
with, interfere in; **mêle-toi de tes
affaires!** mind your own business!

mélodie [melɔdi] nf melody;
mélodieux, -euse adj melodious

melon [məlɔ̃] nm (Bot) (honeydew)
melon; (aussi: **chapeau ~**) bowler
(hat)

membre [mɑ̃bʀ] nm (Anat) limb;
(personne, pays, élément) member ▷ adj
member cpd

mémé [meme] nf (fam) granny

 MOT-CLÉ

même [mɛm] adj 1 (avant le nom)
same; **en même temps** at the same
time; **ils ont les mêmes goûts** they
have the same ou similar tastes
2 (après le nom, renforcement): **il est la
loyauté même** he is loyalty itself; **ce
sont ses paroles/celles-là même**
they are his very words/the very ones
▶ pron: **le (la) même** the same one
▶ adv 1 (renforcement): **il n'a même
pas pleuré** he didn't even cry; **même
lui l'a dit** even HE said it; **ici même** at
this very place; **même si** even if
2: **à même: à même la bouteille**
straight from the bottle; **à même la
peau** next to the skin; **être à même
de faire** to be in a position to do, be
able to do
3: **de même** likewise; **faire de même**
to do likewise ou the same; **lui de
même** so does (ou did ou is) he; **de
même que** just as; **il en va de même
pour** the same goes for

mémoire [memwaʀ] nf memory
▷ nm (Scol) dissertation, paper; **à la
~ de** to the ou in memory of; **de ~**
from memory; **~ morte** read-only
memory, ROM; **~ vive** random
access memory, RAM

mémoires [memwaʀ] nmpl
memoirs

mémorable [memɔʀabl] adj
memorable

menace [mənas] nf threat; **menacer**
/3/ vt to threaten

ménage [menaʒ] nm (travail)
housework; (couple) (married) couple;
(famille, Admin) household; **faire le ~**
to do the housework; **ménagement**
nm care and attention

ménager¹ [menaʒe] vt (traiter avec
mesure) to handle with tact; (utiliser)
to use sparingly; (prendre soin de)
to take (great) care of, look after;
(organiser) to arrange

ménager², -ère adj household cpd,
domestic ▷ nf housewife

mendiant, e [mɑ̃djɑ̃, -ɑ̃t] nm/f
beggar

mendier [mɑ̃dje] /7/ vi to beg ▷ vt
to beg (for)

mener [məne] /5/ vt to lead;
(enquête) to conduct; (affaires) to
manage ▷ vi: **~ à/dans** (emmener)
to take to/into; **~ qch à bonne
fin** ou **à terme** ou **à bien** to see sth
through (to a successful conclusion),
complete sth successfully

meneur, -euse [mənœʀ, -øz] nm/f
leader; (péj) ringleader

méningite [menɛ̃ʒit] nf meningitis
no pl

ménopause [menopoz] nf
menopause

menotte [mənɔt] nf (langage
enfantin) handie; **menottes** nfpl
handcuffs

m

mensonge [mɑ̃sɔ̃ʒ] nm: **le ~** lying no pl; **un ~** a lie; **mensonger, -ère** adj false

mensualité [mɑ̃sɥalite] nf (somme payée) monthly payment

mensuel, le [mɑ̃sɥɛl] adj monthly

mensurations [mɑ̃syRasjɔ̃] nfpl measurements

mental, e, -aux [mɑ̃tal, -o] adj mental; **mentalité** nf mentality

menteur, -euse [mɑ̃tœR, -øz] nm/f liar

menthe [mɑ̃t] nf mint

mention [mɑ̃sjɔ̃] nf (note) note, comment; (Scol): **~ (très) bien/ passable** (very) good/satisfactory pass; **"rayer la ~ inutile"** "delete as appropriate"; **mentionner** /1/ vt to mention

mentir [mɑ̃tiR] /16/ vi to lie

menton [mɑ̃tɔ̃] nm chin

menu, e [məny] adj (mince) slim, slight; (frais, difficulté) minor ▷ adv (couper, hacher) very fine ▷ nm menu; **~ touristique** popular ou tourist menu

menuiserie [mənɥizRi] nf (travail) joinery, carpentry; (d'amateur) woodwork; **menuisier** nm joiner, carpenter

méprendre [mepRɑ̃dR] /58/: **se méprendre** vi: **se ~ sur** to be mistaken about

mépris, e [mepRi, -iz] pp de **méprendre** ▷ nm (dédain) contempt, scorn; **au ~ de** regardless of, in defiance of; **méprisable** adj contemptible, despicable; **méprisant, e** adj scornful; **méprise** nf mistake, error; **mépriser** /1/ vt to scorn, despise; (gloire, danger) to scorn, spurn

mer [mɛR] nf sea; (marée) tide; **en ~** at sea; **en haute** ou **pleine ~** off shore, on the open sea; **la ~ Morte** the Dead Sea; **la ~ Noire** the Black Sea; **la ~ du Nord** the North Sea; **la ~ Rouge** the Red Sea

mercenaire [mɛRsənɛR] nm mercenary, hired soldier

mercerie [mɛRsəRi] nf (boutique) haberdasher's (shop) (BRIT), notions store (US)

merci [mɛRsi] excl thank you ▷ nf: **à la ~ de qn/qch** at sb's mercy/the mercy of sth; **~ beaucoup** thank you very much; **~ de** ou **pour** thank you for; **sans ~** merciless; mercilessly

mercredi [mɛRkRədi] nm Wednesday; **~ des Cendres** Ash Wednesday; voir aussi **lundi**

mercure [mɛRkyR] nm mercury

merde [mɛRd] (!) nf shit (!) ▷ excl (bloody) hell (!)

mère [mɛR] nf mother ▷ adj inv mother cpd; **~ célibataire** single parent, unmarried mother; **~ de famille** housewife, mother

merguez [mɛRgɛz] nf spicy North African sausage

méridional, e, -aux [meRidjɔnal, -o] adj southern ▷ nm/f Southerner

meringue [məRɛ̃g] nf meringue

mérite [meRit] nm merit; **avoir du ~ (à faire qch)** to deserve credit (for doing sth); **mériter** /1/ vt to deserve

merle [mɛRl] nm blackbird

merveille [mɛRvɛj] nf marvel, wonder; **faire ~** ou **des ~s** to work wonders; **à ~** perfectly, wonderfully; **merveilleux, -euse** adj marvellous, wonderful

mes [me] adj poss voir **mon**

mésange [mezɑ̃ʒ] nf tit (mouse)

mésaventure [mezavɑ̃tyR] nf misadventure, misfortune

Mesdames [medam] nfpl voir **Madame**

Mesdemoiselles [medmwazɛl] nfpl voir **Mademoiselle**

mesquin, e [mɛskɛ̃, -in] adj mean, petty; **mesquinerie** nf meanness no pl; (procédé) mean trick

message [mesaʒ] nm message; **~ SMS** text message; **messager, -ère** nm/f messenger; **messagerie** nf

(*Internet*): **messagerie électronique** email; **messagerie instantanée** instant messenger; **messagerie vocale** voice mail
messe [mɛs] *nf* mass; **aller à la ~** to go to mass
Messieurs [mesjø] *nmpl voir* **Monsieur**
mesure [məzyʀ] *nf* (*évaluation, dimension*) measurement; (*étalon, récipient, contenu*) measure; (*Mus: cadence*) time, tempo; (: *division*) bar; (*retenue*) moderation; (*disposition*) measure, step; **sur ~** (*costume*) made-to-measure; **dans la ~ où** insofar as, inasmuch as; **dans une certaine ~** to some *ou* a certain extent; **à ~ que** as; **être en ~ de** to be in a position to
mesurer [məzyʀe] /1/ *vt* to measure; (*juger*) to weigh up, assess; (*modérer: ses paroles etc*) to moderate
métal, -aux [metal, -o] *nm* metal; **métallique** *adj* metallic
météo [meteo] *nf* (*bulletin*) (weather) forecast
météorologie [meteɔʀɔlɔʒi] *nf* meteorology
méthode [metɔd] *nf* method; (*livre, ouvrage*) manual, tutor
méticuleux, -euse [metikylø, -øz] *adj* meticulous
métier [metje] *nm* (*profession: gén*) job; (: *manuel*) trade; (: *artisanal*) craft; (*technique, expérience*) (acquired) skill *ou* technique; (*aussi: ~ à tisser*) (weaving) loom
métrage [metraʒ] *nm*: **long/moyen/court ~** feature *ou* full-length/medium-length/short film
mètre [mɛtʀ] *nm* metre; (*règle*) metre rule; (*ruban*) tape measure; **métrique** *adj* metric
métro [metro] *nm* underground (BRIT), subway (US)
métropole [metrɔpɔl] *nf* (*capitale*) metropolis; (*pays*) home country
mets [mɛ] *nm* dish

metteur [metœʀ] *nm*: **~ en scène** (*Théât*) producer; (*Ciné*) director

 MOT-CLÉ

mettre [mɛtʀ] /56/ *vt* **1** (*placer*) to put; **mettre en bouteille/en sac** to bottle/put in bags *ou* sacks
2 (*vêtements: revêtir*) to put on; (: *porter*) to wear; **mets ton gilet** put your cardigan on; **je ne mets plus mon manteau** I no longer wear my coat
3 (*faire fonctionner: chauffage, électricité*) to put on; (: *réveil, minuteur*) to set; (*installer: gaz, eau*) to put in, lay on; **mettre en marche** to start up
4 (*consacrer*): **mettre du temps/deux heures à faire qch** to take time/two hours to do sth; **y mettre du sien** to pull one's weight
5 (*noter, écrire*) to say, put (down); **qu'est-ce qu'il a mis sur la carte?** what did he say *ou* write on the card?; **mettez au pluriel ...** put ... into the plural
6 (*supposer*): **mettons que ...** let's suppose *ou* say that ...
se mettre *vr* **1** (*se placer*): **vous pouvez vous mettre là** you can sit (*ou* stand) there; **où ça se met?** where does it go?; **se mettre au lit** to get into bed; **se mettre au piano** to sit down at the piano; **se mettre de l'encre sur les doigts** to get ink on one's fingers
2 (*s'habiller*): **se mettre en maillot de bain** to get into *ou* put on a swimsuit; **n'avoir rien à se mettre** to have nothing to wear
3: **se mettre à** to begin, start; **se mettre à faire** to begin *ou* start doing *ou* to do; **se mettre au piano** to start learning the piano; **se mettre au régime** to go on a diet; **se mettre au travail/à l'étude** to get down to work/one's studies

m

meuble [mœbl] *nm* piece of furniture; (*ameublement*) furniture *no pl*; **meublé** *nm* furnished flat (BRIT) *ou* apartment (US); **meubler** /1/ *vt* to furnish; **se meubler** to furnish one's house

meuf [mœf] *nf* (*fam*) woman

meugler [møgle] /1/ *vi* to low, moo

meule [møl] *nf* (*à broyer*) millstone; (*de foin, blé*) stack; (*de fromage*) round

meunier, -ière [mønje, -jɛʀ] *nm* miller ▷ *nf* miller's wife

meurs *etc* [mœʀ] *vb voir* **mourir**

meurtre [mœʀtʀ] *nm* murder; **meurtrier, -ière** *adj* (*arme, épidémie, combat*) deadly; (*fureur, instincts*) murderous ▷ *nm/f* murderer(-ess)

meurtrir [mœʀtʀiʀ] /2/ *vt* to bruise; (*fig*) to wound

meus *etc* [mœ] *vb voir* **mouvoir**

meute [møt] *nf* pack

mexicain, e [mɛksikɛ̃, -ɛn] *adj* Mexican ▷ *nm/f*: **M~, e** Mexican

Mexico [mɛksiko] *n* Mexico City

Mexique [mɛksik] *nm*: **le ~** Mexico

mi [mi] *nm* (*Mus*) E; (*en chantant la gamme*) mi

mi... [mi] *préfixe* half(-), mid-; **à la mi-janvier** in mid-January; **à mi-jambes/-corps** (up *ou* down) to the knees/waist; **à mi-hauteur/-pente** halfway up (*ou* down)/up (*ou* down) the hill

miauler [mjole] /1/ *vi* to miaow

miche [miʃ] *nf* round *ou* cob loaf

mi-chemin [miʃmɛ̃]: **à ~** *adv* halfway, midway

mi-clos, e [miklo, -kloz] *adj* half-closed

micro [mikʀo] *nm* mike, microphone; (*Inform*) micro

microbe [mikʀɔb] *nm* germ, microbe

micro: micro-onde *nf*: **four à micro-ondes** microwave oven; **micro-ordinateur** *nm* microcomputer; **microscope** *nm* microscope; **microscopique** *adj* microscopic

midi [midi] *nm* midday, noon; (*moment du déjeuner*) lunchtime; (*sud*) south; **le M~** the South (of France), the Midi; **à ~** at 12 (o'clock) *ou* midday *ou* noon

mie [mi] *nf* inside (of the loaf)

miel [mjɛl] *nm* honey; **mielleux, -euse** *adj* (*personne*) sugary, syrupy

mien, ne [mjɛ̃, mjɛn] *pron*: **le (la) ~(ne), les ~s** mine; **les ~s** my family

miette [mjɛt] *nf* (*de pain, gâteau*) crumb; (*fig: de la conversation etc*) scrap; **en ~s** in pieces *ou* bits

MOT-CLÉ

mieux [mjø] *adv* **1** (*d'une meilleure façon*): **mieux (que)** better (than); **elle travaille/mange mieux** she works/eats better; **aimer mieux** to prefer; **elle va mieux** she is better; **de mieux en mieux** better and better **2** (*de la meilleure façon*) best; **ce que je sais le mieux** what I know best; **les livres les mieux faits** the best made books

▷ *adj inv* **1** (*plus à l'aise, en meilleure forme*) better; **se sentir mieux** to feel better

2 (*plus satisfaisant*) better; **c'est mieux ainsi** it's better like this; **c'est le mieux des deux** it's the better of the two; **le/la mieux, les mieux** the best; **demandez-lui, c'est le mieux** ask him, it's the best thing

3 (*plus joli*) better-looking; **il est mieux que son frère** (*plus beau*) he's better-looking than his brother; (*plus gentil*) he's nicer than his brother; **il est mieux sans moustache** he looks better without a moustache

4: **au mieux** at best; **au mieux avec** on the best of terms with; **pour le mieux** for the best

▷ *nm* **1** (*progrès*) improvement

2: **de mon/ton mieux** as best I/you can (*ou* could); **faire de son mieux** to do one's best

mignon, ne [miɲɔ̃, -ɔn] *adj* sweet, cute

migraine [migrɛn] *nf* headache; *(Méd)* migraine

mijoter [miʒɔte] /1/ *vt* to simmer; *(préparer avec soin)* to cook lovingly; *(affaire, projet)* to plot, cook up ▷ *vi* to simmer

milieu, x [miljø] *nm (centre)* middle; *(aussi:* **juste ~**) happy medium; *(Bio, Géo)* environment; *(entourage social)* milieu; *(familial)* background; *(pègre)*: **le ~** the underworld; **au ~ de** in the middle of; **au beau** *ou* **en plein ~ (de)** right in the middle (of)

militaire [militɛr] *adj* military, army *cpd* ▷ *nm* serviceman

militant, e [militɑ̃, -ɑ̃t] *adj, nm/f* militant

militer [milite] /1/ *vi* to be a militant

mille [mil] *num* a *ou* one thousand ▷ *nm (mesure)*: **~ (marin)** nautical mile; **mettre dans le ~** *(fig)* to be bang on (target); **millefeuille** *nm* cream *ou* vanilla slice; **millénaire** *nm* millennium ▷ *adj* thousand-year-old; *(fig)* ancient; **mille-pattes** *nm inv* centipede

millet [mijɛ] *nm* millet

milliard [miljar] *nm* milliard, thousand million *(BRIT)*, billion *(US)*; **milliardaire** *nm/f* multimillionaire *(BRIT)*, billionaire *(US)*

millier [milje] *nm* thousand; **un ~ (de)** a thousand or so, about a thousand; **par ~s** in (their) thousands, by the thousand

milligramme [miligram] *nm* milligramme

millimètre [milimɛtr] *nm* millimetre

million [miljɔ̃] *nm* million; **deux ~s de** two million; **millionnaire** *nm/f* millionaire

mime [mim] *nm/f (acteur)* mime(r) ▷ *nm (art)* mime, miming; **mimer** /1/ *vt* to mime; *(singer)* to mimic, take off

minable [minabl] *adj (personne)* shabby(-looking); *(travail)* pathetic

mince [mɛ̃s] *adj* thin; *(personne, taille)* slim, slender; *(fig: profit, connaissances)* slight, small; *(: prétexte)* weak ▷ *excl*: **~ (alors)!** darn it!; **minceur** *nf* thinness; *(d'une personne)* slimness, slenderness; **mincir** /2/ *vi* to get slimmer *ou* thinner

mine [min] *nf (physionomie)* expression, look; *(extérieur)* exterior, appearance; *(de crayon)* lead; *(gisement, exploitation, explosif)* mine; **avoir bonne ~** *(personne)* to look well; *(ironique)* to look an utter idiot; **avoir mauvaise ~** to look unwell; **faire ~ de faire** to make a pretence of doing; **~ de rien** although you wouldn't think so

miner [mine] /1/ *vt (saper)* to undermine, erode; *(Mil)* to mine

minerai [minrɛ] *nm* ore

minéral, e, -aux [mineral, -o] *adj* mineral

minéralogique [mineralɔʒik] *adj*: **plaque ~** number *(BRIT)* *ou* license *(US)* plate; **numéro ~** registration *(BRIT)* *ou* license *(US)* number

minet, te [minɛ, -ɛt] *nm/f (chat)* pussy-cat; *(péj)* young trendy

mineur, e [minœr] *adj* minor ▷ *nm/f (Jur)* minor ▷ *nm (travailleur)* miner

miniature [minjatyr] *adj, nf* miniature

minibus [minibys] *nm* minibus

minier, -ière [minje, -jɛr] *adj* mining

mini-jupe [miniʒyp] *nf* mini-skirt

minime [minim] *adj* minor, minimal

minimiser [minimize] /1/ *vt* to minimize; *(fig)* to play down

minimum [minimɔm] *adj, nm* minimum; **au ~** at the very least

ministère [ministɛr] *nm (cabinet)* government; *(département)* ministry; *(Rel)* ministry

ministre [ministr] *nm* minister *(BRIT)*, secretary; *(Rel)* minister; **~ d'État** senior minister *ou* secretary

Minitel® [minitɛl] nm (former) videotext terminal and service

minoritaire [minɔritɛr] adj minority cpd

minorité [minɔrite] nf minority; **être en ~** to be in the ou a minority

minuit [minɥi] nm midnight

minuscule [minyskyl] adj minute, tiny ▷ nf: **(lettre) ~** small letter

minute [minyt] nf minute; **à la ~** (just) this instant; (passé) there and then; **minuter** /1/ vt to time; **minuterie** nf time switch

minutieux, -euse [minysjø, -øz] adj (personne) meticulous; (travail) requiring painstaking attention to detail

mirabelle [mirabɛl] nf (cherry) plum

miracle [mirakl] nm miracle

mirage [miraʒ] nm mirage

mire [mir] nf: **point de ~** (fig) focal point

miroir [mirwar] nm mirror

miroiter [mirwate] /1/ vi to sparkle, shimmer; **faire ~ qch à qn** to paint sth in glowing colours for sb, dangle sth in front of sb's eyes

mis, e [mi, miz] pp de **mettre** ▷ adj: **bien ~** well dressed ▷ nf (argent: au jeu) stake; (tenue) clothing; attire; **être de ~e** to be acceptable ou in season; **~e de fonds** capital outlay; **~e à jour** update; **~e en plis** set; **~e au point** (fig) clarification; **~e en scène** production

miser [mize] /1/ vt (enjeu) to stake, bet; **~ sur** (cheval, numéro) to bet on; (fig) to bank ou count on

misérable [mizerabl] adj (lamentable, malheureux) pitiful, wretched; (pauvre) poverty-stricken; (insignifiant, mesquin) miserable ▷ nm/f wretch

misère [mizɛr] nf (extreme) poverty, destitution; **misères** nfpl (malheurs) woes, miseries; (ennuis) little troubles; **salaire de ~** starvation wage

missile [misil] nm missile

mission [misjɔ̃] nf mission; **partir en ~** (Admin, Pol) to go on an assignment; **missionnaire** nm/f missionary

mité, e [mite] adj moth-eaten

mi-temps [mitɑ̃] nf inv (Sport: période) half; (: pause) half-time; **à ~** part-time

miteux, -euse [mitø, -øz] adj seedy

mitigé, e [mitiʒe] adj (sentiments) mixed

mitoyen, ne [mitwajɛ̃, -ɛn] adj (mur) common, party cpd; **maisons ~nes** semi-detached houses; (plus de deux) terraced (BRIT) ou row (US) houses

mitrailler [mitraje] /1/ vt to machine-gun; (fig: photographier) to snap away at; **~ qn de** to pelt ou bombard sb with; **mitraillette** nf submachine gun; **mitrailleuse** nf machine gun

mi-voix [mivwa]: **à ~** adv in a low ou hushed voice

mixage [miksaʒ] nm (Ciné) (sound) mixing

mixer [miksœr] nm (food) mixer

mixte [mikst] adj (gén) mixed; (Scol) mixed, coeducational; **cuisinière ~** combined gas and electric cooker

mixture [mikstyr] nf mixture; (fig) concoction

Mlle (pl **Mlles**) abr = **Mademoiselle**

MM abr = **Messieurs**

Mme (pl **Mmes**) abr = **Madame**

mobile [mɔbil] adj mobile; (pièce de machine) moving ▷ nm (motif) motive; (œuvre d'art) mobile; **(téléphone) ~** mobile (phone)

mobilier, -ière [mɔbilje, -jɛr] nm furniture

mobiliser [mɔbilize] /1/ vt to mobilize

mobylette® [mɔbilɛt] nf moped

mocassin [mɔkasɛ̃] nm moccasin

moche [mɔʃ] adj (fam: laid) ugly; (mauvais, méprisable) rotten

modalité [mɔdalite] nf form, mode

mode [mɔd] nf fashion ▷ nm (manière) form, mode; (Ling) mood; (Inform,

Mus) mode; **à la ~** fashionable, in
fashion; **~ d'emploi** directions pl
(for use); **~ de paiement** method of
payment; **~ de vie** way of life

modèle [mɔdɛl] adj ▷ nm model;
(qui pose: de peintre) sitter; **~ déposé**
registered design; **~ réduit** small-
scale model; **modeler** /5/ vt to model

modem [mɔdɛm] nm modem

modéré, e [mɔdeʀe] adj, nm/f
moderate

modérer [mɔdeʀe] /6/ vt to
moderate; **se modérer** vi to restrain
o.s

moderne [mɔdɛʀn] adj
modern ▷ nm (Art) modern style;
(ameublement) modern furniture;
moderniser /1/ vt to modernize

modeste [mɔdɛst] adj modest;
modestie nf modesty

modifier [mɔdifje] /7/ vt to modify,
alter; **se modifier** vi to alter

modique [mɔdik] adj modest

module [mɔdyl] nm module

moelle [mwal] nf marrow

moelleux, -euse [mwalø, -øz] adj
soft; (gâteau) light and moist

mœurs [mœʀ] nfpl (conduite) morals;
(manières) manners; (pratiques
sociales) habits

moi [mwa] pron me; (emphatique):
~, je ... for my part, I ..., I myself ...;
c'est ~ qui l'ai fait I did it, it was me
who did it; **apporte-le-~** bring it to
me; **à ~** mine; (dans un jeu) my turn;
moi-même pron myself; (emphatique)
I myself

moindre [mwɛ̃dʀ] adj lesser;
lower; **le (la) ~, les ~s** the least; the
slightest; **c'est la ~ des choses** it's
nothing at all

moine [mwan] nm monk, friar

moineau, x [mwano] nm sparrow

MOT-CLÉ

moins [mwɛ̃] adv **1** (comparatif):
moins (que) less (than); **moins**

grand que less tall than, not as tall
as; **il a trois ans de moins que
moi** he's three years younger than
me; **moins je travaille, mieux
je me porte** the less I work, the
better I feel

2 (superlatif): **le moins** (the) least;
c'est ce que j'aime le moins it's
what I like (the) least; **le (la) moins
doué(e)** the least gifted; **au moins,
du moins** at least; **pour le moins** at
the very least

3: **moins de** (quantité) less (than);
(nombre) fewer (than); **moins de
sable/d'eau** less sand/water;
moins de livres/gens fewer books/
people; **moins de deux ans** less
than two years; **moins de midi** not
yet midday

4: **de moins, en moins: 100 euros/
3 jours de moins** 100 euros/3 days
less; **trois livres en moins** three
books fewer; three books too few;
de l'argent en moins less money;
le soleil en moins but for the sun,
minus the sun; **de moins en moins**
less and less

5: **à moins de, à moins que** unless;
à moins de faire unless we do (ou
he does etc); **à moins que tu ne
fasses** unless you do; **à moins d'un
accident** barring any accident

▶ prép: **quatre moins deux** four
minus two; **dix heures moins cinq**
five to ten; **il fait moins cinq** it's five
(degrees) below (freezing), it's minus
five; **il est moins cinq** it's five to

mois [mwa] nm month

moisi [mwazi] nm mould, mildew;
odeur de ~ musty smell; **moisir**
/2/ vi to go mouldy; **moisissure** nf
mould no pl

moisson [mwasɔ̃] nf harvest;
moissonner /1/ vt to harvest,
reap; **moissonneuse** nf (machine)
harvester

moite [mwat] adj sweaty, sticky

moitié [mwatje] *nf* half; **la ~** half; **la ~ de** half (of); **la ~ du temps/des gens** half the time/the people; **à la ~ de** halfway through; **à ~** half (*avant le verbe*), half- (*avant l'adjectif*); **à ~ prix** (at) half price

molaire [mɔlɛʀ] *nf* molar

molester [mɔlɛste] /1/ *vt* to manhandle, maul (about)

molle [mɔl] *adj f voir* **mou**; **mollement** *adv* (*péj: travailler*) sluggishly; (*protester*) feebly

mollet [mɔlɛ] *nm* calf ▷ *adj m*: **œuf ~** soft-boiled egg

molletonné, e [mɔltɔne] *adj* fleece-lined

mollir [mɔliʀ] /2/ *vi* (*personne*) to relent; (*substance*) to go soft

mollusque [mɔlysk] *nm* mollusc

môme [mom] *nm/f* (*fam: enfant*) brat

moment [mɔmɑ̃] *nm* moment; **ce n'est pas le ~** this is not the right time; **au même ~** at the same time; (*instant*) at the same moment; **pour un bon ~** for a good while; **pour le ~** for the moment, for the time being; **au ~ de** at the time of; **au ~ où** as; **à tout ~** at any time ou moment; (*continuellement*) constantly, continually; **en ce ~** at the moment; (*aujourd'hui*) at present; **sur le ~** at the time; **par ~s** now and then, at times; **d'un ~ à l'autre** any time (now); **du ~ où** ou **que** seeing that, since; **momentané, e** *adj* temporary, momentary; **momentanément** *adv* for a while

momie [mɔmi] *nf* mummy

mon, ma (*pl* **mes**) [mɔ̃, ma, me] *adj poss* my

Monaco [mɔnako] *nm*: **le ~** Monaco

monarchie [mɔnaʀʃi] *nf* monarchy

monastère [mɔnastɛʀ] *nm* monastery

mondain, e [mɔ̃dɛ̃, -ɛn] *adj* (*soirée, vie*) society *cpd*

monde [mɔ̃d] *nm* world; **le ~** (*personnes mondaines*) (high) society; **il** y a du ~ (*beaucoup de gens*) there are a lot of people; (*quelques personnes*) there are some people; **beaucoup/peu de ~** many/few people; **mettre au ~** to bring into the world; **pas le moins du ~** not in the least; **mondial, e, -aux** *adj* (*population*) world *cpd*; (*influence*) world-wide; **mondialement** *adv* throughout the world; **mondialisation** *nf* globalization

monégasque [mɔnegask] *adj* Monegasque, of ou from Monaco ▷ *nm/f*: **M~** Monegasque

monétaire [mɔnetɛʀ] *adj* monetary

moniteur, -trice [mɔnitœʀ, -tʀis] *nm/f* (*Sport*) instructor (instructress); (*de colonie de vacances*) supervisor ▷ *nm* (*écran*) monitor

monnaie [mɔnɛ] *nf* (*Écon: moyen d'échange*) currency; (*petites pièces*): **avoir de la ~** to have (some) change; **faire de la ~** to get (some) change; **avoir/faire la ~ de 20 euros** to have change of/get change for 20 euros; **rendre à qn la ~ (sur 20 euros)** to give sb the change (from ou out of 20 euros)

monologue [mɔnɔlɔg] *nm* monologue, soliloquy; **monologuer** /1/ *vi* to soliloquize

monopole [mɔnɔpɔl] *nm* monopoly

monotone [mɔnɔtɔn] *adj* monotonous

Monsieur (*pl* **Messieurs**) [məsjø, mesjø] *nm* (*titre*) Mr; **un/le monsieur** (*homme quelconque*) a/the gentleman; **~, ...** (*en tête de lettre*) Dear Sir, ...; *voir aussi* **Madame**

monstre [mɔ̃stʀ] *nm* monster ▷ *adj* (*fam: effet, publicité*) massive; **un travail ~** a fantastic amount of work; **monstrueux, -euse** *adj* monstrous

mont [mɔ̃] *nm*: **par ~s et par vaux** up hill and down dale; **le M~ Blanc** Mont Blanc

montage [mɔ̃taʒ] *nm* (*d'une machine etc*) assembly; (*Photo*) photomontage; (*Ciné*) editing

montagnard, e [mɔ̃taɲaʀ, -aʀd] *adj* mountain *cpd* ▷ *nm/f* mountain-dweller

montagne [mɔ̃taɲ] *nf* (*cime*) mountain; (*région*): **la ~** the mountains *pl*; **~s russes** big dipper *sg*, switchback *sg*; **montagneux, -euse** *adj* mountainous; (*basse montagne*) hilly

montant, e [mɔ̃tɑ̃, -ɑ̃t] *adj* rising; (*robe, corsage*) high-necked ▷ *nm* (*somme, total*) total, (*total*) amount; (*de fenêtre*) upright; (*de lit*) post

monte-charge [mɔ̃tʃaʀʒ] *nm inv* goods lift, hoist

montée [mɔ̃te] *nf* rise; (*escalade*) climb; (*côte*) hill; **au milieu de la ~** halfway up

monter [mɔ̃te] /1/ *vt* (*escalier, côte*) to go (*ou* come) up; (*valise, paquet*) to take (*ou* bring) up; (*étagère*) to raise; (*tente, échafaudage*) to put up; (*machine*) to assemble; (*Ciné*) to edit; (*Théât*) to put on, stage; (*société, coup etc*) to set up ▷ *vi* to go (*ou* come) up; (*chemin, niveau, température, voix, prix*) to go up, rise; (*passager*) to get on; **~ à cheval** (*faire du cheval*) to ride (a horse); **~ sur** to climb up onto; **~ sur** *ou* **à un arbre/une échelle** to climb (up) a tree/ladder; **se ~ à** (*frais etc*) to add up to, come to

montgolfière [mɔ̃gɔlfjɛʀ] *nf* hot-air balloon

montre [mɔ̃tʀ] *nf* watch; **contre la ~** (*Sport*) against the clock

Montréal [mɔ̃real] *n* Montreal

montrer [mɔ̃tʀe] /1/ *vt* to show; **~ qch à qn** to show sb sth

monture [mɔ̃tyʀ] *nf* (*bête*) mount; (*d'une bague*) setting; (*de lunettes*) frame

monument [mɔnymɑ̃] *nm* monument; **~ aux morts** war memorial

moquer [mɔke] /1/: **se ~ de** *vt* to make fun of, laugh at; (*fam: se*

désintéresser de) not to care about; (*tromper*): **se ~ de qn** to take sb for a ride

moquette [mɔkɛt] *nf* fitted carpet

moqueur, -euse [mɔkœʀ, -øz] *adj* mocking

moral, e, -aux [mɔʀal, -o] *adj* moral ▷ *nm* morale ▷ *nf* (*conduite*) morals *pl* (*règles*); (*valeurs*) moral standards *pl*, morality; (*d'une fable etc*) moral; **faire la ~e à** to lecture, preach at; **moralité** *nf* morality; (*conclusion, enseignement*) moral

morceau, x [mɔʀso] *nm* piece, bit; (*d'une œuvre*) passage, extract; (*Mus*) piece; (*Culin: de viande*) cut; (: *de sucre*) lump; **mettre en ~x** to pull to pieces *ou* bits; **manger un ~** to have a bite (to eat)

morceler [mɔʀsəle] /4/ *vt* to break up, divide up

mordant, e [mɔʀdɑ̃, -ɑ̃t] *adj* (*ton, remarque*) scathing, cutting; (*froid*) biting ▷ *nm* (*fougue*) bite, punch

mordiller [mɔʀdije] /1/ *vt* to nibble at, chew at

mordre [mɔʀdʀ] /41/ *vt* to bite ▷ *vi* (*poisson*) to bite; **~ sur** (*fig*) to go over into, overlap into; **~ à l'hameçon** to bite, rise to the bait

mordu, e [mɔʀdy] *nm/f* enthusiast; **un ~ du jazz/de la voile** a jazz/sailing fanatic *ou* buff

morfondre [mɔʀfɔ̃dʀ] /41/: **se morfondre** *vi* to mope

morgue [mɔʀg] *nf* (*arrogance*) haughtiness; (*lieu: de la police*) morgue; (: *à l'hôpital*) mortuary

morne [mɔʀn] *adj* dismal, dreary

morose [mɔʀoz] *adj* sullen, morose

mors [mɔʀ] *nm* bit

morse [mɔʀs] *nm* (*Zool*) walrus; (*Tél*) Morse (code)

morsure [mɔʀsyʀ] *nf* bite

mort¹ [mɔʀ] *nf* death

mort², e [mɔʀ, mɔʀt] *pp de* **mourir** ▷ *adj* dead ▷ *nm/f* (*défunt*) dead man/woman; (*victime*): **il y a eu plusieurs**

m

~s several people were killed; **~ de peur/fatigue** frightened to death/dead tired

mortalité [mɔʀtalite] *nf* mortality, death rate

mortel, le [mɔʀtɛl] *adj* (*poison etc*) deadly, lethal; (*accident, blessure*) fatal; (*silence, ennemi*) deadly; (*danger, frayeur, péché*) mortal; (*ennui, soirée*) deadly (boring)

mort-né, e [mɔʀne] *adj* (*enfant*) stillborn

mortuaire [mɔʀtɥɛʀ] *adj*: **avis ~s** death announcements

morue [mɔʀy] *nf* (*Zool*) cod *inv*

mosaïque [mɔzaik] *nf* mosaic

Moscou [mɔsku] *n* Moscow

mosquée [mɔske] *nf* mosque

mot [mo] *nm* word; (*message*) line, note; **~ à ~** word for word; **~ de passe** password; **~s croisés** crossword (puzzle) *sg*

motard [mɔtaʀ] *nm* biker; (*policier*) motorcycle cop

mot-dièse *nm* (*Inform: Twitter*) hashtag

motel [mɔtɛl] *nm* motel

moteur, -trice [mɔtœʀ, -tʀis] *adj* (*Anat, Physiol*) motor; (*Tech*) driving; (*Auto*): **à 4 roues motrices** 4-wheel drive ▷ *nm* engine, motor; **à ~** power-driven, motor *cpd*; **~ de recherche** search engine

motif [mɔtif] *nm* (*cause*) motive; (*décoratif*) design, pattern, motif; **sans ~** groundless

motivation [mɔtivasjɔ̃] *nf* motivation

motiver [mɔtive] /1/ *vt* (*justifier*) to justify, account for; (*Admin, Jur, Psych*) to motivate

moto [mɔto] *nf* (*motor*)bike; **motocycliste** *nm/f* motorcyclist

motorisé, e [mɔtɔʀize] *adj* (*personne*) having one's own transport

motrice [mɔtʀis] *adj f voir* **moteur**

motte [mɔt] *nf*: **~ de terre** lump of earth, clod (of earth); **~ de beurre** lump of butter

mou (mol), molle [mu, mɔl] *adj* soft; (*personne*) sluggish; (*résistance, protestations*) feeble ▷ *nm*: **avoir du ~** to be slack

mouche [muʃ] *nf* fly

moucher [muʃe] /1/: **se moucher** *vi* to blow one's nose

moucheron [muʃʀɔ̃] *nm* midge

mouchoir [muʃwaʀ] *nm* handkerchief, hanky; **~ en papier** tissue, paper hanky

moudre [mudʀ] /47/ *vt* to grind

moue [mu] *nf* pout; **faire la ~** to pout; (*fig*) to pull a face

mouette [mwɛt] *nf* (sea)gull

moufle [mufl] *nf* (*gant*) mitt(en)

mouillé, e [muje] *adj* wet

mouiller [muje] /1/ *vt* (*humecter*) to wet, moisten; (*tremper*): **~ qn/qch** to make sb/sth wet ▷ *vi* (*Navig*) to lie *ou* be at anchor; **se mouiller** to get wet; (*fam: prendre des risques*) to commit o.s

moulant, e [mulɑ̃, -ɑ̃t] *adj* figure-hugging

moule [mul] *nf* mussel ▷ *nm* (*Culin*) mould; **~ à gâteau** *nm* cake tin (BRIT) *ou* pan (US)

mouler [mule] /1/ *vt* (*vêtement*) to hug, fit closely round

moulin [mulɛ̃] *nm* mill; **~ à café** coffee mill; **~ à eau** watermill; **~ à légumes** (vegetable) shredder; **~ à paroles** (*fig*) chatterbox; **~ à poivre** pepper mill; **~ à vent** windmill

moulinet [mulinɛ] *nm* (*de canne à pêche*) reel; (*mouvement*): **faire des ~s avec qch** to whirl sth around

moulinette® [mulinɛt] *nf* (vegetable) shredder

moulu, e [muly] *pp de* **moudre**

mourant, e [muʀɑ̃, -ɑ̃t] *adj* dying

mourir [muʀiʀ] /1/ *vi* to die; (*civilisation*) to die out; **~ de froid/faim/vieillesse** to die of exposure/hunger/old age; **~ de faim/d'ennui** (*fig*) to be starving/be bored to death; **~ d'envie de faire** to be dying to do

mousse [mus] *nf* (*Bot*) moss; (*de savon*) lather; (*écume: sur eau, bière*) froth, foam; (*Culin*) mousse ▷ *nm* (*Navig*) ship's boy; **~ à raser** shaving foam
mousseline [muslin] *nf* muslin; **pommes ~** creamed potatoes
mousser [muse] /1/ *vi* (*bière, détergent*) to foam; (*savon*) to lather; **mousseux, -euse** *adj* frothy ▷ *nm*: **(vin) mousseux** sparkling wine
mousson [musɔ̃] *nf* monsoon
moustache [mustaʃ] *nf* moustache; **moustaches** *nfpl* (*d'animal*) whiskers *pl*; **moustachu, e** *adj* with a moustache
moustiquaire [mustikɛʀ] *nf* mosquito net
moustique [mustik] *nm* mosquito
moutarde [mutaʀd] *nf* mustard
mouton [mutɔ̃] *nm* sheep *inv*; (*peau*) sheepskin; (*Culin*) mutton
mouvement [muvmɑ̃] *nm* movement; (*geste*) gesture; **avoir un bon ~** to make a nice gesture; **en ~** in motion; on the move; **mouvementé, e** *adj* (*vie, poursuite*) eventful; (*réunion*) turbulent
mouvoir [muvwaʀ] /27/: **se mouvoir** *vi* to move
moyen, ne [mwajɛ̃, -ɛn] *adj* average; (*tailles, prix*) medium; (*de grandeur moyenne*) medium-sized ▷ *nm* (*façon*) means *sg*, way ▷ *nf* average; (*Statistique*) mean; (*Scol: à l'examen*) pass mark; **moyens** *nmpl* (*capacités*) means; **très ~** (*résultats*) pretty poor; **je n'en ai pas les ~s** I can't afford it; **au ~ de** by means of; **par tous les ~s** by every possible means, every possible way; **par ses propres ~s** all by oneself; **~ âge** Middle Ages; **~ de transport** means of transport; **~ne d'âge** average age; **~ne entreprise** (*Comm*) medium-sized firm
moyennant [mwajenɑ̃] *prép* (*somme*) for; (*service, conditions*) in return for; (*travail, effort*) with

Moyen-Orient [mwajɛnɔʀjɑ̃] *nm*: **le ~** the Middle East
moyeu, x [mwajø] *nm* hub
MST *sigle f* (= *maladie sexuellement transmissible*) STD
mû, mue [my] *pp de* **mouvoir**
muer [mɥe] /1/ *vi* (*oiseau, mammifère*) to moult; (*serpent*) to slough (its skin); (*jeune garçon*): **il mue** his voice is breaking
muet, te [mɥɛ, -ɛt] *adj* (*fig*): **~ d'admiration** *etc* speechless with admiration *etc*; (*Ciné*) silent
mufle [myfl] *nm* muzzle; (*goujat*) boor
mugir [myʒiʀ] /2/ *vi* (*bœuf*) to bellow; (*vache*) to low; (*fig*) to howl
muguet [mygɛ] *nm* lily of the valley
mule [myl] *nf* (*Zool*) (she-)mule
mulet [mylɛ] *nm* (*Zool*) (he-)mule; (*poisson*) mullet
multinational, e, -aux [myltinasjɔnal, -o] *adj, nf* multinational
multiple [myltipl] *adj* multiple, numerous; (*varié*) many, manifold; **multiplication** *nf* multiplication; **multiplier** /7/ *vt* to multiply; **se multiplier** *vi* to multiply
municipal, e, -aux [mynisipal, -o] *adj* (*élections, stade*) municipal; (*conseil*) town *cpd*; **piscine/ bibliothèque ~e** public swimming pool/library; **municipalité** *nf* (*corps municipal*) town council; (*commune*) municipality
munir [myniʀ] /2/ *vt*: **~ qn/qch de** to equip sb/sth with; **se ~ de** to provide o.s. with
munitions [mynisjɔ̃] *nfpl* ammunition *sg*
mur [myʀ] *nm* wall; **~ (payant)** (*Inform*) paywall; **~ du son** sound barrier
mûr, e [myʀ] *adj* ripe; (*personne*) mature
muraille [myʀaj] *nf* (high) wall
mural, e, -aux [myʀal, -o] *adj* wall *cpd* ▷ *nm* (*Art*) mural

m

mûre [myʀ] nf blackberry
muret [myʀɛ] nm low wall
mûrir [myʀiʀ] /2/ vi (fruit, blé) to ripen; (abcès, furoncle) to come to a head; (fig: idée, personne) to mature ▷ vt (personne) to (make) mature; (pensée, projet) to nurture
murmure [myʀmyʀ] nm murmur; **murmurer** /1/ vi to murmur
muscade [myskad] nf (aussi: **noix (de) ~**) nutmeg
muscat [myska] nm (raisin) muscat grape; (vin) muscatel (wine)
muscle [myskl] nm muscle; **musclé, e** adj muscular; (fig) strong-arm cpd
museau, x [myzo] nm muzzle; (Culin) brawn
musée [myze] nm museum; (de peinture) art gallery
museler [myzle] /4/ vt to muzzle; **muselière** nf muzzle
musette [myzɛt] nf (sac) lunch bag
musical, e, -aux [myzikal, -o] adj musical
music-hall [myzikol] nm (salle) variety theatre; (genre) variety
musicien, ne [myzisjɛ̃, -ɛn] adj musical ▷ nm/f musician
musique [myzik] nf music
musulman, e [myzylmɑ̃, -an] adj, nm/f Moslem, Muslim
mutation [mytasjɔ̃] nf (Admin) transfer
muter [myte] /1/ vt to transfer, move
mutilé, e [mytile] nm/f person with a disability (through loss of limbs)
mutiler [mytile] /1/ vt to mutilate, maim
mutin, e [mytɛ̃, -in] adj (enfant, air, ton) mischievous, impish ▷ nm/f (Mil, Navig) mutineer; **mutinerie** nf mutiny
mutisme [mytism] nm silence
mutuel, le [mytɥɛl] adj mutual ▷ nf mutual benefit society
myope [mjɔp] adj short-sighted
myosotis [mjɔzɔtis] nm forget-me-not

myrtille [miʀtij] nf blueberry
mystère [mistɛʀ] nm mystery; **mystérieux, -euse** adj mysterious
mystifier [mistifje] /7/ vt to fool
mythe [mit] nm myth
mythologie [mitɔlɔʒi] nf mythology

n

n' [n] *adv voir* **ne**

nacre [nakʀ] *nf* mother-of-pearl

nage [naʒ] *nf* swimming; *(manière)* style of swimming, stroke; **traverser/s'éloigner à la ~** to swim across/away; **en ~** bathed in sweat; **nageoire** *nf* fin; **nager** /3/ *vi* to swim; **nageur, -euse** *nm/f* swimmer

naïf, -ïve [naif, naiv] *adj* naïve

nain, e [nɛ̃, nɛn] *nm/f (péj)* dwarf (!)

naissance [nɛsɑ̃s] *nf* birth; **donner ~ à** to give birth to; *(fig)* to give rise to; **lieu de ~** place of birth

naître [nɛtʀ] /59/ *vi* to be born; *(conflit, complications):* **~ de** to arise from, be born out of; **je suis né en 1960** I was born in 1960; **faire ~** *(fig)* to give rise to, arouse

naïveté [naivte] *nf* naivety

nana [nana] *nf (fam: fille)* bird (BRIT), chick

nappe [nap] *nf* tablecloth; *(de pétrole, gaz)* layer; **napperon** *nm* table-mat

narguer [naʀge] /1/ *vt* to taunt

narine [naʀin] *nf* nostril

natal, e [natal] *adj* native; **natalité** *nf* birth rate

natation [natasjɔ̃] *nf* swimming

natif, -ive [natif, -iv] *adj* native

nation [nasjɔ̃] *nf* nation; **national, e, -aux** *adj* national ⊳ *nf:* **(route) nationale** ≈ A road (BRIT), ≈ state highway (US); **nationaliser** /1/ *vt* to nationalize; **nationalisme** *nm* nationalism; **nationalité** *nf* nationality

natte [nat] *nf (tapis)* mat; *(cheveux)* plait

naturaliser [natyʀalize] /1/ *vt* to naturalize

nature [natyʀ] *nf* nature ⊳ *adj, adv (Culin)* plain, without seasoning or sweetening; *(café, thé)* black; without sugar; *(yaourt)* natural; **payer en ~** to pay in kind; **~ morte** still-life; **naturel, le** *adj* natural ⊳ *nm* naturalness; *(caractère)* disposition, nature; **naturellement** *adv* naturally; *(bien sûr)* of course

naufrage [nofʀaʒ] *nm* (ship)wreck; **faire ~** to be shipwrecked

nausée [noze] *nf* nausea; **avoir la ~** to feel sick

nautique [notik] *adj* nautical, water *cpd*; **sports ~s** water sports

naval, e [naval] *adj* naval; *(industrie)* shipbuilding

navet [navɛ] *nm* turnip; *(péj: film)* third-rate film

navette [navɛt] *nf* shuttle; **faire la ~ (entre)** to go to and fro (between)

navigateur [navigatœʀ] *nm (Navig)* seafarer; *(Inform)* browser

navigation [navigasjɔ̃] *nf* navigation, sailing

naviguer [navige] /1/ *vi* to navigate, sail; **~ sur Internet** to browse the Internet

navire [naviʀ] *nm* ship

navrer [navʀe] /1/ *vt* to upset, distress; **je suis navré (de/de faire/ que)** I'm so sorry (for/for doing/that)

n

ne, n' [nə, n] *adv voir* **pas¹**; **plus²**; **jamais** *etc*; *(sans valeur négative, non traduit)*: **c'est plus loin que je ne le croyais** it's further than I thought

né, e [ne] *pp de* **naître**; **né en 1960** born in 1960; **née Scott** née Scott

néanmoins [neãmwɛ̃] *adv* nevertheless

néant [neã] *nm* nothingness; **réduire à ~** to bring to nought; *(espoir)* to dash

nécessaire [neseseʀ] *adj* necessary ▷ *nm* necessary; *(sac)* kit; **faire le ~** to do the necessary; **~ de couture** sewing kit; **~ de toilette** toilet bag; **nécessité** *nf* necessity; **nécessiter** /1/ *vt* to require

nectar [nɛktaʀ] *nm* nectar

néerlandais, e [neɛʀlãdɛ, -ɛz] *adj* Dutch

nef [nɛf] *nf (d'église)* nave

néfaste [nefast] *adj (nuisible)* harmful; *(funeste)* ill-fated

négatif, -ive [negatif, -iv] *adj* negative ▷ *nm (Photo)* negative

négligé, e [neɡliʒe] *adj (en désordre)* slovenly ▷ *nm (tenue)* negligee

négligeable [neɡliʒabl] *adj* negligible

négligent, e [neɡliʒã, -ãt] *adj* careless; negligent

négliger [neɡliʒe] /3/ *vt (épouse, jardin)* to neglect; *(tenue)* to be careless about; *(avis, précautions)* to disregard; **~ de faire** to fail to do, not bother to do

négociant, e [neɡɔsjã, -jãt] *nm/f* merchant

négociation [neɡɔsjasjɔ̃] *nf* negotiation

négocier [neɡɔsje] /7/ *vi, vt* to negotiate

nègre [nɛɡʀ] *nm (péj)* Negro (!); *(écrivain)* ghost writer

neige [nɛʒ] *nf* snow; **neiger** /3/ *vi* to snow

nénuphar [nenyfaʀ] *nm* water-lily

néon [neɔ̃] *nm* neon

néo-zélandais, e [neɔzelãdɛ, -ɛz] *adj* New Zealand *cpd* ▷ *nm/f*: **N~, e** New Zealander

Népal [nepal] *nm*: **le ~** Nepal

nerf [nɛʀ] *nm* nerve; **être** *ou* **vivre sur les ~s** to live on one's nerves; **nerveux, -euse** *adj* nervous; *(irritable)* touchy, nervy; *(voiture)* nippy, responsive; **nervosité** *nf* excitability, tenseness

n'est-ce pas [nɛspɑ] *adv* isn't it?, won't you? *etc (selon le verbe qui précède)*

net, nette [nɛt] *adj (sans équivoque, distinct)* clear; *(amélioration, différence)* marked, distinct; *(propre)* neat, clean; *(Comm: prix, salaire, poids)* net ▷ *adv (refuser)* flatly ▷ *nm*: **mettre au ~** to copy out; **s'arrêter ~** to stop dead; **nettement** *adv* clearly, decidedly; **netteté** *nf* clearness

nettoyage [netwajaʒ] *nm* cleaning; **~ à sec** dry cleaning

nettoyer [netwaje] /8/ *vt* to clean

neuf¹ [nœf] *num* nine

neuf², neuve [nœf, nœv] *adj* new; **remettre à ~** to do up (as good as new), refurbish; **quoi de ~?** what's new?

neutre [nøtʀ] *adj (Ling)* neuter

neuve [nœv] *adj f voir* **neuf²**

neuvième [nœvjɛm] *num* ninth

neveu, x [nəvø] *nm* nephew

New York [njujɔʀk] *n* New York

nez [ne] *nm* nose; **avoir du ~** to have flair; **~ à ~ avec** face to face with

ni [ni] *conj*: **ni … ni** neither … nor; **je n'aime ni les lentilles ni les épinards** I like neither lentils nor spinach; **il n'a dit ni oui ni non** he didn't say either yes or no; **elles ne sont venues ni l'une ni l'autre** neither of them came; **il n'a rien vu ni entendu** he didn't see or hear anything

niche [niʃ] *nf (du chien)* kennel; *(de mur)* recess, niche; **nicher** /1/ *vi* to nest

nid [ni] *nm* nest; **~ de poule** pothole
nièce [njɛs] *nf* niece
nier [nje] /7/ *vt* to deny
Nil [nil] *nm*: **le ~** the Nile
n'importe [nɛ̃pɔʀt] *adv*: **~ qui/
quoi/où** anybody/anything/
anywhere; **~ quand** any time; **~
quel/quelle** any; **~ lequel/laquelle**
any (one); **~ comment** (*sans soin*)
carelessly
niveau, x [nivo] *nm* level; (*des élèves,
études*) standard; **~ de vie** standard
of living
niveler [nivle] /4/ *vt* to level
noble [nɔbl] *adj* noble; **noblesse** *nf*
nobility; (*d'une action etc*) nobleness
noce [nɔs] *nf* wedding; (*gens*)
wedding party (*ou* guests *pl*); **faire
la ~** (*fam*) to go on a binge; **~s
d'or/d'argent/de diamant** golden/
silver/diamond wedding
nocif, -ive [nɔsif, -iv] *adj* harmful
nocturne [nɔktyʀn] *adj* nocturnal
▷ *nf* late opening
Noël [nɔɛl] *nm* Christmas
nœud [nø] *nm* knot; (*ruban*) bow;
~ papillon bow tie
noir, e [nwaʀ] *adj* black; (*obscur,
sombre*) dark ▷ *nm/f* black man/
woman ▷ *nm*: **dans le ~** in the dark
▷ *nf* (*Mus*) crotchet (BRIT), quarter
note (US); **travailler au ~** to work on
the side; **noircir** /2/ *vt, vi* to blacken
noisette [nwazɛt] *nf* hazelnut
noix [nwa] *nf* walnut; (*Culin*): **une ~
de beurre** a knob of butter; **à la ~**
(*fam*) worthless; **~ de cajou** cashew
nut; **~ de coco** coconut; **~ muscade**
nutmeg
nom [nɔ̃] *nm* name; (*Ling*) noun;
~ de famille surname; **~ de jeune
fille** maiden name; **~ d'utilisateur**
username
nomade [nɔmad] *nm/f* nomad
nombre [nɔ̃bʀ] *nm* number; **venir
en ~** to come in large numbers;
depuis ~ d'années for many
years; **au ~ de mes amis** among

my friends; **nombreux, -euse** *adj*
many, numerous; (*avec nom sg: foule
etc*) large; **peu nombreux** few; **de
nombreux cas** many cases
nombril [nɔ̃bʀi(l)] *nm* navel
nommer [nɔme] /1/ *vt* to name;
(*élire*) to appoint, nominate; **se
nommer** *vr*: **il se nomme Pascal** his
name's Pascal, he's called Pascal
non [nɔ̃] *adv* (*réponse*) no; (*suivi d'un
adjectif, adverbe*) not; **Paul est venu,
~?** Paul came, didn't he?; **~ pas que**
not that; **moi ~ plus** neither do I, I
don't either; **je pense que ~** I don't
think so; **~ alcoolisé** non-alcoholic
nonchalant, e [nɔ̃ʃalɑ̃, -ɑ̃t] *adj*
nonchalant
non-fumeur, -euse [nɔ̃fymœr,
-øz] *nm/f* non-smoker
non-sens [nɔ̃sɑ̃s] *nm* absurdity
nord [nɔʀ] *nm* North ▷ *adj* northern;
north; **au ~** (*situation*) in the north;
(*direction*) to the north; **au ~ de** to the
north of; **nord-africain, e** *adj* North-
African ▷ *nm/f*: **Nord-Africain, e**
North African; **nord-est** *nm* North-
East; **nord-ouest** *nm* North-West
normal, e, -aux [nɔʀmal, -o] *adj*
normal ▷ *nf*: **la ~e** the norm, the
average; **c'est tout à fait ~** it's
perfectly natural; **vous trouvez
ça ~?** does it seem right to you?;
normalement *adv* (*en général*)
normally
normand, e [nɔʀmɑ̃, -ɑ̃d] *adj*
Norman ▷ *nm/f*: **N~, e** (*de Normandie*)
Norman
Normandie [nɔʀmɑ̃di] *nf*: **la ~**
Normandy
norme [nɔʀm] *nf* norm; (*Tech*)
standard
Norvège [nɔʀvɛʒ] *nf*: **la ~** Norway;
norvégien, ne *adj* Norwegian
▷ *nm* (*Ling*) Norwegian ▷ *nm/f*:
Norvégien, ne Norwegian
nos [no] *adj poss voir* **notre**
nostalgie [nɔstalʒi] *nf* nostalgia;
nostalgique *adj* nostalgic

n

notable [nɔtabl] *adj* notable, noteworthy; (*marqué*) noticeable, marked ▷ *nm* prominent citizen

notaire [nɔtɛʀ] *nm* solicitor

notamment [nɔtamɑ̃] *adv* in particular, among others

note [nɔt] *nf* (*écrite, Mus*) note; (*Scol*) mark (*BRIT*), grade; (*facture*) bill; **~ de service** memorandum

noter [nɔte] /1/ *vt* (*écrire*) to write down; (*remarquer*) to note, notice; (*devoir*) to mark, give a grade to

notice [nɔtis] *nf* summary, short article; (*brochure*): **~ explicative** explanatory leaflet, instruction booklet

notifier [nɔtifje] /7/ *vt*: **~ qch à qn** to notify sb of sth, notify sth to sb

notion [nɔsjɔ̃] *nf* notion, idea

notoire [nɔtwaʀ] *adj* widely known; (*en mal*) notorious

notre (*pl* **nos**) [nɔtʀ(ə), no] *adj poss* our

nôtre [notʀ] *adj* ours ▷ *pron*: **le/la ~** ours; **les ~s** ours; (*alliés etc*) our own people; **soyez des ~s** join us

nouer [nwe] /1/ *vt* to tie, knot; (*fig: alliance etc*) to strike up

noueux, -euse [nwø, -øz] *adj* gnarled

nourrice [nuʀis] *nf* ≈ child-minder

nourrir [nuʀiʀ] /2/ *vt* to feed; (*fig: espoir*) to harbour, nurse; **nourrissant, e** *adj* nutritious; **nourrisson** *nm* (unweaned) infant; **nourriture** *nf* food

nous [nu] *pron* (*sujet*) we; (*objet*) us; **nous-mêmes** *pron* ourselves

nouveau (nouvel), -elle, x [nuvo, -ɛl] *adj* new ▷ *nm/f* new pupil (*ou* employee) ▷ *nm*: **il y a du ~** there's something new ▷ *nf* (*piece of*) news *sg*; (*Littérature*) short story; **nouvelles** *nfpl* (*Presse, TV*) news; **de ~**, **à ~** again; **je suis sans nouvelles de lui** I haven't heard from him; **Nouvel An** New Year; **~ venu, nouvelle venue** newcomer; **~x mariés** newly-weds; **nouveau-né, e** *nm/f* newborn

(baby); **nouveauté** *nf* novelty; (*chose nouvelle*) something new

nouvelle: **Nouvelle-Calédonie** [nuvɛlkaledɔni] *nf*: **la Nouvelle-Calédonie** New Caledonia; **Nouvelle-Zélande** [nuvɛlzelɑ̃d] *nf*: **la Nouvelle-Zélande** New Zealand

novembre [nɔvɑ̃bʀ] *nm* November; *voir aussi* **juillet**

● **LE 11 NOVEMBRE**
●
● *Le 11 novembre* is a public holiday
● in France and commemorates
● the signing of the armistice, near
● Compiègne, at the end of the First
● World War.

noyade [nwajad] *nf* drowning *no pl*

noyau, x [nwajo] *nm* (*de fruit*) stone; (*Bio, Physique*) nucleus; (*fig: centre*) core

noyer [nwaje] /8/ *nm* walnut (tree); (*bois*) walnut ▷ *vt* to drown; (*moteur*) to flood; **se noyer** to be drowned, drown; (*suicide*) to drown o.s.

nu, e [ny] *adj* naked; (*membres*) naked, bare; (*chambre, fil, plaine*) bare ▷ *nm* (*Art*) nude; **tout nu** stark naked; **se mettre nu** to strip

nuage [nɥaʒ] *nm* (*aussi Inform*) cloud; **informatique en ~** cloud computing; **nuageux, -euse** *adj* cloudy

nuance [nɥɑ̃s] *nf* (*de couleur, sens*) shade; **il y a une ~ (entre)** there's a slight difference (between); **nuancer** /3/ *vt* (*pensée, opinion*) to qualify

nucléaire [nykleɛʀ] *adj* nuclear ▷ *nm*: **le ~** nuclear power

nudiste [nydist] *nm/f* nudist

nuée [nɥe] *nf*: **une ~ de** a cloud *ou* host *ou* swarm of

nuire [nɥiʀ] /38/ *vi* to be harmful; **~ à** to harm, do damage to; **nuisible** [nɥizibl] *adj* harmful; **(animal) nuisible** pest

nuit [nɥi] *nf* night; **il fait ~** it's dark; **cette ~** (*hier*) last night; (*aujourd'hui*)

tonight; **de ~** (*vol, service*) night *cpd*;
~ blanche sleepless night
nul, nulle [nyl] *adj* (*aucun*) no;
(*minime*) nil, non-existent; (*non
valable*) null; (*péj*) useless, hopeless
▷ *pron* none, no one; **résultat ~,
match ~** draw; **nulle part** nowhere;
nullement *adv* by no means
numérique [nymeʀik] *adj*
numerical; (*affichage, son, télévision*)
digital
numéro [nymeʀo] *nm* number;
(*spectacle*) act, turn; (*Presse*) issue,
number; **~ de téléphone** (tele)phone
number; **~ vert** ≈ Freefone® number
(BRIT), ≈ toll-free number (US);
numéroter /1/ *vt* to number
nuque [nyk] *nf* nape of the neck
nu-tête [nytɛt] *adj inv* bareheaded
nutritif, -ive [nytʀitif, -iv] *adj*
(*besoins, valeur*) nutritional; (*aliment*)
nutritious, nourishing
nylon [nilɔ̃] *nm* nylon

oasis [ɔazis] *nm ou f* oasis
obéir [ɔbeiʀ] /2/ *vi* to obey; **~ à** to
obey; **obéissance** *nf* obedience;
obéissant, e *adj* obedient
obèse [ɔbɛz] *adj* obese; **obésité** *nf*
obesity
objecter [ɔbʒɛkte] /1/ *vt*: **~ (à qn)
que** to object (to sb) that; **objecteur**
nm: **objecteur de conscience**
conscientious objector
objectif, -ive [ɔbʒɛktif, -iv] *adj*
objective ▷ *nm* (*Optique, Photo*) lens
sg; (*Mil, fig*) objective
objection [ɔbʒɛksjɔ̃] *nf* objection
objectivité [ɔbʒɛktivite] *nf*
objectivity
objet [ɔbʒɛ] *nm* object; (*d'une
discussion, recherche*) subject; **être
ou faire l'~ de** (*discussion*) to be the
subject of; (*soins*) to be given *ou*
shown; **sans ~** purposeless; (*sans
fondement*) groundless; **~ d'art** objet
d'art; **~s personnels** personal items;

~s trouvés lost property sg (BRIT), lost-and-found sg (US); **~s de valeur** valuables

obligation [ɔbligasjɔ̃] nf obligation; (Comm) bond, debenture; **obligatoire** adj compulsory, obligatory; **obligatoirement** adv necessarily; (fam: sans aucun doute) inevitably

obliger [ɔbliʒe] /3/ vt (contraindre): **~ qn à faire** to force ou oblige sb to do; **je suis bien obligé (de le faire)** I have to (do it)

oblique [ɔblik] adj oblique; **en ~** diagonally

oblitérer [ɔblitere] /6/ vt (timbre-poste) to cancel

obnubiler [ɔbnybile] /1/ vt to obsess

obscène [ɔpsɛn] adj obscene

obscur, e [ɔpskyʀ] adj dark; (raisons) obscure; **obscurcir** /2/ vt to darken; (fig) to obscure; **s'obscurcir** vi to grow dark; **obscurité** nf darkness; **dans l'obscurité** in the dark, in darkness

obsédé, e [ɔpsede] nm/f fanatic; **~(e) sexuel(le)** sex maniac

obséder [ɔpsede] /6/ vt to obsess, haunt

obsèques [ɔpsɛk] nfpl funeral sg

observateur, -trice [ɔpsɛʀvatœʀ, -tʀis] adj observant, perceptive ▷ nm/f observer

observation [ɔpsɛʀvasjɔ̃] nf observation; (d'un règlement etc) observance; (reproche) reproof; **en ~** (Méd) under observation

observatoire [ɔpsɛʀvatwaʀ] nm observatory

observer [ɔpsɛʀve] /1/ vt (regarder) to observe, watch; (scientifiquement, aussi: règlement, jeûne etc) to observe; (surveiller) to watch; (remarquer) to observe, notice; **faire ~ qch à qn** (dire) to point out sth to sb

obsession [ɔpsesjɔ̃] nf obsession

obstacle [ɔpstakl] nm obstacle; (Équitation) jump, hurdle; **faire ~ à**

(projet) to hinder, put obstacles in the path of

obstiné, e [ɔpstine] adj obstinate

obstiner [ɔpstine] /1/: **s'obstiner** vi to insist, dig one's heels in; **s' ~ à faire** to persist (obstinately) in doing

obstruer [ɔpstʀye] /1/ vt to block, obstruct

obtenir [ɔptəniʀ] /22/ vt to obtain, get; (résultat) to achieve, obtain; **~ de pouvoir faire** to obtain permission to do

obturateur [ɔptyʀatœʀ] nm (Photo) shutter

obus [ɔby] nm shell

occasion [ɔkazjɔ̃] nf (aubaine, possibilité) opportunity; (circonstance) occasion; (Comm: article non neuf) secondhand buy; (: acquisition avantageuse) bargain; **à plusieurs ~s** on several occasions; **à l'~** sometimes, on occasions; **d'~** secondhand; **occasionnel, le** adj occasional

occasionner [ɔkazjɔne] /1/ vt to cause

occident [ɔksidɑ̃] nm: **l'O~** the West; **occidental, e, -aux** adj western; (Pol) Western ▷ nm/f Westerner

occupation [ɔkypasjɔ̃] nf occupation

occupé, e [ɔkype] adj (Mil, Pol) occupied; (personne) busy; (place, sièges) taken; (toilettes) engaged; **la ligne est ~e** the line's engaged (BRIT) ou busy (US)

occuper [ɔkype] /1/ vt to occupy; (poste, fonction) to hold; **s'~ (à qch)** to occupy o.s ou keep o.s. busy (with sth); **s'~ de** (être responsable de) to be in charge of; (se charger de: affaire) to take charge of, deal with; (: clients etc) to attend to

occurrence [ɔkyʀɑ̃s] nf: **en l'~** in this case

océan [ɔseɑ̃] nm ocean

octet [ɔktɛ] nm byte

octobre [ɔktɔbʀ] nm October

oculiste [ɔkylist] nm/f eye specialist

odeur [ɔdœʀ] nf smell

odieux, -euse [ɔdjø, -øz] adj hateful

odorant, e [ɔdɔʀɑ̃, -ɑ̃t] adj sweet-smelling, fragrant

odorat [ɔdɔʀa] nm (sense of) smell

œil [œj] (pl **yeux**) nm eye; **avoir un ~ poché** ou **au beurre noir** to have a black eye; **à l'~** (fam) for free; **à l'~ nu** with the naked eye; **fermer les yeux (sur)** (fig) to turn a blind eye (to); **les yeux fermés** (aussi fig) with one's eyes shut; **ouvrir l'~** (fig) to keep one's eyes open ou an eye out

œillères [œjɛʀ] nfpl blinkers (BRIT), blinders (US)

œillet [œjɛ] nm (Bot) carnation

œuf [œf] nm egg; **~ à la coque/dur/mollet** soft-boiled/hard-boiled/soft-boiled egg; **~ au plat/poché** fried/poached egg; **~s brouillés** scrambled eggs; **~ de Pâques** Easter egg

œuvre [œvʀ] nf (tâche) task, undertaking; (ouvrage achevé, livre, tableau etc) work; (ensemble de la production artistique) works pl ▷ nm (Constr): **le gros ~** the shell; **mettre en ~** (moyens) to make use of; **~ d'art** work of art; **~s de bienfaisance** charitable works

offense [ɔfɑ̃s] nf insult; **offenser** /1/ vt to offend, hurt; **s'offenser de** vi to take offence (BRIT) ou offense (US) at

offert, e [ɔfɛʀ, -ɛʀt] pp de **offrir**

office [ɔfis] nm (agence) bureau, agency; (Rel) service ▷ nm ou f (pièce) pantry; **faire ~ de** to act as; **d'~** automatically; **~ du tourisme** tourist office

officiel, le [ɔfisjɛl] adj, nm/f official

officier [ɔfisje] /7/ nm officer

officieux, -euse [ɔfisjø, -øz] adj unofficial

offrande [ɔfʀɑ̃d] nf offering

offre [ɔfʀ] nf offer; (aux enchères) bid; (Admin: soumission) tender; (Écon): **l'~ et la demande** supply and demand; **~ d'emploi** job advertised;

"~s d'emploi" "situations vacant"; **~ publique d'achat (OPA)** takeover bid

offrir [ɔfʀiʀ] /18/ vt: **~ (à qn)** to offer (to sb); (faire cadeau) to give to (sb); **s'offrir**, vt (vacances, voiture) to treat o.s. to; **~ (à qn) de faire qch** to offer to do sth (for sb); **~ à boire à qn** (chez soi) to offer sb a drink; **je vous offre un verre** I'll buy you a drink

OGM sigle m (= organisme génétiquement modifié) GMO

oie [wa] nf (Zool) goose

oignon [ɔɲɔ̃] nm onion; (de tulipe etc) bulb

oiseau, x [wazo] nm bird; **~ de proie** bird of prey

oisif, -ive [wazif, -iv] adj idle

oléoduc [ɔleɔdyk] nm (oil) pipeline

olive [ɔliv] nf (Bot) olive; **olivier** nm olive (tree)

OLP sigle f (= Organisation de libération de la Palestine) PLO

olympique [ɔlɛ̃pik] adj Olympic

ombragé, e [ɔ̃bʀaʒe] adj shaded, shady

ombre [ɔ̃bʀ] nf (espace non ensoleillé) shade; (ombre portée, tache) shadow; **à l'~** in the shade; **dans l'~** (fig) in the dark; **~ à paupières** eye shadow

omelette [ɔmlɛt] nf omelette; **~ norvégienne** baked Alaska

omettre [ɔmɛtʀ] /56/ vt to omit, leave out

omoplate [ɔmɔplat] nf shoulder blade

MOT-CLÉ

on [ɔ̃] pron **1** (indéterminé) you, one; **on peut le faire ainsi** you ou one can do it like this, it can be done like this **2** (quelqu'un): **on les a attaqués** they were attacked; **on vous demande au téléphone** there's a phone call for you, you're wanted on the phone **3** (nous) we; **on va y aller demain** we're going tomorrow

4 (les gens) they; **autrefois, on croyait ...** they used to believe ..
5: **on ne peut plus** adv: **on ne peut plus stupide** as stupid as can be

oncle [ɔ̃kl] nm uncle
onctueux, -euse [ɔ̃ktɥø, -øz] adj creamy; smooth
onde [ɔ̃d] nf wave; **~s courtes (OC)** short wave sg; **~s moyennes (OM)** medium wave sg; **grandes ~s (GO), ~s longues (OL)** long wave sg
ondée [ɔ̃de] nf shower
on-dit [ɔ̃di] nm inv rumour
onduler [ɔ̃dyle] /1/ vi to undulate; (cheveux) to wave
onéreux, -euse [ɔnerø, -øz] adj costly
ongle [ɔ̃gl] nm nail
ont [ɔ̃] vb voir **avoir**
ONU sigle f (= Organisation des Nations unies) UN(O)
onze ['ɔ̃z] num eleven; **onzième** num eleventh
OPA sigle f = **offre publique d'achat**
opaque [ɔpak] adj opaque
opéra [ɔpera] nm opera; (édifice) opera house
opérateur, -trice [ɔperatœr, -tris] nm/f operator; **~ (de prise de vues)** cameraman
opération [ɔperasjɔ̃] nf operation; (Comm) dealing
opératoire [ɔperatwar] adj (choc etc) post-operative
opérer [ɔpere] /6/ vt (Méd) to operate on; (faire, exécuter) to carry out, make ▷ vi (remède: faire effet) to act, work; (Méd) to operate; **s'opérer** vi (avoir lieu) to occur, take place; **se faire ~** to have an operation
opérette [ɔperɛt] nf operetta, light opera
opinion [ɔpinjɔ̃] nf opinion; **l'~ (publique)** public opinion
opportun, e [ɔpɔrtœ̃, -yn] adj timely, opportune; **opportuniste** [ɔpɔrtynist] nm/f opportunist

opposant, e [ɔpozɑ̃, -ɑ̃t] nm/f opponent
opposé, e [ɔpoze] adj (direction, rive) opposite; (faction) opposing; (opinions, intérêts) conflicting; (contre): **~ à** opposed to, against ▷ nm: **l'~** the other ou opposite side (ou direction); (contraire) the opposite; **à l'~** (fig) on the other hand; **à l'~ de** (fig) contrary to, unlike
opposer [ɔpoze] /1/ vt (personnes, armées, équipes) to oppose; (couleurs, termes, tons) to contrast; **~ qch à** (comme obstacle, défense) to set sth against; (comme objection) to put sth forward against; **s'opposer** vi (équipes) to confront each other; (opinions) to conflict; (couleurs, styles) to contrast; **s'~ à** (interdire, empêcher) to oppose
opposition [ɔpozisjɔ̃] nf opposition; **par ~ à** as opposed to; **entrer en ~ avec** to come into conflict with; **faire ~ à un chèque** to stop a cheque
oppressant, e [ɔpresɑ̃, -ɑ̃t] adj oppressive
oppresser [ɔprese] /1/ vt to oppress; **oppression** nf oppression
opprimer [ɔprime] /1/ vt to oppress
opter [ɔpte] /1/ vi: **~ pour** to opt for; **~ entre** to choose between
opticien, ne [ɔptisjɛ̃, -ɛn] nm/f optician
optimisme [ɔptimism] nm optimism; **optimiste** [ɔptimist] adj optimistic ▷ nm/f optimist
option [ɔpsjɔ̃] nf option; **matière à ~** (Scol) optional subject
optique [ɔptik] adj (nerf) optic; (verres) optical ▷ nf (fig: manière de voir) perspective
or [ɔr] nm gold ▷ conj now, but; **en or** gold cpd; **une affaire en or** a real bargain; **il croyait gagner or il a perdu** he was sure he would win and yet he lost
orage [ɔraʒ] nm (thunder)storm; **orageux, -euse** adj stormy

oral, e, -aux [ɔral, -o] adj oral; (Méd):
par voie ~e orally ▷ nm oral
orange [ɔrɑ̃ʒ] adj inv, nf orange;
orangé, e adj orangey, orange-
coloured; **orangeade** nf orangeade;
oranger nm orange tree
orateur [ɔratœr] nm speaker
orbite [ɔrbit] nf (Anat) (eye-)socket;
(Physique) orbit
Orcades [ɔrkad] nfpl: **les ~** the
Orkneys, the Orkney Islands
orchestre [ɔrkɛstr] nm orchestra;
(de jazz, danse) band; (places) stalls pl
(BRIT), orchestra (US)
orchidée [ɔrkide] nf orchid
ordinaire [ɔrdiner] adj ordinary;
(modèle, qualité) standard; (péj:
commun) common ▷ nm ordinary;
(menus) everyday fare ▷ nf (essence)
≈ two-star (petrol) (BRIT), ≈ regular
(gas) (US); **d'~** usually, normally;
comme à l'~ as usual
ordinateur [ɔrdinatœr] nm
computer; **~ individuel** ou
personnel personal computer;
~ portable laptop (computer)
ordonnance [ɔrdɔnɑ̃s] nf (Méd)
prescription; (Mil) orderly, batman
(BRIT)
ordonné, e [ɔrdɔne] adj tidy, orderly
ordonner [ɔrdɔne] /1/ vt (agencer) to
organize, arrange; (donner un ordre):
~ à qn de faire to order sb to do; (Rel)
to ordain; (Méd) to prescribe
ordre [ɔrdr] nm order; (propreté et
soin) orderliness, tidiness; **à l'~ de**
payable to; (nature): **d'~ pratique** of
a practical nature; **ordres** nmpl (Rel)
holy orders; **mettre en ~** to tidy (up),
put in order; **par ~ alphabétique/
d'importance** in alphabetical order/
in order of importance; **être aux
~s de qn/sous les ~s de qn** to be at
sb's disposal/under sb's command;
jusqu'à nouvel ~ until further notice;
de premier ~ first-rate; **~ du jour**
(d'une réunion) agenda; **à l'~ du jour**
(fig) topical; **~ public** law and order

ordure [ɔrdyr] nf filth no pl; **ordures**
nfpl (balayures, déchets) rubbish sg,
refuse sg; **~s ménagères** household
refuse
oreille [ɔrɛj] nf ear; **avoir de l'~** to
have a good ear (for music)
oreiller [ɔreje] nm pillow
oreillons [ɔrejɔ̃] nmpl mumps sg
ores [ɔr]: **d'~ et déjà** adv already
orfèvrerie [ɔrfevrəri] nf
goldsmith's (ou silversmith's) trade;
(ouvrage) (silver ou gold) plate
organe [ɔrgan] nm organ; (porte-
parole) representative, mouthpiece
organigramme [ɔrganigram] nm
(hiérarchie, structure) organization
chart; (des opérations) flow chart
organique [ɔrganik] adj organic
organisateur, -trice
[ɔrganizatœr, -tris] nm/f organizer
organisation [ɔrganizasjɔ̃] nf
organization; **O~ des Nations
unies (ONU)** United Nations
(Organization) (UN(O))
organiser [ɔrganize] /1/ vt to
organize; (mettre sur pied: service
etc) to set up; **s'organiser** to get
organized
organisme [ɔrganism] nm (Bio)
organism; (corps humain) body;
(Admin, Pol etc) body
organiste [ɔrganist] nm/f organist
orgasme [ɔrgasm] nm orgasm, climax
orge [ɔrʒ] nf barley
orgue [ɔrg] nm organ
orgueil [ɔrgœj] nm pride;
orgueilleux, -euse adj proud
oriental, e, -aux [ɔrjɑ̃tal, -o] adj
(langue, produit) oriental; (frontière)
eastern
orientation [ɔrjɑ̃tasjɔ̃] nf (de
recherches) orientation; (d'une maison
etc) aspect; (d'un journal) leanings pl;
avoir le sens de l'~ to have a (good)
sense of direction; **~ professionnelle**
careers advisory service
orienté, e [ɔrjɑ̃te] adj (fig: article,
journal) slanted; **bien/mal ~**

(*appartement*) well/badly positioned;
~ au sud facing south, with a
southern aspect

orienter [ɔRjɑ̃te] /1/ *vt* (*tourner*:
antenne) to direct, turn; (: *voyageur*,
touriste, *recherches*) to direct; (*fig*:
élève) to orientate; **s'orienter**
(*se repérer*) to find one's bearings; **s'~
vers** (*fig*) to turn towards

origan [ɔRigɑ̃] *nm* oregano

originaire [ɔRiʒinɛR] *adj*: **être ~ de**
to be a native of

original, e, -aux [ɔRiʒinal, -o] *adj*
original; (*bizarre*) eccentric ▷ *nm/f*
eccentric ▷ *nm* (*document etc*, *Art*)
original

origine [ɔRiʒin] *nf* origin; **origines**
nfpl (*d'une personne*) origins; **d'~**
(*pays*) of origin; (*pneus etc*) original;
d'~ française of French origin; **à l'~**
originally; **originel, le** *adj* original

orme [ɔRm] *nm* elm

ornement [ɔRnəmɑ̃] *nm* ornament

orner [ɔRne] /1/ *vt* to decorate,
adorn

ornière [ɔRnjɛR] *nf* rut

orphelin, e [ɔRfəlɛ̃, -in] *adj*
orphan(ed) ▷ *nm/f* orphan; **~ de
père/mère** fatherless/motherless;
orphelinat *nm* orphanage

orteil [ɔRtɛj] *nm* toe; **gros ~** big toe

orthographe [ɔRtɔgRaf] *nf* spelling

ortie [ɔRti] *nf* (stinging) nettle

os [ɔs] *nm* bone; **os à moelle**
marrowbone

osciller [ɔsile] /1/ *vi* (*au vent etc*)
to rock; (*fig*): **~ entre** to waver *ou*
fluctuate between

osé, e [oze] *adj* daring, bold

oseille [ozɛj] *nf* sorrel

oser [oze] /1/ *vi, vt* to dare; **~ faire** to
dare (to) do

osier [ozje] *nm* willow; **d'~, en ~**
wicker(work) *cpd*

osseux, -euse [ɔsø, -øz] *adj* bony;
(*tissu, maladie, greffe*) bone *cpd*

otage [ɔtaʒ] *nm* hostage; **prendre
qn comme ~** to take sb hostage

OTAN *sigle f* (= *Organisation du traité de
l'Atlantique Nord*) NATO

otarie [ɔtaRi] *nf* sea-lion

ôter [ote] /1/ *vt* to remove; (*soustraire*)
to take away; **~ qch à qn** to take sth
(away) from sb; **~ qch de** to remove
sth from

otite [ɔtit] *nf* ear infection

ou [u] *conj* or; **ou ... ou** either ... or;
ou bien or (else)

 MOT-CLÉ

où [u] *pron relatif* **1** (*position, situation*)
where, that (*souvent omis*); **la
chambre où il était** the room (that)
he was in, the room where he was; **la
ville où je l'ai rencontré** the town
where I met him; **la pièce d'où il
est sorti** the room he came out of;
le village d'où je viens the village
I come from; **les villes par où il est
passé** the towns he went through
2 (*temps, état*) that (*souvent omis*); **le
jour où il est parti** the day (that) he
left; **au prix où c'est** at the price it is
▷ *adv* **1** (*interrogation*) where; **où est-
il/va-t-il?** where is he/is he going?;
par où? which way?; **d'où vient
que ...?** how come ...?
2 (*position*) where; **je sais où il est**
I know where he is; **où que l'on aille**
wherever you go

ouate [wat] *nf* cotton wool (BRIT),
cotton (US)

oubli [ubli] *nm* (*acte*): **l'~ de**
forgetting; (*trou de mémoire*) lapse
of memory; (*négligence*) omission,
oversight; **tomber dans l'~** to sink
into oblivion

oublier [ublije] /7/ *vt* to forget; (*ne pas
voir*: *erreurs etc*) to miss; (*laisser quelque
part*: *chapeau etc*) to leave behind

ouest [wɛst] *nm* west ▷ *adj inv* west;
(*région*) western; **à l'~** in the west;
(*direction*) (to the) west, westwards;
à l'~ de (to the) west of

ouf [uf] *excl* phew!

oui [wi] *adv* yes

ouï-dire ['widiʀ]: **par ~** *adv* by hearsay

ouïe [wi] *nf* hearing; **ouïes** *nfpl* (*de poisson*) gills

ouragan [uʀagɑ̃] *nm* hurricane

ourlet [uʀlɛ] *nm* hem

ours [uʀs] *nm* bear; **~ brun/blanc** brown/polar bear; **~ (en peluche)** teddy (bear)

oursin [uʀsɛ̃] *nm* sea urchin

ourson [uʀsɔ̃] *nm* (bear-)cub

ouste [ust] *excl* hop it!

outil [uti] *nm* tool; **outiller** /1/ *vt* to equip

outrage [utʀaʒ] *nm* insult; **~ à la pudeur** indecent behaviour *no pl*

outrance [utʀɑ̃s]: **à ~** *adv* excessively, to excess

outre [utʀ] *prép* besides ▷ *adv*: **passer ~ à** to disregard, take no notice of; **en ~** besides, moreover; **~ mesure** to excess; (*manger, boire*) immoderately; **outre-Atlantique** *adv* across the Atlantic; **outre-mer** *adv* overseas

ouvert, e [uvɛʀ, -ɛʀt] *pp de* **ouvrir** ▷ *adj* open; (*robinet, gaz etc*) on; **ouvertement** *adv* openly; **ouverture** *nf* opening; (*Mus*) overture; **ouverture d'esprit** open-mindedness; **heures d'ouverture** (*Comm*) opening hours

ouvrable [uvʀabl] *adj*: **jour ~** working day, weekday

ouvrage [uvʀaʒ] *nm* (*tâche, de tricot etc*) work *no pl*; (*texte, livre*) work

ouvre-boîte(s) [uvʀəbwat] *nm inv* tin (BRIT) *ou* can opener

ouvre-bouteille(s) [uvʀəbutɛj] *nm inv* bottle-opener

ouvreuse [uvʀøz] *nf* usherette

ouvrier, -ière [uvʀije, -jɛʀ] *nm/f* worker ▷ *adj* working-class; (*problèmes, conflit*) industrial; (*mouvement*) labour *cpd*; **classe ouvrière** working class

ouvrir [uvʀiʀ] /18/ *vt* (*gén*) to open; (*brèche, passage*) to open up; (*commencer l'exploitation de, créer*) to open (up); (*eau, électricité, chauffage, robinet*) to turn on; (*Méd: abcès*) to open up, cut open ▷ *vi* to open; to open up; **s'ouvrir** *vi* to open; **s'~ à qn (de qch)** to open one's heart to sb (about sth); **~ l'appétit à qn** to whet sb's appetite

ovaire [ɔvɛʀ] *nm* ovary

ovale [ɔval] *adj* oval

OVNI [ɔvni] *sigle m* (= *objet volant non identifié*) UFO

oxyder [ɔkside] /1/: **s'oxyder** *vi* to become oxidized

oxygéné, e [ɔksiʒene] *adj*: **eau ~e** hydrogen peroxide

oxygène [ɔksiʒɛn] *nm* oxygen

ozone [ozon] *nm* ozone; **trou dans la couche d'~** hole in the ozone layer

o

P

pacifique [pasifik] *adj* peaceful ▷ *nm*: **le P~, l'océan P~** the Pacific (Ocean)

pack [pak] *nm* pack

pacotille [pakɔtij] *nf* cheap junk *pl*

PACS *sigle m* (= pacte civil de solidarité) ≈ civil partnership; **se pacser** *vi* ≈ to form a civil partnership

pacte [pakt] *nm* pact, treaty

pagaille [pagaj] *nf* mess, shambles *sg*

page [paʒ] *nf* page ▷ *nm* page (boy); **à la ~** (*fig*) up-to-date; **~ d'accueil** (*Inform*) home page; **~ Web** (*Inform*) web page

païen, ne [pajɛ̃, -ɛn] *adj, nm/f* pagan, heathen

paillasson [pajasɔ̃] *nm* doormat

paille [pɑj] *nf* straw

pain [pɛ̃] *nm* (*substance*) bread; (*unité*) loaf (of bread); (*morceau*): **~ de cire** *etc* bar of wax *etc*; **~ bis/ complet** brown/wholemeal (*BRIT*) *ou* wholewheat (*US*) bread; **~ d'épice** ≈ gingerbread; **~ grillé** toast; **~ de mie** sandwich loaf; **~ au chocolat** pain au chocolat; **~ aux raisins** currant pastry

pair, e [pɛR] *adj* (*nombre*) even ▷ *nm* peer; **aller de ~ (avec)** to go hand in hand *ou* together (with); **jeune fille au ~** au pair; **paire** *nf* pair

paisible [pezibl] *adj* peaceful, quiet

paix [pɛ] *nf* peace; **faire la ~ avec** to make peace with; **fiche-lui la ~!** (*fam*) leave him alone!

Pakistan [pakistɑ̃] *nm*: **le ~** Pakistan

palais [palɛ] *nm* palace; (*Anat*) palate

pâle [pɑl] *adj* pale; **bleu ~** pale blue

Palestine [palɛstin] *nf*: **la ~** Palestine

palette [palɛt] *nf* (*de peintre*) palette; (*de produits*) range

pâleur [pɑlœR] *nf* paleness

palier [palje] *nm* (*d'escalier*) landing; (*fig*) level, plateau; **par ~s** in stages

pâlir [pɑliR] /2/ *vi* to turn *ou* go pale; (*couleur*) to fade

pallier [palje] /7/ *vt*: **~ à** to offset, make up for

palme [palm] *nf* (*de plongeur*) flipper; **palmé, e** [palme] *adj* (*pattes*) webbed

palmier [palmje] *nm* palm tree; (*gâteau*) heart-shaped biscuit made of flaky pastry

pâlot, te [pɑlo, -ɔt] *adj* pale, peaky

palourde [paluRd] *nf* clam

palper [palpe] /1/ *vt* to feel, finger

palpitant, e [palpitɑ̃, -ɑ̃t] *adj* thrilling

palpiter [palpite] /1/ *vi* (*cœur, pouls*) to beat (: *plus fort*) to pound, throb

paludisme [palydism] *nm* malaria

pamphlet [pɑ̃flɛ] *nm* lampoon, satirical tract

pamplemousse [pɑ̃pləmus] *nm* grapefruit

pan [pɑ̃] *nm* section, piece ▷ *excl* bang!

panache [panaʃ] *nm* plume; (*fig*) spirit, panache

panaché, e [panaʃe] *nm* (*bière*) shandy; **glace ~e** mixed ice cream

pancarte [pɑ̃kart] nf sign, notice
pancréas [pɑ̃kreas] nm pancreas
pandémie [pɑ̃demi] nf pandemic
pané, e [pane] adj fried in breadcrumbs
panier [panje] nm basket; **mettre au ~ to** chuck away; **~ à provisions** shopping basket; **panier-repas** nm packed lunch
panique [panik] adj panicky ▷ nf panic; **paniquer** /1/ vi to panic
panne [pan] nf breakdown; **être/ tomber en ~ to** have broken down/ break down; **être en ~ d'essence** ou **en ~ sèche** to have run out of petrol (BRIT) ou gas (US); **~ d'électricité** ou **de courant** power ou electrical failure
panneau, x [pano] nm (écriteau) sign, notice; **~ d'affichage** notice (BRIT) ou bulletin (US) board; **~ indicateur** signpost; **~ de signalisation** roadsign
panoplie [panɔpli] nf (jouet) outfit; (d'armes) display; (fig) array
panorama [panɔrama] nm panorama
panse [pɑ̃s] nf paunch
pansement [pɑ̃smɑ̃] nm dressing, bandage; **~ adhésif** sticking plaster
pantacourt [pɑ̃takur] nm cropped trousers pl
pantalon [pɑ̃talɔ̃] nm trousers pl (BRIT), pants pl (US), pair of trousers ou pants; **~ de ski** ski pants pl
panthère [pɑ̃tɛr] nf panther
pantin [pɑ̃tɛ̃] nm puppet
pantoufle [pɑ̃tufl] nf slipper
paon [pɑ̃] nm peacock
papa [papa] nm dad(dy)
pape [pap] nm pope
paperasse [papras] nf (péj) bumf no pl, papers pl; **paperasserie** nf (péj) red tape no pl; paperwork no pl
papeterie [papetri] nf (magasin) stationer's (shop) (BRIT)
papi [papi] nm (fam) granddad
papier [papje] nm paper; (article) article; **papiers** nmpl (aussi: **~s**)

d'identité) (identity) papers; **~ (d') aluminium** aluminium (BRIT) ou aluminum (US) foil, tinfoil; **~ calque** tracing paper; **~ hygiénique** ou **(de) toilette** toilet paper; **~ journal** newspaper; **~ à lettres** writing paper, notepaper; **~ peint** wallpaper; **~ de verre** sandpaper
papillon [papijɔ̃] nm butterfly; (fam: contravention) (parking) ticket; **~ de nuit** moth
papillote [papijɔt] nf: **en ~** cooked in tinfoil
papoter [papɔte] /1/ vi to chatter
paquebot [pakbo] nm liner
pâquerette [pakrɛt] nf daisy
Pâques [pak] nm, nfpl Easter

> **PÂQUES**
>
> In France, Easter eggs are said to
> be brought by the Easter bells or
> cloches de Pâques which fly from
> Rome and drop them in people's
> gardens.

paquet [pakɛ] nm packet; (colis) parcel; (fig: tas): **~ de** pile ou heap of; **paquet-cadeau** nm gift-wrapped parcel
par [par] prép by; **finir** etc **~** to end etc with; **~ amour** out of love; **passer ~ Lyon/la côte** to go via ou through Lyons/along by the coast; **~ la fenêtre** (jeter, regarder) out of the window; **trois ~ jour/personne** three a ou per day/head; **deux ~ deux** in twos; **~ ici** this way; (dans le coin) round here; **~-ci, ~-là** here and there; **~ temps de pluie** in wet weather
parabolique [parabɔlik] adj: **antenne ~** satellite dish
parachute [paraʃyt] nm parachute; **parachutiste** nm/f parachutist; (Mil) paratrooper
parade [parad] nf (spectacle, défilé) parade; (Escrime, Boxe) parry

P

paradis [paʀadi] nm heaven, paradise
paradoxe [paʀadɔks] nm paradox
paraffine [paʀafin] nf paraffin
parages [paʀaʒ] nmpl: **dans les ~ (de)** in the area ou vicinity (of)
paragraphe [paʀagʀaf] nm paragraph
paraître [paʀɛtʀ] /57/ vb copule to seem, look, appear ▷ vi to appear; (être visible) to show; (Presse, Édition) to be published, come out, appear ▷ vb impers: **il paraît que** it seems ou appears that
parallèle [paʀalɛl] adj parallel; (police, marché) unofficial ▷ nm (comparaison): **faire un ~ entre** to draw a parallel between ▷ nf parallel (line)
paralyser [paʀalize] /1/ vt to paralyze
paramédical, e, -aux [paʀamedikal, -o] adj: **personnel ~** paramedics pl, paramedical workers pl
paraphrase [paʀafʀaz] nf paraphrase
parapluie [paʀaplɥi] nm umbrella
parasite [paʀazit] nm parasite; **parasites** nmpl (Tél) interference sg
parasol [paʀasɔl] nm parasol, sunshade
paratonnerre [paʀatɔnɛʀ] nm lightning conductor
parc [paʀk] nm (public) park, gardens pl; (de château etc) grounds pl; (d'enfant) playpen; **~ d'attractions** amusement park; **~ éolien** wind farm; **~ de stationnement** car park; **~ à thème** theme park
parcelle [paʀsɛl] nf fragment, scrap; (de terrain) plot, parcel
parce que [paʀsk] conj because
parchemin [paʀʃəmɛ̃] nm parchment
parc(o)mètre [paʀk(ɔ)mɛtʀ] nm parking meter
parcourir [paʀkuʀiʀ] /11/ vt (trajet, distance) to cover; (article, livre) to skim ou glance through; (lieu) to go

all over, travel up and down; (frisson, vibration) to run through
parcours [paʀkuʀ] nm (trajet) journey; (itinéraire) route
par-dessous [paʀdəsu] prép, adv under(neath)
pardessus [paʀdəsy] nm overcoat
par-dessus [paʀdəsy] prép over (the top of) ▷ adv over (the top); **~ le marché** on top of it all; **~ tout** above all; **en avoir ~ la tête** to have had enough
par-devant [paʀdəvã] adv (passer) round the front
pardon [paʀdɔ̃] nm forgiveness no pl ▷ excl (I'm) sorry; (pour interpeller etc) excuse me; **demander ~ à qn (de)** to apologize to sb (for); **je vous demande ~** I'm sorry; (pour interpeller) excuse me; **pardonner** /1/ vt to forgive; **pardonner qch à qn** to forgive sb for sth
pare: pare-brise nm inv windscreen (BRIT), windshield (US); **pare-chocs** nm inv bumper; **pare-feu** nm inv (de foyer) fireguard; (Inform) firewall ▷ adj inv
pareil, le [paʀɛj] adj (identique) the same, alike; (similaire) similar; (tel): **un courage/livre ~** such courage/a book, courage/a book like this; **de ~s livres** such books; **faire ~** to do the same (thing); **~ à** the same as; similar to; **sans ~** unparalleled, unequalled
parent, e [paʀã, -ãt] nm/f: **un/une ~/e** a relative ou relation; **parents** nmpl (père et mère) parents; **parenté** nf (lien) relationship
parenthèse [paʀãtɛz] nf (ponctuation) bracket, parenthesis; (digression) parenthesis, digression; **entre ~s** in brackets; (fig) incidentally
paresse [paʀɛs] nf laziness; **paresseux, -euse** adj lazy
parfait, e [paʀfɛ, -ɛt] adj perfect ▷ nm (Ling) perfect (tense); **parfaitement** adv perfectly ▷ excl (most) certainly

parfois [paʀfwa] adv sometimes

parfum [paʀfœ̃] nm (produit) perfume, scent; (odeur: de fleur) scent, fragrance; (goût) flavour ; **parfumé, e** adj (fleur, fruit) fragrant; (femme) perfumed; **parfumé au café** coffee-flavoured (BRIT) ou -flavored (US); **parfumer** /1/ vt (odeur, bouquet) to perfume; (crème, gâteau) to flavour ; **parfumerie** nf (produits) perfumes; (boutique) perfume shop (BRIT) ou store (US)

pari [paʀi] nm bet; **parier** /7/ vt to bet

Paris [paʀi] n Paris; **parisien, ne** adj Parisian; (Géo, Admin) Paris cpd ▷ nm/f: **Parisien, ne** Parisian

parité [paʀite] nf: **~ hommes-femmes** (Pol) balanced representation of men and women

parjure [paʀʒyʀ] nm perjury

parking [paʀkiŋ] nm (lieu) car park (BRIT), parking lot (US)

> Attention à ne pas traduire parking par le mot anglais parking.

parlant, e [paʀlɑ̃, -ɑ̃t] adj (comparaison, preuve) eloquent; (Ciné) talking

parlement [paʀləmɑ̃] nm parliament; **parlementaire** adj parliamentary ▷ nm/f ≈ Member of Parliament (BRIT) ou Congress (US)

parler [paʀle] /1/ vi to speak, talk; (avouer) to talk; **~ (à qn) de** to talk ou speak (to sb) about; **~ le/en français** to speak French/in French; **~ affaires** to talk business; **sans ~ de** (fig) not to mention, to say nothing of; **tu parles!** (bien sûr) you bet!

parloir [paʀlwaʀ] nm (d'une prison, d'un hôpital) visiting room

parmi [paʀmi] prép among(st)

paroi [paʀwa] nf wall; (cloison) partition

paroisse [paʀwas] nf parish

parole [paʀɔl] nf (mot, promesse) word; (faculté): **la ~** speech; **paroles** nfpl (Mus) words, lyrics; **tenir ~** to keep one's word; **prendre la ~** to speak; **demander la ~** to ask for permission to speak; **je le crois sur ~** I'll take his word for it

parquet [paʀkɛ] nm (parquet) floor; (Jur) public prosecutor's office; **le ~ (général)** ≈ the Bench

parrain [paʀɛ̃] nm godfather; **parrainer** /1/ vt (nouvel adhérent) to sponsor

pars [paʀ] vb voir **partir**

parsemer [paʀsəme] /5/ vt (feuilles, papiers) to be scattered over; **~ qch de** to scatter sth with

part [paʀ] nf (qui revient à qn) share; (fraction, portie) part; **prendre ~ à** (débat etc) to take part in; (soucis, douleur de qn) to share in; **faire ~ de qch à qn** to announce sth to sb, inform sb of sth; **pour ma ~** as for me, as far as I'm concerned; **à ~ entière** full; **de la ~ de** (au nom de) on behalf of; (donné par) from; **de toute(s) ~(s)** from all sides ou quarters; **de ~ et d'autre** on both sides, on either side; **d'une ~ ... d'autre ~** on the one hand ... on the other hand; **d'autre ~** (de plus) moreover; **à ~** adv separately; (de côté) aside; prép apart from, except for; **faire la ~ des choses** to make allowances

partage [paʀtaʒ] nm sharing (out) no pl, share-out; dividing up

partager [paʀtaʒe] /3/ vt to share; (distribuer, répartir) to share (out); (morceler, diviser) to divide (up); **se partager** vt (héritage etc) to share between themselves (ou ourselves etc)

partenaire [paʀtənɛʀ] nm/f partner

parterre [paʀtɛʀ] nm (de fleurs) (flower) bed; (Théât) stalls pl

parti [paʀti] nm (Pol) party; (décision) course of action; (personne à marier) match; **tirer ~ de** to take advantage of, turn to good account; **prendre ~ (pour/contre)** to take sides ou a stand (for/against); **~ pris** bias

P

partial, e, -aux [paʀsjal, -o] *adj*
biased, partial

participant, e [paʀtisipɑ̃, -ɑ̃t] *nm/f*
participant; *(à un concours)* entrant

participation [paʀtisipasjɔ̃]
nf participation; *(financière)*
contribution

participer [paʀtisipe] /1/: **~ à** *vt*
(course, réunion) to take part in; *(frais
etc)* to contribute to; *(chagrin, succès
de qn)* to share (in)

particularité [paʀtikylaʀite] *nf*
(distinctive) characteristic

particulier, -ière [paʀtikylje, -jɛʀ]
adj (personnel, privé) private; *(étrange)*
peculiar, odd; *(spécial)* special,
particular; *(spécifique)* particular ▷ *nm*
(individu: Admin) private individual;
~ à peculiar to; **en ~** *(surtout)* in
particular, particularly; *(en privé)*
in private; **particulièrement** *adv*
particularly

partie [paʀti] *nf (gén)* part; *(Jur etc:
protagonistes)* party; *(de cartes, tennis
etc)* game; **une ~ de campagne/de
pêche** an outing in the country/a
fishing party *ou* trip; **en ~** partly, in
part; **faire ~ de** to be part of;
prendre qn à ~ to take sb to task;
en grande ~ largely, in the main;
~ civile *(Jur)* party claiming damages in
a criminal case

partiel, le [paʀsjɛl] *adj* partial ▷ *nm*
(Scol) class exam

partir [paʀtiʀ] /16/ *vi (gén)* to go;
(quitter) to go, leave; *(tache)* to go,
come out; **~ de** *(lieu: quitter)* to leave;
(commencer à) to start from; **~ pour/à**
(lieu, pays etc) to leave for/go off to;
à ~ de from

partisan, e [paʀtizɑ̃, -an] *nm/f*
partisan; **être ~ de qch/faire** to
be in favour (BRIT) *ou* favor (US) of
sth/doing

partition [paʀtisjɔ̃] *nf (Mus)* score

partout [paʀtu] *adv* everywhere;
~ où il allait everywhere *ou* wherever
he went

paru [paʀy] *pp de* **paraître**

parution [paʀysjɔ̃] *nf* publication

parvenir [paʀvəniʀ] /22/: **~ à** *vt*
(atteindre) to reach; *(réussir)*: **~ à faire**
to manage to do, succeed in doing;
faire ~ qch à qn to have sth sent to sb

 MOT-CLÉ

pas¹ [pɑ] *adv* **1** *(en corrélation avec
ne, non etc)* not; **il ne pleure pas**
(habituellement) he does not *ou*
doesn't cry; *(maintenant)* he's not *ou*
isn't crying; **il n'a pas pleuré/ne
pleurera pas** he did not *ou* didn't/
will not *ou* won't cry; **ils n'ont pas de
voiture/d'enfants** they haven't got
a car/any children; **il m'a dit de ne
pas le faire** he told me not to do it;
non pas que … not that ..
2 *(employé sans ne etc)*: **pas moi**
not me, I don't *(ou* can't *etc)*; **elle
travaille, (mais) lui pas** *ou* **pas lui**
she works but he doesn't *ou* does
not; **une pomme pas mûre** an
apple which isn't ripe; **pas du tout**
not at all; **pas de sucre, merci** no
sugar, thanks; **ceci est à vous ou
pas?** is this yours or not?, is this yours
or isn't it?
3: **pas mal** *(joli: personne, maison)* not
bad; **pas mal fait** not badly done *ou*
made; **comment ça va? — pas mal**
how are things? — not bad; **pas mal
de** quite a lot of

pas² [pɑ] *nm (enjambée, Danse)* step;
(bruit) (foot)step; *(trace)* footprint;
(allure, mesure) pace; **~ à ~** step
by step; **au ~** at a walking pace;
marcher à grands ~ to stride along;
à ~ de loup stealthily; **faire les cent
~** to pace up and down; **faire les
premiers ~** to make the first move;
sur le ~ de la porte on the doorstep

passage [pɑsaʒ] *nm (fait de passer)*:
voir **passer**; *(lieu, prix de la traversée,
extrait de livre etc)* passage; *(chemin)*

way; **de ~** (touristes) passing through; **~ clouté** pedestrian crossing; **"~ interdit"** "no entry"; **~ à niveau** level (BRIT) ou grade (US) crossing; **~ souterrain** subway (BRIT), underpass

passager, -ère [pasaʒe, -ɛʀ] adj passing ▷ nm/f passenger

passant, e [pasɑ̃, -ɑ̃t] adj (rue, endroit) busy ▷ nm/f passer-by; **remarquer qch en ~** to notice sth in passing

passe [pas] nf (Sport) pass; (Navig) channel; **être en ~ de faire** to be on the way to doing; **être dans une mauvaise ~** to be going through a bad patch

passé, e [pase] adj (événement, temps) past; (dernier: semaine etc) last; (couleur, tapisserie) faded ▷ prép after ▷ nm past; (Ling) past (tense); **~ de mode** out of fashion; **~ composé** perfect (tense); **~ simple** past historic

passe-partout [paspaʀtu] nm inv master ou skeleton key ▷ adj inv all-purpose

passeport [paspɔʀ] nm passport

passer [pase] /1/ vi (se rendre, aller) to go; (voiture, piétons: défiler) to pass (by), go by; (facteur, laitier etc) to come, call; (pour rendre visite) to call ou drop in; (film, émission) to be on; (temps, jours) to pass, go by; (couleur, papier) to fade; (mode) to die out; (douleur) to pass, go away; (Scol): **~ dans la classe supérieure** to go up (to the next class) ▷ vt (frontière, rivière etc) to cross; (douane) to go through; (examen) to sit, take; (visite médicale etc) to have; (journée, temps) to spend; **~ qch à qn** (sel etc) to pass sth to sb; (prêter) to lend sb sth; (lettre, message) to pass sth on to sb; (tolérer) to let sb get away with sth; (enfiler: vêtement) to slip on; (film, pièce) to show, put on; (disque) to play, put on; (commande) to place; (marché, accord) to agree on; **se passer** vi (avoir lieu: scène, action) to take place; (se dérouler: entretien etc) to go; (arriver): **que s'est-il passé?** what happened?; (s'écouler: semaine etc) to pass, go by; **se ~ de** to go ou do without; **~ par** to go through; **~ avant qch/qn** (fig) to come before sth/sb; **un coup de fil à qn** (fam) to give sb a ring; **laisser ~** (air, lumière, personne) to let through; (occasion) to let slip, miss; (erreur) to overlook; **à la radio/télévision** to be on the radio/on television; **~ à table** to sit down to eat; **~ au salon** to go through to ou into the sitting room; **~ son tour** to miss one's turn; **~ la seconde** (Auto) to change into second; **~ le balai/l'aspirateur** to sweep up/hoover; **je vous passe M. Dupont** (je vous mets en communication avec lui) I'm putting you through to Mr Dupont; (je lui passe l'appareil) here is Mr Dupont, I'll hand you over to Mr Dupont

passerelle [pasʀɛl] nf footbridge; (de navire, avion) gangway

passe-temps [pastɑ̃] nm inv pastime

passif, -ive [pasif, -iv] adj passive

passion [pasjɔ̃] nf passion; **passionnant, e** adj fascinating; **passionné, e** adj (personne, tempérament) passionate; (description, récit) impassioned; **être passionné de** ou **pour qch** to have a passion for sth; **passionner** /1/ vt (personne) to fascinate, grip

passoire [paswaʀ] nf sieve; (à légumes) colander; (à thé) strainer

pastèque [pastɛk] nf watermelon

pasteur [pastœʀ] nm (protestant) minister, pastor

pastille [pastij] nf (à sucer) lozenge, pastille

patate [patat] nf spud; **~ douce** sweet potato

patauger [patoʒe] /3/ vi to splash about

pâte [pɑt] *nf* (*à tarte*) pastry; (*à pain*) dough; (*à frire*) batter; **pâtes** *nfpl* (*macaroni etc*) pasta *sg*; **~ d'amandes** almond paste, marzipan; **~ brisée** shortcrust (*BRIT*) *ou* pie crust (*US*) pastry; **~ à choux/feuilletée** choux/ puff *ou* flaky (*BRIT*) pastry; **~ de fruits** crystallized fruit *no pl*; **~ à modeler** modelling clay, Plasticine® (*BRIT*)

pâté [pɑte] *nm* (*charcuterie*) pâté; (*tache*) ink blot; (*de sable*) sandpie; **~ (en croûte)** ≈ meat pie; **~ de maisons** block (of houses)

pâtée [pɑte] *nf* mash, feed

patente [patɑ̃t] *nf* (*Comm*) trading licence (*BRIT*) *ou* license (*US*)

paternel, le [patɛʀnɛl] *adj* (*amour, soins*) fatherly; (*ligne, autorité*) paternal

pâteux, -euse [pɑtø, -øz] *adj* pasty; **avoir la bouche** *ou* **langue pâteuse** to have a furred (*BRIT*) *ou* coated tongue

pathétique [patetik] *adj* moving

patience [pasjɑ̃s] *nf* patience

patient, e [pasjɑ̃, -ɑ̃t] *adj, nm/f* patient; **patienter** /1/ *vi* to wait

patin [patɛ̃] *nm* skate; (*sport*) skating; **~s (à glace)** (ice) skates; **~s à roulettes** roller skates

patinage [patinaʒ] *nm* skating

patiner [patine] /1/ *vi* to skate; (*roue, voiture*) to spin; **se patiner** *vi* (*meuble, cuir*) to acquire a sheen; **patineur, -euse** *nm/f* skater; **patinoire** *nf* skating rink, (ice) rink

pâtir [pɑtiʀ] /2/: **~ de** *vt* to suffer because of

pâtisserie [pɑtisʀi] *nf* (*boutique*) cake shop; (*à la maison*) pastry- *ou* cake-making, baking; **pâtisseries** *nfpl* (*gâteaux*) pastries, cakes; **pâtissier, -ière** *nm/f* pastrycook

patois [patwa] *nm* dialect, patois

patrie [patʀi] *nf* homeland

patrimoine [patʀimwan] *nm* (*culture*) heritage

patriotique [patʀijɔtik] *adj* patriotic

patron, ne [patʀɔ̃, -ɔn] *nm/f* boss; (*Rel*) patron saint ▷ *nm* (*Couture*) pattern; **patronat** *nm* employers *pl*; **patronner** /1/ *vt* to sponsor, support

patrouille [patʀuj] *nf* patrol

patte [pat] *nf* (*jambe*) leg; (*pied: de chien, chat*) paw; (*: d'oiseau*) foot

pâturage [pɑtyʀaʒ] *nm* pasture

paume [pom] *nf* palm

paumé, e [pome] *nm/f* (*fam*) drop-out

paupière [popjɛʀ] *nf* eyelid

pause [poz] *nf* (*arrêt*) break; (*en parlant, Mus*) pause; **~ de midi** lunch break

pauvre [povʀ] *adj* poor; **les ~s** the poor; **pauvreté** *nf* (*état*) poverty

pavé, e [pave] *adj* (*cour*) paved; (*rue*) cobbled ▷ *nm* (*bloc*) paving stone; cobblestone; **~ numérique** keypad

pavillon [pavijɔ̃] *nm* (*de banlieue*) small (detached) house; pavilion; (*Navig*) flag

payant, e [pɛjɑ̃, -ɑ̃t] *adj* (*spectateurs etc*) paying; (*fig: entreprise*) profitable; (*effort*) which pays off; **c'est ~** you have to pay, there is a charge

paye [pɛj] *nf* pay, wages *pl*

payer [peje] /8/ *vt* (*créancier, employé, loyer*) to pay; (*achat, réparations, faute*) to pay for ▷ *vi* to pay; (*métier*) to be well-paid; (*effort, tactique etc*) to pay off; **il me l'a fait ~ 10 euros** he charged me 10 euros for it; **~ qch à qn** to buy sth for sb, buy sb sth; **se ~ la tête de qn** to take the mickey out of sb (*BRIT*)

pays [pei] *nm* country; *(région)* region; **du ~** local

paysage [peiza3] *nm* landscape

paysan, ne [peizã, -an] *nm/f* farmer; *(péj)* peasant ▷ *adj (rural)* country *cpd*; *(agricole)* farming

Pays-Bas [peiba] *nmpl*: **les ~** the Netherlands

PC *sigle m (Inform:* = personal computer) PC; = **permis de construire**; (= **prêt conventionné**) type of loan for house purchase

PDA *sigle m* (= personal digital assistant) PDA

PDG *sigle m* = **président directeur général**

péage [pea3] *nm* toll; *(endroit)* tollgate

peau, x [po] *nf* skin; **gants de ~** leather gloves; **être bien/mal dans sa ~** to be at ease/ill-at-ease; **~ de chamois** *(chiffon)* chamois leather, shammy

péché [pefe] *nm* sin

pêche [pɛʃ] *nf (sport, activité)* fishing; *(poissons pêchés)* catch; *(fruit)* peach; **~ à la ligne** *(en rivière)* angling

pécher [pefe] /6/ *vi (Rel)* to sin

pêcher [pefe] /1/ *vi* to go fishing ▷ *vt (attraper)* to catch; *(chercher)* to fish for ▷ *nm* peach tree

pêcheur, -eresse [peʃœʀ, peʃʀɛs] *nm/f* sinner

pêcheur [peʃœʀ] *nm voir* **pêcher** fisherman; *(à la ligne)* angler

pédagogie [pedagoʒi] *nf* educational methods *pl*, pedagogy; **pédagogique** *adj* educational

pédale [pedal] *nf* pedal

pédalo [pedalo] *nm* pedal-boat

pédant, e [pedã, -ãt] *adj (péj)* pedantic ▷ *nm/f* pedant

pédestre [pedɛstʀ] *adj:* **randonnée ~** ramble; **sentier ~** pedestrian footpath

pédiatre [pedjatʀ] *nm/f* paediatrician, child specialist

pédicure [pedikyʀ] *nm/f* chiropodist

pègre [pɛgʀ] *nf* underworld

peigne [pɛɲ] *nm* comb; **peigner** /1/ *vt* to comb (the hair of); **se peigner** *vi* to comb one's hair; **peignoir** *nm* dressing gown; **peignoir de bain** bathrobe

peindre [pɛ̃dʀ] /52/ *vt* to paint; *(fig)* to portray, depict

peine [pɛn] *nf (affliction)* sorrow, sadness *no pl*; *(mal, effort)* trouble *no pl*, effort; *(difficulté)* difficulty; *(Jur)* sentence; **faire de la ~ à qn** to distress *ou* upset sb; **prendre la ~ de faire** to go to the trouble of doing; **se donner de la ~** to make an effort; **ce n'est pas la ~ de faire** there's no point in doing, it's not worth doing; **avoir de la ~** to be sad; **à ~** scarcely, barely; **à ~ ... que** hardly ... than, no sooner ... than; **~ capitale** capital punishment; **~ de mort** death sentence *ou* penalty; **peiner** [pene] /1/ *vi* to work hard; to struggle; *(moteur, voiture)* to labour (BRIT), labor (US) ▷ *vt* to grieve, sadden

peintre [pɛ̃tʀ] *nm* painter; **~ en bâtiment** painter and decorator

peinture [pɛ̃tyʀ] *nf* painting; *(couche de couleur, couleur)* paint; *(surfaces peintes: aussi:* **~s**) paintwork; **"~ fraîche"** "wet paint"

péjoratif, -ive [peʒɔʀatif, -iv] *adj* pejorative, derogatory

Pékin [pekɛ̃] *n* Beijing

pêle-mêle [pɛlmɛl] *adv* higgledy-piggledy

peler [pəle] /5/ *vt, vi* to peel

pèlerin [pɛlʀɛ̃] *nm* pilgrim

pèlerinage [pɛlʀinaʒ] *nm* pilgrimage

pelle [pɛl] *nf* shovel; *(d'enfant, de terrassier)* spade

pellicule [pelikyl] *nf* film; **pellicules** *nfpl (Méd)* dandruff *sg*

pelote [pəlɔt] *nf (de fil, laine)* ball; **~ basque** pelota

peloton [pəlɔtɔ̃] *nm* group; squad; *(Sport)* pack

pelotonner [pəlɔtɔne] /1/: **se pelotonner** *vi* to curl (o.s.) up

pelouse [pəluz] *nf* lawn

peluche [pəlyʃ] *nf*: **animal en ~** soft toy, fluffy animal; **chien/lapin en ~** fluffy dog/rabbit

pelure [pəlyʀ] *nf* peeling, peel *no pl*

pénal, e, -aux [penal, -o] *adj* penal; **pénalité** *nf* penalty

penchant [pɑ̃ʃɑ̃] *nm*: **un ~ à faire/à qch** a tendency to do/to sth; **un ~ pour qch** a liking *ou* fondness for sth

pencher [pɑ̃ʃe] /1/ *vi* to tilt, lean over ▷ *vt* to tilt; **se pencher** *vi* to lean over; *(se baisser)* to bend down; **se ~ sur** *(fig: problème)* to look into; **~ pour** to be inclined to favour (BRIT) *ou* favor (US)

pendant, e [pɑ̃dɑ̃, -ɑ̃t] *adj* hanging (out) ▷ *prép (au cours de)* during; *(indiquant la durée)* for; **~ que** while

pendentif [pɑ̃dɑ̃tif] *nm* pendant

penderie [pɑ̃dʀi] *nf* wardrobe

pendre [pɑ̃dʀ] /41/ *vt, vi* to hang; **se ~ (à)** *(se suicider)* to hang o.s. (on); **~ qch à** *(mur)* to hang sth (up) on; *(plafond)* to hang sth (up) from

pendule [pɑ̃dyl] *nf* clock ▷ *nm* pendulum

pénétrer [penetʀe] /6/ *vi* to come *ou* get in ▷ *vt* to penetrate; **~ dans** to enter

pénible [penibl] *adj (astreignant)* hard; *(affligeant)* painful; *(personne, caractère)* tiresome; **péniblement** *adv* with difficulty

péniche [peniʃ] *nf* barge

pénicilline [penisilin] *nf* penicillin

péninsule [penɛ̃syl] *nf* peninsula

pénis [penis] *nm* penis

pénitence [penitɑ̃s] *nf (repentir)* penitence; *(peine)* penance; **pénitencier** *nm* penitentiary (US)

pénombre [penɔ̃bʀ] *nf (faible clarté)* half-light; *(obscurité)* darkness

pensée [pɑ̃se] *nf (démarche, doctrine)* thinking *no pl*; *(Bot)* pansy; **en ~** in one's mind

penser [pɑ̃se] /1/ *vi* to think ▷ *vt* to think; **~ à** *(prévoir)* to think of; *(ami,*

vacances) to think of *ou* about; **~ faire qch** to be thinking of doing sth, intend to do sth; **faire ~ à** to remind one of; **pensif, -ive** *adj* pensive, thoughtful

pension [pɑ̃sjɔ̃] *nf (allocation)* pension; *(prix du logement)* board and lodging, bed and board; *(école)* boarding school; **~ alimentaire** *(de divorcée)* maintenance allowance; alimony; **~ complète** full board; **~ de famille** boarding house, guesthouse; **pensionnaire** *nm/f (Scol)* boarder; **pensionnat** *nm* boarding school

pente [pɑ̃t] *nf* slope; **en ~** sloping

Pentecôte [pɑ̃tkot] *nf*: **la ~** Whitsun (BRIT), Pentecost

pénurie [penyʀi] *nf* shortage

pépé [pepe] *nm (fam)* grandad

pépin [pepɛ̃] *nm (Bot: graine)* pip; *(fam: ennui)* snag, hitch

pépinière [pepinjɛʀ] *nf* nursery

perçant, e [pɛʀsɑ̃, -ɑ̃t] *adj (vue, regard, yeux)* sharp; *(cri, voix)* piercing, shrill

perce-neige [pɛʀsənɛʒ] *nm ou f inv* snowdrop

percepteur, -trice [pɛʀsɛptœʀ, -tʀis] *nm/f* tax collector

perception [pɛʀsɛpsjɔ̃] *nf* perception; *(bureau)* tax (collector's) office

percer [pɛʀse] /3/ *vt* to pierce; *(ouverture etc)* to make; *(mystère, énigme)* to penetrate ▷ *vi* to break through; **perceuse** *nf* drill

percevoir [pɛʀsəvwaʀ] /28/ *vt* *(distinguer)* to perceive, detect; *(taxe, impôt)* to collect; *(revenu, indemnité)* to receive

perche [pɛʀʃ] *nf (bâton)* pole

percher [pɛʀʃe] /1/ *vt* to perch; **se percher** *vi* to perch; **perchoir** *nm* perch

perçois *etc* [pɛʀswa] *vb voir* **percevoir**

perçu, e [pɛʀsy] *pp de* **percevoir**

percussion [pɛʀkysjɔ̃] *nf* percussion

percuter [pɛʀkyte] /1/ vt to strike; (véhicule) to crash into

perdant, e [pɛʀdɑ̃, -ɑ̃t] nm/f loser

perdre [pɛʀdʀ] /41/ vt to lose; (gaspiller: temps, argent) to waste; (personne: moralement etc) to ruin ▷ vi to lose; (sur une vente etc) to lose out; **se perdre** vi (s'égarer) to get lost, lose one's way; (se gâter) to go to waste; **je me suis perdu** (et je le suis encore) I'm lost; (et je ne le suis plus) I got lost

perdrix [pɛʀdʀi] nf partridge

perdu, e [pɛʀdy] pp de **perdre** ▷ adj (isolé) out-of-the-way; (Comm: emballage) non-returnable; (malade): **il est ~** there's no hope left for him; **à vos moments ~s** in your spare time

père [pɛʀ] nm father; **~ de famille** father; **le ~ Noël** Father Christmas

perfection [pɛʀfɛksjɔ̃] nf perfection; **à la ~** to perfection; **perfectionné, e** adj sophisticated; **perfectionner** /1/ vt to improve, perfect; **se perfectionner en anglais** to improve one's English

perforer [pɛʀfɔʀe] /1/ vt (ticket, bande, carte) to punch

performant, e [pɛʀfɔʀmɑ̃, -ɑ̃t] adj: **très ~** high-performance cpd

perfusion [pɛʀfyzjɔ̃] nf: **faire une ~ à qn** to put sb on a drip

péril [peʀil] nm peril

périmé, e [peʀime] adj (Admin) out-of-date, expired

périmètre [peʀimɛtʀ] nm perimeter

période [peʀjɔd] nf period; **périodique** adj periodic ▷ nm periodical; **garniture** ou **serviette périodique** sanitary towel (BRIT) ou napkin (US)

périphérique [peʀifeʀik] adj (quartiers) outlying ▷ nm (Auto): **(boulevard) ~** ring road (BRIT), beltway (US)

périr [peʀiʀ] /2/ vi to die, perish

périssable [peʀisabl] adj perishable

perle [pɛʀl] nf pearl; (de plastique, métal, sueur) bead

permanence [pɛʀmanɑ̃s] nf permanence; (local) (duty) office; **assurer une ~** (service public, bureaux) to operate ou maintain a basic service; **être de ~** to be on call ou duty; **en ~** continuously

permanent, e [pɛʀmanɑ̃, -ɑ̃t] adj permanent; (spectacle) continuous ▷ nf perm

perméable [pɛʀmeabl] adj (terrain) permeable; **~ à** (fig) receptive ou open to

permettre [pɛʀmɛtʀ] /56/ vt to allow, permit; **~ à qn de faire/qch** to allow sb to do/sth; **se ~ de faire qch** to take the liberty of doing sth

permis [pɛʀmi] nm permit, licence; **~ (de conduire)** (driving) licence (BRIT), (driver's) license (US); **~ de construire** planning permission (BRIT), building permit (US); **~ de séjour** residence permit; **~ de travail** work permit

permission [pɛʀmisjɔ̃] nf permission; (Mil) leave; **en ~** on leave; **avoir la ~ de faire** to have permission to do

Pérou [peʀu] nm: **le ~** Peru

P

perpétuel, le [pɛʀpetɥɛl] adj perpetual; **perpétuité** nf: **à perpétuité** for life; **être condamné à perpétuité** to be sentenced to life imprisonment

perplexe [pɛʀplɛks] adj perplexed, puzzled

perquisitionner [pɛʀkizisjɔne] /1/ vi to carry out a search

perron [peʀɔ̃] nm steps pl (in front of mansion etc)

perroquet [peʀɔkɛ] nm parrot

perruche [peʀyʃ] nf budgerigar (BRIT), budgie (BRIT), parakeet (US)

perruque [peʀyk] nf wig

persécuter [pɛʀsekyte] /1/ vt to persecute

persévérer [pɛʀseveʀe] /6/ vi to persevere

persil [pɛʀsi] nm parsley

Persique [pɛʀsik] *adj*: **le golfe ~** the (Persian) Gulf

persistant, e [pɛʀsistɑ̃, -ɑ̃t] *adj* persistent

persister [pɛʀsiste] /1/ *vi* to persist; **~ à faire qch** to persist in doing sth

personnage [pɛʀsɔnaʒ] *nm* (*notable*) personality; (*individu*) character, individual; (*de roman, film*) character; (*Peinture*) figure

personnalité [pɛʀsɔnalite] *nf* personality; (*personnage*) prominent figure

personne [pɛʀsɔn] *nf* person ▷ *pron* nobody, no one; (*avec négation en anglais*) anybody, anyone; **~ âgée** elderly person; **personnel, le** *adj* personal; (*égoïste*) selfish ▷ *nm* personnel; **personnellement** *adv* personally

perspective [pɛʀspɛktiv] *nf* (*Art*) perspective; (*vue, coup d'œil*) view; (*point de vue*) viewpoint, angle; (*chose escomptée, envisagée*) prospect; **en ~** in prospect

perspicace [pɛʀspikas] *adj* clear-sighted, gifted with (*ou* showing) insight; **perspicacité** *nf* insight

persuader [pɛʀsɥade] /1/ *vt*: **~ qn (de/de faire)** to persuade sb (of/to do); **persuasif, -ive** *adj* persuasive

perte [pɛʀt] *nf* loss; (*de temps*) waste; (*fig: morale*) ruin; **à ~ de vue** as far as the eye can (*ou* could) see; **~s blanches** (vaginal) discharge *sg*

pertinent, e [pɛʀtinɑ̃, -ɑ̃t] *adj* apt, relevant

perturbation [pɛʀtyʀbasjɔ̃] *nf*: **~ (atmosphérique)** atmospheric disturbance

perturber [pɛʀtyʀbe] /1/ *vt* to disrupt; (*Psych*) to perturb, disturb

pervers, e [pɛʀvɛʀ, -ɛʀs] *adj* perverted

pervertir [pɛʀvɛʀtiʀ] /2/ *vt* to pervert

pesant, e [pəzɑ̃, -ɑ̃t] *adj* heavy; (*fig: présence*) burdensome

pèse-personne [pɛzpɛʀsɔn] *nm* (bathroom) scales *pl*

peser [pəze] /5/ *vt* to weigh ▷ *vi* to be heavy; (*fig: avoir de l'importance*) to carry weight

pessimiste [pesimist] *adj* pessimistic ▷ *nm/f* pessimist

peste [pɛst] *nf* plague

pétale [petal] *nm* petal

pétanque [petɑ̃k] *nf* type of bowls

- **PÉTANQUE**
-
- *Pétanque* is a version of the game
- of 'boules', played on a variety of
- hard surfaces. Standing with their
- feet together, players throw steel
- bowls at a wooden jack. *Pétanque*
- originated in the South of France
- and is still very much associated
- with that area.

pétard [petaʀ] *nm* banger (BRIT), firecracker

péter [pete] /6/ *vi* (*fam: casser, sauter*) to bust; (*fam!*) to fart (*!*)

pétillant, e [petijɑ̃, -ɑ̃t] *adj* (*eau*) sparkling

pétiller [petije] /1/ *vi* (*flamme, bois*) to crackle; (*mousse, champagne*) to bubble; (*yeux*) to sparkle

petit, e [pəti, -it] *adj* small; (*avec nuance affective*) little; (*voyage*) short, little; (*bruit etc*) faint, slight ▷ *nm/f* (*petit enfant*) little one, child; **petits** *nmpl* (*d'un animal*) young *pl*; **faire des ~s** to have kittens (*ou* puppies *etc*); **la classe des ~s** the infant class; **les tout-~s** toddlers; **~ à ~** bit by bit, gradually; **~(e) ami(e)** boyfriend/girlfriend; **les ~es annonces** the small ads; **~ déjeuner** breakfast; **~ four** petit four; **~ pain** (bread) roll; **~s pois** garden peas; **petite-fille** *nf* granddaughter; **petit-fils** *nm* grandson

pétition [petisjɔ̃] *nf* petition

petits-enfants [pətizɑ̃fɑ̃] *nmpl* grandchildren

pétrin [petʀɛ̃] nm (fig): **dans le ~** in a jam ou fix
pétrir [petʀiʀ] /2/ vt to knead
pétrole [petʀɔl] nm oil; (pour lampe, réchaud etc) paraffin; **pétrolier, -ière** nm oil tanker

Attention à ne pas traduire pétrole par le mot anglais petrol.

O **MOT-CLÉ**

peu [pø] adv 1 (modifiant verbe, adjectif, adverbe): **il boit peu** he doesn't drink (very) much; **il est peu bavard** he's not very talkative; **peu avant/après** shortly before/afterwards
2 (modifiant nom): **peu de: peu de gens/d'arbres** few ou not (very) many people/trees; **il a peu d'espoir** he hasn't (got) much hope, he has little hope; **pour peu de temps** for (only) a short while
3: **peu à peu** little by little; **à peu près** just about, more or less; **à peu près 10 kg/10 euros** approximately 10 kg/10 euros
▶ nm 1: **le peu de gens qui** the few people who; **le peu de sable qui** what little sand, the little sand which
2: **un peu** a little; **un petit peu** a little bit; **un peu d'espoir** a little hope; **elle est un peu bavarde** she's rather talkative; **un peu plus de** slightly more than; **un peu moins de** slightly less than; (avec pluriel) slightly fewer than
▶ pron: **peu le savent** few know (it); **de peu** (only) just

peuple [pœpl] nm people; **peupler** /1/ vt (pays, région) to populate; (étang) to stock; (hommes, poissons) to inhabit
peuplier [pøplije] nm poplar (tree)
peur [pœʀ] nf fear; **avoir ~ (de/ de faire/que)** to be frightened ou afraid (of/of doing/that); **faire ~ à** to frighten; **de ~ de/que** for fear of/

that; **peureux, -euse** adj fearful, timorous
peut [pø] vb voir **pouvoir**
peut-être [pøtɛtʀ] adv perhaps, maybe; **~ que** perhaps, maybe; **~ bien qu'il fera/est** he may well do/be
phare [faʀ] nm (en mer) lighthouse; (de véhicule) headlight
pharmacie [faʀmasi] nf (magasin) chemist's (BRIT), pharmacy; (armoire) medicine chest ou cupboard; **pharmacien, ne** nm/f pharmacist, chemist (BRIT)
phénomène [fenɔmɛn] nm phenomenon
philosophe [filɔzɔf] nm/f philosopher ▷ adj philosophical
philosophie [filɔzɔfi] nf philosophy
phobie [fɔbi] nf phobia
phoque [fɔk] nm seal
phosphorescent, e [fɔsfɔʀesɑ̃, -ɑ̃t] adj luminous
photo [fɔto] nf photo; **prendre en ~** to take a photo of; **aimer la/ faire de la ~** to like taking/take photos; **~ d'identité** passport photo; **photocopie** nf photocopy; **photocopier** /7/ vt to photocopy
photocopieur [fɔtɔkɔpjœʀ] nm, **photocopieuse** [fɔtɔkɔpjøz] nf (photo)copier
photo: photographe nm/f photographer; **photographie** nf (procédé, technique) photography; (cliché) photograph; **photographier** /7/ vt to photograph
phrase [fʀɑz] nf sentence
physicien, ne [fizisjɛ̃, -ɛn] nm/f physicist
physique [fizik] adj physical ▷ nm physique ▷ nf physics sg; **au ~** physically; **physiquement** adv physically
pianiste [pjanist] nm/f pianist
piano [pjano] nm piano; **pianoter** /1/ vi to tinkle away (at the piano)
pic [pik] nm (instrument) pick(axe); (montagne) peak; (Zool) woodpecker;

P

à ~ vertically; (fig: tomber, arriver) just at the right time
pichet [piʃɛ] nm jug
picorer [pikɔʀe] /1/ vt to peck
pie [pi] nf magpie
pièce [pjɛs] nf (d'un logement) room; (Théât) play; (de mécanisme, machine) part; (de monnaie) coin; (document) document; (de drap, fragment, d'une collection) piece; **deux euros ~** two euros each; **vendre à la ~** to sell separately ou individually; **travailler/payer à la ~** to do piecework/pay piece rate; **un maillot une ~** a one-piece swimsuit; **un deux-~s cuisine** a two-room(ed) flat (BRIT) ou apartment (US) with kitchen; **~ à conviction** exhibit; **~ d'eau** ornamental lake ou pond; **~ d'identité: avez-vous une ~ d'identité?** have you got any (means of) identification?; **~ jointe** (Inform) attachment; **~ montée** tiered cake; **~ de rechange** spare (part); **~s détachées** spares, (spare) parts; **~s justificatives** supporting documents
pied [pje] nm foot; (de table) leg; (de lampe) base; **~s nus** barefoot; **à ~** on foot; **au ~ de la lettre** literally; **avoir ~** to be able to touch the bottom, not to be out of one's depth; **avoir le ~ marin** to be a good sailor; **sur ~** (debout, rétabli) up and about; **mettre sur ~** (entreprise) to set up; **c'est le ~!** it's brilliant!; **mettre les ~s dans le plat** (fam) to put one's foot in it; **il se débrouille comme un ~** (fam) he's completely useless; **pied-noir** nm Algerian-born Frenchman
piège [pjɛʒ] nm trap; **prendre au ~** to trap; **piéger** /3, 6/ vt (avec une bombe) to booby-trap; **lettre/voiture piégée** letter-/car-bomb
piercing [pjɛʀsiŋ] nm piercing
pierre [pjɛʀ] nf stone; **~ tombale** tombstone; **pierreries** nfpl gems, precious stones

piétiner [pjetine] /1/ vi (trépigner) to stamp (one's foot); (fig) to be at a standstill ▷ vt to trample on
piéton, ne [pjetɔ̃, -ɔn] nm/f pedestrian; **piétonnier, -ière** adj pedestrian cpd
pieu, x [pjø] nm post; (pointu) stake
pieuvre [pjœvʀ] nf octopus
pieux, -euse [pjø, -øz] adj pious
pigeon [piʒɔ̃] nm pigeon
piger [piʒe] /3/ vi (fam) to get it ▷ vt (fam) to get
pigiste [piʒist] nm/f freelance journalist (paid by the line)
pignon [piɲɔ̃] nm (de mur) gable
pile [pil] nf (tas, pilier) pile; (Élec) battery ▷ adv (net, brusquement) dead; **à deux heures ~** at two on the dot; **jouer à ~ ou face** to toss up (for it); **~ ou face?** heads or tails?
piler [pile] /1/ vt to crush, pound
pilier [pilje] nm pillar
piller [pije] /1/ vt to pillage, plunder, loot
pilote [pilɔt] nm pilot; (de char, voiture) driver ▷ adj pilot cpd; **~ de chasse/d'essai/de ligne** fighter/test/airline pilot; **~ de course** racing driver; **piloter** /1/ vt (navire) to pilot; (avion) to fly; (automobile) to drive
pilule [pilyl] nf pill; **prendre la ~** to be on the pill
piment [pimɑ̃] nm (Bot) pepper, capsicum; (fig) spice, piquancy; **~ rouge** (Culin) chilli; **pimenté, e** adj (plat) hot and spicy
pin [pɛ̃] nm pine (tree)
pinard [pinaʀ] nm (fam) (cheap) wine, plonk (BRIT)
pince [pɛ̃s] nf (outil) pliers pl; (de homard, crabe) pincer, claw; (Couture: pli) dart; **~ à épiler** tweezers pl; **~ à linge** clothes peg (BRIT) ou pin (US)
pincé, e [pɛ̃se] adj (air) stiff
pinceau, x [pɛ̃so] nm (paint)brush
pincer [pɛ̃se] /3/ vt to pinch; (fam) to nab

pinède [pinɛd] nf pinewood, pine forest

pingouin [pɛ̃gwɛ̃] nm penguin

ping-pong [piŋpɔ̃g] nm table tennis

pinson [pɛ̃sɔ̃] nm chaffinch

pintade [pɛ̃tad] nf guinea-fowl

pion, ne [pjɔ̃, pjɔn] nm/f (Scol: péj) student paid to supervise schoolchildren ▷ nm (Échecs) pawn; (Dames) piece

pionnier [pjɔnje] nm pioneer

pipe [pip] nf pipe; **fumer la** ou **une ~** to smoke a pipe

piquant, e [pikã, -ãt] adj (barbe, rosier etc) prickly; (saveur, sauce) hot, pungent; (fig: détail) titillating; (: mordant, caustique) biting ▷ nm (épine) thorn, prickle; (fig) spiciness, spice

pique [pik] nf pike; (fig): **envoyer** ou **lancer des ~s à qn** to make cutting remarks to sb ▷ nm (Cartes) spades pl

pique-nique [piknik] nm picnic; **pique-niquer** /1/ vi to (have a) picnic

piquer /1/ vt (percer) to prick; (Méd) to give an injection to; (: animal blessé etc) to put to sleep; (insecte, fumée, ortie) to sting; (moustique) to bite; (froid) to bite; (intérêt etc) to arouse; (fam: voler) to pinch ▷ vi (oiseau, avion) to go into a dive

piquet [pikɛ] nm (pieu) post, stake; (de tente) peg

piqûre [pikyr] nf (d'épingle) prick; (d'ortie) sting; (de moustique) bite; (Méd) injection, shot (US); **faire une ~ à qn** to give sb an injection

pirate [pirat] adj ▷ nm pirate; **~ de l'air** hijacker

pire [pir] adj worse; (superlatif): **le (la) ~ ...** the worst ... ▷ nm: **le ~ (de)** the worst (of); **au ~** at (the very) worst

pis [pi] nm (de vache) udder ▷ adj, adv worse; **de mal en ~** from bad to worse

piscine [pisin] nf (swimming) pool; **~ couverte** indoor (swimming) pool

pissenlit [pisɑ̃li] nm dandelion

pistache [pistaʃ] nf pistachio (nut)

piste [pist] nf (d'un animal, sentier) track, trail; (indice) lead; (de stade, de magnétophone) track; (de cirque) ring; (de danse) floor; (de patinage) rink; (de ski) run; (Aviat) runway; **~ cyclable** cycle track

pistolet [pistɔlɛ] nm (arme) pistol, gun; (à peinture) spray gun; **pistolet-mitrailleur** nm submachine gun

piston [pistɔ̃] nm (Tech) piston; **avoir du ~** (fam) to have friends in the right places; **pistonner** /1/ vt (candidat) to pull strings for

piteux, -euse [pitø, -øz] adj pitiful, sorry (avant le nom); **en ~ état** in a sorry state

pitié [pitje] nf pity; **il me fait ~** I feel sorry for him; **avoir ~ de** (compassion) to pity, feel sorry for; (merci) to have pity ou mercy on

pitoyable [pitwajabl] adj pitiful

pittoresque [pitɔrɛsk] adj picturesque

pizza [pidza] nf pizza

PJ sigle f (= police judiciaire) ≈ CID (BRIT), ≈ FBI (US)

placard [plakar] nm (armoire) cupboard; (affiche) poster, notice

place [plas] nf (emplacement, situation, classement) place; (de ville, village) square; (espace libre) room, space; (de parking) space; (siège: de train, cinéma, voiture) seat; (emploi) job; **en ~** (mettre) in its place; **sur ~** on the spot; **faire ~ à** to give way to; **ça prend de la ~** it takes up a lot of room ou space; **à la ~ de** in place of, instead of; **à votre ~ ...** if I were you ...; **se mettre à la ~ de qn** to put o.s. in sb's place ou in sb's shoes

placé, e [plase] adj: **haut ~** (fig) high-ranking; **être bien/mal ~** to be well/badly placed; (spectateur) to have a good/bad seat; **il est bien ~ pour le savoir** he is in a position to know

placement [plasmɑ̃] nm (Finance) investment; **agence** ou **bureau de ~** employment agency

P

placer [plase] /3/ vt to place; (convive, spectateur) to seat; (capital, argent) to place, invest; **se ~ au premier rang** to go and stand (ou sit) in the first row

plafond [plafɔ̃] nm ceiling

plage [plaʒ] nf beach; **~ arrière** (Auto) parcel ou back shelf

plaider [plede] /1/ vi (avocat) to plead ▷ vt to plead; **se ~ pour** (fig) to speak for; **plaidoyer** nm (Jur) speech for the defence (BRIT) ou defense (US); (fig) plea

plaie [plɛ] nf wound

plaignant, e [plɛɲɑ̃, -ɑ̃t] nm/f plaintiff

plaindre [plɛ̃dʀ] /52/ vt to pity, feel sorry for; **se plaindre** vi (gémir) to moan; (protester, rouspéter): **se ~ (à qn) (de)** to complain (to sb) (about); **se ~ de** (souffrir) to complain of

plaine [plɛn] nf plain

plain-pied [plɛ̃pje] adv: **de ~ (avec)** on the same level (as)

plaint, e [plɛ̃, -ɛ̃t] pp de **plaindre** ▷ nf (gémissement) moan, groan; (doléance) complaint; **porter ~e** to lodge a complaint

plaire [plɛʀ] /54/ vi to be a success, be successful; **cela me plaît** I like it; **ça plaît beaucoup aux jeunes** it's very popular with young people; **se ~ quelque part** to like being somewhere; **s'il vous plaît, s'il te plaît** please

plaisance [plɛzɑ̃s] nf (aussi: **navigation de ~**) (pleasure) sailing, yachting

plaisant, e [plɛzɑ̃, -ɑ̃t] adj pleasant; (histoire, anecdote) amusing

plaisanter [plɛzɑ̃te] /1/ vi to joke; **plaisanterie** nf joke

plaisir [plɛziʀ] nm pleasure; **faire ~ à qn** (délibérément) to be nice to sb, please sb; (cadeau, nouvelle) **ça me fait ~** I'm delighted ou very pleased with this; **j'espère que ça te fera ~** I hope you'll like it; **pour le** ou **pour son** ou **par ~** for pleasure

plaît [plɛ] vb voir **plaire**

plan, e [plɑ̃, -an] adj flat ▷ nm plan; (fig) level, plane; (Ciné) shot; **au premier/second ~** in the foreground/ middle distance; **à l'arrière ~** in the background; **~ d'eau** lake

planche [plɑ̃ʃ] nf (pièce de bois) plank, (wooden) board; (illustration) plate; **~ à repasser** ironing board; **~ (à roulettes)** skateboard; **~ à voile** (sport) windsurfing

plancher [plɑ̃ʃe] /1/ nm floor; (planches) floorboards pl ▷ vi to work hard

planer [plane] /1/ vi to glide; (fam: rêveur) to have one's head in the clouds; **~ sur** (danger) to hang over

planète [planɛt] nf planet

planeur [planœʀ] nm glider

planifier [planifje] /7/ vt to plan

planning [planiŋ] nm programme, schedule; **~ familial** family planning

plant [plɑ̃] nm seedling, young plant

plante [plɑ̃t] nf plant; **~ d'appartement** house ou pot plant; **~ du pied** sole (of the foot); **~ verte** house plant

planter [plɑ̃te] /1/ vt (plante) to plant; (enfoncer) to hammer ou drive in; (tente) to put up, pitch; (fam: mettre) to dump; **se planter** vi (fam: se tromper) to get it wrong; (: ordinateur) to crash

plaque [plak] nf plate; (de verglas, d'eczéma) patch; (avec inscription) plaque; **~ chauffante** hotplate; **~ de chocolat** bar of chocolate; **~ tournante** (fig) centre

plaqué, e [plake] adj: **~ or/argent** gold-/silver-plated

plaquer [plake] /1/ vt (Rugby) to bring down; (fam: laisser tomber) to drop

plaquette [plakɛt] nf (de chocolat) bar; (de beurre) packet; **~ de frein** brake pad

plastique [plastik] adj ▷ nm plastic ▷ nf plastic arts pl; (d'une statue) modelling; **plastiquer** /1/ vt to blow up

plat, e [pla, -at] adj flat; (style) flat, dull ▷ nm (récipient, Culin) dish; (d'un repas) course; **à ~ ventre** face down; **à ~** (pneu, batterie) flat; (fam: fatigué) dead beat; **~ cuisiné** pre-cooked meal (ou dish); **~ du jour** dish of the day; **~ principal** ou **de résistance** main course

platane [platan] nm plane tree

plateau, x [plato] nm (support) tray; (Géo) plateau; (Ciné) set; **~ à fromages** cheeseboard

plate-bande [platbɑ̃d] nf flower bed

plate-forme [platfɔrm] nf platform; **~ de forage/pétrolière** drilling/oil rig

platine [platin] nm platinum ▷ nf (d'un tourne-disque) turntable; **~ laser** ou **compact-disc** compact disc (player)

plâtre [plɑtr] nm (matériau) plaster; (statue) plaster statue; (Méd) (plaster) cast; **avoir un bras dans le ~** to have an arm in plaster

plein, e [plɛ̃, -ɛn] adj full ▷ nm: **faire le ~ (d'essence)** to fill up (with petrol (BRIT) ou gas (US)); **à ~es mains** (ramasser) in handfuls; **à ~ temps** full-time; **en ~ air** in the open air; **en ~ soleil** in direct sunlight; **en ~e nuit/rue** in the middle of the night/street; **en ~ jour** in broad daylight

pleurer [plœre] /1/ vi to cry; (yeux) to water ▷ vt to mourn (for); **~ sur** to lament (over), bemoan

pleurnicher [plœrniʃe] /1/ vi to snivel, whine

pleurs [plœr] nmpl: **en ~** in tears

pleut [plø] vb voir **pleuvoir**

pleuvoir [pløvwar] /23/ vb impers to rain ▷ vi (coups) to rain down; (critiques, invitations) to shower down; **il pleut** it's raining; **il pleut des cordes** ou **à verse** ou **à torrents** it's pouring (down), it's raining cats and dogs

pli [pli] nm fold; (de jupe) pleat; (de pantalon) crease

pliant, e [plijɑ̃, -ɑ̃t] adj folding

plier [plije] /7/ vt to fold; (pour ranger) to fold up; (genou, bras) to bend ▷ vi to bend; (fig) to yield; **se ~ à** to submit to

plisser [plise] /1/ vt (yeux) to screw up; (front) to furrow; (jupe) to put pleats in

plomb [plɔ̃] nm (métal) lead; (d'une cartouche) (lead) shot; (Pêche) sinker; (Élec) fuse; **sans ~** (essence) unleaded

plomberie [plɔ̃bri] nf plumbing

plombier [plɔ̃bje] nm plumber

plonge [plɔ̃ʒ] nf: **faire la ~** to be a washer-up (BRIT) ou dishwasher (person)

plongeant, e [plɔ̃ʒɑ̃, -ɑ̃t] adj (vue) from above; (tir, décolleté) plunging

plongée [plɔ̃ʒe] nf (Sport) diving no pl; (: sans scaphandre) skin diving; **~ sous-marine** diving

plongeoir [plɔ̃ʒwar] nm diving board

plongeon [plɔ̃ʒɔ̃] nm dive

plonger [plɔ̃ʒe] /3/ vi to dive ▷ vt: **~ qch dans** to plunge sth into; **se ~ dans** (études, lecture) to bury ou immerse o.s. in; **plongeur, -euse** [plɔ̃ʒœr, -øz] nm/f diver

plu [ply] pp de **plaire; pleuvoir**

pluie [plɥi] nf rain

plume [plym] nf feather; (pour écrire) (pen) nib; (fig) pen

plupart [plypar]: **la ~** pron the majority, most (of them); **la ~ des** most, the majority of; **la ~ du temps/d'entre nous** most of the time/of us; **pour la ~** for the most part, mostly

pluriel [plyrjɛl] nm plural

plus¹ [ply] vb voir **plaire**

MOT-CLÉ

plus² [ply] adv 1 (forme négative): **ne ... plus** no more, no longer; **je n'ai plus d'argent** I've got no more money ou no money left; **il ne travaille plus** he's no longer working, he doesn't work any more

2 [ply, plyz + *voyelle*] (*comparatif*) more, ...+er; (*superlatif*): **le plus** the most, the ...+est; **plus grand/ intelligent (que)** bigger/more intelligent (than); **le plus grand/ intelligent** the biggest/most intelligent; **tout au plus** at the very most

3 [plys, plyz + *voyelle*] (*davantage*) more; **il travaille plus (que)** he works more (than); **plus il travaille, plus il est heureux** the more he works, the happier he is; **plus de 10 personnes/trois heures/quatre kilos** more than *ou* over 10 people/ three hours/four kilos; **trois heures de plus que** three hours more than; **de plus** what's more, moreover; **il a trois ans de plus que moi** he's three years older than me; **trois kilos en plus** three kilos more; **en plus de** in addition to; **de plus en plus** more and more; **plus ou moins** more or less; **ni plus ni moins** no more, no less
▷ *prép* [plys]: **quatre plus deux** four plus two

plusieurs [plyzjœr] *adj*, *pron* several; **ils sont ~** there are several of them
plus-value [plyvaly] *nf* (*bénéfice*) capital gain
plutôt [plyto] *adv* rather; **je ferais ~ ceci** I'd rather *ou* sooner do this; **~ que (de) faire** rather than *ou* instead of doing
pluvieux, -euse [plyvjø, -øz] *adj* rainy, wet
PME *sigle fpl* (= *petites et moyennes entreprises*) small businesses
PMU *sigle m* (= *pari mutuel urbain*) (*dans un café*) betting agency
PNB *sigle m* (= *produit national brut*) GNP
pneu [pnø] *nm* tyre (BRIT), tire (US)

pneumonie [pnømɔni] *nf* pneumonia
poche [pɔʃ] *nf* pocket; (*sous les yeux*) bag, pouch; **argent de ~** pocket money
pochette [pɔʃɛt] *nf* (*d'aiguilles etc*) case; (*de femme*) clutch bag; (*mouchoir*) breast pocket handkerchief; **~ de disque** record sleeve
podcast [pɔdkast] *nm* podcast; **podcaster** /1/ *vi* to podcast
poêle [pwal] *nm* stove ▷ *nf*: **~ (à frire)** frying pan
poème [pɔɛm] *nm* poem
poésie [pɔezi] *nf* (*poème*) poem; (*art*): **la ~** poetry
poète [pɔɛt] *nm* poet
poids [pwa] *nm* weight; (*Sport*) shot; **vendre au ~** to sell by weight; **perdre/prendre du ~** to lose/put on weight; **~ lourd** (*camion*) (big) lorry (BRIT), truck (US)
poignant, e [pwaɲɑ̃, -ɑ̃t] *adj* poignant
poignard [pwaɲar] *nm* dagger; **poignarder** /1/ *vt* to stab, knife
poigne [pwaɲ] *nf* grip; **avoir de la ~** (*fig*) to rule with a firm hand
poignée [pwaɲe] *nf* (*de sel etc, fig*) handful; (*de couvercle, porte*) handle; **~ de main** handshake
poignet [pwaɲe] *nm* (*Anat*) wrist; (*de chemise*) cuff
poil [pwal] *nm* (*Anat*) hair; (*de pinceau, brosse*) bristle; (*de tapis, tissu*) strand; (*pelage*) coat; **à ~** (*fam*) starkers; **au ~** (*fam*) hunky-dory; **poilu, e** *adj* hairy
poinçonner [pwɛ̃sɔne] /1/ *vt* (*bijou etc*) to hallmark; (*billet, ticket*) to punch
poing [pwɛ̃] *nm* fist; **coup de ~** punch
point [pwɛ̃] *nm* dot; (*de ponctuation*) full stop, period (US); (*Couture, Tricot*) stitch ▷ *adv* = **pas¹**; **faire le ~** (*fig*) to take stock (of the situation); **sur le ~ de faire** (just) about to do; **à tel ~ que** so much so that; **mettre au ~** (*mécanisme, procédé*) to develop;

(affaire) to settle; **à ~** (Culin: viande) medium; **à ~ (nommé)** just at the right time; **deux ~s** colon; **~ (de côté)** stitch (pain); **~ d'exclamation** exclamation mark; **~ faible** weak spot; **~ final** full stop, period (US); **~ d'interrogation** question mark; **~ mort**; **au ~ mort** (Auto) in neutral; **~ de repère** landmark; (dans le temps) point of reference; **~ de vente** retail outlet; **~ de vue** viewpoint; (fig: opinion) point of view; **~s cardinaux** cardinal points; **~s de suspension** suspension points

pointe [pwɛ̃t] nf point; (clou) tack; **une ~ d'ail/d'accent** a touch ou hint of garlic/of an accent; **être à la ~ de** (fig) to be in the forefront of; **sur la ~ des pieds** on tiptoe; **en ~** adj pointed, tapered; **de ~** (technique etc) leading; **heures/jours de ~** peak hours/days

pointer [pwɛ̃te] /1/ vt (diriger: canon, longue-vue, doigt): **~ vers qch, ~ sur qch** to point at sth ▷ vi (employé) to clock in ou on

pointeur, -euse [pwɛ̃tœʀ, -øz] nf timeclock ▷ nm (Inform) cursor

pointillé [pwɛ̃tije] nm (trait) dotted line

pointilleux, -euse [pwɛ̃tijø, -øz] adj particular, pernickety

pointu, e [pwɛ̃ty] adj pointed; (voix) shrill; (analyse) precise

pointure [pwɛ̃tyʀ] nf size

point-virgule [pwɛ̃viʀgyl] nm semi-colon

poire [pwaʀ] nf pear; (fam, péj) mug

poireau, x [pwaʀo] nm leek

poirier [pwaʀje] nm pear tree

pois [pwa] nm (Bot) pea; (sur une étoffe) dot, spot; **à ~** (cravate etc) spotted, polka-dot cpd; **~ chiche** chickpea

poison [pwazɔ̃] nm poison

poisseux, -euse [pwasø, -øz] adj sticky

poisson [pwasɔ̃] nm fish gén inv; **les P~s** (Astrologie: signe) Pisces; **~ d'avril** April fool; (blague) April fool's day trick; see note **"poisson d'avril"**; **~ rouge** goldfish; **poissonnerie** nf fishmonger's; **poissonnier, -ière** nm/f fishmonger (BRIT), fish merchant (US)

⬤ **POISSON D'AVRIL**
⬤
⬤ The traditional April Fools'
⬤ Day prank in France involves
⬤ attaching a cut-out paper fish,
⬤ known as a 'poisson d'avril', to the
⬤ back of one's victim, without being
⬤ caught.

poitrine [pwatʀin] nf chest; (seins) bust, bosom; (Culin) breast

poivre [pwavʀ] nm pepper

poivron [pwavʀɔ̃] nm pepper, capsicum

polaire [pɔlɛʀ] adj polar

pôle [pol] nm (Géo, Élec) pole; **le ~ Nord/Sud** the North/South Pole

poli, e [pɔli] adj polite; (lisse) smooth

police [pɔlis] nf police; **~ judiciaire (PJ)** ≈ Criminal Investigation Department (CID) (BRIT), ≈ Federal Bureau of Investigation (FBI) (US); **~ secours** ≈ emergency services pl (BRIT), ≈ paramedics pl (US); **policier, -ière** adj police cpd ▷ nm policeman; (aussi: **roman policier**) detective novel

polir [pɔliʀ] /2/ vt to polish

politesse [pɔlitɛs] nf politeness

politicien, ne [pɔlitisjɛ̃, -ɛn] nm/f (péj) politician

politique [pɔlitik] adj political ▷ nf politics sg; (principes, tactique) policies pl

politiquement [pɔlitikmɑ̃] adv politically; **~ correct** politically correct

pollen [pɔlɛn] nm pollen

polluant, e [pɔlɥɑ̃, -ɑ̃t] adj polluting ▷ nm pollutant; **non ~** non-polluting

P

polluer [pɔlɥe] /1/ vt to pollute;
  pollution nf pollution
polo [pɔlo] nm (tricot) polo shirt
Pologne [pɔlɔɲ] nf: **la ~** Poland;
  polonais, e adj Polish ▷ nm (Ling)
  Polish ▷ nm/f: **Polonais, e** Pole
poltron, ne [pɔltʀɔ̃, -ɔn] adj
  cowardly
polycopier [pɔlikɔpje] /7/ vt to
  duplicate
Polynésie [pɔlinezi] nf: **la ~** Polynesia;
  la ~ française French Polynesia
polyvalent, e [pɔlivalɑ̃, -ɑ̃t] adj
  (rôle) varied; (salle) multi-purpose
pommade [pɔmad] nf ointment,
  cream
pomme [pɔm] nf apple; **tomber
  dans les ~s** (fam) to pass out;
  ~ d'Adam Adam's apple; **~ de pin**
  pine ou fir cone; **~ de terre** potato; **~s
  vapeur** boiled potatoes
pommette [pɔmɛt] nf cheekbone
pommier [pɔmje] nm apple tree
pompe [pɔ̃p] nf pump; (faste)
  pomp (and ceremony); **~ à eau/
  essence** water/petrol pump; **~s
  funèbres** undertaker's sg, funeral
  parlour sg; **pomper** /1/ vt to pump;
  (aspirer) to pump up; (absorber) to
  soak up
pompeux, -euse [pɔ̃pø, -øz] adj
  pompous
pompier [pɔ̃pje] nm fireman
pompiste [pɔ̃pist] nm/f petrol (BRIT)
  ou gas (US) pump attendant
poncer [pɔ̃se] /3/ vt to sand (down)
ponctuation [pɔ̃ktɥasjɔ̃] nf
  punctuation
ponctuel, le [pɔ̃ktɥɛl] adj punctual
pondéré, e [pɔ̃deʀe] adj level-
  headed, composed
pondre [pɔ̃dʀ] /41/ vt to lay
poney [pɔnɛ] nm pony
pont [pɔ̃] nm bridge; (Navig) deck;
  faire le ~ to take the extra day off;
  see note **"faire le pont"**; **~ suspendu**
  suspension bridge; **pont-levis** nm
  drawbridge

FAIRE LE PONT

The expression 'faire le pont' refers
to the practice of taking a Monday
or Friday off to make a long
weekend if a public holiday falls on
a Tuesday or Thursday. The French
commonly take an extra day off
work to give four consecutive days'
holiday at 'l'Ascension', 'le 14 juillet'
and the '15 août'.

pop [pɔp] adj inv pop
populaire [pɔpylɛʀ] adj popular;
  (manifestation) mass cpd; (milieux,
  clientèle) working-class; (mot etc) used
  by the lower classes (of society)
popularité [pɔpylaʀite] nf
  popularity
population [pɔpylasjɔ̃] nf population
populeux, -euse [pɔpylø, -øz] adj
  densely populated
porc [pɔʀ] nm pig; (Culin) pork
porcelaine [pɔʀsəlɛn] nf porcelain,
  china; (objet) piece of china(ware)
porc-épic [pɔʀkepik] nm porcupine
porche [pɔʀʃ] nm porch
porcherie [pɔʀʃəʀi] nf pigsty
pore [pɔʀ] nm pore
porno [pɔʀno] adj porno ▷ nm porn
port [pɔʀ] nm harbour, port; (ville)
  port; (de l'uniforme etc) wearing;
  (pour lettre) postage; (pour colis,
  aussi: posture) carriage; **~ d'arme**
  (Jur) carrying of a firearm; **~ payé**
  postage paid
portable [pɔʀtabl] adj (portatif)
  portable; (téléphone) mobile
  ▷ nm (Inform) laptop (computer);
  (téléphone) mobile (phone)
portail [pɔʀtaj] nm gate
portant, e [pɔʀtɑ̃, -ɑ̃t] adj: **bien/
  mal ~** in good/poor health
portatif, -ive [pɔʀtatif, -iv] adj
  portable
porte [pɔʀt] nf door; (de ville,
  forteresse) gate; **mettre à la ~** to
  throw out; **~ d'entrée** front door

porté, e [pɔʀte] *adj*: **être ~ à faire qch** to be apt to do sth; **être ~ sur qch** to be partial to sth

porte: **porte-avions** *nm inv* aircraft carrier; **porte-bagages** *nm inv* luggage rack (*ou* basket *etc*); **porte-bonheur** *nm inv* lucky charm; **porte-clefs** *nm inv* key ring; **porte-documents** *nm inv* attaché *ou* document case

portée [pɔʀte] *nf* (*d'une arme*) range; (*fig: importance*) impact, import; (*: capacités*) scope, capability; (*de chatte etc*) litter; (*Mus*) stave, staff; **à/ hors de ~ (de)** within/out of reach (of); **à ~ de (la) main** within (arm's) reach; **à la ~ de qn** (*fig*) at sb's level, within sb's capabilities

porte: **portefeuille** *nm* wallet; **portemanteau, x** *nm* coat rack; (*cintre*) coat hanger; **porte-monnaie** *nm inv* purse; **porte-parole** *nm inv* spokesperson

porter [pɔʀte] /1/ *vt* to carry; (*sur soi: vêtement, barbe, bague*) to wear; (*fig: responsabilité etc*) to bear, carry; (*inscription, marque, titre, patronyme, fruits, fleurs*) to bear; (*coup*) to deal; (*attention*) to turn; (*apporter*): **~ qch quelque part/à qn** to take sth somewhere/to sb ▷ *vi* to carry; (*coup, argument*) to hit home; **se porter** *vi* (*se sentir*): **se ~ bien/mal** to be well/unwell; **~ sur** (*conférence etc*) to concern; **se faire ~ malade** to report sick

porteur, -euse [pɔʀtœʀ, -øz] *nm/f* ▷ *nm* (*de bagages*) porter; (*de chèque*) bearer

porte-voix [pɔʀtəvwa] *nm inv* megaphone

portier [pɔʀtje] *nm* doorman

portière [pɔʀtjɛʀ] *nf* door

portion [pɔʀsjɔ̃] *nf* (*part*) portion, share; (*partie*) portion, section

porto [pɔʀto] *nm* port (wine)

portrait [pɔʀtʀɛ] *nm* portrait; (*photographie*) photograph; **portrait- robot** *nm* Identikit® *ou* Photo-fit® (BRIT) picture

portuaire [pɔʀtɥɛʀ] *adj* port *cpd*, harbour *cpd*

portugais, e [pɔʀtygɛ, -ɛz] *adj* Portuguese ▷ *nm* (*Ling*) Portuguese ▷ *nm/f*: **P~, e** Portuguese

Portugal [pɔʀtygal] *nm*: **le ~** Portugal

pose [poz] *nf* (*de moquette*) laying; (*attitude, d'un modèle*) pose; (*Photo*) exposure

posé, e [poze] *adj* calm

poser [poze] /1/ *vt* (*place*) to put down, to put; (*déposer, installer: moquette, carrelage*) to lay; (*rideaux, papier peint*) to hang; (*question*) to ask; (*principe, conditions*) to lay *ou* set down; (*problème*) to formulate; (*difficulté*) to pose ▷ *vi* (*modèle*) to pose; **se poser** *vi* (*oiseau, avion*) to land; (*question*) to arise; **~ qch (sur)** to put sth down (on); **~ qn à** to drop sb at; **~ qch sur qch/quelque part** to put sth on sth/somewhere; **~ sa candidature à un poste** to apply for a post

positif, -ive [pozitif, -iv] *adj* positive

position [pozisjɔ̃] *nf* position; **prendre ~** (*fig*) to take a stand

posologie [pozɔlɔʒi] *nf* dosage

posséder [pɔsede] /6/ *vt* to own, possess; (*qualité, talent*) to have, possess; (*sexuellement*) to possess; **possession** *nf* ownership *no pl*; possession; **être en possession de qch** to be in possession of sth; **prendre possession de qch** to take possession of sth

possibilité [pɔsibilite] *nf* possibility; **possibilités** *nfpl* potential *sg*

possible [pɔsibl] *adj* possible; (*projet, entreprise*) feasible ▷ *nm*: **faire son ~** to do all one can, do one's utmost; **le plus/moins de livres ~** as many/ few books as possible; **le plus vite ~** as quickly as possible; **dès que ~** as soon as possible

P

postal, e, -aux [pɔstal, -o] *adj* postal

poste¹ [pɔst] *nf* (*service*) post, postal service; (*administration, bureau*) post office; **mettre à la ~** to post; **~ restante (PR)** poste restante (*BRIT*), general delivery (*US*)

poste² [pɔst] *nm* (*fonction, Mil*) post; (*Tél*) extension; (*de radio etc*) set; **~ d'essence** filling station; **~ d'incendie** fire point; **~ de pilotage** cockpit, flight deck; **~ (de police)** police station; **~ de secours** first-aid post

poster /1/ *vt* [pɔste] to post ▷ *nm* [pɔstɛʀ] poster

postérieur, e [pɔsteʀjœʀ] *adj* (*date*) later; (*partie*) back ▷ *nm* (*fam*) behind

postuler [pɔstyle] /1/ *vi*: **~ à** *ou* **pour un emploi** to apply for a job

pot [po] *nm* (*en verre*) jar; (*en terre*) pot; (*en plastique, carton*) carton; (*en métal*) tin; (*fam: chance*) luck; **avoir du ~** to be lucky; **boire** *ou* **prendre un ~** (*fam*) to have a drink; **petit ~ (pour bébé)** (jar of) baby food; **~ catalytique** catalytic converter; **~ d'échappement** exhaust pipe

potable [pɔtabl] *adj*: **eau (non) ~** (not) drinking water

potage [pɔtaʒ] *nm* soup; **potager, -ère** *adj*: **(jardin) potager** kitchen *ou* vegetable garden

pot-au-feu [pɔtofø] *nm inv* (beef) stew

pot-de-vin [pɔdvɛ̃] *nm* bribe

pote [pɔt] *nm* (*fam*) pal

poteau, x [pɔto] *nm* post; **~ indicateur** signpost

potelé, e [pɔtle] *adj* plump, chubby

potentiel, le [pɔtɑ̃sjɛl] *adj, nm* potential

poterie [pɔtʀi] *nf* pottery; (*objet*) piece of pottery

potier, -ière [pɔtje, -jɛʀ] *nm/f* potter

potiron [pɔtiʀɔ̃] *nm* pumpkin

pou, x [pu] *nm* louse

poubelle [pubɛl] *nf* (dust)bin

pouce [pus] *nm* thumb

poudre [pudʀ] *nf* powder; (*fard*) (face) powder; (*explosif*) gunpowder; **en ~: café en ~** instant coffee; **lait en ~** dried *ou* powdered milk

poudreux, -euse [pudʀø, -øz] *adj* dusty; (*neige*) powder *cpd*

poudre: poudrier [pudʀije] *nm* (powder) compact

pouffer [pufe] /1/ *vi*: **~ (de rire)** to burst out laughing

poulailler [pulaje] *nm* henhouse

poulain [pulɛ̃] *nm* foal; (*fig*) protégé

poule [pul] *nf* hen; (*Culin*) (boiling) fowl; **~ mouillée** coward

poulet [pulɛ] *nm* chicken; (*fam*) cop

poulie [puli] *nf* pulley

pouls [pu] *nm* pulse; **prendre le ~ de qn** to take sb's pulse

poumon [pumɔ̃] *nm* lung

poupée [pupe] *nf* doll

pour [puʀ] *prép* ▷ *nm*: **le ~ et le contre** the pros and cons; **~ faire** (so as) to do, in order to do; **~ avoir fait** for having done; **~ que** so that, in order that; **fermé ~ (cause de) travaux** closed for refurbishment *ou* alterations; **c'est ~ ça que ...** that's why ...; **~ quoi faire?** what for?; **~ 20 euros d'essence** 20 euros' worth of petrol; **~ cent** per cent; **~ ce qui est de** as for

pourboire [puʀbwaʀ] *nm* tip

pourcentage [puʀsɑ̃taʒ] *nm* percentage

pourchasser [puʀʃase] /1/ *vt* to pursue

pourparlers [puʀpaʀle] *nmpl* talks, negotiations

pourpre [puʀpʀ] *adj* crimson

pourquoi [puʀkwa] *adv, conj* why ▷ *nm inv*: **le ~ (de)** the reason (for)

pourrai *etc* [puʀe] *vb voir* **pouvoir**

pourri, e [puʀi] *adj* rotten

pourrir [puʀiʀ] /2/ *vi* to rot; (*fruit*) to go rotten *ou* bad ▷ *vt* to rot; (*fig*) to spoil thoroughly; **pourriture** *nf* rot

poursuite [puʀsɥit] *nf* pursuit, chase; **poursuites** *nfpl* (*Jur*) legal proceedings

poursuivre [puʀsɥivʀ] /40/ *vt* to pursue, chase (after); (*obséder*) to haunt; (*Jur*) to bring proceedings against, prosecute (: *au civil*) to sue; (*but*) to strive towards; (*voyage, études*) to carry on with, continue; **se poursuivre** *vi* to go on, continue

pourtant [puʀtɑ̃] *adv* yet; **c'est ~ facile** (and) yet it's easy

pourtour [puʀtuʀ] *nm* perimeter

pourvoir [puʀvwaʀ] /25/ *vt*: **~ qch/ qn de** to equip sth/sb with ▷ *vi*: **~ à** to provide for; **pourvu, e** *adj*: **pourvu de** equipped with; **pourvu que** (*si*) provided that, so long as; (*espérons que*) let's hope (that)

pousse [pus] *nf* growth; (*bourgeon*) shoot

poussée [puse] *nf* thrust; (*d'acné*) eruption; (*fig: prix*) upsurge

pousser [puse] /1/ *vt* to push; (*émettre: cri etc*) to give; (*stimuler: élève*) to urge on; (*poursuivre: études, discussion*) to carry on ▷ *vi* to push; (*croître*) to grow; **se pousser** *vi* to move over; **~ qn à faire qch** (*inciter*) to urge *ou* press sb to do sth; **faire ~** (*plante*) to grow

poussette [puset] *nf* pushchair (BRIT), stroller (US)

poussière [pusjɛʀ] *nf* dust; **poussiéreux, -euse** *adj* dusty

poussin [pusɛ̃] *nm* chick

poutre [putʀ] *nf* beam

MOT-CLÉ

pouvoir [puvwaʀ] /33/ *nm* power; (*dirigeants*): **le pouvoir** those in power; **les pouvoirs publics** the authorities; **pouvoir d'achat** purchasing power

▷ *vb aux* **1** (*être en état de*) can, be able to; **je ne peux pas le réparer** I can't *ou* I am not able to repair it; **déçu de ne pas pouvoir le faire** disappointed not to be able to do it

2 (*avoir la permission*) can, may, be allowed to; **vous pouvez aller au cinéma** you can *ou* may go to the pictures

3 (*probabilité, hypothèse*) may, might, could; **il a pu avoir un accident** he may *ou* might *ou* could have had an accident; **il aurait pu le dire!** he might *ou* could have said (so)!

▷ *vb impers* may, might, could; **il peut arriver que** it may *ou* might *ou* could happen that; **il pourrait pleuvoir** it might rain

▷ *vt* can, be able to; **j'ai fait tout ce que j'ai pu** I did all I could; **je n'en peux plus** (*épuisé*) I'm exhausted; (*à bout*) I can't take any more

se pouvoir *vi*: **il se peut que** it may *ou* might be that; **cela se pourrait** that's quite possible

prairie [pʀeʀi] *nf* meadow

praline [pʀalin] *nf* sugared almond

praticable [pʀatikabl] *adj* passable; practicable

pratiquant, e [pʀatikɑ̃, -ɑ̃t] *nm/f* (regular) churchgoer

pratique [pʀatik] *nf* practice ▷ *adj* practical; **pratiquement** *adv* (*pour ainsi dire*) practically, virtually; **pratiquer** /1/ *vt* to practise; (*l'équitation, la pêche*) to go in for; (*le golf, football*) to play; (*intervention, opération*) to carry out

pré [pʀe] *nm* meadow

préalable [pʀealabl] *adj* preliminary; **au ~** beforehand

préambule [pʀeɑ̃byl] *nm* preamble; (*fig*) prelude; **sans ~** straight away

préau, x [pʀeo] *nm* (*d'une cour d'école*) covered playground

préavis [pʀeavi] *nm* notice

précaution [pʀekosjɔ̃] *nf* precaution; **avec ~** cautiously; **par ~** as a precaution

précédemment [pʀesedamɑ̃] *adv* before, previously

P

précédent, e [pʀesedɑ̃, -ɑ̃t] adj
previous ▷ nm precedent; **sans ~**
unprecedented; **le jour ~** the day
before, the previous day

précéder [pʀesede] /6/ vt to precede

prêcher [pʀeʃe] /1/ vt to preach

précieux, -euse [pʀesjø, -øz] adj
precious; (collaborateur, conseils)
invaluable

précipice [pʀesipis] nm drop, chasm

précipitamment [pʀesipitamɑ̃]
adv hurriedly, hastily

précipitation [pʀesipitasjɔ̃] nf
(hâte) haste

précipité, e [pʀesipite] adj hurried;
hasty

précipiter [pʀesipite] /1/ vt (hâter:
départ) to hasten; **se précipiter** vi
to speed up; **~ qn/qch du haut de**
(faire tomber) to throw ou hurl sb/sth
off ou from; **se ~ sur/vers** to rush
at/towards

précis, e [pʀesi, -iz] adj precise;
(tir, mesures) accurate, precise; **à
4 heures ~es** at 4 o'clock sharp;
précisément adv precisely; **préciser**
/1/ vt (expliquer) to be more specific
about, clarify; (spécifier) to state,
specify; **se préciser** vi to become
clear(er); **précision** nf precision;
(détail) point ou detail (made clear or
to be clarified)

précoce [pʀekɔs] adj early; (enfant)
precocious

préconçu, e [pʀekɔ̃sy] adj
preconceived

préconiser [pʀekɔnize] /1/ vt to
advocate

prédécesseur [pʀedesesœʀ] nm
predecessor

prédilection [pʀedilɛksjɔ̃] nf: **avoir
une ~ pour** to be partial to

prédire [pʀediʀ] /37/ vt to predict

prédominer [pʀedɔmine] /1/ vi to
predominate

préface [pʀefas] nf preface

préfecture [pʀefɛktyʀ] nf prefecture;
~ de police police headquarters

préférable [pʀefeʀabl] adj
preferable

préféré, e [pʀefeʀe] adj, nm/f
favourite

préférence [pʀefeʀɑ̃s] nf
preference; **de ~** preferably

préférer [pʀefeʀe] /6/ vt: **~ qn/qch
(à)** to prefer sb/sth (to), like sb/sth
better (than); **~ faire** to prefer to do;
je préférerais du thé I would rather
have tea, I'd prefer tea

préfet [pʀefɛ] nm prefect

préhistorique [pʀeistɔʀik] adj
prehistoric

préjudice [pʀeʒydis] nm (matériel)
loss; (moral) harm no pl; **porter ~ à** to
harm, be detrimental to; **au ~ de** at
the expense of

préjugé [pʀeʒyʒe] nm prejudice;
avoir un ~ contre to be prejudiced
against

prélasser [pʀelɑse] /1/: **se prélasser**
vi to lounge

prélèvement [pʀelɛvmɑ̃] nm
(montant) deduction; **faire un ~ de
sang** to take a blood sample

prélever [pʀelve] /5/ vt (échantillon)
to take; **~ (sur)** (argent) to deduct
(from); (sur son compte) to withdraw
(from)

prématuré, e [pʀematyʀe] adj
premature ▷ nm premature baby

premier, -ière [pʀəmje, -jɛʀ] adj
first; (rang) front; (fig: fondamental)
basic ▷ nf (Rail, Aviat etc) first
class; (Scol) year 12 (BRIT), eleventh
grade (US); **de ~ ordre** first-rate;
le ~ venu the first person to come
along; **P~ Ministre** Prime Minister;
premièrement adv firstly

prémonition [pʀemɔnisjɔ̃] nf
premonition

prenant, e [pʀənɑ̃, -ɑ̃t] adj
absorbing, engrossing

prénatal, e [pʀenatal] adj (Méd)
antenatal

prendre [pʀɑ̃dʀ] /58/ vt to take;
(repas) to have; (aller chercher) to

get; (*malfaiteur, poisson*) to catch; (*passager*) to pick up; (*personnel*) to take on; (*traiter: enfant, problème*) to handle; (*voix, ton*) to put on; (*ôter*): **~ qch à** to take sth from; (*coincer*): **se ~ les doigts dans** to get one's fingers caught in ▷ *vi* (*liquide, ciment*) to set; (*greffe, vaccin*) to take; (*feu: foyer*) to go; (*se diriger*): **~ à gauche** to turn (to the) left; **~ froid** to catch cold; **se ~ pour** to think one is; **s'en ~ à** to attack; **se ~ d'amitié/d'affection pour** to befriend/become fond of; **s'y ~** (*procéder*) to set about it

preneur [pʀənœʀ] *nm*: **être ~** to be willing to buy; **trouver ~** to find a buyer

prénom [pʀenɔ̃] *nm* first name

préoccupation [pʀeɔkypasjɔ̃] *nf* (*souci*) concern; (*idée fixe*) preoccupation

préoccuper [pʀeɔkype] /1/ *vt* (*tourmenter, tracasser*) to concern; (*absorber, obséder*) to preoccupy; **se ~ de qch** to be concerned about sth

préparatifs [pʀepaʀatif] *nmpl* preparations

préparation [pʀepaʀasjɔ̃] *nf* preparation

préparer [pʀepaʀe] /1/ *vt* to prepare; (*café, repas*) to make; (*examen*) to prepare for; (*voyage, entreprise*) to plan; **se préparer** *vi* (*orage, tragédie*) to brew, be in the air; **se ~ (à qch/à faire)** to prepare (o.s.) *ou* get ready (for sth/to do); **~ qch à qn** (*surprise etc*) to have sth in store for sb

prépondérant, e [pʀepɔ̃deʀɑ̃, -ɑ̃t] *adj* major, dominating

préposé, e [pʀepoze] *nm/f* employee; (*facteur*) postman/woman

préposition [pʀepozisjɔ̃] *nf* preposition

près [pʀɛ] *adv* near, close; **~ de** near (to), close to; (*environ*) nearly, almost; **de ~** closely; **à cinq kg ~** to within about five kg; **il n'est pas à 10 minutes ~** he can spare 10 minutes

présage [pʀezaʒ] *nm* omen

presbyte [pʀɛsbit] *adj* long-sighted

presbytère [pʀɛsbiteʀ] *nm* presbytery

prescription [pʀɛskʀipsjɔ̃] *nf* prescription

prescrire [pʀɛskʀiʀ] /39/ *vt* to prescribe

présence [pʀezɑ̃s] *nf* presence; (*au bureau etc*) attendance

présent, e [pʀezɑ̃, -ɑ̃t] *adj, nm* present; **à ~ que** now that

présentation [pʀezɑ̃tasjɔ̃] *nf* presentation; (*de nouveau venu*) introduction; (*allure*) appearance; **faire les ~s** to do the introductions

présenter [pʀezɑ̃te] /1/ *vt* to present; (*invité, candidat*) to introduce; (*félicitations, condoléances*) to offer; **~ qn à** to introduce sb to ▷ *vi*: **~ mal/bien** to have an unattractive/a pleasing appearance; **se présenter** *vi* (*à une élection*) to stand; (*occasion*) to arise; **se ~ à un examen** to sit an exam; **je vous présente Nadine** this is Nadine

préservatif [pʀezɛʀvatif] *nm* condom, sheath

préserver [pʀezɛʀve] /1/ *vt*: **~ de** (*protéger*) to protect from

président [pʀezidɑ̃] *nm* (Pol) president; (*d'une assemblée, Comm*) chairman; **~ directeur général** chairman and managing director

présidentiel, le [pʀezidɑ̃sjɛl] *adj* presidential; **présidentielles** *nfpl* presidential election(s)

présider [pʀezide] /1/ *vt* to preside over; (*dîner*) to be the guest of honour (BRIT) *ou* honor (US) at

presque [pʀɛsk] *adv* almost, nearly; **~ rien** hardly anything; **~ pas** hardly (at all); **~ pas de** hardly any; **personne, ou ~** next to nobody, hardly anyone

presqu'île [pʀɛskil] *nf* peninsula

pressant, e [pʀesɑ̃, -ɑ̃t] *adj* urgent

presse [pʀɛs] *nf* press; (*affluence*): **heures de ~** busy times

pressé, e [prese] *adj* in a hurry; *(besogne)* urgent; **orange ~e** freshly squeezed orange juice

pressentiment [presãtimã] *nm* foreboding, premonition

pressentir [presãtir] /16/ *vt* to sense

presse-papiers [prespapje] *nm inv* paperweight

presser [prese] /1/ *vt (fruit, éponge)* to squeeze; *(interrupteur, bouton)* to press; *(allure, affaire)* to speed up; *(inciter)*: **~ qn de faire** to urge *ou* press sb to do ▷ *vi* to be urgent; **se presser** *vi (se hâter)* to hurry (up); **rien ne presse** there's no hurry; **se ~ contre qn** to squeeze up against sb; **le temps presse** there's not much time

pressing [presiŋ] *nm (magasin)* dry-cleaner's

pression [presjõ] *nf* pressure; *(bouton)* press stud (BRIT), snap fastener (US); *(fam: bière)* draught beer; **faire ~ sur** to put pressure on; **sous ~** pressurized, under pressure; *(fig)* keyed up; **~ artérielle** blood pressure

prestataire [prestater] *nm/f* person receiving benefits; **~ de services** provider of services

prestation [prestasjõ] *nf (allocation)* benefit; *(d'une entreprise)* service provided; *(d'un joueur, artiste)* performance

prestidigitateur, -trice [prestidiʒitatœr, -tris] *nm/f* conjurer

prestige [presti ʒ] *nm* prestige; **prestigieux, -euse** *adj* prestigious

présumer [prezyme] /1/ *vt*: **~ que** to presume *ou* assume that

prêt, e [prɛ, prɛt] *adj* ready ▷ *nm (somme prêtée)* loan; **prêt-à-porter** *nm* ready-to-wear *ou* off-the-peg (BRIT) clothes *pl*

prétendre [pretãdr] /41/ *vt (affirmer)*: **~ que** to claim that; **~ faire qch** *(avoir l'intention de)* to mean *ou*

intend to do sth; **prétendu, e** *adj (supposé)* so-called

▎ Attention à ne pas traduire *prétendre* par *to pretend*.

prétentieux, -euse [pretãsjø, -øz] *adj* pretentious

prétention [pretãsjõ] *nf* pretentiousness; *(exigence, ambition)* claim

prêter [prete] /1/ *vt*: **~ qch à qn** *(livres, argent)* to lend sth to sb; *(caractère, propos)* to attribute sth to sb

prétexte [pretɛkst] *nm* pretext, excuse; **sous aucun ~** on no account; **prétexter** [pretɛkste] /1/ *vt* to give as a pretext *ou* an excuse

prêtre [prɛtr] *nm* priest

preuve [prœv] *nf* proof; *(indice)* proof, evidence *no pl*; **faire ~ de** to show; **faire ses ~s** to prove o.s. *(ou* itself)

prévaloir [prevalwar] /29/ *vi* to prevail

prévenant, e [prevnã, -ãt] *adj* thoughtful, kind

prévenir [prevnir] /22/ *vt (éviter: catastrophe etc)* to avoid, prevent; *(anticiper: désirs, besoins)* to anticipate; **~ qn (de)** *(avertir)* to warn sb (about); *(informer)* to tell *ou* inform sb (about)

préventif, -ive [prevãtif, -iv] *adj* preventive

prévention [prevãsjõ] *nf* prevention; **~ routière** road safety

prévenu, e [prevny] *nm/f (Jur)* defendant, accused

prévision [previzjõ] *nf*: **~s** predictions; *(météorologiques, économiques)* forecast *sg*; **en ~ de** in anticipation of; **~s météorologiques** *ou* **du temps** weather forecast *sg*

prévoir [prevwar] /24/ *vt (deviner)* to foresee; *(s'attendre à)* to expect, reckon on; *(organiser: voyage etc)* to plan; *(préparer, réserver)* to

allow; **comme prévu** as planned;
prévoyant, e adj gifted with (ou
showing) foresight; **prévu, e** pp de
prévoir

prier [pʀije] /7/ vi to pray ▷ vt
(Dieu) to pray to; (implorer) to beg;
(demander): **~ qn de faire** to ask sb
to do; **se faire ~** to need coaxing ou
persuading; **je vous en prie** (allez-y)
please do; (de rien) don't mention it;
prière nf prayer; **"prière de faire ..."**
"please do ..."

primaire [pʀimɛʀ] adj primary ▷ nm
(Scol) primary education

prime [pʀim] nf (bonification) bonus;
(subside) allowance; (Comm: cadeau)
free gift; (Assurances, Bourse) premium
▷ adj: **de ~ abord** at first glance;
primer /1/ vt (récompenser) to award a
prize to ▷ vi to dominate

primevère [pʀimvɛʀ] nf primrose

primitif, -ive [pʀimitif, -iv] adj
primitive; (originel) original

prince [pʀɛ̃s] nm prince; **princesse**
nf princess

principal, e, -aux [pʀɛ̃sipal, -o]
adj principal, main ▷ nm (Scol) head
(teacher) (BRIT), principal (US);
(essentiel) main thing

principe [pʀɛ̃sip] nm principle; **par ~**
on principle; **en ~** (habituellement) as a
rule; (théoriquement) in principle

printemps [pʀɛ̃tɑ̃] nm spring

priorité [pʀijɔʀite] nf priority;
(Auto)**~ à droite** right of way to
vehicles coming from the right

pris, e [pʀi, pʀiz] pp de **prendre**
▷ adj (place) taken; (journée, mains)
full; (personne) busy; **avoir le nez/
la gorge ~(e)** to have a stuffy nose/a
bad throat; **être ~ de peur/de
fatigue/de panique** to be stricken
with fear/overcome with fatigue/
panic-stricken

prise [pʀiz] nf (d'une ville) capture;
(Pêche, Chasse) catch; (point d'appui ou
pour empoigner) hold; (Élec: fiche) plug;
(: femelle) socket; **être aux ~s avec**

to be grappling with; **~ de courant**
power point; **~ multiple** adaptor;
~ de sang blood test

priser [pʀize] /1/ vt (estimer) to
prize, value

prison [pʀizɔ̃] nf prison; **aller/être
en ~** to go to/be in prison ou jail;
prisonnier, -ière nm/f prisoner ▷ adj
captive

privé, e [pʀive] adj private; (en
punition): **tu es ~ de télé!** no TV for
you! ▷ nm (Comm) private sector; **en
~** in private

priver [pʀive] /1/ vt: **~ qn de** to deprive
sb of; **se ~ de** to go ou do without

privilège [pʀivilɛʒ] nm privilege

prix [pʀi] nm price; (récompense, Scol)
prize; **hors de ~** exorbitantly priced;
à aucun ~ not at any price; **à tout ~**
at all costs

probable [pʀɔbabl] adj likely,
probable; **probablement** adv
probably

problème [pʀɔblɛm] nm problem

procédé [pʀɔsede] nm (méthode)
process; (comportement) behaviour
no pl

procéder [pʀɔsede] /6/ vi to
proceed; (moralement) to behave; **~ à**
to carry out

procès [pʀɔsɛ] nm trial (poursuites)
proceedings pl; **être en ~ avec** to be
involved in a lawsuit with

processus [pʀɔsesys] nm process

procès-verbal, -aux [pʀɔsɛvɛʀbal,
-o] nm (de réunion) minutes pl; (aussi:
PV): **avoir un ~** to get a parking
ticket

prochain, e [pʀɔʃɛ̃, -ɛn] adj next;
(proche: départ, arrivée) impending
▷ nm fellow man; **la ~e fois/semaine
~e** next time/week; **prochainement**
adv soon, shortly

proche [pʀɔʃ] adj nearby; (dans
le temps) imminent; (parent, ami)
close; **proches** nmpl (parents) close
relatives; **être ~ (de)** to be near, be
close (to)

proclamer [pʀɔklame] /1/ vt to proclaim

procuration [pʀɔkyʀasjɔ̃] nf proxy

procurer [pʀɔkyʀe] /1/ vt (fournir): **~ qch à qn** (obtenir) to get ou obtain sth for sb; (plaisir etc) to bring ou give sb sth; **se procurer** vt to get; **procureur** nm public prosecutor

prodige [pʀɔdiʒ] nm marvel, wonder; (personne) prodigy; **prodiguer** /1/ vt (soins, attentions): **prodiguer qch à qn** to lavish sth on sb

producteur, -trice [pʀɔdyktœʀ, -tʀis] nm/f producer

productif, -ive [pʀɔdyktif, -iv] adj productive

production [pʀɔdyksjɔ̃] nf production; (rendement) output

productivité [pʀɔdyktivite] nf productivity

produire [pʀɔdɥiʀ] /38/ vt to produce; **se produire** vi (acteur) to perform, appear; (événement) to happen, occur

produit, e [pʀɔdɥi, -it] nm product; **~ chimique** chemical; **~ d'entretien** cleaning product; **~s agricoles** farm produce sg; **~s de beauté** beauty products, cosmetics

prof [pʀɔf] nm (fam) teacher

proférer [pʀɔfeʀe] /6/ vt to utter

professeur, e [pʀɔfesœʀ] nm/f teacher; (titulaire d'une chaire) professor; **~ (de faculté)** (university) lecturer

profession [pʀɔfesjɔ̃] nf (libérale) profession; (gén) occupation; **"sans ~"** "unemployed"; **professionnel, le** adj, nm/f professional

profil [pʀɔfil] nm profile; **de ~** in profile

profit [pʀɔfi] nm (avantage) benefit, advantage; (Comm, Finance) profit; **au ~ de** in aid of; **tirer** ou **retirer ~ de** to profit from; **profitable** adj (utile) beneficial; (lucratif) profitable; **profiter** /1/ vi: **profiter de** (situation, occasion) to take advantage of; (vacances, jeunesse etc) to make the most of

profond, e [pʀɔfɔ̃, -ɔ̃d] adj deep; (méditation, mépris) profound; **profondément** adv deeply; **il dort profondément** he is sound asleep; **profondeur** nf depth; **l'eau a quelle profondeur?** how deep is the water?

programme [pʀɔgʀam] nm programme; (Scol) syllabus, curriculum; (Inform) program; **programmer** /1/ vt (organiser, prévoir: émission) to schedule; (Inform) to program; **programmeur, -euse** nm/f (computer) programmer

progrès [pʀɔgʀɛ] nm progress no pl; **faire des/être en ~** to make/ be making progress; **progresser** /1/ vi to progress; **progressif, -ive** adj progressive

proie [pʀwa] nf prey no pl

projecteur [pʀɔʒɛktœʀ] nm projector; (de théâtre, cirque) spotlight

projectile [pʀɔʒɛktil] nm missile

projection [pʀɔʒɛksjɔ̃] nf projection; (séance) showing

projet [pʀɔʒɛ] nm plan; (ébauche) draft; **~ de loi** bill; **projeter** /4/ vt (envisager) to plan; (film, photos) to project; (ombre, lueur) to throw, cast; (jeter) to throw up (ou off ou out)

prolétaire [pʀɔletɛʀ] adj, nm/f proletarian

prolongement [pʀɔlɔ̃ʒmɑ̃] nm extension; **dans le ~ de** running on from

prolonger [pʀɔlɔ̃ʒe] /3/ vt (débat, séjour) to prolong; (délai, billet, rue) to extend; **se prolonger** vi to go on

promenade [pʀɔmnad] nf walk (ou drive ou ride); **faire une ~** to go for a walk; **une ~ (à pied)/en voiture/à vélo** a walk/drive/(bicycle) ride

promener [pʀɔmne] /5/ vt (personne, chien) to take out for a walk; (doigts, regard): **~ qch sur** to run sth over; **se promener** vi to go for (ou be out for) a walk

promesse [pʀɔmɛs] nf promise

promettre [pRɔmɛtR] /56/ vt to promise ▷ vi to look promising; **~ à qn de faire** to promise sb that one will do

promiscuité [pRɔmiskɥite] nf lack of privacy

promontoire [pRɔmɔ̃twaR] nm headland

promoteur, -trice [pRɔmɔtœR, -tRis] nm/f: **~ (immobilier)** property developer (BRIT), real estate promoter (US)

promotion [pRɔmosjɔ̃] nf promotion; **en ~** on (special) offer

promouvoir [pRɔmuvwaR] /27/ vt to promote

prompt, e [pRɔ̃, pRɔ̃t] adj swift, rapid

prôner [pRone] /1/ vt (préconiser) to advocate

pronom [pRɔnɔ̃] nm pronoun

prononcer [pRɔnɔ̃se] /3/ vt to pronounce; (dire) to utter; (discours) to deliver; **se prononcer** vi to be pronounced; **se ~ (sur)** (se décider) to reach a decision (on ou about), give a verdict (on); **ça se prononce comment?** how do you pronounce this?; **prononciation** nf pronunciation

pronostic [pRɔnɔstik] nm (Méd) prognosis; (fig: aussi: **~s**) forecast

propagande [pRɔpagɑ̃d] nf propaganda

propager [pRɔpaʒe] /3/ vt to spread; **se propager** vi to spread

prophète, prophétesse [pRɔfɛt, pRɔfetɛs] nm/f prophet(ess)

prophétie [pRɔfesi] nf prophecy

propice [pRɔpis] adj favourable

proportion [pRɔpɔRsjɔ̃] nf proportion; **toute(s) ~(s) gardée(s)** making due allowance(s)

propos [pRɔpo] nm (paroles) talk no pl, remark; (intention, but) intention, aim; (sujet): **à quel ~?** what about?; **à ~ de** about, regarding; **à tout ~** for no reason at all; **à ~** by the way; (opportunément) (just) at the right moment

proposer [pRɔpoze] /1/ vt to propose; **~ qch (à qn)/de faire** (suggérer) to suggest sth (to sb)/doing, propose sth (to sb)/(to) do; (offrir) to offer (sb) sth/to do; **se ~ (pour faire)** to offer one's services (to do); **proposition** nf suggestion; proposal; (Ling) clause

propre [pRɔpR] adj clean; (net) neat, tidy; (possessif) own; (sens) literal; (particulier): **~ à** peculiar to; (approprié): **~ à** suitable ou appropriate for ▷ nm: **recopier au ~** to make a fair copy of; **proprement** adv (avec propreté) cleanly; **à proprement parler** strictly speaking; **le village proprement dit** the village itself; **propreté** nf cleanliness

propriétaire [pRɔpRijetɛR] nm/f owner; (pour le locataire) landlord(-lady)

propriété [pRɔpRijete] nf (droit) ownership; (objet, immeuble etc) property

propulser [pRɔpylse] /1/ vt to propel

prose [pRoz] nf prose (style)

prospecter [pRɔspɛkte] /1/ vt to prospect; (Comm) to canvass

prospectus [pRɔspɛktys] nm leaflet

prospère [pRɔspɛR] adj prosperous; **prospérer** /6/ vi to thrive

prosterner [pRɔstɛRne] /1/: **se prosterner** vi to bow low, prostrate o.s.

prostituée [pRɔstitɥe] nf prostitute

prostitution [pRɔstitysjɔ̃] nf prostitution

protecteur, -trice [pRɔtɛktœR, -tRis] adj protective; (air, ton: péj) patronizing ▷ nm/f protector

protection [pRɔtɛksjɔ̃] nf protection; (d'un personnage influent: aide) patronage

protéger [pRɔteʒe] /6, 3/ vt to protect; **se ~ de/contre** to protect o.s. from

protège-slip [pRɔtɛʒslip] nm panty liner

P

protéine [pʁɔtein] nf protein

protestant, e [pʁɔtɛstɑ̃, -ɑ̃t] adj, nm/f Protestant

protestation [pʁɔtɛstasjɔ̃] nf (plainte) protest

protester [pʁɔteste] /1/ vi: ~ **(contre)** to protest (against ou about); ~ **de** (son innocence, sa loyauté) to protest

prothèse [pʁɔtɛz] nf: ~ **dentaire** denture

protocole [pʁɔtɔkɔl] nm (fig) etiquette

proue [pʁu] nf bow(s pl), prow

prouesse [pʁuɛs] nf feat

prouver [pʁuve] /1/ vt to prove

provenance [pʁɔvnɑ̃s] nf origin; **avion en ~ de** plane (arriving) from

provenir [pʁɔvniʁ] /22/: ~ **de** vt to come from

proverbe [pʁɔvɛʁb] nm proverb

province [pʁɔvɛ̃s] nf province

proviseur [pʁɔvizœʁ] nm ≈ head (teacher) (BRIT), ≈ principal (US)

provision [pʁɔvizjɔ̃] nf (réserve) stock, supply; **provisions** nfpl (vivres) provisions, food no pl

provisoire [pʁɔvizwaʁ] adj temporary; **provisoirement** adv temporarily

provocant, e [pʁɔvɔkɑ̃, -ɑ̃t] adj provocative

provoquer [pʁɔvɔke] /1/ vt (défier) to provoke; (causer) to cause, bring about; (inciter): ~ **qn à** to incite sb to

proxénète [pʁɔksenɛt] nm procurer

proximité [pʁɔksimite] nf nearness, closeness; (dans le temps) imminence, closeness; **à ~** near ou close by; **à ~ de** near (to), close to

prudemment [pʁydamɑ̃] adv carefully; wisely, sensibly

prudence [pʁydɑ̃s] nf carefulness; **avec ~** carefully; **par (mesure de) ~** as a precaution

prudent, e [pʁydɑ̃, -ɑ̃t] adj (pas téméraire) careful (: en général) safety-conscious; (sage, conseillé) wise, sensible; **c'est plus ~** it's wiser

prune [pʁyn] nf plum

pruneau, x [pʁyno] nm prune

prunier [pʁynje] nm plum tree

PS sigle m = **parti socialiste**; (= post-scriptum) PS

pseudonyme [psødɔnim] nm (gén) fictitious name; (d'écrivain) pseudonym, pen name

psychanalyse [psikanaliz] nf psychoanalysis

psychiatre [psikjatʁ] nm/f psychiatrist; **psychiatrique** adj psychiatric

psychique [psiʃik] adj psychological

psychologie [psikɔlɔʒi] nf psychology; **psychologique** adj psychological; **psychologue** nm/f psychologist

pu [py] pp de **pouvoir**

puanteur [pɥɑ̃tœʁ] nf stink, stench

pub [pyb] nf (fam) = **publicité**; **la ~** advertising

public, -ique [pyblik] adj public; (école, instruction) state cpd ▷ nm public; (assistance) audience; **en ~** in public

publicitaire [pyblisitɛʁ] adj advertising cpd; (film, voiture) publicity cpd

publicité [pyblisite] nf (méthode, profession) advertising; (annonce) advertisement; (révélations) publicity

publier [pyblije] /7/ vt to publish

publipostage [pyblipɔstaʒ] nm (mass) mailing

publique [pyblik] adj f voir **public**

puce [pys] nf flea; (Inform) chip; **carte à ~** smart card; **(marché aux) ~s** flea market sg

pudeur [pydœʁ] nf modesty; **pudique** adj (chaste) modest; (discret) discreet

puer [pɥe] /1/ (péj) vi to stink

puéricultrice [pɥeʁikyltʁis] nf ≈ paediatric nurse

puéril, e [pɥeʁil] adj childish

puis [pɥi] vb voir **pouvoir** ▷ adv then

puiser [pɥize] /1/ vt: ~ **(dans)** to draw (from)

puisque [pɥisk] conj since

puissance [pɥisɑ̃s] nf power; **en ~** adj potential

puissant, e [pɥisɑ̃, -ɑ̃t] adj powerful

puits [pɥi] nm well

pull(-over) [pyl(ɔvœʀ)] nm sweater

pulluler [pylyle] /1/ vi to swarm

pulpe [pylp] nf pulp

pulvériser [pylveʀize] /1/ vt to pulverize; (liquide) to spray

punaise [pynɛz] nf (Zool) bug; (clou) drawing pin (BRIT), thumb tack (US)

punch [pɔ̃ʃ] nm (boisson) punch

punir [pyniʀ] /2/ vt to punish; **punition** nf punishment

pupille [pypij] nf (Anat) pupil ▷ nm/f (enfant) ward

pupitre [pypitʀ] nm (Scol) desk

pur, e [pyʀ] adj pure; (vin) undiluted; (whisky) neat; **en ~e perte** to no avail; **c'est de la folie ~e** it's sheer madness

purée [pyʀe] nf: ~ **(de pommes de terre)** ≈ mashed potatoes pl; ~ **de marrons** chestnut purée

purement [pyʀmɑ̃] adv purely

purgatoire [pyʀgatwaʀ] nm purgatory

purger [pyʀʒe] /3/ vt (Méd, Pol) to purge; (Jur: peine) to serve

pur-sang [pyʀsɑ̃] nm inv thoroughbred

pus [py] nm pus

putain [pytɛ̃] nf (!) whore (!)

puzzle [pœzl] nm jigsaw (puzzle)

PV sigle m = **procès-verbal**

pyjama [piʒama] nm pyjamas pl (BRIT), pajamas pl (US)

pyramide [piʀamid] nf pyramid

Pyrénées [piʀene] nfpl: **les ~** the Pyrenees

QI sigle m (= quotient intellectuel) IQ

quadragénaire [kadraʒeneʀ] nm/f man/woman in his/her forties

quadruple [k(w)adʀypl] nm: **le ~ de** four times as much as

quai [ke] nm (de port) quay; (de gare) platform; **être à ~** (navire) to be alongside

qualification [kalifikasjɔ̃] nf qualification

qualifier [kalifje] /7/ vt to qualify; ~ **qch/qn de** to describe sth/sb as; **se qualifier** vi to qualify

qualité [kalite] nf quality

quand [kɑ̃] conj, adv when; ~ **je serai riche** when I'm rich; ~ **même** all the same; ~ **même, il exagère!** really, he overdoes it!; ~ **bien même** even though

quant [kɑ̃]: ~ **à** prép (pour ce qui est de) as for, as to; (au sujet de) regarding

quantité [kɑ̃tite] nf quantity, amount; **une** ou **des ~(s) de** (grand nombre) a great deal of

quarantaine [kaʀɑ̃tɛn] nf
(isolement) quarantine; **une ~ (de)**
forty or so, about forty; **avoir la ~**
(âge) to be around forty
quarante [kaʀɑ̃t] num forty
quart [kaʀ] nm (fraction) quarter;
(surveillance) watch; **un ~ de vin** a
quarter litre of wine; **le ~ de** a quarter
of; **~ d'heure** quarter of an hour; **~s
de finale** quarter finals
quartier [kaʀtje] nm (de ville) district,
area; (de bœuf, de la lune) quarter;
(de fruit, fromage) piece; **cinéma/
salle de ~** local cinema/hall; **avoir
~ libre** to be free; **~ général (QG)**
headquarters (HQ)
quartz [kwaʀts] nm quartz
quasi [kazi] adv almost, nearly;
quasiment adv almost, (very) nearly;
quasiment jamais hardly ever
quatorze [katɔʀz] num fourteen
quatorzième [katɔʀzjɛm] num
fourteenth
quatre [katʀ] num four; **à ~ pattes**
on all fours; **se mettre en ~ pour
qn** to go out of one's way for sb;
~ à ~ (monter, descendre) four at
a time; **quatre-vingt-dix** num
ninety; **quatre-vingts** num eighty;
quatrième num fourth ▷ nf (Scol)
year 9 (BRIT), eighth grade (US)
quatuor [kwatyɔʀ] nm quartet(te)

MOT-CLÉ

que [kə] conj **1** (introduisant complétive)
that; **il sait que tu es là** he knows
(that) you're here; **je veux que tu
acceptes** I want you to accept; **il
a dit que oui** he said he would (ou
it was etc)
2 (reprise d'autres conjonctions): **quand
il rentrera et qu'il aura mangé**
when he gets back and (when) he has
eaten; **si vous y allez ou que vous
...** if you go there or if you ...
3 (en tête de phrase, hypothèse, souhait
etc): **qu'il le veuille ou non** whether

he likes it or not; **qu'il fasse ce qu'il
voudra!** let him do as he pleases!
4 (but): **tenez-le qu'il ne tombe pas**
hold it so (that) it doesn't fall
5 (après comparatif) than, as; voir aussi
plus², **aussi**, **autant** etc
6 (seulement): **ne ... que** only; **il ne
boit que de l'eau** he only drinks
water
7 (temps): **il y a quatre ans qu'il est
parti** it is four years since he left, he
left four years ago
▶ adv (exclamation): **qu'il** ou **qu'est-ce
qu'il est bête/court vite!** he's so
silly!/he runs so fast!; **que de livres!**
what a lot of books!
▶ pron **1** (relatif: personne) whom;
(: chose) that, which; **l'homme que
je vois** the man (whom) I see; **le livre
que tu vois** the book (that ou which)
you see; **un jour que j'étais ...** a day
when I was ...
2 (interrogatif) what; **que fais-tu?**,
qu'est-ce que tu fais? what are you
doing?; **qu'est-ce que c'est?** what
is it?, what's that?; **que faire?** what
can one do?

Québec [kebɛk] nm: **le ~** Quebec
(Province)
québécois, e adj Quebec cpd ▷ nm
(Ling) Quebec French ▷ nm/f: **Q~, e**
Quebecois, Quebec(k)er

MOT-CLÉ

quel, quelle [kɛl] adj **1** (interrogatif:
personne) who; (: chose) what; **quel
est cet homme?** who is this man?;
quel est ce livre? what is this
book?; **quel livre/homme?** what
book/man?; (parmi un certain choix)
which book/man?; **quels acteurs
préférez-vous?** which actors do you
prefer?; **dans quels pays êtes-vous
allé?** which ou what countries did
you go to?
2 (exclamatif): **quelle surprise/**

coïncidence! what a surprise/coincidence!

3: **quel que soit le coupable** whoever is guilty; **quel que soit votre avis** whatever your opinion (may be)

quelconque [kɛlkɔ̃k] *adj* (*médiocre: repas*) indifferent, poor; (*sans attrait*) ordinary, plain; (*indéfini*): **un ami/prétexte ~** some friend/pretext or other

 MOT-CLÉ

quelque [kɛlk] *adj* **1** (*au singulier*) some; (*au pluriel*) a few, some; (*tournure interrogative*) any; **quelque espoir** some hope; **il a quelques amis** he has a few *ou* some friends; **a-t-il quelques amis?** does he have any friends?; **les quelques livres qui** the few books which; **20 kg et quelque(s)** a bit over 20 kg
2: **quelque ... que**: **quelque livre qu'il choisisse** whatever (*ou* whichever) book he chooses
3: **quelque chose** something; (*tournure interrogative*) anything; **quelque chose d'autre** something else; anything else; **quelque part** somewhere; anywhere; **en quelque sorte** as it were
▶ *adv* **1** (*environ*): **quelque 100 mètres** some 100 metres
2: **quelque peu** rather, somewhat

quelquefois [kɛlkəfwa] *adv* sometimes
quelques-uns, -unes [kɛlkəzœ̃, -yn] *pron* some, a few
quelqu'un [kɛlkœ̃] *pron* someone, somebody; (*+ tournure interrogative ou négative*) anyone, anybody; **~ d'autre** someone *ou* somebody else; anybody else
qu'en dira-t-on [kɑ̃diʀatɔ̃] *nm inv*: **le ~** gossip, what people say

querelle [kəʀɛl] *nf* quarrel; **quereller** /1/: **se quereller** *vi* to quarrel
qu'est-ce que [kɛskə] *voir* **que**
qu'est-ce qui [kɛski] *voir* **qui**
question [kɛstjɔ̃] *nf* question; (*fig*) matter; issue; **il a été ~ de** we (*ou* they) spoke about; **de quoi est-il ~?** what is it about?; **il n'en est pas ~** there's no question of it; **en ~** in question; **hors de ~** out of the question; **(re)mettre en ~** to question; **questionnaire** *nm* questionnaire; **questionner** /1/ *vt* to question
quête [kɛt] *nf* collection; (*recherche*) quest, search; **faire la ~** (*à l'église*) to take the collection; (*artiste*) to pass the hat round
quetsche [kwɛtʃ] *nf* damson
queue [kø] *nf* tail; (*fig: du classement*) bottom; (: *de poêle*) handle; (: *de fruit, feuille*) stalk; (: *de train, colonne, file*) rear; **faire la ~** to queue (up) (*BRIT*), line up (*US*); **~ de cheval** ponytail; **~ de poisson: faire une ~ de poisson à qn** (*Auto*) to cut in front of sb

 MOT-CLÉ

qui [ki] *pron* **1** (*interrogatif: personne*) who; (: *chose*) **qu'est-ce qui est sur la table?** what is on the table?; **qui est-ce qui?** who?; **qui est-ce que?** who?; **à qui est ce sac?** whose bag is this?; **à qui parlais-tu?** who were you talking to?, to whom were you talking?; **chez qui allez-vous?** whose house are you going to?
2 (*relatif: personne*) who; (+*prép*) whom; **l'ami de qui je vous ai parlé** the friend I told you about; **la dame chez qui je suis allé** the lady whose house I went to
3 (*sans antécédent*): **amenez qui vous voulez** bring who you like; **qui que ce soit** whoever it may be

quiche [kiʃ] *nf* quiche

q

quiconque [kikɔ̃k] pron (celui qui) whoever, anyone who; (n'importe qui, personne) anyone, anybody

quille [kij] nf: **(jeu de) ~s** skittles sg (BRIT), bowling (US)

quincaillerie [kɛ̃kajʀi] nf (ustensiles) hardware; (magasin) hardware shop ou store (US)

quinquagénaire [kɛ̃kaʒenɛʀ] nm/f man/woman in his/her fifties

quinquennat [kɛ̃kena] nm five year term of office (of French President)

quinte [kɛ̃t] nf: **~ (de toux)** coughing fit

quintuple [kɛ̃typl] nm: **le ~ de** five times as much as

quinzaine [kɛ̃zɛn] nf: **une ~ (de)** about fifteen, fifteen or so; **une ~ (de jours)** a fortnight (BRIT), two weeks

quinze [kɛ̃z] num fifteen; **dans ~ jours** in a fortnight('s time) (BRIT), in two weeks(' time)

quinzième [kɛ̃zjɛm] num fifteenth

quittance [kitɑ̃s] nf (reçu) receipt

quitte [kit] adj: **être ~ envers qn** to be no longer in sb's debt; (fig) to be quits with sb; **~ à faire** even if it means doing

quitter [kite] /1/ vt to leave; (vêtement) to take off; **se quitter** vi (couples, interlocuteurs) to part; **ne quittez pas** (au téléphone) hold the line

qui-vive [kiviv] nm inv: **être sur le ~** to be on the alert

○ MOT-CLÉ

quoi [kwa] pron interrog 1 what; **~ de neuf?** what's new?; **~?** (qu'est-ce que tu dis?) what?

2 (avec prép): **à ~ tu penses?** what are you thinking about?; **de ~ parlez-vous?** what are you talking about?; **à ~ bon?** what's the use?

▶ pron relatif: **as-tu de ~ écrire?** do you have anything to write with?; **il n'y a pas de ~** (please) don't mention it; **il n'y a pas de ~ rire** there's nothing to laugh about

▶ pron (locutions): **~ qu'il arrive** whatever happens; **~ qu'il en soit** be that as it may; **~ que ce soit** anything at all

▶ excl what!

quoique [kwak] conj (al)though

quotidien, ne [kɔtidjɛ̃, -ɛn] adj daily; (banal) everyday ▷ nm (journal) daily (paper); **quotidiennement** adv daily, every day

R, r *abr* = **route**; **rue**

rab [Rab] *nm (fam: nourriture)* extra; **est-ce qu'il y a du ~?** are there any seconds?

rabâcher [Rabɑʃe] /1/ *vt* to keep on repeating

rabais [Rabɛ] *nm* reduction, discount; **rabaisser** /1/ *vt (rabattre: prix)* to reduce; *(dénigrer)* to belittle

Rabat [Raba(t)] *n* Rabat

rabattre [Rabatʀ] /41/ *vt (couvercle, siège)* to pull down; *(déduire)* to reduce; **se rabattre** *vi (bords, couvercle)* to fall shut; *(véhicule, coureur)* to cut in; **se ~ sur** to fall back on

rabbin [Rabɛ̃] *nm* rabbi

rabougri, e [Rabugri] *adj* stunted

raccommoder [Rakɔmɔde] /1/ *vt* to mend, repair

raccompagner [Rakɔ̃paɲe] /1/ *vt* to take *ou* see back

raccord [RakɔR] *nm* link; *(retouche)* touch-up; **raccorder** /1/ *vt* to join (up), link up; *(pont etc)* to connect, link

raccourci [Rakursi] *nm* short cut

raccourcir [Rakursir] /2/ *vt* to shorten ▷ *vi (jours)* to grow shorter, draw in

raccrocher [Rakrɔʃe] /1/ *vt (tableau, vêtement)* to hang back up; *(récepteur)* to put down ▷ *vi (Tél)* to hang up, ring off

race [Ras] *nf* race; *(d'animaux, fig)* breed; **de ~** purebred, pedigree

rachat [Raʃa] *nm* buying; *(du même objet)* buying back

racheter [Raʃte] /5/ *vt (article perdu)* to buy another; *(davantage)* to buy more; *(après avoir vendu)* to buy back; *(d'occasion)* to buy; *(Comm: part, firme)* to buy up; **se racheter** *(gén)* to make amends; **~ du lait/trois œufs** to buy more milk/another three eggs

racial, e, -aux [Rasjal, -o] *adj* racial

racine [Rasin] *nf* root; **~ carrée/ cubique** square/cube root

racisme [Rasism] *nm* racism

raciste [Rasist] *adj, nm/f* racist

racket [Rakɛt] *nm* racketeering *no pl*

raclée [Rɑkle] *nf (fam)* hiding, thrashing

racler [Rɑkle] /1/ *vt (os, plat)* to scrape; **se ~ la gorge** to clear one's throat

racontars [Rakɔ̃taR] *nmpl* stories, gossip *sg*

raconter [Rakɔ̃te] /1/ *vt*: **~ (à qn)** *(décrire)* to relate (to sb), tell (sb) about; *(dire)* to tell (sb); **~ une histoire** to tell a story

radar [RadaR] *nm* radar; **~ (automatique)** *(Auto)* speed camera

rade [Rad] *nf* (natural) harbour; **rester en ~** *(fig)* to be left stranded

radeau, x [Rado] *nm* raft

radiateur [Radjatœr] *nm* radiator, heater; *(Auto)* radiator; **~ électrique/à gaz** electric/gas heater *ou* fire

radiation [Radjasjɔ̃] *nf (Physique)* radiation

radical, e, -aux [Radikal, -o] *adj* radical

radieux, -euse [ʀadjø, -øz] *adj*
radiant

radin, e [ʀadɛ̃, -in] *adj* (*fam*) stingy

radio [ʀadjo] *nf* radio; (*Méd*) X-ray
▷ *nm* radio operator; **à la ~** on
the radio; **radioactif, -ive** *adj*
radioactive; **radiocassette** *nf*
cassette radio; **radiographie**
nf radiography; (*photo*) X-ray
photograph; **radiophonique** *adj*
radio *cpd*; **radio-réveil** (*pl* **radios-
réveils**) *nm* radio alarm (clock)

radis [ʀadi] *nm* radish

radoter [ʀadɔte] /1/ *vi* to ramble on

radoucir [ʀadusiʀ] /2/: **se radoucir**
vi (*se réchauffer*) to become milder; (*se
calmer*) to calm down

rafale [ʀafal] *nf* (*vent*) gust (of wind);
(*de balles, d'applaudissements*) burst

raffermir [ʀafɛʀmiʀ] /2/ *vt*, **se
raffermir** *vi* to firm up

raffiner [ʀafine] /1/ *vt* to refine;
raffinerie *nf* refinery

raffoler [ʀafɔle] /1/: **~ de** *vt* to be
very keen on

rafle [ʀafl] *nf* (*de police*) raid; **rafler** /1/
vt (*fam*) to swipe, nick

rafraîchir [ʀafʀeʃiʀ] /2/ *vt*
(*atmosphère, température*) to cool
(down); (*boisson*) to chill; (*fig: rénover*)
to brighten up; **se rafraîchir** *vi* to
grow cooler; (*en se lavant*) to freshen
up; (*en buvant etc*) to refresh o.s.;
rafraîchissant, e *adj* refreshing;
rafraîchissement *nm* (*boisson*)
cool drink; **rafraîchissements** *nmpl*
(*boissons, fruits etc*) refreshments

rage [ʀaʒ] *nf* (*Méd*): **la ~** rabies; (*fureur*)
rage, fury; **faire ~** to rage; **~ de dents**
(raging) toothache

ragot [ʀago] *nm* (*fam*) malicious
gossip *no pl*

ragoût [ʀagu] *nm* stew

raide [ʀɛd] *adj* (*tendu*) taut, tight;
(*escarpé*) steep; (*droit: cheveux*)
straight; (*ankylosé, dur, guindé*) stiff;
(*fam: sans argent*) flat broke; (*osé,
licencieux*) daring ▷ *adv* (*en pente*)

steeply; **~ mort** stone dead; **raideur**
nf (*rigidité*) stiffness; **avec raideur**
(*répondre*) stiffly, abruptly; **raidir** /2/
vt (*muscles*) to stiffen; **se raidir** *vi* to
stiffen; (*personne*) to tense up; (: *se
préparer moralement*) to brace o.s.; (*fig:
devenir intransigeant*) to harden

raie [ʀɛ] *nf* (*Zool*) skate, ray; (*rayure*)
stripe; (*des cheveux*) parting

raifort [ʀefɔʀ] *nm* horseradish

rail [ʀaj] *nm* rail; (*chemins de fer*)
railways *pl*; **par ~** by rail

railler [ʀaje] /1/ *vt* to scoff at, jeer at

rainure [ʀenyʀ] *nf* groove

raisin [ʀezɛ̃] *nm* (*aussi*: **~s**) grapes *pl*;
~s secs raisins

raison [ʀezɔ̃] *nf* reason; **avoir ~** to be
right; **donner ~ à qn** to agree with
sb; (*fait*) to prove sb right; **se faire
une ~** to learn to live with it; **perdre
la ~** to become insane; **~ de plus** all
the more reason; **à plus forte ~** all
the more so; **sans ~** for no reason;
en ~ de because of; **à ~ de** at the
rate of; **~ sociale** corporate name;
raisonnable *adj* reasonable, sensible

raisonnement [ʀezɔnmɑ̃] *nm*
reasoning; argument

raisonner [ʀezɔne] /1/ *vi* (*penser*) to
reason; (*argumenter, discuter*) to argue
▷ *vt* (*personne*) to reason with

rajeunir [ʀaʒœniʀ] /2/ *vt* (*en
recrutant*) to inject new blood into
▷ *vi* to become (*ou* look) younger; **~
qn** (*coiffure, robe*) to make sb look
younger

rajouter [ʀaʒute] /1/ *vt* to add

rajuster [ʀaʒyste] /1/ *vt* (*vêtement*) to
straighten, tidy; (*salaires*) to adjust

ralenti [ʀalɑ̃ti] *nm*: **au ~** (*fig*) at a
slower pace; **tourner au ~** (*Auto*) to
tick over, idle

ralentir [ʀalɑ̃tiʀ] /2/ *vt, vi*, **se
ralentir** *vi* to slow down

râler [ʀale] /1/ *vi* to groan; (*fam*) to
grouse, moan (and groan)

rallier [ʀalje] /7/ *vt* (*rejoindre*) to
rejoin; (*gagner à sa cause*) to win over

rallonge [Ralɔ̃ʒ] nf (de table) (extra) leaf

rallonger [Ralɔ̃ʒe] /3/ vt to lengthen

rallye [Rali] nm rally; (Pol) march

ramassage [Ramɑsaʒ] nm: ~ **scolaire** school bus service

ramasser [Ramɑse] /1/ vt (objet tombé ou par terre) to pick up; (recueillir: copies, ordures) to collect; (récolter) to gather; **ramassis** nm (péj: de voyous) bunch; (de choses) jumble

rambarde [Rɑ̃baRd] nf guardrail

rame [Ram] nf (aviron) oar; (de métro) train; (de papier) ream

rameau, x [Ramo] nm (small) branch; **les R~x** (Rel) Palm Sunday sg

ramener [Ramne] /5/ vt to bring back; (reconduire) to take back; ~ **qch à** (réduire à) to reduce sth to

ramer [Rame] /1/ vi to row

ramollir [Ramɔliʀ] /2/ vt to soften; **se ramollir** vi to get (ou go) soft

rampe [Rɑ̃p] nf (d'escalier) banister(s pl); (dans un garage, d'un terrain) ramp; **la ~** (Théât) the footlights pl; ~ **de lancement** launching pad

ramper [Rɑ̃pe] /1/ vi to crawl

rancard [Rɑ̃kaR] nm (fam) date

rancart [Rɑ̃kaR] nm: **mettre au ~** to scrap

rance [Rɑ̃s] adj rancid

rancœur [Rɑ̃kœR] nf rancour

rançon [Rɑ̃sɔ̃] nf ransom

rancune [Rɑ̃kyn] nf grudge, rancour; **garder ~ à qn (de qch)** to bear sb a grudge (for sth); **sans ~!** no hard feelings!; **rancunier, -ière** adj vindictive, spiteful

randonnée [Rɑ̃dɔne] nf ride; (à pied) walk, ramble; (en montagne) hike, hiking no pl; **la ~** (activité) hiking, walking; **une ~ à cheval** a pony trek

rang [Rɑ̃] nm (rangée) row; (grade, condition sociale, classement) rank; **rangs** nmpl (Mil) ranks; **se mettre en ~s/sur un ~** to get into ou form rows/a line; **au premier ~** in the first row; (fig) ranking first

rangé, e [Rɑ̃ʒe] adj (vie) well-ordered; (sérieux: personne) steady

rangée [Rɑ̃ʒe] nf row

ranger [Rɑ̃ʒe] /3/ vt (classer, grouper) to order, arrange; (mettre à sa place) to put away; (mettre de l'ordre dans) to tidy up; (fig: classer): ~ **qn/qch parmi** to rank sb/sth among; (véhicule, conducteur) to pull over or in; (piéton) to step aside; (s'asseoir) to settle down; **se ~ à** (avis) to come round to

ranimer [Ranime] /1/ vt (personne évanouie) to bring round; (douleur, souvenir) to revive; (feu) to rekindle

rapace [Rapas] nm bird of prey

râpe [Rɑp] nf (Culin) grater; **râper** /1/ vt (Culin) to grate

rapide [Rapid] adj fast; (prompt: intelligence, coup d'œil, mouvement) quick ▷ nm express (train); (de cours d'eau) rapid; **rapidement** adv fast; quickly

rapiécer [Rapjese] /3, 6/ vt to patch

rappel [Rapɛl] nm (Théât) curtain call; (Méd: vaccination) booster; (d'une aventure, d'un nom) reminder; **rappeler** /4/ vt to call back; (ambassadeur, Mil) to recall; (faire se souvenir): **rappeler qch à qn** to remind sb of sth; **se rappeler** vt (se souvenir de) to remember, recall

rapport [RapɔR] nm (compte rendu) report; (profit) yield, return; (lien, analogie) relationship; (corrélation) connection; **rapports** nmpl (entre personnes, pays) relations; **avoir ~ à** to have something to do with; **être/ se mettre en ~ avec qn** to be/get in touch with sb; **par ~ à** in relation to; **~s (sexuels)** (sexual) intercourse sg; **~ qualité-prix** value (for money)

rapporter [RapɔRte] /1/ vt (rendre, ramener) to bring back; (investissement) to yield; (relater) to report ▷ vi (investissement) to give a good return ou yield; (activité) to be very profitable; **se ~ à** to relate to

r

rapprochement [ʀapʀɔʃmɑ̃] *nm*
(*de nations, familles*) reconciliation;
(*analogie, rapport*) parallel

rapprocher [ʀapʀɔʃe] /1/ *vt* (*deux
objets*) to bring closer together;
(*ennemis, partis etc*) to bring together;
(*comparer*) to establish a parallel
between; (*chaise d'une table*): ~
qch (de) to bring sth closer (to);
se rapprocher *vi* to draw closer *ou*
nearer; **se ~ de** to come closer to;
(*présenter une analogie avec*) to be
close to

raquette [ʀakɛt] *nf* (*de tennis*) racket;
(*de ping-pong*) bat

rare [ʀɑʀ] *adj* rare; **se faire ~** to
become scarce; **rarement** *adv* rarely,
seldom

ras, e [ʀɑ, ʀɑz] *adj* (*tête, cheveux*)
close-cropped; (*poil, herbe*) short
▷ *adv* short; **en ~e campagne** in
open country; **à ~ bords** to the brim;
en avoir ~ le bol (*fam*) to be fed up

raser [ʀɑze] /1/ *vt* (*barbe, cheveux*) to
shave off; (*menton, personne*) to shave;
(*fam: ennuyer*) to bore; (*démolir*) to raze
(to the ground); (*frôler*) to graze, skim;
se raser *vi* to shave; (*fam*) to be bored
(to tears); **rasoir** *nm* razor

rassasier [ʀasazje] /7/ *vt*: **être
rassasié** to be sated

rassemblement [ʀasɑ̃bləmɑ̃] *nm*
(*groupe*) gathering; (*Pol*) union

rassembler [ʀasɑ̃ble] /1/ *vt* (*réunir*)
to assemble, gather; (*documents,
notes*) to gather together, collect; **se
rassembler** *vi* to gather

rassurer [ʀasyʀe] /1/ *vt* to reassure;
se rassurer *vi* to be reassured;
rassure-toi don't worry

rat [ʀa] *nm* rat

rate [ʀat] *nf* spleen

raté, e [ʀate] *adj* (*tentative*)
unsuccessful, failed ▷ *nm/f* (*fam:
personne*) failure

râteau, x [ʀɑto] *nm* rake

rater [ʀate] /1/ *vi* (*affaire, projet etc*)
to go wrong, fail ▷ *vt* (*cible, train,*

occasion) to miss; (*démonstration, plat*)
to spoil; (*examen*) to fail

ration [ʀasjɔ̃] *nf* ration

RATP *sigle f* (= *Régie autonome des
transports parisiens*) Paris transport
authority

rattacher [ʀataʃe] /1/ *vt* (*animal,
cheveux*) to tie up again; **~ qch à** (*relier*)
to link sth with

rattraper [ʀatʀape] /1/ *vt* (*fugitif*) to
recapture; (*retenir, empêcher de tomber*)
to catch (hold of); (*atteindre, rejoindre*)
to catch up with; (*réparer: erreur*) to
make up for; **se rattraper** *vi* to make
up for it; **se ~ (à)** (*se raccrocher*) to
stop o.s. falling (by catching hold of)

rature [ʀatyʀ] *nf* deletion, erasure

rauque [ʀok] *adj* (*voix*) hoarse

ravages [ʀavaʒ] *nmpl*: **faire des ~** to
wreak havoc

ravi, e [ʀavi] *adj*: **être ~ de/que** to be
delighted with/that

ravin [ʀavɛ̃] *nm* gully, ravine

ravir [ʀaviʀ] /2/ *vt* (*enchanter*) to
delight; **à ~** *adv* beautifully

raviser [ʀavize] /1/: **se raviser** *vi* to
change one's mind

ravissant, e [ʀavisɑ̃, -ɑ̃t] *adj*
delightful

ravisseur, -euse [ʀavisœʀ, -øz]
nm/f abductor, kidnapper

ravitailler [ʀavitaje] /1/ *vt* (*en
vivres, munitions*) to provide with
fresh supplies; (*véhicule*) to refuel; **se
ravitailler** *vi* to get fresh supplies

raviver [ʀavive] /1/ *vt* (*feu*) to
rekindle; (*douleur*) to revive; (*couleurs*)
to brighten up

rayé, e [ʀeje] *adj* (*à rayures*) striped

rayer [ʀeje] /8/ *vt* (*érafler*) to scratch;
(*barrer*) to cross *ou* score out; (*d'une
liste*) to cross *ou* strike off

rayon [ʀejɔ̃] *nm* (*de soleil etc*) ray;
(*Géom*) radius; (*de roue*) spoke;
(*étagère*) shelf; (*de grand magasin*)
department; **dans un ~ de** within a
radius of; **~ de soleil** sunbeam; **~s
X** X-rays

rayonnement [ʀɛjɔnmɑ̃] nm (d'une culture) influence

rayonner [ʀɛjɔne] /1/ vi (fig) to shine forth; (: visage, personne) to be radiant; (touriste) to go touring (from one base)

rayure [ʀejyʀ] nf (motif) stripe; (éraflure) scratch; **à ~s** striped

raz-de-marée [ʀɑdmaʀe] nm inv tidal wave

ré [ʀe] nm (Mus) D; (en chantant la gamme) re

réaction [ʀeaksjɔ̃] nf reaction

réadapter [ʀeadapte] /1/: **se ~ (à)** vi to readjust (to)

réagir [ʀeaʒiʀ] /2/ vi to react

réalisateur, -trice [ʀealizatœʀ, -tʀis] nm/f (TV, Ciné) director

réalisation [ʀealizasjɔ̃] nf realization; (Ciné) production; **en cours de ~** under way

réaliser [ʀealize] /1/ vt (projet, opération) to carry out, realize; (rêve, souhait) to realize, fulfil; (exploit) to achieve; (film) to produce; (se rendre compte de) to realize; **se réaliser** vi to be realized

réaliste [ʀealist] adj realistic

réalité [ʀealite] nf reality; **en ~** in (actual) fact; **dans la ~** in reality

réanimation [ʀeanimasjɔ̃] nf resuscitation; **service de ~** intensive care unit

rébarbatif, -ive [ʀebaʀbatif, -iv] adj forbidding

rebattu, e [ʀəbaty] adj hackneyed

rebelle [ʀəbɛl] nm/f rebel ▷ adj (troupes) rebel; (enfant) rebellious; (mèche etc) unruly

rebeller [ʀəbele] /1/: **se rebeller** vi to rebel

rebondir [ʀəbɔ̃diʀ] /2/ vi (ballon: au sol) to bounce; (: contre un mur) to rebound; (fig) to get moving again

rebord [ʀəbɔʀ] nm edge; **le ~ de la fenêtre** the windowsill

rebours [ʀəbuʀ]: **à ~** adv the wrong way

rebrousser [ʀəbʀuse] /1/ vt: **~ chemin** to turn back

rebuter [ʀəbyte] /1/ vt to put off

récalcitrant, e [ʀekalsitʀɑ̃, -ɑ̃t] adj refractory

récapituler [ʀekapityle] /1/ vt to recapitulate; to sum up

receler [ʀəsəle] /5/ vt (produit d'un vol) to receive; (fig) to conceal; **receleur, -euse** nm/f receiver

récemment [ʀesamɑ̃] adv recently

recensement [ʀəsɑ̃smɑ̃] nm census

recenser [ʀəsɑ̃se] /1/ vt (population) to take a census of; (dénombrer) to list

récent, e [ʀesɑ̃, -ɑ̃t] adj recent

récépissé [ʀesepise] nm receipt

récepteur, -trice [ʀeseptœʀ, -tʀis] adj receiving ▷ nm receiver

réception [ʀesɛpsjɔ̃] nf receiving no pl; (accueil) reception, welcome; (bureau) reception (desk); (réunion mondaine) reception, party; **réceptionniste** nm/f receptionist

recette [ʀəsɛt] nf recipe; (Comm) takings pl; **recettes** nfpl (Comm: rentrées) receipts; **faire ~** (spectacle, exposition) to be a winner

recevoir [ʀəsvwaʀ] /28/ vt to receive; (client, patient, représentant) to see; **être reçu** (à un examen) to pass

rechange [ʀəʃɑ̃ʒ]: **de ~** adj (pièces, roue) spare; (fig: solution) alternative; **des vêtements de ~** a change of clothes

recharge [ʀəʃaʀʒ] nf refill; **rechargeable** adj (stylo etc) refillable; **recharger** /3/ vt (briquet, stylo) to refill; (batterie) to recharge

réchaud [ʀeʃo] nm (portable) stove

réchauffement [ʀeʃofmɑ̃] nm warming (up); **le ~ de la planète** global warming

réchauffer [ʀeʃofe] /1/ vt (plat) to reheat; (mains, personne) to warm; **se réchauffer** vi (température) to get warmer; (personne) to warm o.s. (up)

rêche [ʀɛʃ] adj rough

recherche [ʀəʃɛʀʃ] nf (action): **la ~ de** the search for; (raffinement) studied

r

elegance; (*scientifique etc*): **la ~** research; **recherches** *nfpl* (*de la police*) investigations; (*scientifiques*) research *sg*; **être/se mettre à la ~ de** to be/go in search of

recherché, e [ʀəʃɛʀʃe] *adj* (*rare, demandé*) much sought-after; (*raffiné*) affected; (*tenue*) elegant

rechercher [ʀəʃɛʀʃe] /1/ *vt* (*objet égaré, personne*) to look for; (*causes d'un phénomène, nouveau procédé*) to try to find; (*bonheur etc, l'amitié de qn*) to seek

rechute [ʀəʃyt] *nf* (*Méd*) relapse

récidiver [ʀesidive] /1/ *vi* to commit a second (*ou* subsequent) offence; (*fig*) to do it again

récif [ʀesif] *nm* reef

récipient [ʀesipjɑ̃] *nm* container

réciproque [ʀesipʀɔk] *adj* reciprocal

récit [ʀesi] *nm* story; **récital** *nm* recital; **réciter** /1/ *vt* to recite

réclamation [ʀeklamasjɔ̃] *nf* complaint; **réclamations** *nfpl* complaints department *sg*

réclame [ʀeklam] *nf*: **une ~** an ad(vertisement), an advert (BRIT); **article en ~** special offer; **réclamer** /1/ *vt* to ask for; (*revendiquer*) to claim, demand ▷ *vi* to complain

réclusion [ʀeklyzjɔ̃] *nf* imprisonment

recoin [ʀəkwɛ̃] *nm* nook, corner

reçois *etc* [ʀəswa] *vb voir* **recevoir**

récolte [ʀekɔlt] *nf* harvesting, gathering; (*produits*) harvest, crop; **récolter** /1/ *vt* to harvest, gather (in); (*fig*) to get

recommandé [ʀəkɔmɑ̃de] *nm* (*Postes*): **en ~** by registered mail

recommander [ʀəkɔmɑ̃de] /1/ *vt* to recommend; (*Postes*) to register

recommencer [ʀəkɔmɑ̃se] /3/ *vt* (*reprendre: lutte, séance*) to resume, start again; (*refaire: travail, explications*) to start afresh, start (over) again ▷ *vi* to start again; (*récidiver*) to do it again

récompense [ʀekɔ̃pɑ̃s] *nf* reward; (*prix*) award; **récompenser** /1/ *vt*: **récompenser qn (de** *ou* **pour)** to reward sb (for)

réconcilier [ʀekɔ̃silje] /7/ *vt* to reconcile; **se réconcilier (avec)** to be reconciled (with)

reconduire [ʀəkɔ̃dɥiʀ] /38/ *vt* (*raccompagner*) to take *ou* see back; (*renouveler*) to renew

réconfort [ʀekɔ̃fɔʀ] *nm* comfort; **réconforter** /1/ *vt* (*consoler*) to comfort

reconnaissance [ʀəkɔnɛsɑ̃s] *nf* (*action de reconnaître*) recognition; (*gratitude*) gratitude, gratefulness; (*Mil*) reconnaissance, recce; **reconnaissant, e** *adj* grateful; **je vous serais reconnaissant de bien vouloir** I should be most grateful if you would (kindly)

reconnaître [ʀəkɔnɛtʀ] /57/ *vt* to recognize; (*Mil: lieu*) to reconnoitre; (*Jur: enfant, dette, droit*) to acknowledge; **~ que** to admit *ou* acknowledge that; **~ qn/qch à** (*l'identifier grâce à*) to recognize sb/sth by; **reconnu, e** *adj* (*indiscuté, connu*) recognized

reconstituer [ʀəkɔ̃stitɥe] /1/ *vt* (*fresque, vase brisé*) to piece together, reconstitute; (*événement, accident*) to reconstruct

reconstruire [ʀəkɔ̃strɥiʀ] /38/ *vt* to rebuild

reconvertir [ʀəkɔ̃vɛʀtiʀ] /2/ *vt* to reconvert; **se ~ dans** (*un métier, une branche*) to move into

record [ʀəkɔʀ] *nm, adj* record

recoupement [ʀəkupmɑ̃] *nm*: **par ~** by cross-checking

recouper [ʀəkupe] /1/: **se recouper** *vi* (*témoignages*) to tie *ou* match up

recourber [ʀəkuʀbe] /1/: **se recourber** *vi* to curve (up), bend (up)

recourir [ʀəkuʀiʀ] /11/: **~ à** *vt* (*ami, agence*) to turn *ou* appeal to; (*force, ruse, emprunt*) to resort to

recours [RəkuR] *nm*: **avoir ~ à**
= **recourir à**; **en dernier ~** as a last
resort

recouvrer [RəkuvRe] /1/ *vt (vue,
santé etc)* to recover, regain

recouvrir [RəkuvRiR] /18/ *vt (couvrir
à nouveau)* to re-cover; *(couvrir
entièrement, aussi fig)* to cover

récréation [RekReasjɔ̃] *nf (Scol)*
break

recroqueviller [RəkRɔkvije] /1/:
se recroqueviller *vi (personne)* to
huddle up

recrudescence [RəkRydesɑ̃s] *nf*
fresh outbreak

recruter [RəkRyte] /1/ *vt* to recruit

rectangle [Rɛktɑ̃gl] *nm* rectangle;
rectangulaire *adj* rectangular

rectificatif, -ive [Rɛktifikatif, -iv]
adj corrected ▷ *nm* correction

rectifier [Rɛktifje] /7/ *vt (calcul,
adresse)* to correct; *(erreur, faute)*
to rectify

rectiligne [Rɛktiliɲ] *adj* straight

recto [Rɛkto] *nm* front *(of a sheet
of paper)*; **~ verso** on both sides (of
the page)

reçu, e [Rəsy] *pp de* **recevoir** ▷ *adj
(candidat)* successful; *(admis, consacré)*
accepted ▷ *nm (Comm)* receipt

recueil [Rəkœj] *nm* collection;
recueillir /12/ *vt* to collect; *(voix,
suffrages)* to win; *(accueillir: réfugiés,
chat)* to take in; **se recueillir** *vi* to
gather one's thoughts; to meditate

recul [Rəkyl] *nm (déclin)* decline;
(éloignement) distance; **avoir un
mouvement de ~** to recoil; **prendre
du ~** to stand back; **être en ~** to be on
the decline; **avec le ~** in retrospect;
reculé, e *adj* remote; **reculer** /1/ *vi*
to move back, back away; *(Auto)* to
reverse, back (up); *(fig)* to be (on the
decline ▷ *vt* to move back; *(véhicule)*
to reverse, back (up); *(date, décision)*
to postpone; **reculer devant** *(danger,
difficulté)* to shrink from; **reculons: à
reculons** *adv* backwards

récupérer [RekypeRe] /6/ *vt* to
recover, get back; *(déchets etc)* to
salvage (for reprocessing); *(journée,
heures de travail)* to make up ▷ *vi* to
recover

récurer [RekyRe] /1/ *vt* to scour;
poudre à ~ scouring powder

reçus *etc* [Rəsy] *vb voir* **recevoir**

recycler [Rəsikle] /1/ *vt (matériau)* to
recycle; **se recycler** *vi* to retrain

rédacteur, -trice [Redaktœr, -tRis]
nm/f (journaliste) writer; subeditor;
(d'ouvrage de référence) editor,
compiler

rédaction [Redaksjɔ̃] *nf* writing;
(rédacteurs) editorial staff; *(Scol:
devoir)* essay, composition

redescendre [Rədesɑ̃dR] /41/ *vi*
to go back down ▷ *vt (pente etc)* to
go down

rédiger [Rediʒe] /3/ *vt* to write;
(contrat) to draw up

redire [RədiR] /37/ *vt* to repeat;
trouver à ~ à to find fault with

redoubler [Rəduble] /1/ *vi (tempête,
violence)* to intensify; *(Scol)* to repeat a
year; **~ de patience/prudence** to be
doubly patient/careful

redoutable [Rədutabl] *adj*
formidable, fearsome

redouter [Rədute] /1/ *vt* to dread

redressement [RədRɛsmɑ̃] *nm
(économique)* recovery

redresser [RədRese] /1/ *vt (arbre,
mât)* to set upright; *(pièce tordue)* to
straighten out; *(situation, économie)* to
put right; **se redresser** *vi (personne)*
to sit *(ou* stand) up; *(pays, situation)*
to recover

réduction [Redyksjɔ̃] *nf* reduction

réduire [RedɥiR] /38/ *vt* to reduce;
(prix, dépenses) to cut; reduce; **réduit**
nm tiny room

rééducation [Reedykasjɔ̃] *nf (d'un
membre)* re-education; *(de délinquants,
d'un blessé)* rehabilitation

réel, le [Reɛl] *adj* real; **réellement**
adv really

r

réexpédier [ʀeɛkspedje] /7/ vt
(à l'envoyeur) to return, send back;
(au destinataire) to send on, forward

refaire [ʀəfɛʀ] /60/ vt to do again;
(sport) to take up again; (réparer,
restaurer) to do up

réfectoire [ʀefɛktwaʀ] nm refectory

référence [ʀefeʀɑ̃s] nf reference;
références nfpl (recommandations)
reference sg

référer [ʀefeʀe] /6/: **se ~ à** vt to
refer to

refermer [ʀəfɛʀme] /1/ vt to close
again, shut again; **se refermer** vi
(porte) to close ou shut (again)

refiler [ʀəfile] /1/ vt (fam): **~ qch à qn**
to palm ou fob sth off on sb

réfléchi, e [ʀefleʃi] adj (caractère)
thoughtful; (action) well-thought-
out; (Ling) reflexive; **c'est tout ~** my
mind's made up

réfléchir [ʀefleʃiʀ] /2/ vt to reflect
▷ vi to think; **~ à** ou **sur** to think about

reflet [ʀəflɛ] nm reflection; (sur
l'eau etc) sheen no pl, glint; **refléter**
/6/ vt to reflect; **se refléter** vi to be
reflected

réflexe [ʀeflɛks] adj, nm reflex

réflexion [ʀeflɛksjɔ̃] nf (de la
lumière etc) reflection; (fait de penser)
thought; (remarque) remark; **~ faite,
à la ~** on reflection; **délai de ~**
cooling-off period; **groupe de ~**
think tank

réflexologie [ʀeflɛksɔlɔʒi] nf
reflexology

réforme [ʀefɔʀm] nf reform; (Rel):
la R~ the Reformation; **réformer**
/1/ vt to reform; (Mil) to declare unfit
for service

refouler [ʀəfule] /1/ vt (envahisseurs)
to drive back; (liquide, larmes) to force
back; (désir, colère) to repress

refrain [ʀəfʀɛ̃] nm refrain, chorus

refréner, **réfréner** [ʀəfʀene,
ʀefʀene] vt to curb, check

réfrigérateur [ʀefʀiʒeʀatœʀ] nm
refrigerator

refroidir [ʀəfʀwadiʀ] /2/ vt to
cool; (personne) to put off ▷ vi to cool
(down); **se refroidir** vi (temps) to get
cooler ou colder; (fig: ardeur) to cool
(off); **refroidissement** nm (grippe
etc) chill

refuge [ʀəfyʒ] nm refuge; **réfugié,
e** adj, nm/f refugee; **réfugier** /7/: **se
réfugier** vi to take refuge

refus [ʀəfy] nm refusal; **ce n'est pas
de ~** I won't say no, it's very welcome;
refuser /1/ vt to refuse; (Scol:
candidat) to fail; **refuser qch à qn/
faire** to refuse sb sth/to do; **refuser
du monde** to have to turn people
away; **se refuser à qch** ou **à faire
qch** to refuse to do sth

regagner [ʀəgaɲe] /1/ vt (argent,
faveur) to win back; (lieu) to get back to

régal [ʀegal] nm treat; **régaler** /1/
vt: **régaler qn de** to treat sb to; **se
régaler** vi to have a delicious meal;
(fig) to enjoy o.s.

regard [ʀəgaʀ] nm (coup d'œil) look,
glance; (expression) look (in one's eye);
au ~ de (loi, morale) from the point of
view of; **en ~ de** in comparison with

regardant, e [ʀəgaʀdɑ̃, -ɑ̃t] adj:
très/peu ~ (sur) quite fussy/very
free (about); (économe) very tight-
fisted/quite generous (with)

regarder [ʀəgaʀde] /1/ vt to look
at; (film, télévision, match) to watch;
(concerner) to concern ▷ vi to look;
ne pas ~ à la dépense to spare no
expense; **~ qn/qch comme** to regard
sb/sth as

régie [ʀeʒi] nf (Comm, Industrie)
state-owned company; (Théât, Ciné)
production; (Radio, TV) control room

régime [ʀeʒim] nm (Pol) régime;
(Admin: carcéral, fiscal etc) system;
(Méd) diet; (de bananes, dattes) bunch;
se mettre au/suivre un ~ to go on/
be on a diet

régiment [ʀeʒimɑ̃] nm regiment

région [ʀeʒjɔ̃] nf region; **régional, e,
-aux** adj regional

régir [ReʒiR] /2/ vt to govern
régisseur [ReʒisœR] nm (d'un domaine) steward; (Ciné, TV) assistant director; (Théât) stage manager
registre [RaʒistR] nm register
réglage [Regla ʒ] nm adjustment
réglé, e [Regle] adj well-ordered; (arrangé) settled
règle [Regl] nf (instrument) ruler; (loi, prescription) rule; **règles** nfpl (Physiol) period sg; **en ~** (papiers d'identité) in order; **en ~ générale** as a (general) rule
règlement [Reglamã] nm (paiement) settlement; (arrêté) regulation; (règles, statuts) regulations pl, rules pl; **réglementaire** adj conforming to the regulations; (tenue, uniforme) regulation cpd; **réglementation** nf (règlements) regulations pl; **réglementer** /1/ vt to regulate
régler [Regle] /6/ vt (mécanisme, machine) to regulate, adjust; (thermostat etc) to set, adjust; (question, conflit, facture, dette) to settle; (fournisseur) to settle up with
réglisse [Reglis] nm ou f liquorice
règne [Reɲ] nm (d'un roi etc, fig) reign; **le ~ végétal/animal** the vegetable/animal kingdom; **régner** /6/ vi (roi) to rule, reign; (fig) to reign
regorger [RagɔRʒe] /3/ vi: **~ de** to overflow with, be bursting with
regret [RagRɛ] nm regret; **à ~** with regret; **sans ~** with no regrets; **regrettable** adj regrettable; **regretter** /1/ vt to regret; (personne) to miss; **non, je regrette** no, I'm sorry
regrouper [RagRupe] /1/ vt (grouper) to group together; (contenir) to include, comprise; **se regrouper** vi to gather (together)
régulier, -ière [Regylje, -jɛR] adj (gén) regular; (vitesse, qualité) steady; (répartition, pression) even; (Transports: ligne, service) scheduled, regular; (légal, réglementaire) lawful,

in order; (fam: correct) straight, on the level; **régulièrement** adv regularly; evenly
rehausser [Raose] /1/ vt (relever) to heighten, raise; (fig: souligner) to set off, enhance
rein [Rɛ̃] nm kidney; **reins** nmpl (dos) back sg
reine [Rɛn] nf queen
reine-claude [Rɛnklod] nf greengage
réinscriptible [Reɛ̃skRiptibl] adj (CD, DVD) rewritable
réinsertion [Reɛ̃sɛRsjɔ̃] nf (de délinquant) reintegration, rehabilitation
réintégrer [Reɛ̃tegRe] /6/ vt (lieu) to return to; (fonctionnaire) to reinstate
rejaillir [RaʒajiR] /2/ vi to splash up; **~ sur** (fig) (scandale) to rebound on; (gloire) to be reflected on
rejet [Raʒɛ] nm rejection; **rejeter** /4/ vt (relancer) to throw back; (vomir) to bring ou throw up; (écarter) to reject; (déverser) to throw out, discharge; **rejeter la responsabilité de qch sur qn** to lay the responsibility for sth at sb's door
rejoindre [RaʒwɛdR] /49/ vt (famille, régiment) to rejoin, return to; (lieu) to get (back) to; (route etc) to meet, join; (rattraper) to catch up (with); **se rejoindre** vi to meet; **je te rejoins au café** I'll see ou meet you at the café
réjouir [ReʒwiR] /2/ vt to delight; **se ~ de qch/de faire** to be delighted about sth/to do; **réjouissances** nfpl (fête) festivities
relâche [Ralaʃ]: **sans ~** adv without respite ou a break; **relâché, e** adj loose, lax; **relâcher** /1/ vt (ressort, prisonnier) to release; (étreinte, cordes) to loosen; **se relâcher** vi (discipline) to become slack ou lax; (élève etc) to slacken off
relais [Ralɛ] nm (Sport): **(course de) ~** relay (race); **prendre le ~ (de)** to take

r

over (from); **~ routier** ≈ transport
café (BRIT), ≈ truck stop (US)
relancer [Rəlɑ̃se] /3/ vt (balle)
to throw back (again); (moteur)
to restart; (fig) to boost, revive;
(personne): **~ qn** to pester sb
relatif, -ive [Rəlatif, -iv] adj relative
relation [Rəlasjɔ̃] nf (rapport)
relation(ship); (connaissance)
acquaintance; **relations** nfpl
(rapports) relations; (connaissances)
connections; **être/entrer en ~(s)
avec** to be in contact ou be dealing/
get in contact with
relaxer [Rəlakse] /1/: **se relaxer**
vi to relax
relayer [Rəleje] /8/ vt (collaborateur,
coureur etc) to relieve; **se relayer** vi
(dans une activité) to take it in turns
reléguer [Rəlege] /6/ vt to relegate
relevé, e [Rəlve] adj (manches) rolled-
up; (sauce) highly-seasoned ▷ nm
(lecture) reading; **~ bancaire** ou **de
compte** bank statement
relève [Rəlɛv] nf (personne) relief;
prendre la ~ to take over
relever [Rəlve] /5/ vt (statue, meuble)
to stand up again; (personne tombée)
to help up; (vitre, plafond, niveau de
vie) to raise; (col) to turn up; (style,
conversation) to elevate; (plat, sauce) to
season; (sentinelle, équipe) to relieve;
(fautes, points) to pick out; (défi) to
accept, take up; (noter: adresse etc) to
take down, note; (: plan) to sketch;
(compteur) to read; (ramasser: cahiers,
copies) to collect, take in ▷ vi: **~ de**
(maladie) to be recovering from; (être
du ressort de) to be a matter for; (fig)
to be relevant to; **se relever** vi (se remettre
debout) to get up; **~ qn de** (fonctions)
to relieve sb of; **~ la tête** to look up
relief [Rəljɛf] nm relief; **mettre en ~**
(fig) to bring out, highlight
relier [Rəlje] /7/ vt to link up; (livre) to
bind; **~ qch à** to link sth to
religieux, -euse [Rəliʒjø, -øz] adj
religious ▷ nm monk

religion [Rəliʒjɔ̃] nf religion
relire [Rəlir] /43/ vt (à nouveau)
to reread, read again; (vérifier) to
read over
reluire [Rəlɥir] /38/ vi to gleam
remanier [Rəmanje] /7/ vt to
reshape, recast; (Pol) to reshuffle
remarquable [Rəmarkabl] adj
remarkable
remarque [Rəmark] nf remark;
(écrite) note
remarquer [Rəmarke] /1/ vt (voir)
to notice; **se remarquer** vi to
be noticeable; **se faire ~** to draw
attention to o.s.; **faire ~ (à qn) que**
to point out (to sb) that; **faire ~
qch (à qn)** to point sth out (to sb);
remarquez, ... mind you, ...
rembourrer [Rɑ̃bure] /1/ vt to stuff
remboursement [Rɑ̃bursəmɑ̃]
nm (de dette, d'emprunt) repayment;
(de frais) refund; **rembourser** /1/ vt
to pay back, repay; (frais, billet etc)
to refund; **se faire rembourser** to
get a refund
remède [Rəmɛd] nm (médicament)
medicine; (traitement, fig) remedy,
cure
remémorer [Rəmemɔre] /1/: **se
remémorer** vt to recall, recollect
remerciements [Rəmɛrsimɑ̃] nmpl
thanks; **(avec) tous mes ~** (with)
grateful ou many thanks
remercier [Rəmɛrsje] /7/ vt to
thank; (congédier) to dismiss; **~ qn
de/d'avoir fait** to thank sb for/for
having done
remettre [Rəmɛtr] /56/ vt
(vêtement): **~ qch** to put sth back on;
(replacer): **~ qch quelque part** to
put sth back somewhere; (ajouter):
~ du sel/un sucre to add more salt/
another lump of sugar; (ajourner):
~ qch (à) to postpone sth ou put sth off
(until); **se remettre** vi to get better;
~ qch à qn (donner) to hand over sth
to sb; (prix, décoration) to present sb
with sth; **se ~ de** to recover from;

s'en ~ à to leave it (up) to; **se ~ à faire/qch** to start doing/sth again
remis, e [ʀəmi, -iz] *pp de* **remettre**
▷ *nf* (*rabais*) discount; (*local*) shed; **~e en cause/question** calling into question/challenging; **~e en jeu** (*Football*) throw-in; **~e de peine** remission of sentence; **~e des prix** prize-giving
remontant [ʀəmɔ̃tɑ̃] *nm* tonic, pick-me-up
remonte-pente [ʀəmɔ̃tpɑ̃t] *nm* ski lift
remonter [ʀəmɔ̃te] /1/ *vi* to go back up; (*prix, température*) to go up again; (*en voiture*) to get back in ▷ *vt* (*pente*) to go up; (*fleuve*) to sail (*ou* swim *etc*) up; (*manches, pantalon*) to roll up; (*fam*) to turn up; (*niveau, limite*) to raise; (*fig: personne*) to buck up; (*moteur, meuble*) to put back together, reassemble; (*montre, mécanisme*) to wind up; **~ le moral à qn** to raise sb's spirits; **~ à** (*dater de*) to date *ou* go back to
remords [ʀəmɔʀ] *nm* remorse *no pl*; **avoir des ~** to feel remorse
remorque [ʀəmɔʀk] *nf* trailer; **remorquer** /1/ *vt* to tow; **remorqueur** *nm* tug(boat)
remous [ʀəmu] *nm* (*d'un navire*) (back)wash *no pl*; (*de rivière*) swirl, eddy *pl*; (*fig*) stir *sg*
remparts [ʀɑ̃paʀ] *nmpl* walls, ramparts
remplaçant, e [ʀɑ̃plasɑ̃, -ɑ̃t] *nm/f* replacement, stand-in; (*Scol*) supply (BRIT) *ou* substitute (US) teacher
remplacement [ʀɑ̃plasmɑ̃] *nm* replacement; **faire des ~s** (*professeur*) to do supply *ou* substitute teaching; (*secrétaire*) to temp
remplacer [ʀɑ̃plase] /3/ *vt* to replace; **~ qch/qn par** to replace sth/sb with
rempli, e [ʀɑ̃pli] *adj* (*emploi du temps*) full, busy; **~ de** full of, filled with

remplir [ʀɑ̃pliʀ] /2/ *vt* to fill (up); (*questionnaire*) to fill out *ou* up; (*obligations, fonction, condition*) to fulfil; **se remplir** *vi* to fill up
remporter [ʀɑ̃pɔʀte] /1/ *vt* (*marchandise*) to take away; (*fig*) to win, achieve
remuant, e [ʀəmɥɑ̃, -ɑ̃t] *adj* restless
remue-ménage [ʀəmymenaʒ] *nm inv* commotion
remuer [ʀəmɥe] /1/ *vt* to move; (*café, sauce*) to stir ▷ *vi* to move; **se remuer** *vi* to move; (*fam: s'activer*) to get a move on
rémunérer [ʀemyneʀe] /6/ *vt* to remunerate
renard [ʀənaʀ] *nm* fox
renchérir [ʀɑ̃ʃeʀiʀ] /2/ *vi* (*fig*): **~ (sur)** (*en paroles*) to add something (to)
rencontre [ʀɑ̃kɔ̃tʀ] *nf* meeting; (*imprévue*) encounter; **aller à la ~ de qn** to go and meet sb; **rencontrer** /1/ *vt* to meet; (*mot, expression*) to come across; (*difficultés*) to meet with; **se rencontrer** *vi* to meet
rendement [ʀɑ̃dmɑ̃] *nm* (*d'un travailleur, d'une machine*) output; (*d'une culture, d'un champ*) yield
rendez-vous [ʀɑ̃devu] *nm* appointment; (*d'amoureux*) date; (*lieu*) meeting place; **donner ~ à qn** to arrange to meet sb; **avoir/ prendre ~ (avec)** to have/make an appointment (with)
rendre [ʀɑ̃dʀ] /41/ *vt* (*livre, argent etc*) to give back, return; (*otages, visite, politesse, invitation*) to return; (*sang, aliments*) to bring up; (*exprimer, traduire*) to render; (*faire devenir*): **~ qn célèbre/qch possible** to make sb famous/sth possible; **se rendre** *vi* (*capituler*) to surrender, give o.s. up; (*aller*): **se ~ quelque part** to go somewhere; **se ~ compte de qch** to realize sth; **~ la monnaie** to give change
rênes [ʀɛn] *nfpl* reins

renfermé, e [ʀɑ̃fɛʀme] *adj (fig)* withdrawn ▷ *nm*: **sentir le ~** to smell stuffy

renfermer [ʀɑ̃fɛʀme] /1/ *vt* to contain

renforcer [ʀɑ̃fɔʀse] /3/ *vt* to reinforce; **renfort** *nm*: **renforts** *nmpl* reinforcements; **à grand renfort de** with a great deal of

renfrogné, e [ʀɑ̃fʀɔɲe] *adj* sullen, scowling

renier [ʀənje] /7/ *vt (parents)* to disown, repudiate; *(foi)* to renounce

renifler [ʀənifle] /1/ *vi* to sniff ▷ *vt (odeur)* to sniff

renne [ʀɛn] *nm* reindeer *inv*

renom [ʀənɔ̃] *nm* reputation; *(célébrité)* renown; **renommé, e** *adj* celebrated, renowned ▷ *nf* fame

renoncer [ʀənɔ̃se] /3/: **~ à** *vt* to give up; **~ à faire** to give up the idea of doing

renouer [ʀənwe] /1/ *vt*: **~ avec** *(habitude)* to take up again

renouvelable [ʀ(ə)nuvlabl] *adj (contrat, bail, énergie)* renewable

renouveler [ʀənuvle] /4/ *vt* to renew; *(exploit, méfait)* to repeat; **se renouveler** *vi (incident)* to recur, happen again; **renouvellement** *nm* renewal

rénover [ʀenɔve] /1/ *vt (immeuble)* to renovate, do up; *(quartier)* to redevelop

renseignement [ʀɑ̃sɛɲmɑ̃] *nm* information *no pl*, piece of information; **(guichet des) ~s** information desk; **(service des) ~s** *(Tél)* directory inquiries (BRIT), information (US)

renseigner [ʀɑ̃seɲe] /1/ *vt*: **~ qn (sur)** to give information to sb (about); **se renseigner** *vi* to ask for information, make inquiries

rentabilité [ʀɑ̃tabilite] *nf* profitability

rentable [ʀɑ̃tabl] *adj* profitable

rente [ʀɑ̃t] *nf* income; *(pension)* pension

rentrée [ʀɑ̃tʀe] *nf*: **~ (d'argent)** cash *no pl* coming in; **la ~ (des classes** *ou* **scolaire)** the start of the new school year

rentrer [ʀɑ̃tʀe] /1/ *vi (entrer de nouveau)* to go (*ou* come) back in; *(entrer)* to go (*ou* come) in; *(revenir chez soi)* to go (*ou* come) (back) home; *(air, clou: pénétrer)* to go in; *(revenu, argent)* to come in ▷ *vt* to bring in; *(véhicule)* to put away; *(chemise dans pantalon etc)* to tuck in; *(griffes)* to draw in; **~ le ventre** to pull in one's stomach; **~ dans** *(heurter)* to crash into; **~ dans l'ordre** to get back to normal; **~ dans ses frais** to recover one's expenses (*ou* initial outlay)

renverse [ʀɑ̃vɛʀs]: **à la ~** *adv* backwards

renverser [ʀɑ̃vɛʀse] /1/ *vt (faire tomber: chaise, verre)* to knock over, overturn; *(: piéton)* to knock down; *(: liquide, contenu)* to spill, upset; *(retourner)* to turn upside down; *(: ordre des mots etc)* to reverse; *(fig: gouvernement etc)* to overthrow; *(stupéfier)* to bowl over; **se renverser** *vi (verre, vase)* to fall over; *(contenu)* to spill

renvoi [ʀɑ̃vwa] *nm (d'employé)* dismissal; *(d'élève)* expulsion; *(référence)* cross-reference; *(éructation)* belch; **renvoyer** /8/ *vt* to send back; *(congédier)* to dismiss; *(élève: définitivement)* to expel; *(lumière)* to reflect; *(ajourner)*: **renvoyer qch (à)** to postpone sth (until)

repaire [ʀəpɛʀ] *nm* den

répandre [ʀepɑ̃dʀ] /41/ *vt (renverser)* to spill; *(étaler, diffuser)* to spread; *(chaleur, odeur)* to give off; **se répandre** *vi* to spill; to spread; **répandu, e** *adj (opinion, usage)* widespread

réparateur, -trice [ʀepaʀatœʀ, -tʀis] *nm/f* repairer

réparation [ʀepaʀasjɔ̃] *nf* repair

réparer [ʀepaʀe] /1/ vt to repair; (fig: offense) to make up for, atone for; (: oubli, erreur) to put right

repartie [ʀepaʀti] nf retort; **avoir de la ~** to be quick at repartee

repartir [ʀəpaʀtiʀ] /16/ vi to set off again; (voyageur) to leave again; (fig) to get going again; **~ à zéro** to start from scratch (again)

répartir [ʀepaʀtiʀ] /2/ vt (pour attribuer) to share out; (pour disperser, disposer) to divide up; (poids, chaleur) to distribute; **se répartir** vt (travail, rôles) to share out between themselves; **répartition** nf (des richesses etc) distribution

repas [ʀəpɑ] nm meal

repassage [ʀəpɑsaʒ] nm ironing

repasser [ʀəpɑse] /1/ vi to come (ou go) back ▷ vt (vêtement, tissu) to iron; (examen) to retake, resit; (film) to show again; (leçon, rôle: revoir) to go over (again)

repentir [ʀəpɑ̃tiʀ] /16/ nm repentance; **se repentir** vi to repent; **se ~ d'avoir fait qch** (regretter) to regret having done sth

répercussions [ʀepɛʀkysjɔ̃] nfpl repercussions

répercuter [ʀepɛʀkyte] /1/: **se répercuter** vi (bruit) to reverberate; (fig): **se ~ sur** to have repercussions on

repère [ʀəpɛʀ] nm mark; (monument etc) landmark

repérer [ʀəpeʀe] /6/ vt (erreur, connaissance) to spot; (abri, ennemi) to locate; **se repérer** vi to get one's bearings

répertoire [ʀepɛʀtwaʀ] nm (liste) (alphabetical) list; (carnet) index notebook; (Inform) directory; (d'un théâtre, artiste) repertoire

répéter [ʀepete] /6/ vt to repeat; (préparer: leçon) to learn, go over; (Théât) to rehearse; **se répéter** (redire) to repeat o.s.; (se reproduire) to be repeated, recur

répétition [ʀepetisjɔ̃] nf repetition; (Théât) rehearsal; **~ générale** final dress rehearsal

répit [ʀepi] nm respite; **sans ~** without letting up

replier [ʀəplije] /7/ vt (rabattre) to fold down ou over; **se replier** vi (armée) to withdraw, fall back; **se ~ sur soi-même** to withdraw into oneself

réplique [ʀeplik] nf (repartie, fig) reply; (Théât) line; (copie) replica; **répliquer** /1/ vi to reply; (riposter) to retaliate

répondeur [ʀepɔ̃dœʀ] nm: **~ (automatique)** (Tél) answering machine

répondre [ʀepɔ̃dʀ] /41/ vi to answer, reply; (freins, mécanisme) to respond; **~ à** to reply to, answer; (affection, salut) to return; (provocation) to respond to; (correspondre à) (besoin) to answer; (conditions) to meet; (description) to match; **~ à qn** (avec impertinence) to answer sb back; **~ de** to answer for

réponse [ʀepɔ̃s] nf answer, reply; **en ~ à** in reply to

reportage [ʀəpɔʀtaʒ] nm report

reporter¹ [ʀəpɔʀtɛʀ] nm reporter

reporter² [ʀəpɔʀte] vt (ajourner): **~ qch (à)** to postpone sth (until); (transférer): **~ qch sur** to transfer sth to; **se ~ à** (époque) to think back to; (document) to refer to

repos [ʀəpo] nm rest; (fig) peace (and quiet); (Mil): **~!** (stand) at ease!; **ce n'est pas de tout ~!** it's no picnic!

reposant, e [ʀ(ə)pozɑ̃, -ɑ̃t] adj restful

reposer [ʀəpoze] /1/ vt (verre, livre) to put down; (délasser) to rest ▷ vi: **laisser ~** (pâte) to leave to stand

repoussant, e [ʀəpusɑ̃, -ɑ̃t] adj repulsive

repousser [ʀəpuse] /1/ vi to grow again ▷ vt to repel, repulse; (offre) to turn down, reject; (*tiroir, personne*) to push back; (*différer*) to put back

reprendre [ʀəpʀɑ̃dʀ] /58/ *vt* (*prisonnier, ville*) to recapture; (*firme, entreprise*) to take over; (*emprunter: argument, idée*) to take up, use; (*refaire: article etc*) to go over again; (*jupe etc*) to alter; (*réprimander*) to tell off; (*corriger*) to correct; (*travail, promenade*) to resume; (*chercher*): **je viendrai te ~ à 4 h** I'll come and fetch you *ou* I'll come back for you at 4; (*se resservir de*): **~ du pain/un œuf** to take (*ou* eat) more bread/ another egg ▷ *vi* (*classes, pluie*) to start (up) again; (*activités, travaux, combats*) to resume, start (up) again; (*affaires, industrie*) to pick up; (*dire*): **reprit-il** he went on; **~ des forces** to recover one's strength; **~ courage** to take new heart; **~ la route** to resume one's journey, set off again; **~ haleine** *ou* **son souffle** to get one's breath back

représentant, e [ʀəpʀezɑ̃tɑ̃, -ɑ̃t] *nm/f* representative

représentation [ʀəpʀezɑ̃tasjɔ̃] *nf* representation; (*spectacle*) performance

représenter [ʀəpʀezɑ̃te] /1/ *vt* to represent; (*donner: pièce, opéra*) to perform; **se représenter** *vt* (*se figurer*) to imagine

répression [ʀepʀesjɔ̃] *nf* repression

réprimer [ʀepʀime] /1/ *vt* (*émotions*) to suppress; (*peuple etc*) repress

repris, e [ʀəpʀi, -iz] *pp de* **reprendre** ▷ *nm*: **~ de justice** ex-prisoner, ex-convict

reprise [ʀəpʀiz] *nf* (*recommencement*) resumption; (*économique*) recovery; (*TV*) repeat; (*Comm*) trade-in, part exchange; (*raccommodage*) mend; **à plusieurs ~s** on several occasions

repriser [ʀəpʀize] /1/ *vt* (*chaussette, lainage*) to darn; (*tissu*) to mend

reproche [ʀəpʀɔʃ] *nm* (*remontrance*) reproach; **faire des ~s à qn** to reproach sb; **sans ~(s)** beyond *ou* above reproach; **reprocher** /1/ *vt*: **reprocher qch à qn** to reproach *ou* blame sb for sth; **reprocher qch à** (*machine, théorie*) to have sth against

reproduction [ʀəpʀɔdyksjɔ̃] *nf* reproduction

reproduire [ʀəpʀɔdɥiʀ] /38/ *vt* to reproduce; **se reproduire** *vi* (*Bio*) to reproduce; (*recommencer*) to recur, re-occur

reptile [ʀɛptil] *nm* reptile

république [ʀepyblik] *nf* republic

répugnant, e [ʀepyɲɑ̃, -ɑ̃t] *adj* repulsive

répugner [ʀepyɲe] /1/: **~ à** *vt*: **~ à qn** to repel *ou* disgust sb; **~ à faire** to be loath *ou* reluctant to do

réputation [ʀepytasjɔ̃] *nf* reputation; **réputé, e** *adj* renowned

requérir [ʀəkeʀiʀ] /21/ *vt* (*nécessiter*) to require, call for

requête [ʀəkɛt] *nf* request

requin [ʀəkɛ̃] *nm* shark

requis, e [ʀəki, -iz] *adj* required

RER *sigle m* (= *Réseau express régional*) Greater Paris high-speed train service

rescapé, e [ʀɛskape] *nm/f* survivor

rescousse [ʀɛskus] *nf*: **aller à la ~ de qn** to go to sb's aid *ou* rescue

réseau, x [ʀezo] *nm* network; **~ social** social network

réseautage [ʀezotaʒ] *nm* social networking

réservation [ʀezɛʀvasjɔ̃] *nf* reservation; booking

réserve [ʀezɛʀv] *nf* (*retenue*) reserve; (*entrepôt*) storeroom; (*restriction, aussi: d'Indiens*) reservation; (*de pêche, chasse*) preserve; **de ~** (*provisions etc*) in reserve

réservé, e [ʀezɛʀve] *adj* reserved; (*chasse, pêche*) private

réserver [ʀezɛʀve] /1/ *vt* to reserve; (*chambre, billet etc*) to book, reserve; (*mettre de côté, garder*): **~ qch pour** *ou* **à** to keep *ou* save sth for

réservoir [ʀezɛʀvwaʀ] *nm* tank

résidence [rezidãs] *nf* residence;
~ principale/secondaire main/
second home; **~ universitaire**
hall of residence (BRIT), dormitory
(US); **résidentiel, le** *adj* residential;
résider /1/ *vi*: **résider à** *ou* **dans** *ou*
en to reside in; **résider dans** (*fig*)
to lie in

résidu [rezidy] *nm* residue *no pl*

résigner [reziɲe] /1/: **se résigner** *vi*:
se ~ (à qch/à faire) to resign o.s. (to
sth/to doing)

résilier [rezilje] /7/ *vt* to terminate

résistance [rezistãs] *nf* resistance;
(*de réchaud, bouilloire: fil*) element

résistant, e [rezistã, -ãt] *adj*
(*personne*) robust, tough; (*matériau*)
strong, hard-wearing

résister [reziste] /1/ *vi* to resist; **~ à**
(*assaut, tentation*) to resist; (*matériau,
plante*) to withstand; (*désobéir à*) to
stand up to, oppose

résolu, e [rezɔly] *pp de* **résoudre**
▷ *adj*: **être ~ à qch/faire** to be set
upon sth/doing

résolution [rezɔlysjɔ̃] *nf* (*fermeté,
décision*) resolution; (*d'un problème*)
solution

résolvais *etc* [rezɔlve] *vb voir*
résoudre

résonner [rezɔne] /1/ *vi* (*cloche, pas*)
to reverberate, resound; (*salle*) to be
resonant

résorber [rezɔrbe] /1/: **se résorber**
vi (*Méd*) to be resorbed; (*fig*) to be
absorbed

résoudre [rezudr] /51/ *vt* to solve;
se ~ à faire to bring o.s. to do

respect [rɛspɛ] *nm* respect; **tenir
en ~** to keep at bay; **présenter
ses ~s à qn** to pay one's respects
to sb; **respecter** /1/ *vt* to respect;
respectueux, -euse *adj* respectful

respiration [rɛspirasjɔ̃] *nf*
breathing *no pl*

respirer [rɛspire] /1/ *vi* to breathe;
(*fig: se reposer*) to get one's breath;
(*: être soulagé*) to breathe again ▷ *vt* to
breathe (in), inhale; (*manifester: santé,
calme etc*) to exude

resplendir [rɛsplãdir] /2/ *vi* to
shine; (*fig*): **~ (de)** to be radiant (with)

responsabilité [rɛspɔ̃sabilite] *nf*
responsibility; (*légale*) liability

responsable [rɛspɔ̃sabl] *adj*
responsible ▷ *nm/f* (*personne
coupable*) person responsible; (*du
ravitaillement etc*) person in charge;
(*de parti, syndicat*) official; **~ de**
responsible for

ressaisir [rəsezir] /2/: **se ressaisir**
vi to regain one's self-control

ressasser [rəsase] /1/ *vt* to keep
turning over

ressemblance [rəsãblãs] *nf*
resemblance, similarity, likeness

ressemblant, e [rəsãblã, -ãt] *adj*
(*portrait*) lifelike, true to life

ressembler [rəsãble] /1/: **~ à** *vt* to
be like, resemble; (*visuellement*) to
look like; **se ressembler** *vi* to be (*ou*
look) alike

ressentiment [rəsãtimã] *nm*
resentment

ressentir [rəsãtir] /16/ *vt* to feel; **se
~ de** to feel (*ou* show) the effects of

resserrer [rəsere] /1/ *vt* (*nœud,
boulon*) to tighten (up); (*fig: liens*) to
strengthen

resservir [rəsɛrvir] /14/ *vi* to do *ou*
serve again; **~ qn (d'un plat)** to give
sb a second helping of a dish); **se ~
de** (*plat*) to take a second helping of;
(*outil etc*) to use again

ressort [rəsɔr] *nm* (*pièce*) spring;
(*force morale*) spirit; **en dernier ~** as a
last resort; **être du ~ de** to fall within
the competence of

ressortir [rəsɔrtir] /16/ *vi* to go
(*ou* come) out (again); (*contraster*) to
stand out; **~ de: il ressort de ceci
que** it emerges from this that; **faire ~**
(*fig: souligner*) to bring out

ressortissant, e [rəsɔrtisã, -ãt]
nm/f national

ressources [rəsurs] *nfpl* resources

r

ressusciter [ʀesysite] /1/ vt (fig) to revive, bring back ▷ vi to rise (from the dead)

restant, e [ʀɛstɑ̃, -ɑ̃t] adj remaining ▷ nm: **le ~ (de)** the remainder (of); **un ~ de** (de trop) some leftover

restaurant [ʀɛstɔʀɑ̃] nm restaurant

restauration [ʀɛstɔʀasjɔ̃] nf restoration; (hôtellerie) catering; **~ rapide** fast food

restaurer [ʀɛstɔʀe] /1/ vt to restore; **se restaurer** vi to have something to eat

reste [ʀɛst] nm (restant): **le ~ (de)** the rest (of); (de trop): **un ~ (de)** some leftover; **restes** nmpl leftovers; (d'une cité etc, dépouille mortelle) remains; **du ~, au ~** besides, moreover

rester [ʀɛste] /1/ vi to stay, remain; (subsister) to remain, be left; (durer) to last, live on ▷ vb impers: **il reste du pain/deux œufs** there's some bread/there are two eggs left (over); **il me reste assez de temps** I have enough time left; **il ne me reste plus qu'à ...** I've just got to ...; **restons-en là** let's leave it at that

restituer [ʀɛstitɥe] /1/ vt (objet, somme): **~ qch (à qn)** to return ou restore sth (to sb)

restreindre [ʀɛstʀɛ̃dʀ] /52/ vt to restrict, limit

restriction [ʀɛstʀiksjɔ̃] nf restriction

résultat [ʀezylta] nm result; (d'élection etc) results pl; **résultats** nmpl (d'une enquête) findings

résulter [ʀezylte] /1/: **~ de** vt to result from, be the result of

résumé [ʀezyme] nm summary, résumé; **en ~** in brief; (pour conclure) to sum up

résumer [ʀezyme] /1/ vt (texte) to summarize; (récapituler) to sum up

▪ Attention à ne pas traduire résumer par to resume.

résurrection [ʀezyʀɛksjɔ̃] nf resurrection

rétablir [ʀetabliʀ] /2/ vt to restore, re-establish; **se rétablir** vi (guérir) to recover; (silence, calme) to return, be restored; **rétablissement** nm restoring; (guérison) recovery

retaper [ʀətape] /1/ vt (maison, voiture etc) to do up; (fam: revigorer) to buck up

retard [ʀətaʀ] nm (d'une personne attendue) lateness no pl; (sur l'horaire, un programme, une échéance) delay; (fig: scolaire, mental etc) backwardness; **en ~ (de deux heures)** (two hours) late; **désolé d'être en ~** sorry I'm late; **avoir du ~** to be late; (sur un programme) to be behind (schedule); **prendre du ~** (train, avion) to be delayed; **sans ~** without delay

retardataire [ʀətaʀdatɛʀ] nm/f latecomer

retardement [ʀətaʀdəmɑ̃]: **à ~** adj delayed action cpd; **bombe à ~** time bomb

retarder [ʀətaʀde] /1/ vt to delay; (horloge) to put back; **~ qn (d'une heure)** to delay sb (an hour); (départ, date): **~ qch (de deux jours)** to put sth back (two days) ▷ vi (montre) to be slow

retenir [ʀətniʀ] /22/ vt (garder, retarder) to keep, detain; (maintenir: objet qui glisse, colère, larmes, rire) to hold back; (se rappeler) to retain; (accepter) to accept; (fig: empêcher d'agir): **~ qn (de faire)** to hold sb back (from doing); (prélever): **~ qch (sur)** to deduct sth (from); **se retenir** vi (se raccrocher): **se ~ à** to hold onto; (se contenir): **se ~ de faire** to restrain o.s. from doing; **~ son souffle** ou **haleine** to hold one's breath

retentir [ʀətɑ̃tiʀ] /2/ vi to ring out; **retentissant, e** adj resounding

retenu, e [ʀətny] adj (place) reserved ▷ nf (prélèvement) deduction; (Scol) detention; (modération) (self-)restraint

réticence [ʁetisɑ̃s] nf reticence no pl, reluctance no pl; **réticent, e** adj reticent, reluctant

rétine [ʁetin] nf retina

retiré, e [ʁətiʁe] adj (solitaire) secluded; (éloigné) remote

retirer [ʁətiʁe] /1/ vt (argent, plainte) to withdraw; (vêtement) to take off, remove; (reprendre: billets) to collect, pick up; **~ qn/qch de** to take sb away from/sth out of, remove sb/ sth from

retomber [ʁətɔ̃be] /1/ vi (à nouveau) to fall again; (atterrir: après un saut etc) to land; (échoir): **~ sur qn** to fall on sb

rétorquer [ʁetɔʁke] /1/ vt: **~ (à qn) que** to retort (to sb) that

retouche [ʁətuʃ] nf (sur vêtement) alteration; **retoucher** /1/ vt (photographie, tableau) to touch up; (texte, vêtement) to alter

retour [ʁətuʁ] nm return; **au ~** (en route) on the way back; **à mon/ton ~** on my/your return; **être de ~ (de)** to be back (from); **quand serons-nous de ~?** when do we get back?; **par ~ du courrier** by return of post

retourner [ʁətuʁne] /1/ vt (dans l'autre sens: matelas, crêpe) to turn (over); (: sac, vêtement) to turn inside out; (émouvoir) to shake; (renvoyer, restituer): **~ qch à qn** to return sth to sb ▷ vi (aller, revenir): **~ quelque part/à** to go back ou return somewhere/to; **~ à** (état, activité) to return to, go back to; **se retourner** vi (tourner la tête) to turn round; **se ~ contre** (fig) to turn against

retrait [ʁətʁɛ] nm (d'argent) withdrawal; **en ~** set back; **~ du permis (de conduire)** disqualification from driving (BRIT), revocation of driver's license (US)

retraite [ʁətʁɛt] nf (d'une armée, Rel) retreat; (d'un employé) retirement; (revenu) (retirement) pension; **prendre sa ~** to retire; **~ anticipée**

early retirement; **retraité, e** adj retired ▷ nm/f (old age) pensioner

retrancher [ʁətʁɑ̃ʃe] /1/ vt: **~ qch de** (nombre, somme) to take ou deduct sth from; **se ~ derrière/dans** to take refuge behind/in

rétrécir [ʁetʁesiʁ] /2/ vt (vêtement) to take in ▷ vi to shrink; **se rétrécir** (route, vallée) to narrow

rétro [ʁetʁo] adj inv: **la mode ~** the nostalgia vogue

rétrospectif, -ive [ʁetʁɔspɛktif, -iv] adj retrospective ▷ nf (Art) retrospective; (Ciné) season, retrospective; **rétrospectivement** adv in retrospect

retrousser [ʁətʁuse] /1/ vt to roll up

retrouvailles [ʁətʁuvaj] nfpl reunion sg

retrouver [ʁətʁuve] /1/ vt (fugitif, objet perdu) to find; (calme, santé) to regain; (revoir) to see again; (rejoindre) to meet (again), join; **se retrouver** vi to meet; (s'orienter) to find one's way; **se ~ quelque part** to find o.s. somewhere; **s'y ~** (y voir clair) to make sense of it; (rentrer dans ses frais) to break even

rétroviseur [ʁetʁɔvizœʁ] nm (rear-view) mirror

retweeter [ʁətwite] /1/ vt (Inform: Twitter) to retweet

réunion [ʁeynjɔ̃] nf (séance) meeting

réunir [ʁeyniʁ] /2/ vt (rassembler) to gather together; (inviter: amis, famille) to have round, have in; (cumuler: qualités etc) to combine; (rapprocher: ennemis) to bring together (again), reunite; (rattacher: parties) to join (together); **se réunir** vi (se rencontrer) to meet

réussi, e [ʁeysi] adj successful

réussir [ʁeysiʁ] /2/ vi to succeed, be successful; (à un examen) to pass ▷ vt to make a success of; **~ à faire** to succeed in doing; **~ à qn** (être bénéfique à) to agree with sb; **réussite** nf success; (Cartes) patience

r

revaloir [ʀəvalwaʀ] /29/ vt: **je vous revaudrai cela** I'll repay you some day; (en mal) I'll pay you back for this

revanche [ʀəvɑ̃ʃ] nf revenge; (sport) revenge match; **en ~** on the other hand

rêve [ʀɛv] nm dream; **de ~** dream cpd; **faire un ~** to have a dream

réveil [ʀevɛj] nm waking up no pl; (fig) awakening; (pendule) alarm (clock); **au ~** on waking (up); **réveiller** /1/ vt (personne) to wake up; (fig) to awaken, revive; **se réveiller** vi to wake up

réveillon [ʀevɛjɔ̃] nm Christmas Eve; (de la Saint-Sylvestre) New Year's Eve; **réveillonner** /1/ vi to celebrate Christmas Eve (ou New Year's Eve)

révélateur, -trice [ʀevelatœʀ, -tʀis] adj: **~ (de qch)** revealing (sth)

révéler [ʀevele] /6/ vt to reveal; **se révéler** vi to be revealed, reveal itself; **se ~ facile/faux** to prove (to be) easy/false

revenant, e [ʀəvnɑ̃, -ɑ̃t] nm/f ghost

revendeur, -euse [ʀəvɑ̃dœʀ, -øz] nm/f (détaillant) retailer; (de drogue) (drug-)dealer

revendication [ʀəvɑ̃dikasjɔ̃] nf claim, demand

revendiquer [ʀəvɑ̃dike] /1/ vt to claim, demand; (responsabilité) to claim

revendre [ʀəvɑ̃dʀ] /41/ vt (d'occasion) to resell; (détailler) to sell; **à ~** (en abondance) to spare

revenir [ʀəvniʀ] /22/ vi to come back; **faire ~** (Culin) to brown; **~ cher/à 100 euros (à qn)** to cost (sb) a lot/100 euros; **~ à** (reprendre: études, projet) to return to, go back to; (équivaloir à) to amount to; **~ à qn** (part, honneur) to go to sb, be sb's; (souvenir, nom) to come back to sb; **~ sur** (question, sujet) to go back over; (engagement) to go back on; **~ à soi** to come round; **je n'en**

reviens pas I can't get over it; **~ sur ses pas** to retrace one's steps; **cela revient à dire que/au même** it amounts to saying that/to the same thing

revenu [ʀəvny] nm income; **revenus** nmpl income sg

rêver [ʀeve] /1/ vi, vt to dream; **~ de qch/de faire** to dream of sth/of doing; **~ à** to dream of

réverbère [ʀevɛʀbɛʀ] nm street lamp ou light; **réverbérer** /6/ vt to reflect

revers [ʀəvɛʀ] nm (de feuille, main) back; (d'étoffe) wrong side; (de pièce, médaille) back, reverse; (Tennis, Ping-Pong) backhand; (de veston) lapel; (fig: échec) setback

revêtement [ʀəvɛtmɑ̃] nm (des sols) flooring; (de chaussée) surface

revêtir [ʀəvetiʀ] /20/ vt (habit) to don, put on; (prendre: importance, apparence) to take on; **~ qch de** to cover sth with

rêveur, -euse [ʀɛvœʀ, -øz] adj dreamy ▷ nm/f dreamer

revient [ʀəvjɛ̃] vb voir **revenir**

revigorer [ʀəvigɔʀe] /1/ vt (air frais) to invigorate, brace up; (repas, boisson) to revive, buck up

revirement [ʀəviʀmɑ̃] nm change of mind; (d'une situation) reversal

réviser [ʀevize] /1/ vt to revise; (machine, installation, moteur) to overhaul, service

révision [ʀevizjɔ̃] nf revision; (de voiture) servicing no pl

revivre [ʀəvivʀ] /46/ vi (reprendre des forces) to come alive again ▷ vt (épreuve, moment) to relive

revoir [ʀəvwaʀ] /30/ vt to see again ▷ nm: **au ~** goodbye

révoltant, e [ʀevɔltɑ̃, -ɑ̃t] adj revolting, appalling

révolte [ʀevɔlt] nf rebellion, revolt

révolter [ʀevɔlte] /1/ vt to revolt; **se révolter** vi: **se ~ (contre)** to rebel (against)

révolu, e [Revɔly] adj past; (Admin): **âgé de 18 ans ~s** over 18 years of age

révolution [Revɔlysjɔ̃] nf revolution; **révolutionnaire** adj, nm/f revolutionary

revolver [Revɔlvɛʀ] nm gun; (à barillet) revolver

révoquer [Revɔke] /1/ vt (fonctionnaire) to dismiss; (arrêt, contrat) to revoke

revu, e [Rəvy] pp de **revoir** ▷ nf review; (périodique) review, magazine; (de music-hall) variety show; **passer en ~** (mentalement) to go through

rez-de-chaussée [Redʃose] nm inv ground floor

RF sigle f = **République française**

Rhin [Rɛ̃] nm: **le ~** the Rhine

rhinocéros [Rinɔseʀɔs] nm rhinoceros

Rhône [Ron] nm: **le ~** the Rhone

rhubarbe [Rybaʀb] nf rhubarb

rhum [Rɔm] nm rum

rhumatisme [Rymatism] nm rheumatism no pl

rhume [Rym] nm cold; **~ de cerveau** head cold; **le ~ des foins** hay fever

ricaner [Rikane] /1/ vi (avec méchanceté) to snigger; (bêtement, avec gêne) to giggle

riche [Riʃ] adj rich; (personne, pays) rich, wealthy; **~ en** rich in; **richesse** nf wealth; (fig: de sol, musée etc) richness; **richesses** nfpl (ressources, argent) wealth sg; (fig: trésors) treasures

ricochet [Rikɔʃɛ] nm: **faire des ~s** to skip stones

ride [Rid] nf wrinkle

rideau, x [Rido] nm curtain; **~ de fer** (lit) metal shutter

rider [Ride] /1/ vt to wrinkle; **se rider** vi to become wrinkled

ridicule [Ridikyl] adj ridiculous ▷ nm: **le ~** ridicule; **ridiculiser** /1/ vt to ridicule; **se ridiculiser** vi to make a fool of o.s.

MOT-CLÉ

rien [Rjɛ̃] pron 1: **(ne) … rien** nothing; (tournure négative) anything; **qu'est-ce que vous avez? — rien** what have you got? — nothing; **il n'a rien dit/fait** he said/did nothing, he hasn't said/done anything; **n'avoir peur de rien** to be afraid ou frightened of nothing, not to be afraid ou frightened of anything; **il n'a rien** (n'est pas blessé) he's all right; **ça ne fait rien** it doesn't matter
2 (quelque chose): **a-t-il jamais rien fait pour nous?** has he ever done anything for us?
3: **rien de: rien d'intéressant** nothing interesting; **rien d'autre** nothing else; **rien du tout** nothing at all
4: **rien que** just, only; nothing but; **rien que pour lui faire plaisir** only ou just to please him; **rien que la vérité** nothing but the truth; **rien que cela** that alone
▷ excl: **de rien!** not at all!
▷ nm: **un petit rien** (cadeau) a little something; **des riens** trivia pl; **un rien de** a hint of; **en un rien de temps** in no time at all

rieur, -euse [Rjœʀ, -øz] adj cheerful

rigide [Riʒid] adj stiff; (fig) rigid; (moralement) strict

rigoler [Rigɔle] /1/ vi (rire) to laugh; (s'amuser) to have (some) fun; (plaisanter) to be joking ou kidding; **rigolo, rigolote** adj funny ▷ nm/f comic; (péj) fraud, phoney

rigoureusement [Riguʀøzmɑ̃] adv rigorously

rigoureux, -euse [Riguʀø, -øz] adj rigorous; (climat, châtiment) harsh, severe

rigueur [Rigœʀ] nf rigour; **"tenue de soirée de ~"** "evening dress to be worn"; **à la ~** at a pinch; **tenir ~ à qn de qch** to hold sth against sb

r

rillettes [Rijɛt] *nfpl* ≈ potted meat *sg* (*made from pork or goose*)

rime [Rim] *nf* rhyme

rinçage [Rɛ̃saʒ] *nm* rinsing (out); (*opération*) rinse

rincer [Rɛ̃se] /3/ *vt* to rinse; (*récipient*) to rinse out

ringard, e [Rɛ̃gaR, -aRd] *adj* old-fashioned

riposter [Riposte] /1/ *vi* to retaliate ▷ *vt*: **~ que** to retort that

rire [RiR] /36/ *vi* to laugh; (*se divertir*) to have fun ▷ *nm* laugh; **le ~** laughter; **~ de** to laugh at; **pour ~** (*pas sérieusement*) for a joke *ou* a laugh

risible [Rizibl] *adj* laughable

risque [Risk] *nm* risk; **le ~** danger; **à ses ~s et périls** at his own risk; **risqué, e** *adj* risky; (*plaisanterie*) risqué, daring; **risquer** /1/ *vt* to risk; (*allusion, question*) to venture, hazard; **se risquer** *vi*: **ça ne risque rien** it's quite safe; **il risque de se tuer** he could get *ou* risks getting himself killed; **ce qui risque de se produire** what might *ou* could well happen; **il ne risque pas de recommencer** there's no chance of him doing that again; **se risquer à faire** (*tenter*) to dare to do

rissoler [Risole] /1/ *vi, vt*: **(faire) ~** to brown

ristourne [RistuRn] *nf* discount

rite [Rit] *nm* rite; (*fig*) ritual

rivage [Rivaʒ] *nm* shore

rival, e, -aux [Rival, -o] *adj, nm/f* rival; **rivaliser** /1/ *vi*: **rivaliser avec** to rival, vie with; **rivalité** *nf* rivalry

rive [Riv] *nf* shore; (*de fleuve*) bank; **riverain, e** *nm/f* riverside (*ou* lakeside) resident; (*d'une route*) local *ou* roadside resident

rivière [RivjɛR] *nf* river

riz [Ri] *nm* rice; **rizière** *nf* paddy field

RMI *sigle m* (= *revenu minimum d'insertion*) ≈ income support (BRIT), ≈ welfare (US)

RN *sigle f* = **route nationale**

robe [Rɔb] *nf* dress; (*de juge, d'ecclésiastique*) robe; (*pelage*) coat; **~ de soirée/de mariée** evening/wedding dress; **~ de chambre** dressing gown

robinet [Rɔbinɛ] *nm* tap (BRIT), faucet (US)

robot [Rɔbo] *nm* robot; **~ de cuisine** food processor

robuste [Rɔbyst] *adj* robust, sturdy; **robustesse** *nf* robustness, sturdiness

roc [Rɔk] *nm* rock

rocade [Rɔkad] *nf* bypass

rocaille [Rɔkaj] *nf* loose stones *pl*; (*jardin*) rockery, rock garden

roche [Rɔʃ] *nf* rock

rocher [Rɔʃe] *nm* rock

rocheux, -euse [Rɔʃø, -øz] *adj* rocky

rodage [Rɔdaʒ] *nm*: **en ~** running *ou* breaking in

rôder [Rode] /1/ *vi* to roam *ou* wander about; (*de façon suspecte*) to lurk (about *ou* around); **rôdeur, -euse** *nm/f* prowler

rogne [Rɔɲ] *nf*: **être en ~** to be mad *ou* in a temper

rogner [Rɔɲe] /1/ *vt* to trim; **~ sur** (*fig*) to cut down *ou* back on

rognons [Rɔɲɔ̃] *nmpl* kidneys

roi [Rwa] *nm* king; **le jour** *ou* **la fête des R~s** Twelfth Night

rôle [Rol] *nm* role; part

rollers [RɔlœR] *nmpl* Rollerblades®

romain, e [Rɔmɛ̃, -ɛn] *adj* Roman ▷ *nm/f*: **R~, e** Roman

roman, e [Rɔmɑ̃, -an] *adj* (*Archit*) Romanesque ▷ *nm* novel; **~ policier** detective novel

romancer [Rɔmɑ̃se] /3/ *vt* to romanticize; **romancier, -ière** *nm/f* novelist; **romanesque** *adj* (*amours, aventures*) storybook *cpd*; (*sentimental: personne*) romantic

roman-feuilleton [Rɔmɑ̃fœjtɔ̃] *nm* serialized novel

romanichel, le [Rɔmaniʃɛl] *nm/f* gipsy

romantique [Rɔmɑ̃tik] *adj* romantic

romarin [ʀɔmaʀɛ̃] nm rosemary

Rome [ʀɔm] n Rome

rompre [ʀɔ̃pʀ] /41/ vt to break; (entretien, fiançailles) to break off ▷ vi (fiancés) to break it off; **se rompre** vi to break; **rompu, e** adj (fourbu) exhausted

ronce [ʀɔ̃s] nf bramble branch; **ronces** nfpl brambles

ronchonner [ʀɔ̃ʃɔne] /1/ vi (fam) to grouse, grouch

rond, e [ʀɔ̃, ʀɔ̃d] adj round; (joues, mollets) well-rounded; (fam: ivre) tight ▷ nm (cercle) ring; (fam: sou): **je n'ai plus un ~** I haven't a penny left ▷ nf (gén: de surveillance) rounds pl, patrol; (danse) round (dance); (Mus) semibreve (BRIT), whole note (US); **en ~** (s'asseoir, danser) in a ring; **à la ~e** (alentour): **à 10 km à la ~e** for 10 km round; **rondelet, te** adj plump

rondelle [ʀɔ̃dɛl] nf (Tech) washer; (tranche) slice, round

rond-point [ʀɔ̃pwɛ̃] nm roundabout

ronflement [ʀɔ̃fləmɑ̃] nm snore

ronfler [ʀɔ̃fle] /1/ vi to snore; (moteur, poêle) to hum

ronger [ʀɔ̃ʒe] /3/ vt to gnaw (at); (vers, rouille) to eat into; **se ~ les sangs** to worry o.s. sick; **se ~ les ongles** to bite one's nails; **rongeur, -euse** [ʀɔ̃ʒœʀ, -øz] nm/f rodent

ronronner [ʀɔ̃ʀɔne] /1/ vi to purr

rosbif [ʀɔsbif] nm: **du ~** roasting beef; (cuit) roast beef

rose [ʀoz] nf rose ▷ adj pink; **~ bonbon** adj inv candy pink

rosé, e [ʀoze] adj pinkish; **(vin) ~** rosé (wine)

roseau, x [ʀozo] nm reed

rosée [ʀoze] nf dew

rosier [ʀozje] nm rosebush, rose tree

rossignol [ʀɔsiɲɔl] nm (Zool) nightingale

rotation [ʀɔtasjɔ̃] nf rotation

roter [ʀɔte] /1/ vi (fam) to burp, belch

rôti [ʀoti] nm: **du ~** roasting meat; (cuit) roast meat; **un ~ de bœuf/porc** a joint of beef/pork

rotin [ʀɔtɛ̃] nm rattan (cane); **fauteuil en ~** cane (arm)chair

rôtir [ʀotiʀ] /2/ vt (aussi: **faire ~**) to roast ▷ vi to roast; **rôtisserie** nf (restaurant) steakhouse; (traiteur) roast meat shop; **rôtissoire** nf (roasting) spit

rotule [ʀɔtyl] nf kneecap

rouage [ʀwaʒ] nm cog(wheel), gearwheel; **les ~s de l'État** the wheels of State

roue [ʀu] nf wheel; **~ de secours** spare wheel

rouer [ʀwe] /1/ vt: **~ qn de coups** to give sb a thrashing

rouge [ʀuʒ] adj, nm/f red ▷ nm red; **(vin) ~** red wine; **passer au ~** (signal) to go red; (automobiliste) to go through a red light; **sur la liste ~** ex-directory (BRIT), unlisted (US); **~ à joue** blusher; **~ (à lèvres)** lipstick; **rouge-gorge** nm robin (redbreast)

rougeole [ʀuʒɔl] nf measles sg

rougeoyer [ʀuʒwaje] /8/ vi to glow red

rouget [ʀuʒɛ] nm mullet

rougeur [ʀuʒœʀ] nf redness; **rougeurs** nfpl (Méd) red blotches

rougir [ʀuʒiʀ] /2/ vi to turn red; (de honte, timidité) to blush, flush; (de plaisir, colère) to redden

rouille [ʀuj] nf rust; **rouillé, e** adj rusty; **rouiller** /1/ vt to rust ▷ vi to rust, go rusty

roulant, e [ʀulɑ̃, -ɑ̃t] adj (meuble) on wheels; (surface, trottoir, tapis) moving; **escalier ~** escalator

rouleau, x [ʀulo] nm roll; (à mise en plis, à peinture, vague) roller; **~ à pâtisserie** rolling pin

roulement [ʀulmɑ̃] nm (bruit) rumbling no pl, rumble; (rotation) rotation; **par ~** on a rota (BRIT) ou rotation (US) basis; **~ (à billes)** ball bearings pl; **~ de tambour** drum roll

r

rouler [Rule] /1/ vt to roll; (papier, tapis) to roll up; (Culin: pâte) to roll out; (fam: duper) to do, con ▷ vi (bille, boule) to roll; (voiture, train) to go, run; (automobiliste) to drive; (cycliste) to ride; (bateau) to roll; **se ~ dans** (boue) to roll in; (couverture) to roll o.s. (up) in

roulette [Rulɛt] nf (de table, fauteuil) castor; (de dentiste) drill; (jeu): **la ~** roulette; **à ~s** on castors; **ça a marché comme sur des ~s** (fam) it went off very smoothly

roulotte [Rulɔt] nf caravan

roumain, e [Rumɛ̃, -ɛn] adj Rumanian ▷ nm/f: **R~, e** Rumanian

Roumanie [Rumani] nf: **la ~** Rumania

rouquin, e [Rukɛ̃, -in] nm/f (péj) redhead

rouspéter [Ruspete] /6/ vi (fam) to moan

rousse [Rus] adj f voir **roux**

roussir [Rusir] /2/ vt to scorch ▷ vi (Culin): **faire ~** to brown

route [Rut] nf road; (fig: chemin) way; (itinéraire, parcours) route; (fig: voie) road, path; **il y a trois heures de ~** it's a three-hour ride ou journey; **en ~** on the way; **en ~!** let's go!; **mettre en ~** to start up; **se mettre en ~** to set off; **~ nationale** ≈ A-road (BRIT), ≈ state highway (US)

routeur [Rutœr] nm (Inform) router

routier, -ière [Rutje, -jɛr] adj road cpd ▷ nm (camionneur) (long-distance) lorry (BRIT) ou truck (US) driver; (restaurant) ≈ transport café (BRIT), ≈ truck stop (US)

routine [Rutin] nf routine; **routinier, -ière** [Rutinje, -jɛr] adj (péj: travail) humdrum; (: personne) addicted to routine

rouvrir [Ruvrir] /18/ vt, vi to reopen, open again; **se rouvrir** vi to open up again

roux, rousse [Ru, Rus] adj red; (personne) red-haired ▷ nm/f redhead

royal, e, -aux [Rwajal, -o] adj royal; (fig) fit for a king

royaume [Rwajom] nm kingdom; (fig) realm

Royaume-Uni [Rwajomyni] nm: **le ~** the United Kingdom

royauté [Rwajote] nf (régime) monarchy

ruban [Rybã] nm ribbon; **~ adhésif** adhesive tape

rubéole [Rybeɔl] nf German measles sg, rubella

rubis [Rybi] nm ruby

rubrique [Rybrik] nf (titre, catégorie) heading; (Presse: article) column

ruche [Ryʃ] nf hive

rude [Ryd] adj (barbe, toile) rough; (métier, tâche) hard, tough; (climat) severe, harsh; (bourru) harsh, rough; (fruste: manières) rugged, tough; (fam: fameux) jolly good; **rudement** adv (très) terribly

rudimentaire [Rydimãtɛr] adj rudimentary, basic

rudiments [Rydimã] nmpl: **avoir des ~ d'anglais** to have a smattering of English

rue [Ry] nf street

ruée [Rɥe] nf rush

ruelle [Rɥɛl] nf alley(way)

ruer [Rɥe] /1/ vi (cheval) to kick out; **se ruer** vi: **se ~ sur** to pounce on; **se ~ vers/dans/hors de** to rush towards/into/out of

rugby [Rygbi] nm rugby (football)

rugir [Ryʒir] /2/ vi to roar

rugueux, -euse [Rygø, -øz] adj rough

ruine [Rɥin] nf ruin; **ruiner** /1/ vt to ruin; **ruineux, -euse** adj ruinous

ruisseau, x [Rɥiso] nm stream, brook

ruisseler [Rɥisle] /4/ vi to stream

rumeur [Rymœr] nf (bruit confus) rumbling; (nouvelle) rumour

ruminer [Rymine] /1/ vt (herbe) to ruminate; (fig) to ruminate on ou over, chew over

rupture [Ryptyr] nf (de négociations etc) breakdown; (de contrat) breach;

(*dans continuité*) break; (*séparation, désunion*) break-up, split

rural, e, -aux [ʀyʀal, -o] *adj* rural, country *cpd*

ruse [ʀyz] *nf*: **la ~** cunning, craftiness; (*pour tromper*) trickery; **une ~** a trick, a ruse; **rusé, e** *adj* cunning, crafty

russe [ʀys] *adj* Russian ▷ *nm* (*Ling*) Russian ▷ *nm/f*: **R~** Russian

Russie [ʀysi] *nf*: **la ~** Russia

rustine [ʀystin] *nf* repair patch (*for bicycle inner tube*)

rustique [ʀystik] *adj* rustic

rythme [ʀitm] *nm* rhythm; (*vitesse*) rate (: *de la vie*) pace, tempo; **rythmé, e** *adj* rhythmic(al)

S

s' [s] *pron voir* **se**

sa [sa] *adj poss voir* **son**[1]

sable [sabl] *nm* sand

sablé [sable] *nm* shortbread biscuit

sabler [sable] /1/ *vt* (*contre le verglas*) to grit; **~ le champagne** to drink champagne

sabot [sabo] *nm* clog; (*de cheval, bœuf*) hoof; **~ de frein** brake shoe

saboter [sabɔte] /1/ *vt* (*travail, morceau de musique*) to botch, make a mess of; (*machine, installation, négociation etc*) to sabotage

sac [sak] *nm* bag; (*à charbon etc*) sack; **mettre à ~** to sack; **~ à provisions/ de voyage** shopping/travelling bag; **~ de couchage** sleeping bag; **~ à dos** rucksack; **~ à main** handbag

saccadé, e [sakade] *adj* jerky; (*respiration*) spasmodic

saccager [sakaʒe] /3/ *vt* (*piller*) to sack; (*dévaster*) to create havoc in

saccharine [sakaʀin] *nf* saccharin(e)

sachet [saʃɛ] nm (small) bag; (de lavande, poudre, shampooing) sachet; **~ de thé** tea bag; **du potage en ~** packet soup

sacoche [sakɔʃ] nf (gén) bag; (de bicyclette) saddlebag

sacré, e [sakʀe] adj sacred; (fam: satané) blasted; (: fameux): **un ~ ...** a heck of a ...

sacrement [sakʀəmɑ̃] nm sacrament

sacrifice [sakʀifis] nm sacrifice; **sacrifier** /7/ vt to sacrifice

sacristie [sakʀisti] nf sacristy; (culte protestant) vestry

sadique [sadik] adj sadistic

safran [safʀɑ̃] nm saffron

sage [saʒ] adj wise; (enfant) good

sage-femme [saʒfam] nf midwife

sagesse [saʒɛs] nf wisdom

Sagittaire [saʒitɛʀ] nm: **le ~** Sagittarius

Sahara [saaʀa] nm: **le ~** the Sahara (Desert)

saignant, e [sɛɲɑ̃, -ɑ̃t] adj (viande) rare

saigner [seɲe] /1/ vi to bleed ▷ vt to bleed; (animal) to bleed to death; **~ du nez** to have a nosebleed

saillir [sajiʀ] /13/ vi to project, stick out; (veine, muscle) to bulge

sain, e [sɛ̃, sɛn] adj healthy; **~ et sauf** safe and sound, unharmed; **~ d'esprit** sound in mind, sane

saindoux [sɛ̃du] nm lard

saint, e [sɛ̃, sɛ̃t] adj holy ▷ nm/f saint; **la S~e Vierge** the Blessed Virgin

Saint-Esprit [sɛ̃tɛspʀi] nm: **le ~** the Holy Spirit ou Ghost

sainteté [sɛ̃təte] nf holiness

Saint-Sylvestre [sɛ̃silvɛstʀ] nf: **la ~** New Year's Eve

sais etc [sɛ] vb voir **savoir**

saisie [sezi] nf seizure; **~ (de données)** (data) capture

saisir [seziʀ] /2/ vt to take hold of, grab; (fig: occasion) to seize; (comprendre) to grasp; (entendre) to get, catch; (Inform) to capture; (Culin) to fry quickly; (Jur: biens, publication) to seize; **saisissant, e** adj startling, striking

saison [sɛzɔ̃] nf season; **haute/ basse/morte ~** high/low/slack season; **saisonnier, -ière** adj seasonal

salade [salad] nf (Bot) lettuce etc (generic term); (Culin) (green) salad; (fam: confusion) tangle, muddle; **~ composée** mixed salad; **~ de fruits** fruit salad; **~ verte** green salad; **saladier** nm (salad) bowl

salaire [salɛʀ] nm (annuel, mensuel) salary; (hebdomadaire, journalier) pay, wages pl; **~ minimum interprofessionnel de croissance** index-linked guaranteed minimum wage

salarié, e [salaʀje] nm/f salaried employee; wage-earner

salaud [salo] nm (fam!) sod (!), bastard (!)

sale [sal] adj dirty, filthy; (fig: mauvais) nasty

salé, e [sale] adj (liquide, saveur, mer, goût) salty; (Culin: amandes, beurre etc) salted; (: gâteaux) savoury; (fig: grivois) spicy; (: note, facture) steep

saler [sale] /1/ vt to salt

saleté [salte] nf (état) dirtiness; (crasse) dirt, filth; (tache etc) dirt no pl; (fig: tour) filthy trick; (: chose sans valeur) rubbish no pl; (: obscénité) filth no pl

salière [saljɛʀ] nf saltcellar

salir [saliʀ] /2/ vt to (make) dirty; (fig) to soil the reputation of; **se salir** vi to get dirty; **salissant, e** adj (tissu) which shows the dirt; (métier) dirty, messy

salle [sal] nf room; (d'hôpital) ward; (de restaurant) dining room; (d'un cinéma) auditorium (: public) audience; **~ d'attente** waiting room; **~ de bain(s)** bathroom; **~ de classe** classroom; **~ de concert** concert hall; **~ d'eau** shower-room;

~ d'embarquement (à l'aéroport) departure lounge; **~ de jeux** (pour enfants) playroom; **~ à manger** dining room; **~ des professeurs** staffroom; **~ de séjour** living room; **~ des ventes** saleroom

salon [salɔ̃] nm lounge, sitting room; (mobilier) lounge suite; (exposition) exhibition, show; **~ de coiffure** hairdressing salon; **~ de thé** tearoom

salope [salɔp] nf (fam!) bitch (!); **saloperie** nf (fam!: action) dirty trick; (: chose sans valeur) rubbish no pl

salopette [salɔpɛt] nf dungarees pl; (d'ouvrier) overall(s)

salsifis [salsifi] nm salsify

salubre [salybʀ] adj healthy, salubrious

saluer [salɥe] /1/ vt (pour dire bonjour, fig) to greet; (pour dire au revoir) to take one's leave; (Mil) to salute

salut [saly] nm (sauvegarde) safety; (Rel) salvation; (geste) wave; (parole) greeting; (Mil) salute ▷ excl (fam: pour dire bonjour) hi (there); (: pour dire au revoir) see you!, bye!

salutations [salytasjɔ̃] nfpl greetings; **recevez mes ~ distinguées** ou **respectueuses** yours faithfully

samedi [samdi] nm Saturday

SAMU [samy] sigle m (= service d'assistance médicale d'urgence) ≈ ambulance (service) (BRIT), ≈ paramedics (US)

sanction [sɑ̃ksjɔ̃] nf sanction; **sanctionner** /1/ vt (loi, usage) to sanction; (punir) to punish

sandale [sɑ̃dal] nf sandal

sandwich [sɑ̃dwitʃ] nm sandwich

sang [sɑ̃] nm blood; **en ~** covered in blood; **se faire du mauvais ~** to fret, get in a state; **sang-froid** nm calm, sangfroid; **de sang-froid** in cold blood; **sanglant, e** adj bloody

sangle [sɑ̃gl] nf strap

sanglier [sɑ̃glije] nm (wild) boar

sanglot [sɑ̃glo] nm sob; **sangloter** /1/ vi to sob

sangsue [sɑ̃sy] nf leech

sanguin, e [sɑ̃gɛ̃, -in] adj blood cpd

sanitaire [sanitɛʀ] adj health cpd; **sanitaires** nmpl (salle de bain et w.-c.) bathroom sg

sans [sɑ̃] prép without; **~ qu'il s'en aperçoive** without him ou his noticing; **un pull ~ manches** a sleeveless jumper; **~ faute** without fail; **~ arrêt** without a break; **~ ça** (fam) otherwise; **sans-abri** nmpl homeless; **sans-emploi** nm/f inv unemployed person; **les sans-emploi** the unemployed; **sans-gêne** adj inv inconsiderate

santé [sɑ̃te] nf health; **être en bonne ~** to be in good health; **boire à la ~ de qn** to drink (to) sb's health; **à ta** ou **votre ~!** cheers!

saoudien, ne [saudjɛ̃, -ɛn] adj Saudi (Arabian) ▷ nm/f: **S~, ne** Saudi (Arabian)

saoul, e [su, sul] adj = **soûl**

saper [sape] /1/ vt to undermine, sap

sapeur-pompier [sapœʀpɔ̃pje] nm fireman

saphir [safiʀ] nm sapphire

sapin [sapɛ̃] nm fir (tree); (bois) fir; **~ de Noël** Christmas tree

sarcastique [saʀkastik] adj sarcastic

Sardaigne [saʀdɛɲ] nf: **la ~** Sardinia

sardine [saʀdin] nf sardine

SARL [saʀl] sigle f (= société à responsabilité limitée) ≈ plc (BRIT), ≈ Inc. (US)

sarrasin [saʀazɛ̃] nm buckwheat

satané, e [satane] adj (fam) confounded

satellite [satelit] nm satellite

satin [satɛ̃] nm satin

satire [satiʀ] nf satire; **satirique** adj satirical

satisfaction [satisfaksjɔ̃] nf satisfaction

satisfaire [satisfɛʀ] /60/ vt to satisfy; **~ à** (revendications, conditions)

to meet; **satisfaisant, e** adj
(acceptable) satisfactory; **satisfait,
e** adj satisfied; **satisfait de** happy ou
satisfied with
saturer [satyʀe] /1/ vt to saturate
sauce [sos] nf sauce; (avec un rôti)
gravy; **~ tomate** tomato sauce;
saucière nf sauceboat
saucisse [sosis] nf sausage
saucisson [sosisɔ̃] nm (slicing)
sausage
sauf¹ [sof] prép except; **~ si** (à moins
que) unless; **~ avis contraire** unless
you hear to the contrary; **~ erreur** if
I'm not mistaken
sauf², sauve [sof, sov] adj
unharmed, unhurt; (fig: honneur)
intact, saved; **laisser la vie sauve à
qn** to spare sb's life
sauge [soʒ] nf sage
saugrenu, e [sogʀəny] adj
preposterous
saule [sol] nm willow (tree)
saumon [somɔ̃] nm salmon inv
saupoudrer [supudʀe] /1/ vt: **~ qch
de** to sprinkle sth with
saur [sɔʀ] adj m: **hareng ~** smoked ou
red herring, kipper
saut [so] nm jump; (discipline sportive)
jumping; **faire un ~ chez qn** to pop
over to sb's (place); **~ en hauteur/
longueur** high/long jump; **~ à la
perche** pole vaulting; **~ à l'élastique**
bungee jumping; **~ périlleux**
somersault
sauter [sote] /1/ vi to jump, leap;
(exploser) to blow up, explode;
(: fusibles) to blow; (se détacher) to
pop out (ou off) ▷ vt to jump (over),
leap (over); (fig: omettre) to skip, miss
(out); **faire ~** to blow up; (Culin) to
sauté; **~ à la corde** to skip; **~ au cou
de qn** to fly into sb's arms; **~ sur une
occasion** to jump at an opportunity;
~ aux yeux to be quite obvious
sauterelle [sotʀɛl] nf grasshopper
sautiller [sotije] /1/ vi (oiseau) to hop;
(enfant) to skip

sauvage [sovaʒ] adj (gén) wild;
(peuplade) savage; (farouche)
unsociable; (barbare) wild, savage;
(non officiel) unauthorized, unofficial;
faire du camping ~ to camp in
the wild ▷ nm/f savage; (timide)
unsociable type
sauve [sov] adj f voir **sauf²**
sauvegarde [sovgaʀd] nf
safeguard; (Inform) backup;
sauvegarder /1/ vt to safeguard;
(Inform: enregistrer) to save; (: copier)
to back up
sauve-qui-peut [sovkipø] excl run
for your life!
sauver [sove] /1/ vt to save; (porter
secours à) to rescue; (récupérer) to
salvage, rescue; **se sauver** vi (s'enfuir)
to run away; (fam: partir) to be off;
sauvetage nm rescue; **sauveteur**
nm rescuer; **sauvette: à la sauvette**
adv (se marier etc) hastily, hurriedly;
sauveur nm saviour (BRIT), savior
(US)
savant, e [savɑ̃, -ɑ̃t] adj scholarly,
learned ▷ nm scientist
saveur [savœʀ] nf flavour; (fig)
savour
savoir [savwaʀ] /32/ vt to know; (être
capable de): **il sait nager** he can swim
▷ nm knowledge; **se savoir** vi (être
connu) to be known; **je n'en sais rien**
I (really) don't know; **à ~ (que)** that
is, namely; **faire ~ qch à qn** to let sb
know sth; **pas que je sache** not as
far as I know
savon [savɔ̃] nm (produit) soap;
(morceau) bar ou tablet of soap; (fam):
passer un ~ à qn to give sb a good
dressing-down; **savonner** /1/ vt to
soap; **savonnette** nf bar of soap
savourer [savuʀe] /1/ vt to savour;
savoureux, -euse adj tasty; (fig:
anecdote) spicy, juicy
saxo(phone) [saksɔ(fɔn)] nm
sax(ophone)
scabreux, -euse [skabʀø, -øz] adj
risky; (indécent) improper, shocking

scandale [skɑ̃dal] nm scandal; **faire un ~** (scène) to make a scene; (Jur) create a disturbance; **faire ~** to scandalize people; **scandaleux, -euse** adj scandalous, outrageous
scandinave [skɑ̃dinav] adj Scandinavian ▷ nm/f: **S~** Scandinavian
Scandinavie [skɑ̃dinavi] nf: **la ~** Scandinavia
scarabée [skaʀabe] nm beetle
scarlatine [skaʀlatin] nf scarlet fever
scarole [skaʀɔl] nf endive
sceau, x [so] nm seal
sceller [sele] /1/ vt to seal
scénario [senaʀjo] nm scenario
scène [sɛn] nf (gén) scene; (estrade, fig: théâtre) stage; **entrer en ~** to come on stage; **mettre en ~** (Théât) to stage; (Ciné) to direct; **faire une ~ (à qn)** to make a scene (with sb); **~ de ménage** domestic fight ou scene
sceptique [sɛptik] adj sceptical
schéma [ʃema] nm (diagramme) diagram, sketch; **schématique** adj diagrammatic(al), schematic; (fig) oversimplified
sciatique [sjatik] nf sciatica
scie [si] nf saw
sciemment [sjamɑ̃] adv knowingly
science [sjɑ̃s] nf science; (savoir) knowledge; **~s humaines/sociales** social sciences; **~s naturelles** (Scol) natural science sg, biology sg; **~s po** political science ou studies pl; **science-fiction** nf science fiction; **scientifique** adj scientific ▷ nm/f scientist; (étudiant) science student
scier [sje] /7/ vt to saw; (retrancher) to saw off; **scierie** nf sawmill
scintiller [sɛ̃tije] /1/ vi to sparkle; (étoile) to twinkle
sciure [sjyʀ] nf: **~ (de bois)** sawdust
sclérose [skleʀoz] nf: **~ en plaques (SEP)** multiple sclerosis (MS)
scolaire [skɔlɛʀ] adj school cpd; **scolariser** /1/ vt to provide with

schooling (ou schools); **scolarité** nf schooling
scooter [skutœʀ] nm (motor) scooter
score [skɔʀ] nm score
scorpion [skɔʀpjɔ̃] nm (signe): **le S~** Scorpio
scotch [skɔtʃ] nm (whisky) scotch, whisky; **Scotch®** (adhésif) Sellotape® (BRIT), Scotch tape® (US)
scout, e [skut] adj, nm scout
script [skʀipt] nm (écriture) printing; (Ciné) (shooting) script
scrupule [skʀypyl] nm scruple
scruter [skʀyte] /1/ vt to scrutinize; (l'obscurité) to peer into
scrutin [skʀytɛ̃] nm (vote) ballot; (ensemble des opérations) poll
sculpter [skylte] /1/ vt to sculpt; (érosion) to carve; **sculpteur** nm sculptor; **sculpture** nf sculpture
SDF sigle m (= sans domicile fixe) homeless person; **les ~** the homeless

🔵 **MOT-CLÉ**

se, s' [sə, s] pron 1 (emploi réfléchi) oneself; (: masc) himself; (: fém) herself; (: sujet non humain) itself; (: pl) themselves; **se savonner** to soap o.s.
2 (réciproque) one another, each other; **ils s'aiment** they love one another ou each other
3 (passif): **cela se répare facilement** it is easily repaired
4 (possessif): **se casser la jambe/se laver les mains** to break one's leg/wash one's hands

séance [seɑ̃s] nf (d'assemblée) meeting, session; (de tribunal) sitting, session; (musicale, Ciné, Théât) performance
seau, x [so] nm bucket, pail
sec, sèche [sɛk, sɛʃ] adj dry; (raisins, figues) dried; (insensible: cœur, personne) hard, cold ▷ nm: **tenir au ~** to keep in a dry place ▷ adv hard; **je le**

s

bois ~ I drink it straight *ou* neat; **à ~** (*puits*) dried up

sécateur [sekatœʀ] *nm* secateurs *pl* (BRIT), shears *pl*

sèche [sɛʃ] *adj f voir* **sec**; **sèche-cheveux** *nm inv* hair-drier; **sèche-linge** *nm inv* tumble dryer; **sèchement** *adv* (*répliquer etc*) drily

sécher [seʃe] /6/ *vt* to dry; (*dessécher: peau, blé*) to dry (out); (: *étang*) to dry up; (*fam: classe, cours*) to skip ▷ *vi* to dry; to dry out; to dry up; (*fam: candidat*) to be stumped; **se sécher** *vi* (*après le bain*) to dry o.s.; **sécheresse** *nf* dryness; (*absence de pluie*) drought; **séchoir** *nm* drier

second, e [s(ə)gɔ̃, -ɔ̃d] *adj* second ▷ *nm* (*assistant*) second in command; (*Navig*) first mate ▷ *nf* second; (*Scol*) ≈ year 11 (BRIT), ≈ tenth grade (US); (*Aviat, Rail etc*) second class; **voyager en ~e** to travel second-class; **secondaire** *adj* secondary; **seconder** /1/ *vt* to assist

secouer [s(ə)kwe] /1/ *vt* to shake; (*passagers*) to rock; (*traumatiser*) to shake (up)

secourir [s(ə)kuʀiʀ] /11/ *vt* (*venir en aide à*) to assist, aid; **secourisme** *nm* first aid; **secouriste** *nm/f* first-aid worker

secours [s(ə)kuʀ] *nm* help, aid, assistance ▷ *nmpl* aid *sg*; **au ~!** help!; **appeler au ~** to shout *ou* call for help; **porter ~ à qn** to give sb assistance, help sb; **les premiers ~** first aid *sg*

⚬ **ÉQUIPES DE SECOURS**
⚬
⚬ Emergency phone numbers can
⚬ be dialled free from public phones.
⚬ For the police ('la police') dial 17; for
⚬ medical services ('le SAMU') dial 15;
⚬ for the fire brigade ('les sapeurs—
⚬ pompiers') dial 18.

secousse [s(ə)kus] *nf* jolt, bump; (*électrique*) shock; (*fig: psychologique*) jolt, shock

secret, -ète [səkʀɛ, -ɛt] *adj* secret; (*fig: renfermé*) reticent, reserved ▷ *nm* secret; (*discrétion absolue*): **le ~** secrecy; **en ~** in secret, secretly; **~ professionnel** professional secrecy

secrétaire [səkʀetɛʀ] *nm/f* secretary ▷ *nm* (*meuble*) writing desk; **~ de direction** private *ou* personal secretary; **~ d'État** ≈ junior minister; **secrétariat** *nm* (*profession*) secretarial work; (*bureau*) (secretary's) office; (: *d'organisation internationale*) secretariat

secteur [sɛktœʀ] *nm* sector; (*Admin*) district; (*Élec*) sector: **branché sur le ~** plugged into the mains (supply)

section [sɛksjɔ̃] *nf* section; (*de parcours d'autobus*) fare stage; (*Mil: unité*) platoon; **sectionner** /1/ *vt* to sever

sécu [seky] *nf* = **sécurité sociale**

sécurité [sekyʀite] *nf* (*absence de troubles*) security; (*absence de danger*) safety; **système de ~** security (*ou* safety) system; **être en ~** to be safe; **la ~ routière** road safety; **la ~ sociale** ≈ (the) Social Security (BRIT), ≈ (the) Welfare (US)

sédentaire [sedɑ̃tɛʀ] *adj* sedentary

séduction [sedyksjɔ̃] *nf* seduction; (*charme, attrait*) appeal, charm

séduire [seduiʀ] /38/ *vt* to charm; (*femme: abuser de*) to seduce; **séduisant, e** *adj* (*femme*) seductive; (*homme, offre*) very attractive

ségrégation [segʀegasjɔ̃] *nf* segregation

seigle [sɛgl] *nm* rye

seigneur [sɛɲœʀ] *nm* lord

sein [sɛ̃] *nm* breast; (*entrailles*) womb; **au ~ de** (*équipe, institution*) within

séisme [seism] *nm* earthquake

seize [sɛz] *num* sixteen; **seizième** *num* sixteenth

séjour [seʒuʀ] *nm* stay; (*pièce*) living room; **séjourner** /1/ *vi* to stay

sel [sɛl] *nm* salt; (*fig: piquant*) spice

sélection [selɛksjɔ̃] *nf* selection; **sélectionner** /1/ *vt* to select

self [sɛlf] nm (fam) self-service
selfie [sɛlfi] nm selfie
self-service [sɛlfsɛʀvis] adj self-service ▷ nm self-service (restaurant)
selle [sɛl] nf saddle; **selles** nfpl (Méd) stools; **seller** /1/ vt to saddle
selon [səlɔ̃] prép according to; (en se conformant à) in accordance with; **~ moi** as I see it; **~ que** according to
semaine [səmɛn] nf week; **en ~** during the week, on weekdays
semblable [sɑ̃blabl] adj similar; (de ce genre): **de ~s mésaventures** such mishaps ▷ nm fellow creature ou man; **~ à** similar to, like
semblant [sɑ̃blɑ̃] nm: **un ~ de vérité** a semblance of truth; **faire ~ (de faire)** to pretend (to do)
sembler [sɑ̃ble] /1/ vb copule to seem ▷ vb impers: **il semble (bien) que/inutile de** it (really) seems ou appears that/useless to; **il me semble (bien) que** it (really) seems to me that; **comme bon lui semble** as he sees fit
semelle [səmɛl] nf sole; (intérieure) insole, inner sole
semer [səme] /5/ vt to sow; (fig: éparpiller) to scatter; (: confusion) to spread; (fam: poursuivants) to lose, shake off; **semé de** (difficultés) riddled with
semestre [səmɛstʀ] nm half-year; (Scol) semester
séminaire [seminɛʀ] nm seminar; **~ en ligne** webinar
semi-remorque [səmiʀəmɔʀk] nm articulated lorry (BRIT), semi(trailer) (US)
semoule [səmul] nf semolina
sénat [sena] nm senate; **sénateur** nm senator
Sénégal [senegal] nm: **le ~** Senegal
sens [sɑ̃s] nm (Physiol) sense; (signification) meaning, sense; (direction) direction; **à mon ~** to my mind; **dans le ~ des aiguilles d'une montre** clockwise; **dans le ~ contraire des aiguilles d'une**

montre anticlockwise; **dans le mauvais ~** (aller) the wrong way; in the wrong direction; **bon ~** good sense; **~ dessus dessous** upside down; **~ interdit, ~ unique** one-way street
sensation [sɑ̃sasjɔ̃] nf sensation; **faire ~** to cause a sensation, create a stir; **à ~** (péj) sensational; **sensationnel, le** adj sensational, fantastic
sensé, e [sɑ̃se] adj sensible
sensibiliser [sɑ̃sibilize] /1/ vt: **~ qn (à)** to make sb sensitive (to)
sensibilité [sɑ̃sibilite] nf sensitivity
sensible [sɑ̃sibl] adj sensitive; (aux sens) perceptible; (appréciable: différence, progrès) appreciable, noticeable; **~ à** sensitive to; **sensiblement** adv (à peu près): **ils ont sensiblement le même poids** they weigh approximately the same; **sensiblerie** nf sentimentality

Attention à ne pas traduire sensible par le mot anglais sensible.

sensuel, le [sɑ̃sɥɛl] adj (personne) sensual; (musique) sensuous
sentence [sɑ̃tɑ̃s] nf (Jur) sentence
sentier [sɑ̃tje] nm path
sentiment [sɑ̃timɑ̃] nm feeling; **recevez mes ~s respectueux** (personne nommée) yours sincerely; (personne non nommée) yours faithfully; **sentimental, e, -aux** adj sentimental; (vie, aventure) love cpd
sentinelle [sɑ̃tinɛl] nf sentry
sentir [sɑ̃tiʀ] /16/ vt (par l'odorat) to smell; (par le goût) to taste; (au toucher, fig) to feel; (répandre une odeur de) to smell of (: ressemblance) to smell like ▷ vi to smell; **~ mauvais** to smell bad; **se ~ bien** to feel good; **se ~ mal** (être indisposé) to feel unwell ou ill; **se ~ le courage/la force de faire** to feel brave/strong enough to do; **il ne peut pas le ~** (fam) he can't stand him; **je ne me sens pas bien** I don't feel well

S

séparation [separasjɔ̃] nf
separation; (cloison) division,
partition

séparé, e [separe] adj (appartements,
pouvoirs) separate; (époux) separated;
séparément adv separately

séparer [separe] /1/ vt to separate;
(désunir) to drive apart; (détacher):
~ qch de to pull sth (off) from; **se
séparer** vi (époux) to separate, part;
(prendre congé: amis etc) to part; (se
diviser: route, tige etc) to divide; **se ~
de** (époux) to separate ou part from;
(employé, objet personnel) to part with

sept [sɛt] num seven; **septante** num
(BELGIQUE, SUISSE) seventy

septembre [sɛptɑ̃bʀ] nm
September

septicémie [sɛptisemi] nf blood
poisoning, septicaemia

septième [sɛtjɛm] num seventh

séquelles [sekɛl] nfpl after-effects;
(fig) aftermath sg

serbe [sɛʀb] adj Serbian

Serbie [sɛʀbi] nf: **la ~** Serbia

serein, e [səʀɛ̃, -ɛn] adj serene

sergent [sɛʀʒɑ̃] nm sergeant

série [seʀi] nf series inv; (de clés,
casseroles, outils) set; (catégorie:
Sport) rank; **en ~** in quick succession;
(Comm) mass cpd; **de ~** (voiture)
standard; **hors ~** (Comm) custom-
built; **~ noire** (crime) thriller

sérieusement [seʀjøzmɑ̃] adv
seriously

sérieux, -euse [seʀjø, -øz] adj
serious; (élève, employé) reliable,
responsible; (client, maison) reliable,
dependable ▷ nm seriousness; (d'une
entreprise etc) reliability; **garder son ~**
to keep a straight face; **prendre qch/
qn au ~** to take sth/sb seriously

serin [səʀɛ̃] nm canary

seringue [səʀɛ̃g] nf syringe

serment [sɛʀmɑ̃] nm (juré) oath;
(promesse) pledge, vow

sermon [sɛʀmɔ̃] nm sermon

séropositif, -ive [seʀopozitif, -iv]
adj HIV positive

serpent [sɛʀpɑ̃] nm snake;
serpenter /1/ vi to wind

serpillière [sɛʀpijɛʀ] nf floorcloth

serre [sɛʀ] nf (Agr) greenhouse;
serres nfpl (griffes) claws, talons

serré, e [seʀe] adj (réseau) dense;
(habits) tight; (fig: lutte, match) tight,
close-fought; (passagers etc) (tightly)
packed; **avoir le cœur ~** to have a
heavy heart

serrer [seʀe] /1/ vt (tenir) to grip
ou hold tight; (comprimer, coincer)
to squeeze; (poings, mâchoires) to
clench; (vêtement) to be too tight for;
(ceinture, nœud, frein, vis) to tighten
▷ vi: **~ à droite** to keep to the right

serrure [seʀyʀ] nf lock; **serrurier** nm
locksmith

sers, sert [sɛʀ] vb voir **servir**

servante [sɛʀvɑ̃t] nf (maid)servant

serveur, -euse [sɛʀvœʀ, -øz] nm/f
waiter (waitress)

serviable [sɛʀvjabl] adj obliging,
willing to help

service [sɛʀvis] nm service; (série
de repas): **premier ~** first sitting;
(assortiment de vaisselle) set, service;
(bureau: de la vente etc) department,
section; **faire le ~** to serve; **rendre
~ à qn** to help sb; **rendre un ~ à qn**
to do sb a favour; **être de ~** to be on
duty; **être/mettre en ~** to be in/put
into service ou operation; **~ compris/
non compris** service included/
not included; **hors ~** out of order;
~ après-vente after-sales service;
~ militaire military service; see
note **"service militaire"**; **~ d'ordre**
police (ou stewards) in charge of
maintaining order; **~s secrets** secret
service sg

● **SERVICE MILITAIRE**
●
● Until 1997, French men over
● the age of 18 who were passed
● as fit, and who were not in

full-time higher education, were required to do ten months' 'service militaire'. Conscientious objectors were required to do two years' community service. Since 1997, military service has been suspended in France. However, all sixteen-year-olds, both male and female, are required to register for a compulsory one-day training course, the 'JDC' ('journée défense et citoyenneté'), which covers basic information on the principles and organization of defence in France, and also advises on career opportunities in the military and in the voluntary sector. Young people must attend the training day before their eighteenth birthday.

serviette [sɛʀvjɛt] nf (de table) (table) napkin, serviette; (de toilette) towel; (porte-documents) briefcase; **~ hygiénique** sanitary towel

servir [sɛʀviʀ] /14/ vt to serve; (au restaurant) to wait on; (au magasin) to serve, attend to ▷ vi (Tennis) to serve; (Cartes) to deal; **se servir** vi (prendre d'un plat) to help o.s.; **vous êtes servi?** are you being served?; **sers-toi!** help yourself!; **se ~ de** (plat) to help o.s. to; (voiture, outil, relations) to use; **~ à qn** (diplôme, livre) to be of use to sb; **~ à qch/à faire** (outil etc) to be used for sth/for doing; **ça ne sert à rien** it's no use; **~ (à qn) de ...** to serve as ... (for sb)

serviteur [sɛʀvitœʀ] nm servant

ses [se] adj poss voir **son**[1]

seuil [sœj] nm doorstep; (fig) threshold

seul, e [sœl] adj (sans compagnie) alone; (unique): **un ~ livre** only one book, a single book; **le ~ livre** the only book ▷ adv (vivre) alone, on one's own; **faire qch (tout) ~** to do sth (all) on one's own ou (all) by oneself ▷ nm/f: **il en reste un(e) ~(e)** there's

only one left; **à lui (tout) ~** single-handed, on his own; **se sentir ~** to feel lonely; **parler tout ~** to talk to oneself; **seulement** adv only; **non seulement ... mais aussi** ou **encore** not only ... but also

sève [sɛv] nf sap

sévère [sevɛʀ] adj severe

sexe [sɛks] nm sex; (organe mâle) member; **sexuel, le** adj sexual

shampooing [ʃɑ̃pwɛ̃] nm shampoo

Shetland [ʃɛtlɑ̃d] n: **les îles ~** the Shetland Islands, Shetland

shopping [ʃɔpiŋ] nm: **faire du ~** to go shopping

short [ʃɔʀt] nm (pair of) shorts pl

MOT-CLÉ

si [si] adv 1 (oui) yes; **"Paul n'est pas venu"** — **"si!"** "Paul hasn't come" — "Yes he has!"; **je vous assure que si** I assure you he did/she is etc
2 (tellement) so; **si gentil/rapidement** so kind/fast; **(tant et) si bien que** so much so that; **si rapide qu'il soit** however fast he may be
▷ conj if; **si tu veux** if you want; **je me demande si** I wonder if ou whether; **si seulement** if only
▷ nm (Mus) B; (: en chantant la gamme) ti

Sicile [sisil] nf: **la ~** Sicily

sida [sida] nm (= syndrome immuno-déficitaire acquis) AIDS sg

sidéré, e [sideʀe] adj staggered

sidérurgie [sideʀyʀʒi] nf steel industry

siècle [sjɛkl] nm century

siège [sjɛʒ] nm seat; (d'entreprise) head office; (d'organisation) headquarters pl; (Mil) siege; **~ social** registered office; **siéger** /3, 6/ vi to sit

sien, ne [sjɛ̃, sjɛn] pron: **le (la) ~(ne), les ~(ne)s** (d'un homme) his; (d'une femme) hers; (d'une chose) its

S

sieste [sjɛst] nf (afternoon) snooze ou nap; **faire la ~** to have a snooze ou nap

sifflement [sifləmɑ̃] nm whistle

siffler [sifle] /1/ vi (gén) to whistle; (en respirant) to wheeze; (serpent, vapeur) to hiss ▷ vt (chanson) to whistle; (chien etc) to whistle for; (fille) to whistle at; (pièce, orateur) to hiss, boo; (fin du match, départ) to blow one's whistle for; (fam: verre, bouteille) to guzzle

sifflet [siflɛ] nm whistle; **coup de ~** whistle

siffloter [siflɔte] /1/ vi, vt to whistle

sigle [sigl] nm acronym

signal, -aux [siɲal, -o] nm signal; (indice, écriteau) sign; **donner le ~ de** to give the signal for; **~ d'alarme** alarm signal; **signalement** nm description, particulars pl

signaler [siɲale] /1/ vt to indicate; (vol, perte) to report; (personne, faire un signe) to signal; **~ qch à qn/à qn que** to point out sth to sb/to sb that

signature [siɲatyʀ] nf signature; (action) signing

signe [siɲ] nm sign; (Typo) mark; **faire un ~ de la main/tête** to give a sign with one's hand/shake one's head; **faire ~ à qn** (fig: contacter) to get in touch with sb; **faire ~ à qn d'entrer** to motion (to) sb to come in; **signer** /1/ vt to sign; **se signer** vi to cross o.s.

significatif, -ive [siɲifikatif, -iv] adj significant

signification [siɲifikasjɔ̃] nf meaning

signifier [siɲifje] /7/ vt (vouloir dire) to mean; (faire connaître): **~ qch (à qn)** to make sth known (to sb)

silence [silɑ̃s] nm silence; (Mus) rest; **garder le ~ (sur qch)** to keep silent (about sth), say nothing (about sth); **silencieux, -euse** adj quiet, silent ▷ nm silencer

silhouette [silwɛt] nf outline, silhouette; (figure) figure

sillage [sijaʒ] nm wake

sillon [sijɔ̃] nm furrow; (de disque) groove; **sillonner** /1/ vt to criss-cross

simagrées [simagʀe] nfpl fuss sg

similaire [similɛʀ] adj similar; **similicuir** nm imitation leather; **similitude** nf similarity

simple [sɛ̃pl] adj simple; (non multiple) single; **~ messieurs/dames** nm (Tennis) men's/ladies' singles sg; **~ d'esprit** nm/f simpleton; **~ soldat** private

simplicité [sɛ̃plisite] nf simplicity; **en toute ~** quite simply

simplifier [sɛ̃plifje] /7/ vt to simplify

simuler [simyle] /1/ vt to sham, simulate

simultané, e [simyltane] adj simultaneous

sincère [sɛ̃sɛʀ] adj sincere; **sincèrement** adv sincerely; genuinely; **sincérité** nf sincerity

Singapour [sɛ̃gapuʀ] nm: Singapore

singe [sɛ̃ʒ] nm monkey; (de grande taille) ape; **singer** /3/ vt to ape, mimic; **singeries** nfpl antics

singulariser [sɛ̃gylaʀize] /1/: **se singulariser** vi to call attention to o.s.

singularité [sɛ̃gylaʀite] nf peculiarity

singulier, -ière [sɛ̃gylje, -jɛʀ] adj remarkable, singular ▷ nm singular

sinistre [sinistʀ] adj sinister ▷ nm (incendie) blaze; (catastrophe) disaster; (Assurances) damage (giving rise to a claim); **sinistré, e** adj disaster-stricken ▷ nm/f disaster victim

sinon [sinɔ̃] conj (autrement, sans quoi) otherwise, or else; (sauf) except, other than; (si ce n'est) if not

sinueux, -euse [sinɥø, -øz] adj winding

sinus [sinys] nm (Anat) sinus; (Géom) sine; **sinusite** nf sinusitis

sirène [siʀɛn] nf siren; **~ d'alarme** fire alarm; (pendant la guerre) air-raid siren

sirop [siʀo] *nm (à diluer: de fruit etc)* syrup; *(pharmaceutique)* syrup, mixture; **~ contre la toux** cough syrup *ou* mixture

siroter [siʀote] /1/ *vt* to sip

sismique [sismik] *adj* seismic

site [sit] *nm (paysage, environnement)* setting; *(d'une ville etc: emplacement)* site; **~ (pittoresque)** beauty spot; **~s touristiques** places of interest; **~ web** *(Inform)* website

sitôt [sito] *adv*: **~ parti** as soon as he *etc* had left; **pas de ~** not for a long time; **~ (après) que** as soon as

situation [situasjɔ̃] *nf* situation; *(d'un édifice, d'une ville)* position; location; **~ de famille** marital status

situé, e [sitɥe] *adj*: **bien ~** well situated

situer [sitɥe] /1/ *vt* to site, situate; *(en pensée)* to set, place; **se situer** *vi*: **se ~ à/près de** to be situated at/near

six [sis] *num* six; **sixième** *num* sixth ▷ *nf (Scol)* year 7

skaï® [skaj] *nm* ≈ Leatherette®

skate [sket], **skate-board** [sketbɔʀd] *nm (sport)* skateboarding; *(planche)* skateboard

ski [ski] *nm (objet)* ski; *(sport)* skiing; **faire du ~** to ski; **~ de fond** cross-country skiing; **~ nautique** water-skiing; **~ de piste** downhill skiing; **~ de randonnée** cross-country skiing; **skier** /7/ *vi* to ski; **skieur, -euse** *nm/f* skier

slip [slip] *nm (sous-vêtement)* pants *pl (BRIT)*, briefs *pl*; *(de bain: d'homme)* trunks *pl*; *(: du bikini)* (bikini) briefs *pl*

slogan [slɔgã] *nm* slogan

Slovaquie [slɔvaki] *nf*: **la ~** Slovakia

SMIC [smik] *sigle m* = **salaire minimum interprofessionnel de croissance**

smoking [smɔkiŋ] *nm* dinner *ou* evening suit

SMS *sigle m (= short message service) (service)* SMS; *(message)* text (message)

SNCF *sigle f (= Société nationale des chemins de fer français)* French railways

snob [snɔb] *adj* snobbish ▷ *nm/f* snob; **snobisme** *nm* snobbery, snobbishness

sobre [sɔbʀ] *adj (personne)* temperate, abstemious; *(élégance, style)* sober

sobriquet [sɔbʀikɛ] *nm* nickname

social, e, -aux [sɔsjal, -o] *adj* social

socialisme [sɔsjalism] *nm* socialism; **socialiste** *nm/f* socialist

société [sɔsjete] *nf* society; *(sportive)* club; *(Comm)* company; **la ~ d'abondance/de consommation** the affluent/consumer society; **~ anonyme** ≈ limited company *(BRIT)*, ≈ incorporated company *(US)*

sociologie [sɔsjɔlɔʒi] *nf* sociology

socle [sɔkl] *nm (de colonne, statue)* plinth, pedestal; *(de lampe)* base

socquette [sɔkɛt] *nf* ankle sock

sœur [sœʀ] *nf* sister; *(religieuse)* nun, sister

soi [swa] *pron* oneself; **en ~** *(intrinsèquement)* in itself; **cela va de ~** that *ou* it goes without saying; **soi-disant** *adj inv* so-called ▷ *adv* supposedly

soie [swa] *nf* silk; **soierie** *nf (tissu)* silk

soif [swaf] *nf* thirst; **avoir ~** to be thirsty; **donner ~ à qn** to make sb thirsty

soigné, e [swaɲe] *adj (tenue)* well-groomed, neat; *(travail)* careful, meticulous

soigner [swaɲe] /1/ *vt (malade, maladie: docteur)* to treat; *(: infirmière, mère)* to nurse, look after; *(travail, détails)* to take care over; *(jardin, chevelure, invités)* to look after; **soigneux, -euse** *adj* tidy, neat; *(méticuleux)* painstaking, careful

soi-même [swamɛm] *pron* oneself

soin [swɛ̃] *nm (application)* care; *(propreté, ordre)* tidiness, neatness; **soins** *nmpl (à un malade, blessé)* treatment *sg*, medical attention *sg*; *(hygiène)* care *sg*; **avoir** *ou* **prendre ~**

S

de to take care of, look after; **avoir** ou **prendre ~ de faire** to take care to do; **les premiers ~s** first aid sg

soir [swaʀ] nm evening; **ce ~** this evening, tonight; **à ce ~!** see you this evening (ou tonight)!; **sept/dix heures du ~** seven in the evening/ ten at night; **demain ~** tomorrow evening, tomorrow night; **soirée** nf evening; (réception) party

soit [swa] vb voir **être** ▷ conj (à savoir) namely; (ou): **~ ... ~** either ... or ▷ adv so be it, very well; **~ que ... ~ que** ou **ou que** whether ... or whether

soixantaine [swasɑ̃tɛn] nf: **une ~ (de)** sixty or so, about sixty; **avoir la ~ (âge)** to be around sixty

soixante [swasɑ̃t] num sixty; **soixante-dix** num seventy

soja [sɔʒa] nm soya; (graines) soya beans pl; **germes de ~** beansprouts

sol [sɔl] nm ground; (de logement) floor; (Agr, Géo) soil; (Mus) G (: en chantant la gamme) so(h)

solaire [sɔlɛʀ] adj (énergie etc) solar; (crème etc) sun cpd

soldat [sɔlda] nm soldier

solde [sɔld] nf pay ▷ nm (Comm) balance; **soldes** nmpl ou nfpl (Comm) sales; **en ~** at sale price; **solder** /1/ vt (marchandise) to sell at sale price, sell off

sole [sɔl] nf sole inv (fish)

soleil [sɔlɛj] nm sun; (lumière) sun(light); (temps ensoleillé) sun(shine); **il y a** ou **il fait du ~** it's sunny; **au ~** in the sun

solennel, le [sɔlanɛl] adj solemn

solfège [sɔlfɛʒ] nm rudiments pl of music

solidaire [sɔlidɛʀ] adj: **être ~s** (personnes) to show solidarity, stand ou stick together; **être ~ de** (collègues) to stand by; **solidarité** nf solidarity; **par solidarité (avec)** in sympathy (with)

solide [sɔlid] adj solid; (mur, maison, meuble) solid, sturdy; (connaissances, argument) sound; (personne) robust, sturdy ▷ nm solid

soliste [sɔlist] nm/f soloist

solitaire [sɔlitɛʀ] adj (sans compagnie) solitary, lonely; (lieu) lonely ▷ nm/f (ermite) recluse; (fig: ours) loner

solitude [sɔlityd] nf loneliness; (paix) solitude

solliciter [sɔlisite] /1/ vt (personne) to appeal to; (emploi, faveur) to seek

sollicitude [sɔlisityd] nf concern

soluble [sɔlybl] adj soluble

solution [sɔlysjɔ̃] nf solution; **~ de facilité** easy way out

solvable [sɔlvabl] adj solvent

sombre [sɔ̃bʀ] adj dark; (fig) gloomy; **sombrer** /1/ vi (bateau) to sink; **sombrer dans** (misère, désespoir) to sink into

sommaire [sɔmɛʀ] adj (simple) basic; (expéditif) summary ▷ nm summary

somme [sɔm] nf (Math) sum; (fig) amount; (argent) sum, amount ▷ nm: **faire un ~** to have a (short) nap; **en ~, ~ toute** all in all

sommeil [sɔmɛj] nm sleep; **avoir ~** to be sleepy; **sommeiller** /1/ vi to doze

sommet [sɔmɛ] nm top; (d'une montagne) summit, top; (fig: de la perfection, gloire) height

sommier [sɔmje] nm bed base

somnambule [sɔmnɑ̃byl] nm/f sleepwalker

somnifère [sɔmnifɛʀ] nm sleeping drug; sleeping pill ou tablet

somnoler [sɔmnɔle] /1/ vi to doze

somptueux, -euse [sɔ̃ptɥø, -øz] adj sumptuous

son¹, sa (pl ses) [sɔ̃, sa, se] adj poss (antécédent humain: mâle) his (: femelle) her; (: valeur indéfinie) one's, his (her); (: non humain) its

son² [sɔ̃] nm sound; (de blé etc) bran

sondage [sɔ̃daʒ] nm: **~ (d'opinion)** (opinion) poll

sonde [sɔ̃d] *nf* (Navig) lead *ou* sounding line; (Méd) probe; (Tech: de forage, sondage) drill

sonder [sɔ̃de] /1/ *vt* (Navig) to sound; (Tech) to bore, drill; (fig: personne) to sound out; **~ le terrain** (fig) to see how the land lies

songe [sɔ̃ʒ] *nm* dream; **songer** /3/ *vi*: **songer à** (rêver à) to think over; (envisager) to contemplate, think of; **songer que** to think that; **songeur, -euse** *adj* pensive

sonnant, e [sɔnɑ̃, -ɑ̃t] *adj*: **à huit heures ~es** on the stroke of eight

sonné, e [sɔne] *adj* (fam) cracked; **il est midi ~** it's gone twelve

sonner [sɔne] /1/ *vi* to ring ▷ *vt* (cloche) to ring; (glas, tocsin) to sound; (portier, infirmière) to ring for; **~ faux** (instrument) to sound out of tune; (rire) to ring false

sonnerie [sɔnri] *nf* (son) ringing; (sonnette) bell; (de portable) ringtone; **~ d'alarme** alarm bell

sonnette [sɔnɛt] *nf* bell; **~ d'alarme** alarm bell

sonore [sɔnɔʀ] *adj* (voix) sonorous, ringing; (salle, métal) resonant; (ondes, film, signal) sound *cpd*; **sonorisation** *nf* (équipement: de salle de conférences) public address system, P.A. system; (: de discothèque) sound system; **sonorité** *nf* (de piano, violon) tone; (d'une salle) acoustics *pl*

sophistiqué, e [sɔfistike] *adj* sophisticated

sorbet [sɔʀbɛ] *nm* water ice, sorbet

sorcier, -ière [sɔʀsje, -jɛʀ] *nm/f* sorcerer (witch *ou* sorceress)

sordide [sɔʀdid] *adj* (lieu) squalid; (action) sordid

sort [sɔʀ] *nm* (fortune, destinée) fate; (condition, situation) lot; (magique): **jeter un ~** to cast a spell; **tirer au ~** to draw lots

sorte [sɔʀt] *nf* sort, kind; **de la ~** in that way; **en quelque ~** in a way; **de (telle) ~ que** so that; **faire en ~ que** to see to it that

sortie [sɔʀti] *nf* (issue) way out, exit; (verbale) sally; (promenade) outing; (le soir, au restaurant etc) night out; (Comm: d'un disque) release; (: d'un livre) publication; (: d'un modèle) launching; **~ de bain** (vêtement) bathrobe; **~ de secours** emergency exit

sortilège [sɔʀtilɛʒ] *nm* (magic) spell

sortir [sɔʀtiʀ] /16/ *vi* (gén) to come out; (partir, se promener, aller au spectacle etc) to go out; (bourgeon, plante, numéro gagnant) to come up ▷ *vt* (gén) to take out; (produit, ouvrage, modèle) to bring out; (fam: dire) to come out with; **~ avec qn** to be going out with sb; **~ de** (endroit) to go (ou come) out of, leave; (cadre, compétence) to be outside; (provenir de) to come from; **s'en ~** (malade) to pull through; (d'une difficulté etc) to get through

sosie [sozi] *nm* double

sot, sotte [so, sɔt] *adj* silly, foolish ▷ *nm/f* fool; **sottise** *nf* silliness *no pl*, foolishness *no pl*; (propos, acte) silly *ou* foolish thing (to do *ou* say)

sou [su] *nm*: **près de ses ~s** tight-fisted; **sans le ~** penniless

soubresaut [subʀəso] *nm* start; (cahot) jolt

souche [suʃ] *nf* (d'arbre) stump; (de carnet) counterfoil (BRIT), stub

souci [susi] *nm* (inquiétude) worry; (préoccupation) concern; (Bot) marigold; **se faire du ~** to worry; **soucier** /7/: **se soucier de** *vt* to care about; **soucieux, -euse** *adj* concerned, worried

soucoupe [sukup] *nf* saucer; **~ volante** flying saucer

soudain, e [sudɛ̃, -ɛn] *adj* (douleur, mort) sudden ▷ *adv* suddenly, all of a sudden

Soudan [sudɑ̃] *nm*: **le ~** Sudan

soude [sud] *nf* soda

S

souder [sude] /1/ vt (avec fil à souder) to solder; (par soudure autogène) to weld; (fig) to bind ou knit together

soudure [sudyʀ] nf soldering; welding; (joint) soldered joint; weld

souffle [sufl] nm (en expirant) breath; (en soufflant) puff, blow; (respiration) breathing; (d'explosion, de ventilateur) blast; (du vent) blowing; **être à bout de ~** to be out of breath; **un ~ d'air** ou **de vent** a breath of air

soufflé, e [sufle] adj (fam: ahuri, stupéfié) staggered ▷ nm (Culin) soufflé

souffler [sufle] /1/ vi (gén) to blow; (haleter) to puff (and blow) ▷ vt (feu, bougie) to blow out; (chasser: poussière etc) to blow away; (Tech: verre) to blow; (dire): **~ qch à qn** to whisper sth to sb

souffrance [sufʀɑ̃s] nf suffering; **en ~** (affaire) pending

souffrant, e [sufʀɑ̃, -ɑ̃t] adj unwell

souffre-douleur [sufʀədulœʀ] nm inv butt, underdog

souffrir [sufʀiʀ] /18/ vi to suffer; (éprouver des douleurs) to be in pain ▷ vt to suffer, endure; (supporter) to bear, stand; **~ de** (maladie, froid) to suffer from; **elle ne peut pas le ~** she can't stand ou bear him

soufre [sufʀ] nm sulphur

souhait [swɛ] nm wish; **tous nos ~s pour la nouvelle année** (our) best wishes for the New Year; **souhaitable** adj desirable

souhaiter [swete] /1/ vt to wish for; **~ la bonne année à qn** to wish sb a happy New Year; **~ que** to hope that

soûl, e [su, sul] adj drunk ▷ nm: **tout son ~** to one's heart's content

soulagement [sulaʒmɑ̃] nm relief

soulager [sulaʒe] /3/ vt to relieve

soûler [sule] /1/ vt: **~ qn** to get sb drunk; (boisson) to make sb drunk; (fig) to make sb's head spin ou reel; **se soûler** vi to get drunk

soulever [sulve] /5/ vt to lift; (vagues, poussière) to send up; (enthousiasme) to arouse; (question, débat, protestations, difficultés) to raise; **se soulever** vi (peuple) to rise up; (personne couchée) to lift o.s. up

soulier [sulje] nm shoe

souligner [suliɲe] /1/ vt to underline; (fig) to emphasize, stress

soumettre [sumɛtʀ] /56/ vt (pays) to subject, subjugate; (rebelles) to put down, subdue; **~ qch à qn** (projet etc) to submit sth to sb; **se ~ (à)** to submit (to)

soumis, e [sumi, -iz] adj submissive; **soumission** nf submission

soupçon [supsɔ̃] nm suspicion; (petite quantité): **un ~ de** a hint ou touch of; **soupçonner** /1/ vt to suspect; **soupçonneux, -euse** adj suspicious

soupe [sup] nf soup

souper [supe] /1/ vi to have supper ▷ nm supper

soupeser [supəze] /5/ vt to weigh in one's hand(s); (fig) to weigh up

soupière [supjɛʀ] nf (soup) tureen

soupir [supiʀ] nm sigh; **pousser un ~ de soulagement** to heave a sigh of relief

soupirer [supiʀe] /1/ vi to sigh

souple [supl] adj supple; (fig: règlement, caractère) flexible; (: démarche, taille) lithe, supple; **souplesse** nf suppleness; (de caractère) flexibility

source [suʀs] nf (point d'eau) spring; (d'un cours d'eau, fig) source; **tenir qch de bonne ~/de ~ sûre** to have sth on good authority/from a reliable source

sourcil [suʀsij] nm (eye)brow; **sourciller** /1/ vi: **sans sourciller** without turning a hair ou batting an eyelid

sourd, e [suʀ, suʀd] adj deaf; (bruit, voix) muffled; (douleur) dull ▷ nm/f deaf person; **faire la ~e oreille** to turn a deaf ear; **sourdine** nf (Mus) mute; **en sourdine** softly, quietly; **sourd-muet, sourde-muette** adj with a speech and hearing impairment

souriant, e [suʀjɑ̃, -ɑ̃t] adj cheerful
sourire [suʀiʀ] /36/ nm smile ▷ vi to
smile; **~ à qn** to smile at sb; (fig: plaire
à) to appeal to sb; (chance) to smile on
sb; **garder le ~** to keep smiling
souris [suʀi] nf mouse
sournois, e [suʀnwa, -waz] adj
deceitful, underhand
sous [su] prép under; **~ la pluie/le
soleil** in the rain/sunshine; **~ terre**
underground; **~ peu** shortly, before
long; **sous-bois** nm inv undergrowth
souscrire [suskʀiʀ] /39/: **~ à** vt to
subscribe to
sous: sous-directeur, -trice nm/f
assistant manager/manageress;
sous-entendre /41/ vt to imply,
infer; **sous-entendu, e** adj implied
▷ nm innuendo, insinuation; **sous-
estimer** /1/ vt to underestimate;
sous-jacent, e adj underlying;
sous-louer /1/ vt to sublet;
sous-marin, e adj (flore, volcan)
submarine; (navigation, pêche, explosif)
underwater ▷ nm submarine;
sous-pull nm thin poloneck sweater;
soussigné, e adj: **je soussigné**
I the undersigned; **sous-sol** nm
basement; **sous-titre** [sutitʀ] nm
subtitle
soustraction [sustʀaksjɔ̃] nf
subtraction
soustraire [sustʀɛʀ] /50/ vt to
subtract, take away; (dérober): **~ qch
à qn** to remove sth from sb; **se ~ à**
(autorité, obligation, devoir) to elude,
escape from
sous: sous-traitant nm
subcontractor; **sous-traiter** /1/ vt, vi
to subcontract; **sous-vêtement** nm
item of underwear; **sous-vêtements**
nmpl underwear sg
soutane [sutan] nf cassock, soutane
soute [sut] nf hold
soutenir [sutniʀ] /22/ vt to support;
(assaut, choc, regard) to stand up to,
withstand; (intérêt, effort) to keep
up; (assurer): **~ que** to maintain that;

soutenu, e adj (efforts) sustained,
unflagging; (style) elevated
souterrain, e [suteʀɛ̃, -ɛn] adj
underground ▷ nm underground
passage
soutien [sutjɛ̃] nm support; **soutien-
gorge** nm bra
soutirer [sutiʀe] /1/ vt: **~ qch à qn** to
squeeze ou get sth out of sb
souvenir [suvniʀ] /22/ nm
(réminiscence) memory; (cadeau)
souvenir ▷ vb: **se ~ de** to remember;
se ~ que to remember that; **en ~ de**
in memory ou remembrance of; **avec
mes affectueux/meilleurs ~s, ...**
with love from, .../regards, ...
souvent [suvɑ̃] adv often; **peu ~**
seldom, infrequently
souverain, e [suvʀɛ̃, -ɛn] nm/f
sovereign, monarch
soyeux, -euse [swajø, -øz] adj silky
spacieux, -euse [spasjø, -øz] adj
spacious; roomy
spaghettis [spageti] nmpl
spaghetti sg
sparadrap [spaʀadʀa] nm adhesive ou
sticking (BRIT) plaster, bandaid® (US)
spatial, e, -aux [spasjal, -o] adj
(Aviat) space cpd
speaker, ine [spikœʀ, -kʀin] nm/f
announcer
spécial, e, -aux [spesjal, -o]
adj special; (bizarre) peculiar;
spécialement adv especially,
particularly; (tout exprès) specially;
spécialiser /1/: **se spécialiser**
vi to specialize; **spécialiste** nm/f
specialist; **spécialité** nf speciality;
(Scol) special field
spécifier [spesifje] /7/ vt to specify,
state
spécimen [spesimɛn] nm specimen
spectacle [spɛktakl] nm (tableau,
scène) sight; (représentation)
show; (industrie) show business;
spectaculaire adj spectacular
spectateur, -trice [spɛktatœʀ,
-tʀis] nm/f (Ciné etc) member of the

S

audience; (*Sport*) spectator; (*d'un événement*) onlooker, witness

spéculer [spekyle] /1/ *vi* to speculate

spéléologie [speleɔlɔʒi] *nf* potholing

sperme [spɛʀm] *nm* semen, sperm

sphère [sfɛʀ] *nf* sphere

spirale [spiʀal] *nf* spiral

spirituel, le [spiʀityɛl] *adj* spiritual; (*fin, piquant*) witty

splendide [splɑ̃did] *adj* splendid

spontané, e [spɔ̃tane] *adj* spontaneous; **spontanéité** *nf* spontaneity

sport [spɔʀ] *nm* sport ▷ *adj inv* (*vêtement*) casual; **faire du ~** to do sport; **~s d'hiver** winter sports; **sportif, -ive** *adj* (*journal, association, épreuve*) sports *cpd*; (*allure, démarche*) athletic; (*attitude, esprit*) sporting

spot [spɔt] *nm* (*lampe*) spot(light); (*annonce*): **~ (publicitaire)** commercial (break)

square [skwaʀ] *nm* public garden(s)

squelette [skəlɛt] *nm* skeleton; **squelettique** *adj* scrawny

SRAS [sʀas] *sigle m* (= *syndrome respiratoire aigu sévère*) SARS

Sri Lanka [sʀilɑ̃ka] *nm*: **le ~** Sri Lanka

stabiliser [stabilize] /1/ *vt* to stabilize

stable [stabl] *adj* stable, steady

stade [stad] *nm* (*Sport*) stadium; (*phase, niveau*) stage

stage [staʒ] *nm* (*cours*) training course; **~ de formation (professionnelle)** vocational (training) course; **~ de perfectionnement** advanced training course; **stagiaire** [staʒjɛʀ] *nm/f, adj* trainee

▌ Attention à ne pas traduire *stage* par le mot anglais *stage*.

stagner [stagne] /1/ *vi* to stagnate

stand [stɑ̃d] *nm* (*d'exposition*) stand; (*de foire*) stall; **~ de tir** (*à la foire, Sport*) shooting range

standard [stɑ̃daʀ] *adj inv* standard ▷ *nm* switchboard; **standardiste** *nm/f* switchboard operator

standing [stɑ̃diŋ] *nm* standing; **de grand ~** luxury

starter [staʀtɛʀ] *nm* (*Auto*) choke

station [stasjɔ̃] *nf* station; (*de bus*) stop; (*de villégiature*) resort; **~ de ski** ski resort; **~ de taxis** taxi rank (BRIT) *ou* stand (US); **stationnement** *nm* parking; **stationner** /1/ *vi* to park; **station-service** *nf* service station

statistique [statistik] *nf* (*science*) statistics *sg*; (*rapport, étude*) statistic ▷ *adj* statistical

statue [staty] *nf* statue

statu quo [statykwo] *nm* status quo

statut [staty] *nm* status; **statuts** *nmpl* (*Jur, Admin*) statutes; **statutaire** *adj* statutory

Sté *abr* (= *société*) soc

steak [stɛk] *nm* steak; **~ haché** hamburger

sténo [stenɔ] *nf* (*aussi*: **~graphie**) shorthand

stérile [steʀil] *adj* sterile

stérilet [steʀilɛ] *nm* coil, loop

stériliser [steʀilize] /1/ *vt* to sterilize

stimulant, e [stimylɑ̃, -ɑ̃t] *adj* stimulating ▷ *nm* (*Méd*) stimulant; (*fig*) stimulus, incentive

stimuler [stimyle] /1/ *vt* to stimulate

stipuler [stipyle] /1/ *vt* to stipulate

stock [stɔk] *nm* stock; **stocker** /1/ *vt* to stock

stop [stɔp] *nm* (*Auto: écriteau*) stop sign; (: *signal*) brake-light; **faire du ~** (*fam*) to hitch(hike); **stopper** /1/ *vt* to stop ▷ *vi* to stop, halt

store [stɔʀ] *nm* blind; (*de magasin*) shade, awning

strabisme [stʀabism] *nm* squint(ing)

strapontin [stʀapɔ̃tɛ̃] *nm* jump *ou* foldaway seat

stratégie [stʀateʒi] *nf* strategy; **stratégique** *adj* strategic

stress [stʀɛs] *nm inv* stress;
stressant, e *adj* stressful; **stresser**
/1/ *vt*: **stresser qn** to make sb (feel)
tense

strict, e [stʀikt] *adj* strict; (*tenue,
décor*) severe, plain; **le ~ nécessaire/
minimum** the bare essentials/
minimum

strident, e [stʀidã, -ãt] *adj* shrill,
strident

strophe [stʀɔf] *nf* verse, stanza

structure [stʀyktyʀ] *nf* structure; **~s
d'accueil/touristiques** reception/
tourist facilities

studieux, -euse [stydjø, -øz] *adj*
studious

studio [stydjo] *nm* (*logement*) studio
flat (BRIT) *ou* apartment (US);
(*d'artiste, TV etc*) studio

stupéfait, e [stypefɛ, -ɛt] *adj*
astonished

stupéfiant, e [stypefjã, -ãt] *adj*
(*étonnant*) stunning, astonishing
▷ *nm* (*Méd*) drug, narcotic

stupéfier [stypefje] /7/ *vt* (*étonner*)
to stun, astonish

stupeur [stypœʀ] *nf* astonishment

stupide [stypid] *adj* stupid;
stupidité *nf* stupidity *no pl*; (*parole,
acte*) stupid thing (to say *ou* do)

style [stil] *nm* style

stylé, e [stile] *adj* well-trained

styliste [stilist] *nm/f* designer

stylo [stilo] *nm*: **~ (à encre)**
(fountain) pen; **~ (à) bille** ballpoint
pen

su, e [sy] *pp de* **savoir** ▷ *nm*: **au su de**
with the knowledge of

suave [sɥav] *adj* sweet

subalterne [sybaltɛʀn] *adj* (*employé,
officier*) junior; (*rôle*) subordinate,
subsidiary ▷ *nm/f* subordinate

subconscient [sypkɔ̃sjã] *nm*
subconscious

subir [sybiʀ] /2/ *vt* (*affront, dégâts,
mauvais traitements*) to suffer;
(*traitement, opération, châtiment*) to
undergo

subit, e [sybi, -it] *adj* sudden;
subitement *adv* suddenly, all of a
sudden

subjectif, -ive [sybʒɛktif, -iv] *adj*
subjective

subjonctif [sybʒɔ̃ktif] *nm*
subjunctive

subjuguer [sybʒyge] /1/ *vt* to
subjugate

submerger [sybmɛʀʒe] /3/ *vt* to
submerge; (*fig*) to overwhelm

subordonné, e [sybɔʀdɔne] *adj,
nm/f* subordinate

subrepticement [sybʀɛptismã]
adv surreptitiously

subside [sypsid] *nm* grant

subsidiaire [sypsidjɛʀ] *adj*:
question ~ deciding question

subsister [sybziste] /1/ *vi* (*rester*) to
remain, subsist; (*survivre*) to live on

substance [sypstãs] *nf* substance

substituer [sypstitɥe] /1/ *vt*: **~ qn/
qch à** to substitute sb/sth for; **se ~ à
qn** (*évincer*) to substitute o.s. for sb

substitut [sypstity] *nm* (*succédané*)
substitute

subterfuge [sybtɛʀfyʒ] *nm* subterfuge

subtil, e [sybtil] *adj* subtle

subvenir [sybvəniʀ] /22/: **~ à** *vt*
to meet

subvention [sybvãsjɔ̃] *nf* subsidy,
grant; **subventionner** /1/ *vt* to
subsidize

suc [syk] *nm* (*Bot*) sap; (*de viande,
fruit*) juice

succéder [syksede] /6/: **~ à** *vt* to
succeed; **se succéder** *vi* (*accidents,
années*) to follow one another

succès [syksɛ] *nm* success; **avoir du
~** to be a success, be successful; **à ~**
successful; **~ de librairie** bestseller

successeur [syksesœʀ] *nm*
successor

successif, -ive [syksesif, -iv] *adj*
successive

succession [syksesjɔ̃] *nf* (*série, Pol*)
succession; (*Jur: patrimoine*) estate,
inheritance

succomber [sykɔ̃be] /1/ vi to die, succumb; (fig): **~ à** to succumb to
succulent, e [sykylɑ̃, -ɑ̃t] adj delicious
succursale [sykyrsal] nf branch
sucer [syse] /3/ vt to suck; **sucette** nf (bonbon) lollipop; (de bébé) dummy (BRIT), pacifier (US)
sucre [sykr] nm (substance) sugar; (morceau) lump of sugar, sugar lump ou cube; **~ en morceaux/cristallisé/en poudre** lump ou cube/granulated/caster sugar; **~ glace** icing sugar (BRIT), confectioner's sugar (US); **~ d'orge** barley sugar; **sucré, e** adj (produit alimentaire) sweetened; (au goût) sweet; **sucrer** /1/ vt (thé, café) to sweeten, put sugar in; **sucrerie** nf sugar refinery; **sucreries** nfpl (bonbons) sweets, sweet things; **sucrier** nm (récipient) sugar bowl ou basin
sud [syd] nm: **le ~** the south ▷ adj inv south; (côte) south, southern; **au ~** (situation) in the south; (direction) to the south; **au ~ de** (to the) south of; **sud-africain, e** adj South African ▷ nm/f: **Sud-Africain, e** South African; **sud-américain, e** adj South American ▷ nm/f: **Sud-Américain, e** South American; **sud-est** nm, adj inv south-east; **sud-ouest** nm, adj inv south-west
Suède [sɥɛd] nf: **la ~** Sweden; **suédois, e** adj Swedish ▷ nm (Ling) Swedish ▷ nm/f: **Suédois, e** Swede
suer [sɥe] /1/ vi to sweat; (suinter) to ooze; **sueur** nf sweat; **en sueur** sweating, in a sweat; **avoir des sueurs froides** to be in a cold sweat
suffire [syfir] /37/ vi (être assez): **~ (à qn/pour qch/pour faire)** to be enough ou sufficient (for sb/for sth/to do); **il suffit d'une négligence/qu'on oublie pour que …** it only takes one act of carelessness/one only needs to forget for …; **ça suffit!** that's enough!

suffisamment [syfizamɑ̃] adv sufficiently, enough; **~ de** sufficient, enough
suffisant, e [syfizɑ̃, -ɑ̃t] adj sufficient; (résultats) satisfactory; (vaniteux) self-important, bumptious
suffixe [syfiks] nm suffix
suffoquer [syfɔke] /1/ vt to choke, suffocate; (stupéfier) to stagger, astound ▷ vi to choke, suffocate
suffrage [syfraʒ] nm (Pol: voix) vote
suggérer [sygʒere] /6/ vt to suggest; **suggestion** nf suggestion
suicide [sɥisid] nm suicide; **suicider** /1/: **se suicider** vi to commit suicide
suie [sɥi] nf soot
suisse [sɥis] adj Swiss ▷ nm/f: **S~** Swiss inv ▷ nf: **la S~** Switzerland; **la S~ romande/allemande** French-speaking/German-speaking Switzerland
suite [sɥit] nf (continuation: d'énumération etc) rest, remainder; (: de feuilleton) continuation; (: second film etc sur le même thème) sequel; (série) series, succession; (conséquence) result; (ordre, liaison logique) coherence; (appartement, Mus) suite; (escorte) retinue, suite; **suites** nfpl (d'une maladie etc) effects; **une ~ de** a series ou succession of; **prendre la ~ de** (directeur etc) to succeed, take over from; **donner ~ à** (requête, projet) to follow up; **faire ~ à** to follow; **(faisant) ~ à votre lettre du** further to your letter of the; **de ~** (d'affilée) in succession; (immédiatement) at once; **par la ~** afterwards, subsequently; **à la ~** one after the other; **à la ~ de** (derrière) behind; (en conséquence de) following
suivant, e [sɥivɑ̃, -ɑ̃t] adj next, following ▷ prép (selon) according to; **au ~!** next!
suivi, e [sɥivi] adj (effort, qualité) consistent; (cohérent) coherent; **très/peu ~** (cours) well-/poorly-attended

suivre [sɥivʀ] /40/ vt (gén) to follow; (Scol: cours) to attend; (: programme) to keep up with; (Comm: article) to continue to stock ▷ vi to follow; (élève: assimiler le programme) to keep up; **se suivre** vi (accidents, personnes, voitures etc) to follow one after the other; **faire ~** (lettre) to forward; **"à ~"** "to be continued"

sujet, te [syʒɛ, -ɛt] adj: **être ~ à** (vertige etc) to be liable ou subject to ▷ nm/f (d'un souverain) subject ▷ nm subject; **au ~ de** about; **~ de conversation** topic ou subject of conversation; **~ d'examen** (Scol) examination question

super [sypɛʀ] adj inv great, fantastic

superbe [sypɛʀb] adj magnificent, superb

superficie [sypɛʀfisi] nf (surface) area

superficiel, le [sypɛʀfisjɛl] adj superficial

superflu, e [sypɛʀfly] adj superfluous

supérieur, e [sypeʀjœʀ] adj (lèvre, étages, classes) upper; **~ (à)** (plus élevé: température, niveau) higher (than); (meilleur: qualité, produit) superior (to); (excellent, hautain) superior ▷ nm/f superior; **supériorité** nf superiority

supermarché [sypɛʀmaʀʃe] nm supermarket

superposer [sypɛʀpoze] /1/ vt (faire chevaucher) to superimpose; **lits superposés** bunk beds

superpuissance [sypɛʀpɥisɑ̃s] nf superpower

superstitieux, -euse [sypɛʀstisjø, -øz] adj superstitious

superviser [sypɛʀvize] /1/ vt to supervise

supplanter [syplɑ̃te] /1/ vt to supplant

suppléant, e [sypleɑ̃, -ɑ̃t] adj (juge, fonctionnaire) deputy cpd; (professeur) supply cpd (BRIT), substitute cpd (US) ▷ nm/f (professeur) supply ou substitute teacher

suppléer [syplee] /1/ vt (ajouter: mot manquant etc) to supply, provide; (compenser: lacune) to fill in; **~ à** to make up for

supplément [syplemɑ̃] nm supplement; **un ~ de travail** extra ou additional work; **un ~ de frites** etc an extra portion of chips etc; **le vin est en ~** wine is extra; **payer un ~** to pay an additional charge; **supplémentaire** adj additional, further; (train, bus) relief cpd, extra

supplication [syplikasjɔ̃] nf supplication; **supplications** nfpl pleas, entreaties

supplice [syplis] nm torture no pl

supplier [syplije] /7/ vt to implore, beseech

support [sypɔʀ] nm support; **~ audio-visuel** audio-visual aid; **~ publicitaire** advertising medium

supportable [sypɔʀtabl] adj (douleur, température) bearable

supporter¹ [sypɔʀtɛʀ] nm supporter, fan

supporter² [sypɔʀte] vt (conséquences, épreuve) to bear, endure; (défauts, personne) to tolerate, put up with; (chose, chaleur etc) to withstand; (personne, chaleur, vin) to take

⬛ Attention à ne pas traduire *supporter* par to support.

S

supposer [sypoze] /1/ vt to suppose; (impliquer) to presuppose; **en supposant** ou **à ~ que** supposing (that)

suppositoire [sypozitwaʀ] nm suppository

suppression [sypʀesjɔ̃] nf (voir supprimer) removal; deletion; cancellation

supprimer [sypʀime] /1/ vt (cloison, cause, anxiété) to remove; (clause, mot) to delete; (congés, service d'autobus etc) to cancel; (emplois, privilèges, témoin gênant) to do away with

suprême [sypʀɛm] adj supreme

⊙ MOT-CLÉ

sur [syr] *prép* **1** (*position*) on; (: *par-dessus*) over; (: *au-dessus*) above; **pose-le sur la table** put it on the table; **je n'ai pas d'argent sur moi** I haven't any money on me
2 (*direction*) towards; **en allant sur Paris** going towards Paris; **sur votre droite** on *ou* to your right
3 (*à propos de*) on, about; **un livre/ une conférence sur Balzac** a book/ lecture on *ou* about Balzac
4 (*proportion, mesures*) out of; **un sur 10** one in 10; (*Scol*) one out of 10; **4 m sur 2** 4 m by 2; **avoir accident sur accident** to have one accident after another

sûr, e [syr] *adj* sure, certain; (*digne de confiance*) reliable; (*sans danger*) safe; **~ de soi** self-assured, self-confident; **le plus ~ est de** the safest thing is to
surcharge [syrʃarʒ] *nf* (*de passagers, marchandises*) excess load; **surcharger** /3/ *vt* to overload; (*décoration*) to overdo
surcroît [syrkrwa] *nm*: **~ de qch** additional sth; **par** *ou* **de ~** moreover; **en ~** in addition
surdité [syrdite] *nf* deafness
sûrement [syrmɑ̃] *adv* (*sans risques*) safely; (*certainement*) certainly
surenchère [syrɑ̃ʃɛr] *nf* (*aux enchères*) higher bid; **surenchérir** /2/ *vi* to bid higher; (*fig*) to try and outbid each other
surestimer [syrɛstime] /1/ *vt* to overestimate
sûreté [syrte] *nf* (*exactitude: de renseignements etc*) reliability; (*sécurité*) safety; (*d'un geste*) steadiness; **mettre en ~** to put in a safe place; **pour plus de ~** as an extra precaution; to be on the safe side
surf [sœrf] *nm* surfing
surface [syrfas] *nf* surface; (*superficie*) surface area; **une**

grande ~ a supermarket; **faire ~** to surface; **en ~** near the surface; (*fig*) superficially
surfait, e [syrfɛ, -ɛt] *adj* overrated
surfer [sœrfe] /1/ *vi* to surf; **~ sur Internet** to surf *ou* browse the Internet
surgelé, e [syrʒəle] *adj* (deep-)frozen ⊳ *nm*: **les ~s** (deep-)frozen food
surgir [syrʒir] /2/ *vi* to appear suddenly; (*fig: problème, conflit*) to arise
sur: surhumain, e *adj* superhuman; **sur-le-champ** *adv* immediately; **surlendemain** *nm*: **le surlendemain (soir)** two days later (in the evening); **le surlendemain de** two days after; **surmenage** *nm* overwork; **surmener** /5/: **se surmener** *vi* to overwork
surmonter [syrmɔ̃te] /1/ *vt* (*vaincre*) to overcome; (*être au-dessus de*) to top
surnaturel, le [syrnatyrɛl] *adj*, *nm* supernatural
surnom [syrnɔ̃] *nm* nickname
surnombre [syrnɔ̃br] *nm*: **être en ~** to be too many (*ou* one too many)
surpeuplé, e [syrpœple] *adj* overpopulated
surplace [syrplas] *nm*: **faire du ~** to mark time
surplomber [syrplɔ̃be] /1/ *vi* to be overhanging ⊳ *vt* to overhang
surplus [syrply] *nm* (*Comm*) surplus; (*reste*): **~ de bois** wood left over
surprenant, e [syrprənɑ̃, -ɑ̃t] *adj* amazing
surprendre [syrprɑ̃dr] /58/ *vt* (*étonner, prendre à l'improviste*) to amaze; (*tomber sur: intrus etc*) to catch; (*conversation*) to overhear
surpris, e [syrpri, -iz] *adj*: **~ (de/ que)** amazed *ou* surprised (at/that); **surprise** *nf* surprise; **faire une surprise à qn** to give sb a surprise; **surprise-partie** *nf* party
sursaut [syrso] *nm* start, jump; **~ de** (*énergie, indignation*) sudden fit *ou*

burst of; **en ~** with a start; **sursauter** /1/ vi to (give a) start, jump

sursis [syʀsi] nm (Jur: gén) suspended sentence; (aussi fig) reprieve

surtout [syʀtu] adv (avant tout, d'abord) above all; (spécialement, particulièrement) especially; **~, ne dites rien!** whatever you do, don't say anything!; **~ pas!** certainly ou definitely not!; **~ que ...** especially as ...

surveillance [syʀvejɑ̃s] nf watch; (Police, Mil) surveillance; **sous ~ médicale** under medical supervision

surveillant, e [syʀvejɑ̃, -ɑ̃t] nm/f (de prison) warder; (Scol) monitor

surveiller [syʀveje] /1/ vt (enfant, élèves, bagages) to watch, keep an eye on; (prisonnier, suspect) to keep (a) watch on; (territoire, bâtiment) to (keep) watch over; (travaux, cuisson) to supervise; (Scol: examen) to invigilate; **~ son langage/sa ligne** to watch one's language/figure

survenir [syʀvəniʀ] /22/ vi (incident, retards) to occur, arise; (événement) to take place

survêt [syʀvɛt], **survêtement** [syʀvɛtmɑ̃] nm tracksuit

survie [syʀvi] nf survival; **survivant, e** nm/f survivor; **survivre** /46/ vi to survive; **survivre à** (accident etc) to survive

survoler [syʀvɔle] /1/ vt to fly over; (fig: livre) to skim through

survolté, e [syʀvɔlte] adj (fig) worked up

sus [sy(s)]: **en ~ de** prép in addition to, over and above; **en ~** in addition

susceptible [sysɛptibl] adj touchy, sensitive; **~ de faire** (probabilité) liable to do

susciter [sysite] /1/ vt (admiration) to arouse; (obstacles, ennuis): **~ (à qn)** to create (for sb)

suspect, e [syspɛ(kt), -ɛkt] adj suspicious; (témoignage, opinions, vin etc) suspect ▷ nm/f suspect;

suspecter /1/ vt to suspect; (honnêteté de qn) to question, have one's suspicions about

suspendre [syspɑ̃dʀ] /41/ vt (interrompre, démettre) to suspend; (accrocher: vêtement): **~ qch (à)** to hang sth up (on)

suspendu, e [syspɑ̃dy] adj (accroché): **~ à** hanging on (ou from); (perché): **~ au-dessus de** suspended over

suspens [syspɑ̃]: **en ~** adv (affaire) in abeyance; **tenir en ~** to keep in suspense

suspense [syspɑ̃s] nm suspense

suspension [syspɑ̃sjɔ̃] nf suspension; (lustre) pendant light fitting

suture [sytyʀ] nf: **point de ~** stitch

svelte [svɛlt] adj slender, svelte

SVP abr (= s'il vous plaît) please

sweat [swit] nm (fam) sweatshirt

sweat-shirt (pl **sweat-shirts**) [switʃœʀt] nm sweatshirt

syllabe [silab] nf syllable

symbole [sɛ̃bɔl] nm symbol; **symbolique** adj symbolic; (geste, offrande) token cpd; **symboliser** /1/ vt to symbolize

symétrique [simetʀik] adj symmetrical

sympa [sɛ̃pa] adj inv (fam) nice; **sois ~, prête-le moi** be a pal and lend it to me

sympathie [sɛ̃pati] nf (inclination) liking; (affinité) fellow feeling; (condoléances) sympathy; **avoir de la ~ pour qn** to like sb; **sympathique** adj nice, friendly

> Attention à ne pas traduire sympathique par sympathetic.

sympathisant, e [sɛ̃patizɑ̃, -ɑ̃t] nm/f sympathizer

sympathiser [sɛ̃patize] /1/ vi (voisins etc: s'entendre) to get on (BRIT) ou along (US) (well)

symphonie [sɛ̃fɔni] nf symphony

symptôme [sɛ̃ptom] nm symptom

S

synagogue [sinagɔg] *nf* synagogue
syncope [sɛ̃kɔp] *nf* (*Méd*) blackout;
  tomber en ~ to faint, pass out
syndic [sɛ̃dik] *nm* managing agent
syndical, e, -aux [sɛ̃dikal, -o] *adj*
  (trade-)union *cpd*; **syndicaliste** *nm/f*
  trade unionist
syndicat [sɛ̃dika] *nm* (*d'ouvriers,*
  employés) (trade(s)) union; **~**
  d'initiative tourist office *ou* bureau;
  syndiqué, e *adj* belonging to a
  (trade) union; **syndiquer** /1/: **se**
  syndiquer *vi* to form a trade union;
  (*adhérer*) to join a trade union
synonyme [sinɔnim] *adj*
  synonymous ▷ *nm* synonym; **~ de**
  synonymous with
syntaxe [sɛ̃taks] *nf* syntax
synthèse [sɛ̃tɛz] *nf* synthesis
synthétique [sɛ̃tetik] *adj* synthetic
Syrie [siʀi] *nf*: **la ~** Syria
systématique [sistematik] *adj*
  systematic
système [sistɛm] *nm* system; **le ~ D**
  resourcefulness

t' [t] *pron voir* **te**
ta [ta] *adj poss voir* **ton¹**
tabac [taba] *nm* tobacco; (*aussi*: **débit**
  ou **bureau de ~**) tobacconist's (shop)
tabagisme [tabaʒism] *nm*: **~ passif**
  passive smoking
table [tabl] *nf* table; **à ~!** dinner
  etc is ready!; **se mettre à ~** to sit
  down to eat; **mettre** *ou* **dresser/**
  desservir la ~ to lay *ou* set/clear
  the table; **~ à repasser** ironing
  board; **~ de cuisson** hob; **~ des**
  matières (table of) contents *pl*; **~**
  de nuit *ou* **de chevet** bedside table;
  ~ d'orientation viewpoint indicator;
  ~ roulante (tea) trolley (*BRIT*), tea
  wagon (*US*)
tableau, x [tablo] *nm* (*Art*) painting;
  (*reproduction, fig*) picture; (*panneau*)
  board; (*schéma*) table, chart;
  ~ d'affichage notice board; **~ de**
  bord dashboard; (*Aviat*) instrument
  panel; **~ noir** blackboard

tablette [tablɛt] nf (planche) shelf; **~ de chocolat** bar of chocolate; **~ tactile** (Inform) tablet

tablier [tablije] nm apron

tabou [tabu] nm taboo

tabouret [taburɛ] nm stool

tac [tak] nm: **du ~ au ~** tit for tat

tache [taʃ] nf (saleté) stain, mark; (Art, de couleur, lumière) spot; **~ de rousseur** ou **de son** freckle

tâche [taʃ] nf task

tacher [taʃe] /1/ vt to stain, mark

tâcher [taʃe] /1/ vi: **~ de faire** to try to do, endeavour (BRIT) ou endeavor (US) to do

tacheté, e [taʃte] adj: **~ de** speckled ou spotted with

tact [takt] nm tact; **avoir du ~** to be tactful

tactique [taktik] adj tactical ▷ nf (technique) tactics sg; (plan) tactic

taie [tɛ] nf: **~ (d'oreiller)** pillowslip, pillowcase

taille [taj] nf cutting; (d'arbre) pruning; (milieu du corps) waist; (hauteur) height; (grandeur) size; **de ~ à faire** capable of doing; **de ~** sizeable

taille-crayon(s) [tajkRɛjɔ̃] nm inv pencil sharpener

tailler [taje] /1/ vt (pierre, diamant) to cut; (arbre, plante) to prune; (vêtement) to cut out; (crayon) to sharpen

tailleur [tajœR] nm (couturier) tailor; (vêtement) suit; **en ~** (assis) cross-legged

taillis [taji] nm copse

taire [tɛR] /54/ vi: **faire ~ qn** to make sb be quiet; **se taire** vi to be silent ou quiet; **taisez-vous!** be quiet!

Taiwan [tajwan] nf Taiwan

talc [talk] nm talc, talcum powder

talent [talɑ̃] nm talent

talkie-walkie [tɔkiwɔki] nm walkie-talkie

talon [talɔ̃] nm heel; (de chèque, billet) stub, counterfoil (BRIT); **~s plats/ aiguilles** flat/stiletto heels

talus [taly] nm embankment

tambour [tɑ̃buR] nm (Mus, Tech) drum; (musicien) drummer; (porte) revolving door(s pl); **tambourin** nm tambourine

Tamise [tamiz] nf: **la ~** the Thames

tamisé, e [tamize] adj (fig) subdued, soft

tampon [tɑ̃pɔ̃] nm (de coton, d'ouate) pad; (aussi: **~ hygiénique** ou **périodique**) tampon; (amortisseur, Inform: aussi: **mémoire ~**) buffer; (bouchon) plug, stopper; (cachet, timbre) stamp; **tamponner** /1/ vt (timbres) to stamp; (heurter) to crash ou ram into; **tamponneuse** adj f: **autos tamponneuses** dodgems

tandem [tɑ̃dɛm] nm tandem

tandis [tɑ̃di]: **~ que** conj while

tanguer [tɑ̃ge] /1/ vi to pitch (and toss)

tant [tɑ̃] adv so much; **~ de** (sable, eau) so much; (gens, livres) so many; **~ que** as long as; **~ que** as much as; **~ mieux** that's great; (avec une certaine réserve) so much the better; **~ pis** too bad; (conciliant) never mind; **~ bien que mal** as well as can be expected

tante [tɑ̃t] nf aunt

tantôt [tɑ̃to] adv (parfois): **tantôt … tantôt** now … now; (cet après-midi) this afternoon

taon [tɑ̃] nm horsefly

tapage [tapaʒ] nm uproar, din

tapageur, -euse [tapaʒœR, -øz] adj noisy; (voyant) loud, flashy

tape [tap] nf slap

tape-à-l'œil [tapalœj] adj inv flashy, showy

taper [tape] /1/ vt (porte) to bang, slam; (enfant) to slap; (dactylographier) to type (out); (fam: emprunter): **~ qn de 10 euros** to touch sb for 10 euros ▷ vi (soleil) to beat down; **se taper** vt (fam: travail) to get landed with; (: boire, manger) to down; **~ sur qn** to thump sb; (fig) to run sb down; **~ sur qch** (clou etc) to hit sth; (table etc) to bang on sth; **~ à** (porte etc) to knock on; **~ dans** (se servir) to dig into; **~ des mains/pieds** to clap one's hands/stamp one's feet; **~ (à la machine)** to type

tapi, e [tapi] adj: **~ dans/derrière** (caché) hidden away in/behind

tapis [tapi] nm carpet; (petit) rug; **~ roulant** (pour piétons) moving walkway; (pour bagages) carousel; **~ de sol** (de tente) groundsheet; **~ de souris** (Inform) mouse mat

tapisser [tapise] /1/ vt (avec du papier peint) to paper; (recouvrir): **~ qch (de)** to cover sth (with); **tapisserie** nf (tenture, broderie) tapestry; (papier peint) wallpaper

tapissier, -ière [tapisje, -jɛʀ] nm/f: **~-décorateur** interior decorator

tapoter [tapɔte] /1/ vt (joue, main) to pat; (objet) to tap

taquiner [takine] /1/ vt to tease

tard [taʀ] adv late ▷ nm: **sur le ~** late in life; **plus ~** later (on); **au plus ~** at the latest; **il est trop ~** it's too late

tarder [taʀde] /1/ vi (chose) to be a long time coming; (personne): **~ à faire** to delay doing; **il me tarde d'être** I am longing to be; **sans (plus) ~** without (further) delay

tardif, -ive [taʀdif, -iv] adj late

tarif [taʀif] nm: **~ des consommations** price list; **~s postaux/douaniers** postal/customs rates; **des taxis** taxi fares; **~ plein/réduit** (train) full/reduced fare; (téléphone) peak/off-peak rate

tarir [taʀiʀ] /2/ vi to dry up, run dry

tarte [taʀt] nf tart; **~ aux pommes/à la crème** apple/custard tart; **~ Tatin** ≈ apple upside-down tart

tartine [taʀtin] nf slice of bread (and butter (ou jam)); **~ de miel** slice of bread and honey; **tartiner** /1/ vt to spread; **fromage à tartiner** cheese spread

tartre [taʀtʀ] nm (des dents) tartar; (de chaudière) fur, scale

tas [tɑ] nm heap, pile; **un ~ de** (fig) heaps of, lots of; **en ~** in a heap ou pile; **formé sur le ~** trained on the job

tasse [tɑs] nf cup; **~ à café/thé** coffee/teacup

tassé, e [tɑse] adj: **bien ~** (café etc) strong

tasser [tɑse] /1/ vt (terre, neige) to pack down; (entasser): **~ qch dans** to cram sth into; **se tasser** vi (se serrer) to squeeze up; (s'affaisser) to settle; (personne: avec l'âge) to shrink; (fig) to sort itself out, settle down

tâter [tɑte] /1/ vt to feel; (fig) to try out; **~ de** (prison etc) to have a taste of; **se tâter** (hésiter) to be in two minds

tatillon, ne [tatijɔ̃, -ɔn] adj pernickety

tâtonnement [tɑtɔnmɑ̃] nm: **par ~s** (fig) by trial and error

tâtonner [tɑtɔne] /1/ vi to grope one's way along

tâtons [tɑtɔ̃]: **à ~** adv: **chercher/avancer à ~** to grope around for/grope one's way forward

tatouage [tatwaʒ] nm tattoo

tatouer [tatwe] /1/ vt to tattoo

taudis [todi] nm hovel, slum

taule [tol] nf (fam) nick (BRIT), jail

taupe [top] nf mole

taureau, x [tɔʀo] nm bull; (signe): **le T~** Taurus

taux [to] nm rate; (d'alcool) level; **~ d'intérêt** interest rate

taxe [taks] nf tax; (douanière) duty; **toutes ~s comprises** inclusive of tax; **la boutique hors ~s** the duty-free shop; **~ de séjour** tourist tax; **~ à ou sur la valeur ajoutée** value added tax

taxer [takse] /1/ vt (personne) to tax; (produit) to put a tax on, tax

taxi [taksi] nm taxi; (chauffeur: fam) taxi driver

Tchécoslovaquie [tʃekɔslɔvaki] nf: **la ~** Czechoslovakia; **tchèque** adj Czech ▷ nm (Ling) Czech ▷ nm/f:

Tchèque Czech; **la République tchèque** the Czech Republic

Tchétchénie [tʃetʃeni] nf: **la ~** Chechnya

te, t' [tə] pron you; (réfléchi) yourself

technicien, ne [tɛknisjɛ̃, -ɛn] nm/f technician

technico-commercial, e, -aux [tɛknikokɔmɛʀsjal, -o] adj: **agent ~** sales technician

technique [tɛknik] adj technical ▷ nf technique; **techniquement** adv technically

techno [tɛkno] nf: **la (musique) ~** techno (music)

technologie [tɛknɔlɔʒi] nf technology; **technologique** adj technological

teck [tɛk] nm teak

tee-shirt [tiʃœʀt] nm T-shirt, tee-shirt

teindre [tɛ̃dʀ] /52/ vt to dye; **se ~ (les cheveux)** to dye one's hair; **teint, e** adj dyed ▷ nm (du visage) complexion; (: momentané) colour ▷ nf shade; **grand teint** colourfast

teinté, e [tɛ̃te] adj: **~ de** (fig) tinged with

teinter [tɛ̃te] /1/ vt (verre) to tint; (bois) to stain

teinture [tɛ̃tyʀ] nf dye; **~ d'iode** tincture of iodine; **teinturerie** nf dry cleaner's; **teinturier, -ière** nm/f dry cleaner

tel, telle [tɛl] adj (pareil) such; (comme): **~ un/des ...** like a/like ...; (indéfini) such-and-such a; (intensif): **un ~/de ~s ...** such (a)/such ...; **venez ~ jour** come on such-and-such a day; **rien de ~** nothing like it; **~ que** like, such as; **~ quel** as it is ou stands (ou was etc)

télé [tele] nf (fam) TV; **à la ~** on TV ou telly; **télécabine** nf (benne) cable car; **télécarte** nf phonecard; **téléchargeable** adj downloadable; **téléchargement** nm (action) downloading; (fichier) download;

télécharger /3/ vt (recevoir) to download; (transmettre) to upload; **télécommande** nf remote control; **télécopieur** nm fax (machine); **télédistribution** nf cable TV; **télégramme** nm telegram; **télégraphier** /7/ vt to telegraph, cable; **téléguider** /1/ vt to operate by remote control; **télématique** nf telematics sg; **téléobjectif** nm telephoto lens sg; **télépathie** nf telepathy; **téléphérique** nm cable-car

téléphone [telefɔn] nm telephone; **avoir le ~** to be on the (tele)phone; **au ~** on the phone; **~ sans fil** cordless (tele)phone; **téléphoner** /1/ vi to make a phone call; **téléphoner à** to phone, call up; **téléphonique** adj (tele)phone cpd

téléréalité [teleʀealite] nf reality TV

télescope [telɛskɔp] nm telescope

télescoper [telɛskɔpe] /1/ vt to smash up; **se télescoper** (véhicules) to concertina

télé: téléscripteur nm teleprinter; **télésiège** nm chairlift; **téléski** nm ski-tow; **téléspectateur, -trice** nm/f (television) viewer; **télétravail** nm telecommuting; **télévente** nf telesales; **téléviseur** nm television set; **télévision** nf television; **à la télévision** on television; **télévision numérique** digital TV; **télévision par câble/satellite** cable/satellite television

télex [telɛks] nm telex

telle [tɛl] adj f voir **tel**; **tellement** adv (tant) so much; (si) so; **tellement de** (sable, eau) so much; (gens, livres) so many; **il s'est endormi tellement il était fatigué** he was so tired (that) he fell asleep; **pas tellement** not really; **pas tellement fort/lentement** not (all) that strong/slowly; **il ne mange pas tellement** he doesn't eat (all that) much

téméraire [temeʀɛʀ] adj reckless, rash

témoignage [temwaɲaʒ] nm (Jur: déclaration) testimony no pl, evidence no pl; (rapport, récit) account; (fig: d'affection etc) token, mark; (geste) expression

témoigner [temwaɲe] /1/ vt (intérêt, gratitude) to show ▷ vi (Jur) to testify, give evidence; **~ de** to bear witness to, testify to

témoin [temwɛ̃] nm witness ▷ adj: **appartement-~** show flat; **être ~ de** to witness; **~ oculaire** eyewitness

tempe [tɑ̃p] nf temple

tempérament [tɑ̃peʀamɑ̃] nm temperament, disposition; **à ~** (vente) on deferred (payment) terms; (achat) by instalments, hire purchase cpd

température [tɑ̃peʀatyʀ] nf temperature; **avoir ou faire de la ~** to be running ou have a temperature

tempête [tɑ̃pɛt] nf storm; **~ de sable/neige** sand/snowstorm

temple [tɑ̃pl] nm temple; (protestant) church

temporaire [tɑ̃pɔʀɛʀ] adj temporary

temps [tɑ̃] nm (atmosphérique) weather; (durée) time; (époque) time, times pl; (Ling) tense; (Mus) beat; (Tech) stroke; **un ~ de chien** (fam) rotten weather; **quel ~ fait-il?** what's the weather like?; **il fait beau/mauvais ~** the weather is fine/bad; **avoir le ~/tout le ~/juste le ~** to have time/plenty of time/just enough time; **en ~ de paix/guerre** in peacetime/wartime; **en ~ utile ou voulu** in due time ou course; **ces derniers ~** lately; **dans quelque ~** in a (little) while; **de ~ en ~, de ~ à autre** from time to time; **à ~** (partir, arriver) in time; **à ~ complet, à plein ~** adv, adj full-time; **quel ~ partiel, à mi-~** adv, adj part-time; **dans le ~** at one time; **~ d'arrêt** pause, halt; **~ libre** free ou spare time; **~ mort** (Comm) slack period

tenable [tənabl] adj bearable

tenace [tənas] adj persistent

tenant, e [tənɑ̃, -ɑ̃t] nm/f (Sport): **~ du titre** title-holder

tendance [tɑ̃dɑ̃s] nf (opinions) leanings pl, sympathies pl; (inclination) tendency; (évolution) trend ▷ adj inv trendy; **avoir ~ à** to have a tendency to, tend to

tendeur [tɑ̃dœʀ] nm (attache) elastic strap

tendre [tɑ̃dʀ] /41/ adj tender; (bois, roche, couleur) soft ▷ vt (élastique, peau) to stretch; (corde) to tighten; (muscle) to tense; (donner): **~ qch à qn** to hold sth out to sb; (offrir) to offer sb sth; (fig: piège) to set, lay; **se tendre** vi (corde) to tighten; (relations) to become strained; **~ à qch/à faire** to tend towards sth/to do; **~ l'oreille** to prick up one's ears; **~ la main/le bras** to hold out one's hand/stretch out one's arm; **tendrement** adv tenderly; **tendresse** nf tenderness

tendu, e [tɑ̃dy] pp de **tendre** ▷ adj (corde) tight; (muscles) tensed; (relations) strained

ténèbres [tenɛbʀ] nfpl darkness sg

teneur [tənœʀ] nf content; (d'une lettre) terms pl, content

tenir [təniʀ] /22/ vt to hold; (magasin, hôtel) to run; (promesse) to keep ▷ vi to hold; (neige, gel) to last; **se tenir** vi (avoir lieu) to be held, take place; (être: personne) to stand; **se ~ droit** to stand up (ou sit up) straight; **bien se ~** to behave well; **se ~ à qch** to hold on to sth; **s'en ~ à qch** to confine o.s. to sth; **~ à** (personne, objet) to be attached to, care about (ou for); (réputation) to care about; **~ à faire** to want to do; **~ de** (ressembler à) to take after; **ça ne tient qu'à lui** it is entirely up to him; **~ qn pour** to take sb for; **~ qch de qn** (histoire) to have heard ou learnt sth from sb; (qualité, défaut) to have inherited ou got sth from sb; **~ dans** to fit into; **~ compte de qch** to take sth into account; **~ les**

comptes to keep the books; **~ le coup** to hold out; **~ bon** to stand ou hold fast; **~ au chaud/à l'abri** to keep hot/under shelter ou cover; **un manteau qui tient chaud** a warm coat; **tiens (ou tenez), voilà le stylo** there's the pen!; **tiens, voilà Alain!** look, here's Alain!; **tiens?** (surprise) really?

tennis [tenis] nm tennis; (aussi: **court de ~**) tennis court ▷ nmpl, nfpl (aussi: **chaussures de ~**) tennis ou gym shoes; **~ de table** table tennis; **tennisman** nm tennis player

tension [tɑ̃sjɔ̃] nf tension; (Méd) blood pressure; **faire** ou **avoir de la ~** to have high blood pressure

tentation [tɑ̃tasjɔ̃] nf temptation

tentative [tɑ̃tativ] nf attempt

tente [tɑ̃t] nf tent

tenter [tɑ̃te] /1/ vt (éprouver, attirer) to tempt; (essayer): **~ qch/de faire** to attempt ou try sth/to do; **~ sa chance** to try one's luck

tenture [tɑ̃tyʀ] nf hanging

tenu, e [təny] pp de **tenir** ▷ adj: **bien ~** (maison, comptes) well-kept; **~ de faire** (obligé) under an obligation to do ▷ nf (vêtements) clothes pl; (comportement) manners pl, behaviour; (d'une maison) upkeep; **en petite ~e** scantily dressed ou clad

ter [tɛʀ] adj: **16 ~** 16b ou B

terme [tɛʀm] nm term; (fin) end; **être en bons/mauvais ~s avec qn** to be on good/bad terms with sb; **à court/long ~** adj short-/long-term ou -range; adv in the short/long term; **avant ~** (Méd) prematurely; **mettre un ~ à** to put an end ou a stop to

terminaison [tɛʀminɛzɔ̃] nf (Ling) ending

terminal, e, -aux [tɛʀminal, -o] nm terminal ▷ nf (Scol) ≈ year 13 (BRIT), ≈ twelfth grade (US)

terminer [tɛʀmine] /1/ vt to finish; **se terminer** vi to end

terne [tɛʀn] adj dull

ternir [tɛʀniʀ] /2/ vt to dull; (fig) to sully, tarnish; **se ternir** vi to become dull

terrain [teʀɛ̃] nm (sol, fig) ground; (Comm: étendue de terre) land no pl; (: parcelle) plot (of land); (: à bâtir) site; **sur le ~** (fig) on the field; **~ de football/rugby** football/rugby pitch (BRIT) ou field (US); **~ d'aviation** airfield; **~ de camping** campsite; **~ de golf** golf course; **~ de jeu** (pour les petits) playground; (Sport) games field; **~ de sport** sports ground; **~ vague** waste ground no pl

terrasse [teʀas] nf terrace; **à la ~** (café) outside; **terrasser** /1/ vt (adversaire) to floor; (maladie etc) to lay low

terre [tɛʀ] nf (gén, aussi Élec) earth; (substance) soil, earth; (opposé à mer) land no pl; (contrée) land; **terres** nfpl (terrains) lands, land sg; **en ~** (pipe, poterie) clay cpd; **à** ou **par ~** (mettre, être, s'asseoir) on the ground (ou floor); (jeter, tomber) to the ground, down; **~ à ~** adj inv down-to-earth; **~ cuite** terracotta; **la ~ ferme** dry land; **~ glaise** clay

terreau [teʀo] nm compost

terre-plein [tɛʀplɛ̃] nm platform; (sur chaussée) central reservation

terrestre [teʀɛstʀ] adj (surface) earth's, of the earth; (Bot, Zool, Mil) land cpd; (Rel) earthly

terreur [teʀœʀ] nf terror no pl

terrible [teʀibl] adj terrible, dreadful; (fam) terrific; **pas ~** nothing special

terrien, ne [teʀjɛ̃, -ɛn] adj: **propriétaire ~** landowner ▷ nm/f (non martien etc) earthling

terrier [teʀje] nm burrow, hole; (chien) terrier

terrifier [teʀifje] /7/ vt to terrify

terrine [teʀin] nf (récipient) terrine; (Culin) pâté

territoire [teʀitwaʀ] nm territory

terroriser [teʀɔʀize] /1/ vt to terrorize

t

terrorisme [tɛʀɔʀism] *nm* terrorism;
terroriste [tɛʀɔʀist] *nm/f* terrorist
tertiaire [tɛʀsjɛʀ] *adj* tertiary ▷ *nm*
(*Écon*) service industries *pl*
tes [te] *adj poss voir* **ton¹**
test [tɛst] *nm* test
testament [tɛstamɑ̃] *nm* (*Jur*) will;
(*fig*) legacy; (*Rel*): **T~** Testament
tester [tɛste] /1/ *vt* to test
testicule [tɛstikyl] *nm* testicle
tétanos [tetanos] *nm* tetanus
têtard [tɛtaʀ] *nm* tadpole
tête [tɛt] *nf* head; (*cheveux*) hair *no
pl*; (*visage*) face; **de ~** *adj* (*wagon etc*)
front *cpd* ▷ *adv* (*calculer*) in one's head,
mentally; **perdre la ~** (*fig*) (*s'affoler*)
to lose one's head; (*devenir fou*) to go off
one's head; **tenir ~ à qn** to stand up
to *ou* defy sb; **la ~ en bas** with one's
head down; **la ~ la première** (*tomber*)
head-first; **faire une ~** (*Football*) to
head the ball; **faire la ~** (*fig*) to sulk;
en ~ (*Sport*) in the lead; **à la ~ de** at
the head of; **à ~ reposée** in a more
leisurely moment; **n'en faire qu'à
sa ~** to do as one pleases; **en avoir
par-dessus la ~** to be fed up; **en ~
à ~** in private, alone together; **de la
~ aux pieds** from head to toe; **~ de
lecture** (playback) head; **~ de liste**
(*Pol*) chief candidate; **~ de mort**
skull and crossbones; **~ de série**
(*Tennis*) seeded player, seed; **~ de
Turc** (*fig*) whipping boy (*BRIT*), butt;
tête-à-queue *nm inv*: **faire un tête-
à-queue** to spin round; **tête-à-tête**
nm inv: **en tête-à-tête** in private,
alone together
téter [tete] /6/ *vt*: **~ (sa mère)** to
suck at one's mother's breast, feed
tétine [tetin] *nf* teat; (*sucette*)
dummy (*BRIT*), pacifier (*US*)
têtu, e [tety] *adj* stubborn, pigheaded
texte [tɛkst] *nm* text; (*morceau choisi*)
passage
texter [tɛkste] /1/ *vi, vt* to text
textile [tɛkstil] *adj* textile *cpd* ▷ *nm*
textile; (*industrie*) textile industry

Texto [tɛksto] *nm* text (message)
textoter [tɛkstɔte] /1/ *vi, vt* to text
texture [tɛkstyʀ] *nf* texture
TGV *sigle m* = **train à grande vitesse**
thaïlandais, e [tailɑ̃dɛ, -ɛz] *adj* Thai
▷ *nm/f*: **T~, e** Thai
Thaïlande [tailɑ̃d] *nf*: **la ~** Thailand
thé [te] *nm* tea; **prendre le ~** to have
tea; **~ au lait/citron** tea with milk/
lemon; **faire le ~** to make the tea
théâtral, e, -aux [teatʀal, -o] *adj*
theatrical
théâtre [teatʀ] *nm* theatre; (*péj*)
playacting; (*fig: lieu*): **le ~ de** the scene
of; **faire du ~** to act
théière [tejɛʀ] *nf* teapot
thème [tɛm] *nm* theme; (*Scol:
traduction*) prose (composition)
théologie [teɔlɔʒi] *nf* theology
théorie [teɔʀi] *nf* theory; **théorique**
adj theoretical
thérapie [teʀapi] *nf* therapy
thermal, e, -aux [tɛʀmal, -o] *adj*:
station ~e spa; **cure ~e** water cure
thermomètre [tɛʀmɔmɛtʀ] *nm*
thermometer
thermos® [tɛʀmos] *nm ou f*:
(bouteille) ~ vacuum *ou* Thermos®
flask : *BRIT ou* bottle (*US*)
thermostat [tɛʀmɔsta] *nm*
thermostat
thèse [tɛz] *nf* thesis
thon [tɔ̃] *nm* tuna (fish)
thym [tɛ̃] *nm* thyme
Tibet [tibɛ] *nm*: **le ~** Tibet
tibia [tibja] *nm* shin; shinbone, tibia
TIC *sigle fpl* (= *technologies de l'information
et de la communication*) ICT *sg*
tic [tik] *nm* tic, (nervous) twitch; (*de
langage etc*) mannerism
ticket [tikɛ] *nm* ticket; **~ de caisse**
till receipt
tiède [tjɛd] *adj* lukewarm; (*vent, air*)
mild, warm; **tiédir** /2/ *vi* (*se réchauffer*)
to grow warmer; (*refroidir*) to cool
tien, tienne [tjɛ̃, tjɛn] *pron*: **le (la)
~(ne)** yours; **les ~(ne)s** yours; **à la
~ne!** cheers!

tiens [tjɛ̃] vb, excl voir **tenir**

tiercé [tjɛʀse] nm system of forecast betting giving first three horses

tiers, tierce [tjɛʀ, tjɛʀs] adj third ▷ nm (Jur) third party; (fraction) third; **le ~ monde** the third world

tige [tiʒ] nf stem; (baguette) rod

tignasse [tiɲas] nf (péj) shock ou mop of hair

tigre [tigʀ] nm tiger; **tigré, e** adj (rayé) striped; (tacheté) spotted; (chat) tabby; **tigresse** nf tigress

tilleul [tijœl] nm lime (tree), linden (tree); (boisson) lime(-blossom) tea

timbre [tɛ̃bʀ] nm (tampon) stamp; (aussi: **~-poste**) (postage) stamp; (Mus: de voix, instrument) timbre, tone

timbré, e [tɛ̃bʀe] adj (fam) cracked

timide [timid] adj shy; (timoré) timid; **timidement** adv shyly; timidly; **timidité** nf shyness; timidity

tintamarre [tɛ̃tamaʀ] nm din, uproar

tinter [tɛ̃te] /1/ vi to ring, chime; (argent, clés) to jingle

tique [tik] nf tick (insect)

tir [tiʀ] nm (sport) shooting; (fait ou manière de tirer) firing no pl; (rafale) fire; (stand) shooting gallery; **~ à l'arc** archery

tirage [tiʀaʒ] nm (action) printing; (Photo) print; (de journal) circulation; (de livre) (print-)run; edition; (de loterie) draw; **~ au sort** drawing lots

tire [tiʀ] nf: **vol à la ~** pickpocketing

tiré, e [tiʀe] adj (visage, traits) drawn; **~ par les cheveux** far-fetched

tire-bouchon [tiʀbuʃɔ̃] nm corkscrew

tirelire [tiʀliʀ] nf moneybox

tirer [tiʀe] /1/ vt (gén) to pull; (ligne, trait) to draw; (rideau) to draw; (carte, conclusion, chèque) to draw; (en faisant feu: balle, coup) to fire; (: animal) to shoot; (journal, livre, photo) to print; (Football: corner etc) to take ▷ vi (faire feu) to fire; (faire du tir, Football) to shoot; **se tirer** vi (fam) to push off;

(aussi: **s'en ~**) (éviter le pire) to get off; (survivre) to pull through; (se débrouiller) to manage; (extraire): **~ qch de** to take ou pull sth out of; **~ sur** (corde, poignée) to pull on ou at; (faire feu sur) to shoot ou fire at; (pipe) to draw on; (fig: avoisiner) to verge ou border on; **~ qn de** (embarras etc) to help ou get sb out of; **~ à l'arc/la carabine** to shoot with a bow and arrow/with a rifle; **~ à sa fin** to be drawing to an end; **~ qch au clair** to clear sth up; **~ au sort** to draw lots; **~ parti de** to take advantage of; **~ profit de** to profit from; **~ les cartes** to read ou tell the cards

tiret [tiʀe] nm dash

tireur [tiʀœʀ] nm gunman; **~ d'élite** marksman

tiroir [tiʀwaʀ] nm drawer; **tiroir-caisse** nm till

tisane [tizan] nf herb tea

tisser [tise] /1/ vt to weave

tissu [tisy] nm fabric, material, cloth no pl; (Anat, Bio) tissue; **tissu-éponge** nm (terry) towelling no pl

titre [titʀ] nm (gén) title; (de journal) headline; (diplôme) qualification; (Comm) security; **en ~** (champion, responsable) official; **à juste ~** rightly; **à quel ~?** on what grounds?; **à aucun ~** on no account; **au même ~ (que)** in the same way (as); **à ~ d'information** for (your) information; **à ~ gracieux** free of charge; **à ~ d'essai** on a trial basis; **à ~ privé** in a private capacity; **~ de propriété** title deed; **~ de transport** ticket

tituber [titybe] /1/ vi to stagger ou reel (along)

titulaire [titylɛʀ] adj (Admin) with tenure ▷ nm/f (de permis) holder; **être ~ de** (diplôme, permis) to hold

toast [tost] nm slice ou piece of toast; (de bienvenue) (welcoming) toast; **porter un ~ à qn** to propose ou drink a toast to sb

toboggan [tɔbɔgɑ̃] nm slide; (Auto) flyover

toc [tɔk] nm: **en toc** imitation cpd ▷ excl: **toc, toc** knock knock

tocsin [tɔksɛ̃] nm alarm (bell)

tohu-bohu [tɔybɔy] nm commotion

toi [twa] pron you

toile [twal] nf (tableau) canvas; **de** ou **en ~** (pantalon) cotton; (sac) canvas; **~ d'araignée** cobweb; **la T~** (Internet) the Web; **~ cirée** oilcloth; **~ de fond** (fig) backdrop

toilette [twalɛt] nf (habits) outfit; **toilettes** nfpl toilet sg; **faire sa ~** to have a wash, get washed; **articles de ~** toiletries

toi-même [twamɛm] pron yourself

toit [twa] nm roof; **~ ouvrant** sun roof

toiture [twatyʀ] nf roof

Tokyo [tɔkjo] n Tokyo

tôle [tol] nf (plaque) steel (ou iron) sheet; **~ ondulée** corrugated iron

tolérable [tɔleʀabl] adj tolerable

tolérant, e [tɔleʀɑ̃, -ɑ̃t] adj tolerant

tolérer [tɔleʀe] /6/ vt to tolerate; (Admin: hors taxe etc) to allow

tollé [tɔle] nm: **un ~ (de protestations)** a general outcry

tomate [tɔmat] nf tomato; **~s farcies** stuffed tomatoes

tombe [tɔ̃b] nf (sépulture) grave; (avec monument) tomb

tombeau, x [tɔ̃bo] nm tomb

tombée [tɔ̃be] nf: **à la ~ du jour** ou **de la nuit** at nightfall

tomber [tɔ̃be] /1/ vi to fall; (fièvre, vent) to drop ▷ vt: **laisser ~** (objet) to drop; (personne) to let down; (activité) to give up; **laisse ~!** forget it!; **faire ~** to knock over; **~ sur** (rencontrer) to come across; **~ de fatigue/sommeil** to drop from exhaustion/be falling asleep on one's feet; **~ à l'eau** (projet etc) to fall through; **~ en panne** to break down; **~ en ruine** to fall into ruins; **ça tombe bien/mal** (fig) that's come at the right/wrong time; **il**

est bien/mal tombé (fig) he's been lucky/unlucky

tombola [tɔ̃bɔla] nf raffle

tome [tɔm] nm volume

ton¹, ta [tɔ̃, ta, te] (pl **tes**) adj poss your

ton² [tɔ̃] nm (gén) tone; (couleur) shade, tone; **de bon ~** in good taste

tonalité [tɔnalite] nf (au téléphone) dialling tone

tondeuse [tɔ̃døz] nf (à gazon) (lawn) mower; (du coiffeur) clippers pl; (pour la tonte) shears pl

tondre [tɔ̃dʀ] /41/ vt (pelouse, herbe) to mow; (haie) to cut, clip; (mouton, toison) to shear; (cheveux) to crop

tongs [tɔ̃g] nfpl flip-flops

tonifier [tɔnifje] /7/ vt (peau, organisme) to tone up

tonique [tɔnik] adj fortifying ▷ nm tonic

tonne [tɔn] nf metric ton, tonne

tonneau, x [tɔno] nm (à vin, cidre) barrel; **faire des ~x** (voiture, avion) to roll over

tonnelle [tɔnɛl] nf bower, arbour

tonner [tɔne] /1/ vi to thunder; **il tonne** it is thundering, there's some thunder

tonnerre [tɔnɛʀ] nm thunder

tonus [tɔnys] nm energy

top [tɔp] nm: **au troisième ~** at the third stroke ▷ adj: **~ secret** top secret

topinambour [tɔpinɑ̃buʀ] nm Jerusalem artichoke

torche [tɔʀʃ] nf torch

torchon [tɔʀʃɔ̃] nm cloth; (à vaisselle) tea towel ou cloth

tordre [tɔʀdʀ] /41/ vt (chiffon) to wring; (barre, fig: visage) to twist; **se tordre** vi; **se ~ le poignet/la cheville** to twist one's wrist/ankle; **se ~ de douleur/rire** to writhe in pain/be doubled up with laughter; **tordu, e** adj (fig) twisted; (fig) crazy

tornade [tɔʀnad] nf tornado

torrent [tɔʀɑ̃] nm mountain stream

torsade [tɔʀsad] *nf*: **un pull à ~s** a cable sweater

torse [tɔʀs] *nm* chest; (*Anat, Sculpture*) torso; **~ nu** stripped to the waist

tort [tɔʀ] *nm* (*défaut*) fault; **torts** *nmpl* (*Jur*) fault *sg*; **avoir ~** to be wrong; **être dans son ~** to be in the wrong; **donner ~ à qn** to lay the blame on sb; **causer du ~ à** to harm; **à ~** wrongly; **à ~ et à travers** wildly

torticolis [tɔʀtikɔli] *nm* stiff neck

tortiller [tɔʀtije] /1/ *vt* to twist; (*moustache*) to twirl; **se tortiller** *vi* to wriggle; (*en dansant*) to wiggle

tortionnaire [tɔʀsjɔnɛʀ] *nm* torturer

tortue [tɔʀty] *nf* tortoise; (*d'eau douce*) terrapin; (*d'eau de mer*) turtle

tortueux, -euse [tɔʀtɥø, -øz] *adj* (*rue*) twisting; (*fig*) tortuous

torture [tɔʀtyʀ] *nf* torture; **torturer** /1/ *vt* to torture; (*fig*) to torment

tôt [to] *adv* early; **~ ou tard** sooner or later; **si ~** so early; (*déjà*) so soon; **au plus ~** at the earliest; **plus ~** earlier

total, e, -aux [tɔtal, -o] *adj, nm* total; **au ~** in total *ou* all; (*fig*) on the whole; **faire le ~** to work out the total; **totalement** *adv* totally; **totaliser** /1/ *vt* to total (up); **totalitaire** *adj* totalitarian; **totalité** *nf*: **la totalité de: la totalité des élèves** all (of) the pupils; **la totalité de la population/classe** the whole population/class; **en totalité** entirely

toubib [tubib] *nm* (*fam*) doctor

touchant, e [tuʃɑ̃, -ɑ̃t] *adj* touching

touche [tuʃ] *nf* (*de piano, de machine à écrire*) key; (*de téléphone*) button; (*Peinture etc*) stroke, touch; (*fig: de couleur, nostalgie*) touch; (*Football: aussi*: **remise en ~**) throw-in; (*aussi*: **ligne de ~**) touch-line; (*Escrime*) hit; **~ dièse** (*de téléphone, clavier*) hash key

toucher [tuʃe] /1/ *nm* touch ▷ *vt* to touch; (*palper*) to feel; (*atteindre: d'un coup de feu etc*) to hit; (*concerner*) to concern, affect; (*contacter*) to reach, contact; (*recevoir: récompense*) to receive, get; (*: salaire*) to draw, get; (*chèque*) to cash; (*aborder: problème, sujet*) to touch on; **au ~** to the touch; **~ à** to touch; (*traiter de, concerner*) to have to do with, concern; **je vais lui en ~ un mot** I'll have a word with him about it; **~ au but** (*fig*) to near one's goal; **~ à sa fin** to be drawing to a close

touffe [tuf] *nf* tuft

touffu, e [tufy] *adj* thick, dense

toujours [tuʒuʀ] *adv* always; (*encore*) still; (*constamment*) forever; **essaie ~** (you can) try anyway; **pour ~** forever; **~ est-il que** the fact remains that; **~ plus** more and more

toupie [tupi] *nf* (spinning) top

tour [tuʀ] *nf* tower; (*immeuble*) high-rise block (BRIT) *ou* building (US); (*Échecs*) castle, rook ▷ *nm* (*excursion: à pied*) stroll, walk; (*: en voiture etc*) run, ride; (*: plus long*) trip; (*Sport: aussi*: **~ de piste**) lap; (*d'être servi ou de jouer etc*) turn; (*de roue etc*) revolution; (*Pol: aussi*: **~ de scrutin**) ballot; (*ruse, de prestidigitation, de cartes*) trick; (*de potier*) wheel; (*à bois, métaux*) lathe; (*circonférence*): **de 3 m de ~** 3 m round, with a circumference *ou* girth of 3 m; **faire le ~ de** to go (a)round; (*à pied*) to walk (a)round; **faire un ~** to go for a walk; **c'est au ~ de Renée** it's Renée's turn; **à ~ de rôle, ~ à ~** in turn; **~ de taille/tête** *nm* waist/head measurement; **~ de chant** *nm* song recital; **~ de contrôle** *nf* control tower; **la ~ Eiffel** the Eiffel Tower; **le T~ de France** the Tour de France; **~ de force** *nm* tour de force; **~ de garde** *nm* spell of duty; **un 33 ~s** an LP; **un 45 ~s** a single; **~ d'horizon** *nm* (*fig*) general survey

tourbe [tuʀb] *nf* peat

tourbillon [tuʀbijɔ̃] *nm* whirlwind; (*d'eau*) whirlpool; (*fig*) whirl, swirl;

tourbillonner /1/ vi to whirl ou twirl round

tourelle [turɛl] nf turret

tourisme [turism] nm tourism; **agence de ~** tourist agency; **faire du ~** to go touring; (en ville) to go sightseeing; **touriste** nm/f tourist; **touristique** adj tourist cpd; (région) touristic (péj)

tourment [turmã] nm torment; **tourmenter** /1/ vt to torment; **se tourmenter** to fret, worry o.s.

tournage [turnaʒ] nm (d'un film) shooting

tournant, e [turnã, -ãt] adj (feu, scène) revolving ▷ nm (de route) bend ; (fig) turning point

tournée [turne] nf (du facteur etc) round; (d'artiste, politicien) tour; (au café) round (of drinks)

tourner [turne] /1/ vt to turn; (sauce, mélange) to stir; (Ciné: faire les prises de vues) to shoot; (: produire) to make ▷ vi to turn; (moteur) to run; (compteur) to tick away; (lait etc) to turn (sour); **se tourner** vi to turn (a)round; **se ~ vers** to turn to; to turn towards; **mal ~** to go wrong; **~ autour de** to go (a)round; (péj) to hang (a)round; **~ à/en** to turn into; **~ en ridicule** to ridicule; **~ le dos à** (mouvement) to turn one's back on; (position) to have one's back to; **se ~ les pouces** to twiddle one's thumbs; **~ de l'œil** to pass out

tournesol [turnəsɔl] nm sunflower

tournevis [turnəvis] nm screwdriver

tournoi [turnwa] nm tournament

tournure [turnyr] nf (Ling) turn of phrase; **la ~ de qch** (évolution) the way sth is developing; **~ d'esprit** turn ou cast of mind

tourte [turt] nf pie

tourterelle [turtərɛl] nf turtledove

tous [tu, tus] adj, pron voir **tout**

Toussaint [tusɛ̃] nf: **la ~** All Saints' Day

tousser [tuse] /1/ vi to cough

MOT-CLÉ

tout, e (mpl **tous**, fpl **toutes**) [tu, tut, tus, tut] adj **1** (avec article singulier) all; **tout le lait** all the milk; **toute la nuit** all night, the whole night; **tout le livre** the whole book; **tout un pain** a whole loaf; **tout le temps** all the time, the whole time; **c'est tout le contraire** it's quite the opposite **2** (avec article pluriel) every; all; **tous les livres** all the books; **toutes les nuits** every night; **toutes les fois** every time; **toutes les trois/deux semaines** every third/other ou second week, every three/two weeks; **tous les deux** both ou each of us (ou them ou you); **toutes les trois** all three of us (ou them ou you) **3** (sans article): **à tout âge** at any age; **pour toute nourriture, il avait ...** his only food was ...
▶ pron everything, all; **il a tout fait** he's done everything; **je les vois tous** I can see them all ou all of them; **nous y sommes tous allés** all of us went, we all went; **c'est tout** that's all; **en tout** in all; **tout ce qu'il sait** all he knows
▶ nm whole; **le tout** all of it (ou them); **le tout est de ...** the main thing is to ...; **pas du tout** not at all
▶ adv **1** (très, complètement) very; **tout près** ou **à côté** very near; **le tout premier** the very first; **tout seul** all alone; **le livre tout entier** the whole book; **tout en haut** right at the top; **tout droit** straight ahead

2: **tout en** while; **tout en travaillant** while working, as he *etc* works
3: **tout d'abord** first of all; **tout à coup** suddenly; **tout à fait** absolutely; **tout à l'heure** a short while ago; (*futur*) in a short while, shortly; **à tout à l'heure!** see you later!; **tout de même** all the same; **tout le monde** everybody; **tout simplement** quite simply; **tout de suite** immediately, straight away

toutefois [tutfwa] *adv* however
toutes [tut] *adj, pron voir* **tout**
tout-terrain [tuterɛ̃] *adj*: **vélo ~** mountain bike; **véhicule ~** four-wheel drive
toux [tu] *nf* cough
toxicomane [tɔksikɔman] *nm/f* drug addict
toxique [tɔksik] *adj* toxic
trac [trak] *nm* (*aux examens*) nerves *pl*; (*Théât*) stage fright; **avoir le ~** (*aux examens*) to get an attack of nerves; (*Théât*) to have stage fright
tracasser [trakase] /1/ *vt* to worry, bother; **se tracasser** to worry (o.s.)
trace [tras] *nf* (*empreintes*) tracks *pl*; (*marques, fig*) mark; (*restes, vestige*) trace; **~s de pas** footprints
tracer [trase] /3/ *vt* to draw; (*piste*) to open up
tract [trakt] *nm* tract, pamphlet
tracteur [traktœr] *nm* tractor
traction [traksjɔ̃] *nf*: **~ avant/ arrière** front-wheel/rear-wheel drive
tradition [tradisjɔ̃] *nf* tradition; **traditionnel, le** *adj* traditional
traducteur, -trice [tradyktœr, -tris] *nm/f* translator
traduction [tradyksjɔ̃] *nf* translation
traduire [traduir] /38/ *vt* to translate; (*exprimer*) to convey; **~ en français** to translate into French; **~ en justice** to bring before the courts
trafic [trafik] *nm* traffic; **~ d'armes** arms dealing; **trafiquant, e** *nm/f*

trafficker; (*d'armes*) dealer; **trafiquer** /1/ *vt* (*péj: vin*) to doctor; (: *moteur, document*) to tamper with
tragédie [traʒedi] *nf* tragedy; **tragique** *adj* tragic
trahir [trair] /2/ *vt* to betray; **trahison** *nf* betrayal; (*Jur*) treason
train [trɛ̃] *nm* (*Rail*) train; (*allure*) pace; **être en ~ de faire qch** to be doing sth; **~ à grande vitesse** high-speed train; **~ d'atterrissage** undercarriage; **~ électrique** (*jouet*) (electric) train set; **~ de vie** style of living
traîne [trɛn] *nf* (*de robe*) train; **être à la ~** to lag behind
traîneau, x [trɛno] *nm* sleigh, sledge
traîner [trene] /1/ *vt* (*remorque*) to pull; (*enfant, chien*) to drag ou trail along ▷ *vi* (*robe, manteau*) to trail; (*être en désordre*) to lie around; (*marcher lentement*) to dawdle (along); (*vagabonder*) to hang about; (*durer*) to drag on; **se traîner** *vi*: **se ~ par terre** to crawl (on the ground); **~ les pieds** to drag one's feet
train-train [trɛ̃trɛ̃] *nm* humdrum routine
traire [trɛr] /50/ *vt* to milk
trait, e [trɛ, -ɛt] *nm* (*ligne*) line; (*de dessin*) stroke; (*caractéristique*) feature, trait; **traits** *nmpl* (*du visage*) features; **d'un ~** (*boire*) in one gulp; **de ~** (*animal*) draught; **avoir ~ à** to concern; **~ d'union** hyphen
traitant, e [trɛtã, -ãt] *adj*: **votre médecin ~** your usual ou family doctor; **shampooing ~** medicated shampoo
traite [trɛt] *nf* (*Comm*) draft; (*Agr*) milking; **d'une (seule) ~** without stopping (once)
traité [trete] *nm* treaty
traitement [trɛtmã] *nm* treatment; (*salaire*) salary; **~ de données** ou **de l'information** data processing; **~ de texte** word processing; (*logiciel*) word processing package

traiter [tʀɛte] /1/ vt to treat; (*qualifier*): **~ qn d'idiot** to call sb a fool ▷ vi to deal; **~ de** to deal with
traiteur [tʀɛtœʀ] nm caterer
traître, -esse [tʀɛtʀ, -tʀɛs] adj (*dangereux*) treacherous ▷ nm/f traitor (traitress)
trajectoire [tʀaʒɛktwaʀ] nf path
trajet [tʀaʒɛ] nm (*parcours, voyage*) journey; (*itinéraire*) route; (*distance à parcourir*) distance; **il y a une heure de ~** the journey takes one hour
trampoline [tʀɑ̃pɔlin] nm trampoline
tramway [tʀamwɛ] nm tram(way); (*voiture*) tram(car) (BRIT), streetcar (US)
tranchant, e [tʀɑ̃ʃɑ̃, -ɑ̃t] adj sharp; (*fig*) peremptory ▷ nm (*d'un couteau*) cutting edge; (*de la main*) edge; **à double ~** double-edged
tranche [tʀɑ̃ʃ] nf (*morceau*) slice; (*arête*) edge; **~ d'âge/de salaires** age/wage bracket
tranché, e [tʀɑ̃ʃe] adj (*couleurs*) distinct; (*opinions*) clear-cut
trancher [tʀɑ̃ʃe] /1/ vt to cut, sever ▷ vi to be decisive; **~ avec** to contrast sharply with
tranquille [tʀɑ̃kil] adj quiet; (*rassuré*) easy in one's mind, with one's mind at rest; **se tenir ~** (*enfant*) to be quiet; **avoir la conscience ~** to have an easy conscience; **laisse-moi/laisse-ça ~** leave me/it alone; **tranquillisant** nm tranquillizer; **tranquillité** nf peace (and quiet); **tranquillité d'esprit** peace of mind
transférer [tʀɑ̃sfeʀe] /6/ vt to transfer; **transfert** nm transfer
transformation [tʀɑ̃sfɔʀmasjɔ̃] nf change, alteration; (*radicale*) transformation; (*Rugby*) conversion; **transformations** nfpl (*travaux*) alterations
transformer [tʀɑ̃sfɔʀme] /1/ vt to change; (*radicalement*) to transform; (*vêtement*) alter; (*matière première,*

appartement, Rugby) to convert; **~ en** to turn into
transfusion [tʀɑ̃sfyzjɔ̃] nf: **~ sanguine** blood transfusion
transgénique [tʀɑ̃sʒenik] adj transgenic
transgresser [tʀɑ̃sgʀese] /1/ vt to contravene
transi, e [tʀɑ̃zi] adj numb (with cold), chilled to the bone
transiger [tʀɑ̃ziʒe] /3/ vi to compromise
transit [tʀɑ̃zit] nm transit; **transiter** /1/ vi to pass in transit
transition [tʀɑ̃zisjɔ̃] nf transition; **transitoire** adj transitional
transmettre [tʀɑ̃smɛtʀ] /56/ vt (*passer*): **~ qch à qn** to pass sth on to sb; (*Tech, Tél, Méd*) to transmit; (*TV, Radio: retransmettre*) to broadcast; **transmission** nf transmission
transparent, e [tʀɑ̃spaʀɑ̃, -ɑ̃t] adj transparent
transpercer [tʀɑ̃spɛʀse] /3/ vt (*froid, pluie*) to go through, pierce; (*balle*) to go through
transpiration [tʀɑ̃spiʀasjɔ̃] nf perspiration
transpirer [tʀɑ̃spiʀe] /1/ vi to perspire
transplanter [tʀɑ̃splɑ̃te] /1/ vt (*Méd, Bot*) to transplant
transport [tʀɑ̃spɔʀ] nm transport; **~s en commun** public transport sg; **transporter** /1/ vt to carry, move; (*Comm*) to transport, convey; **transporteur** nm haulage contractor (BRIT), trucker (US)
transvaser [tʀɑ̃svaze] /1/ vt to decant
transversal, e, -aux [tʀɑ̃svɛʀsal, -o] adj (*mur, chemin, rue*) running at right angles; **coupe ~e** cross section
trapèze [tʀapɛz] nm (*au cirque*) trapeze
trappe [tʀap] nf trap door
trapu, e [tʀapy] adj squat, stocky
traquenard [tʀaknaʀ] nm trap

traquer [tʀake] /1/ vt to track down; (*harceler*) to hound

traumatiser [tʀomatize] /1/ vt to traumatize

travail, -aux [tʀavaj, -o] nm (*gén*) work; (*tâche, métier*) work no pl, job; (*Écon, Méd*) labour; **travaux** nmpl (*de réparation, agricoles etc*) work sg; (*sur route*) roadworks; (*de construction*) building (work) sg; **être sans ~** (*employé*) to be out of work; **~ (au) noir** moonlighting; **travaux des champs** farmwork sg; **travaux dirigés** (*Scol*) supervised practical work sg; **travaux forcés** hard labour sg; **travaux manuels** (*Scol*) handicrafts; **travaux ménagers** housework sg; **travaux pratiques** (*gén*) practical work sg; (*en laboratoire*) lab work sg

travailler [tʀavaje] /1/ vi to work; (*bois*) to warp ▷ vt (*bois, métal*) to work; (*objet d'art, discipline*) to work on; **cela le travaille** it is on his mind; **travailleur, -euse** adj hard-working ▷ nm/f worker; **travailleur social** social worker; **travailliste** adj ≈ Labour cpd

travaux [tʀavo] nmpl voir **travail**

travers [tʀavɛʀ] nm fault, failing; **en ~ (de)** across; **au ~ (de)** through; **de ~** (*nez, bouche*) crooked; (*chapeau*) askew; **à ~** through; **regarder de ~** (*fig*) to look askance at; **comprendre de ~** to misunderstand

traverse [tʀavɛʀs] nf (*de voie ferrée*) sleeper; **chemin de ~** shortcut

traversée [tʀavɛʀse] nf crossing

traverser [tʀavɛʀse] /1/ vt (*gén*) to cross; (*ville, tunnel, aussi percer, fig*) to go through; (*ligne, trait*) to run across

traversin [tʀavɛʀsɛ̃] nm bolster

travesti [tʀavɛsti] nm transvestite

trébucher [tʀebyʃe] /1/ vi: **~ (sur)** to stumble (over), trip (over)

trèfle [tʀɛfl] nm (*Bot*) clover; (*Cartes: couleur*) clubs pl; (*: carte*) club; **~ à quatre feuilles** four-leaf clover

treize [tʀɛz] num thirteen; **treizième** num thirteenth

tréma [tʀema] nm diaeresis

tremblement [tʀɑ̃bləmɑ̃] nm: **~ de terre** earthquake

trembler [tʀɑ̃ble] /1/ vi to tremble, shake; **~ de** (*froid, fièvre*) to shiver ou tremble with; (*peur*) to shake ou tremble with; **~ pour qn** to fear for sb

trémousser [tʀemuse] /1/: **se trémousser** vi to jig about, wriggle about

trempé, e [tʀɑ̃pe] adj soaking (wet), drenched; (*Tech*): **acier ~** tempered steel

tremper [tʀɑ̃pe] /1/ vt to soak, drench; (*aussi*: **faire ~, mettre à ~**) to soak ▷ vi to soak; (*fig*): **~ dans** to be involved ou have a hand in; **se tremper** vi to have a quick dip

tremplin [tʀɑ̃plɛ̃] nm springboard; (*Ski*) ski jump

trentaine [tʀɑ̃tɛn] nf (*âge*): **avoir la ~** to be around thirty; **une ~ (de)** thirty or so, about thirty

trente [tʀɑ̃t] num thirty; **être/ se mettre sur son ~ et un** to be wearing/put on one's Sunday best; **trentième** num thirtieth

trépidant, e [tʀepidɑ̃, -ɑ̃t] adj (*fig: rythme*) pulsating; (*: vie*) hectic

trépigner [tʀepiɲe] /1/ vi to stamp (one's feet)

très [tʀɛ] adv very; **~ beau/bien** very beautiful/well; **~ critiqué** much criticized; **~ industrialisé** highly industrialized

trésor [tʀezɔʀ] nm treasure; **~ (public)** public revenue; **trésorerie** nf (*gestion*) accounts pl; (*bureaux*) accounts department; **difficultés de trésorerie** cash problems, shortage of cash ou funds; **trésorier, -ière** nm/f treasurer

tressaillir [tʀesajiʀ] /13/ vi to shiver, shudder

t

tressauter [tresote] /1/ vi to start, jump

tresse [tres] nf braid, plait; **tresser** /1/ vt (cheveux) to braid, plait; (fil, jonc) to plait; (corbeille) to weave; (corde) to twist

trêve [trev] nf (Mil, Pol) truce; (fig) respite; **~ de ...** enough of this ...

tri [tri] nm: **faire le ~ (de)** to sort out; **le (bureau de) ~** (Postes) the sorting office

triangle [trijɑ̃gl] nm triangle; **triangulaire** adj triangular

tribord [tribɔr] nm: **à ~** to starboard, on the starboard side

tribu [triby] nf tribe

tribunal, -aux [tribynal, -o] nm (Jur) court; (Mil) tribunal

tribune [tribyn] nf (estrade) platform, rostrum; (débat) forum; (d'église, de tribunal) gallery; (de stade) stand

tribut [triby] nm tribute

tributaire [tribyter] adj: **être ~ de** to be dependent on

tricher [triʃe] /1/ vi to cheat; **tricheur, -euse** nm/f cheat

tricolore [trikɔlɔr] adj three-coloured; (français) red, white and blue

tricot [triko] nm (technique, ouvrage) knitting no pl; (vêtement) jersey, sweater; **~ de corps, ~ de peau** vest; **tricoter** /1/ vt to knit

tricycle [trisikl] nm tricycle

trier [trije] /7/ vt to sort (out); (Postes, Inform, fruits) to sort

trimestre [trimestr] nm (Scol) term; (Comm) quarter; **trimestriel, le** adj quarterly; (Scol) end-of-term

trinquer [trɛ̃ke] /1/ vi to clink glasses

triomphe [trijɔ̃f] nm triumph; **triompher** /1/ vi to triumph, win; **triompher de** to triumph over, overcome

tripes [trip] nfpl (Culin) tripe sg

triple [tripl] adj triple ▷ nm: **le ~ (de)** (comparaison) three times as much

(as); **en ~ exemplaire** in triplicate; **tripler** /1/ vi, vt to triple, treble

triplés, -ées [triple] nm/f pl triplets

tripoter [tripɔte] /1/ vt to fiddle with

triste [trist] adj sad; (couleur, temps, journée) dreary; (péj): **~ personnage/ affaire** sorry individual/affair; **tristesse** nf sadness

trivial, e, -aux [trivjal, -o] adj coarse, crude; (commun) mundane

troc [trɔk] nm barter

trognon [trɔɲɔ̃] nm (de fruit) core; (de légume) stalk

trois [trwa] num three; **troisième** num third ▷ nf (Scol) year 10 (Brit), ninth grade (us); **le troisième âge** (période de vie) one's retirement years; (personnes âgées) senior citizens pl

troll [trɔl] nm, **trolleur, -euse** [trɔlœr, -øz] nm/f (Inform) troll

trombe [trɔ̃b] nf: **des ~s d'eau** a downpour; **en ~** like a whirlwind

trombone [trɔ̃bɔn] nm (Mus) trombone; (de bureau) paper clip

trompe [trɔ̃p] nf (d'éléphant) trunk; (Mus) trumpet, horn

tromper [trɔ̃pe] /1/ vt to deceive; (vigilance, poursuivants) to elude; **se tromper** vi to make a mistake, be mistaken; **se ~ de voiture/jour** to take the wrong car/get the day wrong; **se ~ de 3 cm/20 euros** to be out by 3 cm/20 euros

trompette [trɔ̃pet] nf trumpet; **en ~** (nez) turned-up

trompeur, -euse [trɔ̃pœr, -øz] adj deceptive

tronc [trɔ̃] nm (Bot, Anat) trunk; (d'église) collection box

tronçon [trɔ̃sɔ̃] nm section; **tronçonner** /1/ vt to saw up; **tronçonneuse** nf chainsaw

trône [tron] nm throne

trop [tro] adv too; (avec verbe) too much; (aussi: **~ nombreux**) too many; (aussi: **~ souvent**) too often; **~ peu (nombreux)** too few; **~ longtemps** (for) too long; **~ de**

(nombre) too many; (quantité) too much; **de ~, en ~: des livres en ~** a few books too many; **du lait en ~** too much milk; **trois livres/cinq euros de ~** three books too many/five euros too much; **ça coûte ~ cher** it's too expensive

tropical, e, -aux [tʀɔpikal, -o] adj tropical

tropique [tʀɔpik] nm tropic

trop-plein [tʀɔplɛ̃] nm (tuyau) overflow ou outlet (pipe); (liquide) overflow

troquer [tʀɔke] /1/ vt: **~ qch contre** to barter ou trade sth for; (fig) to swap sth for

trot [tʀo] nm trot; **trotter** /1/ vi to trot

trottinette [tʀɔtinɛt] nf (child's) scooter

trottoir [tʀɔtwaʀ] nm pavement (BRIT), sidewalk (US); **faire le ~** (péj) to walk the streets; **~ roulant** moving walkway, travelator

trou [tʀu] nm hole; (fig) gap; (Comm) deficit; **~ d'air** air pocket; **~ de mémoire** blank, lapse of memory

troublant, e [tʀublɑ̃, -ɑ̃t] adj disturbing

trouble [tʀubl] adj (liquide) cloudy; (image, photo) blurred; (affaire) shady, murky ▷ adv: **voir ~** to have blurred vision ▷ nm agitation; **troubles** nmpl (Pol) disturbances, troubles, unrest sg; (Méd) trouble sg, disorders; **trouble-fête** nm/f inv spoilsport

troubler [tʀuble] /1/ vt to disturb; (liquide) to make cloudy; (intriguer) to bother; **se troubler** vi (personne) to become flustered ou confused

trouer [tʀue] /1/ vt to make a hole (ou holes) in

trouille [tʀuj] nf (fam): **avoir la ~** to be scared stiff

troupe [tʀup] nf troop; **~ (de théâtre)** (theatrical) company

troupeau, x [tʀupo] nm (de moutons) flock; (de vaches) herd

trousse [tʀus] nf case, kit; (d'écolier) pencil case; **aux ~s de** (fig) on the heels ou tail of; **~ à outils** toolkit; **~ de toilette** toilet bag

trousseau, x [tʀuso] nm (de mariée) trousseau; **~ de clefs** bunch of keys

trouvaille [tʀuvaj] nf find

trouver [tʀuve] /1/ vt to find; (rendre visite): **aller/venir ~ qn** to go/come and see sb; **se trouver** vi (être) to be; **je trouve que** I find ou think that; **~ à boire/critiquer** to find something to drink/criticize; **se ~ mal** to pass out

truand [tʀyɑ̃] nm villain; **truander** /1/ vt: **se faire truander** to be swindled

truc [tʀyk] nm (astuce) way; (de cinéma, prestidigitateur) trick effect; (chose) thing; thingumajig; **avoir le ~** to have the knack; **c'est pas son (ou mon etc) ~** (fam) it's not really his (ou my etc) thing

truffe [tʀyf] nf truffle; (nez) nose

truffé, e [tʀyfe] adj (Culin) garnished with truffles

truie [tʀyi] nf sow

truite [tʀyit] nf trout inv

truquage [tʀyka3] nm special effects pl

truquer [tʀyke] /1/ vt (élections, serrure, dés) to fix

TSVP abr (= tournez s'il vous plaît) PTO

TTC abr (= toutes taxes comprises) inclusive of tax

tu¹ [ty] pron you ▷ nm: **employer le tu** to use the "tu" form

tu², e [ty] pp de **taire**

tuba [tyba] nm (Mus) tuba; (Sport) snorkel

tube [tyb] nm tube; (chanson, disque) hit song ou record

tuberculose [tybɛʀkyloz] nf tuberculosis

tuer [tɥe] /1/ vt to kill; **se tuer** (se suicider) to kill o.s.; (dans un accident) to be killed; **se ~ au travail** (fig) to work o.s. to death; **tuerie** nf slaughter no pl

tue-tête [tytɛt]: **à ~** adv at the top of one's voice

tueur [tɥœʀ] nm killer; **~ à gages** hired killer

tuile [tɥil] nf tile; (fam) spot of bad luck, blow

tulipe [tylip] nf tulip

tuméfié, e [tymefje] adj puffy, swollen

tumeur [tymœʀ] nf growth, tumour

tumulte [tymylt] nm commotion; **tumultueux, -euse** adj stormy, turbulent

tunique [tynik] nf tunic

Tunis [tynis] n Tunis

Tunisie [tynizi] nf: **la ~** Tunisia; **tunisien, ne** adj Tunisian ▷ nm/f: **Tunisien, ne** Tunisian

tunnel [tynɛl] nm tunnel; **le ~ sous la Manche** the Channel Tunnel

turbulent, e [tyʀbylɑ̃, -ɑ̃t] adj boisterous, unruly

turc, turque [tyʀk] adj Turkish ▷ nm (Ling) Turkish ▷ nm/f: **Turc, Turque** Turk/Turkish woman

turf [tyʀf] nm racing; **turfiste** nm/f racegoer

Turquie [tyʀki] nf: **la ~** Turkey

turquoise [tyʀkwaz] nf, adj inv turquoise

tutelle [tytɛl] nf (Jur) guardianship; (Pol) trusteeship; **sous la ~ de** (fig) under the supervision of

tuteur, -trice [tytœʀ, -tʀis] nm/f (Jur) guardian; (de plante) stake, support

tutoyer [tytwaje] /8/ vt: **~ qn** to address sb as "tu"

tuyau, x [tɥijo] nm pipe; (flexible) tube; (fam) tip; **~ d'arrosage** hosepipe; **~ d'échappement** exhaust pipe; **tuyauterie** nf piping no pl

TVA sigle f (= taxe à ou sur la valeur ajoutée) VAT

tweet [twit] nm (aussi Internet: Twitter) tweet; **tweeter** /1/ vi (Internet: Twitter) to tweet

tympan [tɛ̃pɑ̃] nm (Anat) eardrum

type [tip] nm type; (fam) chap, guy ▷ adj typical, standard

typé, e [tipe] adj ethnic (euphémisme)

typique [tipik] adj typical

tyran [tiʀɑ̃] nm tyrant; **tyrannique** adj tyrannical

tzigane [dzigan] adj gipsy, tzigane

u

ulcère [ylsɛʀ] *nm* ulcer
ultérieur, e [ylteʀjœʀ] *adj* later, subsequent; **remis à une date ~e** postponed to a later date; **ultérieurement** *adv* later, subsequently
ultime [yltim] *adj* final

MOT-CLÉ

un, une [œ̃, yn] *art indéf* a; (*devant voyelle*) an; **un garçon/vieillard** a boy/an old man; **une fille** a girl ▶ *pron* one; **l'un des meilleurs** one of the best; **l'un ..., l'autre** (the) one ..., the other; **les uns ..., les autres** some ..., others; **l'un et l'autre** both (of them); **l'un ou l'autre** either (of them); **l'un l'autre, les uns les autres** each other, one another; **pas un seul** not a single one; **un par un** one by one ▶ *num* one; **une pomme seulement**

one apple only, just one apple
▶ *nf*: **la une** (*Presse*) the front page

unanime [ynanim] *adj* unanimous; **unanimité** *nf*: **à l'unanimité** unanimously
uni, e [yni] *adj* (*ton, tissu*) plain; (*surface*) smooth, even; (*famille*) close(-knit); (*pays*) united
unifier [ynifje] /7/ *vt* to unite, unify
uniforme [ynifɔʀm] *adj* uniform; (*surface, ton*) even ▶ *nm* uniform; **uniformiser** /1/ *vt* (*systèmes*) to standardize
union [ynjɔ̃] *nf* union; **~ de consommateurs** consumers' association; **~ libre: vivre en ~ libre** (*en concubinage*) to cohabit; **l'U~ européenne** the European Union; **l'U~ soviétique** the Soviet Union
unique [ynik] *adj* (*seul*) only; (*exceptionnel*) unique; **un prix/système ~** a single price/system; **fils/fille ~** only son/daughter, only child; **sens ~** one-way street; **uniquement** *adv* only, solely; (*juste*) only, merely
unir [yniʀ] /2/ *vt* (*nations*) to unite; (*en mariage*) to unite, join together; **s'unir** *vi* to unite; (*en mariage*) to be joined together
unitaire [ynitɛʀ] *adj*: **prix ~** unit price
unité [ynite] *nf* (*harmonie, cohésion*) unity; (*Math*) unit
univers [ynivɛʀ] *nm* universe; **universel, le** *adj* universal
universitaire [yniveʀsitɛʀ] *adj* university *cpd*; (*diplôme, études*) academic, university *cpd* ▶ *nm/f* academic
université [yniveʀsite] *nf* university
urbain, e [yʀbɛ̃, -ɛn] *adj* urban, city *cpd*, town *cpd*; **urbanisme** *nm* town planning
urgence [yʀʒɑ̃s] *nf* urgency; (*Méd etc*) emergency; **d'~** *adj* emergency *cpd* ▶ *adv* as a matter of urgency; **service des ~s** emergency service

urgent, e [yRʒɑ̃, -ɑ̃t] *adj* urgent
urine [yRin] *nf* urine; **urinoir** *nm* (public) urinal
urne [yRn] *nf* (*électorale*) ballot box; (*vase*) urn
urticaire [yRtikɛR] *nf* nettle rash
us [ys] *nmpl*: **us et coutumes** (habits and) customs
usage [yzaʒ] *nm* (*emploi, utilisation*) use; (*coutume*) custom; **à l'~** with use; **à l'~ de** (*pour*) for (use of); **en ~** in use; **hors d'~** out of service; **à ~ interne** (*Méd*) to be taken (internally); **à ~ externe** (*Méd*) for external use only; **usagé, e** *adj* (*usé*) worn; **usager, -ère** *nm/f* user
usé, e [yze] *adj* worn (down *ou* out *ou* away); (*banal: argument etc*) hackneyed
user [yze] /1/ *vt* (*outil*) to wear down; (*vêtement*) to wear out; (*matière*) to wear away; (*consommer: charbon etc*) to use; **s'user** *vi* (*tissu, vêtement*) to wear out; **~ de** (*moyen, procédé*) to use, employ; (*droit*) to exercise
usine [yzin] *nf* factory
usité, e [yzite] *adj* common
ustensile [ystɑ̃sil] *nm* implement; **~ de cuisine** kitchen utensil
usuel, le [yzɥɛl] *adj* everyday, common
usure [yzyR] *nf* wear
utérus [yteRys] *nm* uterus, womb
utile [ytil] *adj* useful
utilisation [ytilizasjɔ̃] *nf* use
utiliser [ytilize] /1/ *vt* to use
utilitaire [ytilitɛR] *adj* utilitarian
utilité [ytilite] *nf* usefulness *no pl*; **de peu d'~** of little use *ou* help
utopie [ytɔpi] *nf* utopia

va [va] *vb voir* **aller**
vacance [vakɑ̃s] *nf* (*Admin*) vacancy; **vacances** *nfpl* holiday(s) *pl* (BRIT), vacation *sg* (US); **les grandes ~s** the summer holidays *ou* vacation; **prendre des/ses ~s** to take a holiday *ou* vacation/ one's holiday(s) *ou* vacation; **aller en ~s** to go on holiday *ou* vacation; **vacancier, -ière** *nm/f* holidaymaker
vacant, e [vakɑ̃, -ɑ̃t] *adj* vacant
vacarme [vakaRm] *nm* row, din
vaccin [vaksɛ̃] *nm* vaccine; (*opération*) vaccination; **vaccination** *nf* vaccination; **vacciner** /1/ *vt* to vaccinate; **être vacciné** (*fig*) to be immune
vache [vaʃ] *nf* (*Zool*) cow; (*cuir*) cowhide ▷ *adj* (*fam*) rotten, mean; **vachement** *adv* (*fam*) really; **vacherie** *nf* (*action*) dirty trick; (*propos*) nasty remark

vaciller [vasije] /1/ vi to sway, wobble; (*bougie, lumière*) to flicker; (*fig*) to be failing, falter

VAE *sigle m* (= vélo (à assistance) électrique) e-bike

va-et-vient [vaevjɛ̃] *nm inv* comings and goings *pl*

vagabond, e [vagabɔ̃, -ɔ̃d] *adj* wandering ▷ *nm* (*rôdeur*) tramp, vagrant; (*voyageur*) wanderer; **vagabonder** /1/ vi to roam, wander

vagin [vaʒɛ̃] *nm* vagina

vague [vag] *nf* wave ▷ *adj* vague; (*regard*) faraway; (*manteau, robe*) loose(-fitting); (*quelconque*) **un ~ bureau/cousin** some office/cousin or other; **~ de fond** ground swell; **~ de froid** cold spell

vaillant, e [vajɑ̃, -ɑ̃t] *adj* (*courageux*) gallant; (*robuste*) hale and hearty

vain, e [vɛ̃, vɛn] *adj* vain; **en ~** in vain

vaincre [vɛ̃kʀ] /42/ vt to defeat; (*fig*) to conquer, overcome; **vaincu, e** *nm/f* defeated party; **vainqueur** *nm* victor; (*Sport*) winner

vaisseau, x [vɛso] *nm* (*Anat*) vessel; (*Navig*) ship, vessel; **~ spatial** spaceship

vaisselier [vɛsəlje] *nm* dresser

vaisselle [vɛsɛl] *nf* (*service*) crockery; (*plats etc à laver*) (dirty) dishes *pl*; **faire la ~** to do the dishes

valable [valabl] *adj* valid; (*acceptable*) decent, worthwhile

valet [valɛ] *nm* valet; (*Cartes*) jack

valeur [valœʀ] *nf* (*gén*) value; (*mérite*) worth, merit; (*Comm: titre*) security; **valeurs** *nfpl* (*morales*) values; **mettre en ~** (*fig*) to highlight; to show off to advantage; **avoir de la ~** to be valuable; **prendre de la ~** to go up *ou* gain in value; **sans ~** worthless

valide [valid] *adj* (*en bonne santé*) fit; (*valable*) valid; **valider** /1/ vt to validate

valise [valiz] *nf* (suit)case; **faire sa ~** to pack one's (suit)case

vallée [vale] *nf* valley

vallon [valɔ̃] *nm* small valley

valoir [valwaʀ] /29/ vi (*être valable*) to hold, apply ▷ vt (*prix, valeur, effort*) to be worth; (*causer*): **~ qch à qn** to earn sb sth; **se valoir** to be of equal merit; (*péj*) to be two of a kind; **faire ~** (*droits, prérogatives*) to assert; **se faire ~** to make the most of o.s.; **à ~ sur** to be deducted from; **vaille que vaille** somehow or other; **cela ne me dit rien qui vaille** I don't like the look of it at all; **ce climat ne me vaut rien** this climate doesn't suit me; **~ la peine** to be worth the trouble, be worth it; **~ mieux: il vaut mieux se taire** it's better to say nothing; **ça ne vaut rien** it's worthless; **que vaut ce candidat?** how good is this applicant?

valse [vals] *nf* waltz

vandalisme [vɑ̃dalism] *nm* vandalism

vanille [vanij] *nf* vanilla

vanité [vanite] *nf* vanity; **vaniteux, -euse** *adj* vain, conceited

vanne [van] *nf* gate; (*fam*) dig

vantard, e [vɑ̃taʀ, -aʀd] *adj* boastful

vanter [vɑ̃te] /1/ vt to speak highly of, praise; **se vanter** vi to boast, brag; **se ~ de** to pride o.s. on; (*péj*) to boast of

vapeur [vapœʀ] *nf* steam; (*émanation*) vapour , fumes *pl*; **vapeurs** *nfpl* (*bouffées*) vapours; **à ~** steam-powered, steam *cpd*; **cuit à la ~** steamed; **vaporeux, -euse** *adj* (*flou*) hazy, misty; (*léger*) filmy; **vaporisateur** *nm* spray; **vaporiser** /1/ vt (*parfum etc*) to spray

vapoter [vapɔte] /1/ vi to smoke an e-cigarette

varappe [vaʀap] *nf* rock climbing

vareuse [vaʀøz] *nf* (*blouson*) pea jacket; (*d'uniforme*) tunic

variable [vaʀjabl] *adj* variable; (*temps, humeur*) changeable; (*divers: résultats*) varied, various

varice [vaʀis] *nf* varicose vein

varicelle [vaʀisɛl] *nf* chickenpox

V

varié, e [vaʁje] *adj* varied; (*divers*) various; **hors-d'œuvre ~s** selection of hors d'œuvres

varier [vaʁje] /7/ *vi* to vary; (*temps, humeur*) to change ▷ *vt* to vary; **variété** *nf* variety; **spectacle de variétés** variety show

variole [vaʁjɔl] *nf* smallpox

Varsovie [vaʁsɔvi] *n* Warsaw

vas [va] *vb voir* **aller**; **~-y!** go on!

vase [vɑz] *nm* vase ▷ *nf* silt, mud; **vaseux, -euse** *adj* silty, muddy; (*fig: confus*) woolly, hazy; (: *fatigué*) peaky

vasistas [vazistas] *nm* fanlight

vaste [vast] *adj* vast, immense

vautour [votuʁ] *nm* vulture

vautrer [votʁe] /1/: **se vautrer** *vi*: **se ~ dans** to wallow in; **se ~ sur** to sprawl on

va-vite [vavit]: **à la ~** *adv* in a rush

VDQS *sigle m* (= *vin délimité de qualité supérieure*) *label guaranteeing quality of wine*

veau, x [vo] *nm* (*Zool*) calf; (*Culin*) veal; (*peau*) calfskin

vécu, e [veky] *pp de* **vivre**

vedette [vədɛt] *nf* (*artiste etc*) star; (*canot*) patrol boat; (*police*) launch

végétal, e, -aux [veʒetal, -o] *adj* vegetable ▷ *nm* vegetable, plant; **végétalien, ne** *adj, nm/f* vegan

végétarien, ne [veʒetaʁjɛ̃, -ɛn] *adj, nm/f* vegetarian

végétation [veʒetasjɔ̃] *nf* vegetation; **végétations** *nfpl* (*Méd*) adenoids

véhicule [veikyl] *nm* vehicle; **~ utilitaire** commercial vehicle

veille [vɛj] *nf* (*Psych*) wakefulness; (*jour*): **la ~** the day before; **la ~ au soir** the previous evening; **la ~ de** the day before; **la ~ de Noël** Christmas Eve; **la ~ du jour de l'An** New Year's Eve; **à la ~ de** on the eve of

veillée [veje] *nf* (*soirée*) evening; (*réunion*) evening gathering; **~ (funèbre)** wake

veiller [veje] /1/ *vi* to stay *ou* sit up ▷ *vt* (*malade, mort*) to watch over, sit up with; **~ à** to attend to, see to; **~ à ce que** to make sure that; **~ sur** to keep a watch *ou* an eye on; **veilleur** *nm*: **veilleur de nuit** night watchman; **veilleuse** *nf* (*lampe*) night light; (*Auto*) sidelight; (*flamme*) pilot light

veinard, e [vɛnaʁ, -aʁd] *nm/f* lucky devil

veine [vɛn] *nf* (*Anat, du bois etc*) vein; (*filon*) vein, seam; **avoir de la ~** (*fam*) (*chance*) to be lucky

véliplanchiste [veliplɑ̃ʃist] *nm/f* windsurfer

vélo [velo] *nm* bike, cycle; **faire du ~** to go cycling; **vélomoteur** *nm* moped

velours [v(ə)luʁ] *nm* velvet; **~ côtelé** corduroy; **velouté, e** *adj* velvety ▷ *nm*: **velouté d'asperges/ de tomates** cream of asparagus/ tomato soup

velu, e [vəly] *adj* hairy

vendange [vɑ̃dɑ̃ʒ] *nf* (*aussi*: **~s**) grape harvest; **vendanger** /3/ *vi* to harvest the grapes

vendeur, -euse [vɑ̃dœʁ, -øz] *nm/f* shop *ou* sales assistant ▷ *nm* (*Jur*) vendor, seller

vendre [vɑ̃dʁ] /41/ *vt* to sell; **~ qch à qn** to sell sb sth; **"à ~"** "for sale"

vendredi [vɑ̃dʁədi] *nm* Friday; **V- saint** Good Friday

vénéneux, -euse [venenø, -øz] *adj* poisonous

vénérien, ne [veneʁjɛ̃, -ɛn] *adj* venereal

vengeance [vɑ̃ʒɑ̃s] *nf* vengeance *no pl*, revenge *no pl*

venger [vɑ̃ʒe] /3/ *vt* to avenge; **se venger** *vi* to avenge o.s.; **se ~ de qch** to avenge o.s. for sth; to take one's revenge for sth; **se ~ de qn** to take revenge on sb; **se ~ sur** to take revenge on

venimeux, -euse [vənimø, -øz] *adj* poisonous, venomous; (*fig: haineux*) venomous, vicious

venin [vənɛ̃] *nm* venom, poison

venir [v(ə)niʀ] /22/ *vi* to come; **~ de** to come from; **~ de faire: je viens d'y aller/de le voir** I've just been there/seen him; **s'il vient à pleuvoir** if it should rain; **où veux-tu en ~?** what are you getting at?; **faire ~** (*docteur, plombier*) to call (out)

vent [vɑ̃] *nm* wind; **il y a du ~** it's windy; **c'est du ~** it's all hot air; **dans le ~** (*fam*) trendy

vente [vɑ̃t] *nf* sale; **la ~** (*activité*) selling; (*secteur*) sales *pl*; **mettre en ~** to put on sale; (*objets personnels*) to put up for sale; **~ aux enchères** auction sale; **~ de charité** jumble (BRIT) *ou* rummage (US) sale

venteux, -euse [vɑ̃tø, -øz] *adj* windy

ventilateur [vɑ̃tilatœʀ] *nm* fan

ventiler [vɑ̃tile] /1/ *vt* to ventilate

ventouse [vɑ̃tuz] *nf* (*de caoutchouc*) suction pad

ventre [vɑ̃tʀ] *nm* (*Anat*) stomach; (*fig*) belly; **avoir mal au ~** to have (a) stomach ache

venu, e [v(ə)ny] *pp de* **venir** ▷ *adj*: **être mal ~ à** *ou* **de faire** to have no grounds for doing, be in no position to do; **mal ~** ill-timed; **bien ~** timely

ver [vɛʀ] *nm* worm; (*des fruits etc*) maggot; (*du bois*) woodworm *no pl*; **~ luisant** glow-worm; **~ à soie** silkworm; **~ solitaire** tapeworm; **~ de terre** earthworm

verbe [vɛʀb] *nm* verb

verdâtre [vɛʀdɑtʀ] *adj* greenish

verdict [vɛʀdik(t)] *nm* verdict

verdir [vɛʀdiʀ] /2/ *vi, vt* to turn green; **verdure** *nf* greenery

véreux, -euse [veʀø, -øz] *adj* worm-eaten; (*malhonnête*) shady, corrupt

verge [vɛʀʒ] *nf* (*Anat*) penis

verger [vɛʀʒe] *nm* orchard

verglacé, e [vɛʀglase] *adj* icy, iced-over

verglas [vɛʀgla] *nm* (black) ice

véridique [veʀidik] *adj* truthful

vérification [veʀifikasjɔ̃] *nf* checking *no pl*, check

vérifier [veʀifje] /7/ *vt* to check; (*corroborer*) to confirm, bear out

véritable [veʀitabl] *adj* real; (*ami, amour*) true; **un ~ désastre** an absolute disaster

vérité [veʀite] *nf* truth; **en ~** to tell the truth

verlan [vɛʀlɑ̃] *nm* (back) slang

vermeil, le [vɛʀmɛj] *adj* ruby red

vermine [vɛʀmin] *nf* vermin *pl*

vermoulu, e [vɛʀmuly] *adj* worm-eaten

verni, e [vɛʀni] *adj* (*fam*) lucky; **cuir ~** patent leather

vernir [vɛʀniʀ] /2/ *vt* (*bois, tableau, ongles*) to varnish; (*poterie*) to glaze; **vernis** *nm* (*enduit*) varnish; glaze; (*fig*) veneer; **vernis à ongles** nail varnish (BRIT) *ou* polish; **vernissage** *nm* (*d'une exposition*) preview

vérole [veʀɔl] *nf* (*variole*) smallpox

verre [vɛʀ] *nm* glass; (*de lunettes*) lens *sg*; **boire** *ou* **prendre un ~** to have a drink; **~s de contact** contact lenses; **verrière** *nf* (*grand vitrage*) window; (*toit vitré*) glass roof

verrou [veʀu] *nm* (*targette*) bolt; **mettre qn sous les ~s** to put sb behind bars; **verrouillage** *nm* locking mechanism; **verrouillage central** *ou* **centralisé** central locking; **verrouiller** /1/ *vt* to bolt; to lock

verrue [veʀy] *nf* wart

vers [vɛʀ] *nm* line ▷ *nmpl* (*poésie*) verse *sg* ▷ *prép* (*en direction de*) toward(s); (*près de*) around (about); (*temporel*) about, around

versant [vɛʀsɑ̃] *nm* slopes *pl*, side

versatile [vɛʀsatil] *adj* fickle, changeable

verse [vɛʀs]: **à ~** *adv*: **il pleut à ~** it's pouring (with rain)

V

Verseau [vɛrso] *nm*: **le ~** Aquarius

versement [vɛrsəmɑ̃] *nm* payment; **en trois ~s** in three instalments

verser [vɛrse] /1/ *vt* (*liquide, grains*) to pour; (*larmes, sang*) to shed; (*argent*) to pay; **~ sur un compte** to pay into an account

version [vɛrsjɔ̃] *nf* version; (*Scol*) translation (*into the mother tongue*); **film en ~ originale** film in the original language

verso [vɛrso] *nm* back; **voir au ~** see over(leaf)

vert, e [vɛr, vɛrt] *adj* green; (*vin*) young; (*vigoureux*) sprightly ▷ *nm* green; **les V~s** (*Pol*) the Greens

vertèbre [vɛrtɛbr] *nf* vertebra

vertement [vɛrtəmɑ̃] *adv* (*réprimander*) sharply

vertical, e, -aux [vɛrtikal, -o] *adj* vertical; **verticale** *nf* vertical; **à la verticale** vertically; **verticalement** *adv* vertically

vertige [vɛrtiʒ] *nm* (*peur du vide*) vertigo; (*étourdissement*) dizzy spell; (*fig*) fever; **vertigineux, -euse** *adj* breathtaking

vertu [vɛrty] *nf* virtue; **en ~ de** in accordance with; **vertueux, -euse** *adj* virtuous

verve [vɛrv] *nf* witty eloquence; **être en ~** to be in brilliant form

verveine [vɛrvɛn] *nf* (*Bot*) verbena, vervain; (*infusion*) verbena tea

vésicule [vezikyl] *nf* vesicle; **~ biliaire** gall-bladder

vessie [vesi] *nf* bladder

veste [vɛst] *nf* jacket; **~ droite/ croisée** single-/double-breasted jacket

vestiaire [vɛstjɛr] *nm* (*au théâtre etc*) cloakroom; (*de stade etc*) changing-room (BRIT), locker-room (US)

vestibule [vɛstibyl] *nm* hall

vestige [vɛstiʒ] *nm* relic; (*fig*) vestige; **vestiges** *nmpl* (*d'une ville*) remains

vestimentaire [vɛstimɑ̃tɛr] *adj* (*détail*) of dress; (*élégance*) sartorial; **dépenses ~s** clothing expenditure

veston [vɛstɔ̃] *nm* jacket

vêtement [vɛtmɑ̃] *nm* garment, item of clothing; **vêtements** *nmpl* clothes

vétérinaire [veterinɛr] *nm/f* vet, veterinary surgeon

vêtir [vetir] /20/ *vt* to clothe, dress

vêtu, e [vety] *pp de* **vêtir** ▷ *adj*: **~ de** dressed in, wearing

vétuste [vetyst] *adj* ancient, timeworn

veuf, veuve [vœf, vœv] *adj* widowed ▷ *nm* widower ▷ *nf* widow

vexant, e [vɛksɑ̃, -ɑ̃t] *adj* (*contrariant*) annoying; (*blessant*) upsetting

vexation [vɛksasjɔ̃] *nf* humiliation

vexer [vɛkse] /1/ *vt* to hurt; **se vexer** *vi* to be offended

viable [vjabl] *adj* viable; (*économie, industrie etc*) sustainable

viande [vjɑ̃d] *nf* meat; **je ne mange pas de ~** I don't eat meat

vibrer [vibre] /1/ *vi* to vibrate; (*son, voix*) to be vibrant; (*fig*) to be stirred; **faire ~** to (cause to) vibrate; to stir, thrill

vice [vis] *nm* vice; (*défaut*) fault; **~ de forme** legal flaw *ou* irregularity

vicié, e [visje] *adj* (*air*) polluted, tainted; (*Jur*) invalidated

vicieux, -euse [visjø, -øz] *adj* (*pervers*) dirty(-minded); (*méchant*) nasty ▷ *nm/f* lecher

vicinal, e, -aux [visinal, -o] *adj*: **chemin ~** byroad, byway

victime [viktim] *nf* victim; (*d'accident*) casualty

victoire [viktwar] *nf* victory

victuailles [viktɥɑj] *nfpl* provisions

vidange [vidɑ̃ʒ] *nf* (*d'un fossé, réservoir*) emptying; (*Auto*) oil change; (*de lavabo: bonde*) waste outlet; **vidanges** *nfpl* (*matières*) sewage *sg*; **vidanger** /3/ *vt* to empty

vide [vid] adj empty ▷ nm (Physique) vacuum; (espace) (empty) space, gap; (futilité, néant) void; **emballé sous ~** vacuum-packed; **avoir peur du ~** to be afraid of heights; **à ~** (sans occupants) empty; (sans charge) unladen

vidéo [video] nf video; **cassette ~** video cassette; **vidéoclip** nm music video; **vidéoconférence** nf videoconference

vide-ordures [vidɔRdyR] nm inv (rubbish) chute

vider [vide] /1/ vt to empty; (Culin: volaille, poisson) to gut, clean out; **se vider** vi to empty; **~ les lieux** to quit ou vacate the premises; **videur** nm (de boîte de nuit) bouncer

vie [vi] nf life; **être en ~** to be alive; **sans ~** lifeless; **à ~** for life; **que faites-vous dans la ~?** what do you do?

vieil [vjɛj] adj m voir **vieux**; **vieillard** nm old man; **vieille** adj f, nf voir **vieux**; **vieilleries** nfpl old things ou stuff sg; **vieillesse** nf old age; **vieillir** /2/ vi (prendre de l'âge) to grow old; (population, vin) to age; (doctrine, auteur) to become dated ▷ vt to age; **se vieillir** to make o.s. older; **vieillissement** nm growing old; ageing

Vienne [vjɛn] n Vienna

viens [vjɛ̃] vb voir **venir**

vierge adj virgin; (page) clean, blank ▷ nf virgin; (signe): **la V~** Virgo

Viêtnam, Vietnam [vjɛtnam] nm: **le ~** Vietnam; **vietnamien, ne** adj Vietnamese ▷ nm/f: **Vietnamien, ne** Vietnamese

vieux (vieil), vieille [vjø, vjɛj] adj old ▷ nm/f old man/woman ▷ nmpl: **les ~** (pej) old people; **un petit ~** a little old man; **mon ~/ ma vieille** (fam) old man/girl; **prendre un coup de ~** to put years on; **~ garçon** bachelor; **~ jeu** adj inv old-fashioned

vif, vive [vif, viv] adj (animé) lively; (alerte) sharp; (lumière, couleur) brilliant; (air) crisp; (vent, émotion) keen; (fort: regret, déception) great, deep; (vivant): **brûlé ~** burnt alive; **de vive voix** personally; **avoir l'esprit ~** to be quick-witted; **piquer qn au ~** to cut sb to the quick; **à ~** (plaie) open; **avoir les nerfs à ~** to be on edge

vigne [viɲ] nf (plante) vine; (plantation) vineyard; **vigneron** nm wine grower

vignette [viɲɛt] nf (pour voiture) ≈ (road) tax disc (BRIT), ≈ license plate sticker (US); (sur médicament) price label (on medicines for reimbursement by Social Security)

vignoble [viɲɔbl] nm (plantation) vineyard; (vignes d'une région) vineyards pl

vigoureux, -euse [viguRø, -øz] adj vigorous, robust

vigueur [vigœR] nf vigour; **être/ entrer en ~** to be in/come into force; **en ~** current

vilain, e [vilɛ̃, -ɛn] adj (laid) ugly; (affaire, blessure) nasty; (pas sage: enfant) naughty; **~ mot** bad word

villa [vila] nf (detached) house; **~ en multipropriété** time-share villa

village [vilaʒ] nm village; **villageois, e** adj village cpd ▷ nm/f villager

ville [vil] nf town; (importante) city; (administration): **la ~** ≈ the (town) council; **~ d'eaux** spa; **~ nouvelle** new town

vin [vɛ̃] nm wine; **avoir le ~ gai/ triste** to get happy/miserable after a few drinks; **~ d'honneur** reception (with wine and snacks); **~ ordinaire** ou **de table** table wine; **~ de pays** local wine

vinaigre [vinɛgR] nm vinegar; **vinaigrette** nf vinaigrette, French dressing

vindicatif, -ive [vɛ̃dikatif, -iv] adj vindictive

V

vingt [vɛ̃, vɛ̃t] (2nd pron used when followed by a vowel) num twenty; **~-quatre heures sur ~-quatre** twenty-four hours a day, round the clock; **vingtaine** nf: **une vingtaine (de)** around twenty, twenty or so; **vingtième** num twentieth

vinicole [vinikɔl] adj wine cpd; wine-growing

vinyle [vinil] nm vinyl

viol [vjɔl] nm (d'une femme) rape; (d'un lieu sacré) violation

violacé, e [vjɔlase] adj purplish, mauvish

violemment [vjɔlamɑ̃] adv violently

violence [vjɔlɑ̃s] nf violence

violent, e [vjɔlɑ̃, -ɑ̃t] adj violent; (remède) drastic

violer [vjɔle] /1/ vt (femme) to rape; (sépulture) to desecrate; (loi, traité) to violate

violet, te [vjɔlɛ, -ɛt] adj, nm purple, mauve ▷ nf (fleur) violet

violon [vjɔlɔ̃] nm violin; (fam: prison) lock-up; **~ d'Ingres** (artistic) hobby; **violoncelle** nm cello; **violoniste** nm/f violinist

virage [viraʒ] nm (d'un véhicule) turn; (d'une route, piste) bend

viral, e, -aux [viral, -o] adj (aussi Inform) viral

virée [vire] nf run; (à pied) walk; (longue) hike

virement [virmɑ̃] nm (Comm) transfer

virer [vire] /1/ vt (Comm) to transfer; (fam: renvoyer) to sack ▷ vi to turn; (Chimie) to change colour (BRIT) ou color (US); **~ au bleu** to turn blue; **~ de bord** to tack

virevolter [virvɔlte] /1/ vi to twirl around

virgule [virgyl] nf comma; (Math) point

viril, e [viril] adj (propre à l'homme) masculine; (énergique, courageux) manly, virile

virtuel, le [virtɥɛl] adj potential; (théorique) virtual

virtuose [virtɥoz] nm/f (Mus) virtuoso; (gén) master

virus [virys] nm virus

vis vb [vi] voir **voir, vivre** ▷ nf [vis] screw

visa [viza] nm (sceau) stamp; (validation de passeport) visa

visage [vizaʒ] nm face

vis-à-vis [vizavi]: **~ de** prép towards; **en ~** facing ou opposite each other

visée [vize] nf aiming; **visées** nfpl (intentions) designs

viser [vize] /1/ vi to aim ▷ vt to aim at; (concerner) to be aimed ou directed at; (apposer un visa sur) to stamp, visa; **~ à qch/faire** to aim at sth/at doing ou to do

visibilité [vizibilite] nf visibility

visible [vizibl] adj visible; (disponible): **est-il ~?** can he see me?, will he see visitors?

visière [vizjɛr] nf (de casquette) peak; (qui s'attache) eyeshade

vision [vizjɔ̃] nf vision; (sens) (eye)sight, vision; (fait de voir): **la ~ de** the sight of; **visionneuse** nf viewer

visiophone [vizjɔfɔn] nm videophone

visite [vizit] nf visit; **~ médicale** medical examination; **~ accompagnée** ou **guidée** guided tour; **faire une ~ à qn** to call on sb, pay sb a visit; **rendre ~ à qn** to visit sb, pay sb a visit; **être en ~ (chez qn)** to be visiting (sb); **avoir de la ~** to have visitors; **heures de ~** (hôpital, prison) visiting hours

visiter [vizite] /1/ vt to visit; **visiteur, -euse** nm/f visitor

vison [vizɔ̃] nm mink

visser [vise] /1/ vt: **~ qch** (fixer, serrer) to screw sth on

visuel, le [vizɥɛl] adj visual

vital, e, -aux [vital, -o] adj vital

vitamine [vitamin] nf vitamin

vite [vit] adv (rapidement) quickly, fast; (sans délai) quickly; soon; **~!** quick!; **faire ~** to be quick

vitesse [vitɛs] *nf* speed; (*Auto: dispositif*) gear; **prendre de la ~** to pick up *ou* gather speed; **à toute ~** at full *ou* top speed; **en ~** quickly

● **LIMITE DE VITESSE**
●
● The speed limit in France is 50
● km/h in built-up areas, 90 km/h
● on main roads, and 130 km/h on
● motorways (110 km/h when it is
● raining).

viticulteur [vitikyltœʀ] *nm* wine grower
vitrage [vitʀaʒ] *nm*: **double ~** double glazing
vitrail, -aux [vitʀaj, -o] *nm* stained-glass window
vitre [vitʀ] *nf* (window) pane; (*de portière, voiture*) window; **vitré, e** *adj* glass *cpd*
vitrine [vitʀin] *nf* (shop) window; (*petite armoire*) display cabinet; **en ~** in the window
vivable [vivabl] *adj* (*personne*) livable-with; (*maison*) fit to live in
vivace [vivas] *adj* (*arbre, plante*) hardy; (*fig*) enduring
vivacité [vivasite] *nf* liveliness, vivacity
vivant, e [vivɑ̃, -ɑ̃t] *adj* (*qui vit*) living, alive; (*animé*) lively; (*preuve, exemple*) living ▷ *nm*: **du ~ de qn** in sb's lifetime; **les ~s et les morts** the living and the dead
vive [viv] *adj f voir* **vif** ▷ *vb voir* **vivre** ▷ *excl*: **~ le roi!** long live the king!; **vivement** *adv* sharply ▷ *excl*: **vivement les vacances!** roll on the holidays!
vivier [vivje] *nm* (*au restaurant etc*) fish tank; (*étang*) fishpond
vivifiant, e [vivifjɑ̃, -ɑ̃t] *adj* invigorating
vivoter [vivɔte] /1/ *vi* (*personne*) to scrape a living, get by; (*fig: affaire etc*) to struggle along

vivre [vivʀ] /46/ *vi*, *vt* to live; **vivres** *nmpl* provisions, food supplies; **il vit encore** he is still alive; **se laisser ~** to take life as it comes; **ne plus ~** (*être anxieux*) to live on one's nerves; **il a vécu** (*eu une vie aventureuse*) he has seen life; **être facile à ~** to be easy to get on with; **faire ~ qn** (*pourvoir à sa subsistance*) to provide (a living) for sb; **~ de** to live on
vlan [vlɑ̃] *excl* wham!, bang!
VO *sigle f* = **version originale**; **voir un film en VO** to see a film in its original language
vocabulaire [vɔkabylɛʀ] *nm* vocabulary
vocation [vɔkasjɔ̃] *nf* vocation, calling
vœu, x [vø] *nm* wish; (*à Dieu*) vow; **faire ~ de** to take a vow of; **avec tous nos ~x** with every good wish *ou* our best wishes
vogue [vɔg] *nf* fashion, vogue; **en ~** in fashion, in vogue
voici [vwasi] *prép* (*pour introduire, désigner*) here is (+ *sg*); here are (+ *pl*); **et ~ que ...** and now it (*ou* he) ...; *voir aussi* **voilà**
voie [vwa] *nf* way; (*Rail*) track, line; (*Auto*) lane; **par ~ buccale** *ou* **orale** orally; **être en bonne ~** to be shaping *ou* going well; **mettre qn sur la ~** to put sb on the right track; **être en ~ d'achèvement/de rénovation** to be nearing completion/in the process of renovation; **à ~ unique** single-track; **route à deux/trois ~s** two-/three-lane road; **~ express** expressway; **~ ferrée** track; railway line (*BRIT*), railroad (*US*); **~ de garage** (*Rail*) siding; **la ~ lactée** the Milky Way; **la ~ publique** the public highway
voilà [vwala] *prép* (*en désignant*) there is (+ *sg*); there are (+ *pl*); **les ~** *ou* **voici** here *ou* there they are; **en ~** *ou* **voici un** here's one, there's one; **voici mon frère et ~ ma sœur** this is my brother

V

and that's my sister; **~** ou **voici deux ans** two years ago; **~** ou **voici deux ans que** it's two years since; **et ~!** there we are!; **~ tout** that's all; **"~** ou **voici"** (en offrant etc) "there ou here you are"; **tiens! ~ Paul** look! there's Paul

voile [vwal] nm veil; (tissu léger) net ▷ nf sail; (sport) sailing; **voiler** /1/ vt to veil; (fausser: roue) to buckle; (: bois) to warp; **se voiler** vi (lune, regard) to mist over; (voix) to become husky; (roue, disque) to buckle; (planche) to warp; **voilier** nm sailing ship; (de plaisance) sailing boat; **voilure** nf (de voilier) sails pl

voir [vwaʀ] /30/ vi, vt to see; **se voir**: cela se voit (c'est visible) that's obvious, it shows; **faire ~ qch à qn** to show sb sth; **en faire ~ à qn** (fig) to give sb a hard time; **ne pas pouvoir ~ qn** not to be able to stand sb; **voyons!** let's see now; (indignation etc) come (along) now!; **ça n'a rien à ~ avec lui** that has nothing to do with him

voire [vwaʀ] adv or even

voisin, e [vwazɛ̃, -in] adj (proche) neighbouring ; next; (ressemblant) connected ▷ nm/f neighbour; **voisinage** nm (proximité) proximity; (environs) vicinity; (quartier, voisins) neighbourhood

voiture [vwatyʀ] nf car; (wagon) coach, carriage; **~ de course** racing car; **~ de sport** sports car

voix [vwa] nf voice; (Pol) vote; **à haute ~** aloud; **à ~ basse** in a low voice; **à deux/quatre ~** (Mus) in two/four parts; **avoir ~ au chapitre** to have a say in the matter

vol [vɔl] nm (trajet, voyage, groupe d'oiseaux) flight; (mode d'appropriation) theft, stealing; (larcin) theft; **à ~ d'oiseau** as the crow flies; **au ~: attraper qch au ~** to catch sth as it flies past; **en ~** in flight; **~ libre** hang-gliding; **~ à main armée** armed

robbery; **~ régulier** scheduled flight; **~ à voile** gliding

volage [vɔlaʒ] adj fickle

volaille [vɔlaj] nf (oiseaux) poultry pl; (viande) poultry no pl; (oiseau) fowl

volant, e [vɔlɑ̃, -ɑ̃t] adj flying ▷ nm (d'automobile) (steering) wheel; (de commande) wheel; (objet lancé) shuttlecock; (bande de tissu) flounce

volcan [vɔlkɑ̃] nm volcano

volée [vɔle] nf (Tennis) volley; **à la ~: rattraper à la ~** to catch in midair; **à toute ~** (sonner les cloches) vigorously; (lancer un projectile) with full force

voler [vɔle] /1/ vi (avion, oiseau, fig) to fly; (voleur) to steal ▷ vt (objet) to steal; (personne) to rob; **~ qch à qn** to steal sth from sb; **on m'a volé mon portefeuille** my wallet (BRIT) ou billfold (US) has been stolen; **il ne l'a pas volé!** he asked for it!

volet [vɔle] nm (de fenêtre) shutter; (Aviat) flap; (de feuillet, document) section; (fig) facet

voleur, -euse [vɔlœʀ, -øz] nm/f thief ▷ adj thieving; **"au ~!"** "stop thief!"

volley [vɔlɛ], **volley-ball** [vɔlɛbol] nm volleyball

volontaire [vɔlɔ̃tɛʀ] adj (acte, activité) voluntary; (délibéré) deliberate; (caractère, personne: décidé) self-willed ▷ nm/f volunteer

volonté [vɔlɔ̃te] nf (faculté de vouloir) will; (énergie, fermeté) will (power); (souhait, désir) wish; **se servir/boire à ~** to take/drink as much as one likes; **bonne ~** goodwill, willingness; **mauvaise ~** lack of goodwill, unwillingness

volontiers [vɔlɔ̃tje] adv (avec plaisir) willingly, gladly; (habituellement, souvent) readily, willingly; **"~"** "with pleasure"

volt [vɔlt] nm volt

volte-face [vɔltəfas] nf inv: **faire ~** to do an about-turn

voltige [vɔltiʒ] nf (Équitation) trick riding; (au cirque) acrobatics sg;

voltiger [vɔltiʒe] /3/ vi to flutter (about)

volubile [vɔlybil] adj voluble

volume [vɔlym] nm volume; (Géom: solide) solid; **volumineux, -euse** adj voluminous, bulky

volupté [vɔlypte] nf sensual delight ou pleasure

vomi [vɔmi] nm vomit; **vomir** /2/ vi to vomit, be sick ▷ vt to vomit, bring up; (fig) to belch out, spew out; (exécrer) to loathe, abhor

vorace [vɔʀas] adj voracious

vos [vo] adj poss voir **votre**

vote [vɔt] nm vote; **~ par correspondance/procuration** postal/proxy vote; **voter** [vɔte] /1/ vi to vote ▷ vt (loi, décision) to vote for

votre [vɔtʀ] (pl **vos**) adj poss your

vôtre [votʀ] pron: **le ~, la ~, les ~s** yours; **les ~s** (fig) your family ou folks; **à la ~** (toast) your (good) health!

vouer [vwe] /1/ vt: **~ sa vie/son temps à** (étude, cause etc) to devote one's life/time to; **~ une haine/amitié éternelle à qn** to vow undying hatred/friendship to sb

○ **MOT-CLÉ**

vouloir [vulwaʀ] /31/ vt **1** (exiger, désirer) to want; **vouloir faire/que qn fasse** to want to do/sb to do; **voulez-vous du thé?** would you like ou do you want some tea?; **que me veut-il?** what does he want with me?; **sans le vouloir** (involontairement) without meaning to, unintentionally; **je voudrais ceci/faire** I would ou I'd like this/to do; **le hasard a voulu que ...** as fate would have it, ...; **la tradition veut que ...** tradition demands that ...
2 (consentir): **je veux bien** (bonne volonté) I'll be happy to; (concession) fair enough, that's fine; **oui, si on veut** (en quelque sorte) yes, if you like; **veuillez attendre** please

wait; **veuillez agréer ...** (formule épistolaire) yours faithfully
3: **en vouloir à qn** to bear sb a grudge; **s'en vouloir (de)** to be annoyed with o.s. (for); **il en veut à mon argent** he's after my money
4: **vouloir de: l'entreprise ne veut plus de lui** the firm doesn't want him any more; **elle ne veut pas de son aide** she doesn't want his help
5: **vouloir dire** to mean
▷ nm: **le bon vouloir de qn** sb's goodwill; sb's pleasure

voulu, e [vuly] pp de **vouloir** ▷ adj (requis) required, requisite; (délibéré) deliberate, intentional

vous [vu] pron you; (objet indirect) (to) you; (réfléchi: sg) yourself; (: pl) yourselves; (réciproque) each other ▷ nm: **employer le ~** (vouvoyer) to use the "vous" form; **~-même** yourself; **~-mêmes** yourselves

vouvoyer [vuvwaje] /8/ vt: **~ qn** to address sb as "vous"

voyage [vwajaʒ] nm journey, trip; (fait de voyager): **le ~** travel(ling); **partir/être en ~** to go off/be away on a journey ou trip; **faire bon ~** to have a good journey; **~ d'agrément/d'affaires** pleasure/business trip; **~ de noces** honeymoon; **~ organisé** package tour

voyager [vwajaʒe] /3/ vi to travel; **voyageur, -euse** nm/f traveller; (passager) passenger; **voyageur (de commerce)** commercial traveller

voyant, e [vwajɑ̃, -ɑ̃t] adj (couleur) loud, gaudy ▷ nm (signal) (warning) light

voyelle [vwajɛl] nf vowel

voyou [vwaju] nm hoodlum

vrac [vʀak]: **en ~** adv loose; (Comm) in bulk

vrai, e [vʀɛ] adj (véridique: récit, faits) true; (non factice, authentique) real; **à ~ dire** to tell the truth; **vraiment** adv really;

vraisemblable *adj* likely; (*excuse*) plausible; **vraisemblablement** *adv* in all likelihood, very likely; **vraisemblance** *nf* likelihood; (*romanesque*) verisimilitude

vrombir [vʀɔ̃biʀ] /2/ *vi* to hum

VRP *sigle m* (= *voyageur, représentant, placier*) (sales) rep (*fam*)

VTT *sigle m* (= *vélo tout-terrain*) mountain bike

vu¹ [vy] *prép* (*en raison de*) in view of; **vu que** in view of the fact that

vu², e [vy] *pp de* **voir** ▷ *adj*: **bien/mal vu** (*personne*) well/poorly thought of

vue [vy] *nf* (*sens, faculté*) sight; (*panorama, image, photo*) view; **la ~ de** (*spectacle*) the sight of; **vues** *nfpl* (*idées*) views; (*dessein*) designs; **perdre la ~** to lose one's (eye)sight; **perdre de ~** to lose sight of; **hors de ~** out of sight; **à première ~** at first sight; **tirer à ~** to shoot on sight; **à ~ d'œil** visibly; **avoir ~ sur** to have a view of; **en ~** (*visible*) in sight; (*célèbre*) in the public eye; **en ~ de faire** with a view to doing; **~ d'ensemble** overall view

vulgaire [vylgɛʀ] *adj* (*grossier*) vulgar, coarse; (*trivial*) commonplace, mundane; (*péj: quelconque*): **de ~s touristes/chaises de cuisine** common tourists/kitchen chairs; (*Bot, Zool: non latin*) common; **vulgariser** /1/ *vt* to popularize

vulnérable [vylneʀabl] *adj* vulnerable

wagon [vagɔ̃] *nm* (*de voyageurs*) carriage; (*de marchandises*) truck, wagon; **wagon-lit** *nm* sleeper, sleeping car; **wagon-restaurant** *nm* restaurant *ou* dining car

wallon, ne [walɔ̃, -ɔn] *adj* Walloon ▷ *nm* (*Ling*) Walloon ▷ *nm/f*: **W~, ne** Walloon

watt [wat] *nm* watt

WC [vese] *nmpl* toilet *sg*

Web [wɛb] *nm inv*: **le ~** the (World Wide) Web; **webcam** *nf* webcam; **webmaster, webmestre** *nm/f* webmaster

week-end [wikɛnd] *nm* weekend

western [wɛstɛʀn] *nm* western

whisky [wiski] (*pl* **whiskies**) *nm* whisky

wifi [wifi] *nm inv* wifi

WWW *sigle m* (= *World Wide Web*) WWW

xénophobe [gzenɔfɔb] *adj* xenophobic ▷ *nm/f* xenophobe
xérès [gzeʀɛs] *nm* sherry
xylophone [gzilɔfɔn] *nm* xylophone

y [i] *adv* (*à cet endroit*) there; (*dessus*) on it (*ou* them); (*dedans*) in it (*ou* them) ▷ *pron* (about *ou* on *ou* of) it (*vérifier la syntaxe du verbe employé*); **j'y pense** I'm thinking about it; **ça y est!** that's it!; *voir aussi* **aller, avoir**
yacht [jɔt] *nm* yacht
yaourt [jauʀt] *nm* yogurt; **~ nature/ aux fruits** plain/fruit yogurt
yeux [jø] *nmpl de* **œil**
yoga [jɔga] *nm* yoga
yoghourt [jɔguʀt] *nm* = **yaourt**
yougoslave [jugɔslav] *adj* Yugoslav(ian) ▷ *nm/f*: **Y~** Yugoslav(ian)
Yougoslavie [jugɔslavi] *nf*: **la ~** Yugoslavia; **l'ex-~** the former Yugoslavia

Z

zone [zon] *nf* zone, area;
(*quartiers pauvres*): **la ~** the slums;
~ bleue ≈ restricted parking area;
~ industrielle (ZI) industrial estate
zoo [zoo] *nm* zoo
zoologie [zɔɔlɔʒi] *nf* zoology;
zoologique *adj* zoological
zut [zyt] *excl* dash (it)! (BRIT), nuts!
(US)

zapper [zape] /1/ *vi* to zap
zapping [zapiŋ] *nm*: **faire du ~** to
flick through the channels
zèbre [zɛbʀ] *nm* (*Zool*) zebra; **zébré, e**
adj striped, streaked
zèle [zɛl] *nm* zeal; **faire du ~** (*péj*) to
be over-zealous; **zélé, e** *adj* zealous
zéro [zeʀo] *nm* zero, nought (BRIT);
au-dessous de ~ below zero
(Centigrade), below freezing; **partir
de ~** to start from scratch; **trois
(buts) à ~** three (goals to) nil
zeste [zɛst] *nm* peel, zest
zézayer [zezeje] /8/ *vi* to have a lisp
zigzag [zigzag] *nm* zigzag; **zigzaguer**
/1/ *vi* to zigzag (along)
Zimbabwe [zimbabwe] *nm*: **le ~**
Zimbabwe
zinc [zɛ̃g] *nm* (*Chimie*) zinc
zipper [zipe] /1/ *vt* (*Inform*) to zip
zizi [zizi] *nm* (*fam*) willy
zodiaque [zɔdjak] *nm* zodiac
zona [zona] *nm* shingles *sg*

French in focus

Introduction

French in focus gives you a fascinating introduction to the French-speaking world. The following pages look at where French is spoken throughout the world, helping you to get to know the language and the people that speak it. Practical language tips and notes on common translation difficulties will allow you to become more confident in French and a useful correspondence section gives you all the information you need to be able to communicate effectively.

We've also included a number of links to useful websites, which will give you the opportunity to read and learn more about French-speaking countries and the French language.

We hope that you will enjoy using your *French in focus* supplement. We are sure that it will help you to find out more about French-speaking countries and become more confident in writing and speaking French.

Allez-y!

France and its regions

ROYAUME-UNI

BELGIQUE

ALLEMAGNE

LUXEMBOURG

•Lille

HAUTS-DE-FRANCE

•Rouen

Seine

NORMANDIE

ÎLE-DE-FRANCE

GRAND EST

•Strasbourg

Rhin

•Paris

Vosges

BRETAGNE

•Rennes

Orléans•

Loire

Dijon•

Jura

SUISSE

PAYS DE LA LOIRE

CENTRE - VAL DE LOIRE

BOURGOGNE - FRANCHE-COMTE

•Nantes

NOUVELLE AQUITAINE

•Lyon

Alpes

AUVERGNE - RHÔNE-ALPES

ITALIE

Massif central

•Bordeaux

Rhône

Garonne

OCCITANIE

PROVENCE - ALPES CÔTE D'AZUR

MONACO•

•Toulouse

•Marseille

P y r é n é e s

ESPAGNE

ANDORRE

CORSE

©Collins Bartholomew Ltd 2016

Ajaccio•

France and its regions

French speakers often refer to mainland France as *l'Hexagone* because of its shape. The head of state is the President (*le Président de la République*), who is elected for five years. The President appoints a Prime Minister (*le Premier Ministre*), who heads the government.

France is organized into thirteen areas called *régions*. Each *région* is made up of several smaller *départements*, four of which lie far beyond Europe's borders.

The overseas *Départements* (*Départements d'outre-mer – DOM –* and *Régions d'outre-mer – ROM*) consist of:
• the Caribbean islands of *Martinique* and *Guadeloupe*
• *Mayotte* in the Indian Ocean
• *Réunion* in the Indian Ocean
• *Guyane française* in South America

They have the same legal system as mainland France.

France's overseas territories (*Collectivités d'outre-mer – COM*) consist of:
• *Polynésie française, Wallis-et-Futuna* and *Nouvelle-Calédonie* in the South Pacific
• *Saint-Pierre et Miquelon*
• *Terres Australes et antarctiques françaises*, polar territories in the Antarctic
• *Saint-Barthélemy* and *Saint-Martin* in the West Indies

Useful links:
www.gouvernement.fr
  Offical website of the French government.
www.service-public.fr
  Links to most government departments.
www.outre-mer.gouv.fr
  Information on the DOM-ROM and COM.

A snapshot of France

- France is the biggest country by area in Western Europe, covering 544,000 km² (well over twice the size of the UK).

- The Loire is the longest river in France, and is around 1010 km long. It rises in the Cévennes mountains and flows into the Atlantic Ocean at Saint-Nazaire.

- The highest mountain in the Alps, Mont Blanc (4810 m), lies just within France's border with Italy.

- 64.4 million people live in metropolitan France, and there are another 2.2 million in the overseas *départements*.

- France is the world's sixth largest economy after the US, China, Japan, the UK and Germany.

- The main religion in France is Roman Catholicism; Islam is the second largest religion.

- After Italy, France is the world's biggest wine-producing country.

- The Tour de France is the world's most famous cycle race. Competitors cover approximately 3500 km nationwide.

A useful link:
www.insee.fr
The French statistical office.

The French-speaking world

océ

Canada

QUÉBEC

SAINT-PIERRE
ET MIQUELON

NOUVEAU
BRUNSWICK

FR

Louisiane

M

Haïti

GUADELOUPE   Mauritani

MARTINIQUE   Sénégal

Guinée

GUYANE   Burkina Faso
                  Côte d'Ivoire

océan
Pacifique   océan
                                 Atlanti

WALLIS ET FUTUNA

POLYNÉSIE   Norc
FRANÇAISE
                        Ouest

                        Sud

_r c t i q u e_

ique
Luxembourg
uisse
Val d'Aoste
MONACO
ore
unisie

Liban   Égypte

océan
Pacifique

ger
Tchad
Djibouti
Cameroun
in.
République
o
centrafricaine
Guinée équatoriale
République du Congo
Rwanda
Burundi   •Seychelles

océan
Indien

Comores
MAYOTTE

épublique
ocratique
du Congo

•Madagascar
•Île Maurice
LA RÉUNION

Laos
Cambodge   •Vietnam

Vanuatu •
•
NOUVELLE-
CALÉDONIE

©Collins Bartholomew Ltd 2016

COUNTRIES OR REGIONS WHERE FRENCH IS THE MOTHER TONGUE

Countries where French is one of the official languages

Countries or regions where French is used

7

Varieties of French

French is the native language of over 75 million people and it is spoken by around 270 million people worldwide. 49 million people are learning French as a foreign language. It is the fastest-growing language in Africa.

Outside France, French is mostly spoken in:

• Belgium and Switzerland

• Algeria, Morocco, Tunisia, Cameroon, Côte d'Ivoire and the Democratic Republic of the Congo

• Canada

A useful link:
www.academie-francaise.fr
   The Académie française website.

Le Québec
Québec is the largest Canadian province, with an area of 1,542,000 km². Over 80% of the province's inhabitants speak French as their first language, although it is rather different from the language of mainland France. The French spoken in Québec is called *québécois*.

French regional languages

Other languages spoken within France:

Language	French name	Brief description	Where spoken
Alsatian	l'alsacien	Close to German	Near the border with Germany
Breton	le breton	A Celtic language	Brittany in north-west France
Basque	le basque	Not related to any other known language	Near the border with Spain
Catalan	le catalan	Close to Spanish	Near the border with Spain
Corsican	le corse	Close to Italian	The island of Corsica
Flemish	le flamand	Close to Dutch	Near the border with Belgium
Occitan	l'occitan	Close to Spanish and French	The southern part of France

Words that have crossed the Channel

When the Normans invaded England in 1066, French became the language of the ruling classes. Since then, it has played a central part in the development of English.

English has absorbed thousands of French words over time, for example, 'beef' comes from *bœuf*, 'marriage' comes from *mariage* and so on.

However, English also uses words that come directly from French and don't change at all: for example, 'au pair', 'eau de toilette' and 'rendez-vous'.

With the spread of English as a global means of communication, English terms have become more widespread in the French language.

Some of these terms mean the same in both languages:

le brunch	*un cocktail*
un boycott	*une interview*
un self-service	*le stress*
un tee-shirt	*les WC*
le Web	*le week-end*
un western	*un yacht*

Others have different meanings in French and English:

un agenda	diary
les baskets	trainers (BRIT), sneakers (US)
les chips	crisps (BRIT), chips (US)
la lecture	reading
un parking	a car park
un smoking	a dinner jacket
un stop	a stop sign, a brake-light

> *Be careful!*
> Some words are singular in French but plural in English and vice versa:
>
> *un jean* (a pair of) jeans
> *un short* (a pair of) shorts
> *les WC* the WC

A useful link:
www.academie-francaise.fr
   The Académie française website.

Some informal French

We all use different language styles – more relaxed, more formal – depending on the situation we find ourselves in.

When you visit a French-speaking country, you're sure to hear some informal expressions in everyday situations.

Here are some examples of French informal words:

la bagnole	car
le boulot	work
dingue	crazy
génial	fantastic
le mec	guy
moche	ugly, rotten
le prof	teacher

Informal language is marked very clearly in the dictionary to help you choose the appropriate word or phrase.

Be careful when using items marked 'informal' (*fam*) in your dictionary, and avoid ones marked 'offensive' (*fam!*) altogether.

> *Le verlan*
> *Verlan* is a kind of slang in which words are invented by swapping round syllables and often chopping off the end of the new word: for example, *femme* becomes *meuf*, and *Arabe* becomes *beur*.

Improving your pronunciation

There are a number of different methods you can use to improve your pronunciation and increase your confidence in speaking French:

- read out loud to yourself to improve your confidence
- listen to French radio
- watch French-language films
- chat with French-speakers

Some points to help you with your pronunciation

- **Silent consonant endings and *liaison*.** Consonants at the end of words are not normally pronounced but you do pronounce them when the following word starts with a vowel (*mes amis* sounds like 'may**z**amee', *c'est ici* sounds like 'se**t**eesee'). This is called *liaison*.

- **Elision.** When the words *je, le, la, me, te, se, ce* and *ne* are immediately followed by a word starting with any vowel, the *e* is dropped (and replaced by an apostrophe in writing): *j'adore l'été, elle s'habille, je t'aime.*

- **Letter *h*.** The letter *h* is never pronounced at the beginning of French words. So, *haricot* is pronounced 'areeko' and *hôtel* as 'otel'.

Words beginning with *h* can behave in one of two ways as regards pronunciation.

In some cases, the word behaves as if it began with a vowel, and preceding words like *le* and *la* are shortened: *à l'hôtel, l'huile, ils l'hébergent.* For such words liaison also takes place: *les hôtels* is pronounced as 'lay**z**otel'.

In other cases, *le, la* and similar words are not shortened: *la Hollande, le haricot,* and liaison does not happen: *les haricots* is pronounced as 'lay ariko' and not 'layzariko'. Words which behave like this are preceded by an apostrophe in the dictionary: *'hasard.*

Improving your fluency

Conversational words and phrases

In English we insert lots of words and phrases, such as *so, then, by the way*, into our conversation, to give our thoughts a structure and often to show our attitude. The French words shown below do the same thing. If you use them they will make you sound more fluent and natural.

- *alors*

  Tu as fini? **Alors** je m'en vais. (= then)

  Alors tu viens (oui ou non)? (= well, then)

- *bon*

  Bon! J'y vais. (= right!)

  Bon! Ça suffit maintenant. (= OK!)

- *ah bon*

  Je pars aux États-Unis demain. – **Ah bon**? (= really?)

- *c'est ça*

  Vous avez vingt-cinq ans, alors? – Oui, **c'est ça**. (= that's right)

- *donc*

  Voilà **donc** la solution. (= so, then)

  C'était **donc** un espion? (= then, so)

- *enfin*

  Enfin, vous voyez, c'est la catastrophe! (= in a word)

  Enfin, tu aurais pu le faire! (= even so)

- *de toute façon*

  De toute façon, je ne veux pas y aller. (= anyway)

  Tu peux m'appeler, je serai à la maison **de toute façon**. (= in any case)

- *au fait*

  Au fait, est-ce que tu as aimé le film? (= by the way)

  C'est quand, **au fait**, ton anniversaire? (= in fact)

- *en fait*

  En fait, je n'ai pas beaucoup de temps. (= actually)

  En fait, on devrait partir maintenant. (= in fact)

- *quand même*

  C'est **quand même** ennuyeux. (= after all)

  Merci **quand même**. (= all the same)

Improving your fluency

Varying the words you use to get your message across will make you sound more fluent in French. For example, you already know *J'aime bien les gâteaux*, but for a change you could say *J'adore les gâteaux* to mean the same thing. Here are some other suggestions:

Saying what you like or dislike

J'ai bien aimé le film.	I liked ...
La visite des vignobles m'a beaucoup plu.	I really enjoyed ...
Je n'aime pas (du tout) le poisson.	I don't like ... (at all).
J'ai horreur du sport.	I loathe ...

Expressing your opinion

Je pense que c'est trop cher.	I think ...
Je trouve que c'est normal.	I think ...
Je crois que c'est un peu tard.	I think ...
Je suis certain/sûr que Marc va gagner.	I'm sure ...
À mon avis, il n'a pas changé.	In my opinion ...

Agreeing or disagreeing

Je trouve que vous avez raison.	I think you're right.
Je suis d'accord avec vous.	I agree with you.
Il a tort.	He's wrong.
Je ne suis pas d'accord.	I disagree.

Correspondence

The following section on correspondence has been designed to help you communicate confidently in written as well as spoken French. Sample letters, emails and sections on text messaging and making telephone calls will ensure that you have all the vocabulary you need to correspond successfully in French.

Text messaging

Texto	French	English
@+	à plus tard	see you later
@2m1	à demain	see you tomorrow
bi1to	bientôt	soon
cpg	c'est pas grave	it's no big deal
dsl	désolé	I'm sorry
entouk	en tout cas	in any case
G la N	J'ai la haine	I'm gutted
je t'M	je t'aime	I love you
mdr	mort de rire	LOL (laughing out loud)
mr6	merci	thanks
MSG	message	message
p2k	pas de quoi	you're welcome
pcq	parce que	because
qqn	quelqu'un	someone
ri1	rien	nothing
svp	s'il vous plaît	please
TOK	t'es OK?	are you OK?
TOQP	t'es occupé?	are you busy?
we	week-end	weekend
Xlnt	excellent	excellent

Writing an email

Fichier	Edition	Affichage	Outils	**Composer**	Aide	Envoyer

A: michel@europost.fr

| Nouveau message |
| Répondre |
| Répondre à tous |
| Faire suivre |
| Fichier joint |

Cc:

Copie cachée:

Object: Demain soir

Tu veux sortir demain soir? Le nouveau James Bond passe à l'Odéon, si ça t'intéresse.

Si tu ne peux pas demain, je suis libre samedi midi. On pourrait déjeuner ensemble.

Grosses bises

Nadia

Saying your email address
In French, when you tell someone your email address, you say:
michel arobase europost point ef-ayr

fichier (m)	file	*répondre à tous*	reply to all
édition (f)	edit	*faire suivre*	forward
affichage (m)	view	*fichier (m) joint*	attachment
outils (mpl)	tools	*à*	to
composer	compose	*cc*	cc (carbon copy)
aide (f)	help	*copie (f) cachée*	bcc (blind carbon copy)
envoyer	send	*objet (m)*	subject
nouveau message (m)	new message	*de*	from
répondre	reply	*date (f)*	date

Here is some additional useful Internet vocabulary:

barre (f) de défilement	scroll bar		*imprimer*	to print
base (f) de données	database		*l'Internet (m)*	the Internet
clavier (m)	keyboard		*liens (mpl)*	links
clic (m) droit	right click		*menu (m)*	menu
cliquer	to click		*moniteur (m)*	monitor
coller	to paste		*moteur (m) de recherche*	search engine
copier	to copy		*navigateur (m)*	browser
corbeille (f)	recycle bin		*page (f) d'accueil*	home page
couper	to cut		*page (f) Web*	web page
déconnecter	to log off		*précédente*	back
dossier (m)	folder		*rechercher*	to search
double-cliquer	to double click		*sauvegarder*	to save
envoyé	sent		*se connecter*	to log on
FAQ	FAQs		*site (m) Web*	website
favoris	favourites		*suivante*	forward
fenêtre (f)	window		*surfer sur Internet*	to surf the Net
feuille (f) de calcul	spreadsheet		*télécharger*	to download
fournisseur (m) d'accès à Internet	Internet Service Provider		*transmission (f) à haut débit*	broadband
historique	history		*le Web*	the (World-Wide) Web
icône (f)	icon			

Writing a personal letter

Guy Leduc
18, rue des Tulipes
65004 Gervais

Your own name and address ➝

Town/city you are writing from, and the date ➝ Gervais, le 14 février 2017

Salut Frédéric !

Merci beaucoup pour les livres que tu m'as envoyés. Tu as vraiment bien choisi puisqu'il s'agit de mes deux écrivains préférés: j'ai hâte de les lire!

Sinon, rien de nouveau ici. Je passe presque tout mon temps à préparer mes examens qui commencent dans quinze jours. J'espère que je les réussirai tous, mais j'ai le trac pour mon examen de maths: c'est la matière que j'aime le moins.

Maman m'a dit que tu pars en Crète avec ta famille la semaine prochaine. Je te souhaite de très bonnes vacances, et je suis sûr que tu reviendras tout bronzé.

À bientôt!

Maxime

Writing a personal letter

Other ways of starting a personal letter	Other ways of ending a personal letter
Chers Jean et Sylvie *Chère tante Laure* *Mon cher Laurent*	*Affectueusement* *Je t'embrasse* *Grosses bises* (informal)

Some useful phrases

Je te remercie de ta lettre.	Thank you for your letter.
J'ai été très content d'avoir de tes nouvelles.	It was great to hear from you.
Je suis désolé de ne pas vous avoir répondu plus vite.	I'm sorry I didn't reply sooner.
Transmettez mes amitiés à Sophie.	Give my regards to Sophie.
Dis bonjour à Martin de ma part.	Say hello to Martin for me.
Maman t'embrasse.	Mum sends her love.

Writing a formal letter

Jeanne Judon ◄ Your own name and address
89, bd des Tertres
75008 Paris

Hôtel Renoir

Name and address of the
person/company you are → 15, av. Jean Médecin
writing to 06000 Nice

Paris, le 2 juin 2017 ◄ Town/city you are writing
from, and the date

Madame ou Monsieur,

Suite à notre conversation téléphonique de ce
matin, je vous écris afin de confirmer ma réservation
pour une chambre avec salle de bains pour deux
nuits du mercredi 4 au jeudi 5 juillet 2017 inclus.

Comme convenu, veuillez trouver ci-joint un chèque
de 30€ correspondant au montant des arrhes.

Je vous prie de croire, Madame, Monsieur, à
l'assurance de mes sentiments distingués.

Jeanne Judon

Writing a formal letter

Other ways of starting a formal letter	Other ways of ending a formal letter
Monsieur le Directeur (or le Maire etc) *Madame le Directeur* *Messieurs* *Madame* *Cher Monsieur* *Chère Madame*	*Veuillez accepter, [...]*, l'expression de mes sentiments distingués.* *Fill in the brackets with the words you used to start your letter: *Messieurs, chère Madame* etc.

Some useful phrases

Je vous serais reconnaissant de ...	I would be grateful if you would ...
Je vous prie de ...	Please ...
Nous vous remercions de votre lettre.	Thank you for your letter.
Dans l'attente de votre réponse ...	I look forward to hearing from you ...
Je vous remercie dès à présent de ...	Thank you in advance for ...

Monsieur Léon Mougeot
45, avenue de la République
75101 Paris
FRANCE

There should always be a comma between the street number and street name.

The postcode comes before the name of the town.

Making a call

Asking for information

Quel est l'indicatif de Bordeaux?	What's the code for Bordeaux?
Comment fait-on pour avoir une ligne extérieure?	How do I get an outside line?
Pouvez-vous me donner le numéro du poste de M Durand?	Could you give me the extension number for Mr Durand?

When your number answers

Bonjour! J'aimerais parler à Valérie.	Hello! Could I speak to Valérie, please?
Pourriez-vous me passer le docteur Leduc, s'il vous plaît?	Could you put me through to Dr Leduc, please?
Pourriez-vous lui demander de me rappeler, s'il vous plaît?	Would you ask him/her to call me back, please?
Je rappellerai dans une demi-heure.	I'll call back in half an hour.
Je peux laisser un message, s'il vous plaît?	Could I leave a message, please?

When you answer the telephone

Allô! C'est Marc à l'appareil.	Hello! It's Marc speaking.
C'est moi.	Speaking.
Qui est à l'appareil?	Who's speaking?

What you may hear

C'est de la part de qui?	Who shall I say is calling?
Je vous le/la passe.	I'm putting you through (to him/her).
Ne quittez pas.	Please hold.
Ça ne répond pas.	There's no reply.
Voulez-vous laisser un message?	Would you like to leave a message?

Making a call

If you have a problem

Je suis désolé, j'ai dû faire un faux numéro.	I'm sorry, I must have dialled the wrong number.
La ligne est très mauvaise.	This is a very bad line.
Ça coupe.	You're breaking up.
Ma batterie est presque à plat.	My battery's low.
Je ne t'entends plus.	I can't hear you.

Saying your phone number

To tell someone your phone number in French, you divide the number up into pairs instead of saying each digit separately. For example:

01 40 32 37 12

zéro-un / quarante / trente-deux / trente-sept / douze

If there's one extra number, you say that first:

0 26 23 84 47 46

zéro / vingt-six / vingt-trois / quatre-vingt-quatre / quarante-sept / quarante-six

French phrases and sayings

In French, as in many languages, people use vivid expressions based on images from their experience of real life. We've grouped the common expressions below according to the type of image they use. For fun, we have given you the word-for-word translation as well as the true English equivalent.

Fruit and vegetables

Ce ne sont pas mes oignons!
    word for word:
→ This is none of my business!
these aren't my onions

C'est la fin des haricots.
    word for word:
→ It's the last straw.
it's the end of beans

être haut comme trois pommes
    word for word:
→ to be knee-high to a grasshopper
to be high as three apples

tomber dans les pommes
    word for word:
→ to faint
to fall into the apples

Animals and insects

donner sa langue au chat
    word for word:
→ to give in or up (when guessing)
to give one's tongue to the cat

appeler un chat un chat
    word for word:
→ to call a spade a spade
to call a cat a cat

quand les poules auront des dents
    word for word:
→ pigs might fly
when hens have teeth

passer du coq à l'âne
    word for word:
→ to jump from one subject to another
to go from the cockerel to the donkey

avoir un chat dans la gorge
    word for word:
→ to have a frog in one's throat
to have a cat in one's throat

French phrases and sayings

Ce n'est pas la mer à boire. → It's not the end of the world.

      word for word: *it's not like having to drink the sea*

Je ne suis pas tombé de la dernière → I wasn't born yesterday.
pluie.

      word for word: *I didn't come down with the last
          shower of rain*

passer entre les gouttes → to come through without a scratch

      word for word: *to run between the raindrops*

pleuvoir des cordes → to be bucketing down

      word for word: *to be raining ropes*

Ça ne me fait ni chaud ni froid. → It doesn't make any difference to me.

      word for word: *it makes me neither hot nor cold*

avoir une dent contre quelqu'un → to have a grudge against somebody

      word for word: *to have a tooth against somebody*

Il n'a pas la langue dans sa poche. → He's never at a loss for words.

      word for word: *he doesn't keep his tongue in his pocket*

avoir un poil dans la main → to be bone idle

      word for word: *to have a hair in one's hand*

gagner les doigts dans le nez → to win hands down

      word for word: *to win with one's fingers up one's nose*

French phrases and sayings

changer d'avis comme de chemise → to be always changing one's mind
      word for word: *to change one's mind as often as*
                              one's shirt

trouver chaussure à son pied → to find a suitable match
      word for word: *to find a shoe for one's foot*

Lâche-moi la chemise! or **Lâche-moi** → Get off my back!
les baskets!

      word for word: *let go of my shirt, let go of my trainers*

C'est bonnet blanc et blanc bonnet. → It's six of one and half a dozen of
                              the other.
      word for word: *it's white hat and hat white*

voir tout en rose → to see life through rose-tinted
                              spectacles
      word for word: *to see everything in pink*

avoir une peur bleue de quelque → to be scared stiff of something
chose

      word for word: *to have a blue fear of something*

regarder qn dans le blanc des yeux → to look somebody straight in the eye
      word for word: *to look into the whites of somebody's*
                              eyes

Some common translation difficulties

On the following pages we have shown some of the translation difficulties that you are most likely to come across. We hope that the tips we have given will help you to avoid these common pitfalls when writing and speaking French.

Tu or vous?

In French the word for 'you' depends on who you are talking to:

• To a person you know well, use **tu**:

Will **you** lend me this book? ➔ **Tu** me prêtes ce livre?

• To a person you do not know so well, use **vous**:

Have **you** met my wife? ➔ **Vous** connaissez ma femme?

• To more than one person, whether you know them well or not, use **vous**:

Do **you** understand, children? ➔ **Vous** comprenez, les enfants?

Getting friendly

When you get to know someone, they may ask you:

On se tutoie? ➔ Shall we use 'tu' to each other?

On is the usual way of saying 'we' in conversation.

On est allé voir la Tour Eiffel. ➔ We went to see the Eiffel Tower.

Some common translation difficulties

Showing possession

In English -'**s** is a common way of showing who or what something belongs to. In French you have to use *de*:

my brother**'s** car	→	*la voiture **de** mon frère*
the children**'s** bedroom	→	*la chambre **des** enfants*

Singular versus plural

A word that is singular in English may be plural in French, and vice versa. Check in the dictionary if you are not sure:

Singular:		*Plural:*
luggage	→	*les bagages*
Plural:		*Singular:*
my trouser**s**	→	*mon pantalon*

'There is' and 'there are'

In French these are both translated by *il y a*:

There is someone at the door.	→	*Il y a quelqu'un à la porte.*
There are five books on the table.	→	*Il y a cinq livres sur la table.*

Some common translation difficulties

Using *en*

When the word *en* is used with numbers, it is often not translated in English but it can <u>never</u> be missed out in French:

I want **two (of them)**. → *J'**en** veux **deux**.*

Have you got a dictionary? – Yes, I've got **one**. → *Tu as un dictionnaire? – Oui, j'**en** ai **un**.*

Translating 'to'

'To' is generally translated by *à*, but remember:

• When you are talking about the time, use *moins*:

  five **to** ten → *dix heures **moins** cinq*

• In front of verbs, it is shown by the verb ending:

  to eat → *mang**er***
  to leave → *part**ir***
  to wait → *attend**re***

• When you mean 'in order to', use *pour*:

  He's going into town **(in order) to** buy a present. → *Il va en ville **pour** acheter un cadeau.*

Using *ne ... pas* and other negatives

You often find the verb 'do' in English negatives, but *faire* is never used like this. You use set word pairs instead:

English negative with 'do': French negative word pair:

I do**n't** smoke. → *Je **ne** fume **pas**.*

Do**n't** change **anything**. → ***Ne** changez **rien**.*

Some common translation difficulties

'To be' usually corresponds to *être*, but remember:

• In phrases describing how you feel, use *avoir*:

to be warm/cold	→ *avoir* chaud/froid
to be hungry/thirsty	→ *avoir* faim/soif
to be afraid	→ *avoir* peur

• To describe the weather, use *faire*:

It**'s** lovely weather today.	→ Il *fait* beau aujourd'hui.

• To say your age, use *avoir*:

I**'m** fifteen.	→ J'*ai* quinze ans.

• To talk about your health, use *aller*:

I**'m** very well, thank you.	→ Je *vais* très bien, merci.

Translating verbs

Many English verbs can be followed by a preposition or adverb such as 'on' or 'back' – 'to go on', 'to give back'. These additions often give the verb a new meaning. There is no similar way of doing this in French – you just use a different word, for example:

Verb (+ preposition/adverb):		Translation:
to go	→	aller
to go on	→	continuer
to give	→	donner
to give back	→	rendre

30

Some common translation difficulties

Sentences that contain a verb and preposition in English might not contain a preposition in French, and vice versa. The dictionary can help you with these. For example:

• Verb + preposition:

    to pay **for** something

Verb without preposition:

→   *payer quelque chose*

• Verb without preposition:

    to change something

Verb + preposition:

→   *changer **de** quelque chose*

A [eɪ] *n* (*Mus*) la *m*

○ **KEYWORD**

a [eɪ, ə] (*before vowel and silent h* **an**) *indef art* **1** un(e); **a book** un livre; **an apple** une pomme; **she's a doctor** elle est médecin

2 (*instead of the number "one"*) un(e); **a year ago** il y a un an; **a hundred/ thousand** *etc* **pounds** cent/mille *etc* livres

3 (*in expressing ratios, prices etc*): **three a day/week** trois par jour/semaine; **10 km an hour** 10 km à l'heure; **£5 a person** 5£ par personne; **30p a kilo** 30p le kilo

A2 *n* (*BRIT Scol*) deuxième partie de l'examen équivalent au baccalauréat
A.A. *n abbr* (*BRIT*: = *Automobile Association*) ≈ ACF *m*; (= *Alcoholics Anonymous*) AA

A.A.A. *n abbr* (= *American Automobile Association*) ≈ ACF *m*
aback [ə'bæk] *adv*: **to be taken ~** être décontenancé(e)
abandon [ə'bændən] *vt* abandonner
abattoir ['æbətwɑːʳ] *n* (*BRIT*) abattoir *m*
abbey ['æbɪ] *n* abbaye *f*
abbreviation [əbriːvɪ'eɪʃən] *n* abréviation *f*
abdomen ['æbdəmən] *n* abdomen *m*
abduct [æb'dʌkt] *vt* enlever
abide [ə'baɪd] *vt* souffrir, supporter; **I can't ~ it/him** je ne le supporte pas; **abide by** *vt fus* observer, respecter
ability [ə'bɪlɪtɪ] *n* compétence *f*; capacité *f*; (*skill*) talent *m*
able ['eɪbl] *adj* compétent(e); **to be ~ to do sth** pouvoir faire qch, être capable de faire qch
abnormal [æb'nɔːməl] *adj* anormal(e)
aboard [ə'bɔːd] *adv* à bord ▷ *prep* à bord de; (*train*) dans
abolish [ə'bɒlɪʃ] *vt* abolir
abolition [æbə'lɪʃən] *n* abolition *f*
abort [ə'bɔːt] *vt* (*Med*) faire avorter; (*Comput, fig*) abandonner; **abortion** [ə'bɔːʃən] *n* avortement *m*; **to have an abortion** se faire avorter

 KEYWORD

about [ə'baut] *adv* **1** (*approximately*) environ, à peu près; **about a hundred/thousand** *etc* environ cent/mille *etc*, une centaine (de)/ un millier (de) *etc*; **it takes about 10 hours** ça prend environ *or* à peu près 10 heures; **at about 2 o'clock** vers 2 heures; **I've just about finished** j'ai presque fini

2 (*referring to place*) çà et là, de-ci de-là; **to run about** courir çà et là; **to walk about** se promener, aller et venir; **they left all their things lying about** ils ont laissé traîner toutes leurs affaires

3: **to be about to do sth** être sur le point de faire qch
▶ prep **1** (relating to) au sujet de, à propos de; **a book about London** un livre sur Londres; **what is it about?** de quoi s'agit-il?; **we talked about it** nous en avons parlé; **what** or **how about doing this?** et si nous faisions ceci?
2 (referring to place) dans; **to walk about the town** se promener dans la ville

above [ə'bʌv] adv au-dessus ▷ prep au-dessus de; (more than) plus de; **mentioned ~** mentionné ci-dessus; **~ all** par-dessus tout, surtout
abroad [ə'brɔːd] adv à l'étranger
abrupt [ə'brʌpt] adj (steep, blunt) abrupt(e); (sudden, gruff) brusque
abscess ['æbsɪs] n abcès m
absence ['æbsəns] n absence f
absent ['æbsənt] adj absent(e); **absent-minded** adj distrait(e)
absolute ['æbsəluːt] adj absolu(e); **absolutely** [æbsə'luːtlɪ] adv absolument
absorb [əb'zɔːb] vt absorber; **to be ~ed in a book** être plongé(e) dans un livre; **absorbent cotton** n (US) coton m hydrophile; **absorbing** adj absorbant(e); (book, film etc) captivant(e)
abstain [əb'steɪn] vi: **to ~ (from)** s'abstenir (de)
abstract ['æbstrækt] adj abstrait(e)
absurd [əb'sɜːd] adj absurde
abundance [ə'bʌndəns] n abondance f
abundant [ə'bʌndənt] adj abondant(e)
abuse n [ə'bjuːs] (insults) insultes fpl, injures fpl; (ill-treatment) mauvais traitements mpl; (of power etc) abus m ▷ vt [ə'bjuːz] (insult) insulter; (ill-treat) malmener; (power etc) abuser de; **abusive** adj grossier(-ière), injurieux(-euse)

abysmal [ə'bɪzməl] adj exécrable; (ignorance etc) sans bornes
academic [ækə'dɛmɪk] adj universitaire; (person: scholarly) intellectuel(le); (pej: issue) oiseux(-euse), purement théorique ▷ n universitaire m/f; **academic year** n (University) année f universitaire; (Scol) année scolaire
academy [ə'kædəmɪ] n (learned body) académie f; (school) collège m; **~ of music** conservatoire m
accelerate [æk'sɛləreɪt] vt, vi accélérer; **acceleration** [æksɛlə'reɪʃən] n accélération f; **accelerator** n (BRIT) accélérateur m
accent ['æksɛnt] n accent m
accept [ək'sɛpt] vt accepter; **acceptable** adj acceptable; **acceptance** n acceptation f
access ['æksɛs] n accès m; **to have ~ to** (information, library etc) avoir accès à, pouvoir utiliser or consulter; (person) avoir accès auprès de; **accessible** [æk'sɛsəbl] adj accessible
accessory [æk'sɛsərɪ] n accessoire m; **~ to** (Law) accessoire à
accident ['æksɪdənt] n accident m; (chance) hasard m; **I've had an ~** j'ai eu un accident; **by ~** (by chance) par hasard; (not deliberately) accidentellement; **accidental** [æksɪ'dɛntl] adj accidentel(le); **accidentally** [æksɪ'dɛntəlɪ] adv accidentellement; **Accident and Emergency Department** n (BRIT) service m des urgences; **accident insurance** n assurance f accident
acclaim [ə'kleɪm] vt acclamer ▷ n acclamations fpl
accommodate [ə'kɔmədeɪt] vt loger, recevoir; (oblige, help) obliger; (car etc) contenir
accommodation, (US) **accommodations** [əkɔmə'deɪʃən(z)] n, npl logement m
accompaniment [ə'kʌmpənɪmənt] n accompagnement m

accompany [ə'kʌmpənı] vt accompagner

accomplice [ə'kʌmplıs] n complice m/f

accomplish [ə'kʌmplıʃ] vt accomplir; **accomplishment** n (skill: gen pl) talent m; (completion) accomplissement m; (achievement) réussite f

accord [ə'kɔːd] n accord m ▷ vt accorder; **of his own ~** de son plein gré; **accordance** n: **in accordance with** conformément à; **according: according to** prep selon; **accordingly** adv (appropriately) en conséquence; (as a result) par conséquent

account [ə'kaunt] n (Comm) compte m; (report) compte rendu, récit m; **accounts** npl (Comm: records) comptabilité f, comptes; **of no ~** sans importance; **on ~** en acompte; **to buy sth on ~** acheter qch à crédit; **on no ~** en aucun cas; **on ~ of** à cause de; **to take into ~, take ~ of** tenir compte de; **account for** vt fus (explain) expliquer, rendre compte de; (represent) représenter; **accountable** adj: **accountable (for/to)** responsable (de/devant); **accountant** n comptable m/f; **account number** n numéro m de compte

accumulate [ə'kjuːmjuleıt] vt accumuler, amasser ▷ vi s'accumuler, s'amasser

accuracy ['ækjurəsı] n exactitude f, précision f

accurate ['ækjurıt] adj exact(e), précis(e); (device) précis; **accurately** adv avec précision

accusation [ækju'zeıʃən] n accusation f

accuse [ə'kjuːz] vt: **to ~ sb (of sth)** accuser qn (de qch); **accused** n (Law) accusé(e)

accustomed [ə'kʌstəmd] adj: **~ to** habitué(e) or accoutumé(e) à

ace [eıs] n as m

ache [eık] n mal m, douleur f ▷ vi (be sore) faire mal, être douloureux(-euse); **my head ~s** j'ai mal à la tête

achieve [ə'tʃiːv] vt (aim) atteindre; (victory, success) remporter, obtenir; **achievement** n exploit m, réussite f; (of aims) réalisation f

acid ['æsıd] adj, n acide (m)

acknowledge [ək'nɔlıdʒ] vt (also: **~ receipt of**) accuser réception de; (fact) reconnaître; **acknowledgement** n (of letter) accusé m de réception

acne ['æknı] n acné m

acorn ['eıkɔːn] n gland m

acoustic [ə'kuːstık] adj acoustique

acquaintance [ə'kweıntəns] n connaissance f

acquire [ə'kwaıər] vt acquérir; **acquisition** [ækwı'zıʃən] n acquisition f

acquit [ə'kwıt] vt acquitter; **to ~ o.s. well** s'en tirer très honorablement

acre ['eıkər] n acre f (= 4047 m²)

acronym ['ækrənım] n acronyme m

across [ə'krɔs] prep (on the other side) de l'autre côté de; (crosswise) en travers de ▷ adv de l'autre côté; en travers; **to run/swim ~** traverser en courant/à la nage; **~ from** en face de

acrylic [ə'krılık] adj, n acrylique (m)

act [ækt] n acte m, action f; (Theat: part of play) acte; (: of performer) numéro m; (Law) loi f ▷ vi agir; (Theat) jouer; (pretend) jouer la comédie ▷ vt (role) jouer, tenir; **to catch sb in the ~** prendre qn sur le fait or en flagrant délit; **to ~ as** servir de; **act up** (inf) vi (person) se conduire mal; (knee, back, injury) jouer des tours; (machine) être capricieux(-ieuse); **acting** adj suppléant(e), par intérim ▷ n (activity): **to do some acting** faire du théâtre (or du cinéma)

action ['ækʃən] n action f; (Mil) combat(s) m(pl); (Law) procès m, action en justice; **out of ~** hors de

combat; (*machine etc*) hors d'usage;
to take ~ agir, prendre des mesures;
action replay *n* (*BRIT TV*) ralenti *m*
activate ['æktɪveɪt] *vt* (*mechanism*)
actionner, faire fonctionner
active ['æktɪv] *adj* actif(-ive);
(*volcano*) en activité; **actively** *adv*
activement; (*discourage*) vivement
activist ['æktɪvɪst] *n* activiste *m/f*
activity [æk'tɪvɪtɪ] *n* activité *f*;
activity holiday *n* vacances actives
actor ['æktə'] *n* acteur *m*
actress ['æktrɪs] *n* actrice *f*
actual ['æktjuəl] *adj* réel(le),
véritable; (*emphatic use*) lui-même
(elle-même)

⬛ Be careful not to translate *actual*
by the French word *actuel*.

actually ['æktjuəlɪ] *adv* réellement,
véritablement; (*in fact*) en fait

⬛ Be careful not to translate
actually by the French word
actuellement.

acupuncture ['ækjupʌŋktfə'] *n*
acuponcture *f*
acute [ə'kju:t] *adj* aigu(ë); (*mind,*
observer) pénétrant(e)
ad [æd] *n abbr* = **advertisement**
A.D. *adv abbr* (= *Anno Domini*) ap. J.-C.
adamant ['ædəmənt] *adj* inflexible
adapt [ə'dæpt] *vt* adapter ▷ *vi*: **to ~**
(to) s'adapter (à); **adapter, adaptor**
n (*Elec*) adaptateur *m*; (*for several*
plugs) prise *f* multiple
add [æd] *vt* ajouter; (*figures: also:* **to ~**
up) additionner; **it doesn't ~ up** (*fig*)
cela ne rime à rien; **add up to** *vt fus*
(*Math*) s'élever à; (*fig: mean*) signifier
addict ['ædɪkt] *n* toxicomane
m/f; (*fig*) fanatique *m/f*; **addicted**
[ə'dɪktɪd] *adj*: **to be addicted to**
(*drink, drugs*) être adonné(e) à; (*fig:*
football etc) être un(e) fanatique
de; **addiction** [ə'dɪkʃən] *n* (*Med*)
dépendance *f*; **addictive** [ə'dɪktɪv]
adj qui crée une dépendance
addition [ə'dɪʃən] *n* (*adding up*)
addition *f*; (*thing added*) ajout *m*; **in ~**

de plus, de surcroît; **in ~ to** en plus de;
additional *adj* supplémentaire
additive ['ædɪtɪv] *n* additif *m*
address [ə'drɛs] *n* adresse *f*; (*talk*)
discours *m*, allocution *f* ▷ *vt* adresser;
(*speak to*) s'adresser à; **my ~ is ...** mon
adresse, c'est ...; **address book** *n*
carnet *m* d'adresses
adequate ['ædɪkwɪt] *adj*
(*enough*) suffisant(e); (*satisfactory*)
satisfaisant(e)
adhere [əd'hɪə'] *vi*: **to ~ to** adhérer à;
(*fig: rule, decision*) se tenir à
adhesive [əd'hi:zɪv] *n* adhésif *m*;
adhesive tape *n* (*BRIT*) ruban *m*
adhésif; (*US Med*) sparadrap *m*
adjacent [ə'dʒeɪsənt] *adj*
adjacent(e), contigu(ë); **~ to**
adjacent à
adjective ['ædʒɛktɪv] *n* adjectif *m*
adjoining [ə'dʒɔɪnɪŋ] *adj* voisin(e),
adjacent(e), attenant(e)
adjourn [ə'dʒə:n] *vt* ajourner ▷ *vi*
suspendre la séance; lever la séance;
clore la session
adjust [ə'dʒʌst] *vt* (*machine*) ajuster,
régler; (*prices, wages*) rajuster ▷ *vi*:
to ~ (to) s'adapter (à); **adjustable** *adj*
réglable; **adjustment** *n* (*of machine*)
ajustage *m*, réglage *m*; (*of prices, wages*)
rajustement *m*; (*of person*) adaptation *f*
administer [əd'mɪnɪstə'] *vt*
administrer; **administration**
[ədmɪnɪs'treɪʃən] *n* (*management*)
administration *f*; (*government*)
gouvernement *m*; **administrative**
[əd'mɪnɪstrətɪv] *adj*
administratif(-ive)
administrator [əd'mɪnɪstreɪtə'] *n*
administrateur(-trice)
admiral ['ædmərəl] *n* amiral *m*
admiration [ædmə'reɪʃən] *n*
admiration *f*
admire [əd'maɪə'] *vt* admirer;
admirer *n* (*fan*) admirateur(-trice)
admission [əd'mɪʃən] *n* admission
f; (*to exhibition, night club etc*) entrée *f*;
(*confession*) aveu *m*

admit [əd'mɪt] *vt* laisser entrer; admettre; *(agree)* reconnaître, admettre; *(crime)* reconnaître avoir commis; **"children not ~ted"** "entrée interdite aux enfants"; **admit to** *vt fus* reconnaître, avouer; **admittance** *n* admission *f*, droit *m* d'entrée *f*; **admittedly** *adv* il faut en convenir

adolescent [ædəu'lɛsnt] *adj, n* adolescent(e)

adopt [ə'dɔpt] *vt* adopter; **adopted** *adj* adoptif(-ive), adopté(e); **adoption** [ə'dɔpʃən] *n* adoption *f*

adore [ə'dɔːʳ] *vt* adorer

adorn [ə'dɔːn] *vt* orner

Adriatic (Sea) [eɪdrɪ'ætɪk-] *n*: **the Adriatic (Sea)** la mer Adriatique, l'Adriatique *f*

adrift [ə'drɪft] *adv* à la dérive

ADSL *n abbr* (= *asymmetric digital subscriber line*) ADSL *m*

adult ['ædʌlt] *n* adulte *m/f* ▷ *adj* (*grown-up*) adulte; (*for adults*) pour adultes; **adult education** *n* éducation *f* des adultes

adultery [ə'dʌltərɪ] *n* adultère *m*

advance [əd'vɑːns] *n* avance *f* ▷ *vt* avancer ▷ *vi* s'avancer; **in ~** en avance, d'avance; **to make ~s to sb** (*amorously*) faire des avances à qn; **~ booking** location *f*; **~ notice, ~ warning** préavis *m*; (*verbal*) avertissement *m*; **do I need to book in ~?** est-ce qu'il faut réserver à l'avance?; **advanced** *adj* avancé(e); (*Scol: studies*) supérieur(e)

advantage [əd'vɑːntɪdʒ] *n* (*also Tennis*) avantage *m*; **to take ~ of** (*person*) exploiter; (*opportunity*) profiter de

advent ['ædvənt] *n* avènement *m*, venue *f*; **A~** (*Rel*) avent *m*

adventure [əd'vɛntʃəʳ] *n* aventure *f*; **adventurous** [əd'vɛntʃərəs] *adj* aventureux(-euse)

adverb ['ædvəːb] *n* adverbe *m*

adversary ['ædvəsərɪ] *n* adversaire *m/f*

adverse ['ædvəːs] *adj* adverse; (*effect*) négatif(-ive); (*weather, publicity*) mauvais(e); (*wind*) contraire

advert ['ædvəːt] *n abbr* (BRIT) = **advertisement**

advertise ['ædvətaɪz] *vi* faire de la publicité or de la réclame; (*in classified ads etc*) mettre une annonce ▷ *vt* faire de la publicité or de la réclame pour; (*in classified ads etc*) mettre une annonce pour vendre; **to ~ for** (*staff*) recruter par (voie d')annonce; **advertisement** [əd'vəːtɪsmənt] *n* publicité *f*, réclame *f*; (*in classified ads etc*) annonce *f*; **advertiser** *n* annonceur *m*; **advertising** *n* publicité *f*

advice [əd'vaɪs] *n* conseils *mpl*; (*notification*) avis *m*; **a piece of ~** un conseil; **to take legal ~** consulter un avocat

advisable [əd'vaɪzəbl] *adj* recommandable, indiqué(e)

advise [əd'vaɪz] *vt* conseiller; **to ~ sb of sth** aviser or informer qn de qch; **to ~ against sth/doing sth** déconseiller qch/conseiller de ne pas faire qch; **adviser, advisor** *n* conseiller(-ère); **advisory** *adj* consultatif(-ive)

advocate *n* ['ædvəkɪt] (*lawyer*) avocat (plaidant); (*upholder*) défenseur *m*, avocat(e) ▷ *vt* ['ædvəkeɪt] recommander, prôner; **to be an ~ of** être partisan(e) de

Aegean [iː'dʒiːən] *n, adj*: **the ~ (Sea)** la mer Égée, l'Égée *f*

aerial ['ɛərɪəl] *n* antenne *f* ▷ *adj* aérien(ne)

aerobics [ɛə'rəubɪks] *n* aérobic *m*

aeroplane ['ɛərəpleɪn] *n* (BRIT) avion *m*

aerosol ['ɛərəsɔl] *n* aérosol *m*

affair [ə'fɛəʳ] *n* affaire *f*; (*also*: **love ~**) liaison *f*; aventure *f*

affect [ə'fɛkt] *vt* affecter; (*subj: disease*) atteindre; **affected** *adj* affecté(e); **affection** *n* affection *f*; **affectionate** *adj* affectueux(-euse)

afflict [ə'flɪkt] vt affliger
affluent ['æfluənt] adj aisé(e), riche; **the ~ society** la société d'abondance
afford [ə'fɔːd] vt (behaviour) se permettre; (provide) fournir, procurer; **can we ~ a car?** avons-nous de quoi acheter or les moyens d'acheter une voiture?; **affordable** adj abordable
Afghanistan [æf'gænɪstæn] n Afghanistan m
afraid [ə'freɪd] adj effrayé(e); **to be ~ of or to** avoir peur de; **I am ~ that** je crains que + sub; **I'm ~ so/not** oui/non, malheureusement
Africa ['æfrɪkə] n Afrique f; **African** adj africain(e) ▷ n Africain(e); **African-American** adj afro-américain(e) ▷ n Afro-Américain(e)
after ['ɑːftəʳ] prep, adv après ▷ conj après que; **it's quarter ~ two** (us) il est deux heures et quart; **~ having done/~ he left** après avoir fait/après son départ; **to name sb ~ sb** donner à qn le nom de qn; **to ask ~ sb** demander des nouvelles de qn; **what/who are you ~?** que/qui cherchez-vous?; **~ you!** après vous!; **~ all** après tout; **after-effects** npl (of disaster, radiation, drink etc) répercussions fpl; (of illness) séquelles fpl, suites fpl; **aftermath** n conséquences fpl; **afternoon** n après-midi m/f; **after-shave (lotion)** n lotion f après-rasage; **aftersun (cream/lotion)** n après-soleil m inv; **afterwards**, (us) **afterward** ['ɑːftəwəd(z)] adv après
again [ə'gɛn] adv de nouveau, encore (une fois); **to do sth ~** refaire qch; **~ and ~** à plusieurs reprises
against [ə'gɛnst] prep contre; (compared to) par rapport à
age [eɪdʒ] n âge m ▷ vt, vi vieillir; **he is 20 years of ~** il a 20 ans; **to come of ~** atteindre sa majorité; **it's been ~s since I saw you** ça fait une éternité que je ne t'ai pas vu
aged adj âgé(e); **~ 10** âgé de 10 ans

age: age group n tranche f d'âge; **age limit** n limite f d'âge
agency ['eɪdʒənsɪ] n agence f
agenda [ə'dʒɛndə] n ordre m du jour
Be careful not to translate agenda by the French word agenda.
agent ['eɪdʒənt] n agent m; (firm) concessionnaire m
aggravate ['ægrəveɪt] vt (situation) aggraver; (annoy) exaspérer, agacer
aggression [ə'grɛʃən] n agression f
aggressive [ə'grɛsɪv] adj agressif(-ive)
agile ['ædʒaɪl] adj agile
AGM n abbr (= annual general meeting) AG f
ago [ə'gəu] adv: **two days ~** il y a deux jours; **not long ~** il n'y a pas longtemps; **how long ~?** il y a combien de temps (de cela)?
agony ['ægənɪ] n (pain) douleur f atroce; (distress) angoisse f; **to be in ~** souffrir le martyre
agree [ə'griː] vt (price) convenir de ▷ vi: **to ~ with** (person) être d'accord avec; (statements etc) concorder avec; (Ling) s'accorder avec; **to ~ to do** accepter de or consentir à faire; **to ~ to sth** consentir à qch; **to ~ that** (admit) convenir or reconnaître que; **garlic doesn't ~ with me** je ne supporte pas l'ail; **agreeable** adj (pleasant) agréable; (willing) consentant(e), d'accord; **agreed** adj (time, place) convenu(e); **agreement** n accord m; **in agreement** d'accord
agricultural [ægrɪ'kʌltʃərəl] adj agricole
agriculture ['ægrɪkʌltʃəʳ] n agriculture f
ahead [ə'hɛd] adv en avant; devant; **go right or straight ~** (direction) allez tout droit; **go ~!** (permission) allez-y!; **~ of** devant; (fig: schedule etc) en avance sur; **~ of time** en avance
aid [eɪd] n aide f; (device) appareil m ▷ vt aider; **in ~ of** en faveur de
aide [eɪd] n (person) assistant(e)

AIDS [eɪdz] n abbr (= acquired immune (or immuno-)deficiency syndrome) SIDA m

ailing ['eɪlɪŋ] adj (person) souffreteux(euse); (economy) malade

ailment ['eɪlmənt] n affection f

aim [eɪm] n (objective) but m; (skill): **his ~ is bad** il vise mal ▷ vi (also: **to take ~**) viser ▷ vt: **to ~ sth (at)** (gun, camera) braquer or pointer qch (sur); (missile) lancer qch (à or contre or en direction de); (remark, blow) destiner or adresser qch (à); **to ~ at** viser; (fig) viser (à); **to ~ to do** avoir l'intention de faire

ain't [eɪnt] (inf) = **am not; aren't; isn't**

air [ɛəʳ] n air m ▷ vt aérer; (idea, grievance, views) mettre sur le tapis ▷ cpd (currents, attack etc) aérien(ne); **to throw sth into the ~** (ball etc) jeter qch en l'air; **by ~** par avion; **to be on the ~** (Radio, TV: programme) être diffusé(e); (: station) émettre; **airbag** n airbag m; **airbed** n (BRIT) matelas m pneumatique; **airborne** adj (plane) en vol; **as soon as the plane was airborne** dès que l'avion eut décollé; **air-conditioned** adj climatisé(e), à air conditionné; **air conditioning** n climatisation f; **aircraft** n inv avion m; **airfield** n terrain m d'aviation; **Air Force** n Armée f de l'air; **air hostess** n (BRIT) hôtesse f de l'air; **airing cupboard** n (BRIT) placard qui contient la chaudière et dans lequel on met le linge à sécher; **airlift** n pont aérien; **airline** n ligne aérienne, compagnie aérienne; **airliner** n avion m de ligne; **airmail** n: **by airmail** par avion; **airplane** n (US) avion m; **airport** n aéroport m; **air raid** n attaque aérienne; **airsick** adj: **to be airsick** avoir le mal de l'air; **airspace** n espace m aérien; **airstrip** n terrain m d'atterrissage; **air terminal** n aérogare f; **airtight** adj hermétique; **air-traffic controller** n aiguilleur m du ciel; **airy** adj bien aéré(e); (manners) dégagé(e)

aisle [aɪl] n (of church: central) allée f centrale; (: side) nef f latérale, bas-côté m; (in theatre, supermarket) allée f; (on plane) couloir m; **aisle seat** n place f côté couloir

ajar [ə'dʒɑːʳ] adj entrouvert(e)

à la carte [ælæ'kɑːt] adv à la carte

alarm [ə'lɑːm] n alarme f ▷ vt alarmer; **alarm call** n coup m de fil pour réveiller; **could I have an alarm call at 7 am, please?** pouvez-vous me réveiller à 7 heures, s'il vous plaît?; **alarm clock** n réveille-matin m inv, réveil m; **alarmed** adj (frightened) alarmé(e); (protected by an alarm) protégé(e) par un système d'alarme; **alarming** adj alarmant(e)

Albania [æl'beɪnɪə] n Albanie f

albeit [ɔːl'biːɪt] conj bien que + sub, encore que + sub

album ['ælbəm] n album m

alcohol ['ælkəhɔl] n alcool m; **alcohol-free** adj sans alcool; **alcoholic** [ælkə'hɔlɪk] adj, n alcoolique (m/f)

alcove ['ælkəuv] n alcôve f

ale [eɪl] n bière f

alert [ə'ləːt] adj alerte, vif (vive); (watchful) vigilant(e) ▷ n alerte f ▷ vt alerter; **on the ~** sur le qui-vive; (Mil) en état d'alerte

algebra ['ældʒɪbrə] n algèbre m

Algeria [æl'dʒɪərɪə] n Algérie f

Algerian [æl'dʒɪərɪən] adj algérien(ne) ▷ n Algérien(ne)

Algiers [æl'dʒɪəz] n Alger

alias ['eɪlɪəs] adv alias ▷ n faux nom, nom d'emprunt

alibi ['ælɪbaɪ] n alibi m

alien ['eɪlɪən] n (from abroad) étranger(-ère); (from outer space) extraterrestre ▷ adj: **~ (to)** étranger(-ère) (à); **alienate** vt aliéner; (subj: person) s'aliéner

alight [ə'laɪt] adj en feu ▷ vi mettre pied à terre; (passenger) descendre; (bird) se poser

align [ə'laɪn] vt aligner

alike [əˈlaɪk] *adj* semblable, pareil(le)
▷ *adv* de même; **to look ~** se
ressembler

alive [əˈlaɪv] *adj* vivant(e); (*active*)
plein(e) de vie

🔵 **KEYWORD**

all [ɔ:l] *adj* (*singular*) tout(e); (*plural*)
tous (toutes); **all day** toute la
journée; **all night** toute la nuit; **all
men** tous les hommes; **all five** tous
les cinq; **all the books** tous les livres;
all his life toute sa vie
▷ *pron* 1 tout; **I ate it all, I ate all
of it** j'ai tout mangé; **all of us went**
nous y sommes tous allés; **all of the
boys went** tous les garçons y sont
allés; **is that all?** c'est tout?; (*in shop*)
ce sera tout?
2 (*in phrases*): **above all** surtout,
par-dessus tout; **after all** après
tout; **at all: not at all** (*in answer to
question*) pas du tout; (*in answer to
thanks*) je vous en prie!; **I'm not at all
tired** je ne suis pas du tout fatigué(e);
anything at all will do n'importe
quoi fera l'affaire; **all in all** tout bien
considéré, en fin de compte
▷ *adv*: **all alone** tout(e) seul(e); **it's
not as hard as all that** ce n'est pas
si difficile que ça; **all the more/
the better** d'autant plus/mieux;
all but presque, pratiquement;
the score is 2 all le score est de 2
partout

Allah [ˈælə] *n* Allah *m*
allegation [ælɪˈgeɪʃən] *n* allégation *f*
alleged [əˈlɛdʒd] *adj* prétendu(e);
allegedly *adv* à ce que l'on prétend,
paraît-il
allegiance [əˈliːdʒəns] *n* fidélité *f*,
obéissance *f*
allergic [əˈlɜːdʒɪk] *adj*: **~ to**
allergique à; **I'm ~ to penicillin** je
suis allergique à la pénicilline
allergy [ˈælədʒɪ] *n* allergie *f*

alleviate [əˈliːvɪeɪt] *vt* soulager,
adoucir
alley [ˈælɪ] *n* ruelle *f*
alliance [əˈlaɪəns] *n* alliance *f*
allied [ˈælaɪd] *adj* allié(e)
alligator [ˈælɪgeɪtər] *n* alligator *m*
all-in [ˈɔːlɪn] *adj*, *adv* (BRIT: *charge*)
tout compris
allocate [ˈæləkeɪt] *vt* (*share out*)
répartir, distribuer; **to ~ sth to**
(*duties*) assigner or attribuer qch à;
(*sum, time*) allouer qch à
allot [əˈlɒt] *vt* (*share out*) répartir,
distribuer; **to ~ sth to** (*time*) allouer
qch à; (*duties*) assigner qch à
all-out [ˈɔːlaut] *adj* (*effort etc*) total(e)
allow [əˈlau] *vt* (*practice, behaviour*)
permettre, autoriser; (*sum to spend
etc*) accorder, allouer; (*sum, time
estimated*) compter, prévoir; (*claim,
goal*) admettre; (*concede*): **to ~
that** convenir que; **to ~ sb to do**
permettre à qn de faire, autoriser qn
à faire; **he is ~ed to ...** on lui permet
de ...; **allow for** *vt fus* tenir compte
de; **allowance** *n* (*money received*)
allocation *f* (: *from parent etc*) subside
m; (: *for expenses*) indemnité *f*; (*us:
pocket money*) argent *m* de poche;
(*Tax*) somme *f* déductible du revenu
imposable, abattement *m*; **to make
allowances for** (*person*) essayer de
comprendre; (*thing*) tenir compte de
all right *adv* (*feel, work*) bien; (*as
answer*) d'accord
ally [ˈælaɪ] *n* allié *m* ▷ *vt* [əˈlaɪ]: **to ~
o.s. with** s'allier avec
almighty [ɔːlˈmaɪtɪ] *adj* tout(e)-
puissant(e); (*tremendous*) énorme
almond [ˈɑːmənd] *n* amande *f*
almost [ˈɔːlməust] *adv* presque
alone [əˈləun] *adj*, *adv* seul(e); **to
leave sb ~** laisser qn tranquille; **to
leave sth ~** ne pas toucher à qch; **let
~ ...** sans parler de ...; encore moins ...
along [əˈlɒŋ] *prep* le long de ▷ *adv*: **is
he coming ~ with us?** vient-il avec
nous?; **he was hopping/limping ~**

il venait or avançait en sautillant/
boitant; **~ with** avec, en plus de;
(person) en compagnie de; **all ~** (all the
time) depuis le début; **alongside** prep
(along) le long de; (beside) à côté de
▷ adv bord à bord; côte à côte
aloof [ə'lu:f] adj distant(e) ▷ adv: **to
stand ~** se tenir à l'écart or à distance
aloud [ə'laud] adv à haute voix
alphabet ['ælfəbɛt] n alphabet m
Alps [ælps] npl: **the ~** les Alpes fpl
already [ɔːl'rɛdɪ] adv déjà
alright ['ɔːl'raɪt] adv (BRIT) = **all right**
also ['ɔːlsəu] adv aussi
altar ['ɔltər] n autel m
alter ['ɔltər] vt, vi changer; **alteration**
[ɔltə'reɪʃən] n changement m,
modification f; **alterations** npl
(Sewing) retouches fpl; (Archit)
modifications fpl
alternate adj [ɔl'tə:nɪt] alterné(e),
alternant(e), alternatif(-ive); (us)
= **alternative** ▷ vi ['ɔltə:neɪt]
alterner; **to ~ with** alterner avec;
on ~ days un jour sur deux, tous les
deux jours
alternative [ɔl'tə:nətɪv]
adj (solution, plan) autre, de
remplacement; (lifestyle) parallèle
▷ n (choice) alternative f; (other
possibility) autre possibilité f; **~
medicine** médecine alternative,
médecine douce; **alternatively** adv:
alternatively one could ... une
autre or l'autre solution serait de ...
although [ɔːl'ðəu] conj bien que + sub
altitude ['æltɪtju:d] n altitude f
altogether [ɔːltə'gɛðər] adv
entièrement, tout à fait; (on the whole)
tout compte fait; (in all) en tout
aluminium [ælju'mɪnɪəm],
(us) **aluminum** [ə'lu:mɪnəm] n
aluminium m
always ['ɔːlweɪz] adv toujours
Alzheimer's (disease)
['æltshaɪməz-] n maladie f
d'Alzheimer
am [æm] vb see **be**

a.m. adv abbr (= ante meridiem) du
matin
amalgamate [ə'mælgəmeɪt] vt,
vi fusionner
amass [ə'mæs] vt amasser
amateur ['æmətər] n amateur m
amaze [ə'meɪz] vt stupéfier; **to be ~d
(at)** être stupéfait(e) (de); **amazed**
adj stupéfait(e); **amazement** n
surprise f, étonnement m; **amazing**
adj étonnant(e), incroyable; (bargain,
offer) exceptionnel(le)
Amazon ['æməzən] n (Geo)
Amazone f
ambassador [æm'bæsədər] n
ambassadeur m
amber ['æmbər] n ambre m; **at ~**
(BRIT Aut) à l'orange
ambiguous [æm'bɪgjuəs] adj
ambigu(ë)
ambition [æm'bɪʃən] n ambition
f; **ambitious** [æm'bɪʃəs] adj
ambitieux(-euse)
ambulance ['æmbjuləns] n
ambulance f; **call an ~!** appelez une
ambulance!
ambush ['æmbuʃ] n embuscade f
▷ vt tendre une embuscade à
amen ['ɑː'mɛn] excl amen
amend [ə'mɛnd] vt (law) amender;
(text) corriger; **to make ~s** réparer
ses torts, faire amende honorable;
amendment n (to law) amendement
m; (to text) correction f
amenities [ə'mi:nɪtɪz] npl
aménagements mpl, équipements
mpl
America [ə'mɛrɪkə] n Amérique
f; **American** adj américain(e) ▷ n
Américain(e); **American football** n
(BRIT) football m américain
amicable ['æmɪkəbl] adj amical(e);
(Law) à l'amiable
amid(st) [ə'mɪd(st)] prep parmi, au
milieu de
ammunition [æmju'nɪʃən] n
munitions fpl
amnesty ['æmnɪstɪ] n amnistie f

among(st) [ə'mʌŋ(st)] *prep* parmi, entre

amount [ə'maunt] *n* (*sum of money*) somme *f*; (*total*) montant *m*; (*quantity*) quantité *f*; nombre *m* ▷ *vi*: **to ~ to** (*total*) s'élever à; (*be same as*) équivaloir à, revenir à

amp(ère) ['æmp(εə')] *n* ampère *m*

ample ['æmpl] *adj* ample, spacieux(-euse); (*enough*): **this is ~** c'est largement suffisant; **to have ~ time/room** avoir bien assez de temps/place

amplifier ['æmplɪfaɪə'] *n* amplificateur *m*

amputate ['æmpjuteɪt] *vt* amputer

Amtrak ['æmtræk] (*US*) *n société mixte de transports ferroviaires interurbains pour voyageurs*

amuse [ə'mju:z] *vt* amuser; **amusement** *n* amusement *m*; (*pastime*) distraction *f*; **amusement arcade** *n* salle *f* de jeu; **amusement park** *n* parc *m* d'attractions

amusing [ə'mju:zɪŋ] *adj* amusant(e), divertissant(e)

an [æn, ən, n] *indef art see* **a**

anaemia, (*US*) **anemia** [ə'ni:mɪə] *n* anémie *f*

anaemic, (*US*) **anemic** [ə'ni:mɪk] *adj* anémique

anaesthetic, (*US*) **anesthetic** [ænɪs'θεtɪk] *n* anesthésique *m*

analog(ue) ['ænəlɔg] *adj* (*watch, computer*) analogique

analogy [ə'nælədʒɪ] *n* analogie *f*

analyse, (*US*) **analyze** ['ænəlaɪz] *vt* analyser; **analysis** (*pl* **analyses**) [ə'næləsɪs, -si:z] *n* analyse *f*; **analyst** ['ænəlɪst] *n* (*political analyst etc*) analyste *m/f*; (*US*) psychanalyste *m/f*

analyze ['ænəlaɪz] *vt* (*US*) = **analyse**

anarchy ['ænəkɪ] *n* anarchie *f*

anatomy [ə'nætəmɪ] *n* anatomie *f*

ancestor ['ænsɪstə'] *n* ancêtre *m*, aïeul *m*

anchor ['æŋkə'] *n* ancre *f* ▷ *vi* (*also*: **to drop ~**) jeter l'ancre, mouiller ▷ *vt*

mettre à l'ancre; (*fig*): **to ~ sth to** fixer qch à

anchovy ['æntʃəvɪ] *n* anchois *m*

ancient ['eɪnʃənt] *adj* ancien(ne), antique; (*person*) d'un âge vénérable; (*car*) antédiluvien(ne)

and [ænd] *conj* et; **~ so on** et ainsi de suite; **try ~ come** tâchez de venir; **come ~ sit here** venez vous asseoir ici; **he talked ~ talked** il a parlé pendant des heures; **better ~ better** de mieux en mieux; **more ~ more** de plus en plus

Andorra [æn'dɔːrə] *n* (principauté *f* d')Andorre *f*

anemia *etc* [ə'ni:mɪə] *n* (*US*) = **anaemia** *etc*

anesthetic [ænɪs'θεtɪk] *n, adj* (*US*) = **anaesthetic**

angel ['eɪndʒəl] *n* ange *m*

anger ['æŋgə'] *n* colère *f*

angina [æn'dʒaɪnə] *n* angine *f* de poitrine

angle ['æŋgl] *n* angle *m*; **from their ~** de leur point de vue

angler ['æŋglə'] *n* pêcheur(-euse) à la ligne

Anglican ['æŋglɪkən] *adj, n* anglican(e)

angling ['æŋglɪŋ] *n* pêche *f* à la ligne

angrily ['æŋgrɪlɪ] *adv* avec colère

angry ['æŋgrɪ] *adj* en colère, furieux(-euse); (*wound*) enflammé(e); **to be ~ with sb/at sth** être furieux contre qn/de qch; **to get ~** se fâcher, se mettre en colère

anguish ['æŋgwɪʃ] *n* angoisse *f*

animal ['ænɪməl] *n* animal *m* ▷ *adj* animal(e)

animated ['ænɪmeɪtɪd] *adj* animé(e)

animation [ænɪ'meɪʃən] *n* (*of person*) entrain *m*; (*of street, Cine*) animation *f*

aniseed ['ænɪsi:d] *n* anis *m*

ankle ['æŋkl] *n* cheville *f*

annex ['ænεks] *n* (*BRIT: also*: **~e**) annexe *f* ▷ *vt* [ə'nεks] annexer

anniversary [ænɪ'vəːsərɪ] *n* anniversaire *m*

announce [ə'nauns] vt annoncer; (birth, death) faire part de; **announcement** n annonce f; (for births etc: in newspaper) avis m de faire-part; (: letter, card) faire-part m; **announcer** n (Radio, TV: between programmes) speaker(ine); (: in a programme) présentateur(-trice)

annoy [ə'nɔɪ] vt agacer, ennuyer, contrarier; **don't get ~ed!** ne vous fâchez pas!; **annoying** adj agaçant(e), contrariant(e)

annual ['ænjuəl] adj annuel(le) ▷ n (Bot) plante annuelle; (book) album m; **annually** adv annuellement

annum ['ænəm] n see **per**

anonymous [ə'nɔnɪməs] adj anonyme

anorak ['ænəræk] n anorak m

anorexia [ænə'rɛksɪə] n (also: ~ **nervosa**) anorexie f

anorexic [ænə'rɛksɪk] adj, n anorexique (m/f)

another [ə'nʌðə^r] adj: ~ **book** (one more) un autre livre, encore un livre, un livre de plus; (a different one) un autre livre ▷ pron un(e) autre, encore un(e), un(e) de plus; see also **one**

answer ['ɑ:nsə^r] n réponse f; (to problem) solution f ▷ vi répondre ▷ vt (reply to) répondre à; (problem) résoudre; (prayer) exaucer; **in ~ to your letter** suite à or en réponse à votre lettre; **to ~ the phone** répondre (au téléphone); **to ~ the bell** or **the door** aller or venir ouvrir (la porte); **answer back** vi répliquer, répondre; **answerphone** n (esp BRIT) répondeur m (téléphonique)

ant [ænt] n fourmi f

Antarctic [ænt'ɑ:ktɪk] n: **the ~** l'Antarctique m

antelope ['æntɪləup] n antilope f

antenatal ['æntɪ'neɪtl] adj prénatal(e)

antenna (pl **antennae**) [æn'tɛnə, -ni:] n antenne f

anthem ['ænθəm] n: **national ~** hymne national

anthology [æn'θɔlədʒɪ] n anthologie f

anthropology [ænθrə'pɔlədʒɪ] n anthropologie f

anti ['æntɪ] prefix anti-; **antibiotic** ['æntɪbaɪ'ɔtɪk] n antibiotique m; **antibody** ['æntɪbɔdɪ] n anticorps m

anticipate [æn'tɪsɪpeɪt] vt s'attendre à, prévoir; (wishes, request) aller au devant de, devancer; **anticipation** [æntɪsɪ'peɪʃən] n attente f

anticlimax [æntɪ'klaɪmæks] n déception f

anticlockwise ['æntɪ'klɔkwaɪz] (BRIT) adv dans le sens inverse des aiguilles d'une montre

antics ['æntɪks] npl singeries fpl

anti: antidote ['æntɪdəut] n antidote m, contrepoison m; **antifreeze** ['æntɪfri:z] n antigel m; **antiglobalization** n antimondialisation f; **antihistamine** [æntɪ'hɪstəmɪn] n antihistaminique m; **antiperspirant** [æntɪ'pə:spɪrənt] n déodorant m

antique [æn'ti:k] n (ornament) objet m d'art ancien; (furniture) meuble ancien ▷ adj ancien(ne); **antique shop** n magasin m d'antiquités

antiseptic [æntɪ'sɛptɪk] adj, n antiseptique (m)

antisocial ['æntɪ'səuʃəl] adj (unfriendly) insociable; (against society) antisocial(e)

antivirus [æntɪ'vaɪrəs] adj (Comput) antivirus inv; **~ software** (logiciel m) antivirus

antlers ['æntləz] npl bois mpl, ramure f

anxiety [æŋ'zaɪətɪ] n anxiété f; (keenness): **~ to do** grand désir or impatience f de faire

anxious ['æŋkʃəs] adj (très) inquiet(-ète); (always worried) anxieux(-euse); (worrying) angoissant(e); **~ to do/that** (keen)

qui tient beaucoup à faire/à ce que
+ *sub*; impatient(e) de faire/que + *sub*

 KEYWORD

any ['ɛnɪ] *adj* **1** (*in questions etc*:
singular) du, de l', de la; (: *plural*) des;
**do you have any butter/children/
ink?** avez-vous du beurre/des
enfants/de l'encre?
2 (*with negative*) de, d'; **I don't have
any money/books** je n'ai pas
d'argent/de livres
3 (*no matter which*) n'importe quel(le);
(*each and every*) tout(e), chaque;
choose any book you like vous
pouvez choisir n'importe quel livre;
any teacher you ask will tell you
n'importe quel professeur vous le dira
4 (*in phrases*): **in any case** de toute
façon; **any day now** d'un jour à
l'autre; **at any moment** à tout
moment, d'un instant à l'autre; **at
any rate** en tout cas; **any time**
n'importe quand; **he might come
(at) any time** il pourrait venir
n'importe quand; **come (at) any
time** venez quand vous voulez
▶ *pron* **1** (*in questions etc*) en; **have
you got any?** est-ce que vous en
avez?; **can any of you sing?** est-ce
que parmi vous il y en a qui savent
chanter?
2 (*with negative*) en; **I don't have
any (of them)** je n'en ai pas, je n'en
ai aucun
3 (*no matter which one(s)*) n'importe
lequel (*or* laquelle); (*anybody*)
n'importe qui; **take any of those
books (you like)** vous pouvez
prendre n'importe lequel de ces livres
▶ *adv* **1** (*in questions etc*): **do you
want any more soup/sandwiches?**
voulez-vous encore de la soupe/des
sandwichs?; **are you feeling any
better?** est-ce que vous vous sentez
mieux?
2 (*with negative*): **I can't hear him**

any more je ne l'entends plus;
don't wait any longer n'attendez
pas plus longtemps; **anybody**
pron n'importe qui; (*in interrogative
sentences*) quelqu'un; (*in negative
sentences*): **I don't see anybody** je ne
vois personne; **if anybody should
phone …** si quelqu'un téléphone
…; **anyhow** *adv* quoi qu'il en soit;
(*haphazardly*) n'importe comment;
do it anyhow you like faites-le
comme vous voulez; **she leaves
things just anyhow** elle laisse
tout traîner; **I shall go anyhow**
j'irai de toute façon; **anyone** *pron*
= **anybody**; **anything** *pron* (*no matter
what*) n'importe quoi; (*in questions*)
quelque chose; (*with negative*) ne
… rien; **can you see anything?** tu
vois quelque chose?; **if anything
happens to me …** s'il m'arrive quoi
que ce soit …; **you can say anything
you like** vous pouvez dire ce que vous
voulez; **anything will do** n'importe
quoi fera l'affaire; **he'll eat anything**
il mange de tout; **anytime** *adv* (*at
any moment*) d'un moment à l'autre;
(*whenever*) n'importe quand; **anyway**
adv de toute façon; **anyway, I
couldn't come even if I wanted
to** de toute façon, je ne pouvais pas
venir même si je le voulais; **I shall
go anyway** j'irai quand même; **why
are you phoning, anyway?** au
fait, pourquoi tu me téléphones?;
anywhere *adv* n'importe où; (*in
interrogative sentences*) quelque part;
(*in negative sentences*): **I can't see him
anywhere** je ne le vois nulle part;
can you see him anywhere? tu le
vois quelque part?; **put the books
down anywhere** pose les livres
n'importe où; **anywhere in the
world** (*no matter where*) n'importe où
dans le monde

apart [ə'pɑːt] *adv* (*to one side*) à
part; de côté; à l'écart; (*separately*)

séparément; **to take/pull ~**
démonter; **10 miles/a long way ~** à
10 miles/très éloignés l'un de l'autre;
~ from prep à part, excepté
apartment [əˈpɑːtmənt] n (US)
appartement m, logement m; (room)
chambre f; **apartment building** n
(US) immeuble m; maison divisée en
appartements
apathy [ˈæpəθɪ] n apathie f,
indifférence f
ape [eɪp] n (grand) singe ▷ vt singer
aperitif [əˈpɛrɪtɪf] n apéritif m
aperture [ˈæpətʃjuəʳ] n orifice m,
ouverture f; (Phot) ouverture (du
diaphragme)
APEX [ˈeɪpɛks] n abbr (Aviat: = advance
purchase excursion) APEX m
apologize [əˈpɒlədʒaɪz] vi: **to ~ (for
sth to sb)** s'excuser (de qch auprès
de qn), présenter des excuses (à qn
pour qch)
apology [əˈpɒlədʒɪ] n excuses fpl
apostrophe [əˈpɒstrəfɪ] n
apostrophe f
app n abbr (inf: Comput: = application)
appli f
appal, (US) **appall** [əˈpɔːl] vt
consterner, atterrer; horrifier;
appalling adj épouvantable;
(stupidity) consternant(e)
apparatus [æpəˈreɪtəs] n appareil m,
dispositif m; (in gymnasium) agrès mpl
apparent [əˈpærənt] adj
apparent(e); **apparently** adv
apparemment
appeal [əˈpiːl] vi (Law) faire or
interjeter appel ▷ n (Law) appel m;
(request) appel m; prière f; (charm) attrait
m, charme m; **to ~ for** demander
(instamment); implorer; **to ~ to** (beg)
faire appel à; (be attractive) plaire à;
it doesn't ~ to me cela ne m'attire
pas; **appealing** adj (attractive)
attrayant(e)
appear [əˈpɪəʳ] vi apparaître,
se montrer; (Law) comparaître;
(publication) paraître, sortir, être

publié(e); (seem) paraître, sembler; **it
would ~ that** il semble que; **to ~ in
Hamlet** jouer dans Hamlet; **to ~ on
TV** passer à la télé; **appearance** n
apparition f; parution f; (look, aspect)
apparence f, aspect m
appendices [əˈpɛndɪsiːz] npl of
appendix
appendicitis [əpɛndɪˈsaɪtɪs] n
appendicite f
appendix (pl **appendices**)
[əˈpɛndɪks, -siːz] n appendice m
appetite [ˈæpɪtaɪt] n appétit m
appetizer [ˈæpɪtaɪzəʳ] n (food)
amuse-gueule m; (drink) apéritif m
applaud [əˈplɔːd] vt, vi applaudir
applause [əˈplɔːz] n
applaudissements mpl
apple [ˈæpl] n pomme f; **apple pie** n
tarte f aux pommes
appliance [əˈplaɪəns] n appareil m
applicable [əˈplɪkəbl] adj applicable;
to be ~ to (relevant) valoir pour
applicant [ˈæplɪkənt] n: **~ (for)**
candidat(e) (à)
application [æplɪˈkeɪʃən] n (also
Comput) application f; (for a job, a
grant etc) demande f; candidature f;
application form n formulaire m de
demande
apply [əˈplaɪ] vt: **to ~ (to)** (paint,
ointment) appliquer (sur); (law, etc)
appliquer (à) ▷ vi: **to ~ to** (ask)
s'adresser à; (be suitable for, relevant
to) s'appliquer à; **to ~ (for)** (permit,
grant) faire une demande (en vue
d'obtenir); (job) poser sa candidature
(pour), faire une demande
d'emploi (concernant); **to ~ o.s. to**
s'appliquer à
appoint [əˈpɔɪnt] vt (to post)
nommer, engager; (date, place)
fixer, désigner; **appointment** n (to
post) nomination f; (job) poste m;
(arrangement to meet) rendez-vous
m; **to have an appointment**
avoir un rendez-vous; **to make
an appointment (with)** prendre

rendez-vous (avec); **I'd like to make an appointment** je voudrais prendre rendez-vous

appraisal [əˈpreɪzl] *n* évaluation *f*

appreciate [əˈpriːʃɪeɪt] *vt* (*like*) apprécier, faire cas de; (*be grateful for*) être reconnaissant(e) de; (*be aware of*) comprendre, se rendre compte de ▷ *vi* (*Finance*) prendre de la valeur; **appreciation** [əpriːʃɪˈeɪʃən] *n* appréciation *f*; (*gratitude*) reconnaissance *f*; (*Finance*) hausse *f*, valorisation *f*

apprehension [æprɪˈhenʃən] *n* appréhension *f*, inquiétude *f*

apprehensive [æprɪˈhensɪv] *adj* inquiet(-ète), appréhensif(-ive)

apprentice [əˈprentɪs] *n* apprenti *m*

approach [əˈprəʊtʃ] *vi* approcher ▷ *vt* (*come near*) approcher de; (*ask, apply to*) s'adresser à; (*subject, passer-by*) aborder ▷ *n* approche *f*; accès *m*, abord *m*; (*intellectual*) démarche *f*

appropriate *adj* [əˈprəʊprɪɪt] (*tool etc*) qui convient, approprié(e); (*moment, remark*) opportun(e) ▷ *vt* [əˈprəʊprɪeɪt] (*take*) s'approprier

approval [əˈpruːvəl] *n* approbation *f*; **on ~** (*Comm*) à l'examen

approve [əˈpruːv] *vt* approuver; **approve of** *vt fus* (*thing*) approuver; (*person*): **they don't ~ of her** ils n'ont pas bonne opinion d'elle

approximate [əˈprɔksɪmɪt] *adj* approximatif(-ive); **approximately** *adv* approximativement

Apr. *abbr* = **April**

apricot [ˈeɪprɪkɔt] *n* abricot *m*

April [ˈeɪprəl] *n* avril *m*; **April Fools' Day** *n* le premier avril

⬤ **APRIL FOOLS' DAY**
⬤
⬤ *April Fools' Day* est le 1er avril, à
⬤ l'occasion duquel on fait des farces
⬤ de toutes sortes. Les victimes de
⬤ ces farces sont les "April fools".

⬤ Traditionnellement, on n'est censé
⬤ faire des farces que jusqu'à midi.

apron [ˈeɪprən] *n* tablier *m*

apt [æpt] *adj* (*suitable*) approprié(e); **~ to do** (*likely*) susceptible de faire; ayant tendance à faire

aquarium [əˈkwɛərɪəm] *n* aquarium *m*

Aquarius [əˈkwɛərɪəs] *n* le Verseau

Arab [ˈærəb] *n* Arabe *m/f* ▷ *adj* arabe

Arabia [əˈreɪbɪə] *n* Arabie *f*; **Arabian** *adj* arabe; **Arabic** [ˈærəbɪk] *adj*, *n* arabe (*m*)

arbitrary [ˈɑːbɪtrərɪ] *adj* arbitraire

arbitration [ɑːbɪˈtreɪʃən] *n* arbitrage *m*

arc [ɑːk] *n* arc *m*

arcade [ɑːˈkeɪd] *n* arcade *f*; (*passage with shops*) passage *m*, galerie *f*; (*with games*) salle *f* de jeu

arch [ɑːtʃ] *n* arche *f*; (*of foot*) cambrure *f*, voûte *f* plantaire ▷ *vt* arquer, cambrer

archaeology, (*US*) **archeology** [ɑːkɪˈɔlədʒɪ] *n* archéologie *f*

archbishop [ɑːtʃˈbɪʃəp] *n* archevêque *m*

archeology [ɑːkɪˈɔlədʒɪ] (*US*) *n* = **archaeology**

architect [ˈɑːkɪtɛkt] *n* architecte *m*; **architectural** [ɑːkɪˈtɛktʃərəl] *adj* architectural(e); **architecture** *n* architecture *f*

archive [ˈɑːkaɪv] *n* (*often pl*) archives *fpl*

Arctic [ˈɑːktɪk] *adj* arctique ▷ *n*: **the ~** l'Arctique *m*

are [ɑːʳ] *vb see* **be**

area [ˈɛərɪə] *n* (*Geom*) superficie *f*; (*zone*) région *f* (*: smaller*) secteur *m*; (*in room*) coin *m*; (*knowledge, research*) domaine *m*; **area code** (*US*) *n* (*Tel*) indicatif *m* de zone

arena [əˈriːnə] *n* arène *f*

aren't [ɑːnt] = **are not**

Argentina [ɑːdʒənˈtiːnə] *n* Argentine *f*; **Argentinian**

[ɑːdʒən'tɪnɪən] *adj* argentin(e) ▷ *n* Argentin(e)

arguably ['ɑːgjuəblɪ] *adv*: **it is ~ ...** on peut soutenir que c'est ...

argue ['ɑːgjuː] *vi* (*quarrel*) se disputer; (*reason*) argumenter; **to ~ that** objecter or alléguer que, donner comme argument que

argument ['ɑːgjumənt] *n* (*quarrel*) dispute *f*, discussion *f*; (*reasons*) argument *m*

Aries ['ɛərɪz] *n* le Bélier

arise (*pt* **arose**, *pp* **arisen**) [ə'raɪz, ə'rəuz, ə'rɪzn] *vi* survenir, se présenter

arithmetic [ə'rɪθmətɪk] *n* arithmétique *f*

arm [ɑːm] *n* bras *m* ▷ *vt* armer; **arms** *npl* (*weapons*, *Heraldry*) armes *fpl*; **~ in ~** bras dessus bras dessous; **armchair** ['ɑːmtʃɛər] *n* fauteuil *m*

armed [ɑːmd] *adj* armé(e); **armed forces** *npl*: **the armed forces** les forces armées; **armed robbery** *n* vol *m* à main armée

armour, (*us*) **armor** ['ɑːmər] *n* armure *f*; (*Mil: tanks*) blindés *mpl*

armpit ['ɑːmpɪt] *n* aisselle *f*

armrest ['ɑːmrɛst] *n* accoudoir *m*

army ['ɑːmɪ] *n* armée *f*

A road *n* (*BRIT*) ≈ route nationale

aroma [ə'rəumə] *n* arôme *m*; **aromatherapy** *n* aromathérapie *f*

arose [ə'rəuz] *pt of* **arise**

around [ə'raund] *adv* (tout) autour; (*nearby*) dans les parages ▷ *prep* autour de; (*near*) près de; (*fig: about*) environ; (: *date, time*) vers; **is he ~?** est-il dans les parages or là?

arouse [ə'rauz] *vt* (*sleeper*) éveiller; (*curiosity, passions*) éveiller, susciter; (*anger*) exciter

arrange [ə'reɪndʒ] *vt* arranger; **to ~ to do sth** prévoir de faire qch; **arrangement** *n* arrangement *m*; **arrangements** *npl* (*plans etc*) arrangements *mpl*, dispositions *fpl*

array [ə'reɪ] *n* (*of objects*) déploiement *m*, étalage *m*

arrears [ə'rɪəz] *npl* arriéré *m*; **to be in ~ with one's rent** devoir un arriéré de loyer

arrest [ə'rɛst] *vt* arrêter; (*sb's attention*) retenir, attirer ▷ *n* arrestation *f*; **under ~** en état d'arrestation

arrival [ə'raɪvl] *n* arrivée *f*; **new ~** nouveau venu/nouvelle venue; (*baby*) nouveau-né(e)

arrive [ə'raɪv] *vi* arriver; **arrive at** *vt fus* (*decision, solution*) parvenir à

arrogance ['ærəgəns] *n* arrogance *f*

arrogant ['ærəgənt] *adj* arrogant(e)

arrow ['ærəu] *n* flèche *f*

arse [ɑːs] *n* (*BRIT inf!*) cul *m* (!)

arson ['ɑːsn] *n* incendie criminel

art [ɑːt] *n* art *m*; **Arts** *npl* (*Scol*) les lettres *fpl*; **art college** *n* école *f* des beaux-arts

artery ['ɑːtərɪ] *n* artère *f*

art gallery *n* musée *m* d'art; (*saleroom*) galerie *f* de peinture

arthritis [ɑː'θraɪtɪs] *n* arthrite *f*

artichoke ['ɑːtɪtʃəuk] *n* artichaut *m*; **Jerusalem ~** topinambour *m*

article ['ɑːtɪkl] *n* article *m*

articulate *adj* [ɑː'tɪkjulɪt] (*person*) qui s'exprime clairement et aisément; (*speech*) bien articulé(e), prononcé(e) clairement ▷ *vi* [ɑː'tɪkjuleɪt] articuler, parler distinctement ▷ *vt* articuler

artificial [ɑːtɪ'fɪʃəl] *adj* artificiel(le)

artist ['ɑːtɪst] *n* artiste *m/f*; **artistic** [ɑː'tɪstɪk] *adj* artistique

art school *n* ≈ école *f* des beaux-arts

KEYWORD

as [æz] *conj* **1** (*time: moment*) comme, alors que; à mesure que; **he came in as I was leaving** il est arrivé comme je partais; **as the years went by** à mesure que les années passaient; **as from tomorrow** à partir de demain **2** (*because*) comme, puisque; **he left early as he had to be home by**

10 comme il or puisqu'il devait être de retour avant 10h, il est parti de bonne heure

3 (referring to manner, way) comme; **do as you wish** faites comme vous voudrez; **as she said** comme elle disait

▶ adv **1** (in comparisons): **as big as** aussi grand que; **twice as big as** deux fois plus grand que; **as much** or **many as** autant que; **as much money/many books as** autant d'argent/de livres que; **as soon as** dès que

2 (concerning): **as for** or **to that** quant à cela, pour ce qui est de cela

3: **as if** or **though** comme si; **he looked as if he was ill** il avait l'air d'être malade; see also **long; such; well**

▶ prep (in the capacity of) en tant que, en qualité de; **he works as a driver** il travaille comme chauffeur; **as chairman of the company, he …** en tant que président de la société, il …; **he gave me it as a present** il me l'a offert, il m'en a fait cadeau

a.s.a.p. abbr = **as soon as possible**

asbestos [æz'bɛstəs] n asbeste m, amiante m

ascent [ə'sɛnt] n (climb) ascension f

ash [æʃ] n (dust) cendre f; (also: **~ tree**) frêne m

ashamed [ə'ʃeɪmd] adj honteux(-euse), confus(e); **to be ~ of** avoir honte de

ashore [ə'ʃɔːʳ] adv à terre

ashtray [ˈæʃtreɪ] n cendrier m

Ash Wednesday n mercredi m des Cendres

Asia [ˈeɪʃə] n Asie f; **Asian** n (from Asia) Asiatique m/f; (BRIT: from Indian subcontinent) Indo-Pakistanais(e) ▷ adj asiatique; indo-pakistanais(e)

aside [ə'saɪd] adv de côté; à l'écart ▷ n aparté m

ask [ɑːsk] vt demander; (invite) inviter; **to ~ sb sth/to do sth** demander à qn qch/de faire qch; **to ~ sb about sth** questionner qn au sujet de qch; se renseigner auprès de qn au sujet de qch; **to ~ (sb) a question** poser une question (à qn); **to ~ sb out to dinner** inviter qn au restaurant; **ask for** vt fus demander; **it's just ~ing for trouble** or **for it** ce serait chercher des ennuis

asleep [ə'sliːp] adj endormi(e); **to fall ~** s'endormir

AS level n abbr (= Advanced Subsidiary level) première partie de l'examen équivalent au baccalauréat

asparagus [əs'pærəgəs] n asperges fpl

aspect [ˈæspɛkt] n aspect m; (direction in which a building etc faces) orientation f, exposition f

aspire [əs'paɪəʳ] vi: **to ~ to** aspirer à

aspirin [ˈæsprɪn] n aspirine f

ass [æs] n âne m; (inf) imbécile m/f; (US inf!) cul m (!)

assassin [ə'sæsɪn] n assassin m; **assassinate** vt assassiner

assault [ə'sɔːlt] n (Mil) assaut m; (gen: attack) agression f ▷ vt attaquer; (sexually) violenter

assemble [ə'sɛmbl] vt assembler ▷ vi s'assembler, se rassembler

assembly [ə'sɛmblɪ] n (meeting) rassemblement m; (parliament) assemblée f; (construction) assemblage m

assert [ə'səːt] vt affirmer, déclarer; (authority) faire valoir; (innocence) protester de; **assertion** [ə'səːʃən] n assertion f, affirmation f

assess [ə'sɛs] vt évaluer, estimer; (tax, damages) établir or fixer le montant de; (person) juger la valeur de; **assessment** n évaluation f, estimation f; (of tax) fixation f

asset [ˈæsɛt] n avantage m, atout m; (person) atout; **assets** npl (Comm) capital m; avoir(s) m(pl); actif m

assign [ə'saɪn] vt (date) fixer, arrêter; **to ~ sth to** (task) assigner

qch à; (*resources*) affecter qch à;
assignment *n* (*task*) mission *f*;
(*homework*) devoir *m*

assist [ə'sɪst] *vt* aider, assister;
assistance *n* aide *f*, assistance *f*;
assistant *n* assistant(e), adjoint(e);
(BRIT: *also*: **shop assistant**)
vendeur(-euse)

associate *adj*, *n* [ə'səʊʃɪɪt]
associé(e) ▷ *vt* [ə'səʊʃɪeɪt] associer
▷ *vi* [ə'səʊʃɪeɪt]: **to ~ with sb**
fréquenter qn

association [əsəʊsɪ'eɪʃən] *n*
association *f*

assorted [ə'sɔ:tɪd] *adj* assorti(e)

assortment [ə'sɔ:tmənt] *n*
assortiment *m*; (*of people*) mélange *m*

assume [ə'sju:m] *vt* supposer;
(*responsibilities etc*) assumer; (*attitude*,
name) prendre, adopter

assumption [ə'sʌmpʃən] *n*
supposition *f*, hypothèse *f*; (*of power*)
assomption *f*, prise *f*

assurance [ə'ʃʊərəns] *n* assurance *f*

assure [ə'ʃʊə^r] *vt* assurer

asterisk ['æstərɪsk] *n* astérisque *m*

asthma ['æsmə] *n* asthme *m*

astonish [ə'stɒnɪʃ] *vt* étonner,
stupéfier; **astonished** *adj*
étonné(e); **to be astonished at**
être étonné(e) de; **astonishing**
adj étonnant(e), stupéfiant(e);
I find it astonishing that ...
je trouve incroyable que ... +
sub; **astonishment** *n* (grand)
étonnement, stupéfaction *f*

astound [ə'staʊnd] *vt* stupéfier,
sidérer

astray [ə'streɪ] *adv*: **to go ~** s'égarer;
(*fig*) quitter le droit chemin; **to lead ~**
(*morally*) détourner du droit chemin

astrology [əs'trɒlədʒɪ] *n* astrologie *f*

astronaut ['æstrənɔ:t] *n*
astronaute *m/f*

astronomer [əs'trɒnəmə^r] *n*
astronome *m*

astronomical [æstrə'nɔmɪkl] *adj*
astronomique

astronomy [əs'trɒnəmɪ] *n*
astronomie *f*

astute [əs'tju:t] *adj* astucieux(-euse),
malin(-igne)

asylum [ə'saɪləm] *n* asile *m*; **asylum
seeker** [-si:kə^r] *n* demandeur(-euse)
d'asile

KEYWORD

at [æt] *prep* **1** (*referring to position*,
direction) à; **at the top** au sommet;
at home/school à la maison *or* chez
soi/à l'école; **at the baker's** à la
boulangerie, chez le boulanger; **to
look at sth** regarder qch
2 (*referring to time*): **at 4 o'clock** à 4
heures; **at Christmas** à Noël; **at night**
la nuit; **at times** par moments, parfois
3 (*referring to rates, speed etc*) à; **at £1
a kilo** une livre le kilo; **two at a time**
deux à la fois; **at 50 km/h** à 50 km/h
4 (*referring to manner*): **at a stroke**
d'un seul coup; **at peace** en paix
5 (*referring to activity*): **to be at
work** (*in the office etc*) être au travail;
(*working*) travailler; **to play at
cowboys** jouer aux cowboys; **to be
good at sth** être bon en qch
6 (*referring to cause*): **shocked/
surprised/annoyed at sth** choqué
par/étonné de/agacé par qch; **I went
at his suggestion** j'y suis allé sur
son conseil
▶ *n* (@ *symbol*) arobase *f*

ate [eɪt] *pt of* **eat**

atheist ['eɪθɪɪst] *n* athée *m/f*

Athens ['æθɪnz] *n* Athènes

athlete ['æθli:t] *n* athlète *m/f*

athletic [æθ'lɛtɪk] *adj* athlétique;
athletics *n* athlétisme *m*

Atlantic [ət'læntɪk] *adj* atlantique
▷ *n*: **the ~ (Ocean)** l'(océan *m*)
Atlantique *m*

atlas ['ætləs] *n* atlas *m*

A.T.M. *n abbr* (= *Automated Telling
Machine*) guichet *m* automatique

atmosphere ['ætməsfɪəʳ] n (air)
atmosphère f; (fig: of place etc)
atmosphère, ambiance f
atom ['ætəm] n atome m; **atomic**
[ə'tɒmɪk] adj atomique; **atom(ic)
bomb** n bombe f atomique
atrocity [ə'trɒsɪtɪ] n atrocité f
attach [ə'tætʃ] vt (gen) attacher;
(document, letter) joindre; **to be ~ed
to sb/sth** (to like) être attaché à qn/
qch; **to ~ a file to an email** joindre
un fichier à un e-mail; **attachment**
n (tool) accessoire m; (Comput) fichier
m joint; (love): **attachment (to)**
affection f (pour), attachement m (à)
attack [ə'tæk] vt attaquer; (task etc)
s'attaquer à ▷ n attaque f; **heart
~** crise f cardiaque; **attacker** n
attaquant m; agresseur m
attain [ə'teɪn] vt (also: **to ~ to**)
parvenir à, atteindre; (knowledge)
acquérir
attempt [ə'tɛmpt] n tentative f ▷ vt
essayer, tenter
attend [ə'tɛnd] vt (course) suivre;
(meeting, talk) assister à; (school,
church) aller à, fréquenter; (patient)
soigner, s'occuper de; **attend to**
vt fus (needs, affairs etc) s'occuper
de; (customer) s'occuper de, servir;
attendance n (being present)
présence f; (people present) assistance
f; **attendant** n employé(e);
gardien(ne) ▷ adj concomitant(e), qui
accompagne or s'ensuit

▌ Be careful not to translate attend
by the French word attendre.

attention [ə'tɛnʃən] n attention f
▷ excl (Mil) garde-à-vous!; **for the ~ of**
(Admin) à l'attention de
attic ['ætɪk] n grenier m, combles mpl
attitude ['ætɪtjuːd] n attitude f
attorney [ə'təːnɪ] n (US: lawyer)
avocat m; **Attorney General** n (BRIT)
≈ procureur général; (US) ≈ garde m
des Sceaux, ministre m de la Justice
attract [ə'trækt] vt attirer;
attraction [ə'trækʃən] n (gen pl:

pleasant things) attraction f, attrait
m; (Physics) attraction; (fig: towards
sb, sth) attirance f; **attractive** adj
séduisant(e), attrayant(e)
attribute n ['ætrɪbjuːt] attribut m
▷ vt [ə'trɪbjuːt]: **to ~ sth to** attribuer
qch à
aubergine ['əubəʒiːn] n aubergine f
auburn ['ɔːbən] adj auburn inv,
châtain roux inv
auction ['ɔːkʃən] n (also: **sale by ~**)
vente f aux enchères ▷ vt (also: **to sell
by ~**) vendre aux enchères
audible ['ɔːdɪbl] adj audible
audience ['ɔːdɪəns] n (people)
assistance f, public m; (on radio)
auditeurs mpl; (at theatre) spectateurs
mpl; (interview) audience f
audit ['ɔːdɪt] vt vérifier
audition [ɔː'dɪʃən] n audition f
auditor ['ɔːdɪtəʳ] n vérificateur m
des comptes
auditorium [ɔːdɪ'tɔːrɪəm] n
auditorium m, salle f de concert or
de spectacle
Aug. abbr = **August**
August ['ɔːgəst] n août m
aunt [ɑːnt] n tante f; **auntie, aunty** n
diminutive of **aunt**
au pair ['əu'pɛəʳ] n (also: **~ girl**) jeune
fille f au pair
aura ['ɔːrə] n atmosphère f; (of person)
aura f
austerity [ɒs'tɛrɪtɪ] n austérité f
Australia [ɒs'treɪlɪə] n Australie f;
Australian adj australien(ne) ▷ n
Australien(ne)
Austria ['ɒstrɪə] n Autriche f;
Austrian adj autrichien(ne) ▷ n
Autrichien(ne)
authentic [ɔː'θɛntɪk] adj
authentique
author ['ɔːθəʳ] n auteur m
authority [ɔː'θɒrɪtɪ] n autorité f;
(permission) autorisation (formelle);
the authorities les autorités fpl,
l'administration f
authorize ['ɔːθəraɪz] vt autoriser

auto [ˈɔːtəu] n (US) auto f, voiture f; **autobiography** [ɔːtəbaɪˈɒɡrəfɪ] n autobiographie f; **autograph** [ˈɔːtəɡrɑːf] n autographe m ▷ vt signer, dédicacer; **automatic** [ɔːtəˈmætɪk] adj automatique ▷ n (gun) automatique m; (car) voiture f à transmission automatique; **automatically** adv automatiquement; **automobile** [ˈɔːtəməbiːl] n (US) automobile f; **autonomous** [ɔːˈtɒnəməs] adj autonome; **autonomy** [ɔːˈtɒnəmɪ] n autonomie f

autumn [ˈɔːtəm] n automne m

auxiliary [ɔːɡˈzɪlɪərɪ] adj, n auxiliaire (m/f)

avail [əˈveɪl] vt: **to ~ o.s. of** user de; profiter de ▷ n: **to no ~** sans résultat, en vain, en pure perte

availability [əveɪləˈbɪlɪtɪ] n disponibilité f

available [əˈveɪləbl] adj disponible

avalanche [ˈævəlɑːnʃ] n avalanche f

Ave. abbr = **avenue**

avenue [ˈævənjuː] n avenue f; (fig) moyen m

average [ˈævərɪdʒ] n moyenne f ▷ adj moyen(ne) ▷ vt (a certain figure) atteindre or faire etc en moyenne; **on ~** en moyenne

avert [əˈvəːt] vt (danger) prévenir, écarter; (one's eyes) détourner

avid [ˈævɪd] adj avide

avocado [ævəˈkɑːdəu] n (BRIT: also: ~ **pear**) avocat m

avoid [əˈvɔɪd] vt éviter

await [əˈweɪt] vt attendre

awake [əˈweɪk] (pt **awoke**, pp **awoken**) adj éveillé(e) ▷ vt éveiller ▷ vi s'éveiller; **to be ~** être réveillé(e)

award [əˈwɔːd] n (for bravery) récompense f; (prize) prix m; (Law: damages) dommages-intérêts mpl ▷ vt (prize) décerner; (Law: damages) accorder

aware [əˈwɛəʳ] adj: **~ of** (conscious) conscient(e) de; (informed) au courant de; **to become ~ of/that** prendre conscience de/que; se rendre compte de/que; **awareness** n conscience f, connaissance f

away [əˈweɪ] adv (au) loin; (movement): **she went ~** elle est partie ▷ adj (not in, not here) absent(e); **far ~** (au) loin; **two kilometres ~** à (une distance de) deux kilomètres, à deux kilomètres de distance; **two hours ~ by car** à deux heures de voiture or de route; **the holiday was two weeks ~** il restait deux semaines jusqu'aux vacances; **he's ~ for a week** il est parti (pour) une semaine; **to take sth ~ from sb** prendre qch à qn; **to take sth ~ from sth** (subtract) ôter qch de qch; **to work/pedal ~** travailler/pédaler à cœur joie; **to fade ~** (colour) s'estomper; (sound) s'affaiblir

awe [ɔː] n respect mêlé de crainte, effroi mêlé d'admiration; **awesome** [ˈɔːsəm] (US) adj (inf: excellent) génial(e)

awful [ˈɔːfəl] adj affreux(-euse); **an ~ lot of** énormément de; **awfully** adv (very) terriblement, vraiment

awkward [ˈɔːkwəd] adj (clumsy) gauche, maladroit(e); (inconvenient) peu pratique; (embarrassing) gênant

awoke [əˈwəuk] pt of **awake**

awoken [əˈwəukən] pp of **awake**

axe, (US) **ax** [æks] n hache f ▷ vt (project etc) abandonner; (jobs) supprimer

axle [ˈæksl] n essieu m

ay(e) [aɪ] excl (yes) oui

azalea [əˈzeɪlɪə] n azalée f

B [biː] *n* (*Mus*) si *m*
B.A. *abbr* (*Scol*) = **Bachelor of Arts**
baby ['beɪbɪ] *n* bébé *m*; **baby carriage** *n* (*US*) voiture *f* d'enfant; **baby-sit** *vi* garder les enfants; **baby-sitter** *n* baby-sitter *m/f*; **baby wipe** *n* lingette *f* (*pour bébé*)
bachelor ['bætʃələʳ] *n* célibataire *m*; **B~ of Arts/Science (BA/BSc)** ≈ licencié(e) ès *or* en lettres/sciences
back [bæk] *n* (*of person, horse*) dos *m*; (*of hand*) dos, revers *m*; (*of house*) derrière *m*; (*of car, train*) arrière *m*; (*of chair*) dossier *m*; (*of page*) verso *m*; (*Football*) arrière *m* ▷ *vt* (*financially*) soutenir (financièrement); (*candidate: also:* ~ **up**) soutenir, appuyer; (*horse: at races*) parier *or* miser sur; (*car*) (faire) reculer ▷ *vi* reculer; (*car etc*) faire marche arrière ▷ *adj* (*in compounds*) de derrière, à l'arrière ▷ *adv* (*not forward*) en arrière; (*returned*): **he's ~** il est rentré, il est de retour; **can**

the people at the ~ hear me properly? est-ce que les gens du fond m'entendent?; ~ **to front** à l'envers; ~ **seat/wheel** (*Aut*) siège *m*/roue *f* arrière *inv*; ~ **payments/rent** arriéré *m* de paiements/loyer; ~ **garden/room** jardin/pièce sur l'arrière; **he ran ~** il est revenu en courant; **throw the ball ~** renvoie la balle; **can I have it ~?** puis-je le ravoir?, peux-tu me le rendre?; **he called ~** (*again*) il a rappelé; **back down** *vi* rabattre de ses prétentions; **back out** *vi* (*of promise*) se dédire; **back up** *vt* (*person*) soutenir; (*Comput*) faire une copie de sauvegarde de; **backache** *n* mal *m* au dos; **backbencher** *n* (BRIT) membre du parlement sans portefeuille; **backbone** *n* colonne vertébrale, épine dorsale; **back door** *n* porte *f* de derrière; **backfire** *vi* (*Aut*) pétarader; (*plans*) mal tourner; **backgammon** *n* trictrac *m*; **background** *n* arrière-plan *m*; (*of events*) situation *f*, conjoncture *f*; (*basic knowledge*) éléments *mpl* de base; (*experience*) formation *f*; **family background** milieu familial; **backing** *n* (*fig*) soutien *m*, appui *m*; **backlog** *n*: **backlog of work** travail *m* en retard; **backpack** *n* sac *m* à dos; **backpacker** *n* randonneur(-euse); **backslash** *n* barre oblique inversée; **backstage** *adv* dans les coulisses; **backstroke** *n* dos crawlé; **backup** *adj* (*train, plane*) supplémentaire, de réserve; (*Comput*) de sauvegarde ▷ *n* (*support*) appui *m*, soutien *m*; (*Comput: also:* **backup file**) sauvegarde *f*; **backward** *adj* (*movement*) en arrière; (*person, country*) arriéré(e), attardé(e); **backwards** *adv* (*move, go*) en arrière; (*read a list*) à l'envers, à rebours; (*fall*) à la renverse; (*walk*) à reculons; **backyard** *n* arrière-cour *f*
bacon ['beɪkən] *n* bacon *m*, lard *m*
bacteria [bæk'tɪərɪə] *npl* bactéries *fpl*
bad [bæd] *adj* mauvais(e); (*child*) vilain(e); (*mistake, accident*) grave;

(*meat, food*) gâté(e), avarié(e); **his ~ leg** sa jambe malade; **to go ~** (*meat, food*) se gâter; (*milk*) tourner

bade [bæd] *pt of* **bid**

badge [bædʒ] *n* insigne *m*; (*of policeman*) plaque *f*; (*stick-on, sew-on*) badge *m*

badger ['bædʒə'] *n* blaireau *m*

badly ['bædlɪ] *adv* (*work, dress etc*) mal; **to reflect ~ on sb** donner une mauvaise image de qn; **~ wounded** grièvement blessé; **he needs it ~** il en a absolument besoin; **~ off** *adj, adv* dans la gêne

bad-mannered ['bæd'mænəd] *adj* mal élevé(e)

badminton ['bædmɪntən] *n* badminton *m*

bad-tempered ['bæd'tɛmpəd] *adj* (*by nature*) ayant mauvais caractère; (*on one occasion*) de mauvaise humeur

bag [bæg] *n* sac *m*; **~s of** (*inf: lots of*) des tas de; **baggage** *n* bagages *mpl*; **baggage allowance** *n* franchise *f* de bagages; **baggage reclaim** *n* (*at airport*) livraison *f* des bagages; **baggy** *adj* avachi(e), qui fait des poches; **bagpipes** *npl* cornemuse *f*

bail [beɪl] *n* caution *f* ⊳ *vt* (*prisoner: also*: **grant ~ to**) mettre en liberté sous caution; (*boat: also*: **~ out**) écoper; **to be released on ~** être libéré(e) sous caution; **bail out** *vt* (*prisoner*) payer la caution de qn

bait [beɪt] *n* appât *m* ⊳ *vt* appâter; (*fig: tease*) tourmenter

bake [beɪk] *vt* (faire) cuire au four ⊳ *vi* (*bread etc*) cuire (au four); (*make cakes etc*) faire de la pâtisserie; **baked beans** *npl* haricots blancs à la sauce tomate; **baked potato** *n* pomme *f* de terre en robe des champs; **baker** *n* boulanger *m*; **bakery** *n* boulangerie *f*; **baking** *n* (*process*) cuisson *f*; **baking powder** *n* levure *f* (chimique)

balance ['bæləns] *n* équilibre *m*; (*Comm: sum*) solde *m*; (*remainder*) reste *m*; (*scales*) balance *f* ⊳ *vt* mettre or faire tenir en équilibre; (*pros and cons*) peser; (*budget*) équilibrer; (*account*) balancer; (*compensate*) compenser, contrebalancer; **~ of trade/ payments** balance commerciale/ des comptes *or* paiements; **balanced** *adj* (*personality, diet*) équilibré(e); (*report*) objectif(-ive); **balance sheet** *n* bilan *m*

balcony ['bælkənɪ] *n* balcon *m*; **do you have a room with a ~?** avez-vous une chambre avec balcon?

bald [bɔːld] *adj* chauve; (*tyre*) lisse

ball [bɔːl] *n* boule *f*; (*football*) ballon *m*; (*for tennis, golf*) balle *f*; (*dance*) bal *m*; **to play ~** jouer au ballon (*or* à la balle); (*fig*) coopérer

ballerina [bælə'riːnə] *n* ballerine *f*

ballet ['bæleɪ] *n* ballet *m*; (*art*) danse *f* (classique); **ballet dancer** *n* danseur(-euse) de ballet

balloon [bə'luːn] *n* ballon *m*

ballot ['bælət] *n* scrutin *m*

ballpoint (pen) ['bɔːlpɔɪnt-] *n* stylo *m* à bille

ballroom ['bɔːlrum] *n* salle *f* de bal

Baltic [bɔːltɪk] *n*: **the ~ (Sea)** la (mer) Baltique

bamboo [bæm'buː] *n* bambou *m*

ban [bæn] *n* interdiction *f* ⊳ *vt* interdire

banana [bə'nɑːnə] *n* banane *f*

band [bænd] *n* bande *f*; (*at a dance*) orchestre *m*; (*Mil*) musique *f*, fanfare *f*

bandage ['bændɪdʒ] *n* bandage *m*, pansement *m* ⊳ *vt* (*wound, leg*) mettre un pansement *or* une bandage sur

Band-Aid® ['bændeɪd] *n* (*US*) pansement adhésif

B. & B. *n abbr* = **bed and breakfast**

bandit ['bændɪt] *n* bandit *m*

bang [bæŋ] *n* détonation *f*; (*of door*) claquement *m*; (*blow*) coup (violent) ⊳ *vt* frapper (violemment); (*door*) claquer ⊳ *vi* détoner; claquer

Bangladesh [bæŋglə'dɛʃ] *n* Bangladesh *m*

Bangladeshi [bæŋglə'dɛʃɪ] *adj* du Bangladesh ▷ *n* habitant(e) du Bangladesh

bangle ['bæŋgl] *n* bracelet *m*

bangs [bæŋz] *npl* (*us: fringe*) frange *f*

banish ['bænɪʃ] *vt* bannir

banister(s) ['bænɪstə(z)] *n(pl)* rampe *f* (d'escalier)

banjo ['bændʒəu] (*pl* **banjoes** or **banjos**) *n* banjo *m*

bank [bæŋk] *n* banque *f*; (*of river, lake*) bord *m*, rive *f*; (*of earth*) talus *m*, remblai *m* ▷ *vi* (*Aviat*) virer sur l'aile; **bank on** *vt fus* miser or tabler sur; **bank account** *n* compte *m* en banque; **bank balance** *n* solde *m* bancaire; **bank card** (BRIT) *n* carte *f* d'identité bancaire; **bank charges** *npl* (BRIT) frais *mpl* de banque; **banker** *n* banquier *m*; **bank holiday** *n* (BRIT) jour férié (*où les banques sont fermées*); *voir article* **"bank holiday"**; **banking** *n* opérations *fpl* bancaires; profession *f* de banquier; **bank manager** *n* directeur *m* d'agence (bancaire); **banknote** *n* billet *m* de banque

● **BANK HOLIDAY**
●
● Le terme *bank holiday* s'applique
● au Royaume-Uni aux jours fériés
● pendant lesquels banques et
● commerces sont fermés. Les
● principaux *bank holidays* à part Noël
● et Pâques se situent au mois de
● mai et fin août, et contrairement
● aux pays de tradition catholique,
● ne coïncident pas nécessairement
● avec une fête religieuse.

bankrupt ['bæŋkrʌpt] *adj* en faillite; **to go ~** faire faillite; **bankruptcy** *n* faillite *f*

bank statement *n* relevé *m* de compte

banner ['bænər] *n* bannière *f*

bannister(s) ['bænɪstə(z)] *n(pl)* = **banister(s)**

banquet ['bæŋkwɪt] *n* banquet *m*, festin *m*

baptism ['bæptɪzəm] *n* baptême *m*

baptize [bæp'taɪz] *vt* baptiser

bar [bɑːr] *n* (*pub*) bar *m*; (*counter*) comptoir *m*, bar; (*rod: of metal etc*) barre *f*; (*: of window etc*) barreau *m*; (*of chocolate*) tablette *f*, plaque *f*; (*fig: obstacle*) obstacle *m*; (*prohibition*) mesure *f* d'exclusion; (*Mus*) mesure *f* ▷ *vt* (*road*) barrer; (*person*) exclure; (*activity*) interdire; **~ of soap** savonnette *f*; **behind ~s** (*prisoner*) derrière les barreaux; **the B~** (*Law*) le barreau; **~ none** sans exception

barbaric [bɑː'bærɪk] *adj* barbare

barbecue ['bɑːbɪkjuː] *n* barbecue *m*

barbed wire ['bɑːbd-] *n* fil *m* de fer barbelé

barber ['bɑːbər] *n* coiffeur *m* (pour hommes); **barber's (shop)**, (*us*) **barber shop** *n* salon *m* de coiffure (pour hommes)

bar code *n* code *m* à barres, code-barre *m*

bare [bɛər] *adj* nu(e) ▷ *vt* mettre à nu, dénuder; (*teeth*) montrer; **barefoot** *adj*, *adv* nu-pieds, (les) pieds nus; **barely** *adv* à peine

bargain ['bɑːgɪn] *n* (*transaction*) marché *m*; (*good buy*) affaire *f*, occasion *f* ▷ *vi* (*haggle*) marchander; (*negotiate*) négocier, traiter; **into the ~** par-dessus le marché; **bargain for** *vt fus* (*inf*): **he got more than he ~ed for!** il en a eu pour son argent!

barge [bɑːdʒ] *n* péniche *f*; **barge in** *vi* (*walk in*) faire irruption; (*interrupt talk*) intervenir mal à propos

bark [bɑːk] *n* (*of tree*) écorce *f*; (*of dog*) aboiement *m* ▷ *vi* aboyer

barley ['bɑːlɪ] *n* orge *f*

barmaid ['bɑːmeɪd] *n* serveuse *f* (de bar), barmaid *f*

barman ['bɑːmən] (*irreg*) *n* serveur *m* (de bar), barman *m*

barn [bɑːn] *n* grange *f*

barometer [bəˈrɔmɪtəʳ] n
baromètre m

baron [ˈbærən] n baron m; **baroness**
n baronne f

barracks [ˈbærəks] npl caserne f

barrage [ˈbærɑːʒ] n (Mil) tir m de
barrage; (dam) barrage m; (of criticism)
feu m

barrel [ˈbærəl] n tonneau m; (of gun)
canon m

barren [ˈbærən] adj stérile

barrette [bəˈrɛt] (US) n barrette f

barricade [bærɪˈkeɪd] n barricade f

barrier [ˈbærɪəʳ] n barrière f

barring [ˈbɑːrɪŋ] prep sauf

barrister [ˈbærɪstəʳ] n (BRIT) avocat
(plaidant)

barrow [ˈbærəu] n (cart) charrette
f à bras

bartender [ˈbɑːtɛndəʳ] n (US) serveur
m (de bar), barman m

base [beɪs] n base f ▷ vt (opinion,
belief): **to ~ sth on** baser or fonder qch
sur ▷ adj vil(e), bas(se)

baseball [ˈbeɪsbɔːl] n base-ball
m; **baseball cap** n casquette f de
base-ball

Basel [bɑːl] n = **Basle**

basement [ˈbeɪsmənt] n sous-sol m

bases [ˈbeɪsiːz] npl of **basis**

bash [bæʃ] vt (inf) frapper, cogner

basic [ˈbeɪsɪk] adj (precautions, rules)
élémentaire; (principles, research)
fondamental(e); (vocabulary, salary) de
base; (minimal) réduit(e) au minimum,
rudimentaire; **basically** adv (in fact) en
fait; (essentially) fondamentalement;
basics npl; **the basics** l'essentiel m

basil [ˈbæzl] n basilic m

basin [ˈbeɪsn] n (vessel, also Geo)
cuvette f, bassin m; (BRIT: for food) bol
m; (also: **wash~**) lavabo m

basis (pl **bases**) [ˈbeɪsɪs, -siːz] n base
f; **on a part-time/trial ~** à temps
partiel/à l'essai

basket [ˈbɑːskɪt] n corbeille f; (with
handle) panier m; **basketball** n
basket-ball m

Basle [bɑːl] n Bâle

Basque [bæsk] adj basque ▷ n
Basque m/f; **the ~ Country** le Pays
basque

bass [beɪs] n (Mus) basse f

bastard [ˈbɑːstəd] n enfant
naturel(le), bâtard(e); (inf!) salaud m (!)

bat [bæt] n chauve-souris f; (for
baseball etc) batte f; (BRIT: for table
tennis) raquette f ▷ vt: **he didn't ~ an
eyelid** il n'a pas sourcillé or bronché

batch [bætʃ] n (of bread) fournée f; (of
papers) liasse f; (of applicants, letters)
paquet m

bath (pl **baths**) [bɑːθ, bɑːðz] n bain
m; (bathtub) baignoire f ▷ vt baigner,
donner un bain à; **to have a ~**
prendre un bain; see also **baths**

bathe [beɪð] vi se baigner ▷ vt
baigner; (wound etc) laver

bathing [ˈbeɪðɪŋ] n baignade f;
bathing costume, (US) **bathing suit**
n maillot m (de bain)

bath: bathrobe n peignoir m de bain;
bathroom n salle f de bains; **baths**
[bɑːðz] npl (BRIT: also: **swimming
baths**) piscine f; **bath towel** n
serviette f de bain; **bathtub** n
baignoire f

baton [ˈbætən] n bâton m; (Mus)
baguette f; (club) matraque f

batter [ˈbætəʳ] vt battre ▷ n pâte
f à frire; **battered** adj (hat, pan)
cabossé(e); **battered wife/child**
épouse/enfant maltraité(e) or
martyr(e)

battery [ˈbætərɪ] n (for torch, radio)
pile f; (Aut, Mil) batterie f; **battery
farming** n élevage m en batterie

battle [ˈbætl] n bataille f, combat m
▷ vi se battre, lutter; **battlefield** n
champ m de bataille

bay [beɪ] n (of sea) baie f; (BRIT: for
parking) place f de stationnement;
(: for loading) aire f de chargement;
B~ of Biscay golfe m de Gascogne;
to hold sb at ~ tenir qn à distance
or en échec

bay leaf n laurier m
bazaar [bə'zɑːʳ] n (shop, market) bazar m; (sale) vente f de charité
BBC n abbr (= British Broadcasting Corporation) office de la radiodiffusion et télévision britannique
B.C. adv abbr (= before Christ) av. J.-C.

 KEYWORD

be [biː] (pt **was**, **were**, pp **been**) aux vb **1** (with present participle, forming continuous tenses): **what are you doing?** que faites-vous?; **they're coming tomorrow** ils viennent demain; **I've been waiting for you for 2 hours** je t'attends depuis 2 heures
2 (with pp, forming passives) être; **to be killed** être tué(e); **the box had been opened** la boîte avait été ouverte; **he was nowhere to be seen** on ne le voyait nulle part
3 (in tag questions): **it was fun, wasn't it?** c'était drôle, n'est-ce pas?; **he's good-looking, isn't he?** il est beau, n'est-ce pas?; **she's back, is she?** elle est rentrée, n'est-ce pas or alors?
4 (+to +infinitive): **the house is to be sold** (necessity) la maison doit être vendue; (future) la maison va être vendue; **he's not to open it** il ne doit pas l'ouvrir
▸ vb + complement **1** (gen) être; **I'm English** je suis anglais(e); **I'm tired** je suis fatigué(e); **I'm hot/cold** j'ai chaud/froid; **he's a doctor** il est médecin; **be careful/good/quiet!** faites attention/soyez sages/taisez-vous!; **2 and 2 are 4** 2 et 2 font 4
2 (of health) aller; **how are you?** comment allez-vous?; **I'm better now** je vais mieux maintenant; **he's very ill** il est très malade
3 (of age) avoir; **how old are you?** quel âge avez-vous?; **I'm sixteen (years old)** j'ai seize ans

4 (cost) coûter; **how much was the meal?** combien a coûté le repas?; **that'll be £5, please** ça fera 5 livres, s'il vous plaît; **this shirt is £17** cette chemise coûte 17 livres
▸ vi **1** (exist, occur etc) être, exister; **the prettiest girl that ever was** la fille la plus jolie qui ait jamais existé; **is there a God?** y a-t-il un dieu?; **be that as it may** quoi qu'il en soit; **so be it** soit
2 (referring to place) être, se trouver; **I won't be here tomorrow** je ne serai pas là demain
3 (referring to movement) aller; **where have you been?** où êtes-vous allé(s)?
▸ impers vb **1** (referring to time) être; **it's 5 o'clock** il est 5 heures; **it's the 28th of April** c'est le 28 avril
2 (referring to distance): **it's 10 km to the village** le village est à 10 km
3 (referring to the weather) faire; **it's too hot/cold** il fait trop chaud/froid; **it's windy today** il y a du vent aujourd'hui
4 (emphatic): **it's me/the postman** c'est moi/le facteur; **it was Maria who paid the bill** c'est Maria qui a payé la note

beach [biːtʃ] n plage f ▷ vt échouer
beacon ['biːkən] n (lighthouse) fanal m; (marker) balise f
bead [biːd] n perle f; (of dew, sweat) goutte f; **beads** npl (necklace) collier m
beak [biːk] n bec m
beam [biːm] n (Archit) poutre f; (of light) rayon m ▷ vi rayonner
bean [biːn] n haricot m; (of coffee) grain m; **beansprouts** npl pousses fpl or germes mpl de soja
bear [bɛəʳ] n ours m ▷ vt (pt **bore**, pp **borne**) porter; (endure) supporter; (interest) rapporter ▷ vi: **to ~ right/left** obliquer à droite/gauche, se diriger vers la droite/gauche
beard [bɪəd] n barbe f

b

bearer [ˈbɛərəʳ] n porteur m; (of passport etc) titulaire m/f

bearing [ˈbɛərɪŋ] n maintien m, allure f; (connection) rapport m; **(ball) bearings** npl (Tech) roulement m (à billes)

beast [biːst] n bête f; (inf: person) brute f

beat [biːt] n battement m; (Mus) temps m, mesure f; (of policeman) ronde f ▷ vt, vi (pt **beat**, pp **beaten**) battre; **off the ~en track** hors des chemins or sentiers battus; **to ~ it** (inf) ficher le camp; **beat up** vt (inf: person) tabasser; **beating** n raclée f

beautiful [ˈbjuːtɪful] adj beau (belle); **beautifully** adv admirablement

beauty [ˈbjuːtɪ] n beauté f; **beauty parlour**, (US) **beauty parlor** n institut m de beauté; **beauty salon** n institut m de beauté; **beauty spot** n (on skin) grain m de beauté; (BRIT Tourism) site naturel (d'une grande beauté)

beaver [ˈbiːvəʳ] n castor m

became [bɪˈkeɪm] pt of **become**

because [bɪˈkɔz] conj parce que; **~ of** prep à cause de

beckon [ˈbɛkən] vt (also: **~ to**) faire signe (de venir) à

become [bɪˈkʌm] vi devenir; **to ~ fat/thin** grossir/maigrir; **to ~ angry** se mettre en colère

bed [bɛd] n lit m; (of flowers) parterre m; (of coal, clay) couche f; (of sea, lake) fond m; **to go to ~** aller se coucher; **bed and breakfast** n (terms) chambre et petit déjeuner; (place) ≈ chambre f d'hôte; voir article **"bed and breakfast"**; **bedclothes** npl couvertures fpl et draps mpl; **bedding** n literie f; **bed linen** n draps mpl de lit (et taies fpl d'oreillers), literie f; **bedroom** n chambre f (à coucher); **bedside** n: **at sb's bedside** au chevet de qn; **bedside lamp** n lampe f de chevet; **bedside table** n table f de chevet; **bedsit(ter)** n (BRIT) chambre

meublée, studio m; **bedspread** n couvre-lit m; **bedtime** n: **it's bedtime** c'est l'heure de se coucher

BED AND BREAKFAST

Un bed and breakfast est une petite pension dans une maison particulière ou une ferme où l'on peut louer une chambre avec petit déjeuner compris pour un prix modique par rapport à ce que l'on paierait dans un hôtel. Ces établissements sont communément appelés "B & B", et sont signalés par une pancarte dans le jardin ou au-dessus de la porte.

bee [biː] n abeille f

beech [biːtʃ] n hêtre m

beef [biːf] n bœuf m; **roast ~** rosbif m; **beefburger** n hamburger m

been [biːn] pp of **be**

beer [bɪəʳ] n bière f; **beer garden** n (BRIT) jardin m d'un pub (où l'on peut emmener ses consommations)

beet [biːt] n (vegetable) betterave f; (US: also: **red ~**) betterave (potagère)

beetle [ˈbiːtl] n scarabée m, coléoptère m

beetroot [ˈbiːtruːt] n (BRIT) betterave f

before [bɪˈfɔːʳ] prep (of time) avant; (of space) devant ▷ conj avant que + sub; avant de ▷ adv avant; **~ going** avant de partir; **~ she goes** avant qu'elle (ne) parte; **the week ~** la semaine précédente or d'avant; **I've never seen it ~** c'est la première fois que je le vois; **beforehand** adv au préalable, à l'avance

beg [bɛg] vi mendier ▷ vt mendier; (forgiveness, mercy etc) demander; (entreat) supplier; **to ~ sb to do sth** supplier qn de faire qch; see also **pardon**

began [bɪ'gæn] pt of **begin**

beggar ['bɛgə'] n mendiant(e)

begin [bɪ'gɪn] (pt **began**, pp **begun**) vt, vi commencer; **to ~ doing** or **to do sth** commencer à faire qch; **beginner** n débutant(e); **beginning** n commencement m, début m

begun [bɪ'gʌn] pp of **begin**

behalf [bɪ'hɑ:f] n **on ~ of**, (US) **in ~ of** (representing) de la part de; (for benefit of) pour le compte de; **on my/his ~** de ma/sa part

behave [bɪ'heɪv] vi se conduire, se comporter; (well: also: **~ o.s.**) se conduire bien or comme il faut; **behaviour**, (US) **behavior** n comportement m, conduite f

behind [bɪ'haɪnd] prep derrière; (time) en retard sur; (supporting): **to be ~ sb** soutenir qn ▷ adv derrière; en retard ▷ n derrière m; **~ the scenes** dans les coulisses; **to be ~ (schedule) with sth** être en retard dans qch

beige [beɪʒ] adj beige

Beijing ['beɪ'dʒɪŋ] n Pékin

being ['biːɪŋ] n être m; **to come into ~** prendre naissance

belated [bɪ'leɪtɪd] adj tardif(-ive)

belch [bɛltʃ] vi avoir un renvoi, roter ▷ vt (smoke etc: also: **~ out**) vomir, cracher

Belgian ['bɛldʒən] adj belge, de Belgique ▷ n Belge m/f

Belgium ['bɛldʒəm] n Belgique f

belief [bɪ'liːf] n (opinion) conviction f; (trust, faith) foi f

believe [bɪ'liːv] vt, vi croire, estimer; **to ~ in** (God) croire en; (ghosts, method) croire à; **believer** n (in idea, activity) partisan(e); (Rel) croyant(e)

bell [bɛl] n cloche f; (small) clochette f, grelot m; (on door) sonnette f; (electric) sonnerie f

bellboy ['bɛlbɔɪ], (US) **bellhop** ['bɛlhɔp] n groom m, chasseur m

bellow ['bɛləu] vi (bull) meugler; (person) brailler

bell pepper n (esp US) poivron m

belly ['bɛlɪ] n ventre m; **belly button** (inf) n nombril m

belong [bɪ'lɔŋ] vi: **to ~ to** appartenir à; (club etc) faire partie de; **this book ~s here** ce livre va ici, la place de ce livre est ici; **belongings** npl affaires fpl, possessions fpl

beloved [bɪ'lʌvɪd] adj (bien-)aimé(e), chéri(e)

below [bɪ'ləu] prep sous, au-dessous de ▷ adv en dessous; en contre-bas; **see ~** voir plus bas or plus loin or ci-dessous

belt [bɛlt] n ceinture f; (Tech) courroie f ▷ vt (thrash) donner une raclée à; **beltway** n (US Aut) route f de ceinture; (: motorway) périphérique m

bemused [bɪ'mjuːzd] adj médusé(e)

bench [bɛntʃ] n banc m; (in workshop) établi m; **the B~** (Law: judges) la magistrature, la Cour

bend [bɛnd] (pt, pp **bent**) vt courber; (leg, arm) plier ▷ vi se courber ▷ n (in road) virage m, tournant m; (in pipe, river) coude m; **bend down** vi se baisser; **bend over** vi se pencher

beneath [bɪ'niːθ] prep sous, au-dessous de; (unworthy of) indigne de ▷ adv dessous, au-dessous, en bas

beneficial [bɛnɪ'fɪʃəl] adj: **~ (to)** salutaire (pour), bénéfique (à)

benefit ['bɛnɪfɪt] n avantage m, profit m; (allowance of money) allocation f ▷ vt faire du bien à, profiter à ▷ vi: **he'll ~ from it** cela lui fera du bien, il y gagnera or s'en trouvera bien

Benelux ['bɛnɪlʌks] n Bénélux m

benign [bɪ'naɪn] adj (person, smile) bienveillant(e), affable; (Med) bénin(-igne)

bent [bɛnt] pt, pp of **bend** ▷ n inclination f, penchant m ▷ adj: **to be ~ on** être résolu(e) à

bereaved [bɪ'riːvd] n: **the ~** la famille du disparu

beret ['bɛreɪ] n béret m

Berlin [bə:'lɪn] n Berlin

Bermuda [bə:ˈmjuːdə] n Bermudes fpl

Bern [bə:n] n Berne

berry [ˈbɛrɪ] n baie f

berth [bə:θ] n (bed) couchette f; (for ship) poste m d'amarrage, mouillage m ▷ vi (in harbour) venir à quai; (at anchor) mouiller

beside [bɪˈsaɪd] prep à côté de; (compared with) par rapport à; **that's ~ the point** ça n'a rien à voir; **to be ~ o.s. (with anger)** être hors de soi; **besides** adv en outre, de plus ▷ prep en plus de; (except) excepté

best [bɛst] adj meilleur(e) ▷ adv le mieux; **the ~ part of** (quantity) le plus clair de, la plus grande partie de; **at ~** au mieux; **to make the ~ of sth** s'accommoder de qch (du mieux que l'on peut); **to do one's ~** faire de son mieux; **to the ~ of my knowledge** pour autant que je sache; **to the ~ of my ability** du mieux que je pourrai; **best-before date** n date f de limite d'utilisation or de consommation; **best man** (irreg) n garçon m d'honneur; **bestseller** n best-seller m, succès m de librairie

bet [bɛt] n pari m ▷ vt, vi (pt bet, pp betted) parier; **to ~ sb sth** parier qch à qn

betray [bɪˈtreɪ] vt trahir

better [ˈbɛtəʳ] adj meilleur(e) ▷ adv mieux ▷ vt améliorer ▷ n: **to get the ~ of** triompher de, l'emporter sur; **you had ~ do it** vous feriez mieux de le faire; **he thought ~ of it** il s'est ravisé; **to get ~** (Med) aller mieux; (improve) s'améliorer

betting [ˈbɛtɪŋ] n paris mpl; **betting shop** n (BRIT) bureau m de paris

between [bɪˈtwiːn] prep entre ▷ adv au milieu, dans l'intervalle

beverage [ˈbɛvərɪdʒ] n boisson f (gén sans alcool)

beware [bɪˈwɛəʳ] vi: **to ~ (of)** prendre garde (à); **"~ of the dog"** (attention) chien méchant"

bewildered [bɪˈwɪldəd] adj dérouté(e), ahuri(e)

beyond [bɪˈjɔnd] prep (in space, time) au-delà de; (exceeding) au-dessus de ▷ adv au-delà; **~ doubt** hors de doute; **~ repair** irréparable

bias [ˈbaɪəs] n (prejudice) préjugé m, parti pris m; (preference) prévention f; **bias(s)ed** adj partial(e), montrant un parti pris

bib [bɪb] n bavoir m

Bible [ˈbaɪbl] n Bible f

bicarbonate of soda [baɪˈkɑːbənɪt-] n bicarbonate m de soude

biceps [ˈbaɪsɛps] n biceps m

bicycle [ˈbaɪsɪkl] n bicyclette f; **bicycle pump** n pompe f à vélo

bid [bɪd] n offre f; (at auction) enchère f; (attempt) tentative f ▷ vi (pt, pp bid) faire une enchère or offre ▷ vt (pt bade, pp bidden) faire une enchère or offre de; **to ~ sb good day** souhaiter le bonjour à qn; **bidder** n: **the highest bidder** le plus offrant

bidet [ˈbiːdeɪ] n bidet m

big [bɪg] adj (in height: person, building, tree) grand(e); (in bulk, amount: person, parcel, book) gros(se); **Big Apple** n voir article **"Big Apple"**; **bigheaded** adj prétentieux(-euse); **big toe** n gros orteil

● BIG APPLE
●
● Si l'on sait que "The Big Apple"
● désigne la ville de New York ("apple"
● est en réalité un terme d'argot
● signifiant "grande ville"), on connaît
● moins les surnoms donnés aux
● autres grandes villes américaines.
● Chicago est surnommée "Windy
● City" à cause des rafales soufflant
● du lac Michigan, La Nouvelle-
● Orléans doit son sobriquet
● de "Big Easy" à son style de
● vie décontracté, et l'industrie

◉ automobile a donné à Detroit son
◉ surnom de "Motown".

bike [baɪk] n vélo m; **bike lane** n piste
f cyclable
bikini [bɪˈkiːnɪ] n bikini m
bilateral [baɪˈlætərl] adj bilatéral(e)
bilingual [baɪˈlɪŋgwəl] adj bilingue
bill [bɪl] n note f, facture f; (in restaurant)
addition f, note f; (Pol) projet m de loi;
(US: banknote) billet m (de banque);
(notice) affiche f; (of bird) bec m; **put it
on my ~** mettez-le sur mon compte;
"post no ~s" "défense d'afficher"; **to fit
or fill the ~** (fig) faire l'affaire; **billboard**
n (US) panneau m d'affichage; **billfold**
[ˈbɪlfəuld] n (US) portefeuille m
billiards [ˈbɪljədz] n billard m
billion [ˈbɪljən] n (BRIT) billion m
(million de millions); (US) milliard m
bin [bɪn] n boîte f; (BRIT: also: **dust~**,
litter~) poubelle f; (for coal) coffre m
bind (pt, pp **bound**) [baɪnd, baund] vt
attacher; (book) relier; (oblige) obliger,
contraindre ▷ n (inf: nuisance) scie f
binge [bɪndʒ] n (inf): **to go on a ~**
faire la bringue
bingo [ˈbɪŋgəu] n sorte de jeu de loto
pratiqué dans des établissements publics
binoculars [bɪˈnɔkjuləz] npl
jumelles fpl
bio…: **biochemistry** [baɪəˈkɛmɪstrɪ]
n biochimie f; **biodegradable**
[ˈbaɪəudɪˈgreɪdəbl] adj biodégradable;
biodiesel [ˈbaɪəudiːzl] n biogazole m,
biodiesel m; **biofuel** [ˈbaɪəufjuəl] n
biocarburant; **biography** [baɪˈɔgrəfɪ]
n biographie f; **biological** adj
biologique; **biology** [baɪˈɔlədʒɪ] n
biologie f; **biometric** [baɪəˈmɛtrɪk]
adj biométrique
bipolar [baɪˈpəuləʳ] adj bipolaire
birch [bəːtʃ] n bouleau m
bird [bəːd] n oiseau m; (BRIT inf: girl)
nana f; **bird flu** n grippe f aviaire;
bird of prey n oiseau m de proie;
birdwatching n ornithologie f
(d'amateur)

Biro® [ˈbaɪərəu] n stylo m à bille
birth [bəːθ] n naissance f; **to
give ~ to** donner naissance
à, mettre au monde; (animal)
mettre bas; **birth certificate**
n acte m de naissance; **birth
control** n (policy) limitation f des
naissances; (methods) méthode(s)
contraceptive(s); **birthday** n
anniversaire m ▷ cpd (cake, card etc)
d'anniversaire; **birthmark** n envie
f, tache f de vin; **birthplace** n lieu m
de naissance
biscuit [ˈbɪskɪt] n (BRIT) biscuit m; (US)
petit pain au lait
bishop [ˈbɪʃəp] n évêque m; (Chess)
fou m
bistro [ˈbiːstrəu] n petit restaurant
m, bistrot m
bit [bɪt] pt of **bite** ▷ n morceau m;
(Comput) bit m, élément m binaire; (of
tool) mèche f; (of horse) mors m; **a ~ of**
un peu de; **a ~ mad/dangerous** un
peu fou/risqué; **~ by ~** petit à petit
bitch [bɪtʃ] n (dog) chienne f; (offensive)
salope f (!), garce f
bite [baɪt] vt, vi (pt **bit**, pp **bitten**)
mordre; (insect) piquer ▷ n morsure
f; (insect bite) piqûre f; (mouthful)
bouchée f; **let's have a ~ (to eat)**
mangeons un morceau; **to ~ one's
nails** se ronger les ongles
bitten [ˈbɪtn] pp of **bite**
bitter [ˈbɪtəʳ] adj amer(-ère);
(criticism) cinglant(e); (icy: weather,
wind) glacial(e) ▷ n (BRIT: beer) bière f
(à forte teneur en houblon)
bizarre [bɪˈzɑːʳ] adj bizarre
black [blæk] adj noir(e) ▷ n (colour)
noir m ▷ vt (BRIT Industry) boycotter;
to give sb a ~ eye pocher l'œil à qn,
faire un œil au beurre noir à qn; **to
be in the ~** (in credit) avoir un compte
créditeur; **~ and blue** (bruised)
couvert(e) de bleus; **black out** vi
(faint) s'évanouir; **blackberry** n mûre
f; **blackbird** n merle m; **blackboard**
n tableau noir; **black coffee** n café

noir; **blackcurrant** n cassis m; **black ice** n verglas m; **blackmail** n chantage m ▷ vt faire chanter, soumettre au chantage; **black market** n marché noir; **blackout** n panne f d'électricité; (in wartime) black-out m; (TV) interruption f d'émission; (fainting) syncope f; **black pepper** n poivre noir; **black pudding** n boudin (noir); **Black Sea** n: **the Black Sea** la mer Noire

bladder ['blædər] n vessie f

blade [bleɪd] n lame f; (of propeller) pale f; **a ~ of grass** un brin d'herbe

blame [bleɪm] n faute f, blâme m ▷ vt: **to ~ sb/sth for sth** attribuer à qn/qch la responsabilité de qch; reprocher qch à qn/qch; **I'm not to ~** ce n'est pas ma faute

bland [blænd] adj (taste, food) doux (douce), fade

blank [blæŋk] adj blanc (blanche); (look) sans expression, dénué(e) d'expression ▷ n espace m vide, blanc m; (cartridge) cartouche f à blanc; **his mind was a ~** il avait la tête vide

blanket ['blæŋkɪt] n couverture f; (of snow, cloud) couche f

blast [blɑːst] n explosion f; (shock wave) souffle m; (of air, steam) bouffée f ▷ vt faire sauter or exploser

blatant ['bleɪtənt] adj flagrant(e), criant(e)

blaze [bleɪz] n (fire) incendie m; (fig) flamboiement m ▷ vi (fire) flamber; (fig) flamboyer, resplendir ▷ vt: **to ~ a trail** (fig) montrer la voie; **in a ~ of publicity** à grand renfort de publicité

blazer ['bleɪzər] n blazer m

bleach [bliːtʃ] n (also: **household ~**) eau f de Javel ▷ vt (linen) blanchir; **bleachers** npl (us Sport) gradins mpl (en plein soleil)

bleak [bliːk] adj morne, désolé(e); (weather) triste, maussade; (smile) lugubre; (prospect, future) morose

bled [blɛd] pt, pp of **bleed**

bleed (pt, pp **bled**) [bliːd, blɛd] vt saigner; (brakes, radiator) purger ▷ vi saigner; **my nose is ~ing** je saigne du nez

blemish ['blɛmɪʃ] n défaut m; (on reputation) tache f

blend [blɛnd] n mélange m ▷ vt mélanger ▷ vi (colours etc: also: **~ in**) se mélanger, se fondre, s'allier; **blender** n (Culin) mixeur m

bless (pt, pp **blessed** or **blest**) [blɛs, blɛst] vt bénir; **~ you!** (after sneeze) à tes souhaits!; **blessing** n bénédiction f; (godsend) bienfait m

blew [bluː] pt of **blow**

blight [blaɪt] vt (hopes etc) anéantir, briser

blind [blaɪnd] adj aveugle ▷ n (for window) store m ▷ vt aveugler; **~ people** les aveugles mpl; **blind alley** n impasse f; **blindfold** n bandeau m ▷ adj, adv les yeux bandés ▷ vt bander les yeux à

blink [blɪŋk] vi cligner des yeux; (light) clignoter

bliss [blɪs] n félicité f, bonheur m sans mélange

blister ['blɪstər] n (on skin) ampoule f, cloque f; (on paintwork) boursouflure f ▷ vi (paint) se boursoufler, se cloquer

blizzard ['blɪzəd] n blizzard m, tempête f de neige

bloated ['bləutɪd] adj (face) bouffi(e); (stomach, person) gonflé(e)

blob [blɔb] n (drop) goutte f; (stain, spot) tache f

block [blɔk] n bloc m; (in pipes) obstruction f; (toy) cube m; (of buildings) pâté m (de maisons) ▷ vt bloquer; (fig) faire obstacle à; **the sink is ~ed** l'évier est bouché; **~ of flats** (BRIT) immeuble (locatif); **mental ~** blocage m; **block up** vt boucher; **blockade** [blɔ'keɪd] n blocus m ▷ vt faire le blocus de; **blockage** n obstruction f; **blockbuster** n (film, book) grand succès; **block capitals** npl majuscules *fpl* d'imprimerie; **block letters** *npl* majuscules *fpl*

blog [blɒg] *n* blog *m* ▷ *vi* bloguer

blogger [ˈblɒgəʳ] *n* blogueur(-euse)

blogosphere [ˈblɒgəsfɪəʳ] *n* blogosphère *f*

bloke [bləuk] *n* (BRIT inf) type *m*

blond(e) [blɒnd] *adj*, *n* blond(e)

blood [blʌd] *n* sang *m*; **blood donor** *n* donneur(-euse) de sang; **blood group** *n* groupe sanguin; **blood poisoning** *n* empoisonnement *m* du sang; **blood pressure** *n* tension (artérielle); **bloodshed** *n* effusion *f* de sang, carnage *m*; **bloodshot** *adj*: **bloodshot eyes** yeux injectés de sang; **bloodstream** *n* sang *m*, système sanguin; **blood test** *n* analyse *f* de sang; **blood transfusion** *n* transfusion *f* de sang; **blood type** *n* groupe sanguin; **blood vessel** *n* vaisseau sanguin; **bloody** *adj* sanglant(e); (BRIT inf!): **this bloody ...** ce foutu ..., ce putain de ... (!) ▷ *adv*: **bloody strong/good** (BRIT inf!) vachement *or* sacrément fort/bon

bloom [bluːm] *n* fleur *f* ▷ *vi* être en fleur

blossom [ˈblɒsəm] *n* fleur(s) *f(pl)* ▷ *vi* être en fleurs; (fig) s'épanouir

blot [blɒt] *n* tache *f* ▷ *vt* tacher; (ink) sécher

blouse [blauz] *n* (feminine garment) chemisier *m*, corsage *m*

blow [bləu] (pt **blew**, pp **blown**) *n* coup *m* ▷ *vi* souffler ▷ *vt* (instrument) jouer de; (fuse) faire sauter; **to ~ one's nose** se moucher; **blow away** *vi* s'envoler ▷ *vt* chasser, faire s'envoler; **blow out** *vi* (fire, flame) s'éteindre; (tyre) éclater; (fuse) sauter; **blow up** *vi* exploser, sauter ▷ *vt* faire sauter; (tyre) gonfler; (Phot) agrandir; **blow-dry** *n* (hairstyle) brushing *m*

blue [bluː] *adj* bleu(e); (depressed) triste; **~ film/joke** film *m*/histoire *f* pornographique; **out of the ~** (fig) à l'improviste, sans qu'on s'y attende; **bluebell** *n* jacinthe *f* des bois;

blueberry *n* myrtille *f*, airelle *f*; **blue cheese** *n* (fromage) bleu *m*; **blues** *npl*: **the blues** (Mus) le blues; **to have the blues** (inf: feeling) avoir le cafard

bluff [blʌf] *vi* bluffer ▷ *n* bluff *m*; **to call sb's ~** mettre qn au défi d'exécuter ses menaces

blunder [ˈblʌndəʳ] *n* gaffe *f*, bévue *f* ▷ *vi* faire une gaffe *or* une bévue

blunt [blʌnt] *adj* (knife) émoussé(e), peu tranchant(e); (pencil) mal taillé(e); (person) brusque, ne mâchant pas ses mots

blur [bləːʳ] *n* (shape): **to become a ~** devenir flou ▷ *vt* brouiller, rendre flou(e); **blurred** *adj* flou(e)

blush [blʌʃ] *vi* rougir ▷ *n* rougeur *f*; **blusher** *n* rouge *m* à joues

board [bɔːd] *n* (wooden) planche *f*; (on wall) panneau *m*; (for chess etc) plateau *m*; (cardboard) carton *m*; (committee) conseil *m*, comité *m*; (in firm) conseil d'administration; (Naut, Aviat): **on ~** à bord ▷ *vt* (ship) monter à bord de; (train) monter dans; **full ~** (BRIT) pension complète; **half ~** (BRIT) demi-pension *f*; **~ and lodging** *n* chambre *f* avec pension; **to go by the ~** (hopes, principles) être abandonné(e); **board game** *n* jeu *m* de société; **boarding card** *n* (Aviat, Naut) carte *f* d'embarquement; **boarding pass** *n* (BRIT) = **boarding card**; **boarding school** *n* internat *m*, pensionnat *m*; **board room** *n* salle *f* du conseil d'administration

boast [bəust] *vi*: **to ~ (about or of)** se vanter (de)

boat [bəut] *n* bateau *m*; (small) canot *m*; barque *f*

bob [bɒb] *vi* (boat, cork on water: also: **~ up and down**) danser, se balancer

bobby pin [ˈbɒbɪ-] *n* (US) pince *f* à cheveux

body [ˈbɒdɪ] *n* corps *m*; (of car) carrosserie *f*; (fig: society) organe *m*, organisme *m*; **body-building** *n* body-building *m*, culturisme *m*; **bodyguard**

n garde m du corps; **bodywork** n carrosserie f

bog [bɔg] n tourbière f ▷ vt: **to get ~ged down (in)** (fig) s'enliser (dans)

bogus ['bəʊgəs] adj bidon inv; fantôme

boil [bɔɪl] vt (faire) bouillir ▷ vi bouillir ▷ n (Med) furoncle m; **to come to the** or (US) **a ~** bouillir; **boil down** vi (fig): **to ~ down to** se réduire or ramener à; **boil over** vi déborder; **boiled egg** n œuf m à la coque; **boiler** n chaudière f; **boiling** ['bɔɪlɪŋ] adj: **I'm boiling (hot)** (inf) je crève de chaud; **boiling point** n point m d'ébullition

bold [bəʊld] adj hardi(e), audacieux(-euse); (pej) effronté(e); (outline, colour) franc (franche), tranché(e), marqué(e)

bollard ['bɔləd] n (BRIT Aut) borne lumineuse or de signalisation

bolt [bəʊlt] n verrou m; (with nut) boulon m ▷ adv: **~ upright** droit(e) comme un piquet ▷ vt (door) verrouiller; (food) engloutir ▷ vi se sauver, filer (comme une flèche); (horse) s'emballer

bomb [bɔm] n bombe f ▷ vt bombarder; **bombard** [bɔm'bɑːd] vt bombarder; **bomber** n (Aviat) bombardier m; (terrorist) poseur m de bombes; **bomb scare** n alerte f à la bombe

bond [bɔnd] n lien m; (binding promise) engagement m, obligation f; (Finance) obligation; **bonds** npl (chains) chaînes fpl; **in ~** (of goods) en entrepôt

bone [bəʊn] n os m; (of fish) arête f ▷ vt désosser; ôter les arêtes de

bonfire ['bɔnfaɪər] n feu m (de joie); (for rubbish) feu

bonnet ['bɔnɪt] n bonnet m; (BRIT: of car) capot m

bonus ['bəʊnəs] n (money) prime f; (advantage) avantage m

boo [buː] excl hou!, peuh! ▷ vt huer

book [buk] n livre m; (of stamps, tickets etc) carnet m ▷ vt (ticket) prendre;

(seat, room) réserver; (football player) prendre le nom de, donner un carton à; **books** npl (Comm) comptes mpl, comptabilité f; **I ~ed a table in the name of ...** j'ai réservé une table au nom de ...; **book in** vi (BRIT: at hotel) prendre sa chambre; **book up** vt réserver; **the hotel is ~ed up** l'hôtel est complet; **bookcase** n bibliothèque f (meuble); **booking** n (BRIT) réservation f; **I confirmed my booking by fax/email** j'ai confirmé ma réservation par fax/e-mail; **booking office** n (BRIT) bureau m de location; **book-keeping** n comptabilité f; **booklet** n brochure f; **bookmaker** n bookmaker m; **bookmark** n (for book) marque-page m; (Comput) signet m; **bookseller** n libraire m/f; **bookshelf** n (single) étagère f (à livres); (bookcase) bibliothèque f; **bookshop, bookstore** n librairie f

boom [buːm] n (noise) grondement m; (in prices, population) forte augmentation; (busy period) boom m, vague f de prospérité ▷ vi gronder; prospérer

boost [buːst] n stimulant m, remontant m ▷ vt stimuler

boot [buːt] n botte f; (for hiking) chaussure f (de marche); (ankle boot) bottine f; (BRIT: of car) coffre m ▷ vt (Comput) lancer, mettre en route; **to ~** (in addition) par-dessus le marché, en plus

booth [buːð] n (at fair) baraque (foraine); (of telephone etc) cabine f; (also: **voting ~**) isoloir m

booze [buːz] (inf) n boissons fpl alcooliques, alcool m

border ['bɔːdər] n bordure f; bord m; (of a country) frontière f; **borderline** n (fig) ligne f de démarcation

bore [bɔːr] pt of **bear** ▷ vt (person) ennuyer, raser; (hole) percer; (well, tunnel) creuser ▷ n (person) raseur(-euse); (boring thing) barbe f;

(*of gun*) calibre m; **bored** *adj*: **to be bored** s'ennuyer; **boredom** *n* ennui m
boring ['bɔːrɪŋ] *adj* ennuyeux(-euse)
born [bɔːn] *adj*: **to be ~** naître; **I was ~ in 1960** je suis né en 1960
borne [bɔːn] *pp of* **bear**
borough ['bʌrə] *n* municipalité f
borrow ['bɔrəu] *vt*: **to ~ sth (from sb)** emprunter qch (à qn)
Bosnian ['bɒznɪən] *adj* bosniaque, bosnien(ne) ▷ *n* Bosniaque m/f, Bosnien(ne)
bosom ['buzəm] *n* poitrine f; (*fig*) sein m
boss [bɒs] *n* patron(ne) ▷ *vt* (*also*: **~ about, ~ around**) mener à la baguette; **bossy** *adj* autoritaire
both [bəuθ] *adj* les deux, l'un(e) et l'autre ▷ *pron*: **~ (of them)** les deux, tous (toutes) (les) deux, l'un(e) et l'autre; **~ of us went, we ~ went** nous y sommes allés tous les deux ▷ *adv*: **~ A and B** A et B
bother ['bɒðər] *vt* (*worry*) tracasser; (*needle, bait*) importuner, ennuyer; (*disturb*) déranger ▷ *vi* (*also*: **~ o.s.**) se tracasser, se faire du souci ▷ *n* (*trouble*) ennuis mpl; **to ~ doing** prendre la peine de faire; **don't ~** ce n'est pas la peine; **it's no ~** aucun problème
bottle ['bɒtl] *n* bouteille f; (*baby's*) biberon m; (*of perfume, medicine*) flacon m ▷ *vt* mettre en bouteille(s); **bottle bank** *n* conteneur m (de bouteilles); **bottle-opener** *n* ouvre-bouteille m
bottom ['bɒtəm] *n* (*of container, sea etc*) fond m; (*buttocks*) derrière m; (*of page, list*) bas m; (*of mountain, tree, hill*) pied m ▷ *adj* (*shelf, step*) du bas
bought [bɔːt] *pt, pp of* **buy**
boulder ['bəuldər] *n* gros rocher (*gén lisse, arrondi*)
bounce [bauns] *vi* (*ball*) rebondir; (*cheque*) être refusé (*étant sans provision*) ▷ *vt* faire rebondir ▷ *n* (*rebound*) rebond m; **bouncer** *n* (*inf: at dance, club*) videur m

bound [baund] *pt, pp of* **bind** ▷ *n* (*gen pl*) limite f; (*leap*) bond m ▷ *vi* (*leap*) bondir ▷ *vt* (*limit*) borner ▷ *adj*: **to be ~ to do sth** (*obliged*) être obligé(e) or avoir obligation de faire qch; **he's ~ to fail** (*likely*) il est sûr d'échouer, son échec est inévitable or assuré; **~ by** (*law, regulation*) engagé(e) par; **~ for** à destination de; **out of ~s** dont l'accès est interdit
boundary ['baundrɪ] *n* frontière f
bouquet ['bukeɪ] *n* bouquet m
bourbon ['buəbən] *n* (*US: also*: **~ whiskey**) bourbon m
bout [baut] *n* période f; (*of malaria etc*) accès m, crise f, attaque f; (*Boxing etc*) combat m, match m
boutique [buːˈtiːk] *n* boutique f
bow¹ [bəu] *n* nœud m; (*weapon*) arc m; (*Mus*) archet m
bow² [bau] *n* (*with body*) révérence f, inclination f (du buste or corps); (*Naut: also*: **~s**) proue f ▷ *vi* faire une révérence, s'incliner
bowels [bauəlz] *npl* intestins mpl; (*fig*) entrailles fpl
bowl [bəul] *n* (*for eating*) bol m; (*for washing*) cuvette f; (*ball*) boule f ▷ *vi* (*Cricket*) lancer (la balle); **bowler** *n* (*Cricket*) lanceur m (de la balle); (*BRIT: also*: **bowler hat**) (chapeau m) melon m; **bowling** *n* (*game*) jeu m de boules, jeu de quilles; **bowling alley** *n* bowling m; **bowling green** *n* terrain m de boules (*gazonné et carré*); **bowls** *n* (jeu m de) boules fpl
bow tie [bəu-] *n* nœud m papillon
box [bɒks] *n* boîte f; (*also*: **cardboard ~**) carton m; (*Theat*) loge f ▷ *vt* mettre en boîte ▷ *vi* boxer, faire de la boxe; **boxer** ['bɒksər] *n* (*person*) boxeur m; **boxer shorts** *npl* caleçon m; **boxing** ['bɒksɪŋ] *n* (*sport*) boxe f; **Boxing Day** *n* (*BRIT*) le lendemain de Noël; *voir article* **"Boxing Day"**; **boxing gloves** *npl* gants mpl de boxe; **boxing ring** *n* ring m; **box office** *n* bureau m de location

● **BOXING DAY**
●
● *Boxing Day* est le lendemain de
● Noël, férié en Grande-Bretagne. Ce
● nom vient d'une coutume du XIXe
● siècle qui consistait à donner des
● cadeaux de Noël (dans des boîtes) à
● ses employés etc le 26 décembre.

boy [bɔɪ] *n* garçon *m*; **boy band** *n*
boys band *m*
boycott ['bɔɪkɒt] *n* boycottage *m* ▷ *vt*
boycotter
boyfriend ['bɔɪfrɛnd] *n* (petit) ami
bra [brɑː] *n* soutien-gorge *m*
brace [breɪs] *n* (*support*) attache
f, agrafe *f*; (BRIT: *also*: **~s** : *on
teeth*) appareil *m* (dentaire);
(*tool*) vilebrequin *m* ▷ *vt* (*support*)
consolider, soutenir; **braces** *npl* (BRIT:
for trousers) bretelles *fpl*; **to ~ o.s.** (*fig*)
se préparer mentalement
bracelet ['breɪslɪt] *n* bracelet *m*
bracket ['brækɪt] *n* (*Tech*) tasseau
m, support *m*; (*group*) classe *f*,
tranche *f*; (*also*: **brace ~**)
accolade *f*; (*also*: **round ~**) parenthèse *f*; (*also*:
square ~) crochet *m* ▷ *vt* mettre entre
parenthèses; **in ~s** entre parenthèses
or crochets
brag [bræg] *vi* se vanter
braid [breɪd] *n* (*trimming*) galon *m*; (*of
hair*) tresse *f*, natte *f*
brain [breɪn] *n* cerveau *m*; **brains** *npl*
(*intellect, food*) cervelle *f*
braise [breɪz] *vt* braiser
brake [breɪk] *n* frein *m* ▷ *vt*, *vi* freiner;
brake light *n* feu *m* de stop
bran [bræn] *n* son *m*
branch [brɑːntʃ] *n* branche *f*; (*Comm*)
succursale *f* (: *of bank*) agence *f*;
branch off *vi* (*road*) bifurquer;
branch out *vi* diversifier ses activités
brand [brænd] *n* marque
(commerciale) ▷ *vt* (*cattle*) marquer
(au fer rouge); **brand name** *n* nom *m*
de marque; **brand-new** *adj* tout(e)
neuf (neuve), flambant neuf (neuve)

brandy ['brændɪ] *n* cognac *m*
brash [bræʃ] *adj* effronté(e)
brass [brɑːs] *n* cuivre *m* (jaune), laiton
m; **the ~** (*Mus*) les cuivres; **brass
band** *n* fanfare *f*
brat [bræt] *n* (*pej*) mioche *m/f*,
môme *m/f*
brave [breɪv] *adj* courageux(-euse),
brave ▷ *vt* braver, affronter; **bravery**
n bravoure *f*, courage *m*
brawl [brɔːl] *n* rixe *f*, bagarre *f*
Brazil [brə'zɪl] *n* Brésil *m*; **Brazilian**
adj brésilien(ne) ▷ *n* Brésilien(ne)
breach [briːtʃ] *vt* ouvrir une brèche
dans ▷ *n* (*gap*) brèche *f*; (*breaking*): **~
of contract** rupture *f* de contrat; **~ of
the peace** attentat *m* à l'ordre public
bread [brɛd] *n* pain *m*; **breadbin**
n (BRIT) boîte *f* or huche *f* à pain;
breadbox *n* (US) boîte *f* or huche *f* à
pain; **breadcrumbs** *npl* miettes *fpl* de
pain; (*Culin*) chapelure *f*, panure *f*
breadth [brɛtθ] *n* largeur *f*
break [breɪk] (*pt* **broke**, *pp* **broken**)
vt casser, briser; (*promise*) rompre;
(*law*) violer ▷ *vi* se casser, se briser;
(*weather*) tourner; (*storm*) éclater;
(*day*) se lever ▷ *n* (*gap*) brèche *f*;
(*fracture*) cassure *f*; (*rest*) interruption
f, arrêt *m* (: *short*) pause *f*; (: *at school*)
récréation *f*; (*chance*) chance *f*,
occasion *f* favorable; **to ~ one's
leg** *etc* se casser la jambe *etc*; **to ~ a
record** battre un record; **to ~ the
news to sb** annoncer la nouvelle
à qn; **break down** *vt* (*door etc*)
enfoncer; (*figures, data*) décomposer,
analyser ▷ *vi* s'effondrer; (*Med*) faire
une dépression (nerveuse); (*Aut*)
tomber en panne; **my car has
broken down** ma voiture est en
panne; **break in** *vt* (*horse etc*) dresser
▷ *vi* (*burglar*) entrer par effraction;
(*interrupt*) interrompre; **break into**
vt fus (*house*) s'introduire *or* pénétrer
par effraction dans; **break off** *vi*
(*speaker*) s'interrompre; (*branch*)
se rompre ▷ *vt* (*talks, engagement*)

b

rompre; **break out** vi éclater, se
déclarer; (*prisoner*) s'évader; **to ~ out
in spots** se couvrir de boutons; **break
up** vi (*partnership*) cesser, prendre fin;
(*marriage*) se briser; (*crowd, meeting*)
se séparer; (*ship*) se disloquer; (*Scol:
pupils*) être en vacances; (*line*) couper
▷ vt fracasser, casser; (*fight etc*)
interrompre, faire cesser; (*marriage*)
désunir; **the line's** or **you're ~ing
up** ça coupe; **breakdown** n (*Aut*)
panne f; (*in communications, marriage*)
rupture f; (*Med: also:* **nervous
breakdown**) dépression (nerveuse);
(*of figures*) ventilation f, répartition f;
breakdown van, (US) **breakdown
truck** n dépanneuse f
breakfast ['brɛkfəst] n petit
déjeuner m; **what time is ~?** le petit
déjeuner est à quelle heure?
break: break-in n cambriolage m;
breakthrough n percée f
breast [brɛst] n (*of woman*) sein m;
(*chest*) poitrine f; (*of chicken, turkey*)
blanc m; **breast-feed** vt, vi (*irreg:
like* **feed**) allaiter; **breast-stroke** n
brasse f
breath [brɛθ] n haleine f, souffle m;
to take a deep ~ respirer à fond; **out
of ~** à bout de souffle, essoufflé(e)
Breathalyser® ['brɛθəlaɪzəʳ] (*BRIT*)
n alcootest m
breathe [briːð] vt, vi respirer;
breathe in vi aspirer ▷ vt aspirer;
breathe out vt, vi expirer; **breathing**
n respiration f
breath: breathless adj essoufflé(e),
haletant(e); **breathtaking** adj
stupéfiant(e), à vous couper le
souffle; **breath test** n alcootest m
bred [brɛd] pt, pp of **breed**
breed [briːd] (*pt, pp* **bred**) vt élever,
faire l'élevage de ▷ vi se reproduire ▷ n
race f, variété f
breeze [briːz] n brise f
breezy ['briːzɪ] adj (*day, weather*)
venteux(-euse); (*manner*) désinvolte;
(*person*) jovial(e)

brew [bruː] vt (*tea*) faire infuser; (*beer*)
brasser ▷ vi (*fig*) se préparer, couver;
brewery n brasserie f (*fabrique*)
bribe [braɪb] n pot-de-vin m ▷ vt
acheter; soudoyer; **bribery** n
corruption f
bric-a-brac ['brɪkəbræk] n bric-
à-brac m
brick [brɪk] n brique f; **bricklayer** n
maçon m
bride [braɪd] n mariée f, épouse f;
bridegroom n marié m, époux m;
bridesmaid n demoiselle f d'honneur
bridge [brɪdʒ] n pont m; (*Naut*)
passerelle f (de commandement); (*of
nose*) arête f; (*Cards, Dentistry*) bridge
m ▷ vt (*gap*) combler
bridle ['braɪdl] n bride f
brief [briːf] adj bref (brève) ▷ n
(*Law*) dossier m, cause f; (*gen*) tâche
f ▷ vt mettre au courant; **briefs**
npl slip m; **briefcase** n serviette f;
porte-documents m inv; **briefing** n
instructions fpl; (*Press*) briefing m;
briefly adv brièvement
brigadier [brɪgə'dɪəʳ] n brigadier
général
bright [braɪt] adj brillant(e); (*room,
weather*) clair(e); (*person: clever*)
intelligent(e), doué(e); (: *cheerful*)
gai(e); (*idea*) génial(e); (*colour*) vif
(vive)
brilliant ['brɪljənt] adj brillant(e);
(*light, sunshine*) éclatant(e); (*inf:
great*) super
brim [brɪm] n bord m
brine [braɪn] n (*Culin*) saumure f
bring [brɪŋ] (*pt, pp* **brought**) [brɔːt]
vt (*thing*) apporter; (*person*) amener;
bring about vt provoquer, entraîner;
bring back vt rapporter; (*person*)
ramener; **bring down** vt (*lower*)
abaisser; (*shoot down*) abattre;
(*government*) faire s'effondrer; **bring
in** vt (*person*) faire entrer; (*object*)
rentrer; (*Pol: legislation*) introduire;
(*produce: income*) rapporter; **bring
on** vt (*illness, attack*) provoquer;

(*player, substitute*) amener; **bring out**
vt sortir; (*meaning*) faire ressortir,
mettre en relief; **bring up** *vt* élever;
(*carry up*) monter; (*question*) soulever;
(*food: vomit*) vomir, rendre

brink [brɪŋk] *n* bord *m*

brisk [brɪsk] *adj* vif (vive); (*abrupt*)
brusque; (*trade etc*) actif(-ive)

bristle ['brɪsl] *n* poil *m* ▷ *vi* se hérisser

Brit [brɪt] *n abbr* (*inf*: = *British person*)
Britannique *m/f*

Britain ['brɪtən] *n* (*also*: **Great ~**) la
Grande-Bretagne

British ['brɪtɪʃ] *adj* britannique ▷ *npl*;
the ~ les Britanniques *mpl*; **British
Isles** *npl*; **the British Isles** les îles *fpl*
Britanniques

Briton ['brɪtən] *n* Britannique *m/f*

Brittany ['brɪtənɪ] *n* Bretagne *f*

brittle ['brɪtl] *adj* cassant(e), fragile

broad [brɔ:d] *adj* large; (*distinction*)
général(e); (*accent*) prononcé(e); **in ~
daylight** en plein jour

B road *n* (BRIT) ≈ route
départementale

broad: broadband *n* transmission
f à haut débit; **broad bean** *n* fève
f; **broadcast** (*pt, pp* broadcast) *n*
émission *f* ▷ *vt* (*Radio*) radiodiffuser;
(*TV*) téléviser ▷ *vi* émettre; **broaden**
vt élargir; **to broaden one's mind**
élargir ses horizons ▷ *vi* s'élargir;
broadly *adv* en gros, généralement;
broad-minded *adj* large d'esprit

broccoli ['brɔkəlɪ] *n* brocoli *m*

brochure ['brəʊʃjʊəʳ] *n*
prospectus *m*, dépliant *m*

broil [brɔɪl] *vt* (US) rôtir

broke [brəʊk] *pt* of **break** ▷ *adj* (*inf*)
fauché(e)

broken ['brəʊkn] *pp* of **break** ▷ *adj*
(*stick, leg etc*) cassé(e); (*machine*:
also: **~ down**) fichu(e); **in ~ French/
English** dans un français/anglais
approximatif *or* hésitant

broker ['brəʊkəʳ] *n* courtier *m*

bronchitis [brɔŋ'kaɪtɪs] *n* bronchite *f*

bronze [brɔnz] *n* bronze *m*

brooch [brəʊtʃ] *n* broche *f*

brood [bru:d] *n* couvée *f* ▷ *vi* (*person*)
méditer (sombrement), ruminer

broom [brum] *n* balai *m*; (*Bot*)
genêt *m*

Bros. *abbr* (*Comm*: = *brothers*) Frères

broth [brɔθ] *n* bouillon *m* de viande et
de légumes

brothel ['brɔθl] *n* maison close,
bordel *m*

brother ['brʌðəʳ] *n* frère *m*; **brother-
in-law** *n* beau-frère *m*

brought [brɔ:t] *pt, pp* of **bring**

brow [braʊ] *n* front *m*; (*eyebrow*)
sourcil *m*; (*of hill*) sommet *m*

brown [braʊn] *adj* brun(e), marron
inv; (*hair*) châtain *inv*; (*tanned*)
bronzé(e) ▷ *n* (*colour*) brun *m*, marron
m ▷ *vt* brunir; (*Culin*) faire dorer, faire
roussir; **brown bread** *n* pain *m* bis

Brownie ['braʊnɪ] *n* jeannette *f*
éclaireuse (cadette)

brown rice *n* riz *m* complet

brown sugar *n* cassonade *f*

browse [braʊz] *vi* (*in shop*) regarder
(*sans acheter*); **to ~ through a
book** feuilleter un livre; **browser** *n*
(*Comput*) navigateur *m*

bruise [bru:z] *n* bleu *m*, ecchymose
f, contusion *f* ▷ *vt* contusionner,
meurtrir

brunette [bru:'nɛt] *n* (*femme*) brune

brush [brʌʃ] *n* brosse *f*; (*for painting*)
pinceau *m*; (*for shaving*) blaireau *m*;
(*quarrel*) accrochage *m*, prise *f* de bec
▷ *vt* brosser; (*also*: **~ past, ~ against**)
effleurer, frôler

Brussels ['brʌslz] *n* Bruxelles

Brussels sprout *n* chou *m* de
Bruxelles

brutal ['bru:tl] *adj* brutal(e)

B.Sc. *n abbr* = **Bachelor of Science**

BSE *n abbr* (= *bovine spongiform
encephalopathy*) ESB *f*, BSE *f*

bubble ['bʌbl] *n* bulle *f* ▷ *vi*
bouillonner, faire des bulles;
(*sparkle, fig*) pétiller; **bubble bath**
n bain moussant; **bubble gum** *n*

chewing-gum m; **bubblejet printer** ['bʌbldʒɛt-] n imprimante f à bulle d'encre

buck [bʌk] n mâle m (d'un lapin, lièvre, daim etc); (US inf) dollar m ▷ vi ruer, lancer une ruade; **to pass the ~ (to sb)** se décharger de la responsabilité (sur qn)

bucket ['bʌkɪt] n seau m; **bucket list** n liste f de choses à faire avant de mourir

buckle ['bʌkl] n boucle f ▷ vt (belt etc) boucler, attacher ▷ vi (warp) tordre, gauchir (: wheel) se voiler

bud [bʌd] n bourgeon m; (of flower) bouton m ▷ vi bourgeonner; (flower) éclore

Buddhism ['budɪzəm] n bouddhisme m

Buddhist ['budɪst] adj bouddhiste ▷ n Bouddhiste m/f

buddy ['bʌdɪ] n (US) copain m

budge [bʌdʒ] vt faire bouger ▷ vi bouger

budgerigar ['bʌdʒərɪgɑːʳ] n perruche f

budget ['bʌdʒɪt] n budget m ▷ vi: **to ~ for sth** inscrire qch au budget

budgie ['bʌdʒɪ] n = **budgerigar**

buff [bʌf] adj (couleur f) chamois m ▷ n (inf: enthusiast) mordu(e)

buffalo ['bʌfələu] (pl **buffalo** or **buffaloes**) n (BRIT) buffle m; (US) bison m

buffer ['bʌfəʳ] n tampon m; (Comput) mémoire f tampon

buffet n ['bʌfeɪ] (food, BRIT: bar) buffet m ▷ vt ['bʌfɪt] secouer, ébranler; **buffet car** n (BRIT Rail) voiture-bar f

bug [bʌg] n (bedbug etc) punaise f; (esp US: any insect) insecte m, bestiole f; (fig: germ) virus m, microbe m; (spy device) dispositif m d'écoute (électronique), micro clandestin; (Comput: of program) erreur f ▷ vt (room) poser des micros dans; (inf: annoy) embêter

buggy ['bʌgɪ] n poussette f

build [bɪld] n (of person) carrure f, charpente f ▷ vt (pt, pp **built**)

construire, bâtir; **build up** vt accumuler, amasser; (business) développer; (reputation) bâtir; **builder** n entrepreneur m; **building** n (trade) construction f; (structure) bâtiment m, construction (: residential, offices) immeuble m; **building site** n chantier m (de construction); **building society** n (BRIT) société f de crédit immobilier

built [bɪlt] pt, pp of **build**; **built-in** adj (cupboard) encastré(e); (device) incorporé(e); intégré(e); **built-up** adj: **built-up area** zone urbanisée

bulb [bʌlb] n (Bot) bulbe m, oignon m; (Elec) ampoule f

Bulgaria [bʌl'gɛərɪə] n Bulgarie f; **Bulgarian** adj bulgare ▷ n Bulgare m/f

bulge [bʌldʒ] n renflement m, gonflement m ▷ vi faire saillie; présenter un renflement; (pocket, file): **to be bulging with** être plein(e) à craquer de

bulimia [bə'lɪmɪə] n boulimie f

bulimic [bju:'lɪmɪk] adj, n boulimique m/f

bulk [bʌlk] n masse f, volume m; **in ~** (Comm) en gros, en vrac; **the ~ of** la plus grande or grosse partie de; **bulky** adj volumineux(-euse), encombrant(e)

bull [bul] n taureau m; (male elephant, whale) mâle m

bulldozer ['buldəuzəʳ] n bulldozer m

bullet ['bulɪt] n balle f (de fusil etc)

bulletin ['bulɪtɪn] n bulletin m, communiqué m; (also: **news ~**) (bulletin d')informations fpl; **bulletin board** n (Comput) messagerie f (électronique)

bullfight ['bulfaɪt] n corrida f, course f de taureaux; **bullfighter** n torero m; **bullfighting** n tauromachie f

bully ['bulɪ] n brute f, tyran m ▷ vt tyranniser, rudoyer

bum [bʌm] n (inf: BRIT: backside) derrière m; (esp US: tramp) vagabond(e), traîne-savates *m/f inv*; (*idler*) glandeur *m*

bumblebee ['bʌmblbiː] *n* bourdon *m*

bump [bʌmp] *n* (*blow*) coup *m*, choc *m*; (*jolt*) cahot *m*; (*on road etc, on head*) bosse *f* ▷ *vt* heurter, cogner; (*car*) emboutir; **bump into** *vt fus* rentrer dans, tamponner; (*inf: meet*) tomber sur; **bumper** *n* pare-chocs *m inv* ▷ *adj*: **bumper crop/harvest** récolte/moisson exceptionnelle; **bumpy** *adj* (*road*) cahoteux(-euse); **it was a bumpy flight/ride** on a été secoués dans l'avion/la voiture

bun [bʌn] *n* (*cake*) petit gâteau; (*bread*) petit pain au lait; (*of hair*) chignon *m*

bunch [bʌntʃ] *n* (*of flowers*) bouquet *m*; (*of keys*) trousseau *m*; (*of bananas*) régime *m*; (*of people*) groupe *m*; **bunches** *npl* (*in hair*) couettes *fpl*; **~ of grapes** grappe *f* de raisin

bundle ['bʌndl] *n* paquet *m* ▷ *vt* (*also*: **~ up**) faire un paquet de; (*put*): **to ~ sth/sb into** fourrer *or* enfourner qch/qn dans

bungalow ['bʌŋgələu] *n* bungalow *m*

bungee jumping ['bʌndʒiː'dʒʌmpɪŋ] *n* saut *m* à l'élastique

bunion ['bʌnjən] *n* oignon *m* (*au pied*)

bunk [bʌŋk] *n* couchette *f*; **bunk beds** *npl* lits superposés

bunker ['bʌŋkəʳ] *n* (*coal store*) soute *f* à charbon; (*Mil, Golf*) bunker *m*

bunny ['bʌnɪ] *n* (*also*: **~ rabbit**) lapin *m*

buoy [bɔɪ] *n* bouée *f*; **buoyant** *adj* (*ship*) flottable; (*carefree*) gai(e), plein(e) d'entrain; (*Comm: market, economy*) actif(-ive)

burden ['bəːdn] *n* fardeau *m*, charge *f* ▷ *vt* charger; (*oppress*) accabler, surcharger

bureau (*pl* **bureaux**) ['bjuərəu, -z] *n* (*BRIT: writing desk*) bureau *m*, secrétaire *m*; (*US: chest of drawers*) commode *f*; (*office*) bureau, office *m*

bureaucracy [bjuə'rɔkrəsɪ] *n* bureaucratie *f*

bureaucrat ['bjuərəkræt] *n* bureaucrate *m/f*, rond-de-cuir *m*

bureau de change [-də'ʃɑ̃ʒ] (*pl* **bureaux de change**) *n* bureau *m* de change

bureaux ['bjuərəuz] *npl of* **bureau**

burger ['bəːgəʳ] *n* hamburger *m*

burglar ['bəːgləʳ] *n* cambrioleur *m*; **burglar alarm** *n* sonnerie *f* d'alarme; **burglary** *n* cambriolage *m*

Burgundy ['bəːgəndɪ] *n* Bourgogne *f*

burial ['berɪəl] *n* enterrement *m*

burn [bəːn] *vt*, *vi* (*pt* **burned**, *pp* **burnt**) brûler ▷ *n* brûlure *f*; **burn down** *vt* incendier, détruire par le feu; **burn out** *vt* (*writer etc*): **to ~ o.s. out** s'user (à force de travailler); **burning** *adj* (*building, forest*) en flammes; (*issue, question*) brûlant(e); (*ambition*) dévorant(e)

Burns' Night [bəːnz-] *n* fête écossaise à la mémoire du poète Robert Burns

- **BURNS' NIGHT**
-
- *Burns' Night* est une fête qui a lieu
- le 25 janvier, à la mémoire du poète
- écossais Robert Burns (1759–1796),
- à l'occasion de laquelle les Écossais
- partout dans le monde organisent
- un souper, en général arrosé
- de whisky. Le plat principal est
- toujours le haggis, servi avec de la
- purée de pommes de terre et de la
- purée de rutabagas. On apporte
- le haggis au son des cornemuses
- et au cours du repas on lit des
- poèmes de Burns et on chante ses
- chansons.

burnt [bəːnt] *pt*, *pp of* **burn**

burp [bəːp] (*inf*) *n* rot *m* ▷ *vi* roter

burrow ['bʌrəu] *n* terrier *m* ▷ *vi* (*rabbit*) creuser un terrier; (*rummage*) fouiller

burst [bəːst] (*pt*, *pp* **burst**) *vt* faire éclater; (*river: banks etc*) rompre ▷ *vi*

éclater; (tyre) crever ▷ n explosion f;
(also: **~ pipe**) fuite f (due à une rupture);
a ~ of enthusiasm/energy un accès
d'enthousiasme/d'énergie; **to ~ into
flames** s'enflammer soudainement;
to ~ out laughing éclater de rire;
to ~ into tears fondre en larmes;
to ~ open vi s'ouvrir violemment
or soudainement; **to be ~ing with**
(container) être plein(e) (à craquer) de,
regorger de; (fig) être débordant(e)
de; **burst into** vt fus (room etc) faire
irruption dans
bury ['bɛrɪ] vt enterrer
bus (pl **buses**) [bʌs, 'bʌsɪz] n
(auto) bus m; **bus conductor** n
receveur(-euse) m/f de bus
bush [bʊʃ] n buisson m; (scrub land)
brousse f; **to beat about the ~**
tourner autour du pot
business ['bɪznɪs] n (matter, firm)
affaire f; (trading) affaires fpl; (job,
duty) travail m; **to be away on ~**
être en déplacement d'affaires; **it's
none of my ~** cela ne me regarde
pas, ce ne sont pas mes affaires;
he means ~ il ne plaisante pas, il
est sérieux; **business class** n (on
plane) classe f affaires; **businesslike**
adj sérieux(-euse), efficace;
businessman (irreg) n homme m
d'affaires; **business trip** n voyage m
d'affaires; **businesswoman** (irreg) n
femme f d'affaires
busker ['bʌskəʳ] n (BRIT) artiste
ambulant(e)
bus: bus pass n carte f de bus; **bus
shelter** n abribus m; **bus station** n
gare routière; **bus stop** n arrêt m
d'autobus
bust [bʌst] n buste m; (measurement)
tour m de poitrine ▷ adj (inf: broken)
fichu(e), fini(e); **to go ~** (inf) faire
faillite
bustling ['bʌslɪŋ] adj (town) très
animé(e)
busy ['bɪzɪ] adj occupé(e); (shop,
street) très fréquenté(e); (US:

telephone, line) occupé ▷ vt: **to ~ o.s.**
s'occuper; **busy signal** n (US) tonalité
f occupé inv

but [bʌt] conj mais; **I'd love to come,
but I'm busy** j'aimerais venir mais
je suis occupé; **he's not English
but French** il n'est pas anglais
mais français; **but that's far too
expensive!** mais c'est bien trop cher!
▶ prep (apart from, except) sauf,
excepté; **nothing but** rien d'autre
que; **we've had nothing but
trouble** nous n'avons eu que des
ennuis; **no-one but him can do
it** lui seul peut le faire; **who but a
lunatic would do such a thing?**
qui sinon un fou ferait une chose
pareille?; **but for you/your help**
sans toi/ton aide; **anything but
that** tout sauf or excepté ça, tout
mais pas ça
▶ adv (just, only) ne … que; **she's but
a child** elle n'est qu'une enfant; **had I
but known** si seulement j'avais su; **I
can but try** je peux toujours essayer;
all but finished pratiquement
terminé

butcher ['bʊtʃəʳ] n boucher m ▷ vt
massacrer; (cattle etc for meat) tuer;
butcher's (shop) n boucherie f
butler ['bʌtləʳ] n maître m d'hôtel
butt [bʌt] n (cask) gros tonneau m; (of
gun) crosse f; (of cigarette) mégot m;
(BRIT fig: target) cible f ▷ vt donner un
coup de tête à
butter ['bʌtəʳ] n beurre m ▷ vt
beurrer; **buttercup** n bouton m d'or
butterfly ['bʌtəflaɪ] n papillon m;
(Swimming: also: **~ stroke**) brasse
f papillon
buttocks ['bʌtəks] npl fesses fpl
button ['bʌtn] n bouton m; (US:
badge) pin m ▷ vt (also: **~ up**)
boutonner ▷ vi se boutonner

buy [baɪ] (pt, pp **bought**) vt acheter ▷ n achat m; **to ~ sb sth/sth from sb** acheter qch à qn; **to ~ sb a drink** offrir un verre or à boire à qn; **can I ~ you a drink?** je vous offre un verre?; **where can I ~ some postcards?** où est-ce que je peux acheter des cartes postales?; **buy out** vt (partner) désintéresser; **buy up** vt acheter en bloc, rafler; **buyer** n acheteur(-euse) m/f

buzz [bʌz] n bourdonnement m; (inf: phone call): **to give sb a ~** passer un coup de fil à qn ▷ vi bourdonner; **buzzer** n timbre m électrique

○ **KEYWORD**

by [baɪ] prep 1 (referring to cause, agent) par, de; **killed by lightning** tué par la foudre; **surrounded by a fence** entouré d'une barrière; **a painting by Picasso** un tableau de Picasso
2 (referring to method, manner, means): **by bus/car** en autobus/voiture; **by train** par le or en train; **to pay by cheque** payer par chèque; **by moonlight/candlelight** à la lueur de la lune/d'une bougie; **by saving hard, he ...** à force d'économiser, il ...
3 (via, through) par; **we came by Dover** nous sommes venus par Douvres
4 (close to, past) à côté de; **the house by the school** la maison à côté de l'école; **a holiday by the sea** des vacances au bord de la mer; **she went by me** elle est passée à côté de moi; **I go by the post office every day** je passe devant la poste tous les jours
5 (with time: not later than) avant; (: during): **by daylight** à la lumière du jour; **by night** la nuit, de nuit; **by 4 o'clock** avant 4 heures; **by this time tomorrow** d'ici demain à la même heure; **by the time I got here it was too late** lorsque je suis arrivé il était déjà trop tard
6 (amount) à; **by the kilo/metre** au kilo/au mètre; **paid by the hour** payé à l'heure
7 (Math: measure): **to divide/multiply by 3** diviser/multiplier par 3; **a room 3 metres by 4** une pièce de 3 mètres sur 4; **it's broader by a metre** c'est plus large d'un mètre
8 (according to) d'après, selon; **it's 3 o'clock by my watch** il est 3 heures à ma montre; **it's all right by me** je n'ai rien contre
9: **(all) by oneself** etc tout(e) seul(e)
▷ adv 1 see **go**; **pass** etc
2: **by and by** un peu plus tard, bientôt; **by and large** dans l'ensemble

bye(-bye) ['baɪ-] excl au revoir!, salut!
by-election ['baɪɪlekʃən] n (BRIT) élection (législative) partielle
bypass ['baɪpɑːs] n rocade f; (Med) pontage m ▷ vt éviter
byte [baɪt] n (Comput) octet m

C [siː] n (Mus) do m

cab [kæb] n taxi m; (of train, truck) cabine f

cabaret ['kæbəreɪ] n (show) spectacle m de cabaret

cabbage ['kæbɪdʒ] n chou m

cabin ['kæbɪn] n (house) cabane f, hutte f; (on ship) cabine f; (on plane) compartiment m; **cabin crew** n (Aviat) équipage m

cabinet ['kæbɪnɪt] n (Pol) cabinet m; (furniture) petit meuble à tiroirs et rayons; (also: **display ~**) vitrine f, petite armoire vitrée; **cabinet minister** n ministre m (membre du cabinet)

cable ['keɪbl] n câble m ▷ vt câbler, télégraphier; **cable car** n téléphérique m; **cable television** n télévision f par câble

cactus (pl **cacti**) ['kæktəs, -taɪ] n cactus m

café ['kæfeɪ] n ≈ café(-restaurant) m (sans alcool)

cafeteria [kæfɪ'tɪərɪə] n cafétéria f

caffeine ['kæfiːn] n caféine f

cage [keɪdʒ] n cage f

cagoule [kə'guːl] n K-way® m

Cairo ['kaɪərəu] n Le Caire

cake [keɪk] n gâteau m; **~ of soap** savonnette f

calcium ['kælsɪəm] n calcium m

calculate ['kælkjuleɪt] vt calculer; (estimate: chances, effect) évaluer; **calculation** [kælkju'leɪʃən] n calcul m; **calculator** n calculatrice f

calendar ['kæləndəʳ] n calendrier m

calf (pl **calves**) [kɑːf, kɑːvz] n (of cow) veau m; (of other animals) petit m; (also: **~skin**) veau m, vachette f; (Anat) mollet m

calibre, (US) **caliber** ['kælɪbəʳ] n calibre m

call [kɔːl] vt appeler; (meeting) convoquer ▷ vi appeler; (visit: also: **~ in, ~ round**) passer ▷ n (shout) appel m, cri m; (also: **telephone ~**) coup m de téléphone; **to be on ~** être de permanence; **to be ~ed** s'appeler; **can I make a ~ from here?** est-ce que je peux téléphoner d'ici?; **call back** vi (return) repasser; (Tel) rappeler ▷ vt (Tel) rappeler; **can you ~ back later?** pouvez-vous rappeler plus tard?; **call for** vt fus (demand) demander; (fetch) passer prendre; **call in** vt (doctor, expert, police) appeler, faire venir; **call off** vt annuler; **call on** vt fus (visit) rendre visite à, passer voir; (request): **to ~ on sb to do** inviter qn à faire; **call out** vi pousser un cri or des cris; **call up** vt (Mil) appeler, mobiliser; (Tel) appeler; **call box** n (BRIT) cabine f téléphonique; **call centre**, (US) **call center** n centre m d'appels; **caller** n (Tel) personne f qui appelle; (visitor) visiteur m

callous ['kæləs] adj dur(e), insensible

calm [kɑːm] adj calme ▷ n calme m ▷ vt calmer, apaiser; **calm down** vi se calmer, s'apaiser ▷ vt calmer, apaiser; **calmly** ['kɑːmlɪ] adv calmement, avec calme

Calor gas® ['kælə^r-] n (BRIT) butane m, butagaz® m

calorie ['kælərɪ] n calorie f

calves [kɑːvz] npl of **calf**

Cambodia [kæm'bəʊdɪə] n Cambodge m

camcorder ['kæmkɔːdə^r] n caméscope m

came [keɪm] pt of **come**

camel ['kæməl] n chameau m

camera ['kæmərə] n appareil photo m; (Cine, TV) caméra f; **in ~** à huis clos, en privé; **cameraman** (irreg) n caméraman m; **camera phone** n téléphone m avec appareil photo

camouflage ['kæməflɑːʒ] n camouflage m ▷ vt camoufler

camp [kæmp] n camp m ▷ vi camper ▷ adj (man) efféminé(e)

campaign [kæm'peɪn] n (Mil, Pol) campagne f ▷ vi (also fig) faire campagne; **campaigner** n: **campaigner for** partisan(e) de; **campaigner against** opposant(e) à

camp: camp bed n (BRIT) lit m de camp; **camper** n campeur(-euse); (vehicle) camping-car m; **camping** n camping m; **to go camping** faire du camping; **campsite** n (terrain m de) camping m

campus ['kæmpəs] n campus m

can¹ [kæn] n (of milk, oil, water) bidon m; (tin) boîte f (de conserve) ▷ vt mettre en conserve

⊙ **KEYWORD**

can² [kæn] (negative **cannot** or **can't**, conditional, pt **could**) aux vb **1** (be able to) pouvoir; **you can do it if you try** vous pouvez le faire si vous essayez; **I can't hear you** je ne t'entends pas **2** (know how to) savoir; **I can swim/ play tennis/drive** je sais nager/jouer au tennis/conduire; **can you speak French?** parlez-vous français? **3** (may) pouvoir; **can I use your phone?** puis-je me servir de votre

téléphone? **4** (expressing disbelief, puzzlement etc): **it can't be true!** ce n'est pas possible!; **what can he want?** qu'est-ce qu'il peut bien vouloir? **5** (expressing possibility, suggestion etc): **he could be in the library** il est peut-être dans la bibliothèque; **she could have been delayed** il se peut qu'elle ait été retardée

Canada ['kænədə] n Canada m; **Canadian** [kə'neɪdɪən] adj canadien(ne) ▷ n Canadien(ne)

canal [kə'næl] n canal m

canary [kə'nɛərɪ] n canari m, serin m

cancel ['kænsəl] vt annuler; (train) supprimer; (party, appointment) décommander; (cross out) barrer, rayer; (cheque) faire opposition à; **I would like to ~ my booking** je voudrais annuler ma réservation; **cancellation** [kænsə'leɪʃən] n annulation f; suppression f

Cancer ['kænsə^r] n (Astrology) le Cancer

cancer ['kænsə^r] n cancer m

candidate ['kændɪdeɪt] n candidat(e)

candle ['kændl] n bougie f; (in church) cierge m; **candlestick** n (also: **candle holder**) bougeoir m; (bigger, ornate) chandelier m

candy ['kændɪ] n sucre candi; (US) bonbon m; **candy bar** (US) n barre f chocolatée; **candyfloss** n (BRIT) barbe f à papa

cane [keɪn] n canne f; (for baskets, chairs etc) rotin m ▷ vt (BRIT Scol) administrer des coups de bâton à

canister ['kænɪstə^r] n boîte f (gén en métal); (of gas) bombe f

cannabis ['kænəbɪs] n (drug) cannabis m

canned ['kænd] adj (food) en boîte, en conserve; (inf: music) enregistré(e); (BRIT inf: drunk) bourré(e); (US inf: worker) mis(e) à la porte

cannon ['kænən] (*pl* **cannon** or
  cannons) *n* (*gun*) canon *m*
cannot ['kænɔt] = **can not**
canoe [kə'nu:] *n* pirogue *f*; (*Sport*)
  canoë *m*; **canoeing** *n* (*sport*) canoë *m*
canon ['kænən] *n* (*clergyman*)
  chanoine *m*; (*standard*) canon *m*
can-opener [-'əupnə^r] *n* ouvre-
  boîte *m*
can't [kɑ:nt] = **can not**
canteen [kæn'ti:n] *n* (*eating place*)
  cantine *f*; (BRIT: *of cutlery*) ménagère *f*
canter ['kæntə^r] *vi* aller au petit
  galop
canvas ['kænvəs] *n* toile *f*
canvass ['kænvəs] *vi* (*Pol*): **to ~ for**
  faire campagne pour ▷ *vt* sonder
canyon ['kænjən] *n* cañon *m*, gorge
  (profonde)
cap [kæp] *n* casquette *f*; (*for
  swimming*) bonnet *m* de bain; (*of pen*)
  capuchon *m*; (*of bottle*) capsule *f*;
  (BRIT: *contraceptive: also:* **Dutch ~**)
  diaphragme *m* ▷ *vt* (*outdo*) surpasser;
  (*put limit on*) plafonner
capability [keɪpə'bɪlɪtɪ] *n* aptitude
  f, capacité *f*
capable ['keɪpəbl] *adj* capable
capacity [kə'pæsɪtɪ] *n* (*of container*)
  capacité *f*, contenance *f*; (*ability*)
  aptitude *f*
cape [keɪp] *n* (*garment*) cape *f*; (*Geo*)
  cap *m*
caper ['keɪpə^r] *n* (*Culin: gen pl*) câpre *f*;
  (*prank*) farce *f*
capital ['kæpɪtl] *n* (*also:* **~ city**)
  capitale *f*; (*money*) capital *m*; (*also:*
  ~ letter) majuscule *f*; **capitalism**
  n capitalisme *m*; **capitalist** *adj, n*
  capitaliste *m/f*; **capital punishment**
  n peine capitale
Capitol ['kæpɪtl] *n*: **the ~** le Capitole
Capricorn ['kæprɪkɔ:n] *n* le
  Capricorne
capsize [kæp'saɪz] *vt* faire chavirer
  ▷ *vi* chavirer
capsule ['kæpsju:l] *n* capsule *f*
captain ['kæptɪn] *n* capitaine *m*

caption ['kæpʃən] *n* légende *f*
captivity [kæp'tɪvɪtɪ] *n* captivité *f*
capture ['kæptʃə^r] *vt* (*prisoner, animal*)
  capturer; (*town*) prendre; (*attention*)
  capter; (*Comput*) saisir ▷ *n* capture *f*;
  (*of data*) saisie *f* de données
car [kɑ:^r] *n* voiture *f*, auto *f*; (US *Rail*)
  wagon *m*, voiture
caramel ['kærəməl] *n* caramel *m*
carat ['kærət] *n* carat *m*
caravan ['kærəvæn] *n* caravane *f*;
  caravan site *n* (BRIT) camping *m*
  pour caravanes
carbohydrate [kɑ:bəu'haɪdreɪt]
  n hydrate *m* de carbone; (*food*)
  féculent *m*
carbon ['kɑ:bən] *n* carbone *m*;
  carbon dioxide [-daɪ'ɔksaɪd] *n* gaz
  m carbonique, dioxyde *m* de carbone;
  carbon footprint *n* empreinte
  f carbone; **carbon monoxide**
  [-mɔ'nɔksaɪd] *n* oxyde *m* de carbone;
  carbon-neutral *adj* neutre en carbone
car boot sale *n* voir article **"car
  boot sale"**

● **CAR BOOT SALE**
●
● Type de brocante très populaire, où
● chacun vide sa cave ou son grenier.
● Les articles sont présentés dans
● des coffres de voitures et la vente
● a souvent lieu sur un parking ou
● dans un champ. Les brocanteurs
● d'un jour doivent s'acquitter d'une
● petite contribution pour participer
● à la vente.

carburettor, (US) **carburetor**
  [kɑ:bju'retə^r] *n* carburateur *m*
card [kɑ:d] *n* carte *f*; (*material*) carton
  m; **cardboard** *n* carton *m*; **card
  game** *n* jeu *m* de cartes
cardigan ['kɑ:dɪgən] *n* cardigan *m*
cardinal ['kɑ:dɪnl] *adj* cardinal(e);
  (*importance*) capital(e) ▷ *n* cardinal *m*
cardphone ['kɑ:dfəun] *n* téléphone
  m à carte (magnétique)

care [kɛəʳ] n soin m, attention f; (worry) souci m ▷ vi: **to ~ about** (feel interest for) se soucier de, s'intéresser à; (person: love) être attaché(e) à; **in sb's ~** à la garde de qn, confié à qn; **~ of** (on letter) chez; **to take ~** faire attention (à faire); **to take ~ of** vt s'occuper de; **I don't ~** ça m'est bien égal, peu m'importe; **I couldn't ~ less** cela m'est complètement égal, je m'en fiche complètement; **care for** vt fus s'occuper de; (like) aimer

career [kə'rɪəʳ] n carrière f ▷ vi (also: **~ along**) aller à toute allure

care: carefree adj sans souci, insouciant(e); **careful** adj soigneux(-euse); (cautious) prudent(e); **(be) careful!** (fais) attention!; **carefully** adv avec soin, soigneusement; prudemment; **caregiver** n (us) (professional) travailleur social; (unpaid) personne qui s'occupe d'un proche qui est malade; **careless** adj négligent(e); (heedless) insouciant(e); **carelessness** n manque m de soin, négligence f; insouciance f; **carer** ['kɛərəʳ] n (professional) travailleur social; (unpaid) personne qui s'occupe d'un proche qui est malade; **caretaker** n gardien(ne), concierge m/f

car-ferry ['kɑːfɛrɪ] n (on sea) ferry(-boat) m; (on river) bac m

cargo ['kɑːgəu] (pl **cargoes**) n cargaison f, chargement m

car hire n (BRIT) location f de voitures

Caribbean [kærɪ'biːən] adj, n: **the ~ (Sea)** la mer des Antilles or des Caraïbes

caring ['kɛərɪŋ] adj (person) bienveillant(e); (society, organization) humanitaire

carnation [kɑː'neɪʃən] n œillet m

carnival ['kɑːnɪvl] n (public celebration) carnaval m; (us: funfair) fête foraine

carol ['kærəl] n: **(Christmas) ~** chant m de Noël

carousel [kærə'sɛl] n (for luggage) carrousel m; (us) manège m

car park (BRIT) n parking m, parc m de stationnement

carpenter ['kɑːpɪntəʳ] n charpentier m; (joiner) menuisier m

carpet ['kɑːpɪt] n tapis m ▷ vt recouvrir (d'un tapis); **fitted ~** (BRIT) moquette f

car rental n (us) location f de voitures

carriage ['kærɪdʒ] n (BRIT Rail) wagon m; (horse-drawn) voiture f; (of goods) transport m (: cost) port m; **carriageway** n (BRIT: part of road) chaussée f

carrier ['kærɪəʳ] n transporteur m, camionneur m; (company) entreprise f de transport; (Med) porteur(-euse); **carrier bag** n (BRIT) sac m en papier or en plastique

carrot ['kærət] n carotte f

carry ['kærɪ] vt (subj: person) porter; (: vehicle) transporter; (involve: responsibilities etc) comporter, impliquer; (Med: disease) être porteur de ▷ vi (sound) porter; **to get carried away** (fig) s'emballer, s'enthousiasmer; **carry on** vi (continue) continuer ▷ vt (conduct: business) diriger; (: conversation) entretenir; (continue: business, conversation) continuer; **to ~ on with sth/doing** continuer qch/à faire; **carry out** vt (orders) exécuter; (investigation) effectuer

cart [kɑːt] n charrette f ▷ vt (inf) transporter

carton ['kɑːtən] n (box) carton m; (of yogurt) pot m (en carton)

cartoon [kɑː'tuːn] n (Press) dessin m (humoristique); (satirical) caricature f; (comic strip) bande dessinée; (Cine) dessin animé

cartridge ['kɑːtrɪdʒ] n (for gun, pen) cartouche f

carve [kɑːv] vt (meat: also: **~ up**) découper; (wood, stone) tailler, sculpter; **carving** n (in wood etc) sculpture f

car wash n station f de lavage (de voitures)

case [keɪs] n cas m; (Law) affaire f, procès m; (box) caisse f, boîte f; (for glasses) étui m; (BRIT: also: **suit~**) valise f; **in ~ of** en cas de; **in ~ he** au cas où il; **just in ~** à tout hasard; **in any ~** en tout cas, de toute façon

cash [kæʃ] n argent m; (Comm: argent m) liquide m ▷ vt encaisser; **to pay (in) ~** payer (en argent) comptant or en espèces; **~ with order/on delivery** (Comm) payable or paiement à la commande/livraison; **I haven't got any ~** je n'ai pas de liquide; **cashback** n (discount) remise f; (at supermarket etc) retrait m (à la caisse); **cash card** n carte f de retrait; **cash desk** n (BRIT) caisse f; **cash dispenser** n distributeur m automatique de billets

cashew [kæ'ʃuː] n (also: **~ nut**) noix f de cajou

cashier [kæ'ʃɪər] n caissier(-ère)

cashmere ['kæʃmɪər] n cachemire m

cash point n distributeur m automatique de billets

cash register n caisse enregistreuse

casino [kə'siːnəu] n casino m

casket ['kɑːskɪt] n coffret m; (US: coffin) cercueil m

casserole ['kæsərəul] n (pot) cocotte f; (food) ragoût m (en cocotte)

cassette [kæ'sɛt] n cassette f; **cassette player** n lecteur m de cassettes

cast [kɑːst] (vb: pt, pp **cast**) vt (throw) jeter; (shadow: lit) projeter; (: fig) jeter; (glance) jeter ▷ n (Theat) distribution f; (also: **plaster ~**) plâtre m; **to ~ sb as Hamlet** attribuer à qn le rôle d'Hamlet; **to ~ one's vote** voter, exprimer son suffrage; **to ~ doubt on** jeter un doute sur; **cast off** vi (Naut) larguer les amarres; (Knitting) arrêter les mailles

castanets [kæstə'nɛts] npl castagnettes fpl

caster sugar ['kɑːstə-] n (BRIT) sucre m semoule

cast-iron ['kɑːstaɪən] adj (lit) de or en fonte; (fig: will) de fer; (alibi) en béton

castle ['kɑːsl] n château m; (fortress) château-fort m; (Chess) tour f

casual ['kæʒjul] adj (by chance) de hasard, fait(e) au hasard, fortuit(e); (irregular: work etc) temporaire; (unconcerned) désinvolte; **~ wear** vêtements mpl sport inv

casualty ['kæʒjultɪ] n accidenté(e), blessé(e); (dead) victime f, mort(e); (BRIT Med: department) urgences fpl

cat [kæt] n chat m

Catalan ['kætəlæn] adj catalan(e)

catalogue, (US) **catalog** ['kætələg] n catalogue m ▷ vt cataloguer

catalytic converter [kætə'lɪtɪkkən'vəːtər] n pot m catalytique

cataract ['kætərækt] n (also Med) cataracte f

catarrh [kə'tɑːr] n rhume m chronique, catarrhe f

catastrophe [kə'tæstrəfɪ] n catastrophe f

catch [kætʃ] (pt, pp **caught**) vt attraper; (person: by surprise) prendre, surprendre; (understand) saisir; (get entangled) accrocher ▷ vi (fire) prendre; (get entangled) s'accrocher ▷ n (fish etc) prise f; (hidden problem) attrape f; (Tech) loquet m; cliquet m; **to ~ sb's attention** or **eye** attirer l'attention de qn; **to ~ fire** prendre feu; **to ~ sight of** apercevoir; **catch up** vi (with work) se rattraper, combler son retard ▷ vt (also: **~ up with**) rattraper; **catching** ['kætʃɪŋ] adj (Med) contagieux(-euse)

category ['kætɪgərɪ] n catégorie f

cater ['keɪtər] vi: **to ~ for** (BRIT: needs) satisfaire, pourvoir à; (readers, consumers) s'adresser à, pourvoir aux besoins de; (Comm: parties etc) préparer des repas pour

caterpillar ['kætəpɪləʳ] n chenille f
cathedral [kə'θiːdrəl] n cathédrale f
Catholic ['kæθəlɪk] (Rel) adj
catholique ▷ n catholique m/f
cattle ['kætl] npl bétail m, bestiaux mpl
catwalk ['kætwɔːk] n passerelle f; (for models) podium m (de défilé de mode)
caught [kɔːt] pt, pp of **catch**
cauliflower ['kɔlɪflauəʳ] n chou-fleur m
cause [kɔːz] n cause f ▷ vt causer
caution ['kɔːʃən] n prudence f; (warning) avertissement m ▷ vt avertir, donner un avertissement à; **cautious** adj prudent(e)
cave [keɪv] n caverne f, grotte f; **cave in** vi (roof etc) s'effondrer
caviar(e) ['kævɪɑːʳ] n caviar m
cavity ['kævɪtɪ] n cavité f; (Med) carie f
cc abbr (= cubic centimetre) cm³; (on letter etc = carbon copy) cc
CCTV n abbr = **closed-circuit television**
CD n abbr (= compact disc) CD m; **CD burner** n graveur m de CD; **CD player** n platine f laser; **CD-ROM** [siː'diː'rɔm] n abbr (= compact disc read-only memory) CD-ROM m inv; **CD writer** n graveur m de CD
cease [siːs] vt, vi cesser; **ceasefire** n cessez-le-feu m
cedar ['siːdəʳ] n cèdre m
ceilidh ['keɪlɪ] n bal m folklorique écossais or irlandais
ceiling ['siːlɪŋ] n (also fig) plafond m
celebrate ['sɛlɪbreɪt] vt, vi célébrer; **celebration** [sɛlɪ'breɪʃən] n célébration f
celebrity [sɪ'lɛbrɪtɪ] n célébrité f
celery ['sɛlərɪ] n céleri m (en branches)
cell [sɛl] n (gen) cellule f; (Elec) élément m (de pile)
cellar ['sɛləʳ] n cave f
cello ['tʃɛləu] n violoncelle m
Cellophane® ['sɛləfeɪn] n cellophane® f

cellphone ['sɛlfəun] n (téléphone m) portable m, mobile m
Celsius ['sɛlsɪəs] adj Celsius inv
Celtic ['kɛltɪk, 'sɛltɪk] adj celte, celtique
cement [sə'mɛnt] n ciment m
cemetery ['sɛmɪtrɪ] n cimetière m
censor ['sɛnsəʳ] n censeur m ▷ vt censurer; **censorship** n censure f
census ['sɛnsəs] n recensement m
cent [sɛnt] n (unit of dollar, euro) cent m (= un centième du dollar, de l'euro); see also **per cent**
centenary [sɛn'tiːnərɪ], (US) **centennial** [sɛn'tɛnɪəl] n centenaire m
center ['sɛntəʳ] (US) = **centre**
centi... ['sɛntɪ]: **centigrade** adj centigrade; **centimetre**, (US) **centimeter** n centimètre m; **centipede** ['sɛntɪpiːd] n mille-pattes m inv
central ['sɛntrəl] adj central(e); **Central America** n Amérique centrale; **central heating** n chauffage central; **central reservation** n (BRIT Aut) terre-plein central
centre, (US) **center** ['sɛntəʳ] n centre m ▷ vt centrer; **centre-forward** n (Sport) avant-centre m; **centre-half** n (Sport) demi-centre m
century ['sɛntjurɪ] n siècle m; **in the twentieth ~** au vingtième siècle
CEO n abbr (US) = **chief executive officer**
ceramic [sɪ'ræmɪk] adj céramique
cereal ['siːrɪəl] n céréale f
ceremony ['sɛrɪmənɪ] n cérémonie f; **to stand on ~** faire des façons
certain ['sɜːtən] adj certain(e); **to make ~ of** s'assurer de; **for ~** certainement, sûrement; **certainly** adv certainement; **certainty** n certitude f
certificate [sə'tɪfɪkɪt] n certificat m
certify ['sɜːtɪfaɪ] vt certifier; (award diploma to) conférer un diplôme etc

à; (*declare insane*) déclarer malade mental(e)

cf. *abbr* (= *compare*) cf., voir

CFC *n abbr* (= *chlorofluorocarbon*) CFC *m*

chain [tʃeɪn] *n* (*gen*) chaîne *f* ▷ *vt* (*also*: ~ **up**) enchaîner, attacher (avec une chaîne); **chain-smoke** *vi* fumer cigarette sur cigarette

chair [tʃɛəʳ] *n* chaise *f*; (*armchair*) fauteuil *m*; (*of university*) chaire *f*; (*of meeting*) présidence *f* ▷ *vt* (*meeting*) présider; **chairlift** *n* télésiège *m*; **chairman** (*irreg*) *n* président *m*; **chairperson** (*irreg*) *n* président(e); **chairwoman** (*irreg*) *n* présidente *f*

chalet ['ʃæleɪ] *n* chalet *m*

chalk [tʃɔːk] *n* craie *f*

challenge ['tʃælɪndʒ] *n* défi *m* ▷ *vt* défier; (*statement, right*) mettre en question, contester; **to ~ sb to do** mettre qn au défi de faire; **challenging** *adj* (*task, career*) qui représente un défi or une gageure; (*tone, look*) de défi, provocateur(-trice)

chamber ['tʃeɪmbəʳ] *n* chambre *f*; (*BRIT Law: gen pl*) cabinet *m*; ~ **of commerce** chambre de commerce; **chambermaid** *n* femme *f* de chambre

champagne [ʃæm'peɪn] *n* champagne *m*

champion ['tʃæmpɪən] *n* (*also of cause*) champion(ne); **championship** *n* championnat *m*

chance [tʃɑːns] *n* (*luck*) hasard *m*; (*opportunity*) occasion *f*, possibilité *f*; (*hope, likelihood*) chance *f*; (*risk*) risque *m* ▷ *vt* (*risk*) risquer ▷ *adj* fortuit(e), de hasard; **to take a ~** prendre un risque; **by ~** par hasard; **to ~ it** risquer le coup, essayer

chancellor ['tʃɑːnsələʳ] *n* chancelier *m*; **Chancellor of the Exchequer** [-ɪks'tʃɛkəʳ] (*BRIT*) *n* chancelier *m* de l'Échiquier

chandelier [ʃændə'lɪəʳ] *n* lustre *m*

change [tʃeɪndʒ] *vt* (*alter, replace: Comm: money*) changer; (*switch,* *substitute: hands, trains, clothes, one's name etc*) changer de ▷ *vi* (*gen*) changer; (*change clothes*) se changer; (*be transformed*): **to ~ into** se changer or transformer en ▷ *n* changement *m*; (*money*) monnaie *f*; **to ~ gear** (*Aut*) changer de vitesse; **to ~ one's mind** changer d'avis; **a ~ of clothes** des vêtements de rechange; **for a ~** pour changer; **do you have ~ for £10?** vous avez la monnaie de 10 livres?; **where can I ~ some money?** où est-ce que je peux changer de l'argent?; **keep the ~!** gardez la monnaie!; **change over** *vi* (*swap*) échanger; (*change: drivers etc*) changer; (*change sides: players etc*) changer de côté; **to ~ over from sth to sth** passer de qch à qch; **changeable** *adj* (*weather*) variable; **change machine** *n* distributeur *m* de monnaie; **changing room** *n* (*BRIT: in shop*) salon *m* d'essayage (: *Sport*) vestiaire *m*

channel ['tʃænl] *n* (*TV*) chaîne *f*; (*waveband, groove, fig: medium*) canal *m*; (*of river, sea*) chenal *m* ▷ *vt* canaliser; **the (English) C~** la Manche; **Channel Islands** *npl*; **the Channel Islands** les îles *fpl* Anglo-Normandes; **Channel Tunnel** *n*: **the Channel Tunnel** le tunnel sous la Manche

chant [tʃɑːnt] *n* chant *m*; (*Rel*) psalmodie *f* ▷ *vt* chanter, scander

chaos ['keɪɔs] *n* chaos *m*

chaotic [keɪ'ɔtɪk] *adj* chaotique

chap [tʃæp] *n* (*BRIT inf: man*) type *m*

chapel ['tʃæpl] *n* chapelle *f*

chapped [tʃæpt] *adj* (*skin, lips*) gercé(e)

chapter ['tʃæptəʳ] *n* chapitre *m*

character ['kærɪktəʳ] *n* caractère *m*; (*in novel, film*) personnage *m*; (*eccentric person*) numéro *m*, phénomène *m*; **characteristic** ['kærɪktə'rɪstɪk] *adj*, *n* caractéristique (*f*); **characterize** ['kærɪktəraɪz] *vt* caractériser

charcoal ['tʃɑːkəul] n charbon m de bois; (Art) charbon

charge [tʃɑːdʒ] n (accusation) accusation f; (Law) inculpation f; (cost) prix (demandé) ▷ vt (gun, battery, Mil: enemy) charger; (customer, sum) faire payer ▷ vi foncer; **charges** npl (costs) frais mpl; **to reverse the ~s** (BRIT Tel) téléphoner en PCV; **to take ~ of** se charger de; **to be in ~ of** être responsable de, s'occuper de; **to ~ sb (with)** (Law) inculper qn (de); **charge card** n carte f de client (émise par un grand magasin); **charger** n (also: **battery charger**) chargeur m

charismatic [kærɪzˈmætɪk] adj charismatique

charity ['tʃærɪtɪ] n charité f; (organization) institution f charitable or de bienfaisance, œuvre f (de charité); **charity shop** n (BRIT) boutique vendant des articles d'occasion au profit d'une organisation caritative

charm [tʃɑːm] n charme m; (on bracelet) breloque f ▷ vt charmer, enchanter; **charming** adj charmant(e)

chart [tʃɑːt] n tableau m, diagramme m; graphique m; (map) carte marine ▷ vt dresser or établir la carte de; (sales, progress) établir la courbe de; **charts** npl (Mus) hit-parade m; **to be in the ~s** (record, pop group) figurer au hit-parade

charter ['tʃɑːtə'] vt (plane) affréter ▷ n (document) charte f; **chartered accountant** n (BRIT) expert-comptable m; **charter flight** n charter m

chase [tʃeɪs] vt poursuivre, pourchasser; (also: **~ away**) chasser ▷ n poursuite f, chasse f

chat [tʃæt] vi (also: **have a ~**) bavarder, causer; (on Internet) chatter ▷ n conversation f; (on Internet) chat m; **chat up** vt (BRIT inf: girl) baratiner; **chat room** n (Internet) salon m de discussion; **chat show** n (BRIT) talk-show m

chatter ['tʃætə'] vi (person) bavarder, papoter ▷ n bavardage m, papotage m; **my teeth are ~ing** je claque des dents

chauffeur ['ʃəufə'] n chauffeur m (de maître)

chauvinist ['ʃəuvɪnɪst] n (also: **male ~**) phallocrate m, macho m; (nationalist) chauvin(e)

cheap [tʃiːp] adj bon marché inv, pas cher (chère); (reduced: ticket) à prix réduit; (: fare) réduit(e); (joke) facile, d'un goût douteux; (poor quality) à bon marché, de qualité médiocre ▷ adv à bon marché, pour pas cher; **can you recommend a ~ hotel/ restaurant, please?** pourriez-vous m'indiquer un hôtel/restaurant bon marché?; **cheap day return** n billet m d'aller et retour réduit (valable pour la journée); **cheaply** adv à bon marché, à bon compte

cheat [tʃiːt] vi tricher; (in exam) copier ▷ vt tromper, duper; (rob): **to ~ sb out of sth** escroquer qch à qn ▷ n tricheur(-euse) m/f; escroc m; **cheat on** vt fus tromper

Chechnya [tʃɪtʃˈnjɑː] n Tchétchénie f

check [tʃɛk] vt vérifier; (passport, ticket) contrôler; (halt) enrayer; (restrain) maîtriser ▷ vi (official etc) se renseigner ▷ n vérification f; contrôle m; (curb) frein m; (BRIT: bill) addition f; (US) = **cheque**; (pattern: gen pl) carreaux mpl; **to ~ with sb** demander à qn; **check in** vi (in hotel) remplir sa fiche (d'hôtel); (at airport) se présenter à l'enregistrement ▷ vt (luggage) (faire) enregistrer; **check off** vt (tick off) cocher; **check out** vi (in hotel) régler sa note ▷ vt (investigate: story) vérifier; **check up** vi: **to ~ up (on sth)** vérifier (qch); **to ~ up on sb** se renseigner sur le compte de qn; **checkbook** n (US) = **chequebook**; **checked** adj (pattern, cloth) à carreaux; **checkers** n (US) jeu m de dames; **check-in** n (at airport: also:

check-in desk) enregistrement m;
checking account n (US) compte
courant; **checklist** n liste f de
contrôle; **checkmate** n échec et
mat m; **checkout** n (in supermarket)
caisse f; **checkpoint** n contrôle
m; **checkroom** (US) n consigne f;
checkup n (Med) examen médical,
check-up m

cheddar ['tʃedəʳ] n (also: ~ **cheese**)
cheddar m

cheek [tʃiːk] n joue f; (impudence)
toupet m, culot m; **what a ~!** quel
toupet!; **cheekbone** n pommette f;
cheeky adj effronté(e), culotté(e)

cheer [tʃɪəʳ] vt acclamer, applaudir;
(gladden) réjouir, réconforter ▷ vi
applaudir ▷ n (gen pl) acclamations
fpl, applaudissements mpl; bravos
mpl, hourras mpl; **~s!** à la vôtre!;
cheer up vi se dérider, reprendre
courage ▷ vt remonter le moral à
or de, dérider, égayer; **cheerful** adj
gai(e), joyeux(-euse)

cheerio [tʃɪərɪˈəu] excl (BRIT) salut!,
au revoir!

cheerleader ['tʃɪəliːdəʳ] n membre
d'un groupe de majorettes qui chantent
et dansent pour soutenir leur équipe
pendant les matchs de football américain

cheese [tʃiːz] n fromage m;
cheeseburger n cheeseburger m;
cheesecake n tarte f au fromage

chef [ʃef] n chef (cuisinier)

chemical ['kemɪkl] adj chimique ▷ n
produit m chimique

chemist ['kemɪst] n (BRIT:
pharmacist) pharmacien(ne);
(scientist) chimiste m/f; **chemistry** n
chimie f; **chemist's (shop)** n (BRIT)
pharmacie f

cheque, (US) **check** [tʃek] n chèque
m; **chequebook**, (US) **checkbook** n
chéquier m, carnet m de chèques;
cheque card n (BRIT) carte f
(d'identité) bancaire

cherry ['tʃerɪ] n cerise f; (also: ~ **tree**)
cerisier m

chess [tʃes] n échecs mpl

chest [tʃest] n poitrine f; (box) coffre
m, caisse f

chestnut ['tʃesnʌt] n châtaigne f;
(also: ~ **tree**) châtaignier m

chest of drawers n commode f

chew [tʃuː] vt mâcher; **chewing gum**
n chewing-gum m

chic [ʃiːk] adj chic inv, élégant(e)

chick [tʃɪk] n poussin m; (inf) fille f

chicken ['tʃɪkɪn] n poulet m; (inf:
coward) poule mouillée; **chicken out**
vi (inf) se dégonfler; **chickenpox** n
varicelle f

chickpea ['tʃɪkpiː] n pois m chiche

chief [tʃiːf] n chef m ▷ adj
principal(e); **chief executive**,
(US) **chief executive officer** n
directeur(-trice) général(e); **chiefly**
adv principalement, surtout

child (pl **children**) [tʃaɪld,
'tʃɪldrən] n enfant m/f; **child
abuse** n maltraitance f d'enfants;
(sexual) abus mpl sexuels sur des
enfants; **child benefit** n (BRIT) ≈
allocations familiales; **childbirth** n
accouchement m; **childcare** n (for
working parents) garde f des enfants
(pour les parents qui travaillent);
childhood n enfance f; **childish** adj
puéril(e), enfantin(e); **child minder**
n (BRIT) garde f d'enfants; **children**
['tʃɪldrən] npl of **child**

Chile ['tʃɪlɪ] n Chili m

chill [tʃɪl] n (of water) froid m; (of air)
fraîcheur f; (Med) refroidissement
m, coup m de froid ▷ vt (person) faire
frissonner; (Culin) mettre au frais,
rafraîchir; **chill out** vi (inf: esp US)
se relaxer

chil(l)i ['tʃɪlɪ] n piment m (rouge)

chilly ['tʃɪlɪ] adj froid(e), glacé(e);
(sensitive to cold) frileux(-euse)

chimney ['tʃɪmnɪ] n cheminée f

chimpanzee [tʃɪmpænˈziː] n
chimpanzé m

chin [tʃɪn] n menton m

China ['tʃaɪnə] n Chine f

china ['tʃaɪnə] n (material) porcelaine f; (crockery) vaisselle f en porcelaine
Chinese [tʃaɪ'niːz] adj chinois(e) ▷ n (pl inv) Chinois(e); (Ling) chinois m
chip [tʃɪp] n (gen pl: Culin: BRIT) frite f; (: US: also: **potato ~**) chip m; (of wood) copeau m; (of glass, stone) éclat m; (also: **micro~**) puce f; (in gambling) fiche f ▷ vt (cup, plate) ébrécher; **chip shop** n (BRIT) friterie f

- **CHIP SHOP**
-
- Un *chip shop*, que l'on appelle
- également un "fish-and-chip shop",
- est un magasin où l'on vend des
- plats à emporter. Les *chip shops* sont
- d'ailleurs à l'origine des "takeaways".
- On y achète en particulier du
- poisson frit et des frites, mais
- on y trouve également des plats
- traditionnels britanniques ("steak
- pies", saucisses, etc). Tous les plats
- étaient à l'origine emballés dans du
- papier journal. Dans certains de ces
- magasins, on peut s'asseoir pour
- consommer sur place.

chiropodist [kɪ'rɒpədɪst] n (BRIT) pédicure m/f
chisel ['tʃɪzl] n ciseau m
chives [tʃaɪvz] npl ciboulette f, civette f
chlorine ['klɔːriːn] n chlore m
choc-ice ['tʃɒkaɪs] n (BRIT) esquimau® m
chocolate ['tʃɒklɪt] n chocolat m
choice [tʃɔɪs] n choix m ▷ adj de choix
choir ['kwaɪə'] n chœur m, chorale f
choke [tʃəuk] vi étouffer ▷ vt étrangler; étouffer; (block) boucher, obstruer ▷ n (Aut) starter m
cholesterol [kə'lɛstərɒl] n cholestérol m
chook [tʃuk] n (AUST, NZ inf) poule f
choose (pt **chose**, pp **chosen**) [tʃuːz, tʃəuz, 'tʃəuzn] vt choisir; **to ~ to do** décider de faire, juger bon de faire

chop [tʃɒp] vt (wood) couper (à la hache); (Culin: also: **~ up**) couper (fin), émincer, hacher (en morceaux) ▷ n (Culin) côtelette f; **chop down** vt (tree) abattre; **chop off** vt trancher; **chopsticks** ['tʃɒpstɪks] npl baguettes fpl
chord [kɔːd] n (Mus) accord m
chore [tʃɔː'] n travail m de routine; **household ~s** travaux mpl du ménage
chorus ['kɔːrəs] n chœur m; (repeated part of song, also fig) refrain m
chose [tʃəuz] pt of **choose**
chosen ['tʃəuzn] pp of **choose**
Christ [kraɪst] n Christ m
christen ['krɪsn] vt baptiser; **christening** n baptême m
Christian ['krɪstɪən] adj, n chrétien(ne); **Christianity** [krɪstɪ'ænɪtɪ] n christianisme m; **Christian name** n prénom m
Christmas ['krɪsməs] n Noël m or f; **happy** or **merry ~!** joyeux Noël!; **Christmas card** n carte f de Noël; **Christmas carol** n chant m de Noël; **Christmas Day** n le jour de Noël; **Christmas Eve** n la veille de Noël; la nuit de Noël; **Christmas pudding** n (esp BRIT) Christmas m pudding; **Christmas tree** n arbre m de Noël
chrome [krəum] n chrome m
chronic ['krɒnɪk] adj chronique
chrysanthemum [krɪ'sænθəməm] n chrysanthème m
chubby ['tʃʌbɪ] adj potelé(e), rondelet(te)
chuck [tʃʌk] vt (inf) lancer, jeter; (job) lâcher; **chuck out** vt (inf: person) flanquer dehors or à la porte; (: rubbish etc) jeter
chuckle ['tʃʌkl] vi glousser
chum [tʃʌm] n copain (copine)
chunk [tʃʌŋk] n gros morceau
church [tʃəːtʃ] n église f; **churchyard** n cimetière m
churn [tʃəːn] n (for butter) baratte f; (also: **milk ~**) (grand) bidon à lait

C

chute [ʃuːt] n goulotte f; (also: **rubbish ~**) vide-ordures m inv; (BRIT: children's slide) toboggan m

chutney ['tʃʌtnɪ] n chutney m

CIA n abbr (= Central Intelligence Agency) CIA f

CID n abbr (= Criminal Investigation Department) ≈ P.J. f

cider ['saɪdər] n cidre m

cigar [sɪ'gɑːr] n cigare m

cigarette [sɪgə'rɛt] n cigarette f; **cigarette lighter** n briquet m

cinema ['sɪnəmə] n cinéma m

cinnamon ['sɪnəmən] n cannelle f

circle ['səːkl] n cercle m; (in cinema) balcon m ▷ vi faire or décrire des cercles ▷ vt (surround) entourer, encercler; (move round) faire le tour de, tourner autour de

circuit ['səːkɪt] n circuit m; (lap) tour m

circular ['səːkjulər] adj circulaire ▷ n circulaire f; (as advertisement) prospectus m

circulate ['səːkjuleɪt] vi circuler ▷ vt faire circuler; **circulation** [səːkju'leɪʃən] n circulation f; (of newspaper) tirage m

circumstances ['səːkəmstənsɪz] npl circonstances fpl; (financial condition) moyens mpl, situation financière

circus ['səːkəs] n cirque m

cite [saɪt] vt citer

citizen ['sɪtɪzn] n (Pol) citoyen(ne); (resident): **the ~s of this town** les habitants de cette ville; **citizenship** n citoyenneté f; (BRIT Scol) ≈ éducation f civique

citrus fruits ['sɪtrəs-] npl agrumes mpl

city ['sɪtɪ] n (grande) ville f; **the C~** la Cité de Londres (centre des affaires); **city centre** n centre ville m; **city technology college** n (BRIT) établissement m d'enseignement technologique (situé dans un quartier défavorisé)

civic ['sɪvɪk] adj civique; (authorities) municipal(e)

civil ['sɪvɪl] adj civil(e); (polite) poli(e), civil(e); **civilian** [sɪ'vɪlɪən] adj, n civil(e)

civilization [sɪvɪlaɪ'zeɪʃən] n civilisation f

civilized ['sɪvɪlaɪzd] adj civilisé(e); (fig) où règnent les bonnes manières

civil: civil law n code civil; (study) droit civil; **civil rights** npl droits mpl civiques; **civil servant** n fonctionnaire m/f; **Civil Service** n fonction publique, administration f; **civil war** n guerre civile

CJD n abbr (= Creutzfeldt-Jakob disease) MCJ f

claim [kleɪm] vt (rights etc) revendiquer; (compensation) réclamer; (assert) déclarer, prétendre ▷ vi (for insurance) faire une déclaration de sinistre ▷ n revendication f; prétention f; (right) droit m; **(insurance) ~** demande f d'indemnisation, déclaration f de sinistre; **claim form** n (gen) formulaire m de demande

clam [klæm] n palourde f

clamp [klæmp] n crampon m; (on workbench) valet m; (on car) sabot m de Denver ▷ vt attacher; (car) mettre un sabot à; **clamp down on** vt fus sévir contre, prendre des mesures draconiennes à l'égard de

clan [klæn] n clan m

clap [klæp] vi applaudir

claret ['klærət] n (vin m de) bordeaux m (rouge)

clarify ['klærɪfaɪ] vt clarifier

clarinet [klærɪ'nɛt] n clarinette f

clarity ['klærɪtɪ] n clarté f

clash [klæʃ] n (sound) choc m, fracas m; (with police) affrontement m; (fig) conflit m ▷ vi se heurter; être or entrer en conflit; (colours) jurer; (dates, events) tomber en même temps

clasp [klɑːsp] n (of necklace, bag) fermoir m ▷ vt serrer, étreindre

class [klɑːs] n (gen) classe f; (group, category) catégorie f ▷ vt classer, classifier

classic ['klæsɪk] adj classique ▷ n (author, work) classique m; **classical** adj classique

classification [klæsɪfɪ'keɪʃən] n classification f

classify ['klæsɪfaɪ] vt classifier, classer

classmate ['klɑːsmeɪt] n camarade m/f de classe

classroom ['klɑːsrum] n (salle f de) classe f; **classroom assistant** n assistant(e) d'éducation

classy ['klɑːsɪ] (inf) adj classe (inf)

clatter ['klætəʳ] n cliquetis m ▷ vi cliqueter

clause [klɔːz] n clause f; (Ling) proposition f

claustrophobic [klɔːstrə'fəubɪk] adj (person) claustrophobe; (place) où l'on se sent claustrophobe

claw [klɔː] n griffe f; (of bird of prey) serre f; (of lobster) pince f

clay [kleɪ] n argile f

clean [kliːn] adj propre; (clear, smooth) net(te); (record, reputation) sans tache; (joke, story) correct(e) ▷ vt nettoyer; **clean up** vt nettoyer, remettre de l'ordre dans; **cleaner** n (person) nettoyeur(-euse), femme f de ménage; (product) détachant m; **cleaner's** n (also: **dry cleaner's**) teinturier m; **cleaning** n nettoyage m

cleanser ['klɛnzəʳ] n (for face) démaquillant m

clear [klɪəʳ] adj clair(e); (glass, plastic) transparent(e); (road, way) libre, dégagé(e); (profit, majority) net(te); (conscience) tranquille; (skin) frais (fraîche); (sky) dégagé(e) ▷ vt (road) dégager, déblayer; (table) débarrasser; (room etc: of people) faire évacuer; (cheque) compenser; (Law: suspect) innocenter; (obstacle) franchir or sauter sans heurter ▷ vi (weather) s'éclaircir; (fog) se dissiper ▷ adv: **~ of** à distance de, à l'écart de; **to ~ the table** débarrasser la table, desservir; **clear away** vt (things, clothes etc) enlever, retirer; **to ~ away the dishes** débarrasser la table; **clear up** vt ranger, mettre en ordre; (mystery) éclaircir, résoudre; **clearance** n (removal) déblayage m; (permission) autorisation f; **clear-cut** adj précis(e), nettement défini(e); **clearing** n (in forest) clairière f; **clearly** adv clairement; (obviously) de toute évidence; **clearway** n (BRIT) route f à stationnement interdit

clench [klɛntʃ] vt serrer

clergy ['kləːdʒɪ] n clergé m

clerk [klɑːk, US kləːrk] n (BRIT) employé(e) de bureau; (US: salesman/woman) vendeur(-euse)

clever ['klɛvəʳ] adj (intelligent) intelligent(e); (skilful) habile, adroit(e); (device, arrangement) ingénieux(-euse), astucieux(-euse)

cliché ['kliːʃeɪ] n cliché m

click [klɪk] n (Comput) clic m ▷ vi (Comput) cliquer ▷ vt: **to ~ one's tongue** faire claquer sa langue; **to ~ one's heels** claquer des talons; **to ~ on an icon** cliquer sur une icône

client ['klaɪənt] n client(e)

cliff [klɪf] n falaise f

climate ['klaɪmɪt] n climat m; **climate change** n changement m climatique

climax ['klaɪmæks] n apogée m, point culminant; (sexual) orgasme m

climb [klaɪm] vi grimper, monter; (plane) prendre de l'altitude ▷ vt (stairs) monter; (mountain) escalader; (tree) grimper à ▷ n montée f, escalade f; **to ~ over a wall** passer par dessus un mur; **climb down** vi (re)descendre; (BRIT fig) rabattre de ses prétentions; **climber** n (also: **rock climber**) grimpeur(-euse), varappeur(-euse); (plant) plante grimpante; **climbing** n (also: **rock climbing**) escalade f, varappe f

clinch [klɪntʃ] vt (deal) conclure, sceller

cling (pt, pp **clung**) [klɪŋ, klʌŋ] vi: **to ~ (to)** se cramponner (à), s'accrocher (à); (clothes) coller (à); **clingfilm** n film m alimentaire

clinic ['klɪnɪk] n clinique f; centre médical

clip [klɪp] n (for hair) barrette f; (also: **paper ~**) trombone m; (TV, Cine) clip m ▷ vt (also: **~ together**: papers) attacher; (hair, nails) couper; (hedge) tailler; **clipping** n (from newspaper) coupure f de journal

cloak [kləuk] n grande cape ▷ vt (fig) masquer, cacher; **cloakroom** n (for coats etc) vestiaire m; (BRIT: W.C.) toilettes fpl

clock [klɔk] n (large) horloge f; (small) pendule f; **clock in, clock on** (BRIT) vi (with card) pointer (en arrivant); (start work) commencer à travailler; **clock off, clock out** (BRIT) vi (with card) pointer (en partant); (leave work) quitter le travail; **clockwise** adv dans le sens des aiguilles d'une montre; **clockwork** n rouages mpl, mécanisme m; (of clock) mouvement m (d'horlogerie) ▷ adj (toy, train) mécanique

clog [klɔg] n sabot m ▷ vt boucher, encrasser ▷ vi (also: **~ up**) se boucher, s'encrasser

clone [kləun] n clone m ▷ vt cloner

close¹ [kləus] adj (contact, link, watch) étroit(e); (examination) attentif(-ive), minutieux(-euse); (contest) très serré(e); (weather) lourd(e), étouffant(e); (near): **~ (to)** près (de), proche (de) ▷ adv près, à proximité; **~ to** prep près de; **~ by, ~ at hand** adj, adv tout(e) près; **a ~ friend** un ami intime; **to have a ~ shave** (fig) l'échapper belle

close² [kləuz] vt fermer ▷ vi (shop etc) fermer; (lid, door etc) se fermer; (end) se terminer, se conclure ▷ n (end) conclusion f; **what time do you ~?** à quelle heure fermez-vous?; **close**

down vi fermer (définitivement); **closed** adj (shop etc) fermé(e)

closely ['kləuslɪ] adv (examine, watch) de près

closet ['klɔzɪt] n (cupboard) placard m, réduit m

close-up ['kləusʌp] n gros plan

closing time n heure f de fermeture

closure ['kləuʒər] n fermeture f

clot [klɔt] n (of blood, milk) caillot m; (inf: person) ballot m ▷ vi (external bleeding) se coaguler

cloth [klɔθ] n (material) tissu m, étoffe f; (BRIT: also: **tea ~**) torchon m; lavette f; (also: **table~**) nappe f

clothes [kləuðz] npl vêtements mpl, habits mpl; **clothes line** n corde f (à linge); **clothes peg**, (US) **clothes pin** n pince f à linge

clothing ['kləuðɪŋ] n = **clothes**

cloud [klaud] n (also Comput) nuage m; **cloud computing** n (Comput) informatique f en nuage; **cloud over** vi se couvrir; (fig) s'assombrir; **cloudy** adj nuageux(-euse), couvert(e); (liquid) trouble

clove [kləuv] n clou m de girofle; **a ~ of garlic** une gousse d'ail

clown [klaun] n clown m ▷ vi (also: **~ about, ~ around**) faire le clown

club [klʌb] n (society) club m; (weapon) massue f, matraque f; (also: **golf ~**) club ▷ vt matraquer ▷ vi: **to ~ together** s'associer; **clubs** npl (Cards) trèfle m; **club class** n (Aviat) classe f club

clue [kluː] n indice m; (in crosswords) définition f; **I haven't a ~** je n'en ai pas la moindre idée

clump [klʌmp] n: **~ of trees** bouquet m d'arbres

clumsy ['klʌmzɪ] adj (person) gauche, maladroit(e); (object) malcommode, peu maniable

clung [klʌŋ] pt, pp of **cling**

cluster ['klʌstər] n (petit) groupe; (of flowers) grappe f ▷ vi se rassembler

clutch [klʌtʃ] n (Aut) embrayage m; (grasp): **~es** étreinte f, prise f ▷ vt (*grasp*) agripper; (*hold tightly*) serrer fort; (*hold on to*) se cramponner à

cm *abbr* (= *centimetre*) cm

Co. *abbr* = **company, county**

c/o *abbr* (= *care of*) c/o, aux bons soins de

coach [kəʊtʃ] *n* (*bus*) autocar *m*; (*horse-drawn*) diligence *f*; (*of train*) voiture *f*, wagon *m*; (*Sport: trainer*) entraîneur(-euse); (*school: tutor*) répétiteur(-trice) ▷ *vt* (*Sport*) entraîner; (*student*) donner des leçons particulières à; **coach station** (*BRIT*) *n* gare routière; **coach trip** *n* excursion *f* en car

coal [kəʊl] *n* charbon *m*

coalition [kəʊəˈlɪʃən] *n* coalition *f*

coarse [kɔːs] *adj* grossier(-ère), rude; (*vulgar*) vulgaire

coast [kəʊst] *n* côte *f* ▷ *vi* (*car, cycle*) descendre en roue libre; **coastal** *adj* côtier(-ère); **coastguard** *n* garde-côte *m*; **coastline** *n* côte *f*, littoral *m*

coat [kəʊt] *n* manteau *m*; (*of animal*) pelage *m*, poil *m*; (*of paint*) couche *f* ▷ *vt* couvrir, enduire; **coat hanger** *n* cintre *m*; **coating** *n* couche *f*, enduit *m*

coax [kəʊks] *vt* persuader par des cajoleries

cob [kɔb] *n see* **corn**

cobbled [ˈkɔbld] *adj* pavé(e)

cobweb [ˈkɔbwɛb] *n* toile *f* d'araignée

cocaine [kəˈkeɪn] *n* cocaïne *f*

cock [kɔk] *n* (*rooster*) coq *m*; (*male bird*) mâle *m* ▷ *vt* (*gun*) armer; **cockerel** *n* jeune coq *m*

cockney [ˈkɔknɪ] *n* cockney *m/f* (*habitant des quartiers populaires de l'East End de Londres*), ≈ faubourien(ne)

cockpit [ˈkɔkpɪt] *n* (*in aircraft*) poste *m* de pilotage, cockpit *m*

cockroach [ˈkɔkrəʊtʃ] *n* cafard *m*, cancrelat *m*

cocktail [ˈkɔkteɪl] *n* cocktail *m*

cocoa [ˈkəʊkəʊ] *n* cacao *m*

coconut [ˈkəʊkənʌt] *n* noix *f* de coco

cod [kɔd] *n* morue fraîche, cabillaud *m*

C.O.D. *abbr* = **cash on delivery**

code [kəʊd] *n* code *m*; (*Tel: area code*) indicatif *m*

coeducational [ˈkəʊɛdjuˈkeɪʃənl] *adj* mixte

coffee [ˈkɔfɪ] *n* café *m*; **coffee bar** *n* (*BRIT*) café *m*; **coffee bean** *n* grain *m* de café; **coffee break** *n* pause-café *f*; **coffee maker** *n* cafetière *f*; **coffeepot** *n* cafetière *f*; **coffee shop** *n* café *m*; **coffee table** *n* (petite) table basse

coffin [ˈkɔfɪn] *n* cercueil *m*

cog [kɔg] *n* (*wheel*) roue dentée; (*tooth*) dent *f* (d'engrenage)

cognac [ˈkɔnjæk] *n* cognac *m*

coherent [kəʊˈhɪərənt] *adj* cohérent(e)

coil [kɔɪl] *n* rouleau *m*, bobine *f*; (*contraceptive*) stérilet *m* ▷ *vt* enrouler

coin [kɔɪn] *n* pièce *f* (de monnaie) ▷ *vt* (*word*) inventer

coincide [kəʊɪnˈsaɪd] *vi* coïncider; **coincidence** [kəʊˈɪnsɪdəns] *n* coïncidence *f*

Coke® [kəʊk] *n* coca *m*

coke [kəʊk] *n* (*coal*) coke *m*

colander [ˈkɔləndəʳ] *n* passoire *f* (à légumes)

cold [kəʊld] *adj* froid(e) ▷ *n* froid *m*; (*Med*) rhume *m*; **it's ~** il fait froid; **to be ~** (*person*) avoir froid; **to catch a ~** s'enrhumer, attraper un rhume; **in ~ blood** de sang-froid; **cold sore** *n* bouton *m* de fièvre

coleslaw [ˈkəʊlslɔː] *n* sorte de salade de chou cru

colic [ˈkɔlɪk] *n* colique(s) *f(pl)*

collaborate [kəˈlæbəreɪt] *vi* collaborer

collapse [kəˈlæps] *vi* s'effondrer, s'écrouler; (*Med*) avoir un malaise ▷ *n* effondrement *m*, écroulement *m*; (*of government*) chute *f*

collar [ˈkɔləʳ] *n* (*of coat, shirt*) col *m*; (*for dog*) collier *m*; **collarbone** *n* clavicule *f*

colleague [ˈkɔliːg] *n* collègue *m/f*

collect [kə'lɛkt] vt rassembler; (pick up) ramasser; (as a hobby) collectionner; (BRIT: call for) (passer) prendre; (mail) faire la levée de, ramasser; (money owed) encaisser; (donations, subscriptions) recueillir ▷ vi (people) se rassembler; (dust, dirt) s'amasser; **to call ~** (US Tel) téléphoner en PCV; **collection** [kə'lɛkʃən] n collection f; (of mail) levée f; (for money) collecte f, quête f; **collective** [kə'lɛktɪv] adj collectif(-ive); **collector** n collectionneur m

college ['kɔlɪdʒ] n collège m; (of technology, agriculture etc) institut m

collide [kə'laɪd] vi: **to ~ (with)** entrer en collision (avec)

collision [kə'lɪʒən] n collision f, heurt m

cologne [kə'ləun] n (also: **eau de ~**) eau f de cologne

colon ['kəulən] n (sign) deux-points mpl; (Med) côlon m

colonel ['kə:nl] n colonel m

colonial [kə'ləuniəl] adj colonial(e)

colony ['kɔləni] n colonie f

colour, (US) **color** ['kʌlər] n couleur f ▷ vt colorer; (dye) teindre; (paint) peindre; (with crayons) colorier; (news) fausser, exagérer ▷ vi (blush) rougir; **I'd like a different ~** je le voudrais dans un autre coloris; **colour in** vt colorier; **colour-blind**, (US) **color-blind** adj daltonien(ne); **coloured**, (US) **colored** adj coloré(e); (photo) en couleur; **colour film**, (US) **color film** n (for camera) pellicule f (en) couleur; **colourful**, (US) **colorful** adj coloré(e), vif (vive); (personality) pittoresque, haut(e) en couleurs; **colouring**, (US) **coloring** n colorant m; (complexion) teint m; **colour television**, (US) **color television** n télévision f (en) couleur

column ['kɔləm] n colonne f; (fashion column, sports column etc) rubrique f

coma ['kəumə] n coma m

comb [kəum] n peigne m ▷ vt (hair) peigner; (area) ratisser, passer au peigne fin

combat ['kɔmbæt] n combat m ▷ vt combattre, lutter contre

combination [kɔmbɪ'neɪʃən] n (gen) combinaison f

combine [kəm'baɪn] vt combiner ▷ vi s'associer; (Chem) se combiner ▷ n ['kɔmbaɪn] (Econ) trust m; (also: **~ harvester**) moissonneuse-batteuse(-lieuse) f; **to ~ sth with sth** (one quality with another) joindre ou allier qch à qch

KEYWORD

come (pt **came**, pp **come**) [kʌm, keɪm] vi **1** (movement towards) venir; **to come running** arriver en courant; **he's come here to work** il est venu ici pour travailler; **come with me** suivez-moi

2 (arrive) arriver; **to come home** rentrer (chez soi or à la maison); **we've just come from Paris** nous arrivons de Paris

3 (reach): **to come to** (decision etc) parvenir à, arriver à; **the bill came to £40** la note s'est élevée à 40 livres

4 (occur): **an idea came to me** il m'est venu une idée

5 (be, become): **to come loose/undone** se défaire/desserrer; **I've come to like him** j'ai fini par bien l'aimer

come across vt fus rencontrer par hasard, tomber sur

come along vi (BRIT: pupil, work) faire des progrès, avancer

come back vi revenir

come down vi descendre; (prices) baisser; (buildings) s'écrouler; (: be demolished) être démoli(e)

come from vt fus (source) venir de; (place) venir de, être originaire de

come in vi entrer; (train) arriver;

(*fashion*) entrer en vogue; (*on deal etc*) participer

come off *vi* (*button*) se détacher; (*attempt*) réussir

come on *vi* (*lights, electricity*) s'allumer; (*central heating*) se mettre en marche; (*pupil, work, project*) faire des progrès, avancer; **come on!** viens!; allons!, allez!

come out *vi* sortir; (*sun*) se montrer; (*book*) paraître; (*stain*) s'enlever; (*strike*) cesser le travail, se mettre en grève

come round *vi* (*after faint, operation*) revenir à soi, reprendre connaissance

come to *vi* revenir à soi

come up *vi* monter; (*sun*) se lever; (*problem*) se poser; (*event*) survenir; (*in conversation*) être soulevé

come up with *vt fus* (*money*) fournir; **he came up with an idea** il a eu une idée, il a proposé quelque chose

comeback ['kʌmbæk] *n* (*Theat*) rentrée *f*

comedian [kə'miːdɪən] *n* (*comic*) comique *m*; (*Theat*) comédien *m*

comedy ['kɒmɪdɪ] *n* comédie *f*; (*humour*) comique *m*

comet ['kɒmɪt] *n* comète *f*

comfort ['kʌmfət] *n* confort *m*, bien-être *m*; (*solace*) consolation *f*, réconfort *m* ▷ *vt* consoler, réconforter; **comfortable** *adj* confortable; (*person*) à l'aise; (*financially*) aisé(e); (*patient*) dont l'état est stationnaire; **comfort station** *n* (*US*) toilettes *fpl*

comic ['kɒmɪk] *adj* (*also*: **~al**) comique ▷ *n* (*person*) comique *m*; (*BRIT: magazine: for children*) magazine *m* de bandes dessinées *or* de BD; (: *for adults*) illustré *m*; **comic book** *n* (*US: for children*) magazine *m* de bandes dessinées *or* de BD; (: *for adults*) illustré *m*; **comic strip** *n* bande dessinée

comma ['kɒmə] *n* virgule *f*

command [kə'mɑːnd] *n* ordre *m*, commandement *m*; (*Mil: authority*) commandement; (*mastery*) maîtrise *f* ▷ *vt* (*troops*) commander; **to ~ sb to do** donner l'ordre *or* commander à qn de faire; **commander** *n* (*Mil*) commandant *m*

commemorate [kə'mɛməreɪt] *vt* commémorer

commence [kə'mɛns] *vt*, *vi* commencer

commend [kə'mɛnd] *vt* louer; (*recommend*) recommander

comment ['kɒmɛnt] *n* commentaire *m* ▷ *vi*: **to ~ on** faire des remarques sur; **"no ~"** "je n'ai rien à déclarer"; **commentary** ['kɒməntərɪ] *n* commentaire *m*; (*Sport*) reportage *m* (en direct); **commentator** ['kɒmənteɪtəʳ] *n* commentateur *m*; (*Sport*) reporter *m*

commerce ['kɒməːs] *n* commerce *m*

commercial [kə'məːʃəl] *adj* commercial(e) ▷ *n* (*Radio, TV*) annonce *f* publicitaire, spot *m* (publicitaire); **commercial break** *n* (*Radio, TV*) spot *m* (publicitaire)

commission [kə'mɪʃən] *n* (*committee, fee*) commission *f* ▷ *vt* (*work of art*) commander, charger un artiste de l'exécution de; **out of ~** (*machine*) hors service; **commissioner** *n* (*Police*) préfet *m* (de police)

commit [kə'mɪt] *vt* (*act*) commettre; (*resources*) consacrer; (*to sb's care*) confier (à); **to ~ o.s. (to do)** s'engager (à faire); **to ~ suicide** se suicider; **commitment** *n* engagement *m*; (*obligation*) responsabilité(s) *f(pl)*

committee [kə'mɪtɪ] *n* comité *m*; commission *f*

commodity [kə'mɒdɪtɪ] *n* produit *m*, marchandise *f*, article *m*

common ['kɒmən] *adj* (*gen*) commun(e); (*usual*) courant(e) ▷ *n* terrain communal; **commonly** *adv* communément, généralement; couramment; **commonplace** *adj* banal(e), ordinaire; **Commons**

npl (BRIT *Pol*): **the (House of) Commons** la chambre des Communes; **common sense** *n* bon sens; **Commonwealth** *n*: **the Commonwealth** le Commonwealth

communal ['kɔmjuːnl] *adj* (*life*) communautaire; (*for common use*) commun(e)

commune *n* ['kɔmjuːn] (*group*) communauté *f* ▷ *vi* [kə'mjuːn]: **to ~ with** (*nature*) communier avec

communicate [kə'mjuːnɪkeɪt] *vt* communiquer, transmettre ▷ *vi*: **to ~ (with)** communiquer (avec)

communication [kəmjuːnɪ'keɪʃən] *n* communication *f*

communion [kə'mjuːnɪən] *n* (*also*: **Holy C~**) communion *f*

communism ['kɔmjunɪzəm] *n* communisme *m*; **communist** *adj*, *n* communiste *m/f*

community [kə'mjuːnɪtɪ] *n* communauté *f*; **community centre**, (US) **community center** *n* foyer socio-éducatif, centre *m* de loisirs; **community service** *n* ≈ travail *m* d'intérêt général, TIG *m*

commute [kə'mjuːt] *vi* faire le trajet journalier (*de son domicile à un lieu de travail assez éloigné*) ▷ *vt* (*Law*) commuer; **commuter** *n* banlieusard(e) (*qui fait un trajet journalier pour se rendre à son travail*)

compact *adj* [kəm'pækt] compact(e) ▷ *n* ['kɔmpækt] (*also*: **powder ~**) poudrier *m*; **compact disc** *n* disque compact; **compact disc player** *n* lecteur *m* de disques compacts

companion [kəm'pænjən] *n* compagnon (compagne)

company ['kʌmpənɪ] *n* compagnie *f*; **to keep sb ~** tenir compagnie à qn; **company car** *n* voiture *f* de fonction; **company director** *n* administrateur(-trice)

comparable ['kɔmpərəbl] *adj* comparable

comparative [kəm'pærətɪv] *adj* (*study*) comparatif(-ive); (*relative*) relatif(-ive); **comparatively** *adv* (*relatively*) relativement

compare [kəm'pɛəʳ] *vt*: **to ~ sth/sb with** *or* **to** comparer qch/qn avec *or* à ▷ *vi*: **to ~ (with)** se comparer (à); être comparable (à); **comparison** [kəm'pærɪsn] *n* comparaison *f*

compartment [kəm'pɑːtmənt] *n* (*also* Rail) compartiment *m*; **a non-smoking ~** un compartiment non-fumeurs

compass ['kʌmpəs] *n* boussole *f*; **compasses** *npl* (*Math*) compas *m*

compassion [kəm'pæʃən] *n* compassion *f*, humanité *f*

compatible [kəm'pætɪbl] *adj* compatible

compel [kəm'pɛl] *vt* contraindre, obliger; **compelling** *adj* (*fig*: *argument*) irrésistible

compensate ['kɔmpənseɪt] *vt* indemniser, dédommager ▷ *vi*: **to ~ for** compenser; **compensation** [kɔmpən'seɪʃən] *n* compensation *f*; (*money*) dédommagement *m*, indemnité *f*

compete [kəm'piːt] *vi* (*take part*) concourir; (*vie*): **to ~ (with)** rivaliser (avec), faire concurrence (à)

competent ['kɔmpɪtənt] *adj* compétent(e), capable

competition [kɔmpɪ'tɪʃən] *n* (*contest*) compétition *f*, concours *m*; (*Econ*) concurrence *f*

competitive [kəm'pɛtɪtɪv] *adj* (*Econ*) concurrentiel(le); (*sports*) de compétition; (*person*) qui a l'esprit de compétition

competitor [kəm'pɛtɪtəʳ] *n* concurrent(e)

complacent [kəm'pleɪsnt] *adj* (*trop*) content(e) de soi

complain [kəm'pleɪn] *vi*: **to ~ (about)** se plaindre (de); (*in shop etc*) réclamer (au sujet de); **complaint** *n*

plainte f; (in shop etc) réclamation f;
(Med) affection f

complement ['kɔmplɪmənt] n
complément m; (esp of ship's crew
etc) effectif complet ▷ vt (enhance)
compléter; **complementary**
[kɔmplɪ'mɛntərɪ] adj complémentaire

complete [kəm'pliːt] adj
complet(-ète); (finished) achevé(e)
▷ vt achever, parachever; (set,
group) compléter; (a form) remplir;
completely adv complètement;
completion [kəm'pliːʃən] n
achèvement m; (of contract)
exécution f

complex ['kɔmplɛks] adj complexe
▷ n (Psych, buildings etc) complexe m

complexion [kəm'plɛkʃən] n (of
face) teint m

compliance [kəm'plaɪəns] n
(submission) docilité f; (agreement):
~ **with** le fait de se conformer
à; **in ~ with** en conformité avec,
conformément à

complicate ['kɔmplɪkeɪt] vt
compliquer; **complicated** adj
compliqué(e); **complication**
[kɔmplɪ'keɪʃən] n complication f

compliment n ['kɔmplɪmənt]
compliment m ▷ vt ['kɔmplɪmɛnt]
complimenter; **complimentary**
[kɔmplɪ'mɛntərɪ] adj flatteur(-euse);
(free) à titre gracieux

comply [kəm'plaɪ] vi: **to ~ with** se
soumettre à, se conformer à

component [kəm'pəunənt] adj
composant(e), constituant(e) ▷ n
composant m, élément m

compose [kəm'pəuz] vt composer;
(form): **to be ~d of** se composer de;
to ~ o.s. se calmer, se maîtriser;
composer n (Mus) compositeur m;
composition [kɔmpə'zɪʃən] n
composition f

composure [kəm'pəuʒər] n calme m,
maîtrise f de soi

compound ['kɔmpaund] n (Chem,
Ling) composé m; (enclosure) enclos m,
enceinte f ▷ adj composé(e); (fracture)
compliqué(e)

comprehension [kɔmprɪ'hɛnʃən] n
compréhension f

comprehensive [kɔmprɪ'hɛnsɪv]
adj (très) complet(-ète); **~ policy**
(Insurance) assurance f tous risques;
comprehensive (school) n (BRIT)
école secondaire non sélective avec
libre circulation d'une section à l'autre,
≈ CES m

> Be careful not to translate
> comprehensive by the French word
> compréhensif.

compress vt [kəm'prɛs] comprimer;
(text, information) condenser ▷ n
['kɔmprɛs] (Med) compresse f

comprise [kəm'praɪz] vt (also: **be
~d of**) comprendre; (constitute)
constituer, représenter

compromise ['kɔmprəmaɪz] n
compromis m ▷ vt compromettre ▷ vi
transiger, accepter un compromis

compulsive [kəm'pʌlsɪv] adj
(Psych) compulsif(-ive); (book, film etc)
captivant(e)

compulsory [kəm'pʌlsərɪ] adj
obligatoire

computer [kəm'pjuːtər] n ordinateur
m; **computer game** n jeu m vidéo;
computer-generated adj de
synthèse; **computerize** vt (data)
traiter par ordinateur; (system,
office) informatiser; **computer
programmer** n programmeur(-euse);
computer programming n
programmation f; **computer science**
n informatique f; **computer studies**
npl informatique f; **computing**
[kəm'pjuːtɪŋ] n informatique f

con [kɔn] vt duper; (cheat) escroquer
▷ n escroquerie f

conceal [kən'siːl] vt cacher,
dissimuler

concede [kən'siːd] vt concéder
▷ vi céder

conceited [kən'siːtɪd] adj
vaniteux(-euse), suffisant(e)

conceive [kən'siːv] vt, vi concevoir
concentrate ['kɔnsəntreɪt] vi se
concentrer ▷ vt concentrer
concentration [kɔnsən'treɪʃən] n
concentration f
concept ['kɔnsɛpt] n concept m
concern [kən'səːn] n affaire f;
(Comm) entreprise f, firme f; (anxiety)
inquiétude f, souci m ▷ vt (worry)
inquiéter; (involve) concerner;
(relate to) se rapporter à; **to be
~ed (about)** s'inquiéter (de),
être inquiet(-ète) (au sujet de);
concerning prep en ce qui concerne,
à propos de
concert ['kɔnsət] n concert m;
concert hall n salle f de concert
concerto [kən'tʃəːtəu] n concerto m
concession [kən'sɛʃən] n
(compromise) concession f; (reduced
price) réduction f; **tax ~** dégrèvement
fiscal; **"~s"** tarif réduit
concise [kən'saɪs] adj concis(e)
conclude [kən'kluːd] vt conclure;
conclusion [kən'kluːʒən] n
conclusion f
concrete ['kɔnkriːt] n béton m ▷ adj
concret(-ète); (Constr) en béton
concussion [kən'kʌʃən] n (Med)
commotion (cérébrale)
condemn [kən'dɛm] vt condamner
condensation [kɔndɛn'seɪʃən] n
condensation f
condense [kən'dɛns] vi se condenser
▷ vt condenser
condition [kən'dɪʃən] n condition
f; (disease) maladie f ▷ vt déterminer,
conditionner; **on ~ that** à
condition que + sub, à condition
de; **conditional** [kən'dɪʃənl] adj
conditionnel(le); **conditioner** n (for
hair) baume démêlant; (for fabrics)
assouplissant m
condo ['kɔndəu] n (US inf)
= **condominium**
condom ['kɔndəm] n préservatif m
condominium [kɔndə'mɪnɪəm]
n (US: building) immeuble m (en

copropriété); (: rooms) appartement
m (dans un immeuble en copropriété)
condone [kən'dəun] vt fermer les
yeux sur, approuver (tacitement)
conduct n ['kɔndʌkt] conduite f ▷ vt
[kən'dʌkt] conduire; (manage) mener,
diriger; (Mus) diriger; **to ~ o.s.** se
conduire, se comporter; **conductor**
n (of orchestra) chef m d'orchestre; (on
bus) receveur m; (US: on train) chef m
de train; (Elec) conducteur m
cone [kəun] n cône m; (for ice-cream)
cornet m; (Bot) pomme f de pin, cône
confectionery [kən'fɛkʃənrɪ] n
(sweets) confiserie f
confer [kən'fəːʳ] vt: **to ~ sth
on** conférer qch à ▷ vi conférer,
s'entretenir
conference ['kɔnfərns] n
conférence f
confess [kən'fɛs] vt confesser,
avouer ▷ vi (admit sth) avouer; (Rel) se
confesser; **confession** [kən'fɛʃən] n
confession f
confide [kən'faɪd] vi: **to ~ in** s'ouvrir
à, se confier à
confidence ['kɔnfɪdns] n confiance
f; (also: **self-~**) assurance f,
confiance en soi; (secret) confidence
f; **in ~** (speak, write) en confidence,
confidentiellement; **confident** adj
(self-assured) sûr(e) de soi; (sure) sûr;
confidential [kɔnfɪ'dɛnʃəl] adj
confidentiel(le)
confine [kən'faɪn] vt limiter,
borner; (shut up) confiner, enfermer;
confined adj (space) restreint(e),
réduit(e)
confirm [kən'fəːm] vt (report, Rel)
confirmer; (appointment) ratifier;
confirmation [kɔnfə'meɪʃən] n
confirmation f; ratification f
confiscate ['kɔnfɪskeɪt] vt confisquer
conflict n ['kɔnflɪkt] conflit m, lutte
f ▷ vi [kən'flɪkt] (opinions) s'opposer,
se heurter
conform [kən'fɔːm] vi: **to ~ (to)** se
conformer (à)

confront [kən'frʌnt] vt (two people) confronter; (enemy, danger) affronter, faire face à; (problem) faire face à; **confrontation** [kɔnfrən'teɪʃən] n confrontation f

confuse [kən'fju:z] vt (person) troubler; (situation) embrouiller; (one thing with another) confondre; **confused** adj (person) dérouté(e), désorienté(e); (situation) embrouillé(e); **confusing** adj peu clair(e), déroutant(e); **confusion** [kən'fju:ʒən] n confusion f

congestion [kən'dʒɛstʃən] n (Med) congestion f; (fig: traffic) encombrement m

congratulate [kən'grætjuleɪt] vt: **to ~ sb (on)** féliciter qn (de); **congratulations** [kəngrætju'leɪʃənz] npl; **congratulations (on)** félicitations fpl (pour) ▷ excl: **congratulations!** (toutes mes) félicitations!

congregation [kɔngrɪ'geɪʃən] n assemblée f (des fidèles)

congress ['kɔngrɛs] n congrès m; (Pol): **C~** Congrès m; **congressman** (irreg) n membre m du Congrès; **congresswoman** (irreg) n membre m du Congrès

conifer ['kɔnɪfər] n conifère m

conjugate ['kɔndʒugeɪt] vt conjuguer

conjugation [kɔndʒə'geɪʃən] n conjugaison f

conjunction [kən'dʒʌŋkʃən] n conjonction f; **in ~ with** (conjointement) avec

conjure ['kʌndʒər] vi faire des tours de passe-passe

connect [kə'nɛkt] vt joindre, relier; (Elec) connecter; (Tel: caller) mettre en connexion; (: subscriber) brancher; (fig) établir un rapport entre, faire un rapprochement entre ▷ vi (train): **to ~ with** assurer la correspondance avec; **to be ~ed with** avoir un rapport avec; (have dealings with) avoir

des rapports avec, être en relation avec; **connecting flight** n (vol m de) correspondance f; **connection** [kə'nɛkʃən] n relation f, lien m; (Elec) connexion f; (Tel) communication f; (train etc) correspondance f

conquer ['kɔŋkər] vt conquérir; (feelings) vaincre, surmonter

conquest ['kɔŋkwɛst] n conquête f

cons [kɔnz] npl see **convenience; pro**

conscience ['kɔnʃəns] n conscience f

conscientious [kɔnʃɪ'ɛnʃəs] adj consciencieux(-euse)

conscious ['kɔnʃəs] adj conscient(e); (deliberate: insult, error) délibéré(e); **consciousness** n conscience f; (Med) connaissance f

consecutive [kən'sɛkjutɪv] adj consécutif(-ive); **on three ~ occasions** trois fois de suite

consensus [kən'sɛnsəs] n consensus m

consent [kən'sɛnt] n consentement m ▷ vi: **to ~ (to)** consentir (à)

consequence ['kɔnsɪkwəns] n suites fpl, conséquence f; (significance) importance f

consequently ['kɔnsɪkwəntlɪ] adv par conséquent, donc

conservation [kɔnsə'veɪʃən] n préservation f, protection f; (also: **nature ~**) défense f de l'environnement

Conservative [kən'sə:vətɪv] adj, n (BRIT Pol) conservateur(-trice)

conservative adj conservateur(-trice); (cautious) prudent(e)

conservatory [kən'sə:vətrɪ] n (room) jardin m d'hiver; (Mus) conservatoire m

consider [kən'sɪdər] vt (study) considérer, réfléchir à; (take into account) penser à, prendre en considération; (regard, judge) considérer, estimer; **to ~ doing sth** envisager de faire qch; **considerable** adj considérable; **considerably** adv nettement; **considerate** adj

prévenant(e), plein(e) d'égards;
consideration [kənsɪdə'reɪʃən] *n*
considération *f*; (*reward*) rétribution
f, rémunération *f*; **considering**
prep: **considering (that)** étant
donné (que)
consignment [kən'saɪnmənt] *n*
arrivage *m*, envoi *m*
consist [kən'sɪst] *vi*: **to ~ of** consister
en, se composer de
consistency [kən'sɪstənsɪ] *n*
(*thickness*) consistance *f*; (*fig*)
cohérence *f*
consistent [kən'sɪstənt] *adj* logique,
cohérent(e)
consolation [kɒnsə'leɪʃən] *n*
consolation *f*
console¹ [kən'səul] *vt* consoler
console² ['kɒnsəul] *n* console *f*
consonant ['kɒnsənənt] *n*
consonne *f*
conspicuous [kən'spɪkjuəs] *adj*
voyant(e), qui attire l'attention
conspiracy [kən'spɪrəsɪ] *n*
conspiration *f*, complot *m*
constable ['kʌnstəbl] *n* (BRIT) ≈
agent *m* de police, gendarme *m*; **chief
~** ≈ préfet *m* de police
constant ['kɒnstənt] *adj*
constant(e); incessant(e);
constantly *adv* constamment,
sans cesse
constipated ['kɒnstɪpeɪtɪd]
adj constipé(e); **constipation**
[kɒnstɪ'peɪʃən] *n* constipation *f*
constituency [kən'stɪtjuənsɪ] *n*
(*Pol: area*) circonscription électorale;
(*: electors*) électorat *m*
constitute ['kɒnstɪtjuːt] *vt*
constituer
constitution [kɒnstɪ'tjuːʃən] *n*
constitution *f*
constraint [kən'streɪnt] *n*
contrainte *f*
construct [kən'strʌkt] *vt* construire;
construction [kən'strʌkʃən] *n*
construction *f*; **constructive** *adj*
constructif(-ive)

consul ['kɒnsl] *n* consul *m*;
consulate ['kɒnsjulɪt] *n* consulat *m*
consult [kən'sʌlt] *vt* consulter;
consultant *n* (*Med*) médecin
consultant; (*other specialist*)
consultant *m*, (expert-)conseil *m*;
consultation [kɒnsəl'teɪʃən] *n*
consultation *f*; **consulting room** *n*
(BRIT) cabinet *m* de consultation
consume [kən'sjuːm] *vt*
consommer; (*subj: flames, hatred,
desire*) consumer; **consumer** *n*
consommateur(-trice)
consumption [kən'sʌmpʃən] *n*
consommation *f*
cont. *abbr* (= *continued*) suite
contact ['kɒntækt] *n* contact *m*;
(*person*) connaissance *f*, relation *f* ▷ *vt*
se mettre en contact *or* en rapport
avec; **~ number** numéro *m* de
téléphone; **contact lenses** *npl* verres
mpl de contact
contagious [kən'teɪdʒəs] *adj*
contagieux(-euse)
contain [kən'teɪn] *vt* contenir;
to ~ o.s. se contenir, se maîtriser;
container *n* récipient *m*; (*for shipping
etc*) conteneur *m*
contaminate [kən'tæmɪneɪt] *vt*
contaminer
cont'd *abbr* (= *continued*) suite
contemplate ['kɒntəmpleɪt] *vt*
contempler; (*consider*) envisager
contemporary [kən'tempərərɪ] *adj*
contemporain(e); (*design, wallpaper*)
moderne ▷ *n* contemporain(e)
contempt [kən'tempt] *n* mépris *m*,
dédain *m*; **~ of court** (*Law*) outrage *m*
à l'autorité de la justice
contend [kən'tend] *vt*: **to ~ that**
soutenir *or* prétendre que ▷ *vi*: **to
~ with** (*compete*) rivaliser avec;
(*struggle*) lutter avec
content [kən'tent] *adj* content(e),
satisfait(e) ▷ *vt* contenter, satisfaire
▷ *n* ['kɒntent] contenu *m*; (*of fat,
moisture*) teneur *f*; **contents** *npl* (*of
container etc*) contenu *m*; **(table of)**

~s table *f* des matières; **contented** *adj* content(e), satisfait(e)

contest *n* ['kɔntest] combat *m*, lutte *f*; (*competition*) concours *m* ▷ *vt* [kən'test] contester, discuter; (*compete for*) disputer; (*Law*) attaquer; **contestant** [kən'testənt] *n* concurrent(e); (*in fight*) adversaire *m/f*

context ['kɔntekst] *n* contexte *m*

continent ['kɔntɪnənt] *n* continent *m*; **the C~** (BRIT) l'Europe continentale; **continental** [kɔntɪ'nentl] *adj* continental(e); **continental breakfast** *n* café (or thé) complet; **continental quilt** *n* (BRIT) couette *f*

continual [kən'tɪnjuəl] *adj* continuel(le); **continually** *adv* continuellement, sans cesse

continue [kən'tɪnju:] *vi* continuer ▷ *vt* continuer; (*start again*) reprendre

continuity [kɔntɪ'nju:ɪtɪ] *n* continuité *f*; (TV) enchaînement *m*

continuous [kən'tɪnjuəs] *adj* continu(e), permanent(e); (Ling) progressif(-ive); **continuous assessment** (BRIT) *n* contrôle continu; **continuously** *adv* (*repeatedly*) continuellement; (*uninterruptedly*) sans interruption

contour ['kɔntuəʳ] *n* contour *m*, profil *m*; (*also*: **~ line**) courbe *f* de niveau

contraception [kɔntrə'sepʃən] *n* contraception *f*

contraceptive [kɔntrə'septɪv] *adj* contraceptif(-ive), anticonceptionnel(le) ▷ *n* contraceptif *m*

contract *n* ['kɔntrækt] contrat *m* ▷ *vi* [kən'trækt] (*become smaller*) se contracter, se resserrer ▷ *vt* contracter; (*Comm*): **to ~ to do sth** s'engager (par contrat) à faire qch; **contractor** *n* entrepreneur *m*

contradict [kɔntrə'dɪkt] *vt* contredire; **contradiction** [kɔntrə'dɪkʃən] *n* contradiction *f*

contrary¹ ['kɔntrərɪ] *adj* contraire, opposé(e) ▷ *n* contraire *m*; **on the ~** au contraire; **unless you hear to the ~** sauf avis contraire

contrary² [kən'trɛərɪ] *adj* (*perverse*) contrariant(e), entêté(e)

contrast *n* ['kɔntrɑ:st] contraste *m* ▷ *vt* [kən'trɑ:st] mettre en contraste, contraster; **in ~ to** *or* **with** contrairement à, par opposition à

contribute [kən'trɪbju:t] *vi* contribuer ▷ *vt*: **to ~ £10/an article to** donner 10 livres/un article à; **to ~ to** (*gen*) contribuer à; (*newspaper*) collaborer à; (*discussion*) prendre part à; **contribution** [kɔntrɪ'bju:ʃən] *n* contribution *f*; (BRIT: *for social security*) cotisation *f*; (*to publication*) article *m*; **contributor** *n* (*to newspaper*) collaborateur(-trice); (*of money, goods*) donateur(-trice)

control [kən'trəul] *vt* (*process, machinery*) commander; (*temper*) maîtriser; (*disease*) enrayer ▷ *n* maîtrise *f*; (*power*) autorité *f*; **controls** *npl* (*of machine etc*) commandes *fpl*; (*on radio*) boutons *mpl* de réglage; **to be in ~ of** être maître de, maîtriser; (*in charge of*) être responsable de; **everything is under ~** j'ai (*or* il a *etc*) la situation en main; **the car went out of ~** j'ai (*or* il a *etc*) perdu le contrôle du véhicule; **control tower** *n* (*Aviat*) tour *f* de contrôle

controversial [kɔntrə'və:ʃl] *adj* discutable, controversé(e)

controversy ['kɔntrəvə:sɪ] *n* controverse *f*, polémique *f*

convenience [kən'vi:nɪəns] *n* commodité *f*; **at your ~** quand *or* comme cela vous convient; **all modern ~s, all mod cons** (BRIT) avec tout le confort moderne, tout confort

convenient [kən'vi:nɪənt] *adj* commode

convent ['kɔnvənt] *n* couvent *m*

convention [kən'vɛnʃən] n
convention f; (custom) usage m;
conventional adj conventionnel(le)

conversation [kɔnvə'seɪʃən] n
conversation f

conversely [kɔn'və:slɪ] adv
inversement, réciproquement

conversion [kən'və:ʃən] n
conversion f; (BRIT: of house)
transformation f, aménagement m;
(Rugby) transformation f

convert vt [kən'və:t] (Rel, Comm)
convertir; (alter) transformer; (house)
aménager ▷ n ['kɔnvə:t] converti(e);
convertible adj convertible ▷ n
(voiture f) décapotable f

convey [kən'veɪ] vt transporter;
(thanks) transmettre; (idea)
communiquer; **conveyor belt** n
convoyeur m tapis roulant

convict vt [kən'vɪkt] déclarer (or
reconnaître) coupable ▷ n ['kɔnvɪkt]
forçat m, convict m; **conviction**
[kən'vɪkʃən] n (Law) condamnation f;
(belief) conviction f

convince [kən'vɪns] vt convaincre,
persuader; **convinced** adj:
convinced of/that convaincu(e) de/
que; **convincing** adj persuasif(-ive),
convaincant(e)

convoy ['kɔnvɔɪ] n convoi m

cook [kuk] vt (faire) cuire ▷ vi
cuire; (person) faire la cuisine ▷ n
cuisinier(-ière); **cookbook** n livre
m de cuisine; **cooker** n cuisinière f;
cookery n cuisine f; **cookery book**
n (BRIT) = cookbook; **cookie** n (US)
biscuit m, petit gâteau sec; **cooking**
n cuisine f

cool [ku:l] adj frais (fraîche); (not
afraid) calme; (unfriendly) froid(e);
(inf: trendy) cool inv (inf); (: great)
super inv (inf) ▷ vt, vi rafraîchir,
refroidir; **cool down** vi refroidir; (fig:
person, situation) se calmer; **cool off**
vi (become calmer) se calmer; (lose
enthusiasm) perdre son enthousiasme

cop [kɔp] n (inf) flic m

cope [kəup] vi s'en sortir, tenir le
coup; **to ~ with** (problem) faire face à

copper ['kɔpər] n cuivre m; (BRIT inf:
policeman) flic m

copy ['kɔpɪ] n copie f; (book etc)
exemplaire m ▷ vt copier; (imitate)
imiter; **copyright** n droit m d'auteur,
copyright m

coral ['kɔrəl] n corail m

cord [kɔ:d] n corde f; (fabric)
velours côtelé; (Elec) cordon m
(d'alimentation), fil m (électrique);
cords npl (trousers) pantalon m de
velours côtelé; **cordless** adj sans fil

corduroy ['kɔ:dərɔɪ] n velours côtelé

core [kɔ:r] n (of fruit) trognon m,
cœur m; (fig: of problem etc) cœur ▷ vt
enlever le trognon or le cœur de

coriander [kɔrɪ'ændər] n coriandre f

cork [kɔ:k] n (material) liège m; (of
bottle) bouchon m; **corkscrew** n
tire-bouchon m

corn [kɔ:n] n (BRIT: wheat) blé m; (US:
maize) maïs m; (on foot) cor m; **~ on the
cob** (Culin) épi m de maïs au naturel

corned beef ['kɔ:nd-] n corned-
beef m

corner ['kɔ:nər] n coin m; (in road)
tournant m, virage m; (Football)
corner m ▷ vt (trap: prey) acculer; (fig)
coincer; (Comm: market) accaparer
▷ vi prendre un virage; **corner shop**
(BRIT) n magasin m du coin

cornflakes ['kɔ:nfleɪks] npl
cornflakes mpl

cornflour ['kɔ:nflauər] n (BRIT) farine
f de maïs, maïzena® f

cornstarch ['kɔ:nstɑ:tʃ] n (US) farine
f de maïs, maïzena® f

Cornwall ['kɔ:nwəl] n Cornouailles f

coronary ['kɔrənərɪ] n:
~ (thrombosis) infarctus m (du
myocarde), thrombose f coronaire

coronation [kɔrə'neɪʃən] n
couronnement m

coroner ['kɔrənər] n coroner m,
officier de police judiciaire chargé de
déterminer les causes d'un décès

corporal ['kɔ:pǝrl] n caporal m, brigadier m ▷ adj: **~ punishment** châtiment corporel

corporate ['kɔ:pǝrɪt] adj (action, ownership) en commun; (Comm) de la société

corporation [kɔ:pǝ'reɪʃǝn] n (of town) municipalité f, conseil municipal; (Comm) société f

corps (pl **corps**) [kɔ:ʳ, kɔ:z] n corps m; **the diplomatic ~** le corps diplomatique; **the press ~** la presse

corpse [kɔ:ps] n cadavre m

correct [kǝ'rɛkt] adj (accurate) correct(e), exact(e); (proper) correct, convenable ▷ vt corriger; **correction** [kǝ'rɛkʃǝn] n correction f

correspond [kɔrɪs'pɔnd] vi correspondre; **to ~ to sth** (be equivalent to) correspondre à qch; **correspondence** n correspondance f; **correspondent** n correspondant(e); **corresponding** adj correspondant(e)

corridor ['kɔrɪdɔ:ʳ] n couloir m, corridor m

corrode [kǝ'rǝud] vt corroder, ronger ▷ vi se corroder

corrupt [kǝ'rʌpt] adj corrompu(e); (Comput) altéré(e) ▷ vt corrompre; (Comput) altérer; **corruption** n corruption f; (Comput) altération f (de données)

Corsica ['kɔ:sɪkǝ] n Corse f

cosmetic [kɔz'mɛtɪk] n produit m de beauté, cosmétique m ▷ adj (fig: reforms) symbolique, superficiel(le); **cosmetic surgery** n chirurgie f esthétique

cosmopolitan [kɔzmǝ'pɔlɪtn] adj cosmopolite

cost [kɔst] (pt, pp **cost**) n coût m ▷ vi coûter ▷ vt établir or calculer le prix de revient de; **costs** npl (Comm) frais mpl; (Law) dépens mpl; **how much does it ~?** combien ça coûte?; **to ~ sb time/effort** demander du temps/un effort à qn; **it ~ him his life/job** ça lui

a coûté la vie/son emploi; **at all ~s** coûte que coûte, à tout prix

co-star ['kǝustɑ:ʳ] n partenaire m/f

costly ['kɔstlɪ] adj coûteux(-euse)

cost of living n coût m de la vie

costume ['kɔstju:m] n costume m; (BRIT: also: **swimming ~**) maillot m (de bain)

cosy, (US) **cozy** ['kǝuzɪ] adj (room, bed) douillet(te); **to be ~** (person) être bien (au chaud)

cot [kɔt] n (BRIT: child's) lit m d'enfant, petit lit; (US: campbed) lit de camp

cottage ['kɔtɪdʒ] n petite maison (à la campagne), cottage m; **cottage cheese** n fromage blanc (maigre)

cotton ['kɔtn] n coton m; (thread) fil m (de coton); **cotton on** vi (inf): **to ~ on (to sth)** piger (qch); **cotton bud** (BRIT) n coton-tige® m; **cotton candy** (US) n barbe f à papa; **cotton wool** n (BRIT) ouate f, coton m hydrophile

couch [kautʃ] n canapé m; divan m

cough [kɔf] vi tousser ▷ n toux f; **I've got a ~** j'ai la toux; **cough mixture, cough syrup** n sirop m pour la toux

could [kud] pt of **can²**; **couldn't = could not**

council ['kaunsl] n conseil m; **city or town ~** conseil municipal; **council estate** n (BRIT) (quartier m or zone f de) logements loués à/par la municipalité; **council house** n (BRIT) maison f (à loyer modéré) louée par la municipalité; **councillor**, (US) **councilor** n conseiller(-ère); **council tax** n (BRIT) impôts locaux

counsel ['kaunsl] n conseil m; (lawyer) avocat(e) ▷ vt: **to ~ (sb to do sth)** conseiller (à qn de faire qch); **counselling**, (US) **counseling** n (Psych) aide psychosociale; **counsellor**, (US) **counselor** n conseiller(-ère); (US Law) avocat m

count [kaunt] vt, vi compter ▷ n compte m; (nobleman) comte m; **count in** vt (inf): **to ~ sb in on sth**

inclure qn dans qch; **count on** vt fus compter sur; **countdown** n compte m à rebours

counter ['kauntər] n comptoir m; (in post office, bank) guichet m; (in game) jeton m ▷ vt aller à l'encontre de, opposer ▷ adv: **~ to** à l'encontre de; contrairement à; **counterclockwise** (us) adv en sens inverse des aiguilles d'une montre

counterfeit ['kauntəfɪt] n faux m, contrefaçon f ▷ vt contrefaire ▷ adj faux (fausse)

counterpart ['kauntəpɑːt] n (of person) homologue m/f

countess ['kauntɪs] n comtesse f

countless ['kauntlɪs] adj innombrable

country ['kʌntrɪ] n pays m; (native land) patrie f; (as opposed to town) campagne f; (region) région f, pays; **country and western (music)** n musique f country; **country house** n manoir m, (petit) château; **countryside** n campagne f

county ['kauntɪ] n comté m

coup (pl **coups**) [kuː, kuːz] n (achievement) beau coup; (also: **~ d'état**) coup d'État

couple ['kʌpl] n couple m; **a ~ of** (two) deux; (a few) deux ou trois

coupon ['kuːpɔn] n (voucher) bon m de réduction; (detachable form) coupon m détachable, coupon-réponse m

courage ['kʌrɪdʒ] n courage m; **courageous** [kə'reɪdʒəs] adj courageux(-euse)

courgette [kuə'ʒet] n (BRIT) courgette f

courier ['kurɪər] n messager m, courrier m; (for tourists) accompagnateur(-trice)

course [kɔːs] n cours m; (of ship) route f; (for golf) terrain m; (part of meal) plat m; **of ~** adv bien sûr; **(no,) of ~ not!** bien sûr que non!, évidemment que non!; **~ of treatment** (Med) traitement m

court [kɔːt] n cour f; (Law) cour, tribunal m; (Tennis) court m ▷ vt (woman) courtiser, faire la cour à; **to take to ~** actionner or poursuivre en justice

courtesy ['kəːtəsɪ] n courtoisie f, politesse f; **(by) ~ of** avec l'aimable autorisation de; **courtesy bus, courtesy coach** n navette gratuite

court: court-house ['kɔːthaus] n (us) palais m de justice; **courtroom** ['kɔːtrum] n salle f de tribunal; **courtyard** ['kɔːtjɑːd] n cour f

cousin ['kʌzn] n cousin(e); **first ~** cousin(e) germain(e)

cover ['kʌvər] vt couvrir; (Press: report on) faire un reportage sur; (feelings, mistake) cacher; (include) englober; (discuss) traiter ▷ n (of book, Comm) couverture f; (of pan) couvercle m; (over furniture) housse f; (shelter) abri m; **covers** npl (on bed) couvertures; **to take ~** se mettre à l'abri; **under ~** à l'abri; **under ~ of darkness** à la faveur de la nuit; **under separate ~** (Comm) sous pli séparé; **cover up** vi: **to ~ up for sb** (fig) couvrir qn; **coverage** n (in media) reportage m; **cover charge** n couvert m (supplément à payer); **cover-up** n tentative f pour étouffer une affaire

cow [kau] n vache f ▷ vt effrayer, intimider

coward ['kauəd] n lâche m/f; **cowardly** adj lâche

cowboy ['kaubɔɪ] n cow-boy m

cozy ['kəuzɪ] adj (us) = **cosy**

crab [kræb] n crabe m

crack [kræk] n (split) fente f, fissure f; (in cup, bone) fêlure f; (in wall) lézarde f; (noise) craquement m, coup (sec); (Drugs) crack m ▷ vt fendre, fissurer; fêler; lézarder; (whip) faire claquer; (nut) casser; (problem) résoudre; (code) déchiffrer ▷ cpd (athlete) de première classe, d'élite; **crack down on** vt fus (crime) sévir contre, réprimer; **cracked** adj (cup, bone) fêlé(e); (*broken*) cassé(e); (*wall*) lézardé(e); (*surface*) craquelé(e); (*inf*) toqué(e), timbré(e); **cracker** *n* (*also*: **Christmas cracker**) pétard *m*; (*biscuit*) biscuit (salé), craquelin *m*

crackle ['krækl] *vi* crépiter, grésiller

cradle ['kreɪdl] *n* berceau *m*

craft [krɑːft] *n* métier (artisanal); (*cunning*) ruse *f*, astuce *f*; (*boat: pl inv*) embarcation *f*, barque *f*; (*plane: pl inv*) appareil *m*; **craftsman** (*irreg*) *n* artisan *m* ouvrier (qualifié); **craftsmanship** *n* métier *m*, habileté *f*

cram [kræm] *vt*: **to ~ sth with** (*fill*) bourrer qch de; **to ~ sth into** (*put*) fourrer qch dans ▷ *vi* (*for exams*) bachoter

cramp [kræmp] *n* crampe *f*; **I've got ~ in my leg** j'ai une crampe à la jambe; **cramped** *adj* à l'étroit, très serré(e)

cranberry ['krænbərɪ] *n* canneberge *f*

crane [kreɪn] *n* grue *f*

crap [kræp] *n* (*inf!: nonsense*) conneries *fpl* (!); (: *excrement*) merde *f* (!)

crash [kræʃ] *n* (*noise*) fracas *m*; (*of car, plane*) collision *f*; (*of business*) faillite *f* ▷ *vt* (*plane*) écraser ▷ *vi* (*plane*) s'écraser; (*two cars*) se percuter, s'emboutir; (*business*) s'effondrer; **to ~ into** se jeter *or* se fracasser contre; **crash course** *n* cours intensif; **crash helmet** *n* casque (protecteur)

crate [kreɪt] *n* cageot *m*; (*for bottles*) caisse *f*

crave [kreɪv] *vt, vi*: **to ~ (for)** avoir une envie irrésistible de

crawl [krɔːl] *vi* ramper; (*vehicle*) avancer au pas ▷ *n* (*Swimming*) crawl *m*

crayfish ['kreɪfɪʃ] *n* (*pl inv: freshwater*) écrevisse *f*; (: *saltwater*) langoustine *f*

crayon ['kreɪən] *n* crayon *m* (de couleur)

craze [kreɪz] *n* engouement *m*

crazy ['kreɪzɪ] *adj* fou (folle); **to be ~ about sb/sth** (*inf*) être fou de qn/qch

creak [kriːk] *vi* (*hinge*) grincer; (*floor, shoes*) craquer

cream [kriːm] *n* crème *f* ▷ *adj* (*colour*) crème *inv*; **cream cheese** *n* fromage *m* à la crème, fromage blanc; **creamy** *adj* crémeux(-euse)

crease [kriːs] *n* pli *m* ▷ *vt* froisser, chiffonner ▷ *vi* se froisser, se chiffonner

create [kriːˈeɪt] *vt* créer; **creation** [kriːˈeɪʃən] *n* création *f*; **creative** *adj* créatif(-ive); **creator** *n* créateur(-trice)

creature ['kriːtʃəʳ] *n* créature *f*

crèche [krɛʃ] *n* garderie *f*, crèche *f*

credentials [krɪˈdɛnʃlz] *npl* (*references*) références *fpl*; (*identity papers*) pièce *f* d'identité

credibility [krɛdɪˈbɪlɪtɪ] *n* crédibilité *f*

credible ['krɛdɪbl] *adj* digne de foi, crédible

credit ['krɛdɪt] *n* crédit *m*; (*recognition*) honneur *m*; (*Scol*) unité *f* de valeur ▷ *vt* (*Comm*) créditer; (*believe: also*: **give ~ to**) ajouter foi à, croire; **credits** *npl* (*Cine*) générique *m*; **to be in ~** (*person, bank account*) être créditeur(-trice); **to ~ sb with** (*fig*) prêter *or* attribuer à qn; **credit card** *n* carte *f* de crédit; **do you take credit cards?** acceptez-vous les cartes de crédit?; **credit crunch** *n* crise *f* du crédit

creek [kriːk] *n* (*inlet*) crique *f*, anse *f*; (*us: stream*) ruisseau *m*, petit cours d'eau

creep (*pt, pp* **crept**) [kriːp, krɛpt] *vi* ramper

cremate [krɪˈmeɪt] *vt* incinérer

crematorium (*pl* **crematoria**) [krɛməˈtɔːrɪəm, -ˈtɔːrɪə] *n* four *m* crématoire

crept [krɛpt] *pt, pp* of **creep**

crescent ['krɛsnt] *n* croissant *m*; (*street*) rue *f* (en arc de cercle)

cress [krɛs] *n* cresson *m*

crest [krɛst] *n* crête *f*; (*of coat of arms*) timbre *m*

crew [kru:] n équipage m; (Cine)
équipe f (de tournage); **crew-neck**
n col ras

crib [krɪb] n lit m d'enfant; (for baby)
berceau m ▷ vt (inf) copier

cricket ['krɪkɪt] n (insect) grillon
m, cri-cri m inv; (game) cricket m;
cricketer n joueur m de cricket

crime [kraɪm] n crime m; **criminal**
['krɪmɪnl] adj, n criminel(le)

crimson ['krɪmzn] adj cramoisi(e)

cringe [krɪndʒ] vi avoir un
mouvement de recul

cripple ['krɪpl] n (pej) boiteux(-euse),
infirme m/f ▷ vt (person) estropier,
paralyser; (ship, plane) immobiliser;
(production, exports) paralyser

crisis (pl **crises**) ['kraɪsɪs, -si:z] n crise f

crisp [krɪsp] adj croquant(e);
(weather) vif (vive); (manner etc)
brusque; **crisps** (BRIT) npl (pommes
fpl) chips fpl; **crispy** adj croustillant(e)

criterion (pl **criteria**) [kraɪ'tɪərɪən,
-'tɪərɪə] n critère m

critic ['krɪtɪk] n critique m/f; **critical**
adj critique; **criticism** ['krɪtɪsɪzəm]
n critique f; **criticize** ['krɪtɪsaɪz] vt
critiquer

Croat ['krəuæt] adj, n = **Croatian**

Croatia [krəu'eɪʃə] n Croatie f;
Croatian adj croate ▷ n Croate m/f;
(Ling) croate m

crockery ['krɔkərɪ] n vaisselle f

crocodile ['krɔkədaɪl] n crocodile m

crocus ['krəukəs] n crocus m

croissant ['krwasɑ̃] n croissant m

crook [kruk] n (inf) escroc m; (of
shepherd) houlette f; **crooked**
['krukɪd] adj courbé(e), tordu(e);
(action) malhonnête

crop [krɔp] n (produce) culture f;
(amount produced) récolte f; (riding
crop) cravache f ▷ vt (hair) tondre;
crop up vi surgir, se présenter,
survenir

cross [krɔs] n croix f; (Biol) croisement
m ▷ vt (street etc) traverser; (arms,
legs, Biol) croiser; (cheque) barrer

▷ adj en colère, fâché(e); **cross off,
cross out** vt barrer, rayer; **cross
over** vi traverser; **cross-Channel
ferry** ['krɔs'tʃænl-] n ferry m qui fait
la traversée de la Manche; **cross-
country (race)** n cross(-country) m;
crossing n (sea passage) traversée f;
(also: **pedestrian crossing**) passage
clouté; **how long does the crossing
take?** combien de temps dure la
traversée?; **crossing guard** n (US)
contractuel qui fait traverser la rue aux
enfants; **crossroads** n carrefour m;
crosswalk n (US) passage clouté;
crossword n mots mpl croisés

crotch [krɔtʃ] n (of garment)
entrejambe m; (Anat) entrecuisse m

crouch [krautʃ] vi s'accroupir; (hide)
se tapir; (before springing) se ramasser

crouton ['kru:tɔn] n croûton m

crow [krəu] n (bird) corneille f; (of
cock) chant m du coq, cocorico m ▷ vi
(cock) chanter

crowd [kraud] n foule f ▷ vt bourrer,
remplir ▷ vi affluer, s'attrouper,
s'entasser; **crowded** adj bondé(e)

crown [kraun] n couronne f; (of head)
sommet m de la tête; (of hill) sommet
m ▷ vt (also tooth) couronner; **crown
jewels** npl joyaux mpl de la Couronne

crucial ['kru:ʃl] adj crucial(e),
décisif(-ive)

crucifix ['kru:sɪfɪks] n crucifix m

crude [kru:d] adj (materials)
brut(e); non raffiné(e); (basic)
rudimentaire, sommaire; (vulgar)
cru(e), grossier(-ière) ▷ n (also: **~ oil**)
(pétrole m) brut m

cruel ['kruəl] adj cruel(le); **cruelty**
n cruauté f

cruise [kru:z] n croisière f ▷ vi (ship)
croiser; (car) rouler; (aircraft) voler

crumb [krʌm] n miette f

crumble ['krʌmbl] vt émietter ▷ vi
(plaster etc) s'effriter; (land, earth)
s'ébouler; (building) s'écrouler,
crouler; (fig) s'effondrer

crumpet ['krʌmpɪt] n petite crêpe (épaisse)

crumple ['krʌmpl] vt froisser, friper

crunch [krʌntʃ] vt croquer; (underfoot) faire craquer, écraser; faire crisser ▷ n (fig) instant m or moment m critique, moment de vérité; **crunchy** adj croquant(e), croustillant(e)

crush [krʌʃ] n (crowd) foule f, cohue f; (love): **to have a ~ on sb** avoir le béguin pour qn; (drink): **lemon ~** citron pressé ▷ vt écraser; (crumple) froisser; (grind, break up: garlic, ice) piler; (: grapes) presser; (hopes) anéantir

crust [krʌst] n croûte f; **crusty** adj (bread) croustillant(e); (inf: person) revêche, bourru(e)

crutch [krʌtʃ] n béquille f; (of garment) entrejambe m; (Anat) entrecuisse m

cry [kraɪ] vi pleurer; (shout: also: ~ out) crier ▷ n cri m; **cry out** vi (call out, shout) pousser un cri ▷ vt crier

crystal ['krɪstl] n cristal m

cub [kʌb] n petit m (d'un animal); (also: ~ scout) louveteau m

Cuba ['kjuːbə] n Cuba m

cube [kjuːb] n cube m ▷ vt (Math) élever au cube

cubicle ['kjuːbɪkl] n (in hospital) box m; (at pool) cabine f

cuckoo ['kuku] n coucou m

cucumber ['kjuːkʌmbər] n concombre m

cuddle ['kʌdl] vt câliner, caresser ▷ vi se blottir l'un contre l'autre

cue [kjuː] n queue f de billard; (Theat etc) signal m

cuff [kʌf] n (BRIT: of shirt, coat etc) poignet m, manchette f; (US: on trousers) revers m; (blow) gifle f; **off the ~** adv à l'improviste; **cufflinks** n boutons m de manchette

cuisine [kwɪ'ziːn] n cuisine f

cul-de-sac ['kʌldəsæk] n cul-de-sac m, impasse f

cull [kʌl] vt sélectionner ▷ n (of animals) abattage sélectif

culminate ['kʌlmɪneɪt] vi: **to ~ in** finir or se terminer par; (lead to) mener à

culprit ['kʌlprɪt] n coupable m/f

cult [kʌlt] n culte m

cultivate ['kʌltɪveɪt] vt cultiver

cultural ['kʌltʃərəl] adj culturel(le)

culture ['kʌltʃər] n culture f

cumin ['kʌmɪn] n (spice) cumin m

cunning ['kʌnɪŋ] n ruse f, astuce f ▷ adj rusé(e), malin(-igne); (clever: device, idea) astucieux(-euse)

cup [kʌp] n tasse f; (prize, event) coupe f; (of bra) bonnet m

cupboard ['kʌbəd] n placard m

cup final n (BRIT Football) finale f de la coupe

curator [kjuə'reɪtər] n conservateur m (d'un musée etc)

curb [kəːb] vt refréner, mettre un frein à ▷ n (fig) frein m; (US) bord m du trottoir

curdle ['kəːdl] vi (se) cailler

cure [kjuər] vt guérir; (Culin: salt) saler; (: smoke) fumer; (: dry) sécher ▷ n remède m

curfew ['kəːfjuː] n couvre-feu m

curiosity [kjuərɪ'ɒsɪtɪ] n curiosité f

curious ['kjuərɪəs] adj curieux(-euse); **I'm ~ about him** il m'intrigue

curl [kəːl] n boucle f (de cheveux) ▷ vt, vi boucler; (tightly) friser; **curl up** vi s'enrouler; (person) se pelotonner; **curler** n bigoudi m, rouleau m; **curly** adj bouclé(e); (tightly curled) frisé(e)

currant ['kʌrnt] n raisin m de Corinthe, raisin sec; (fruit) groseille f

currency ['kʌrnsɪ] n monnaie f; **to gain ~** (fig) s'accréditer

current ['kʌrnt] n courant m ▷ adj (common) courant(e); (tendency, price, event) actuel(le); **current account** n (BRIT) compte courant; **current affairs** npl (questions fpl d')actualité f; **currently** adv actuellement

curriculum (*pl* **curriculums** *or* **curricula**) [kə'rɪkjʊləm, -lə] *n* programme *m* d'études; **curriculum vitae** [-'viːtaɪ] *n* curriculum vitae (CV) *m*

curry ['kʌrɪ] *n* curry *m* ▷ *vt*: **to ~ favour with** chercher à gagner la faveur *or* à s'attirer les bonnes grâces de; **curry powder** *n* poudre *f* de curry

curse [kəːs] *vi* jurer, blasphémer ▷ *vt* maudire ▷ *n* (*spell*) malédiction *f*; (*problem, scourge*) fléau *m*; (*swearword*) juron *m*

cursor ['kəːsər] *n* (*Comput*) curseur *m*

curt [kəːt] *adj* brusque, sec (sèche)

curtain ['kəːtn] *n* rideau *m*

curve [kəːv] *n* courbe *f*; (*in the road*) tournant *m*, virage *m* ▷ *vi* se courber; (*road*) faire une courbe; **curved** *adj* courbe

cushion ['kʊʃən] *n* coussin *m* ▷ *vt* (*fall, shock*) amortir

custard ['kʌstəd] *n* (*for pouring*) crème anglaise

custody ['kʌstədɪ] *n* (*of child*) garde *f*; (*for offenders*): **to take sb into ~** placer qn en détention préventive

custom ['kʌstəm] *n* coutume *f*, usage *m*; (*Comm*) clientèle *f*

customer ['kʌstəmər] *n* client(e)

customized ['kʌstəmaɪzd] *adj* personnalisé(e); (*car etc*) construit(e) sur commande

customs ['kʌstəmz] *npl* douane *f*; **customs officer** *n* douanier *m*

cut [kʌt] (*pt, pp* **cut**) *vt* couper; (*meat*) découper; (*reduce*) réduire ▷ *vi* couper ▷ *n* (*gen*) coupure *f*; (*of clothes*) coupe *f*; (*in salary etc*) réduction *f*; (*of meat*) morceau *m*; **to ~ a tooth** percer une dent; **to ~ one's finger** se couper le doigt; **to get one's hair ~** se faire couper les cheveux; **I've ~ myself** je me suis coupé; **cut back** *vt* (*plants*) tailler; (*production, expenditure*) réduire; **cut down** *vt* (*tree*) abattre; (*reduce*) réduire; **cut off** *vt* couper; (*fig*) isoler; **cut out** *vt* (*picture etc*)

découper; (*remove*) supprimer; **cut up** *vt* découper; **cutback** *n* réduction *f*

cute [kjuːt] *adj* mignon(ne), adorable

cutlery ['kʌtlərɪ] *n* couverts *mpl*

cutlet ['kʌtlɪt] *n* côtelette *f*

cut-price ['kʌt'praɪs], (*US*) **cut-rate** ['kʌt'reɪt] *adj* au rabais, à prix réduit

cutting ['kʌtɪŋ] *adj* (*fig*) cinglant(e) ▷ *n* (*BRIT: from newspaper*) coupure *f* (de journal); (*from plant*) bouture *f*

CV *n abbr* = **curriculum vitae**

cyberbullying ['saɪbəbulɪɪŋ] *n* harcèlement *m* virtuel

cyberspace ['saɪbəspeɪs] *n* cyberespace *m*

cycle ['saɪkl] *n* cycle *m*; (*bicycle*) bicyclette *f*, vélo *m* ▷ *vi* faire de la bicyclette; **cycle hire** *n* location *f* de vélos; **cycle lane, cycle path** *n* piste *f* cyclable; **cycling** *n* cyclisme *m*; **cyclist** *n* cycliste *m/f*

cyclone ['saɪkləʊn] *n* cyclone *m*

cylinder ['sɪlɪndər] *n* cylindre *m*

cymbals ['sɪmblz] *npl* cymbales *fpl*

cynical ['sɪnɪkl] *adj* cynique

Cypriot ['sɪprɪət] *adj* cypriote, chypriote ▷ *n* Cypriote *m/f*, Chypriote *m/f*

Cyprus ['saɪprəs] *n* Chypre *f*

cyst [sɪst] *n* kyste *m*; **cystitis** [sɪs'taɪtɪs] *n* cystite *f*

czar [zɑːr] *n* tsar *m*

Czech [tʃɛk] *adj* tchèque ▷ *n* Tchèque *m/f*; (*Ling*) tchèque *m*; **Czech Republic** *n*: **the Czech Republic** la République tchèque

d

D [diː] n (Mus) ré m
dab [dæb] vt (eyes, wound) tamponner; (paint, cream) appliquer (par petites touches or rapidement)
dad, daddy [dæd, 'dædɪ] n papa m
daffodil ['dæfədɪl] n jonquille f
daft [dɑːft] adj (inf) idiot(e), stupide
dagger ['dægəʳ] n poignard m
daily ['deɪlɪ] adj quotidien(ne), journalier(-ière) ▷ adv tous les jours
dairy ['dɛərɪ] n (shop) crémerie f, laiterie f; (on farm) laiterie f; **dairy produce** n produits laitiers
daisy ['deɪzɪ] n pâquerette f
dam [dæm] n (wall) barrage m; (water) réservoir m, lac m de retenue ▷ vt endiguer
damage ['dæmɪdʒ] n dégâts mpl, dommages mpl; (fig) tort m ▷ vt endommager, abîmer; (fig) faire du tort à; **damages** npl (Law) dommages-intérêts mpl
damn [dæm] vt condamner; (curse) maudire ▷ n (inf): **I don't give a ~** je

m'en fous ▷ adj (inf: also: **~ed**): **this ~ ...** ce sacré or foutu ...; **~ (it)!** zut!
damp [dæmp] adj humide ▷ n humidité f ▷ vt (also: **~en**: cloth, rag) humecter; (: enthusiasm etc) refroidir
dance [dɑːns] n danse f; (ball) bal m ▷ vi danser; **dance floor** n piste f de danse; **dancer** n danseur(-euse); **dancing** n danse f
dandelion ['dændɪlaɪən] n pissenlit m
dandruff ['dændrəf] n pellicules fpl
D & T n abbr (BRIT Scol) = **design and technology**
Dane [deɪn] n Danois(e)
danger ['deɪndʒəʳ] n danger m; **~!** (on sign) danger!; **in ~** en danger; **he was in ~ of falling** il risquait de tomber; **dangerous** adj dangereux(-euse)
dangle ['dæŋgl] vt balancer ▷ vi pendre, se balancer
Danish ['deɪnɪʃ] adj danois(e) ▷ n (Ling) danois m
dare [dɛəʳ] vt: **to ~ sb to do** défier qn or mettre qn au défi de faire ▷ vi: **to ~ (to) do sth** oser faire qch; **I ~ say he'll turn up** il est probable qu'il viendra; **daring** adj hardi(e), audacieux(-euse) ▷ n audace f, hardiesse f
dark [dɑːk] adj (night, room) obscur(e), sombre; (colour, complexion) foncé(e), sombre ▷ n: **in the ~** dans le noir; **to be in the ~ about** (fig) ignorer tout de; **after ~** après la tombée de la nuit; **darken** vt obscurcir, assombrir ▷ vi s'obscurcir, s'assombrir; **darkness** n obscurité f; **darkroom** n chambre noire
darling ['dɑːlɪŋ] adj, n chéri(e)
dart [dɑːt] n fléchette f; (in sewing) pince f ▷ vi: **to ~ towards** se précipiter or s'élancer vers; **dartboard** n cible f (de jeu de fléchettes); **darts** n jeu m de fléchettes
dash [dæʃ] n (sign) tiret m; (small quantity) goutte f, larme f ▷ vt (throw)

jeter or lancer violemment; (*hopes*) anéantir ▷ vi: **to ~ towards** se précipiter or se ruer vers
dashboard ['dæʃbɔːd] *n* (*Aut*) tableau *m* de bord
data ['deɪtə] *npl* données *fpl*; **database** *n* base *f* de données; **data processing** *n* traitement *m* des données
date [deɪt] *n* date *f*; (*with sb*) rendez-vous *m*; (*fruit*) datte *f* ▷ vt dater; (*person*) sortir avec; **~ of birth** date de naissance; **to ~** *adv* à ce jour; **out of ~** périmé(e); **up to ~** à la page, mis(e) à jour, moderne; **dated** *adj* démodé(e)
daughter ['dɔːtər] *n* fille *f*; **daughter-in-law** *n* belle-fille *f*, bru *f*
daunting ['dɔːntɪŋ] *adj* décourageant(e), intimidant(e)
dawn [dɔːn] *n* aube *f*, aurore *f* ▷ vi (*day*) se lever, poindre; **it ~ed on him that ...** il lui vint à l'esprit que ...
day [deɪ] *n* jour *m*; (*as duration*) journée *f*; (*period of time, age*) époque *f*, temps *m*; **the ~ before** la veille, le jour précédent; **the ~ after, the following ~** le lendemain, le jour suivant; **the ~ before yesterday** avant-hier; **the ~ after tomorrow** après-demain; **by ~** de jour; **day-care centre** ['deɪkɛə-] *n* (*for elderly etc*) centre *m* d'accueil de jour; (*for children*) garderie *f*; **daydream** *vi* rêver (tout éveillé); **daylight** *n* (lumière *f* du) jour *m*; **day return** *n* (*BRIT*) billet *m* d'aller-retour (*valable pour la journée*); **daytime** *n* jour *m*, journée *f*; **day-to-day** *adj* (*routine, expenses*) journalier(-ière); **day trip** *n* excursion *f* (d'une journée)
dazed [deɪzd] *adj* abruti(e)
dazzle ['dæzl] *vt* éblouir, aveugler; **dazzling** *adj* (*light*) aveuglant(e), éblouissant(e); (*fig*) éblouissant(e)
DC *abbr* (*Elec*) = **direct current**
dead [dɛd] *adj* mort(e); (*numb*) engourdi(e), insensible; (*battery*) à plat ▷ *adv* (*completely*) absolument,

complètement; (*exactly*) juste; **he was shot ~** il a été tué d'un coup de revolver; **~ tired** éreinté(e), complètement fourbu(e); **to stop ~** s'arrêter pile or net; **the line is ~** (*Tel*) la ligne est coupée; **dead end** *n* impasse *f*; **deadline** *n* date *f* or heure *f* limite; **deadly** *adj* mortel(le); (*weapon*) meurtrier(-ière); **Dead Sea** *n*: **the Dead Sea** la mer Morte
deaf [dɛf] *adj* sourd(e); **deafen** *vt* rendre sourd(e); **deafening** *adj* assourdissant(e)
deal [diːl] *n* affaire *f*, marché *m* ▷ vt (*pt, pp* **dealt**) (*blow*) porter; (*cards*) donner, distribuer; **a great ~ of** beaucoup de; **deal with** *vt fus* (*handle*) s'occuper or se charger de; (*be about*) traiter de; **dealer** *n* (*Comm*) marchand *m*; (*Cards*) donneur *m*; **dealings** *npl* (*in goods, shares*) opérations *fpl*, transactions *fpl*; (*relations*) relations *fpl*, rapports *mpl*
dealt [dɛlt] *pt, pp of* **deal**
dean [diːn] *n* (*Rel, BRIT Scol*) doyen *m*; (*US Scol*) conseiller principal (conseillère principale) d'éducation
dear [dɪər] *adj* cher (chère); (*expensive*) cher, coûteux(-euse) ▷ *n*: **my ~** mon cher (ma chère) ▷ *excl*: **~ me!** mon Dieu!; **D~ Sir/Madam** (*in letter*) Monsieur/Madame; **D~ Mr/Mrs X** Cher Monsieur/Chère Madame X; **dearly** *adv* (*love*) tendrement; (*pay*) cher
death [dɛθ] *n* mort *f*; (*Admin*) décès *m*; **death penalty** *n* peine *f* de mort; **death sentence** *n* condamnation *f* à mort
debate [dɪ'beɪt] *n* discussion *f*, débat *m* ▷ vt discuter, débattre
debit ['dɛbɪt] *n* débit *m* ▷ vt: **to ~ a sum to sb** or **to sb's account** porter une somme au débit de qn, débiter qn d'une somme; **debit card** *n* carte *f* de paiement
debris ['dɛbriː] *n* débris *mpl*, décombres *mpl*

debt [dɛt] n dette f; **to be in ~** avoir des dettes, être endetté(e)

debug [diː'bʌg] vt (Comput) déboguer

debut ['deɪbjuː] n début(s) m(pl)

Dec. abbr (= December) déc

decade ['dɛkeɪd] n décennie f, décade f

decaffeinated [dɪ'kæfɪneɪtɪd] adj décaféiné(e)

decay [dɪ'keɪ] n (of food, wood etc) décomposition f, pourriture f; (of building) délabrement m; (also: **tooth ~**) carie f (dentaire) ▷ vi (rot) se décomposer, pourrir; (teeth) se carier

deceased [dɪ'siːst] n: **the ~** le (la) défunt(e)

deceit [dɪ'siːt] n tromperie f, supercherie f; **deceive** [dɪ'siːv] vt tromper

December [dɪ'sɛmbəʳ] n décembre m

decency ['diːsənsɪ] n décence f

decent ['diːsənt] adj (proper) décent(e), convenable

deception [dɪ'sɛpʃən] n tromperie f

deceptive [dɪ'sɛptɪv] adj trompeur(-euse)

decide [dɪ'saɪd] vt (subj: person) décider; (question, argument) trancher, régler ▷ vi se décider, décider; **to ~ to do/that** décider de faire/que; **to ~ on** décider, se décider pour

decimal ['dɛsɪməl] adj décimal(e) ▷ n décimale f

decision [dɪ'sɪʒən] n décision f

decisive [dɪ'saɪsɪv] adj décisif(-ive); (manner, person) décidé(e), catégorique

deck [dɛk] n (Naut) pont m; (of cards) jeu m; (record deck) platine f; (of bus): **top ~** impériale f; **deckchair** n chaise longue

declaration [dɛklə'reɪʃən] n déclaration f

declare [dɪ'klɛəʳ] vt déclarer

decline [dɪ'klaɪn] n (decay) déclin m; (lessening) baisse f ▷ vt refuser, décliner ▷ vi décliner; (business) baisser

decorate ['dɛkəreɪt] vt (adorn, give a medal to) décorer; (paint and paper) peindre et tapisser; **decoration** [dɛkə'reɪʃən] n (medal etc, adornment) décoration f; **decorator** n peintre m en bâtiment

decrease n ['diːkriːs] diminution f ▷ vt, vi [diː'kriːs] diminuer

decree [dɪ'kriː] n (Pol, Rel) décret m; (Law) arrêt m, jugement m

dedicate ['dɛdɪkeɪt] vt consacrer; (book etc) dédier; **dedicated** adj (person) dévoué(e); (Comput) spécialisé(e), dédié(e); **dedicated word processor** station f de traitement de texte; **dedication** [dɛdɪ'keɪʃən] n (devotion) dévouement m; (in book) dédicace f

deduce [dɪ'djuːs] vt déduire, conclure

deduct [dɪ'dʌkt] vt: **to ~ sth (from)** déduire qch (de), retrancher qch (de); **deduction** [dɪ'dʌkʃən] n (deducting, deducing) déduction f; (from wage etc) prélèvement m, retenue f

deed [diːd] n action f, acte m; (Law) acte notarié, contrat m

deem [diːm] vt (formal) juger, estimer

deep [diːp] adj profond(e); (voice) grave ▷ adv: **spectators stood 20 ~** il y avait 20 rangs de spectateurs; **4 metres ~** de 4 mètres de profondeur; **how ~ is the water?** l'eau a quelle profondeur?; **deep-fry** vt faire frire (dans une friteuse); **deeply** adv profondément; (regret, interested) vivement

deer [dɪəʳ] n (pl inv): **(red) ~** cerf m; **(fallow) ~** daim m; **(roe) ~** chevreuil m

default [dɪ'fɔːlt] n (Comput: also: **~ value**) valeur f par défaut; **by ~** (Law) par défaut, par contumace; (Sport) par forfait

defeat [dɪ'fiːt] n défaite f ▷ vt (team, opponents) battre

defect n ['diːfɛkt] défaut m ▷ vi [dɪ'fɛkt]: **to ~ to the enemy/the West** passer à l'ennemi/l'Ouest;

defective [dɪ'fɛktɪv] *adj* défectueux(-euse)

defence, *(us)* **defense** [dɪ'fɛns] *n* défense *f*

defend [dɪ'fɛnd] *vt* défendre; **defendant** *n* défendeur(-deresse); *(in criminal case)* accusé(e), prévenu(e); **defender** *n* défenseur *m*

defense [dɪ'fɛns] *n (us)* = **defence**

defensive [dɪ'fɛnsɪv] *adj* défensif(-ive) ▷ *n*: **on the ~** sur la défensive

defer [dɪ'fəː'] *vt (postpone)* différer, ajourner

defiance [dɪ'faɪəns] *n* défi *m*; **in ~ of** au mépris de; **defiant** [dɪ'faɪənt] *adj* provocant(e), de défi; *(person)* rebelle, intraitable

deficiency [dɪ'fɪʃənsɪ] *n (lack)* insuffisance *f*; (: *Med)* carence *f*; *(flaw)* faiblesse *f*; **deficient** [dɪ'fɪʃənt] *adj (inadequate)* insuffisant(e); **to be deficient in** manquer de

deficit ['dɛfɪsɪt] *n* déficit *m*

define [dɪ'faɪn] *vt* définir

definite ['dɛfɪnɪt] *adj (fixed)* défini(e), (bien) déterminé(e); *(clear, obvious)* net(te), manifeste; *(certain)* sûr(e); **he was ~ about it** il a été catégorique; **definitely** *adv* sans aucun doute

definition [dɛfɪ'nɪʃən] *n* définition *f*; *(clearness)* netteté *f*

deflate [diː'fleɪt] *vt* dégonfler

deflect [dɪ'flɛkt] *vt* détourner, faire dévier

defraud [dɪ'frɔːd] *vt*: **to ~ sb of sth** escroquer qch à qn

defriend [diː'frɛnd] *vt (Internet)* supprimer de sa liste d'amis

defrost [diː'frɔst] *vt (fridge)* dégivrer; *(frozen food)* décongeler

defuse [diː'fjuːz] *vt* désamorcer

defy [dɪ'faɪ] *vt* défier; *(efforts etc)* résister à; **it defies description** cela défie toute description

degree [dɪ'griː] *n* degré *m*; *(Scol)* diplôme *m* (universitaire); **a (first) ~ in maths** *(BRIT)* une licence en maths; **by ~s** *(gradually)* par degrés;

to some ~ jusqu'à un certain point, dans une certaine mesure

dehydrated [diːhaɪ'dreɪtɪd] *adj* déshydraté(e); *(milk, eggs)* en poudre

de-icer ['diː'aɪsə'] *n* dégivreur *m*

delay [dɪ'leɪ] *vt* retarder; *(payment)* différer ▷ *vi* s'attarder ▷ *n* délai *m*, retard *m*; **to be ~ed** être en retard

delegate *n* ['dɛlɪgɪt] délégué(e) ▷ *vt* ['dɛlɪgeɪt] déléguer

delete [dɪ'liːt] *vt* rayer, supprimer; *(Comput)* effacer

deli ['dɛlɪ] *n* épicerie fine

deliberate *adj* [dɪ'lɪbərɪt] *(intentional)* délibéré(e); *(slow)* mesuré(e) ▷ *vi* [dɪ'lɪbəreɪt] délibérer, réfléchir; **deliberately** *adv (on purpose)* exprès, délibérément

delicacy ['dɛlɪkəsɪ] *n* délicatesse *f*; *(choice food)* mets fin *or* délicat, friandise *f*

delicate ['dɛlɪkɪt] *adj* délicat(e)

delicatessen [dɛlɪkə'tɛsn] *n* épicerie fine

delicious [dɪ'lɪʃəs] *adj* délicieux(-euse)

delight [dɪ'laɪt] *n* (grande) joie, grand plaisir ▷ *vt* enchanter; **she's a ~ to work with** c'est un plaisir de travailler avec elle; **to take ~ in** prendre grand plaisir à; **delighted** *adj*: **delighted (at *or* with sth)** ravi(e) (de qch); **to be delighted to do sth/that** être enchanté(e) *or* ravi(e) de faire qch/que; **delightful** *adj (person)* adorable; *(meal, evening)* merveilleux(-euse)

delinquent [dɪ'lɪŋkwənt] *adj, n* délinquant(e)

deliver [dɪ'lɪvə'] *vt (mail)* distribuer; *(goods)* livrer; *(message)* remettre; *(speech)* prononcer; *(Med: baby)* mettre au monde; **delivery** *n (of mail)* distribution *f*; *(of goods)* livraison *f*; *(of speaker)* élocution *f*; *(Med)* accouchement *m*; **to take delivery of** prendre livraison de

delusion [dɪ'luːʒən] *n* illusion *f*

de luxe [də'lʌks] *adj* de luxe

delve [dɛlv] *vi*: **to ~ into** fouiller dans

demand [dɪ'mɑːnd] vt réclamer, exiger ▷ n exigence f; (claim) revendication f; (Econ) demande f; **in ~** demandé(e), recherché(e); **on ~** sur demande; **demanding** adj (person) exigeant(e); (work) astreignant(e)

> Be careful not to translate to demand by the French word demander.

demise [dɪ'maɪz] n décès m

demo ['dɛməu] n abbr (inf: = demonstration) (protest) manif f; (Comput) démonstration f

democracy [dɪ'mɔkrəsɪ] n démocratie f; **democrat** ['dɛməkræt] n démocrate m/f; **democratic** [dɛmə'krætɪk] adj démocratique

demolish [dɪ'mɔlɪʃ] vt démolir

demolition [dɛmə'lɪʃən] n démolition f

demon ['diːmən] n démon m

demonstrate ['dɛmənstreɪt] vt démontrer, prouver; (show) faire une démonstration de ▷ vi: **to ~ (for/against)** manifester (en faveur de/contre); **demonstration** [dɛmən'streɪʃən] n démonstration f; (Pol etc) manifestation f; **demonstrator** n (Pol etc) manifestant(e)

demote [dɪ'məut] vt rétrograder

den [dɛn] n (of lion) tanière f; (room) repaire m

denial [dɪ'naɪəl] n (of accusation) démenti m; (of rights, guilt, truth) dénégation f

denim ['dɛnɪm] n jean m; **denims** npl (blue-)jeans mpl

Denmark ['dɛnmɑːk] n Danemark m

denomination [dɪnɔmɪ'neɪʃən] n (money) valeur f; (Rel) confession f

denounce [dɪ'nauns] vt dénoncer

dense [dɛns] adj dense; (inf: stupid) obtus(e)

density ['dɛnsɪtɪ] n densité f

dent [dɛnt] n bosse f ▷ vt (also: **make a ~ in**) cabosser

dental ['dɛntl] adj dentaire; **dental floss** [-flɔs] n fil m dentaire; **dental surgery** n cabinet m de dentiste

dentist ['dɛntɪst] n dentiste m/f

dentures ['dɛntʃəz] npl dentier msg

deny [dɪ'naɪ] vt nier; (refuse) refuser

deodorant [diː'əudərənt] n déodorant m

depart [dɪ'pɑːt] vi partir; **to ~ from** (fig: differ from) s'écarter de

department [dɪ'pɑːtmənt] n (Comm) rayon m; (Scol) section f; (Pol) ministère m, département m; **department store** n grand magasin

departure [dɪ'pɑːtʃə] n départ m; **a new ~** une nouvelle voie; **departure lounge** n salle f de départ

depend [dɪ'pɛnd] vi: **to ~ (up)on** dépendre de; (rely on) compter sur; **it ~s** cela dépend; **~ing on the result ...** selon le résultat ...; **dependant** n personne f à charge; **dependent** adj: **to be dependent (on)** dépendre (de) ▷ n = **dependant**

depict [dɪ'pɪkt] vt (in picture) représenter; (in words) (dé)peindre, décrire

deport [dɪ'pɔːt] vt déporter, expulser

deposit [dɪ'pɔzɪt] n (Chem, Comm, Geo) dépôt m; (of ore, oil) gisement m; (part payment) arrhes fpl, acompte m; (on bottle etc) consigne f; (for hired goods etc) cautionnement m, garantie f ▷ vt déposer; **deposit account** n compte m sur livret

depot ['dɛpəu] n dépôt m; (US Rail) gare f

depreciate [dɪ'priːʃɪeɪt] vi se déprécier, se dévaloriser

depress [dɪ'prɛs] vt déprimer; (press down) appuyer sur, abaisser; (wages etc) faire baisser; **depressed** adj (person) déprimé(e); (area) en déclin, touché(e) par le sous-emploi; **depressing** adj déprimant(e); **depression** [dɪ'prɛʃən] n dépression f

deprive [dɪ'praɪv] vt: **to ~ sb of** priver qn de; **deprived** adj déshérité(e)

dept. *abbr* (= *department*) dép, dépt
depth [dɛpθ] *n* profondeur *f*; **to be in the ~s of despair** être au plus profond du désespoir; **to be out of one's ~** (BRIT: *swimmer*) ne plus avoir pied; (*fig*) être dépassé(e), nager
deputy ['dɛpjʊtɪ] *n* (*second in command*) adjoint(e); (*Pol*) député *m*; (US: *also*: **~ sheriff**) shérif adjoint ▷ *adj*: **~ head** (*Scol*) directeur(-trice) adjoint(e), sous-directeur(-trice)
derail [dɪ'reɪl] *vt*: **to be ~ed** dérailler
derelict ['dɛrɪlɪkt] *adj* abandonné(e), à l'abandon
derive [dɪ'raɪv] *vt*: **to ~ sth from** tirer qch de; trouver qch dans ▷ *vi*: **to ~ from** provenir de, dériver de
descend [dɪ'sɛnd] *vt, vi* descendre; **to ~ from** descendre de, être issu(e) de; **to ~ to** s'abaisser à; **descendant** *n* descendant(e); **descent** *n* descente *f*; (*origin*) origine *f*
describe [dɪs'kraɪb] *vt* décrire; **description** [dɪs'krɪpʃən] *n* description *f*; (*sort*) sorte *f*, espèce *f*
desert *n* ['dɛzət] désert *m* ▷ *vt* [dɪ'zəːt] déserter, abandonner ▷ *vi* (*Mil*) déserter; **deserted** [dɪ'zəːtɪd] *adj* désert(e)
deserve [dɪ'zəːv] *vt* mériter
design [dɪ'zaɪn] *n* (*sketch*) plan *m*, dessin *m*; (*layout, shape*) conception *f*, ligne *f*; (*pattern*) dessin, motif(s) *m(pl)*; (*of dress, car*) modèle *m*; (*art*) design *m*, stylisme *m*; (*intention*) dessein *m* ▷ *vt* dessiner; (*plan*) concevoir; **design and technology** *n* (BRIT Scol) technologie *f*
designate *vt* ['dɛzɪgneɪt] désigner ▷ *adj* ['dɛzɪgnɪt] désigné(e)
designer [dɪ'zaɪnəʳ] *n* (*Archit, Art*) dessinateur(-trice); (*Industry*) concepteur *m*, designer *m*; (*Fashion*) styliste *m/f*
desirable [dɪ'zaɪərəbl] *adj* (*property, location, purchase*) attrayant(e)
desire [dɪ'zaɪəʳ] *n* désir *m* ▷ *vt* désirer, vouloir

desk [dɛsk] *n* (*in office*) bureau *m*; (*for pupil*) pupitre *m*; (BRIT: *in shop, restaurant*) caisse *f*; (*in hotel, at airport*) réception *f*; **desktop** ['dɛsktɒp] *n* bureau *m*; **desktop publishing** *n* publication assistée par ordinateur, PAO *f*
despair [dɪs'pɛəʳ] *n* désespoir *m* ▷ *vi*: **to ~ of** désespérer de
despatch [dɪs'pætʃ] *n, vt* = **dispatch**
desperate ['dɛspərɪt] *adj* désespéré(e); (*fugitive*) prêt(e) à tout; **to be ~ for sth/to do sth** avoir désespérément besoin de qch/de faire qch; **desperately** *adv* désespérément; (*very*) terriblement, extrêmement; **desperation** [dɛspə'reɪʃən] *n* désespoir *m*; **in (sheer) desperation** en désespoir de cause
despise [dɪs'paɪz] *vt* mépriser
despite [dɪs'paɪt] *prep* malgré, en dépit de
dessert [dɪ'zəːt] *n* dessert *m*; **dessertspoon** *n* cuiller *f* à dessert
destination [dɛstɪ'neɪʃən] *n* destination *f*
destined ['dɛstɪnd] *adj*: **~ for London** à destination de Londres
destiny ['dɛstɪnɪ] *n* destinée *f*, destin *m*
destroy [dɪs'trɔɪ] *vt* détruire; (*injured horse*) abattre; (*dog*) faire piquer
destruction [dɪs'trʌkʃən] *n* destruction *f*
destructive [dɪs'trʌktɪv] *adj* destructeur(-trice)
detach [dɪ'tætʃ] *vt* détacher; **detached** *adj* (*attitude*) détaché(e); **detached house** *n* pavillon *m*, maison(nette) (individuelle)
detail ['diːteɪl] *n* détail *m* ▷ *vt* raconter en détail, énumérer; **in ~** en détail; **detailed** *adj* détaillé(e)
detain [dɪ'teɪn] *vt* retenir; (*in captivity*) détenir
detect [dɪ'tɛkt] *vt* déceler, percevoir; (*Med, Police*) dépister; (*Mil, Radar, Tech*) détecter; **detection** [dɪ'tɛkʃən] *n*

découverte f; **detective** n policier m; **private detective** détective privé; **detective story** n roman policier

detention [dɪ'tɛnʃən] n détention f; (Scol) retenue f, consigne f

deter [dɪ'tə:ʳ] vt dissuader

detergent [dɪ'tə:dʒənt] n détersif m, détergent m

deteriorate [dɪ'tɪərɪəreɪt] vi se détériorer, se dégrader

determination [dɪtə:mɪ'neɪʃən] n détermination f

determine [dɪ'tə:mɪn] vt déterminer; **to ~ to do** résoudre de faire, se déterminer à faire; **determined** adj (person) déterminé(e), décidé(e); **determined to do** bien décidé à faire

deterrent [dɪ'tɛrənt] n effet m de dissuasion; force f de dissuasion

detest [dɪ'tɛst] vt détester, avoir horreur de

detour ['di:tuəʳ] n détour m; (us Aut: diversion) déviation f

detox ['di:tɔks] n détox f

detract [dɪ'trækt] vt: **to ~ from** (quality, pleasure) diminuer; (reputation) porter atteinte à

detrimental [dɛtrɪ'mɛntl] adj: **~ to** préjudiciable or nuisible à

devastating ['dɛvəsteɪtɪŋ] adj dévastateur(-trice); (news) accablant(e)

develop [dɪ'vɛləp] vt (gen) développer; (disease) commencer à souffrir de; (resources) mettre en valeur, exploiter; (land) aménager ▷ vi se développer; (situation, disease: evolve) évoluer; (facts, symptoms: appear) se manifester, se produire; **can you ~ this film?** pouvez-vous développer cette pellicule? **developing country** n pays m en voie de développement; **development** n développement m; (of land) exploitation f; (new fact, event) rebondissement m, fait(s) nouveau(x)

device [dɪ'vaɪs] n (apparatus) appareil m, dispositif m

devil ['dɛvl] n diable m; démon m

devious ['di:vɪəs] adj (person) sournois(e), dissimulé(e)

devise [dɪ'vaɪz] vt imaginer, concevoir

devote [dɪ'vəut] vt: **to ~ sth to** consacrer qch à; **devoted** adj dévoué(e); **to be devoted to** être dévoué(e) or très attaché(e) à; (book etc) être consacré(e) à; **devotion** n dévouement m, attachement m; (Rel) dévotion f, piété f

devour [dɪ'vauəʳ] vt dévorer

devout [dɪ'vaut] adj pieux(-euse)

dew [dju:] n rosée f

diabetes [daɪə'bi:ti:z] n diabète m

diabetic [daɪə'bɛtɪk] n diabétique m/f ▷ adj (person) diabétique

diagnose [daɪəg'nəuz] vt diagnostiquer

diagnosis (pl **diagnoses**) [daɪəg'nəusɪs, -si:z] n diagnostic m

diagonal [daɪ'ægənl] adj diagonal(e) ▷ n diagonale f

diagram ['daɪəgræm] n diagramme m, schéma m

dial ['daɪəl] n cadran m ▷ vt (number) faire, composer

dialect ['daɪəlɛkt] n dialecte m

dialling code ['daɪəlɪŋ-], (us) **dial code** n indicatif m (téléphonique); **what's the ~ for Paris?** quel est l'indicatif de Paris?

dialling tone ['daɪəlɪŋ-], (us) **dial tone** n tonalité f

dialogue, (us) **dialog** ['daɪəlɔg] n dialogue m

diameter [daɪ'æmɪtəʳ] n diamètre m

diamond ['daɪəmənd] n diamant m; (shape) losange m; **diamonds** npl (Cards) carreau m

diaper ['daɪəpəʳ] n (us) couche f

diarrhoea, (us) **diarrhea** [daɪə'ri:ə] n diarrhée f

diary ['daɪərɪ] n (daily account) journal m; (book) agenda m

dice [daɪs] n (pl inv) dé m ▷ vt (Culin) couper en dés or en cubes

d

dictate vt [dɪk'teɪt] dicter; **dictation** [dɪk'teɪʃən] n dictée f

dictator [dɪk'teɪtə^r] n dictateur m

dictionary ['dɪkʃənrɪ] n dictionnaire m

did [dɪd] pt of **do**

didn't [dɪdnt] = **did not**

die [daɪ] vi mourir; **to be dying for sth** avoir une envie folle de qch; **to be dying to do sth** mourir d'envie de faire qch; **die down** vi se calmer, s'apaiser; **die out** vi disparaître, s'éteindre

diesel ['diːzl] n (vehicle) diesel m; (also: **~ oil**) carburant m diesel, gas-oil m

diet ['daɪət] n alimentation f; (restricted food) régime m ▷ vi (also: **be on a ~**) suivre un régime

differ ['dɪfə^r] vi: **to ~ from sth** (be different) être différent(e) de qch, différer de qch; **to ~ from sb over sth** ne pas être d'accord avec qn au sujet de qch; **difference** n différence f; (quarrel) différend m, désaccord m; **different** adj différent(e); **differentiate** [dɪfə'renʃɪeɪt] vi: **to differentiate between** faire une différence entre; **differently** adv différemment

difficult ['dɪfɪkəlt] adj difficile; **difficulty** n difficulté f

dig [dɪg] vt (pt, pp **dug**) (hole) creuser; (garden) bêcher ▷ n (prod) coup m de coude; (fig: remark) coup de griffe or de patte; (Archaeology) fouille f; **to ~ one's nails into** enfoncer ses ongles dans; **dig up** vt déterrer

digest vt [daɪ'dʒest] digérer ▷ n ['daɪdʒest] sommaire m, résumé m; **digestion** [dɪ'dʒestʃən] n digestion f

digit ['dɪdʒɪt] n (number) chiffre m (de 0 à 9); (finger) doigt m; **digital** adj (system, recording, radio) numérique, digital(e); (watch) à affichage numérique or digital; **digital camera** n appareil m photo numérique; **digital TV** n télévision f numérique

dignified ['dɪgnɪfaɪd] adj digne

dignity ['dɪgnɪtɪ] n dignité f

digs [dɪgz] npl (BRIT inf) piaule f, chambre meublée

dilemma [daɪ'lemə] n dilemme m

dill [dɪl] n aneth m

dilute [daɪ'luːt] vt diluer

dim [dɪm] adj (light, eyesight) faible; (memory, outline) vague, indécis(e); (room) sombre; (inf: stupid) borné(e), obtus(e) ▷ vt (light) réduire, baisser; (us Aut) mettre en code, baisser

dime [daɪm] n (US) pièce f de 10 cents

dimension [daɪ'menʃən] n dimension f

diminish [dɪ'mɪnɪʃ] vt, vi diminuer

din [dɪn] n vacarme m

dine [daɪn] vi dîner; **diner** n (person) dîneur(-euse); (US: eating place) petit restaurant

dinghy ['dɪŋgɪ] n youyou m; (inflatable) canot m pneumatique; (also: **sailing ~**) voilier m, dériveur m

dingy ['dɪndʒɪ] adj miteux(-euse), minable

dining car ['daɪnɪŋ-] n (BRIT) voiture-restaurant f, wagon-restaurant m

dining room ['daɪnɪŋ-] n salle f à manger

dining table [daɪnɪŋ-] n table f de (la) salle à manger

dinkum ['dɪŋkʌm] adj (AUST, NZ inf) vrai(e); **fair ~** vrai(e)

dinner ['dɪnə^r] n (evening meal) dîner m; (lunch) déjeuner m; (public) banquet m; **dinner jacket** n smoking m; **dinner party** n dîner m; **dinner time** n (evening) heure f du dîner; (midday) heure du déjeuner

dinosaur ['daɪnəsɔː^r] n dinosaure m

dip [dɪp] n (slope) déclivité f; (in sea) baignade f, bain m; (Culin) ≈ sauce f ▷ vt tremper, plonger; (BRIT Aut: lights) mettre en code, baisser ▷ vi plonger

diploma [dɪ'pləumə] n diplôme m

diplomacy [dɪ'pləuməsɪ] n diplomatie f

diplomat ['dɪpləmæt] n diplomate m; **diplomatic** [dɪplə'mætɪk] adj diplomatique

dipstick ['dɪpstɪk] n (BRIT Aut) jauge f de niveau d'huile

dire [daɪəʳ] adj (poverty) extrême; (awful) affreux(-euse)

direct [daɪ'rɛkt] adj direct(e) ▷ vt (tell way) diriger, orienter; (letter, remark) adresser; (Cine, TV) réaliser; (Theat) mettre en scène; (order): **to ~ sb to do sth** ordonner à qn de faire qch ▷ adv directement; **can you ~ me to …?** pouvez-vous m'indiquer le chemin de …?; **direct debit** n (BRIT Banking) prélèvement m automatique

direction [dɪ'rɛkʃən] n direction f; **directions** npl (to a place) indications fpl; **~s for use** mode m d'emploi; **sense of ~** sens m de l'orientation

directly [dɪ'rɛktlɪ] adv (in straight line) directement, tout droit; (at once) tout de suite, immédiatement

director [dɪ'rɛktəʳ] n directeur m; (Theat) metteur m en scène; (Cine, TV) réalisateur(-trice)

directory [dɪ'rɛktərɪ] n annuaire m; (Comput) répertoire m; **directory enquiries**, (US) **directory assistance** n (Tel: service) renseignements mpl

dirt [də:t] n saleté f; (mud) boue f; **dirty** adj sale; (joke) cochon(ne) ▷ vt salir

disability [dɪsə'bɪlɪtɪ] n invalidité f, infirmité f

disabled [dɪs'eɪbld] adj handicapé(e); (maimed) mutilé(e)

disadvantage [dɪsəd'vɑːntɪdʒ] n désavantage m, inconvénient m

disagree [dɪsə'griː] vi (differ) ne pas concorder; (be against, think otherwise): **to ~ (with)** ne pas être d'accord (avec); **disagreeable** adj désagréable; **disagreement** n désaccord m, différend m

disappear [dɪsə'pɪəʳ] vi disparaître; **disappearance** n disparition f

disappoint [dɪsə'pɔɪnt] vt décevoir; **disappointed** adj déçu(e); **disappointing** adj décevant(e); **disappointment** n déception f

disapproval [dɪsə'pruːvəl] n désapprobation f

disapprove [dɪsə'pruːv] vi: **to ~ of** désapprouver

disarm [dɪs'ɑːm] vt désarmer; **disarmament** [dɪs'ɑːməmənt] n désarmement m

disaster [dɪ'zɑːstəʳ] n catastrophe f, désastre m; **disastrous** adj désastreux(-euse)

disbelief ['dɪsbə'liːf] n incrédulité f

disc [dɪsk] n disque m; (Comput) = **disk**

discard [dɪs'kɑːd] vt (old things) se débarrasser de; (fig) écarter, renoncer à

discharge vt [dɪs'tʃɑːdʒ] (duties) s'acquitter de; (waste etc) déverser; décharger; (patient) renvoyer (chez lui); (employee, soldier) congédier, licencier ▷ n ['dɪstʃɑːdʒ] (Elec, Med) émission f; (dismissal) renvoi m licenciement m

discipline ['dɪsɪplɪn] n discipline f ▷ vt discipliner; (punish) punir

disc jockey n disque-jockey m (DJ)

disclose [dɪs'kləuz] vt révéler, divulguer

disco ['dɪskəu] n abbr discothèque f

discoloured, (US) **discolored** [dɪs'kʌləd] adj décoloré(e), jauni(e)

discomfort [dɪs'kʌmfət] n malaise m, gêne f; (lack of comfort) manque m de confort

disconnect [dɪskə'nɛkt] vt (Elec, Radio) débrancher; (gas, water) couper

discontent [dɪskən'tɛnt] n mécontentement m

discontinue [dɪskən'tɪnjuː] vt cesser, interrompre; **"~d"** (Comm) "fin de série"

discount n ['dɪskaunt] remise f, rabais m ▷ vt [dɪs'kaunt] (report etc) ne pas tenir compte de

d

discourage [dɪs'kʌrɪdʒ] vt
décourager

discover [dɪs'kʌvər] vt découvrir;
discovery n découverte f

discredit [dɪs'krɛdɪt] vt (idea) mettre
en doute; (person) discréditer

discreet [dɪ'skriːt] adj discret(-ète)

discrepancy [dɪ'skrɛpənsɪ] n
divergence f, contradiction f

discretion [dɪ'skrɛʃən] n discrétion f;
at the ~ of à la discrétion de

discriminate [dɪ'skrɪmɪneɪt] vi: **to
~ between** établir une distinction
entre, faire la différence entre; **to ~
against** pratiquer une discrimination
contre; **discrimination**
[dɪskrɪmɪ'neɪʃən] n discrimination f;
(judgment) discernement m

discuss [dɪ'skʌs] vt discuter de;
(debate) discuter; **discussion**
[dɪ'skʌʃən] n discussion f

disease [dɪ'ziːz] n maladie f

disembark [dɪsɪm'bɑːk] vt, vi
débarquer

disgrace [dɪs'greɪs] n honte f;
(disfavour) disgrâce f ▷ vt déshonorer,
couvrir de honte; **disgraceful** adj
scandaleux(-euse), honteux(-euse)

disgruntled [dɪs'grʌntld] adj
mécontent(e)

disguise [dɪs'gaɪz] n déguisement m
▷ vt déguiser; **in ~** déguisé(e)

disgust [dɪs'gʌst] n dégoût m,
aversion f ▷ vt dégoûter, écœurer

disgusted [dɪs'gʌstɪd] adj
dégoûté(e), écœuré(e)

disgusting [dɪs'gʌstɪŋ] adj
dégoûtant(e)

dish [dɪʃ] n plat m; **to do** or **wash the
~es** faire la vaisselle; **dishcloth** n
(for drying) torchon m; (for washing)
lavette f

dishonest [dɪs'ɔnɪst] adj
malhonnête

dishtowel ['dɪʃtauəl] n (US) torchon
m (à vaisselle)

dishwasher ['dɪʃwɔʃər] n lave-
vaisselle m

disillusion [dɪsɪ'luːʒən] vt
désabuser, désenchanter

disinfectant [dɪsɪn'fɛktənt] n
désinfectant m

disintegrate [dɪs'ɪntɪgreɪt] vi se
désintégrer

disk [dɪsk] n (Comput) disquette f;
single-/double-sided ~ disquette
une face/double face; **disk drive** n
lecteur m de disquette; **diskette** n
(Comput) disquette f

dislike [dɪs'laɪk] n aversion f,
antipathie f ▷ vt ne pas aimer

dislocate ['dɪsləkeɪt] vt disloquer,
déboîter

disloyal [dɪs'lɔɪəl] adj déloyal(e)

dismal ['dɪzml] adj (gloomy) lugubre,
maussade; (very bad) lamentable

dismantle [dɪs'mæntl] vt démonter

dismay [dɪs'meɪ] n consternation f
▷ vt consterner

dismiss [dɪs'mɪs] vt congédier,
renvoyer; (idea) écarter; (Law) rejeter;
dismissal n renvoi m

disobedient [dɪsə'biːdɪənt] adj
désobéissant(e), indiscipliné(e)

disobey [dɪsə'beɪ] vt désobéir à

disorder [dɪs'ɔːdər] n désordre
m; (rioting) désordres mpl; (Med)
troubles mpl

disorganized [dɪs'ɔːgənaɪzd] adj
désorganisé(e)

disown [dɪs'əun] vt renier

dispatch [dɪs'pætʃ] vt expédier,
envoyer ▷ n envoi m, expédition f;
(Mil, Press) dépêche f

dispel [dɪs'pɛl] vt dissiper, chasser

dispense [dɪs'pɛns] vt (medicine)
préparer (et vendre); **dispense with**
vt fus se passer de; **dispenser** n
(device) distributeur m

disperse [dɪs'pəːs] vt disperser ▷ vi
se disperser

display [dɪs'pleɪ] n (of goods) étalage
m; affichage m; (Comput: information)
visualisation f; (: device) visuel m; (of
feeling) manifestation f ▷ vt montrer;
(goods) mettre à l'étalage, exposer;

(*results, departure times*) afficher; (*pej*) faire étalage de

displease [dɪs'pliːz] *vt* mécontenter, contrarier

disposable [dɪs'pəuzəbl] *adj* (*pack etc*) jetable; (*income*) disponible

disposal [dɪs'pəuzl] *n* (*of rubbish*) évacuation *f*, destruction *f*; (*of property etc: by selling*) vente *f*; (*: by giving away*) cession *f*; **at one's ~** à sa disposition

dispose [dɪs'pəuz] *vi*: **to ~ of** (*unwanted goods*) se débarrasser de, se défaire de; (*problem*) expédier; **disposition** [dɪspə'zɪʃən] *n* disposition *f*; (*temperament*) naturel *m*

disproportionate [dɪsprə'pɔːʃənət] *adj* disproportionné(e)

dispute [dɪs'pjuːt] *n* discussion *f*; (*also*: **industrial ~**) conflit *m* ▷ *vt* (*question*) contester; (*matter*) discuter

disqualify [dɪs'kwɔlɪfaɪ] *vt* (*Sport*) disqualifier; **to ~ sb for sth/from doing** rendre qn inapte à qch/à faire

disregard [dɪsrɪ'gɑːd] *vt* ne pas tenir compte de

disrupt [dɪs'rʌpt] *vt* (*plans, meeting, lesson*) perturber, déranger; **disruption** [dɪs'rʌpʃən] *n* perturbation *f*, dérangement *m*

dissatisfaction [dɪssætɪs'fækʃən] *n* mécontentement *m*, insatisfaction *f*

dissatisfied [dɪs'sætɪsfaɪd] *adj*: **~ (with)** insatisfait(e) (de)

dissect [dɪ'sɛkt] *vt* disséquer

dissent [dɪ'sɛnt] *n* dissentiment *m*, différence *f* d'opinion

dissertation [dɪsə'teɪʃən] *n* (*Scol*) mémoire *m*

dissolve [dɪ'zɔlv] *vt* dissoudre ▷ *vi* se dissoudre, fondre; **to ~ in(to) tears** fondre en larmes

distance ['dɪstns] *n* distance *f*; **in the ~** au loin

distant ['dɪstnt] *adj* lointain(e), éloigné(e); (*manner*) distant(e), froid(e)

distil, (*us*) **distill** [dɪs'tɪl] *vt* distiller; **distillery** *n* distillerie *f*

distinct [dɪs'tɪŋkt] *adj* distinct(e); (*clear*) marqué(e); **as ~ from** par opposition à; **distinction** [dɪs'tɪŋkʃən] *n* distinction *f*; (*in exam*) mention *f* très bien; **distinctive** *adj* distinctif(-ive)

distinguish [dɪs'tɪŋgwɪʃ] *vt* distinguer; **to ~ o.s.** se distinguer; **distinguished** *adj* (*eminent, refined*) distingué(e)

distort [dɪs'tɔːt] *vt* déformer

distract [dɪs'trækt] *vt* distraire, déranger; **distracted** *adj* (*not concentrating*) distrait(e); (*worried*) affolé(e); **distraction** [dɪs'trækʃən] *n* distraction *f*

distraught [dɪs'trɔːt] *adj* éperdu(e)

distress [dɪs'trɛs] *n* détresse *f* ▷ *vt* affliger; **distressing** *adj* douloureux(-euse), pénible

distribute [dɪs'trɪbjuːt] *vt* distribuer; **distribution** [dɪstrɪ'bjuːʃən] *n* distribution *f*; **distributor** *n* (*gen, Tech*) distributeur *m*; (*Comm*) concessionnaire *m/f*

district ['dɪstrɪkt] *n* (*of country*) région *f*; (*of town*) quartier *m*; (*Admin*) district *m*; **district attorney** *n* (*us*) ≈ procureur *m* de la République

distrust [dɪs'trʌst] *n* méfiance *f*, doute *m* ▷ *vt* se méfier de

disturb [dɪs'təːb] *vt* troubler; (*inconvenience*) déranger; **disturbance** *n* dérangement *m*; (*political etc*) troubles *mpl*; **disturbed** *adj* (*worried, upset*) agité(e), troublé(e); **to be emotionally disturbed** avoir des problèmes affectifs; **disturbing** *adj* troublant(e), inquiétant(e)

ditch [dɪtʃ] *n* fossé *m*; (*for irrigation*) rigole *f* ▷ *vt* (*inf*) abandonner; (*person*) plaquer

ditto ['dɪtəu] *adv* idem

dive [daɪv] *n* plongeon *m*; (*of submarine*) plongée *f* ▷ *vi* plonger; **to ~ into** (*bag etc*) plonger la main dans; (*place*) se précipiter dans; **diver** *n* plongeur *m*

diverse [daɪ'və:s] *adj* divers(e)
diversion [daɪ'və:ʃən] *n* (BRIT
Aut) déviation *f*; (*distraction, Mil*)
diversion *f*
diversity [daɪ'və:sɪtɪ] *n* diversité
f, variété *f*
divert [daɪ'və:t] *vt* (BRIT: *traffic*)
dévier; (*plane*) dérouter; (*train, river*)
détourner
divide [dɪ'vaɪd] *vt* diviser; (*separate*)
séparer ▷ *vi* se diviser; **divided
highway** (US) *n* route *f* à quatre voies
divine [dɪ'vaɪn] *adj* divin(e)
diving ['daɪvɪŋ] *n* plongée (sous-
marine); **diving board** *n* plongeoir *m*
division [dɪ'vɪʒən] *n* division *f*;
(*separation*) séparation *f*; (*Comm*)
service *m*
divorce [dɪ'vɔːs] *n* divorce *m* ▷ *vt*
divorcer d'avec; **divorced** *adj*
divorcé(e); **divorcee** [dɪvɔː'siː] *n*
divorcé(e)
DIY *adj, n abbr* (BRIT) = **do-it-yourself**
dizzy ['dɪzɪ] *adj*: **I feel ~** la tête me
tourne, j'ai la tête qui tourne
DJ *n abbr* = **disc jockey**
DNA *n abbr* (= *deoxyribonucleic acid*)
ADN *m*

 KEYWORD

do [duː] *n* (*inf*: *party etc*) soirée *f*, fête *f*
▷ *aux vb* (*pt* **did**, *pp* **done**) **1** (*in negative
constructions*) *non traduit*; **I don't
understand** je ne comprends pas
2 (*to form questions*) *non traduit*;
didn't you know? vous ne le saviez
pas?; **what do you think?** qu'en
pensez-vous?
3 (*for emphasis, in polite expressions*):
**people do make mistakes
sometimes** on peut toujours se
tromper; **she does seem rather
late** je trouve qu'elle est bien en
retard; **do sit down/help yourself**
asseyez-vous/servez-vous je vous
en prie; **do take care!** faites bien
attention à vous!

4 (*used to avoid repeating vb*): **she
swims better than I do** elle nage
mieux que moi; **do you agree?
— yes, I do/no I don't** vous êtes
d'accord? — oui/non; **she lives
in Glasgow — so do I** elle habite
Glasgow — moi aussi; **he didn't like
it and neither did we** il n'a pas aimé
ça, et nous non plus; **who broke
it? — I did** qui l'a cassé? — c'est moi;
he asked me to help him and I did
il m'a demandé de l'aider, et c'est ce
que j'ai fait
5 (*in question tags*): **you like him,
don't you?** vous l'aimez bien, n'est-ce
pas?; **I don't know him, do I?** je ne
crois pas le connaître
▷ *vt* (*pt* **did**, *pp* **done**) **1** (*gen*: *carry out,
perform etc*) faire; (*visit*: *city, museum*)
faire, visiter; **what are you doing
tonight?** qu'est-ce que vous faites
ce soir?; **what do you do?** (*job*)
que faites-vous dans la vie?; **what
can I do for you?** que puis-je faire
pour vous?; **to do the cooking/
washing-up** faire la cuisine/la
vaisselle; **to do one's teeth/hair/
nails** se brosser les dents/se coiffer/
se faire les ongles
2 (*Aut etc*: *distance*) faire; (: *speed*) faire
du; **we've done 200 km already**
nous avons déjà fait 200 km; **the
car was doing 100** la voiture faisait
du 100 (à l'heure); **he can do 100 in
that car** il peut faire du 100 (à l'heure)
dans cette voiture-là
▷ *vi* (*pt* **did**, *pp* **done**) **1** (*act, behave*)
faire; **do as I do** faites comme moi
2 (*get on, fare*) marcher; **the firm
is doing well** l'entreprise marche
bien; **he's doing well/badly at
school** ça marche bien/mal pour lui
à l'école; **how do you do?** comment
allez-vous?; (*on being introduced*)
enchanté(e)!
3 (*suit*) aller; **will it do?** est-ce que
ça ira?
4 (*be sufficient*) suffire, aller; **will £10**

do? est-ce que 10 livres suffiront?; **that'll do** ça suffit, ça ira; **that'll do!** (in annoyance) ça va or suffit comme ça!; **to make do (with)** se contenter (de)

do up vt (laces, dress) attacher; (buttons) boutonner; (zip) fermer; (renovate: room) refaire; (: house) remettre à neuf

do with vt fus (need): **I could do with a drink/some help** quelque chose à boire/un peu d'aide ne serait pas de refus; **it could do with a wash** ça ne lui ferait pas de mal d'être lavé; (be connected with): **that has nothing to do with you** cela ne vous concerne pas; **I won't have anything to do with it** je ne veux pas m'en mêler

do without vi s'en passer; **if you're late for tea then you'll do without** si vous êtes en retard pour le dîner il faudra vous en passer ▷ vt fus se passer de; **I can do without a car** je peux me passer de voiture

dock [dɔk] n dock m; (wharf) quai m; (Law) banc m des accusés ▷ vi se mettre à quai; (Space) s'arrimer; **docks** npl (Naut) docks

doctor ['dɔktə^r] n médecin m, docteur m; (PhD etc) docteur ▷ vt (drink) frelater; **call a ~!** appelez un docteur or un médecin!; **Doctor of Philosophy** n (degree) doctorat m; (person) titulaire m/f d'un doctorat

document ['dɔkjumənt] n document m; **documentary** [dɔkju'mɛntərɪ] adj, n documentaire (m); **documentation** [dɔkjumən'teɪʃən] n documentation f

dodge [dɔdʒ] n truc m; combine f ▷ vt esquiver, éviter

dodgy ['dɔdʒɪ] adj (BRIT inf: uncertain) douteux(-euse); (: shady) louche

does [dʌz] vb see **do**

doesn't ['dʌznt] = **does not**

dog [dɔg] n chien(ne) ▷ vt (follow closely) suivre de près; (fig: memory etc) poursuivre, harceler; **doggy bag** ['dɔgɪ-] n petit sac pour emporter les restes

do-it-yourself ['duːɪtjɔː'sɛlf] n bricolage m

dole [dəul] n (BRIT: payment) allocation f de chômage; **on the ~** au chômage

doll [dɔl] n poupée f

dollar ['dɔlə^r] n dollar m

dolphin ['dɔlfɪn] n dauphin m

dome [dəum] n dôme m

domestic [də'mɛstɪk] adj (duty, happiness) familial(e); (policy, affairs, flight) intérieur(e); (animal) domestique

dominant ['dɔmɪnənt] adj dominant(e)

dominate ['dɔmɪneɪt] vt dominer

domino ['dɔmɪnəu] (pl **dominoes**) n domino m; **dominoes** n (game) dominos mpl

donate [də'neɪt] vt faire don de, donner; **donation** [də'neɪʃən] n donation f, don m

done [dʌn] pp of **do**

dongle ['dɔŋgl] n (Comput) dongle m

donkey ['dɔŋkɪ] n âne m

donor ['dəunə^r] n (of blood etc) donneur(-euse); (to charity) donateur(-trice); **donor card** n carte f de don d'organes

don't [dəunt] = **do not**

donut ['dəunʌt] (US) n = **doughnut**

doodle ['duːdl] vi gribouiller

doom [duːm] n (fate) destin m ▷ vt: **to be ~ed to failure** être voué(e) à l'échec

door [dɔː^r] n porte f; (Rail, car) portière f; **doorbell** n sonnette f; **door handle** n poignée f de porte; (of car) poignée de portière; **doorknob** n poignée f or bouton m de porte; **doorstep** n pas m de (la) porte, seuil m; **doorway** n (embrasure f de) porte f

dope [dəup] n (inf: drug) drogue f; (: person) andouille f ▷ vt (horse etc) doper

dormitory ['dɔːmɪtrɪ] *n* (BRIT)
dortoir *m*; (US: *hall of residence*)
résidence *f* universitaire

DOS [dɔs] *n abbr* (= *disk operating
system*) DOS *m*

dosage ['dəʊsɪdʒ] *n* dose *f*; dosage *m*;
(*on label*) posologie *f*

dose [dəʊs] *n* dose *f*

dot [dɔt] *n* point *m*; (*on material*) pois
m ▷ *vt*: **~ted with** parsemé(e) de; **on
the ~** à l'heure tapante; **dotcom** *n*
point com *m*, pointcom *m*; **dotted
line** ['dɔtɪd-] *n* ligne pointillée; **to
sign on the dotted line** signer
à l'endroit indiqué *or* sur la ligne
pointillée

double ['dʌbl] *adj* double ▷ *adv*
(*twice*): **to cost ~ (sth)** coûter le
double (de qch) *or* deux fois plus (que
qch) ▷ *n* double *m*; (*Cine*) doublure *f*
▷ *vt* doubler; (*fold*) plier en deux ▷ *vi*
doubler; **on the ~, at the ~** au pas
de course; **double back** *vi* (*person*)
revenir sur ses pas; **double bass** *n*
contrebasse *f*; **double bed** *n* grand
lit; **double-check** *vt* revérifier;
double-click *vi* (*Comput*) double-
cliquer; **double-cross** *vt* doubler,
trahir; **double-decker** *n* autobus *m*
à impériale; **double glazing** *n* (BRIT)
double vitrage *m*; **double room** *n*
chambre *f* pour deux; **doubles** *n*
(*Tennis*) double *m*; **double yellow
lines** *npl* (BRIT Aut) double bande jaune
marquant l'interdiction de stationner

doubt [daʊt] *n* doute *m* ▷ *vt* douter
de; **no ~** sans doute; **to ~ that**
douter que + *sub*; **doubtful** *adj*
douteux(-euse); (*person*) incertain(e);
doubtless *adv* sans doute, sûrement

dough [dəʊ] *n* pâte *f*; **doughnut**, (US)
donut *n* beignet *m*

dove [dʌv] *n* colombe *f*

Dover ['dəʊvə'] *n* Douvres

down [daʊn] *n* (*fluff*) duvet *m* ▷ *adv*
en bas, vers le bas; (*on the ground*) par
terre ▷ *prep* en bas de; (*along*) le long
de ▷ *vt* (*inf: drink*) siffler; **to walk ~**

a hill descendre une colline; **to run
~ the street** descendre la rue en
courant; **~ with X!** à bas X!; **down-
and-out** *n* (*tramp*) clochard(e);
downfall *n* chute *f*; ruine *f*; **downhill**
adv: **to go downhill** descendre;
(*business*) péricliter

Downing Street ['daʊnɪŋ-] *n*
(BRIT): **10 ~** résidence du Premier ministre

DOWNING STREET

Downing Street est une rue de
Westminster (à Londres) où se
trouvent la résidence officielle
du Premier ministre et celle du
ministre des Finances. Le nom
Downing Street est souvent utilisé
pour désigner le gouvernement
britannique.

down: download *vt* (*Comput*)
télécharger; **downloadable** *adj*
(*Comput*) téléchargeable; **downright**
adj (*lie etc*) effronté(e); (*refusal*)
catégorique

Down's syndrome [daʊnz-] *n*
trisomie *f*

down: downstairs *adv* (*on or to
ground floor*) au rez-de-chaussée; (*on
or to floor below*) à l'étage inférieur;
down-to-earth *adj* terre à terre *inv*;
downtown *adv* en ville; **down under**
adv en Australie *or* Nouvelle Zélande;
downward ['daʊnwəd] *adj, adv*
le bas; **downwards** ['daʊnwədz] *adv*
vers le bas

doz. *abbr* = **dozen**

doze [dəʊz] *vi* sommeiller

dozen ['dʌzn] *n* douzaine *f*; **a ~ books**
une douzaine de livres; **~s of** des
centaines de

Dr. *abbr* (= *doctor*) Dr; (*in street names*);
= **drive**

drab [dræb] *adj* terne, morne

draft [drɑːft] *n* (*of letter, school work*)
brouillon *m*; (*of literary work*) ébauche
f; (*Comm*) traite *f*; (US Mil: *call-up*)

conscription f ▷ vt faire le brouillon de; (*Mil: send*) détacher; *see also* **draught**

drag [dræg] vt traîner; (*river*) draguer ▷ vi traîner ▷ n (*inf*) casse-pieds m/f; (: *women's clothing*): **in ~** (en) travesti; **to ~ and drop** (*Comput*) glisser-poser

dragonfly ['drægənflaɪ] n libellule f

drain [dreɪn] n égout m; (*on resources*) saignée f ▷ vt (*land, marshes*) assécher; (*vegetables*) égoutter; (*reservoir etc*) vider ▷ vi (*water*) s'écouler; **drainage** n (*system*) système m d'égouts; (*act*) drainage m; **drainpipe** n tuyau m d'écoulement

drama ['drɑːmə] n (*art*) théâtre m, art m dramatique; (*play*) pièce f; (*event*) drame m; **dramatic** [drə'mætɪk] adj dramatique; (*impressive*) spectaculaire

drank [dræŋk] pt of **drink**

drape [dreɪp] vt draper; **drapes** npl (*us*) rideaux mpl

drastic ['dræstɪk] adj (*measures*) d'urgence, énergique; (*change*) radical(e)

draught, (*us*) **draft** [drɑːft] n courant m d'air; **on ~** (*beer*) à la pression; **draught beer** n bière f (à la) pression; **draughts** n (*BRIT: game*) (jeu m de) dames fpl

draw [drɔː] (*vb: pt* **drew**, *pp* **drawn**) vt tirer; (*picture*) dessiner; (*attract*) attirer; (*line, circle*) tracer; (*money*) retirer; (*wages*) toucher ▷ vi (*Sport*) faire match nul ▷ n match nul; (*lottery*) loterie f; (*picking of ticket*) tirage m au sort; **draw out** vi (*lengthen*) s'allonger ▷ vt (*money*) retirer; **draw up** vi (*stop*) s'arrêter ▷ vt (*document*) établir, dresser; (*plan*) formuler, dessiner; (*chair*) approcher; **drawback** n inconvénient m, désavantage m

drawer [drɔː^r] n tiroir m

drawing ['drɔːɪŋ] n dessin m; **drawing pin** n (*BRIT*) punaise f; **drawing room** n salon m

drawn [drɔːn] pp of **draw**

dread [drɛd] n épouvante f, effroi m ▷ vt redouter, appréhender; **dreadful** adj épouvantable, affreux(-euse)

dream [driːm] n rêve m ▷ vt, vi (*pt* **dreamed**, *pp* **dreamt**) rêver; **dreamer** n rêveur(-euse)

dreamt [drɛmt] pt, pp of **dream**

dreary ['drɪərɪ] adj triste; monotone

drench [drɛntʃ] vt tremper

dress [drɛs] n robe f; (*clothing*) habillement m, tenue f ▷ vt habiller; (*wound*) panser ▷ vi: **to get ~ed** s'habiller; **dress up** vi s'habiller; (*in fancy dress*) se déguiser; **dress circle** n (*BRIT*) premier balcon; **dresser** n (*furniture*) vaisselier m (: *us*) coiffeuse f, commode f; **dressing** n (*Med*) pansement m; (*Culin*) sauce f, assaisonnement m; **dressing gown** n (*BRIT*) robe f de chambre; **dressing room** n (*Theat*) loge f; (*Sport*) vestiaire m; **dressing table** n coiffeuse f; **dressmaker** n couturière f

drew [druː] pt of **draw**

dribble ['drɪbl] vi (*baby*) baver ▷ vt (*ball*) dribbler

dried [draɪd] adj (*fruit, beans*) sec (sèche); (*eggs, milk*) en poudre

drier ['draɪə^r] n = **dryer**

drift [drɪft] n (*of current etc*) force f; direction f; (*of snow*) rafale f; coulée f (*on ground*) congère f; (*general meaning*) sens général ▷ vi (*boat*) aller à la dérive, dériver; (*sand, snow*) s'amonceler, s'entasser

drill [drɪl] n perceuse f; (*bit*) foret m; (*of dentist*) roulette f, fraise f; (*Mil*) exercice m ▷ vt percer; (*troops*) entraîner ▷ vi (*for oil*) faire un ou des forage(s)

drink [drɪŋk] n boisson f; (*alcoholic*) verre m ▷ vt, vi (*pt* **drank**, *pp* **drunk**) boire; **to have a ~** boire quelque chose, boire un verre; **a ~ of water** un verre d'eau; **would you like a ~?** tu veux boire quelque chose?; **drink-driving** n conduite f en état d'ivresse;

drinker n buveur(-euse); **drinking water** n eau f potable

drip [drɪp] n (drop) goutte f; (Med: device) goutte-à-goutte m inv; (: liquid) perfusion f ▷ vi tomber goutte à goutte; (tap) goutter

drive [draɪv] (pt **drove**, pp **driven**) n promenade f or trajet m en voiture; (also: **~way**) allée f; (energy) dynamisme m, énergie f; (push) effort (concerté) campagne f; (Comput: also: **disk ~**) lecteur m de disquette ▷ vt conduire; (nail) enfoncer; (push) chasser, pousser; (Tech: motor) actionner; entraîner ▷ vi (be at the wheel) conduire; (travel by car) aller en voiture; **left-/right-hand ~** (Aut) conduite f à gauche/droite; **to ~ sb mad** rendre qn fou (folle); **drive out** vt (force out) chasser; **drive-in** adj, n (esp US) drive-in m

driven ['drɪvn] pp of **drive**

driver ['draɪvəʳ] n conducteur(-trice); (of taxi, bus) chauffeur m; **driver's license** n (US) permis m de conduire

driveway ['draɪvweɪ] n allée f

driving ['draɪvɪŋ] n conduite f; **driving instructor** n moniteur m d'auto-école; **driving lesson** n leçon f de conduite; **driving licence** n (BRIT) permis m de conduire; **driving test** n examen m du permis de conduire

drizzle ['drɪzl] n bruine f, crachin m

droop [druːp] vi (flower) commencer à se faner; (shoulders, head) tomber

drop [drɔp] n (of liquid) goutte f; (fall) baisse f; (also: **parachute ~**) saut m ▷ vt laisser tomber; (voice, eyes, price) baisser; (passenger) déposer ▷ vi tomber; **drop in** vi (inf: visit): **to ~ in (on)** faire un saut (chez), passer (chez); **drop off** vi (sleep) s'assoupir ▷ vt (passenger) déposer; **drop out** vi (withdraw) se retirer; (student etc) abandonner, décrocher

drought [draut] n sécheresse f

drove [drəuv] pt of **drive**

drown [draun] vt noyer ▷ vi se noyer

drowsy ['drauzɪ] adj somnolent(e)

drug [drʌg] n médicament m; (narcotic) drogue f ▷ vt droguer; **to be on ~s** se droguer; **drug addict** n toxicomane m/f; **drug dealer** n revendeur(-euse) de drogue; **druggist** n (US) pharmacien(ne)-droguiste; **drugstore** n (US) pharmacie-droguerie f, drugstore m

drum [drʌm] n tambour m; (for oil, petrol) bidon m; **drums** npl (Mus) batterie f; **drummer** n (joueur m de) tambour m

drunk [drʌŋk] pp of **drink** ▷ adj ivre, soûl(e) ▷ n (also: **~ard**) ivrogne m/f; **to get ~** se soûler; **drunken** adj ivre, soûl(e); (rage, stupor) ivrogne, d'ivrogne

dry [draɪ] adj sec (sèche); (day) sans pluie ▷ vt sécher; (clothes) faire sécher ▷ vi sécher; **dry off** vi, vt sécher; **dry up** vi (river, supplies) se tarir; **dry-cleaner's** n teinturerie f; **dry-cleaning** n (process) nettoyage m à sec; **dryer** n (tumble-dryer) sèche-linge m inv; (for hair) sèche-cheveux m inv

DSS n abbr (BRIT) = **Department of Social Security**

DTP n abbr (= desktop publishing) PAO f

dual ['djuəl] adj double; **dual carriageway** n (BRIT) route f à quatre voies

dubious ['djuːbɪəs] adj hésitant(e), incertain(e); (reputation, company) douteux(-euse)

duck [dʌk] n canard m ▷ vi se baisser vivement, baisser subitement la tête

due [djuː] adj (money, payment) dû (due); (expected) attendu(e); (fitting) qui convient ▷ adv: **~ north** droit vers le nord; **~ to** (because of) en raison de; (caused by) dû à; **the train is ~ at 8 a.m.** le train est attendu à 8 h; **she is ~ back tomorrow** elle doit rentrer demain; **he is ~ £10** on lui doit 10 livres; **to give sb his or her ~** être juste envers qn

duel ['djuəl] *n* duel *m*

duet [dju:'ɛt] *n* duo *m*

dug [dʌg] *pt, pp of* **dig**

duke [dju:k] *n* duc *m*

dull [dʌl] *adj* (*boring*) ennuyeux(-euse); (*not bright*) morne, terne; (*sound, pain*) sourd(e); (*weather, day*) gris(e), maussade ▷ *vt* (*pain, grief*) atténuer; (*mind, senses*) engourdir

dumb [dʌm] *adj* (!) muet(te); (*stupid*) bête

dummy ['dʌmɪ] *n* (*tailor's model*) mannequin *m*; (*mock-up*) factice *m*, maquette *f*; (BRIT: *for baby*) tétine *f* ▷ *adj* faux (fausse), factice

dump [dʌmp] *n* (*also:* **rubbish ~**) décharge (publique); (*inf: place*) trou *m* ▷ *vt* (*put down*) déposer; déverser; (*get rid of*) se débarrasser de; (*Comput*) lister

dumpling ['dʌmplɪŋ] *n* boulette *f* (de pâte)

dune [dju:n] *n* dune *f*

dungarees [dʌŋgə'ri:z] *npl* bleu(s) *m*(*pl*); (*for child, woman*) salopette *f*

dungeon ['dʌndʒən] *n* cachot *m*

duplex ['dju:plɛks] *n* (US: *also:* **~ apartment**) duplex *m*

duplicate *n* ['dju:plɪkət] double *m* ▷ *vt* ['dju:plɪkeɪt] faire un double de; (*on machine*) polycopier; **in ~** en deux exemplaires, en double

durable ['djuərəbl] *adj* durable; (*clothes, metal*) résistant(e), solide

duration [djuə'reɪʃən] *n* durée *f*

during ['djuərɪŋ] *prep* pendant, au cours de

dusk [dʌsk] *n* crépuscule *m*

dust [dʌst] *n* poussière *f* ▷ *vt* (*furniture*) essuyer, épousseter; (*cake etc*): **to ~ with** saupoudrer de; **dustbin** *n* (BRIT) poubelle *f*; **duster** *n* chiffon *m*; **dustman** (*irreg*) *n* (BRIT) boueux *m*, éboueur *m*; **dustpan** *n* pelle *f* à poussière; **dusty** *adj* poussiéreux(-euse)

Dutch [dʌtʃ] *adj* hollandais(e), néerlandais(e) ▷ *n* (*Ling*) hollandais *m*, néerlandais *m* ▷ *adv*: **to go ~** or **dutch** (*inf*) partager les frais; **the Dutch** *npl* les Hollandais, les Néerlandais; **Dutchman** (*irreg*) *n* Hollandais *m*; **Dutchwoman** (*irreg*) *n* Hollandaise *f*

duty ['dju:tɪ] *n* devoir *m*; (*tax*) droit *m*, taxe *f*; **on ~** de service; (*at night etc*) de garde; **off ~** libre, pas de service or de garde; **duty-free** *adj* exempté(e) de douane, hors-taxe

duvet ['du:veɪ] *n* (BRIT) couette *f*

DVD *n abbr* (= *digital versatile or video disc*) DVD *m*; **DVD burner** *n* graveur *m* de DVD; **DVD player** *n* lecteur *m* de DVD; **DVD writer** *n* graveur *m* de DVD

dwarf (*pl* **dwarves**) [dwɔ:f, dwɔ:vz] *n* (*pej*) nain(e) ▷ *vt* écraser

dwell (*pt, pp* **dwelt**) [dwɛl, dwɛlt] *vi* demeurer; **dwell on** *vt fus* s'étendre sur

dwelt [dwɛlt] *pt, pp of* **dwell**

dwindle ['dwɪndl] *vi* diminuer, décroître

dye [daɪ] *n* teinture *f* ▷ *vt* teindre

dying ['daɪɪŋ] *adj* mourant(e), agonisant(e)

dynamic [daɪ'næmɪk] *adj* dynamique

dynamite ['daɪnəmaɪt] *n* dynamite *f*

dyslexia [dɪs'lɛksɪə] *n* dyslexie *f*

dyslexic [dɪs'lɛksɪk] *adj, n* dyslexique *m/f*

E [iː] n (Mus) mi m
each [iːtʃ] adj chaque ▷ pron
chacun(e); **~ other** l'un l'autre;
they hate ~ other ils se détestent
(mutuellement); **they have 2
books ~** ils ont 2 livres chacun;
they cost £5 ~ ils coûtent 5 livres
(la) pièce
eager [ˈiːgər] adj (person, buyer)
empressé(e); (keen: pupil, worker)
enthousiaste; **to be ~ to do sth**
(impatient) brûler de faire qch; (keen)
désirer vivement faire qch; **to be
~ for** (event) désirer vivement;
(vengeance, affection, information) être
avide de
eagle [ˈiːgl] n aigle m
ear [ɪər] n oreille f; (of corn) épi m;
earache n mal m aux oreilles;
eardrum n tympan m
earl [əːl] n comte m
earlier [ˈəːlɪər] adj (date etc) plus
rapproché(e); (edition etc) plus

ancien(ne), antérieur(e) ▷ adv
plus tôt
early [ˈəːlɪ] adv tôt, de bonne heure;
(ahead of time) en avance; (near the
beginning) au début ▷ adj précoce,
qui se manifeste (or se fait) tôt or de
bonne heure; (Christians, settlers)
premier(-ière); (reply) rapide; (death)
prématuré(e); (work) de jeunesse; **to
have an ~ night/start** se coucher/
partir tôt or de bonne heure; **in the
~** or **~ in the spring/19th century**
au début or commencement du
printemps/19ème siècle; **early
retirement** n retraite anticipée
earmark [ˈɪəmɑːk] vt: **to ~ sth for**
réserver or destiner qch à
earn [əːn] vt gagner; (Comm: yield)
rapporter; **to ~ one's living** gagner
sa vie
earnest [ˈəːnɪst] adj sérieux(-euse)
▷ n: **in ~** adv sérieusement, pour
de bon
earnings [ˈəːnɪŋz] npl salaire m;
gains mpl; (of company etc) profits mpl,
bénéfices mpl
ear: earphones npl écouteurs mpl;
earplugs npl boules fpl Quiès®; (to
keep out water) protège-tympans mpl;
earring n boucle f d'oreille
earth [əːθ] n (gen, also BRIT Elec)
terre f ▷ vt (BRIT Elec) relier à la terre;
earthquake n tremblement m de
terre, séisme m
ease [iːz] n facilité f, aisance f;
(comfort) bien-être m ▷ vt (soothe:
mind) tranquilliser; (reduce: pain,
problem) atténuer; (: tension) réduire;
(loosen) relâcher, détendre; (help pass):
to ~ sth in/out faire pénétrer/sortir
qch délicatement or avec douceur,
faciliter la pénétration/la sortie de
qch; **at ~** à l'aise; (Mil) au repos
easily [ˈiːzɪlɪ] adv facilement; (by
far) de loin
east [iːst] n est m ▷ adj (wind) d'est;
(side) est inv ▷ adv à l'est, vers l'est;
the E~ l'Orient m; (Pol) les pays mpl de

l'Est; **eastbound** adj en direction de l'est; (carriageway) est inv

Easter ['iːstəʳ] n Pâques fpl; **Easter egg** n œuf m de Pâques

eastern ['iːstən] adj de l'est, oriental(e)

Easter Sunday n le dimanche de Pâques

easy ['iːzɪ] adj facile; (manner) aisé(e) ▷ adv: **to take it** or **things ~** (rest) ne pas se fatiguer; (not worry) ne pas (trop) s'en faire; **easy-going** adj accommodant(e), facile à vivre

eat (pt **ate**, pp **eaten**) [iːt, eɪt, 'iːtn] vt, vi manger; **can we have something to ~?** est-ce qu'on peut manger quelque chose?; **eat out** vi manger au restaurant

eavesdrop ['iːvzdrɔp] vi: **to ~ (on)** écouter de façon indiscrète

e-bike ['iːbaɪk] n VAE m

e-book ['iːbuk] n livre m électronique

e-business ['iːbɪznɪs] n (company) entreprise f électronique; (commerce) commerce m électronique

eccentric [ɪk'sentrɪk] adj, n excentrique m/f

echo ['ekəu] (pl **echoes**) n écho m ▷ vt répéter ▷ vi résonner; faire écho

e-cigarette ['iːsɪgəret] n cigarette f électronique

eclipse [ɪ'klɪps] n éclipse f

eco-friendly [iːkəu'frendlɪ] adj non nuisible à l'environnement

ecological [iːkə'lɔdʒɪkəl] adj écologique

ecology [ɪ'kɔlədʒɪ] n écologie f

e-commerce ['iːkɔməːs] n commerce m électronique

economic [iːkə'nɔmɪk] adj économique; (profitable) rentable; **economical** adj économique; (person) économe; **economics** n (Scol) économie f politique ▷ npl (of project etc) côté m or aspect m économique

economist [ɪ'kɔnəmɪst] n économiste m/f

economize [ɪ'kɔnəmaɪz] vi économiser, faire des économies

economy [ɪ'kɔnəmɪ] n économie f; **economy class** n (Aviat) classe f touriste; **economy class syndrome** n syndrome m de la classe économique

ecstasy ['ekstəsɪ] n extase f; (Drugs) ecstasy m; **ecstatic** [eks'tætɪk] adj extatique, en extase

eczema ['eksɪmə] n eczéma m

edge [edʒ] n bord m; (of knife etc) tranchant m, fil m ▷ vt border; **on ~** (fig) crispé(e), tendu(e)

edgy ['edʒɪ] adj crispé(e), tendu(e)

edible ['edɪbl] adj comestible; (meal) mangeable

Edinburgh ['edɪnbərə] n Édimbourg; voir article **"Edinburgh Festival"**

edit ['edɪt] vt (text, book) éditer; (report) préparer; (film) monter; (magazine) diriger; (newspaper) être le rédacteur or la rédactrice en chef de; **edition** [ɪ'dɪʃən] n édition f; **editor** n (of newspaper) rédacteur(-trice), rédacteur(-trice) en chef; (of sb's work) éditeur(-trice); (also: **film editor**) monteur(-euse); **political/foreign editor** rédacteur politique/au service étranger; **editorial** [edɪ'tɔːrɪəl] adj de la rédaction ▷ n éditorial m

educate ['ɛdjukeɪt] vt (teach)
instruire; (bring up) éduquer;
educated ['ɛdjukeɪtɪd] adj (person)
cultivé(e)

education [ɛdju'keɪʃən] n éducation
f; (studies) études fpl; (teaching)
enseignement m, instruction f;
educational adj pédagogique;
(institution) scolaire; (game, toy)
éducatif(-ive)

eel [i:l] n anguille f

eerie ['ɪərɪ] adj inquiétant(e),
spectral(e), surnaturel(le)

effect [ɪ'fɛkt] n effet m ▷ vt effectuer;
effects npl (property) effets, affaires
fpl; **to take ~** (Law) entrer en
vigueur, prendre effet; (drug) agir,
faire son effet; **in ~** en fait; **effective**
adj efficace; (actual) véritable;
effectively adv efficacement; (in
reality) effectivement, en fait

efficiency [ɪ'fɪʃənsɪ] n efficacité f; (of
machine, car) rendement m

efficient [ɪ'fɪʃənt] adj efficace;
(machine, car) d'un bon rendement;
efficiently adv efficacement

effort ['ɛfət] n effort m; **effortless**
adj sans effort, aisé(e); (achievement)
facile

e.g. adv abbr (= exempli gratia) par
exemple, p. ex.

egg [ɛg] n œuf m; **hard-boiled/soft-
boiled ~** œuf dur/à la coque; **eggcup**
n coquetier m; **egg plant** (us) n
aubergine f; **eggshell** n coquille f
d'œuf; **egg white** n blanc m d'œuf;
egg yolk n jaune m d'œuf

ego ['i:gəu] n (self-esteem) amour-
propre m; (Psych) moi m

Egypt ['i:dʒɪpt] n Égypte f; **Egyptian**
[ɪ'dʒɪpʃən] adj égyptien(ne) ▷ n
Égyptien(ne)

Eiffel Tower ['aɪfəl-] n tour f Eiffel

eight [eɪt] num huit; **eighteen**
num dix-huit; **eighteenth** num
dix-huitième; **eighth** num huitième;
eightieth ['eɪtɪɪθ] num quatre-
vingtième

eighty ['eɪtɪ] num quatre-vingt(s)

Eire ['ɛərə] n République f d'Irlande

either ['aɪðə] adj l'un ou l'autre; (both,
each) chaque ▷ pron: **~ (of them)** l'un
ou l'autre ▷ adv non plus ▷ conj: **~
good or bad** soit bon soit mauvais;
on ~ side de chaque côté; **I don't
like ~** je n'aime ni l'un ni l'autre; **no,
I don't ~** moi non plus; **which bike
do you want? — ~ will do** quel vélo
voulez-vous? — n'importe lequel;
answer with ~ yes or no répondez
par oui ou par non

eject [ɪ'dʒɛkt] vt (tenant etc) expulser;
(object) éjecter

elaborate adj [ɪ'læbərɪt]
compliqué(e), recherché(e),
minutieux(-euse) ▷ vt [ɪ'læbəreɪt]
élaborer ▷ vi entrer dans les détails

elastic [ɪ'læstɪk] adj, n élastique (m);
elastic band n (BRIT) élastique m

elbow ['ɛlbəu] n coude m

elder ['ɛldə] adj aîné(e) ▷ n (tree)
sureau m; **one's ~s** ses aînés; **elderly**
adj âgé(e); **~ people** les personnes
âgées

eldest ['ɛldɪst] adj, n: **the ~ (child)**
l'aîné(e) (des enfants)

elect [ɪ'lɛkt] vt élire; (choose): **to
~ to do** choisir de faire ▷ adj: **the
president ~** le président désigné;
election n élection f; **electoral** adj
électoral(e); **electorate** n électorat m

electric [ɪ'lɛktrɪk] adj électrique;
electrical adj électrique; **electric
blanket** n couverture chauffante;
electric fire n (BRIT) radiateur m
électrique; **electrician** [ɪlɛk'trɪʃən] n
électricien m; **electricity** [ɪlɛk'trɪsɪtɪ]
n électricité f; **electric shock** n choc
m or décharge f électrique; **electrify**
[ɪ'lɛktrɪfaɪ] vt (Rail) électrifier;
(audience) électriser

electronic [ɪlɛk'trɒnɪk] adj
électronique; **electronic mail** n
courrier m électronique; **electronics**
n électronique f

elegance ['ɛlɪgəns] n élégance f

elegant ['ɛlɪgənt] adj élégant(e)

element ['ɛlɪmənt] n (gen) élément m; (of heater, kettle etc) résistance f

elementary [ɛlɪ'mɛntərɪ] adj élémentaire; (school, education) primaire; **elementary school** n (US) école f primaire

elephant ['ɛlɪfənt] n éléphant m

elevate ['ɛlɪveɪt] vt élever

elevator ['ɛlɪveɪtə'] n (in warehouse etc) élévateur m, monte-charge m inv; (US: lift) ascenseur m

eleven [ɪ'lɛvn] num onze; **eleventh** num onzième

eligible ['ɛlɪdʒəbl] adj éligible; (for membership) admissible; **an ~ young man** un beau parti; **to be ~ for sth** remplir les conditions requises pour qch

eliminate [ɪ'lɪmɪneɪt] vt éliminer

elm [ɛlm] n orme m

eloquent ['ɛləkwənt] adj éloquent(e)

else [ɛls] adv: **something ~** quelque chose d'autre, autre chose; **somewhere ~** ailleurs, autre part; **everywhere ~** partout ailleurs; **everyone ~** tous les autres; **nothing ~** rien d'autre; **where ~?** à quel autre endroit?; **little ~** pas grand-chose d'autre; **elsewhere** adv ailleurs, autre part

elusive [ɪ'lu:sɪv] adj insaisissable

email ['i:meɪl] n abbr (= electronic mail) (e-)mail m, courriel m ▷ vt: **to ~ sb** envoyer un (e-)mail or un courriel à qn; **email account** n compte m (e-)mail; **email address** n adresse f (e-)mail or électronique

embankment [ɪm'bæŋkmənt] n (of road, railway) remblai m, talus m; (of river) berge f, quai m; (dyke) digue f

embargo [ɪm'bɑːgəu] (pl **embargoes**) n (Comm, Naut) embargo m; (prohibition) interdiction f

embark [ɪm'bɑːk] vi embarquer ▷ vt embarquer; **to ~ on** (journey etc) commencer, entreprendre; (fig) se lancer or s'embarquer dans

embarrass [ɪm'bærəs] vt embarrasser, gêner; **embarrassed** adj gêné(e); **embarrassing** adj gênant(e), embarrassant(e); **embarrassment** n embarras m, gêne f; (embarrassing thing, person) source f d'embarras

embassy ['ɛmbəsɪ] n ambassade f

embrace [ɪm'breɪs] vt embrasser, étreindre; (include) embrasser ▷ vi s'embrasser, s'étreindre ▷ n étreinte f

embroider [ɪm'brɔɪdə'] vt broder; **embroidery** n broderie f

embryo ['ɛmbrɪəu] n (also fig) embryon m

emerald ['ɛmərəld] n émeraude f

emerge [ɪ'məːdʒ] vi apparaître; (from room, car) surgir; (from sleep, imprisonment) sortir

emergency [ɪ'məːdʒənsɪ] n (crisis) cas m d'urgence; (Med) urgence f; **in an ~** en cas d'urgence; **state of ~** état m d'urgence; **emergency brake** (US) n frein m à main; **emergency exit** n sortie f de secours; **emergency landing** n atterrissage forcé; **emergency room** n (US Med) urgences fpl; **emergency services** npl; **the emergency services** (fire, police, ambulance) les services mpl d'urgence

emigrate ['ɛmɪgreɪt] vi émigrer; **emigration** [ɛmɪ'greɪʃən] n émigration f

eminent ['ɛmɪnənt] adj éminent(e)

emissions [ɪ'mɪʃənz] npl émissions fpl

emit [ɪ'mɪt] vt émettre

emoticon [ɪ'məutɪkən] n (Comput) émoticone m

emotion [ɪ'məuʃən] n sentiment m; **emotional** adj (person) émotif(-ive), très sensible; (needs) affectif(-ive); (scene) émouvant(e); (tone, speech) qui fait appel aux sentiments

emperor ['ɛmpərə'] n empereur m

emphasis (pl **emphases**) ['ɛmfəsɪs, -siːz] n accent m; **to lay** or **place**

~ on sth (*fig*) mettre l'accent sur, insister sur
emphasize ['ɛmfəsaɪz] *vt* (*syllable, word, point*) appuyer *or* insister sur; (*feature*) souligner, accentuer
empire ['ɛmpaɪəʳ] *n* empire *m*
employ [ɪm'plɔɪ] *vt* employer;
    employee [ɪmplɔɪ'i:] *n* employé(e);
    employer *n* employeur(-euse);
    employment *n* emploi *m*;
    employment agency *n* agence *for* bureau *m* de placement
empower [ɪm'pauəʳ] *vt*: **to ~ sb to do** autoriser *or* habiliter qn à faire
empress ['ɛmprɪs] *n* impératrice *f*
emptiness ['ɛmptɪnɪs] *n* vide *m*; (*of area*) aspect *m* désertique
empty ['ɛmptɪ] *adj* vide; (*street, area*) désert(e); (*threat, promise*) en l'air, vain(e) ▷ *vt* vider ▷ *vi* se vider; (*liquid*) s'écouler; **empty-handed** *adj* les mains vides
EMU *n abbr* (= *European Monetary Union*) UME *f*
emulsion [ɪ'mʌlʃən] *n* émulsion *f*; (*also:* **~ paint**) peinture mate
enable [ɪ'neɪbl] *vt*: **to ~ sb to do** permettre à qn de faire
enamel [ɪ'næməl] *n* émail *m*; (*also:* **~ paint**) (peinture *f*) laque *f*
enchanting [ɪn'tʃɑ:ntɪŋ] *adj* ravissant(e), enchanteur(-eresse)
encl. *abbr* (*on letters etc* = *enclosed*) ci-joint(e); (: = *enclosure*) PJ *f*
enclose [ɪn'kləuz] *vt* (*land*) clôturer; (*space, object*) entourer; (*letter etc*) **to ~ (with)** joindre (à); **please find ~d** veuillez trouver ci-joint
enclosure [ɪn'kləuʒəʳ] *n* enceinte *f*
encore [ɔŋ'kɔːʳ] *excl, n* bis (*m*)
encounter [ɪn'kauntəʳ] *n* rencontre *f* ▷ *vt* rencontrer
encourage [ɪn'kʌrɪdʒ] *vt* encourager
encouraging [ɪn'kʌrɪdʒɪŋ] *adj* encourageant(e)
encyclop(a)edia [ɛnsaɪkləu'pi:dɪə] *n* encyclopédie *f*

end [ɛnd] *n* fin *f*; (*of table, street, rope etc*) bout *m*, extrémité *f* ▷ *vt* terminer; (*also:* **bring to an ~, put an ~ to**) mettre fin à ▷ *vi* se terminer, finir; **in the ~** finalement; **on ~** (*object*) debout, dressé(e); **to stand on ~** (*hair*) se dresser sur la tête; **for hours on ~** pendant des heures (et des heures); **end up** *vi*: **to ~ up in** (*condition*) finir *or* se terminer par; (*place*) finir *or* aboutir à
endanger [ɪn'deɪndʒəʳ] *vt* mettre en danger; **an ~ed species** une espèce en voie de disparition
endearing [ɪn'dɪərɪŋ] *adj* attachant(e)
endeavour, (*us*) **endeavor** [ɪn'dɛvəʳ] *n* effort *m*; (*attempt*) tentative *f* ▷ *vt*: **to ~ to do** tenter *or* s'efforcer de faire
ending ['ɛndɪŋ] *n* dénouement *m*, conclusion *f*; (*Ling*) terminaison *f*
endless ['ɛndlɪs] *adj* sans fin, interminable
endorse [ɪn'dɔ:s] *vt* (*cheque*) endosser; (*approve*) appuyer, approuver, sanctionner; **endorsement** *n* (*approval*) appui *m*, aval *m*; (*brit: on driving licence*) contravention *f* (*portée au permis de conduire*)
endurance [ɪn'djuərəns] *n* endurance *f*
endure [ɪn'djuəʳ] *vt* (*bear*) supporter, endurer ▷ *vi* (*last*) durer
enemy ['ɛnəmɪ] *adj, n* ennemi(e)
energetic [ɛnə'dʒɛtɪk] *adj* énergique; (*activity*) très actif(-ive), qui fait se dépenser (physiquement)
energy ['ɛnədʒɪ] *n* énergie *f*
enforce [ɪn'fɔːs] *vt* (*law*) appliquer, faire respecter
engaged [ɪn'geɪdʒd] *adj* (*brit: busy, in use*) occupé(e); (*betrothed*) fiancé(e); **to get ~** se fiancer; **the line's ~** la ligne est occupée; **engaged tone** *n* (*brit Tel*) tonalité *f* occupé *inv*

engagement [ɪn'geɪdʒmənt]
n (undertaking) obligation f,
engagement m; (appointment) rendez-
vous m inv; (to marry) fiançailles fpl;
engagement ring n bague f de
fiançailles

engaging [ɪn'geɪdʒɪŋ] adj
engageant(e), attirant(e)

engine ['endʒɪn] n (Aut) moteur m;
(Rail) locomotive f

■ Be careful not to translate engine
by the French word engin.

engineer [endʒɪ'nɪəʳ] n ingénieur m;
(BRIT: repairer) dépanneur m; (Navy,
US Rail) mécanicien m; **engineering**
n engineering m, ingénierie f; (of
bridges, ships) génie m; (of machine)
mécanique f

England ['ɪŋɡlənd] n Angleterre f

English ['ɪŋɡlɪʃ] adj anglais(e) ▷ n
(Ling) anglais m; **the ~** npl les Anglais;
English Channel n: **the English
Channel** la Manche; **Englishman**
(irreg) n Anglais m; **Englishwoman**
(irreg) n Anglaise f

engrave [ɪn'greɪv] vt graver

engraving [ɪn'greɪvɪŋ] n gravure f

enhance [ɪn'hɑːns] vt rehausser,
mettre en valeur

enjoy [ɪn'dʒɔɪ] vt aimer, prendre
plaisir à; (have benefit of: health,
fortune) jouir de; (: success) connaître;
to ~ o.s. s'amuser; **enjoyable** adj
agréable; **enjoyment** n plaisir m

enlarge [ɪn'lɑːdʒ] vt accroître;
(Phot) agrandir ▷ vi: **to ~ on** (subject)
s'étendre sur; **enlargement** n (Phot)
agrandissement m

enlist [ɪn'lɪst] vt recruter; (support)
s'assurer ▷ vi s'engager

enormous [ɪ'nɔːməs] adj énorme

enough [ɪ'nʌf] adj: **~ time/
books** assez or suffisamment de
temps/livres ▷ adv: **big ~** assez or
suffisamment grand ▷ pron: **have
you got ~?** (en) avez-vous assez?;
~ to eat assez à manger; **that's
~, thanks** cela suffit or c'est assez,

merci; **I've had ~ of him** j'en ai
assez de lui; **he has not worked
~** il n'a pas assez or suffisamment
travaillé, il n'a pas travaillé assez or
suffisamment; **... which, funnily** or
oddly or **strangely ~ ...** qui, chose
curieuse, ...

enquire [ɪn'kwaɪəʳ] vt, vi = **inquire**

enquiry [ɪn'kwaɪərɪ] n = **inquiry**

enrage [ɪn'reɪdʒ] vt mettre en fureur
or en rage, rendre furieux(-euse)

enrich [ɪn'rɪtʃ] vt enrichir

enrol, (US) **enroll** [ɪn'rəul] vt inscrire
▷ vi s'inscrire; **enrolment**, (US)
enrollment n inscription f

en route [ɔn'ruːt] adv en route, en
chemin

en suite ['ɔnswiːt] adj: **with ~
bathroom** avec salle de bains en
attenante

ensure [ɪn'ʃuəʳ] vt assurer, garantir

entail [ɪn'teɪl] vt entraîner, nécessiter

enter ['entəʳ] vt (room) entrer dans,
pénétrer dans; (club, army) entrer à;
(competition) s'inscrire à or pour; (sb
for a competition) (faire) inscrire; (write
down) inscrire, noter; (Comput) entrer,
introduire ▷ vi entrer

enterprise ['entəpraɪz] n
(company, undertaking) entreprise
f; (initiative) (esprit m d')initiative
f; **free ~** libre entreprise; **private
~** entreprise privée; **enterprising**
adj entreprenant(e), dynamique;
(scheme) audacieux(-euse)

entertain [entə'teɪn] vt amuser,
distraire; (invite) recevoir (à dîner);
(idea, plan) envisager; **entertainer** n
artiste m/f de variétés; **entertaining**
adj amusant(e), distrayant(e);
entertainment n (amusement)
distraction f, divertissement m,
amusement m; (show) spectacle m

enthusiasm [ɪn'θuːzɪæzəm] n
enthousiasme m

enthusiast [ɪn'θuːzɪæst] n
enthousiaste m/f; **enthusiastic**
[ɪnθuːzɪ'æstɪk] adj enthousiaste;

to be enthusiastic about être enthousiasmé(e) par

entire [ɪn'taɪə'] *adj* (tout) entier(-ère); **entirely** *adv* entièrement

entitle [ɪn'taɪtl] *vt*: **to ~ sb to sth** donner droit à qch à qn; **entitled** *adj* (*book*) intitulé(e); **to be entitled to do** avoir le droit de faire

entrance *n* ['ɛntrns] entrée *f* ▷ *vt* [ɪn'trɑːns] enchanter, ravir; **where's the ~?** où est l'entrée?; **to gain ~ to** (*university etc*) être admis à; **entrance examination** *n* examen *m* d'entrée *or* d'admission; **entrance fee** *n* (*to museum etc*) prix *m* d'entrée; (*to join club etc*) droit *m* d'inscription; **entrance ramp** *n* (*US Aut*) bretelle *f* d'accès; **entrant** *n* (*in race etc*) participant(e), concurrent(e); (*BRIT: in exam*) candidat(e)

entrepreneur ['ɔntrəprə'nəː'] *n* entrepreneur *m*

entrust [ɪn'trʌst] *vt*: **to ~ sth to** confier qch à

entry ['ɛntrɪ] *n* entrée *f*; (*in register, diary*) inscription *f*; **"no ~"** "défense d'entrer", "entrée interdite"; (*Aut*) "sens interdit"; **entry phone** *n* (*BRIT*) interphone *m* (*à l'entrée d'un immeuble*)

envelope ['ɛnvələup] *n* enveloppe *f*

envious ['ɛnvɪəs] *adj* envieux(-euse)

environment [ɪn'vaɪərnmənt] *n* (*social, moral*) milieu *m*; (*natural world*): **the ~** l'environnement *m*; **environmental** [ɪnvaɪərn'mɛntl] *adj* (*of surroundings*) du milieu; (*issue, disaster*) écologique; **environmentally** [ɪnvaɪərn'mɛntlɪ] *adv*: **environmentally sound/ friendly** qui ne nuit pas à l'environnement

envisage [ɪn'vɪzɪdʒ] *vt* (*foresee*) prévoir

envoy ['ɛnvɔɪ] *n* envoyé(e); (*diplomat*) ministre *m* plénipotentiaire

envy ['ɛnvɪ] *n* envie *f* ▷ *vt* envier; **to ~ sb sth** envier qch à qn

epic ['ɛpɪk] *n* épopée *f* ▷ *adj* épique

epidemic [ɛpɪ'dɛmɪk] *n* épidémie *f*

epilepsy ['ɛpɪlɛpsɪ] *n* épilepsie *f*; **epileptic** *adj*, *n* épileptique *m/f*; **epileptic fit** *n* crise *f* d'épilepsie

episode ['ɛpɪsəud] *n* épisode *m*

equal ['iːkwl] *adj* égal(e) ▷ *vt* égaler; **~ to** (*task*) à la hauteur de; **equality** [iː'kwɔlɪtɪ] *n* égalité *f*; **equalize** *vt*, *vi* (*Sport*) égaliser; **equally** *adv* également; (*share*) en parts égales; (*treat*) de la même façon; (*pay*) autant; (*just as*) tout aussi

equation [ɪ'kweɪʃən] *n* (*Math*) équation *f*

equator [ɪ'kweɪtə'] *n* équateur *m*

equip [ɪ'kwɪp] *vt* équiper; **to ~ sb/ sth with** équiper *or* munir qn/ qch de; **equipment** *n* équipement *m*; (*electrical etc*) appareillage *m*, installation *f*

equivalent [ɪ'kwɪvəlnt] *adj* équivalent(e) ▷ *n* équivalent *m*; **to be ~ to** équivaloir à, être équivalent(e) à

ER *abbr* (*BRIT*: = *Elizabeth Regina*) la reine Élisabeth; (*US Med*: = *emergency room*) urgences *fpl*

era ['ɪərə] *n* ère *f*, époque *f*

erase [ɪ'reɪz] *vt* effacer; **eraser** *n* gomme *f*

e-reader ['iːriːdə'] *n* liseuse *f*

erect [ɪ'rɛkt] *adj* droit(e) ▷ *vt* construire; (*monument*) ériger, élever; (*tent etc*) dresser; **erection** [ɪ'rɛkʃən] *n* (*Physiol*) érection *f*; (*of building*) construction *f*

ERM *n abbr* (= *Exchange Rate Mechanism*) mécanisme *m* des taux de change

erode [ɪ'rəud] *vt* éroder; (*metal*) ronger

erosion [ɪ'rəuʒən] *n* érosion *f*

erotic [ɪ'rɔtɪk] *adj* érotique

errand ['ɛrnd] *n* course *f*, commission *f*

erratic [ɪ'rætɪk] *adj* irrégulier(-ière), inconstant(e)

error ['ɛrə'] *n* erreur *f*

erupt [ɪ'rʌpt] vi entrer en éruption;
(fig) éclater; **eruption** [ɪ'rʌpʃən]
n éruption f; (of anger, violence)
explosion f

escalate ['ɛskəleɪt] vi s'intensifier;
(costs) monter en flèche

escalator ['ɛskəleɪtə^r] n escalier
roulant

escape [ɪ'skeɪp] n évasion f, fuite f;
(of gas etc) fuite f ▷ vi s'échapper, fuir;
(from jail) s'évader; (fig) s'en tirer;
(leak) s'échapper ▷ vt échapper à; **to
~ from** (person) échapper à; (place)
s'échapper de; (fig) fuir; **his name ~s
me** son nom m'échappe

escort vt [ɪ'skɔːt] escorter ▷ n
['ɛskɔːt] (Mil) escorte f

especially [ɪ'spɛʃlɪ] adv (particularly)
particulièrement; (above all) surtout

espionage ['ɛspɪɑnɑːʒ] n
espionnage m

essay ['ɛseɪ] n (Scol) dissertation f;
(Literature) essai m

essence ['ɛsns] n essence f; (Culin)
extrait m

essential [ɪ'sɛnʃl] adj essentiel(le);
(basic) fondamental(e); **essentials**
npl éléments essentiels; **essentially**
adv essentiellement

establish [ɪ'stæblɪʃ] vt établir;
(business) fonder, créer; (one's power
etc) asseoir, affermir; **establishment**
n établissement m; (founding) création
f; (institution) établissement; **the
Establishment** les pouvoirs établis;
l'ordre établi

estate [ɪ'steɪt] n (land) domaine
m, propriété f; (Law) biens mpl,
succession f; (BRIT: also: **housing ~**)
lotissement m; **estate agent** n (BRIT)
agent immobilier; **estate car** n (BRIT)
break m

estimate n ['ɛstɪmət] estimation
f; (Comm) devis m ▷ vt ['ɛstɪmeɪt]
estimer

etc abbr (= et cetera) etc

eternal [ɪ'təːnl] adj éternel(le)

eternity [ɪ'təːnɪtɪ] n éternité f

ethical ['ɛθɪkl] adj moral(e); **ethics**
['ɛθɪks] n éthique f ▷ npl moralité f

Ethiopia [iːθɪ'əupɪə] n Éthiopie f

ethnic ['ɛθnɪk] adj ethnique; (clothes,
food) folklorique, exotique, propre aux
minorités ethniques non-occidentales;
ethnic minority n minorité f
ethnique

e-ticket ['iːtɪkɪt] n billet·m
électronique

etiquette ['ɛtɪkɛt] n convenances
fpl, étiquette f

EU n abbr (= European Union) UE f

euro ['juərəu] n (currency) euro m

Europe ['juərəp] n Europe f;
European [juərə'piːən] adj
européen(ne) ▷ n Européen(ne);
European Community n
Communauté européenne;
European Union n Union
européenne

Eurostar® ['juərəustɑː^r] n
Eurostar® m

evacuate [ɪ'vækjueɪt] vt évacuer

evade [ɪ'veɪd] vt échapper à; (question
etc) éluder; (duties) se dérober à

evaluate [ɪ'væljueɪt] vt évaluer

evaporate [ɪ'væpəreɪt] vi s'évaporer;
(fig: hopes, fear) s'envoler; (anger) se
dissiper

eve [iːv] n: **on the ~ of** à la veille de

even ['iːvn] adj (level, smooth)
régulier(-ière); (equal) égal(e);
(number) pair(e) ▷ adv même; **~ if**
même si + indic; **~ though** alors
même que + cond; **~ more** encore
plus; **~ faster** encore plus vite; **~
so** quand même; **not ~** pas même;
~ he was there même lui était là;
~ on Sundays même le dimanche;
to get ~ with sb prendre sa
revanche sur qn

evening ['iːvnɪŋ] n soir m; (as
duration, event) soirée f; **in the ~** le
soir; **evening class** n cours m du soir;
evening dress n (man's) tenue f de
soirée, smoking m; (woman's) robe
f de soirée

event [ɪ'vɛnt] n événement m; (Sport) épreuve f; **in the ~ of** en cas de; **eventful** adj mouvementé(e)

eventual [ɪ'vɛntʃuəl] adj final(e)

Be careful not to translate *eventual* by the French word *éventuel*.

eventually [ɪ'vɛntʃuəlɪ] adv finalement

Be careful not to translate *eventually* by the French word *éventuellement*.

ever ['ɛvəʳ] adv jamais; (at all times) toujours; **why ~ not?** mais enfin, pourquoi pas?; **the best ~** le meilleur qu'on ait jamais vu; **have you ~ seen it?** l'as-tu déjà vu?, as-tu eu l'occasion or t'est-il arrivé de le voir?; **~ since** (as adv) depuis; (as conj) depuis que; **~ so pretty** si joli; **evergreen** n arbre m à feuilles persistantes

 KEYWORD

every ['ɛvrɪ] adj **1** (each) chaque; **every one of them** tous (sans exception); **every shop in town was closed** tous les magasins en ville étaient fermés

2 (all possible) tous (toutes) les; **I gave you every assistance** j'ai fait tout mon possible pour vous aider; **I have every confidence in him** j'ai entièrement or pleinement confiance en lui; **we wish you every success** nous vous souhaitons beaucoup de succès

3 (showing recurrence) tous les; **every day** tous les jours, chaque jour; **every other car** une voiture sur deux; **every other/third day** tous les deux/trois jours; **every now and then** de temps en temps; **everybody** pron = **everyone**; **everyday** adj (expression) courant(e), d'usage courant; (use) courant(e); (clothes, life) de tous les jours; (occurrence, problem) quotidien(ne); **everyone** pron tout

le monde, tous pl; **everything** pron tout; **everywhere** adv partout; **everywhere you go you meet ...** où qu'on aille on rencontre ...

evict [ɪ'vɪkt] vt expulser

evidence ['ɛvɪdns] n (proof) preuve(s) f(pl); (of witness) témoignage m; (sign): **to show ~ of** donner des signes de; **to give ~** témoigner, déposer

evident ['ɛvɪdnt] adj évident(e); **evidently** adv de toute évidence; (apparently) apparemment

evil ['i:vl] adj mauvais(e) ▷ n mal m

evoke [ɪ'vəuk] vt évoquer

evolution [i:və'lu:ʃən] n évolution f

evolve [ɪ'vɔlv] vt élaborer ▷ vi évoluer, se transformer

ewe [ju:] n brebis f

ex [ɛks] n (inf): **my ex** mon ex

ex- [ɛks] prefix ex-

exact [ɪg'zækt] adj exact(e) ▷ vt: **to ~ sth (from)** (signature, confession) extorquer qch (à); (apology) exiger qch (de); **exactly** adv exactement

exaggerate [ɪg'zædʒəreɪt] vt, vi exagérer; **exaggeration** [ɪgzædʒə'reɪʃən] n exagération f

exam [ɪg'zæm] n abbr (Scol); = **examination**

examination [ɪgzæmɪ'neɪʃən] n (Scol, Med) examen m; **to take** or **sit an ~** (BRIT) passer un examen

examine [ɪg'zæmɪn] vt (gen) examiner; (Scol, Law: person) interroger; **examiner** n examinateur(-trice)

example [ɪg'zɑ:mpl] n exemple m; **for ~** par exemple

exasperated [ɪg'zɑ:spəreɪtɪd] adj exaspéré(e)

excavate ['ɛkskəveɪt] vt (site) fouiller, excaver; (object) mettre au jour

exceed [ɪk'si:d] vt dépasser; (one's powers) outrepasser; **exceedingly** adv extrêmement

excel [ɪk'sɛl] *vi* exceller ▷ *vt*
surpasser; **to ~ o.s.** se surpasser
excellence ['ɛksələns] *n* excellence *f*
excellent ['ɛksələnt] *adj* excellent(e)
except [ɪk'sɛpt] *prep* (*also:* **~ for,
~ing**) sauf, excepté, à l'exception
de ▷ *vt* excepter; **~ if/when** sauf
si/quand; **~ that** excepté que, si ce
n'est que; **exception** [ɪk'sɛpʃən]
n exception *f*; **to take exception
to** s'offusquer de; **exceptional**
[ɪk'sɛpʃənl] *adj* exceptionnel(le);
exceptionally [ɪk'sɛpʃənəlɪ] *adv*
exceptionnellement
excerpt ['ɛksəːpt] *n* extrait *m*
excess [ɪk'sɛs] *n* excès *m*; **excess
baggage** *n* excédent *m* de bagages;
excessive *adj* excessif(-ive)
exchange [ɪks'tʃeɪndʒ] *n* échange
m; (*also:* **telephone ~**) central *m*
▷ *vt*: **to ~ (for)** échanger (contre);
could I ~ this, please? est-ce que je
peux échanger ceci, s'il vous plaît?;
exchange rate *n* taux *m* de change
excite [ɪk'saɪt] *vt* exciter; **excited**
adj (tout) excité(e); **to get excited**
s'exciter; **excitement** *n* excitation *f*;
exciting *adj* passionnant(e)
exclaim [ɪk'skleɪm] *vi* s'exclamer;
exclamation [ɛksklə'meɪʃən] *n*
exclamation *f*; **exclamation mark**,
(*us*) **exclamation point** *n* point *m*
d'exclamation
exclude [ɪk'skluːd] *vt* exclure
excluding [ɪk'skluːdɪŋ] *prep*: **~ VAT**
la TVA non comprise
exclusion [ɪk'skluːʒən] *n* exclusion *f*
exclusive [ɪk'skluːsɪv] *adj*
exclusif(-ive); (*club, district*) sélect(e);
(*item of news*) en exclusivité; **~ of VAT**
TVA non comprise; **exclusively** *adv*
exclusivement
excruciating [ɪk'skruːʃɪeɪtɪŋ]
adj (*pain*) atroce, déchirant(e);
(*embarrassing*) pénible
excursion [ɪk'skəːʃən] *n* excursion *f*
excuse *n* [ɪk'skjuːs] excuse *f* ▷ *vt*
[ɪk'skjuːz] (*forgive*) excuser; **to ~ sb**

from (*activity*) dispenser qn de; **~
me!** excusez-moi!, pardon!; **now if you
will ~ me, ...** maintenant, si vous (le)
permettez ...
ex-directory ['ɛksdɪ'rɛktərɪ] *adj*
(*brit*) sur la liste rouge
execute ['ɛksɪkjuːt] *vt* exécuter;
execution [ɛksɪ'kjuːʃən] *n*
exécution *f*
executive [ɪg'zɛkjutɪv] *n* (*person*)
cadre *m*; (*managing group*) bureau *m*;
(*Pol*) exécutif *m* ▷ *adj* exécutif(-ive);
(*position, job*) de cadre
exempt [ɪg'zɛmpt] *adj*: **~ from**
exempté(e) or dispensé(e) de ▷ *vt*: **to ~
sb from** exempter or dispenser qn de
exercise ['ɛksəsaɪz] *n* exercice *m* ▷ *vt*
exercer; (*patience etc*) faire preuve de;
(*dog*) promener ▷ *vi* (*also:* **to take ~**)
prendre de l'exercice; **exercise book**
n cahier *m*
exert [ɪg'zəːt] *vt* exercer, employer;
to ~ o.s. se dépenser; **exertion**
[ɪg'zəːʃən] *n* effort *m*
exhale [ɛks'heɪl] *vt* exhaler ▷ *vi*
expirer
exhaust [ɪg'zɔːst] *n* (*also:* **~ fumes**)
gaz *mpl* d'échappement; (*also:* **~
pipe**) tuyau *m* d'échappement ▷ *vt*
épuiser; **exhausted** *adj* épuisé(e);
exhaustion [ɪg'zɔːstʃən] *n*
épuisement *m*; **nervous exhaustion**
fatigue nerveuse
exhibit [ɪg'zɪbɪt] *n* (*Art*) objet
exposé, pièce exposée; (*Law*) pièce
à conviction ▷ *vt* (*Art*) exposer;
(*courage, skill*) faire preuve de;
exhibition [ɛksɪ'bɪʃən] *n* exposition *f*
exhilarating [ɪg'zɪləreɪtɪŋ] *adj*
grisant(e), stimulant(e)
exile ['ɛksaɪl] *n* exil *m*; (*person*) exilé(e)
▷ *vt* exiler
exist [ɪg'zɪst] *vi* exister; **existence** *n*
existence *f*; **existing** *adj* actuel(le)
exit ['ɛksɪt] *n* sortie *f* ▷ *vi* (*Comput,
Theat*) sortir; **where's the ~?** où est la
sortie?; **exit ramp** *n* (*us Aut*) bretelle
f d'accès

exotic [ɪgˈzɒtɪk] *adj* exotique
expand [ɪkˈspænd] *vt* (*area*) agrandir; (*quantity*) accroître ▷ *vi* (*trade, etc*) se développer, s'accroître; (*gas, metal*) se dilater
expansion [ɪkˈspænʃən] *n* (*territorial, economic*) expansion *f*; (*of trade, influence etc*) développement *m*; (*of production*) accroissement *m*; (*of population*) croissance *f*; (*of gas, metal*) expansion, dilatation *f*
expect [ɪkˈspɛkt] *vt* (*anticipate*) s'attendre à, s'attendre à ce que + *sub*; (*count on*) compter sur, escompter; (*require*) demander, exiger; (*suppose*) supposer; (*await: also baby*) attendre ▷ *vi*: **to be ~ing** (*pregnant woman*) être enceinte; **expectation** [ɛkspɛkˈteɪʃən] *n* (*hope*) attente *f*, espérance(s) *f(pl)*; (*belief*) attente
expedition [ɛkspəˈdɪʃən] *n* expédition *f*
expel [ɪkˈspɛl] *vt* chasser, expulser; (*Scol*) renvoyer, exclure
expenditure [ɪkˈspɛndɪtʃəʳ] *n* (*act of spending*) dépense *f*; (*money spent*) dépenses *fpl*
expense [ɪkˈspɛns] *n* (*high cost*) coût *m*; (*spending*) dépense *f*, frais *mpl*; **expenses** *npl* frais *mpl*; dépenses; **at the ~ of** (*fig*) aux dépens de; **expense account** *n* (*note f de*) frais *mpl*
expensive [ɪkˈspɛnsɪv] *adj* cher (chère), coûteux(-euse); **it's too ~** ça coûte trop cher
experience [ɪkˈspɪərɪəns] *n* expérience *f* ▷ *vt* connaître; (*feeling*) éprouver; **experienced** *adj* expérimenté(e)
experiment [ɪkˈspɛrɪmənt] *n* expérience *f* ▷ *vi* faire une expérience; **experimental** [ɪksperɪˈmɛntl] *adj* expérimental(e)
expert [ˈɛkspəːt] *adj* expert(e) ▷ *n* expert *m*; **expertise** [ɛkspəːˈtiːz] *n* (grande) compétence
expire [ɪkˈspaɪəʳ] *vi* expirer; **expiry** *n* expiration *f*; **expiry date** *n* date

f d'expiration; (*on label*) à utiliser avant …
explain [ɪkˈspleɪn] *vt* expliquer; **explanation** [ɛkspləˈneɪʃən] *n* explication *f*
explicit [ɪkˈsplɪsɪt] *adj* explicite; (*definite*) formel(le)
explode [ɪkˈspləʊd] *vi* exploser
exploit *n* [ˈɛksplɔɪt] exploit *m* ▷ *vt* [ɪkˈsplɔɪt] exploiter; **exploitation** [ɛksplɔɪˈteɪʃən] *n* exploitation *f*
explore [ɪkˈsplɔːʳ] *vt* explorer; (*possibilities*) étudier, examiner; **explorer** *n* explorateur(-trice)
explosion [ɪkˈspləʊʒən] *n* explosion *f*; **explosive** [ɪkˈspləʊsɪv] *adj* explosif(-ive) ▷ *n* explosif *m*
export *vt* [ɛkˈspɔːt] exporter ▷ *n* [ˈɛkspɔːt] exportation *f* ▷ *cpd* [ˈɛkspɔːt] d'exportation; **exporter** *n* exportateur *m*
expose [ɪkˈspəʊz] *vt* exposer; (*unmask*) démasquer, dévoiler; **exposed** *adj* (*land, house*) exposé(e); **exposure** [ɪkˈspəʊʒəʳ] *n* exposition *f*; (*publicity*) couverture *f*; (*Phot: speed*) (temps *m* de) pose *f*; (: *shot*) pose; **to die of exposure** (*Med*) mourir de froid
express [ɪkˈsprɛs] *adj* (*definite*) formel(le), exprès(-esse); (BRIT: *letter etc*) exprès *inv* ▷ *n* (*train*) rapide *m* ▷ *vt* exprimer; **expression** [ɪkˈsprɛʃən] *n* expression *f*; **expressway** *n* (US) voie *f* express (à plusieurs files)
exquisite [ɛkˈskwɪzɪt] *adj* exquis(e)
extend [ɪkˈstɛnd] *vt* (*visit, street*) prolonger; remettre; (*building*) agrandir; (*offer*) présenter, offrir; (*hand, arm*) tendre ▷ *vi* (*land*) s'étendre; **extension** *n* (*of visit, street*) prolongation *f*; (*building*) annexe *f*; (*telephone: in offices*) poste *m*; (: *in private house*) téléphone *m* supplémentaire; **extension cable, extension lead** *n* (*Elec*) rallonge *f*; **extensive** *adj* étendu(e), vaste; (*damage, alterations*) considérable; (*inquiries*) approfondi(e)

extent [ɪk'stɛnt] n étendue f; **to some ~** dans une certaine mesure; **to the ~ of ...** au point de ...; **to what ~?** dans quelle mesure?, jusqu'à quel point?; **to such an ~ that ...** à tel point que ...

exterior [ɛk'stɪərɪəʳ] adj extérieur(e) ▷ n extérieur m

external [ɛk'stə:nl] adj externe

extinct [ɪk'stɪŋkt] adj (volcano) éteint(e); (species) disparu(e); **extinction** n extinction f

extinguish [ɪk'stɪŋgwɪʃ] vt éteindre

extra ['ɛkstrə] adj supplémentaire, de plus ▷ adv (in addition) en plus ▷ n supplément m; (perk) à-coté m; (Cine, Theat) figurant(e)

extract vt [ɪk'strækt] extraire; (tooth) arracher; (money, promise) soutirer ▷ n ['ɛkstrækt] extrait m

extradite ['ɛkstrədaɪt] vt extrader

extraordinary [ɪk'strɔ:dnrɪ] adj extraordinaire

extravagance [ɪk'strævəgəns] n (excessive spending) prodigalités fpl; (thing bought) folie f, dépense excessive; **extravagant** adj extravagant(e); (in spending: person) prodigue, dépensier(-ière); (: tastes) dispendieux(-euse)

extreme [ɪk'stri:m] adj, n extrême (m); **extremely** adv extrêmement

extremist [ɪk'stri:mɪst] adj, n extrémiste m/f

extrovert ['ɛkstrəvə:t] n extraverti(e)

eye [aɪ] n œil m; (of needle) trou m, chas m ▷ vt examiner; **to keep an ~ on** surveiller; **eyeball** n globe m oculaire; **eyebrow** n sourcil m; **eye drops** npl gouttes fpl pour les yeux; **eyelash** n cil m; **eyelid** n paupière f; **eyeliner** n eye-liner m; **eye shadow** n ombre f à paupières; **eyesight** n vue f; **eye witness** n témoin m oculaire

F [ɛf] n (Mus) fa m

fabric ['fæbrɪk] n tissu m

fabulous ['fæbjuləs] adj fabuleux(-euse); (inf: super) formidable, sensationnel(le)

face [feɪs] n visage m, figure f; (expression) air m; (of clock) cadran m; (of cliff) paroi f; (of mountain) face f; (of building) façade f ▷ vt faire face à; (facts etc) accepter; **~ down** (person) à plat ventre; (card) face en dessous; **to lose/save ~** perdre/sauver la face; **to pull a ~** faire une grimace; **in the ~ of** (difficulties etc) face à, devant; **on the ~ of it** à première vue; **~ to ~** face à face; **face up to** vt fus faire face à, affronter; **face cloth** n (BRIT) gant m de toilette; **face pack** n (BRIT) masque m (de beauté)

facial ['feɪʃl] adj facial(e) ▷ n soin complet du visage

facilitate [fə'sɪlɪteɪt] vt faciliter

facilities [fə'sɪlɪtɪz] *npl* installations *fpl*, équipement *m*; **credit ~** facilités de paiement

fact [fækt] *n* fait *m*; **in ~** en fait

faction ['fækʃən] *n* faction *f*

factor ['fæktə^r] *n* facteur *m*; (*of sun cream*) indice *m* (de protection); **I'd like a ~ 15 suntan lotion** je voudrais une crème solaire d'indice 15

factory ['fæktərɪ] *n* usine *f*, fabrique *f*

factual ['fæktjuəl] *adj* basé(e) sur les faits

faculty ['fækəltɪ] *n* faculté *f*; (*us: teaching staff*) corps enseignant

fad [fæd] *n* (*personal*) manie *f*; (*craze*) engouement *m*

fade [feɪd] *vi* se décolorer, passer; (*light, sound*) s'affaiblir; (*flower*) se faner; **fade away** *vi* (*sound*) s'affaiblir

fag [fæg] *n* (BRIT inf: *cigarette*) clope *f*

Fahrenheit ['fɑːrənhaɪt] *n* Fahrenheit *m inv*

fail [feɪl] *vt* (*exam*) échouer à; (*candidate*) recaler; (*subj: courage, memory*) faire défaut à ▷ *vi* échouer; (*eyesight, health, light: also:* **be ~ing**) baisser, s'affaiblir; (*brakes*) lâcher; **to ~ to do sth** (*neglect*) négliger de *or* ne pas faire qch; (*be unable*) ne pas arriver *or* parvenir à faire qch; **without ~** à coup sûr; sans faute; **failing** *n* défaut *m* ▷ *prep* faute de; **failing that** à défaut, sinon; **failure** ['feɪljə^r] *n* échec *m*; (*person*) raté(e); (*mechanical etc*) défaillance *f*

faint [feɪnt] *adj* faible; (*recollection*) vague; (*mark*) à peine visible ▷ *n* évanouissement *m* ▷ *vi* s'évanouir; **to feel ~** défaillir; **faintest** *adj:* **I haven't the faintest idea** je n'en ai pas la moindre idée; **faintly** *adv* faiblement; (*vaguely*) vaguement

fair [fɛə^r] *adj* équitable, juste; (*hair*) blond(e); (*skin, complexion*) pâle, blanc (blanche); (*weather*) beau (belle); (*good enough*) assez bon(ne); (*sizeable*) considérable ▷ *adv:* **to play ~** jouer franc jeu ▷ *n* foire *f*; (BRIT: *funfair*) fête

(foraine); **fairground** *n* champ *m* de foire; **fair-haired** *adj* (*person*) aux cheveux clairs, blond(e); **fairly** *adv* (*justly*) équitablement; (*quite*) assez; **fair trade** *n* commerce *m* équitable; **fairway** *n* (*Golf*) fairway *m*

fairy ['fɛərɪ] *n* fée *f*; **fairy tale** *n* conte *m* de fées

faith [feɪθ] *n* foi *f*; (*trust*) confiance *f*; (*sect*) culte *m*, religion *f*; **faithful** *adj* fidèle; **faithfully** *adv* fidèlement; **yours faithfully** (BRIT: *in letters*) veuillez agréer l'expression de mes salutations les plus distinguées

fake [feɪk] *n* (*painting etc*) faux *m*; (*person*) imposteur *m* ▷ *adj* faux (fausse) ▷ *vt* (*emotions*) simuler; (*painting*) faire un faux de

falcon ['fɔːlkən] *n* faucon *m*

fall [fɔːl] *n* chute *f*; (*decrease*) baisse *f*; (*us: autumn*) automne *m* ▷ *vi* (*pt* **fell**, *pp* **fallen**) tomber; (*price, temperature, dollar*) baisser; **falls** *npl* (*waterfall*) chute *f* d'eau, cascade *f*; **to ~ flat** *vi* (*on one's face*) tomber de tout son long, s'étaler; (*joke*) tomber à plat; (*plan*) échouer; **fall apart** *vi* (*object*) tomber en morceaux; **fall down** *vi* (*person*) tomber; (*building*) s'effondrer, s'écrouler; **fall for** *vt* (*trick*) se laisser prendre à; (*person*) tomber amoureux(-euse) de; **fall off** *vi* tomber; (*diminish*) baisser, diminuer; **fall out** *vi* (*friends etc*) se brouiller; (*hair, teeth*) tomber; **fall over** *vi* tomber (par terre); **fall through** *vi* (*plan, project*) tomber à l'eau

fallen ['fɔːlən] *pp of* **fall**

fallout ['fɔːlaut] *n* retombées (radioactives)

false [fɔːls] *adj* faux (fausse); **under ~ pretences** sous un faux prétexte; **false alarm** *n* fausse alerte; **false teeth** *npl* (BRIT) fausses dents, dentier *m*

fame [feɪm] *n* renommée *f*, renom *m*

familiar [fə'mɪlɪə^r] *adj* familier(-ière); **to be ~ with sth** connaître qch;

familiarize [fəˈmɪlɪəraɪz] vt: **to familiarize o.s. with** se familiariser avec

family [ˈfæmɪlɪ] n famille f; **family doctor** n médecin m de famille; **family planning** n planning familial

famine [ˈfæmɪn] n famine f

famous [ˈfeɪməs] adj célèbre

fan [fæn] n (folding) éventail m; (Elec) ventilateur m; (person) fan m, admirateur(-trice); (Sport) supporter m/f ▷ vt éventer; (fire, quarrel) attiser

fanatic [fəˈnætɪk] n fanatique m/f

fan belt n courroie f de ventilateur

fan club n fan-club m

fancy [ˈfænsɪ] n (whim) fantaisie f, envie f; (imagination) imagination f ▷ adj (luxury) de luxe; (elaborate: jewellery, packaging) fantaisie inv ▷ vt (feel like, want) avoir envie de; (imagine) imaginer; **to take a ~ to** se prendre d'affection pour; s'enticher de; **he fancies her** elle lui plaît; **fancy dress** n déguisement m, travesti m

fan heater n (BRIT) radiateur soufflant

fantasize [ˈfæntəsaɪz] vi fantasmer

fantastic [fænˈtæstɪk] adj fantastique

fantasy [ˈfæntəsɪ] n imagination f, fantaisie f; (unreality) fantasme m

fanzine [ˈfænziːn] n fanzine m

FAQ n abbr (= frequently asked question) FAQ f inv, faq f inv

far [fɑːʳ] adj (distant) lointain(e), éloigné(e) ▷ adv loin; **the ~ side/end** l'autre côté/bout; **it's not ~ (from here)** ce n'est pas loin (d'ici); **~ away, ~ off** au loin, dans le lointain; **~ better** beaucoup mieux; **~ from** loin de; **by ~** de loin, de beaucoup; **go as ~ as the bridge** allez jusqu'au pont; **as ~ as I know** pour autant que je sache; **how ~ is it to …?** combien y a-t-il d'ici à …?; **how ~ have you got with your work?** où en êtes-vous dans votre travail?

farce [fɑːs] n farce f

fare [fɛəʳ] n (on trains, buses) prix m du billet; (in taxi) prix de la course; (food) table f, chère f; **half ~** demi-tarif; **full ~** plein tarif

Far East n: **the ~** l'Extrême-Orient m

farewell [fɛəˈwɛl] excl, n adieu m

farm [fɑːm] n ferme f ▷ vt cultiver; **farmer** n fermier(-ière); **farmhouse** n (maison f de) ferme f; **farming** n agriculture f; (of animals) élevage m; **farmyard** n cour f de ferme

far-reaching [ˈfɑːˈriːtʃɪŋ] adj d'une grande portée

fart [fɑːt] (infl) vi péter

farther [ˈfɑːðəʳ] adv plus loin ▷ adj plus éloigné(e), plus lointain(e)

farthest [ˈfɑːðɪst] superlative of **far**

fascinate [ˈfæsɪneɪt] vt fasciner, captiver

fascinating [ˈfæsɪneɪtɪŋ] adj fascinant(e)

fascination [fæsɪˈneɪʃən] n fascination f

fascist [ˈfæʃɪst] adj, n fasciste m/f

fashion [ˈfæʃən] n mode f; (manner) façon f, manière f ▷ vt façonner; **in ~** à la mode; **out of ~** démodé(e); **fashionable** adj à la mode; **fashion show** n défilé m de mannequins or de mode

fast [fɑːst] adj rapide; (clock): **to be ~** avancer; (dye, colour) grand or bon teint inv ▷ adv vite, rapidement; (stuck, held) solidement ▷ n jeûne m ▷ vi jeûner; **~ asleep** profondément endormi

fasten [ˈfɑːsn] vt attacher, fixer; (coat) attacher, fermer ▷ vi se fermer, s'attacher

fast food n fast food m, restauration f rapide

fat [fæt] adj gros(se) ▷ n graisse f; (on meat) gras m; (for cooking) matière grasse

fatal [ˈfeɪtl] adj (mistake) fatal(e); (injury) mortel(le); **fatality** [fəˈtælɪtɪ] n (road death etc) victime f, décès m;

fatally adv fatalement; (injured) mortellement

fate [feɪt] n destin m; (of person) sort m

father ['fɑːðəʳ] n père m; **Father Christmas** n le Père Noël; **father-in-law** n beau-père m

fatigue [fə'tiːg] n fatigue f

fattening ['fætnɪŋ] adj (food) qui fait grossir

fatty ['fætɪ] adj (food) gras(se) ▷ n (inf) gros (grosse)

faucet ['fɔːsɪt] n (US) robinet m

fault [fɔːlt] n faute f; (defect) défaut m; (Geo) faille f ▷ vt trouver des défauts à, prendre en défaut; **it's my ~** c'est de ma faute; **to find ~ with** trouver à redire or à critiquer à; **at ~** fautif(-ive), coupable; **faulty** adj défectueux(-euse)

fauna ['fɔːnə] n faune f

favour, (US) **favor** ['feɪvəʳ] n faveur f; (help) service m ▷ vt (proposition) être en faveur de; (pupil etc) favoriser; (team, horse) donner gagnant; **to do sb a ~** rendre un service à qn; **in ~ of** en faveur de; **to find ~ with sb** trouver grâce aux yeux de qn; **favourable**, (US) **favorable** adj favorable; **favourite**, (US) **favorite** ['feɪvrɪt] adj, n favori(te)

fawn [fɔːn] n (deer) faon m ▷ adj (also: **~-coloured**) fauve ▷ vi: **to ~ (up)on** flatter servilement

fax [fæks] n (document) télécopie f; (machine) télécopieur m ▷ vt envoyer par télécopie

FBI n abbr (US: = Federal Bureau of Investigation) FBI m

fear [fɪəʳ] n crainte f, peur f ▷ vt craindre; **for ~ of** de peur que + sub or de + infinitive; **fearful** adj craintif(-ive); (sight, noise) affreux(-euse), épouvantable; **fearless** adj intrépide

feasible ['fiːzəbl] adj faisable, réalisable

feast [fiːst] n festin m, banquet m; (Rel: also: **~ day**) fête f ▷ vi festoyer

feat [fiːt] n exploit m, prouesse f

feather ['fɛðəʳ] n plume f

feature ['fiːtʃəʳ] n caractéristique f; (article) chronique f, rubrique f ▷ vt (film) avoir pour vedette(s) ▷ vi figurer (en bonne place); **features** npl (of face) traits mpl; **a (special) ~ on sth/sb** un reportage sur qch/qn; **feature film** n long métrage

Feb. abbr (= February) fév

February ['fɛbruərɪ] n février m

fed [fɛd] pt, pp of **feed**

federal ['fɛdərəl] adj fédéral(e)

federation [fɛdə'reɪʃən] n fédération f

fed up adj: **to be ~ (with)** en avoir marre or plein le dos (de)

fee [fiː] n rémunération f; (of doctor, lawyer) honoraires mpl; (of school, college etc) frais mpl de scolarité; (for examination) droits mpl

feeble ['fiːbl] adj faible; (attempt, excuse) pauvre; (joke) piteux(-euse)

feed [fiːd] n (of animal) nourriture f, pâture f; (on printer) mécanisme m d'alimentation ▷ vt (pt, pp **fed**) (person) nourrir; (BRIT: baby: breastfeed) allaiter; (: with bottle) donner le biberon à; (horse etc) donner à manger à; (machine) alimenter; (data etc): **to ~ sth into** enregistrer qch dans; **feedback** n (Elec) effet m Larsen; (from person) réactions fpl

feel [fiːl] n (sensation) sensation f; (impression) impression f ▷ vt (pt, pp **felt**) (touch) toucher; (explore) tâter, palper; (cold, pain) sentir; (grief, anger) ressentir, éprouver; (think, believe): **to ~ (that)** trouver que; **to ~ hungry/cold** avoir faim/froid; **to ~ lonely/better** se sentir seul/mieux; **I don't ~ well** je ne me sens pas bien; **it ~s soft** c'est doux au toucher; **to ~ like** (want) avoir envie de; **feeling** n (physical) sensation f; (emotion, impression) sentiment m; **to hurt sb's feelings** froisser qn

feet [fiːt] npl of **foot**

fell [fɛl] pt of **fall** ▷ vt (tree) abattre

fellow ['fɛləu] n type m; (comrade) compagnon m; (of learned society) membre m ▷ cpd: **their ~ prisoners/students** leurs camarades prisonniers/étudiants; **fellow citizen** n concitoyen(ne); **fellow countryman** (irreg) n compatriote m; **fellow men** npl semblables mpl; **fellowship** n (society) association f; (comradeship) amitié f, camaraderie f; (Scol) sorte de bourse universitaire

felony ['fɛlənɪ] n crime m, forfait m

felt [fɛlt] pt, pp of **feel** ▷ n feutre m; **felt-tip** n (also: **felt-tip pen**) stylo-feutre m

female ['fi:meɪl] n (Zool) femelle f; (pej: woman) bonne femme f ▷ adj (Biol) femelle; (sex, character) féminin(e); (vote etc) des femmes

feminine ['fɛmɪnɪn] adj féminin(e)

feminist ['fɛmɪnɪst] n féministe m/f

fence [fɛns] n barrière f ▷ vi faire de l'escrime; **fencing** n (sport) escrime m

fend [fɛnd] vi: **to ~ for o.s.** se débrouiller (tout seul); **fend off** vt (attack etc) parer; (questions) éluder

fender ['fɛndər] n garde-feu m inv; (on boat) défense f; (US: of car) aile f

fennel ['fɛnl] n fenouil m

ferment vi [fə'mɛnt] fermenter ▷ n ['fə:mɛnt] (fig) agitation f, effervescence f

fern [fə:n] n fougère f

ferocious [fə'rəuʃəs] adj féroce

ferret ['fɛrɪt] n furet m

ferry ['fɛrɪ] n (small) bac m; (large: also: **~-boat**) ferry(-boat m) m ▷ vt transporter

fertile ['fə:taɪl] adj fertile; (Biol) fécond(e); **fertilize** ['fə:tɪlaɪz] vt fertiliser; (Biol) féconder; **fertilizer** n engrais m

festival ['fɛstɪvəl] n (Rel) fête f; (Art, Mus) festival m

festive ['fɛstɪv] adj de fête; **the ~ season** (BRIT: Christmas) la période des fêtes

fetch [fɛtʃ] vt aller chercher; (BRIT: sell for) rapporter

fête [feɪt] n fête f, kermesse f

fetus ['fi:təs] n (US) = **foetus**

feud [fju:d] n querelle f, dispute f

fever ['fi:vər] n fièvre f; **feverish** adj fiévreux(-euse), fébrile

few [fju:] adj (not many) peu de ▷ pron peu; **a ~** (as adj) quelques; (as pron) quelques-uns(-unes); **quite a ~ ...** adj un certain nombre de ..., pas mal de ...; **in the past ~ days** ces derniers jours; **fewer** adj moins de; **fewest** adj le moins nombreux

fiancé [fɪ'ɑ̃:nseɪ] n fiancé m; **fiancée** n fiancée f

fiasco [fɪ'æskəu] n fiasco m

fib [fɪb] n bobard m

fibre, (US) **fiber** ['faɪbər] n fibre f; **fibreglass**, (US) **Fiberglass®** n fibre f de verre

fickle ['fɪkl] adj inconstant(e), volage, capricieux(-euse)

fiction ['fɪkʃən] n romans mpl, littérature f romanesque; (invention) fiction f; **fictional** adj fictif(-ive)

fiddle ['fɪdl] n (Mus) violon m; (cheating) combine f; escroquerie f ▷ vt (BRIT: accounts) falsifier, maquiller; **fiddle with** vt fus tripoter

fidelity [fɪ'dɛlɪtɪ] n fidélité f

fidget ['fɪdʒɪt] vi se trémousser, remuer

field [fi:ld] n champ m; (fig) domaine m, champ m; (Sport: ground) terrain m; **field marshal** n maréchal m

fierce [fɪəs] adj (look, animal) féroce, sauvage; (wind, attack, person) (très) violent(e); (fighting, enemy) acharné(e)

fifteen [fɪf'ti:n] num quinze; **fifteenth** num quinzième

fifth [fɪfθ] num cinquième

fiftieth ['fɪftɪθ] num cinquantième

fifty ['fɪftɪ] num cinquante; **fifty-fifty** adv moitié-moitié ▷ adj: **to have a fifty-fifty chance (of success)** avoir une chance sur deux (de réussir)

fig | 400

fig [fɪg] n figue f

fight [faɪt] (pt, pp **fought**) n (between persons) bagarre f; (argument) dispute f; (Mil) combat m; (against cancer etc) lutte f ▷ vt se battre contre; (cancer, alcoholism, emotion) combattre, lutter contre; (election) se présenter à ▷ vi se battre; (argue) se disputer; (fig): **to ~ (for/against)** lutter (pour/contre); **fight back** vi rendre les coups; (after illness) reprendre le dessus ▷ vt (tears) réprimer; **fight off** vt repousser; (disease, sleep, urge) lutter contre; **fighting** n combats mpl; (brawls) bagarres fpl

figure ['fɪgəʳ] n (Drawing, Geom) figure f; (number) chiffre m; (body, outline) silhouette f; (person's shape) ligne f, formes fpl; (person) personnage m ▷ vt (us: think) supposer ▷ vi (appear) figurer; (us: make sense) s'expliquer; **figure out** vt (understand) arriver à comprendre; (plan) calculer

file [faɪl] n (tool) lime f; (dossier) dossier m; (folder) dossier, chemise f (: binder) classeur m; (Comput) fichier m; (row) file f ▷ vt (nails, wood) limer; (papers) classer; (Law: claim) faire enregistrer; déposer; **filing cabinet** n classeur m (meuble)

Filipino [fɪlɪ'piːnəu] adj philippin(e) ▷ n (person) Philippin(e)

fill [fɪl] vt remplir; (vacancy) pourvoir à ▷ n: **to eat one's ~** manger à sa faim; **to ~ with** remplir de; **fill in** vt (hole) boucher; (form) remplir; **fill out** vt (form, receipt) remplir; **fill up** vt remplir ▷ vi (Aut) faire le plein

fillet ['fɪlɪt] n filet m; **fillet steak** n filet m de bœuf, tournedos m

filling ['fɪlɪŋ] n (Culin) garniture f, farce f; (for tooth) plombage m; **filling station** n station-service f, station f d'essence

film [fɪlm] n film m; (Phot) pellicule f, film; (of powder, liquid) couche f, pellicule ▷ vt (scene) filmer ▷ vi tourner; **I'd like a 36-exposure ~** je voudrais une pellicule de 36 poses; **film star** n vedette f de cinéma

filter ['fɪltəʳ] n filtre m ▷ vt filtrer; **filter lane** n (BRIT Aut: at traffic lights) voie f de dégagement; (: on motorway) voie f de sortie

filth [fɪlθ] n saleté f; **filthy** adj sale, dégoûtant(e); (language) ordurier(-ière), grossier(-ière)

fin [fɪn] n (of fish) nageoire f; (of shark) aileron m; (of diver) palme f

final ['faɪnl] adj final(e), dernier(-ière); (decision, answer) définitif(-ive) ▷ n (BRIT Sport) finale f; **finals** npl (us) (Scol) examens mpl de dernière année; (Sport) finale f; **finale** [fɪ'nɑːlɪ] n finale m; **finalist** n (Sport) finaliste m/f; **finalize** vt mettre au point; **finally** adv (eventually) enfin, finalement; (lastly) en dernier lieu

finance [faɪ'næns] n finance f ▷ vt financer; **finances** npl finances fpl; **financial** [faɪ'nænʃəl] adj financier(-ière); **financial year** n année f budgétaire

find [faɪnd] vt (pt, pp **found**) trouver; (lost object) retrouver ▷ n trouvaille f, découverte f; **to ~ sb guilty** (Law) déclarer qn coupable; **find out** vt se renseigner sur; (truth, secret) découvrir; (person) démasquer ▷ vi: **to ~ out about** (make enquiries) se renseigner sur; (by chance) apprendre; **findings** npl (Law) conclusions fpl, verdict m; (of report) constatations fpl

fine [faɪn] adj (weather) beau (belle); (excellent) excellent(e); (thin, subtle, not coarse) fin(e); (acceptable) bien inv ▷ adv (well) très bien; (small) fin, finement ▷ n (Law) amende f; contravention f ▷ vt (Law) condamner à une amende; donner une contravention à; **he's ~** il va bien; **the weather is ~** il fait beau; **fine arts** npl beaux-arts mpl

finger ['fɪŋgəʳ] n doigt m ▷ vt palper, toucher; **index ~** index m; **fingernail** n ongle m (de la main); **fingerprint** n empreinte digitale; **fingertip** n bout m du doigt

finish ['fɪnɪʃ] n fin f; (Sport) arrivée f; (polish etc) finition f ▷ vt finir, terminer ▷ vi finir, se terminer; **to ~ doing sth** finir de faire qch; **to ~ third** arriver or terminer troisième; **when does the show ~?** quand est-ce que le spectacle se termine?; **finish off** vt finir, terminer; (kill) achever; **finish up** vi, vt finir

Finland ['fɪnlənd] n Finlande f; **Finn** n Finnois(e), Finlandais(e); **Finnish** adj finnois(e), finlandais(e) ▷ n (Ling) finnois m

fir [fəː¹] n sapin m

fire ['faɪə¹] n feu m; (accidental) incendie m; (heater) radiateur m ▷ vt (discharge): **to ~ a gun** tirer un coup de feu; (fig: interest) enflammer, animer; (inf: dismiss) mettre à la porte, renvoyer ▷ vi (shoot) tirer, faire feu; **~!** au feu!; **on ~** en feu; **to set ~ to sth, set sth on ~** mettre le feu à qch; **fire alarm** n avertisseur m d'incendie; **firearm** n arme f à feu; **fire brigade** n (régiment m de sapeurs-)pompiers mpl; **fire engine** n (BRIT) pompe f à incendie; **fire escape** n escalier m de secours; **fire exit** n issue f or sortie f de secours; **fire extinguisher** n extincteur m; **fireman** (irreg) n pompier m; **fireplace** n cheminée f; **fire station** n caserne f de pompiers; **fire truck** n (US) = **fire engine**; **firewall** n (Internet) pare-feu m; **firewood** n bois m de chauffage; **fireworks** npl (display) feu(x) m(pl) d'artifice

firm [fəːm] adj ferme ▷ n compagnie f, firme f; **firmly** adv fermement

first [fəːst] adj premier(-ière) ▷ adv (before other people) le premier, la première; (before other things) en premier, d'abord; (when listing reasons etc) en premier lieu, premièrement; (in the beginning) au début ▷ n (person: in race) premier(-ière); (BRIT Scol) mention f très bien; (Aut) première f; **the ~ of January** le premier janvier; **at ~** au commencement, au début; **~ of all** tout d'abord, pour commencer; **first aid** n premiers secours or soins; **first-aid kit** n trousse f à pharmacie; **first-class** adj (ticket etc) de première classe; (excellent) excellent(e), exceptionnel(le); (post) en tarif prioritaire; **first-hand** adj de première main; **first lady** n (US) femme f du président; **firstly** adv premièrement, en premier lieu; **first name** n prénom m; **first-rate** adj excellent(e)

fiscal ['fɪskl] adj fiscal(e); **fiscal year** n exercice financier

fish [fɪʃ] n (pl inv) poisson m ▷ vt, vi pêcher; **~ and chips** poisson frit et frites; **fisherman** (irreg) n pêcheur m; **fish fingers** npl (BRIT) bâtonnets mpl de poisson (congelés); **fishing** n pêche f; **to go fishing** aller à la pêche; **fishing boat** n barque f de pêche; **fishing line** n ligne f (de pêche); **fishmonger** n (BRIT) marchand m de poisson; **fishmonger's (shop)** n (BRIT) poissonnerie f; **fish sticks** npl (US) = **fish fingers**; **fishy** adj (inf) suspect(e), louche

fist [fɪst] n poing m

fit [fɪt] adj (Med, Sport) en (bonne) forme; (proper) convenable; approprié(e) ▷ vt (subj: clothes) aller à; (put in, attach) installer, poser; (equip) équiper, garnir, munir; (suit) convenir à ▷ vi (clothes) aller; (parts) s'adapter; (in space, gap) entrer, s'adapter ▷ n (Med) accès m, crise f; (of anger) accès; (of hysterics, jealousy) crise; **~ to** (ready to) en état de; **~ for** (worthy) digne de; (capable) apte à; **to keep ~** se maintenir en forme; **this dress is a tight/good ~** cette robe est un peu juste/(me) va très bien; **a ~ of coughing** une quinte de toux; **by ~s and starts** par à-coups;

fit in vi (add up) cadrer; (integrate) s'intégrer; (to new situation) s'adapter; **fitness** n (Med) forme f physique; **fitted** adj (jacket, shirt) ajusté(e); **fitted carpet** n moquette f; **fitted kitchen** n (BRIT) cuisine équipée; **fitted sheet** n drap-housse m; **fitting** adj approprié(e) ▷ n (of dress) essayage m; (of piece of equipment) pose f, installation f; **fitting room** n (in shop) cabine f d'essayage; **fittings** npl installations fpl

five [faɪv] num cinq; **fiver** n (inf: US) billet de cinq dollars; (: BRIT) billet m de cinq livres

fix [fɪks] vt (date, amount etc) fixer; (sort out) arranger; (mend) réparer; (make ready: meal, drink) préparer ▷ n: **to be in a ~** être dans le pétrin; **fix up** vt (meeting) arranger; **to ~ sb up with sth** faire avoir qch à qn; **fixed** adj (prices etc) fixe; **fixture** n installation f (fixe); (Sport) rencontre f (au programme)

fizzy ['fɪzɪ] adj pétillant(e), gazeux(-euse)

flag [flæg] n drapeau m; (also: **~stone**) dalle f ▷ vi faiblir; fléchir; **flag down** vt héler, faire signe (de s'arrêter) à; **flagpole** n mât m

flair [flɛəʳ] n flair m

flak [flæk] n (Mil) tir antiaérien; (inf: criticism) critiques fpl

flake [fleɪk] n (of rust, paint) écaille f; (of snow, soap powder) flocon m ▷ vi (also: **~ off**) s'écailler

flamboyant [flæm'bɔɪənt] adj flamboyant(e), éclatant(e); (person) haut(e) en couleur

flame [fleɪm] n flamme f

flamingo [flə'mɪŋɡəu] n flamant m (rose)

flammable ['flæməbl] adj inflammable

flan [flæn] n (BRIT) tarte f

flank [flæŋk] n flanc m ▷ vt flanquer

flannel ['flænl] n (BRIT: also: **face ~**) gant m de toilette; (fabric) flanelle f

flap [flæp] n (of pocket, envelope) rabat m ▷ vt (wings) battre (de) ▷ vi (sail, flag) claquer

flare [flɛəʳ] n (signal) signal lumineux; (Mil) fusée éclairante; (in skirt etc) évasement m; **flares** npl (trousers) pantalon m à pattes d'éléphant; **flare up** vi s'embraser; (fig: person) se mettre en colère, s'emporter; (: revolt) éclater

flash [flæʃ] n éclair m; (also: **news ~**) flash m (d'information); (Phot) flash m ▷ vt (switch on) allumer (brièvement); (direct): **to ~ sth at** braquer qch sur; (send: message) câbler; (smile) lancer ▷ vi briller; jeter des éclairs; (light on ambulance etc) clignoter; **a ~ of lightning** un éclair; **in a ~** en un clin d'œil; **to ~ one's headlights** faire un appel de phares; **he ~ed by** or **past** il passa (devant nous) comme un éclair; **flashback** n flashback m, retour m en arrière; **flashbulb** n ampoule f de flash; **flashlight** n lampe f de poche

flask [flɑːsk] n flacon m, bouteille f; (also: **vacuum ~**) bouteille f thermos®

flat [flæt] adj plat(e); (tyre) dégonflé(e), à plat; (beer) éventé(e); (battery) à plat; (denial) catégorique; (Mus) bémol inv (: voice) faux (fausse) ▷ n (BRIT: apartment) appartement m; (Aut) crevaison f, pneu crevé; (Mus) bémol m; **~ out** (work) sans relâche; (race) à fond; **flatten** vt (also: **flatten out**) aplatir; (crop) coucher; (house, city) raser

flatter ['flætəʳ] vt flatter; **flattering** adj flatteur(-euse); (clothes etc) seyant(e)

flaunt [flɔːnt] vt faire étalage de

flavour, (US) **flavor** ['fleɪvəʳ] n goût m, saveur f; (of ice cream etc) parfum m ▷ vt parfumer, aromatiser; **vanilla-~ed** à l'arôme de vanille, vanillé(e); **what ~s do you have?** quels parfums avez-vous?; **flavouring**, (US) **flavoring** n arôme m (synthétique)

flaw [flɔ:] n défaut m; **flawless** adj
sans défaut

flea [fli:] n puce f; **flea market** n
marché m aux puces

fled [flɛd] pt, pp of **flee**

flee (pt, pp **fled**) [fli:, flɛd] vt fuir,
s'enfuir de ▷ vi fuir, s'enfuir

fleece [fli:s] n (of sheep) toison f;
(top) (laine f) polaire f ▷ vt (inf) voler,
filouter

fleet [fli:t] n flotte f; (of lorries, cars etc)
parc m; convoi m

fleeting ['fli:tɪŋ] adj fugace,
fugitif(-ive); (visit) très bref (brève)

Flemish ['flɛmɪʃ] adj flamand(e)
▷ n (Ling) flamand m; **the ~** npl les
Flamands

flesh [flɛʃ] n chair f

flew [flu:] pt of **fly**

flex [flɛks] n fil m or câble m électrique
(souple) ▷ vt (knee) fléchir; (muscles)
bander; **flexibility** n flexibilité f;
flexible adj flexible; (person, schedule)
souple; **flexitime**, (us) **flextime** n
horaire m variable or à la carte

flick [flɪk] n petit coup; (with finger)
chiquenaude f ▷ vt donner un petit
coup à; (switch) appuyer sur; **flick
through** vt fus feuilleter

flicker ['flɪkə'] vi (light, flame) vaciller

flies [flaɪz] npl of **fly**

flight [flaɪt] n vol m; (escape) fuite f;
(also: **~ of steps**) escalier m; **flight
attendant** n steward m, hôtesse
f de l'air

flimsy ['flɪmzɪ] adj peu solide;
(clothes) trop léger(-ère); (excuse)
pauvre, mince

flinch [flɪntʃ] vi tressaillir; **to ~ from**
se dérober à, reculer devant

fling [flɪŋ] vt (pt, pp **flung**) jeter,
lancer

flint [flɪnt] n silex m; (in lighter) pierre
f (à briquet)

flip [flɪp] vt (throw) donner une
chiquenaude à; (switch) appuyer sur;
(us: pancake) faire sauter; **to ~ sth
over** retourner qch

flip-flops ['flɪpflɔps] npl (esp BRIT)
tongs fpl

flipper ['flɪpə'] n (of animal) nageoire
f; (for swimmer) palme f

flirt [flə:t] vi flirter ▷ n flirteur(-euse)

float [fləut] n flotteur m; (in
procession) char m; (sum of money)
réserve f ▷ vi flotter

flock [flɔk] n (of sheep) troupeau m; (of
birds) vol m; (of people) foule f

flood [flʌd] n inondation f; (of letters,
refugees etc) flot m ▷ vt inonder ▷ vi
(place) être inondé; (people): **to ~ into**
envahir; **flooding** n inondation f;
floodlight n projecteur m

floor [flɔ:ʳ] n sol m; (storey) étage
m; (of sea, valley) fond m ▷ vt (knock
down) terrasser; (baffle) désorienter;
ground ~, (us) **first ~** rez-de-
chaussée m; **first ~**, (us) **second ~**
premier étage; **what ~ is it on?**
c'est à quel étage?; **floorboard** n
planche f (du plancher); **flooring** n
sol m; (wooden) plancher m; (covering)
revêtement m de sol; **floor show** n
spectacle m de variétés

flop [flɔp] n fiasco m ▷ vi (fail) faire
fiasco; (fall) s'affaler, s'effondrer;
floppy adj lâche, flottant(e)
▷ n (Comput: also: **floppy disk**)
disquette f

flora ['flɔ:rə] n flore f

floral ['flɔ:rl] adj floral(e); (dress)
à fleurs

florist ['flɔrɪst] n fleuriste m/f;
florist's (shop) n magasin m or
boutique f de fleuriste

flotation [fləu'teɪʃən] n (of shares)
émission f; (of company) lancement m
(en Bourse)

flour ['flauəʳ] n farine f

flourish ['flʌrɪʃ] vi prospérer ▷ n
(gesture) moulinet m

flow [fləu] n (of water, traffic etc)
écoulement m; (tide, influx) flux
m; (of blood, Elec) circulation f; (of
river) courant m ▷ vi couler; (traffic)
s'écouler; (robes, hair) flotter

flower ['flauə'] n fleur f ▷ vi fleurir;
  flower bed n plate-bande f;
  flowerpot n pot m (à fleurs)
flown [fləun] pp of **fly**
fl. oz. abbr = **fluid ounce**
flu [flu:] n grippe f
fluctuate ['flʌktjueɪt] vi varier,
  fluctuer
fluent ['flu:ənt] adj (speech, style)
  coulant(e), aisé(e); **he speaks ~
  French, he's ~ in French** il parle le
  français couramment
fluff [flʌf] n duvet m; (on jacket, carpet)
  peluche f; **fluffy** adj duveteux(-euse);
  (toy) en peluche
fluid ['flu:ɪd] n fluide m; (in diet)
  liquide m ▷ adj fluide; **fluid ounce** n
  (BRIT) = 0.028 l; 0.05 pints
fluke [flu:k] n coup m de veine
flung [flʌŋ] pt, pp of **fling**
fluorescent [fluə'rɛsnt] adj
  fluorescent(e)
fluoride ['fluəraɪd] n fluor m
flurry ['flʌrɪ] n (of snow) rafale f,
  bourrasque f; **a ~ of activity** un
  affairement soudain
flush [flʌʃ] n (on face) rougeur f; (fig:
  of youth etc) éclat m ▷ vt nettoyer à
  grande eau ▷ vi rougir ▷ adj (level):
  ~ with au ras de, au niveau avec; **to ~
  the toilet** tirer la chasse (d'eau)
flute [flu:t] n flûte f
flutter ['flʌtə'] n (of panic, excitement)
  agitation f; (of wings) battement m
  ▷ vi (bird) battre des ailes, voleter
fly [flaɪ] (pt **flew**, pp **flown**) n (insect)
  mouche f; (on trousers: also: **flies**)
  braguette f ▷ vt (plane) piloter;
  (passengers, cargo) transporter (par
  avion); (distance) parcourir ▷ vi voler;
  (passengers) aller en avion; (escape)
  s'enfuir, fuir; (flag) se déployer; **fly
  away, fly off** vi s'envoler; **fly-drive**
  n formule f avion plus voiture; **flying**
  n (activity) aviation f; (action) vol
  m ▷ adj: **flying visit** visite f éclair
  inv; **with flying colours** haut la
  main; **flying saucer** n soucoupe

volante; **flyover** n (BRIT: overpass)
  pont routier
FM abbr (Radio: = frequency modulation)
  FM
foal [fəul] n poulain m
foam [fəum] n écume f; (on beer)
  mousse f; (also: **~ rubber**) caoutchouc
  m mousse ▷ vi (liquid) écumer; (soapy
  water) mousser
focus ['fəukəs] n (pl **focuses**) foyer
  m; (of interest) centre m ▷ vt (field
  glasses etc) mettre au point ▷ vi: **to
  ~ (on)** (with camera) régler la mise au
  point (sur); (with eyes) fixer son regard
  (sur); **out of/in ~** (picture) flou(e)/
  net(te); (camera) pas au point/
  au point
foetus, (US) **fetus** ['fi:təs] n fœtus m
fog [fɔg] n brouillard m; **foggy** adj:
  it's foggy il y a du brouillard; **fog
  lamp**, (US) **fog light** n (Aut) phare m
  anti-brouillard
foil [fɔɪl] vt déjouer, contrecarrer ▷ n
  feuille f de métal; (kitchen foil) papier
  m d'alu(minium); **to act as a ~** (fig)
  servir de repoussoir à
fold [fəuld] n (bend, crease) pli m; (Agr)
  parc m à moutons; (fig) bercail m ▷ vt
  plier; **to ~ one's arms** croiser les
  bras; **fold up** vi (map etc) se plier, se
  replier; (business) fermer boutique
  ▷ vt (map etc) plier, replier; **folder** n
  (for papers) chemise f (: binder) classeur
  m; (Comput) dossier m; **folding** adj
  (chair, bed) pliant(e)
foliage ['fəulɪɪdʒ] n feuillage m
folk [fəuk] npl gens mpl ▷ cpd
  folklorique; **folks** npl (inf: parents)
  famille f, parents mpl; **folklore**
  ['fəuklɔ:'] n folklore m; **folk music** n
  musique f folklorique; (contemporary)
  musique folk, folk m; **folk song** n
  chanson f folklorique; (contemporary)
  chanson folk inv
follow ['fɔləu] vt suivre; (on Twitter)
  s'abonner aux tweets de ▷ vi suivre;
  (result) s'ensuivre; **to ~ suit** (fig) faire

de même; **follow up** vt (letter, offer) donner suite à; (case) suivre; **follower** n disciple m/f, partisan(e); **following** adj suivant(e) ▷ n partisans mpl, disciples mpl; **follow-up** n suite f; (on file, case) suivi m

fond [fɔnd] adj (memory, look) tendre, affectueux(-euse); (hopes, dreams) un peu fou (folle); **to be ~ of** aimer beaucoup

food [fuːd] n nourriture f; **food mixer** n mixeur m; **food poisoning** n intoxication f alimentaire; **food processor** n robot m de cuisine; **food stamp** n (US) bon m de nourriture (pour indigents)

fool [fuːl] n idiot(e); (Culin) mousse f de fruits ▷ vt berner, duper; **fool about, fool around** vi (pej: waste time) traînailler, glandouiller; (: behave foolishly) faire l'idiot or l'imbécile; **foolish** adj idiot(e), stupide; (rash) imprudent(e); **foolproof** adj (plan etc) infaillible

foot (pl **feet**) [fut, fiːt] n pied m; (of animal) patte f; (measure) pied (= 30.48 cm; 12 inches) ▷ vt (bill) payer; **on ~** à pied; **footage** n (Cine: length) ≈ métrage m; (: material) séquences fpl; **foot-and-mouth (disease)** [futənd'mauθ-] n fièvre aphteuse; **football** n (ball) ballon m (de football); (sport: BRIT) football m; (: US) football américain; **footballer** n (BRIT) = **football player**; **football match** n (BRIT) match m de foot(ball); **football player** n footballeur(-euse), joueur(-euse) de football; (US) joueur(-euse) de football américain; **footbridge** n passerelle f; **foothills** npl contreforts mpl; **foothold** n prise f (de pied); **footing** n (fig) position f; **to lose one's footing** perdre pied; **footnote** n note f (en bas de page); **footpath** n sentier m; **footprint** n trace f (de pied); **footstep** n pas m; **footwear** n chaussures fpl

for [fɔːʳ] prep **1** (indicating destination, intention, purpose) pour; **the train for London** le train pour (or à destination de) Londres; **he left for Rome** il est parti pour Rome; **he went for the paper** il est allé chercher le journal; **is this for me?** c'est pour moi?; **it's time for lunch** c'est l'heure du déjeuner; **what's it for?** ça sert à quoi?; **what for?** (why?) pourquoi?; (to what end?) pour quoi faire?, à quoi bon?; **for sale** à vendre; **to pray for peace** prier pour la paix
2 (on behalf of, representing) pour; **the MP for Hove** le député de Hove; **to work for sb/sth** travailler pour qn/qch; **I'll ask him for you** je vais lui demander pour toi; **G for George** G comme Georges
3 (because of) pour; **for this reason** pour cette raison; **for fear of being criticized** de peur d'être critiqué
4 (with regard to) pour; **it's cold for July** il fait froid pour juillet; **a gift for languages** un don pour les langues
5 (in exchange for): **I sold it for £5** je l'ai vendu 5 livres; **to pay 50 pence for a ticket** payer un billet 50 pence
6 (in favour of) pour; **are you for or against us?** êtes-vous pour ou contre nous?; **I'm all for it** je suis tout à fait pour; **vote for X** votez pour X
7 (referring to distance) pendant, sur; **there are roadworks for 5 km** il y a des travaux sur or pendant 5 km; **we walked for miles** nous avons marché pendant des kilomètres
8 (referring to time) pendant; depuis; pour; **he was away for 2 years** il a été absent pendant 2 ans; **she will be away for a month** elle sera absente (pendant) un mois; **it hasn't rained for 3 weeks** ça fait 3 semaines qu'il ne pleut pas, il ne pleut pas depuis 3 semaines; **I have known her for years** je la connais

depuis des années; **can you do it for tomorrow?** est-ce que tu peux le faire pour demain?
9 (with infinitive clauses): **it is not for me to decide** ce n'est pas à moi de décider; **it would be best for you to leave** le mieux serait que vous partiez; **there is still time for you to do it** vous avez encore le temps de le faire; **for this to be possible ...** pour que cela soit possible ..
10 (in spite of): **for all that** malgré cela, néanmoins; **for all his work/ efforts** malgré tout son travail/tous ses efforts; **for all his complaints, he's very fond of her** il a beau se plaindre, il l'aime beaucoup
▶ conj (since, as: formal) car

forbid (pt **forbad** or **forbade**, pp **forbidden**) [fə'bɪd, -'bæd, -'bɪdn] vt défendre, interdire; **to ~ sb to do** défendre or interdire à qn de faire; **forbidden** adj défendu(e)
force [fɔːs] n force f ▷ vt forcer; (push) pousser (de force); **to ~ o.s. to do** se forcer à faire; **in ~** (rule, law, prices) en vigueur; (in large numbers) en force; **forced** adj forcé(e); **forceful** adj énergique
ford [fɔːd] n gué m
fore [fɔː'] n: **to the ~** en évidence; **forearm** n avant-bras m inv; **forecast** n prévision f; (also: **weather forecast**) prévisions fpl météorologiques, météo f ▷ vt (irreg: like **cast**) prévoir; **forecourt** n (of garage) devant m; **forefinger** n index m; **forefront** n: **in the forefront of** au premier rang or plan de; **foreground** n premier plan; **forehead** ['fɔrɪd] n front m
foreign ['fɔrɪn] adj étranger(-ère); (trade) extérieur(e); (travel) à l'étranger; **foreign currency** n devises étrangères; **foreigner** n étranger(-ère); **foreign exchange** n (system) change m; (money) devises

fpl; **Foreign Office** n (BRIT) ministère m des Affaires étrangères; **Foreign Secretary** n (BRIT) ministre m des Affaires étrangères
fore: foreman (irreg) n (in construction) contremaître m; **foremost** adj le (la) plus en vue, premier(-ière) ▷ adv: **first and foremost** avant tout, tout d'abord; **forename** n prénom m
forensic [fə'rɛnsɪk] adj: **~ medicine** médecine légale
foresee (pt **foresaw**, pp **foreseen**) [fɔː'siː, -'sɔː, -'siːn] vt prévoir; **foreseeable** adj prévisible
foreseen [fɔː'siːn] pp of **foresee**
forest ['fɔrɪst] n forêt f; **forestry** n sylviculture f
forever [fə'rɛvə'] adv pour toujours; (fig: endlessly) continuellement
foreword ['fɔːwəd] n avant-propos m inv
forfeit ['fɔːfɪt] vt perdre
forgave [fə'geɪv] pt of **forgive**
forge [fɔːdʒ] n forge f ▷ vt (signature) contrefaire; (wrought iron) forger; **to ~ money** (BRIT) fabriquer de la fausse monnaie; **forger** n faussaire m; **forgery** n faux m, contrefaçon f
forget (pt **forgot**, pp **forgotten**) [fə'gɛt, -'gɔt, -'gɔtn] vt, vi oublier; **I've forgotten my key/passport** j'ai oublié ma clé/mon passeport; **forgetful** adj distrait(e), étourdi(e)
forgive (pt **forgave**, pp **forgiven**) [fə'gɪv, -'geɪv, -'gɪvn] vt pardonner; **to ~ sb for sth/for doing sth** pardonner qch à qn/à qn de faire qch
forgot [fə'gɔt] pt of **forget**
forgotten [fə'gɔtn] pp of **forget**
fork [fɔːk] n (for eating) fourchette f; (for gardening) fourche f; (of roads) bifurcation f ▷ vi (in road) bifurquer
forlorn [fə'lɔːn] adj (deserted) abandonné(e); (hope, attempt) désespéré(e)
form [fɔːm] n forme f; (Scol) classe f; (questionnaire) formulaire m ▷ vt former; (habit) contracter; **to ~ part**

of sth faire partie de qch; **on top ~** en pleine forme

formal ['fɔːməl] adj (offer, receipt) en bonne et due forme; (person) cérémonieux(-euse); (occasion, dinner) officiel(le); (garden) à la française; (clothes) de soirée; **formality** [fɔː'mælɪtɪ] n formalité f

format ['fɔːmæt] n format m ▷ vt (Comput) formater

formation [fɔː'meɪʃən] n formation f

former ['fɔːmər] adj ancien(ne); (before n) précédent(e); **the ~ ... the latter** le premier ... le second, celui-là ... celui-ci; **formerly** adv autrefois

formidable ['fɔːmɪdəbl] adj redoutable

formula ['fɔːmjulə] n formule f

fort [fɔːt] n fort m

forthcoming [fɔːθ'kʌmɪŋ] adj qui va paraître or avoir lieu prochainement; (character) ouvert(e), communicatif(-ive); (available) disponible

fortieth ['fɔːtɪɪθ] num quarantième

fortify ['fɔːtɪfaɪ] vt (city) fortifier; (person) remonter

fortnight ['fɔːtnaɪt] n (BRIT) quinzaine f, quinze jours mpl; **fortnightly** adj bimensuel(le) ▷ adv tous les quinze jours

fortress ['fɔːtrɪs] n forteresse f

fortunate ['fɔːtʃənɪt] adj heureux(-euse); (person) chanceux(-euse); **it is ~ that** c'est une chance que, il est heureux que; **fortunately** adv heureusement, par bonheur

fortune ['fɔːtʃən] n chance f; (wealth) fortune f; **fortune-teller** n diseuse f de bonne aventure

forty ['fɔːtɪ] num quarante

forum ['fɔːrəm] n forum m, tribune f

forward ['fɔːwəd] adj (movement, position) en avant, vers l'avant; (not shy) effronté(e); (in time) en avance ▷ adv (also: **~s**) en avant ▷ n (Sport) avant m ▷ vt (letter) faire suivre; (parcel, goods) expédier; (fig) promouvoir, favoriser; **to move ~**

avancer; **forwarding address** n adresse f de réexpédition; **forward slash** n barre f oblique

fossick ['fɔsɪk] vi (AUST, NZ inf) chercher; **to ~ around for** fouiner (inf) pour trouver

fossil ['fɔsl] adj, n fossile m

foster ['fɔstər] vt (encourage) encourager, favoriser; (child) élever (sans adopter); **foster child** n enfant élevé dans une famille d'accueil

fought [fɔːt] pt, pp of **fight**

foul [faul] adj (weather, smell, food) infect(e); (language) ordurier(-ière) ▷ n (Football) faute f ▷ vt (dirty) salir, encrasser; **he's got a ~ temper** il a un caractère de chien; **foul play** n (Law) acte criminel

found [faund] pt, pp of **find** ▷ vt (establish) fonder; **foundation** [faun'deɪʃən] n (act) fondation f; (base) fondement m; (also: **foundation cream**) fond m de teint; **foundations** npl (of building) fondations fpl

founder ['faundər] n fondateur m ▷ vi couler, sombrer

fountain ['fauntɪn] n fontaine f; **fountain pen** n stylo m (à encre)

four [fɔːr] num quatre; **on all ~s** à quatre pattes; **four-letter word** n obscénité f, gros mot; **four-poster** n (also: **four-poster bed**) lit m à baldaquin; **fourteen** num quatorze; **fourteenth** num quatorzième; **fourth** num quatrième ▷ n (Aut: also: **fourth gear**) quatrième f; **four-wheel drive** n (Aut: car) voiture f à quatre roues motrices

fowl [faul] n volaille f

fox [fɔks] n renard m ▷ vt mystifier

foyer ['fɔɪeɪ] n (in hotel) vestibule m; (Theat) foyer m

fracking ['frækɪŋ] n fracturation f hydraulique

fraction ['frækʃən] n fraction f

fracture ['fræktʃər] n fracture f ▷ vt fracturer

fragile ['frædʒaɪl] *adj* fragile
fragment ['frægmənt] *n* fragment *m*
fragrance ['freɪɡrəns] *n* parfum *m*
frail [freɪl] *adj* fragile, délicat(e);
(*person*) frêle
frame [freɪm] *n* (*of building*)
charpente *f*; (*of human, animal*)
charpente, ossature *f*; (*of
picture*) cadre *m*; (*of door, window*)
encadrement *m*, chambranle *m*;
(*of spectacles: also*: **~s**) monture *f*
▷ *vt* (*picture*) encadrer; **~ of mind**
disposition *f* d'esprit; **framework** *n*
structure *f*
France [frɑːns] *n* la France
franchise ['fræntʃaɪz] *n* (*Pol*) droit *m*
de vote; (*Comm*) franchise *f*
frank [fræŋk] *adj* franc (franche)
▷ *vt* (*letter*) affranchir; **frankly** *adv*
franchement
frantic ['fræntɪk] *adj* (*hectic*)
frénétique; (*distraught*) hors de soi
fraud [frɔːd] *n* (*eccentric person*)
supercherie *f*, fraude *f*,
tromperie *f*; (*person*) imposteur *m*
fraught [frɔːt] *adj* (*tense: person*)
très tendu(e); (: *situation*) pénible;
~ with (*difficulties etc*) chargé(e) de,
plein(e) de
fray [freɪ] *vt* effilocher ▷ *vi* s'effilocher
freak [friːk] *n* (*eccentric person*)
phénomène *m*; (*unusual event*) hasard
m extraordinaire; (*pej: fanatic*):
health food ~ fana *m/f* or obsédé(e)
de l'alimentation saine ▷ *adj* (*storm*)
exceptionnel(le); (*accident*) bizarre
freckle ['frɛkl] *n* tache *f* de rousseur
free [friː] *adj* libre; (*gratis*) gratuit(e)
▷ *vt* (*prisoner etc*) libérer; (*jammed
object or person*) dégager; **is this seat
~?** la place est libre?; **~ (of charge)**
gratuitement; **freedom** *n* liberté *f*;
Freefone® *n* numéro vert; **free gift**
n prime *f*; **free kick** *n* (*Sport*) coup
franc; **freelance** *adj* (*journalist etc*)
indépendant(e), free-lance *inv* ▷ *adv*
en free-lance; **freely** *adv* librement;
(*liberally*) libéralement; **Freepost®** *n*
(BRIT) port payé; **free-range** *adj* (*egg*)

de ferme; (*chicken*) fermier; **freeway**
n (US) autoroute *f*; **free will** *n* libre
arbitre *m*; **of one's own free will** de
son plein gré
freeze [friːz] (*pt* **froze**, *pp* **frozen**)
vi geler ▷ *vt* geler; (*food*) congeler;
(*prices, salaries*) bloquer, geler ▷ *n*
gel *m*; (*of prices, salaries*) blocage *m*;
freezer *n* congélateur *m*; **freezing**
adj: **freezing (cold)** (*room etc*)
glacial(e); (*person, hands*) gelé(e),
glacé(e) ▷ *n*: **3 degrees below
freezing** 3 degrés au-dessous de
zéro; **it's freezing** il fait un froid
glacial; **freezing point** *n* point *m* de
congélation
freight [freɪt] *n* (*goods*) fret *m*,
cargaison *f*; (*money charged*) fret, prix
m du transport; **freight train** *n* (US)
train *m* de marchandises
French [frɛntʃ] *adj* français(e)
▷ *n* (*Ling*) français *m*; **the ~** *npl* les
Français; **what's the ~ (word) for
...?** comment dit-on ... en français?;
French bean *n* (BRIT) haricot vert;
French bread *n* pain *m* français;
French dressing *n* (*Culin*) vinaigrette
f; **French fried potatoes**, **French
fries** (US) *npl* (pommes de terre
fpl) frites *fpl*; **Frenchman** (*irreg*)
n Français *m*; **French stick** *n* ≈
baguette *f*; **French window** *n* porte-
fenêtre *f*; **Frenchwoman** (*irreg*) *n*
Française *f*
frenzy ['frɛnzɪ] *n* frénésie *f*
frequency ['friːkwənsɪ] *n*
fréquence *f*
frequent *adj* ['friːkwənt] fréquent(e)
▷ *vt* [frɪ'kwɛnt] fréquenter;
frequently ['friːkwəntlɪ] *adv*
fréquemment
fresh [frɛʃ] *adj* frais (fraîche);
(*new*) nouveau (nouvelle); (*cheeky*)
familier(-ière), culotté(e); **freshen** *vi*
(*wind, air*) fraîchir; **freshen up** *vi* faire
un brin de toilette; **fresher** *n* (BRIT
University: inf*) bizuth *m*, étudiant(e)
de première année; **freshly** *adv*

nouvellement, récemment;
freshman (*irreg*) *n* (*US*) = **fresher**;
freshwater *adj* (*fish*) d'eau douce
fret [frɛt] *vi* s'agiter, se tracasser
friction ['frɪkʃən] *n* friction *f*,
frottement *m*
Friday ['fraɪdɪ] *n* vendredi *m*
fridge [frɪdʒ] *n* (BRIT) frigo *m*,
frigidaire® *m*
fried [fraɪd] *adj* frit(e); **~ egg** œuf *m*
sur le plat
friend [frɛnd] *n* ami(e) ▷ *vt* (*Internet*)
ajouter comme ami(e); **friendly**
adj amical(e); (*kind*) sympathique,
gentil(le); (*place*) accueillant(e); (*Pol:
country*) ami(e) ▷ *n* (*also:* **friendly
match**) match amical; **friendship**
n amitié *f*
fries [fraɪz] (*esp US*) *npl* = **chips**
frigate ['frɪɡɪt] *n* frégate *f*
fright [fraɪt] *n* peur *f*, effroi *m*; **to
give sb a ~** faire peur à qn; **to take
~** prendre peur, s'effrayer; **frighten**
vt effrayer, faire peur à; **frightened**
adj: **to be frightened (of)** avoir peur
(de); **frightening** *adj* effrayant(e);
frightful *adj* affreux(-euse)
frill [frɪl] *n* (*of dress*) volant *m*; (*of shirt*)
jabot *m*
fringe [frɪndʒ] *n* (BRIT: *of hair*) frange
f; (*edge: of forest etc*) bordure *f*
Frisbee® ['frɪzbɪ] *n* Frisbee® *m*
fritter ['frɪtə^r] *n* beignet *m*
frivolous ['frɪvələs] *adj* frivole
fro [frəʊ] *adv see* **to**
frock [frɒk] *n* robe *f*
frog [frɒɡ] *n* grenouille *f*; **frogman**
(*irreg*) *n* homme-grenouille *m*

KEYWORD

from [frɒm] *prep* **1** (*indicating starting
place, origin etc*) de; **where do you
come from?, where are you from?**
d'où venez-vous?; **where has he
come from?** d'où arrive-t-il?; **from
London to Paris** de Londres à Paris;
to escape from sb/sth échapper

à qn/qch; **a letter/telephone call
from my sister** une lettre/un appel
de ma sœur; **to drink from the
bottle** boire (à même) la bouteille;
tell him from me that … dites-lui de
ma part que …
2 (*indicating time*) (à partir) de; **from
one o'clock to** *or* **until** *or* **till two**
d'une heure à deux heures; **from
January (on)** à partir de janvier
3 (*indicating distance*) de; **the hotel
is one kilometre from the beach**
l'hôtel est à un kilomètre de la plage
4 (*indicating price, number etc*) de;
prices range from £10 to £50 les prix
varient entre 10 livres et 50 livres; **the
interest rate was increased from
9% to 10%** le taux d'intérêt est passé
de 9% à 10%
5 (*indicating difference*) de; **he can't
tell red from green** il ne peut pas
distinguer le rouge du vert; **to be
different from sb/sth** être différent
de qn/qch
6 (*because of, on the basis of*): **from
what he says** d'après ce qu'il dit;
weak from hunger affaibli par
la faim

front [frʌnt] *n* (*of house, dress*)
devant *m*; (*of coach, train*) avant *m*;
(*promenade: also:* **sea ~**) bord *m* de
mer; (*Mil, Pol, Meteorology*) front
m; (*fig: appearances*) contenance *f*,
façade *f* ▷ *adj* de devant; (*seat, wheel*)
avant *inv* ▷ *vi*: **in ~ (of)** devant;
front door *n* porte *f* d'entrée; (*of car*)
portière *f* avant; **frontier** ['frʌntɪə^r]
n frontière *f*; **front page** *n* première
page; **front-wheel drive** *n* traction
f avant
frost [frɒst] *n* gel *m*, gelée *f*; (*also:*
hoar~) givre *m*; **frostbite** *n* gelures
fpl; **frosting** *n* (*esp US: on cake*)
glaçage *m*; **frosty** *adj* (*window*)
couvert(e) de givre; (*weather, welcome*)
glacial(e)
froth [frɒθ] *n* mousse *f*; écume *f*

frown [fraun] *n* froncement *m* de sourcils ▷ *vi* froncer les sourcils

froze [frəuz] *pt of* **freeze**

frozen ['frəuzn] *pp of* **freeze** ▷ *adj* (*food*) congelé(e); (*person, also assets*) gelé(e)

fruit [fru:t] *n* (*pl inv*) fruit *m*; **fruit juice** *n* jus *m* de fruit; **fruit machine** *n* (BRIT) machine *f* à sous; **fruit salad** *n* salade *f* de fruits

frustrate [frʌs'treɪt] *vt* frustrer; **frustrated** *adj* frustré(e)

fry (*pt, pp* **fried**) [fraɪ, -d] *vt* (faire) frire ▷ *n*: **small ~** le menu fretin; **frying pan** *n* poêle *f* (à frire)

ft. *abbr* = **foot; feet**

fudge [fʌdʒ] *n* (Culin) sorte de confiserie à base de sucre, de beurre et de lait

fuel [fjuəl] *n* (*for heating*) combustible *m*; (*for engine*) carburant *m*; **fuel tank** *n* (*in vehicle*) réservoir *m* de or à carburant

fulfil, (US) **fulfill** [ful'fɪl] *vt* (*function, condition*) remplir; (*order*) exécuter; (*wish, desire*) satisfaire, réaliser

full [ful] *adj* plein(e); (*details, hotel, bus*) complet(-ète); (*busy: day*) chargé(e); (*skirt*) ample, large ▷ *adv*: **to know ~ well that** savoir fort bien que; **I'm ~ (up)** j'ai bien mangé; **~ employment/ fare** plein emploi/tarif; **a ~ two hours** deux bonnes heures; **at ~ speed** à toute vitesse; **in ~** (*reproduce, quote, pay*) intégralement; (*write name etc*) en toutes lettres; **full-length** *adj* (*portrait*) en pied; (*coat*) long(ue); **full-length film** long métrage; **full moon** *n* pleine lune; **full-scale** *adj* (*model*) grandeur nature *inv*; (*search, retreat*) complet(-ète), total(e); **full stop** *n* point *m*; **full-time** *adj, adv* (*work*) à plein temps; **fully** *adv* entièrement, complètement

fumble ['fʌmbl] *vi* fouiller, tâtonner; **fumble with** *vt fus* tripoter

fume [fju:m] *vi* (*rage*) rager; **fumes** [fju:mz] *npl* vapeurs *fpl*, émanations *fpl*, gaz *mpl*

fun [fʌn] *n* amusement *m*, divertissement *m*; **to have ~** s'amuser; **for ~** pour rire; **to make ~ of** se moquer de

function ['fʌŋkʃən] *n* fonction *f*; (*reception, dinner*) cérémonie *f*, soirée officielle ▷ *vi* fonctionner

fund [fʌnd] *n* caisse *f*, fonds *m*; (*source, store*) source *f*, mine *f*; **funds** *npl* (*money*) fonds *mpl*

fundamental [fʌndə'mɛntl] *adj* fondamental(e)

funeral ['fju:nərəl] *n* enterrement *m*, obsèques *fpl* (*more formal occasion*); **funeral director** *n* entrepreneur *m* des pompes funèbres; **funeral parlour** *n* (BRIT) dépôt *m* mortuaire

funfair ['fʌnfɛəʳ] *n* (BRIT) fête (foraine)

fungus (*pl* **fungi**) ['fʌŋgəs, -gaɪ] *n* champignon *m*; (*mould*) moisissure *f*

funnel ['fʌnl] *n* entonnoir *m*; (*of ship*) cheminée *f*

funny ['fʌnɪ] *adj* amusant(e), drôle; (*strange*) curieux(-euse), bizarre

fur [fəːʳ] *n* fourrure *f*; (BRIT: *in kettle etc*) (dépôt *m* de) tartre *m*; **fur coat** *n* manteau *m* de fourrure

furious ['fjuərɪəs] *adj* furieux(-euse); (*effort*) acharné(e)

furnish ['fəːnɪʃ] *vt* meubler; (*supply*) fournir; **furnishings** *npl* mobilier *m*, articles *mpl* d'ameublement

furniture ['fəːnɪtʃəʳ] *n* meubles *mpl*, mobilier *m*; **piece of ~** meuble *m*

furry ['fəːrɪ] *adj* (*animal*) à fourrure; (*toy*) en peluche

further ['fəːðəʳ] *adj* supplémentaire, autre; nouveau (nouvelle) ▷ *adv* plus loin; (*more*) davantage; (*moreover*) de plus ▷ *vt* faire avancer or progresser, promouvoir; **further education** *n* enseignement *m* postscolaire (*recyclage, formation professionnelle*); **furthermore** *adv* de plus, en outre

furthest ['fəːðɪst] *superlative of* **far**

fury ['fjuərɪ] *n* fureur *f*

fuse, (US) **fuze** [fju:z] n fusible m;
(for bomb etc) amorce f, détonateur m
▷ vt, vi (metal) fondre; (BRIT Elec): **to
~ the lights** faire sauter les fusibles
or les plombs; **fuse box** n boîte f à
fusibles
fusion ['fju:ʒən] n fusion f
fuss [fʌs] n (anxiety, excitement) chichis
mpl, façons fpl; (commotion) tapage m;
(complaining, trouble) histoire(s) f(pl);
to make a ~ faire des façons (or des
histoires); **to make a ~ of sb** dorloter
qn; **fussy** adj (person) tatillon(ne),
difficile, chichiteux(-euse); (dress,
style) tarabiscoté(e)
future ['fju:tʃəʳ] adj futur(e) ▷ n
avenir m; (Ling) futur m; **futures** npl
(Comm) opérations fpl à terme; **in
(the) ~** à l'avenir
fuze [fju:z] n, vt, vi (US) = **fuse**
fuzzy ['fʌzɪ] adj (Phot) flou(e); (hair)
crépu(e)
FYI abbr = **for your information**

g

G [dʒi:] n (Mus) sol m
g. abbr (= gram) g
gadget ['gædʒɪt] n gadget m
Gaelic ['geɪlɪk] adj, n (Ling) gaélique
(m)
gag [gæg] n (on mouth) bâillon m; (joke)
gag m ▷ vt (prisoner etc) bâillonner
gain [geɪn] n (improvement) gain m;
(profit) gain, profit m ▷ vt gagner
▷ vi (watch) avancer; **to ~ from/by**
gagner de/à; **to ~ on sb** (catch up)
rattraper qn; **to ~ 3lbs (in weight)**
prendre 3 livres; **to ~ ground** gagner
du terrain
gal. abbr = **gallon**
gala ['gɑːlə] n gala m
galaxy ['gæləksɪ] n galaxie f
gale [geɪl] n coup m de vent
gall bladder ['gɔːl-] n vésicule f
biliaire
gallery ['gælərɪ] n (also: art ~) musée
m; (private) galerie; (in theatre) dernier
balcon

gallon ['gæln] n gallon m (Brit = 4.543 l; US = 3.785 l)

gallop ['gæləp] n galop m ▷ vi galoper

gallstone ['gɔ:lstəun] n calcul m (biliaire)

gamble ['gæmbl] n pari m, risque calculé ▷ vt, vi jouer; **to ~ on** (fig) miser sur; **gambler** n joueur m; **gambling** n jeu m

game [geɪm] n jeu m; (event) match m; (of tennis, chess, cards) partie f; (Hunting) gibier m ▷ adj (willing): **to be ~ (for)** être prêt(e) (à or pour); **games** npl (Scol) sport m; (sport event) jeux; **big ~** gros gibier; **games console** ['geɪmz-] n console f de jeux vidéo; **game show** n jeu télévisé

gammon ['gæmən] n (bacon) quartier m de lard fumé; (ham) jambon fumé or salé

gang [gæŋ] n bande f; (of workmen) équipe f

gangster ['gæŋstə^r] n gangster m

gap [gæp] n trou m; (in time) intervalle m; (difference): **~ (between)** écart m (entre)

gape [geɪp] vi (person) être or rester bouche bée; (hole, shirt) être ouvert(e)

gap year n année que certains étudiants prennent pour voyager ou pour travailler avant d'entrer à l'université

garage ['gærɑ:ʒ] n garage m; **garage sale** n vide-grenier m

garbage ['gɑ:bɪdʒ] n (US: rubbish) ordures fpl, détritus mpl; (inf: nonsense) âneries fpl; **garbage can** n (US) poubelle f, boîte f à ordures; **garbage collector** n (US) éboueur m

garden ['gɑ:dn] n jardin m; **gardens** npl (public) jardin public; (private) parc m; **garden centre** (BRIT) n pépinière f, jardinerie f; **gardener** n jardinier m; **gardening** n jardinage m

garlic ['gɑ:lɪk] n ail m

garment ['gɑ:mənt] n vêtement m

garnish ['gɑ:nɪʃ] (Culin) vt garnir ▷ n décoration f

gas [gæs] n gaz m; (US: gasoline) essence f ▷ vt asphyxier; **I can**

smell **~** ça sent le gaz; **gas cooker** n (BRIT) cuisinière f à gaz; **gas cylinder** n bouteille f de gaz; **gas fire** n (BRIT) radiateur m à gaz

gasket ['gæskɪt] n (Aut) joint m de culasse

gasoline ['gæsəli:n] n (US) essence f

gasp [gɑ:sp] n halètement m; (of shock etc): **she gave a small ~ of pain** la douleur lui coupa le souffle ▷ vi haleter; (fig) avoir le souffle coupé

gas: gas pedal n (US) accélérateur m; **gas station** n (US) station-service f; **gas tank** n (US Aut) réservoir m d'essence

gastric band ['gæstrɪk-] n anneau m gastrique

gate [geɪt] n (of garden) portail m; (of field, at level crossing) barrière f; (of building, town, at airport) porte f

gateau (pl **gateaux**) ['gætəu, -z] n gros gâteau à la crème

gatecrash ['geɪtkræʃ] vt s'introduire sans invitation dans

gateway ['geɪtweɪ] n porte f

gather ['gæðə^r] vt (flowers, fruit) cueillir; (pick up) ramasser; (assemble: objects) rassembler; (: people) réunir; (: information) recueillir; (understand) comprendre; (Sewing) froncer ▷ vi (assemble) se rassembler; **to ~ speed** prendre de la vitesse; **gathering** n rassemblement m

gauge [geɪdʒ] n (instrument) jauge f ▷ vt jauger; (fig) juger de

gave [geɪv] pt of **give**

gay [geɪ] adj homosexuel(le); (colour) gai, vif (vive)

gaze [geɪz] n regard m fixe ▷ vi: **to ~ at** fixer du regard

GB abbr = **Great Britain**

GCSE n abbr (BRIT: = General Certificate of Secondary Education) examen passé à l'âge de 16 ans sanctionnant les connaissances de l'élève

gear [gɪə^r] n matériel m, équipement m; (Tech) engrenage m; (Aut) vitesse f

f ▷ vt (fig: adapt) adapter; **top** or
(US) **high/low ~** quatrième (or
cinquième)/première vitesse; **in ~** en
prise; **gear up** vi: **to ~ up (to do)** se
préparer (à faire); **gear box** n boîte
f de vitesse; **gear lever** n levier m de
vitesse; **gear shift** (US), **gear stick**
(BRIT) n = **gear lever**

geese [giːs] npl of **goose**

gel [dʒɛl] n gelée f

gem [dʒɛm] n pierre précieuse

Gemini ['dʒɛmɪnaɪ] n les Gémeaux
mpl

gender ['dʒɛndər] n genre m; (person's
sex) sexe m

gene [dʒiːn] n (Biol) gène m

general ['dʒɛnərl] n général m
▷ adj général(e); **in ~** en général;
general anaesthetic, (US)
general anesthetic n anesthésie
générale; **general election** n
élection(s) législative(s); **generalize**
vi généraliser; **generally** adv
généralement; **general practitioner**
n généraliste m/f; **general store** n
épicerie f

generate ['dʒɛnəreɪt] vt engendrer;
(electricity) produire

generation [dʒɛnə'reɪʃən] n
génération f; (of electricity etc)
production f

generator ['dʒɛnəreɪtər] n
générateur m

generosity [dʒɛnə'rɔsɪtɪ] n
générosité f

generous ['dʒɛnərəs] adj
généreux(-euse); (copious)
copieux(-euse)

genetic [dʒɪ'nɛtɪk] adj génétique;
~ engineering ingénierie m
génétique; **~ fingerprinting** système
m d'empreinte génétique; **genetically
modified** adj (food etc) génétiquement
modifié(e); **genetics** n génétique f

Geneva [dʒɪ'niːvə] n Genève

genitals ['dʒɛnɪtlz] npl organes
génitaux

genius ['dʒiːnɪəs] n génie m

genome ['dʒiːnəʊm] n génome m

gent [dʒɛnt] n abbr (BRIT inf)
= **gentleman**

gentle ['dʒɛntl] adj doux (douce);
(breeze, touch) léger(-ère)

gentleman ['dʒɛntlmən] (irreg)
n monsieur m; (well-bred man)
gentleman m

gently ['dʒɛntlɪ] adv doucement

gents [dʒɛnts] n W.-C. mpl (pour
hommes)

genuine ['dʒɛnjuɪn] adj véritable,
authentique; (person, emotion)
sincère; **genuinely** adv sincèrement,
vraiment

geographic(al) [dʒɪə'ɡræfɪk(l)-] adj
géographique

geography [dʒɪ'ɔɡrəfɪ] n
géographie f

geology [dʒɪ'ɔlədʒɪ] n géologie f

geometry [dʒɪ'ɔmətrɪ] n géométrie f

geranium [dʒɪ'reɪnɪəm] n
géranium m

geriatric [dʒɛrɪ'ætrɪk] adj
gériatrique ▷ n patient(e) gériatrique

germ [dʒəːm] n (Med) microbe m

German ['dʒəːmən] adj allemand(e)
▷ n Allemand(e); (Ling) allemand m;
German measles n rubéole f

Germany ['dʒəːmənɪ] n Allemagne f

gesture ['dʒɛstjər] n geste m

KEYWORD

get [ɡɛt] (pt, pp **got**, (US) pp **gotten**)
vi **1** (become, be) devenir; **to get old/
tired** devenir vieux/fatigué, vieillir/se
fatiguer; **to get drunk** s'enivrer; **to
get dirty** se salir; **to get married** se
marier; **when do I get paid?** quand
est-ce que je serai payé?; **it's getting
late** il se fait tard
2 (go): **to get to/from** aller à/de;
to get home rentrer chez soi; **how
did you get here?** comment es-tu
arrivé ici?
3 (begin) commencer or se mettre
à; **to get to know sb** apprendre à

connaître qn; **I'm getting to like him** je commence à l'apprécier; **let's get going** or **started** allons-y
4 (*modal aux vb*): **you've got to do it** il faut que vous le fassiez; **I've got to tell the police** je dois le dire à la police
▶ *vt* **1**: **to get sth done** (*do*) faire qch; (*have done*) faire faire qch; **to get sth/sb ready** préparer qch/qn; **to get one's hair cut** se faire couper les cheveux; **to get the car going** or **to go** (*faire*) démarrer la voiture; **to get sb to do sth** faire faire qch à qn
2 (*obtain: money, permission, results*) obtenir, avoir; (*buy*) acheter; (*find: job, flat*) trouver; (*fetch: person, doctor, object*) aller chercher; **to get sth for sb** procurer qch à qn; **get me Mr Jones, please** (*on phone*) passez-moi Mr Jones, s'il vous plaît; **can I get you a drink?** est-ce que je peux vous servir à boire?
3 (*receive: present, letter*) recevoir, avoir; (*acquire: reputation*) avoir; (*: prize*) obtenir; **what did you get for your birthday?** qu'est-ce que tu as eu pour ton anniversaire?; **how much did you get for the painting?** combien avez-vous vendu le tableau?
4 (*catch*) prendre, saisir, attraper; (*hit: target etc*) atteindre; **to get sb by the arm/throat** prendre or saisir or attraper qn par le bras/à la gorge; **get him!** arrête-le!; **the bullet got him in the leg** il a pris la balle dans la jambe
5 (*take, move*): **to get sth to sb** faire parvenir qch à qn; **do you think we'll get it through the door?** on arrivera à le faire passer par la porte?
6 (*catch, take: plane, bus etc*) prendre; **where do we get the train for Birmingham?** où prend-on le train pour Birmingham?
7 (*understand*) comprendre, saisir; (*hear*) entendre; **I've got it!** j'ai compris!; **I don't get your meaning**

je ne vois or comprends pas ce que vous voulez dire; **I didn't get your name** je n'ai pas entendu votre nom
8 (*have, possess*): **to have got** avoir; **how many have you got?** vous en avez combien?
9 (*illness*) avoir; **I've got a cold** j'ai le rhume; **she got pneumonia and died** elle a fait une pneumonie et elle en est morte
get away *vi* partir, s'en aller; (*escape*) s'échapper
get away with *vt fus* (*punishment*) en être quitte pour; (*crime etc*) se faire pardonner
get back *vi* (*return*) rentrer ▶ *vt* récupérer, recouvrer; **when do we get back?** quand serons-nous de retour?
get in *vi* entrer; (*arrive home*) rentrer; (*train*) arriver
get into *vt fus* entrer dans; (*car, train etc*) monter dans; (*clothes*) mettre, enfiler, endosser; **to get into bed/a rage** se mettre au lit/en colère
get off *vi* (*from train etc*) descendre; (*depart: person, car*) s'en aller ▶ *vt* (*remove: clothes, stain*) enlever ▶ *vt fus* (*train, bus*) descendre de; **where do I get off?** où est-ce que je dois descendre?
get on *vi* (*at exam etc*) se débrouiller; (*agree*): **to get on (with)** s'entendre (avec); **how are you getting on?** comment ça va? ▶ *vt fus* monter dans; (*horse*) monter sur
get out *vi* sortir; (*of vehicle*) descendre ▶ *vt* sortir
get out of *vt fus* sortir de; (*duty etc*) échapper à, se soustraire à
get over *vt fus* (*illness*) se remettre de
get through *vi* (*Tel*) avoir la communication; **to get through to sb** atteindre qn
get up *vi* (*rise*) se lever ▶ *vt fus* monter
getaway ['gɛtəweɪ] *n* fuite *f*

Ghana ['gɑ:nə] n Ghana m

ghastly ['gɑ:stlɪ] adj atroce, horrible

ghetto ['gɛtəu] n ghetto m

ghost [gəust] n fantôme m, revenant m

giant ['dʒaɪənt] n géant(e) ▷ adj géant(e), énorme

gift [gɪft] n cadeau m; (donation, talent) don m; **gifted** adj doué(e); **gift shop**, (US) **gift store** n boutique f de cadeaux; **gift token, gift voucher** n chèque-cadeau m

gig [gɪg] n (inf: concert) concert m

gigabyte ['dʒɪgəbaɪt] n gigaoctet m

gigantic [dʒaɪ'gæntɪk] adj gigantesque

giggle ['gɪgl] vi pouffer, ricaner sottement

gills [gɪlz] npl (of fish) ouïes fpl, branchies fpl

gilt [gɪlt] n dorure f ▷ adj doré(e)

gimmick ['gɪmɪk] n truc m

gin [dʒɪn] n gin m

ginger ['dʒɪndʒəʳ] n gingembre m

gipsy ['dʒɪpsɪ] n = **gypsy**

giraffe [dʒɪ'rɑ:f] n girafe f

girl [gə:l] n fille f, fillette f; (young unmarried woman) jeune fille; (daughter) fille; **an English ~** une jeune Anglaise; **girl band** n girls band m; **girlfriend** n (of girl) amie f; (of boy) petite amie; **Girl Guide** n (BRIT) éclaireuse f; (Roman Catholic) guide f; **Girl Scout** n (US) = **Girl Guide**

gist [dʒɪst] n essentiel m

give [gɪv] (pt **gave**, pp **given**) vt donner ▷ vi (break) céder; (stretch: fabric) se prêter; **to ~ sb sth, ~ sth to sb** donner qch à qn; (gift) offrir qch à qn; (message) transmettre qch à qn; **to ~ sb a call/kiss** appeler/embrasser qn; **to ~ a cry/sigh** pousser un cri/un soupir; **give away** vt donner; (give free) faire cadeau de; (betray) donner, trahir; (disclose) révéler; **give back** vt rendre; **give in** vi céder ▷ vt donner; **give out** vt (food etc) distribuer; **give up** vi

renoncer ▷ vt renoncer à; **to ~ up smoking** arrêter de fumer; **to ~ o.s. up** se rendre

given ['gɪvn] pp of **give** ▷ adj (fixed: time, amount) donné(e), déterminé(e) ▷ conj: **~ the circumstances ...** étant donné les circonstances ..., vu les circonstances ...; **~ that ...** étant donné que ...

glacier ['glæsɪəʳ] n glacier m

glad [glæd] adj content(e); **gladly** ['glædlɪ] adv volontiers

glamorous ['glæmərəs] adj (person) séduisant(e); (job) prestigieux(-euse)

glamour, (US) **glamor** ['glæməʳ] n éclat m, prestige m

glance [glɑ:ns] n coup m d'œil ▷ vi: **to ~ at** jeter un coup d'œil à

gland [glænd] n glande f

glare [glɛəʳ] n (of anger) regard furieux; (of light) lumière éblouissante; (of publicity) feux mpl ▷ vi briller d'un éclat aveuglant; **to ~ at** lancer un regard or des regards furieux à; **glaring** adj (mistake) criant(e), qui saute aux yeux

glass [glɑ:s] n verre m; **glasses** npl (spectacles) lunettes fpl

glaze [gleɪz] vt (door) vitrer; (pottery) vernir ▷ n vernis m

gleam [gli:m] vi luire, briller

glen [glɛn] n vallée f

glide [glaɪd] vi glisser; (Aviat, bird) planer; **glider** n (Aviat) planeur m

glimmer ['glɪməʳ] n lueur f

glimpse [glɪmps] n vision passagère, aperçu m ▷ vt entrevoir, apercevoir

glint [glɪnt] vi étinceler

glisten ['glɪsn] vi briller, luire

glitter ['glɪtəʳ] vi scintiller, briller

global ['gləubl] adj (world-wide) mondial(e); (overall) global(e); **globalization** n mondialisation f; **global warming** n réchauffement m de la planète

globe [gləub] n globe m

gloom [glu:m] n obscurité f; (sadness) tristesse f, mélancolie f; **gloomy**

adj (*person*) morose; (*place, outlook*) sombre

glorious [ˈɡlɔːrɪəs] *adj* glorieux(-euse); (*beautiful*) splendide

glory [ˈɡlɔːrɪ] *n* gloire *f*; splendeur *f*

gloss [ɡlɔs] *n* (*shine*) brillant *m*, vernis *m*; (*also:* **~ paint**) peinture brillante

glossary [ˈɡlɔsərɪ] *n* glossaire *m*, lexique *m*

glossy [ˈɡlɔsɪ] *adj* brillant(e), luisant(e) ▷ *n* (*also:* **~ magazine**) revue *f* de luxe

glove [ɡlʌv] *n* gant *m*; **glove compartment** *n* (*Aut*) boîte *f* à gants, vide-poches *m inv*

glow [ɡləu] *vi* rougeoyer; (*face*) rayonner; (*eyes*) briller

glucose [ˈɡluːkəus] *n* glucose *m*

glue [ɡluː] *n* colle *f* ▷ *vt* coller

GM *abbr* (= *genetically modified*) génétiquement modifié(e)

gm *abbr* (= *gram*) g

GM crop *n* culture *f* OGM

GMO *n abbr* (= *genetically modified organism*) OGM *m*

GMT *abbr* (= *Greenwich Mean Time*) GMT

gnaw [nɔː] *vt* ronger

go [ɡəu] (*pt* **went**, *pp* **gone**) *vi* aller; (*depart*) partir, s'en aller; (*work*) marcher; (*break*) céder; (*time*) passer; (*be sold*): **to go for £10** se vendre 10 livres; (*become*): **to go pale/mouldy** pâlir/moisir ▷ *n* (*pl* **goes**): **to have a go (at)** essayer (de faire); **to be on the go** être en mouvement; **whose go is it?** à qui est-ce de jouer?; **he's going to do it** il va le faire, il est sur le point de le faire; **to go for a walk** aller se promener; **to go dancing/shopping** aller danser/faire les courses; **to go and see sb, go to see sb** aller voir qn; **how did it go?** comment est-ce que ça s'est passé?; **to go round the back/by the shop** passer par derrière/devant le magasin; **... to go** (*us: food*) ... à emporter; **go ahead** *vi* (*take place*) avoir lieu; (*get going*) y aller; **go away**

vi partir, s'en aller; **go back** *vi* rentrer; revenir; (*go again*) retourner; **go by** *vi* (*years, time*) passer, s'écouler ▷ *vt fus* s'en tenir à; (*believe*) en croire; **go down** *vi* descendre; (*number, price, amount*) baisser; (*ship*) couler; (*sun*) se coucher ▷ *vt fus* descendre; **go for** *vt fus* (*fetch*) aller chercher; (*like*) aimer; (*attack*) s'en prendre à; attaquer; **go in** *vi* entrer; **go into** *vt fus* entrer dans; (*investigate*) étudier, examiner; (*embark on*) se lancer dans; **go off** *vi* partir, s'en aller; (*food*) se gâter; (*milk*) tourner; (*bomb*) sauter; (*alarm clock*) sonner; (*alarm*) se déclencher; (*lights etc*) s'éteindre; (*event*) se dérouler ▷ *vt fus* ne plus aimer; **the gun went off** le coup est parti; **go on** *vi* continuer; (*happen*) se passer; (*lights*) s'allumer ▷ *vt fus*: **to go on doing** continuer à faire; **go out** *vi* sortir; (*fire, light*) s'éteindre; (*tide*) descendre; **to go out with sb** sortir avec qn; **go over** *vi, vt fus* (*check*) revoir, vérifier; **go past** *vt fus*: **to go past sth** passer devant qch; **go round** *vi* (*circulate: news, rumour*) circuler; (*revolve*) tourner; (*suffice*) suffire (pour tout le monde); **to go round to sb's** passer chez qn; aller chez qn; (*make a detour*): **to go round (by)** faire un détour (par); **go through** *vt fus* (*town etc*) traverser; (*search through*) fouiller; (*visit*) subir; **go up** *vi* monter; (*price*) augmenter ▷ *vt fus* gravir; **go with** *vt fus* aller avec; **go without** *vt fus* se passer de

go-ahead [ˈɡəuəhɛd] *adj* dynamique, entreprenant(e) ▷ *n* feu vert

goal [ɡəul] *n* but *m*; **goalkeeper** *n* gardien *m* de but; **goal-post** *n* poteau *m* de but

goat [ɡəut] *n* chèvre *f*

gobble [ˈɡɔbl] *vt* (*also:* **~ down, ~ up**) engloutir

god [ɡɔd] *n* dieu *m*; **God** Dieu; **godchild** *n* filleul(e); **goddaughter**

n filleule *f*; **goddess** *n* déesse *f*;
godfather *n* parrain *m*; **godmother**
n marraine *f*; **godson** *n* filleul *m*

goggles ['gɔglz] *npl* (for skiing etc)
lunettes (protectrices); (for swimming)
lunettes de piscine

going ['gəuɪŋ] *n* (conditions) état *m*
du terrain ▷ *adj*: **the ~ rate** le tarif
(en vigueur)

gold [gəuld] *n* or *m* ▷ *adj* en or;
(reserves) d'or; **golden** *adj* (made of
gold) en or; (gold in colour) doré(e);
goldfish *n* poisson *m* rouge;
goldmine *n* mine *f* d'or; **gold-plated**
adj plaqué(e) or *inv*

golf [gɔlf] *n* golf *m*; **golf ball** *n* balle
f de golf; (on typewriter) boule *f*; **golf
club** *n* club *m* de golf; (stick) club *m*,
crosse *f* de golf; **golf course** *n* terrain
m de golf; **golfer** *n* joueur(-euse)
de golf

gone [gɔn] *pp of* **go**

gong [gɔŋ] *n* gong *m*

good [gud] *adj* bon(ne); (kind)
gentil(le); (child) sage; (weather)
beau (belle) ▷ *n* bien *m*; **goods** *npl*
marchandise *f*, articles *mpl*; **~!** bon!,
très bien!; **to be ~ at** être bon en;
to be ~ for être bon pour; **it's no
~ complaining** cela ne sert à rien
de se plaindre; **to make ~** (deficit)
combler; (losses) compenser; **for ~**
(for ever) pour de bon, une fois pour
toutes; **would you be ~ enough to
…?** auriez-vous la bonté or l'amabilité
de …?; **is this any ~?** (will it do?)
est-ce que ceci fera l'affaire?, est-ce
que cela peut vous rendre service?;
(what's it like?) qu'est-ce que ça vaut?;
a ~ deal (of) beaucoup (de); **a ~
many** beaucoup (de); **~ morning/
afternoon!** bonjour!; **~ evening!**
bonsoir!; **~ night!** bonsoir!; (on going
to bed) bonne nuit!; **goodbye** *excl* au
revoir!; **to say goodbye to sb** dire au
revoir à qn; **Good Friday** *n* Vendredi
saint; **good-looking** *adj* beau (belle),
bien *inv*; **good-natured** *adj* (person)

qui a un bon naturel; **goodness** *n* (of
person) bonté *f*; **for goodness sake!**
je vous en prie!; **goodness gracious!**
mon Dieu!; **goods train** *n* (BRIT)
train *m* de marchandises; **goodwill** *n*
bonne volonté

google ['gugl] *vi* faire une recheche
Google® ▷ *vt* googler

goose (*pl* **geese**) [gu:s, gi:s] *n* oie *f*

gooseberry ['guzbəri] *n* groseille *f*
à maquereau; **to play ~** (BRIT) tenir
la chandelle

goose bumps, goose pimples
npl chair *f* de poule

gorge [gɔ:dʒ] *n* gorge *f* ▷ *vt*: **to ~ o.s.
(on)** se gorger (de)

gorgeous ['gɔ:dʒəs] *adj* splendide,
superbe

gorilla [gə'rɪlə] *n* gorille *m*

gosh [gɔʃ] (inf) *excl* mince alors!

gospel ['gɔspl] *n* évangile *m*

gossip ['gɔsɪp] *n* (chat) bavardages
mpl; (malicious) commérage *m*,
cancans *mpl*; (person) commère
f ▷ *vi* bavarder; cancaner, faire des
commérages; **gossip column** *n*
(Press) échos *mpl*

got [gɔt] *pt, pp of* **get**

gotten ['gɔtn] (US) *pp of* **get**

gourmet ['guəmeɪ] *n* gourmet *m*,
gastronome *m/f*

govern ['gʌvən] *vt* gouverner;
(influence) déterminer; **government**
n gouvernement *m*; (BRIT: ministers)
ministère *m*; **governor** *n* (of colony,
state, bank) gouverneur *m*; (of school,
hospital etc) administrateur(-trice);
(BRIT: of prison) directeur(-trice)

gown [gaun] *n* robe *f*; (of teacher, BRIT:
of judge) toge *f*

GP *n abbr* (Med) = **general
practitioner**

GPS *n abbr* (= global positioning system)
GPS *m*

grab [græb] *vt* saisir, empoigner ▷ *vi*:
to ~ at essayer de saisir

grace [greɪs] *n* grâce *f* ▷ *vt* (honour)
honorer; (adorn) orner; **5 days'**

~ un répit de 5 jours; **graceful** adj
gracieux(-euse), élégant(e); **gracious**
['greɪʃəs] adj bienveillant(e)
grade [greɪd] n (Comm: quality)
qualité f; (: size) calibre m; (: type)
catégorie f; (in hierarchy) grade m,
échelon m; (Scol) note f; (us: school
class) classe f; (: gradient) pente f
▷ vt classer; (by size) calibrer; **grade
crossing** n (us) passage m à niveau;
grade school n (us) école f primaire
gradient ['greɪdɪənt] n inclinaison
f, pente f
gradual ['grædjuəl] adj graduel(le),
progressif(-ive); **gradually** adv peu à
peu, graduellement
graduate n ['grædjuɪt] diplômé(e)
d'université, (us: of high school)
diplômé(e) de fin d'études ▷ vi
['grædjueɪt] obtenir un diplôme
d'université (or de fin d'études);
graduation [grædju'eɪʃən] n
cérémonie f de remise des diplômes
graffiti [grə'fi:tɪ] npl graffiti mpl
graft [grɑ:ft] n (Agr, Med) greffe f;
(bribery) corruption f ▷ vt greffer;
hard ~ (BRIT inf) boulot acharné
grain [greɪn] n (single piece) grain
m; (no pl: cereals) céréales fpl; (us:
corn) blé m
gram [græm] n gramme m
grammar ['græmər] n grammaire f;
grammar school n (BRIT) ≈ lycée m
gramme [græm] n = **gram**
gran [græn] (inf) n (BRIT) mamie f (inf),
mémé f (inf)
grand [grænd] adj magnifique,
splendide; (gesture etc) noble;
grandad n (inf) = **granddad**;
grandchild (pl **grandchildren**)
n petit-fils m, petite-fille f;
grandchildren npl petits-enfants;
granddad n (inf) papy m (inf), papi m
(inf), pépé m (inf); **granddaughter** n
petite-fille f; **grandfather** n grand-
père m; **grandma** n (inf) = **gran**;
grandmother n grand-mère f;
grandpa n (inf) = **granddad**;

grandparents npl grands-parents
mpl; **grand piano** n piano m à queue;
Grand Prix ['grɑ̃:'pri:] n (Aut)
grand prix automobile; **grandson** n
petit-fils m
granite ['grænɪt] n granit m
granny ['grænɪ] n (inf) = **gran**
grant [grɑ:nt] vt accorder; (a request)
accéder à; (admit) concéder ▷ n
(Scol) bourse f; (Admin) subside m,
subvention f; **to take sth for ~ed**
considérer qch comme acquis;
to take sb for ~ed considérer qn
comme faisant partie du décor
grape [greɪp] n raisin m
grapefruit ['greɪpfru:t] n
pamplemousse m
graph [grɑ:f] n graphique m, courbe
f; **graphic** ['græfɪk] adj graphique;
(vivid) vivant(e); **graphics** n (art) arts
mpl graphiques; (process) graphisme
m ▷ npl (drawings) illustrations fpl
grasp [grɑ:sp] vt saisir ▷ n (grip)
prise f; (fig) compréhension f,
connaissance f
grass [grɑ:s] n herbe f; (lawn) gazon
m; **grasshopper** n sauterelle f
grate [greɪt] n grille f de cheminée
▷ vi grincer ▷ vt (Culin) râper
grateful ['greɪtful] adj
reconnaissant(e)
grater ['greɪtər] n râpe f
gratitude ['grætɪtjuːd] n gratitude f
grave [greɪv] n tombe f ▷ adj grave,
sérieux(-euse)
gravel ['grævl] n gravier m
gravestone ['greɪvstəun] n pierre
tombale
graveyard ['greɪvjɑ:d] n
cimetière m
gravity ['grævɪtɪ] n (Physics) gravité f,
pesanteur f; (seriousness) gravité
gravy ['greɪvɪ] n jus m (de viande),
sauce f (au jus de viande)
gray [greɪ] adj (us) = **grey**
graze [greɪz] vi paître, brouter ▷ vt
(touch lightly) frôler, effleurer; (scrape)
écorcher ▷ n écorchure f

grease [griːs] n (fat) graisse f; (lubricant) lubrifiant m ▷ vt graisser; lubrifier; **greasy** adj gras(se), graisseux(-euse); (hands, clothes) graisseux

great [greɪt] adj grand(e); (heat, pain etc) très fort(e), intense; (inf) formidable; **Great Britain** n Grande-Bretagne f; **great-grandfather** n arrière-grand-père m; **great-grandmother** n arrière-grand-mère f; **greatly** adv très, grandement; (with verbs) beaucoup

Greece [griːs] n Grèce f

greed [griːd] n (also: **~iness**) avidité f; (for food) gourmandise f; **greedy** adj avide; (for food) gourmand(e)

Greek [griːk] adj grec (grecque) ▷ n Grec (Grecque); (Ling) grec m

green [griːn] adj vert(e); (inexperienced) (bien) jeune, naïf(-ive); (ecological: product etc) écologique ▷ n (colour) vert m; (on golf course) green m; (stretch of grass) pelouse f; **greens** npl (vegetables) légumes verts; **green card** n (Aut) carte verte; (US: work permit) permis m de travail; **greengage** n reine-claude f; **greengrocer** n (BRIT) marchand m de fruits et légumes; **greengrocer's (shop)** n magasin m de fruits et légumes; **greenhouse** n serre f; **the greenhouse effect** l'effet m de serre

Greenland ['griːnlənd] n Groenland m

green salad n salade verte

green tax n écotaxe f

greet [griːt] vt accueillir; **greeting** n salutation f; **Christmas/birthday greetings** souhaits mpl de Noël/de bon anniversaire; **greeting(s) card** n carte f de vœux

grew [gruː] pt of **grow**

grey, (US) **gray** [greɪ] adj gris(e); (dismal) sombre; **grey-haired**, (US) **gray-haired** adj aux cheveux gris; **greyhound** n lévrier m

grid [grɪd] n grille f; (Elec) réseau m; **gridlock** n (traffic jam) embouteillage m

grief [griːf] n chagrin m, douleur f

grievance ['griːvəns] n doléance f, grief m; (cause for complaint) grief

grieve [griːv] vi avoir du chagrin; se désoler ▷ vt faire de la peine à, affliger; **to ~ for sb** pleurer qn

grill [grɪl] n (on cooker) gril m; (also: **mixed ~**) grillade(s) f(pl) ▷ vt (Culin) griller; (inf: question) cuisiner

grille [grɪl] n grillage m; (Aut) calandre f

grim [grɪm] adj sinistre, lugubre; (serious, stern) sévère

grime [graɪm] n crasse f

grin [grɪn] n large sourire m ▷ vi sourire

grind [graɪnd] (pt, pp **ground**) vt écraser; (coffee, pepper etc) moudre; (US: meat) hacher ▷ n (work) corvée f

grip [grɪp] n (handclasp) poigne f; (control) prise f; (handle) poignée f; (holdall) sac m de voyage ▷ vt saisir, empoigner; (viewer, reader) captiver; **to come to ~s with** se colleter avec, en venir aux prises avec; **to ~ the road** (Aut) adhérer à la route; **gripping** adj prenant(e), palpitant(e)

grit [grɪt] n gravillon m; (courage) cran m ▷ vt (road) sabler; **to ~ one's teeth** serrer les dents

grits [grɪts] npl (US) gruau m de maïs

groan [grəun] n (of pain) gémissement m ▷ vi gémir

grocer ['grəusə'] n épicier m; **groceries** npl provisions fpl; **grocer's (shop), grocery** n épicerie f

groin [grɔɪn] n aine f

groom [gruːm] n (for horses) palefrenier m; (also: **bride~**) marié m ▷ vt (horse) panser; (fig): **to ~ sb for** former qn pour

groove [gruːv] n sillon m, rainure f

grope [grəup] vi tâtonner; **to ~ for** chercher à tâtons

gross [grəus] *adj* grossier(-ière);
(Comm) brut(e); **grossly** *adv* (greatly)
très, grandement

grotesque [grə'tɛsk] *adj* grotesque

ground [graund] *pt, pp of* **grind** ▷ *n*
sol *m*, terre *f*; (land) terrain *m*, terres
fpl; (Sport) terrain; (reason: gen pl)
raison *f*; (us: also: **~ wire**) terre *f* ▷ *vt*
(plane) empêcher de décoller, retenir
au sol; (us Elec) équiper d'une prise
de terre; **grounds** *npl* (gardens etc)
parc *m*, domaine *m*; (of coffee) marc
m; **on the ~, to the ~** par terre;
to gain/lose ~ gagner/perdre
du terrain; **ground floor** *n* (BRIT)
rez-de-chaussée *m*; **groundsheet** *n*
(BRIT) tapis *m* de sol; **groundwork** *n*
préparation *f*

group [gruːp] *n* groupe *m* ▷ *vt* (also:
~ together) grouper ▷ *vi* (also: **~
together**) se grouper

grouse [graus] *n* (pl inv: bird) grouse *f*
(sorte de coq de bruyère) ▷ *vi* (complain)
rouspéter, râler

grovel ['grɔvl] *vi* (fig): **to ~ (before)**
ramper (devant)

grow (pt **grew**, pp **grown**) [grəu,
gruː, grəun] *vi* (plant) pousser,
croître; (person) grandir; (increase)
augmenter, se développer; (become)
devenir; **to ~ rich/weak** s'enrichir/
s'affaiblir ▷ *vt* cultiver, faire pousser;
(hair, beard) laisser pousser; **grow on**
vt fus: **that painting is ~ing on me**
je finirai par aimer ce tableau; **grow
up** *vi* grandir

growl [graul] *vi* grogner

grown [grəun] *pp of* **grow**; **grown-
up** *n* adulte *m/f*, grande personne

growth [grəuθ] *n* croissance *f*,
développement *m*; (what has grown)
pousse *f*, poussée *f*; (Med) grosseur
f, tumeur *f*

grub [grʌb] *n* larve *f*; (inf: food) bouffe *f*

grubby ['grʌbɪ] *adj* crasseux(-euse)

grudge [grʌdʒ] *n* rancune *f* ▷ *vt*: **to
~ sb sth** (in giving) donner qch à qn
à contre-cœur; (resent) reprocher

qch à qn; **to bear sb a ~ (for)** garder
rancune *or* en vouloir à qn (de)

gruelling, (us) **grueling** ['gruəlɪŋ]
adj exténuant(e)

gruesome ['gruːsəm] *adj* horrible

grumble ['grʌmbl] *vi* rouspéter,
ronchonner

grumpy ['grʌmpɪ] *adj*
grincheux(-euse)

grunt [grʌnt] *vi* grogner

guarantee [gærən'tiː] *n* garantie *f*
▷ *vt* garantir

guard [gɑːd] *n* garde *f*; (one man)
garde *m*; (BRIT Rail) chef *m* de train;
(safety device: on machine) dispositif
m de sûreté; (also: **fire~**) garde-feu *m*
inv ▷ *vt* garder, surveiller; (protect):
to ~ sb/sth (against *or* **from)**
protéger qn/qch (contre); **to be
on one's ~** (fig) être sur ses gardes;
guardian *n* gardien(ne); (of minor)
tuteur(-trice)

guerrilla [gə'rɪlə] *n* guérillero *m*

guess [gɛs] *vi* deviner ▷ *vt* deviner;
(estimate) évaluer; (us) croire, penser
▷ *n* supposition *f*, hypothèse *f*; **to
take** *or* **have a ~** essayer de deviner

guest [gɛst] *n* invité(e); (in hotel)
client(e); **guest house** *n* pension *f*;
guest room *n* chambre *f* d'amis

guidance ['gaɪdəns] *n* (advice)
conseils *mpl*

guide [gaɪd] *n* (person) guide
m/f; (book) guide *m*; (also: **Girl
G~**) éclaireuse *f*; (Roman Catholic)
guide *f* ▷ *vt* guider; **is there an
English-speaking ~?** est-ce que
l'un des guides parle anglais?;
guidebook *n* guide *m*; **guide dog**
n chien *m* d'aveugle; **guided tour**
n visite guidée; **what time does
the guided tour start?** la visite
guidée commence à quelle heure?;
guidelines *npl* (advice) instructions
générales, conseils *mpl*

guild [gɪld] *n* (Hist) corporation
f; (sharing interests) cercle *m*,
association *f*

guilt [gɪlt] n culpabilité f; **guilty** adj coupable
guinea pig ['gɪnɪ-] n cobaye m
guitar [gɪ'tɑːʳ] n guitare f; **guitarist** n guitariste m/f
gulf [gʌlf] n golfe m; (abyss) gouffre m
gull [gʌl] n mouette f
gulp [gʌlp] vi avaler sa salive; (from emotion) avoir la gorge serrée, s'étrangler ▷ vt (also: **~ down**) avaler
gum [gʌm] n (Anat) gencive f; (glue) colle f; (also: **chewing-~**) chewing-gum m ▷ vt coller
gun [gʌn] n (small) revolver m, pistolet m; (rifle) fusil m, carabine f; (cannon) canon m; **gunfire** n fusillade f; **gunman** (irreg) n bandit armé; **gunpoint** n: **at gunpoint** sous la menace du pistolet (or fusil); **gunpowder** n poudre f à canon; **gunshot** n coup m de feu
gush [gʌʃ] vi jaillir; (fig) se répandre en effusions
gust [gʌst] n (of wind) rafale f
gut [gʌt] n intestin m, boyau m; **guts** npl (inf: Anat) boyaux mpl; (: courage) cran m
gutter ['gʌtəʳ] n (of roof) gouttière f; (in street) caniveau m
guy [gaɪ] n (inf: man) type m; (also: **~rope**) corde f; (figure) effigie de Guy Fawkes
Guy Fawkes' Night [gaɪ'fɔːks-] n voir article **"Guy Fawkes' Night"**

● GUY FAWKES' NIGHT
●
● Guy Fawkes' Night, que l'on appelle
● également "bonfire night",
● commémore l'échec du complot (le
● "Gunpowder Plot") contre James
● Ier et son parlement le 5 novembre
● 1605. L'un des conspirateurs, Guy
● Fawkes, avait été surpris dans
● les caves du parlement alors
● qu'il s'apprêtait à y mettre le feu.
● Chaque année pour le 5 novembre,
● les enfants préparent à l'avance
● une effigie de Guy Fawkes et ils
● demandent aux passants "un
● penny pour le guy" avec lequel ils
● pourront s'acheter des fusées de
● feu d'artifice. Beaucoup de gens
● font encore un feu dans leur jardin
● sur lequel ils brûlent le "guy".

gym [dʒɪm] n (also: **~nasium**) gymnase m; (also: **~nastics**) gym f; **gymnasium** n gymnase m; **gymnast** n gymnaste m/f; **gymnastics** n, npl gymnastique f; **gym shoes** npl chaussures fpl de gym(nastique)
gynaecologist, (us) **gynecologist** [gaɪnɪ'kɔlədʒɪst] n gynécologue m/f
gypsy ['dʒɪpsɪ] n gitan(e), bohémien(ne)

h

haberdashery [hæbə'dæʃərɪ] *n*
(BRIT) mercerie *f*
habit ['hæbɪt] *n* habitude *f*; (*costume:*
Rel) habit *m*
habitat ['hæbɪtæt] *n* habitat *m*
hack [hæk] *vt* hacher, tailler ▷ *n* (*pej:*
writer) nègre *m*; **hacker** *n* (*Comput*)
pirate *m* (informatique)
had [hæd] *pt, pp of* **have**
haddock ['hædək] (*pl* **haddock** *or*
haddocks) *n* églefin *m*; **smoked ~**
haddock *m*
hadn't ['hædnt] = **had not**
haemorrhage, (US) **hemorrhage**
['hemərɪdʒ] *n* hémorragie *f*
haemorrhoids, (US)
hemorrhoids ['hemərɔɪdz] *npl*
hémorroïdes *fpl*
haggle ['hægl] *vi* marchander
Hague [heɪg] *n*: **The ~** La Haye
hail [heɪl] *n* grêle *f* ▷ *vt* (*call*) héler;
(*greet*) acclamer ▷ *vi* grêler; **hailstone**
n grêlon *m*

hair [hɛəʳ] *n* cheveux *mpl*; (*on body*)
poils *mpl*; (*of animal*) pelage *m*; (*single*
hair: on head) cheveu *m*; (: *on body,*
of animal) poil *m*; **to do one's ~** se
coiffer; **hairband** *n* (*elasticated*)
bandeau *m*; (*plastic*) serre-tête *m*;
hairbrush *n* brosse *f* à cheveux;
haircut *n* coupe *f* (de cheveux);
hairdo *n* coiffure *f*; **hairdresser** *n*
coiffeur(-euse); **hairdresser's** *n*
salon *m* de coiffure, coiffeur *m*; **hair**
dryer *n* sèche-cheveux *m*, séchoir *m*;
hair gel *n* gel *m* pour cheveux; **hair**
spray *n* laque *f* (pour les cheveux);
hairstyle *n* coiffure *f*; **hairy** *adj*
poilu(e), chevelu(e); (*inf: frightening*)
effrayant(e)
haka ['hɑːkə] *n* (NZ) haka *m*
hake [heɪk] (*pl* **hake** *or* **hakes**) *n* colin
m, merlu *m*
half [hɑːf] *n* (*pl* **halves**) moitié *f*; (*of*
beer: also: **~ pint**) ≈ demi *m*; (*Rail, bus:*
also: **~ fare**) demi-tarif *m*; (*Sport: of*
match) mi-temps *f* ▷ *adj* demi(e) ▷ *adv*
(à) moitié, à demi; **~ an hour** une
demi-heure; **~ a dozen** une demi-
douzaine; **~ a pound** une demi-livre,
≈ 250 g; **two and a ~** deux et demi;
to cut sth in ~ couper qch en deux;
half board *n* (BRIT: *in hotel*) demi-
pension *f*; **half-brother** *n* demi-frère
m; **half day** *n* demi-journée *f*; **half**
fare *n* demi-tarif *m*; **half-hearted** *adj*
tiède, sans enthousiasme; **half-hour**
n demi-heure *f*; **half-price** *adj* à
moitié prix ▷ *adv* (*also:* **at half-price**)
à moitié prix; **half term** *n* (BRIT
Scol) vacances *fpl* (de demi-trimestre);
half-time *n* mi-temps *f*; **halfway** *adv*
à mi-chemin; **halfway through sth**
au milieu de qch
hall [hɔːl] *n* salle *f*; (*entrance way: big*)
hall *m*; (: *small*) entrée *f*; (US: *corridor*)
couloir *m*; (*mansion*) château *m*,
manoir *m*
hallmark ['hɔːlmɑːk] *n* poinçon *m*;
(*fig*) marque *f*
hallo [hə'ləʊ] *excl* = **hello**

hall of residence n (BRIT) pavillon m
or résidence f universitaire
Hallowe'en, Halloween
['hæləu'i:n] n veille f de la Toussaint

Selon la tradition, *Hallowe'en*
est la nuit des fantômes et des
sorcières. En Écosse et aux États-
Unis surtout (et de plus en plus en
Angleterre) les enfants, pour fêter
Hallowe'en, se déguisent ce soir-là
et ils vont ainsi de porte en porte
en demandant de petits cadeaux
(du chocolat, etc).

hallucination [həlu:sɪ'neɪʃən] n
hallucination f
hallway ['hɔ:lweɪ] n (entrance)
vestibule m; (corridor) couloir m
halo ['heɪləu] n (of saint etc) auréole f
halt [hɔ:lt] n halte f, arrêt m ▷ vt faire
arrêter; (progress etc) interrompre ▷ vi
faire halte, s'arrêter
halve [hɑ:v] vt (apple etc) partager or
diviser en deux; (reduce by half) réduire
de moitié
halves [hɑ:vz] npl of **half**
ham [hæm] n jambon m
hamburger ['hæmbə:gəʳ] n
hamburger m
hamlet ['hæmlɪt] n hameau m
hammer ['hæməʳ] n marteau m
▷ vt (nail) enfoncer; (fig) éreinter,
démolir ▷ vi (at door) frapper à
coups redoublés; **to ~ a point
home to sb** faire rentrer qch dans
la tête de qn
hammock ['hæmək] n hamac m
hamper ['hæmpəʳ] vt gêner ▷ n
panier m (d'osier)
hamster ['hæmstəʳ] n hamster m
hamstring ['hæmstrɪŋ] n (Anat)
tendon m du jarret
hand [hænd] n main f; (of clock)
aiguille f; (handwriting) écriture f; (at
cards) jeu m; (worker) ouvrier(-ière)

▷ vt passer, donner; **to give sb a ~**
donner un coup de main à qn; **at ~**
à portée de la main; **in ~** (situation)
en main; (work) en cours; **to be on ~**
(person) être disponible; (emergency
services) se tenir prêt(e) (à intervenir);
to ~ (information etc) sous la main,
à portée de la main; **on the one ~
..., on the other ~** d'une part ...,
d'autre part; **hand down** vt passer;
(tradition, heirloom) transmettre; (US:
sentence, verdict) prononcer; **hand in**
vt remettre; **hand out** vt distribuer;
hand over vt remettre; (powers
etc) transmettre; **handbag** n sac m
à main; **hand baggage** n = **hand
luggage**; **handbook** n manuel
m; **handbrake** n frein m à main;
handcuffs npl menottes fpl; **handful**
n poignée f
handicap ['hændɪkæp] n handicap
m ▷ vt handicaper
handkerchief ['hæŋkətʃɪf] n
mouchoir m
handle ['hændl] n (of door etc)
poignée f; (of cup etc) anse f; (of knife
etc) manche m; (of saucepan) queue f;
(for winding) manivelle f ▷ vt toucher,
manier; (deal with) s'occuper de;
(treat: people) prendre; **"~ with care"**
"fragile"; **to fly off the ~** s'énerver;
handlebar(s) n(pl) guidon m
hand: hand luggage n bagages mpl
à main; **handmade** adj fait(e) à la
main; **handout** n (money) aide f, don
m; (leaflet) prospectus m; (at lecture)
polycopié m; **hands-free** adj mains
libres inv ▷ n (also: **hands-free kit**) kit
m mains libres inv
handsome ['hænsəm] adj beau
(belle); (profit) considérable
handwriting ['hændraɪtɪŋ] n
écriture f
handy ['hændɪ] adj (person)
adroit(e); (close at hand) sous la main;
(convenient) pratique
hang (pt, pp **hung**) [hæŋ, hʌŋ] vt
accrocher; (criminal) pendre ▷ vi

pendre; (*hair, drapery*) tomber ▷ *n*: **to get the ~ of (doing) sth** (*inf*) attraper le coup pour faire qch; **hang about, hang around** *vi* traîner; **hang down** *vi* pendre; **hang on** *vi* (*wait*) attendre; **hang out** *vt* (*washing*) étendre (dehors) ▷ *vi* (*inf: live*) habiter, percher; (: *spend time*) traîner; **hang round** *vi* = **hang about**; **hang up** *vi* (*Tel*) raccrocher ▷ *vt* (*coat, painting etc*) accrocher, suspendre

hanger ['hæŋəʳ] *n* cintre *m*, portemanteau *m*

hang-gliding ['hæŋglaɪdɪŋ] *n* vol *m* libre *or* sur aile delta

hangover ['hæŋəʊvəʳ] *n* (*after drinking*) gueule *f* de bois

hankie, hanky ['hæŋkɪ] *n abbr* = **handkerchief**

happen ['hæpən] *vi* arriver, se passer, se produire; **what's ~ing?** que se passe-t-il?; **she ~ed to be free** il s'est trouvé (*or* se trouvait) qu'elle était libre; **as it ~s** justement

happily ['hæpɪlɪ] *adv* heureusement; (*cheerfully*) joyeusement

happiness ['hæpɪnɪs] *n* bonheur *m*

happy ['hæpɪ] *adj* heureux(-euse); **~ with** (*arrangements etc*) satisfait(e) de; **to be ~ to do** faire volontiers; **~ birthday!** bon anniversaire!

harass ['hærəs] *vt* accabler, tourmenter; **harassment** *n* tracasseries *fpl*

harbour, (*US*) **harbor** ['hɑːbəʳ] *n* port *m* ▷ *vt* héberger, abriter; (*hopes, suspicions*) entretenir

hard [hɑːd] *adj* dur(e); (*question, problem*) difficile; (*facts, evidence*) concret(-ète) ▷ *adv* (*work*) dur; (*think, try*) sérieusement; **to look ~ at** regarder fixement; (*thing*) regarder de près; **no ~ feelings!** sans rancune!; **to be ~ of hearing** être dur(e) d'oreille; **to be ~ done by** être traité(e) injustement; **hardback** *n* livre relié; **hardboard** *n* Isorel® *m*; **hard disk** *n* (*Comput*) disque dur;

harden *vt* durcir; (*fig*) endurcir ▷ *vi* (*substance*) durcir

hardly ['hɑːdlɪ] *adv* (*scarcely*) à peine; (*harshly*) durement; **~ anywhere/ ever** presque nulle part/jamais

hard-: **hardship** *n* (*difficulties*) épreuves *fpl*; (*deprivation*) privations *fpl*; **hard shoulder** *n* (BRIT *Aut*) accotement stabilisé; **hard-up** *adj* (*inf*) fauché(e); **hardware** *n* quincaillerie *f*; (*Comput, Mil*) matériel *m*; **hardware shop**, (*US*) **hardware store** *n* quincaillerie *f*; **hard-working** *adj* travailleur(-euse)

hardy ['hɑːdɪ] *adj* robuste; (*plant*) résistant(e) au gel

hare [hɛəʳ] *n* lièvre *m*

harm [hɑːm] *n* mal *m*; (*wrong*) tort *m* ▷ *vt* (*person*) faire du mal *or* du tort à; (*thing*) endommager; **out of ~'s way** à l'abri du danger, en lieu sûr; **harmful** *adj* nuisible; **harmless** *adj* inoffensif(-ive)

harmony ['hɑːmənɪ] *n* harmonie *f*

harness ['hɑːnɪs] *n* harnais *m* ▷ *vt* (*horse*) harnacher; (*resources*) exploiter

harp [hɑːp] *n* harpe *f* ▷ *vi*: **to ~ on about** revenir toujours sur

harsh [hɑːʃ] *adj* (*hard*) dur(e); (*severe*) sévère; (*unpleasant: sound*) discordant(e); (: *light*) cru(e)

harvest ['hɑːvɪst] *n* (*of corn*) moisson *f*; (*of fruit*) récolte *f*; (*of grapes*) vendange *f* ▷ *vt* moissonner; récolter; vendanger

has [hæz] *vb see* **have**

hashtag ['hæʃtæg] *n* (*on Twitter*) mot-dièse *m*, hashtag *m*

hasn't ['hæznt] = **has not**

hassle ['hæsl] *n* (*inf: fuss*) histoire(s) *f(pl)*

haste [heɪst] *n* hâte *f*, précipitation *f*; **hasten** ['heɪsn] *vt* hâter, accélérer ▷ *vi* se hâter, s'empresser; **hastily** *adv* à la hâte; (*leave*) précipitamment; **hasty** *adj* (*decision, action*) hâtif(-ive); (*departure, escape*) précipité(e)

hat [hæt] *n* chapeau *m*

hatch [hætʃ] n (Naut: also: **~way**)
écoutille f; (BRIT: also: **service ~**)
passe-plats m inv ▷ vi éclore
hatchback ['hætʃbæk] n (Aut)
modèle m avec hayon arrière
hate [heɪt] vt haïr, détester ▷ n haine
f; **hatred** ['heɪtrɪd] n haine f
haul [hɔːl] vt traîner, tirer ▷ n (of fish)
prise f; (of stolen goods etc) butin m
haunt [hɔːnt] vt (subj: ghost, fear)
hanter; (: person) fréquenter ▷ n
repaire m; **haunted** adj (castle etc)
hanté(e); (look) égaré(e), hagard(e)

 KEYWORD

have [hæv] (pt, pp **had**) aux vb
1 (gen) avoir; être; **to have eaten/
slept** avoir mangé/dormi; **to have
arrived/gone** être arrivé(e)/allé(e);
having finished or **when he had
finished, he left** quand il a eu fini, il
est parti; **we'd already eaten** nous
avions déjà mangé
2 (in tag questions): **you've done
it, haven't you?** vous l'avez fait,
n'est-ce pas?
3 (in short answers and questions): **no I
haven't!/yes we have!** mais non!/
mais si!; **so I have!** ah oui!, oui c'est
vrai!; **I've been there before, have
you?** j'y suis déjà allé, et vous?
▷ modal aux vb (be obliged): **to have
(got) to do sth** devoir faire qch,
être obligé(e) de faire qch; **she has
(got) to do it** elle doit le faire, il faut
qu'elle le fasse; **you haven't to tell
her** vous n'êtes pas obligé de le lui
dire; (must not) ne le lui dites surtout
pas; **do you have to book?** il faut
réserver?
▷ vt **1** (possess) avoir; **he has (got)
blue eyes/dark hair** il a les yeux
bleus/les cheveux bruns
2 (referring to meals etc): **to have
breakfast** prendre le petit déjeuner;
to have dinner/lunch dîner/
déjeuner; **to have a drink** prendre

un verre; **to have a cigarette** fumer
une cigarette
3 (receive) avoir, recevoir; (obtain)
avoir; **may I have your address?**
puis-je avoir votre adresse?; **you can
have it for £5** vous pouvez l'avoir
pour 5 livres; **I must have it for
tomorrow** il me le faut pour demain;
to have a baby avoir un bébé
4 (maintain, allow): **I won't have it!**
ça ne se passera pas comme ça!; **we
can't have that** nous ne tolérerons
pas ça
5 (by sb else): **to have sth done** faire
faire qch; **to have one's hair cut** se
faire couper les cheveux; **to have sb
do sth** faire faire qch à qn
6 (experience, suffer) avoir; **to have a
cold/flu** avoir un rhume/la grippe;
to have an operation se faire
opérer; **she had her bag stolen** elle
s'est fait voler son sac
7 (+noun): **to have a swim/walk**
nager/se promener; **to have a
bath/shower** prendre un bain/une
douche; **let's have a look** regardons;
to have a meeting se réunir; **to
have a party** organiser une fête; **let
me have a try** laissez-moi essayer

haven ['heɪvn] n port m; (fig) havre m
haven't ['hævnt] = **have not**
havoc ['hævək] n ravages mpl
Hawaii [hə'waɪː] n (îles fpl) Hawaï m
hawk [hɔːk] n faucon m
hawthorn ['hɔːθɔːn] n aubépine f
hay [heɪ] n foin m; **hay fever** n rhume
m des foins; **haystack** n meule f
de foin
hazard ['hæzəd] n (risk) danger
m, risque m ▷ vt risquer, hasarder;
hazardous adj hasardeux(-euse),
risqué(e); **hazard warning lights** npl
(Aut) feux mpl de détresse
haze [heɪz] n brume f
hazel ['heɪzl] n (tree) noisetier m
▷ adj (eyes) noisette inv; **hazelnut** n
noisette f

hazy ['heɪzɪ] *adj* brumeux(-euse); (*idea*) vague

he [hi:] *pron* il; **it is he who ...** c'est lui qui ...; **here he is** le voici

head [hɛd] *n* tête *f*; (*leader*) chef *m*; (*of school*) directeur(-trice); (*of secondary school*) proviseur *m* ▷ *vt* (*list*) être en tête de; (*group, company*) être à la tête de; **~s or tails** pile ou face; **~ first** la tête la première; **~ over heels in love** follement *or* éperdument amoureux(-euse); **to ~ the ball** faire une tête; **head for** *vt fus* se diriger vers; (*disaster*) aller à; **head off** *vt* (*threat, danger*) détourner; **headache** *n* mal *m* de tête; **to have a headache** avoir mal à la tête; **heading** *n* titre *m*; (*subject title*) rubrique *f*; **headlamp** (*BRIT*) *n* = **headlight**; **headlight** *n* phare *m*; **headline** *n* titre *m*; **head office** *n* siège *m*, bureau *m* central; **headphones** *npl* casque *m* (à écouteurs); **headquarters** *npl* (*of business*) bureau *or* siège central; (*Mil*) quartier général; **headroom** *n* (*in car*) hauteur *f* de plafond; (*under bridge*) hauteur limite; **headscarf** *n* foulard *m*; **headset** *n* = **headphones**; **headteacher** *n* directeur(-trice); (*of secondary school*) proviseur *m*; **head waiter** *n* maître *m* d'hôtel

heal [hi:l] *vt, vi* guérir

health [hɛlθ] *n* santé *f*; **health care** *n* services médicaux; **health centre** *n* (*BRIT*) centre *m* de santé; **health food** *n* aliment(s) naturel(s); **Health Service** *n*: **the Health Service** (*BRIT*) ≈ la Sécurité Sociale; **healthy** *adj* (*person*) en bonne santé; (*climate, food, attitude etc*) sain(e)

heap [hi:p] *n* tas *m* ▷ *vt* (*also*: **~ up**) entasser, amonceler; **she ~ed her plate with cakes** elle a chargé son assiette de gâteaux; **~s (of)** (*inf*: *lots*) des tas (de)

hear (*pt, pp* **heard**) [hɪər, hə:d] *vt* entendre; (*news*) apprendre ▷ *vi* entendre; **to ~ about** entendre parler de; (*have news of*) avoir des nouvelles de; **to ~ from sb** recevoir des nouvelles de qn

heard [hə:d] *pt, pp of* **hear**

hearing ['hɪərɪŋ] *n* (*sense*) ouïe *f*; (*of witnesses*) audition *f*; (*of a case*) audience *f*; **hearing aid** *n* appareil *m* acoustique

hearse [hə:s] *n* corbillard *m*

heart [hɑ:t] *n* cœur *m*; **hearts** *npl* (*Cards*) cœur; **at ~** au fond; **by ~** (*learn, know*) par cœur; **to lose/ take ~** perdre/prendre courage; **heart attack** *n* crise *f* cardiaque; **heartbeat** *n* battement *m* de cœur; **heartbroken** *adj*: **to be heartbroken** avoir beaucoup de chagrin; **heartburn** *n* brûlures *fpl* d'estomac; **heart disease** *n* maladie *f* cardiaque

hearth [hɑ:θ] *n* foyer *m*, cheminée *f*

heartless ['hɑ:tlɪs] *adj* (*person*) sans cœur, insensible; (*treatment*) cruel(le)

hearty ['hɑ:tɪ] *adj* chaleureux(-euse); (*appetite*) solide; (*dislike*) cordial(e); (*meal*) copieux(-euse)

heat [hi:t] *n* chaleur *f*; (*Sport: also*: **qualifying ~**) éliminatoire *f* ▷ *vt* chauffer; **heat up** *vi* (*liquid*) chauffer; (*room*) se réchauffer ▷ *vt* réchauffer; **heated** *adj* chauffé(e); (*fig*) passionné(e), échauffé(e), excité(e); **heater** *n* appareil *m* de chauffage; radiateur *m*; (*in car*) chauffage *m*; (*water heater*) chauffe-eau *m*

heather ['hɛðər] *n* bruyère *f*

heating ['hi:tɪŋ] *n* chauffage *m*

heatwave ['hi:tweɪv] *n* vague *f* de chaleur

heaven ['hɛvn] *n* ciel *m*, paradis *m*; (*fig*) paradis; **heavenly** *adj* céleste, divin(e)

heavily ['hɛvɪlɪ] *adv* lourdement; (*drink, smoke*) beaucoup; (*sleep, sigh*) profondément

heavy ['hɛvɪ] *adj* lourd(e); (*work, rain, user, eater*) gros(se); (*drinker, smoker*) grand(e); (*schedule, week*) chargé(e)

Hebrew ['hi:bru:] *adj* hébraïque ▷ *n* (*Ling*) hébreu *m*

Hebrides ['hɛbrɪdi:z] *npl*; **the ~** les Hébrides *fpl*

hectare ['hɛktɑː^r] *n* (*BRIT*) hectare *m*

hectic ['hɛktɪk] *adj* (*schedule*) très chargé(e); (*day*) mouvementé(e); (*lifestyle*) trépidant(e)

he'd [hi:d] = **he would; he had**

hedge [hɛdʒ] *n* haie *f* ▷ *vi* se dérober ▷ *vt*: **to ~ one's bets** (*fig*) se couvrir

hedgehog ['hɛdʒhɔg] *n* hérisson *m*

heed [hi:d] *vt* (*also*: **take ~ of**) tenir compte de, prendre garde à

heel [hi:l] *n* talon *m* ▷ *vt* retalonner

hefty ['hɛftɪ] *adj* (*person*) costaud(e); (*parcel*) lourd(e); (*piece, price*) gros(se)

height [haɪt] *n* (*of person*) taille *f*, grandeur *f*; (*of object*) hauteur *f*; (*of plane, mountain*) altitude *f*; (*high ground*) hauteur, éminence *f*; (*fig: of glory, fame, power*) sommet *m*; (*: of luxury, stupidity*) comble *m*; **at the ~ of summer** au cœur de l'été; **heighten** *vt* hausser, surélever; (*fig*) augmenter

heir [ɛə^r] *n* héritier *m*; **heiress** *n* héritière *f*

held [hɛld] *pt, pp of* **hold**

helicopter ['hɛlɪkɔptə^r] *n* hélicoptère *m*

hell [hɛl] *n* enfer *m*; **oh ~!** (*inf*) merde!

he'll [hi:l] = **he will; he shall**

hello [hə'ləu] *excl* bonjour!; (*to attract attention*) hé!; (*surprise*) tiens!

helmet ['hɛlmɪt] *n* casque *m*

help [hɛlp] *n* aide *f*; (*cleaner etc*) femme *f* de ménage ▷ *vt, vi* aider; **~!** au secours!; **~ yourself** servez-vous; **can you ~ me?** pouvez-vous m'aider?; **can I ~ you?** (*in shop*) vous désirez?; **he can't ~ it** il n'y peut rien; **help out** *vi* aider ▷ *vt*: **to ~ sb out** aider qn; **helper** *n* aide *m/f*, assistant(e); **helpful** *adj* serviable, obligeant(e); (*useful*) utile; **helping** *n* portion *f*; **helpless** *adj* impuissant(e); (*baby*) sans défense; **helpline** *n* service *m* d'assistance téléphonique; (*free*) ≈ numéro vert

hem [hɛm] *n* ourlet *m* ▷ *vt* ourler

hemisphere ['hɛmɪsfɪə^r] *n* hémisphère *m*

hemorrhage ['hɛmərɪdʒ] *n* (*US*) = **haemorrhage**

hemorrhoids ['hɛmərɔɪdz] *npl* (*US*) = **haemorrhoids**

hen [hɛn] *n* poule *f*; (*female bird*) femelle *f*

hence [hɛns] *adv* (*therefore*) d'où, de là; **2 years ~** d'ici 2 ans

hen night, hen party *n* soirée *f* entre filles (*avant le mariage de l'une d'elles*)

hepatitis [hɛpə'taɪtɪs] *n* hépatite *f*

her [hə:^r] *pron* (*direct*) la, l' + *vowel or h mute*; (*indirect*) lui; (*stressed, after prep*) elle ▷ *adj* son (sa), ses *pl*; *see also* **me, my**

herb [hə:b] *n* herbe *f*; **herbal** *adj* à base de plantes; **herbal tea** *n* tisane *f*

herd [hə:d] *n* troupeau *m*

here [hɪə^r] *adv* ici; (*time*) alors ▷ *excl* tiens!, tenez!; **~!** (*present*) présent!; **~ is, ~ are** voici; **~ he/she is** le (la) voici

hereditary [hɪ'rɛdɪtrɪ] *adj* héréditaire

heritage ['hɛrɪtɪdʒ] *n* héritage *m*, patrimoine *m*

hernia ['hə:nɪə] *n* hernie *f*

hero ['hɪərəu] (*pl* **heroes**) *n* héros *m*; **heroic** [hɪ'rəuɪk] *adj* héroïque

heroin ['hɛrəuɪn] *n* héroïne *f* (*drogue*)

heroine ['hɛrəuɪn] *n* héroïne *f* (*femme*)

heron ['hɛrən] *n* héron *m*

herring ['hɛrɪŋ] *n* hareng *m*

hers [hə:z] *pron* le sien(ne), les siens (siennes); *see also* **mine¹**

herself [hə:'sɛlf] *pron* (*reflexive*) se; (*emphatic*) elle-même; (*after prep*) elle; *see also* **oneself**

he's [hi:z] = **he is; he has**

hesitant ['hɛzɪtənt] *adj* hésitant(e), indécis(e)

h

hesitate ['hɛzɪteɪt] vi: **to ~ (about/to do)** hésiter (sur/à faire); **hesitation** [hɛzɪ'teɪʃən] n hésitation f

heterosexual ['hɛtərəu'sɛksjuəl] adj, n hétérosexuel(le)

hexagon ['hɛksəgən] n hexagone m

hey [heɪ] excl hé!

heyday ['heɪdeɪ] n: **the ~ of** l'âge m d'or de, les beaux jours de

HGV n abbr = **heavy goods vehicle**

hi [haɪ] excl salut!; (to attract attention) hé!

hibernate ['haɪbəneɪt] vi hiberner

hiccough, hiccup ['hɪkʌp] vi hoqueter ▷ n: **to have (the) ~s** avoir le hoquet

hid [hɪd] pt of **hide**

hidden ['hɪdn] pp of **hide** ▷ adj: **~ agenda** intentions non déclarées

hide [haɪd] (pt **hid**, pp **hidden**) n (skin) peau f ▷ vt cacher ▷ vi: **to ~ (from sb)** se cacher (de qn)

hideous ['hɪdɪəs] adj hideux(-euse), atroce

hiding ['haɪdɪŋ] n (beating) correction f, volée f de coups; **to be in ~** (concealed) se tenir caché(e)

hi-fi ['haɪfaɪ] adj, n abbr (= high fidelity) hi-fi f inv

high [haɪ] adj haut(e); (speed, respect, number) grand(e); (price) élevé(e); (wind) fort(e), violent(e); (voice) aigu(ë) ▷ adv haut, en haut; **20 m ~** haut(e) de 20 m; **~ in the air** haut dans le ciel; **highchair** n (child's) chaise haute; **high-class** adj (neighbourhood, hotel) chic inv, de grand standing; **higher education** n études supérieures; **high heels** npl talons hauts, hauts talons; **high jump** n (Sport) saut m en hauteur; **highlands** ['haɪləndz] npl région montagneuse; **the Highlands** (in Scotland) les Highlands mpl; **highlight** n (fig: of event) point culminant ▷ vt (emphasize) faire ressortir, souligner; **highlights** npl (in hair) reflets mpl; **highlighter** n (pen) surligneur (lumineux); **highly** adv extrêmement, très; (unlikely) fort; (recommended, skilled, qualified) hautement; **to speak highly of** dire beaucoup de bien de; **highness** n: **His/Her Highness** son Altesse f; **high-rise** n (also: **high-rise block, high-rise building**) tour f (d'habitation); **high school** n lycée m; (US) établissement m d'enseignement supérieur; **high season** n (BRIT) haute saison; **high street** n (BRIT) grand-rue f; **high-tech** (inf) adj de pointe; **highway** n (BRIT) route f; (US) route nationale; **Highway Code** n (BRIT) code m de la route

hijack ['haɪdʒæk] vt détourner (par la force); **hijacker** n auteur m d'un détournement d'avion, pirate m de l'air

hike [haɪk] vi faire des excursions à pied ▷ n excursion f à pied, randonnée f; **hiker** n promeneur(-euse), excursionniste m/f; **hiking** n excursions fpl à pied, randonnée f

hilarious [hɪ'lɛərɪəs] adj (behaviour, event) désopilant(e)

hill [hɪl] n colline f; (fairly high) montagne f; (on road) côte f; **hillside** n (flanc m de) coteau m; **hill walking** n randonnée f de basse montagne; **hilly** adj vallonné(e), montagneux(-euse)

him [hɪm] pron (direct) le, l' + vowel or h mute; (stressed, indirect, after prep) lui; see also **me**; **himself** pron (reflexive) se; (emphatic) lui-même; (after prep) lui; see also **oneself**

hind [haɪnd] adj de derrière

hinder ['hɪndə'] vt gêner; (delay) retarder

hindsight ['haɪndsaɪt] n: **with (the benefit of) ~** avec du recul, rétrospectivement

Hindu ['hɪnduː] n Hindou(e); **Hinduism** n (Rel) hindouisme m

hinge [hɪndʒ] n charnière f ▷ vi (fig):
to ~ on dépendre de

hint [hɪnt] n allusion f; (advice) conseil
m; (clue) indication f ▷ vt: **to ~ that**
insinuer que ▷ vi: **to ~ at** faire une
allusion à

hip [hɪp] n hanche f

hippie, hippy ['hɪpɪ] n hippie m/f

hippo ['hɪpəʊ] (pl **hippos**) n
hippopotame m

hippopotamus (pl
hippopotamuses or **hippopotami**)
[hɪpə'pɔtəməs, hɪpə'pɔtəmaɪ] n
hippopotame m

hippy ['hɪpɪ] n = **hippie**

hire ['haɪə'] vt (BRIT: car, equipment)
louer; (worker) embaucher, engager
▷ n location f; **for ~** à louer; (taxi)
libre; **I'd like to ~ a car** je voudrais
louer une voiture; **hire(d) car** n
(BRIT) voiture f de location; **hire
purchase** n (BRIT) achat m (or vente f)
à tempérament or crédit

his [hɪz] pron le sien(ne), les siens
(siennes) ▷ adj son (sa), ses pl;
mine¹; my

Hispanic [hɪs'pænɪk] adj (in US)
hispano-américain(e) ▷ n Hispano-
Américain(e)

hiss [hɪs] vi siffler

historian [hɪ'stɔːrɪən] n
historien(ne)

historic(al) [hɪ'stɔrɪk(l)] adj
historique

history ['hɪstərɪ] n histoire f

hit [hɪt] vt (pt, pp **hit**) frapper; (reach:
target) atteindre, toucher; (collide
with: car) entrer en collision avec,
heurter; (fig: affect) toucher ▷ n coup
m; (success) succès m; (song) tube m;
(to website) visite f; (on search engine)
résultat m de recherche; **to ~ it off
with sb** bien s'entendre avec qn; **hit
back** vi: **to ~ back at sb** prendre sa
revanche sur qn

hitch [hɪtʃ] vt (fasten) accrocher,
attacher; (also: **~ up**) remonter d'une
saccade ▷ vi faire de l'autostop ▷ n

(difficulty) anicroche f, contretemps
m; **to ~ a lift** faire du stop; **hitch-hike**
vi faire de l'auto-stop; **hitch-hiker** n
auto-stoppeur(-euse); **hitch-hiking**
n auto-stop m, stop m (inf)

hi-tech ['haɪ'tɛk] adj de pointe

hitman ['hɪtmæn] (irreg) n (inf) tueur
m à gages

HIV n abbr (= human immunodeficiency
virus) HIV m, VIH m; **~-negative**
séronégatif(-ive); **~-positive**
séropositif(-ive)

hive [haɪv] n ruche f

hoard [hɔːd] n (of food) provisions
fpl, réserves fpl; (of money) trésor m
▷ vt amasser

hoarse [hɔːs] adj enroué(e)

hoax [həʊks] n canular m

hob [hɔb] n plaque chauffante

hobble ['hɔbl] vi boitiller

hobby ['hɔbɪ] n passe-temps favori

hobo ['həʊbəʊ] n (US) vagabond m

hockey ['hɔkɪ] n hockey m; **hockey
stick** n crosse f de hockey

hog [hɔg] n porc (châtré) m ▷ vt (fig)
accaparer; **to go the whole ~** aller
jusqu'au bout

Hogmanay [hɔgmə'neɪ] n réveillon
m du jour de l'An, Saint-Sylvestre f

- HOGMANAY
-
-
- La Saint-Sylvestre ou "New Year's
- Eve" se nomme Hogmanay en
- Écosse. En cette occasion, la
- famille et les amis se réunissent
- pour entendre sonner les douze
- coups de minuit et pour fêter le
- "first-footing", une coutume qui
- veut qu'on se rende chez ses amis et
- voisins en apportant quelque chose
- à boire (du whisky en général) et
- un morceau de charbon en gage de
- prospérité pour la nouvelle année.

hoist [hɔɪst] n palan m ▷ vt hisser

hold [həʊld] (pt, pp **held**) vt tenir;
(contain) contenir; (meeting)

h

tenir; (*keep back*) retenir; (*believe*) considérer; (*possess*) avoir ▷ *vi* (*withstand pressure*) tenir (bon); (*be valid*) valoir; (*on telephone*) attendre ▷ *n* prise *f*; (*find*) influence *f*; (*Naut*) cale *f*; **to catch** *or* **get (a) ~ of** saisir; **to get ~ of** (*find*) trouver; **~ the line!** (*Tel*) ne quittez pas!; **to ~ one's own** (*fig*) (bien) se défendre; **hold back** *vt* retenir; (*secret*) cacher; **hold on** *vi* tenir bon; (*wait*) attendre; **~ on!** (*Tel*) ne quittez pas!; **to ~ on to sth** (*grasp*) se crammponner à qch; (*keep*) conserver *or* garder qch; **hold out** *vt* offrir ▷ *vi* (*resist*): **to ~ out (against)** résister (devant), tenir bon (devant); **hold up** *vt* (*raise*) lever; (*support*) soutenir; (*delay*) retarder (: *traffic*) ralentir; (*rob*) braquer; **holdall** *n* (BRIT) fourre-tout *m inv*; **holder** *n* (*container*) support *m*; (*of ticket, record*) détenteur(-trice); (*of office, title, passport etc*) titulaire *m/f*
hole [həʊl] *n* trou *m*
holiday ['hɔlədɪ] *n* (BRIT: *vacation*) vacances *fpl*; (*day off*) jour *m* de congé; (*public*) jour férié; **to be on ~** être en vacances; **I'm here on ~** je suis ici en vacances; **holiday camp** *n* (*also*: **holiday centre**) camp *m* de vacances; **holiday job** *n* (BRIT) boulot *m* (*inf*) de vacances; **holiday-maker** *n* (BRIT) vacancier(-ière); **holiday resort** *n* centre *m* de villégiature *or* de vacances
Holland ['hɔlənd] *n* Hollande *f*
hollow ['hɔləʊ] *adj* creux(-euse); (*fig*) faux (fausse) ▷ *n* creux *m*; (*in land*) dépression *f* (de terrain), cuvette *f* ▷ *vt*: **to ~ out** creuser, évider
holly ['hɔlɪ] *n* houx *m*
holocaust ['hɔləkɔːst] *n* holocauste *m*
holy ['həʊlɪ] *adj* saint(e); (*bread, water*) bénit(e); (*ground*) sacré(e)
home [həʊm] *n* foyer *m*, maison *f*; (*country*) pays natal, patrie *f*; (*institution*) maison ▷ *adj* de famille; (*Econ, Pol*) national(e), intérieur(e);

(*Sport: team*) qui reçoit; (: *match, win*) sur leur (*or* notre) terrain ▷ *adv* chez soi, à la maison; au pays natal; (*right in: nail etc*) à fond; **at ~** chez soi, à la maison; **to go** (*or* **come**) **~** rentrer (chez soi), rentrer à la maison (*or* au pays); **make yourself at ~** faites comme chez vous; **home address** *n* domicile permanent; **homeland** *n* patrie *f*; **homeless** *adj* sans foyer, sans abri; **homely** *adj* (*plain*) simple, sans prétention; (*welcoming*) accueillant(e); **home-made** *adj* fait(e) à la maison; **home match** *n* match *m* à domicile; **Home Office** *n* (BRIT) ministère *m* de l'Intérieur; **home owner** *n* propriétaire occupant; **home page** *n* (*Comput*) page *f* d'accueil; **Home Secretary** *n* (BRIT) ministre *m* de l'Intérieur; **homesick** *adj*: **to be homesick** avoir le mal du pays; (*missing one's family*) s'ennuyer de sa famille; **home town** *n* ville natale; **homework** *n* devoirs *mpl*
homicide ['hɔmɪsaɪd] *n* (US) homicide *m*
homoeopathic, (US) **homeopathic** [həʊmɪəʊ'pæθɪk] *adj* (*medicine*) homéopathique; (*doctor*) homéopathe
homoeopathy, (US) **homeopathy** [həʊmɪ'ɔpəθɪ] *n* homéopathie *f*
homosexual [hɔmə'sɛksjuəl] *adj*, *n* homosexuel(le)
honest ['ɔnɪst] *adj* honnête; (*sincere*) franc (franche); **honestly** *adv* honnêtement; franchement; **honesty** *n* honnêteté *f*
honey ['hʌnɪ] *n* miel *m*; **honeymoon** *n* lune *f* de miel, voyage *m* de noces; **we're on honeymoon** nous sommes en voyage de noces; **honeysuckle** *n* chèvrefeuille *m*
Hong Kong ['hɔŋ'kɔŋ] *n* Hong Kong
honorary ['ɔnərərɪ] *adj* honoraire; (*duty, title*) honorifique; **~ degree** diplôme *m* honoris causa

honour, (us) **honor** ['ɔnəʳ] vt honorer ▷ n honneur m; **to graduate with ~s** obtenir sa licence avec mention; **honourable**, (us) **honorable** adj honorable; **honours degree** n (Scol) ≈ licence f avec mention

hood [hud] n capuchon m; (of cooker) hotte f; (BRIT Aut) capote f; (us Aut) capot m; **hoodie** ['hudɪ] n (top) sweat m à capuche

hoof (pl **hoofs** or **hooves**) [hu:f, hu:vz] n sabot m

hook [huk] n crochet m; (on dress) agrafe f; (for fishing) hameçon m ▷ vt accrocher; **off the ~** (Tel) décroché

hooligan ['hu:lɪgən] n voyou m

hoop [hu:p] n cerceau m

hoot [hu:t] vi (BRIT Aut) klaxonner; (siren) mugir; (owl) hululer

Hoover® ['hu:vəʳ] (BRIT) n aspirateur m ▷ vt: **to hoover** (room) passer l'aspirateur dans; (carpet) passer l'aspirateur sur

hooves [hu:vz] npl of **hoof**

hop [hɔp] vi sauter; (on one foot) sauter à cloche-pied; (bird) sautiller

hope [həup] vt, vi espérer ▷ n espoir m; **I ~ so** je l'espère; **I ~ not** j'espère que non; **hopeful** adj (person) plein(e) d'espoir; (situation) prometteur(-euse), encourageant(e); **hopefully** adv (expectantly) avec espoir, avec optimisme; (one hopes) avec un peu de chance; **hopeless** adj désespéré(e); (useless) nul(le)

hops [hɔps] npl houblon m

horizon [hə'raɪzn] n horizon m; **horizontal** [hɔrɪ'zɔntl] adj horizontal(e)

hormone ['hɔ:məun] n hormone f

horn [hɔ:n] n corne f; (Mus) cor m; (Aut) klaxon m

horoscope ['hɔrəskəup] n horoscope m

horrendous [hə'rɛndəs] adj horrible, affreux(-euse)

horrible ['hɔrɪbl] adj horrible, affreux(-euse)

horrid ['hɔrɪd] adj (person) détestable; (weather, place, smell) épouvantable

horrific [hɔ'rɪfɪk] adj horrible

horrifying ['hɔrɪfaɪɪŋ] adj horrifiant(e)

horror ['hɔrəʳ] n horreur f; **horror film** n film m d'épouvante

hors d'œuvre [ɔ:'də:vrə] n hors d'œuvre m

horse [hɔ:s] n cheval m; **horseback**: **on horseback** adj, adv à cheval; **horse chestnut** n (nut) marron m (d'Inde); (tree) marronnier m (d'Inde); **horsepower** n puissance f (en chevaux); (unit) cheval-vapeur m (CV); **horse-racing** n courses fpl de chevaux; **horseradish** n raifort m; **horse riding** n (BRIT) équitation f

hose [həuz] n tuyau m; (also: **garden ~**) tuyau d'arrosage; **hosepipe** n tuyau m; (in garden) tuyau d'arrosage

hospital ['hɔspɪtl] n hôpital m; **in ~** à l'hôpital; **where's the nearest ~?** où est l'hôpital le plus proche?

hospitality [hɔspɪ'tælɪtɪ] n hospitalité f

host [həust] n hôte m; (TV, Radio) présentateur(-trice); (large number): **a ~ of** une foule de; (Rel) hostie f

hostage ['hɔstɪdʒ] n otage m

hostel ['hɔstl] n foyer m; (also: **youth ~**) auberge f de jeunesse

hostess ['həustɪs] n hôtesse f; (BRIT: also: **air ~**) hôtesse de l'air; (TV, Radio) présentatrice f

hostile ['hɔstaɪl] adj hostile

hostility [hɔ'stɪlɪtɪ] n hostilité f

hot [hɔt] adj chaud(e); (as opposed to only warm) très chaud; (spicy) fort(e); (fig: contest) acharné(e); (topic) brûlant(e); (temper) violent(e), passionné(e); **to be ~** (person) avoir chaud; (thing) être (très) chaud; **it's ~** (weather) il fait chaud; **hot dog** n hot-dog m

hotel [həu'tɛl] n hôtel m

h

hotspot ['hɔtspɔt] n (Comput: also: **wireless ~**) borne f wifi, hotspot m

hot-water bottle [hɔt'wɔːtə-] n bouillotte f

hound [haund] vt poursuivre avec acharnement ▷ n chien courant

hour ['auə^r] n heure f; **hourly** adj toutes les heures; (rate) horaire

house n [haus] maison f; (Pol) chambre f; (Theat) salle f; auditoire m ▷ vt [hauz] (person) loger, héberger; **on the ~** (fig) aux frais de la maison; **household** n (Admin etc) ménage m; (people) famille f, maisonnée f; **householder** n propriétaire m/f; (head of house) chef m de famille; **housekeeper** n gouvernante f; **housekeeping** n (work) ménage m; **housewife** (irreg) n ménagère f; femme f au foyer; **house wine** n cuvée f maison or du patron; **housework** n (travaux mpl du) ménage m

housing ['hauzɪŋ] n logement m; **housing development, housing estate** (BRIT) n (blocks of flats) cité f; (houses) lotissement m

hover ['hɔvə^r] vi planer; **hovercraft** n aéroglisseur m, hovercraft m

how [hau] adv comment; **~ are you?** comment allez-vous?; **~ do you do?** bonjour; (on being introduced) enchanté(e); **~ long have you been here?** depuis combien de temps êtes-vous là?; **~ lovely/awful!** que or comme c'est joli/affreux!; **~ much time/many people?** combien de temps/gens?; **~ much does it cost?** ça coûte combien?; **~ old are you?** quel âge avez-vous?; **~ tall is he?** combien mesure-t-il?; **~ is school?** ça va à l'école?; **~ was the film?** comment était le film?

however [hau'ɛvə^r] conj pourtant, cependant ▷ adv: **~ I do it** de quelque manière que je m'y prenne; **~ cold it is** même s'il fait très froid; **~ did you do it?** comment y êtes-vous donc arrivé?

howl [haul] n hurlement m ▷ vi hurler; (wind) mugir

H.P. n abbr (BRIT) = **hire purchase**

h.p. abbr (Aut) = **horsepower**

HQ n abbr (= headquarters) QG m

hr abbr (= hour) h

hrs abbr (= hours) h

HTML n abbr (= hypertext markup language) HTML m

hubcap ['hʌbkæp] n (Aut) enjoliveur m

huddle ['hʌdl] vi: **to ~ together** se blottir les uns contre les autres

huff [hʌf] n: **in a ~** fâché(e)

hug [hʌg] vt serrer dans ses bras; (shore, kerb) serrer ▷ n: **to give sb a ~** serrer qn dans ses bras

huge [hjuːdʒ] adj énorme, immense

hull [hʌl] n (of ship) coque f

hum [hʌm] vt (tune) fredonner ▷ vi fredonner; (insect) bourdonner; (plane, tool) vrombir

human ['hjuːmən] adj humain(e) ▷ n (also: **~ being**) être humain

humane [hjuː'meɪn] adj humain(e), humanitaire

humanitarian [hjuːmænɪ'tɛərɪən] adj humanitaire

humanity [hjuː'mænɪtɪ] n humanité f

human rights npl droits mpl de l'homme

humble ['hʌmbl] adj humble, modeste

humid ['hjuːmɪd] adj humide; **humidity** [hjuː'mɪdɪtɪ] n humidité f

humiliate [hjuː'mɪlɪeɪt] vt humilier

humiliating [hjuː'mɪlɪeɪtɪŋ] adj humiliant(e)

humiliation [hjuːmɪlɪ'eɪʃən] n humiliation f

hummus ['huməs] n houm(m)ous m

humorous ['hjuːmərəs] adj humoristique

humour, (US) **humor** ['hjuːmə^r] n humour m; (mood) humeur f ▷ vt (person) faire plaisir à; se prêter aux caprices de

hump [hʌmp] n bosse f
hunch [hʌntʃ] n (premonition) intuition f
hundred ['hʌndrəd] num cent; **~s of** des centaines de; **hundredth** ['hʌndrədɪdθ] num centième
hung [hʌŋ] pt, pp of **hang**
Hungarian [hʌŋ'gɛərɪən] adj hongrois(e) ▷ n Hongrois(e); (Ling) hongrois m
Hungary ['hʌŋgərɪ] n Hongrie f
hunger ['hʌŋgəʳ] n faim f ▷ vi: **to ~ for** avoir faim de, désirer ardemment
hungry ['hʌŋgrɪ] adj affamé(e); **to be ~** avoir faim; **~ for** (fig) avide de
hunt [hʌnt] vt (seek) chercher; (Sport) chasser ▷ vi (search): **to ~ for** chercher (partout); (Sport) chasser ▷ n (Sport) chasse f; **hunter** n chasseur m; **hunting** n chasse f
hurdle ['həːdl] n (Sport) haie f; (fig) obstacle m
hurl [həːl] vt lancer (avec violence); (abuse, insults) lancer
hurrah, hurray [hu'rɑː, hu'reɪ] excl hourra!
hurricane ['hʌrɪkən] n ouragan m
hurry ['hʌrɪ] n hâte f, précipitation f ▷ vi se presser, se dépêcher ▷ vt (person) faire presser, faire se dépêcher; (work) presser; **to be in a ~** être pressé(e); **to do sth in a ~** faire qch en vitesse; **hurry up** vi se dépêcher
hurt [həːt] (pt, pp **hurt**) vt (cause pain to) faire mal à; (injure, fig) blesser ▷ vi faire mal ▷ adj blessé(e); **my arm ~s** j'ai mal au bras; **to ~ o.s.** se faire mal
husband ['hʌzbənd] n mari m
hush [hʌʃ] n calme m, silence m ▷ vt faire taire; **~!** chut!
husky ['hʌskɪ] adj (voice) rauque ▷ n chien m esquimau or de traîneau
hut [hʌt] n hutte f; (shed) cabane f
hyacinth ['haɪəsɪnθ] n jacinthe f
hydrofoil ['haɪdrəfɔɪl] n hydrofoil m
hydrogen ['haɪdrədʒən] n hydrogène m

hygiene ['haɪdʒiːn] n hygiène f; **hygienic** [haɪ'dʒiːnɪk] adj hygiénique
hymn [hɪm] n hymne m; cantique m
hype [haɪp] n (inf) matraquage m publicitaire or médiatique
hyperlink ['haɪpəlɪŋk] n hyperlien m
hypermarket ['haɪpəmɑːkɪt] (BRIT) n hypermarché m
hyphen ['haɪfn] n trait m d'union
hypnotize ['hɪpnətaɪz] vt hypnotiser
hypocrite ['hɪpəkrɪt] n hypocrite m/f
hypocritical [hɪpə'krɪtɪkl] adj hypocrite
hypothesis (pl **hypotheses**) [haɪ'pɔθɪsɪs, -siːz] n hypothèse f
hysterical [hɪ'stɛrɪkl] adj hystérique; (funny) hilarant(e)
hysterics [hɪ'stɛrɪks] npl; **to be in/have ~** (anger, panic) avoir une crise de nerfs; (laughter) attraper un fou rire

h

I [aɪ] *pron* je; (*before vowel*) j'; (*stressed*) moi

ice [aɪs] *n* glace *f*; (*on road*) verglas *m* ▷ *vt* (*cake*) glacer ▷ *vi* (*also:* **~ over**) geler; (*also:* **~ up**) se givrer; **iceberg** *n* iceberg *m*; **ice cream** *n* glace *f*; **ice cube** *n* glaçon *m*; **ice hockey** *n* hockey *m* sur glace

Iceland ['aɪslənd] *n* Islande *f*; **Icelander** *n* Islandais(e); **Icelandic** [aɪs'lændɪk] *adj* islandais(e) ▷ *n* (*Ling*) islandais *m*

ice: ice lolly *n* (*BRIT*) esquimau *m*; **ice rink** *n* patinoire *f*; **ice skating** *n* patinage *m* (sur glace)

icing ['aɪsɪŋ] *n* (*Culin*) glaçage *m*; **icing sugar** *n* (*BRIT*) sucre *m* glace

icon ['aɪkɔn] *n* icône *f*

ICT *n abbr* (*BRIT Scol:* = *information and communications technology*) TIC *fpl*

icy ['aɪsɪ] *adj* glacé(e); (*road*) verglacé(e); (*weather, temperature*) glacial(e)

I'd [aɪd] = **I would; I had**

ID card *n* carte *f* d'identité

idea [aɪ'dɪə] *n* idée *f*

ideal [aɪ'dɪəl] *n* idéal *m* ▷ *adj* idéal(e); **ideally** [aɪ'dɪəlɪ] *adv* (*preferably*) dans l'idéal; (*perfectly*): **he is ideally suited to the job** il est parfait pour ce poste

identical [aɪ'dɛntɪkl] *adj* identique

identification [aɪdɛntɪfɪ'keɪʃən] *n* identification *f*; **means of ~** pièce *f* d'identité

identify [aɪ'dɛntɪfaɪ] *vt* identifier

identity [aɪ'dɛntɪtɪ] *n* identité *f*; **identity card** *n* carte *f* d'identité; **identity theft** *n* usurpation *f* d'identité

ideology [aɪdɪ'ɔlədʒɪ] *n* idéologie *f*

idiom ['ɪdɪəm] *n* (*phrase*) expression *f* idiomatique; (*style*) style *m*

idiot ['ɪdɪət] *n* idiot(e), imbécile *m/f*

idle ['aɪdl] *adj* (*doing nothing*) sans occupation, désœuvré(e); (*lazy*) oisif(-ive), paresseux(-euse); (*unemployed*) au chômage; (*machinery*) au repos; (*question, pleasures*) vain(e), futile ▷ *vi* (*engine*) tourner au ralenti

idol ['aɪdl] *n* idole *f*

idyllic [ɪ'dɪlɪk] *adj* idyllique

i.e. *abbr* (= *id est: that is*) c. à d., c'est-à-dire

if [ɪf] *conj* si; **if necessary** si nécessaire, le cas échéant; **if so** si c'est le cas; **if not** sinon; **if only I could!** si seulement je pouvais!; *see also* **as; even**

ignite [ɪg'naɪt] *vt* mettre le feu à, enflammer ▷ *vi* s'enflammer

ignition [ɪg'nɪʃən] *n* (*Aut*) allumage *m*; **to switch on/off the ~** mettre/couper le contact

ignorance ['ɪgnərəns] *n* ignorance *f*

ignorant ['ɪgnərənt] *adj* ignorant(e); **to be ~ of** (*subject*) ne rien connaître en; (*events*) ne pas être au courant de

ignore [ɪg'nɔːr] *vt* ne tenir aucun compte de; (*mistake*) ne pas relever;

(person: pretend to not see) faire
semblant de ne pas reconnaître; (: pay
no attention to) ignorer
ill [ɪl] adj (sick) malade; (bad)
mauvais(e) ▷ n mal m ▷ adv: **to
speak/think ~ of sb** dire/penser du
mal de qn; **to be taken ~** tomber
malade
I'll [aɪl] = **I will; I shall**
illegal [ɪ'li:gl] adj illégal(e)
illegible [ɪ'lɛdʒɪbl] adj illisible
illegitimate [ɪlɪ'dʒɪtɪmət] adj
illégitime
ill health n mauvaise santé
illiterate [ɪ'lɪtərət] adj illettré(e)
illness ['ɪlnɪs] n maladie f
illuminate [ɪ'lu:mɪneɪt] vt (room,
street) éclairer; (for special effect)
illuminer
illusion [ɪ'lu:ʒən] n illusion f
illustrate ['ɪləstreɪt] vt illustrer
illustration [ɪlə'streɪʃən] n illustration f
I'm [aɪm] = **I am**
image ['ɪmɪdʒ] n image f; (public face)
image de marque
imaginary [ɪ'mædʒɪnərɪ] adj
imaginaire
imagination [ɪmædʒɪ'neɪʃən] n
imagination f
imaginative [ɪ'mædʒɪnətɪv] adj
imaginatif(-ive); (person) plein(e)
d'imagination
imagine [ɪ'mædʒɪn] vt s'imaginer;
(suppose) imaginer, supposer
imam [ɪ'mɑːm] n imam m
imbalance [ɪm'bæləns] n
déséquilibre m
imitate ['ɪmɪteɪt] vt imiter;
imitation [ɪmɪ'teɪʃən] n imitation f
immaculate [ɪ'mækjulət] adj
impeccable; (Rel) immaculé(e)
immature [ɪmə'tjuəʳ] adj (fruit) qui
n'est pas mûr(e); (person) qui manque
de maturité
immediate [ɪ'miːdɪət] adj
immédiat(e); **immediately** adv (at
once) immédiatement; **immediately
next to** juste à côté de

immense [ɪ'mɛns] adj immense,
énorme
immerse [ɪ'məːs] vt immerger,
plonger; **to be ~d in** (fig) être plongé
dans
immigrant ['ɪmɪgrənt] n
immigrant(e); (already established)
immigré(e); **immigration**
[ɪmɪ'greɪʃən] n immigration f
imminent ['ɪmɪnənt] adj
imminent(e)
immoral [ɪ'mɔrl] adj immoral(e)
immortal [ɪ'mɔːtl] adj, n
immortel(le)
immune [ɪ'mjuːn] adj: **~ (to)**
immunisé(e) (contre); **immune
system** n système m immunitaire
immunize ['ɪmjunaɪz] vt immuniser
impact ['ɪmpækt] n choc m, impact
m; (fig) impact
impair [ɪm'pɛəʳ] vt détériorer,
diminuer
impartial [ɪm'pɑːʃl] adj impartial(e)
impatience [ɪm'peɪʃəns] n
impatience f
impatient [ɪm'peɪʃənt] adj
impatient(e); **to get** or **grow ~**
s'impatienter
impeccable [ɪm'pɛkəbl] adj
impeccable, parfait(e)
impending [ɪm'pɛndɪŋ] adj
imminent(e)
imperative [ɪm'pɛrətɪv] adj
(need) urgent(e), pressant(e);
(tone) impérieux(-euse) ▷ n (Ling)
impératif m
imperfect [ɪm'pəːfɪkt] adj
imparfait(e); (goods etc)
défectueux(-euse) ▷ n (Ling: also:
~ tense) imparfait m
imperial [ɪm'pɪərɪəl] adj impérial(e);
(BRIT: measure) légal(e)
impersonal [ɪm'pəːsənl] adj
impersonnel(le)
impersonate [ɪm'pəːsəneɪt] vt se
faire passer pour; (Theat) imiter
impetus ['ɪmpətəs] n impulsion f; (of
runner) élan m

i

implant [ɪm'plɑːnt] vt (Med)
implanter; (fig: idea, principle)
inculquer

implement n ['ɪmplɪmənt] outil m,
instrument m; (for cooking) ustensile
m ▷ vt ['ɪmplɪmɛnt] exécuter

implicate ['ɪmplɪkeɪt] vt impliquer,
compromettre

implication [ɪmplɪ'keɪʃən] n
implication f; **by ~** indirectement

implicit [ɪm'plɪsɪt] adj implicite;
(complete) absolu(e), sans réserve

imply [ɪm'plaɪ] vt (hint) suggérer,
laisser entendre; (mean) indiquer,
supposer

impolite [ɪmpə'laɪt] adj impoli(e)

import vt [ɪm'pɔːt] importer ▷ n
['ɪmpɔːt] (Comm) importation f;
(meaning) portée f, signification f

importance [ɪm'pɔːtns] n
importance f

important [ɪm'pɔːtnt] adj
important(e); **it's not ~** c'est sans
importance, ce n'est pas important

importer [ɪm'pɔːtə'] n
importateur(-trice)

impose [ɪm'pəʊz] vt imposer ▷ vi:
to ~ on sb abuser de la gentillesse
de qn; **imposing** adj imposant(e),
impressionnant(e)

impossible [ɪm'pɔsɪbl] adj
impossible

impotent ['ɪmpətnt] adj
impuissant(e)

impoverished [ɪm'pɔvərɪʃt] adj
pauvre, appauvri(e)

impractical [ɪm'præktɪkl] adj pas
pratique; (person) qui manque d'esprit
pratique

impress [ɪm'prɛs] vt impressionner,
faire impression sur; (mark) imprimer,
marquer; **to ~ sth on sb** faire bien
comprendre qch à qn

impression [ɪm'prɛʃən] n
impression f; (of stamp, seal)
empreinte f; (imitation) imitation
f; **to be under the ~ that** avoir
l'impression que

impressive [ɪm'prɛsɪv] adj
impressionnant(e)

imprison [ɪm'prɪzn] vt emprisonner,
mettre en prison; **imprisonment**
n emprisonnement m; (period):
**to sentence sb to 10 years'
imprisonment** condamner qn à 10
ans de prison

improbable [ɪm'prɔbəbl] adj
improbable; (excuse) peu plausible

improper [ɪm'prɔpə'] adj (unsuitable)
déplacé(e), de mauvais goût;
(indecent) indécent(e); (dishonest)
malhonnête

improve [ɪm'pruːv] vt améliorer
▷ vi s'améliorer; (pupil etc) faire
des progrès; **improvement** n
amélioration f; (of pupil etc)
progrès m

improvise ['ɪmprəvaɪz] vt, vi
improviser

impulse ['ɪmpʌls] n impulsion f;
on ~ impulsivement, sur un coup
de tête; **impulsive** [ɪm'pʌlsɪv] adj
impulsif(-ive)

 KEYWORD

in [ɪn] prep **1** (indicating place, position)
dans; **in the house/the fridge** dans
la maison/le frigo; **in the garden**
dans le or au jardin; **in town** en ville;
in the country à la campagne; **in
school** à l'école; **in here/there** ici/là

2 (with place names, of town, region,
country): **in London** à Londres; **in
England** en Angleterre; **in Japan**
au Japon; **in the United States** aux
États-Unis

3 (indicating time: during): **in spring**
au printemps; **in summer** en été;
in May/2005 en mai/2005; **in the
afternoon** (dans) l'après-midi; **at 4
o'clock in the afternoon** à 4 heures
de l'après-midi

4 (indicating time: in the space of) en;
(: future) dans; **I did it in 3 hours/
days** je l'ai fait en 3 heures/jours; **I'll**

see you in 2 weeks or **in 2 weeks'
time** je te verrai dans 2 semaines
5 (*indicating manner etc*) à; **in a loud/
soft voice** à voix haute/basse; **in
pencil** au crayon; **in writing** par
écrit; **in French** en français; **the boy
in the blue shirt** le garçon à or avec la
chemise bleue
6 (*indicating circumstances*): **in
the sun** au soleil; **in the shade** à
l'ombre; **in the rain** sous la pluie; **a
change in policy** un changement
de politique
7 (*indicating mood, state*): **in tears** en
larmes; **in anger** sous le coup de la
colère; **in despair** au désespoir; **in
good condition** en bon état; **to live
in luxury** vivre dans le luxe
8 (*with ratios, numbers*): **1 in 10
households, 1 household in 10** 1
ménage sur 10; **20 pence in the
pound** 20 pence par livre sterling;
they lined up in twos ils se mirent
en rangs (deux) par deux; **in
hundreds** par centaines
9 (*referring to people, works*) chez; **the
disease is common in children**
c'est une maladie courante chez les
enfants; **in (the works of) Dickens**
chez Dickens, dans (l'œuvre de)
Dickens
10 (*indicating profession etc*) dans;
to be in teaching être dans
l'enseignement
11 (*after superlative*) de; **the best
pupil in the class** le meilleur élève
de la classe
12 (*with present participle*): **in saying
this** en disant ceci
▷ *adv*: **to be in** (*person: at home,
work*) être là; (*train, ship, plane*) être
arrivé(e); (*in fashion*) être à la mode;
to ask sb in inviter qn à entrer; **to
run/limp etc in** entrer en courant/
boitant *etc*
▷ *n*: **the ins and outs (of)** (*of
proposal, situation etc*) les tenants et
aboutissants (de)

inability [ɪnə'bɪlɪtɪ] *n* incapacité f;
~ to pay incapacité de payer
inaccurate [ɪn'ækjurət] *adj*
inexact(e); (*person*) qui manque de
précision
inadequate [ɪn'ædɪkwət] *adj*
insuffisant(e), inadéquat(e)
inadvertently [ɪnəd'vɜ:tntlɪ] *adv*
par mégarde
inappropriate [ɪnə'prəuprɪət] *adj*
inopportun(e), mal à propos; (*word,
expression*) impropre
inaugurate [ɪ'nɔ:gjureɪt] *vt*
inaugurer; (*president, official*) investir
de ses fonctions
Inc. *abbr* = **incorporated**
incapable [ɪn'keɪpəbl] *adj*: **~ (of)**
incapable (de)
incense *n* ['ɪnsɛns] encens *m* ▷ *vt*
[ɪn'sɛns] (*anger*) mettre en colère
incentive [ɪn'sɛntɪv] *n*
encouragement *m*, raison f de se
donner de la peine
inch [ɪntʃ] *n* pouce *m* (= 25 mm; 12 in a
foot); **within an ~ of** à deux doigts de;
he wouldn't give an ~ (*fig*) il n'a pas
voulu céder d'un pouce
incidence ['ɪnsɪdns] *n* (*of crime,
disease*) fréquence f
incident ['ɪnsɪdnt] *n* incident *m*
incidentally [ɪnsɪ'dɛntəlɪ] *adv* (*by
the way*) à propos
inclination [ɪnklɪ'neɪʃən] *n*
inclination f; (*desire*) envie f
incline *n* ['ɪnklaɪn] pente f, plan
incliné ▷ *vt* [ɪn'klaɪn] incliner ▷ *vi*
(*surface*) s'incliner; **to be ~d to do**
(*have a tendency to do*) avoir tendance
à faire
include [ɪn'klu:d] *vt* inclure,
comprendre; **service is/is not
~d** le service est compris/n'est pas
compris; **including** *prep* y compris;
inclusion *n* inclusion f; **inclusive** *adj*
inclus(e), compris(e); **inclusive of
tax** taxes comprises
income ['ɪnkʌm] *n* revenu *m*; (*from
property etc*) rentes fpl; **income**

support n (BRIT) ≈ revenu m minimum d'insertion, RMI m; **income tax** n impôt m sur le revenu

incoming ['ɪnkʌmɪŋ] adj (passengers, mail) à l'arrivée; (government, tenant) nouveau (nouvelle)

incompatible [ɪnkəm'pætɪbl] adj incompatible

incompetence [ɪn'kɔmpɪtns] n incompétence f, incapacité f

incompetent [ɪn'kɔmpɪtnt] adj incompétent(e), incapable

incomplete [ɪnkəm'pliːt] adj incomplet(-ète)

inconsistent [ɪnkən'sɪstnt] adj qui manque de constance; (work) irrégulier(-ière); (statement) peu cohérent(e); ~ **with** en contradiction avec

inconvenience [ɪnkən'viːnjəns] n inconvénient m; (trouble) dérangement m ▷ vt déranger

inconvenient [ɪnkən'viːnjənt] adj malcommode; (time, place) mal choisi(e), qui ne convient pas; (visitor) importun(e)

incorporate [ɪn'kɔːpəreɪt] vt incorporer; (contain) contenir

incorporated [ɪn'kɔːpəreɪtɪd] adj: ~ **company** (US) ≈ société f anonyme

incorrect [ɪnkə'rɛkt] adj incorrect(e); (opinion, statement) inexact(e)

increase n ['ɪnkriːs] augmentation f ▷ vi, vt [ɪn'kriːs] augmenter; **increasingly** adv de plus en plus

incredible [ɪn'krɛdɪbl] adj incroyable; **incredibly** adv incroyablement

incur [ɪn'kəːʳ] vt (expenses) encourir; (anger, risk) s'exposer à; (debt) contracter; (loss) subir

indecent [ɪn'diːsnt] adj indécent(e), inconvenant(e)

indeed [ɪn'diːd] adv (confirming, agreeing) en effet, effectivement; (for emphasis) vraiment; (furthermore) d'ailleurs; **yes ~!** certainement!

indefinitely [ɪn'dɛfɪnɪtlɪ] adv (wait) indéfiniment

independence [ɪndɪ'pɛndns] n indépendance f; **Independence Day** n (US) fête de l'Indépendance américaine

INDEPENDENCE DAY

L'*Independence Day* est la fête nationale aux États-Unis, le 4 juillet. Il commémore l'adoption de la déclaration d'Indépendance, en 1776, écrite par Thomas Jefferson et proclamant la séparation des 13 colonies américaines de la Grande-Bretagne.

independent [ɪndɪ'pɛndnt] adj indépendant(e); (radio) libre; **independent school** n (BRIT) école privée

index ['ɪndɛks] n (pl **indexes**) (in book) index m; (in library etc) catalogue m; (pl **indices**) (ratio, sign) indice m

India ['ɪndɪə] n Inde f; **Indian** adj indien(ne) ▷ n Indien(ne); **(American) Indian** Indien(ne) (d'Amérique)

indicate ['ɪndɪkeɪt] vt indiquer ▷ vi (BRIT Aut): **to ~ left/right** mettre son clignotant à gauche/à droite; **indication** [ɪndɪ'keɪʃən] n indication f, signe m; **indicative** [ɪn'dɪkətɪv] adj: **to be indicative of sth** être symptomatique de qch ▷ n (Ling) indicatif m; **indicator** n (sign) indicateur m; (Aut) clignotant m

indices ['ɪndɪsiːz] npl of **index**

indict [ɪn'daɪt] vt accuser; **indictment** n accusation f

indifference [ɪn'dɪfrəns] n indifférence f

indifferent [ɪn'dɪfrənt] adj indifférent(e); (poor) médiocre, quelconque

indigenous [ɪn'dɪdʒɪnəs] adj indigène

indigestion [ɪndɪ'dʒɛstʃən] *n*
indigestion *f*, mauvaise digestion
indignant [ɪn'dɪgnənt] *adj*: **~ (at
sth/with sb)** indigné(e) (de qch/
contre qn)
indirect [ɪndɪ'rɛkt] *adj* indirect(e)
indispensable [ɪndɪ'spɛnsəbl] *adj*
indispensable
individual [ɪndɪ'vɪdjuəl] *n* individu
m ▷ *adj* individuel(le); (*characteristic*)
particulier(-ière), original(e);
individually *adv* individuellement
Indonesia [ɪndə'niːzɪə] *n* Indonésie *f*
indoor ['ɪndɔː'] *adj* d'intérieur; (*plant*)
d'appartement; (*swimming pool*)
couvert(e); (*sport, games*) pratiqué(e)
en salle; **indoors** [ɪn'dɔːz] *adv* à
l'intérieur
induce [ɪn'djuːs] *vt* (*persuade*)
persuader; (*bring about*) provoquer;
(*labour*) déclencher
indulge [ɪn'dʌldʒ] *vt* (*whim*) céder à,
satisfaire; (*child*) gâter ▷ *vi*: **to ~ in
sth** (*luxury*) s'offrir qch, se permettre
qch; (*fantasies etc*) se livrer à qch;
indulgent *adj* indulgent(e)
industrial [ɪn'dʌstrɪəl] *adj*
industriel(le); (*injury*) du travail;
(*dispute*) ouvrier(-ière); **industrial
estate** *n* (BRIT) zone industrielle;
industrialist *n* industriel *m*;
industrial park *n* (US) zone
industrielle
industry ['ɪndəstrɪ] *n* industrie *f*;
(*diligence*) zèle *m*, application *f*
inefficient [ɪnɪ'fɪʃənt] *adj* inefficace
inequality [ɪnɪ'kwɔlɪtɪ] *n* inégalité *f*
inevitable [ɪn'ɛvɪtəbl] *adj* inévitable;
inevitably *adv* inévitablement,
fatalement
inexpensive [ɪnɪk'spɛnsɪv] *adj* bon
marché *inv*
inexperienced [ɪnɪk'spɪərɪənst] *adj*
inexpérimenté(e)
inexplicable [ɪnɪk'splɪkəbl] *adj*
inexplicable
infamous ['ɪnfəməs] *adj* infâme,
abominable

infant ['ɪnfənt] *n* (*baby*) nourrisson *m*;
(*young child*) petit(e) enfant
infantry ['ɪnfəntrɪ] *n* infanterie *f*
infant school *n* (BRIT) classes *fpl*
préparatoires (*entre 5 et 7 ans*)
infect [ɪn'fɛkt] *vt* (*wound*) infecter;
(*person, blood*) contaminer; **infection**
[ɪn'fɛkʃən] *n* infection *f*; (*contagion*)
contagion *f*; **infectious** [ɪn'fɛkʃəs]
adj infectieux(-euse); (*also fig*)
contagieux(-euse)
infer [ɪn'fəː'] *vt*: **to ~ (from)** conclure
(de), déduire (de)
inferior [ɪn'fɪərɪə'] *adj* inférieur(e);
(*goods*) de qualité inférieure ▷ *n*
inférieur(e); (*in rank*) subalterne *m/f*
infertile [ɪn'fəːtaɪl] *adj* stérile
infertility [ɪnfəː'tɪlɪtɪ] *n* infertilité
f, stérilité *f*
infested [ɪn'fɛstɪd] *adj*: **~ (with)**
infesté(e) (de)
infinite ['ɪnfɪnɪt] *adj* infini(e); (*time,
money*) illimité(e); **infinitely** *adv*
infiniment
infirmary [ɪn'fəːmərɪ] *n* hôpital *m*;
(*in school, factory*) infirmerie *f*
inflamed [ɪn'fleɪmd] *adj*
enflammé(e)
inflammation [ɪnflə'meɪʃən] *n*
inflammation *f*
inflatable [ɪn'fleɪtəbl] *adj* gonflable
inflate [ɪn'fleɪt] *vt* (*tyre, balloon*)
gonfler; (*fig: exaggerate*) grossir;
(: *increase*) gonfler; **inflation**
[ɪn'fleɪʃən] *n* (*Econ*) inflation *f*
inflexible [ɪn'flɛksɪbl] *adj* inflexible,
rigide
inflict [ɪn'flɪkt] *vt*: **to ~ on** infliger à
influence ['ɪnfluəns] *n* influence
f ▷ *vt* influencer; **under the ~ of
alcohol** en état d'ébriété; **influential**
[ɪnflu'ɛnʃl] *adj* influent(e)
influenza [ɪnflu'ɛnzə] *n* grippe *f*
influx ['ɪnflʌks] *n* afflux *m*
info ['ɪnfəu] (*inf*) *n* (= *information*)
renseignements *mpl*
inform [ɪn'fɔːm] *vt*: **to ~ sb (of)**
informer *or* avertir qn (de) ▷ *vi*: **to**

~ on sb dénoncer qn, informer contre qn

informal [ɪnˈfɔːml] *adj* (*person, manner, party*) simple; (*visit, discussion*) dénué(e) de formalités; (*announcement, invitation*) non officiel(le); (*colloquial*) familier(-ère)

information [ɪnfəˈmeɪʃən] *n* information(s) *f(pl)*; renseignements *mpl*; (*knowledge*) connaissances *fpl*; **a piece of ~** un renseignement; **information office** *n* bureau *m* de renseignements; **information technology** *n* informatique *f*

informative [ɪnˈfɔːmətɪv] *adj* instructif(-ive)

infra-red [ɪnfrəˈrɛd] *adj* infrarouge

infrastructure [ˈɪnfrəstrʌktʃəʳ] *n* infrastructure *f*

infrequent [ɪnˈfriːkwənt] *adj* peu fréquent(e), rare

infuriate [ɪnˈfjuərɪeɪt] *vt* mettre en fureur

infuriating [ɪnˈfjuərɪeɪtɪŋ] *adj* exaspérant(e)

ingenious [ɪnˈdʒiːnjəs] *adj* ingénieux(-euse)

ingredient [ɪnˈɡriːdɪənt] *n* ingrédient *m*; (*fig*) élément *m*

inhabit [ɪnˈhæbɪt] *vt* habiter; **inhabitant** *n* habitant(e)

inhale [ɪnˈheɪl] *vt* inhaler; (*perfume*) respirer; (*smoke*) avaler ▷ *vi* (*breathe in*) aspirer; (*in smoking*) avaler la fumée; **inhaler** *n* inhalateur *m*

inherent [ɪnˈhɪərənt] *adj*: **~ (in or to)** inhérent(e) (à)

inherit [ɪnˈhɛrɪt] *vt* hériter (de); **inheritance** *n* héritage *m*

inhibit [ɪnˈhɪbɪt] *vt* (*Psych*) inhiber; (*growth*) freiner; **inhibition** [ɪnhɪˈbɪʃən] *n* inhibition *f*

initial [ɪˈnɪʃl] *adj* initial(e) ▷ *n* initiale *f* ▷ *vt* parafer; **initials** *npl* initiales *fpl*; (*as signature*) parafe *m*; **initially** *adv* initialement, au début

initiate [ɪˈnɪʃɪeɪt] *vt* (*start*) entreprendre; amorcer; (*enterprise*)

lancer; (*person*) initier; **to ~ proceedings against sb** (*Law*) intenter une action à qn, engager des poursuites contre qn

initiative [ɪˈnɪʃətɪv] *n* initiative *f*

inject [ɪnˈdʒɛkt] *vt* injecter; (*person*): **to ~ sb with sth** faire une piqûre de qch à qn; **injection** [ɪnˈdʒɛkʃən] *n* injection *f*, piqûre *f*

injure [ˈɪndʒəʳ] *vt* blesser; (*damage: reputation etc*) compromettre; **to ~ o.s.** se blesser; **injured** *adj* (*person, leg etc*) blessé(e); **injury** *n* blessure *f*; (*wrong*) tort *m*

injustice [ɪnˈdʒʌstɪs] *n* injustice *f*

ink [ɪŋk] *n* encre *f*; **ink-jet printer** [ˈɪŋkdʒɛt-] *n* imprimante *f* à jet d'encre

inland *adj* [ˈɪnlənd] intérieur(e) ▷ *adv* [ɪnˈlænd] à l'intérieur, dans les terres; **Inland Revenue** *n* (BRIT) fisc *m*

in-laws [ˈɪnlɔːz] *npl* beaux-parents *mpl*; belle famille

inmate [ˈɪnmeɪt] *n* (*in prison*) détenu(e); (*in asylum*) interné(e)

inn [ɪn] *n* auberge *f*

inner [ˈɪnəʳ] *adj* intérieur(e); **inner-city** *adj* (*schools, problems*) de quartiers déshérités

inning [ˈɪnɪŋ] *n* (US Baseball) tour *m* de batte; **innings** *npl* (Cricket) tour de batte

innocence [ˈɪnəsns] *n* innocence *f*

innocent [ˈɪnəsnt] *adj* innocent(e)

innovation [ɪnəuˈveɪʃən] *n* innovation *f*

innovative [ˈɪnəuˌveɪtɪv] *adj* novateur(-trice); (*product*) innovant(e)

in-patient [ˈɪnpeɪʃənt] *n* malade hospitalisé(e)

input [ˈɪnput] *n* (*contribution*) contribution *f*; (*resources*) ressources *fpl*; (*Comput*) entrée *f* (de données) (*: data*) données *fpl* ▷ *vt* (*Comput*) introduire, entrer

inquest [ˈɪnkwɛst] *n* enquête (criminelle); (*coroner's*) enquête judiciaire

inquire [ɪnˈkwaɪəʳ] vi demander ▷ vt demander; **to ~ about** s'informer de, se renseigner sur; **to ~ when/ where/whether** demander quand/ où/si; **inquiry** n demande f de renseignements; (Law) enquête f, investigation f; **"inquiries"** "renseignements"

ins. abbr = **inches**

insane [ɪnˈseɪn] adj fou (folle); (Med) aliéné(e)

insanity [ɪnˈsænɪtɪ] n folie f; (Med) aliénation (mentale)

insect [ˈɪnsɛkt] n insecte m; **insect repellent** n crème f anti-insectes

insecure [ɪnsɪˈkjuəʳ] adj (person) anxieux(-euse); (job) précaire; (building etc) peu sûr(e)

insecurity [ɪnsɪˈkjuərɪtɪ] n insécurité f

insensitive [ɪnˈsɛnsɪtɪv] adj insensible

insert vt [ɪnˈsəːt] insérer ▷ n [ˈɪnsəːt] insertion f

inside [ˈɪnˈsaɪd] n intérieur m ▷ adj intérieur(e) ▷ adv à l'intérieur, dedans ▷ prep à l'intérieur de; (of time): **~ 10 minutes** en moins de 10 minutes; **to go ~** rentrer; **inside lane** n (Aut: in Britain) voie f de gauche; (: in US, Europe) voie f de droite; **inside out** adv à l'envers; (know) à fond; **to turn sth inside out** retourner qch

insight [ˈɪnsaɪt] n perspicacité f; (glimpse, idea) aperçu m

insignificant [ɪnsɪgˈnɪfɪknt] adj insignifiant(e)

insincere [ɪnsɪnˈsɪəʳ] adj hypocrite

insist [ɪnˈsɪst] vi insister; **to ~ on doing** insister pour faire; **to ~ on sth** exiger qch; **to ~ that** (claim) maintenir or soutenir que; **insistent** adj insistant(e), pressant(e); (noise, action) ininterrompu(e)

insomnia [ɪnˈsɒmnɪə] n insomnie f

inspect [ɪnˈspɛkt] vt inspecter; (BRIT: ticket) contrôler; **inspection** [ɪnˈspɛkʃən] n inspection f; (BRIT: of tickets) contrôle m; **inspector** n inspecteur(-trice); (BRIT: on buses, trains) contrôleur(-euse)

inspiration [ɪnspəˈreɪʃən] n inspiration f; **inspire** [ɪnˈspaɪəʳ] vt inspirer; **inspiring** adj inspirant(e)

instability [ɪnstəˈbɪlɪtɪ] n instabilité f

install, (US) **instal** [ɪnˈstɔːl] vt installer; **installation** [ɪnstəˈleɪʃən] n installation f

instalment, (US) **installment** [ɪnˈstɔːlmənt] n (payment) acompte m, versement partiel; (of TV serial etc) épisode m; **in ~s** (pay) à tempérament; (receive) en plusieurs fois

instance [ˈɪnstəns] n exemple m; **for ~** par exemple; **in the first ~** tout d'abord, en premier lieu

instant [ˈɪnstənt] n instant m ▷ adj immédiat(e), urgent(e); (coffee, food) instantané(e), en poudre; **instantly** adv immédiatement, tout de suite; **instant messaging** n messagerie f instantanée

instead [ɪnˈstɛd] adv au lieu de cela; **~ of** au lieu de; **~ of sb** à la place de qn

instinct [ˈɪnstɪŋkt] n instinct m; **instinctive** adj instinctif(-ive)

institute [ˈɪnstɪtjuːt] n institut m ▷ vt instituer, établir; (inquiry) ouvrir; (proceedings) entamer

institution [ɪnstɪˈtjuːʃən] n institution f; (school) établissement m (scolaire); (for care) établissement (psychiatrique etc)

instruct [ɪnˈstrʌkt] vt: **to ~ sb in sth** enseigner qch à qn; **to ~ sb to do** charger qn or ordonner à qn de faire; **instruction** [ɪnˈstrʌkʃən] n instruction f; **instructions** npl (orders) directives fpl; **instructions for use** mode m d'emploi; **instructor** n professeur m; (for skiing, driving) moniteur m

instrument [ˈɪnstrumənt] n instrument m; **instrumental**

[ɪnstrʊˈmɛntl] *adj* (*Mus*) instrumental(e); **to be instrumental in sth/in doing sth** contribuer à qch/à faire qch

insufficient [ɪnsəˈfɪʃənt] *adj* insuffisant(e)

insulate [ˈɪnsjuleɪt] *vt* isoler; (*against sound*) insonoriser; **insulation** [ɪnsjuˈleɪʃən] *n* isolation *f*; (*against sound*) insonorisation *f*

insulin [ˈɪnsjʊlɪn] *n* insuline *f*

insult *n* [ˈɪnsʌlt] insulte *f*, affront *m* ▷ *vt* [ɪnˈsʌlt] insulter, faire un affront à; **insulting** *adj* insultant(e), injurieux(-euse)

insurance [ɪnˈʃuərəns] *n* assurance *f*; **fire/life ~** assurance-incendie/-vie; **insurance company** *n* compagnie *f* or société *f* d'assurances; **insurance policy** *n* police *f* d'assurance

insure [ɪnˈʃuəʳ] *vt* assurer; **to ~ (o.s.) against** (*fig*) parer à

intact [ɪnˈtækt] *adj* intact(e)

intake [ˈɪnteɪk] *n* (*Tech*) admission *f*; (*consumption*) consommation *f*; (*BRIT Scol*) **an ~ of 200 a year** 200 admissions par an

integral [ˈɪntɪɡrəl] *adj* (*whole*) intégral(e); (*part*) intégrant(e)

integrate [ˈɪntɪɡreɪt] *vt* intégrer ▷ *vi* s'intégrer

integrity [ɪnˈtɛɡrɪtɪ] *n* intégrité *f*

intellect [ˈɪntəlɛkt] *n* intelligence *f*; **intellectual** [ɪntəˈlɛktjuəl] *adj, n* intellectuel(le)

intelligence [ɪnˈtɛlɪdʒəns] *n* intelligence *f*; (*Mil*) informations *fpl*, renseignements *mpl*

intelligent [ɪnˈtɛlɪdʒənt] *adj* intelligent(e)

intend [ɪnˈtɛnd] *vt* (*gift etc*) **to ~ sth for** destiner qch à; **to ~ to do** avoir l'intention de faire

intense [ɪnˈtɛns] *adj* intense; (*person*) véhément(e)

intensify [ɪnˈtɛnsɪfaɪ] *vt* intensifier

intensity [ɪnˈtɛnsɪtɪ] *n* intensité *f*

intensive [ɪnˈtɛnsɪv] *adj* intensif(-ive); **intensive care** *n*: **to be in intensive care** être en réanimation; **intensive care unit** *n* service *m* de réanimation

intent [ɪnˈtɛnt] *n* intention *f* ▷ *adj* attentif(-ive), absorbé(e); **to all ~s and purposes** en fait, pratiquement; **to be ~ on doing sth** être (bien) décidé à faire qch

intention [ɪnˈtɛnʃən] *n* intention *f*; **intentional** *adj* intentionnel(le), délibéré(e)

interact [ɪntərˈækt] *vi* avoir une action réciproque; (*people*) communiquer; **interaction** [ɪntərˈækʃən] *n* interaction *f*; **interactive** *adj* (*Comput*) interactif, conversationnel(le)

intercept [ɪntəˈsɛpt] *vt* intercepter; (*person*) arrêter au passage

interchange *n* [ˈɪntətʃeɪndʒ] (*exchange*) échange *m*; (*on motorway*) échangeur *m*

intercourse [ˈɪntəkɔːs] *n*: **sexual ~** rapports sexuels

interest [ˈɪntrɪst] *n* intérêt *m*; (*Comm: stake, share*) participation *f*, intérêts *mpl* ▷ *vt* intéresser; **interested** *adj* intéressé(e); **to be interested in sth** s'intéresser à qch; **I'm interested in going** ça m'intéresse d'y aller; **interesting** *adj* intéressant(e); **interest rate** *n* taux *m* d'intérêt

interface [ˈɪntəfeɪs] *n* (*Comput*) interface *f*

interfere [ɪntəˈfɪəʳ] *vi*: **to ~ in** (*quarrel*) s'immiscer dans; (*other people's business*) se mêler de; **to ~ with** (*object*) tripoter, toucher à; (*plans*) contrecarrer; (*duty*) être en conflit avec; **interference** *n* (*gen*) ingérence *f*; (*Radio, TV*) parasites *mpl*

interim [ˈɪntərɪm] *adj* provisoire; (*post*) intérimaire ▷ *n*: **in the ~** dans l'intérim

interior [ɪnˈtɪərɪəʳ] *n* intérieur *m* ▷ *adj* intérieur(e); (*minister, department*)

de l'intérieur; **interior design** n
architecture f d'intérieur
intermediate [ɪntə'miːdɪət] adj
intermédiaire; (Scol: course, level)
moyen(ne)
intermission [ɪntə'mɪʃən] n pause f;
(Theat, Cine) entracte m
intern vt [ɪn'tə:n] interner ▷ n
['ɪntə:n] (US) interne m/f
internal [ɪn'tə:nl] adj interne; (dispute,
reform etc) intérieur(e); **Internal
Revenue Service** n (US) fisc m
international [ɪntə'næʃənl] adj
international(e) ▷ n (BRIT Sport)
international m
Internet [ɪntə'nɛt] n: **the ~** l'Internet
m; **Internet café** n cybercafé m;
Internet Service Provider n
fournisseur m d'accès à Internet;
Internet user n internaute m/f
interpret [ɪn'tə:prɪt] vt
interpréter ▷ vi servir d'interprète;
interpretation [ɪntə:prɪ'teɪʃən]
n interprétation f; **interpreter** n
interprète m/f; **could you act as an
interpreter for us?** pourriez-vous
nous servir d'interprète?
interrogate [ɪn'tɛrəugeɪt] vt
interroger; (suspect etc) soumettre
à un interrogatoire; **interrogation**
[ɪntɛrəu'geɪʃən] n interrogation f; (by
police) interrogatoire m
interrogative [ɪntə'rɔgətɪv] adj
interrogateur(-trice) ▷ n (Ling)
interrogatif m
interrupt [ɪntə'rʌpt] vt, vi
interrompre; **interruption**
[ɪntə'rʌpʃən] n interruption f
intersection [ɪntə'sekʃən] n (of
roads) croisement m
interstate ['ɪntərsteɪt] (US) n
autoroute f (qui relie plusieurs États)
interval ['ɪntəvl] n intervalle m;
(BRIT: Theat) entracte m; (: Sport)
mi-temps f; **at ~s** par intervalles
intervene [ɪntə'vi:n] vi (time)
s'écouler (entre-temps); (event)
survenir; (person) intervenir

interview ['ɪntəvju:] n (Radio, TV)
interview f; (for job) entrevue f ▷ vt
interviewer, avoir une entrevue
avec; **interviewer** n (Radio, TV)
interviewer m
intimate adj ['ɪntɪmət] intime;
(friendship) profond(e); (knowledge)
approfondi(e) ▷ vt ['ɪntɪmeɪt]
suggérer, laisser entendre; (announce)
faire savoir
intimidate [ɪn'tɪmɪdeɪt] vt intimider
intimidating [ɪn'tɪmɪdeɪtɪŋ] adj
intimidant(e)
into ['ɪntu] prep dans; **~ pieces/
French** en morceaux/français
intolerant [ɪn'tɔlərnt] adj: **~ (of)**
intolérant(e) (de)
intranet [ɪn'trənɛt] n intranet m
intransitive [ɪn'trænsɪtɪv] adj
intransitif(-ive)
intricate ['ɪntrɪkət] adj complexe,
compliqué(e)
intrigue [ɪn'tri:g] n intrigue f ▷ vt
intriguer; **intriguing** adj fascinant(e)
introduce [ɪntrə'dju:s] vt introduire;
(TV show etc) présenter; **to ~ sb
(to sb)** présenter qn (à qn); **to ~
sb to** (pastime, technique) initier qn
à; **introduction** [ɪntrə'dʌkʃən]
n introduction f; (of person)
présentation f; (to new experience)
initiation f; **introductory**
[ɪntrə'dʌktərɪ] adj préliminaire,
introductif(-ive)
intrude [ɪn'tru:d] vi (person) être
importun(e); **to ~ on** or **into**
(conversation etc) s'immiscer dans;
intruder n intrus(e)
intuition [ɪntju:'ɪʃn] n intuition f
inundate ['ɪnʌndeɪt] vt: **to ~ with**
inonder de
invade [ɪn'veɪd] vt envahir
invalid n ['ɪnvəlɪd] malade m/f;
(with disability) invalide m/f ▷ adj
[ɪn'vælɪd] (not valid) invalide, non
valide
invaluable [ɪn'væljuəbl] adj
inestimable, inappréciable

invariably [ɪn'vɛərɪəblɪ] *adv* invariablement; **she is ~ late** elle est toujours en retard

invasion [ɪn'veɪʒən] *n* invasion *f*

invent [ɪn'vɛnt] *vt* inventer; **invention** [ɪn'vɛnʃən] *n* invention *f*; **inventor** *n* inventeur(-trice)

inventory ['ɪnvəntrɪ] *n* inventaire *m*

inverted commas [ɪn'vəːtɪd-] *npl* (BRIT) guillemets *mpl*

invest [ɪn'vɛst] *vt* investir ▷ *vi*: **to ~ in** placer de l'argent *or* investir dans; (*fig*: *acquire*) s'offrir, faire l'acquisition de

investigate [ɪn'vɛstɪgeɪt] *vt* étudier, examiner; (*crime*) faire une enquête sur; **investigation** [ɪnvɛstɪ'geɪʃən] *n* (*of crime*) enquête *f*, investigation *f*

investigator [ɪn'vɛstɪgeɪtə²] *n* investigateur(-trice); **private ~** détective privé

investment [ɪn'vɛstmənt] *n* investissement *m*, placement *m*

investor [ɪn'vɛstə²] *n* épargnant(e); (*shareholder*) actionnaire *m/f*

invisible [ɪn'vɪzɪbl] *adj* invisible

invitation [ɪnvɪ'teɪʃən] *n* invitation *f*

invite [ɪn'vaɪt] *vt* inviter; (*opinions etc*) demander; **inviting** *adj* engageant(e), attrayant(e)

invoice ['ɪnvɔɪs] *n* facture *f* ▷ *vt* facturer

involve [ɪn'vɔlv] *vt* (*entail*) impliquer; (*concern*) concerner; (*require*) nécessiter; **to ~ sb in** (*theft etc*) impliquer qn dans; (*activity, meeting*) faire participer qn à; **involved** *adj* (*complicated*) complexe; **to be involved in** (*take part*) participer à; **involvement** *n* (*personal role*) rôle *m*; (*participation*) participation *f*; (*enthusiasm*) enthousiasme *m*

inward ['ɪnwəd] *adj* (*movement*) vers l'intérieur; (*thought, feeling*) profond(e), intime ▷ *adv* = **inwards**; **inwards** *adv* vers l'intérieur

iPod® ['aɪpɔd] *n* iPod® *m*

IQ *n abbr* (= *intelligence quotient*) Q.I. *m*

IRA *n abbr* (= *Irish Republican Army*) IRA *f*

Iran [ɪ'rɑːn] *n* Iran *m*; **Iranian** [ɪ'reɪnɪən] *adj* iranien(ne) ▷ *n* Iranien(ne)

Iraq [ɪ'rɑːk] *n* Irak *m*; **Iraqi** *adj* irakien(ne) ▷ *n* Irakien(ne)

Ireland ['aɪələnd] *n* Irlande *f*

iris, irises ['aɪrɪs, -ɪz] *n* iris *m*

Irish ['aɪrɪʃ] *adj* irlandais(e) ▷ *npl*: **the ~** les Irlandais; **Irishman** (*irreg*) *n* Irlandais *m*; **Irishwoman** (*irreg*) *n* Irlandaise *f*

iron ['aɪən] *n* fer *m*; (*for clothes*) fer *m* à repasser ▷ *adj* de or en fer ▷ *vt* (*clothes*) repasser

ironic(al) [aɪ'rɔnɪk(l)] *adj* ironique; **ironically** *adv* ironiquement

ironing ['aɪənɪŋ] *n* (*activity*) repassage *m*; (*clothes: ironed*) linge repassé; (*: to be ironed*) linge à repasser; **ironing board** *n* planche *f* à repasser

irony ['aɪrənɪ] *n* ironie *f*

irrational [ɪ'ræʃənl] *adj* irrationnel(le); (*person*) qui n'est pas rationnel

irregular [ɪ'rɛgjulə²] *adj* irrégulier(-ière); (*surface*) inégal(e); (*action, event*) peu orthodoxe

irrelevant [ɪ'rɛləvənt] *adj* sans rapport, hors de propos

irresistible [ɪrɪ'zɪstɪbl] *adj* irrésistible

irresponsible [ɪrɪ'spɔnsɪbl] *adj* (*act*) irréfléchi(e); (*person*) qui n'a pas le sens des responsabilités

irrigation [ɪrɪ'geɪʃən] *n* irrigation *f*

irritable ['ɪrɪtəbl] *adj* irritable

irritate ['ɪrɪteɪt] *vt* irriter; **irritating** *adj* irritant(e); **irritation** [ɪrɪ'teɪʃən] *n* irritation *f*

IRS *n abbr* (US) = **Internal Revenue Service**

is [ɪz] *vb see* **be**

ISDN *n abbr* (= *Integrated Services Digital Network*) RNIS *m*

Islam ['ɪzlɑːm] *n* Islam *m*; **Islamic** [ɪz'lɑːmɪk] *adj* islamique

island ['aɪlənd] n île f; (also: **traffic ~**) refuge m (pour piétons); **islander** n habitant(e) d'une île, insulaire m/f

isle [aɪl] n île f

isn't ['ɪznt] = **is not**

isolated ['aɪsəleɪtɪd] adj isolé(e)

isolation [aɪsə'leɪʃən] n isolement m

ISP n abbr = **Internet Service Provider**

Israel ['ɪzreɪl] n Israël m; **Israeli** [ɪz'reɪlɪ] adj israélien(ne) ▷ n Israélien(ne)

issue ['ɪʃuː] n question f, problème m; (of banknotes) émission f; (of newspaper) numéro m; (of book) publication f, parution f ▷ vt (rations, equipment) distribuer; (orders) donner; (statement) publier, faire; (certificate, passport) délivrer; (banknotes, cheques, stamps) émettre, mettre en circulation; **at ~** en jeu, en cause; **to take ~ with sb (over sth)** exprimer son désaccord avec qn (sur qch)

IT n abbr = **information technology**

○ **KEYWORD**

it [ɪt] pron 1 (specific: subject) il (elle); (: direct object) le (la, l'); (: indirect object) lui; **it's on the table** c'est or il (or elle) est sur la table; **I can't find it** je n'arrive pas à le trouver; **give it to me** donne-le-moi

2 (after prep): **about/from/of it** en; **I spoke to him about it** je lui en ai parlé; **what did you learn from it?** qu'est-ce que vous en avez retiré?; **I'm proud of it** j'en suis fier; **in/to it** y; **put the book in it** mettez-y le livre; **he agreed to it** il y a consenti; **did you go to it?** (party, concert etc) est-ce que vous y êtes allé(s)?

3 (impersonal) il; ce, cela, ça; **it's Friday tomorrow** demain, c'est vendredi or nous sommes vendredi; **it's 6 o'clock** il est 6 heures; **how far is it? — it's 10 miles** c'est loin? — c'est à 10 miles; **who is it? — it's me** qui

est-ce? — c'est moi; **it's raining** il pleut

Italian [ɪ'tæljən] adj italien(ne) ▷ n Italien(ne); (Ling) italien m

italics [ɪ'tælɪks] npl italique m

Italy ['ɪtəlɪ] n Italie f

itch [ɪtʃ] n démangeaison f ▷ vi (person) éprouver des démangeaisons; (part of body) démanger; **I'm ~ing to do** l'envie me démange de faire; **itchy** adj: **my back is itchy** j'ai le dos qui me démange

it'd ['ɪtd] = **it would; it had**

item ['aɪtəm] n (gen) article m; (on agenda) question f, point m; (also: **news ~**) nouvelle f

itinerary [aɪ'tɪnərərɪ] n itinéraire m

it'll ['ɪtl] = **it will; it shall**

its [ɪts] adj son (sa), ses pl

it's [ɪts] = **it is; it has**

itself [ɪt'sɛlf] pron (reflexive) se; (emphatic) lui-même (elle-même)

ITV n abbr (BRIT: = Independent Television) chaîne de télévision commerciale

I've [aɪv] = **I have**

ivory ['aɪvərɪ] n ivoire m

ivy ['aɪvɪ] n lierre m

jab [dʒæb] vt: **to ~ sth into** enfoncer or planter qch dans ▷ n (Med: inf) piqûre f
jack [dʒæk] n (Aut) cric m; (Cards) valet m
jacket ['dʒækɪt] n veste f, veston m; (of book) couverture f, jaquette f; **jacket potato** n pomme f de terre en robe des champs
jackpot ['dʒækpɒt] n gros lot
Jacuzzi® [dʒə'ku:zɪ] n jacuzzi® m
jagged ['dʒægɪd] adj dentelé(e)
jail [dʒeɪl] n prison f ▷ vt emprisonner, mettre en prison; **jail sentence** n peine f de prison
jam [dʒæm] n confiture f; (also: **traffic ~**) embouteillage m ▷ vt (passage etc) encombrer, obstruer; (mechanism, drawer etc) bloquer, coincer; (Radio) brouiller ▷ vi (mechanism, sliding part) se coincer, se bloquer; (gun) s'enrayer; **to be in a ~** (inf) être dans le pétrin; **to ~ sth into** (stuff) entasser or comprimer qch dans; (thrust) enfoncer qch dans
Jamaica [dʒə'meɪkə] n Jamaïque f
jammed [dʒæmd] adj (window etc) coincé(e)
janitor ['dʒænɪtər] n (caretaker) concierge m
January ['dʒænjuərɪ] n janvier m
Japan [dʒə'pæn] n Japon m; **Japanese** [dʒæpə'ni:z] adj japonais(e) ▷ n (pl inv) Japonais(e); (Ling) japonais m
jar [dʒɑːr] n (stone, earthenware) pot m; (glass) bocal m ▷ vi (sound) produire un son grinçant or discordant; (colours etc) détonner, jurer
jargon ['dʒɑːgən] n jargon m
javelin ['dʒævlɪn] n javelot m
jaw [dʒɔː] n mâchoire f
jazz [dʒæz] n jazz m
jealous ['dʒɛləs] adj jaloux(-ouse); **jealousy** n jalousie f
jeans [dʒiːnz] npl jean m
Jello® ['dʒɛləu] (US) n gelée f
jelly ['dʒɛlɪ] n (dessert) gelée f; (US: jam) confiture f; **jellyfish** n méduse f
jeopardize ['dʒɛpədaɪz] vt mettre en danger or péril
jerk [dʒə:k] n secousse f, saccade f; (of muscle) spasme m; (inf) pauvre type m ▷ vt (shake) donner une secousse à; (pull) tirer brusquement ▷ vi (vehicles) cahoter
jersey ['dʒə:zɪ] n tricot m; (fabric) jersey m
Jesus ['dʒiːzəs] n Jésus
jet [dʒɛt] n (of gas, liquid) jet m; (Aviat) avion m à réaction, jet m; **jet lag** n décalage m horaire; **jet-ski** vi faire du jet-ski or scooter des mers
jetty ['dʒɛtɪ] n jetée f, digue f
Jew [dʒuː] n Juif m
jewel ['dʒuːəl] n bijou m, joyau m; (in watch) rubis m; **jeweller,** (US) **jeweler** n bijoutier(-ière), joaillier m; **jeweller's (shop)** n (BRIT) bijouterie f, joaillerie f; **jewellery,** (US) **jewelry** n bijoux mpl
Jewish ['dʒuːɪʃ] adj juif (juive)

jigsaw ['dʒɪgsɔ:] n (also: **~ puzzle**) puzzle m

job [dʒɔb] n (chore, task) travail m, tâche f; (employment) emploi m, poste m, place f; **it's a good ~ that ...** c'est heureux or c'est une chance que ... + sub; **just the ~!** (c'est) juste or exactement ce qu'il faut!; **job centre** (BRIT) n ≈ ANPE f, ≈ Agence nationale pour l'emploi; **jobless** adj sans travail, au chômage

jockey ['dʒɔkɪ] n jockey m ▷ vi: **to ~ for position** manœuvrer pour être bien placer

jog [dʒɔg] vt secouer ▷ vi (Sport) faire du jogging; **to ~ sb's memory** rafraîchir la mémoire de qn; **jogging** n jogging m

join [dʒɔɪn] vt (put together) unir, assembler; (become member of) s'inscrire à; (meet) rejoindre, retrouver; (queue) se joindre à ▷ vi (roads, rivers) se rejoindre, se rencontrer ▷ n raccord m; **join in** vi se mettre de la partie ▷ vt fus se mêler à; **join up** vi (meet) se rejoindre; (Mil) s'engager

joiner ['dʒɔɪnə^r] (BRIT) n menuisier m

joint [dʒɔɪnt] n (Tech) jointure f; joint m; (Anat) articulation f, jointure; (BRIT Culin) rôti m; (inf: place) boîte f; (of cannabis) joint ▷ adj commun(e); (committee) mixte, paritaire; (winner) ex aequo; **joint account** n compte joint; **jointly** adv ensemble, en commun

joke [dʒəuk] n plaisanterie f; (also: **practical ~**) farce f ▷ vi plaisanter; **to play a ~ on** jouer un tour à, faire une farce à; **joker** n (Cards) joker m

jolly ['dʒɔlɪ] adj gai(e), enjoué(e); (enjoyable) amusant(e), plaisant(e) ▷ adv (BRIT inf) rudement, drôlement

jolt [dʒəult] n cahot m, secousse f; (shock) choc m ▷ vt cahoter, secouer

Jordan [dʒɔ:dən] n (country) Jordanie f

journal ['dʒə:nl] n journal m; **journalism** n journalisme m; **journalist** n journaliste m/f

journey ['dʒə:nɪ] n voyage m; (distance covered) trajet m; **the ~ takes two hours** le trajet dure deux heures; **how was your ~?** votre voyage s'est bien passé?

joy [dʒɔɪ] n joie f; **joyrider** n voleur(-euse) de voiture (qui fait une virée dans le véhicule volé); **joy stick** n (Aviat) manche m à balai; (Comput) manche à balai, manette f (de jeu)

Jr abbr = **junior**

judge [dʒʌdʒ] n juge m ▷ vt juger; (estimate: weight, size etc) apprécier; (consider) estimer

judo ['dʒu:dəu] n judo m

jug [dʒʌg] n pot m, cruche f

juggle ['dʒʌgl] vi jongler; **juggler** n jongleur m

juice [dʒu:s] n jus m; **juicy** adj juteux(-euse)

July [dʒu:'laɪ] n juillet m

jumble ['dʒʌmbl] n fouillis m ▷ vt (also: **~ up, ~ together**) mélanger, brouiller; **jumble sale** n (BRIT) vente f de charité

⬤ **JUMBLE SALE**

⬤
⬤ Les jumble sales ont lieu dans les
⬤ églises, salles des fêtes ou halls
⬤ d'écoles, et l'on y vend des articles
⬤ de toutes sortes, en général bon
⬤ marché et surtout d'occasion, pour
⬤ collecter des fonds pour une œuvre
⬤ de charité, une école (par exemple,
⬤ pour acheter des ordinateurs), ou
⬤ encore une église (pour réparer
⬤ un toit etc).

jumbo ['dʒʌmbəu] adj (also: **~ jet**) (avion) gros porteur (à réaction)

jump [dʒʌmp] vi sauter, bondir; (with fear etc) sursauter; (increase) monter en flèche ▷ vt sauter, franchir ▷ n saut m, bond m; (with fear etc) sursaut m; (fence) obstacle m; **to ~ the queue** (BRIT) passer avant son tour

jumper ['dʒʌmpə^r] n (BRIT: pullover)
pull-over m; (US: pinafore dress) robe-
chasuble f
jump leads, (US)**jumper cables**
npl câbles mpl de démarrage
Jun. abbr = **June; junior**
junction ['dʒʌŋkʃən] n (BRIT:
of roads) carrefour m; (of rails)
embranchement m
June [dʒuːn] n juin m
jungle ['dʒʌŋgl] n jungle f
junior ['dʒuːnɪə^r] adj, n: **he's ~ to me
(by two years), he's my ~ (by two
years)** il est mon cadet (de deux ans),
il est plus jeune que moi (de deux
ans); **he's ~ to me** (seniority) il est en
dessous de moi (dans la hiérarchie),
j'ai plus d'ancienneté que lui; **junior
high school** n (US) ≈ collège m
d'enseignement secondaire; see also
high school; junior school n (BRIT)
école f primaire
junk [dʒʌŋk] n (rubbish) camelote f;
(cheap goods) bric-à-brac m inv; **junk
food** n snacks vite prêts (sans valeur
nutritive)
junkie ['dʒʌŋkɪ] n (inf) junkie m,
drogué(e)
junk mail n prospectus mpl; (Comput)
messages mpl publicitaires
Jupiter ['dʒuːpɪtə^r] n (planet) Jupiter f
jurisdiction [dʒuərɪs'dɪkʃən] n
juridiction f; **it falls** or **comes
within/outside our ~** cela est/n'est
pas de notre compétence or ressort
jury ['dʒuərɪ] n jury m
just [dʒʌst] adj juste ▷ adv: **he's ~
done it/left** il vient de le faire/partir;
~ right/two o'clock exactement or
juste ce qu'il faut/deux heures; **we
were ~ going** nous partions; **I was ~
about to phone** j'allais téléphoner;
~ as he was leaving au moment
or à l'instant précis où il partait;
~ before/enough/here juste avant/
assez/là; **it's ~ me/a mistake** ce
n'est que moi/(rien) qu'une erreur;
~ missed/caught manqué/attrapé

de justesse; **~ listen to this!** écoutez
un peu ça!; **she's ~ as clever as
you** elle est tout aussi intelligente
que vous; **it's ~ as well that you
...** heureusement que vous ...; **~ a
minute!, ~ one moment!** un instant
(s'il vous plaît)!
justice ['dʒʌstɪs] n justice f; (US: judge)
juge m de la Cour suprême
justification [dʒʌstɪfɪ'keɪʃən] n
justification f
justify ['dʒʌstɪfaɪ] vt justifier
jut [dʒʌt] vi (also: ~ **out**) dépasser,
faire saillie
juvenile ['dʒuːvənaɪl] adj juvénile;
(court, books) pour enfants ▷ n
adolescent(e)

K

K, k [keɪ] *abbr* (= *one thousand*) K
kangaroo [kæŋgəˈruː] *n* kangourou *m*
karaoke [kɑːrəˈəʊkɪ] *n* karaoké *m*
karate [kəˈrɑːtɪ] *n* karaté *m*
kebab [kəˈbæb] *n* kebab *m*
keel [kiːl] *n* quille *f*; **on an even ~**
(*fig*) à flot
keen [kiːn] *adj* (*eager*) plein(e)
d'enthousiasme; (*interest, desire,
competition*) vif (vive); (*eye, intelligence*)
pénétrant(e); (*edge*) effilé(e); **to be ~ to
do** *or* **on doing sth** désirer vivement
faire qch, tenir beaucoup à faire qch; **to
be ~ on sth/sb** aimer beaucoup qch/qn
keep [kiːp] (*pt, pp* **kept**) *vt* (*retain,
preserve*) garder; (*hold back*) retenir;
(*shop, accounts, promise, diary*) tenir;
(*support*) entretenir; (*chickens, bees,
pigs etc*) élever ▷ *vi* (*food*) se conserver;
(*remain: in a certain state or place*)
rester ▷ *n* (*of castle*) donjon *m*; (*food
etc*): **enough for his ~** assez pour
(assurer) sa subsistance; **to ~ doing
sth** (*continue*) continuer à faire qch;
(*repeatedly*) ne pas arrêter de faire
qch; **to ~ sb from doing/sth from
happening** empêcher qn de faire *or*
que qn (ne) fasse/que qch (n')arrive;
to ~ sb happy/a place tidy faire
que qn soit content/qu'un endroit
reste propre; **to ~ sth to o.s.** garder
qch pour soi, tenir qch secret; **to
~ sth from sb** cacher qch à qn; **to
~ time** (*clock*) être à l'heure, ne pas
retarder; **for ~s** (*inf*) pour de bon,
pour toujours; **keep away** *vt*: **to ~
sth/sb away from sb** tenir qch/qn
éloigné de qn ▷ *vi*: **to ~ away (from)**
ne pas s'approcher (de); **keep back** *vt*
(*crowds, tears, money*) retenir; (*conceal:
information*): **to ~ sth back from sb**
cacher qch à qn ▷ *vi* rester en arrière;
keep off *vt* (*dog, person*) éloigner ▷ *vi*:
if the rain ~s off s'il ne pleut pas; **~
your hands off!** pas touche! (*inf*);
"~ off the grass" "pelouse interdite";
keep on *vi* continuer; **to ~ on doing**
continuer à faire; **don't ~ on about
it!** arrête (d'en parler)!; **keep out** *vt*
empêcher d'entrer ▷ *vi* (*stay out*) rester
en dehors; **"~ out"** "défense d'entrer";
keep up *vi* (*fig: in comprehension*)
suivre ▷ *vt* continuer, maintenir; **to ~
up with sb** (*in work etc*) se maintenir
au même niveau que qn; (*in race etc*)
aller aussi vite que qn; **keeper** *n*
gardien(ne); **keep-fit** *n* gymnastique *f*
(d'entretien); **keeping** *n* (*care*) garde *f*;
in keeping with en harmonie avec
kennel [ˈkɛnl] *n* niche *f*; **kennels** *npl*
(*for boarding*) chenil *m*
Kenya [ˈkɛnjə] *n* Kenya *m*
kept [kɛpt] *pt, pp of* **keep**
kerb [kəːb] *n* (*BRIT*) bordure *f* du trottoir
kerosene [ˈkɛrəsiːn] *n* kérosène *m*
ketchup [ˈkɛtʃəp] *n* ketchup *m*
kettle [ˈkɛtl] *n* bouilloire *f*
key [kiː] *n* (*gen, Mus*) clé *f*; (*of piano,
typewriter*) touche *f*; (*on map*) légende
f ▷ *adj* (*factor, role, area*) clé *inv* ▷ *vt*
(*also: ~ in*) (*text*) saisir; **can I have my**

~? je peux avoir ma clé?; **a ~ issue** un problème fondamental; **keyboard** n clavier m; **keyhole** n trou m de la serrure; **keypad** n pavé m numérique; (of smartphone) clavier m; **keyring** n porte-clés m

kg abbr (= kilogram) K

khaki ['kɑːkɪ] adj, n kaki m

kick [kɪk] vt donner un coup de pied à ▷ vi (horse) ruer ▷ n coup m de pied; (inf: thrill): **he does it for ~s** il le fait parce que ça l'excite, il le fait pour le plaisir; **to ~ the habit** (inf) arrêter; **kick off** vi (Sport) donner le coup d'envoi; **kick-off** n (Sport) coup m d'envoi

kid [kɪd] n (inf: child) gamin(e), gosse m/f; (animal, leather) chevreau m ▷ vi (inf) plaisanter, blaguer

kidnap ['kɪdnæp] vt enlever, kidnapper; **kidnapping** n enlèvement m

kidney ['kɪdnɪ] n (Anat) rein m; (Culin) rognon m; **kidney bean** n haricot m rouge

kill [kɪl] vt tuer ▷ n mise f à mort; **to ~ time** tuer le temps; **killer** n tueur(-euse); (murderer) meurtrier(-ière); **killing** n meurtre m; (of group of people) tuerie f, massacre m; (inf): **to make a killing** se remplir les poches, réussir un beau coup

kiln [kɪln] n four m

kilo ['kiːləu] n kilo m; **kilobyte** n (Comput) kilo-octet m; **kilogram(me)** n kilogramme m; **kilometre**, (us) **kilometer** ['kɪləmiːtər] n kilomètre m; **kilowatt** n kilowatt m

kilt [kɪlt] n kilt m

kin [kɪn] n see **next-of-kin**

kind [kaɪnd] adj gentil(le), aimable ▷ n sorte f, espèce f; (species) genre m; **to be two of a ~** se ressembler; **in ~** (Comm) en nature; **~ of** (inf: rather) plutôt; **a ~ of** une sorte de; **what ~ of …?** quelle sorte de …?

kindergarten ['kɪndəgɑːtn] n jardin m d'enfants

kindly ['kaɪndlɪ] adj bienveillant(e), plein(e) de gentillesse ▷ adv avec

bonté; **will you ~ …** auriez-vous la bonté or l'obligeance de …

kindness ['kaɪndnɪs] n (quality) bonté f, gentillesse f

king [kɪŋ] n roi m; **kingdom** n royaume m; **kingfisher** n martin-pêcheur m; **king-size(d) bed** n grand lit (de 1,95 m de large)

kiosk ['kiːɔsk] n kiosque m; (BRIT: also: **telephone ~**) cabine f (téléphonique)

kipper ['kɪpər] n hareng fumé et salé

kiss [kɪs] n baiser m ▷ vt embrasser; **to ~ (each other)** s'embrasser; **kiss of life** n (BRIT) bouche à bouche m

kit [kɪt] n équipement m, matériel m; (set of tools etc) trousse f; (for assembly) kit m

kitchen ['kɪtʃɪn] n cuisine f

kite [kaɪt] n (toy) cerf-volant m

kitten ['kɪtn] n petit chat, chaton m

kitty ['kɪtɪ] n (money) cagnotte f

kiwi ['kiːwiː] n (also: **~ fruit**) kiwi m

km abbr (= kilometre) km

km/h abbr (= kilometres per hour) km/h

knack [næk] n: **to have the ~ (of doing)** avoir le coup (pour faire)

knee [niː] n genou m; **kneecap** n rotule f

kneel (pt, pp knelt) [niːl, nɛlt] vi (also: **~ down**) s'agenouiller

knelt [nɛlt] pt, pp of **kneel**

knew [njuː] pt of **know**

knickers ['nɪkəz] npl (BRIT) culotte f (de femme)

knife (pl knives) [naɪf, naɪvz] n couteau m ▷ vt poignarder, frapper d'un coup de couteau

knight [naɪt] n chevalier m; (Chess) cavalier m

knit [nɪt] vt tricoter ▷ vi tricoter; (broken bones) se ressouder; **to ~ one's brows** froncer les sourcils; **knitting** n tricot m; **knitting needle** n aiguille f à tricoter; **knitwear** n tricots mpl, lainages mpl

knives [naɪvz] npl of **knife**

knob [nɔb] n bouton m; (BRIT): **a ~ of butter** une noix de beurre

knock [nɔk] vt frapper; (bump into) heurter; (inf: fig) dénigrer ▷ vi (at door *etc*): **to ~ at/on** frapper à/sur ▷ *n* coup *m*; **knock down** *vt* renverser; (*price*) réduire; **knock off** *vi* (*inf: finish*) s'arrêter (de travailler) ▷ *vt* (*vase, object*) faire tomber; (*inf: steal*) piquer; (*fig: from price etc*): **to ~ off £10** faire une remise de 10 livres; **knock out** *vt* assommer; (*Boxing*) mettre k.-o.; (*in competition*) éliminer; **knock over** *vt* (*object*) faire tomber; (*pedestrian*) renverser; **knockout** *n* (*Boxing*) knock-out *m*, K.-O. *m*; **knockout competition** (BRIT) compétition *f* avec épreuves éliminatoires

knot [nɔt] *n* (*gen*) nœud *m* ▷ *vt* nouer

know [nəu] (*pt* **knew**, *pp* **known**) *vt* savoir; (*person, place*) connaître; **to ~ that** savoir que; **to ~ how to do** savoir faire; **to ~ how to swim** savoir nager; **to ~ about/of sth** (*event*) être au courant de qch; (*subject*) connaître qch; **I don't ~** je ne sais pas; **do you ~ where I can …?** savez-vous où je peux …?; **know-all** *n* (BRIT *pej*) je-sais-tout *m/f*; **know-how** *n* savoir-faire *m*, technique *f*, compétence *f*; **knowing** *adj* (*look etc*) entendu(e); **knowingly** *adv* (*on purpose*) sciemment; (*smile, look*) d'un air entendu; **know-it-all** *n* (US) = **know-all**

knowledge ['nɔlɪdʒ] *n* connaissance *f*; (*learning*) connaissances, savoir *m*; **without my ~** à mon insu; **knowledgeable** *adj* bien informé(e)

known [nəun] *pp of* **know** ▷ *adj* (*thief, facts*) notoire; (*expert*) célèbre

knuckle ['nʌkl] *n* articulation *f* (des phalanges), jointure *f*

koala [kəu'ɑ:lə] *n* (*also:* **~ bear**) koala *m*

Koran [kɔ'rɑ:n] *n* Coran *m*

Korea [kə'rɪə] *n* Corée *f*; **Korean** *adj* coréen(ne) ▷ *n* Coréen(ne)

kosher ['kəuʃə'] *adj* kascher *inv*

Kosovar, Kosovan ['kɔsəvɑ:', 'kɔsəvən] *adj* kosovar(e)

Kosovo ['kɔsɔvəu] *n* Kosovo *m*

Kuwait [ku'weɪt] *n* Koweït *m*

L *abbr* (BRIT *Aut:* = *learner*) *signale un conducteur débutant*

l. *abbr* (= *litre*) l

lab [læb] *n abbr* (= *laboratory*) labo *m*

label ['leɪbl] *n* étiquette *f*; (*brand: of record*) marque *f* ▷ *vt* étiqueter

labor *etc* ['leɪbə'] (US) *n* = **labour**

laboratory [lə'bɔrətərɪ] *n* laboratoire *m*

Labor Day *n* (US, CANADA) fête *f* du travail (*le premier lundi de septembre*)

● **LABOR DAY**
●
● *Labor Day* aux États-Unis et au
● Canada est fixée au premier lundi
● de septembre. Instituée par le
● Congrès en 1894 après avoir été
● réclamée par les mouvements
● ouvriers pendant douze ans, elle
● a perdu une grande partie de son
● caractère politique pour devenir
● un jour férié assez ordinaire et

● l'occasion de partir pour un long
● week-end avant la rentrée des
● classes.

labor union n (us) syndicat m
Labour ['leɪbə^r] n (BRIT Pol: also:
the ~ Party) le parti travailliste, les
travaillistes mpl
labour, (us) **labor** ['leɪbə^r] n (work)
travail m; (workforce) main-d'œuvre f
▷ vi: **to ~ (at)** travailler dur (à), peiner
(sur) ▷ vt: **to ~ a point** insister sur un
point; **in ~** (Med) en travail; **labourer**,
(us) **laborer** n manœuvre m; **farm
labourer** ouvrier m agricole
lace [leɪs] n dentelle f; (of shoe etc)
lacet m ▷ vt (shoe: also: **~ up**) lacer
lack [læk] n manque m ▷ vt manquer
de; **through** or **for ~ of** faute de, par
manque de; **to be ~ing** manquer,
faire défaut; **to be ~ing in** manquer
de
lacquer ['lækə^r] n laque f
lacy ['leɪsɪ] adj (made of lace) en
dentelle; (like lace) comme de la
dentelle
lad [læd] n garçon m, gars m
ladder ['lædə^r] n échelle f; (BRIT:
in tights) maille filée ▷ vt, vi (BRIT:
tights) filer
ladle ['leɪdl] n louche f
lady ['leɪdɪ] n dame f; **"ladies and
gentlemen …"** "Mesdames (et)
Messieurs …"; **young ~** jeune fille f;
(married) jeune femme f; **the ladies'
(room)** les toilettes fpl des dames;
ladybird n, (us) **ladybug** n coccinelle f
lag [læg] n retard m ▷ vi (also: ~
behind) rester en arrière, traîner;
(fig) rester à la traîne ▷ vt (pipes)
calorifuger
lager ['lɑ:gə^r] n bière blonde
lagoon [lə'gu:n] n lagune f
laid [leɪd] pt, pp of **lay**; **laid back** adj
(inf) relaxe, décontracté(e)
lain [leɪn] pp of **lie**
lake [leɪk] n lac m
lamb [læm] n agneau m

lame [leɪm] adj (also fig)
boiteux(-euse)
lament [lə'mɛnt] n lamentation f
▷ vt pleurer, se lamenter sur
lamp [læmp] n lampe f; **lamppost**
n (BRIT) réverbère m; **lampshade** n
abat-jour m inv
land [lænd] n (as opposed to sea) terre
f (ferme); (country) pays m; (soil)
terre; (piece of land) terrain m; (estate)
terre(s), domaine(s) m(pl) ▷ vi (from
ship) débarquer; (Aviat) atterrir; (fig:
fall) (re)tomber ▷ vt (passengers,
goods) débarquer; (obtain) décrocher;
to ~ sb with sth (inf) coller qch à qn;
landing n (from ship) débarquement
m; (Aviat) atterrissage m; (of staircase)
palier m; **landing card** n carte f
de débarquement; **landlady** n
propriétaire f, logeuse f; (of pub)
patronne f; **landline** n ligne f fixe;
landlord n propriétaire m, logeur
m; (of pub etc) patron m; **landmark**
n (point m de) repère m; **to be a
landmark** (fig) faire date or époque;
landowner n propriétaire foncier
or terrien; **landscape** n paysage
m; **landslide** n (Geo) glissement m
(de terrain); (fig: Pol) raz-de-marée
(électoral)
lane [leɪn] n (in country) chemin m;
(Aut: of road) voie f; (: line of traffic) file
f; (in race) couloir m
language ['læŋgwɪdʒ] n langue f;
(way one speaks) langage m; **what ~s
do you speak?** quelles langues parlez-
vous?; **bad ~** grossieretés fpl, langage
grossier; **language laboratory** n
laboratoire m de langues; **language
school** n école f de langue
lantern ['læntn] n lanterne f
lap [læp] n (of track) tour m (de piste);
(of body): **in** or **on one's ~** sur les
genoux ▷ vt (also: **~ up**) laper ▷ vi
(waves) clapoter
lapel [lə'pɛl] n revers m
lapse [læps] n défaillance f; (in
behaviour) écart m (de conduite)

▷ *vi* (*Law*) cesser d'être en vigueur; (*contract*) expirer; **to ~ into bad habits** prendre de mauvaises habitudes; **~ of time** laps *m* de temps, intervalle *m*

laptop (computer) ['læptɔp-] *n* (ordinateur *m*) portable *m*

lard [lɑːd] *n* saindoux *m*

larder ['lɑːdəʳ] *n* garde-manger *m inv*

large [lɑːdʒ] *adj* grand(e); (*person, animal*) gros (grosse); **at ~** (*free*) en liberté; (*generally*) en général; pour la plupart; *see also* **by**; **largely** *adv* en grande partie; (*principally*) surtout; **large-scale** *adj* (*map, drawing etc*) à grande échelle; (*fig*) important(e)

lark [lɑːk] *n* (*bird*) alouette *f*; (*joke*) blague *f*, farce *f*

larrikin ['lærɪkɪn] *n* (*AUST, NZ inf*) fripon *m* (*inf*)

laryngitis [lærɪn'dʒaɪtɪs] *n* laryngite *f*

lasagne [lə'zænjə] *n* lasagne *f*

laser ['leɪzəʳ] *n* laser *m*; **laser printer** *n* imprimante *f* laser

lash [læʃ] *n* coup *m* de fouet; (*also:* **eye~**) cil *m* ▷ *vt* fouetter; (*tie*) attacher; **lash out** *vi*: **to ~ out (at** *or* **against sb/sth)** attaquer violemment (qn/qch)

lass [læs] (*BRIT*) *n* (jeune) fille *f*

last [lɑːst] *adj* dernier(-ière) ▷ *adv* en dernier; (*most recently*) la dernière fois; (*finally*) finalement ▷ *vi* durer; **~ week** la semaine dernière; **~ night** (*evening*) hier soir; (*night*) la nuit dernière; **at ~** enfin; **~ but one** avant-dernier(-ière); **lastly** *adv* en dernier lieu, pour finir; **last-minute** *adj* de dernière minute

latch [lætʃ] *n* loquet *m*; **latch onto** *vt fus* (*cling to: person, group*) s'accrocher à; (: *idea*) se mettre en tête

late [leɪt] *adj* (*not on time*) en retard; (*far on in day etc*) tardif(-ive) (: *edition, delivery*) dernier(-ière); (*dead*) défunt(e) ▷ *adv* tard; (*behind time, schedule*) en retard; **to be 10**

minutes ~ avoir 10 minutes de retard; **sorry I'm ~** désolé d'être en retard; **it's too ~** il est trop tard; **of ~** dernièrement; **in ~ May** vers la fin (du mois) de mai, fin mai; **the ~ Mr X** feu M. X; **latecomer** *n* retardataire *m/f*; **lately** *adv* récemment; **later** *adj* (*date etc*) ultérieur(e); (*version etc*) plus récent(e) ▷ *adv* plus tard; **latest** ['leɪtɪst] *adj* tout(e) dernier(-ière); **at the latest** au plus tard

lather ['lɑːðəʳ] *n* mousse *f* (de savon) ▷ *vt* savonner

Latin ['lætɪn] *n* latin *m* ▷ *adj* latin(e); **Latin America** *n* Amérique latine; **Latin American** *adj* latino-américain(e), d'Amérique latine ▷ *n* Latino-Américain(e)

latitude ['lætɪtjuːd] *n* (*also fig*) latitude *f*

latter ['lætəʳ] *adj* deuxième, dernier(-ière) ▷ *n*: **the ~** ce dernier, celui-ci

laugh [lɑːf] *n* rire *m* ▷ *vi* rire; **(to do sth) for a ~** (faire qch) pour rire; **laugh at** *vt fus* se moquer de; (*joke*) rire de; **laughter** *n* rire *m*; (*of several people*) rires *mpl*

launch [lɔːntʃ] *n* lancement *m*; (*also:* **motor ~**) vedette *f* ▷ *vt* (*ship, rocket, plan*) lancer; **launch into** *vt fus* se lancer dans

launder ['lɔːndəʳ] *vt* laver; (*fig: money*) blanchir

Launderette® [lɔːn'drɛt], (*US*) **Laundromat®** ['lɔːndrəmæt] *n* laverie *f* (automatique)

laundry ['lɔːndrɪ] *n* (*clothes*) linge *m*; (*business*) blanchisserie *f*; (*room*) buanderie *f*; **to do the ~** faire la lessive

lava ['lɑːvə] *n* lave *f*

lavatory ['lævətərɪ] *n* toilettes *fpl*

lavender ['lævəndəʳ] *n* lavande *f*

lavish ['lævɪʃ] *adj* (*amount*) copieux(-euse); (*person: giving freely*): **~ with** prodigue de ▷ *vt*: **to ~ sth on sb** prodiguer qch à qn; (*money*) dépenser qch sans compter pour qn

law [lɔ:] n loi f; (science) droit m; **lawful** adj légal(e), permis(e); **lawless** adj (action) illégal(e); (place) sans loi

lawn [lɔ:n] n pelouse f; **lawnmower** n tondeuse f à gazon

lawsuit ['lɔ:su:t] n procès m

lawyer ['lɔ:jəʳ] n (consultant, with company) juriste m; (for sales, wills etc) ≈ notaire m; (partner, in court) ≈ avocat m

lax [læks] adj relâché(e)

laxative ['læksətɪv] n laxatif m

lay [leɪ] pt of **lie** ▷ adj laïque; (not expert) profane ▷ vt (pt, pp **laid**) poser, mettre; (eggs) pondre; (trap) tendre; (plans) élaborer; **to ~ the table** mettre la table; **lay down** vt poser; (rules etc) établir; **to ~ down the law** (fig) faire la loi; **lay off** vt (workers) licencier; **lay on** vt (provide: meal etc) fournir; **lay out** vt (design) dessiner, concevoir; (display) disposer; (spend) dépenser; **lay-by** n (BRIT) aire f de stationnement (sur le bas-côté)

layer ['leɪəʳ] n couche f

layman ['leɪmən] (irreg) n (Rel) laïque m; (non-expert) profane m

layout ['leɪaut] n disposition f, plan m, agencement m; (Press) mise f en page

lazy ['leɪzɪ] adj paresseux(-euse)

lb. abbr (weight) = **pound**

lead¹ (pt, pp **led**) [li:d, lɛd] n (front position) tête f; (distance, time ahead) avance f; (clue) piste f; (Elec) fil m; (for dog) laisse f; (Theat) rôle principal ▷ vt (guide) mener, conduire; (be leader of) être à la tête de ▷ vi (Sport) mener, être en tête; **to ~ to** (road, pipe) mener à, conduire à; (result in) conduire à; aboutir à; **to be in the ~** (Sport) (in race) mener, être en tête; (in match) mener (à la marque); **to ~ sb to do sth** amener qn à faire qch; **to ~ the way** vt montrer le chemin; **lead up to** vt conduire à; (in conversation) en venir à

lead² [lɛd] n (metal) plomb m; (in pencil) mine f

leader ['li:dəʳ] n (of team) chef m; (of party etc) dirigeant(e), leader m; (Sport: in league) leader; (: in race) coureur m de tête; **leadership** n (position) direction f; **under the leadership of ...** sous la direction de ...; **qualities of leadership** qualités fpl de chef or de meneur

lead-free ['lɛdfri:] adj sans plomb

leading ['li:dɪŋ] adj de premier plan; (main) principal(e); (in race) de tête

lead singer [li:d-] n (in pop group) (chanteur m) vedette f

leaf (pl **leaves**) [li:f, li:vz] n feuille f; (of table) rallonge f; **to turn over a new ~** (fig) changer de conduite or d'existence; **leaf through** vt (book) feuilleter

leaflet ['li:flɪt] n prospectus m, brochure f; (Pol, Rel) tract m

league [li:g] n ligue f; (Football) championnat m; **to be in ~ with** avoir partie liée avec, être de mèche avec

leak [li:k] n (lit, fig) fuite f ▷ vi (pipe, liquid etc) fuir; (shoes) prendre l'eau; (ship) faire eau ▷ vt (liquid) répandre; (information) divulguer

lean (pt, pp **leaned** or **leant**) [li:n, lɛnt] adj maigre ▷ vt: **to ~ sth on** appuyer qch sur ▷ vi (slope) pencher; (rest): **to ~ against** s'appuyer contre; être appuyé(e) contre; **to ~ on** s'appuyer sur; **lean forward** vi se pencher en avant; **lean over** vi se pencher; **leaning** n: **leaning (towards)** penchant m (pour)

leant [lɛnt] pt, pp of **lean**

leap (pt, pp **leaped** or **leapt**) [li:p, lɛpt] n bond m, saut m ▷ vi bondir, sauter

leapt [lɛpt] pt, pp of **leap**

leap year n année f bissextile

learn (pt, pp **learned** or **learnt**) [lə:n, lə:nt] vt, vi apprendre; **to ~ (how) to do sth** apprendre à faire qch; **to ~ about sth** (Scol) étudier qch; (hear, read) apprendre qch; **learner** n débutant(e); (BRIT: also: **learner**

driver) (conducteur(-trice))
débutant(e); **learning** n savoir m
learnt [lə:nt] pp of **learn**
lease [li:s] n bail m ▷ vt louer à bail
leash [li:ʃ] n laisse f
least [li:st] adj: **the ~** (+ noun) le (la)
plus petit(e), le (la) moindre; (smallest
amount of) le moins de ▷ pron: **(the)
~** le moins (+ adv or + verb) le moins; (+
adj): **the ~** le (la) moins; **the ~ money**
le moins d'argent; **the ~ expensive** le
(la) moins cher (chère) **the ~ possible
effort** le moins d'effort possible; **at
~** au moins; (or rather) du moins; **you
could at ~ have written** tu aurais au
moins pu écrire; **not in the ~** pas le
moins du monde
leather ['lɛðəʳ] n cuir m
leave (pt, pp **left**) [li:v, lɛft] vt
laisser; (go away from) quitter; (forget)
oublier ▷ vi partir, s'en aller ▷ n
(time off) congé m; (Mil, also consent)
permission f; **what time does the
train/bus ~?** le train/le bus part à
quelle heure?; **to ~ sth to sb** (money
etc) laisser qch à qn; **to be left** rester;
there's some milk left over il reste
du lait; **~ it to me!** laissez-moi faire!,
je m'en occupe!; **on ~** en permission;
leave behind vt (also fig) laisser;
(forget) laisser, oublier; **leave out** vt
oublier, omettre
leaves [li:vz] npl of **leaf**
Lebanon ['lɛbənən] n Liban m
lecture ['lɛktʃəʳ] n conférence f;
(Scol) cours (magistral) ▷ vi donner
des cours; enseigner ▷ vt (scold)
sermonner, réprimander; **to give
a ~ (on)** faire une conférence (sur),
faire un cours (sur); **lecture hall**
n amphithéâtre m; **lecturer** n
(speaker) conférencier(-ière); (BRIT: at
university) professeur m (d'université),
prof m/f de fac (inf); **lecture theatre**
n = **lecture hall**

Be careful not to translate lecture
by the French word lecture.

led [lɛd] pt, pp of **lead**[1]

ledge [lɛdʒ] n (of window, on wall)
rebord m; (of mountain) saillie f,
corniche f
leek [li:k] n poireau m
left [lɛft] pt, pp of **leave** ▷ adj gauche
▷ adv à gauche ▷ n gauche f; **there
are two ~** il en reste deux; **on the
~, to the ~** à gauche; **the L~** (Pol)
la gauche; **left-hand** adj: **the left-
hand side** la gauche, le côté gauche;
left-hand drive n (vehicle) véhicule
m avec la conduite à gauche; **left-
handed** adj gaucher(-ère); (scissors
etc) pour gauchers; **left-luggage
locker** n (BRIT) (casier m à) consigne f
automatique; **left-luggage (office)**
n (BRIT) consigne f; **left-overs** npl
restes mpl; **left-wing** adj (Pol) de
gauche
leg [lɛg] n jambe f; (of animal) patte f;
(of furniture) pied m; (Culin: of chicken)
cuisse f; (of journey) étape f; **1st/2nd
~** (Sport) match m aller/retour; **~ of
lamb** (Culin) gigot m d'agneau
legacy ['lɛgəsɪ] n (also fig) héritage
m, legs m
legal ['li:gl] adj (permitted by law)
légal(e); (relating to law) juridique;
legal holiday n (US) n jour férié;
legalize vt légaliser; **legally** adv
légalement
legend ['lɛdʒənd] n légende f;
legendary ['lɛdʒəndərɪ] adj
légendaire
leggings ['lɛgɪŋz] npl caleçon m
legible ['lɛdʒəbl] adj lisible
legislation [lɛdʒɪs'leɪʃən] n
législation f
legislative ['lɛdʒɪslətɪv] adj
législatif(-ive)
legitimate [lɪ'dʒɪtɪmət] adj
légitime
leisure ['lɛʒəʳ] n (free time) temps
libre, loisirs mpl; **at ~** (tout) à loisir; **at
your ~** (later) à tête reposée; **leisure
centre** n (BRIT) centre m de loisirs;
leisurely adj tranquille, fait(e) sans
se presser

lemon ['lɛmən] n citron m;
lemonade n (fizzy) limonade f;
lemon tea n thé m au citron

lend (pt, pp **lent**) [lɛnd, lɛnt] vt: **to ~
sth (to sb)** prêter qch (à qn); **could
you ~ me some money?** pourriez-
vous me prêter de l'argent?

length [lɛŋθ] n longueur f; (section:
of road, pipe etc) morceau m, bout m;
~ of time durée f; **it is 2 metres in ~**
cela fait 2 mètres de long; **at ~** (at last)
enfin, à la fin; (lengthily) longuement;
lengthen vt allonger, prolonger ▷ vi
s'allonger; **lengthways** adv dans le
sens de la longueur, en long; **lengthy**
adj (très) long (longue)

lens [lɛnz] n lentille f; (of spectacles)
verre m; (of camera) objectif m

Lent [lɛnt] n carême m

lent [lɛnt] pt, pp of **lend**

lentil ['lɛntl] n lentille f

Leo ['liːəu] n le Lion

leopard ['lɛpəd] n léopard m

leotard ['liːətɑːd] n justaucorps m

leprosy ['lɛprəsɪ] n lèpre f

lesbian ['lɛzbɪən] n lesbienne f ▷ adj
lesbien(ne)

less [lɛs] adj moins de ▷ pron, adv
moins ▷ prep: **~ tax/10% discount**
avant impôt/moins 10% de remise;
~ than that/you moins que cela/
vous; **~ than half** moins de la moitié;
~ than ever moins que jamais; **~ and
~** de moins en moins; **the ~ he works
…** moins il travaille …; **lessen** vi
diminuer, s'amoindrir, s'atténuer ▷ vt
diminuer, réduire, atténuer; **lesser**
['lɛsər] adj moindre; **to a lesser
extent** or **degree** à un degré moindre

lesson ['lɛsn] n leçon f; **to teach sb a
~** (fig) donner une bonne leçon à qn

let (pt, pp **let**) [lɛt] vt laisser; (BRIT:
lease) louer); **to ~ sb do sth** laisser
qn faire qch; **to ~ sb know sth**
faire savoir qch à qn, prévenir qn de
qch; **to ~ go** lâcher prise; **to ~ go of
sth, to ~ sth go** lâcher qch; **~'s go**
allons-y; **~ him come** qu'il vienne;

"to ~" (BRIT) "à louer"; **let down** vt
(lower) baisser; (BRIT: tyre) dégonfler;
(disappoint) décevoir; **let in** vt laisser
entrer; (visitor etc) faire entrer; **let
off** vt (allow to leave) laisser partir;
(not punish) ne pas punir; (firework etc)
faire partir; (bomb) faire exploser; **let
out** vt laisser sortir; (scream) laisser
échapper; (BRIT: rent out) louer

lethal ['liːθl] adj mortel(le), fatal(e);
(weapon) meurtrier(-ère)

letter ['lɛtər] n lettre f; **letterbox** n
(BRIT) boîte f aux or à lettres

lettuce ['lɛtɪs] n laitue f, salade f

leukaemia, (US) **leukemia**
[luːˈkiːmɪə] n leucémie f

level ['lɛvl] adj (flat) plat(e), plan(e),
uni(e); (horizontal) horizontal(e) ▷ n
niveau m ▷ vt niveler, aplanir; **A ~s**
npl (BRIT) ≈ baccalauréat m; **to be ~
with** être au même niveau que; **to
draw ~ with** (runner, car) arriver à la
hauteur de, rattraper; **on the ~** (fig:
honest) régulier(-ière); **level crossing**
n (BRIT) passage m à niveau

lever ['liːvər] n levier m; **leverage** n
(influence): **leverage (on** or **with)**
prise f (sur)

levy ['lɛvɪ] n taxe f, impôt m ▷ vt (tax)
lever; (fine) infliger

liability [laɪəˈbɪlɪtɪ] n responsabilité
f; (handicap) handicap m

liable ['laɪəbl] adj (subject): **~ to**
sujet(te) à, passible de; (responsible):
~ (for) responsable (de); (likely): **~ to
do** susceptible de faire

liaise [liːˈeɪz] vi: **to ~ with** assurer la
liaison avec

liar ['laɪər] n menteur(-euse)

libel ['laɪbl] n diffamation f;
(document) écrit m diffamatoire ▷ vt
diffamer

liberal ['lɪbərl] adj libéral(e);
(generous): **~ with** prodigue de,
généreux(-euse) avec ▷ n: **L~** (Pol)
libéral(e); **Liberal Democrat** n (BRIT)
libéral(e)-démocrate m/f

liberate ['lɪbəreɪt] vt libérer

liberation [lɪbə'reɪʃən] n libération f

liberty ['lɪbətɪ] n liberté f; **to be at ~** (criminal) être en liberté; **at ~ to do** libre de faire; **to take the ~ of** prendre la liberté de, se permettre de

Libra ['liːbrə] n la Balance

librarian [laɪ'brɛərɪən] n bibliothécaire m/f

library ['laɪbrərɪ] n bibliothèque f

Be careful not to translate library by the French word librairie.

Libya ['lɪbɪə] n Libye f

lice [laɪs] npl of **louse**

licence, (US) **license** ['laɪsns] n autorisation f, permis m; (Comm) licence f; (Radio, TV) redevance f; **driving ~**, (US) **driver's license** permis m (de conduire)

license ['laɪsns] n (US) = **licence**; **licensed** adj (for alcohol) patenté(e) pour la vente des spiritueux, qui a une patente de débit de boissons; (car) muni(e) de la vignette; **license plate** n (US Aut) plaque f minéralogique; **licensing hours** (BRIT) npl heures fpl d'ouvertures (des pubs)

lick [lɪk] vt lécher; (inf: defeat) écraser, flanquer une piquette or raclée à; **to ~ one's lips** (fig) se frotter les mains

lid [lɪd] n couvercle m; (eyelid) paupière f

lie [laɪ] n mensonge m ▷ vi (pt, pp **lied**) (tell lies) mentir; (pt **lay**, pp **lain**) (rest) être étendu(e) or allongé(e) or couché(e) (: object: be situated) se trouver, être; **to ~ low** (fig) se cacher, rester caché(e); **to tell ~s** mentir; **lie about, lie around** vi (things) traîner; (BRIT: person) traînasser, flemmarder; **lie down** vi se coucher, s'étendre

Liechtenstein ['lɪktənstaɪn] n Liechtenstein m

lie-in ['laɪɪn] n (BRIT): **to have a ~** faire la grasse matinée

lieutenant [lɛf'tɛnənt, US luː'tɛnənt] n lieutenant m

life (pl **lives**) [laɪf, laɪvz] n vie f; **to come to ~** (fig) s'animer; **life assurance** n (BRIT) = **life insurance**; **lifeboat** n canot m or chaloupe f de sauvetage; **lifeguard** n surveillant m de baignade; **life insurance** n assurance-vie f; **life jacket** n gilet m or ceinture f de sauvetage; **lifelike** adj qui semble vrai(e) or vivant(e), ressemblant(e); (painting) réaliste; **life preserver** n (US) gilet m or ceinture f de sauvetage; **life sentence** n condamnation f à vie or à perpétuité; **lifestyle** n style m de vie; **lifetime** n: **in his lifetime** de son vivant

lift [lɪft] vt soulever, lever; (end) supprimer, lever ▷ vi (fog) se lever ▷ n (BRIT: elevator) ascenseur m; **to give sb a ~** (BRIT) emmener or prendre qn en voiture; **can you give me a ~ to the station?** pouvez-vous m'emmener à la gare?; **lift up** vt soulever; **lift-off** n décollage m

light [laɪt] n lumière f; (lamp) lampe f; (Aut: rear light) feu m; (: headlamp) phare m; (for cigarette etc): **have you got a ~?** avez-vous du feu? ▷ vt (pt, pp **lit**) (candle, cigarette, fire) allumer; (room) éclairer ▷ adj (room, colour) clair(e); (not heavy, also fig) léger(-ère); (not strenuous) peu fatigant(e); **lights** npl (traffic lights) feux mpl; **to come to ~** être dévoilé(e) or découvert(e); **in the ~ of** à la lumière de; étant donné; **light up** vi s'allumer; (face) s'éclairer; (smoke) allumer une cigarette or une pipe etc ▷ vt (illuminate) éclairer, illuminer; **light bulb** n ampoule f; **lighten** vt (light up) éclairer; (make lighter) éclaircir; (make less heavy) alléger; **lighter** n (also: **cigarette lighter**) briquet m; **light-hearted** adj gai(e), joyeux(-euse), enjoué(e); **lighthouse** n phare m; **lighting** n éclairage m; (in theatre) éclairages; **lightly** adv légèrement; **to get off lightly** s'en tirer à bon compte

lightning ['laɪtnɪŋ] n foudre f; (flash) éclair m

lightweight ['laɪtweɪt] *adj* (*suit*) léger(-ère) ▷ *n* (*Boxing*) poids léger

like [laɪk] *vt* aimer (bien) ▷ *prep* comme ▷ *adj* semblable, pareil(le) ▷ *n*: **the ~** (*pej*) (d')autres du même genre *or* acabit; **his ~s and dislikes** ses goûts *mpl or* préférences *fpl*; **I would ~, I'd ~** je voudrais, j'aimerais; **would you ~ a coffee?** voulez-vous du café?; **to be/look ~ sb/sth** ressembler à qn/qch; **what's he ~?** comment est-il?; **what does it look ~?** de quoi est-ce que ça a l'air?; **what does it taste ~?** quel goût est-ce que ça a?; **that's just ~ him** c'est bien de lui, ça lui ressemble; **do it ~ this** fais-le comme ceci; **it's nothing ~ …** ce n'est pas du tout comme …; **likeable** *adj* sympathique, agréable

likelihood ['laɪklɪhud] *n* probabilité *f*

likely ['laɪklɪ] *adj* (*result, outcome*) probable; (*excuse*) plausible; **he's ~ to leave** il va sûrement partir, il risque fort de partir; **not ~!** (*inf*) pas de danger!

likewise ['laɪkwaɪz] *adv* de même, pareillement

liking ['laɪkɪŋ] *n* (*for person*) affection *f*; (*for thing*) penchant *m*, goût *m*; **to be to sb's ~** être au goût de qn, plaire à qn

lilac ['laɪlək] *n* lilas *m*

Lilo® ['laɪləu] *n* matelas *m* pneumatique

lily ['lɪlɪ] *n* lis *m*; **~ of the valley** muguet *m*

limb [lɪm] *n* membre *m*

limbo ['lɪmbəu] *n*: **to be in ~** (*fig*) être tombé(e) dans l'oubli

lime [laɪm] *n* (*tree*) tilleul *m*; (*fruit*) citron vert, lime *f*; (*Geo*) chaux *f*

limelight ['laɪmlaɪt] *n*: **in the ~** (*fig*) en vedette, au premier plan

limestone ['laɪmstəun] *n* pierre *f* à chaux; (*Geo*) calcaire *m*

limit ['lɪmɪt] *n* limite *f* ▷ *vt* limiter; **limited** *adj* limité(e), restreint(e);

to be limited to se limiter à, ne concerner que

limousine ['lɪməzi:n] *n* limousine *f*

limp [lɪmp] *n*: **to have a ~** boiter ▷ *vi* boiter ▷ *adj* mou (molle)

line [laɪn] *n* (*gen*) ligne *f*; (*stroke*) trait *m*; (*wrinkle*) ride *f*; (*rope*) corde *f*; (*wire*) fil *m*; (*of poem*) vers *m*; (*row, series*) rangée *f*; (*of people*) file *f*, queue *f*; (*railway track*) voie *f*; (*Comm: series of goods*) article(s) *m(pl)*, ligne de produits; (*work*) métier *m* ▷ *vt* (*subj: trees, crowd*) border; **to ~ (with)** (*clothes*) doubler (de); (*box*) garnir *or* tapisser (de); **to stand in ~** (*US*) faire la queue; **in his ~ of business** dans sa partie, dans son rayon; **to be in ~ for sth** (*fig*) être en lice pour qch; **in ~ with** en accord avec, en conformité avec; **in a ~** aligné(e); **line up** *vi* s'aligner, se mettre en rang(s); (*in queue*) faire la queue ▷ *vt* aligner; (*event*) prévoir; (*find*) trouver; **to have sb/sth ~d up** avoir qn/qch en vue *or* de prévu(e)

linear ['lɪnɪəʳ] *adj* linéaire

linen ['lɪnɪn] *n* linge *m* (de corps *or* de maison); (*cloth*) lin *m*

liner ['laɪnəʳ] *n* (*ship*) paquebot *m* de ligne; (*for bin*) sac-poubelle *m*

line-up ['laɪnʌp] *n* (*US: queue*) file *f*; (*also*: **police ~**) parade *f* d'identification; (*Sport*) (*composition f* de l')équipe *f*

linger ['lɪŋgəʳ] *vi* s'attarder; traîner; (*smell, tradition*) persister

lingerie ['lænʒəri:] *n* lingerie *f*

linguist ['lɪŋgwɪst] *n* linguiste *m/f*; **to be a good ~** être doué(e) pour les langues; **linguistic** *adj* linguistique

lining ['laɪnɪŋ] *n* doublure *f*; (*of brakes*) garniture *f*

link [lɪŋk] *n* (*connection*) lien *m*, rapport *m*; (*Internet*) lien; (*of a chain*) maillon *m* ▷ *vt* relier, lier, unir; **links** *npl* (*Golf*) (terrain *m* de) golf *m*; **link up** *vt* relier ▷ *vi* (*people*) se rejoindre; (*companies etc*) s'associer

lion ['laɪən] n lion m; **lioness** n lionne f

lip [lɪp] n lèvre f; (of cup etc) rebord m; **lip-read** vi (irreg: like **read**) lire sur les lèvres; **lip salve** [-sælv] n pommade f pour les lèvres, pommade rosat; **lipstick** n rouge m à lèvres

liqueur [lɪ'kjuər] n liqueur f

liquid ['lɪkwɪd] n liquide m ▷ adj liquide; **liquidizer** ['lɪkwɪdaɪzər] n (BRIT Culin) mixer m

liquor ['lɪkər] n spiritueux m, alcool m; **liquor store** (US) n magasin m de vins et spiritueux

Lisbon ['lɪzbən] n Lisbonne

lisp [lɪsp] n zézaiement m ▷ vi zézayer

list [lɪst] n liste f ▷ vt (write down) inscrire; (make list of) faire la liste de; (enumerate) énumérer

listen ['lɪsn] vi écouter; **to ~ to** écouter; **listener** n auditeur(-trice)

lit [lɪt] pt, pp of **light**

liter ['liːtər] n (US) = **litre**

literacy ['lɪtərəsɪ] n degré m d'alphabétisation, fait m de savoir lire et écrire; (BRIT Scol) enseignement m de la lecture et de l'écriture

literal ['lɪtərl] adj littéral(e); **literally** adv littéralement; (really) réellement

literary ['lɪtərərɪ] adj littéraire

literate ['lɪtərət] adj qui sait lire et écrire; (educated) instruit(e)

literature ['lɪtrɪtʃər] n littérature f; (brochures etc) copie f publicitaire, prospectus mpl

litre, (US) **liter** ['liːtər] n litre m

litter ['lɪtər] n (rubbish) détritus mpl; (dirtier) ordures fpl; (young animals) portée f; **litter bin** n (BRIT) poubelle f

little ['lɪtl] adj (small) petit(e); (not much): **~ milk** peu de lait ▷ adv peu; **a ~ milk** un peu de lait; **a ~ bit** un peu; **as ~ as possible** le moins possible; **~ by ~** petit à petit, peu à peu; **little finger** n auriculaire m, petit doigt

live¹ [laɪv] adj (animal) vivant(e), en vie; (wire) sous tension; (broadcast) (transmis(e)) en direct; (unexploded) non explosé(e)

live² [lɪv] vi vivre; (reside) vivre, habiter; **to ~ in London** habiter (à) Londres; **where do you ~?** où habitez-vous?; **live together** vi vivre ensemble, cohabiter; **live up to** vt fus se montrer à la hauteur de

livelihood ['laɪvlɪhud] n moyens mpl d'existence

lively ['laɪvlɪ] adj vif (vive), plein(e) d'entrain; (place, book) vivant(e)

liven up ['laɪvn-] vt (room etc) égayer; (discussion, evening) animer ▷ vi s'animer

liver ['lɪvər] n foie m

lives [laɪvz] npl of **life**

livestock ['laɪvstɔk] n cheptel m, bétail m

living ['lɪvɪŋ] adj vivant(e), en vie ▷ n: **to earn** or **make a ~** gagner sa vie; **living room** n salle f de séjour

lizard ['lɪzəd] n lézard m

load [ləud] n (weight) poids m; (thing carried) chargement m, charge f; (Elec, Tech) charge ▷ vt charger; (also: **~ up**): **to ~ (with)** (lorry, ship) charger (de); (gun, camera) charger (avec); **a ~ of, ~s of** (fig) un or des tas de, des masses de; **to talk a ~ of rubbish** (inf) dire des bêtises; **loaded** adj (dice) pipé(e); (question) insidieux(-euse); (inf: rich) bourré(e) de fric

loaf (pl **loaves**) [ləuf, ləuvz] n pain m, miche f ▷ vi (also: **~ about, ~ around**) fainéanter, traîner

loan [ləun] n prêt m ▷ vt prêter; **on ~** prêté(e), en prêt

loathe [ləuð] vt détester, avoir en horreur

loaves [ləuvz] npl of **loaf**

lobby ['lɔbɪ] n hall m, entrée f; (Pol) groupe m de pression, lobby m ▷ vt faire pression sur

lobster ['lɔbstər] n homard m

local ['ləukl] adj local(e) ▷ n (BRIT: pub) pub m or café m du coin; **the locals** npl les gens mpl du pays or du coin; **local anaesthetic**, (US) **local anesthetic** n anesthésie locale; **local authority** n collectivité locale, municipalité f; **local government** n administration locale or municipale; **locally** ['ləukəlı] adv localement, dans les environs or la région

locate [ləu'keɪt] vt (find) trouver, repérer; (situate) situer; **to be ~d in** être situé à or en

location [ləu'keɪʃən] n emplacement m; **on ~** (Cine) en extérieur

> Be careful not to translate location by the French word location.

loch [lɔx] n lac m, loch m

lock [lɔk] n (of door, box) serrure f; (of canal) écluse f; (of hair) mèche f, boucle f ▷ vt (with key) fermer à clé ▷ vi (door etc) fermer à clé; (wheels) se bloquer; **lock in** vt enfermer; **lock out** vt enfermer dehors; (on purpose) mettre à la porte; **lock up** vt (person) enfermer; (house) fermer à clé ▷ vi tout fermer (à clé)

locker ['lɔkəʳ] n casier m; (in station) consigne f automatique; **locker-room** ['lɔkəʳruːm] (US) n (Sport) vestiaire m

locksmith ['lɔksmɪθ] n serrurier m

locomotive [ləukə'məutɪv] n locomotive f

locum ['ləukəm] n (Med) suppléant(e) de médecin etc

lodge [lɔdʒ] n pavillon m (de gardien); (also: **hunting ~**) pavillon de chasse ▷ vi (person): **to ~ with** être logé(e) chez, être en pension chez; (bullet) se loger ▷ vt (appeal etc) présenter; déposer; **to ~ a complaint** porter plainte; **lodger** n locataire m/f; (with room and meals) pensionnaire m/f

lodging ['lɔdʒɪŋ] n logement m

loft [lɔft] n grenier m; (apartment) grenier aménagé m en appartement (gén dans ancien entrepôt ou fabrique)

log [lɔg] n (of wood) bûche f; (Naut) livre m or journal m de bord; (of car) ≈

carte grise ▷ vt enregistrer; **log in, log on** vi (Comput) ouvrir une session, entrer dans le système; **log off, log out** vi (Comput) clore une session, sortir du système

logic ['lɔdʒɪk] n logique f; **logical** adj logique

login ['lɔgɪn] n (Comput) identifiant m

Loire [lwaː] n: **the (River) ~** la Loire

lollipop ['lɔlɪpɔp] n sucette f; **lollipop man/lady** (irreg) (BRIT) n contractuel(le) qui fait traverser la rue aux enfants

lolly ['lɔlɪ] n (inf: ice) esquimau m; (: lollipop) sucette f

London ['lʌndən] n Londres; **Londoner** n Londonien(ne)

lone [ləun] adj solitaire

loneliness ['ləunlɪnɪs] n solitude f, isolement m

lonely ['ləunlɪ] adj seul(e); (childhood etc) solitaire; (place) solitaire, isolé(e)

long [lɔŋ] adj long (longue) ▷ adv longtemps ▷ vi: **to ~ for sth/to do sth** avoir très envie de qch/de faire qch, attendre qch avec impatience/ attendre avec impatience de faire qch; **how ~ is this river/course?** quelle est la longueur de ce fleuve/ la durée de ce cours?; **6 metres ~** (long) de 6 mètres; **6 months ~** qui dure 6 mois, de 6 mois; **all night ~** toute la nuit; **he no ~er comes** il ne vient plus; **I can't stand it any ~er** je ne peux plus le supporter; **~ before** longtemps avant; **before ~** (+ future) avant peu, dans peu de temps; (+ past) peu de temps après; **don't be ~!** fais vite!, dépêche-toi!; **I shan't be ~** je n'en ai pas pour longtemps; **at ~ last** enfin; **so** or **as ~ as** à condition que + sub; **long-distance** adj (race) de fond; (call) interurbain(e); **long-haul** adj (flight) long-courrier; **longing** n désir m, envie f; (nostalgia) nostalgie f ▷ adj plein(e) d'envie or de nostalgie

longitude ['lɔŋgɪtjuːd] n longitude f

long: **long jump** n saut m en longueur; **long-life** adj (batteries etc) longue durée inv; (milk) longue conservation; **long-sighted** adj (BRIT) presbyte; (fig) prévoyant(e); **long-standing** adj de longue date; **long-term** adj à long terme

loo [lu:] n (BRIT inf) w.-c. mpl, petit coin

look [luk] vi (seem) sembler, paraître, avoir l'air; (building etc): **to ~ south/on to the sea** donner au sud/sur la mer ▷ n regard m; (appearance) air m, allure f, aspect m; **looks** npl (good looks) physique m, beauté f; **to ~ like** ressembler à; **to have a ~** regarder; **to have a ~ at sth** jeter un coup d'œil à qch; **~ (here)!** (annoyance) écoutez!; **look after** vt fus s'occuper de; (luggage etc: watch over) garder, surveiller; **look around** vi regarder autour de soi; **look at** vt fus regarder; (problem etc) examiner; **look back** vi: **to ~ back at sth/sb** se retourner pour regarder qch/qn; **to ~ back on** (event, period) évoquer, repenser à; **look down on** vt fus (fig) regarder de haut, dédaigner; **look for** vt fus chercher; **we're ~ing for a hotel/restaurant** nous cherchons un hôtel/restaurant; **look forward to** vt fus attendre avec impatience; **~ing forward to hearing from you** (in letter) dans l'attente de vous lire; **look into** vt fus (matter, possibility) examiner, étudier; **look out** vi (beware): **to ~ out (for)** prendre garde (à), faire attention (à); **~ out!** attention!; **look out for** vt fus (seek) être à la recherche de; (try to spot) guetter; **look round** vt fus (house, shop) faire le tour de ▷ vi (turn) regarder derrière soi, se retourner; **look through** vt fus (papers, book) examiner (: briefly) parcourir; **look up** vi lever les yeux; (improve) s'améliorer ▷ vt (word) chercher; **look up to** vt fus avoir du respect pour; **lookout** n (tower etc) poste m de guet; (person)

guetteur m; **to be on the lookout (for)** guetter

loom [lu:m] vi (also: ~ up) surgir; (event) paraître imminent(e); (threaten) menacer

loony ['lu:nɪ] adj, n (inf) timbré(e), cinglé(e) m/f

loop [lu:p] n boucle f ▷ vt: **to ~ sth round sth** passer qch autour de qch; **loophole** n (fig) porte f de sortie; échappatoire f

loose [lu:s] adj (knot, screw) desserré(e); (clothes) vague, ample, lâche; (hair) dénoué(e), épars(e); (not firmly fixed) pas solide; (morals, discipline) relâché(e); (translation) approximatif(-ive) ▷ n: **to be on the ~** être en liberté; **~ connection** (Elec) mauvais contact; **to be at a ~ end** or (US) **at ~ ends** (fig) ne pas trop savoir quoi faire; **loosely** adv sans serrer; (imprecisely) approximativement; **loosen** vt desserrer, relâcher, défaire

loot [lu:t] n butin m ▷ vt piller

lop-sided ['lɔp'saɪdɪd] adj de travers, asymétrique

lord [lɔːd] n seigneur m; **L~ Smith** lord Smith; **the L~** (Rel) le Seigneur; **my L~** (to noble) Monsieur le comte/le baron; (to judge) Monsieur le juge; (to bishop) Monseigneur; **good L~!** mon Dieu!; **Lords** npl (BRIT Pol): **the (House of) Lords** la Chambre des Lords

lorry ['lɔrɪ] n (BRIT) camion m; **lorry driver** n (BRIT) camionneur m, routier m

lose (pt, pp **lost**) [lu:z, lɔst] vt perdre ▷ vi perdre; **I've lost my wallet/passport** j'ai perdu mon portefeuille/passeport; **to ~ (time)** (clock) retarder; **lose out** vi être perdant(e); **loser** n perdant(e)

loss [lɔs] n perte f; **to make a ~** enregistrer une perte; **to be at a ~** être perplexe or embarrassé(e)

lost [lɔst] pt, pp of **lose** ▷ adj perdu(e); **to get ~** vi se perdre;

I'm ~ je me suis perdu; ~ **and found property** n (US) objets trouvés; ~ **and found** n (US) (bureau m des) objets trouvés; **lost property** n (BRIT) objets trouvés; **lost property office** or **department** (bureau m des) objets trouvés

lot [lɔt] n (at auctions, set) lot m; (destiny) sort m, destinée f; **the ~** (everything) le tout; (everyone) tous mpl, toutes fpl; **a ~** beaucoup; **a ~ of** beaucoup de; **~s of** des tas de; **to draw ~s (for sth)** tirer (qch) au sort

lotion ['ləʊʃən] n lotion f

lottery ['lɔtərɪ] n loterie f

loud [laʊd] adj bruyant(e), sonore; (voice) fort(e); (condemnation etc) vigoureux(-euse); (gaudy) voyant(e), tapageur(-euse) ▷ adv (speak etc) fort; **out ~** tout haut; **loudly** adv fort, bruyamment; **loudspeaker** n haut-parleur m

lounge [laʊndʒ] n salon m; (of airport) salle f; (BRIT: also: ~ **bar**) (salle de) café m or bar m ▷ vi (also: ~ **about**, ~ **around**) se prélasser, paresser

louse (pl **lice**) [laʊs, laɪs] n pou m

lousy ['laʊzɪ] (inf) adj (bad quality) infect(e), moche; **I feel ~** je suis mal fichu(e)

love [lʌv] n amour m ▷ vt aimer; (caringly, kindly) aimer beaucoup; **I ~ chocolate** j'adore le chocolat; **to ~ to do** aimer beaucoup or adorer faire; **"15 ~"** (Tennis) "15 à rien or zéro"; **to be/fall in ~ with** être/tomber amoureux(-euse) de; **to make ~** faire l'amour; **~ from Anne, ~, Anne** affectueusement, Anne; **I ~ you** je t'aime; **love affair** n liaison (amoureuse); **love life** n vie sentimentale

lovely ['lʌvlɪ] adj (pretty) ravissant(e); (friend, wife) charmant(e); (holiday, surprise) très agréable, merveilleux(-euse)

lover ['lʌvəʳ] n amant m; (person in love) amoureux(-euse); (amateur): **a ~**

of un(e) ami(e) de, un(e) amoureux(-euse) de

loving ['lʌvɪŋ] adj affectueux(-euse), tendre, aimant(e)

low [ləʊ] adj bas (basse); (quality) mauvais(e), inférieur(e) ▷ adv bas ▷ n (Meteorology) dépression f; **to feel ~** se sentir déprimé(e); **he's very ~** (ill) il est bien bas or très affaibli; **to turn (down) ~** vt baisser; **to be ~ on** (supplies etc) être à court de; **to reach a new** or **an all-time ~** tomber au niveau le plus bas; **low-alcohol** adj à faible teneur en alcool, peu alcoolisé(e); **low-calorie** adj hypocalorique

lower ['ləʊəʳ] adj inférieur(e) ▷ vt baisser; (resistance) diminuer; **to ~ o.s. to** s'abaisser à

low-fat ['ləʊ'fæt] adj maigre

loyal ['lɔɪəl] adj loyal(e), fidèle; **loyalty** n loyauté f, fidélité f; **loyalty card** n carte f de fidélité

L-plates ['ɛlpleɪts] npl (BRIT) plaques fpl (obligatoires) d'apprenti conducteur

Lt abbr (= lieutenant) Lt.

Ltd abbr (Comm: = limited) ≈ SA

luck [lʌk] n chance f; **bad ~** malchance f, malheur m; **good ~!** bonne chance!; **bad** or **hard** or **tough ~!** pas de chance!; **luckily** adv heureusement, par bonheur; **lucky** adj (person) qui a de la chance; (coincidence) heureux(-euse); (number etc) qui porte bonheur

lucrative ['lu:krətɪv] adj lucratif(-ive), rentable, qui rapporte

ludicrous ['lu:dɪkrəs] adj ridicule, absurde

luggage ['lʌgɪdʒ] n bagages mpl; **our ~ hasn't arrived** nos bagages ne sont pas arrivés; **could you send someone to collect our ~?** pourriez-vous envoyer quelqu'un chercher nos bagages?; **luggage rack** n (in train) porte-bagages m inv; (on car) galerie f

lukewarm ['lu:kwɔ:m] adj tiède

lull [lʌl] n accalmie f; (in conversation) pause f ▷ vt: **to ~ sb to sleep** bercer qn pour qu'il s'endorme; **to be ~ed into a false sense of security** s'endormir dans une fausse sécurité

lullaby ['lʌləbaɪ] n berceuse f

lumber ['lʌmbə'] n (wood) bois m de charpente; (junk) bric-à-brac m inv ▷ vt (BRIT inf): **to ~ sb with sth/sb** coller or refiler qch/qn à qn

luminous ['luːmɪnəs] adj lumineux(-euse)

lump [lʌmp] n morceau m; (in sauce) grumeau m; (swelling) grosseur f ▷ vt (also: **~ together**) réunir, mettre en tas; **lump sum** n somme globale or forfaitaire; **lumpy** adj (sauce) qui a des grumeaux; (bed) défoncé(e), peu confortable

lunatic ['luːnətɪk] n fou (folle), dément(e) ▷ adj fou (folle), dément(e)

lunch [lʌntʃ] n déjeuner m ▷ vi déjeuner; **lunch break, lunch hour** n pause f de midi, heure f du déjeuner; **lunchtime** n: **it's lunchtime** c'est l'heure du déjeuner

lung [lʌŋ] n poumon m

lure [luə'] n (attraction) attrait m, charme m; (in hunting) appât m, leurre m ▷ vt attirer or persuader par la ruse

lurk [ləːk] vi se tapir, se cacher

lush [lʌʃ] adj luxuriant(e)

lust [lʌst] n (sexual) désir (sexuel); (Rel) luxure f; (fig): **~ for** soif f de

Luxembourg ['lʌksəmbəːg] n Luxembourg m

luxurious [lʌg'zjuərɪəs] adj luxueux(-euse)

luxury ['lʌkʃərɪ] n luxe m ▷ cpd de luxe

Lycra® ['laɪkrə] n Lycra® m

lying ['laɪɪŋ] n mensonge(s) m(pl) ▷ adj (statement, story) mensonger(-ère), faux (fausse); (person) menteur(-euse)

Lyons ['ljɔ̃] n Lyon m

lyrics ['lɪrɪks] npl (of song) paroles fpl

m. abbr (= metre) m; (= million) M; (= mile) mi

ma [mɑː] (inf) n maman f

M.A. n abbr (Scol) = **Master of Arts**

mac [mæk] n (BRIT) imper(méable m) m

macaroni [mækə'rəunɪ] n macaronis mpl

Macedonia [mæsɪ'dəunɪə] n Macédoine f; **Macedonian** [mæsɪ'dəunɪən] adj macédonien(ne) ▷ n Macédonien(ne); (Ling) macédonien m

machine [mə'ʃiːn] n machine f ▷ vt (dress etc) coudre à la machine; (Tech) usiner; **machine gun** n mitrailleuse f; **machinery** n machinerie f, machines fpl; (fig) mécanisme(s) m(pl); **machine washable** adj (garment) lavable en machine

macho ['mætʃəu] adj macho inv

mackerel ['mækrl] n (pl inv) maquereau m

mackintosh ['mækɪntɔʃ] n (BRIT) imperméable m

mad [mæd] *adj* fou (folle); (*foolish*) insensé(e); (*angry*) furieux(-euse); **to be ~ (keen) about** *or* **on sth** (*inf*) être follement passionné de qch, être fou de qch

Madagascar [mædəˈɡæskəʳ] *n* Madagascar *m*

madam [ˈmædəm] *n* madame *f*

mad cow disease *n* maladie *f* des vaches folles

made [meɪd] *pt, pp of* **make; made-to-measure** *adj* (BRIT) fait(e) sur mesure; **made-up** [ˈmeɪdʌp] *adj* (*story*) inventé(e), fabriqué(e)

madly [ˈmædlɪ] *adv* follement; **~ in love** éperdument amoureux(-euse)

madman [ˈmædmən] (*irreg*) *n* fou *m*, aliéné *m*

madness [ˈmædnɪs] *n* folie *f*

Madrid [məˈdrɪd] *n* Madrid

Mafia [ˈmæfɪə] *n* maf(f)ia *f*

mag [mæg] *n abbr* (BRIT inf: = *magazine*) magazine *m*

magazine [mægəˈziːn] *n* (*Press*) magazine *m*, revue *f*; (*Radio, TV*) magazine

maggot [ˈmæɡət] *n* ver *m*, asticot *m*

magic [ˈmædʒɪk] *n* magie *f* ▷ *adj* magique; **magical** *adj* magique; (*experience, evening*) merveilleux(-euse); **magician** [məˈdʒɪʃən] *n* magicien(ne)

magistrate [ˈmædʒɪstreɪt] *n* magistrat *m*; juge *m*

magnet [ˈmæɡnɪt] *n* aimant *m*; **magnetic** [mæɡˈnɛtɪk] *adj* magnétique

magnificent [mæɡˈnɪfɪsnt] *adj* superbe, magnifique; (*splendid: robe, building*) somptueux(-euse), magnifique

magnify [ˈmæɡnɪfaɪ] *vt* grossir; (*sound*) amplifier; **magnifying glass** *n* loupe *f*

magpie [ˈmæɡpaɪ] *n* pie *f*

mahogany [məˈhɔɡənɪ] *n* acajou *m*

maid [meɪd] *n* bonne *f*; (*in hotel*) femme *f* de chambre; **old ~** (*pej*) vieille fille

maiden name *n* nom *m* de jeune fille

mail [meɪl] *n* poste *f*; (*letters*) courrier *m* ▷ *vt* envoyer (par la poste); **by ~** par la poste; **mailbox** *n* (US, also Comput) boîte *f* aux lettres; **mailing list** *n* liste *f* d'adresses; **mailman** *n* (US) facteur *m*; **mail-order** *n* vente *f* or achat *m* par correspondance

main [meɪn] *adj* principal(e) ▷ *n* (*pipe*) conduite principale, canalisation *f*; **the ~s** (*Elec*) le secteur; **the ~ thing** l'essentiel *m*; **in the ~** dans l'ensemble; **main course** *n* (*Culin*) plat *m* de résistance; **mainland** *n* continent *m*; **mainly** *adv* principalement, surtout; **main road** *n* grand axe, route nationale; **mainstream** *n* (*fig*) courant principal; **main street** *n* rue *f* principale

maintain [meɪnˈteɪn] *vt* entretenir; (*continue*) maintenir, préserver; (*affirm*) soutenir; **maintenance** [ˈmeɪntənəns] *n* entretien *m*; (*Law: alimony*) pension *f* alimentaire

maisonette [meɪzəˈnɛt] *n* (BRIT) appartement *m* en duplex

maize [meɪz] *n* (BRIT) maïs *m*

majesty [ˈmædʒɪstɪ] *n* majesté *f*; (*title*): **Your M~** Votre Majesté

major [ˈmeɪdʒəʳ] *n* (*Mil*) commandant *m* ▷ *adj* (*important*) important(e); (*most important*) principal(e); (*Mus*) majeur(e) ▷ *vi* (US Scol): **to ~ (in)** se spécialiser (en)

Majorca [məˈjɔːkə] *n* Majorque *f*

majority [məˈdʒɔrɪtɪ] *n* majorité *f*

make [meɪk] *vt* (*pt, pp* **made**) faire; (*manufacture*) faire, fabriquer; (*earn*) gagner; (*decision*) prendre; (*friend*) se faire; (*speech*) faire, prononcer; (*cause to be*): **to ~ sb sad** *etc* rendre qn triste *etc*; (*force*): **to ~ sb do sth** obliger qn à faire qch, faire faire qch à qn; (*equal*): **2 and 2 ~ 4** 2 et 2 font 4 ▷ *n* (*manufacture*) fabrication *f*; (*brand*) marque *f*; **to ~ the bed** faire le lit; **to ~ a fool of sb** (*ridicule*) ridiculiser qn; (*trick*) avoir or duper qn; **to ~ a profit** faire un or des bénéfice(s); **to ~ a loss** essuyer une perte; **to ~ it** (in time etc) y arriver; (succeed) réussir; **what time do you ~ it?** quelle heure avez-vous?; **I ~ it £249** d'après mes calculs ça fait 249 livres; **to be made of** être en; **to ~ do with** se contenter de; se débrouiller avec; **make off** vi filer; **make out** vt (write out: cheque) faire; (decipher) déchiffrer; (understand) comprendre; (see) distinguer; (claim, imply) prétendre, vouloir faire croire; **make up** vt (invent) inventer, imaginer; (constitute) constituer; (parcel, bed) faire ▷ vi se réconcilier; (with cosmetics) se maquiller, se farder; **to be made up of** se composer de; **make up for** vt fus compenser; (lost time) rattraper; **makeover** ['meɪkəʊvə'] n (by beautician) soins mpl de maquillage; (change of image) changement m d'image; **maker** n fabricant m; (of film, programme) réalisateur(-trice); **makeshift** adj provisoire, improvisé(e); **make-up** n maquillage m

making ['meɪkɪŋ] n (fig): **in the ~** en formation or gestation; **to have the ~s of** (actor, athlete) avoir l'étoffe de

malaria [mə'lɛərɪə] n malaria f, paludisme m

Malaysia [mə'leɪzɪə] n Malaisie f

male [meɪl] n (Biol, Elec) mâle m ▷ adj (sex, attitude) masculin(e); (animal) mâle; (child etc) du sexe masculin

malicious [mə'lɪʃəs] adj méchant(e), malveillant(e)

  Be careful not to translate malicious by the French word malicieux.

malignant [mə'lɪgnənt] adj (Med) malin(-igne)

mall [mɔːl] n (also: **shopping ~**) centre commercial

mallet ['mælɪt] n maillet m

malnutrition [mælnjuː'trɪʃən] n malnutrition f

malpractice [mæl'præktɪs] n faute professionnelle; négligence f

malt [mɔːlt] n malt m ▷ cpd (whisky) pur malt

Malta ['mɔːltə] n Malte f; **Maltese** [mɔːl'tiːz] adj maltais(e) ▷ n (pl inv) Maltais(e)

mammal ['mæml] n mammifère m

mammoth ['mæməθ] n mammouth m ▷ adj géant(e), monstre

man (pl **men**) [mæn, mɛn] n homme m; (Sport) joueur m; (Chess) pièce f ▷ vt (Naut: ship) garnir d'hommes; (machine) assurer le fonctionnement de; (Mil: gun) servir; (: post) être de service à; **an old ~** un vieillard; **~ and wife** mari et femme

manage ['mænɪdʒ] vi se débrouiller; (succeed) y arriver, réussir ▷ vt (business) gérer; (team, operation) diriger; (control: ship) manier, manœuvrer; (: person) savoir s'y prendre avec; **to ~ to do** se débrouiller pour faire; (succeed) réussir à faire; **manageable** adj maniable; (task etc) faisable; (number) raisonnable; **management** n (running) administration f, direction f; (people in charge: of business, firm) dirigeants mpl, cadres mpl; (: of hotel, shop, theatre) direction; **manager** n (of business) directeur m; (of institution etc) administrateur m; (of department, unit) responsable m/f, chef m; (of hotel etc) gérant m; (Sport) manager m; (of artist) impresario m; **manageress** n directrice f; (of hotel etc) gérante f; **managerial** [mænɪ'dʒɪərɪəl] adj directorial(e); (skills) de cadre, de gestion; **managing director** n directeur général

mandarin ['mændərɪn] n (also: **~ orange**) mandarine f

mandate ['mændeɪt] n mandat m

mandatory ['mændətərɪ] adj obligatoire

mane [meɪn] n crinière f

m

maneuver [məˈnuːvəʳ] (US) n
= **manoeuvre**

mangetout [ˈmɔ̃ŋʒˈtuː] n mangetout m inv

mango [ˈmæŋgəu] (pl **mangoes**) n
mangue f

man: **manhole** n trou m d'homme;
manhood n (age) âge m d'homme;
(manliness) virilité f

mania [ˈmeɪnɪə] n manie f; **maniac**
[ˈmeɪnɪæk] n maniaque m/f; (fig)
fou (folle)

manic [ˈmænɪk] adj maniaque

manicure [ˈmænɪkjuəʳ] n manucure f

manifest [ˈmænɪfest] vt manifester
▷ adj manifeste, évident(e)

manifesto [mænɪˈfestəu] n (Pol)
manifeste m

manipulate [məˈnɪpjuleɪt] vt
manipuler; (system, situation)
exploiter

man: mankind [mænˈkaɪnd] n
humanité f, genre humain; **manly** adj
viril(e); **man-made** adj artificiel(le);
(fibre) synthétique

manner [ˈmænəʳ] n manière f,
façon f; (behaviour) attitude f,
comportement m; **manners** npl
(good) ~s (bonnes) manières f; **bad ~s**
mauvaises manières f; **all ~ of** toutes
sortes de

manoeuvre, (US) **maneuver**
[məˈnuːvəʳ] vt (move) manœuvrer;
(manipulate: person) manipuler;
(: situation) exploiter ▷ n manœuvre f

manpower [ˈmænpauəʳ] n main-
d'œuvre f

mansion [ˈmænʃən] n château m,
manoir m

manslaughter [ˈmænslɔːtəʳ] n
homicide m involontaire

mantelpiece [ˈmæntlpiːs] n
cheminée f

manual [ˈmænjuəl] adj manuel(le)
▷ n manuel m

manufacture [mænjuˈfæktʃəʳ]
vt fabriquer ▷ n fabrication f;
manufacturer n fabricant m

manure [məˈnjuəʳ] n fumier m;
(artificial) engrais m

manuscript [ˈmænjuskrɪpt] n
manuscrit m

many [ˈmɛnɪ] adj beaucoup de, de
nombreux(-euses) ▷ pron beaucoup,
un grand nombre; **a great ~** un grand
nombre (de); **~ a ...** bien des ..., plus
d'un(e) ...

map [mæp] n carte f; (of town) plan
m; **can you show it to me on the
~?** pouvez-vous me l'indiquer sur la
carte?; **map out** vt tracer; (fig: task)
planifier

maple [ˈmeɪpl] n érable m

mar [mɑːʳ] vt gâcher, gâter

marathon [ˈmærəθən] n
marathon m

marble [ˈmɑːbl] n marbre m; (toy)
bille f

March [mɑːtʃ] n mars m

march [mɑːtʃ] vi marcher au pas;
(demonstrators) défiler ▷ n marche f;
(demonstration) manifestation f

mare [mɛəʳ] n jument f

margarine [mɑːdʒəˈriːn] n
margarine f

margin [ˈmɑːdʒɪn] n marge f;
marginal adj marginal(e); **marginal
seat** (Pol) siège disputé; **marginally**
adv très légèrement, sensiblement

marigold [ˈmærɪgəuld] n souci m

marijuana [mærɪˈwɑːnə] n
marijuana f

marina [məˈriːnə] n marina f

marinade n [mærɪˈneɪd] marinade f

marinate [ˈmærɪneɪt] vt (faire)
mariner

marine [məˈriːn] adj marin(e) ▷ n
fusilier marin; (US) marine m

marital [ˈmærɪtl] adj matrimonial(e);
marital status n situation f de
famille

maritime [ˈmærɪtaɪm] adj maritime

marjoram [ˈmɑːdʒərəm] n
marjolaine f

mark [mɑːk] n marque f; (of skid
etc) trace f; (BRIT Scol) note f; (oven

temperature): **(gas) ~ 4** thermostat
m 4 ▷ vt *(also Sport: player)* marquer;
(stain) tacher; *(BRIT Scol)* corriger,
noter; **to ~ time** marquer le pas;
marked *adj (obvious)* marqué(e),
net(te); **marker** n *(sign)* jalon m;
(bookmark) signet m
market ['mɑːkɪt] n marché m ▷ vt
(Comm) commercialiser; **marketing**
n marketing m; **marketplace** n
place f du marché; *(Comm)* marché
m; **market research** n étude f de
marché
marmalade ['mɑːməleɪd] n
confiture f d'oranges
maroon [mə'ruːn] vt: **to be ~ed** être
abandonné(e); *(fig)* être bloqué(e)
▷ adj *(colour)* bordeaux inv
marquee [mɑː'kiː] n chapiteau m
marriage ['mærɪdʒ] n mariage m;
marriage certificate n extrait m
d'acte de mariage
married ['mærɪd] adj marié(e); *(life,
love)* conjugal(e)
marrow ['mærəu] n *(of bone)* moelle
f; *(vegetable)* courge f
marry ['mærɪ] vt épouser, se marier
avec; *(subj: father, priest etc)* marier
▷ vi *(also: **get married**)* se marier
Mars [mɑːz] n *(planet)* Mars f
Marseilles [mɑː'seɪ] n Marseille
marsh [mɑːʃ] n marais m,
marécage m
marshal ['mɑːʃl] n maréchal m;
(US: fire, police) ≈ capitaine m; *(for
demonstration, meeting)* membre m du
service d'ordre ▷ vt rassembler
martyr ['mɑːtər] n martyr(e)
marvel ['mɑːvl] n merveille f
▷ vi: **to ~ (at)** s'émerveiller (de);
marvellous, *(US)* **marvelous** adj
merveilleux(-euse)
Marxism ['mɑːksɪzəm] n
marxisme m
Marxist ['mɑːksɪst] adj, n marxiste
(m/f)
marzipan ['mɑːzɪpæn] n pâte f
d'amandes

mascara [mæs'kɑːrə] n mascara m
mascot ['mæskət] n mascotte f
masculine ['mæskjulɪn] adj
masculin(e) ▷ n masculin m
mash [mæʃ] vt *(Culin)* faire une purée
de; **mashed potato(es)** n(pl) purée f
de pommes de terre
mask [mɑːsk] n masque m ▷ vt
masquer
mason ['meɪsn] n *(also: **stone~**)*
maçon m; *(also: **free~**)* franc-maçon
m; **masonry** n maçonnerie f
mass [mæs] n multitude f, masse
f; *(Physics)* masse; *(Rel)* messe f
▷ cpd *(communication)* de masse;
(unemployment) massif(-ive) ▷ vi se
masser; **masses** npl: **the ~es** les
masses; **~es of** *(inf)* des tas de
massacre ['mæsəkər] n massacre m
massage ['mæsɑːʒ] n massage m
▷ vt masser
massive ['mæsɪv] adj énorme,
massif(-ive)
mass media npl mass-media mpl
mass-produce ['mæsprə'djuːs] vt
fabriquer en série
mast [mɑːst] n mât m; *(Radio, TV)*
pylône m
master ['mɑːstər] n maître m; *(in
secondary school)* professeur m; *(in
primary school)* instituteur m; *(title for
boys)*: **M~ X** Monsieur X ▷ vt maîtriser;
(learn) apprendre à fond; **Master of Arts/
Science (MA/MSc)** n ≈ titulaire m/f
d'une maîtrise (en lettres/science);
**M~ of Arts/Science degree (MA/
MSc)** n ≈ maîtrise f; **mastermind** n
esprit supérieur ▷ vt diriger, être le
cerveau de; **masterpiece** n chef-
d'œuvre m
masturbate ['mæstəbeɪt] vi se
masturber
mat [mæt] n petit tapis; *(also: **door~**)*
paillasson m; *(also: **table~**)* set m de
table ▷ adj = **matt**
match [mætʃ] n allumette f; *(game)*
match m, partie f; *(fig)* égal(e) ▷ vt
*(also: **~ up**)* assortir; *(go well with)*

aller bien avec, s'assortir à; (*equal*) égaler, valoir ▷ vi être assorti(e); **to be a good ~** être bien assorti(e); **matchbox** n boîte f d'allumettes; **matching** adj assorti(e)

mate [meɪt] n (*inf*) copain (copine); (*animal*) partenaire m/f, mâle (femelle); (*in merchant navy*) second m ▷ vi s'accoupler

material [mə'tɪərɪəl] n (*substance*) matière f, matériau m; (*cloth*) tissu m, étoffe f; (*information, data*) données fpl ▷ adj matériel(le); (*relevant: evidence*) pertinent(e); **materials** npl (*equipment*) matériaux mpl

materialize [mə'tɪərɪəlaɪz] vi se matérialiser, se réaliser

maternal [mə'tə:nl] adj maternel(le)

maternity [mə'tə:nɪtɪ] n maternité f; **maternity hospital** n maternité f; **maternity leave** n congé m de maternité

math [mæθ] n (*us: = mathematics*) maths fpl

mathematical [mæθə'mætɪkl] adj mathématique

mathematician [mæθəmə'tɪʃən] n mathématicien(ne)

mathematics [mæθə'mætɪks] n mathématiques fpl

maths [mæθs] n abbr (BRIT: = mathematics) maths fpl

matinée ['mætɪneɪ] n matinée f

matron ['meɪtrən] n (*in hospital*) infirmière-chef f; (*in school*) infirmière f

matt [mæt] adj mat(e)

matter ['mætər] n question f; (*Physics*) matière f, substance f; (*Med: pus*) pus m ▷ vi importer; **matters** npl (*affairs, situation*) la situation; **it doesn't ~** cela n'a pas d'importance; (*I don't mind*) cela ne fait rien; **what's the ~?** qu'est-ce qu'il y a?, qu'est-ce qui ne va pas?; **no ~ what** quoi qu'il arrive; **as a ~ of course** tout naturellement; **as a ~ of fact** en fait; **reading ~** (BRIT) de quoi lire, de la lecture

mattress ['mætrɪs] n matelas m

mature [mə'tjuər] adj mûr(e); (*cheese*) fait(e); (*wine*) arrive(e) à maturité ▷ vi mûrir; (*cheese, wine*) se faire; **mature student** n étudiant(e) plus âgé(e) que la moyenne; **maturity** n maturité f

maul [mɔ:l] vt lacérer

mauve [məuv] adj mauve

max abbr = **maximum**

maximize ['mæksɪmaɪz] vt (*profits etc, chances*) maximiser

maximum (pl **maxima**) ['mæksɪməm, -mə] adj maximum ▷ n maximum m

May [meɪ] n mai m

may [meɪ] (*conditional* **might**) vi (*indicating possibility*): **he ~ come** il se peut qu'il vienne; (*be allowed to*): **~ I smoke?** puis-je fumer?; (*wishes*): **~ God bless you!** (que) Dieu vous bénisse!; **you ~ as well go** vous feriez aussi bien d'y aller

maybe ['meɪbi:] adv peut-être; **~ he'll ...** peut-être qu'il ...

May Day n le Premier mai

mayhem ['meɪhɛm] n grabuge m

mayonnaise [meɪə'neɪz] n mayonnaise f

mayor [mɛər] n maire m; **mayoress** n (*female mayor*) maire m; (*wife of mayor*) épouse f du maire

maze [meɪz] n labyrinthe m, dédale m

MD n abbr (Comm) = **managing director**

me [mi:] pron me, m' + *vowel or h mute*; (*stressed, after prep*) moi; **it's me** c'est moi; **he heard me** il m'a entendu; **give me a book** donnez-moi un livre; **it's for me** c'est pour moi

meadow ['mɛdəu] n prairie f, pré m

meagre, (*us*) **meager** ['mi:gər] adj maigre

meal [mi:l] n repas m; (*flour*) farine f; **mealtime** n heure f du repas

mean [mi:n] adj (*with money*) avare, radin(e); (*unkind*) mesquin(e), méchant(e); (*shabby*) misérable;

(*average*) moyen(ne) ▷ vt (*pt, pp* **meant**) (*signify*) signifier, vouloir dire; (*refer to*) faire allusion à, parler de; (*intend*): **to ~ to do** avoir l'intention de faire ▷ n moyenne f; **means** npl (*way, money*) moyens mpl; **to be ~t for** être destiné(e) à; **do you ~ it?** vous êtes sérieux?; **what do you ~?** que voulez-vous dire?; **by ~s of** (*instrument*) au moyen de; **by all ~s** je vous en prie

meaning ['mi:nɪŋ] n signification f, sens m; **meaningful** adj significatif(-ive); (*relationship*) valable; **meaningless** adj dénué(e) de sens

meant [mɛnt] pt, pp of **mean**

meantime ['mi:ntaɪm] adv (*also*: **in the ~**) pendant ce temps

meanwhile ['mi:nwaɪl] adv = **meantime**

measles ['mi:zlz] n rougeole f

measure ['mɛʒəʳ] vt, vi mesurer ▷ n mesure f; (*ruler*) règle (graduée)

measurements ['mɛʒəməntz] npl mesures fpl; **chest/hip ~** tour m de poitrine/hanches

meat [mi:t] n viande f; **I don't eat ~** je ne mange pas de viande; **cold ~s** (BRIT) viandes froides; **meatball** n boulette f de viande

Mecca ['mɛkə] n la Mecque

mechanic [mɪ'kænɪk] n mécanicien m; **can you send a ~?** pouvez-vous nous envoyer un mécanicien?; **mechanical** adj mécanique

mechanism ['mɛkənɪzəm] n mécanisme m

medal ['mɛdl] n médaille f; **medallist**, (US) **medalist** n (*Sport*) médaillé(e)

meddle ['mɛdl] vi: **to ~ in** se mêler de, s'occuper de; **to ~ with** toucher à

media ['mi:dɪə] npl media mpl ▷ npl of **medium**

mediaeval [mɛdɪ'i:vl] adj = **medieval**

mediate ['mi:dɪeɪt] vi servir d'intermédiaire

medical ['mɛdɪkl] adj médical(e) ▷ n (*also*: **~ examination**) visite médicale; (*private*) examen médical; **medical certificate** n certificat médical

medicated ['mɛdɪkeɪtɪd] adj traitant(e), médicamenteux(-euse)

medication [mɛdɪ'keɪʃən] n (*drugs etc*) médication f

medicine ['mɛdsɪn] n médecine f; (*drug*) médicament m

medieval [mɛdɪ'i:vl] adj médiéval(e)

mediocre [mi:dɪ'əʊkəʳ] adj médiocre

meditate ['mɛdɪteɪt] vi: **to ~ (on)** méditer (sur)

meditation [mɛdɪ'teɪʃən] n méditation f

Mediterranean [mɛdɪtə'reɪnɪən] adj méditerranéen(ne); **the ~ (Sea)** la (mer) Méditerranée

medium ['mi:dɪəm] adj moyen(ne) ▷ n (pl **media**) (*means*) moyen m; (*person*) médium m; **the happy ~** le juste milieu; **medium-sized** adj de taille moyenne; **medium wave** n (*Radio*) ondes moyennes, petites ondes

meek [mi:k] adj doux (douce), humble

meet (*pt, pp* met) [mi:t, mɛt] vt rencontrer; (*by arrangement*) retrouver, rejoindre; (*for the first time*) faire la connaissance de; (*go and fetch*): **I'll ~ you at the station** j'irai te chercher à la gare; (*opponent, danger, problem*) faire face à; (*requirements*) satisfaire à, répondre à ▷ vi (*friends*) se rencontrer; se retrouver; (*in session*) se réunir; (*join: lines, roads*) se joindre; **nice ~ing you** ravi d'avoir fait votre connaissance; **meet up** vi: **to ~ up with sb** rencontrer qn; **meet with** vt fus (*difficulty*) rencontrer; **to ~ with success** être couronné(e) de succès; **meeting** n (*of group of people*) réunion f; (*between individuals*) rendez-vous m; **she's at** or **in a meeting** (*Comm*) elle est en réunion; **meeting place** n lieu

m

m de (la) réunion; (*for appointment*) lieu de rendez-vous

megabyte ['mɛgəbaɪt] *n* (*Comput*) méga-octet *m*

megaphone ['mɛgəfəun] *n* porte-voix *m inv*

megapixel ['mɛgəpɪksl] *n* mégapixel *m*

melancholy ['mɛlənkəlɪ] *n* mélancolie *f* ▷ *adj* mélancolique

melody ['mɛlədɪ] *n* mélodie *f*

melon ['mɛlən] *n* melon *m*

melt [mɛlt] *vi* fondre ▷ *vt* faire fondre

member ['mɛmbər] *n* membre *m*; **M~ of the European Parliament** eurodéputé *m*; **M~ of Parliament** (*BRIT*) député *m*; **membership** *n* (*becoming a member*) adhésion *f*; admission *f*; (*members*) membres *mpl*, adhérents *mpl*; **membership card** *n* carte *f* de membre

memento [mə'mɛntəu] *n* souvenir *m*

memo ['mɛməu] *n* note *f* (de service)

memorable ['mɛmərəbl] *adj* mémorable

memorandum (*pl* **memoranda**) [mɛmə'rændəm, -də] *n* note *f* (de service)

memorial [mɪ'mɔːrɪəl] *n* mémorial *m* ▷ *adj* commémoratif(-ive)

memorize ['mɛməraɪz] *vt* apprendre *or* retenir par cœur

memory ['mɛmərɪ] *n* (*also Comput*) mémoire *f*; (*recollection*) souvenir *m*; **in ~ of** à la mémoire de; **memory card** *n* (*for digital camera*) carte *f* mémoire; **memory stick** *n* (*Comput: flash pen*) clé *f* USB; (: *card*) carte *f* mémoire

men [mɛn] *npl of* **man**

menace ['mɛnɪs] *n* menace *f*; (*inf: nuisance*) peste *f*, plaie *f* ▷ *vt* menacer

mend [mɛnd] *vt* réparer; (*darn*) raccommoder, repriser ▷ *n* **on the ~** en voie de guérison; **to ~ one's ways** s'amender

meningitis [mɛnɪn'dʒaɪtɪs] *n* méningite *f*

menopause ['mɛnəupɔːz] *n* ménopause *f*

men's room (*us*) *n*: **the ~** les toilettes *fpl* pour hommes

menstruation [mɛnstru'eɪʃən] *n* menstruation *f*

menswear ['mɛnzwɛər] *n* vêtements *mpl* d'hommes

mental ['mɛntl] *adj* mental(e); **mental hospital** *n* (*pej*) hôpital *m* psychiatrique; **mentality** [mɛn'tælɪtɪ] *n* mentalité *f*; **mentally** *adv*: **mentally ill people** les malades mentaux

menthol ['mɛnθɔl] *n* menthol *m*

mention ['mɛnʃən] *n* mention *f* ▷ *vt* mentionner, faire mention de; **don't ~ it!** je vous en prie, il n'y a pas de quoi!

menu ['mɛnjuː] *n* (*set menu, Comput*) menu *m*; (*list of dishes*) carte *f*

MEP *n abbr* = **Member of the European Parliament**

mercenary ['məːsɪnərɪ] *adj* (*person*) intéressé(e), mercenaire ▷ *n* mercenaire *m*

merchandise ['məːtʃəndaɪz] *n* marchandises *fpl*

merchant ['məːtʃənt] *n* négociant *m*, marchand *m*; **merchant bank** *n* (*BRIT*) banque *f* d'affaires; **merchant navy**, (*us*) **merchant marine** *n* marine marchande

merciless ['məːsɪlɪs] *adj* impitoyable, sans pitié

mercury ['məːkjurɪ] *n* mercure *m*

mercy ['məːsɪ] *n* pitié *f*, merci *f*; (*Rel*) miséricorde *f*; **at the ~ of** à la merci de

mere [mɪər] *adj* simple; (*chance*) pur(e); **a ~ two hours** seulement deux heures; **merely** *adv* simplement, purement

merge [məːdʒ] *vt* unir; (*Comput*) fusionner, interclasser ▷ *vi* (*colours, shapes, sounds*) se mêler; (*roads*) se joindre; (*Comm*) fusionner; **merger** *n* (*Comm*) fusion *f*

meringue [mə'ræŋ] *n* meringue *f*

merit ['mɛrɪt] *n* mérite *m*, valeur *f* ▷ *vt* mériter

mermaid ['mə:meɪd] *n* sirène *f*

merry ['mɛrɪ] *adj* gai(e); **M~ Christmas!** joyeux Noël!; **merry-go-round** *n* manège *m*

mesh [mɛʃ] *n* mailles *fpl*

mess [mɛs] *n* désordre *m*, fouillis *m*, pagaille *f*; (*muddle: of life*) gâchis *m*; (: *of economy*) pagaille *f*; (*dirt*) saleté *f*; (*Mil*) mess *m*, cantine *f*; **to be (in) a ~** être en désordre; **to be/get o.s. in a ~** (*fig*) être/se mettre dans le pétrin; **mess about, mess around** (*inf*) *vi* perdre son temps; **mess up** *vt* (*inf: dirty*) salir; (*spoil*) gâcher; **mess with** (*inf*) *vt fus* (*challenge, confront*) se frotter à; (*interfere with*) toucher à

message ['mɛsɪdʒ] *n* message *m*; **can I leave a ~?** est-ce que je peux laisser un message?; **are there any ~s for me?** est-ce que j'ai des messages?

messenger ['mɛsɪndʒəʳ] *n* messager *m*

Messrs, Messrs. ['mɛsəz] *abbr* (*on letters*: = *messieurs*) MM

messy ['mɛsɪ] *adj* (*dirty*) sale; (*untidy*) en désordre

met [mɛt] *pt, pp of* **meet**

metabolism [mɛ'tæbəlɪzəm] *n* métabolisme *m*

metal ['mɛtl] *n* métal *m* ▷ *cpd* en métal; **metallic** [mɛ'tælɪk] *adj* métallique

metaphor ['mɛtəfəʳ] *n* métaphore *f*

meteor ['mi:tɪəʳ] *n* météore *m*; **meteorite** ['mi:tɪəraɪt] *n* météorite *m/f*

meteorology [mi:tɪə'rɔlədʒɪ] *n* météorologie *f*

meter ['mi:təʳ] *n* (*instrument*) compteur *m*; (*also*: **parking ~**) parc(o)mètre *m*; (*us: unit*) = **metre** ▷ *vt* (*us Post*) affranchir à la machine

method ['mɛθəd] *n* méthode *f*; **methodical** [mɪ'θɔdɪkl] *adj* méthodique

methylated spirit ['mɛθɪleɪtɪd-] *n* (*BRIT*) alcool *m* à brûler

meticulous [mɛ'tɪkjuləs] *adj* méticuleux(-euse)

metre, (*us*) **meter** ['mi:təʳ] *n* mètre *m*

metric ['mɛtrɪk] *adj* métrique

metro ['mɛtrəu] *n* métro *m*

metropolitan [mɛtrə'pɔlɪtən] *adj* métropolitain(e); **the M~ Police** (*BRIT*) la police londonienne

Mexican ['mɛksɪkən] *adj* mexicain(e) ▷ *n* Mexicain(e)

Mexico ['mɛksɪkəu] *n* Mexique *m*

mg *abbr* (= *milligram*) mg

mice [maɪs] *npl of* **mouse**

micro... [maɪkrəu] *prefix* micro...; **microchip** *n* (*Elec*) puce *f*; **microphone** *n* microphone *m*; **microscope** *n* microscope *m*

mid [mɪd] *adj*: **~ May** la mi-mai; **~ afternoon** le milieu de l'après-midi; **in ~ air** en plein ciel; **he's in his ~ thirties** il a dans les trente-cinq ans; **midday** *n* midi *m*

middle ['mɪdl] *n* milieu *m*; (*waist*) ceinture *f*, taille *f* ▷ *adj* du milieu; (*average*) moyen(ne); **in the ~ of the night** au milieu de la nuit; **middle-aged** *adj* d'un certain âge, ni vieux ni jeune; **Middle Ages** *npl*: **the Middle Ages** le moyen âge; **middle class(es)** *n(pl)*: **the middle class(es)** ≈ les classes moyennes; **middle-class** *adj* bourgeois(e); **Middle East** *n*: **the Middle East** le Proche-Orient, le Moyen-Orient; **middle name** *n* second prénom; **middle school** *n* (*us*) école pour les enfants de 12 à 14 ans ≈ collège *m*; (*BRIT*) école pour les enfants de 8 à 14 ans

midge [mɪdʒ] *n* moucheron *m*

midget ['mɪdʒɪt] *n* (*pej*) nain(e)

midnight ['mɪdnaɪt] *n* minuit *m*

midst [mɪdst] *n*: **in the ~ of** au milieu de

midsummer [mɪd'sʌmə^r] *n* milieu *m* de l'été

midway [mɪd'weɪ] *adj, adv*: **~ (between)** à mi-chemin (entre); **~ through ...** au milieu de ..., en plein(e) ...

midweek [mɪd'wi:k] *adv* au milieu de la semaine, en pleine semaine

midwife (*pl* **midwives**) ['mɪdwaɪf, -vz] *n* sage-femme *f*

midwinter [mɪd'wɪntə^r] *n* milieu *m* de l'hiver

might [maɪt] *vb see* **may** ▷ *n* puissance *f*, force *f*; **mighty** *adj* puissant(e)

migraine ['mi:greɪn] *n* migraine *f*

migrant ['maɪgrənt] *n* (*bird, animal*) migrateur *m*; (*person*) migrant(e) ▷ *adj* migrateur(-trice); migrant(e); (*worker*) saisonnier(-ière)

migrate [maɪ'greɪt] *vi* migrer

migration [maɪ'greɪʃən] *n* migration *f*

mike [maɪk] *n abbr* (= *microphone*) micro *m*

mild [maɪld] *adj* doux (douce); (*reproach, infection*) léger(-ère); (*illness*) bénin(-igne); (*interest*) modéré(e); (*taste*) peu relevé(e); **mildly** ['maɪldlɪ] *adv* doucement; légèrement; **to put it mildly** (*inf*) c'est le moins qu'on puisse dire

mile [maɪl] *n* mil(l)e *m* (= 1609 *m*); **mileage** *n* distance *f* en milles, ≈ kilométrage *m*; **mileometer** [maɪ'lɔmɪtə^r] *n* compteur *m* kilométrique; **milestone** *n* borne *f*; (*fig*) jalon *m*

military ['mɪlɪtərɪ] *adj* militaire

militia [mɪ'lɪʃə] *n* milice *f*

milk [mɪlk] *n* lait *m* ▷ *vt* (*cow*) traire; (*fig: person*) dépouiller, plumer; (: *situation*) exploiter à fond; **milk chocolate** *n* chocolat *m* au lait; **milkman** (*irreg*) *n* laitier *m*; **milky** *adj* (*drink*) au lait; (*colour*) laiteux(-euse)

mill [mɪl] *n* moulin *m*; (*factory*) usine *f*, fabrique *f*; (*spinning mill*) filature *f*; (*flour mill*) minoterie *f* ▷ *vt* moudre, broyer ▷ *vi* (*also*: **~ about**) grouiller

millennium (*pl* **millenniums** *or* **millennia**) [mɪ'lɛnɪəm, -'lɛnɪə] *n* millénaire *m*

milli... ['mɪlɪ] *prefix* milli...; **milligram(me)** *n* milligramme *m*; **millilitre**, (*US*) **milliliter** *n* millilitre *m*; **millimetre**, (*US*) **millimeter** *n* millimètre *m*

million ['mɪljən] *n* million *m*; **a ~ pounds** un million de livres sterling; **millionaire** [mɪljə'nɛə^r] *n* millionnaire *m*; **millionth** [mɪljə'nθ] *num* millionième

milometer [maɪ'lɔmɪtə^r] *n* = **mileometer**

mime [maɪm] *n* mime *m* ▷ *vt, vi* mimer

mimic ['mɪmɪk] *n* imitateur(-trice) ▷ *vt, vi* imiter, contrefaire

min. *abbr* (= *minute(s)*) mn.; (= *minimum*) min.

mince [mɪns] *vt* hacher ▷ *n* (*BRIT Culin*) viande hachée, hachis *m*; **mincemeat** *n* hachis de fruits secs utilisés en pâtisserie; (*US*) viande hachée, hachis *m*; **mince pie** *n* sorte de tarte aux fruits secs

mind [maɪnd] *n* esprit *m* ▷ *vt* (*attend to, look after*) s'occuper de; (*be careful*) faire attention à; (*object to*): **I don't ~ the noise** je ne crains pas le bruit, le bruit ne me dérange pas; **it is on my ~** cela me préoccupe; **to change one's ~** changer d'avis; **to my ~** à mon avis, selon moi; **to bear sth in ~** tenir compte de qch; **to have sb/sth in ~** avoir qn/qch en tête; **to make up one's ~** se décider; **do you ~ if ...?** est-ce que cela vous gêne si ...?; **I don't ~** cela ne me dérange pas; (*don't care*) ça m'est égal; **~ you, ...** remarquez, ...; **never ~** peu importe, ça ne fait rien; (*don't worry*) ne vous en faites pas; **"~ the step"** "attention à la marche"; **mindless** *adj* irréfléchi(e); (*violence, crime*) insensé(e); (*boring: job*) idiot(e)

mine¹ [maɪn] *pron* le (la) mien(ne), les miens (miennes); **a friend of ~** de mes amis, un ami à moi; **this book is ~** ce livre est à moi

mine² [maɪn] *n* mine f ▷ *vt* (*coal*) extraire; (*ship, beach*) miner; **minefield** *n* champ *m* de mines; **miner** *n* mineur *m*

mineral ['mɪnərəl] *adj* minéral(e) ▷ *n* minéral *m*; **mineral water** *n* eau minérale

mingle ['mɪŋgl] *vi*: **to ~ with** se mêler à

miniature ['mɪnətʃəʳ] *adj* (en) miniature ▷ *n* miniature f

minibar ['mɪnɪbɑːʳ] *n* minibar *m*

minibus ['mɪnɪbʌs] *n* minibus *m*

minicab ['mɪnɪkæb] *n* (BRIT) taxi *m* indépendant

minimal ['mɪnɪml] *adj* minimal(e)

minimize ['mɪnɪmaɪz] *vt* (*reduce*) réduire au minimum; (*play down*) minimiser

minimum ['mɪnɪməm] *n* (*pl* **minima**) minimum *m* ▷ *adj* minimum

mining ['maɪnɪŋ] *n* exploitation minière

miniskirt ['mɪnɪskəːt] *n* mini-jupe f

minister ['mɪnɪstəʳ] *n* (BRIT Pol) ministre *m*; (*Rel*) pasteur *m*

ministry ['mɪnɪstrɪ] *n* (BRIT Pol) ministère *m*; (*Rel*): **to go into the ~** devenir pasteur

minor ['maɪnəʳ] *adj* petit(e), de peu d'importance; (*Mus, poet, problem*) mineur(e) ▷ *n* (*Law*) mineur(e)

minority [maɪ'nɔrɪtɪ] *n* minorité f

mint [mɪnt] *n* (*plant*) menthe f; (*sweet*) bonbon *m* à la menthe ▷ *vt* (*coins*) battre; **the (Royal) M~, the (US) M~** ≈ l'hôtel *m* de la Monnaie; **in ~ condition** à l'état de neuf

minus ['maɪnəs] *n* (*also*: **~ sign**) signe *m* moins ▷ *prep* moins; **12 ~ 6 equals 6** 12 moins 6 égal 6; **~ 24°C** moins 24°C

minute¹ ['mɪnɪt] *n* minute f; **minutes** *npl* (*of meeting*) procès-verbal *m*, compte rendu; **wait a ~!**

(attendez) un instant!; **at the last ~** à la dernière minute

minute² [maɪ'njuːt] *adj* minuscule; (*detailed*) minutieux(-euse); **in ~ detail** par le menu

miracle ['mɪrəkl] *n* miracle *m*

miraculous [mɪ'rækjuləs] *adj* miraculeux(-euse)

mirage ['mɪrɑːʒ] *n* mirage *m*

mirror ['mɪrəʳ] *n* miroir *m*, glace f; (*in car*) rétroviseur *m*

misbehave [mɪsbɪ'heɪv] *vi* mal se conduire

misc. *abbr* = **miscellaneous**

miscarriage ['mɪskærɪdʒ] *n* (*Med*) fausse couche; **~ of justice** erreur f judiciaire

miscellaneous [mɪsɪ'leɪnɪəs] *adj* (*items, expenses*) divers(es); (*selection*) varié(e)

mischief ['mɪstʃɪf] *n* (*naughtiness*) sottises *fpl*; (*playfulness*) espièglerie f; (*harm*) mal *m*, dommage *m*; (*maliciousness*) méchanceté f; **mischievous** ['mɪstʃɪvəs] *adj* (*playful, naughty*) coquin(e), espiègle

misconception ['mɪskən'sɛpʃən] *n* idée fausse

misconduct [mɪs'kɔndʌkt] *n* inconduite f; **professional ~** faute professionnelle

miser ['maɪzəʳ] *n* avare *m/f*

miserable ['mɪzərəbl] *adj* (*person, expression*) malheureux(-euse); (*conditions*) misérable; (*weather*) maussade; (*offer, donation*) minable; (*failure*) pitoyable

misery ['mɪzərɪ] *n* (*unhappiness*) tristesse f; (*pain*) souffrances *fpl*; (*wretchedness*) misère f

misfortune [mɪs'fɔːtʃən] *n* malchance f, malheur *m*

misgiving [mɪs'gɪvɪŋ] *n* (*apprehension*) craintes *fpl*; **to have ~s about sth** avoir des doutes quant à qch

misguided [mɪs'gaɪdɪd] *adj* malavisé(e)

m

mishap ['mɪshæp] n mésaventure f
misinterpret [mɪsɪn'tɜːprɪt] vt mal
interpréter
misjudge [mɪs'dʒʌdʒ] vt méjuger, se
méprendre sur le compte de
mislay [mɪs'leɪ] vt (irreg: like **lay**)
égarer
mislead [mɪs'liːd] vt (irreg: like **lead¹**)
induire en erreur; **misleading** adj
trompeur(-euse)
misplace [mɪs'pleɪs] vt égarer; **to be
~d** (trust etc) être mal placé(e)
misprint ['mɪsprɪnt] n faute f
d'impression
misrepresent [mɪsrɛprɪ'zɛnt] vt
présenter sous un faux jour
Miss [mɪs] n Mademoiselle
miss [mɪs] vt (fail to get, attend, see)
manquer, rater; (regret the absence
of): **I ~ him/it** il/cela me manque ▷ vi
manquer ▷ n (shot) coup manqué; **we
~ed our train** nous avons raté notre
train; **you can't ~ it** vous ne pouvez
pas vous tromper; **miss out** vt (BRIT)
oublier; **miss out on** vt fus (fun, party)
rater, manquer; (chance, bargain)
laisser passer
missile ['mɪsaɪl] n (Aviat) missile m;
(object thrown) projectile m
missing ['mɪsɪŋ] adj manquant(e);
(after escape, disaster: person)
disparu(e); **to go ~** disparaître; **~ in
action** (Mil) porté(e) disparu(e)
mission ['mɪʃən] n mission f; **on
a ~ to sb** en mission auprès de qn;
missionary n missionnaire m/f
misspell ['mɪs'spɛl] vt (irreg: like
spell) mal orthographier
mist [mɪst] n brume f ▷ vi (also: **~
over, ~ up**) devenir brumeux(-euse);
(BRIT: windows) s'embuer
mistake [mɪs'teɪk] n erreur f, faute
f ▷ vt (irreg: like **take**) (meaning)
mal comprendre; (intentions)
se méprendre sur; **to ~ for**
prendre pour; **by ~** par erreur, par
inadvertance; **to make a ~** (in
writing) faire une faute; (in calculating

etc) faire une erreur; **there must be
some ~** il doit y avoir une erreur, se
tromper; **mistaken** pp of **mistake**
▷ adj (idea etc) erroné(e); **to be
mistaken** faire erreur, se tromper
mister ['mɪstə'] n (inf) Monsieur
m; see **Mr**
mistletoe ['mɪsltəu] n gui m
mistook [mɪs'tuk] pt of **mistake**
mistress ['mɪstrɪs] n maîtresse f;
(BRIT: in primary school) institutrice f;
(: in secondary school) professeur m
mistrust [mɪs'trʌst] vt se méfier de
misty ['mɪstɪ] adj brumeux(-euse);
(glasses, window) embué(e)
misunderstand [mɪsʌndə'stænd]
vt, vi (irreg: like **understand**) mal
comprendre; **misunderstanding** n
méprise f, malentendu m; **there's
been a misunderstanding** il y a eu
un malentendu
misunderstood [mɪsʌndə'stud] pt,
pp of **misunderstand** ▷ adj (person)
incompris(e)
misuse n [mɪs'juːs] mauvais emploi;
(of power) abus m ▷ vt [mɪs'juːz] mal
employer; abuser de
mitt(en) ['mɪt(n)] n moufle f;
(fingerless) mitaine f
mix [mɪks] vt mélanger; (sauce,
drink etc) préparer ▷ vi se mélanger;
(socialize): **he doesn't ~ well** il est
peu sociable ▷ n mélange m; **to ~ sth
with sth** mélanger qch à qch; **cake
~** préparation f pour gâteau; **mix up**
vt mélanger; (confuse) confondre; **to
be ~ed up in sth** être mêlé(e) à qch
or impliqué(e) dans qch; **mixed** adj
(feelings, reactions) contradictoire;
(school, marriage) mixte; **mixed grill**
n (BRIT) assortiment m de grillades;
mixed salad n salade f de crudités;
mixed-up adj (person) désorienté(e),
embrouillé(e); **mixer** n (for food)
batteur m, mixeur m; (drink) boisson
gazeuse (servant à couper un alcool);
(person): **he is a good mixer** il est
très sociable; **mixture** n assortiment

m, mélange *m*; (*Med*) préparation *f*;
mix-up *n*: **there was a mix-up** il y a
eu confusion
ml *abbr* (= *millilitre(s)*) ml
mm *abbr* (= *millimetre*) mm
moan [məun] *n* gémissement *m* ▷ *vi*
gémir; (*inf: complain*): **to ~ (about)** se
plaindre (de)
moat [məut] *n* fossé *m*, douves *fpl*
mob [mɔb] *n* foule *f*; (*disorderly*) cohue
f ▷ *vt* assaillir
mobile ['məubaɪl] *adj* mobile ▷ *n*
(*Art*) mobile *m*; (BRIT *inf: phone*)
(téléphone *m*) portable *m*, mobile *m*;
mobile home *n* caravane *f*; **mobile
phone** *n* (téléphone *m*) portable *m*,
mobile *m*
mobility [məu'bɪlɪtɪ] *n* mobilité *f*
mobilize ['məubɪlaɪz] *vt*, *vi* mobiliser
mock [mɔk] *vt* ridiculiser; (*laugh at*)
se moquer de ▷ *adj* faux (fausse);
mocks *npl* (BRIT *Scol*) examens blancs;
mockery *n* moquerie *f*, raillerie *f*
mod cons ['mɔd'kɔnz] *npl abbr*
(BRIT) = **modern conveniences**; *see*
convenience
mode [məud] *n* mode *m*; (*of transport*)
moyen *m*
model ['mɔdl] *n* modèle *m*; (*person:
for fashion*) mannequin *m*; (: *for artist*)
modèle ▷ *vt* (*with clay etc*) modeler
▷ *vi* travailler comme mannequin
▷ *adj* (*railway: toy*) modèle réduit *inv*;
(*child, factory*) modèle; **to ~ clothes**
présenter des vêtements; **to ~ o.s.
on** imiter
modem ['məudɛm] *n* modem *m*
moderate ['mɔdərət] *adj* modéré(e);
(*amount, change*) peu important(e)
▷ *vi* ['mɔdəreɪt] se modérer, se calmer
▷ *vt* ['mɔdəreɪt] modérer
moderation [mɔdə'reɪʃən] *n*
modération *f*, mesure *f*; **in ~** à dose
raisonnable, pris(e) or pratiqué(e)
modérément
modern ['mɔdən] *adj* moderne;
modernize *vt* moderniser; **modern
languages** *npl* langues vivantes

modest ['mɔdɪst] *adj* modeste;
modesty *n* modestie *f*
modification [mɔdɪfɪ'keɪʃən] *n*
modification *f*
modify ['mɔdɪfaɪ] *vt* modifier
module ['mɔdjuːl] *n* module *m*
mohair ['məuhɛə'] *n* mohair *m*
Mohammed [mə'hæmɛd] *n*
Mahomet *m*
moist [mɔɪst] *adj* humide, moite;
moisture ['mɔɪstʃə'] *n* humidité
f; (*on glass*) buée *f*; **moisturizer**
['mɔɪstʃəraɪzə'] *n* crème hydratante
mold *etc* [məuld] (us) *n* = **mould**
mole [məul] *n* (*animal, spy*) taupe *f*;
(*spot*) grain *m* de beauté
molecule ['mɔlɪkjuːl] *n* molécule *f*
molest [məu'lɛst] *vt* (*assault sexually*)
attenter à la pudeur de
molten ['məultən] *adj* fondu(e);
(*rock*) en fusion
mom [mɔm] *n* (us) = **mum**
moment ['məumənt] *n* moment *m*,
instant *m*; **at the ~** en ce moment;
momentarily *adv* momentanément;
(us: *soon*) bientôt; **momentary** *adj*
momentané(e), passager(-ère);
momentous [məu'mɛntəs] *adj*
important(e), capital(e)
momentum [məu'mɛntəm] *n* élan
m, vitesse acquise; (*fig*) dynamique *f*;
to gather ~ prendre de la vitesse; (*fig*)
gagner du terrain
mommy ['mɔmɪ] *n* (us: *mother*)
maman *f*
Monaco ['mɔnəkəu] *n* Monaco *f*
monarch ['mɔnək] *n* monarque *m*;
monarchy *n* monarchie *f*
monastery ['mɔnəstərɪ] *n*
monastère *m*
Monday ['mʌndɪ] *n* lundi *m*
monetary ['mʌnɪtərɪ] *adj* monétaire
money ['mʌnɪ] *n* argent *m*; **to
make ~** (*person*) gagner de l'argent;
(*business*) rapporter; **money belt** *n*
ceinture-portefeuille *f*; **money order**
n mandat *m*
mongrel ['mʌŋgrəl] *n* (*dog*) bâtard *m*

m

monitor [ˈmɒnɪtə^r] n (TV, Comput) écran m, moniteur m ▷ vt contrôler; (foreign station) être à l'écoute de; (progress) suivre de près

monk [mʌŋk] n moine m

monkey [ˈmʌŋkɪ] n singe m

monologue [ˈmɒnəlɒɡ] n monologue m

monopoly [məˈnɒpəlɪ] n monopole m

monosodium glutamate [ˌmɒnəˈsəʊdɪəm ˈgluːtəmeɪt] n glutamate m de sodium

monotonous [məˈnɒtənəs] adj monotone

monsoon [mɒnˈsuːn] n mousson f

monster [ˈmɒnstə^r] n monstre m

month [mʌnθ] n mois m; **monthly** adj mensuel(le) ▷ adv mensuellement

Montreal [mɒntrɪˈɔːl] n Montréal

monument [ˈmɒnjumənt] n monument m

mood [muːd] n humeur f, disposition f; **to be in a good/bad ~** être de bonne/mauvaise humeur; **moody** adj (variable) d'humeur changeante, lunatique; (sullen) morose, maussade

moon [muːn] n lune f; **moonlight** n clair m de lune

moor [muə^r] n lande f ▷ vt (ship) amarrer ▷ vi mouiller

moose [muːs] n (pl inv) élan m

mop [mɒp] n balai m à laver; (for dishes) lavette f à vaisselle ▷ vt éponger, essuyer; **~ of hair** tignasse f; **mop up** vt éponger

mope [məup] vi avoir le cafard, se morfondre

moped [ˈməupɛd] n cyclomoteur m

moral [ˈmɒrl] adj moral(e) ▷ n morale f; **morals** npl moralité f

morale [mɒˈrɑːl] n moral m

morality [məˈrælɪtɪ] n moralité f

morbid [ˈmɔːbɪd] adj morbide

KEYWORD

more [mɔː^r] adj **1** (greater in number etc) plus (de), davantage (de); **more people/work (than)** plus de gens/de travail (que)

2 (additional) encore (de); **do you want (some) more tea?** voulez-vous encore du thé?; **is there any more wine?** reste-t-il du vin?; **I have no** or **I don't have any more money** je n'ai plus d'argent; **it'll take a few more weeks** ça prendra encore quelques semaines ▷ pron plus, davantage; **more than 10** plus de 10; **it cost more than we expected** cela a coûté plus que prévu; **I want more** j'en veux plus or davantage; **is there any more?** est-ce qu'il en reste?; **there's no more** il n'y en a plus; **a little more** un peu plus; **many/much more** beaucoup plus, bien davantage ▷ adv plus; **more dangerous/easily (than)** plus dangereux/facilement (que); **more and more expensive** de plus en plus cher; **more or less** plus ou moins; **more than ever** plus que jamais; **once more** encore une fois, une fois de plus

moreover [mɔːˈrəuvə^r] adv de plus

morgue [mɔːɡ] n morgue f

morning [ˈmɔːnɪŋ] n matin m; (as duration) matinée f ▷ cpd matinal(e); (paper) du matin; **in the ~** le matin; **7 o'clock in the ~** 7 heures du matin; **morning sickness** n nausées matinales

Moroccan [məˈrɒkən] adj marocain(e) ▷ n Marocain(e)

Morocco [məˈrɒkəu] n Maroc m

moron [ˈmɔːrɒn] n (offensive) idiot(e), minus m/f

morphine [ˈmɔːfiːn] n morphine f

morris dancing [ˈmɒrɪs-] n (BRIT) danses folkloriques anglaises

● **MORRIS DANCING**
●
● Le morris dancing est une
● danse folklorique anglaise
● traditionnellement réservée aux

hommes. Habillés tout en blanc
et portant des clochettes, ils
exécutent différentes figures avec
des mouchoirs et de longs bâtons.
Cette danse est très populaire dans
les fêtes de village.

Morse [mɔːs] n (also: ~ **code**) morse m
mortal ['mɔːtl] adj, n mortel(le)
mortar ['mɔːtəʳ] n mortier m
mortgage ['mɔːɡɪdʒ] n hypothèque
f; (loan) prêt m (or crédit m)
hypothécaire ▷ vt hypothéquer
mortician [mɔː'tɪʃən] n (US)
entrepreneur m de pompes funèbres
mortified ['mɔːtɪfaɪd] adj mort(e)
de honte
mortuary ['mɔːtjuərɪ] n morgue f
mosaic [məu'zeɪɪk] n mosaïque f
Moscow ['mɔskəu] n Moscou
Moslem ['mɔzləm] adj, n = **Muslim**
mosque [mɔsk] n mosquée f
mosquito [mɔs'kiːtəu] (pl
mosquitoes) n moustique m
moss [mɔs] n mousse f
most [məust] adj (majority of) la
plupart de; (greatest amount of) le plus
de ▷ pron la plupart ▷ adv le plus;
(very) très, extrêmement; **the ~** le
plus; **~ fish** la plupart des poissons;
**the ~ beautiful woman in the
world** la plus belle femme du monde;
~ of (with plural) la plupart de; (with
singular) la plus grande partie de; **~ of
them** la plupart d'entre eux; **~ of
the time** la plupart du temps; **I saw
~** (a lot but not all) j'en ai vu la plupart;
(more than anyone else) c'est moi qui
en ai vu le plus; **at the (very) ~** au
plus; **to make the ~ of** profiter au
maximum de; **mostly** adv (chiefly)
surtout, principalement; (usually)
généralement
MOT n abbr (BRIT: = Ministry of
Transport): **the ~ (test)** visite
technique (annuelle) obligatoire des
véhicules à moteur
motel [məu'tɛl] n motel m

moth [mɔθ] n papillon m de nuit; (in
clothes) mite f
mother ['mʌðəʳ] n mère f ▷ vt
(pamper, protect) dorloter;
motherhood n maternité f; **mother-
in-law** n belle-mère f; **mother-of-
pearl** n nacre f; **Mother's Day** n fête
f des Mères; **mother-to-be** n future
maman; **mother tongue** n langue
maternelle
motif [məu'tiːf] n motif m
motion ['məuʃən] n mouvement m;
(gesture) geste m; (at meeting) motion
f ▷ vt, vi: **to ~ (to) sb to do** faire
signe à qn de faire; **motionless** adj
immobile, sans mouvement; **motion
picture** n film m
motivate ['məutɪveɪt] vt motiver
motivation [məutɪ'veɪʃən] n
motivation f
motive ['məutɪv] n motif m, mobile m
motor ['məutəʳ] n moteur m; (BRIT
inf: vehicle) auto f; **motorbike** n moto
f; **motorboat** n bateau m à moteur;
motorcar n (BRIT) automobile f;
motorcycle n moto f; **motorcyclist**
n motocycliste m/f; **motoring** (BRIT)
n tourisme m automobile; **motorist**
n automobiliste m/f; **motor racing** n
(BRIT) course f automobile;
motorway n (BRIT) autoroute f
motto ['mɔtəu] (pl **mottoes**) n
devise f
mould, (US) **mold** [məuld] n moule
m; (mildew) moisissure f ▷ vt mouler,
modeler; (fig) façonner; **mouldy**, (US)
moldy adj moisi(e); (smell) de moisi
mound [maund] n monticule m,
tertre m
mount [maunt] n (hill) mont m,
montagne f; (horse) monture f;
(for picture) carton m de montage
▷ vt monter; (horse) monter à;
(bike) monter sur; (picture) monter
sur carton ▷ vi (inflation, tension)
augmenter; **mount up** vi s'élever,
monter; (bills, problems, savings)
s'accumuler

mountain ['mauntɪn] n
montagne f ▷ cpd de (la) montagne;
mountain bike n VTT m, vélo
m tout terrain; **mountaineer** n
alpiniste m/f; **mountaineering** n
alpinisme m; **mountainous** adj
montagneux(-euse); **mountain
range** n chaîne f de montagnes

mourn [mɔ:n] vt pleurer ▷ vi: **to
~ for sb** pleurer qn; **to ~ for sth**
se lamenter sur qch; **mourner** n
parent(e) or ami(e) du défunt;
personne f en deuil or venue rendre
hommage au défunt; **mourning** n
deuil m; **in mourning** en deuil

mouse (pl **mice**) [maus, maɪs] n
(also Comput) souris f; **mouse mat** n
(Comput) tapis m de souris

moussaka [mu'sɑ:kə] n moussaka f

mousse [mu:s] n mousse f

moustache, (us) **mustache**
[məs'tɑ:ʃ] n moustache(s) f(pl)

mouth (pl **mouths**) [mauθ, mauðz]
n bouche f; (of dog, cat) gueule f; (of
river) embouchure f; (of hole, cave)
ouverture f; **mouthful** n bouchée
f; **mouth organ** n harmonica m;
mouthpiece n (of musical instrument)
bec m, embouchure f; (spokesperson)
porte-parole m inv; **mouthwash** n
eau f dentifrice

move [mu:v] n (movement)
mouvement m; (in game) coup m
(: turn to play) tour m; (change of
house) déménagement m; (change
of job) changement m d'emploi ▷ vt
déplacer, bouger; (emotionally)
émouvoir; (Pol: resolution etc)
proposer ▷ vi (gen) bouger, remuer;
(traffic) circuler; (also: **~ house**)
déménager; (in game) jouer; **can you
~ your car, please?** pouvez-vous
déplacer votre voiture, s'il vous
plaît?; **to ~ sb to do sth** pousser
or inciter qn à faire qch; **to get a ~
on** se dépêcher, se remuer; **move
back** vi revenir, retourner; **move in**
vi (to a house) emménager; (police,

soldiers) intervenir; **move off** vi
s'éloigner, s'en aller; **move on** vi
se remettre en route; **move out** vi
(of house) déménager; **move over**
vi se pousser, se déplacer; **move
up** vi avancer; (employee) avoir de
l'avancement; (pupil) passer dans
la classe supérieure; **movement** n
mouvement m

movie ['mu:vɪ] n film m; **movies** npl;
the ~s le cinéma; **movie theater** (us)
n cinéma m

moving ['mu:vɪŋ] adj en
mouvement; (touching)
émouvant(e)

mow (pt **mowed**, pp **mowed** or
mown) [məu, -d, -n] vt faucher;
(lawn) tondre; **mower** n (also:
lawnmower) tondeuse f à gazon

mown [məun] pp of **mow**

Mozambique [məuzəm'bi:k] n
Mozambique m

MP n abbr (BRIT) = **Member of
Parliament**

MP3 n mp3 m; **MP3 player** n baladeur
m numérique, lecteur m mp3

mpg n abbr = **miles per gallon**
(30 mpg = 9,4 l. aux 100 km)

m.p.h. abbr = **miles per hour** (60 mph
= 96 km/h)

Mr, (us) **Mr.** ['mɪstə'] n: **~ X** Monsieur
X, M. X

Mrs, (us) **Mrs.** ['mɪsɪz] n: **~ X**
Madame X, Mme X

Ms, (us) **Ms.** [mɪz] n (Miss or Mrs): **~ X**
Madame X, Mme X

MSP n abbr (= Member of the Scottish
Parliament) député m au Parlement
écossais

Mt abbr (Geo: = mount) Mt

much [mʌtʃ] adj beaucoup de ▷ adv,
n, pron beaucoup; **we don't have
~ time** nous n'avons pas beaucoup
de temps; **how ~ is it?** combien
est-ce que ça coûte?; **it's not ~** ce
n'est pas beaucoup; **too ~** trop (de);
so ~ tant (de); **I like it very/so ~**
j'aime beaucoup/tellement ça; **as ~**

as autant de; **that's ~ better** c'est beaucoup mieux

muck [mʌk] *n* (*mud*) boue *f*; (*dirt*) ordures *fpl*; **muck up** *vt* (*inf: ruin*) gâcher, esquinter; (*dirty*) salir; (*exam, interview*) se planter à; **mucky** *adj* (*dirty*) boueux(-euse), sale

mucus ['mjuːkəs] *n* mucus *m*

mud [mʌd] *n* boue *f*

muddle ['mʌdl] *n* (*mess*) pagaille *f*, fouillis *m*; (*mix-up*) confusion *f* ▷ *vt* (*also:* **~ up**) brouiller, embrouiller; **to get in a ~** (*while explaining etc*) s'embrouiller

muddy ['mʌdɪ] *adj* boueux(-euse)

mudguard ['mʌdɡɑːd] *n* garde-boue *m inv*

muesli ['mjuːzlɪ] *n* muesli *m*

muffin ['mʌfɪn] *n* (*roll*) petit pain rond et plat; (*cake*) petit gâteau au chocolat ou aux fruits

muffled ['mʌfld] *adj* étouffé(e), voilé(e)

muffler ['mʌflə'] *n* (*scarf*) cache-nez *m inv*; (*US Aut*) silencieux *m*

mug [mʌɡ] *n* (*cup*) tasse *f* (*sans soucoupe*); (: *for beer*) chope *f*; (*inf: face*) bouille *f*; (: *fool*) poire *f* ▷ *vt* (*assault*) agresser; **mugger** ['mʌɡə'] *n* agresseur *m*; **mugging** *n* agression *f*

muggy ['mʌɡɪ] *adj* lourd(e), moite

mule [mjuːl] *n* mule *f*

multicoloured, (*US*) **multicolored** ['mʌltɪkʌləd] *adj* multicolore

multimedia ['mʌltɪ'miːdɪə] *adj* multimédia *inv*

multinational [mʌltɪ'næʃənl] *n* multinationale *f* ▷ *adj* multinational(e)

multiple ['mʌltɪpl] *adj* multiple ▷ *n* multiple *m*; **multiple choice (test)** *n* QCM *m*, questionnaire *m* à choix multiple; **multiple sclerosis** [-sklɪ'rəusɪs] *n* sclérose *f* en plaques

multiplex (cinema) ['mʌltɪplɛks-] *n* (cinéma *m*) multisalles *m*

multiplication [mʌltɪplɪ'keɪʃən] *n* multiplication *f*

multiply ['mʌltɪplaɪ] *vt* multiplier ▷ *vi* se multiplier

multistorey ['mʌltɪ'stɔːrɪ] *adj* (BRIT: *building*) à étages; (: *car park*) à étages or niveaux multiples

mum [mʌm] *n* (BRIT) maman *f* ▷ *adj*: **to keep ~** ne pas souffler mot

mumble ['mʌmbl] *vt*, *vi* marmotter, marmonner

mummy ['mʌmɪ] *n* (BRIT: *mother*) maman *f*; (*embalmed*) momie *f*

mumps [mʌmps] *n* oreillons *mpl*

munch [mʌntʃ] *vt*, *vi* mâcher

municipal [mjuː'nɪsɪpl] *adj* municipal(e)

mural ['mjuərl] *n* peinture murale

murder ['məːdə'] *n* meurtre *m*, assassinat *m* ▷ *vt* assassiner; **murderer** *n* meurtrier *m*, assassin *m*

murky ['məːkɪ] *adj* sombre, ténébreux(-euse); (*water*) trouble

murmur ['məːmə'] *n* murmure *m* ▷ *vt*, *vi* murmurer

muscle ['mʌsl] *n* muscle *m*; (*fig*) force *f*; **muscular** ['mʌskjulə'] *adj* musculaire; (*person, arm*) musclé(e)

museum [mjuː'zɪəm] *n* musée *m*

mushroom ['mʌʃrum] *n* champignon *m* ▷ *vi* (*fig*) pousser comme un (*or des*) champignon(s)

music ['mjuːzɪk] *n* musique *f*; **musical** *adj* musical(e); (*person*) musicien(ne) ▷ *n* (*show*) comédie musicale; **musical instrument** *n* instrument *m* de musique; **musician** [mjuː'zɪʃən] *n* musicien(ne)

Muslim ['mʌzlɪm] *adj*, *n* musulman(e)

muslin ['mʌzlɪn] *n* mousseline *f*

mussel ['mʌsl] *n* moule *f*

must [mʌst] *aux vb* (*obligation*): **I ~ do it** je dois le faire, il faut que je le fasse; (*probability*): **he ~ be there by now** il doit y être maintenant, il est probablement maintenant; (*suggestion, invitation*): **you ~ come and see me** il faut que vous veniez me voir ▷ *n* nécessité *f*, impératif *m*;

m

it's a ~ c'est indispensable; **I ~ have made a mistake** j'ai dû me tromper

mustache ['mʌstæʃ] *n (US)* = **moustache**

mustard ['mʌstəd] *n* moutarde *f*

mustn't ['mʌsnt] = **must not**

mutilate ['mjuːtɪleɪt] *vt* mutiler

mutiny ['mjuːtɪnɪ] *n* mutinerie *f* ▷ *vi* se mutiner

mutter ['mʌtər] *vt, vi* marmonner, marmotter

mutton ['mʌtn] *n* mouton *m*

mutual ['mjuːtʃuəl] *adj* mutuel(le), réciproque; (*benefit, interest*) commun(e)

muzzle ['mʌzl] *n* museau *m*; (*protective device*) muselière *f*; (*of gun*) gueule *f* ▷ *vt* museler

my [maɪ] *adj* mon (ma), mes *pl*; **my house/car/gloves** ma maison/ma voiture/mes gants; **I've washed my hair/cut my finger** je me suis lavé les cheveux/coupé le doigt; **is this my pen or yours?** c'est mon stylo ou c'est le vôtre?

myself [maɪ'sɛlf] *pron (reflexive)* me; (*emphatic*) moi-même; (*after prep*) moi; *see also* **oneself**

mysterious [mɪs'tɪərɪəs] *adj* mystérieux(-euse)

mystery ['mɪstərɪ] *n* mystère *m*

mystical ['mɪstɪkl] *adj* mystique

mystify ['mɪstɪfaɪ] *vt (deliberately)* mystifier; (*puzzle*) ébahir

myth [mɪθ] *n* mythe *m*; **mythology** [mɪ'θɔlədʒɪ] *n* mythologie *f*

n/a *abbr (= not applicable)* n.a.

nag [næg] *vt (scold)* être toujours après, reprendre sans arrêt

nail [neɪl] *n (human)* ongle *m*; (*metal*) clou *m* ▷ *vt* clouer; **to ~ sth to sth** clouer qch à qch; **to ~ sb down to a date/price** contraindre qn à accepter or donner une date/un prix; **nailbrush** *n* brosse *f* à ongles; **nailfile** *n* lime *f* à ongles; **nail polish** *n* vernis *m* à ongles; **nail polish remover** *n* dissolvant *m*; **nail scissors** *npl* ciseaux *mpl* à ongles; **nail varnish** *n (BRIT)* = **nail polish**

naïve [naɪ'iːv] *adj* naïf(-ïve)

naked ['neɪkɪd] *adj* nu(e)

name [neɪm] *n* nom *m*; (*reputation*) réputation *f* ▷ *vt* nommer; (*identify: accomplice etc*) citer; (*price, date*) fixer, donner; **by ~** par son nom; de nom; **in the ~ of** au nom de; **what's your ~?** comment vous appelez-vous?, quel est votre nom?; **namely** *adv* à savoir

nanny ['nænɪ] *n* bonne *f* d'enfants

nap [næp] n (sleep) (petit) somme
napkin ['næpkɪn] n serviette f (de table)
nappy ['næpɪ] n (BRIT) couche f
narcotics [nɑː'kɔtɪkz] npl (illegal drugs) stupéfiants mpl
narrative ['nærətɪv] n récit m ▷ adj narratif(-ive)
narrator [nə'reɪtəʳ] n narrateur(-trice)
narrow ['nærəu] adj étroit(e); (fig) restreint(e), limité(e) ▷ vi (road) devenir plus étroit, se rétrécir; (gap, difference) se réduire; **to have a ~ escape** l'échapper belle; **narrow down** vt restreindre; **narrowly** adv: **he narrowly missed injury/the tree** il a failli se blesser/rentrer dans l'arbre; **he only narrowly missed the target** il a manqué la cible de peu or de justesse; **narrow-minded** adj à l'esprit étroit, borné(e); (attitude) borné(e)
nasal ['neɪzl] adj nasal(e)
nasty ['nɑːstɪ] adj (person: malicious) méchant(e); (: rude) très désagréable; (smell) dégoûtant(e); (wound, situation) mauvais(e), vilain(e)
nation ['neɪʃən] n nation f
national ['næʃənl] adj national(e) ▷ n (abroad) ressortissant(e); (when home) national(e); **national anthem** n hymne national; **national dress** n costume national; **National Health Service** n (BRIT) service national de santé, ≈ Sécurité Sociale; **National Insurance** n (BRIT) ≈ Sécurité Sociale; **nationalist** adj, n nationaliste m/f; **nationality** [næʃə'nælɪtɪ] n nationalité f; **nationalize** vt nationaliser; **national park** n parc national; **National Trust** n (BRIT) ≈ Caisse f nationale des monuments historiques et des sites

● **NATIONAL TRUST**
●
● Le National Trust est un organisme
● indépendant, à but non lucratif,
● dont la mission est de protéger et
● de mettre en valeur les monuments
● et les sites britanniques en raison
● de leur intérêt historique ou de leur
● beauté naturelle.

nationwide ['neɪʃənwaɪd] adj s'étendant à l'ensemble du pays; (problem) à l'échelle du pays entier
native ['neɪtɪv] n habitant(e) du pays, autochtone m/f ▷ adj du pays, indigène; (country) natal(e); (language) maternel(le); (ability) inné(e); **Native American** n Indien(ne) d'Amérique ▷ adj amérindien(ne); **native speaker** n locuteur natif
NATO ['neɪtəu] n abbr (= North Atlantic Treaty Organization) OTAN f
natural ['nætʃrəl] adj naturel(le); **natural gas** n gaz naturel; **natural history** n histoire naturelle; **naturally** adv naturellement; **natural resources** npl ressources naturelles
nature ['neɪtʃəʳ] n nature f; **by ~** par tempérament, de nature; **nature reserve** n (BRIT) réserve naturelle
naughty ['nɔːtɪ] adj (child) vilain(e), pas sage
nausea ['nɔːsɪə] n nausée f
naval ['neɪvl] adj naval(e)
navel ['neɪvl] n nombril m
navigate ['nævɪgeɪt] vt (steer) diriger, piloter ▷ vi naviguer; (Aut) indiquer la route à suivre; **navigation** [nævɪ'geɪʃən] n navigation f
navy ['neɪvɪ] n marine f
navy-blue ['neɪvɪ'bluː] adj bleu marine inv
Nazi ['nɑːtsɪ] n Nazi(e)
NB abbr (= nota bene) NB
near [nɪəʳ] adj proche ▷ adv près ▷ prep (also: **~ to**) près de ▷ vt approcher de; **in the ~ future** dans un proche avenir; **nearby** [nɪə'baɪ] adj proche ▷ adv tout près, à proximité; **nearly** adv presque; **I nearly fell** j'ai failli tomber; **it's not**

nearly big enough ce n'est vraiment pas assez grand, c'est loin d'être assez grand; **near-sighted** adj myope

neat [niːt] adj (person, work) soigné(e); (room etc) bien tenu(e) or rangé(e); (solution, plan) habile; (spirits) pur(e); **neatly** adv avec soin or ordre; (skilfully) habilement

necessarily ['nɛsɪsərɪlɪ] adv nécessairement; **not ~** pas nécessairement or forcément

necessary ['nɛsɪsrɪ] adj nécessaire; **if ~** si besoin est, le cas échéant

necessity [nɪ'sɛsɪtɪ] n nécessité f; chose nécessaire or essentielle

neck [nɛk] n cou m; (of horse, garment) encolure f; (of bottle) goulot m; **~ and ~** à égalité; **necklace** ['nɛklɪs] n collier m; **necktie** ['nɛktaɪ] n (esp us) cravate f

nectarine ['nɛktərɪn] n brugnon m, nectarine f

need [niːd] n besoin m ▷ vt avoir besoin de; **to ~ to do** devoir faire; avoir besoin de faire; **you don't ~ to go** vous n'avez pas besoin or vous n'êtes pas obligé de partir; **a signature is ~ed** il faut une signature; **there's no ~ to do ....** il n'y a pas lieu de faire ..., il n'est pas nécessaire de faire ...

needle ['niːdl] n aiguille f ▷ vt (inf) asticoter, tourmenter

needless ['niːdlɪs] adj inutile; **~ to say, ...** inutile de dire que ...

needlework ['niːdlwəːk] n (activity) travaux mpl d'aiguille; (object) ouvrage m

needn't ['niːdnt] = need not

needy ['niːdɪ] adj nécessiteux(-euse)

negative ['nɛgətɪv] n (Phot, Elec) négatif m; (Ling) terme m de négation ▷ adj négatif(-ive)

neglect [nɪ'glɛkt] vt négliger; (garden) ne pas entretenir; (duty) manquer à ▷ n (of person, duty, garden) le fait de négliger; **(state of) ~** abandon m; **to ~ to do sth** négliger

or omettre de faire qch; **to ~ one's appearance** se négliger

negotiate [nɪ'gəʊʃɪeɪt] vi négocier ▷ vt négocier; (obstacle) franchir, négocier; **to ~ with sb for sth** négocier avec qn en vue d'obtenir qch

negotiation [nɪgəʊʃɪ'eɪʃən] n négociation f, pourparlers mpl

negotiator [nɪ'gəʊʃɪeɪtəʳ] n négociateur(-trice)

neighbour, (us) **neighbor** ['neɪbəʳ] n voisin(e); **neighbourhood**, (us) **neighborhood** n (place) quartier m; (people) voisinage m; **neighbouring**, (us) **neighboring** adj voisin(e), avoisinant(e)

neither ['naɪðəʳ] adj, pron aucun(e) (des deux), ni l'un(e) ni l'autre ▷ conj: **~ do I** moi non plus ▷ adv: **~ good nor bad** ni bon ni mauvais; **~ of them** ni l'un ni l'autre

neon ['niːɔn] n néon m

Nepal [nɪ'pɔːl] n Népal m

nephew ['nɛvjuː] n neveu m

nerve [nəːv] n nerf m; (bravery) sang-froid m, courage m; (cheek) aplomb m, toupet m; **nerves** npl (nervousness) nervosité f; **he gets on my ~s** il m'énerve

nervous ['nəːvəs] adj nerveux(-euse); (anxious) inquiet(-ète), plein(e) d'appréhension; (timid) intimidé(e); **nervous breakdown** n dépression nerveuse

nest [nɛst] n nid m ▷ vi (se) nicher, faire son nid

Net [nɛt] n (Comput): **the ~** (Internet) le Net

net [nɛt] n filet m; (fabric) tulle f ▷ adj net(te) ▷ vt (fish etc) prendre au filet; **netball** n netball m

Netherlands ['nɛðələndz] npl; **the ~** les Pays-Bas mpl

nett [nɛt] adj = **net**

nettle ['nɛtl] n ortie f

network ['nɛtwəːk] n réseau m; **there's no ~ coverage here** (Tel) il n'y a pas de réseau ici

neurotic [njuə'rɔtɪk] adj névrosé(e)
neuter ['nju:tər] adj neutre ▷ vt (cat etc) châtrer, couper
neutral ['nju:trəl] adj neutre ▷ n (Aut) point mort
never ['nɛvər] adv (ne …) jamais; **I ~ went** je n'y suis pas allé; **I've ~ been to Spain** je ne suis jamais allé en Espagne; **~ again** plus jamais; **~ in my life** jamais de ma vie; see also **mind**; **never-ending** adj interminable; **nevertheless** [nɛvəðə'lɛs] adv néanmoins, malgré tout
new [nju:] adj nouveau (nouvelle); (brand new) neuf (neuve); **New Age** n New Age m; **newborn** adj nouveau-né(e); **newcomer** ['nju:kʌmər] n nouveau venu (nouvelle venue); **newly** adv nouvellement, récemment
news [nju:z] n nouvelle(s) f(pl); (Radio, TV) informations fpl, actualités fpl; **a piece of ~** une nouvelle; **news agency** n agence f de presse; **newsagent** n (BRIT) marchand m de journaux; **newscaster** n (Radio, TV) présentateur(-trice); **newsletter** n bulletin m; **newspaper** n journal m; **newsreader** n = **newscaster**
newt [nju:t] n triton m
New Year n Nouvel An; **Happy ~!** Bonne Année!; **New Year's Day** n le jour de l'An; **New Year's Eve** n la Saint-Sylvestre
New York [-'jɔ:k] n New York
New Zealand [-'zi:lənd] n Nouvelle-Zélande f; **New Zealander** n Néo-Zélandais(e)
next [nɛkst] adj (in time) prochain(e); (seat, room) voisin(e), d'à côté; (meeting, bus stop) suivant(e) ▷ adv la fois suivante, la prochaine fois; (afterwards) ensuite; **~ to** prep à côté de; **~ to nothing** presque rien; **~ time** adv la prochaine fois; **the ~ day** le lendemain, le jour suivant or d'après; **~ year** l'année prochaine; **please!** (at doctor's etc) au suivant!;

the week after ~ dans deux semaines; **next door** adv à côté ▷ adj (neighbour) d'à côté; **next-of-kin** n parent m le plus proche
NHS n abbr (BRIT) = **National Health Service**
nibble ['nɪbl] vt grignoter
nice [naɪs] adj (holiday, trip, taste) agréable; (flat, picture) joli(e); (person) gentil(le); (distinction, point) subtil(e); **nicely** adv agréablement; joliment; gentiment; subtilement
niche [ni:ʃ] n (Archit) niche f
nick [nɪk] n (indentation) encoche f; (wound) entaille f; (BRIT inf): **in good ~** en bon état ▷ vt (cut): **to ~ o.s.** se couper; (BRIT inf: steal) faucher, piquer; **in the ~ of time** juste à temps
nickel ['nɪkl] n nickel m; (US) pièce f de 5 cents
nickname ['nɪkneɪm] n surnom m ▷ vt surnommer
nicotine ['nɪkəti:n] n nicotine f
niece [ni:s] n nièce f
Nigeria [naɪ'dʒɪərɪə] n Nigéria m/f
night [naɪt] n nuit f; (evening) soir m; **at ~** la nuit; **by ~** de nuit; **last ~** (evening) hier soir; (night-time) la nuit dernière; **night club** n boîte f de nuit; **nightdress** n chemise f de nuit; **nightie** ['naɪtɪ] n chemise f de nuit; **nightlife** n vie f nocturne; **nightly** adj (news) du soir; (by night) nocturne ▷ adv (every evening) tous les soirs; (every night) toutes les nuits; **nightmare** n cauchemar m; **night school** n cours mpl du soir; **night shift** n équipe f de nuit; **night-time** n nuit f
nil [nɪl] n (BRIT Sport) zéro m
nine [naɪn] num neuf; **nineteen** num dix-neuf; **nineteenth** [naɪn'ti:nθ] num dix-neuvième; **ninetieth** ['naɪntɪɪθ] num quatre-vingt-dixième; **ninety** num quatre-vingt-dix
ninth [naɪnθ] num neuvième
nip [nɪp] vt pincer ▷ vi (BRIT inf): **to ~ out/down/up** sortir/descendre/monter en vitesse

n

nipple ['nɪpl] n (Anat) mamelon m,
bout m du sein
nitrogen ['naɪtrədʒən] n azote m

KEYWORD

no [nəu] adv (opposite of "yes") non;
are you coming? — no (I'm not)
est-ce que vous venez? — non;
**would you like some more? — no
thank you** vous en voulez encore?
— non merci
▶ adj (not any) (ne ...) pas de, (ne
...) aucun(e); **I have no money/
books** je n'ai pas d'argent/de livres;
no student would have done it
aucun étudiant ne l'aurait fait; **"no
smoking"** "défense de fumer"; **"no
dogs"** "les chiens ne sont pas admis"
▶ n (pl **noes**) non m

nobility [nəu'bɪlɪtɪ] n noblesse f
noble ['nəubl] adj noble
nobody ['nəubədɪ] pron (ne ...)
personne
nod [nɔd] vi faire un signe de (la) tête
(affirmatif ou amical); (sleep) somnoler
▶ vt: **to ~ one's head** faire un signe
de (la) tête; (in agreement) faire signe
que oui ▶ n signe m de (la) tête; **nod
off** vi s'assoupir
noise [nɔɪz] n bruit m; **I can't sleep
for the ~** je n'arrive pas à dormir à
cause du bruit; **noisy** adj bruyant(e)
nominal ['nɔmɪnl] adj (rent, fee)
symbolique; (value) nominal(e)
nominate ['nɔmɪneɪt] vt (propose)
proposer; (appoint) nommer;
nomination [nɔmɪ'neɪʃən] n
nomination f; **nominee** [nɔmɪ'ni:] n
candidat agréé; personne nommée
none [nʌn] pron aucun(e); **~ of you**
aucun d'entre vous, personne parmi
vous; **I have ~ left** je n'en ai plus;
he's ~ the worse for it il ne s'en porte
pas plus mal
nonetheless ['nʌnðə'lɛs] adv
néanmoins

non-fiction [nɔn'fɪkʃən] n
littérature f non romanesque
nonsense ['nɔnsəns] n absurdités fpl,
idioties fpl; **~!** ne dites pas d'idioties!
non: non-smoker n non-fumeur m;
non-smoking adj non-fumeur; **non-
stick** adj qui n'attache pas
noodles ['nu:dlz] npl nouilles fpl
noon [nu:n] n midi m
no-one ['nəuwʌn] pron = **nobody**
nor [nɔ:ʳ] conj = **neither** ▶ adv see
neither
norm [nɔ:m] n norme f
normal ['nɔ:ml] adj normal(e);
normally adv normalement
Normandy ['nɔ:məndɪ] n
Normandie f
north [nɔ:θ] n nord m ▶ adj nord
inv; (wind) du nord ▶ adv au or vers
le nord; **North Africa** n Afrique f
du Nord; **North African** adj nord-
africain(e), d'Afrique du Nord ▶ n
Nord-Africain(e); **North America**
n Amérique f du Nord; **North
American** n Nord-Américain(e) ▶ adj
nord-américain(e), d'Amérique du
Nord; **northbound** ['nɔ:θbaund]
adj (traffic) en direction du nord;
(carriageway) nord inv; **north-east** n
nord-est m; **northern** ['nɔ:ðən] adj
du nord, septentrional(e); **Northern
Ireland** n Irlande f du Nord; **North
Korea** n Corée f du Nord; **North
Pole** n: **the North Pole** le pôle Nord;
North Sea n: **the North Sea** la mer
du Nord; **north-west** n nord-ouest m
Norway ['nɔ:weɪ] n Norvège f;
Norwegian [nɔ:'wi:dʒən] adj
norvégien(ne) ▶ n Norvégien(ne);
(Ling) norvégien m
nose [nəuz] n nez m; (of dog, cat)
museau m; (fig) flair m; **nose about,
nose around** vi fouiner or fureter
(partout); **nosebleed** n saignement m
de nez; **nosey** adj (inf) curieux(-euse)
nostalgia [nɔs'tældʒɪə] n nostalgie f
nostalgic [nɔs'tældʒɪk] adj
nostalgique

nostril ['nɔstrɪl] n narine f; (of horse) naseau m

nosy ['nəuzɪ] (inf) adj = **nosey**

not [nɔt] adv (ne …) pas; **he is ~** or **isn't here** il n'est pas ici; **you must ~** or **mustn't do that** tu ne dois pas faire ça; **I hope ~** j'espère que non; **~ at all** pas du tout; (after thanks) de rien; **it's too late, isn't it?** c'est trop tard, n'est-ce pas?; **~ yet/now** pas encore/maintenant; see also **only**

notable ['nəutəbl] adj notable; **notably** adv (particularly) en particulier; (markedly) spécialement

notch [nɔtʃ] n encoche f

note [nəut] n note f; (letter) mot m; (banknote) billet m ⊳ vt (also: **~ down**) noter; (notice) constater; **notebook** n carnet m; (for shorthand etc) bloc-notes m; **noted** ['nəutɪd] adj réputé(e); **notepad** n bloc-notes m; **notepaper** n papier m à lettres

nothing ['nʌθɪŋ] n rien m; **he does ~** il ne fait rien; **~ new** rien de nouveau; **for ~** (free) pour rien, gratuitement; (in vain) pour rien; **~ at all** rien du tout; **~ much** pas grand-chose

notice ['nəutɪs] n (announcement, warning) avis m ⊳ vt remarquer, s'apercevoir de; **advance ~** préavis m; **at short ~** dans un délai très court; **until further ~** jusqu'à nouvel ordre; **to give ~, hand in one's ~** (employee) donner sa démission, démissionner; **to take ~ of** prêter attention à; **to bring sth to sb's ~** porter qch à la connaissance de qn; **noticeable** adj visible

notice board n (BRIT) panneau m d'affichage

notify ['nəutɪfaɪ] vt: **to ~ sb of sth** avertir qn de qch

notion ['nəuʃən] n idée f; (concept) notion f; **notions** npl (US: haberdashery) mercerie f

notorious [nəu'tɔ:rɪəs] adj notoire (souvent en mal)

notwithstanding [nɔtwɪθ'stændɪŋ] adv néanmoins ⊳ prep en dépit de

nought [nɔ:t] n zéro m

noun [naun] n nom m

nourish ['nʌrɪʃ] vt nourrir; **nourishment** n nourriture f

Nov. abbr (= November) nov

novel ['nɔvl] n roman m ⊳ adj nouveau (nouvelle), original(e); **novelist** n romancier m; **novelty** n nouveauté f

November [nəu'vɛmbər] n novembre m

novice ['nɔvɪs] n novice m/f

now [nau] adv maintenant ⊳ conj: **~ (that)** maintenant (que); **right ~** tout de suite; **by ~** à l'heure qu'il est; **that's the fashion just ~** c'est la mode en ce moment or maintenant; **~ and then, ~ and again** de temps en temps; **from ~ on** dorénavant; **nowadays** ['nauədeɪz] adv de nos jours

nowhere ['nəuwɛər] adv (ne …) nulle part

nozzle ['nɔzl] n (of hose) jet m, lance f; (of vacuum cleaner) suceur m

nr abbr (BRIT) = **near**

nuclear ['nju:klɪər] adj nucléaire

nucleus (pl **nuclei**) ['nju:klɪəs, 'nju:klɪaɪ] n noyau m

nude [nju:d] adj nu(e) ⊳ n (Art) nu m; **in the ~** (tout(e)) nu(e)

nudge [nʌdʒ] vt donner un (petit) coup de coude à

nudist ['nju:dɪst] n nudiste m/f

nudity ['nju:dɪtɪ] n nudité f

nuisance ['nju:sns] n: **it's a ~** c'est (très) ennuyeux or gênant; **he's a ~** il est assommant or casse-pieds; **what a ~!** quelle barbe!

numb [nʌm] adj engourdi(e); (with fear) paralysé(e)

number ['nʌmbər] n nombre m; (numeral) chiffre m; (of house, car, telephone, newspaper) numéro m ⊳ vt numéroter; (amount to) compter;

n

a ~ of un certain nombre de; **they were seven in ~** ils étaient (au nombre de) sept; **to be ~ed among** compter parmi; **number plate** n (BRIT Aut) plaque f minéralogique or d'immatriculation; **Number Ten** n (BRIT: 10 Downing Street) résidence du Premier ministre

numerical [nju:'mɛrɪkl] adj numérique

numerous ['nju:mərəs] adj nombreux(-euse)

nun [nʌn] n religieuse f, sœur f

nurse [nəːs] n infirmière f; (also: **~maid**) bonne f d'enfants ▷ vt (patient, cold) soigner

nursery ['nəːsərɪ] n (room) nursery f; (institution) crèche f, garderie f; (for plants) pépinière f; **nursery rhyme** n comptine f, chansonnette f pour enfants; **nursery school** n école maternelle; **nursery slope** n (BRIT Ski) piste f pour débutants

nursing ['nəːsɪŋ] n (profession) profession f d'infirmière; (care) soins mpl; **nursing home** n clinique f; (for convalescence) maison f de convalescence or de repos; (for old people) maison de retraite

nurture ['nəːtʃəʳ] vt élever

nut [nʌt] n (of metal) écrou m; (fruit: walnut) noix f; (: hazelnut) noisette f; (: peanut) cacahuète f (terme générique en anglais)

nutmeg ['nʌtmɛg] n (noix f) muscade f

nutrient ['nju:trɪənt] n substance nutritive

nutrition [nju:'trɪʃən] n nutrition f, alimentation f

nutritious [nju:'trɪʃəs] adj nutritif(-ive), nourrissant(e)

nuts [nʌts] (inf) adj dingue

NVQ n abbr (BRIT) = **National Vocational Qualification**

nylon ['naɪlɔn] n nylon m ▷ adj de or en nylon

O

oak [əuk] n chêne m ▷ cpd de or en (bois de) chêne

O.A.P. n abbr (BRIT) = **old age pensioner**

oar [ɔːʳ] n aviron m, rame f

oasis (pl **oases**) [əu'eɪsɪs, əu'eɪsiːz] n oasis f

oath [əuθ] n serment m; (swear word) juron m; **on** (BRIT) or **under ~** sous serment; assermenté(e)

oatmeal ['əutmiːl] n flocons mpl d'avoine

oats [əuts] n avoine f

obedience [ə'biːdɪəns] n obéissance f

obedient [ə'biːdɪənt] adj obéissant(e)

obese [əu'biːs] adj obèse

obesity [əu'biːsɪtɪ] n obésité f

obey [ə'beɪ] vt obéir à; (instructions, regulations) se conformer à ▷ vi obéir

obituary [ə'bɪtjuərɪ] n nécrologie f

object n ['ɔbdʒɪkt] objet m; (purpose) but m, objet; (Ling) complément

m d'objet ▷ *vi* [əb'dʒɛkt]: **to ~ to**
(*attitude*) désapprouver; (*proposal*)
protester contre, élever une objection
contre; **I ~!** je proteste!; **he ~ed that
...** il a fait valoir *or* a objecté que ...;
money is no ~ l'argent n'est pas un
problème; **objection** [əb'dʒɛkʃən]
n objection *f*; **if you have no
objection** si vous n'y voyez pas
d'inconvénient; **objective** *n* objectif
m ▷ *adj* objectif(-ive)
obligation [ɔblɪ'ɡeɪʃən] *n* obligation
f, devoir *m*; (*debt*) dette *f* (de
reconnaissance)
obligatory [ə'blɪɡətərɪ] *adj*
obligatoire
oblige [ə'blaɪdʒ] *vt* (*force*): **to ~ sb to do**
obliger *or* forcer qn à faire; (*do a favour*)
rendre service à, obliger; **to be ~d to
sb for sth** être obligé(e) à qn de qch
oblique [ə'bliːk] *adj* oblique; (*allusion*)
indirect(e)
obliterate [ə'blɪtəreɪt] *vt* effacer
oblivious [ə'blɪvɪəs] *adj*: **~ of**
oublieux(-euse) de
oblong [ɔblɔŋ] *adj* oblong(ue) ▷ *n*
rectangle *m*
obnoxious [əb'nɔkʃəs] *adj*
odieux(-euse); (*smell*) nauséabond(e)
oboe ['əubəu] *n* hautbois *m*
obscene [əb'siːn] *adj* obscène
obscure [əb'skjuəʳ] *adj* obscur(e) ▷ *vt*
obscurcir; (*hide: sun*) cacher
observant [əb'zɜːvnt] *adj*
observateur(-trice)
observation [ɔbzə'veɪʃən] *n*
observation *f*; (*by police etc*)
surveillance *f*
observatory [əb'zɜːvətrɪ] *n*
observatoire *m*
observe [əb'zɜːv] *vt* observer;
(*remark*) faire observer *or* remarquer;
observer *n* observateur(-trice)
obsess [əb'sɛs] *vt* obséder;
obsession [əb'sɛʃən] *n* obsession *f*;
obsessive *adj* obsédant(e)
obsolete ['ɔbsəliːt] *adj* dépassé(e),
périmé(e)

obstacle ['ɔbstəkl] *n* obstacle *m*
obstinate ['ɔbstɪnɪt] *adj* obstiné(e);
(*pain, cold*) persistant(e)
obstruct [əb'strʌkt] *vt* (*block*)
boucher, obstruer; (*hinder*) entraver;
obstruction [əb'strʌkʃən] *n*
obstruction *f*; (*to plan, progress*)
obstacle *m*
obtain [əb'teɪn] *vt* obtenir
obvious ['ɔbvɪəs] *adj* évident(e),
manifeste; **obviously** *adv*
manifestement; **obviously!** bien
sûr!; **obviously not!** évidemment
pas!, bien sûr que non!
occasion [ə'keɪʒən] *n* occasion *f*;
(*event*) événement *m*; **occasional**
adj pris(e) (*or* fait(e) *etc*) de temps
en temps; (*worker, spending*)
occasionnel(le); **occasionally** *adv* de
temps en temps, quelquefois
occult [ɔ'kʌlt] *adj* occulte ▷ *n*: **the ~**
le surnaturel
occupant ['ɔkjupənt] *n* occupant *m*
occupation [ɔkju'peɪʃən] *n*
occupation *f*; (*job*) métier *m*,
profession *f*
occupy ['ɔkjupaɪ] *vt* occuper; **to
~ o.s. with** *or* **by doing** s'occuper
à faire
occur [ə'kɜːʳ] *vi* se produire;
(*difficulty, opportunity*) se présenter;
(*phenomenon, error*) se rencontrer;
to ~ to sb venir à l'esprit de qn;
occurrence [ə'kʌrəns] *n* (*existence*)
présence *f*, existence *f*; (*event*) cas
m, fait *m*
ocean ['əuʃən] *n* océan *m*
o'clock [ə'klɔk] *adv*: **it is 5 ~** il est
5 heures
Oct. *abbr* (= *October*) oct
October [ɔk'təubəʳ] *n* octobre *m*
octopus ['ɔktəpəs] *n* pieuvre *f*
odd [ɔd] *adj* (*strange*) bizarre,
curieux(-euse); (*number*) impair(e);
(*not of a set*) dépareillé(e); **60-~**
60 et quelques; **at ~ times** de
temps en temps; **the ~ one out**
l'exception *f*; **oddly** *adv* bizarrement,

o

curieusement; **odds** npl (in betting) cote f; **it makes no odds** cela n'a pas d'importance; **odds and ends** de petites choses; **at odds** en désaccord

odometer [ɔ'dɒmɪtər] n (US) odomètre m

odour, (US) **odor** ['əudər] n odeur f

KEYWORD

of [ɔv, əv] prep 1 (gen) de; **a friend of ours** un de nos amis; **a boy of 10** un garçon de 10 ans; **that was kind of you** c'était gentil de votre part
2 (expressing quantity, amount, dates etc) de; **a kilo of flour** un kilo de farine; **how much of this do you need?** combien vous en faut-il?; **there were three of them** (people) ils étaient 3; (objects) il y en avait 3; **three of us went** 3 d'entre nous y sont allé(e)s; **the 5th of July** le 5 juillet; **a quarter of 4** (US) 4 heures moins le quart
3 (from, out of) en, de; **a statue of marble** une statue de or en marbre; **made of wood** (fait) en bois

off [ɔf] adj, adv (engine) coupé(e); (light, TV) éteint(e); (tap) fermé(e); (BRIT: food) mauvais(e), avancé(e); (: milk) tourné(e); (absent) absent(e); (cancelled) annulé(e); (removed): **the lid was ~** le couvercle était retiré or n'était pas mis; (away): **to run/drive ~** partir en courant/en voiture ▷ prep de; **to be ~** (to leave) partir, s'en aller; **to be ~ sick** être absent pour cause de maladie; **a day ~** un jour de congé; **to have an ~ day** n'être pas en forme; **he had his coat ~** il avait enlevé son manteau; **10% ~** (Comm) 10% de rabais; **5 km ~ (the road)** à 5 km (de la route); **~ the coast** au large de la côte; **it's a long way ~** c'est loin (d'ici); **I'm ~ meat** je ne mange plus de viande; je n'aime plus la viande; **on**

the ~ chance à tout hasard; **~ and on, on and ~** de temps à autre

offence, (US) **offense** [ə'fɛns] n (crime) délit m, infraction f; **to take ~ at** se vexer de, s'offenser de

offend [ə'fɛnd] vt (person) offenser, blesser; **offender** n délinquant(e); (against regulations) contrevenant(e)

offense [ə'fɛns] n (US) = **offence**

offensive [ə'fɛnsɪv] adj offensant(e), choquant(e); (smell etc) très déplaisant(e); (weapon) offensif(-ive) ▷ n (Mil) offensive f

offer ['ɔfər] n offre f, proposition f ▷ vt offrir, proposer; **"on ~"** (Comm) "en promotion"

offhand [ɔf'hænd] adj désinvolte ▷ adv spontanément

office ['ɔfɪs] n (place) bureau m; (position) charge f, fonction f; **doctor's ~** (US) cabinet (médical); **to take ~** entrer en fonctions; **office block**, (US) **office building** n immeuble m de bureaux; **office hours** npl heures fpl de bureau; (US Med) heures de consultation

officer ['ɔfɪsər] n (Mil etc) officier m; (also: **police ~**) agent m (de police); (of organization) membre m du bureau directeur

office worker n employé(e) de bureau

official [ə'fɪʃl] adj (authorized) officiel(le) ▷ n officiel m; (civil servant) fonctionnaire m/f; (of railways, post office, town hall) employé(e)

off: off-licence n (BRIT: shop) débit m de vins et de spiritueux; **off-line** adj (Comput) (en mode) autonome (: switched off) non connecté(e); **off-peak** adj aux heures creuses; (electricity, ticket) au tarif heures creuses; **off-putting** adj (BRIT) (remark) rébarbatif(-ive); (person) rebutant(e), peu engageant(e); **off-season** adj, adv hors-saison inv

offset ['ɔfsɛt] vt (irreg: like **set**) (counteract) contrebalancer, compenser

offshore [ɔfʃɔːʳ] *adj* (*breeze*) de terre; (*island*) proche du littoral; (*fishing*) côtier(-ière)

offside [ɔfˈsaɪd] *adj* (*Sport*) hors jeu; (*Aut: in Britain*) de droite; (: *in US, Europe*) de gauche

offspring [ˈɔfsprɪŋ] *n* progéniture *f*

often [ˈɔfn] *adv* souvent; **how ~ do you go?** vous y allez tous les combien?; **every so ~** de temps en temps, de temps à autre

oh [əu] *excl* ô!, oh!, ah!

oil [ɔɪl] *n* huile *f*; (*petroleum*) pétrole *m*; (*for central heating*) mazout *m* ▷ *vt* (*machine*) graisser; **oil filter** *n* (*Aut*) filtre *m* à huile; **oil painting** *n* peinture *f* à l'huile; **oil refinery** *n* raffinerie *f* de pétrole; **oil rig** *n* derrick *m*; (*at sea*) plate-forme pétrolière; **oil slick** *n* nappe *f* de mazout; **oil tanker** *n* (*ship*) pétrolier *m*; (*truck*) camion-citerne *m*; **oil well** *n* puits *m* de pétrole; **oily** *adj* huileux(-euse); (*food*) gras(se)

ointment [ˈɔɪntmənt] *n* onguent *m*

O.K., okay [ˈəuˈkeɪ] (*inf*) *excl* d'accord! ▷ *vt* approuver, donner son accord à ▷ *adj* (*not bad*) pas mal; **is it ~?, are you ~?** ça va?

old [əuld] *adj* vieux (vieille); (*person*) vieux, âgé(e); (*former*) ancien(ne), vieux; **how ~ are you?** quel âge avez-vous?; **he's 10 years ~** il a 10 ans, il est âgé de 10 ans; **~er brother/ sister** frère/sœur aîné(e); **old age** *n* vieillesse *f*; **old-age pensioner** *n* (BRIT) retraité(e); **old-fashioned** *adj* démodé(e); (*person*) vieux jeu *inv*; **old people's home** *n* (*esp* BRIT) maison *f* de retraite

olive [ˈɔlɪv] *n* (*fruit*) olive *f*; (*tree*) olivier *m* ▷ *adj* (*also*: **~-green**) (vert) olive *inv*; **olive oil** *n* huile *f* d'olive

Olympic [əuˈlɪmpɪk] *adj* olympique; **the ~ Games, the ~s** les Jeux *mpl* olympiques

omelet(te) [ˈɔmlɪt] *n* omelette *f*

omen [ˈəumən] *n* présage *m*

ominous [ˈɔmɪnəs] *adj* menaçant(e), inquiétant(e); (*event*) de mauvais augure

omit [əuˈmɪt] *vt* omettre

KEYWORD

on [ɔn] *prep* **1** (*indicating position*) sur; **on the table** sur la table; **on the wall** sur le *or* au mur; **on the left** à gauche
2 (*indicating means, method, condition etc*): **on foot** à pied; **on the train/ plane** (*be*) dans le train/l'avion; (*go*) en train/avion; **on the telephone/ radio/television** au téléphone/à la radio/à la télévision; **to be on drugs** se droguer; **on holiday**, (US) **on vacation** en vacances
3 (*referring to time*): **on Friday** vendredi; **on Fridays** le vendredi; **on June 20th** le 20 juin; **a week on Friday** vendredi en huit; **on arrival** à l'arrivée; **on seeing this** en voyant cela
4 (*about, concerning*) sur, de; **a book on Balzac/physics** un livre sur Balzac/de physique
▶ *adv* **1** (*referring to dress*): **to have one's coat on** avoir (mis) son manteau; **to put one's coat on** mettre son manteau; **what's she got on?** qu'est-ce qu'elle porte?
2 (*referring to covering*): **screw the lid on tightly** vissez bien le couvercle
3 (*further, continuously*): **to walk** *etc* **on** continuer à marcher *etc*; **from that day on** depuis ce jour
▶ *adj* **1** (*in operation: machine*) en marche; (: *radio, TV, light*) allumé(e); (: *tap, gas*) ouvert(e); (: *brakes*) mis(e); **is the meeting still on?** (*not cancelled*) est-ce que la réunion a bien lieu?; **when is this film on?** quand passe ce film?
2 (*inf*): **that's not on!** (*not acceptable*) cela ne se fait pas!; (*not possible*) pas question!

o

once [wʌns] *adv* une fois; *(formerly)*
autrefois ▷ *conj* une fois que + *sub*;
~ he had left/it was done une fois
qu'il fut parti/ que ce fut terminé;
at ~ tout de suite, immédiatement;
(simultaneously) à la fois; **all at ~** *adv*
tout d'un coup; **~ a week** une fois par
semaine; **~ more** encore une fois;
~ and for all une fois pour toutes;
~ upon a time there was ... il y avait
une fois ..., il était une fois ...

oncoming [ˈɒnkʌmɪŋ] *adj (traffic)*
venant en sens inverse

KEYWORD

one [wʌn] *num* un(e); **one hundred
and fifty** cent cinquante; **one by
one** un(e) à *or* par un(e); **one day**
un jour

▶ *adj* **1** *(sole)* seul(e), unique; **the
one book which** l'unique *or* le seul
livre qui; **the one man who** le seul
(homme) qui
2 *(same)* même; **they came in the
one car** ils sont venus dans la même
voiture
▶ *pron* **1**: **this one** celui-ci (celle-ci);
that one celui-là (celle-là); **I've
already got one/a red one** j'en ai
déjà un(e)/un(e) rouge; **which one
do you want?** lequel voulez-vous?
2: **one another** l'un(e) l'autre; **to
look at one another** se regarder
3 *(impersonal)*: **one never knows**
on ne sait jamais; **to cut one's finger**
se couper le doigt; **one needs to eat**
il faut manger

one-off [wʌnˈɒf] *n* (BRIT *inf*)
exemplaire *m* unique
oneself [wʌnˈsɛlf] *pron* se; *(after prep,
also emphatic)* soi-même; **to hurt ~**
se faire mal; **to keep sth for ~** garder
qch pour soi; **to talk to ~** se parler à
soi-même; **by ~** tout seul
one: one-shot [wʌnˈʃɒt] (US) *n*
= **one-off**; **one-sided** *adj (argument,*

decision) unilatéral(e); **one-to-one**
adj (relationship) univoque; **one-way**
adj (street, traffic) à sens unique
ongoing [ˈɒngəʊɪŋ] *adj* en cours;
(relationship) suivi(e)
onion [ˈʌnjən] *n* oignon *m*
on-line [ˈɒnlaɪn] *adj* (Comput) en ligne
(: *switched on*) connecté(e)
onlooker [ˈɒnlʊkəʳ] *n*
spectateur(-trice)
only [ˈəʊnlɪ] *adv* seulement ▷ *adj*
seul(e), unique ▷ *conj* seulement,
mais; **an ~ child** un enfant unique;
not ~ ... but also non seulement
... mais aussi; **I ~ took one** j'en ai
seulement pris un, je n'en ai pris qu'un
on-screen [ɒnˈskriːn] *adj* à l'écran
onset [ˈɒnsɛt] *n* début *m*; *(of winter, old
age)* approche *f*
onto [ˈɒntu] *prep* sur
onward(s) [ˈɒnwəd(z)] *adv (move)* en
avant; **from that time ~** à partir de
ce moment
oops [ʊps] *excl* houp!
ooze [uːz] *vi* suinter
opaque [əʊˈpeɪk] *adj* opaque
open [ˈəʊpn] *adj* ouvert(e); *(car)*
découvert(e); *(road, view)* dégagé(e);
(meeting) public(-ique); *(admiration)*
manifeste ▷ *vt* ouvrir ▷ *vi (flower,
eyes, door, debate)* s'ouvrir; *(shop,
bank, museum)* ouvrir; *(book etc:
commence)* commencer, débuter;
is it ~ to public? est-ce ouvert au
public?; **what time do you ~?** à
quelle heure ouvrez-vous?; **in the ~
(air)** en plein air; **open up** *vt* ouvrir;
(blocked road) dégager ▷ *vi* s'ouvrir;
open-air *adj* en plein air; **opening** *n*
ouverture *f*; *(opportunity)* occasion
f; *(work)* débouché *m*; *(job)* poste
vacant; **opening hours** *npl* heures
fpl d'ouverture; **open learning** *n*
enseignement universitaire à la carte,
notamment par correspondance;
(distance learning) télé-enseignement
m; **openly** *adv* ouvertement;
open-minded *adj* à l'esprit ouvert;

open-necked adj à col ouvert;
open-plan adj sans cloisons; **Open
University** n (BRIT) cours universitaires
par correspondance

● **OPEN UNIVERSITY**
●
● L'Open University a été fondée en
● 1969. L'enseignement comprend
● des cours (certaines plages horaires
● sont réservées à cet effet à la
● télévision et à la radio), des devoirs
● qui sont envoyés par l'étudiant
● à son directeur ou sa directrice
● d'études, et un séjour obligatoire en
● université d'été. Il faut préparer un
● certain nombre d'unités de valeur
● pendant une période de temps
● déterminée et obtenir la moyenne
● à un certain nombre d'entre elles
● pour recevoir le diplôme visé.

opera ['ɔpərə] n opéra m; **opera
house** n opéra m; **opera singer** n
chanteur(-euse) d'opéra
operate ['ɔpəreɪt] vt (machine)
faire marcher, faire fonctionner ▷ vi
fonctionner; **to ~ on sb (for)** (Med)
opérer qn (de)
operating room n (US Med) salle f
d'opération
operating theatre n (BRIT Med)
salle f d'opération
operation [ɔpə'reɪʃən] n opération
f; (of machine) fonctionnement m; **to
have an ~ (for)** se faire opérer (de);
to be in ~ (machine) être en service;
(system) être en vigueur; **operational**
adj opérationnel(le); (ready for use) en
état de marche
operative ['ɔpərətɪv] adj (measure) en
vigueur ▷ n (in factory) ouvrier(-ière)
operator ['ɔpəreɪtə'] n (of
machine) opérateur(-trice); (Tel)
téléphoniste m/f
opinion [ə'pɪnjən] n opinion f, avis
m; **in my ~** à mon avis; **opinion poll** n
sondage m d'opinion

opponent [ə'pəunənt] n adversaire
m/f
opportunity [ɔpə'tjuːnɪtɪ] n
occasion f; **to take the ~ to do** or **of
doing** profiter de l'occasion pour faire
oppose [ə'pəuz] vt s'opposer à; **to be
~d to sth** être opposé(e) à qch; **as ~d
to** par opposition à
opposite ['ɔpəzɪt] adj opposé(e);
(house etc) d'en face ▷ adv en face
▷ prep en face de ▷ n opposé m,
contraire m; (of word) contraire
opposition [ɔpə'zɪʃən] n opposition f
oppress [ə'prɛs] vt opprimer
opt [ɔpt] vi: **to ~ for** opter pour; **to ~
to do** choisir de faire; **opt out** vi: **to ~
out of** choisir de ne pas participer à or
de ne pas faire
optician [ɔp'tɪʃən] n opticien(ne)
optimism ['ɔptɪmɪzəm] n
optimisme m
optimist ['ɔptɪmɪst] n optimiste
m/f; **optimistic** [ɔptɪ'mɪstɪk] adj
optimiste
optimum ['ɔptɪməm] adj optimum
option ['ɔpʃən] n choix m, option f;
(Scol) matière f à option; **optional** adj
facultatif(-ive)
or [ɔː'] conj ou; (with negative): **he
hasn't seen or heard anything** il
n'a rien vu ni entendu; **or else** sinon;
ou bien
oral ['ɔːrəl] adj oral(e) ▷ n oral m
orange ['ɔrɪndʒ] n (fruit) orange f
▷ adj orange inv; **orange juice** n jus
m d'orange
orbit ['ɔːbɪt] n orbite f ▷ vt graviter
autour de
orchard ['ɔːtʃəd] n verger m
orchestra ['ɔːkɪstrə] n orchestre m;
(US: seating) (fauteuils mpl d')orchestre
orchid ['ɔːkɪd] n orchidée f
ordeal [ɔː'diːl] n épreuve f
order ['ɔːdə'] n ordre m; (Comm)
commande f ▷ vt ordonner;
(Comm) commander; **in ~** en ordre;
(document) en règle; **out of ~**
(not in correct order) en désordre;

o

(*machine*) hors service; (*telephone*) en dérangement; **a machine in working ~** une machine en état de marche; **in ~ to do/that** pour faire/que + *sub*; **could I ~ now, please?** je peux commander, s'il vous plaît?; **to be on ~** être en commande; **to ~ sb to do** ordonner à qn de faire; **order form** *n* bon *m* de commande; **orderly** *n* (*Mil*) ordonnance *f*; (*Med*) garçon *m* de salle ▷ *adj* (*room*) en ordre; (*mind*) méthodique; (*person*) qui a de l'ordre

ordinary ['ɔːdnrɪ] *adj* ordinaire, normal(e); (*pej*) ordinaire, quelconque; **out of the ~** exceptionnel(le)

ore [ɔːʳ] *n* minerai *m*

oregano [ɒrɪ'gɑːnəʊ] *n* origan *m*

organ ['ɔːgən] *n* organe *m*; (*Mus*) orgue *m*, orgues *fpl*; **organic** [ɔː'gænɪk] *adj* organique; (*crops etc*) biologique, naturel(le); **organism** *n* organisme *m*

organization [ɔːgənaɪ'zeɪʃən] *n* organisation *f*

organize ['ɔːgənaɪz] *vt* organiser; **organized** [ɔːgənaɪzd] *adj* (*planned*) organisé(e); (*efficient*) bien organisé(e); **organizer** *n* organisateur(-trice)

orgasm ['ɔːgæzəm] *n* orgasme *m*

orgy ['ɔːdʒɪ] *n* orgie *f*

oriental [ɔːrɪ'ɛntl] *adj* oriental(e)

orientation [ɔːrɪen'teɪʃən] *n* (*attitudes*) tendance *f*; (*in job*) orientation *f*; (*of building*) orientation, exposition *f*

origin ['ɒrɪdʒɪn] *n* origine *f*

original [ə'rɪdʒɪnl] *adj* original(e); (*earliest*) originel(le) ▷ *n* original *m*; **originally** *adv* (*at first*) à l'origine

originate [ə'rɪdʒɪneɪt] *vi*: **to ~ from** être originaire de; (*suggestion*) provenir de; **to ~ in** (*custom*) prendre naissance dans, avoir son origine dans

Orkney ['ɔːknɪ] *n* (*also*: **the ~s, the ~ Islands**) les Orcades *fpl*

ornament ['ɔːnəmənt] *n* ornement *m*; (*trinket*) bibelot *m*; **ornamental** [ɔːnə'mɛntl] *adj* décoratif(-ive); (*garden*) d'agrément

ornate [ɔː'neɪt] *adj* très orné(e)

orphan ['ɔːfn] *n* orphelin(e)

orthodox ['ɔːθədɒks] *adj* orthodoxe

orthopaedic, (*us*) **orthopedic** [ɔːθə'piːdɪk] *adj* orthopédique

osteopath ['ɒstɪəpæθ] *n* ostéopathe *m/f*

ostrich ['ɒstrɪtʃ] *n* autruche *f*

other ['ʌðəʳ] *adj* autre ▷ *pron*: **the ~ (one)** l'autre; **~s** (*other people*) d'autres ▷ *adv*: **~ than** autrement que; à part; **the ~ day** l'autre jour; **otherwise** *adv*, *conj* autrement

Ottawa ['ɒtəwə] *n* Ottawa

otter ['ɒtəʳ] *n* loutre *f*

ouch [autʃ] *excl* aïe!

ought [ɔːt] *aux vb*: **I ~ to do it** je devrais le faire, il faudrait que je le fasse; **this ~ to have been corrected** cela aurait dû être corrigé; **he ~ to win** (*probability*) il devrait gagner

ounce [auns] *n* once *f* (28.35g; 16 in a pound)

our ['auəʳ] *adj* notre, nos *pl*; *see also* **my**; **ours** *pron* le (la) nôtre, les nôtres; *see also* **mine¹**; **ourselves** *pl pron* (*reflexive, after preposition*) nous; (*emphatic*) nous-mêmes; *see also* **oneself**

oust [aust] *vt* évincer

out [aut] *adv* dehors; (*published, not at home etc*) sorti(e); (*light, fire*) éteint(e); **~ there** là-bas; **he's ~** (*absent*) il est sorti; **to be ~ in one's calculations** s'être trompé dans ses calculs; **to run/back etc ~** sortir en courant/en reculant *etc*; **~ loud** *adv* à haute voix; **~ of** *prep* (*outside*) en dehors de; (*because of: anger etc*) par; (*from among*) **10 ~ of 10** 10 sur 10; (*without*): **~ of petrol** sans essence, à court d'essence; **~ of order** (*machine*) en panne; (*Tel: line*) en dérangement; **outback** n (in Australia) intérieur m; **outbound** adj: **outbound (from/for)** en partance (de/pour); **outbreak** n (of violence) éruption f, explosion f; (of disease) de nombreux cas; **the outbreak of war south of the border** la guerre qui s'est déclarée au sud de la frontière; **outburst** n explosion f, accès m; **outcast** n exilé(e); (socially) paria m; **outcome** n issue f, résultat m; **outcry** n tollé (général); **outdated** adj démodé(e); **outdoor** adj de or en plein air; **outdoors** adv dehors; au grand air

outer ['autə^r] adj extérieur(e); **outer space** n espace m cosmique

outfit ['autfɪt] n (clothes) tenue f

out: outgoing adj (president, tenant) sortant(e); (character) ouvert(e), extraverti(e); **outgoings** npl (BRIT: expenses) dépenses fpl; **outhouse** n appentis m, remise f

outing ['autɪŋ] n sortie f; excursion f

out: outlaw n hors-la-loi m inv ▷ vt (person) mettre hors la loi; (practice) proscrire; **outlay** n dépenses fpl; (investment) mise f de fonds; **outlet** n (for liquid etc) issue f, sortie f; (for emotion) exutoire m; (also: **retail outlet**) point m de vente; (us Elec) prise f de courant; **outline** n (shape) contour m; (summary) esquisse f, grandes lignes ▷ vt (fig: theory, plan) exposer à grands traits; **outlook** n perspective f; (point of view) attitude f; **outnumber** vt surpasser en nombre; **out-of-date** adj (passport, ticket) périmé(e); (theory, idea) dépassé(e); (custom) désuet(-ète); (clothes) démodé(e); **out-of-doors** adv = **outdoors**; **out-of-the-way** adj loin de tout; **out-of-town** adj (shopping centre etc) en périphérie; **outpatient** n malade m/f en consultation externe; **outpost** n avant-poste m; **output** n rendement m, production f; (Comput) sortie f ▷ vt (Comput) sortir

outrage ['autreɪdʒ] n (anger) indignation f; (violent act) atrocité f, acte m de violence; (scandal) scandale m ▷ vt outrager; **outrageous** [aut'reɪdʒəs] adj atroce; (scandalous) scandaleux(-euse)

outright adv [aut'raɪt] complètement; (deny, refuse) catégoriquement; (ask) carrément; (kill) sur le coup ▷ adj ['autraɪt] complet(-ète); catégorique

outset ['autsɛt] n début m

outside [aut'saɪd] n extérieur m ▷ adj extérieur(e) ▷ adv (au) dehors, à l'extérieur ▷ prep hors de, à l'extérieur de; (in front of) devant; **at the ~** (fig) au plus or maximum; **outside lane** n (Aut: in Britain) voie f de droite; (: in US, Europe) voie de gauche; **outside line** n (Tel) ligne extérieure; **outsider** n (stranger) étranger(-ère)

out: outsize adj énorme; (clothes) grande taille inv; **outskirts** npl faubourgs mpl; **outspoken** adj très franc (franche); **outstanding** adj remarquable, exceptionnel(le); (unfinished: work, business) en suspens, en souffrance; (debt) impayé(e); (problem) non réglé(e)

outward ['autwəd] adj (sign, appearances) extérieur(e); (journey) (d')aller; **outwards** adv (esp BRIT) = **outward**

outweigh [aut'weɪ] vt l'emporter sur

oval ['əuvl] adj, n ovale m

ovary ['əuvərɪ] n ovaire m

oven ['ʌvn] n four m; **oven glove** n gant m de cuisine; **ovenproof** adj allant au four; **oven-ready** adj prêt(e) à cuire

over ['əuvə^r] adv (par-)dessus ▷ adj (finished) fini(e), terminé(e); (too much) en plus ▷ prep sur; par-dessus; (above) au-dessus de; (on the other side of) de l'autre côté de; (more than) plus de; (during) pendant; (about, concerning): **they fell out ~ money/ her** ils se sont brouillés pour des questions d'argent/à cause d'elle; **~ here** ici; **~ there** là-bas; **all ~** (everywhere) partout; **~ and ~ (again)** à plusieurs reprises; **~ and above** en plus de; **to ask sb ~** inviter qn (à passer); **to fall ~** tomber; **to turn sth ~** retourner qch

overall ['əʊvərɔːl] *adj (length)* total(e); *(study, impression)* d'ensemble ▷ *n (BRIT)* blouse *f* ▷ *adv* [əʊvər'ɔːl] dans l'ensemble, en général; **overalls** *npl (boiler suit)* bleus *mpl* (de travail)

overboard ['əʊvəbɔːd] *adv (Naut)* par-dessus bord

overcame [əʊvə'keɪm] *pt of* **overcome**

overcast ['əʊvəkɑːst] *adj* couvert(e)

overcharge [əʊvə'tʃɑːdʒ] *vt*: **to ~ sb for sth** faire payer qch trop cher à qn

overcoat ['əʊvəkəʊt] *n* pardessus *m*

overcome [əʊvə'kʌm] *vt (irreg: like* **come**) *(defeat)* triompher de; *(difficulty)* surmonter ▷ *adj (emotionally)* bouleversé(e); **~ with grief** accablé(e) de douleur

over: overcrowded *adj* bondé(e); *(city, country)* surpeuplé(e); **overdo** *vt (irreg: like* **do**) exagérer; *(overcook)* trop cuire; **to overdo it, to overdo things** *(work too hard)* en faire trop, se surmener; **overdone** [əʊvə'dʌn] *adj (vegetables, steak)* trop cuit(e); **overdose** *n* dose excessive; **overdraft** *n* découvert *m*; **overdrawn** *adj (account)* à découvert; **overdue** *adj* en retard; *(bill)* impayé(e); *(change)* qui tarde; **overestimate** *vt* surestimer

overflow *vi* [əʊvə'fləʊ] déborder ▷ *n* ['əʊvəfləʊ] *(also:* **~ pipe**) tuyau *m* d'écoulement, trop-plein *m*

overgrown [əʊvə'grəʊn] *adj (garden)* envahi(e) par la végétation

overhaul *vt* [əʊvə'hɔːl] réviser ▷ *n* ['əʊvəhɔːl] révision *f*

overhead *adv* [əʊvə'hɛd] au-dessus ▷ *adj* ['əʊvəhɛd] aérien(ne); *(lighting)*

vertical(e) ▷ *n* ['əʊvəhɛd] *(US)* = **overheads**; **overhead projector** *n* rétroprojecteur *m*; **overheads** *npl* *(BRIT)* frais généraux

over: overhear *vt (irreg: like* **hear**) entendre (par hasard); **overheat** *vi (engine)* chauffer; **overland** *adj, adv* par voie de terre; **overlap** *vi* se chevaucher; **overleaf** *adv* au verso; **overload** *vt* surcharger; **overlook** *vt (have view of)* donner sur; *(miss)* oublier, négliger; *(forgive)* fermer les yeux sur

overnight *adv* [əʊvə'naɪt] *(happen)* durant la nuit; *(fig)* soudain ▷ *adj* ['əʊvənaɪt] d'une *(or* de) nuit; soudain(e); **to stay ~ (with sb)** passer la nuit (chez qn); **overnight bag** *n* nécessaire *m* de voyage

overpass ['əʊvəpɑːs] *n (US: for cars)* pont autoroutier; *(for pedestrians)* passerelle *f*, pont *m*

overpower [əʊvə'paʊə^r] *vt* vaincre; *(fig)* accabler; **overpowering** *adj* irrésistible; *(heat, stench)* suffocant(e)

over: overreact [əʊvəriː'ækt] *vi* réagir de façon excessive; **overrule** *vt (decision)* annuler; *(claim)* rejeter; *(person)* rejeter l'avis de; **overrun** *vt (irreg: like* **run**) *(Mil: country etc)* occuper; *(time limit etc)* dépasser ▷ *vi* dépasser le temps imparti

overseas [əʊvə'siːz] *adv* outre-mer; *(abroad)* à l'étranger ▷ *adj (trade)* extérieur(e); *(visitor)* étranger(-ère)

oversee [əʊvə'siː] *vt (irreg: like* **see**) surveiller

overshadow [əʊvə'ʃædəʊ] *vt (fig)* éclipser

oversight ['əʊvəsaɪt] *n* omission *f*, oubli *m*

oversleep [əʊvə'sliːp] *vi (irreg: like* **sleep**) se réveiller (trop) tard

overspend [əʊvə'spɛnd] *vi (irreg: like* **spend**) dépenser de trop

overt [əʊ'vəːt] *adj* non dissimulé(e)

overtake [əʊvə'teɪk] *vt (irreg: like* **take**) dépasser; *(BRIT Aut)* dépasser, doubler

over: overthrow vt (irreg: like **throw**)
(government) renverser; **overtime**
n heures fpl supplémentaires;
overturn vt renverser; (decision,
plan) annuler ▷ vi se retourner;
overweight adj (person) trop
gros(se); **overwhelm** vt (subj:
emotion) accabler, submerger; (enemy,
opponent) écraser; **overwhelming**
adj (victory, defeat) écrasant(e); (desire)
irrésistible

owe [əu] vt devoir; **to ~ sb sth, to ~
sth to sb** devoir qch à qn; **how much
do I ~ you?** combien est-ce que je
vous dois?; **owing to** prep à cause de,
en raison de

owl [aul] n hibou m

own [əun] vt posséder ▷ adj propre;
a room of my ~ une chambre à moi,
ma propre chambre; **to get one's
~ back** prendre sa revanche; **on
one's ~** tout(e) seul(e); **own up** vi
avouer; **owner** n propriétaire m/f;
ownership n possession f

ox (pl **oxen**) [ɔks, ˈɔksn] n bœuf m

Oxbridge [ˈɔksbrɪdʒ] n (BRIT) les
universités d'Oxford et de Cambridge

oxen [ˈɔksən] npl of **ox**

oxygen [ˈɔksɪdʒən] n oxygène m

oyster [ˈɔɪstəʳ] n huître f

oz. abbr = **ounce; ounces**

ozone [ˈəuzəun] n ozone m; **ozone
friendly** adj qui n'attaque pas or qui
préserve la couche d'ozone; **ozone
layer** n couche f d'ozone

p

p abbr (BRIT) = **penny; pence**

P.A. n abbr = **personal assistant;
public address system**

p.a. abbr = **per annum**

pace [peɪs] n pas m; (speed) allure f;
vitesse f ▷ vi: **to ~ up and down** faire
les cent pas; **to keep ~ with** aller à
la même vitesse que; (events) se tenir
au courant de; **pacemaker** n (Med)
stimulateur m cardiaque; (Sport: also:
pacesetter) meneur(-euse) de train

Pacific [pəˈsɪfɪk] n: **the ~ (Ocean)** le
Pacifique, l'océan m Pacifique

pacifier [ˈpæsɪfaɪəʳ] n (US: dummy)
tétine f

pack [pæk] n paquet m; (of hounds)
meute f; (of thieves, wolves etc) bande
f; (of cards) jeu m; (US: of cigarettes)
paquet; (back pack) sac m à dos ▷ vt
(goods) empaqueter, emballer; (in
suitcase etc) emballer; (box) remplir;
(cram) entasser ▷ vi: **to ~ (one's
bags)** faire ses bagages; **pack in** (BRIT

inf) vi (*machine*) tomber en panne
▷ vt (*boyfriend*) plaquer; **~ it in!** laisse
tomber!; **pack off** vt: **to ~ sb off to**
expédier qn à; **pack up** vi (*BRIT inf*:
machine) tomber en panne; (*person*) se
tirer ▷ vt (*belongings*) ranger; (*goods,
presents*) empaqueter, emballer

package ['pækɪdʒ] n paquet m;
(*also:* **~ deal**) (*agreement*) marché
global; (*purchase*) forfait m; (*Comput*)
progiciel m ▷ vt (*goods*) conditionner;
package holiday n (*BRIT*) vacances
organisées; **package tour** n voyage
organisé

packaging ['pækɪdʒɪŋ] n (*wrapping
materials*) emballage m

packed [pækt] adj (*crowded*)
bondé(e); **packed lunch** (*BRIT*) n
repas froid

packet ['pækɪt] n paquet m

packing ['pækɪŋ] n emballage m

pact [pækt] n pacte m, traité m

pad [pæd] n bloc-notes m) m; (*to
prevent friction*) tampon m ▷ vt
rembourrer; **padded** adj (*jacket*)
matelassé(e); (*bra*) rembourré(e)

paddle ['pædl] n (*oar*) pagaie f;
(*US: for table tennis*) raquette f de
ping-pong ▷ vi (*with feet*) barboter,
faire trempette ▷ vt: **to ~ a canoe** etc
pagayer; **paddling pool** n petit bassin

paddock ['pædək] n enclos m;
(*Racing*) paddock m

padlock ['pædlɔk] n cadenas m

paedophile, (*US*) **pedophile**
['piːdəufaɪl] n pédophile m

page [peɪdʒ] n (*of book*) page f; (*also:*
~ boy) groom m, chasseur m; (*at
wedding*) garçon m d'honneur ▷ vt (*in
hotel etc*) (faire) appeler

pager ['peɪdʒər] n bip m (*inf*),
Alphapage® m

paid [peɪd] pt, pp of **pay** ▷ adj (*work,
official*) rémunéré(e); (*holiday*)
payé(e); **to put ~ to** (*BRIT*) mettre fin
à, mettre par terre

pain [peɪn] n douleur f; (*inf: nuisance*)
plaie f; **to be in ~** souffrir, avoir

mal; **to take ~s to do** se donner
du mal pour faire; **painful** adj
douloureux(-euse); (*difficult*) difficile,
pénible; **painkiller** n calmant
m, analgésique m; **painstaking**
['peɪnzteɪkɪŋ] adj (*person*)
soigneux(-euse); (*work*) soigné(e)

paint [peɪnt] n peinture f ▷ vt peindre;
to ~ the door blue peindre la porte
en bleu; **paintbrush** n pinceau m;
painter n peintre m; **painting** n
peinture f; (*picture*) tableau m

pair [peər] n (*of shoes, gloves etc*) paire
f; (*of people*) couple m; **~ of scissors**
(paire de) ciseaux mpl; **~ of trousers**
pantalon m

pajamas [pə'dʒɑːməz] npl (*US*)
pyjama m

Pakistan [pɑːkɪ'stɑːn] n Pakistan
m; **Pakistani** adj pakistanais(e) ▷ n
Pakistanais(e)

pal [pæl] n (*inf*) copain (copine)

palace ['pæləs] n palais m

pale [peɪl] adj pâle; **~ blue** adj bleu
pâle inv

Palestine ['pælɪstaɪn] n Palestine
f; **Palestinian** [pælɪs'tɪnɪən] adj
palestinien(ne) ▷ n Palestinien(ne)

palm [pɑːm] n (*Anat*) paume f; (*also:* **~
tree**) palmier m ▷ vt: **to ~ sth off on
sb** (*inf*) refiler qch à qn

pamper ['pæmpər] vt gâter, dorloter

pamphlet ['pæmflət] n brochure f

pan [pæn] n (*also:* **sauce~**) casserole f;
(*also:* **frying ~**) poêle f

pancake ['pænkeɪk] n crêpe f

panda ['pændə] n panda m

pandemic [pæn'dɛmɪk] n
pandémie f

pane [peɪn] n carreau m (de fenêtre),
vitre f

panel ['pænl] n (*of wood, cloth etc*)
panneau m; (*Radio, TV*) experts m,
invités mpl; (*for interview, exams*) jury m

panhandler ['pænhændlər] n (*US
inf*) mendiant(e)

panic ['pænɪk] n panique f,
affolement m ▷ vi s'affoler, paniquer

panorama [pænə'rɑːmə] *n*
  panorama *m*
pansy ['pænzɪ] *n* (*Bot*) pensée *f*
pant [pænt] *vi* haleter
panther ['pænθəʳ] *n* panthère *f*
panties ['pæntɪz] *npl* slip *m*, culotte *f*
pantomime ['pæntəmaɪm] *n* (BRIT)
  spectacle *m* de Noël

> ● **PANTOMIME**
>
> ● Une *pantomime* (à ne pas confondre
> ● avec le mot tel qu'on l'utilise
> ● en français), que l'on appelle
> ● également de façon familière
> ● "panto", est un genre de farce où le
> ● personnage principal est souvent
> ● un jeune garçon et où il y a toujours
> ● une "dame", c'est-à-dire une vieille
> ● femme jouée par un homme, et
> ● un méchant. La plupart du temps,
> ● l'histoire est basée sur un conte de
> ● fées comme Cendrillon ou Le Chat
> ● botté, et le public est encouragé
> ● à participer en prévenant le héros
> ● d'un danger imminent. Ce genre
> ● de spectacle, qui s'adresse surtout
> ● aux enfants, vise également un
> ● public d'adultes au travers des
> ● nombreuses plaisanteries faisant
> ● allusion à des faits d'actualité.

pants [pænts] *npl* (BRIT: *woman's*)
  culotte *f*, slip *m*; (: *man's*) slip, caleçon
  m; (US: *trousers*) pantalon *m*
pantyhose ['pæntɪhəuz] *npl* (US)
  collant *m*
paper ['peɪpəʳ] *n* papier *m*; (*also*:
  wall~) papier peint; (*also*: **news~**)
  journal *m*; (*academic essay*) article
  m; (*exam*) épreuve écrite ▷ *adj* en or
  de papier ▷ *vt* tapisser (de papier
  peint); **papers** *npl* (*also*: **identity ~s**)
  papiers *mpl* (d'identité); **paperback**
  n livre broché *or* non relié; (*small*) livre
  m de poche; **paper bag** *n* sac *m* en
  papier; **paper clip** *n* trombone *m*;
  paper shop *n* (BRIT) marchand *m* de

journaux; **paperwork** *n* papiers *mpl*;
  (*pej*) paperasserie *f*
paprika ['pæprɪkə] *n* paprika *m*
par [pɑːʳ] *n* pair *m*; (*Golf*) normale *f* du
  parcours; **on a ~ with** à égalité avec,
  au même niveau que
paracetamol [pærə'siːtəmɔl] *n*
  (BRIT) paracétamol *m*
parachute ['pærəʃuːt] *n*
  parachute *m*
parade [pə'reɪd] *n* défilé *m* ▷ *vt* (*fig*)
  faire étalage de ▷ *vi* défiler
paradise ['pærədaɪs] *n* paradis *m*
paradox ['pærədɔks] *n* paradoxe *m*
paraffin ['pærəfɪn] *n* (BRIT): **~ (oil)**
  pétrole (lampant)
paragraph ['pærəgrɑːf] *n*
  paragraphe *m*
parallel ['pærəlɛl] *adj*: **~ (with or to)**
  parallèle (à); (*fig*) analogue (à) ▷ *n*
  (*line*) parallèle *f*; (*fig, Geo*) parallèle *m*
paralysed ['pærəlaɪzd] *adj*
  paralysé(e)
paralysis (*pl* **paralyses**) [pə'rælɪsɪs,
  -siːz] *n* paralysie *f*
paramedic [pærə'mɛdɪk] *n*
  auxiliaire *m/f* médical(e)
paranoid ['pærənɔɪd] *adj* (*Psych*)
  paranoïaque; (*neurotic*) paranoïde
parasite ['pærəsaɪt] *n* parasite *m*
parcel ['pɑːsl] *n* paquet *m*, colis *m* ▷ *vt*
  (*also*: **~ up**) empaqueter
pardon ['pɑːdn] *n* pardon *m*; (*Law*)
  grâce *f* ▷ *vt* pardonner à; (*Law*)
  gracier; **~!** pardon!; **~ me!** (*after
  burping etc*) excusez-moi!; **I beg your
  ~!** (*I'm sorry*) pardon!, je suis désolé!; **(I
  beg your) ~?**, (US) **~ me?** (*what did you
  say?*) pardon?
parent ['pɛərənt] *n* (*father*) père
  m; (*mother*) mère *f*; **parents** *npl*
  parents *mpl*; **parental** [pə'rɛntl] *adj*
  parental(e), des parents
Paris ['pærɪs] *n* Paris
parish ['pærɪʃ] *n* paroisse *f*; (BRIT: *civil*)
  ≈ commune *f*
Parisian [pə'rɪzɪən] *adj* parisien(ne),
  de Paris ▷ *n* Parisien(ne)

P

park [pɑːk] n parc m, jardin public
▷ vt garer ▷ vi se garer; **can I ~ here?**
est-ce que je peux me garer ici?
parking ['pɑːkɪŋ] n stationnement
m; **"no ~"** "stationnement interdit";
parking lot n (US) parking m, parc m
de stationnement; **parking meter**
n parc(o)mètre m; **parking ticket**
n P.-V. m

▌ Be careful not to translate parking
by the French word parking.

parkway ['pɑːkweɪ] n (US) route f
express (en site vert ou aménagé)
parliament ['pɑːləmənt] n
parlement m; **parliamentary**
[pɑːlə'mɛntərɪ] adj parlementaire
Parmesan [pɑːmɪ'zæn] n (also:
~ cheese) Parmesan m
parole [pə'rəʊl] n: **on ~** en liberté
conditionnelle
parrot ['pærət] n perroquet m
parsley ['pɑːslɪ] n persil m
parsnip ['pɑːsnɪp] n panais m
parson ['pɑːsn] n ecclésiastique m;
(Church of England) pasteur m
part [pɑːt] n partie f; (of machine)
pièce f; (Theat) rôle m; (of serial)
épisode m; (US: in hair) raie f ▷ adv
= **partly** ▷ vt séparer ▷ vi (people) se
séparer; (crowd) s'ouvrir; **to take ~ in**
participer à, prendre part à; **to take
sb's ~** prendre le parti de qn, prendre
parti pour qn; **for my ~** en ce qui me
concerne; **for the most ~** en grande
partie; dans la plupart des cas; **in ~**
en partie; **to take sth in good/bad
~** prendre qch du bon/mauvais côté;
part with vt fus (person) se séparer
de; (possessions) se défaire de
partial ['pɑːʃl] adj (incomplete)
partiel(le); **to be ~ to** aimer, avoir un
faible pour
participant [pɑː'tɪsɪpənt] n (in
competition, campaign) participant(e)
participate [pɑː'tɪsɪpeɪt] vi: **to ~
(in)** participer (à), prendre part (à)
particle ['pɑːtɪkl] n particule f; (of
dust) grain m

particular [pə'tɪkjʊləʳ] adj (specific)
particulier(-ière); (special) particulier,
spécial(e); (fussy) difficile, exigeant(e);
(careful) méticuleux(-euse); **in ~** en
particulier, surtout; **particularly** adv
particulièrement; (in particular) en
particulier; **particulars** npl détails
mpl; (information) renseignements mpl
parting ['pɑːtɪŋ] n séparation f; (BRIT:
in hair) raie f
partition [pɑː'tɪʃən] n (Pol) partition
f, division f; (wall) cloison f
partly ['pɑːtlɪ] adv en partie,
partiellement
partner ['pɑːtnəʳ] n (Comm)
associé(e); (Sport) partenaire m/f;
(spouse) conjoint(e); (lover) ami(e); (at
dance) cavalier(-ière); **partnership** n
association f
partridge ['pɑːtrɪdʒ] n perdrix f
part-time ['pɑːt'taɪm] adj, adv à
mi-temps, à temps partiel
party ['pɑːtɪ] n (Pol) parti m;
(celebration) fête f; (: formal) réception
f; (: in evening) soirée f; (group) groupe
m; (Law) partie f
pass [pɑːs] vt (time, object) passer;
(place) passer devant; (friend)
croiser; (exam) être reçu(e) à, réussir;
(overtake) dépasser; (approve)
approuver, accepter ▷ vi passer;
(Scol) être reçu(e) or admis(e), réussir
▷ n (permit) laissez-passer m inv;
(membership card) carte f d'accès
or d'abonnement; (in mountains)
col m; (Sport) passe f; (Scol: also: **~
mark**); **to get a ~** être reçu(e) (sans
mention); **to ~ sb sth** passer qch
à qn; **could you ~ the salt/oil,
please?** pouvez-vous me passer le
sel/l'huile, s'il vous plaît?; **to make
a ~ at sb** (inf) faire des avances à qn;
pass away vi mourir; **pass by** vi
passer ▷ vt (ignore) négliger; **pass on**
vt (hand on): **to ~ on (to)** transmettre
(à); **pass out** vi s'évanouir; **pass over**
vt (ignore) passer sous silence; **pass
up** vt (opportunity) laisser passer;

passable adj (road) praticable; (work) acceptable

> Be careful not to translate to pass an exam by the French expression passer un examen.

passage ['pæsɪdʒ] n (also: **~way**) couloir m; (gen, in book) passage m; (by boat) traversée f

passenger ['pæsɪndʒəʳ] n passager(-ère)

passer-by [pɑːsə'baɪ] n passant(e)

passing place n (Aut) aire f de croisement

passion ['pæʃən] n passion f; **passionate** adj passionné(e); **passion fruit** n fruit m de la passion

passive ['pæsɪv] adj (also: Ling) passif(-ive)

passport ['pɑːspɔːt] n passeport m; **passport control** n contrôle m des passeports; **passport office** n bureau m de délivrance des passeports

password ['pɑːswəːd] n mot m de passe

past [pɑːst] prep (in front of) devant; (further than) au delà de, plus loin que; après; (later than) après ▷ adv: **to run ~** passer en courant ▷ adj passé(e); (president etc) ancien(ne) ▷ n passé m; **he's ~ forty** il a dépassé la quarantaine, il a plus de or passé quarante ans; **ten/quarter ~ eight** (BRIT) huit heures dix/un or et quart; **for the ~ few/3 days** depuis quelques/3 jours; ces derniers/3 derniers jours

pasta ['pæstə] n pâtes fpl

paste [peɪst] n pâte f; (Culin: meat) pâté m (à tartiner); (: tomato) purée f, concentré m; (glue) colle f (de pâte) ▷ vt coller

pastel ['pæstl] adj pastel inv ▷ n (Art: pencil) (crayon m) pastel m; (: drawing) (dessin m au) pastel; (colour) ton m pastel inv

pasteurized ['pæstəraɪzd] adj pasteurisé(e)

pastime ['pɑːstaɪm] n passe-temps m inv, distraction f

pastor ['pɑːstəʳ] n pasteur m

pastry ['peɪstrɪ] n pâte f; (cake) pâtisserie f

pasture ['pɑːstʃəʳ] n pâturage m

pasty¹ n ['pæstɪ] petit pâté (en croûte)

pasty² ['peɪstɪ] adj (complexion) terreux(-euse)

pat [pæt] vt donner une petite tape à; (dog) caresser

patch [pætʃ] n (of material) pièce f; (eye patch) cache m; (spot) tache f; (of land) parcelle f; (on tyre) rustine f ▷ vt (clothes) rapiécer; **a bad ~** (BRIT) une période difficile; **patchy** adj inégal(e); (incomplete) fragmentaire

pâté ['pæteɪ] n pâté m, terrine f

patent ['peɪtnt, US 'pætnt] n brevet m (d'invention) ▷ vt faire breveter ▷ adj patent(e), manifeste

paternal [pə'təːnl] adj paternel(le)

paternity leave [pə'təːnɪtɪ-] n congé m de paternité

path [pɑːθ] n chemin m, sentier m; (in garden) allée f; (of missile) trajectoire f

pathetic [pə'θɛtɪk] adj (pitiful) pitoyable; (very bad) lamentable, minable

pathway ['pɑːθweɪ] n chemin m, sentier m; (in garden) allée f

patience ['peɪʃns] n patience f; (BRIT Cards) réussite f

patient ['peɪʃnt] n malade m/f; (of dentist etc) patient(e) ▷ adj patient(e)

patio ['pætɪəu] n patio m

patriotic [pætrɪ'ɔtɪk] adj patriotique; (person) patriote

patrol [pə'trəul] n patrouille f ▷ vt patrouiller dans; **patrol car** n voiture f de police

patron ['peɪtrən] n (in shop) client(e); (of charity) patron(ne); **~ of the arts** mécène m

patronizing ['pætrənaɪzɪŋ] adj condescendant(e)

P

pattern ['pætən] n (Sewing) patron m; (design) motif m; **patterned** adj à motifs

pause [pɔːz] n pause f, arrêt m ▷ vi faire une pause, s'arrêter

pave [peɪv] vt paver, daller; **to ~ the way for** ouvrir la voie à

pavement ['peɪvmənt] n (BRIT) trottoir m; (US) chaussée f

pavilion [pə'vɪlɪən] n pavillon m; (Sport) stand m

paving ['peɪvɪŋ] n (material) pavé m

paw [pɔː] n patte f

pawn [pɔːn] n (Chess, also fig) pion m ▷ vt mettre en gage; **pawnbroker** n prêteur m sur gages

pay [peɪ] (pt, pp **paid**) n salaire m; (of manual worker) paie f ▷ vt payer ▷ vi payer; (be profitable) être rentable; **can I ~ by credit card?** est-ce que je peux payer par carte de crédit?; **to ~ attention (to)** prêter attention (à); **to ~ sb a visit** rendre visite à qn; **to ~ one's respects to sb** présenter ses respects à qn; **pay back** vt rembourser; **pay for** vt fus payer; **pay in** vt verser; **pay off** vt (debts) régler, acquitter; (person) rembourser ▷ vi (scheme, decision) se révéler payant(e); **pay out** vt (money) payer, sortir de sa poche; **pay up** vt (amount) payer; **payable** adj payable; **to make a cheque payable to sb** établir un chèque à l'ordre de qn; **pay-as-you-go** adj (mobile phone) à carte prépayée; **payday** n jour m de paie; **pay envelope** n (US) paie f; **payment** n paiement m; (of bill) règlement m; (of deposit, cheque) versement m; **monthly payment** mensualité f; **payout** n (from insurance) dédommagement m; (in competition) prix m; **pay packet** n (BRIT) paie f; **pay phone** n cabine f téléphonique, téléphone public; **pay raise** n (US) = **pay rise**; **pay rise** n (BRIT) augmentation f (de salaire); **payroll** n registre m du personnel;

pay slip n (BRIT) bulletin m de paie, feuille f de paie; **pay television** n chaînes fpl payantes; **paywall** n (Comput) mur m (payant)

PC n abbr = **personal computer**; (BRIT) = **police constable** ▷ adj abbr = **politically correct**

p.c. abbr = **per cent**

pcm n abbr (= per calendar month) par mois

PDA n abbr (= personal digital assistant) agenda m électronique

PE n abbr (= physical education) EPS f

pea [piː] n (petit) pois

peace [piːs] n paix f; (calm) calme m, tranquillité f; **peaceful** adj paisible, calme

peach [piːtʃ] n pêche f

peacock ['piːkɔk] n paon m

peak [piːk] n (mountain) pic m, cime f; (of cap) visière f; (fig: highest level) maximum m; (: of career, fame) apogée m; **peak hours** npl heures fpl d'affluence or de pointe

peanut ['piːnʌt] n arachide f, cacahuète f; **peanut butter** n beurre m de cacahuète

pear [pɛər] n poire f

pearl [pəːl] n perle f

peasant ['pɛznt] n paysan(ne)

peat [piːt] n tourbe f

pebble ['pɛbl] n galet m, caillou m

peck [pɛk] vt (also: ~ at) donner un coup de bec à; (food) picorer ▷ n coup m de bec; (kiss) bécot m; **peckish** adj (BRIT inf): **I feel peckish** je mangerais bien quelque chose, j'ai la dent

peculiar [pɪ'kjuːlɪər] adj (odd) étrange, bizarre, curieux(-euse); (particular) particulier(-ière); **~ to** particulier à

pedal ['pɛdl] n pédale f ▷ vi pédaler

pedestal ['pɛdəstl] n piédestal m

pedestrian [pɪ'dɛstrɪən] n piéton m; **pedestrian crossing** n (BRIT) passage clouté; **pedestrianized** adj: **a pedestrianized street** une rue piétonne; **pedestrian precinct,**

(US) **pedestrian zone** n (BRIT) zone piétonne

pedigree ['pɛdɪgri:] n ascendance f; (of animal) pedigree m ▷ cpd (animal) de race

pedophile ['pi:dəʊfaɪl] (US) n = **paedophile**

pee [pi:] vi (inf) faire pipi, pisser

peek [pi:k] vi jeter un coup d'œil (furtif)

peel [pi:l] n pelure f, épluchure f; (of orange, lemon) écorce f ▷ vt peler, éplucher ▷ vi (paint etc) s'écailler; (wallpaper) se décoller; (skin) peler

peep [pi:p] n (look) coup d'œil furtif; (sound) pépiement m ▷ vi jeter un coup d'œil (furtif)

peer [pɪəʳ] vi: **to ~ at** regarder attentivement, scruter ▷ n (noble) pair m; (equal) pair, égal(e)

peg [pɛg] n (for coat etc) patère f; (BRIT: also: **clothes ~**) pince f à linge

pelican ['pɛlɪkən] n pélican m; **pelican crossing** n (BRIT Aut) feu m à commande manuelle

pelt [pɛlt] vt: **to ~ sb (with)** bombarder qn (de) ▷ vi (rain) tomber à seaux; (inf: run) courir à toutes jambes ▷ n peau f

pelvis ['pɛlvɪs] n bassin m

pen [pɛn] n (for writing) stylo m; (for sheep) parc m

penalty ['pɛnltɪ] n pénalité f; sanction f; (fine) amende f; (Sport) pénalisation f; (Football) penalty m; (Rugby) pénalité f

pence [pɛns] npl of **penny**

pencil ['pɛnsl] n crayon m; **pencil in** vt noter provisoirement; **pencil case** n trousse f (d'écolier); **pencil sharpener** n taille-crayon(s) m inv

pendant ['pɛndnt] n pendentif m

pending ['pɛndɪŋ] prep en attendant ▷ adj en suspens

penetrate ['pɛnɪtreɪt] vt pénétrer dans; (enemy territory) entrer en

pen friend n (BRIT) correspondant(e)

penguin ['pɛŋgwɪn] n pingouin m

penicillin [pɛnɪ'sɪlɪn] n pénicilline f

peninsula [pə'nɪnsjulə] n péninsule f

penis ['pi:nɪs] n pénis m, verge f

penitentiary [pɛnɪ'tɛnʃərɪ] n (US) prison f

penknife ['pɛnnaɪf] n canif m

penniless ['pɛnɪlɪs] adj sans le sou

penny (pl **pennies** or **pence**) ['pɛnɪ, 'pɛnɪz, pɛns] n (BRIT) penny m; (US) cent m

pen pal n correspondant(e)

pension ['pɛnʃən] n (from company) retraite f; **pensioner** n (BRIT) retraité(e)

pentagon ['pɛntəgən] n: **the P~** (US Pol) le Pentagone

penthouse ['pɛnthaus] n appartement m (de luxe) en attique

penultimate [pɪ'nʌltɪmət] adj pénultième, avant-dernier(-ière)

people ['pi:pl] npl gens mpl; personnes fpl; (inhabitants) population f; (Pol) peuple m ▷ n (nation, race) peuple m; **several ~ came** plusieurs personnes sont venues; **~ say that ...** on dit or les gens disent que ...

pepper ['pɛpəʳ] n poivre m; (vegetable) poivron m ▷ vt (Culin) poivrer; **peppermint** n (sweet) pastille f de menthe

per [pəːʳ] prep par; **~ hour** (miles etc) à l'heure; (fee) (de) l'heure; **~ kilo** etc le kilo etc; **~ day/person** par jour/personne; **~ annum** par an

perceive [pə'si:v] vt percevoir; (notice) remarquer, s'apercevoir de

per cent adv pour cent

percentage [pə'sɛntɪdʒ] n pourcentage m

perception [pə'sɛpʃən] n perception f; (insight) sensibilité f

perch [pəːtʃ] n (fish) perche f; (for bird) perchoir m ▷ vi (se) percher

percussion [pə'kʌʃən] n percussion f

perennial [pə'rɛnɪəl] n (Bot) (plante f) vivace f, plante pluriannuelle

P

perfect ['pə:fɪkt] adj parfait(e)
▷ n (also: **~ tense**) parfait m ▷ vt
[pə'fɛkt] (technique, skill, work of art)
parfaire; (method, plan) mettre au
point; **perfection** [pə'fɛkʃən] n
perfection f; **perfectly** ['pə:fɪktlɪ]
adv parfaitement

perform [pə'fɔ:m] vt (carry out)
exécuter; (concert etc) jouer,
donner ▷ vi (actor, musician) jouer;
performance n représentation
f, spectacle m; (of an artist)
interprétation f; (Sport: of car,
engine) performance f; (of company,
economy) résultats mpl; **performer** n
artiste m/f

perfume ['pə:fju:m] n parfum m

perhaps [pə'hæps] adv peut-être

perimeter [pə'rɪmɪtər] n
périmètre m

period ['pɪərɪəd] n période f; (Hist)
époque f; (Scol) cours m; (full stop)
point m; (Med) règles fpl ▷ adj
(costume, furniture) d'époque;
periodical [pɪərɪ'ɔdɪkl] n périodique
m; **periodically** adv périodiquement

perish ['pɛrɪʃ] vi périr, mourir; (decay)
se détériorer

perjury ['pə:dʒərɪ] n (Law: in court)
faux témoignage; (breach of oath)
parjure m

perk [pə:k] n (inf) avantage m,
à-côté m

perm [pə:m] n (for hair) permanente f

permanent ['pə:mənənt] adj
permanent(e); **permanently**
adv de façon permanente; (move
abroad) définitivement; (open, closed)
en permanence; (tired, unhappy)
constamment

permission [pə'mɪʃən] n permission
f, autorisation f

permit n ['pə:mɪt] permis m

perplex [pə'plɛks] vt (person) rendre
perplexe

persecute ['pə:sɪkju:t] vt persécuter

persecution [pə:sɪ'kju:ʃən] n
persécution f

persevere [pə:sɪ'vɪər] vi persévérer

Persian ['pə:ʃən] adj persan(e); **the ~
Gulf** le golfe Persique

persist [pə'sɪst] vi: **to ~ (in doing)**
persister (à faire), s'obstiner (à faire);
persistent adj persistant(e), tenace

person ['pə:sn] n personne f; **in
~** en personne; **personal** adj
personnel(le); **personal assistant** n
secrétaire personnel(le); **personal
computer** n ordinateur individuel,
PC m; **personality** [pə:sə'nælɪtɪ]
n personnalité f; **personally** adv
personnellement; **to take sth
personally** se sentir visé(e) par
qch; **personal organizer** n agenda
(personnel); (electronic) agenda
électronique; **personal stereo** n
Walkman® m, baladeur m

personnel [pə:sə'nɛl] n personnel m

perspective [pə'spɛktɪv] n
perspective f

perspiration [pə:spɪ'reɪʃən] n
transpiration f

persuade [pə'sweɪd] vt: **to ~ sb to
do sth** persuader qn de faire qch,
amener or décider qn à faire qch

persuasion [pə'sweɪʒən] n
persuasion f; (creed) conviction f

persuasive [pə'sweɪsɪv] adj
persuasif(-ive)

perverse [pə'və:s] adj pervers(e);
(contrary) entêté(e), contrariant(e)

pervert n ['pə:və:t] perverti(e) ▷ vt
[pə'və:t] pervertir; (words) déformer

pessimism ['pɛsɪmɪzəm] n
pessimisme m

pessimist ['pɛsɪmɪst] n pessimiste
m/f; **pessimistic** [pɛsɪ'mɪstɪk] adj
pessimiste

pest [pɛst] n animal m (or insecte m)
nuisible; (fig) fléau m

pester ['pɛstər] vt importuner,
harceler

pesticide ['pɛstɪsaɪd] n pesticide m

pet [pɛt] n animal familier ▷ cpd
(favourite) favori(e) ▷ vt (stroke)
caresser, câliner; **teacher's ~**

chouchou m du professeur; **~ hate**
bête noire
petal ['pɛtl] n pétale m
petite [pə'tiːt] adj menu(e)
petition [pə'tɪʃən] n pétition f
petrified ['pɛtrɪfaɪd] adj (fig) mort(e)
de peur
petrol ['pɛtrəl] n (BRIT) essence f;
I've run out of ~ je suis en panne
d'essence

> Be careful not to translate petrol
> by the French word pétrole.

petroleum [pə'trəʊlɪəm] n pétrole m
petrol: petrol pump n (BRIT: in car,
at garage) pompe f à essence; **petrol
station** n (BRIT) station-service f;
petrol tank n (BRIT) réservoir m
d'essence
petticoat ['pɛtɪkəʊt] n jupon m
petty ['pɛtɪ] adj (mean) mesquin(e);
(unimportant) insignifiant(e), sans
importance
pew [pjuː] n banc m (d'église)
pewter ['pjuːtə'] n étain m
phantom ['fæntəm] n fantôme m
pharmacist ['faːməsɪst] n
pharmacien(ne)
pharmacy ['faːməsɪ] n pharmacie f
phase [feɪz] n phase f, période
f; **phase in** vt introduire
progressivement; **phase out** vt
supprimer progressivement
Ph.D. abbr = **Doctor of Philosophy**
pheasant ['fɛznt] n faisan m
phenomena [fə'nɒmɪnə] npl of
phenomenon
phenomenal [fɪ'nɒmɪnl] adj
phénoménal(e)
phenomenon (pl **phenomena**)
[fə'nɒmɪnən, -nə] n phénomène m
Philippines ['fɪlɪpiːnz] npl (also:
Philippine Islands): **the ~** les
Philippines fpl
philosopher [fɪ'lɒsəfə'] n
philosophe m
philosophical [fɪlə'sɒfɪkl] adj
philosophique
philosophy [fɪ'lɒsəfɪ] n philosophie f

phlegm [flɛm] n flegme m
phobia ['fəʊbjə] n phobie f
phone [fəʊn] n téléphone m ▷ vt
téléphoner à ▷ vi téléphoner; **to
be on the ~** avoir le téléphone; (be
calling) être au téléphone; **phone
back** vt, vi rappeler; **phone up**
vt téléphoner à ▷ vi téléphoner;
phone book n annuaire m; **phone
box**, (US) **phone booth** n cabine f
téléphonique; **phone call** n coup m
de fil or de téléphone; **phonecard** n
télécarte f; **phone number** n numéro
m de téléphone
phonetics [fə'nɛtɪks] n phonétique f
phoney ['fəʊnɪ] adj faux (fausse),
factice; (person) pas franc (franche)
photo ['fəʊtəʊ] n photo f; **photo
album** n album m de photos;
photocopier n copieur m;
photocopy n photocopie f ▷ vt
photocopier
photograph ['fəʊtəgrɑːf] n
photographie f ▷ vt photographier;
photographer [fə'tɒgrəfə'] n
photographe m/f; **photography**
[fə'tɒgrəfɪ] n photographie f
phrase [freɪz] n expression f; (Ling)
locution f ▷ vt exprimer; **phrase
book** n recueil m d'expressions (pour
touristes)
physical ['fɪzɪkl] adj physique;
physical education n éducation
f physique; **physically** adv
physiquement
physician [fɪ'zɪʃən] n médecin m
physicist ['fɪzɪsɪst] n physicien(ne)
physics ['fɪzɪks] n physique f
physiotherapist [fɪzɪəʊ'θɛrəpɪst] n
kinésithérapeute m/f
physiotherapy [fɪzɪəʊ'θɛrəpɪ] n
kinésithérapie f
physique [fɪ'ziːk] n (appearance)
physique m; (health etc) constitution f
pianist ['piːənɪst] n pianiste m/f
piano [pɪ'ænəʊ] n piano m
pick [pɪk] n (tool: also: **~-axe**) pic m,
pioche f ▷ vt choisir; (gather) cueillir;

(*remove*) prendre; (*lock*) forcer; **take your ~** faites votre choix; **the ~ of** le meilleur(e) de; **to ~ one's nose** se mettre les doigts dans le nez; **to ~ one's teeth** se curer les dents; **to ~ a quarrel with sb** chercher noise à qn; **pick on** vt fus (*person*) harceler; **pick out** vt choisir; (*distinguish*) distinguer; **pick up** vi (*improve*) remonter, s'améliorer ▷ vt ramasser; (*collect*) passer prendre; (*Aut: give lift to*) prendre; (*learn*) apprendre; (*Radio*) capter; **to ~ up speed** prendre de la vitesse; **to ~ o.s. up** se relever

pickle ['pɪkl] n (*also:* **~s**) (*as condiment*) pickles mpl ▷ vt conserver dans du vinaigre or dans de la saumure; **in a ~** (*fig*) dans le pétrin

pickpocket ['pɪkpɔkɪt] n pickpocket m

pick-up ['pɪkʌp] n (*also:* **~ truck**) pick-up m inv

picnic ['pɪknɪk] n pique-nique m ▷ vi pique-niquer; **picnic area** n aire f de pique-nique

picture ['pɪktʃə'] n (*also TV*) image f; (*painting*) peinture f, tableau m; (*photograph*) photo(graphie) f; (*drawing*) dessin m; (*film*) film m; (*fig: description*) description f ▷ vt (*imagine*) se représenter; **pictures** npl; **the ~s** (BRIT) le cinéma; **to take a ~ of sb/ sth** prendre qn/qch en photo; **would you take a ~ of us, please?** pourriez-vous nous prendre en photo, s'il vous plaît?; **picture frame** n cadre m; **picture messaging** n picture messaging m, messagerie f d'images

picturesque [pɪktʃə'rɛsk] adj pittoresque

pie [paɪ] n tourte f; (*of fruit*) tarte f; (*of meat*) pâté m en croûte

piece [piːs] n morceau m; (*item*): **a ~ of furniture/advice** un meuble/ conseil ▷ vt: **to ~ together** rassembler; **to take to ~s** démonter

pie chart n graphique m à secteurs, camembert m

pier [pɪə'] n jetée f

pierce [pɪəs] vt percer, transpercer; **pierced** adj (*ears*) percé(e)

pig [pɪg] n cochon m, porc m; (*pej: unkind person*) mufle m; (: *greedy person*) goinfre m

pigeon ['pɪdʒən] n pigeon m

piggy bank ['pɪgɪ-] n tirelire f

pigsty ['pɪgstaɪ] n porcherie f

pigtail ['pɪgteɪl] n natte f, tresse f

pike [paɪk] n (*fish*) brochet m

pilchard ['pɪltʃəd] n pilchard m (*sorte de sardine*)

pile [paɪl] n (*pillar, of books*) pile f; (*heap*) tas m; (*of carpet*) épaisseur f; **pile up** vi (*accumulate*) s'entasser, s'accumuler ▷ vt (*put in heap*) empiler, entasser; (*accumulate*) accumuler; **piles** npl hémorroïdes fpl; **pile-up** n (*Aut*) télescopage m, collision f en série

pilgrim ['pɪlgrɪm] n pèlerin m; voir article **"Pilgrim Fathers"**

● PILGRIM FATHERS

Les *Pilgrim Fathers* ("Pères pèlerins") sont un groupe de puritains qui quittèrent l'Angleterre en 1620 pour fuir les persécutions religieuses. Ayant traversé l'Atlantique à bord du "Mayflower", ils fondèrent New Plymouth en Nouvelle-Angleterre, dans ce qui est aujourd'hui le Massachusetts. Ces Pères pèlerins sont considérés comme les fondateurs des États-Unis, et l'on commémore chaque année, le jour de "Thanksgiving", la réussite de leur première récolte.

pilgrimage ['pɪlgrɪmɪdʒ] n pèlerinage m

pill [pɪl] n pilule f; **the ~** la pilule

pillar ['pɪlə'] n pilier m

pillow ['pɪləu] n oreiller m; **pillowcase, pillowslip** n taie f d'oreiller

pilot ['paɪlət] n pilote m ▷ cpd (scheme etc) pilote, expérimental(e) ▷ vt piloter; **pilot light** n veilleuse f

pimple ['pɪmpl] n bouton m

PIN n abbr (= personal identification number) code m confidentiel

pin [pɪn] n épingle f; (Tech) cheville f ▷ vt épingler; **~s and needles** fourmis fpl; **to ~ sb down** (fig) coincer qn; **to ~ sth on sb** (fig) mettre qch sur le dos de qn

pinafore ['pɪnəfɔːʳ] n tablier m

pinch [pɪntʃ] n pincement m; (of salt etc) pincée f ▷ vt pincer; (inf: steal) piquer, chiper ▷ vi (shoe) serrer; **at a ~** à la rigueur

pine [paɪn] n (also: **~ tree**) pin m ▷ vi: **to ~ for** aspirer à, désirer ardemment

pineapple ['paɪnæpl] n ananas m

ping [pɪŋ] n (noise) tintement m; **ping-pong®** n ping-pong® m

pink [pɪŋk] adj rose ▷ n (colour) rose m

pinpoint ['pɪnpɔɪnt] vt indiquer (avec précision)

pint [paɪnt] n pinte f (Brit = 0,57 l; US = 0,47 l); (BRIT inf) ≈ demi m, ≈ pot m

pioneer [paɪə'nɪəʳ] n pionnier m

pious ['paɪəs] adj pieux(-euse)

pip [pɪp] n (seed) pépin m; **pips** npl; **the ~s** (BRIT: time signal on radio) le top

pipe [paɪp] n tuyau m, conduite f; (for smoking) pipe f ▷ vt amener par tuyau; **pipeline** n (for gas) gazoduc m, pipeline m; (for oil) oléoduc m, pipeline; **piper** n (flautist) joueur(-euse) de pipeau; (of bagpipes) joueur(-euse) de cornemuse

pirate ['paɪərət] n pirate m ▷ vt (CD, video, book) pirater

Pisces ['paɪsiːz] n les Poissons mpl

piss [pɪs] vi (infl) pisser (!); **pissed** adj (infl: BRIT: drunk) bourré(e); (: US: angry) furieux(-euse)

pistol ['pɪstl] n pistolet m

piston ['pɪstən] n piston m

pit [pɪt] n trou m, fosse f; (also: **coal ~**) puits m de mine; (also: **orchestra ~**) fosse d'orchestre; (US: fruit stone)

noyau m ▷ vt: **to ~ o.s.** or **one's wits against** se mesurer à

pitch [pɪtʃ] n (BRIT Sport) terrain m; (Mus) ton m; (fig: degree) degré m; (tar) poix f ▷ vt (throw) lancer; (tent) dresser ▷ vi (fall): **to ~ into/off** tomber dans/de; **pitch-black** adj noir(e) comme poix

pitfall ['pɪtfɔːl] n piège m

pith [pɪθ] n (of orange etc) intérieur m de l'écorce

pitiful ['pɪtɪful] adj (touching) pitoyable; (contemptible) lamentable

pity ['pɪtɪ] n pitié f ▷ vt plaindre; **what a ~!** quel dommage!

pizza ['piːtsə] n pizza f

placard ['plækɑːd] n affiche f; (in march) pancarte f

place [pleɪs] n endroit m, lieu m; (proper position, job, rank, seat) place f; (home): **at/to his ~** chez lui ▷ vt (position) placer, mettre; (identify) situer; reconnaître; **to take ~** avoir lieu; **to change ~s with sb** changer de place avec qn; **out of ~** (not suitable) déplacé(e), inopportun(e); **in the first ~** d'abord, en premier; **place mat** n set m de table; (in linen etc) napperon m; **placement** n (during studies) stage m

placid ['plæsɪd] adj placide

plague [pleɪg] n (Med) peste f ▷ vt (fig) tourmenter

plaice [pleɪs] n (pl inv) carrelet m

plain [pleɪn] adj (in one colour) uni(e); (clear) clair(e), évident(e); (simple) simple; (not handsome) quelconque, ordinaire ▷ adv franchement, carrément ▷ n plaine f; **plain chocolate** n chocolat m à croquer; **plainly** adv clairement; (frankly) carrément, sans détours

plaintiff ['pleɪntɪf] n plaignant(e)

plait [plæt] n tresse f, natte f

plan [plæn] n plan m; (scheme) projet m ▷ vt (think in advance) projeter; (prepare) organiser ▷ vi faire des projets; **to ~ to do** projeter de faire

plane [pleɪn] n (Aviat) avion m; (also:
~ tree) platane m; (tool) rabot m; (Art,
Math etc) plan m; (fig) niveau m, plan
▷ vt (with tool) raboter
planet ['plænɪt] n planète f
plank [plæŋk] n planche f
planning ['plænɪŋ] n planification f;
family ~ planning familial
plant [plɑːnt] n plante f; (machinery)
matériel m; (factory) usine f ▷ vt
planter; (bomb) déposer, poser;
(microphone, evidence) cacher
plantation [plæn'teɪʃən] n
plantation f
plaque [plæk] n plaque f
plaster ['plɑːstər] n plâtre m; (also:
~ of Paris) plâtre à mouler; (BRIT: also:
sticking ~) pansement adhésif ▷ vt
plâtrer; (cover): **to ~ with** couvrir de;
plaster cast n (Med) plâtre m; (model,
statue) moule m
plastic ['plæstɪk] n plastique m ▷ adj
(made of plastic) en plastique; **plastic
bag** n sac m en plastique; **plastic
surgery** n chirurgie f esthétique
plate [pleɪt] n (dish) assiette f; (sheet of
metal, on door, Phot) plaque f; (in book)
gravure f; (dental) dentier m
plateau (pl **plateaus** or **plateaux**)
['plætəu, -z] n plateau m
platform ['plætfɔːm] n (at meeting)
tribune f; (stage) estrade f; (Rail) quai
m; (Pol) plateforme f
platinum ['plætɪnəm] n platine m
platoon [plə'tuːn] n peloton m
platter ['plætər] n plat m
plausible ['plɔːzɪbl] adj plausible;
(person) convaincant(e)
play [pleɪ] n jeu m; (Theat) pièce f (de
théâtre) ▷ vt (game) jouer à; (team,
opponent) jouer contre; (instrument)
jouer de; (part, piece of music, note)
jouer; (CD etc) passer ▷ vi jouer; **to ~
safe** ne prendre aucun risque; **play
back** vt repasser, réécouter; **play
up** vi (cause trouble) faire des siennes;
player n joueur(-euse); (Mus)
musicien(ne); **playful** adj enjoué(e);

playground n cour f de récréation;
(in park) aire f de jeux; **playgroup** n
garderie f; **playing card** n carte f à
jouer; **playing field** n terrain m de
sport; **playschool** n = **playgroup**;
playtime n (Scol) récréation f;
playwright n dramaturge m
plc abbr (= public limited company)
≈ SARL f
plea [pliː] n (request) appel m; (Law)
défense f
plead [pliːd] vt plaider; (give as
excuse) invoquer ▷ vi (Law) plaider;
(beg): **to ~ with sb (for sth)** implorer
qn (d'accorder qch); **to ~ guilty/
not guilty** plaider coupable/non
coupable
pleasant ['plɛznt] adj agréable
please [pliːz] excl s'il te (or vous)
plaît ▷ vt plaire à ▷ vi (think fit): **do
as you ~** faites comme il vous plaira;
~ yourself! (inf) (faites) comme
vous voulez!; **pleased** adj: **pleased
(with)** content(e) (de); **pleased to
meet you** enchanté (de faire votre
connaissance)
pleasure ['plɛʒər] n plaisir m; **"it's a
~"** "je vous en prie"
pleat [pliːt] n pli m
pledge [plɛdʒ] n (promise) promesse f
▷ vt promettre
plentiful ['plɛntɪful] adj
abondant(e), copieux(-euse)
plenty ['plɛntɪ] n: **~ of** beaucoup de;
(sufficient) (bien) assez de
pliers ['plaɪəz] npl pinces fpl
plight [plaɪt] n situation f critique
plod [plɔd] vi avancer péniblement;
(fig) peiner
plonk [plɔŋk] (inf) n (BRIT: wine)
pinard m, piquette f ▷ vt: **to ~ sth
down** poser brusquement qch
plot [plɔt] n complot m, conspiration
f; (of story, play) intrigue f; (of land) lot
m de terrain, lopin m ▷ vt (mark out)
tracer point par point; (Naut) pointer;
(make graph of) faire le graphique de;
(conspire) comploter ▷ vi comploter

plough, (US) **plow** [plaʊ] n charrue f ▷ vt (earth) labourer; **to ~ money into** investir dans

ploy [plɔɪ] n stratagème m

pls abbr (= please) SVP m

pluck [plʌk] vt (fruit) cueillir; (musical instrument) pincer; (bird) plumer; **to ~ one's eyebrows** s'épiler les sourcils; **to ~ up courage** prendre son courage à deux mains

plug [plʌg] n (stopper) bouchon m, bonde f; (Elec) prise f de courant; (Aut: also: **spark(ing) ~**) bougie f ▷ vt (hole) boucher; (inf: advertise) faire du battage pour, matraquer; **plug in** vt (Elec) brancher; **plughole** n (BRIT) trou m (d'écoulement)

plum [plʌm] n (fruit) prune f

plumber ['plʌmə'] n plombier m

plumbing ['plʌmɪŋ] n (trade) plomberie f; (piping) tuyauterie f

plummet ['plʌmɪt] vi (person, object) plonger; (sales, prices) dégringoler

plump [plʌmp] adj rondelet(te), dodu(e), bien en chair; **plump for** vt fus (inf: choose) se décider pour

plunge [plʌndʒ] n plongeon m; (fig) chute f ▷ vt plonger ▷ vi (fall) tomber, dégringoler; (dive) plonger; **to take the ~** se jeter à l'eau

pluperfect [pluː'pə:fɪkt] n (Ling) plus-que-parfait m

plural ['pluərl] adj pluriel(le) ▷ n pluriel m

plus [plʌs] n (also: **~ sign**) signe m plus; (advantage) atout m ▷ prep plus; **ten/twenty ~** plus de dix/vingt

ply [plaɪ] n (of wool) fil m ▷ vt (a trade) exercer ▷ vi (ship) faire la navette; **to ~ sb with drink** donner continuellement à boire à qn; **plywood** n contreplaqué m

P.M. n abbr (BRIT) = **prime minister**

p.m. adv abbr (= post meridiem) de l'après-midi

PMS n abbr (= premenstrual syndrome) syndrome prémenstruel

PMT n abbr (= premenstrual tension) syndrome prémenstruel

pneumatic drill [njuː'mætɪk-] n marteau-piqueur m

pneumonia [njuː'məʊnɪə] n pneumonie f

poach [pəʊtʃ] vt (cook) pocher; (steal) pêcher (or chasser) sans permis ▷ vi braconner; **poached** adj (egg) poché(e)

P.O. Box n abbr = **post office box**

pocket ['pɔkɪt] n poche f ▷ vt empocher; **to be (£5) out of ~** (BRIT) en être de sa poche (pour 5 livres); **pocketbook** n (US: wallet) portefeuille m; **pocket money** n argent m de poche

pod [pɔd] n cosse f

podcast ['pɔdkɑ:st] n podcast m ▷ vi podcaster

podiatrist [pɔ'di:ətrɪst] n (US) pédicure m/f

poem ['pəʊɪm] n poème m

poet ['pəʊɪt] n poète m; **poetic** [pəʊ'ɛtɪk] adj poétique; **poetry** n poésie f

poignant ['pɔɪnjənt] adj poignant(e) **P**

point [pɔɪnt] n point m; (tip) pointe f; (in time) moment m; (in space) endroit m; (subject, idea) point, sujet m; (purpose) but m; (also: **decimal ~**): **2 ~ 3 (2.3)** 2 virgule 3 (2,3); (BRIT Elec: also: **power ~**) prise f (de courant) ▷ vt (show) indiquer; (gun etc): **to ~ sth at** braquer or diriger qch sur ▷ vi: **to ~ at** montrer du doigt; **points** npl (Rail) aiguillage m; **to make a ~ of doing sth** ne pas manquer de faire qch; **to get/miss the ~** comprendre/ne pas comprendre; **to come to the ~** en venir au fait; **there's no ~ (in doing)** cela ne sert à rien (de faire); **to be on the ~ of doing sth** être sur le point de faire qch; **point out** vt (mention) faire remarquer, souligner; **point-blank** adv (fig) catégoriquement; (also: **at point-blank range**) à bout portant; **pointed** adj (shape) pointu(e); (remark) plein(e) de sous-entendus; **pointer** n (needle) aiguille f; (clue) indication f; (advice) tuyau m; **pointless** adj inutile, vain(e); **point of view** n point m de vue

poison ['pɔɪzn] n poison m ▷ vt empoisonner; **poisonous** adj (snake) venimeux(-euse); (substance, plant) vénéneux(-euse); (fumes) toxique

poke [pəuk] vt (jab with finger, stick etc) piquer; pousser du doigt; (put): **to ~ sth in(to)** fourrer or enfoncer qch dans; **poke about** vi fureter; **poke out** vi (stick out) sortir

poker ['pəukə'] n tisonnier m; (Cards) poker m

Poland ['pəulənd] n Pologne f

polar ['pəulə'] adj polaire; **polar bear** n ours blanc

Pole [pəul] n Polonais(e)

pole [pəul] n (of wood) mât m, perche f; (Elec) poteau m; (Geo) pôle m; **pole bean** n (US) haricot m (à rames); **pole vault** n saut m à la perche

police [pə'li:s] npl police f ▷ vt maintenir l'ordre dans; **police car** n voiture f de police; **police constable** n (BRIT) agent m de police; **police force** n police f, forces fpl de l'ordre; **policeman** (irreg) n agent m de police, policier m; **police officer** n agent m de police; **police station** n commissariat m de police; **policewoman** (irreg) n femme-agent f

policy ['pɔlɪsɪ] n politique f; (also: **insurance ~**) police f (d'assurance)

polio ['pəulɪəu] n polio f

Polish ['pəulɪʃ] adj polonais(e) ▷ n (Ling) polonais m

polish ['pɔlɪʃ] n (for shoes) cirage m; (for floor) cire f, encaustique f; (for nails) vernis m; (shine) éclat m, poli m; (fig: refinement) raffinement m ▷ vt (put polish on: shoes, wood) cirer; (make shiny) astiquer, faire briller; **polish off** vt (food) liquider; **polished** adj (fig) raffiné(e)

polite [pə'laɪt] adj poli(e); **politeness** n politesse f

political [pə'lɪtɪkl] adj politique; **politically** adv politiquement; **politically correct** politiquement correct(e)

politician [pɔlɪ'tɪʃən] n homme/femme politique, politicien(ne)

politics ['pɔlɪtɪks] n politique f

poll [pəul] n scrutin m, vote m; (also: **opinion ~**) sondage m (d'opinion) ▷ vt (votes) obtenir

pollen ['pɔlən] n pollen m

polling station n (BRIT) bureau m de vote

pollute [pə'lu:t] vt polluer

pollution [pə'lu:ʃən] n pollution f

polo ['pəuləu] n polo m; **polo-neck** adj à col roulé ▷ n (sweater) pull m à col roulé; **polo shirt** n polo m

polyester [pɔlɪ'estə'] n polyester m

polystyrene [pɔlɪ'staɪri:n] n polystyrène m

polythene ['pɔlɪθi:n] n (BRIT) polyéthylène m; **polythene bag** n sac m en plastique

pomegranate ['pɔmɪgrænɪt] n grenade f

pompous ['pɔmpəs] adj pompeux(-euse)

pond [pɔnd] n étang m; (stagnant) mare f

ponder ['pɔndə'] vt considérer, peser

pony ['pəunɪ] n poney m; **ponytail** n queue f de cheval; **pony trekking** n (BRIT) randonnée f équestre or à cheval

poodle ['pu:dl] n caniche m

pool [pu:l] n (of rain) flaque f; (pond) mare f; (artificial) bassin m; (also: **swimming ~**) piscine f; (sth shared) fonds commun; (billiards) poule f ▷ vt mettre en commun; **pools** npl (football) ≈ loto sportif

poor [puə'] adj pauvre; (mediocre) médiocre, faible, mauvais(e) ▷ npl: **the ~** les pauvres mpl; **poorly** adv (*badly*) mal, médiocrement ▷ *adj* souffrant(e), malade

pop [pɔp] *n* (*noise*) bruit sec; (*Mus*) musique *f* pop; (*inf: drink*) soda *m*; (*us inf: father*) papa *m* ▷ *vt* (*put*) fourrer, mettre (rapidement) ▷ *vi* éclater; (*cork*) sauter; **pop in** *vi* entrer en passant; **pop out** *vi* sortir; **popcorn** *n* pop-corn *m*

pope [pəup] *n* pape *m*

poplar ['pɔplər] *n* peuplier *m*

popper ['pɔpər] *n* (BRIT) bouton-pression *m*

poppy ['pɔpɪ] *n* (*wild*) coquelicot *m*; (*cultivated*) pavot *m*

Popsicle® ['pɔpsɪkl] *n* (US) esquimau *m* (*glace*)

pop star *n* pop star *f*

popular ['pɔpjulər] *adj* populaire; (*fashionable*) à la mode; **popularity** [pɔpju'lærɪtɪ] *n* popularité *f*

population [pɔpju'leɪʃən] *n* population *f*

pop-up *adj* (*Comput: menu, window*) pop up *inv* ▷ *n* pop up *m inv*, fenêtre *f* pop up

porcelain ['pɔːslɪn] *n* porcelaine *f*

porch [pɔːtʃ] *n* porche *m*; (*us*) véranda *f*

pore [pɔːr] *n* pore *m* ▷ *vi*: **to ~ over** s'absorber dans, être plongé(e) dans

pork [pɔːk] *n* porc *m*; **pork chop** *n* côte *f* de porc; **pork pie** *n* pâté *m* de porc en croûte

porn [pɔːn] *adj* (*inf*) porno ▷ *n* (*inf*) porno *m*; **pornographic** [pɔːnə'græfɪk] *adj* pornographique; **pornography** [pɔː'nɔgrəfɪ] *n* pornographie *f*

porridge ['pɔrɪdʒ] *n* porridge *m*

port [pɔːt] *n* (*harbour*) port *m*; (*Naut: left side*) bâbord *m*; (*wine*) porto *m*; (*Comput*) port *m*, accès *m*; **~ of call** (port d')escale *f*

portable ['pɔːtəbl] *adj* portatif(-ive)

porter ['pɔːtər] *n* (*for luggage*) porteur *m*; (*doorkeeper*) gardien(ne); portier *m*

portfolio [pɔːt'fəuliəu] *n* portefeuille *m*; (*of artist*) portfolio *m*

portion ['pɔːʃən] *n* portion *f*, part *f*

portrait ['pɔːtreɪt] *n* portrait *m*

portray [pɔː'treɪ] *vt* faire le portrait de; (*in writing*) dépeindre, représenter; (*subj: actor*) jouer

Portugal ['pɔːtjugl] *n* Portugal *m*

Portuguese [pɔːtju'giːz] *adj* portugais(e) ▷ *n* (*pl inv*) Portugais(e); (*Ling*) portugais *m*

pose [pəuz] *n* pose *f* ▷ *vi* poser; (*pretend*): **to ~ as** se faire passer pour ▷ *vt* poser; (*problem*) créer

posh [pɔʃ] *adj* (*inf*) chic *inv*

position [pə'zɪʃən] *n* position *f*; (*job, situation*) situation *f* ▷ *vt* mettre en place *or* en position

positive ['pɔzɪtɪv] *adj* positif(-ive); (*certain*) sûr(e), certain(e); (*definite*) formel(le), catégorique; **positively** *adv* (*affirmatively, enthusiastically*) de façon positive; (*inf: really*) carrément

possess [pə'zɛs] *vt* posséder; **possession** [pə'zɛʃən] *n* possession *f*; **possessions** *npl* (*belongings*) affaires *fpl*; **possessive** *adj* possessif(-ive)

possibility [pɔsɪ'bɪlɪtɪ] *n* possibilité *f*; (*event*) éventualité *f*

possible ['pɔsɪbl] *adj* possible; **as big as ~** aussi gros que possible; **possibly** *adv* (*perhaps*) peut-être; **I cannot possibly come** il m'est impossible de venir

post [pəust] *n* (BRIT: *mail*) poste *f*; (*: letters, delivery*) courrier *m*; (*job, situation*) poste *m*; (*pole*) poteau *m*; (*Internet*) post ▷ *vt* (*Internet*) poster; (BRIT: *send by post*) poster; (*appoint*): **to ~ to** affecter à; **where can I ~ these cards?** où est-ce que je peux poster ces cartes postales?; **postage** *n* tarifs *mpl* d'affranchissement; **postal** *adj* postal(e); **postal order** *n* mandat(-poste *m*) *m*; **postbox** *n* (BRIT) boîte *f* aux lettres (*publique*); **postcard** *n* carte postale; **postcode** *n* (BRIT) code postal

P

poster ['pəustə'] n affiche f
postgraduate ['pəust'grædjuət] n
≈ étudiant(e) de troisième cycle
postman ['pəustmən] (irreg) (BRIT)
n facteur m
postmark ['pəustmɑ:k] n cachet m
(de la poste)
post-mortem [pəust'mɔ:təm] n
autopsie f
post office n (building) poste f;
(organization): **the Post Office** les
postes fpl
postpone [pəs'pəun] vt remettre (à
plus tard), reculer
posture ['pɔstʃə'] n posture f; (fig)
attitude f
postwoman [pəust'wumən] (irreg)
(BRIT) n factrice f
pot [pɔt] n (for cooking) marmite f,
casserole f; (teapot) théière f; (for
coffee) cafetière f; (for plants, jam) pot
m; (inf: marijuana) herbe f ⊳ vt (plant)
mettre en pot; **to go to ~** (inf) aller
à vau-l'eau
potato [pə'teɪtəu] (pl **potatoes**) n
pomme f de terre; **potato peeler** n
épluche-légumes m
potent ['pəutnt] adj puissant(e);
(drink) fort(e), très alcoolisé(e);
(man) viril
potential [pə'tɛnʃl] adj potentiel(le)
⊳ n potentiel m
pothole ['pɔthəul] n (in road) nid m
de poule; (BRIT: underground) gouffre
m, caverne f
pot plant n plante f d'appartement
potter ['pɔtə'] n potier m ⊳ vi (BRIT):
to ~ around or **about** bricoler;
pottery n poterie f
potty ['pɔtɪ] n (child's) pot m
pouch [pautʃ] n (Zool) poche f; (for
tobacco) blague f; (for money) bourse f
poultry ['pəultrɪ] n volaille f
pounce [pauns] vi: **to ~ (on)** bondir
(sur), fondre (sur)
pound [paund] n livre f (weight =
453g, 16 ounces; money = 100 pence);
(for dogs, cars) fourrière f ⊳ vt (beat)

bourrer de coups, marteler; (crush)
piler, pulvériser ⊳ vi (heart) battre
violemment, taper; **pound sterling**
n livre f sterling
pour [pɔ:'] vt verser ⊳ vi couler à flots;
(rain) pleuvoir à verse; **to ~ sb a drink**
verser or servir à boire à qn; **pour in** vi
(people) affluer, se précipiter; (news,
letters) arriver en masse; **pour out**
vi (people) sortir en masse ⊳ vt vider;
(fig) déverser; (serve: a drink) verser;
pouring adj: **pouring rain** pluie f
torrentielle
pout [paut] vi faire la moue
poverty ['pɔvətɪ] n pauvreté f, misère f
powder ['paudə'] n poudre f ⊳ vt
poudrer; **powdered milk** n lait m
en poudre
power ['pauə'] n (strength, nation)
puissance f, force f; (ability, Pol: of
party, leader) pouvoir m; (of speech,
thought) faculté f; (Elec) courant
m; **to be in ~** être au pouvoir;
power cut n (BRIT) coupure f de
courant; **power failure** n panne f de
courant; **powerful** adj puissant(e);
(performance etc) très fort(e);
powerless adj impuissant(e); **power
point** n (BRIT) prise f de courant;
power station n centrale f électrique
p.p. abbr (= per procurationem: by
proxy) p.p.
PR n abbr = **public relations**
practical ['præktɪkl] adj pratique;
practical joke n farce f; **practically**
adv (almost) pratiquement
practice ['præktɪs] n pratique f; (of
profession) exercice m; (at football etc)
entraînement m; (business) cabinet m
⊳ vt, vi (US) = **practise**; **in ~** (in reality)
en pratique; **out of ~** rouillé(e)
practise, (US) **practice** ['præktɪs]
vt (work at: piano, backhand etc)
s'exercer à, travailler; (train for: sport)
s'entraîner à; (a sport, religion, method)
pratiquer; (profession) exercer ⊳ vi
s'exercer, travailler; (train) s'entraîner;
(lawyer, doctor) exercer; **practising,**

(US) **practicing** adj (Christian etc)
pratiquant(e); (lawyer) en exercice
practitioner [præk'tɪʃənəʳ] n
praticien(ne)
pragmatic [præg'mætɪk] adj
pragmatique
prairie ['prɛərɪ] n savane f
praise [preɪz] n éloge(s) m(pl),
louange(s) f(pl) ▷ vt louer, faire
l'éloge de
pram [præm] n (BRIT) landau m,
voiture f d'enfant
prank [præŋk] n farce f
prawn [prɔːn] n crevette f (rose);
prawn cocktail n cocktail m de
crevettes
pray [preɪ] vi prier; **prayer** [prɛəʳ]
n prière f
preach [priːtʃ] vi prêcher; **preacher**
n prédicateur m; (US: clergyman)
pasteur m
precarious [prɪ'kɛərɪəs] adj précaire
precaution [prɪ'kɔːʃən] n
précaution f
precede [prɪ'siːd] vt, vi précéder;
precedent ['prɛsɪdənt] n précédent
m; **preceding** [prɪ'siːdɪŋ] adj qui
précède (or précédait)
precinct ['priːsɪŋkt] n (US: district)
circonscription f, arrondissement m;
pedestrian ~ (BRIT) zone piétonnière;
shopping ~ (BRIT) centre commercial
precious ['prɛʃəs] adj précieux(-euse)
precise [prɪ'saɪs] adj précis(e);
precisely adv précisément
precision [prɪ'sɪʒən] n précision f
predator ['prɛdətəʳ] n prédateur m,
rapace m
predecessor ['priːdɪsɛsəʳ] n
prédécesseur m
predicament [prɪ'dɪkəmənt] n
situation f difficile
predict [prɪ'dɪkt] vt prédire;
predictable adj prévisible;
prediction [prɪ'dɪkʃən] n prédiction f
predominantly [prɪ'dɔmɪnəntlɪ]
adv en majeure partie; (especially)
surtout

preface ['prɛfəs] n préface f
prefect ['priːfɛkt] n (BRIT: in school)
élève chargé de certaines fonctions de
discipline
prefer [prɪ'fəːʳ] vt préférer;
preferable ['prɛfrəbl] adj préférable;
preferably ['prɛfrəblɪ] adv de
préférence; **preference** ['prɛfrəns]
n préférence f
prefix ['priːfɪks] n préfixe m
pregnancy ['prɛgnənsɪ] n
grossesse f
pregnant ['prɛgnənt] adj enceinte;
(animal) pleine
prehistoric ['priːhɪs'tɔrɪk] adj
préhistorique
prejudice ['prɛdʒudɪs] n préjugé m;
prejudiced adj (person) plein(e) de
préjugés; (in a matter) partial(e)
preliminary [prɪ'lɪmɪnərɪ] adj
préliminaire
prelude ['prɛljuːd] n prélude m
premature ['prɛmətʃuəʳ] adj
prématuré(e)
premier ['prɛmɪəʳ] adj premier(-ière),
principal(e) ▷ n (Pol: Prime Minister)
premier ministre; (Pol: President) chef
m de l'État
premiere ['prɛmɪɛəʳ] n première f
Premier League n première division
premises ['prɛmɪsɪz] npl locaux mpl;
on the ~ sur les lieux; sur place
premium ['priːmɪəm] n prime f; **to
be at a ~** (fig: housing etc) être très
demandé(e), être rarissime
premonition [prɛmə'nɪʃən] n
prémonition f
preoccupied [priː'ɔkjupaɪd] adj
préoccupé(e)
prepaid [priː'peɪd] adj payé(e)
d'avance
preparation [prɛpə'reɪʃən] n
préparation f; **preparations** npl (for
trip, war) préparatifs mpl
preparatory school n (BRIT) école
primaire privée; (US) lycée privé
prepare [prɪ'pɛəʳ] vt préparer ▷ vi: **to
~ for** se préparer à

P

prepared [prɪˈpɛəd] adj: **~ for**
préparé(e) à; **~ to** prêt(e) à
preposition [prɛpəˈzɪʃən] n
préposition f
prep school n = **preparatory school**
prerequisite [priːˈrɛkwɪzɪt] n
condition f préalable
preschool [ˈpriːskuːl] adj
préscolaire; (child) d'âge préscolaire
prescribe [prɪˈskraɪb] vt prescrire
prescription [prɪˈskrɪpʃən] n (Med)
ordonnance f (: medicine) médicament
m (obtenu sur ordonnance); **could
you write me a ~?** pouvez-vous me
faire une ordonnance?
presence [ˈprɛzns] n présence f; **in
sb's ~** en présence de qn; **~ of mind**
présence d'esprit
present [ˈprɛznt] adj présent(e);
(current) présent, actuel(le) ▷ n cadeau
m; (actuality) présent m ▷ vt [prɪˈzɛnt]
présenter; (prize, medal) remettre;
(give): **to ~ sb with sth** offrir qch à
qn; **at ~** en ce moment; **to give sb a
~** offrir un cadeau à qn; **presentable**
[prɪˈzɛntəbl] adj présentable;
presentation [prɛznˈteɪʃən] n
présentation f; (ceremony) remise f du
cadeau (or de la médaille etc); **present-
day** adj contemporain(e), actuel(le);
presenter [prɪˈzɛntə] n (Brit Radio,
TV) présentateur(-trice); **presently**
adv (soon) tout à l'heure, bientôt; (with
verb in past) peu après; (at present) en
ce moment
preservation [prɛzəˈveɪʃən] n
préservation f, conservation f
preservative [prɪˈzəːvətɪv] n agent
m de conservation
preserve [prɪˈzəːv] vt (keep safe)
préserver, protéger; (maintain)
conserver, garder; (food) mettre en
conserve ▷ n (for game, fish) réserve f;
(often pl: jam) confiture f
preside [prɪˈzaɪd] vi présider
president [ˈprɛzɪdənt] n
président(e); **presidential**
[prɛzɪˈdɛnʃl] adj présidentiel(le)

press [prɛs] n (tool, machine,
newspapers) presse f; (for wine)
pressoir m ▷ vt (push) appuyer sur;
(squeeze) presser, serrer; (clothes:
iron) repasser; (insist): **to ~ sth on
sb** presser qn d'accepter qch; (urge,
entreat): **to ~ sb to do or into doing
sth** pousser qn à faire qch ▷ vi
appuyer; **we are ~ed for time** le
temps nous manque; **to ~ for sth**
faire pression pour obtenir qch; **press
conference** n conférence f de presse;
pressing adj urgent(e), pressant(e);
press stud n (Brit) bouton-pression
m; **press-up** n (Brit) traction f
pressure [ˈprɛʃə] n pression f; (stress)
tension f; **to put ~ on sb (to do sth)**
faire pression sur qn (pour qu'il fasse
qch); **pressure cooker** n cocotte-
minute® f; **pressure group** n groupe
m de pression
prestige [prɛsˈtiːʒ] n prestige m
prestigious [prɛsˈtɪdʒəs] adj
prestigieux(-euse)
presumably [prɪˈzjuːməblɪ] adv
vraisemblablement
presume [prɪˈzjuːm] vt présumer,
supposer
pretence, (US) **pretense** [prɪˈtɛns]
n (claim) prétention f; **under false ~s**
sous des prétextes fallacieux
pretend [prɪˈtɛnd] vt (feign) feindre,
simuler ▷ vi (feign) faire semblant
pretense [prɪˈtɛns] n (US) = **pretence**
pretentious [prɪˈtɛnʃəs] adj
prétentieux(-euse)
pretext [ˈpriːtɛkst] n prétexte m
pretty [ˈprɪtɪ] adj joli(e) ▷ adv assez
prevail [prɪˈveɪl] vi (win) l'emporter,
prévaloir; (be usual) avoir cours;
prevailing adj (widespread)
courant(e), répandu(e); (wind)
dominant(e)
prevalent [ˈprɛvələnt] adj
répandu(e), courant(e)
prevent [prɪˈvɛnt] vt: **to ~
(from doing)** empêcher (de
faire); **prevention** [prɪˈvɛnʃən]

n prévention *f*; **preventive** *adj* préventif(-ive)

preview ['pri:vju:] *n* (*of film*) avant-première *f*

previous ['pri:vɪəs] *adj* (*last*) précédent(e); (*earlier*) antérieur(e); **previously** *adv* précédemment, auparavant

prey [preɪ] *n* proie *f* ▷ *vi*: **to ~ on** s'attaquer à; **it was ~ing on his mind** ça le rongeait or minait

price [praɪs] *n* prix *m* ▷ *vt* (*goods*) fixer le prix de; **priceless** *adj* sans prix, inestimable; **price list** *n* tarif *m*

prick [prɪk] *n* (*sting*) piqûre *f* ▷ *vt* piquer; **to ~ up one's ears** dresser or tendre l'oreille

prickly ['prɪklɪ] *adj* piquant(e), épineux(-euse); (*fig: person*) irritable

pride [praɪd] *n* fierté *f*; (*pej*) orgueil *m* ▷ *vt*: **to ~ o.s. on** se flatter de; s'enorgueillir de

priest [pri:st] *n* prêtre *m*

primarily ['praɪmərɪlɪ] *adv* principalement, essentiellement

primary ['praɪmərɪ] *adj* primaire; (*first in importance*) premier(-ière), primordial(e) ▷ *n* (*us: election*) (élection *f*) primaire *f*; **primary school** *n* (BRIT) école *f* primaire

prime [praɪm] *adj* primordial(e), fondamental(e); (*excellent*) excellent(e) ▷ *vt* (*fig*) mettre au courant ▷ *n*: **in the ~ of life** dans la fleur de l'âge; **Prime Minister** *n* Premier ministre

primitive ['prɪmɪtɪv] *adj* primitif(-ive)

primrose ['prɪmrəuz] *n* primevère *f*

prince [prɪns] *n* prince *m*

princess [prɪn'sɛs] *n* princesse *f*

principal ['prɪnsɪpl] *adj* principal(e) ▷ *n* (*head teacher*) directeur *m*, principal *m*; **principally** *adv* principalement

principle ['prɪnsɪpl] *n* principe *m*; **in ~** en principe; **on ~** par principe

print [prɪnt] *n* (*mark*) empreinte *f*; (*letters*) caractères *mpl*; (*fabric*) imprimé *m*; (*Art*) gravure *f*, estampe *f*; (*Phot*) épreuve *f* ▷ *vt* imprimer; (*publish*) publier; (*write in capitals*) écrire en majuscules; **out of ~** épuisé(e); **print out** *vt* (*Comput*) imprimer; **printer** *n* (*machine*) imprimante *f*; (*person*) imprimeur *m*; **printout** *n* (*Comput*) sortie *f* imprimante

prior ['praɪə'] *adj* antérieur(e), précédent(e); (*more important*) prioritaire ▷ *adv*: **~ to doing** avant de faire

priority [praɪ'ɔrɪtɪ] *n* priorité *f*; **to have** or **take ~ over sth/sb** avoir la priorité sur qch/qn

prison ['prɪzn] *n* prison *f* ▷ *cpd* pénitentiaire; **prisoner** *n* prisonnier(-ière); **prisoner of war** *n* prisonnier(-ière) de guerre

pristine ['prɪsti:n] *adj* virginal(e)

privacy ['prɪvəsɪ] *n* intimité *f*, solitude *f*

private ['praɪvɪt] *adj* (*not public*) privé(e); (*personal*) personnel(le); (*house, car, lesson*) particulier(-ière); (*quiet: place*) tranquille ▷ *n* soldat *m* de deuxième classe; **"~"** (*on envelope*) "personnelle"; (*on door*) "privé"; **in ~** en privé; **privately** *adv* en privé; (*within oneself*) intérieurement; **private property** *n* propriété privée; **private school** *n* école privée

privatize ['praɪvɪtaɪz] *vt* privatiser

privilege ['prɪvɪlɪdʒ] *n* privilège *m*

prize [praɪz] *n* prix *m* ▷ *adj* (*example, idiot*) parfait(e); (*bull, novel*) primé(e) ▷ *vt* priser, faire grand cas de; **prize-giving** *n* distribution *f* des prix; **prizewinner** *n* gagnant(e)

pro [prəu] *n* (*inf: Sport*) professionnel(le) ▷ *prep* pro; **pros** *npl*; **the ~s and cons** le pour et le contre

probability [prɔbə'bɪlɪtɪ] *n* probabilité *f*; **in all ~** très probablement

probable ['prɔbəbl] *adj* probable

probably ['prɔbəblɪ] *adv* probablement

P

probation [prə'beɪʃən] n: **on ~** (employee) à l'essai; (Law) en liberté surveillée

probe [prəub] n (Med, Space) sonde f; (enquiry) enquête f, investigation f ▷ vt sonder, explorer

problem ['prɒbləm] n problème m

procedure [prə'siːdʒəʳ] n (Admin, Law) procédure f; (method) marche f à suivre, façon f de procéder

proceed [prə'siːd] vi (go forward) avancer; (act) procéder; (continue): **to ~ (with)** continuer, poursuivre; **to ~ to do** se mettre à faire; **proceedings** npl (measures) mesures fpl; (Law: against sb) poursuites fpl; (meeting) réunion f, séance f; (records) compte rendu; actes mpl; **proceeds** ['prəusiːdz] npl produit m, recette f

process ['prəuses] n processus m; (method) procédé m ▷ vt traiter

procession [prə'seʃən] n défilé m, cortège m; **funeral ~** (on foot) cortège funèbre; (in cars) convoi m mortuaire

proclaim [prə'kleɪm] vt déclarer, proclamer

prod [prɒd] vt pousser

produce n ['prɒdjuːs] (Agr) produits mpl ▷ vt [prə'djuːs] produire; (show) présenter; (cause) provoquer, causer; (Theat) monter, mettre en scène; (TV: programme) réaliser; (: play, film) mettre en scène; (Radio: programme) réaliser; (: play) mettre en ondes; **producer** n (Theat) metteur m en scène; (Agr, Comm, Cine) producteur m; (TV: of programme) réalisateur m; (: of play, film) metteur en scène; (Radio: of programme) réalisateur m; (: of play) metteur en ondes

product ['prɒdʌkt] n produit m; **production** [prə'dʌkʃən] n production f; (Theat) mise f en scène; **productive** [prə'dʌktɪv] adj productif(-ive); **productivity** [prɒdʌk'tɪvɪtɪ] n productivité f

Prof. [prɒf] abbr (= professor) Prof

profession [prə'fɛʃən] n profession f; **professional** n professionnel(le) ▷ adj professionnel(le); (work) de professionnel

professor [prə'fɛsəʳ] n professeur m (titulaire d'une chaire); (us: teacher) professeur m

profile ['prəufaɪl] n profil m

profit ['prɒfɪt] n (from trading) bénéfice m; (advantage) profit m ▷ vi: **to ~ (by or from)** profiter (de); **profitable** adj lucratif(-ive), rentable

profound [prə'faund] adj profond(e)

programme, (us) **program** ['prəugræm] n (Comput) programme m; (Radio, TV) émission f ▷ vt programmer; **programmer** n programmeur(-euse); **programming**, (us) **programing** n programmation f

progress n ['prəugrɛs] progrès m(pl) ▷ vi [prə'grɛs] progresser, avancer; **in ~** en cours; **progressive** [prə'grɛsɪv] adj progressif(-ive); (person) progressiste

prohibit [prə'hɪbɪt] vt interdire, défendre

project n ['prɒdʒɛkt] (plan) projet m, plan m; (venture) opération f, entreprise f; (Scol: research) étude f, dossier m ▷ vt [prə'dʒɛkt] projeter ▷ vi [prə'dʒɛkt] (stick out) faire saillie, s'avancer; **projection** [prə'dʒɛkʃən] n projection f; (overhang) saillie f; **projector** [prə'dʒɛktəʳ] n projecteur m

prolific [prə'lɪfɪk] adj prolifique

prolong [prə'lɒŋ] vt prolonger

prom [prɒm] n abbr = **promenade**; (us: ball) bal m d'étudiants; **the P~s** série de concerts de musique classique

* **PROM**
*
* En Grande-Bretagne, un promenade
* concert ou prom est un concert de
* musique classique, ainsi appelé
* car, à l'origine, le public restait

debout et se promenait au lieu de rester assis. De nos jours, une partie du public reste debout, mais il y a également des places assises (plus chères). Les *Proms* les plus connus sont les Proms londoniens. La dernière séance (the "Last Night of the Proms") est un grand événement médiatique où se jouent des airs traditionnels et patriotiques. Aux États-Unis et au Canada, le *prom* ou *promenade* est un bal organisé par le lycée.

promenade [prɔmə'nɑːd] *n (by sea)* esplanade *f*, promenade *f*

prominent ['prɔmɪnənt] *adj (standing out)* proéminent(e); *(important)* important(e)

promiscuous [prə'mɪskjuəs] *adj (sexually)* de mœurs légères

promise ['prɔmɪs] *n* promesse *f* ▷ *vt, vi* promettre; **promising** *adj* prometteur(-euse)

promote [prə'məut] *vt* promouvoir; *(new product)* lancer; **promotion** [prə'məuʃən] *n* promotion *f*

prompt [prɔmpt] *adj* rapide ▷ *n (Comput)* message *m* (de guidage) ▷ *vt (cause)* entraîner, provoquer; *(Theat)* souffler (son rôle or ses répliques); **at 8 o'clock ~** à 8 heures précises; **to ~ sb to do** inciter or pousser qn à faire; **promptly** *adv (quickly)* rapidement, sans délai; *(on time)* ponctuellement

prone [prəun] *adj (lying)* couché(e) (face contre terre); *(liable)*: **~ to** enclin(e) à

prong [prɔŋ] *n (of fork)* dent *f*

pronoun ['prəunaun] *n* pronom *m*

pronounce [prə'nauns] *vt* prononcer; **how do you ~ it?** comment est-ce que ça se prononce?

pronunciation [prənʌnsɪ'eɪʃən] *n* prononciation *f*

proof [pruːf] *n* preuve *f* ▷ *adj*: **~ against** à l'épreuve de

prop [prɔp] *n* support *m*, étai *m*; *(fig)* soutien *m* ▷ *vt (also: ~ up)* étayer, soutenir; **props** *npl* accessoires *mpl*

propaganda [prɔpə'gændə] *n* propagande *f*

propeller [prə'pɛlər] *n* hélice *f*

proper ['prɔpər] *adj (suited, right)* approprié(e), bon (bonne); *(seemly)* correct(e), convenable; *(authentic)* vrai(e), véritable; *(referring to place)*: **the village ~** le village proprement dit; **properly** *adv* correctement, convenablement; **proper noun** *n* nom *m* propre

property ['prɔpətɪ] *n (possessions)* biens *mpl*; *(house etc)* propriété *f*; *(land)* terres *fpl*, domaine *m*

prophecy ['prɔfɪsɪ] *n* prophétie *f*

prophet ['prɔfɪt] *n* prophète *m*

proportion [prə'pɔːʃən] *n* proportion *f*; *(share)* part *f*, partie *f*; **proportions** *npl (size)* dimensions *fpl*; **proportional, proportionate** *adj* proportionnel(le)

proposal [prə'pəuzl] *n* proposition *f*, offre *f*; *(plan)* projet *m*; *(of marriage)* demande *f* en mariage

propose [prə'pəuz] *vt* proposer, suggérer ▷ *vi* faire sa demande en mariage; **to ~ to do** avoir l'intention de faire

proposition [prɔpə'zɪʃən] *n* proposition *f*

proprietor [prə'praɪətər] *n* propriétaire *m/f*

prose [prəuz] *n* prose *f*; *(Scol: translation)* thème *m*

prosecute ['prɔsɪkjuːt] *vt* poursuivre; **prosecution** [prɔsɪ'kjuːʃən] *n* poursuites *fpl* judiciaires; *(accusing side: in criminal case)* accusation *f*; *(: in civil case)* la partie plaignante; **prosecutor** *n (lawyer)* procureur *m*; *(also: **public prosecutor**)* ministère public; *(us: plaintiff)* plaignant(e)

prospect *n* ['prɔspɛkt] perspective *f*; *(hope)* espoir *m*, chances *fpl* ▷ *vt, vi*

P

[prə'spɛkt] prospecter; **prospects**
npl (*for work etc*) possibilités *fpl*
d'avenir, débouchés *mpl*; **prospective**
[prə'spɛktɪv] *adj* (*possible*)
éventuel(le); (*future*) futur(e)
prospectus [prə'spɛktəs] *n*
prospectus *m*
prosper ['prɔspər] *vi* prospérer;
prosperity [prɔ'spɛrɪtɪ] *n* prospérité
f; **prosperous** *adj* prospère
prostitute ['prɔstɪtjuːt] *n* prostituée
f; **male ~** prostitué *m*
protect [prə'tɛkt] *vt* protéger;
protection [prə'tɛkʃən] *n* protection
f; **protective** *adj* protecteur(-trice);
(*clothing*) de protection
protein ['prəutiːn] *n* protéine *f*
protest *n* ['prəutɛst] protestation *f*
▷ *vi* [prə'tɛst]: **to ~ against/about**
protester contre/à propos de; **to ~
(that)** protester que
Protestant ['prɔtɪstənt] *adj*, *n*
protestant(e)
protester, protestor [prə'tɛstər] *n*
(*in demonstration*) manifestant(e)
protractor [prə'træktər] *n* (*Geom*)
rapporteur *m*
proud [praud] *adj* fier(-ère); (*pej*)
orgueilleux(-euse)
prove [pruːv] *vt* prouver, démontrer
▷ *vi*: **to ~ correct** *etc* s'avérer juste
etc; **to ~ o.s.** montrer ce dont on
est capable
proverb ['prɔvəːb] *n* proverbe *m*
provide [prə'vaɪd] *vt* fournir; **to
~ sb with sth** fournir qch à qn;
provide for *vt fus* (*person*) subvenir
aux besoins de; (*future event*) prévoir;
provided *conj*: **provided (that)**
à condition que + *sub*; **providing**
[prə'vaɪdɪŋ] *conj* à condition que
+ *sub*
province ['prɔvɪns] *n* province *f*; (*fig*)
domaine *m*; **provincial** [prə'vɪnʃəl]
adj provincial(e)
provision [prə'vɪʒən] *n* (*supplying*)
fourniture *f*; approvisionnement *m*;
(*stipulation*) disposition *f*; **provisions**

npl (*food*) provisions *fpl*; **provisional**
adj provisoire
provocative [prə'vɔkətɪv] *adj*
provocateur(-trice), provocant(e)
provoke [prə'vəuk] *vt* provoquer
prowl [praul] *vi* (*also*: **~ about, ~
around**) rôder
proximity [prɔk'sɪmɪtɪ] *n* proximité *f*
proxy ['prɔksɪ] *n*: **by ~** par
procuration
prudent ['pruːdnt] *adj* prudent(e)
prune [pruːn] *n* pruneau *m* ▷ *vt*
élaguer
pry [praɪ] *vi*: **to ~ into** fourrer son
nez dans
PS *n abbr* (= *postscript*) PS *m*
pseudonym ['sjuːdənɪm] *n*
pseudonyme *m*
PSHE *n abbr* (BRIT Scol: = *personal, social
and health education*) cours d'éducation
personnelle, sanitaire et sociale
préparant à la vie adulte
psychiatric [saɪkɪ'ætrɪk] *adj*
psychiatrique
psychiatrist [saɪ'kaɪətrɪst] *n*
psychiatre *m/f*
psychic ['saɪkɪk] *adj* (*also*: **~al**)
(méta)psychique; (*person*) doué(e) de
télépathie *or* d'un sixième sens
psychoanalysis (*pl*
psychoanalyses) [saɪkəuə'nælɪsɪs,
-siːz] *n* psychanalyse *f*
psychological [saɪkə'lɔdʒɪkl] *adj*
psychologique
psychologist [saɪ'kɔlədʒɪst] *n*
psychologue *m/f*
psychology [saɪ'kɔlədʒɪ] *n*
psychologie *f*
psychotherapy [saɪkəu'θɛrəpɪ] *n*
psychothérapie *f*
pt *abbr* = **pint; pints; point; points**
PTO *abbr* (= *please turn over*) TSVP
PTV *abbr* (US) = **pay television**
pub [pʌb] *n abbr* (= *public house*) pub *m*
puberty ['pjuːbətɪ] *n* puberté *f*
public ['pʌblɪk] *adj* public(-ique) ▷ *n*
public *m*; **in ~** en public; **to make ~**
rendre public

publication [pʌblɪ'keɪʃən] *n*
publication *f*

public: public company *n* société
f anonyme; **public convenience** *n*
(BRIT) toilettes *fpl*; **public holiday**
n (BRIT) jour férié; **public house** *n*
(BRIT) pub *m*

publicity [pʌb'lɪsɪtɪ] *n* publicité *f*

publicize ['pʌblɪsaɪz] *vt* (*make
known*) faire connaître, rendre
public; (*advertise*) faire de la publicité
pour

public: public limited company *n*
≈ société *f* anonyme (SA) (*cotée en
Bourse*); **publicly** *adv* publiquement,
en public; **public opinion** *n* opinion
publique; **public relations** *n or npl*
relations publiques (RP); **public
school** *n* (BRIT) école privée; (US)
école publique; **public transport**,
(US) **public transportation** *n*
transports *mpl* en commun

publish ['pʌblɪʃ] *vt* publier; **publisher**
n éditeur *m*; **publishing** *n* (*industry*)
édition *f*

pub lunch *n* repas *m* de bistrot

pudding ['pudɪŋ] *n* (BRIT: *dessert*)
dessert, entremets *m*; (*sweet dish*)
pudding *m*, gâteau *m*

puddle ['pʌdl] *n* flaque *f* d'eau

puff [pʌf] *n* bouffée *f* ▷ *vt* (*also: ~
out: sails, cheeks*) gonfler ▷ *vi* (*pant*)
haleter; **puff pastry**, (US) **puff paste**
n pâte feuilletée

pull [pul] *n* (*tug*): **to give sth a ~** tirer
sur qch ▷ *vt* tirer; (*trigger*) presser;
(*strain: muscle, tendon*) se claquer
▷ *vi* tirer; **to ~ to pieces** mettre en
morceaux; **to ~ one's punches**
(*also fig*) ménager son adversaire;
to ~ one's weight y mettre du sien;
to ~ o.s. together se ressaisir; **to
~ sb's leg** (*fig*) faire marcher qn;
pull apart *vt* (*break*) mettre en
pièces, démantibuler; **pull away** *vi*
(*vehicle: move off*) partir; (*draw back*)
s'éloigner; **pull back** *vt* (*lever etc*)
tirer sur; (*curtains*) ouvrir ▷ *vi* (*refrain*)

s'abstenir; (*Mil: withdraw*) se retirer;
pull down *vt* baisser, abaisser;
(*house*) démolir; **pull in** *vi* (*Aut*) se
ranger; (*Rail*) entrer en gare; **pull off**
vt enlever, ôter; (*deal etc*) conclure;
pull out *vi* démarrer, partir; (*Aut:
come out of line*) déboîter ▷ *vt* (*from
bag, pocket*) sortir; (*remove*) arracher;
pull over *vi* (*Aut*) se ranger; **pull up** *vi*
(*stop*) s'arrêter ▷ *vt* remonter; (*uproot*)
déraciner, arracher

pulley ['pulɪ] *n* poulie *f*

pullover ['puləuvər] *n* pull-over *m*,
tricot *m*

pulp [pʌlp] *n* (*of fruit*) pulpe *f*; (*for
paper*) pâte *f* à papier

pulpit ['pulpɪt] *n* chaire *f*

pulse [pʌls] *n* (*of blood*) pouls *m*; (*of
heart*) battement *m*; **pulses** *npl* (*Culin*)
légumineuses *fpl*

puma ['pju:mə] *n* puma *m*

pump [pʌmp] *n* pompe *f*; (*shoe*)
escarpin *m* ▷ *vt* pomper; **pump up**
vt gonfler

pumpkin ['pʌmpkɪn] *n* potiron *m*,
citrouille *f*

pun [pʌn] *n* jeu *m* de mots,
calembour *m*

punch [pʌntʃ] *n* (*blow*) coup *m* de
poing; (*tool*) poinçon *m*; (*drink*) punch
m ▷ *vt* (*make a hole in*) poinçonner,
perforer; (*hit*): **to ~ sb/sth** donner un
coup de poing à qn/sur qch; **punch-
up** *n* (BRIT inf) bagarre *f*

punctual ['pʌŋktjuəl] *adj*
ponctuel(le)

punctuation [pʌŋktju'eɪʃən] *n*
ponctuation *f*

puncture ['pʌŋktʃər] *n* (BRIT)
crevaison *f* ▷ *vt* crever

punish ['pʌnɪʃ] *vt* punir; **punishment**
n punition *f*, châtiment *m*

punk [pʌŋk] *n* (*person: also: ~ rocker*)
punk *m/f*; (*music: also: ~ rock*) le
punk; (US inf: *hoodlum*) voyou *m*

pup [pʌp] *n* chiot *m*

pupil ['pju:pl] *n* élève *m/f*; (*of eye*)
pupille *f*

P

puppet ['pʌpɪt] n marionnette f, pantin m

puppy ['pʌpɪ] n chiot m, petit chien

purchase ['pəːtʃɪs] n achat m ▷ vt acheter

pure [pjuə^r] adj pur(e); **purely** adv purement

purify ['pjuərɪfaɪ] vt purifier, épurer

purity ['pjuərɪtɪ] n pureté f

purple ['pəːpl] adj violet(te); (face) cramoisi(e)

purpose ['pəːpəs] n intention f, but m; **on ~** exprès

purr [pəː^r] vi ronronner

purse [pəːs] n (BRIT: for money) porte-monnaie m inv; (US: handbag) sac m (à main) ▷ vt serrer, pincer

pursue [pə'sjuː] vt poursuivre

pursuit [pə'sjuːt] n poursuite f; (occupation) occupation f, activité f

pus [pʌs] n pus m

push [puʃ] n poussée f ▷ vt pousser; (button) appuyer sur; (fig: product) mettre en avant, faire de la publicité pour ▷ vi pousser; **to ~ for** (better pay, conditions) réclamer; **push in** vi s'introduire de force; **push off** vi (inf) filer, ficher le camp; **push on** vi (continue) continuer; **push over** vt renverser; **push through** vi (in crowd) se frayer un chemin; **pushchair** n (BRIT) poussette f; **pusher** n (also: **drug pusher**) revendeur(-euse) (de drogue), ravitailleur(-euse) (en drogue); **push-up** n (US) traction f

pussy(-cat) ['pusi-] n (inf) minet m

put (pt, pp **put**) [put] vt mettre; (place) poser, placer; (say) dire, exprimer; (a question) poser; (case, view) exposer, présenter; (estimate) estimer; **put aside** vt mettre de côté; **put away** vt (store) ranger; **put back** vt (replace) remettre, replacer; (postpone) remettre; **put by** vt (money) mettre de côté, économiser; **put down** vt (parcel etc) poser, déposer; (in writing) mettre par écrit, inscrire; (suppress: revolt etc) réprimer, écraser; (attribute)

attribuer; (animal) abattre; (cat, dog) faire piquer; **put forward** vt (ideas) avancer, proposer; **put in** vt (complaint) soumettre; (time, effort) consacrer; **put off** vt (postpone) remettre à plus tard, ajourner; (discourage) dissuader; **put on** vt (clothes, lipstick, CD) mettre; (light etc) allumer; (play etc) monter; (weight) prendre; (assume: accent, manner) prendre; **put out** vt (take outside) mettre dehors; (one's hand) tendre; (light etc) éteindre; (person: inconvenience) déranger, gêner; **put through** vt (Tel: caller) mettre en communication; (: call) passer; (plan) faire accepter; **put together** vt mettre ensemble; (assemble: furniture) monter, assembler; (: meal) préparer; **put up** vt (raise) lever, relever, remonter; (hang) accrocher; (build) construire, ériger; (increase) augmenter; (accommodate) loger; **put up with** vt fus supporter

putt [pʌt] n putt m; **putting green** n green m

puzzle ['pʌzl] n énigme f, mystère m; (game) jeu m, casse-tête m; (jigsaw) puzzle m; (also: **crossword ~**) mots croisés ▷ vt intriguer, rendre perplexe ▷ vi: **to ~ over** chercher à comprendre; **puzzled** adj perplexe; **puzzling** adj déconcertant(e), inexplicable

pyjamas [pɪ'dʒɑːməz] npl (BRIT) pyjama m

pylon ['paɪlən] n pylône m

pyramid ['pɪrəmɪd] n pyramide f

Pyrenees [pɪrə'niːz] npl Pyrénées fpl

q

quack [kwæk] n (of duck) coin-coin m inv; (pej: doctor) charlatan m

quadruple [kwɔ'dru:pl] vt, vi quadrupler

quail [kweɪl] n (Zool) caille f ▷ vi: **to ~ at** or **before** reculer devant

quaint [kweɪnt] adj bizarre; (old-fashioned) désuet(-ète); (picturesque) au charme vieillot, pittoresque

quake [kweɪk] vi trembler ▷ n abbr = **earthquake**

qualification [kwɔlɪfɪ'keɪʃən] n (often pl: degree etc) diplôme m; (training) qualification(s) f(pl); (ability) compétence(s) f(pl); (limitation) réserve f, restriction f

qualified ['kwɔlɪfaɪd] adj (trained) qualifié(e); (professionally) diplômé(e); (fit, competent) compétent(e), qualifié(e); (limited) conditionnel(le)

qualify ['kwɔlɪfaɪ] vt qualifier; (modify) atténuer, nuancer ▷ vi: **to ~ (as)** obtenir son diplôme (de); **to ~ (for)** remplir les conditions requises (pour); (Sport) se qualifier (pour)

quality ['kwɔlɪtɪ] n qualité f

qualm [kwɑ:m] n doute m; scrupule m

quantify ['kwɔntɪfaɪ] vt quantifier

quantity ['kwɔntɪtɪ] n quantité f

quarantine ['kwɔrnti:n] n quarantaine f

quarrel ['kwɔrl] n querelle f, dispute f ▷ vi se disputer, se quereller

quarry ['kwɔrɪ] n (for stone) carrière f; (animal) proie f, gibier m

quart [kwɔ:t] n ≈ litre m

quarter ['kwɔ:tər] n quart m; (of year) trimestre m; (district) quartier m; (US, CANADA: 25 cents) (pièce f de) vingt-cinq cents mpl ▷ vt partager en quartiers or en quatre; (Mil) caserner, cantonner; **quarters** npl logement m; (Mil) quartiers mpl, cantonnement m; **a ~ of an hour** un quart d'heure; **quarter final** n quart m de finale; **quarterly** adj trimestriel(le) ▷ adv tous les trois mois

quartet(te) [kwɔ:'tɛt] n quatuor m; (jazz players) quartette m

quartz [kwɔ:ts] n quartz m

quay [ki:] n (also: ~side) quai m

queasy ['kwi:zɪ] adj: **to feel ~** avoir mal au cœur

Quebec [kwɪ'bɛk] n (city) Québec; (province) Québec m

queen [kwi:n] n (gen) reine f; (Cards etc) dame f

queer [kwɪər] adj étrange, curieux(-euse); (suspicious) louche ▷ n (offensive) homosexuel m

quench [kwɛntʃ] vt: **to ~ one's thirst** se désaltérer

query ['kwɪərɪ] n question f ▷ vt (disagree with, dispute) mettre en doute, questionner

quest [kwɛst] n recherche f, quête f

question ['kwɛstʃən] n question f ▷ vt (person) interroger; (plan, idea) mettre en question or en doute; **beyond ~** sans aucun doute; **out of the ~** hors de question; **questionable** adj discutable; **question mark** n point m d'interrogation; **questionnaire** [kwɛstʃə'nɛəʳ] n questionnaire m

queue [kjuː] (BRIT) n queue f, file f ▷ vi (also: ~ **up**) faire la queue

quiche [kiːʃ] n quiche f

quick [kwɪk] adj rapide; (mind) vif (vive); (agile) agile, vif (vive) ▷ n: **cut to the ~** (fig) touché(e) au vif; **be ~!** dépêche-toi!; **quickly** adv (fast) vite, rapidement; (immediately) tout de suite

quid [kwɪd] n (pl inv: BRIT inf) livre f

quiet ['kwaɪət] adj tranquille, calme; (voice) bas(se); (ceremony, colour) discret(-ète) ▷ n tranquillité f, calme m; (silence) silence m; **quietly** adv tranquillement; (silently) silencieusement; (discreetly) discrètement

quilt [kwɪlt] n édredon m; (continental quilt) couette f

quirky ['kwɜːkɪ] adj singulier(-ère)

quit [kwɪt] (pt, pp quit or quitted) vt quitter ▷ vi (give up) abandonner, renoncer; (resign) démissionner

quite [kwaɪt] adv (rather) assez, plutôt; (entirely) complètement, tout à fait; **~ a few of them** un assez grand nombre d'entre eux; **that's not ~ right** ce n'est pas tout à fait juste; **~ (so)!** exactement!

quits [kwɪts] adj: **~ (with)** quitte (envers); **let's call it ~** restons-en là

quiver ['kwɪvəʳ] vi trembler, frémir

quiz [kwɪz] n (on TV) jeu-concours m (télévisé); (in magazine etc) test m de connaissances ▷ vt interroger

quota ['kwəʊtə] n quota m

quotation [kwəʊ'teɪʃən] n citation f; (estimate) devis m; **quotation marks** npl guillemets mpl

quote [kwəʊt] n citation f; (estimate) devis m ▷ vt (sentence, author) citer; (price) donner, soumettre ▷ vi: **to ~ from** citer; **quotes** npl (inverted commas) guillemets mpl

r

rabbi ['ræbaɪ] n rabbin m

rabbit ['ræbɪt] n lapin m

rabies ['reɪbiːz] n rage f

RAC n abbr (BRIT: = Royal Automobile Club) ≈ ACF m

rac(c)oon [rə'kuːn] n raton m laveur

race [reɪs] n (species) race f; (competition, rush) course f ▷ vt (person) faire la course avec ▷ vi (compete) faire la course, courir; (pulse) battre très vite; **race car** n (US) = **racing car**; **racecourse** n champ m de courses; **racehorse** n cheval m de course; **racetrack** n piste f

racial ['reɪʃl] adj racial(e)

racing ['reɪsɪŋ] n courses fpl; **racing car** n (BRIT) voiture f de course; **racing driver** n (BRIT) pilote m de course

racism ['reɪsɪzəm] n racisme m; **racist** ['reɪsɪst] adj, n raciste m/f

rack [ræk] n (for guns, tools) râtelier m; (for clothes) portant m; (for bottles) casier m; (also: **luggage ~**) filet m à bagages; (also: **roof ~**) galerie f; (also: **dish ~**) égouttoir m ▷ vt tourmenter; **to ~ one's brains** se creuser la cervelle

racket ['rækɪt] n (for tennis) raquette f; (noise) tapage m, vacarme m; (swindle) escroquerie f

racquet ['rækɪt] n raquette f

radar ['reɪdɑːʳ] n radar m

radiation [reɪdɪ'eɪʃən] n rayonnement m; (radioactive) radiation f

radiator ['reɪdɪeɪtəʳ] n radiateur m

radical ['rædɪkl] adj radical(e)

radio ['reɪdɪəu] n radio f ▷ vt (person) appeler par radio; **on the ~** à la radio; **radioactive** adj radioactif(-ive); **radio station** n station f de radio

radish ['rædɪʃ] n radis m

RAF n abbr (BRIT) = **Royal Air Force**

raffle ['ræfl] n tombola f

raft [rɑːft] n (craft: also: **life ~**) radeau m; (logs) train m de flottage

rag [ræg] n chiffon m; (pej: newspaper) feuille f, torchon m; (for charity) attractions organisées par les étudiants au profit d'œuvres de charité; **rags** npl haillons mpl

rage [reɪdʒ] n (fury) rage f, fureur f ▷ vi (person) être fou (folle) de rage; (storm) faire rage, être déchaîné(e); **it's all the ~** cela fait fureur

ragged ['rægɪd] adj (edge) inégal(e), qui accroche; (clothes) en loques; (appearance) déguenillé(e)

raid [reɪd] n (Mil) raid m; (criminal) hold-up m inv; (by police) descente f, rafle f ▷ vt faire une raid sur or un hold-up dans or une descente dans

rail [reɪl] n (on stair) rampe f; (on bridge, balcony) balustrade f; (of ship) bastingage m; (for train) rail m; **railcard** n (BRIT) carte f de chemin de fer; **railing(s)** n(pl) grille f; **railway**, (US) **railroad** n chemin m de fer; (track) voie f ferrée; **railway line** n (BRIT) ligne f de chemin de fer; (track)

voie ferrée; **railway station** n (BRIT) gare f

rain [reɪn] n pluie f ▷ vi pleuvoir; **in the ~** sous la pluie; **it's ~ing** il pleut; **rainbow** n arc-en-ciel m; **raincoat** n imperméable m; **raindrop** n goutte f de pluie; **rainfall** n chute f de pluie; (measurement) hauteur f des précipitations; **rainforest** n forêt tropicale; **rainy** adj pluvieux(-euse)

raise [reɪz] n augmentation f ▷ vt (lift) lever; hausser; (increase) augmenter; (morale) remonter; (standards) améliorer; (a protest, doubt) provoquer, causer; (a question) soulever; (cattle, family) élever; (crop) faire pousser; (army, funds) rassembler; (loan) obtenir; **to ~ one's voice** élever la voix

raisin ['reɪzn] n raisin sec

rake [reɪk] n (tool) râteau m; (person) débauché m ▷ vt (garden) ratisser

rally ['rælɪ] n (Pol etc) meeting m, rassemblement m; (Aut) rallye m; (Tennis) échange m ▷ vt rassembler, rallier; (support) gagner ▷ vi (sick person) aller mieux; (Stock Exchange) reprendre

RAM [ræm] n abbr (Comput: = random access memory) mémoire vive

ram [ræm] n bélier m ▷ vt (push) enfoncer; (crash into: vehicle) emboutir; (: lamppost etc) percuter

Ramadan [ræmə'dæn] n Ramadan m

ramble ['ræmbl] n randonnée f ▷ vi (walk) se promener, faire une randonnée; (pej: also: **~ on**) discourir, pérorer; **rambler** n promeneur(-euse), randonneur(-euse); **rambling** adj (speech) décousu(e); (house) plein(e) de coins et de recoins; (Bot) grimpant(e)

ramp [ræmp] n (incline) rampe f; (Aut) dénivellation f; (in garage) pont m; **on/off ~** (US Aut) bretelle f d'accès

rampage ['ræmpeɪdʒ] n: **to be on the ~** se déchaîner

r

ran [ræn] pt of **run**

ranch [rɑːntʃ] n ranch m

random ['rændəm] adj fait(e) or établi(e) au hasard; (Comput, Math) aléatoire ▷ n: **at ~** au hasard

rang [ræŋ] pt of **ring**

range [reɪndʒ] n (of mountains) chaîne f; (of missile, voice) portée f; (of products) choix m, gamme f; (also: **shooting ~**) champ m de tir; (also: **kitchen ~**) fourneau m (de cuisine) ▷ vt (place) mettre en rang, placer ▷ vi: **to ~ over** couvrir; **to ~ from ... to** aller de ... à

ranger ['reɪndʒər] n garde m forestier

rank [ræŋk] n rang m; (Mil) grade m; (BRIT: also: **taxi ~**) station f de taxis ▷ vi: **to ~ among** compter or se classer parmi ▷ adj (smell) nauséabond(e); **the ~ and file** (fig) la masse, la base

ransom ['rænsəm] n rançon f; **to hold sb to ~** (fig) exercer un chantage sur qn

rant [rænt] vi fulminer

rap [ræp] n (music) rap m ▷ vt (door) frapper sur or à; (table etc) taper sur

rape [reɪp] n viol m; (Bot) colza m ▷ vt violer

rapid ['ræpɪd] adj rapide; **rapidly** adv rapidement; **rapids** npl (Geo) rapides mpl

rapist ['reɪpɪst] n auteur m d'un viol

rapport [ræ'pɔːr] n entente f

rare [reər] adj rare; (Culin: steak) saignant(e); **rarely** adv rarement

rash [ræʃ] adj imprudent(e), irréfléchi(e) ▷ n (Med) rougeur f, éruption f; (of events) série f (noire)

rasher ['ræʃər] n fine tranche (de lard)

raspberry ['rɑːzbərɪ] n framboise f

rat [ræt] n rat m

rate [reɪt] n (ratio) taux m, pourcentage m; (speed) vitesse f, rythme m; (price) tarif m ▷ vt (price) évaluer, estimer; (people) classer; **rates** npl (BRIT: property tax) impôts

locaux; **to ~ sb/sth as** considérer qn/qch comme

rather ['rɑːðər] adv (somewhat) assez, plutôt; (to some extent) un peu; **it's ~ expensive** c'est assez cher; (too much) c'est un peu cher; **there's ~ a lot** il y en a beaucoup; **I would** or **I'd ~ go** j'aimerais mieux or je préférerais partir; **or ~** (more accurately) ou plutôt

rating ['reɪtɪŋ] n (assessment) évaluation f; (score) classement m; (Finance) cote f; **ratings** npl (Radio) indice(s) m(pl) d'écoute; (TV) Audimat® m

ratio ['reɪʃɪəʊ] n proportion f; **in the ~ of 100 to 1** dans la proportion de 100 contre 1

ration ['ræʃən] n ration f ▷ vt rationner; **rations** npl (food) vivres mpl

rational ['ræʃənl] adj raisonnable, sensé(e); (solution, reasoning) logique; (Med: person) lucide

rat race n foire f d'empoigne

rattle ['rætl] n (of door, window) battement m; (of coins, chain) cliquetis m; (of train, engine) bruit m de ferraille; (for baby) hochet m ▷ vi cliqueter; (car, bus): **to ~ along** rouler en faisant un bruit de ferraille ▷ vt agiter (bruyamment); (inf: disconcert) décontenancer

rave [reɪv] vi (in anger) s'emporter; (with enthusiasm) s'extasier; (Med) délirer ▷ n (inf: party) rave f, soirée f techno

raven ['reɪvən] n grand corbeau

ravine [rə'viːn] n ravin m

raw [rɔː] adj (uncooked) cru(e); (not processed) brut(e); (sore) à vif, irrité(e); (inexperienced) inexpérimenté(e); **~ materials** matières premières

ray [reɪ] n rayon m; **~ of hope** lueur f d'espoir

razor ['reɪzər] n rasoir m; **razor blade** n lame f de rasoir

Rd abbr = **road**

RE n abbr (BRIT: = religious education) instruction religieuse

re [ri:] prep concernant

reach [ri:tʃ] n portée f, atteinte f; (of river etc) étendue f ▷ vt atteindre, arriver à; (conclusion, decision) parvenir à ▷ vi s'étendre; **out of/ within ~** (object) hors de/à portée; **reach out** vt tendre ▷ vi: **to ~ out (for)** allonger le bras (pour prendre)

react [ri:'ækt] vi réagir; **reaction** [ri:'ækʃən] n réaction f; **reactor** [ri:'æktər] n réacteur m

read (pt, pp **read**) [ri:d, rɛd] vi lire ▷ vt lire; (understand) comprendre, interpréter; (study) étudier; (meter) relever; (subj: instrument etc) indiquer, marquer; **read out** vt lire à haute voix; **reader** n lecteur(-trice)

readily ['rɛdɪlɪ] adv volontiers, avec empressement; (easily) facilement

reading ['ri:dɪŋ] n lecture f; (understanding) interprétation f; (on instrument) indications fpl

ready ['rɛdɪ] adj prêt(e); (willing) prêt, disposé(e); (available) disponible ▷ n: **at the ~** (Mil) prêt à faire feu; **when will my photos be ~?** quand est-ce que mes photos seront prêtes?; **to get ~** (as vi) se préparer; (as vt) préparer; **ready-cooked** adj précuit(e); **ready-made** adj tout(e) faite(e)

real [rɪəl] adj (world, life) réel(le); (genuine) véritable; (proper) vrai(e) ▷ adv (US inf: very) vraiment; **real ale** n bière traditionnelle; **real estate** n biens fonciers or immobiliers; **realistic** [rɪə'lɪstɪk] adj réaliste; **reality** [ri:'ælɪtɪ] n réalité f; **reality TV** n téléréalité f

realization [rɪəlaɪ'zeɪʃən] n (awareness) prise f de conscience; (fulfilment, also: of asset) réalisation f

realize ['rɪəlaɪz] vt (understand) se rendre compte de, prendre conscience de; (a project, Comm: asset) réaliser

really ['rɪəlɪ] adv vraiment; **~?** vraiment?, c'est vrai?

realm [rɛlm] n royaume m; (fig) domaine m

realtor ['rɪəltɔːr] n (US) agent immobilier

reappear [ri:ə'pɪər] vi réapparaître, reparaître

rear [rɪər] adj de derrière, arrière inv; (Aut: wheel etc) arrière ▷ n arrière m ▷ vt (cattle, family) élever ▷ vi (also: **~ up**: animal) se cabrer

rearrange [ri:ə'reɪndʒ] vt réarranger

rear: rear-view mirror n (Aut) rétroviseur m; **rear-wheel drive** n (Aut) traction f arrière

reason ['ri:zn] n raison f ▷ vi: **to ~ with sb** raisonner qn, faire entendre raison à qn; **it stands to ~ that** il va sans dire que; **reasonable** adj raisonnable; (not bad) acceptable; **reasonably** adv (behave) raisonnablement; (fairly) assez; **reasoning** n raisonnement m

reassurance [ri:ə'ʃuərəns] n (factual) assurance f, garantie f; (emotional) réconfort m

reassure [ri:ə'ʃuər] vt rassurer

rebate ['ri:beɪt] n (on tax etc) dégrèvement m

rebel n ['rɛbl] rebelle m/f ▷ vi [rɪ'bɛl] se rebeller, se révolter; **rebellion** [rɪ'bɛljən] n rébellion f, révolte f; **rebellious** [rɪ'bɛljəs] adj rebelle

rebuild [ri:'bɪld] vt (irreg: like **build**) reconstruire

recall vt [rɪ'kɔ:l] rappeler; (remember) se rappeler, se souvenir de ▷ n ['ri:kɔl] rappel m; (ability to remember) mémoire f

receipt [rɪ'si:t] n (document) reçu m; (for parcel etc) accusé m de réception; (act of receiving) réception f; **receipts** npl (Comm) recettes fpl; **can I have a ~, please?** je peux avoir un reçu, s'il vous plaît?

receive [rɪ'si:v] vt recevoir; (guest) recevoir, accueillir; **receiver** n (Tel)

r

recent | 524

récepteur *m*, combiné *m*; (*Radio*) récepteur; (*of stolen goods*) receleur *m*; (*for bankruptcies*) administrateur *m* judiciaire

recent ['riːsnt] *adj* récent(e); **recently** *adv* récemment

reception [rɪ'sepʃən] *n* réception *f*; (*welcome*) accueil *m*, réception; **reception desk** *n* réception *f*; **receptionist** *n* réceptionniste *m/f*

recession [rɪ'seʃən] *n* (*Econ*) récession *f*

recharge [riː'tʃaːdʒ] *vt* (*battery*) recharger

recipe ['resɪpɪ] *n* recette *f*

recipient [rɪ'sɪpɪənt] *n* (*of payment*) bénéficiaire *m/f*; (*of letter*) destinataire *m/f*

recital [rɪ'saɪtl] *n* récital *m*

recite [rɪ'saɪt] *vt* (*poem*) réciter

reckless ['rekləs] *adj* (*driver etc*) imprudent(e); (*spender etc*) insouciant(e)

reckon ['rekən] *vt* (*count*) calculer, compter; (*consider*) considérer, estimer; (*think*): **I ~ (that) ...** je pense (que) ..., j'estime (que) ...

reclaim [rɪ'kleɪm] *vt* (*land: from sea*) assécher; (*demand back*) réclamer (le remboursement *or* la restitution de); (*waste materials*) récupérer

recline [rɪ'klaɪn] *vi* être allongé(e) *or* étendu(e)

recognition [rekəg'nɪʃən] *n* reconnaissance *f*; **transformed beyond ~** méconnaissable

recognize ['rekəgnaɪz] *vt*: **to ~ (by/as)** reconnaître (à/comme étant)

recollection [rekə'lekʃən] *n* souvenir *m*

recommend [rekə'mend] *vt* recommander; **can you ~ a good restaurant?** pouvez-vous me conseiller un bon restaurant?; **recommendation** [rekəmen'deɪʃən] *n* recommandation *f*

reconcile ['rekənsaɪl] *vt* (*two people*) réconcilier; (*two facts*) concilier, accorder; **to ~ o.s. to** se résigner à

reconsider [riːkən'sɪdər] *vt* reconsidérer

reconstruct [riːkən'strʌkt] *vt* (*building*) reconstruire; (*crime, system*) reconstituer

record *n* ['rekɔːd] rapport *m*, récit *m*; (*of meeting etc*) procès-verbal *m*; (*register*) registre *m*; (*file*) dossier *m*; (*Comput*) article *m*; (*also:* **police ~**) casier *m* judiciaire; (*Mus: disc*) disque *m*; (*Sport*) record *m* ▷ *adj* ['rekɔːd] record *inv* ▷ *vt* [rɪ'kɔːd] (*set down*) noter; (*Mus: song etc*) enregistrer; **public ~s** archives *fpl*; **in ~ time** dans un temps record; **recorded delivery** *n* (*BRIT Post*): **to send sth recorded delivery** ≈ envoyer qch en recommandé; **recorder** *n* (*Mus*) flûte *f* à bec; **recording** *n* (*Mus*) enregistrement *m*; **record player** *n* tourne-disque *m*

recount [rɪ'kaunt] *vt* raconter

recover [rɪ'kʌvər] *vt* récupérer ▷ *vi* (*from illness*) se rétablir; (*from shock*) se remettre; **recovery** *n* récupération *f*; rétablissement *m*; (*Econ*) redressement *m*

recreate [riːkrɪ'eɪt] *vt* recréer

recreation [rekrɪ'eɪʃən] *n* (*leisure*) récréation *f*, détente *f*; **recreational drug** *n* drogue récréative; **recreational vehicle** *n* (*US*) camping-car *m*

recruit [rɪ'kruːt] *n* recrue *f* ▷ *vt* recruter; **recruitment** *n* recrutement *m*

rectangle ['rektæŋgl] *n* rectangle *m*; **rectangular** [rek'tæŋgjulər] *adj* rectangulaire

rectify ['rektɪfaɪ] *vt* (*error*) rectifier, corriger

rector ['rektər] *n* (*Rel*) pasteur *m*

recur [rɪ'kəːr] *vi* se reproduire; (*idea, opportunity*) se retrouver; (*symptoms*) réapparaître; **recurring** *adj* (*problem*) périodique, fréquent(e); (*Math*) périodique

recyclable [riː'saɪkləbl] *adj* recyclable

recycle [riːˈsaɪkl] *vt, vi* recycler
recycling [riːˈsaɪklɪŋ] *n* recyclage *m*
red [rɛd] *n* rouge *m*; (*Pol: pej*) rouge *m/f* ▷ *adj* rouge; (*hair*) roux (rousse);
in the ~ (*account*) à découvert;
(*business*) en déficit; **Red Cross**
n Croix-Rouge *f*; **redcurrant** *n*
groseille *f* (rouge)
redeem [rɪˈdiːm] *vt* (*debt*)
rembourser; (*sth in pawn*) dégager;
(*fig, also Rel*) racheter
red: red-haired *adj* roux (rousse);
redhead *n* roux (rousse); **red-hot** *adj*
chauffé(e) au rouge, brûlant(e); **red
light** *n*: **to go through a red light**
(*Aut*) brûler un feu rouge; **red-light
district** *n* quartier mal famé
red meat *n* viande *f* rouge
reduce [rɪˈdjuːs] *vt* réduire; (*lower*)
abaisser; **"~ speed now"** (*Aut*)
"ralentir"; **to ~ sb to tears** faire
pleurer qn; **reduced** *adj* réduit(e);
"greatly reduced prices" "gros
rabais"; **at a reduced price** (*goods*)
au rabais; (*ticket etc*) à prix réduit;
reduction [rɪˈdʌkʃən] *n* réduction
f; (*of price*) baisse *f*; (*discount*) rabais
m; réduction; **is there a reduction
for children/students?** y a-t-il
une réduction pour les enfants/les
étudiants?
redundancy [rɪˈdʌndənsɪ] *n* (*BRIT*)
licenciement *m*, mise *f* au chômage
redundant [rɪˈdʌndnt] *adj* (*BRIT:
worker*) licencié(e), mis(e) au
chômage; (*detail, object*) superflu(e);
to be made ~ (*worker*) être licencié,
être mis au chômage
reed [riːd] *n* (*Bot*) roseau *m*
reef [riːf] *n* (*at sea*) récif *m*, écueil *m*
reel [riːl] *n* bobine *f*; (*Fishing*) moulinet
m; (*Cine*) bande *f*; (*dance*) quadrille
écossais ▷ *vi* (*sway*) chanceler
ref [rɛf] *n abbr* (*inf: = referee*) arbitre *m*
refectory [rɪˈfɛktərɪ] *n* réfectoire *m*
refer [rɪˈfəː*] *vt*: **to ~ sb to** (*inquirer,
patient*) adresser qn à; (*reader: to text*)
renvoyer qn à ▷ *vi*: **to ~ to** (*allude to*)

parler de, faire allusion à; (*consult*) se
reporter à; (*apply to*) s'appliquer à
referee [rɛfəˈriː] *n* arbitre *m*; (*BRIT:
for job application*) répondant(e) ▷ *vt*
arbitrer
reference [ˈrɛfrəns] *n* référence *f*,
renvoi *m*; (*mention*) allusion *f*, mention
f; (*for job application: letter*) références;
lettre *f* de recommandation; **with ~
to** en ce qui concerne; (*Comm: in letter*)
me référant à; **reference number** *n*
(*Comm*) numéro *m* de référence
refill *vt* [riːˈfɪl] remplir à nouveau;
(*pen, lighter etc*) recharger ▷ *n* [ˈriːfɪl]
(*for pen etc*) recharge *f*
refine [rɪˈfaɪn] *vt* (*sugar, oil*) raffiner;
(*taste*) affiner; (*idea, theory*) peaufiner;
refined *adj* (*person, taste*) raffiné(e);
refinery *n* raffinerie *f*
reflect [rɪˈflɛkt] *vt* (*light, image*)
réfléchir, refléter ▷ *vi* (*think*) réfléchir,
méditer; **it ~s badly on him** cela le
discrédite; **it ~s well on him** c'est
tout à son honneur; **reflection**
[rɪˈflɛkʃən] *n* réflexion *f*; (*image*) reflet
m; **on reflection** réflexion faite
reflex [ˈriːflɛks] *adj, n* réflexe (*m*)
reform [rɪˈfɔːm] *n* réforme *f* ▷ *vt*
réformer
refrain [rɪˈfreɪn] *vi*: **to ~ from doing**
s'abstenir de faire ▷ *n* refrain *m*
refresh [rɪˈfrɛʃ] *vt* rafraîchir;
(*subj: food, sleep etc*) redonner
des forces à; **refreshing** *adj*
(*drink*) rafraîchissant(e); (*sleep*)
réparateur(-trice); **refreshments** *npl*
rafraîchissements *mpl*
refrigerator [rɪˈfrɪdʒəreɪtə*] *n*
réfrigérateur *m*, frigidaire *m*
refuel [riːˈfjuəl] *vi* se ravitailler en
carburant
refuge [ˈrɛfjuːdʒ] *n* refuge *m*; **to
take ~ in** se réfugier dans; **refugee**
[rɛfjuˈdʒiː] *n* réfugié(e)
refund *n* [ˈriːfʌnd] remboursement *m*
▷ *vt* [rɪˈfʌnd] rembourser
refurbish [riːˈfəːbɪʃ] *vt* remettre
à neuf

r

refusal [rɪˈfjuːzəl] n refus m; **to have first ~ on sth** avoir droit de préemption sur qch

refuse¹ [ˈrɛfjuːs] n ordures fpl, détritus mpl

refuse² [rɪˈfjuːz] vt, vi refuser; **to ~ to do sth** refuser de faire qch

regain [rɪˈgeɪn] vt (lost ground) regagner; (strength) retrouver

regard [rɪˈgɑːd] n respect m, estime f, considération f ▷ vt considérer; **to give one's ~s to** faire ses amitiés à; **"with kindest ~s"** "bien amicalement"; **as ~s, with ~ to** en ce qui concerne; **regarding** prep en ce qui concerne; **regardless** adv quand même; **regardless of** sans se soucier de

regenerate [rɪˈdʒɛnəreɪt] vt régénérer ▷ vi se régénérer

reggae [ˈrɛgeɪ] n reggae m

regiment [ˈrɛdʒɪmənt] n régiment m

region [ˈriːdʒən] n région f; **in the ~ of** (fig) aux alentours de; **regional** adj régional(e)

register [ˈrɛdʒɪstəʳ] n registre m; (also: **electoral ~**) liste électorale ▷ vt enregistrer, inscrire; (birth) déclarer; (vehicle) immatriculer; (letter) envoyer en recommandé; (subj: instrument) marquer ▷ vi s'inscrire; (at hotel) signer le registre; (make impression) être (bien) compris(e); **registered** adj (BRIT: letter) recommandé(e); **registered trademark** n marque déposée

registrar [ˈrɛdʒɪstrɑːʳ] n officier m de l'état civil

registration [rɛdʒɪsˈtreɪʃən] n (act) enregistrement m; (of student) inscription f; (BRIT Aut: also: **~ number**) numéro m d'immatriculation

registry office [ˈrɛdʒɪstrɪ-] n (BRIT) bureau m de l'état civil; **to get married in a ~** ≈ se marier à la mairie

regret [rɪˈgrɛt] n regret m ▷ vt regretter; **regrettable** adj regrettable, fâcheux(-euse)

regular [ˈrɛgjuləʳ] adj régulier(-ière); (usual) habituel(le), normal(e); (soldier) de métier; (Comm: size) ordinaire ▷ n (client etc) habitué(e); **regularly** adv régulièrement

regulate [ˈrɛgjuleɪt] vt régler; **regulation** [rɛgjuˈleɪʃən] n (rule) règlement m; (adjustment) réglage m

rehabilitation [ˈriːəbɪlɪˈteɪʃən] n (of offender) réhabilitation f; (of addict) réadaptation f

rehearsal [rɪˈhəːsəl] n répétition f

rehearse [rɪˈhəːs] vt répéter

reign [reɪn] n règne m ▷ vi régner

reimburse [riːɪmˈbəːs] vt rembourser

rein [reɪn] n (for horse) rêne f

reincarnation [riːɪnkɑːˈneɪʃən] n réincarnation f

reindeer [ˈreɪndɪəʳ] n (pl inv) renne m

reinforce [riːɪnˈfɔːs] vt renforcer; **reinforcements** npl (Mil) renfort(s) m(pl)

reinstate [riːɪnˈsteɪt] vt rétablir, réintégrer

reject n [ˈriːdʒɛkt] (Comm) article m de rebut ▷ vt [rɪˈdʒɛkt] refuser; (idea) rejeter; **rejection** [rɪˈdʒɛkʃən] n rejet m, refus m

rejoice [rɪˈdʒɔɪs] vi: **to ~ (at or over)** se réjouir (de)

relate [rɪˈleɪt] vt (tell) raconter; (connect) établir un rapport entre ▷ vi: **to ~ to** (connect) se rapporter à; **to ~ to sb** (interact) entretenir des rapports avec qn; **related** adj apparenté(e); **related to** (subject) lié(e) à; **relating to** prep concernant

relation [rɪˈleɪʃən] n (person) parent(e); (link) rapport m, lien m; **relations** npl (relatives) famille f; **relationship** n rapport m, lien m; (personal ties) relations fpl, rapports; (also: **family relationship**) lien de parenté; (affair) liaison f

relative ['rɛlətɪv] n parent(e) ▷ adj relatif(-ive); (respective) respectif(-ive); **relatively** adv relativement

relax [rɪ'læks] vi (muscle) se relâcher; (person: unwind) se détendre ▷ vt relâcher; (mind, person) détendre; **relaxation** [riːlæk'seɪʃən] n relâchement m; (of mind) détente f; (recreation) détente, délassement m; **relaxed** adj relâché(e); détendu(e); **relaxing** adj délassant(e)

relay ['riːleɪ] n (Sport) course f de relais ▷ vt (message) retransmettre, relayer

release [rɪ'liːs] n (from prison, obligation) libération f; (of gas etc) émission f; (of film etc) sortie f; (new recording) disque m ▷ vt (prisoner) libérer; (book, film) sortir; (report, news) rendre public, publier; (gas etc) émettre, dégager; (free: from wreckage etc) dégager; (Tech: catch, spring etc) déclencher; (let go: person, animal) relâcher; (: hand, object) lâcher; (: grip, brake) desserrer

relegate ['rɛləgeɪt] vt reléguer; (BRIT Sport): **to be ~d** descendre dans une division inférieure

relent [rɪ'lɛnt] vi se laisser fléchir; **relentless** adj implacable; (non-stop) continuel(le)

relevant ['rɛləvənt] adj (question) pertinent(e); (corresponding) approprié(e); (fact) significatif(-ive); (information) utile

reliable [rɪ'laɪəbl] adj (person, firm) sérieux(-euse), fiable; (method, machine) fiable; (news, information) sûr(e)

relic ['rɛlɪk] n (Rel) relique f; (of the past) vestige m

relief [rɪ'liːf] n (from pain, anxiety) soulagement m; (help, supplies) secours m(pl); (Art, Geo) relief m

relieve [rɪ'liːv] vt (pain, patient) soulager; (fear, worry) dissiper; (bring help) secourir; (take over from: gen) relayer; (: guard) relever; **to ~ sb of sth** débarrasser qn de qch; **to ~ o.s.**

(euphemism) se soulager, faire ses besoins; **relieved** adj soulagé(e)

religion [rɪ'lɪdʒən] n religion f

religious [rɪ'lɪdʒəs] adj religieux(-euse); (book) de piété; **religious education** n instruction religieuse

relish ['rɛlɪʃ] n (Culin) condiment m; (enjoyment) délectation f ▷ vt (food etc) savourer; **to ~ doing** se délecter à faire

relocate [riːləʊ'keɪt] vt (business) transférer ▷ vi se transférer, s'installer or s'établir ailleurs

reluctance [rɪ'lʌktəns] n répugnance f

reluctant [rɪ'lʌktənt] adj peu disposé(e), qui hésite; **reluctantly** adv à contrecœur, sans enthousiasme

rely on [rɪ'laɪ-] vt fus (be dependent on) dépendre de; (trust) compter sur

remain [rɪ'meɪn] vi rester; **remainder** n reste m; (Comm) fin f de série; **remaining** adj qui reste; **remains** npl restes mpl

remand [rɪ'mɑːnd] n: **on ~** en détention préventive ▷ vt: **to be ~ed in custody** être placé(e) en détention préventive

remark [rɪ'mɑːk] n remarque f, observation f ▷ vt (faire) remarquer, dire; **remarkable** adj remarquable

remarry [riː'mærɪ] vi se remarier

remedy ['rɛmədɪ] n: **~ (for)** remède m (contre or à) ▷ vt remédier à

remember [rɪ'mɛmbəʳ] vt se rappeler, se souvenir de; (send greetings): **~ me to him** saluez-le de ma part; **Remembrance Day** [rɪ'mɛmbrəns-] n (BRIT) ≈ (le jour de) l'Armistice m, ≈ le 11 novembre

■ **REMEMBRANCE DAY**

● *Remembrance Day* ou *Remembrance*
● *Sunday* est le dimanche le plus
● proche du 11 novembre, jour où
● la Première Guerre mondiale

r

- a officiellement pris fin. Il rend
- hommage aux victimes des
- deux guerres mondiales. À
- cette occasion, on observe deux
- minutes de silence à 11h, heure de
- la signature de l'armistice avec
- l'Allemagne en 1918; certaines
- membres de la famille royale et
- du gouvernement déposent des
- gerbes de coquelicots au cénotaphe
- de Whitehall, et des couronnes
- sont placées sur les monuments
- aux morts dans toute la Grande-
- Bretagne; par ailleurs, les gens
- portent des coquelicots artificiels
- fabriqués et vendus par des
- membres de la légion britannique
- blessés au combat, au profit des
- blessés de guerre et de leur famille.

remind [rɪ'maɪnd] vt: **to ~ sb of sth**
rappeler qch à qn; **to ~ sb to do** faire
penser à qn à faire, rappeler à qn qu'il
doit faire; **reminder** n (Comm: letter)
rappel m; (note etc) pense-bête m;
(souvenir) souvenir m

reminiscent [rɛmɪ'nɪsnt] adj: **~ of**
qui rappelle, qui fait penser à

remnant ['rɛmnənt] n reste m,
restant m; (of cloth) coupon m

remorse [rɪ'mɔːs] n remords m

remote [rɪ'məʊt] adj éloigné(e),
lointain(e); (person) distant(e);
(possibility) vague; **remote control**
n télécommande f; **remotely** adv au
loin; (slightly) très vaguement

removal [rɪ'muːvəl] n (taking away)
enlèvement m; suppression f; (BRIT:
from house) déménagement m;
(from office: dismissal) renvoi m; (of
stain) nettoyage m; (Med) ablation
f; **removal man** (irreg) n (BRIT)
déménageur m; **removal van** n
(BRIT) camion m de déménagement

remove [rɪ'muːv] vt enlever, retirer;
(employee) renvoyer; (stain) faire
partir; (abuse) supprimer; (doubt)
chasser

Renaissance [rɪ'neɪsɑ̃s] n: **the ~** la
Renaissance

rename [riː'neɪm] vt rebaptiser

render ['rɛndər] vt rendre

rendezvous ['rɒndɪvuː] n rendez-
vous m inv

renew [rɪ'njuː] vt renouveler;
(negotiations) reprendre;
(acquaintance) renouer; **renewable**
adj (energy) renouvelable

renovate ['rɛnəveɪt] vt rénover;
(work of art) restaurer

renowned [rɪ'naʊnd] adj
renommé(e)

rent [rɛnt] n loyer m ▷ vt louer;
rental n (for television, car) (prix m de)
location f

reorganize [riː'ɔːɡənaɪz] vt
réorganiser

rep [rɛp] n abbr (Comm)
= **representative**

repair [rɪ'pɛər] n réparation f ▷ vt
réparer; **in good/bad ~** en bon/
mauvais état; **where can I get
this ~ed?** où est-ce que je peux faire
réparer ceci?; **repair kit** n trousse f de
réparations

repay [riː'peɪ] vt (irreg: like **pay**)
(money, creditor) rembourser; (sb's
efforts) récompenser; **repayment** n
remboursement m

repeat [rɪ'piːt] n (Radio, TV) reprise
f ▷ vt répéter; (promise, attack, also
Comm: order) renouveler; (Scol: a
class) redoubler ▷ vi redouble; **can
you ~ that, please?** pouvez-vous
répéter, s'il vous plaît?; **repeatedly**
adv souvent, à plusieurs reprises;
repeat prescription n (BRIT):
I'd like a repeat prescription
je voudrais renouveler mon
ordonnance

repellent [rɪ'pɛlənt] adj
repoussant(e) ▷ n: **insect ~**
insectifuge m

repercussions [riːpə'kʌʃənz] npl
répercussions fpl

repetition [rɛpɪ'tɪʃən] n répétition f

repetitive [rɪ'pɛtɪtɪv] *adj (movement, work)* répétitif(-ive); *(speech)* plein(e) de redites

replace [rɪ'pleɪs] *vt (put back)* remettre, replacer; *(take the place of)* remplacer; **replacement** *n (substitution)* remplacement *m*; *(person)* remplaçant(e)

replay ['riːpleɪ] *n (of match)* match rejoué; *(of tape, film)* répétition *f*

replica ['rɛplɪkə] *n* réplique *f*, copie exacte

reply [rɪ'plaɪ] *n* réponse *f* ▷ *vi* répondre

report [rɪ'pɔːt] *n* rapport *m*; *(Press etc)* reportage *m*; *(BRIT: also:* **school ~)** bulletin *m (scolaire)*; *(of gun)* détonation *f* ▷ *vt* rapporter, faire un compte rendu de; *(Press etc)* faire un reportage sur; *(notify: accident)* signaler; *(: culprit)* dénoncer ▷ *vi (make a report)* faire un rapport; **I'd like to ~ a theft** je voudrais signaler un vol; **to ~ (to sb)** *(present o.s.)* se présenter *(chez qn)*; **report card** *n (US, SCOTTISH)* bulletin *m (scolaire)*; **reportedly** *adv:* **she is reportedly living in Spain** elle habiterait en Espagne; **he reportedly told them to …** il leur aurait dit de …; **reporter** *n* reporter *m*

represent [rɛprɪ'zɛnt] *vt* représenter; *(view, belief)* présenter, expliquer; *(describe):* **to ~ sth as** présenter *or* décrire qch comme; **representation** [rɛprɪzɛn'teɪʃən] *n* représentation *f*; **representative** *n* représentant(e); *(US Pol)* député *m* ▷ *adj* représentatif(-ive), caractéristique

repress [rɪ'prɛs] *vt* réprimer; **repression** [rɪ'prɛʃən] *n* répression *f*

reprimand ['rɛprɪmɑːnd] *n* réprimande *f* ▷ *vt* réprimander

reproduce [riːprə'djuːs] *vt* reproduire ▷ *vi* se reproduire; **reproduction** [riːprə'dʌkʃən] *n* reproduction *f*

reptile ['rɛptaɪl] *n* reptile *m*

republic [rɪ'pʌblɪk] *n* république *f*; **republican** *adj, n* républicain(e)

reputable ['rɛpjutəbl] *adj* de bonne réputation; *(occupation)* honorable

reputation [rɛpju'teɪʃən] *n* réputation *f*

request [rɪ'kwɛst] *n* demande *f*; *(formal)* requête *f* ▷ *vt:* **to ~ (of** *or* **from sb)** demander (à qn); **request stop** *n (BRIT: for bus)* arrêt facultatif

require [rɪ'kwaɪə^r] *vt (need: subj: person)* avoir besoin de; *(: thing, situation)* nécessiter, demander; *(want)* exiger; *(order):* **to ~ sb to do sth/sth of sb** exiger que qn fasse qch/qch de qn; **requirement** *n (need)* exigence *f*; besoin *m*; *(condition)* condition *f* (requise)

resat [riː'sæt] *pt, pp of* **resit**

rescue ['rɛskjuː] *n (from accident)* sauvetage *m*; *(help)* secours *mpl* ▷ *vt* sauver

research [rɪ'səːtʃ] *n* recherche(s) *f(pl)* ▷ *vt* faire des recherches sur

resemblance [rɪ'zɛmbləns] *n* ressemblance *f*

resemble [rɪ'zɛmbl] *vt* ressembler à

resent [rɪ'zɛnt] *vt* être contrarié(e) par; **resentful** *adj* irrité(e), plein(e) de ressentiment; **resentment** *n* ressentiment *m*

reservation [rɛzə'veɪʃən] *n (booking)* réservation *f*; **to make a ~ (in an hotel/a restaurant/on a plane)** réserver *or* retenir une chambre/une table/une place; **reservation desk** *n (US: in hotel)* réception *f*

reserve [rɪ'zəːv] *n* réserve *f*; *(Sport)* remplaçant(e) ▷ *vt (seats etc)* réserver, retenir; **reserved** *adj* réservé(e)

reservoir ['rɛzəvwɑː^r] *n* réservoir *m*

reshuffle ['riːʃʌfl] *n:* **Cabinet ~** *(Pol)* remaniement ministériel

residence ['rɛzɪdəns] *n* résidence *f*; **residence permit** *n (BRIT)* permis *m* de séjour

r

resident ['rɛzɪdənt] n (of country) résident(e); (of area, house) habitant(e); (in hotel) pensionnaire ▷ adj résident(e); **residential** [rɛzɪ'dɛnʃəl] adj de résidence; (area) résidentiel(le); (course) avec hébergement sur place

residue ['rɛzɪdjuː] n reste m; (Chem, Physics) résidu m

resign [rɪ'zaɪn] vt (one's post) se démettre de ▷ vi démissionner; **to ~ o.s. to** (endure) se résigner à; **resignation** [rɛzɪg'neɪʃən] n (from post) démission f; (state of mind) résignation f

resin ['rɛzɪn] n résine f

resist [rɪ'zɪst] vt résister à; **resistance** n résistance f

resit vt [riː'sɪt] (irreg: like **sit**) (BRIT: exam) repasser ▷ n ['riː'sɪt] deuxième session f (d'un examen)

resolution [rɛzə'luːʃən] n résolution f

resolve [rɪ'zɔlv] n résolution f ▷ vt (problem) résoudre; (decide): **to ~ to do** résoudre or décider de faire

resort [rɪ'zɔːt] n (seaside town) station f balnéaire; (for skiing) station de ski; (recourse) recours m ▷ vi: **to ~ to** avoir recours à; **in the last ~** en dernier ressort

resource [rɪ'sɔːs] n ressource f; **resourceful** adj ingénieux(-euse), débrouillard(e)

respect [rɪs'pɛkt] n respect m ▷ vt respecter; **respectable** adj respectable; (quite good: result etc) honorable; **respectful** adj respectueux(-euse); **respective** adj respectif(-ive); **respectively** adv respectivement

respite ['rɛspaɪt] n répit m

respond [rɪs'pɔnd] vi répondre; (react) réagir; **response** [rɪs'pɔns] n réponse f; (reaction) réaction f

responsibility [rɪspɔnsɪ'bɪlɪtɪ] n responsabilité f

responsible [rɪs'pɔnsɪbl] adj (liable): **~ (for)** responsable (de);

(person) digne de confiance; (job) qui comporte des responsabilités; **responsibly** adv avec sérieux

responsive [rɪs'pɔnsɪv] adj (student, audience) réceptif(-ive); (brakes, steering) sensible

rest [rɛst] n repos m; (stop) arrêt m, pause f; (Mus) silence m; (support) support m, appui m; (remainder) reste m, restant m ▷ vi se reposer; (be supported): **to ~ on** appuyer or reposer sur ▷ vt (lean): **to ~ sth on/against** appuyer qch sur/contre; **the ~ of them** les autres

restaurant ['rɛstərɔn] n restaurant m; **restaurant car** n (BRIT Rail) wagon-restaurant m

restless ['rɛstlɪs] adj agité(e)

restoration [rɛstə'reɪʃən] n (of building) restauration f; (of stolen goods) restitution f

restore [rɪ'stɔːʳ] vt (building) restaurer; (sth stolen) restituer; (peace, health) rétablir; **to ~ to** (former state) ramener à

restrain [rɪs'treɪn] vt (feeling) contenir; (person): **to ~ (from doing)** retenir (de faire); **restraint** n (restriction) contrainte f; (moderation) retenue f; (of style) sobriété f

restrict [rɪs'trɪkt] vt restreindre, limiter; **restriction** [rɪs'trɪkʃən] n restriction f, limitation f

rest room n (US) toilettes fpl

restructure [riː'strʌktʃəʳ] vt restructurer

result [rɪ'zʌlt] n résultat m ▷ vi: **to ~ in** aboutir à, se terminer par; **as a ~ of** à la suite de

resume [rɪ'zjuːm] vt (work, journey) reprendre ▷ vi (work etc) reprendre

résumé ['reɪzjuːmeɪ] n (summary) résumé m; (US: curriculum vitae) curriculum vitae m inv

resuscitate [rɪ'sʌsɪteɪt] vt (Med) réanimer

retail ['riːteɪl] adj de or au détail ▷ adv au détail; **retailer** n détaillant(e)

retain [rɪ'teɪn] *vt* (*keep*) garder, conserver

retaliation [rɪtælɪ'eɪʃən] *n* représailles *fpl*, vengeance *f*

retire [rɪ'taɪəʳ] *vi* (*give up work*) prendre sa retraite; (*withdraw*) se retirer, partir; (*go to bed*) aller se coucher; **retired** *adj* (*person*) retraité(e); **retirement** *n* retraite *f*

retort [rɪ'tɔːt] *vi* riposter

retreat [rɪ'triːt] *n* retraite *f* ▷ *vi* battre en retraite

retrieve [rɪ'triːv] *vt* (*sth lost*) récupérer; (*situation, honour*) sauver; (*error, loss*) réparer; (*Comput*) rechercher

retrospect ['rɛtrəspɛkt] *n*: **in ~** rétrospectivement, après coup; **retrospective** [rɛtrə'spɛktɪv] *adj* rétrospectif(-ive); (*law*) rétroactif(-ive) ▷ *n* (*Art*) rétrospective *f*

return [rɪ'təːn] *n* (*going or coming back*) retour *m*; (*of sth stolen etc*) restitution *f*; (*Finance: from land, shares*) rapport *m* ▷ *cpd* (*journey*) de retour; (*BRIT: ticket*) aller et retour; (*match*) retour ▷ *vi* (*person etc: come back*) revenir; (*: go back*) retourner ▷ *vt* rendre; (*bring back*) rapporter; (*send back*) renvoyer; (*put back*) remettre; (*Pol: candidate*) élire; **returns** *npl* (*Comm*) recettes *fpl*; (*Finance*) bénéfices *mpl*; **many happy ~s (of the day)!** bon anniversaire!; **by ~ (of post)** par retour (du courrier); **in ~ (for)** en échange (de); **a ~ (ticket) for ...** un billet aller et retour pour ...; **return ticket** *n* (*esp BRIT*) billet *m* aller-retour

retweet [riː'twiːt] *vt* (*on Twitter*) retweeter

reunion [riː'juːnɪən] *n* réunion *f*

reunite [riːjuː'naɪt] *vt* réunir

revamp [riː'væmp] *vt* (*house*) retaper; (*firm*) réorganiser

reveal [rɪ'viːl] *vt* (*make known*) révéler; (*display*) laisser voir; **revealing** *adj* révélateur(-trice); (*dress*) au décolleté généreux or suggestif

revel ['rɛvl] *vi*: **to ~ in sth/in doing** se délecter de qch/à faire

revelation [rɛvə'leɪʃən] *n* révélation *f*

revenge [rɪ'vɛndʒ] *n* vengeance *f*; (*in game etc*) revanche *f* ▷ *vt* venger; **to take ~ (on)** se venger (sur)

revenue ['rɛvənjuː] *n* revenu *m*

Reverend ['rɛvərənd] *adj*: **the ~ John Smith** (*Anglican*) le révérend John Smith; (*Catholic*) l'abbé (John) Smith; (*Protestant*) le pasteur (John) Smith

reversal [rɪ'vəːsl] *n* (*of opinion*) revirement *m*; (*of order*) renversement *m*; (*of direction*) changement *m*

reverse [rɪ'vəːs] *n* contraire *m*, opposé *m*; (*back*) dos *m*, envers *m*; (*of paper*) verso *m*; (*of coin*) revers *m*; (*Aut: also:* **~ gear**) marche *f* arrière ▷ *adj* (*order, direction*) opposé(e), inverse ▷ *vt* (*order, position*) changer, inverser; (*direction, policy*) changer complètement de; (*decision*) annuler; (*roles*) renverser ▷ *vi* (*BRIT Aut*) faire marche arrière; **reversing lights** *npl* (*BRIT Aut*) feux *mpl* de marche arrière or de recul

revert [rɪ'vəːt] *vi*: **to ~ to** revenir à, retourner à

review [rɪ'vjuː] *n* revue *f*; (*of book, film*) critique *f*; (*of situation, policy*) examen *m*, bilan *m*; (*US: examination*) examen ▷ *vt* passer en revue; faire la critique de; examiner

revise [rɪ'vaɪz] *vt* réviser, modifier; (*manuscript*) revoir, corriger ▷ *vi* (*study*) réviser; **revision** [rɪ'vɪʒən] *n* révision *f*

revival [rɪ'vaɪvəl] *n* reprise *f*; (*recovery*) rétablissement *m*; (*of faith*) renouveau *m*

revive [rɪ'vaɪv] *vt* (*person*) ranimer; (*custom*) rétablir; (*economy*) relancer; (*hope, courage*) raviver, faire renaître; (*play, fashion*) reprendre ▷ *vi* (*person*) reprendre connaissance (*: from ill health*) se rétablir; (*hope etc*) renaître; (*activity*) reprendre

r

revolt [rɪ'vəʊlt] n révolte f ▷ vi
se révolter, se rebeller ▷ vt
révolter, dégoûter; **revolting** adj
dégoûtant(e)

revolution [revə'lu:ʃən] n révolution
f; (of wheel etc) tour m, révolution;
revolutionary adj, n révolutionnaire
(m/f)

revolve [rɪ'vɒlv] vi tourner

revolver [rɪ'vɒlvəʳ] n revolver m

reward [rɪ'wɔːd] n récompense f
▷ vt: **to ~ (for)** récompenser (de);
rewarding adj (fig) qui (en) vaut la
peine, gratifiant(e)

rewind [riː'waɪnd] vt (irreg: like
wind²) (tape) réembobiner

rewritable [riː'raɪtəbl] adj (CD, DVD)
réinscriptible

rewrite [riː'raɪt] (irreg: like **write**)
vt récrire

rheumatism ['ruːmətɪzəm] n
rhumatisme m

Rhine [raɪn] n: **the (River) ~** le Rhin

rhinoceros [raɪ'nɒsərəs] n
rhinocéros m

rhubarb ['ruːbɑːb] n rhubarbe f

rhyme [raɪm] n rime f; (verse) vers mpl

rhythm ['rɪðm] n rythme m

rib [rɪb] n (Anat) côte f

ribbon ['rɪbən] n ruban m; **in ~s** (torn)
en lambeaux

rice [raɪs] n riz m; **rice pudding** n
riz m au lait

rich [rɪtʃ] adj riche; (gift, clothes)
somptueux(-euse); **to be ~ in sth**
être riche en qch

rid [rɪd] (pt, pp **rid**) vt: **to ~ sb of**
débarrasser qn de; **to get ~ of** se
débarrasser de

ridden ['rɪdn] pp of **ride**

riddle ['rɪdl] n (puzzle) énigme f ▷ vt:
to be ~d with être criblé(e) de; (fig)
être en proie à

ride [raɪd] (pt **rode**, pp **ridden**) n
promenade f, tour m; (distance
covered) trajet m ▷ vi (as sport)
monter (à cheval), faire du cheval;
(go somewhere: on horse, bicycle) aller

(à cheval or bicyclette etc); (travel: on
bicycle, motor cycle, bus) rouler ▷ vt (a
horse) monter; (distance) parcourir,
faire; **to ~ a horse/bicycle** monter à
cheval/à bicyclette; **to take sb for a
~** (fig) faire marcher qn; (cheat) rouler
qn; **rider** n cavalier(-ière); (in race)
jockey m; (on bicycle) cycliste m/f; (on
motorcycle) motocycliste m/f

ridge [rɪdʒ] n (of hill) faîte m; (of roof,
mountain) arête f; (on object) strie f

ridicule ['rɪdɪkjuːl] n ridicule m;
dérision f ▷ vt ridiculiser, tourner en
dérision; **ridiculous** [rɪ'dɪkjuləs]
adj ridicule

riding ['raɪdɪŋ] n équitation f;
riding school n manège m, école f
d'équitation

rife [raɪf] adj répandu(e); **~ with**
abondant(e) en

rifle ['raɪfl] n fusil m (à canon rayé)
▷ vt vider, dévaliser

rift [rɪft] n fente f, fissure f; (fig:
disagreement) désaccord m

rig [rɪg] n (also: **oil ~**: on land) derrick
m; (: at sea) plate-forme pétrolière
▷ vt (election etc) truquer

right [raɪt] adj (true) juste, exact(e);
(correct) bon (bonne); (suitable)
approprié(e), convenable; (just)
juste, équitable; (morally good) bien
inv; (not left) droit(e) ▷ n (moral good)
bien m; (title, claim) droit m; (not left)
droite f ▷ adv (answer) correctement;
(treat) bien, comme il faut; (not on
the left) à droite ▷ vt redresser ▷ excl
bon!; **do you have the ~ time?**
avez-vous l'heure juste or exacte?; **to
be ~** (person) avoir raison; (answer)
être juste or correct(e); **by ~s** en
toute justice; **on the ~** à droite; **to
be in the ~** avoir raison; **~ in the
middle** en plein milieu; **~ away**
immédiatement; **right angle** n
(Math) angle droit; **rightful** adj (heir)
légitime; **right-hand** adj: **the right-
hand side** la droite; **right-hand
drive** n conduite f à droite; (vehicle)

véhicule *m* avec la conduite à droite;
right-handed *adj* (*person*) droitier(-ière); **rightly** *adv* bien, correctement; (*with reason*) à juste titre; **right of way** *n* (*on path etc*) droit *m* de passage; (*Aut*) priorité *f*; **right-wing** *adj* de droite

rigid ['rɪdʒɪd] *adj* rigide; (*principle, control*) strict(e)

rigorous ['rɪgərəs] *adj* rigoureux(-euse)

rim [rɪm] *n* bord *m*; (*of spectacles*) monture *f*; (*of wheel*) jante *f*

rind [raɪnd] *n* (*of bacon*) couenne *f*; (*of lemon etc*) écorce *f*, zeste *m*; (*of cheese*) croûte *f*

ring [rɪŋ] *n* anneau *m*; (*on finger*) bague *f*; (*also:* **wedding ~**) alliance *f*; (*of people, objects*) cercle *m*; (*of spies*) réseau *m*; (*of smoke etc*) rond *m*; (*arena*) piste *f*, arène *f*; (*for boxing*) ring *m*; (*sound of bell*) sonnerie *f* ▷ *vi* (*pt* **rang**, *pp* **rung**) (*telephone, bell*) sonner; (*person: by telephone*) téléphoner; (*ears*) bourdonner; (*also:* **~ out**: *voice, words*) retentir ▷ *vt* (*also:* **~ up**) téléphoner à, appeler; **to ~ the bell** sonner; **to give sb a ~** (*Tel*) passer un coup de téléphone *or* de fil à qn; **ring back** *vt, vi* (*BRIT Tel*) rappeler; **ring off** *vi* (*BRIT Tel*) raccrocher; **ring up** *vt* (*BRIT Tel*) téléphoner à, appeler; **ringing tone** *n* (*BRIT Tel*) tonalité *f* d'appel; **ringleader** *n* (*of gang*) chef *m*, meneur *m*; **ring road** *n* (*BRIT*) rocade *f*; (*motorway*) périphérique *m*; **ringtone** *n* (*on mobile*) sonnerie *f* (*de téléphone portable*)

rink [rɪŋk] *n* (*also:* **ice ~**) patinoire *f*

rinse [rɪns] *n* rinçage *m* ▷ *vt* rincer

riot ['raɪət] *n* émeute *f*, bagarres *fpl* ▷ *vi* (*demonstrators*) manifester avec violence; (*population*) se soulever, se révolter; **to run ~** se déchaîner

rip [rɪp] *n* déchirure *f* ▷ *vt* déchirer ▷ *vi* se déchirer; **rip off** *vt* (*inf: cheat*) arnaquer; **rip up** *vt* déchirer

ripe [raɪp] *adj* (*fruit*) mûr(e); (*cheese*) fait(e)

rip-off ['rɪpɔf] *n* (*inf*): **it's a ~!** c'est du vol manifeste!, c'est de l'arnaque!

ripple ['rɪpl] *n* ride *f*, ondulation *f*; (*of applause, laughter*) cascade *f* ▷ *vi* se rider, onduler

rise [raɪz] *n* (*slope*) côte *f*, pente *f*; (*hill*) élévation *f*; (*increase: in wages*: *BRIT*) augmentation *f*; (: *in prices, temperature*) hausse *f*, augmentation; (*fig: to power etc*) ascension *f* ▷ *vi* (*pt* **rose**, *pp* **risen**) s'élever, monter; (*prices, numbers*) augmenter, monter; (*waters, river*) monter; (*sun, wind, person: from chair, bed*) se lever; (*also:* **~ up**: *tower, building*) s'élever; (: *rebel*) se révolter; se rebeller; (*in rank*) s'élever; **to give ~ to** donner lieu à; **to ~ to the occasion** se montrer à la hauteur; **risen** ['rɪzn] *pp of* **rise**; **rising** *adj* (*increasing: number, prices*) en hausse; (*tide*) montant(e); (*sun, moon*) levant(e)

risk [rɪsk] *n* risque *m* ▷ *vt* risquer; **to take** *or* **run the ~ of doing** courir le risque de faire; **at ~** en danger; **at one's own ~** à ses risques et périls; **risky** *adj* risqué(e)

rite [raɪt] *n* rite *m*; **the last ~s** les derniers sacrements

ritual ['rɪtjuəl] *adj* rituel(le) ▷ *n* rituel *m*

rival ['raɪvl] *n* rival(e); (*in business*) concurrent(e) ▷ *adj* rival(e); qui fait concurrence ▷ *vt* (*match*) égaler; **rivalry** *n* rivalité *f*; (*in business*) concurrence *f*

river ['rɪvər] *n* rivière *f*; (*major: also fig*) fleuve *m* ▷ *cpd* (*port, traffic*) fluvial(e); **up/down ~** en amont/aval; **riverbank** *n* rive *f*, berge *f*

rivet ['rɪvɪt] *n* rivet *m* ▷ *vt* (*fig*) river, fixer

Riviera [rɪvɪ'ɛərə] *n*: **the (French) ~** la Côte d'Azur

road [rəud] *n* route *f*; (*in town*) rue *f*; (*fig*) chemin, voie *f* ▷ *cpd* (*accident*)

r

de la route; **major/minor ~** route principale or à priorité/voie secondaire; **which ~ do I take for …?** quelle route dois-je prendre pour aller à …?; **roadblock** n barrage routier; **road map** n carte routière; **road rage** n comportement très agressif de certains usagers de la route; **road safety** n sécurité routière; **roadside** n bord m de la route, bas-côté m; **road sign** n panneau m de signalisation; **road tax** n (BRIT Aut) taxe f sur les automobiles; **roadworks** npl travaux mpl (de réfection des routes)

roam [rəʊm] vi errer, vagabonder

roar [rɔː'] n rugissement m; (of crowd) hurlements mpl; (of vehicle, thunder, storm) grondement m ▷ vi rugir; hurler; gronder; **to ~ with laughter** rire à gorge déployée

roast [rəʊst] n rôti m ▷ vt (meat) (faire) rôtir; (coffee) griller, torréfier; **roast beef** n rôti m de bœuf, rosbif m

rob [rɒb] vt (person) voler; (bank) dévaliser; **to ~ sb of sth** voler or dérober qch à qn; (fig: deprive) priver qn de qch; **robber** n bandit m, voleur m; **robbery** n vol m

robe [rəʊb] n (for ceremony etc) robe f; (also: **bath~**) peignoir m; (US: rug) couverture f ▷ vt revêtir (d'une robe)

robin ['rɒbɪn] n rouge-gorge m

robot ['rəʊbɒt] n robot m

robust [rəʊ'bʌst] adj robuste; (material, appetite) solide

rock [rɒk] n (substance) roche f, roc m; (boulder) rocher m, roche; (US: small stone) caillou m; (BRIT: sweet) ≈ sucre m d'orge ▷ vt (swing gently: cradle) balancer; (: child) bercer; (shake) ébranler, secouer ▷ vi se balancer, être ébranlé(e) or secoué(e); **on the ~s** (drink) avec des glaçons; (marriage etc) en train de craquer; **rock and roll** n rock (and roll) m, rock'n'roll m; **rock climbing** n varappe f

rocket ['rɒkɪt] n fusée f; (Mil) fusée, roquette f; (Culin) roquette

rocking chair ['rɒkɪŋ-] n fauteuil m à bascule

rocky ['rɒkɪ] adj (hill) rocheux(-euse); (path) rocailleux(-euse)

rod [rɒd] n (metallic) tringle f; (Tech) tige f; (wooden) baguette f; (also: **fishing ~**) canne f à pêche

rode [rəʊd] pt of **ride**

rodent ['rəʊdnt] n rongeur m

rogue [rəʊg] n coquin(e)

role [rəʊl] n rôle m; **role-model** n modèle m à émuler

roll [rəʊl] n rouleau m; (of banknotes) liasse f; (also: **bread ~**) petit pain; (register) liste f; (sound: of drums etc) roulement m ▷ vt rouler; (also: **~ up**) (string) enrouler; (also: **~ out**: pastry) étendre au rouleau, abaisser ▷ vi rouler; **roll over** vi se retourner; **roll up** vi (inf: arrive) arriver, s'amener ▷ vt (carpet, cloth, map) rouler; (sleeves) retrousser; **roller** n rouleau m; (wheel) roulette f; (for road) rouleau compresseur; (for hair) bigoudi m; **roller coaster** n montagnes fpl russes; **roller skates** npl patins mpl à roulettes; **roller-skating** n patin m à roulettes; **to go roller-skating** faire du patin à roulettes; **rolling pin** n rouleau m à pâtisserie

ROM [rɒm] n abbr (Comput: = read-only memory) mémoire morte, ROM f

Roman ['rəʊmən] adj romain(e) ▷ n Romain(e); **Roman Catholic** adj, n catholique (m/f)

romance [rə'mæns] n (love affair) idylle f; (charm) poésie f; (novel) roman m à l'eau de rose

Romania [rəʊ'meɪnɪə] n = **Rumania**

Roman numeral n chiffre romain

romantic [rə'mæntɪk] adj romantique; (novel, attachment) sentimental

Rome [rəʊm] n Rome

roof [ruːf] n toit m; (of tunnel, cave) plafond m ▷ vt couvrir (d'un toit); **the ~ of the mouth** la voûte du palais; **roof rack** n (Aut) galerie f

rook [ruk] n (bird) freux m; (Chess) tour f

room [ru:m] n (in house) pièce f; (also: **bed~**) chambre f (à coucher); (in school etc) salle f; (space) place f; **roommate** n camarade m/f de chambre; **room service** n service m des chambres (dans un hôtel); **roomy** adj spacieux(-euse); (garment) ample

rooster ['ru:stər] n coq m

root [ru:t] n (Bot, Math) racine f; (fig: of problem) origine f, fond m ▷ vi (plant) s'enraciner

rope [rəup] n corde f; (Naut) cordage m ▷ vt (tie up or together) attacher; (climbers: also: **~ together**) encorder; (area: also: **~ off**) interdire l'accès de; (: divide off) séparer; **to know the ~s** (fig) être au courant, connaître les ficelles

rort [rɔ:t] n (AUST, NZ inf) arnaque f (inf) ▷ vt escroquer

rose [rəuz] pt of **rise** ▷ n rose f; (also: **~bush**) rosier m

rosé ['rəuzeɪ] n rosé m

rosemary ['rəuzmərɪ] n romarin m

rosy ['rəuzɪ] adj rose; **a ~ future** un bel avenir

rot [rɒt] n (decay) pourriture f; (fig: pej: nonsense) idioties fpl, balivernes fpl ▷ vt, vi pourrir

rota ['rəutə] n liste f, tableau m de service

rotate [rəu'teɪt] vt (revolve) faire tourner; (change round: crops) alterner; (: jobs) faire à tour de rôle ▷ vi (revolve) tourner

rotten ['rɒtn] adj (decayed) pourri(e); (dishonest) corrompu(e); (inf: bad) mauvais(e), moche; **to feel ~** (ill) être mal fichu(e)

rough [rʌf] adj (cloth, skin) rêche, rugueux(-euse); (terrain) accidenté(e); (path) rocailleux(-euse); (voice) rauque, rude; (person, manner: coarse) rude, fruste; (: violent) brutal(e); (district, weather) mauvais(e); (sea) houleux(-euse); (plan) ébauché(e);

(guess) approximatif(-ive) ▷ n (Golf) rough m ▷ vt: **to ~ it** vivre à la dure; **to sleep ~** (BRIT) coucher à la dure; **roughly** adv (handle) rudement, brutalement; (speak) avec brusquerie; (make) grossièrement; (approximately) à peu près, environ

roulette [ru:'let] n roulette f

round [raund] adj rond(e) ▷ n rond m, cercle m; (BRIT: of toast) tranche f; (duty: of policeman, milkman etc) tournée f; (: of doctor) visites fpl; (game: of cards, in competition) partie f; (Boxing) round m; (of talks) série f ▷ vt (corner) tourner ▷ prep autour de ▷ adv: **right ~, all ~** tout autour; **~ of ammunition** cartouche f; **~ of applause** applaudissements mpl; **~ of drinks** tournée f; **the long way ~** (par) le chemin le plus long; **all (the) year ~** toute l'année; **it's just ~ the corner** (fig) c'est tout près; **to go ~ to sb's (house)** aller chez qn; **go ~ the back** passez par derrière; **enough to go ~** assez pour tout le monde; **she arrived ~ (about) noon** (BRIT) elle est arrivée vers midi; **~ the clock** 24 heures sur 24; **round off** vt (speech etc) terminer; **round up** vt rassembler; (criminals) effectuer une rafle de; (prices) arrondir (au chiffre supérieur); **roundabout** n (BRIT: Aut) rond-point m (à sens giratoire); (: at fair) manège m (de chevaux de bois) ▷ adj (route, means) détourné(e); **round trip** n (voyage m) aller et retour m; **roundup** n rassemblement m; (of criminals) rafle f

rouse [rauz] vt (wake up) réveiller; (stir up) susciter, provoquer; (interest) éveiller; (suspicions) susciter, éveiller

route [ru:t] n itinéraire m; (of bus) parcours m; (of trade, shipping) route f

router n (Comput) routeur m

routine [ru:'ti:n] adj (work) ordinaire, courant(e); (procedure) d'usage ▷ n (habits) habitudes fpl; (pej) train-train m; (Theat) numéro m

r

row¹ [rəʊ] n (line) rangée f; (of people, seats, Knitting) rang m; (behind one another: of cars, people) file f ▷ vi (in boat) ramer; (as sport) faire de l'aviron ▷ vt (boat) faire aller à la rame or à l'aviron; **in a ~** (fig) d'affilée

row² [raʊ] n (noise) vacarme m; (dispute) dispute f, querelle f; (scolding) réprimande f, savon m ▷ vi (also: **to have a ~**) se disputer, se quereller

rowboat ['rəʊbəʊt] n (US) canot m (à rames)

rowing ['rəʊɪŋ] n canotage m; (as sport) aviron m; **rowing boat** n (BRIT) canot m (à rames)

royal ['rɔɪəl] adj royal(e); **royalty** n (royal persons) (membres mpl de la) famille royale; (payment: to author) droits mpl d'auteur; (: to inventor) royalties fpl

rpm abbr (= revolutions per minute) t/mn (= tours/minute)

R.S.V.P. abbr (= répondez s'il vous plaît) RSVP

Rt. Hon. abbr (BRIT: = Right Honourable) titre donné aux députés de la Chambre des communes

rub [rʌb] n: **to give sth a ~** donner un coup de chiffon or de torchon à qch ▷ vt frotter; (person) frictionner; (hands) se frotter; **to ~ sb up** (BRIT) or **to ~ sb** (US) **the wrong way** prendre qn à rebrousse-poil; **rub in** vt (ointment) faire pénétrer; **rub off** vi partir; **rub out** vt effacer

rubber ['rʌbə'] n caoutchouc m; (BRIT: eraser) gomme f (à effacer); **rubber band** n élastique m; **rubber gloves** npl gants mpl en caoutchouc

rubbish ['rʌbɪʃ] n (from household) ordures fpl; (fig: pej) choses fpl sans valeur; camelote f; (nonsense) bêtises fpl, idioties fpl; **rubbish bin** n (BRIT) boîte f à ordures, poubelle f; **rubbish dump** n (BRIT: in town) décharge publique, dépotoir m

rubble ['rʌbl] n décombres mpl; (smaller) gravats mpl; (Constr) blocage m

ruby ['ruːbɪ] n rubis m

rucksack ['rʌksæk] n sac m à dos

rudder ['rʌdə'] n gouvernail m

rude [ruːd] adj (impolite: person) impoli(e); (: word, manners) grossier(-ière); (shocking) indécent(e), inconvenant(e)

ruffle ['rʌfl] vt (hair) ébouriffer; (clothes) chiffonner; (fig: person): **to get ~d** s'énerver

rug [rʌg] n petit tapis; (BRIT: blanket) couverture f

rugby ['rʌgbɪ] n (also: **~ football**) rugby m

rugged ['rʌgɪd] adj (landscape) accidenté(e); (features, character) rude

ruin ['ruːɪn] n ruine f ▷ vt ruiner; (spoil: clothes) abîmer; (: event) gâcher; **ruins** npl (of building) ruine(s)

rule [ruːl] n règle f; (regulation) règlement m; (government) autorité f, gouvernement m ▷ vt (country) gouverner; (person) dominer; (decide) décider ▷ vi commander; **as a ~** normalement, en règle générale; **rule out** vt exclure; **ruler** n (sovereign) souverain(e); (leader) chef m (d'État); (for measuring) règle f; **ruling** adj (party) au pouvoir; (class) dirigeant(e) ▷ n (Law) décision f

rum [rʌm] n rhum m

Rumania [ruːˈmeɪnɪə] n Roumanie f; **Rumanian** adj roumain(e) ▷ n Roumain(e); (Ling) roumain m

rumble ['rʌmbl] n grondement m; (of stomach, pipe) gargouillement m ▷ vi gronder; (stomach, pipe) gargouiller

rumour, (US) **rumor** ['ruːmə'] n rumeur f, bruit m (qui court) ▷ vt: **it is ~ed that** on dit or bruit court que

rump steak n romsteck m

run [rʌn] (pt **ran**, pp **run**) n (race) course f; (outing) tour m or promenade f (en voiture); (distance travelled) parcours m, trajet m; (series) suite f, série f; (Theat) série de représentations; (Ski) piste f; (Cricket, Baseball) point m; (in tights, stockings) maille filée, échelle f ▷ vt (business) diriger; (competition, course) organiser; (hotel, house) tenir; (race) participer à; (Comput: program) exécuter; (to pass: hand, finger) **to ~ sth over** promener or passer qch sur; (water, bath) faire couler; (Press: feature) publier ▷ vi courir; (pass: road etc) passer; (work: machine, factory) marcher; (bus, train) circuler; (continue: play) se jouer, être à l'affiche; (: contract) être valide or en vigueur; (flow: river, bath, nose) couler; (colours, washing) déteindre; (in election) être candidat, se présenter; **at a ~** au pas de course; **to go for a ~** aller courir or faire un peu de course à pied; (in car) faire un tour or une promenade (en voiture); **there was a ~ on** (meat, tickets) les gens se sont rués sur; **in the long ~** à la longue; **on the ~** en fuite; **I'll ~ you to the station** je vais vous emmener or conduire à la gare; **to ~ a risk** courir un risque; **run after** vt fus (to catch up) courir après; (chase) poursuivre; **run away** vi s'enfuir; **run down** vt (Aut: knock over) renverser; (BRIT: reduce: production) réduire progressivement; (: factory/shop) réduire progressivement la production/l'activité de; (criticize) critiquer, dénigrer; **to be ~ down** (tired) être fatigué(e) or à plat; **run into** vt fus (meet: person) rencontrer par hasard; (: trouble) se heurter à; (collide with) heurter; **run off** vi s'enfuir ▷ vt (water) laisser s'écouler; (copies) tirer; **run out** vi (person) sortir en courant; (liquid) couler; (lease) expirer; (money) être épuisé(e); **run out of** vt fus se trouver à court de; **run over** vt (Aut) écraser ▷ vt fus (revise) revoir, reprendre; **run through** vt fus (recap) reprendre, revoir; (play) répéter; **run up** vi: **to ~ up against** (difficulties) se heurter

à; **runaway** adj (horse) emballé(e); (truck) fou (folle); (person) fugitif(-ive); (child) fugueur(-euse)

rung [rʌŋ] pp of **ring** ▷ n (of ladder) barreau m

runner ['rʌnər] n (in race: person) coureur(-euse); (: horse) partant m; (on sledge) patin m; (for drawer etc) coulisseau m; **runner bean** n (BRIT) haricot m (à rames); **runner-up** n second(e)

running ['rʌnɪŋ] n (in race etc) course f; (of business, organization) direction f, gestion f ▷ adj (water) courant(e); (commentary) suivi(e); **6 days ~** 6 jours de suite; **to be in/out of the ~ for sth** être/ne pas être sur les rangs pour qch

runny ['rʌnɪ] adj qui coule

run-up ['rʌnʌp] n (BRIT): **~ to sth** période f précédant qch

runway ['rʌnweɪ] n (Aviat) piste f (d'envol or d'atterrissage)

rupture ['rʌptʃər] n (Med) hernie f

rural ['ruərl] adj rural(e)

rush [rʌʃ] n (of crowd, Comm: sudden demand) ruée f; (hurry) hâte f; (of anger, joy) accès m; (current) flot m; (Bot) jonc m ▷ vt (hurry) transporter or envoyer d'urgence ▷ vi se précipiter; **to ~ sth off** (do quickly) faire qch à la hâte; **rush hour** n heures fpl de pointe or d'affluence

Russia ['rʌʃə] n Russie f; **Russian** adj russe ▷ n Russe m/f; (Ling) russe m

rust [rʌst] n rouille f ▷ vi rouiller

rusty ['rʌstɪ] adj rouillé(e)

ruthless ['ruːθlɪs] adj sans pitié, impitoyable

RV n abbr (US) = **recreational vehicle**

rye [raɪ] n seigle m

r

S

Sabbath ['sæbəθ] n (Jewish) sabbat m; (Christian) dimanche m

sabotage ['sæbətɑːʒ] n sabotage m ▷ vt saboter

saccharin(e) ['sækərɪn] n saccharine f

sachet ['sæʃeɪ] n sachet m

sack [sæk] n (bag) sac m ▷ vt (dismiss) renvoyer, mettre à la porte; (plunder) piller, mettre à sac; **to get the ~** être renvoyé(e) or mis(e) à la porte

sacred ['seɪkrɪd] adj sacré(e)

sacrifice ['sækrɪfaɪs] n sacrifice m ▷ vt sacrifier

sad [sæd] adj (unhappy) triste; (deplorable) triste, fâcheux(-euse); (inf: pathetic: thing) triste, lamentable; (: person) minable

saddle ['sædl] n selle f ▷ vt (horse) seller; **to be ~d with sth** (inf) avoir qch sur les bras

sadistic [sə'dɪstɪk] adj sadique

sadly ['sædlɪ] adv tristement; (unfortunately) malheureusement; (seriously) fort

sadness ['sædnɪs] n tristesse f

s.a.e. n abbr (BRIT: = stamped addressed envelope) enveloppe affranchie pour la réponse

safari [sə'fɑːrɪ] n safari m

safe [seɪf] adj (out of danger) hors de danger, en sécurité; (not dangerous) sans danger; (cautious) prudent(e); (sure: bet) assuré(e) ▷ n coffre-fort m; **~ and sound** sain(e) et sauf; **(just) to be on the ~ side** pour plus de sûreté, par précaution; **safely** adv (assume, say) sans risque d'erreur; (drive, arrive) sans accident; **safe sex** n rapports sexuels protégés

safety ['seɪftɪ] n sécurité f; **safety belt** n ceinture f de sécurité; **safety pin** n épingle f de sûreté or de nourrice

saffron ['sæfrən] n safran m

sag [sæg] vi s'affaisser, fléchir; (hem, breasts) pendre

sage [seɪdʒ] n (herb) sauge f; (person) sage m

Sagittarius [sædʒɪ'tɛərɪəs] n le Sagittaire

Sahara [sə'hɑːrə] n: **the ~ (Desert)** le (désert du) Sahara m

said [sɛd] pt, pp of **say**

sail [seɪl] n (on boat) voile f; (trip): **to go for a ~** faire un tour en bateau ▷ vt (boat) manœuvrer, piloter ▷ vi (travel: ship) avancer, naviguer; (set off) partir, prendre la mer; (Sport) faire de la voile; **they ~ed into Le Havre** ils sont entrés dans le port du Havre; **sailboat** n (US) bateau m à voiles, voilier m; **sailing** n (Sport) voile f; **to go sailing** faire de la voile; **sailing boat** n bateau m à voiles, voilier m; **sailor** n marin m, matelot m

saint [seɪnt] n saint(e)

sake [seɪk] n: **for the ~ of** (out of concern for) pour (l'amour de), dans l'intérêt de; (*out of consideration for*) par égard pour

salad ['sæləd] *n* salade *f*; **salad cream** *n* (BRIT) (sorte *f* de) mayonnaise *f*; **salad dressing** *n* vinaigrette *f*

salami [sə'lɑːmɪ] *n* salami *m*

salary ['sælərɪ] *n* salaire *m*, traitement *m*

sale [seɪl] *n* vente *f*; (*at reduced prices*) soldes *mpl*; **sales** *npl* (*total amount sold*) chiffre *m* de ventes; **"for ~"** "à vendre"; **on ~** en vente; **sales assistant**, (US) **sales clerk** *n* vendeur(-euse); **salesman** (*irreg*) *n* (*in shop*) vendeur *m*; **salesperson** (*irreg*) *n* (*in shop*) vendeur(-euse); **sales rep** *n* (*Comm*) représentant(e) *m/f*; **saleswoman** (*irreg*) *n* (*in shop*) vendeuse *f*

saline ['seɪlaɪn] *adj* salin(e)

saliva [sə'laɪvə] *n* salive *f*

salmon ['sæmən] *n* (*pl inv*) saumon *m*

salon ['sælɔn] *n* salon *m*

saloon [sə'luːn] *n* (US) bar *m*; (BRIT Aut) berline *f*; (*ship's lounge*) salon *m*

salt [sɔːlt] *n* sel *m* ▷ *vt* saler; **saltwater** *adj* (*fish etc*) (d'eau) de mer; **salty** *adj* salé(e)

salute [sə'luːt] *n* salut *m*; (*of guns*) salve *f* ▷ *vt* saluer

salvage ['sælvɪdʒ] *n* (*saving*) sauvetage *m*; (*things saved*) biens sauvés *or* récupérés ▷ *vt* sauver, récupérer

Salvation Army [sæl'veɪʃən-] *n* Armée *f* du Salut

same [seɪm] *adj* même ▷ *pron*: **the ~** le (la) même, les mêmes; **the ~ book as** le même livre que; **at the ~ time** en même temps; (*yet*) néanmoins; **all** *or* **just the ~** tout de même, quand même; **to do the ~** faire de même, en faire autant; **to do the ~ as sb** faire comme qn; **and the ~ to you!** et à vous de même!; (*after insult*) toi-même!

sample ['sɑːmpl] *n* échantillon *m*; (*Med*) prélèvement *m* ▷ *vt* (*food, wine*) goûter

sanction ['sæŋkʃən] *n* approbation *f*, sanction *f* ▷ *vt* cautionner, sanctionner; **sanctions** *npl* (*Pol*) sanctions

sanctuary ['sæŋktjuərɪ] *n* (*holy place*) sanctuaire *m*; (*refuge*) asile *m*; (*for wildlife*) réserve *f*

sand [sænd] *n* sable *m* ▷ *vt* (*also*: **~ down**: *wood etc*) poncer

sandal ['sændl] *n* sandale *f*

sand: sandbox *n* (US: *for children*) tas *m* de sable; **sand castle** *n* château *m* de sable; **sand dune** *n* dune *f* de sable; **sandpaper** *n* papier *m* de verre; **sandpit** *n* (BRIT: *for children*) tas *m* de sable; **sands** *npl* plage *f* (de sable); **sandstone** ['sændstəun] *n* grès *m*

sandwich ['sændwɪtʃ] *n* sandwich *m* ▷ *vt* (*also*: **~ in**) intercaler; **~ed between** pris en sandwich entre; **cheese/ham ~** sandwich au fromage/jambon

sandy ['sændɪ] *adj* sablonneux(-euse); (*colour*) sable *inv*, blond roux *inv*

sane [seɪn] *adj* (*person*) sain(e) d'esprit; (*outlook*) sensé(e), sain(e)

sang [sæŋ] *pt of* **sing**

sanitary towel, (US) **sanitary napkin** ['sænɪtərɪ-] *n* serviette *f* hygiénique

sanity ['sænɪtɪ] *n* santé mentale; (*common sense*) bon sens

sank [sæŋk] *pt of* **sink**

Santa Claus [sæntə'klɔːz] *n* le Père Noël

sap [sæp] *n* (*of plants*) sève *f* ▷ *vt* (*strength*) saper, miner

sapphire ['sæfaɪə] *n* saphir *m*

sarcasm ['sɑːkæzm] *n* sarcasme *m*, raillerie *f*

sarcastic [sɑː'kæstɪk] *adj* sarcastique

sardine [sɑː'diːn] *n* sardine *f*

S

SASE n abbr (US: = self-addressed stamped envelope) enveloppe affranchie pour la réponse

sat [sæt] pt, pp of **sit**

Sat. abbr (= Saturday) sa

satchel ['sætʃl] n cartable m

satellite ['sætəlaɪt] n satellite m; **satellite dish** n antenne f parabolique; **satellite navigation system** n système m de navigation par satellite; **satellite television** n télévision f par satellite

satin ['sætɪn] n satin m ▷ adj en or de satin, satiné(e)

satire ['sætaɪəʳ] n satire f

satisfaction [sætɪs'fækʃən] n satisfaction f

satisfactory [sætɪs'fæktərɪ] adj satisfaisant(e)

satisfied ['sætɪsfaɪd] adj satisfait(e); **to be ~ with sth** être satisfait de qch

satisfy ['sætɪsfaɪ] vt satisfaire, contenter; (convince) convaincre, persuader

Saturday ['sætədɪ] n samedi m

sauce [sɔːs] n sauce f; **saucepan** n casserole f

saucer ['sɔːsəʳ] n soucoupe f

Saudi Arabia ['saudɪ-] n Arabie f Saoudite

sauna ['sɔːnə] n sauna m

sausage ['sɒsɪdʒ] n saucisse f; (salami etc) saucisson m; **sausage roll** n friand m

sautéed ['səuteɪd] adj sauté(e)

savage ['sævɪdʒ] adj (cruel, fierce) brutal(e), féroce; (primitive) primitif(-ive), sauvage ▷ n sauvage m/f ▷ vt attaquer férocement

save [seɪv] vt (person, belongings) sauver; (money) mettre de côté, économiser; (time) (faire) gagner; (keep) garder; (Comput) sauvegarder; (Sport: stop) arrêter; (avoid: trouble) éviter ▷ vi (also: ~ up) mettre de l'argent de côté ▷ n (Sport) arrêt m (du ballon) ▷ prep sauf, à l'exception de

saving ['seɪvɪŋ] n économie f; **savings** npl économies fpl

savings account n compte m d'épargne

savings and loan association (US) n ≈ société f de crédit immobilier

savoury, (US) **savory** ['seɪvərɪ] adj savoureux(-euse); (dish: not sweet) salé(e)

saw [sɔː] pt of **see** ▷ n (tool) scie f ▷ vt (pt **sawed**, pp **sawed** or **sawn**) scier; **sawdust** n sciure f

sawn [sɔːn] pp of **saw**

saxophone ['sæksəfəun] n saxophone m

say [seɪ] vt (pt, pp **said**) dire ▷ n: **to have one's ~** dire ce qu'on a à dire; **to have a ~** avoir voix au chapitre; **could you ~ that again?** pourriez-vous répéter ce que vous venez de dire?; **to ~ yes/no** dire oui/non; **my watch ~s 3 o'clock** ma montre indique 3 heures, il est 3 heures à ma montre; **that is to ~** c'est-à-dire; **that goes without ~ing** cela va sans dire, cela va de soi; **saying** n dicton m, proverbe m

scab [skæb] n croûte f; (pej) jaune m

scaffolding ['skæfəldɪŋ] n échafaudage m

scald [skɔːld] n brûlure f ▷ vt ébouillanter

scale [skeɪl] n (of fish) écaille f; (Mus) gamme f; (of ruler, thermometer etc) graduation f, échelle (graduée); (of salaries, fees etc) barème m; (of map, also size, extent) échelle ▷ vt (mountain) escalader; **scales** npl balance f; (larger) bascule f; (also: **bathroom ~s**) pèse-personne m inv; **~ of charges** tableau m des tarifs; **on a large ~** sur une grande échelle, en grand

scallion ['skæljən] n (US: salad onion) ciboule f

scallop ['skɒləp] n coquille f Saint-Jacques; (Sewing) feston m

scalp [skælp] n cuir chevelu ▷ vt scalper

scalpel ['skælpl] n scalpel m
scam [skæm] n (inf) arnaque f
scampi ['skæmpɪ] npl langoustines (frites), scampi mpl
scan [skæn] vt (examine) scruter, examiner; (glance at quickly) parcourir; (TV, Radar) balayer ▷ n (Med) scanographie f
scandal ['skændl] n scandale m; (gossip) ragots mpl
Scandinavia [skændɪ'neɪvɪə] n Scandinavie f; **Scandinavian** adj scandinave ▷ n Scandinave m/f
scanner ['skænə^r] n (Radar, Med) scanner m, scanographe m; (Comput) scanner
scapegoat ['skeɪpɡəʊt] n bouc m émissaire
scar [skɑː^r] n cicatrice f ▷ vt laisser une cicatrice or une marque à
scarce [skɛəs] adj rare, peu abondant(e); **to make o.s. ~** (inf) se sauver; **scarcely** adv à peine, presque pas
scare [skɛə^r] n peur f, panique f ▷ vt effrayer, faire peur à; **to ~ sb stiff** faire une peur bleue à qn; **bomb ~** alerte f à la bombe; **scarecrow** n épouvantail m; **scared** adj: **to be scared** avoir peur
scarf (pl **scarves**) [skɑːf, skɑːvz] n (long) écharpe f; (square) foulard m
scarlet ['skɑːlɪt] adj écarlate
scarves [skɑːvz] npl of **scarf**
scary ['skɛərɪ] adj (inf) effrayant(e); (film) qui fait peur
scatter ['skætə^r] vt éparpiller, répandre; (crowd) disperser ▷ vi se disperser
scenario [sɪ'nɑːrɪəʊ] n scénario m
scene [siːn] n (Theat, fig etc) scène f; (of crime, accident) lieu(x) m(pl), endroit m; (sight, view) spectacle m, vue f; **scenery** n (Theat) décor(s) m(pl); (landscape) paysage m; **scenic** adj offrant de beaux paysages or panoramas
scent [sɛnt] n parfum m, odeur f; (fig: track) piste f

sceptical, (us) **skeptical** ['skɛptɪkl] adj sceptique
schedule ['ʃɛdjuːl, us 'skɛdjuːl] n programme m, plan m; (of trains) horaire m; (of prices etc) barème m, tarif m ▷ vt prévoir; **on ~** à l'heure (prévue); à la date prévue; **to be ahead of/behind ~** avoir de l'avance/ du retard; **scheduled flight** n vol régulier
scheme [skiːm] n plan m, projet m; (plot) complot m, combine f; (arrangement) arrangement m, classification f; (pension scheme etc) régime m ▷ vt, vi comploter, manigancer
schizophrenic [skɪtsə'frɛnɪk] adj schizophrène
scholar ['skɔlə^r] n érudit(e); (pupil) boursier(-ère); **scholarship** n érudition f; (grant) bourse f (d'études)
school [skuːl] n (gen) école f; (secondary school) collège m; lycée m; (in university) faculté f; (us: university) université f ▷ cpd scolaire; **schoolbook** n livre m scolaire or de classe; **schoolboy** n écolier m; (at secondary school) collégien m; lycéen m; **schoolchildren** npl écoliers mpl; (at secondary school) collégiens mpl; lycéens mpl; **schoolgirl** n écolière f; (at secondary school) collégienne f; lycéenne f; **schooling** n instruction f, études fpl; **schoolteacher** n (primary) instituteur(-trice); (secondary) professeur m
science ['saɪəns] n science f; **science fiction** n science-fiction f; **scientific** [saɪən'tɪfɪk] adj scientifique; **scientist** n scientifique m/f; (eminent) savant m
sci-fi ['saɪfaɪ] n abbr (inf: = science fiction) SF f
scissors ['sɪzəz] npl ciseaux mpl; **a pair of ~** une paire de ciseaux
scold [skəʊld] vt gronder
scone [skɔn] n sorte de petit pain rond au lait

S

scoop [sku:p] n pelle f (à main);
(for ice cream) boule f à glace; (Press)
reportage exclusif or à sensation

scooter ['sku:tə^r] n (motor cycle)
scooter m; (toy) trottinette f

scope [skəup] n (capacity: of plan,
undertaking) portée f, envergure f; (: of
person) compétence f, capacités fpl;
(opportunity) possibilités fpl

scorching ['skɔ:tʃɪŋ] adj torride,
brûlant(e)

score [skɔ:^{r}] n score m, décompte m
des points; (Mus) partition f ⊳ vt (goal,
point) marquer; (success) remporter;
(cut: leather, wood, card) entailler,
inciser ⊳ vi marquer des points;
(Football) marquer un but; (keep score)
compter les points; **on that ~** sur ce
chapitre, à cet égard; **a ~ of** (twenty)
vingt; **~s of** (fig) des tas de; **to ~ 6
out of 10** obtenir 6 sur 10; **score out**
vt rayer, barrer, biffer; **scoreboard** n
tableau m; **scorer** n (Football) auteur
m du but; buteur m; (keeping score)
marqueur m

scorn [skɔ:n] n mépris m, dédain m

Scorpio ['skɔ:pɪəu] n le Scorpion

scorpion ['skɔ:pɪən] n scorpion m

Scot [skɔt] n Écossais(e)

Scotch [skɔtʃ] n whisky m, scotch m

Scotch tape® (US) n scotch® m,
ruban adhésif

Scotland ['skɔtlənd] n Écosse f

Scots [skɔts] adj écossais(e);
Scotsman (irreg) n Écossais m;
Scotswoman (irreg) n Écossaise f;
Scottish ['skɔtɪʃ] adj écossais(e); **the
Scottish Parliament** le Parlement
écossais

scout [skaut] n (Mil) éclaireur m;
(also: **boy ~**) scout m; **girl ~** (US)
guide f

scowl [skaul] vi se renfrogner; **to ~
at** regarder de travers

scramble ['skræmbl] n (rush)
bousculade f, ruée f ⊳ vi grimper/
descendre tant bien que mal; **to ~
for** se bousculer or se disputer pour

(avoir); **to go scrambling** (Sport)
faire du trial; **scrambled eggs** npl
œufs brouillés

scrap [skræp] n bout m, morceau m;
(fight) bagarre f; (also: **~ iron**) ferraille
f ⊳ vt jeter, mettre au rebut; (fig)
abandonner, laisser tomber ⊳ vi se
bagarrer; **scraps** npl (waste) déchets
mpl; **scrapbook** n album m

scrape [skreɪp] vt, vi gratter, racler
⊳ n: **to get into a ~** s'attirer des
ennuis; **scrape through** vi (exam etc)
réussir de justesse

scrap paper n papier m brouillon

scratch [skrætʃ] n égratignure f,
rayure f; (on paint) éraflure f; (from
claw) coup m de griffe ⊳ vt (rub) (se)
gratter; (paint etc) érafler; (with claw,
nail) griffer ⊳ vi (se) gratter; **to start
from ~** partir de zéro; **to be up to
~** être à la hauteur; **scratch card** n
carte f à gratter

scream [skri:m] n cri perçant,
hurlement m ⊳ vi crier, hurler

screen [skri:n] n écran m; (in room)
paravent m; (fig) écran, rideau m ⊳ vt
masquer, cacher; (from the wind etc)
abriter, protéger; (film) projeter;
(candidates etc) filtrer; **screening** n
(of film) projection f; (Med) test m (or
tests) de dépistage; **screenplay** n
scénario m; **screen saver** n (Comput)
économiseur m d'écran; **screenshot**
n (Comput) capture f d'écran

screw [skru:] n vis f ⊳ vt (also: **~ in**)
visser; **screw up** vt (paper etc) froisser;
to ~ up one's eyes se plisser les yeux;
screwdriver n tournevis m

scribble ['skrɪbl] n gribouillage m ⊳ vt
gribouiller, griffonner

script [skrɪpt] n (Cine etc) scénario m,
texte m; (writing) (écriture f) script m

scroll [skrəul] n rouleau m ⊳ vt
(Comput) faire défiler (sur l'écran)

scrub [skrʌb] n (land) broussailles fpl
⊳ vt (floor) nettoyer à la brosse; (pan)
récurer; (washing) frotter

scruffy ['skrʌfɪ] adj débraillé(e)

scrum(mage) ['skrʌm(ɪdʒ)] n
mêlée f

scrutiny ['skru:tɪnɪ] n examen
minutieux

scuba diving ['sku:bə-] n plongée
sous-marine

sculptor ['skʌlptər] n sculpteur m

sculpture ['skʌlptʃər] n sculpture f

scum [skʌm] n écume f, mousse f;
(pej: people) rebut m, lie f

scurry ['skʌrɪ] vi filer à toute allure;
to ~ off détaler, se sauver

sea [si:] n mer f ▷ cpd marin(e), de (la)
mer, maritime; **by** or **beside the ~**
(holiday, town) au bord de la mer; **by ~**
par mer, en bateau; **out to ~** au large;
(out) at ~ en mer; **to be all at ~** (fig)
nager complètement; **seafood** n
fruits mpl de mer; **sea front** n bord m
de mer; **seagull** n mouette f

seal [si:l] n (animal) phoque m;
(stamp) sceau m, cachet m ▷ vt sceller;
(envelope) coller (: with seal) cacheter;
seal off vt (forbid entry to) interdire
l'accès de

sea level n niveau m de la mer

seam [si:m] n couture f; (of coal) veine
f, filon m

search [sɜ:tʃ] n (for person, thing,
Comput) recherche(s) f(pl); (of drawer,
pockets) fouille f; (Law: at sb's home)
perquisition f ▷ vt fouiller; (examine)
examiner minutieusement; scruter
▷ vi: **to ~ for** chercher; **in ~ of** à
la recherche de; **search engine** n
(Comput) moteur m de recherche;
search party n expédition f de
secours

sea: seashore n rivage m, plage f,
bord m de (la) mer; **seasick** adj: **to be
seasick** avoir le mal de mer; **seaside**
n bord m de mer; **seaside resort** n
station f balnéaire

season ['si:zn] n saison f ▷ vt
assaisonner, relever; **to be in/
out of ~** être/ne pas être de saison;
seasonal adj saisonnier(-ière);
seasoning n assaisonnement

m; **season ticket** n carte f
d'abonnement

seat [si:t] n siège m; (in bus, train:
place) place f; (buttocks) postérieur m;
(of trousers) fond m ▷ vt faire asseoir,
placer; (have room for) avoir des places
assises pour, pouvoir accueillir; **to be
~ed** être assis; **seat belt** n ceinture
f de sécurité; **seating** n sièges fpl,
places assises

sea: sea water n eau f de mer;
seaweed n algues fpl

sec. abbr (= second) sec

secluded [sɪ'klu:dɪd] adj retiré(e),
à l'écart

second ['sɛkənd] num deuxième,
second(e) ▷ adv (in race etc) en
seconde position ▷ n (unit of time)
seconde f; (Aut: also: **~ gear**)
seconde; (Comm: imperfect) article
m de second choix; (BRIT Scol) ≈
licence f avec mention ▷ vt (motion)
appuyer; **seconds** npl (inf: food) rab
m (inf); **secondary** adj secondaire;
secondary school n (age 11 to 15)
collège m; (age 15 to 18) lycée m;
second-class adj de deuxième
classe; (Rail) de seconde (classe);
(Post) au tarif réduit; (pej) de qualité
inférieure ▷ adv (Rail) en seconde;
(Post) au tarif réduit; **secondhand** adj
d'occasion; (information) de seconde
main; **secondly** adv deuxièmement;
second-rate adj de deuxième
ordre, de qualité inférieure; **second
thoughts** npl; **to have second
thoughts** changer d'avis; **on second
thoughts** or (US) **thought** à la
réflexion

secrecy ['si:krəsɪ] n secret m

secret ['si:krɪt] adj secret(-ète)
▷ n secret m; **in ~** adv en secret,
secrètement, en cachette

secretary ['sɛkrətrɪ] n secrétaire
m/f; **S~ of State (for)** (Pol) ministre
m (de)

secretive ['si:krətɪv] adj réservé(e);
(pej) cachottier(-ière), dissimulé(e)

S

secret service n services secrets

sect [sɛkt] n secte f

section ['sɛkʃən] n section f; (Comm) rayon m; (of document) section, article m, paragraphe m; (cut) coupe f

sector ['sɛktər] n secteur m

secular ['sɛkjulər] adj laïque

secure [sɪ'kjuər] adj (free from anxiety) sans inquiétude, sécurisé(e); (firmly fixed) solide, bien attaché(e) (or fermé(e) etc); (in safe place) en lieu sûr, en sûreté ▷ vt (fix) fixer, attacher; (get) obtenir, se procurer

security [sɪ'kjuərɪtɪ] n sécurité f, mesures fpl de sécurité; (for loan) caution f, garantie f; **securities** npl (Stock Exchange) valeurs fpl, titres mpl; **security guard** n garde chargé de la sécurité; (transporting money) convoyeur m de fonds

sedan [sə'dæn] n (US Aut) berline f

sedate [sɪ'deɪt] adj calme; posé(e) ▷ vt donner des sédatifs à

sedative ['sɛdɪtɪv] n calmant m, sédatif m

seduce [sɪ'djuːs] vt séduire; **seductive** [sɪ'dʌktɪv] adj séduisant(e); (smile) séducteur(-trice); (fig: offer) alléchant(e)

see [siː] (pt **saw**, pp **seen**) vt (gen) voir; (accompany): **to ~ sb to the door** reconduire or raccompagner qn jusqu'à la porte ▷ vi voir; **to ~ that** (ensure) veiller à ce que + sub, faire en sorte que + sub, s'assurer que; **~ you soon/later/tomorrow!** à bientôt/plus tard/demain!; **see off** vt accompagner (à l'aéroport etc); **see out** vt (take to door) raccompagner à la porte; **see through** vt mener à bonne fin ▷ vt fus voir clair dans; **see to** vt fus s'occuper de, se charger de

seed [siːd] n graine f; (fig) germe m; (Tennis etc) tête f de série; **to go to ~** (plant) monter en graine; (fig) se laisser aller

seeing ['siːɪŋ] conj: **~ (that)** vu que, étant donné que

seek [siːk] (pt, pp **sought**) vt chercher, rechercher

seem [siːm] vi sembler, paraître; **there ~s to be ...** il semble qu'il y a ..., on dirait qu'il y a ...; **seemingly** adv apparemment

seen [siːn] pp of **see**

seesaw ['siːsɔː] n (jeu m de) bascule f

segment ['sɛgmənt] n segment m; (of orange) quartier m

segregate ['sɛgrɪgeɪt] vt séparer, isoler

Seine [seɪn] n: **the (River) ~** la Seine

seize [siːz] vt (grasp) saisir, attraper; (take possession of) s'emparer de; (opportunity) saisir

seizure ['siːʒər] n (Med) crise f, attaque f; (of power) prise f

seldom ['sɛldəm] adv rarement

select [sɪ'lɛkt] adj choisi(e), d'élite; (hotel, restaurant, club) chic inv, sélect inv ▷ vt sélectionner, choisir; **selection** n sélection f, choix m; **selective** adj sélectif(-ive); (school) à recrutement sélectif

self (pl **selves**) [sɛlf, sɛlvz] n: **the ~** le moi inv ▷ prefix auto-; **self-assured** adj sûr(e) de soi, plein(e) d'assurance; **self-catering** adj (BRIT: flat) avec cuisine, où l'on peut faire sa cuisine; (: holiday) en appartement (or chalet etc) loué; **self-centred**, (US) **self-centered** adj égocentrique; **self-confidence** n confiance f en soi; **self-confident** adj sûr(e) de soi, plein(e) d'assurance; **self-conscious** adj timide, qui manque d'assurance; **self-contained** adj (BRIT: flat) avec entrée particulière, indépendant(e); **self-control** n maîtrise f de soi; **self-defence**, (US) **self-defense** n autodéfense f; (Law) légitime défense f; **self-drive** adj (BRIT): **self-drive car** voiture f de location; **self-employed** adj qui travaille à son compte; **self-esteem** n amour-propre m; **self-harm** vi s'automutiler; **self-indulgent** adj qui ne se refuse rien; **self-interest** n intérêt personnel;

selfish *adj* égoïste; **self-pity** *n* apitoiement *m* sur soi-même; **self-raising** [sɛlf'reɪzɪŋ], (*US*) **self-rising** [sɛlf'raɪzɪŋ] *adj*: **self-raising flour** farine *f* pour gâteaux (*avec levure incorporée*); **self-respect** *n* respect *m* de soi, amour-propre *m*; **self-service** *adj*, *n* libre-service (*m*), self-service (*m*)

selfie [sɛlfɪ] *n* selfie *m*

sell (*pt, pp* **sold**) [sɛl, səuld] *vt* vendre ▷ *vi* se vendre; **to ~ at** *or* **for 10 euros** se vendre 10 euros; **sell off** *vt* liquider; **sell out** *vi*: **to ~ out (of sth)** (*use up stock*) vendre tout son stock (de qch); **sell-by date** *n* date *f* limite de vente; **seller** *n* vendeur(-euse), marchand(e)

Sellotape® [ˈsɛləuteɪp] *n* (*BRIT*) scotch® *m*

selves [sɛlvz] *npl of* **self**

semester [sɪˈmɛstəʳ] *n* (*esp US*) semestre *m*

semi... [ˈsɛmɪ] *prefix* semi-, demi-; à demi, à moitié; **semicircle** *n* demi-cercle *m*; **semidetached (house)** *n* (*BRIT*) maison jumelée *or* jumelle; **semi-final** *n* demi-finale *f*

seminar [ˈsɛmɪnɑːʳ] *n* séminaire *m*

semi-skimmed [ˈsɛmɪˈskɪmd] *adj* demi-écrémé(e)

senate [ˈsɛnɪt] *n* sénat *m*; (*US*): **the S~** le Sénat; **senator** *n* sénateur *m*

send (*pt, pp* **sent**) [sɛnd, sɛnt] *vt* envoyer; **send back** *vt* renvoyer; **send for** *vt fus* (*by post*) se faire envoyer, commander par correspondance; **send in** *vt* (*report, application, resignation*) remettre; **send off** *vt* (*goods*) envoyer, expédier; (*BRIT Sport: player*) expulser *or* renvoyer du terrain; **send on** *vt* (*BRIT: letter*) faire suivre; (*luggage etc: in advance*) (faire) expédier à l'avance; **send out** *vt* (*invitation*) envoyer (par la poste); (*emit: light, heat, signal*) émettre; **send up** *vt* (*person, price*) faire monter; (*BRIT: parody*) mettre en boîte, parodier; **sender** *n* expéditeur(-trice); **send-off** *n*: **a good send-off** des adieux chaleureux

senile [ˈsiːnaɪl] *adj* sénile

senior [ˈsiːnɪəʳ] *adj* (*high-ranking*) de haut niveau; (*of higher rank*): **to be ~ to sb** être le supérieur de qn; **senior citizen** *n* personne *f* du troisième âge; **senior high school** *n* (*US*) ≈ lycée *m*

sensation [sɛnˈseɪʃən] *n* sensation *f*; **sensational** *adj* qui fait sensation; (*marvellous*) sensationnel(le)

sense [sɛns] *n* sens *m*; (*feeling*) sentiment *m*; (*meaning*) sens, signification *f*; (*wisdom*) bon sens ▷ *vt* sentir, pressentir; **it makes ~** c'est logique; **senseless** *adj* insensé(e), stupide; (*unconscious*) sans connaissance; **sense of humour**, (*US*) **sense of humor** *n* sens *m* de l'humour

sensible [ˈsɛnsɪbl] *adj* sensé(e), raisonnable; (*shoes etc*) pratique

> Be careful not to translate *sensible* by the French word *sensible*.

sensitive [ˈsɛnsɪtɪv] *adj*: **~ (to)** sensible (à)

sensual [ˈsɛnsjuəl] *adj* sensuel(le)

sensuous [ˈsɛnsjuəs] *adj* voluptueux(-euse), sensuel(le)

sent [sɛnt] *pt, pp of* **send**

sentence [ˈsɛntns] *n* (*Ling*) phrase *f*; (*Law: judgment*) condamnation *f*, sentence *f*; (*: punishment*) peine *f* ▷ *vt*: **to ~ sb to death/to 5 years** condamner qn à mort/à 5 ans

sentiment [ˈsɛntɪmənt] *n* sentiment *m*; (*opinion*) opinion *f*, avis *m*; **sentimental** [sɛntɪˈmɛntl] *adj* sentimental(e)

separate *adj* [ˈsɛprɪt] séparé(e); (*organization*) indépendant(e); (*day, occasion, issue*) différent(e) ▷ *vt* [ˈsɛpəreɪt] séparer; (*distinguish*) distinguer ▷ *vi* [ˈsɛpəreɪt] se séparer; **separately** *adv* séparément; **separates** *npl* (*clothes*) coordonnés *mpl*; **separation** [sɛpəˈreɪʃən] *n* séparation *f*

S

September [sɛp'tɛmbəʳ] *n*
septembre *m*

septic ['sɛptɪk] *adj* (*wound*) infecté(e);
septic tank *n* fosse *f* septique

sequel ['si:kwl] *n* conséquence *f*;
séquelles *fpl*; (*of story*) suite *f*

sequence ['si:kwəns] *n* ordre *m*,
suite *f*; (*in film*) séquence *f*; (*dance*)
numéro *m*

sequin ['si:kwɪn] *n* paillette *f*

Serb [sə:b] *adj*, *n* = **Serbian**

Serbia ['sə:bɪə] *n* Serbie *f*

Serbian ['sə:bɪən] *adj* serbe ▷ *n* Serbe
m/f; (*Ling*) serbe *m*

sergeant ['sɑ:dʒənt] *n* sergent *m*;
(*Police*) brigadier *m*

serial ['sɪərɪəl] *n* feuilleton *m*; **serial
killer** *n* meurtrier *m* tuant en série;
serial number *n* numéro *m* de série

series ['sɪərɪz] *n* série *f*; (*Publishing*)
collection *f*

serious ['sɪərɪəs] *adj* sérieux(-euse);
(*accident etc*) grave; **seriously** *adv*
sérieusement; (*hurt*) gravement

sermon ['sə:mən] *n* sermon *m*

servant ['sə:vənt] *n* domestique *m/f*;
(*fig*) serviteur (servante)

serve [sə:v] *vt* (*employer etc*) servir,
être au service de; (*purpose*) servir
à; (*customer, food, meal*) servir; (*subj:
train*) desservir; (*apprenticeship*) faire,
accomplir; (*prison term*) faire; purger
▷ *vi* (*Tennis*) servir; (*be useful*): **to ~
as/for/to do** servir de/à faire ▷ *n*
(*Tennis*) service *m*; **it ~s him right**
c'est bien fait pour lui; **server** *n*
(*Comput*) serveur *m*

service ['sə:vɪs] *n* (*gen*) service *m*;
(*Aut*) révision *f*; (*Rel*) office *m* ▷ *vt*
(*car etc*) réviser; **services** *npl* (*Econ:
tertiary sector*) (secteur *m*) tertiaire
m, secteur des services; (*BRIT: on
motorway*) station-service *f*; (*Mil*): **the
S~s** *npl* les forces armées; **to be of ~
to sb, to do sb a ~** rendre service à
qn; **~ included/not included** service
compris/non compris; **service area**
n (*on motorway*) aire *f* de services;

service charge *n* (*BRIT*) service *m*;
serviceman (*irreg*) *n* militaire *m*;
service station *n* station-service *f*

serviette [sə:vɪ'ɛt] *n* (*BRIT*) serviette
f (de table)

session ['sɛʃən] *n* (*sitting*) séance *f*;
to be in ~ siéger, être en session *or*
en séance

set [sɛt] (*pt, pp* **set**) *n* série *f*,
assortiment *m*; (*of tools etc*) jeu *m*;
(*Radio, TV*) poste *m*; (*Tennis*) set *m*;
(*group of people*) cercle *m*, milieu *m*;
(*Cine*) plateau *m*; (*Theat: stage*) scène
f; (: *scenery*) décor *m*; (*Math*) ensemble
m; (*Hairdressing*) mise *f* en plis ▷ *adj*
(*fixed*) fixe, déterminé(e); (*ready*)
prêt(e) ▷ *vt* (*place*) mettre, poser,
placer; (*fix, establish*) fixer (: *record*)
établir; (*assign: task, homework*)
donner; (*exam*) composer; (*adjust*)
régler; (*decide: rules etc*) fixer, choisir
▷ *vi* (*sun*) se coucher; (*jam, jelly,
concrete*) prendre; (*bone*) se ressouder;
to be ~ on doing être résolu(e)
à faire; **to ~ to music** mettre en
musique; **to ~ on fire** mettre le feu
à; **to ~ free** libérer; **to ~ sth going**
déclencher qch; **to ~ sail** partir,
prendre la mer; **set aside** *vt* mettre
de côté; (*time*) garder; **set down** *vt*
(*subj: bus, train*) déposer; **set in** *vi*
(*infection, bad weather*) s'installer;
(*complications*) survenir, surgir; **set
off** *vi* se mettre en route, partir ▷ *vt*
(*bomb*) faire exploser; (*cause to start*)
déclencher; (*show up well*) mettre en
valeur, faire valoir; **set out** *vi*: **to ~
out (from)** partir (de) ▷ *vt* (*arrange*)
disposer; (*state*) présenter, exposer;
to ~ out to do entreprendre de
faire; avoir pour but *or* intention de
faire; **set up** *vt* (*organization*) fonder,
créer; **setback** *n* (*hitch*) revers *m*,
contretemps *m*; **set menu** *n* menu *m*

settee [sɛ'ti:] *n* canapé *m*

setting ['sɛtɪŋ] *n* cadre *m*; (*of jewel*)
monture *f*; (*position: of controls*)
réglage *m*

settle ['sɛtl] vt (argument, matter, account) régler; (problem) résoudre; (Med: calm) calmer ▷ vi (bird, dust etc) se poser; **to ~ for sth** accepter qch, se contenter de qch; **to ~ on sth** opter or se décider pour qch; **settle down** vi (get comfortable) s'installer; (become calmer) se calmer; se ranger; **settle in** vi s'installer; **settle up** vi: **to ~ up with sb** régler (ce que l'on doit à) qn; **settlement** n (payment) règlement m; (agreement) accord m; (village etc) village m, hameau m

setup ['sɛtʌp] n (arrangement) manière f dont les choses sont organisées; (situation) situation f, allure f des choses

seven ['sɛvn] num sept; **seventeen** num dix-sept; **seventeenth** [sɛvn'tiːnθ] num dix-septième; **seventh** num septième; **seventieth** ['sɛvntiɪθ] num soixante-dixième; **seventy** num soixante-dix

sever ['sɛvəʳ] vt couper, trancher; (relations) rompre

several ['sɛvərl] adj, pron plusieurs pl; **~ of us** plusieurs d'entre nous

severe [sɪ'vɪəʳ] adj (stern) sévère, strict(e); (serious) grave, sérieux(-euse); (plain) sévère, austère

sew (pt **sewed**, pp **sewn**) [səu, səud, səun] vt, vi coudre

sewage ['suːɪdʒ] n vidange(s) f(pl)

sewer ['suːəʳ] n égout m

sewing ['səuɪŋ] n couture f; (item(s)) ouvrage m; **sewing machine** n machine f à coudre

sewn [səun] pp of **sew**

sex [sɛks] n sexe m; **to have ~ with** avoir des rapports (sexuels) avec; **sexism** ['sɛksɪzəm] n sexisme m; **sexist** adj sexiste; **sexual** ['sɛksjuəl] adj sexuel(le); **sexual intercourse** n rapports sexuels; **sexuality** [sɛksju'ælɪtɪ] n sexualité f; **sexy** adj sexy inv

shabby ['ʃæbɪ] adj miteux(-euse); (behaviour) mesquin(e), méprisable

shack [ʃæk] n cabane f, hutte f

shade [ʃeɪd] n ombre f; (for lamp) abat-jour m inv; (of colour) nuance f, ton m; (us: window shade) store m; (small quantity): **a ~ of** un soupçon de ▷ vt abriter du soleil, ombrager; **shades** npl (us: sunglasses) lunettes fpl de soleil; **in the ~** à l'ombre; **a ~ smaller** un tout petit peu plus petit

shadow ['ʃædəu] n ombre f ▷ vt (follow) filer; **shadow cabinet** n (BRIT Pol) cabinet parallèle formé par le parti qui n'est pas au pouvoir

shady ['ʃeɪdɪ] adj ombragé(e); (fig: dishonest) louche, véreux(-euse)

shaft [ʃɑːft] n (of arrow, spear) hampe f; (Aut, Tech) arbre m; (of mine) puits m; (of lift) cage f; (of light) rayon m, trait m

shake [ʃeɪk] (pt **shook**, pp **shaken**) vt secouer; (bottle, cocktail) agiter; (house, confidence) ébranler ▷ vi trembler; **to ~ one's head** (in refusal etc) dire or faire non de la tête; (in dismay) secouer la tête; **to ~ hands with sb** serrer la main à qn; **shake off** vt secouer; (pursuer) se débarrasser de; **shake up** vt secouer; **shaky** adj (hand, voice) tremblant(e); (building) branlant(e), peu solide

shall [ʃæl] aux vb: **I ~ go** j'irai; **~ I open the door?** j'ouvre la porte?; **I'll get the coffee, ~ I?** je vais chercher le café, d'accord?

shallow ['ʃæləu] adj peu profond(e); (fig) superficiel(le), qui manque de profondeur

sham [ʃæm] n frime f

shambles ['ʃæmblz] n confusion f, pagaïe f, fouillis m

shame [ʃeɪm] n honte f ▷ vt faire honte à; **it is a ~ (that/to do)** c'est dommage (que + sub/de faire); **what a ~!** quel dommage!; **shameful** adj honteux(-euse), scandaleux(-euse); **shameless** adj éhonté(e), effronté(e)

shampoo [ʃæm'puː] n shampooing m ▷ vt faire un shampooing à

shandy ['ʃændɪ] n bière panachée

S

shan't [ʃɑːnt] = **shall not**

shape [ʃeɪp] n forme f ▷ vt façonner, modeler; (sb's ideas, character) former; (sb's life) déterminer ▷ vi (also: **~ up**: events) prendre tournure; (: person) faire des progrès, s'en sortir; **to take ~** prendre forme or tournure

share [ʃɛəʳ] n part f; (Comm) action f ▷ vt partager; (have in common) avoir en commun; **to ~ out (among** or **between)** partager (entre); **shareholder** n (BRIT) actionnaire m/f

shark [ʃɑːk] n requin m

sharp [ʃɑːp] adj (razor, knife) tranchant(e), bien aiguisé(e); (point, voice) aigu(ë); (nose, chin) pointu(e); (outline, increase) net(te); (cold, pain) vif (vive); (taste) piquant(e), âcre; (Mus) dièse; (person: quick-witted) vif (vive), éveillé(e); (: unscrupulous) malhonnête ▷ n (Mus) dièse m ▷ adv: **at 2 o'clock ~** à 2 heures pile or tapantes; **sharpen** vt aiguiser; (pencil) tailler; (fig) aviver; **sharpener** n (also: **pencil sharpener**) taille-crayon(s) m inv; **sharply** adv (turn, stop) brusquement; (stand out) nettement; (criticize, retort) sèchement, vertement

shatter ['ʃætəʳ] vt briser; (fig: upset) bouleverser; (: ruin) briser, ruiner ▷ vi voler en éclats, se briser; **shattered** adj (overwhelmed, grief-stricken) bouleversé(e); (inf: exhausted) éreinté(e)

shave [ʃeɪv] vt raser ▷ vi se raser ▷ n: **to have a ~** se raser; **shaver** n (also: **electric shaver**) rasoir m électrique

shaving cream n crème f à raser

shaving foam n mousse f à raser

shavings ['ʃeɪvɪŋz] npl (of wood etc) copeaux mpl

shawl [ʃɔːl] n châle m

she [ʃiː] pron elle

sheath [ʃiːθ] n gaine f, fourreau m, étui m; (contraceptive) préservatif m

shed [ʃɛd] n remise f, resserre f ▷ vt (pt, pp **shed**) (leaves, fur etc) perdre; (tears) verser, répandre; (workers) congédier

she'd [ʃiːd] = **she had; she would**

sheep [ʃiːp] n (pl inv) mouton m; **sheepdog** n chien m de berger; **sheepskin** n peau f de mouton

sheer [ʃɪəʳ] adj (utter) pur(e), pur et simple; (steep) à pic, abrupt(e); (almost transparent) extrêmement fin(e) ▷ adv à pic, abruptement

sheet [ʃiːt] n (on bed) drap m; (of paper) feuille f; (of glass, metal etc) feuille, plaque f

sheik(h) [ʃeɪk] n cheik m

shelf (pl **shelves**) [ʃɛlf, ʃɛlvz] n étagère f, rayon m

shell [ʃɛl] n (on beach) coquillage m; (of egg, nut etc) coquille f; (explosive) obus m; (of building) carcasse f ▷ vt (peas) écosser; (Mil) bombarder (d'obus)

she'll [ʃiːl] = **she will; she shall**

shellfish ['ʃɛlfɪʃ] n (pl inv: crab etc) crustacé m; (: scallop etc) coquillage m ▷ npl (as food) fruits mpl de mer

shelter ['ʃɛltəʳ] n abri m, refuge m ▷ vt abriter, protéger; (give lodging to) donner asile à ▷ vi s'abriter, se mettre à l'abri; **sheltered** adj (life) retiré(e), à l'abri des soucis; (spot) abrité(e)

shelves ['ʃɛlvz] npl of **shelf**

shelving ['ʃɛlvɪŋ] n (shelves) rayonnage(s) m(pl)

shepherd ['ʃɛpəd] n berger m ▷ vt (guide) guider, escorter; **shepherd's pie** n ≈ hachis m Parmentier

sheriff ['ʃɛrɪf] (US) n shérif m

sherry ['ʃɛrɪ] n xérès m, sherry m

she's [ʃiːz] = **she is; she has**

Shetland ['ʃɛtlənd] n (also: **the ~s, the ~ Isles** or **Islands**) les îles fpl Shetland

shield [ʃiːld] n bouclier m; (protection) écran m de protection ▷ vt: **to ~ (from)** protéger (de or contre)

shift [ʃɪft] n (change) changement m; (work period) période f de travail; (of workers) équipe f, poste m ▷ vt déplacer, changer de place; (*remove*) enlever ▷ *vi* changer de place, bouger

shin [ʃɪn] *n* tibia *m*

shine [ʃaɪn] *n* éclat *m*, brillant *m* ▷ *vi* (*pt, pp* **shone**) briller ▷ *vt* (*pt, pp* **shined**) (*polish*) faire briller *or* reluire; **to ~ sth on sth** (*torch*) braquer qch sur qch

shingles ['ʃɪŋglz] *n* (*Med*) zona *m*

shiny ['ʃaɪnɪ] *adj* brillant(e)

ship [ʃɪp] *n* bateau *m*; (*large*) navire *m* ▷ *vt* transporter (par mer); (*send*) expédier (par mer); **shipment** *n* cargaison *f*; **shipping** *n* (*ships*) navires *mpl*; (*traffic*) navigation *f*; (*the industry*) industrie navale; (*transport*) transport *m*; **shipwreck** *n* épave *f*; (*event*) naufrage *m* ▷ *vt*: **to be shipwrecked** faire naufrage; **shipyard** *n* chantier naval

shirt [ʃəːt] *n* chemise *f*; (*woman's*) chemisier *m*; **in ~ sleeves** en bras de chemise

shit [ʃɪt] *excl* (*inf!*) merde (*!*)

shiver ['ʃɪvəʳ] *n* frisson *m* ▷ *vi* frissonner

shock [ʃɔk] *n* choc *m*; (*Elec*) secousse *f*, décharge *f*; (*Med*) commotion *f*, choc ▷ *vt* (*scandalize*) choquer, scandaliser; (*upset*) bouleverser; **shocking** *adj* (*outrageous*) choquant(e), scandaleux(-euse); (*awful*) épouvantable

shoe [ʃuː] *n* chaussure *f*, soulier *m*; (*also*: **horse~**) fer *m* à cheval ▷ *vt* (*pt, pp* **shod**) (*horse*) ferrer; **shoelace** *n* lacet *m* (de soulier); **shoe polish** *n* cirage *m*; **shoeshop** *n* magasin *m* de chaussures

shone [ʃɔn] *pt, pp of* **shine**

shonky ['ʃɔŋkɪ] *adj* (*AUST, NZ inf*: *untrustworthy*) louche

shook [ʃuk] *pt of* **shake**

shoot [ʃuːt] (*pt, pp* **shot**) *n* (*on branch, seedling*) pousse *f* ▷ *vt* (*game: hunt*) chasser; (: *aim at*) tirer; (: *kill*) abattre; (*person*) blesser/tuer d'un coup de fusil (*or* de revolver); (*execute*) fusiller; (*arrow*) tirer; (*gun*) tirer un coup de; (*Cine*) tourner ▷ *vi* (*with gun, bow*): **to ~ (at)** tirer (sur); (*Football*) shooter, tirer; **shoot down** *vt* (*plane*) abattre; **shoot up** *vi* (*fig: prices etc*) monter en flèche; **shooting** *n* (*shots*) coups *mpl* de feu; (*attack*) fusillade *f*; (*murder*) homicide *m* (*à l'aide d'une arme à feu*); (*Hunting*) chasse *f*

shop [ʃɔp] *n* magasin *m*; (*workshop*) atelier *m* ▷ *vi* (*also*: **go ~ping**) faire ses courses *or* ses achats; **shop assistant** *n* (*BRIT*) vendeur(-euse); **shopkeeper** *n* marchand(e), commerçant(e); **shoplifting** *n* vol *m* à l'étalage; **shopping** *n* (*goods*) achats *mpl*, provisions *fpl*; **shopping bag** *n* sac *m* (à provisions); **shopping centre**, (*US*) **shopping center** *n* centre commercial; **shopping mall** *n* centre commercial; **shopping trolley** *n* (*BRIT*) Caddie® *m*; **shop window** *n* vitrine *f*

shore [ʃɔːʳ] *n* (*of sea, lake*) rivage *m*, rive *f* ▷ *vt*: **to ~ (up)** étayer; **on ~** à terre

short [ʃɔːt] *adj* (*not long*) court(e); (*soon finished*) court, bref (brève); (*person, step*) petit(e); (*curt*) brusque, sec (sèche); (*insufficient*) insuffisant(e) ▷ *n* (*also*: **~ film**) court métrage; (*Elec*) court-circuit *m*; **to be ~ of sth** être à court de *or* manquer de qch; **in ~** bref; en bref; **~ of doing** à moins de faire; **everything ~ of** tout sauf; **it is ~ for** c'est l'abréviation *or* le diminutif de; **to cut ~** (*speech, visit*) abréger, écourter; **to fall ~ of** ne pas être à la hauteur de; **to run ~ of** arriver à court de, venir à manquer de; **to stop ~** s'arrêter net; **to stop ~ of** ne pas aller jusqu'à; **shortage** *n* manque *m*, pénurie *f*; **shortbread** *n* ≈ sablé *m*; **shortcoming** *n* défaut *m*; **short(crust) pastry** *n* (*BRIT*) pâte brisée; **shortcut** *n* raccourci *m*; **shorten** *vt* raccourcir; (*text, visit*) abréger; **shortfall** *n* déficit *m*; **shorthand** *n* (*BRIT*) sténo(graphie)

S

f; **shortlist** n (BRIT: *for job*) liste f des candidats sélectionnés; **short-lived** *adj* de courte durée; **shortly** *adv* bientôt, sous peu; **shorts** *npl*: **(a pair of) shorts** un short; **short-sighted** *adj* (BRIT) myope; (*fig*) qui manque de clairvoyance; **short-sleeved** *adj* à manches courtes; **short story** n nouvelle f; **short-tempered** *adj* qui s'emporte facilement; **short-term** *adj* (*effect*) à court terme

shot [ʃɔt] *pt*, *pp of* **shoot** ▷ n coup m (de feu); (*try*) coup, essai m; (*injection*) piqûre f; (*Phot*) photo f; **to be a good/poor ~** (*person*) tirer bien/mal; **like a ~** comme une flèche; (*very readily*) sans hésiter; **shotgun** n fusil m de chasse

should [ʃʊd] *aux vb*: **I ~ go now** je devrais partir maintenant; **he ~ be there now** il devrait être arrivé maintenant; **I ~ go if I were you** si j'étais vous j'irais; **I ~ like to** volontiers, j'aimerais bien

shoulder ['ʃəʊldəʳ] n épaule f ▷ vt (*fig*) endosser, se charger de; **shoulder blade** n omoplate f

shouldn't ['ʃʊdnt] = **should not**

shout [ʃaʊt] n cri m ▷ vt crier ▷ vi crier, pousser des cris

shove [ʃʌv] vt pousser; (*inf*: *put*): **to ~ sth in** fourrer or ficher qch dans ▷ n poussée f

shovel ['ʃʌvl] n pelle f ▷ vt pelleter, enlever (or enfourner) à la pelle

show [ʃəʊ] (*pt* **showed**, *pp* **shown**) n (*of emotion*) manifestation f, démonstration f; (*semblance*) semblant m, apparence f; (*exhibition*) exposition f, salon m; (*Theat*, *TV*) spectacle m; (*Cine*) séance f ▷ vt montrer; (*film*) passer; (*courage etc*) faire preuve de, manifester; (*exhibit*) exposer ▷ vi se voir, être visible; **can you ~ me where it is, please?** pouvez-vous me montrer où c'est?; **to be on ~** être exposé(e); **it's just for ~** c'est juste pour l'effet; **show in**

vt faire entrer; **show off** vi (*pej*) crâner ▷ vt (*display*) faire valoir; (*pej*) faire étalage de; **show out** vt reconduire à la porte; **show up** vi (*stand out*) ressortir; (*inf*: *turn up*) se montrer ▷ vt (*unmask*) démasquer, dénoncer; (*flaw*) faire ressortir; **show business** n le monde du spectacle

shower ['ʃaʊəʳ] n (*for washing*) douche f; (*rain*) averse f; (*of stones etc*) pluie f, grêle f; (US: *party*) réunion *organisée pour la remise de cadeaux* ▷ vi prendre une douche, se doucher ▷ vt: **to ~ sb with** (*gifts etc*) combler qn de; **to have** or **take a ~** prendre une douche, se doucher; **shower cap** n bonnet m de douche; **shower gel** n gel m douche

showing ['ʃəʊɪŋ] n (*of film*) projection f

show jumping [-dʒʌmpɪŋ] n concours m hippique

shown [ʃəʊn] *pp of* **show**

show: **show-off** n (*inf*: *person*) crâneur(-euse), m'as-tu-vu(-e); **showroom** n magasin m or salle f d'exposition

shrank [ʃræŋk] *pt of* **shrink**

shred [ʃrɛd] n (*gen pl*) lambeau m, petit morceau m; (*fig*: *of truth*, *evidence*) parcelle f ▷ vt mettre en lambeaux, déchirer; (*documents*) détruire; (*Culin*: *grate*) râper; (: *lettuce etc*) couper en lanières

shrewd [ʃruːd] *adj* astucieux(-euse), perspicace; (*business person*) habile

shriek [ʃriːk] n cri perçant or aigu, hurlement m ▷ vt, vi hurler, crier

shrimp [ʃrɪmp] n crevette grise

shrine [ʃraɪn] n (*place*) lieu m de pèlerinage

shrink (*pt* **shrank**, *pp* **shrunk**) [ʃrɪŋk, ʃræŋk, ʃrʌŋk] vi rétrécir; (*fig*) diminuer; (*also*: **~ away**) reculer ▷ vt (*wool*) (faire) rétrécir ▷ n (*inf*, *pej*) psychanalyste m/f; **to ~ from (doing) sth** reculer devant (la pensée de faire) qch

shrivel ['ʃrɪvl], **shrivel up** vt ratatiner, flétrir ▷ vi se ratatiner, se flétrir

shroud [ʃraud] n linceul m ▷ vt: **~ed in mystery** enveloppé(e) de mystère

Shrove Tuesday ['ʃrəuv-] n (le) Mardi gras

shrub [ʃrʌb] n arbuste m

shrug [ʃrʌg] n haussement m d'épaules ▷ vt, vi: **to ~ (one's shoulders)** hausser les épaules; **shrug off** vt faire fi de

shrunk [ʃrʌŋk] pp of **shrink**

shudder ['ʃʌdəʳ] n frisson m, frémissement m ▷ vi frissonner, frémir

shuffle ['ʃʌfl] vt (cards) battre; **to ~ (one's feet)** traîner les pieds

shun [ʃʌn] vt éviter, fuir

shut (pt, pp **shut**) [ʃʌt] vt fermer ▷ vi (se) fermer; **shut down** vt fermer définitivement ▷ vi fermer définitivement; **shut up** vi (inf: keep quiet) se taire ▷ vt (close) fermer; (silence) faire taire; **shutter** n volet m; (Phot) obturateur m

shuttle ['ʃʌtl] n navette f; (also: **~ service**) (service m de) navette f; **shuttlecock** n volant m (de badminton)

shy [ʃaɪ] adj timide

siblings ['sɪblɪŋz] npl (formal) frères et sœurs mpl (de mêmes parents)

Sicily ['sɪsɪlɪ] n Sicile f

sick [sɪk] adj (ill) malade; (BRIT: humour) noir(e), macabre; (vomiting): **to be ~** vomir; **to feel ~** avoir envie de vomir, avoir mal au cœur; **to be ~ of** (fig) en avoir assez de; **sickening** adj (fig) écœurant(e), révoltant(e), répugnant(e); **sick leave** n congé m de maladie; **sickly** adj maladif(-ive), souffreteux(-euse); (causing nausea) écœurant(e); **sickness** n maladie f; (vomiting) vomissement(s) m(pl)

side [saɪd] n côté m; (of lake, road) bord m; (of mountain) versant m; (fig: aspect) côté, aspect m; (team: Sport) équipe f; (TV: channel) chaîne f ▷ adj (door, entrance) latéral(e) ▷ vi: **to ~ with sb** prendre le parti de qn, se ranger du côté de qn; **by the ~ of** au bord de; **~ by ~** côte à côte; **to rock from ~ to ~** se balancer; **to take ~s (with)** prendre parti (pour); **sideboard** n buffet m; **sideboards**, (US) **sideburns** npl (whiskers) pattes fpl; **side effect** n effet m secondaire; **sidelight** n (Aut) veilleuse f; **sideline** n (Sport) (ligne f de) touche f; (fig) activité f secondaire; **side order** n garniture f; **side road** n petite route, route transversale; **side street** n rue transversale; **sidetrack** vt (fig) faire dévier de son sujet; **sidewalk** n (US) trottoir m; **sideways** adv de côté

siege [siːdʒ] n siège m

sieve [sɪv] n tamis m, passoire f ▷ vt tamiser, passer (au tamis)

sift [sɪft] vt passer au tamis or au crible; (fig) passer au crible

sigh [saɪ] n soupir m ▷ vi soupirer, pousser un soupir

sight [saɪt] n (faculty) vue f; (spectacle) spectacle m ▷ vt apercevoir; **in ~** visible; (fig) en vue; **out of ~** hors de vue; **sightseeing** n tourisme m; **to go sightseeing** faire du tourisme

sign [saɪn] n (gen) signe m; (with hand etc) signe, geste m; (notice) panneau m, écriteau m; (also: **road ~**) panneau de signalisation ▷ vt signer; **where do I ~?** où dois-je signer?; **sign for** vt fus (item) signer le reçu pour; **sign in** vi signer le registre (en arrivant); **sign on** vi (BRIT: as unemployed) s'inscrire au chômage; (enrol) s'inscrire ▷ vt (employee) embaucher; **sign over** vt: **to ~ sth over to sb** céder qch par écrit à qn; **sign up** vi (Mil) s'engager; (for course) s'inscrire

signal ['sɪgnl] n signal m ▷ vi (Aut) mettre son clignotant ▷ vt (person) faire signe à; (message) communiquer par signaux

signature ['sɪgnətʃəʳ] n signature f

S

significance [sɪgˈnɪfɪkəns] *n*
signification *f*; importance *f*
significant [sɪgˈnɪfɪkənt] *adj*
significatif(-ive); (*important*)
important(e), considérable
signify [ˈsɪgnɪfaɪ] *vt* signifier
sign language *n* langage *m* par
signes
signpost [ˈsaɪnpəʊst] *n* poteau
indicateur
Sikh [siːk] *adj, n* Sikh *m/f*
silence [ˈsaɪləns] *n* silence *m* ▷ *vt* faire
taire, réduire au silence
silent [ˈsaɪlnt] *adj* silencieux(-euse);
(*film*) muet(te); **to keep** *or* **remain ~**
garder le silence, ne rien dire
silhouette [sɪluːˈɛt] *n* silhouette *f*
silicon chip [ˈsɪlɪkən-] *n* puce *f*
électronique
silk [sɪlk] *n* soie *f* ▷ *cpd* de *or* en soie
silly [ˈsɪlɪ] *adj* stupide, sot(te), bête
silver [ˈsɪlvəʳ] *n* argent *m*; (*money*)
monnaie *f* (en pièces d'argent); (*also*:
~ware) argenterie *f* ▷ *adj* (*made
of silver*) d'argent, en argent; (*in
colour*) argenté(e); **silver-plated** *adj*
plaqué(e) argent
SIM card [ˈsɪm-] *abbr* (*Tel*) carte
f SIM
similar [ˈsɪmɪləʳ] *adj*: **~ (to)**
semblable (à); **similarity**
[sɪmɪˈlærɪtɪ] *n* ressemblance *f*,
similarité *f*; **similarly** *adv* de la même
façon, de même
simmer [ˈsɪməʳ] *vi* cuire à feu doux,
mijoter
simple [ˈsɪmpl] *adj* simple;
simplicity [sɪmˈplɪsɪtɪ] *n* simplicité
f; **simplify** [ˈsɪmplɪfaɪ] *vt* simplifier;
simply *adv* simplement; (*without
fuss*) avec simplicité; (*absolutely*)
absolument
simulate [ˈsɪmjuleɪt] *vt* simuler,
feindre
simultaneous [sɪməlˈteɪnɪəs] *adj*
simultané(e); **simultaneously** *adv*
simultanément
sin [sɪn] *n* péché *m* ▷ *vi* pécher

since [sɪns] *adv, prep* depuis ▷ *conj*
(*time*) depuis que; (*because*) puisque,
étant donné que, comme; **~ then,
ever ~** depuis ce moment-là
sincere [sɪnˈsɪəʳ] *adj* sincère;
sincerely *adv* sincèrement; **yours
sincerely** (*at end of letter*) veuillez
agréer, Monsieur (*or* Madame)
l'expression de mes sentiments
distingués *or* les meilleurs
sing (*pt* **sang**, *pp* **sung**) [sɪŋ, sæŋ, sʌŋ]
vt, vi chanter
Singapore [sɪŋgəˈpɔːʳ] *n*
Singapour *m*
singer [ˈsɪŋəʳ] *n* chanteur(-euse)
singing [ˈsɪŋɪŋ] *n* (*of person, bird*)
chant *m*
single [ˈsɪŋgl] *adj* seul(e), unique;
(*unmarried*) célibataire; (*not double*)
simple ▷ *n* (BRIT: *also*: **~ ticket**) aller *m*
(simple); (*record*) 45 tours *m*; **singles**
npl (*Tennis*) simple *m*; **every ~ day**
chaque jour sans exception; **single
out** *vt* choisir; (*distinguish*) distinguer;
single bed *n* lit *m* d'une personne *or* à
une place; **single file** *n*: **in single file**
en file indienne; **single-handed** *adv*
tout(e) seul(e), sans (aucune) aide;
single-minded *adj* résolu(e), tenace;
single parent *n* parent unique (*or*
célibataire); **single-parent family**
famille monoparentale; **single
room** *n* chambre *f* à un lit *or* pour une
personne
singular [ˈsɪŋgjuləʳ] *adj*
singulier(-ière); (*odd*) singulier,
étrange; (*outstanding*) remarquable;
(*Ling*) (au) singulier, du singulier ▷ *n*
(*Ling*) singulier *m*
sinister [ˈsɪnɪstəʳ] *adj* sinistre
sink [sɪŋk] (*pt* **sank**, *pp* **sunk**) *n*
évier *m*; (*washbasin*) lavabo *m* ▷ *vt*
(*ship*) (faire) couler, faire sombrer;
(*foundations*) creuser ▷ *vi* couler,
sombrer; (*ground etc*) s'affaisser; **to ~
into sth** (*chair*) s'enfoncer dans qch;
sink in *vi* (*explanation*) rentrer (*inf*),
être compris

sinus ['saɪnəs] n (Anat) sinus m inv
sip [sɪp] n petite gorgée ▷ vt boire à petites gorgées
sir [səˤ] n monsieur m; **S~ John Smith** sir John Smith; **yes ~** oui Monsieur
siren ['saɪərən] n sirène f
sirloin ['səːlɔɪn] n (also: **~ steak**) aloyau m
sister ['sɪstəˤ] n sœur f; (nun) religieuse f, (bonne) sœur; (BRIT: nurse) infirmière f en chef; **sister-in-law** n belle-sœur f
sit (pt, pp **sat**) [sɪt, sæt] vi s'asseoir; (be sitting) être assis(e); (assembly) être en séance, siéger; (for painter) poser ▷ vt (exam) passer, se présenter à; **sit back** vi (in seat) bien s'installer, se carrer; **sit down** vi s'asseoir; **sit on** vt fus (jury, committee) faire partie de; **sit up** vi s'asseoir; (straight) se redresser; (not go to bed) rester debout, ne pas se coucher
sitcom ['sɪtkɔm] n abbr (TV: = situation comedy) sitcom f, comédie f de situation
site [saɪt] n emplacement m, site m; (also: **building ~**) chantier m; (Internet) site m web ▷ vt placer
sitting ['sɪtɪŋ] n (of assembly etc) séance f; (in canteen) service m; **sitting room** n salon m
situated ['sɪtjueɪtɪd] adj situé(e)
situation [sɪtju'eɪʃən] n situation f; **"~s vacant/wanted"** (BRIT) "offres/demandes d'emploi"
six [sɪks] num six; **sixteen** num seize; **sixteenth** [sɪks'tiːnθ] num seizième; **sixth** ['sɪksθ] num sixième; **sixth form** n (BRIT) ≈ classes fpl de première et de terminale; **sixth-form college** n lycée n'ayant que des classes de première et de terminale; **sixtieth** ['sɪkstɪɪθ] num soixantième; **sixty** num soixante
size [saɪz] n dimensions fpl; (of person) taille f; (of clothing) taille f; (of shoes) pointure f; (of problem) ampleur f; (glue) colle f; **sizeable** adj assez grand(e); (amount, problem, majority) assez important(e)
sizzle ['sɪzl] vi grésiller
skate [skeɪt] n patin m; (fish: pl inv) raie f ▷ vi patiner; **skateboard** n skateboard m, planche f à roulettes; **skateboarding** n skateboard m; **skater** n patineur(-euse); **skating** n patinage m; **skating rink** n patinoire f
skeleton ['skɛlɪtn] n squelette m; (outline) schéma m
skeptical ['skɛptɪkl] (US) adj = **sceptical**
sketch [skɛtʃ] n (drawing) croquis m, esquisse f; (outline plan) aperçu m; (Theat) sketch m, saynète f ▷ vt esquisser, faire un croquis or une esquisse de; (plan etc) esquisser
skewer ['skjuːəˤ] n brochette f
ski [skiː] n ski m ▷ vi skier, faire du ski; **ski boot** n chaussure f de ski
skid [skɪd] n dérapage m ▷ vi déraper
ski: skier n skieur(-euse); **skiing** n ski m; **to go skiing** (aller) faire du ski
skilful, (US) **skillful** ['skɪlful] adj habile, adroit(e)
ski lift n remonte-pente m inv
skill [skɪl] n (ability) habileté f, adresse f, talent m; (requiring training) compétences fpl; **skilled** adj habile, adroit(e); (worker) qualifié(e)
skim [skɪm] vt (soup) écumer; (glide over) raser, effleurer ▷ vi: **to ~ through** (fig) parcourir; **skimmed milk**, (US) **skim milk** n lait écrémé
skin [skɪn] n peau f ▷ vt (fruit etc) éplucher; (animal) écorcher; **skinhead** n skinhead m; **skinny** adj maigre, maigrichon(ne)
skip [skɪp] n petit bond or saut; (BRIT: container) benne f ▷ vi gambader, sautiller; (with rope) sauter à la corde ▷ vt (pass over) sauter
ski: ski pass n forfait-skieur(s) m; **ski pole** n bâton m de ski
skipper ['skɪpəˤ] n (Naut, Sport) capitaine m; (in race) skipper m

skipping rope ['skɪpɪŋ-], (US) **skip rope** n corde f à sauter

skirt [skəːt] n jupe f ▷ vt longer, contourner

skirting board ['skəːtɪŋ-] n (BRIT) plinthe f

ski slope n piste f de ski

ski suit n combinaison f de ski

skull [skʌl] n crâne m

skunk [skʌŋk] n mouffette f

sky [skaɪ] n ciel m; **skyscraper** n gratte-ciel m inv

slab [slæb] n (of stone) dalle f; (of meat, cheese) tranche épaisse

slack [slæk] adj (loose) lâche, desserré(e); (slow) stagnant(e); (careless) négligent(e), peu sérieux(-euse) or conscientieux(-euse); **slacks** npl pantalon m

slain [sleɪn] pp of **slay**

slam [slæm] vt (door) (faire) claquer; (throw) jeter violemment, flanquer; (inf: criticize) éreinter, démolir ▷ vi claquer

slander ['slɑːndəʳ] n calomnie f; (Law) diffamation f

slang [slæŋ] n argot m

slant [slɑːnt] n inclinaison f; (fig) angle m, point m de vue

slap [slæp] n claque f, gifle f; (on the back) tape f ▷ vt donner une claque or une gifle (or une tape) à ▷ adv (directly) tout droit, en plein; **to ~ on** (paint) appliquer rapidement

slash [slæʃ] vt entailler, taillader; (fig: prices) casser

slate [sleɪt] n ardoise f ▷ vt (fig: criticize) éreinter, démolir

slaughter ['slɔːtəʳ] n carnage m, massacre m; (of animals) abattage m ▷ vt (animal) abattre; (people) massacrer; **slaughterhouse** n abattoir m

Slav [slɑːv] adj slave

slave [sleɪv] n esclave m/f ▷ vi (also: **~ away**) trimer, travailler comme un forçat; **slavery** n esclavage m

slay (pt **slew**, pp **slain**) [sleɪ, sluː, sleɪn] vt (literary) tuer

sleazy ['sliːzɪ] adj miteux(-euse), minable

sled [slɛd] (US) n = **sledge**

sledge [slɛdʒ] n luge f

sleek [sliːk] adj (hair, fur) brillant(e), luisant(e); (car, boat) aux lignes pures or élégantes

sleep [sliːp] n sommeil m ▷ vi (pt, pp **slept**) dormir; **to go to ~** s'endormir; **sleep in** vi (oversleep) se réveiller trop tard; (on purpose) faire la grasse matinée; **sleep together** vi (have sex) coucher ensemble; **sleeper** n (person) dormeur(-euse); (BRIT Rail: on track) traverse f; (: train) train-couchettes m; (: berth) couchette f; **sleeping bag** ['sliːpɪŋ-] n sac m de couchage; **sleeping car** n wagon-lits m, voiture-lits f; **sleeping pill** n somnifère m; **sleepover** n nuit f chez un copain or une copine; **we're having a sleepover at Jo's** nous allons passer la nuit chez Jo; **sleepwalk** vi marcher en dormant; **sleepy** adj (fig) endormi(e)

sleet [sliːt] n neige fondue

sleeve [sliːv] n manche f; (of record) pochette f; **sleeveless** adj (garment) sans manches

sleigh [sleɪ] n traîneau m

slender ['slɛndəʳ] adj svelte, mince; (fig) faible, ténu(e)

slept [slɛpt] pt, pp of **sleep**

slew [sluː] pt of **slay**

slice [slaɪs] n tranche f; (round) rondelle f; (utensil) spatule f; (also: **fish ~**) pelle f à poisson ▷ vt couper en tranches (or en rondelles)

slick [slɪk] adj (skilful) bien ficelé(e); (salesperson) qui a du bagout ▷ n (also: **oil ~**) nappe f de pétrole, marée noire

slide (pt, pp **slid**) [slaɪd, slɪd] n (in playground) toboggan m; (Phot) diapositive f; (BRIT: also: **hair ~**) barrette f; (in prices) chute f, baisse f

▷ *vt* (faire) glisser ▷ *vi* glisser; **sliding** *adj* (door) coulissant(e)

slight [slaɪt] *adj* (slim) mince, menu(e); (frail) frêle; (trivial) faible, insignifiant(e); (small) petit(e), léger(-ère) before n ▷ n offense f, affront m ▷ vt (offend) blesser, offenser; **not in the ~est** pas le moins du monde, pas du tout; **slightly** *adv* légèrement, un peu

slim [slɪm] *adj* mince ▷ *vi* maigrir; (diet) suivre un régime amaigrissant; **slimming** *n* amaigrissement *m* ▷ adj (diet, pills) amaigrissant(e), pour maigrir; (food) qui ne fait pas grossir

slimy ['slaɪmɪ] *adj* visqueux(-euse), gluant(e)

sling [slɪŋ] *n* (Med) écharpe f; (for baby) porte-bébé *m*; (weapon) fronde f, lance-pierre *m* ▷ vt (pt, pp **slung**) lancer, jeter

slip [slɪp] *n* faux pas; (mistake) erreur f, bévue f; (underskirt) combinaison f; (of paper) petite feuille, fiche f ▷ vt (slide) glisser ▷ vi (slide) glisser; (decline) baisser; (move smoothly): **to ~ into/ out of** se glisser or se faufiler dans/ hors de; **to ~ sth on/off** enfiler/ enlever qch; **to give sb the ~** fausser compagnie à qn; **a ~ of the tongue** un lapsus; **slip up** *vi* faire une erreur, gaffer

slipped disc [slɪpt-] *n* déplacement *m* de vertèbre

slipper ['slɪpəʳ] *n* pantoufle f

slippery ['slɪpərɪ] *adj* glissant(e)

slip road *n* (BRIT: to motorway) bretelle f d'accès

slit [slɪt] *n* fente f; (cut) incision f ▷ vt (pt, pp **slit**) fendre; couper, inciser

slog [slɔg] *n* (BRIT: effort) gros effort; (work) tâche fastidieuse ▷ vi travailler très dur

slogan ['sləugən] *n* slogan *m*

slope [sləup] *n* pente f, côte f; (side of mountain) versant *m*; (slant) inclinaison f ▷ vi: **to ~ down** être or descendre en pente; **to ~ up** monter;

sloping *adj* en pente, incliné(e); (handwriting) penché(e)

sloppy ['slɔpɪ] *adj* (work) peu soigné(e), bâclé(e); (appearance) négligé(e), débraillé(e)

slot [slɔt] *n* fente f ▷ vt: **to ~ sth into** encastrer or insérer qch dans; **slot machine** *n* (BRIT: vending machine) distributeur *m* (automatique), machine f à sous; (for gambling) appareil *m* or machine à sous

Slovakia [sləu'vækɪə] *n* Slovaquie f

Slovene [sləu'viːn] *adj* slovène ▷ n Slovène *m/f*; (Ling) slovène *m*

Slovenia [sləu'viːnɪə] *n* Slovénie f; **Slovenian** *adj, n* = **Slovene**

slow [sləu] *adj* lent(e); (watch): **to be ~** retarder ▷ adv lentement ▷ vt, vi ralentir; **"~"** (road sign) "ralentir"; **slow down** *vi* ralentir; **slowly** *adv* lentement; **slow motion** *n*: **in slow motion** au ralenti

slug [slʌg] *n* limace f; (bullet) balle f; **sluggish** *adj* (person) mou (molle), lent(e); (stream, engine, trading) lent(e)

slum [slʌm] *n* (house) taudis *m*; **slums** *npl* (area) quartiers *mpl* pauvres

slump [slʌmp] *n* baisse soudaine, effondrement *m*; (Econ) crise f ▷ vi s'effondrer, s'affaisser

slung [slʌŋ] *pt, pp of* **sling**

slur [sləːʳ] *n* (smear): **~ (on)** atteinte f (à); insinuation f (contre) ▷ vt mal articuler

slush [slʌʃ] *n* neige fondue

sly [slaɪ] *adj* (person) rusé(e); (smile, expression, remark) sournois(e)

smack [smæk] *n* (slap) tape f; (on face) gifle f ▷ vt donner une tape à; (on face) gifler; (on bottom) donner la fessée à ▷ vi: **to ~ of** avoir des relents de, sentir

small [smɔːl] *adj* petit(e); **small ads** *npl* (BRIT) petites annonces; **small change** *n* petite or menue monnaie

smart [smɑːt] *adj* élégant(e), chic *inv*; (clever) intelligent(e); (quick) vif (vive), prompt(e) ▷ vi faire mal, brûler;

smart card n carte f à puce; **smart phone** n smartphone m

smash [smæʃ] n (also: **~-up**) collision f, accident m; (Mus) succès foudroyant ▷ vt casser, briser, fracasser; (opponent) écraser; (Sport: record) pulvériser ▷ vi se briser, se fracasser; s'écraser; **smashing** adj (inf) formidable

smear [smɪəʳ] n (stain) tache f; (mark) trace f; (Med) frottis m ▷ vt enduire; (make dirty) salir; **smear test** n (BRIT Med) frottis m

smell [smɛl] (pt, pp **smelt** or **smelled**) n odeur f; (sense) odorat m ▷ vt sentir ▷ vi (pej) sentir mauvais; **smelly** adj qui sent mauvais, malodorant(e)

smelt [smɛlt] pt, pp of **smell**

smile [smaɪl] n sourire m ▷ vi sourire

smirk [smə:k] n petit sourire suffisant or affecté

smog [smɔg] n brouillard mêlé de fumée

smoke [sməuk] n fumée f ▷ vt, vi fumer; **do you mind if I ~?** ça ne vous dérange pas que je fume?; **smoke alarm** n détecteur m de fumée; **smoked** adj (bacon, glass) fumé(e); **smoker** n (person) fumeur(-euse); (Rail) wagon m fumeurs; **smoking** n: **"no smoking"** (sign) "défense de fumer"; **smoky** adj enfumé(e); (taste) fumé(e)

smooth [smu:ð] adj lisse; (sauce) onctueux(-euse); (flavour, whisky) moelleux(-euse); (movement) régulier(-ière), sans à-coups or heurts; (flight) sans secousses; (pej: person) doucereux(-euse), mielleux(-euse) ▷ vt (also: **~ out**) lisser, défroisser; (creases, difficulties) faire disparaître

smother ['smʌðəʳ] vt étouffer

SMS n abbr (= short message service) SMS m; **SMS message** n (message m) SMS m

smudge [smʌdʒ] n tache f, bavure f ▷ vt salir, maculer

smug [smʌg] adj suffisant(e), content(e) de soi

smuggle ['smʌgl] vt passer en contrebande or en fraude; **smuggling** n contrebande f

snack [snæk] n casse-croûte m inv; **snack bar** n snack(-bar) m

snag [snæg] n inconvénient m, difficulté f

snail [sneɪl] n escargot m

snake [sneɪk] n serpent m

snap [snæp] n (sound) claquement m, bruit sec; (photograph) photo f, instantané m ▷ adj subit(e), fait(e) sans réfléchir ▷ vt (fingers) faire claquer; (break) casser net ▷ vi se casser net or avec un bruit sec; (speak sharply) parler d'un ton brusque; **to ~ open/shut** s'ouvrir/se refermer brusquement; **snap at** vt fus (subj: dog) essayer de mordre; **snap up** vt sauter sur, saisir; **snapshot** n photo f, instantané m

snarl [sna:l] vi gronder

snatch [snætʃ] n ▷ vt saisir (d'un geste vif); (steal) voler; **to ~ some sleep** arriver à dormir un peu

sneak [sni:k] (US: pt, pp **snuck**) vi: **to ~ in/out** entrer/sortir furtivement or à la dérobée ▷ n (inf: pej: informer) faux jeton; **to ~ up on sb** s'approcher de qn sans faire de bruit; **sneakers** npl tennis mpl, baskets fpl

sneer [snɪəʳ] vi ricaner; **to ~ at sb/sth** se moquer de qn/qch avec mépris

sneeze [sni:z] vi éternuer

sniff [snɪf] vi renifler ▷ vt renifler, flairer; (glue, drug) sniffer, respirer

snigger ['snɪgəʳ] vi ricaner

snip [snɪp] n (cut) entaille f; (BRIT inf: bargain) (bonne) occasion or affaire f ▷ vt couper

sniper ['snaɪpəʳ] n tireur embusqué

snob [snɔb] n snob m/f

snooker ['snu:kəʳ] n sorte de jeu de billard

snoop [snu:p] vi: **to ~ about** fureter

snooze [snu:z] n petit somme ▷ vi faire un petit somme

snore [snɔːʳ] vi ronfler ▷ n ronflement m

snorkel ['snɔːkl] n (of swimmer) tuba m

snort [snɔːt] n grognement m ▷ vi grogner; (horse) renâcler

snow [snəu] n neige f ▷ vi neiger; **snowball** n boule f de neige; **snowdrift** n congère f; **snowman** (irreg) n bonhomme m de neige; **snowplough**, (US) **snowplow** n chasse-neige m inv; **snowstorm** n tempête f de neige

snub [snʌb] vt repousser, snober ▷ n rebuffade f

snuck [snʌk] (US) pt, pp of **sneak**

snug [snʌg] adj douillet(te), confortable; (person) bien au chaud

○ **KEYWORD**

so [səu] adv 1 (thus, likewise) ainsi, de cette façon; **if so** si oui; **so do or have I** moi aussi; **it's 5 o'clock — so it is!** il est 5 heures — en effet! or c'est vrai!; **I hope/think so** je l'espère/le crois; **so far** jusqu'ici, jusqu'à maintenant; (in past) jusque-là

2 (in comparisons etc: to such a degree) si, tellement; **so big (that)** si or tellement grand (que); **she's not so clever as her brother** elle n'est pas aussi intelligente que son frère

3: **so much** adj, adv tant (de); **I've got so much work** j'ai tant de travail; **I love you so much** je vous aime tant; **so many** tant (de)

4 (phrases): **10 or so** à peu près or environ 10; **so long!** (inf: goodbye) au revoir!, à un de ces jours!; **so (what)?** (inf) (bon) et alors?, et après?

▷ conj 1 (expressing purpose): **so as to do** pour faire, afin de faire; **so (that)** pour que or afin que + sub

2 (expressing result) donc, par conséquent; **so that** si bien que; **so**

that's the reason! c'est donc (pour) ça!; **so you see, I could have gone** alors tu vois, j'aurais pu y aller

soak [səuk] vt faire or laisser tremper; (drench) tremper ▷ vi tremper; **soak up** vt absorber; **soaking** adj (also: **soaking wet**) trempé(e)

so-and-so ['səuənsəu] n (somebody) un(e) tel(le)

soap [səup] n savon m; **soap opera** n feuilleton télévisé (quotidienneté réaliste ou embellie); **soap powder** n lessive f, détergent m

soar [sɔːʳ] vi monter (en flèche), s'élancer; (building) s'élancer

sob [sɔb] n sanglot m ▷ vi sangloter

sober ['səubəʳ] adj qui n'est pas (or plus) ivre; (serious) sérieux(-euse), sensé(e); (colour, style) sobre, discret(-ète); **sober up** vi se dégriser

so-called ['səu'kɔːld] adj soi-disant inv

soccer ['sɔkəʳ] n football m

sociable ['səuʃəbl] adj sociable

social ['səuʃl] adj social(e); (sociable) sociable ▷ n (petite) fête; **socialism** n socialisme m; **socialist** adj, n socialiste (m/f); **socialize** vi: **to socialize with** (meet often) fréquenter; (get to know) lier connaissance or parler avec; **social life** n vie sociale; **socially** adv socialement, en société; **social media** npl médias mpl sociaux; **social networking** n réseaux mpl sociaux; **social networking site** n site m de réseautage; **social security** n aide sociale; **social services** npl services sociaux; **social work** n assistance sociale; **social worker** n assistant(e) sociale(e)

society [sə'saɪətɪ] n société f; (club) société, association f; (also: **high ~**) (haute) société, grand monde

sociology [səusɪ'ɔlədʒɪ] n sociologie f

sock [sɔk] n chaussette f

S

socket ['sɔkɪt] n cavité f; (Elec: also: **wall ~**) prise f de courant

soda ['səudə] n (Chem) soude f; (also: **~ water**) eau f de Seltz; (us: also: **~ pop**) soda m

sodium ['səudɪəm] n sodium m

sofa ['səufə] n sofa m, canapé m; **sofa bed** n canapé-lit m

soft [sɔft] adj (not rough) doux (douce); (not hard) doux, mou (molle); (not loud) doux, léger(-ère); (kind) doux, gentil(le); **soft drink** n boisson non alcoolisée; **soft drugs** npl drogues douces; **soften** ['sɔfn] vt (r)amollir; (fig) adoucir ▷ vi se ramollir; (fig) s'adoucir; **softly** adv doucement; (touch) légèrement; (kiss) tendrement; **software** n (Comput) logiciel m, software m

soggy ['sɔgɪ] adj (clothes) trempé(e); (ground) détrempé(e)

soil [sɔɪl] n (earth) sol m, terre f ▷ vt salir; (fig) souiller

solar ['səulər] adj solaire; **solar power** n énergie f solaire; **solar system** n système m solaire

sold [səuld] pt, pp of **sell**

soldier ['səuldʒər] n soldat m, militaire m

sold out adj (Comm) épuisé(e)

sole [səul] n (of foot) plante f; (of shoe) semelle f; (fish: pl inv) sole f ▷ adj seul(e), unique; **solely** adv seulement, uniquement

solemn ['sɔləm] adj solennel(le); (person) sérieux(-euse), grave

solicitor [sə'lɪsɪtər] n (BRIT: for wills etc) ≈ notaire m; (: in court) ≈ avocat m

solid ['sɔlɪd] adj (not liquid) solide; (not hollow: mass) compact(e); (: metal, rock, wood) massif(-ive) ▷ n solide m

solitary ['sɔlɪtərɪ] adj solitaire

solitude ['sɔlɪtju:d] n solitude f

solo ['səuləu] n solo m ▷ adv (fly) en solitaire; **soloist** n soliste m/f

soluble ['sɔljubl] adj soluble

solution [sə'lu:ʃən] n solution f

solve [sɔlv] vt résoudre

solvent ['sɔlvənt] adj (Comm) solvable ▷ n (Chem) (dis)solvant m

sombre, (us) **somber** ['sɔmbər] adj sombre, morne

KEYWORD

some [sʌm] adj **1** (a certain amount or number of): **some tea/water/ice cream** du thé/de l'eau/de la glace; **some children/apples** des enfants/pommes; **I've got some money but not much** j'ai de l'argent mais pas beaucoup
2 (certain: in contrasts): **some people say that ...** il y a des gens qui disent que ...; **some films were excellent, but most were mediocre** certains films étaient excellents, mais la plupart étaient médiocres
3 (unspecified): **some woman was asking for you** il y avait une dame qui vous demandait; **he was asking for some book (or other)** il demandait un livre quelconque; **some day** un de ces jours; **some day next week** un jour la semaine prochaine
▶ pron **1** (a certain number) quelques-un(e)s, certain(e)s; **I've got some** (books etc) j'en ai (quelques-uns); **some (of them) have been sold** certains ont été vendus
2 (a certain amount) un peu; **I've got some** (money, milk) j'en ai (un peu); **would you like some?** est-ce que vous en voulez?, en voulez-vous?; **could I have some of that cheese?** pourrais-je avoir un peu de ce fromage?; **I've read some of the book** j'ai lu une partie du livre
▶ adv: **some 10 people** quelque 10 personnes, 10 personnes environ; **somebody** ['sʌmbədɪ] pron = **someone**; **somehow** adv d'une façon ou d'une autre; (for some reason) pour une raison ou une autre; **someone** pron quelqu'un; **someplace** adv (us) = **somewhere**;

something *pron* quelque chose *m*;
something interesting quelque
chose d'intéressant; **something to
do** quelque chose à faire; **sometime**
adv (*in future*) un de ces jours, un jour
ou l'autre; (*in past*): **sometime last
month** au cours du mois dernier;
sometimes *adv* quelquefois, parfois;
somewhat *adv* quelque peu, un
peu; **somewhere** *adv* quelque part;
somewhere else ailleurs, autre part

son [sʌn] *n* fils *m*

song [sɔŋ] *n* chanson *f*; (*of bird*)
chant *m*

son-in-law ['sʌnɪnlɔ:] *n* gendre *m*,
beau-fils *m*

soon [su:n] *adv* bientôt; (*early*)
tôt; **~ afterwards** peu après; *see
also* **as**; **sooner** *adv* (*time*) plus
tôt; (*preference*): **I would sooner
do that** j'aimerais autant *or* je
préférerais faire ça; **sooner or later**
tôt ou tard

soothe [su:ð] *vt* calmer, apaiser

sophisticated [sə'fɪstɪkeɪtɪd] *adj*
raffiné(e), sophistiqué(e); (*machinery*)
hautement perfectionné(e), très
complexe

sophomore ['sɔfəmɔ:ʳ] *n* (*US*)
étudiant(e) de seconde année

soprano [sə'prɑ:nəu] *n* (*singer*)
soprano *m/f*

sorbet ['sɔ:beɪ] *n* sorbet *m*

sordid ['sɔ:dɪd] *adj* sordide

sore [sɔ:ʳ] *adj* (*painful*) douloureux(-
euse), sensible ▷ *n* plaie *f*

sorrow ['sɔrəu] *n* peine *f*, chagrin *m*

sorry ['sɔrɪ] *adj* désolé(e); (*condition,
excuse, tale*) triste, déplorable; **~!**
pardon!, excusez-moi!; **~?** pardon?;
to feel ~ for sb plaindre qn

sort [sɔ:t] *n* genre *m*, espèce *f*, sorte *f*;
(*make: of coffee, car etc*) marque *f* ▷ *vt*
(*also:* **~ out**: *select which to keep*) trier;
(*classify*) classer; (*tidy*) ranger; **sort
out** *vt* (*problem*) résoudre, régler

SOS *n* SOS *m*

so-so ['səusəu] *adv* comme ci
comme ça

sought [sɔ:t] *pt, pp of* **seek**

soul [səul] *n* âme *f*

sound [saund] *adj* (*healthy*) en bonne
santé, sain(e); (*safe, not damaged*)
solide, en bon état; (*reliable, not
superficial*) sérieux(-euse), solide;
(*sensible*) sensé(e) ▷ *adv*: **~ asleep**
profondément endormi(e) ▷ *n* (*noise,
volume*) son *m*; (*louder*) bruit *m*; (*Geo*)
détroit *m*, bras m de mer ▷ *vt* (*alarm*)
sonner ▷ *vi* sonner, retentir; (*fig: seem*)
sembler (être); **to ~ like** ressembler à;
sound bite *n* phrase toute faite (*pour
être citée dans les médias*); **soundtrack**
n (*of film*) bande *f* sonore

soup [su:p] *n* soupe *f*, potage *m*

sour ['sauəʳ] *adj* aigre; **it's ~ grapes**
c'est du dépit

source [sɔ:s] *n* source *f*

south [sauθ] *n* sud *m* ▷ *adj* sud *inv*;
(*wind*) du sud ▷ *adv* au sud, vers le
sud; **South Africa** *n* Afrique *f* du Sud;
South African *adj* sud-africain(e) ▷ *n*
Sud-Africain(e); **South America** *n*
Amérique *f* du Sud; **South American**
adj sud-américain(e) ▷ *n* Sud-
Américain(e); **southbound** *adj* en
direction du sud; (*carriageway*) sud *inv*;
south-east *n* sud-est *m*; **southern**
['sʌðən] *adj* (du) sud; méridional(e);
South Korea *n* Corée *f* du Sud;
South of France *n*: **the South of
France** le Sud de la France, le Midi;
South Pole *n*: **the South Pole** le
Pôle Sud; **southward(s)** *adv* vers le
sud; **south-west** *n* sud-ouest *m*

souvenir [su:vǝ'nɪəʳ] *n* souvenir
m (*objet*)

sovereign ['sɔvrɪn] *adj, n*
souverain(e)

sow¹ (*pt* **sowed**, *pp* **sown**) [səu, səud,
səun] *vt* semer

sow² *n* [sau] truie *f*

soya ['sɔɪə], (*US*) **soy** [sɔɪ] *n*: **~ bean**
graine *f* de soja; **~ sauce** sauce *f*
au soja

spa [spɑː] n (town) station thermale; (us: also: **health ~**) établissement m de cure de rajeunissement

space [speɪs] n (gen) espace m; (room) place f; espace; (length of time) laps m de temps ▷ cpd spatial(e) ▷ vt (also: **~ out**) espacer; **spacecraft** n engin or vaisseau spatial; **spaceship** n = **spacecraft**

spacious ['speɪʃəs] adj spacieux(-euse), grand(e)

spade [speɪd] n (tool) bêche f, pelle f; (child's) pelle; **spades** npl (Cards) pique m

spaghetti [spə'gɛtɪ] n spaghetti mpl

Spain [speɪn] n Espagne f

spam [spæm] n (Comput) pourriel m

span [spæn] n (of bird, plane) envergure f; (of arch) portée f; (in time) espace m de temps, durée f ▷ vt enjamber, franchir; (fig) couvrir, embrasser

Spaniard ['spænjəd] n Espagnol(e)

Spanish ['spænɪʃ] adj espagnol(e), d'Espagne ▷ n (Ling) espagnol m; **the Spanish** npl les Espagnols

spank [spæŋk] vt donner une fessée à

spanner ['spænər] n (BRIT) clé f (de mécanicien)

spare [spɛər] adj de réserve, de rechange; (surplus) de or en trop, de reste ▷ n (part) pièce f de rechange, pièce détachée ▷ vt (do without) se passer de; (afford to give) donner, accorder, passer; (not hurt) épargner; **to ~** (surplus) en surplus, de trop; **spare part** n pièce f de rechange, pièce détachée; **spare room** n chambre f d'ami; **spare time** n moments mpl de loisir; **spare tyre**, (us) **spare tire** n (Aut) pneu m de rechange; **spare wheel** n (Aut) roue f de secours

spark [spɑːk] n étincelle f

sparkle ['spɑːkl] n scintillement m, étincellement m, éclat m ▷ vi étinceler, scintiller

sparkling ['spɑːklɪŋ] adj (wine) mousseux(-euse), pétillant(e); (water) pétillant(e), gazeux(-euse)

spark plug n bougie f

sparrow ['spærəu] n moineau m

sparse [spɑːs] adj clairsemé(e)

spasm ['spæzəm] n (Med) spasme m

spat [spæt] pt, pp of **spit**

spate [speɪt] n (fig): **~ of** avalanche f or torrent m de

spatula ['spætjulə] n spatule f

speak (pt **spoke**, pp **spoken**) [spiːk, spəuk, 'spəukn] vt (language) parler; (truth) dire ▷ vi parler; (make a speech) prendre la parole; **to ~ to sb/of** or **about sth** parler à qn/de qch; **I don't ~ French** je ne parle pas français; **do you ~ English?** parlez-vous anglais?; **can I ~ to …?** est-ce que je peux parler à …?; **speaker** n (in public) orateur m; (also: **loudspeaker**) haut-parleur m; (for stereo etc) baffle m, enceinte f; (Pol): **the Speaker** (BRIT) le président de la Chambre des communes or des représentants; (us) le président de la Chambre

spear [spɪər] n lance f ▷ vt transpercer

special ['spɛʃl] adj spécial(e); **special delivery** n (Post): **by special delivery** en express; **special effects** npl (Cine) effets spéciaux; **specialist** n spécialiste m/f; **speciality** [spɛʃɪ'ælɪtɪ] n (BRIT) spécialité f; **specialize** vi: **to specialize (in)** se spécialiser (dans); **specially** adv spécialement, particulièrement; **special needs** npl (BRIT) difficultés fpl d'apprentissage scolaire; **special offer** n (Comm) réclame f; **special school** n (BRIT) établissement m d'enseignement spécialisé; **specialty** n (us) = **speciality**

species ['spiːʃiːz] n (pl inv) espèce f

specific [spə'sɪfɪk] adj (not vague) précis(e), explicite; (particular) particulier(-ière); **specifically** adv explicitement, précisément;

(*intend, ask, design*) expressément, spécialement

specify ['spεsıfaı] *vt* spécifier, préciser

specimen ['spεsımən] *n* spécimen *m*, échantillon *m*; (*Med: of blood*) prélèvement *m*; (: *of urine*) échantillon *m*

speck [spεk] *n* petite tache, petit point; (*particle*) grain *m*

spectacle ['spεktəkl] *n* spectacle *m*; **spectacles** *npl* (BRIT) lunettes *fpl*; **spectacular** [spεk'tækjuləʳ] *adj* spectaculaire

spectator [spεk'teıtəʳ] *n* spectateur(-trice)

spectrum (*pl* **spectra**) ['spεktrəm, -rə] *n* spectre *m*; (*fig*) gamme *f*

speculate ['spεkjuleıt] *vi* spéculer; (*ponder*): **to ~ about** s'interroger sur

sped [spεd] *pt, pp of* **speed**

speech [spi:tʃ] *n* (*faculty*) parole *f*; (*talk*) discours *m*, allocution *f*; (*manner of speaking*) façon *f* de parler, langage *m*; (*enunciation*) élocution *f*; **speechless** *adj* muet(te)

speed [spi:d] *n* vitesse *f*; (*promptness*) rapidité *f* ▷ *vi* (*pt, pp* **sped**) (*Aut: exceed speed limit*) faire un excès de vitesse; **at full** *or* **top ~** à toute vitesse *or* allure; **speed up** (*pt, pp* **speeded up**) *vi* aller plus vite, accélérer ▷ *vt* accélérer; **speedboat** *n* vedette *f*, hors-bord *m inv*; **speed camera** *n* (*Aut*) radar *m*; **speeding** *n* (*Aut*) excès *m* de vitesse; **speed limit** *n* limitation *f* de vitesse, vitesse maximale permise; **speedometer** [spı'dɔmıtəʳ] *n* compteur *m* (de vitesse); **speedy** *adj* rapide, prompt(e)

spell [spεl] *n* (*also:* **magic ~**) sortilège *m*, charme *m*; (*period of time*) (*courte*) période ▷ *vt* (*pt, pp* **spelled** *or* **spelt**) (*in writing*) écrire, orthographier; (*aloud*) épeler; (*fig*) signifier; **to cast a ~ on sb** jeter un sort à qn; **he can't ~** il fait

des fautes d'orthographe; **spell out** *vt* (*explain*): **to ~ sth out for sb** expliquer qch clairement à qn; **spellchecker** ['spεltʃεkəʳ] *n* (*Comput*) correcteur *m or* vérificateur *m* orthographique; **spelling** *n* orthographe *f*

spelt [spεlt] *pt, pp of* **spell**

spend (*pt, pp* **spent**) [spεnd, spεnt] *vt* (*money*) dépenser; (*time, life*) passer; (*devote*) consacrer; **spending** *n*: **government spending** les dépenses publiques

spent [spεnt] *pt, pp of* **spend** ▷ *adj* (*cartridge, bullets*) vide

sperm [spə:m] *n* spermatozoïde *m*; (*semen*) sperme *m*

sphere [sfıəʳ] *n* sphère *f*; (*fig*) sphère, domaine *m*

spice [spaıs] *n* épice *f* ▷ *vt* épicer

spicy ['spaısı] *adj* épicé(e), relevé(e); (*fig*) piquant(e)

spider ['spaıdəʳ] *n* araignée *f*

spike [spaık] *n* pointe *f*; (*Bot*) épi *m*

spill (*pt, pp* **spilt** *or* **spilled**) [spıl, -t, -d] *vt* renverser; répandre ▷ *vi* se répandre; **spill over** *vi* déborder

spilt [spılt] *pt, pp of* **spill**

spin [spın] (*pt, pp* **spun**) *n* (*revolution of wheel*) tour *m*; (*Aviat*) (*chute f en*) vrille *f*; (*trip in car*) petit tour, balade *f*; (*on ball*) effet *m* ▷ *vt* (*wool etc*) filer; (*wheel*) faire tourner ▷ *vi* (*turn*) tourner, tournoyer

spinach ['spınıtʃ] *n* épinards *mpl*

spinal ['spaınl] *adj* vertébral(e), spinal(e); **spinal cord** *n* moelle épinière

spin doctor *n* (*inf*) personne employée pour présenter un parti politique sous un jour favorable

spin-dryer [spın'draıəʳ] *n* (BRIT) essoreuse *f*

spine [spaın] *n* colonne vertébrale; (*thorn*) épine *f*, piquant *m*

spiral ['spaıərl] *n* spirale *f* ▷ *vi* (*fig: prices etc*) monter en flèche

spire [spaıəʳ] *n* flèche *f*, aiguille *f*

S

spirit ['spɪrɪt] n (soul) esprit m, âme f; (ghost) esprit, revenant m; (mood) esprit, état m d'esprit; (courage) courage m, énergie f; **spirits** npl (drink) spiritueux mpl, alcool m; **in good ~s** de bonne humeur

spiritual ['spɪrɪtjuəl] adj spirituel(le); (religious) religieux(-euse)

spit [spɪt] n (for roasting) broche f; (spittle) crachat m; (saliva) salive f ▷ vi (pt, pp **spat**) cracher; (sound) crépiter; (rain) crachiner

spite [spaɪt] n rancune f, dépit m ▷ vt contrarier, vexer; **in ~ of** en dépit de, malgré; **spiteful** adj malveillant(e), rancunier(-ière)

splash [splæʃ] n (sound) plouf m; (of colour) tache f ▷ vt éclabousser ▷ vi (also: **~ about**) barboter, patauger; **splash out** vi (BRIT) faire une folie

splendid ['splendɪd] adj splendide, superbe, magnifique

splinter ['splɪntər] n (wood) écharde f; (metal) éclat m ▷ vi (wood) se fendre; (glass) se briser

split [splɪt] (pt, pp **split**) n fente f, déchirure f; (fig: Pol) scission f ▷ vt fendre, déchirer; (party) diviser; (work, profits) partager, répartir ▷ vi (break) se fendre, se briser; (divide) se diviser; **split up** vi (couple) se séparer, rompre; (meeting) se disperser

spoil (pt, pp **spoiled** or **spoilt**) [spɔɪl, -d, -t] vt (damage) abîmer; (mar) gâcher; (child) gâter

spoilt [spɔɪlt] pt, pp of **spoil** ▷ adj (child) gâté(e); (ballot paper) nul(le)

spoke [spəuk] pt of **speak** ▷ n rayon m

spoken ['spəukn] pp of **speak**

spokesman ['spəuksmən] (irreg) n porte-parole m inv

spokesperson ['spəukspə:sn] (irreg) n porte-parole m inv

spokeswoman ['spəukswumən] (irreg) n porte-parole m inv

sponge [spʌndʒ] n éponge f; (Culin: also: **~ cake**) ≈ biscuit m de Savoie ▷ vt

éponger ▷ vi: **to ~ off** or **on** vivre aux crochets de; **sponge bag** n (BRIT) trousse f de toilette

sponsor ['spɒnsər] n (Radio, TV, Sport) sponsor m; (for application) parrain m, marraine f; (BRIT: for fund-raising event) donateur(-trice) ▷ vt sponsoriser; parrainer; faire un don à; **sponsorship** n sponsoring m; parrainage m; dons mpl

spontaneous [spɒn'teɪnɪəs] adj spontané(e)

spooky ['spu:kɪ] adj (inf) qui donne la chair de poule

spoon [spu:n] n cuiller f; **spoonful** n cuillerée f

sport [spɔ:t] n sport m; (person) chic type m/chic fille f ▷ vt (wear) arborer; **sport jacket** n (US) = **sports jacket**; **sports car** n voiture f de sport; **sports centre** (BRIT) n centre sportif; **sports jacket** n (BRIT) veste f de sport; **sportsman** (irreg) n sportif m; **sports utility vehicle** n véhicule m de loisirs (de type SUV); **sportswear** n vêtements mpl de sport; **sportswoman** (irreg) n sportive f; **sporty** adj sportif(-ive)

spot [spɒt] n tache f; (dot: on pattern) pois m; (pimple) bouton m; (place) endroit m, coin m ▷ vt (notice) apercevoir, repérer; **on the ~** sur place, sur les lieux; (immediately) sur le champ; **spotless** adj immaculé(e); **spotlight** n projecteur m; (Aut) phare m auxiliaire

spouse [spauz] n époux (épouse)

sprain [spreɪn] n entorse f, foulure f ▷ vt: **to ~ one's ankle** se fouler or se tordre la cheville

sprang [spræŋ] pt of **spring**

sprawl [sprɔ:l] vi s'étaler

spray [spreɪ] n jet m (en fines gouttelettes); (from sea) embruns mpl; (aerosol) vaporisateur m, bombe f; (for garden) pulvérisateur m; (of flowers) petit bouquet ▷ vt vaporiser, pulvériser; (crops) traiter

spread [sprɛd] (pt, pp **spread**) n (distribution) répartition f; (Culin) pâte f à tartiner ▷ (inf: meal) festin m ▷ vt (paste, contents) étendre, étaler; (rumour, disease) répandre, propager; (wealth) répartir ▷ vi s'étendre; se répandre; se propager; (stain) s'étaler; **spread out** vi (people) se disperser; **spreadsheet** n (Comput) tableur m

spree [spri:] n: **to go on a ~** faire la fête

spring [sprɪŋ] (pt **sprang**, pp **sprung**) n (season) printemps m; (leap) bond m, saut m; (coiled metal) ressort m; (of water) source f ▷ vi bondir, sauter; **spring up** vi (problem) se présenter, surgir; (plant, buildings) surgir de terre; **spring onion** n (BRIT) ciboule f, cive f

sprinkle ['sprɪŋkl] vt: **to ~ water etc on, ~ with water** etc asperger d'eau etc; **to ~ sugar etc on, ~ with sugar** etc saupoudrer de sucre etc

sprint [sprɪnt] n sprint m ▷ vi courir à toute vitesse; (Sport) sprinter

sprung [sprʌŋ] pp of **spring**

spun [spʌn] pt, pp of **spin**

spur [spəːʳ] n éperon m; (fig) aiguillon m ▷ vt (also: **~ on**) éperonner aiguillonner; **on the ~ of the moment** sous l'impulsion du moment

spurt [spəːt] n jet m; (of blood) jaillissement m; (of energy) regain m, sursaut m ▷ vi jaillir, gicler

spy [spaɪ] n espion(ne) ▷ vi: **to ~ on** espionner, épier ▷ vt (see) apercevoir

Sq. abbr (in address) = **square**

sq. abbr (Math etc) = **square**

squabble ['skwɔbl] vi se chamailler

squad [skwɔd] n (Mil, Police) escouade f, groupe m; (Football) contingent m

squadron ['skwɔdrn] n (Mil) escadron m; (Aviat, Naut) escadrille f

squander ['skwɔndəʳ] vt gaspiller, dilapider

square [skwɛəʳ] n carré m; (in town) place f ▷ adj carré(e) ▷ vt (arrange)

régler; arranger; (Math) élever au carré; (reconcile) concilier; **all ~** quitte; à égalité; **a ~ meal** un repas convenable; **2 metres ~** (de) 2 mètres sur 2; **1 ~ metre** 1 mètre carré; **square root** n racine carrée

squash [skwɔʃ] n (BRIT Sport) squash m; (US: vegetable) courge f; (drink): **lemon/orange ~** citronnade f/ orangeade f ▷ vt écraser

squat [skwɔt] adj petit(e) et épais(se), ramassé(e) ▷ vi (also: **~ down**) s'accroupir; **squatter** n squatter m

squeak [skwiːk] vi (hinge, wheel) grincer; (mouse) pousser un petit cri

squeal [skwiːl] vi pousser un or des cri(s) aigu(s) or perçant(s); (brakes) grincer

squeeze [skwiːz] n pression f ▷ vt presser; (hand, arm) serrer

squid [skwɪd] n calmar m

squint [skwɪnt] vi loucher

squirm [skwəːm] vi se tortiller

squirrel ['skwɪrəl] n écureuil m

squirt [skwəːt] vi jaillir, gicler ▷ vt faire gicler

Sr abbr = **senior**

Sri Lanka [srɪ'læŋkə] n Sri Lanka m

St abbr = **saint; street**

stab [stæb] n (with knife etc) coup m (de couteau etc); (of pain) lancée f; (inf: try): **to have a ~ at (doing) sth** s'essayer à (faire) qch ▷ vt poignarder

stability [stə'bɪlɪtɪ] n stabilité f

stable ['steɪbl] n écurie f ▷ adj stable

stack [stæk] n tas m, pile f ▷ vt empiler, entasser

stadium ['steɪdɪəm] n stade m

staff [stɑːf] n (work force) personnel m; (BRIT Scol: also: **teaching ~**) professeurs mpl, enseignants mpl, personnel enseignant ▷ vt pourvoir en personnel

stag [stæg] n cerf m

stage [steɪdʒ] n scène f; (platform) estrade f; (point) étape f, stade m; (profession): **the ~** le théâtre ▷ vt

S

(*play*) monter, mettre en scène; (*demonstration*) organiser; **in ~s** par étapes, par degrés

▮ Be careful not to translate *stage* by the French word *stage*.

stagger ['stægə^r] *vi* chanceler, tituber ▷ *vt* (*person: amaze*) stupéfier; (*hours, holidays*) étaler, échelonner; **staggering** *adj* (*amazing*) stupéfiant(e), renversant(e)

stagnant ['stægnənt] *adj* stagnant(e)

stag night, stag party *n* enterrement *m* de vie de garçon

stain [steɪn] *n* tache *f*; (*colouring*) colorant *m* ▷ *vt* tacher; (*wood*) teindre; **stained glass** *n* (*decorative*) verre coloré; (*in church*) vitraux *mpl*; **stainless steel** *n* inox *m*, acier *m* inoxydable

staircase ['steəkeɪs] *n* = **stairway**

stairs [steəz] *npl* escalier *m*

stairway ['steəweɪ] *n* escalier *m*

stake [steɪk] *n* pieu *m*, poteau *m*; (*Comm: interest*) intérêts *mpl*; (*Betting*) enjeu *m* ▷ *vt* risquer, jouer; (*also:* ~ **out**: *area*) marquer, délimiter; **to be at ~** être en jeu

stale [steɪl] *adj* (*bread*) rassis(e); (*food*) pas frais (fraîche); (*beer*) éventé(e); (*smell*) de renfermé; (*air*) confiné(e)

stalk [stɔːk] *n* tige *f* ▷ *vt* traquer

stall [stɔːl] *n* (*in street, market etc*) éventaire *m*, étal *m*; (*in stable*) stalle *f* ▷ *vt* (*Aut*) caler; (*fig: delay*) retarder ▷ *vi* (*Aut*) caler; (*fig*) essayer de gagner du temps; **stalls** *npl* (*BRIT: in cinema, theatre*) orchestre *m*

stamina ['stæmɪnə] *n* vigueur *f*, endurance *f*

stammer ['stæmə^r] *n* bégaiement *m* ▷ *vi* bégayer

stamp [stæmp] *n* timbre *m*; (*also:* **rubber ~**) tampon *m*; (*mark: also fig*) empreinte *f*; (*on document*) cachet *m* ▷ *vi* (*also:* **~ one's foot**) taper du pied ▷ *vt* (*letter*) timbrer; (*with rubber stamp*) tamponner; **stamp out** *vt*

(*fire*) piétiner; (*crime*) éradiquer; (*opposition*) éliminer; **stamped addressed envelope** *n* (*BRIT*) enveloppe affranchie pour la réponse

stampede [stæm'piːd] *n* ruée *f*; (*of cattle*) débandade *f*

stance [stæns] *n* position *f*

stand [stænd] (*pt, pp* **stood**) *n* (*position*) position *f*; (*for taxis*) station *f* (de taxis); (*Comm*) étalage *m*, stand *m*; (*Sport: also:* ~**s**) tribune *f*; (*also:* **music ~**) pupitre *m* ▷ *vi* être or se tenir (debout); (*rise*) se lever, se mettre debout; (*be placed*) se trouver; (*remain: offer etc*) rester valable ▷ *vt* (*place*) mettre, poser; (*tolerate, withstand*) supporter; (*treat, invite*) offrir, payer; **to make a ~** prendre position; **to ~ for parliament** (*BRIT*) se présenter aux élections (*comme candidat à la députation*); **I can't ~ him** je ne peux pas le voir; **stand back** *vi* (*move back*) reculer, s'écarter; **stand by** *vi* (*be ready*) se tenir prêt(e) ▷ *vt fus* (*opinion*) s'en tenir à; (*person*) ne pas abandonner, soutenir; **stand down** *vi* (*withdraw*) se retirer; **stand for** *vt fus* (*signify*) représenter, signifier; (*tolerate*) supporter, tolérer; **stand in for** *vt fus* remplacer; **stand out** *vi* (*be prominent*) ressortir; **stand up** *vi* (*rise*) se lever, se mettre debout; **stand up for** *vt fus* défendre; **stand up to** *vt fus* tenir tête à, résister à

standard ['stændəd] *n* (*norm*) norme *f*, étalon *m*; (*level*) niveau *m* (voulu); (*criterion*) critère *m*; (*flag*) étendard *m* ▷ *adj* (*size etc*) ordinaire, normal(e); (*model, feature*) standard *inv*; (*practice*) courant(e); (*text*) de base; **standards** *npl* (*morals*) morale *f*, principes *mpl*; **standard of living** *n* niveau *m* de vie

stand-by ticket *n* (*Aviat*) billet *m* stand-by

standing ['stændɪŋ] *adj* debout *inv*; (*permanent*) permanent(e) ▷ *n* réputation *f*, rang *m*, standing *m*; **of many years' ~** qui dure or existe depuis longtemps; **standing order** n (BRIT: at bank) virement m automatique, prélèvement m bancaire

stand: standpoint n point m de vue; **standstill** n: **at a standstill** à l'arrêt; (fig) au point mort; **to come to a standstill** s'immobiliser, s'arrêter

stank [stæŋk] pt of **stink**

staple ['steɪpl] n (for papers) agrafe f ▷ adj (food, crop, industry etc) de base principal(e) ▷ vt agrafer

star [stɑːʳ] n étoile f; (celebrity) vedette f ▷ vt (Cine) avoir pour vedette; **stars** npl; **the ~s** (Astrology) l'horoscope m

starboard ['stɑːbəd] n tribord m

starch [stɑːtʃ] n amidon m; (in food) fécule f

stardom ['stɑːdəm] n célébrité f

stare [stɛəʳ] n regard m fixe ▷ vi: **to ~ at** regarder fixement

stark [stɑːk] adj (bleak) désolé(e), morne ▷ adv: **~ naked** complètement nu(e)

start [stɑːt] n commencement m, début m; (of race) départ m; (sudden movement) sursaut m; (advantage) avance f, avantage m ▷ vt commencer; (cause: fight) déclencher; (rumour) donner naissance à; (fashion) lancer; (found: business, newspaper) lancer, créer; (engine) mettre en marche ▷ vi (begin) commencer; (begin journey) partir, se mettre en route; (jump) sursauter; **when does the film ~?** à quelle heure est-ce que le film commence?; **to ~ doing** or **to do sth** se mettre à faire qch; **start off** vi commencer; (leave) partir; **start out** vi (begin) commencer; (set out) partir; **start up** vi commencer; (car) démarrer ▷ vt (fight) déclencher; (business) créer; (car) mettre en marche; **starter** n (Aut) démarreur m; (Sport: official) starter m; (BRIT Culin) entrée f; **starting point** n point m de départ

startle ['stɑːtl] vt faire sursauter; donner un choc à; **startling** adj surprenant(e), saisissant(e)

starvation [stɑːˈveɪʃən] n faim f, famine f

starve [stɑːv] vi mourir de faim ▷ vt laisser mourir de faim

state [steɪt] n état m; (Pol) État ▷ vt (declare) déclarer, affirmer; (specify) indiquer, spécifier; **States** npl; **the S~s** les États-Unis; **to be in a ~** être dans tous ses états; **stately home** ['steɪtlɪ-] n manoir m or château m (ouvert au public); **statement** n déclaration f; (Law) déposition f; **state school** n école publique; **statesman** (irreg) n homme m d'État

static ['stætɪk] n (Radio) parasites mpl; (also: **~ electricity**) électricité f statique ▷ adj statique

station ['steɪʃən] n gare f; (also: **police ~**) poste m or commissariat m (de police) ▷ vt placer, poster

stationary ['steɪʃnərɪ] adj à l'arrêt, immobile

stationer's (shop) n (BRIT) papeterie f

stationery ['steɪʃnərɪ] n papier m à lettres, petit matériel de bureau

station wagon n (US) break m

statistic [stəˈtɪstɪk] n statistique f; **statistics** n (science) statistique f

statue ['stætjuː] n statue f

stature ['stætʃəʳ] n stature f; (fig) envergure f

status ['steɪtəs] n position f, situation f; (prestige) prestige m; (Admin, official position) statut m; **status quo** [-ˈkwəu] n: **the status quo** le statu quo

statutory ['stætjutrɪ] adj statutaire, prévu(e) par un article de loi

staunch [stɔːntʃ] adj sûr(e), loyal(e)

stay [steɪ] n (period of time) séjour m ▷ vi rester; (reside) loger; (spend some time) séjourner; **to ~ put** ne pas bouger; **to ~ the night** passer la nuit; **stay away** vi (from person, building) ne pas s'approcher; (*from event*) ne pas venir; **stay behind** vi rester en arrière; **stay in** vi (*at home*) rester à la maison; **stay on** vi rester; **stay out** vi (*of house*) ne pas rentrer; (*strikers*) rester en grève; **stay up** vi (*at night*) ne pas se coucher

steadily ['stɛdɪlɪ] adv (*regularly*) progressivement; (*firmly*) fermement; (*walk*) d'un pas ferme; (*fixedly: look*) sans détourner les yeux

steady ['stɛdɪ] adj stable, solide, ferme; (*regular*) constant(e), régulier(-ière); (*person*) calme, pondéré(e) ▷ vt assurer, stabiliser; (*nerves*) calmer; **a ~ boyfriend** un petit ami

steak [steɪk] n (*meat*) bifteck m, steak m; (*fish, pork*) tranche f

steal (*pt* **stole**, *pp* **stolen**) [stiːl, stəul, 'stəuln] vt, vi voler; (*move*) se faufiler, se déplacer furtivement; **my wallet has been stolen** on m'a volé mon portefeuille

steam [stiːm] n vapeur f ▷ vt (*Culin*) cuire à la vapeur ▷ vi fumer; **steam up** vi (*window*) se couvrir de buée; **to get ~ed up about sth** (*fig: inf*) s'exciter à propos de qch; **steamy** adj humide; (*window*) embué(e); (*sexy*) torride

steel [stiːl] n acier m ▷ cpd d'acier

steep [stiːp] adj raide, escarpé(e); (*price*) très élevé(e), excessif(-ive) ▷ vt (faire) tremper

steeple ['stiːpl] n clocher m

steer [stɪər] vt diriger; (*boat*) gouverner; (*lead: person*) guider, conduire ▷ vi tenir le gouvernail; **steering** n (*Aut*) conduite f; **steering wheel** n volant m

stem [stɛm] n (*of plant*) tige f; (*of glass*) pied m ▷ vt contenir, endiguer; (*attack, spread of disease*) juguler

step [stɛp] n pas m; (*stair*) marche f; (*action*) mesure f, disposition f ▷ vi: **to ~ forward/back** faire un pas en avant/arrière, avancer/reculer; **steps** npl (BRIT) = **stepladder**; **to**

be in/out of ~ (with) (*fig*) aller dans le sens de/être déphasé(e) (par rapport à); **step down** vi (*fig*) se retirer, se désister; **step in** vi (*fig*) intervenir; **step up** vt (*production, sales*) augmenter; (*campaign, efforts*) intensifier; **stepbrother** n demi-frère m; **stepchild** (*pl* **stepchildren**) n beau-fils m, belle-fille f; **stepdaughter** n belle-fille f; **stepfather** n beau-père m; **stepladder** n (BRIT) escabeau m; **stepmother** n belle-mère f; **stepsister** n demi-sœur f; **stepson** n beau-fils m

stereo ['stɛrɪəu] n (*sound*) stéréo f; (*hi-fi*) chaîne f stéréo ▷ adj (*also:* **~phonic**) stéréo(phonique)

stereotype ['stɪərɪətaɪp] n stéréotype m ▷ vt stéréotyper

sterile ['stɛraɪl] adj stérile; **sterilize** ['stɛrɪlaɪz] vt stériliser

sterling ['stəːlɪŋ] adj (*silver*) de bon aloi, fin(e) ▷ n (*currency*) livre f sterling inv

stern [stəːn] adj sévère ▷ n (*Naut*) arrière m, poupe f

steroid ['stɪərɔɪd] n stéroïde m

stew [stjuː] n ragoût m ▷ vt, vi cuire à la casserole

steward ['stjuəd] n (*Aviat, Naut, Rail*) steward m; **stewardess** n hôtesse f

stick [stɪk] (*pt, pp* **stuck**) n bâton m; (*for walking*) canne f; (*of chalk etc*) morceau m ▷ vt (*glue*) coller; (*thrust*): **to ~ sth into** piquer or planter or enfoncer qch dans; (*inf: put*) mettre, fourrer; (: *tolerate*) supporter ▷ vi (*adhere*) tenir, coller; (*remain*) rester; (*get jammed: door, lift*) se bloquer; **stick out** vi dépasser, sortir; **stick up** vi dépasser, sortir; **stick up for** vt fus défendre; **sticker** n auto-collant m; **sticking plaster** n sparadrap m, pansement adhésif; **stick insect** n phasme m; **stick shift** n (US Aut) levier m de vitesses

sticky ['stɪkɪ] *adj* poisseux(-euse); (*label*) adhésif(-ive); (*fig: situation*) délicat(e)

stiff [stɪf] *adj* (*gen*) raide, rigide; (*door, brush*) dur(e); (*difficult*) difficile, ardu(e); (*cold*) froid(e), distant(e); (*strong, high*) fort(e), élevé(e) ▷ *adv*: **to be bored/scared/frozen ~** s'ennuyer à mourir/être mort(e) de peur/froid

stifling ['staɪflɪŋ] *adj* (*heat*) suffocant(e)

stigma ['stɪgmə] *n* stigmate *m*

stiletto [stɪˈlɛtəu] *n* (BRIT: *also*: **~ heel**) talon *m* aiguille

still [stɪl] *adj* immobile ▷ *adv* (*up to this time*) encore, toujours; (*even*) encore; (*nonetheless*) quand même, tout de même

stimulate ['stɪmjuleɪt] *vt* stimuler

stimulus (*pl* **stimuli**) ['stɪmjuləs, 'stɪmjulaɪ] *n* stimulant *m*; (*Biol, Psych*) stimulus *m*

sting [stɪŋ] *n* piqûre *f*; (*organ*) dard *m* ▷ *vt, vi* (*pt, pp* **stung**) piquer

stink [stɪŋk] *n* puanteur *f* ▷ *vi* (*pt* **stank**, *pp* **stunk**) puer, empester

stir [stəːʳ] *n* agitation *f*, sensation *f* ▷ *vt* remuer ▷ *vi* remuer, bouger; **stir up** *vt* (*trouble*) fomenter, provoquer; **stir-fry** *vt* faire sauter ▷ *n*: **vegetable stir-fry** légumes sautés à la poêle

stitch [stɪtʃ] *n* (*Sewing*) point *m*; (*Knitting*) maille *f*; (*Med*) point de suture; (*pain*) point de côté ▷ *vt* coudre, piquer; (*Med*) suturer

stock [stɔk] *n* réserve *f*, provision *f*; (*Comm*) stock *m*; (*Agr*) cheptel *m*, bétail *m*; (*Culin*) bouillon *m*; (*Finance*) valeurs *fpl*, titres *mpl*; (*descent, origin*) souche *f* ▷ *adj* (*fig: reply etc*) classique ▷ *vt* (*have in stock*) avoir, vendre; **in ~** en stock, en magasin; **out of ~** épuisé(e); **to take ~** (*fig*) faire le point; **~s and shares** valeurs (mobilières), titres; **stockbroker** ['stɔkbrəukəʳ] *n* agent *m* de

change; **stock cube** *n* (BRIT *Culin*) bouillon-cube *m*; **stock exchange** *n* Bourse *f* (des valeurs); **stockholder** ['stɔkhəuldəʳ] *n* (US) actionnaire *m/f*

stocking ['stɔkɪŋ] *n* bas *m*

stock market *n* Bourse *f*, marché financier

stole [stəul] *pt of* **steal** ▷ *n* étole *f*

stolen ['stəuln] *pp of* **steal**

stomach ['stʌmək] *n* estomac *m*; (*abdomen*) ventre *m* ▷ *vt* supporter, digérer; **stomachache** *n* mal *m* à l'estomac *or* au ventre

stone [stəun] *n* pierre *f*; (*pebble*) caillou *m*, galet *m*; (*in fruit*) noyau *m*; (*Med*) calcul *m*; (BRIT: *weight*) = 6.348 kg; 14 pounds ▷ *cpd* de *or* en pierre ▷ *vt* (*person*) lancer des pierres sur, lapider; (*fruit*) dénoyauter

stood [stud] *pt, pp of* **stand**

stool [stuːl] *n* tabouret *m*

stoop [stuːp] *vi* (*also*: **have a ~**) être voûté(e); (*also*: **~ down**: *bend*) se baisser, se courber

stop [stɔp] *n* arrêt *m*; (*in punctuation*) point *m* ▷ *vt* arrêter; (*break off*) interrompre; (*also*: **put a ~ to**) mettre fin à; (*prevent*) empêcher ▷ *vi* s'arrêter; (*rain, noise etc*) cesser, s'arrêter; **to ~ doing sth** cesser or arrêter de faire qch; **to ~ sb (from) doing sth** empêcher qn de faire qch; **~ it!** arrête!; **stop by** *vi* s'arrêter (au passage); **stop off** *vi* faire une courte halte; **stopover** *n* halte *f*; (*Aviat*) escale *f*; **stoppage** *n* (*strike*) arrêt *m* de travail; (*obstruction*) obstruction *f*

storage ['stɔːrɪdʒ] *n* emmagasinage *m*

store [stɔːʳ] *n* (*stock*) provision *f*, réserve *f*; (*depot*) entrepôt *m*; (BRIT: *large shop*) grand magasin; (US: *shop*) magasin *m* ▷ *vt* emmagasiner; (*information*) enregistrer; **stores** *npl* (*food*) provisions; **who knows what is in ~ for us?** qui sait ce que l'avenir nous réserve *or* ce qui nous attend?; **storekeeper** *n* (US) commerçant(e)

S

storey, (US) **story** ['stɔːrɪ] *n* étage *m*
storm [stɔːm] *n* tempête *f*;
(*thunderstorm*) orage *m* ▷ *vi* (*fig*)
fulminer ▷ *vt* prendre d'assaut;
stormy *adj* orageux(-euse)
story ['stɔːrɪ] *n* histoire *f*; (*Press:
article*) article *m*; (US) = **storey**
stout [staut] *adj* (*strong*) solide;
(*fat*) gros(se), corpulent(e) ▷ *n* bière
brune
stove [stəuv] *n* (*for cooking*) fourneau
m (: *small*) réchaud *m*; (*for heating*)
poêle *m*
straight [streɪt] *adj* droit(e);
(*hair*) raide; (*frank*) franc
(franche); (*simple*) simple ▷ *adv* (tout)
droit; (*drink*) sec, sans eau; **to put**
or **get ~** mettre en ordre, mettre de
l'ordre dans; (*fig*) mettre au clair; **~
away, ~ off** (*at once*) tout de suite;
straighten *vt* ajuster; (*bed*) arranger;
straighten out *vt* (*fig*) débrouiller;
straighten up *vi* (*stand up*) se
redresser; **straightforward** *adj*
simple; (*frank*) honnête, direct(e)
strain [streɪn] *n* (*Tech*) tension *f*;
pression *f*; (*physical*) effort *m*; (*mental*)
tension (nerveuse); (*Med*) entorse *f*;
(*breed: of plants*) variété *f*; (: *of animals*)
race *f* ▷ *vt* (*fig: resources etc*) mettre à
rude épreuve, grever; (*hurt: back etc*)
se faire mal à; (*vegetables*) égoutter;
strains *npl* (*Mus*) accords *mpl*, accents
mpl; **strained** *adj* (*muscle*) froissé(e);
(*laugh etc*) forcé(e), contraint(e);
(*relations*) tendu(e); **strainer** *n*
passoire *f*
strait [streɪt] *n* (*Geo*) détroit *m*;
straits *npl*; **to be in dire ~s** (*fig*) avoir
de sérieux ennuis
strand [strænd] *n* (*of thread*) fil *m*, brin
m; (*of rope*) toron *m*; (*of hair*) mèche *f*
▷ *vt* (*boat*) échouer; **stranded** *adj* en
rade, en plan
strange [streɪndʒ] *adj* (*not
known*) inconnu(e); (*odd*)
étrange, bizarre; **strangely** *adv*
étrangement, bizarrement; *see also*

enough; **stranger** *n* (*unknown*)
inconnu(e); (*from somewhere else*)
étranger(-ère)
strangle ['stræŋgl] *vt* étrangler
strap [stræp] *n* lanière *f*, courroie *f*,
sangle *f*; (*of slip, dress*) bretelle *f*
strategic [strə'tiːdʒɪk] *adj*
stratégique
strategy ['strætɪdʒɪ] *n* stratégie *f*
straw [strɔː] *n* paille *f*; **that's the
last ~!** ça c'est le comble!
strawberry ['strɔːbərɪ] *n* fraise *f*
stray [streɪ] *adj* (*animal*) perdu(e),
errant(e); (*scattered*) isolé(e) ▷ *vi*
s'égarer; **~ bullet** balle perdue
streak [striːk] *n* bande *f*, filet *m*; (*in
hair*) raie *f* ▷ *vt* zébrer, strier
stream [striːm] *n* (*brook*) ruisseau *m*;
(*current*) courant *m*, flot *m*; (*of people*)
défilé ininterrompu, flot *m* ▷ *vt* (*Scol*)
répartir par niveau ▷ *vi* ruisseler; **to ~
in/out** entrer/sortir à flots
street [striːt] *n* rue *f*; **streetcar** *n* (US)
tramway *m*; **street light** *n* réverbère
m; **street map**, **street plan** *n* plan
m des rues
strength [strɛŋθ] *n* force *f*; (*of girder,
knot etc*) solidité *f*; **strengthen** *vt*
renforcer; (*muscle*) fortifier; (*building,
Econ*) consolider
strenuous ['strɛnjuəs] *adj*
vigoureux(-euse), énergique; (*tiring*)
ardu(e), fatigant(e)
stress [strɛs] *n* (*force, pressure*)
pression *f*; (*mental strain*) tension
(nerveuse), stress *m*; (*accent*) accent
m; (*emphasis*) insistance *f* ▷ *vt* insister
sur, souligner; (*syllable*) accentuer;
stressed *adj* (*tense*) stressé(e);
(*syllable*) accentué(e); **stressful** *adj*
(*job*) stressant(e)
stretch [strɛtʃ] *n* (*of sand etc*) étendue
f ▷ *vi* s'étirer; (*extend*): **to ~ to** *or* **as
far as** s'étendre jusqu'à ▷ *vt* tendre,
étirer; (*fig*) pousser (au maximum); **at
a ~** d'affilée; **stretch out** *vi* s'étendre
▷ *vt* (*arm etc*) allonger, tendre; (*to
spread*) étendre

stretcher ['strɛtʃəʳ] n brancard m, civière f

strict [strɪkt] adj strict(e); **strictly** adv strictement

stridden ['strɪdn] pp of **stride**

stride [straɪd] n grand pas, enjambée f ▷ vi (pt **strode**, pp **stridden**) marcher à grands pas

strike [straɪk] (pt, pp **struck**) n grève f; (of oil etc) découverte f; (attack) raid m ▷ vt frapper; (oil etc) trouver, découvrir; (make: agreement, deal) conclure ▷ vi faire grève; (attack) attaquer; (clock) sonner; **to go on** or **come out on ~** se mettre en grève, faire grève; **to ~ a match** frotter une allumette; **striker** n gréviste m/f; (Sport) buteur m; **striking** adj frappant(e), saisissant(e); (attractive) éblouissant(e)

string [strɪŋ] n ficelle f, fil m; (row: of beads) rang m; (Mus) corde f ▷ vt (pt, pp **strung**): **to ~ out** échelonner; **to ~ together** enchaîner; **the strings** npl (Mus) les instruments mpl à cordes; **to pull ~s** (fig) faire jouer le piston

strip [strɪp] n bande f; (Sport) tenue f ▷ vt (undress) déshabiller; (paint) décaper; (fig) dégarnir, dépouiller; (also: ~ **down**) (machine) démonter ▷ vi se déshabiller; **strip off** vt (paint etc) décaper ▷ vi (person) se déshabiller

stripe [straɪp] n raie f, rayure f; (Mil) galon m; **striped** adj rayé(e), à rayures

stripper ['strɪpəʳ] n strip-teaseuse f

strip-search ['strɪpsə:tʃ] vt: **to ~ sb** fouiller qn (en le faisant se déshabiller)

strive (pt **strove**, pp **striven**) [straɪv, strəuv, 'strɪvn] vi: **to ~ to do/for sth** s'efforcer de faire/d'obtenir qch

strode [strəud] pt of **stride**

stroke [strəuk] n coup m; (Med) attaque f; (Swimming: style) (sorte f de) nage f ▷ vt caresser; **at a ~** d'un (seul) coup

stroll [strəul] n petite promenade ▷ vi flâner, se promener nonchalamment; **stroller** n (US: for child) poussette f

strong [strɔŋ] adj (gen) fort(e); (healthy) vigoureux(-euse); (heart, nerves) solide; **they are 50 ~** ils sont au nombre de 50; **stronghold** n forteresse f, fort m; (fig) bastion m; **strongly** adv fortement, avec force; vigoureusement; solidement

strove [strəuv] pt of **strive**

struck [strʌk] pt, pp of **strike**

structure ['strʌktʃəʳ] n structure f; (building) construction f

struggle ['strʌgl] n lutte f ▷ vi lutter, se battre

strung [strʌŋ] pt, pp of **string**

stub [stʌb] n (of cigarette) bout m, mégot m; (of ticket etc) talon m ▷ vt: **to ~ one's toe (on sth)** se heurter le doigt de pied (contre qch); **stub out** vt écraser

stubble ['stʌbl] n chaume m; (on chin) barbe f de plusieurs jours

stubborn ['stʌbən] adj têtu(e), obstiné(e), opiniâtre

stuck [stʌk] pt, pp of **stick** ▷ adj (jammed) bloqué(e), coincé(e)

stud [stʌd] n (on boots etc) clou m; (collar stud) bouton m de col; (earring) petite boucle d'oreille; (of horses: also: ~ **farm**) écurie f, haras m; (also: ~ **horse**) étalon m ▷ vt (fig): **~ded with** parsemé(e) or criblé(e) de

student ['stju:dənt] n étudiant(e) ▷ adj (life) estudiantin(e), étudiant(e), d'étudiant; (residence, restaurant) universitaire; (loan, movement) étudiant; **student driver** n (US) (conducteur(-trice)) débutant(e); **students' union** n (BRIT: association) ≈ union f des étudiants; (: building) ≈ foyer m des étudiants

studio ['stju:dɪəu] n studio m, atelier m; (TV etc) studio; **studio flat**, (US) **studio apartment** n studio m

study ['stʌdɪ] n étude f; (room) bureau m ▷ vt étudier; (examine) examiner ▷ vi étudier, faire ses études

stuff [stʌf] n (gen) chose(s) f(pl), truc m; (belongings) affaires fpl, trucs; (substance) substance f ▷ vt rembourrer; (Culin) farcir; (inf: push) fourrer; **stuffing** n bourre f, rembourrage m; (Culin) farce f; **stuffy** adj (room) mal ventilé(e) or aéré(e); (ideas) vieux jeu inv

stumble ['stʌmbl] vi trébucher; **to ~ across** or **on** (fig) tomber sur

stump [stʌmp] n souche f; (of limb) moignon m ▷ vt: **to be ~ed** sécher, ne pas savoir que répondre

stun [stʌn] vt (blow) étourdir; (news) abasourdir, stupéfier

stung [stʌŋ] pt, pp of **sting**

stunk [stʌŋk] pp of **stink**

stunned [stʌnd] adj assommé(e); (fig) sidéré(e)

stunning ['stʌnɪŋ] adj (beautiful) étourdissant(e); (news etc) stupéfiant(e)

stunt [stʌnt] n (in film) cascade f, acrobatie f; (publicity) truc m publicitaire ▷ vt retarder, arrêter

stupid ['stjuːpɪd] adj stupide, bête; **stupidity** [stjuːˈpɪdɪtɪ] n stupidité f, bêtise f

sturdy ['stəːdɪ] adj (person, plant) robuste, vigoureux(-euse); (object) solide

stutter ['stʌtər] n bégaiement m ▷ vi bégayer

style [staɪl] n style m; (distinction) allure f, cachet m, style; (design) modèle m; **stylish** adj élégant(e), chic inv; **stylist** n (hair stylist) coiffeur(-euse)

sub... [sʌb] prefix sub..., sous-; **subconscious** adj subconscient(e)

subdued [səbˈdjuːd] adj (light) tamisé(e); (person) qui a perdu de son entrain

subject n ['sʌbdʒɪkt] sujet m; (Scol) matière f ▷ vt [səbˈdʒɛkt]: **to ~ to** soumettre à; **to be ~ to** (law) être soumis(e) à; **subjective** [səbˈdʒɛktɪv] adj subjectif(-ive); **subject matter** n (content) contenu m

subjunctive [səbˈdʒʌŋktɪv] n subjonctif m

submarine [sʌbməˈriːn] n sous-marin m

submission [səbˈmɪʃən] n soumission f

submit [səbˈmɪt] vt soumettre ▷ vi se soumettre

subordinate [səˈbɔːdɪnət] adj (junior) subalterne; (Grammar) subordonné(e) ▷ n subordonné(e)

subscribe [səbˈskraɪb] vi cotiser; **to ~ to** (opinion, fund) souscrire à; (newspaper) s'abonner à; être abonné(e) à

subscription [səbˈskrɪpʃən] n (to magazine etc) abonnement m

subsequent ['sʌbsɪkwənt] adj ultérieur(e), suivant(e); **subsequently** adv par la suite

subside [səbˈsaɪd] vi (land) s'affaisser; (flood) baisser; (wind, feelings) tomber

subsidiary [səbˈsɪdɪərɪ] adj subsidiaire; accessoire; (Brit Scol: subject) complémentaire ▷ n filiale f

subsidize ['sʌbsɪdaɪz] vt subventionner

subsidy ['sʌbsɪdɪ] n subvention f

substance ['sʌbstəns] n substance f

substantial [səbˈstænʃl] adj substantiel(le); (fig) important(e)

substitute ['sʌbstɪtjuːt] n (person) remplaçant(e); (thing) succédané m ▷ vt: **to ~ sth/sb for** substituer qch/qn à, remplacer par qch/qn; **substitution** n substitution f

subtitles ['sʌbtaɪtlz] npl (Cine) sous-titres mpl

subtle ['sʌtl] adj subtil(e)

subtract [səbˈtrækt] vt soustraire, retrancher

suburb ['sʌbəːb] n faubourg m; **the ~s** la banlieue; **suburban** [səˈbəːbən] adj de banlieue, suburbain(e)

subway ['sʌbweɪ] *n* (BRIT: *underpass*) passage souterrain; (US: *railway*) métro *m*

succeed [sək'siːd] *vi* réussir ▷ *vt* succéder à; **to ~ in doing** réussir à faire

success [sək'sɛs] *n* succès *m*; réussite *f*; **successful** *adj* (*business*) prospère, qui réussit; (*attempt*) couronné(e) de succès; **to be successful (in doing)** réussir (à faire); **successfully** *adv* avec succès

succession [sək'sɛʃən] *n* succession *f*

successive [sək'sɛsɪv] *adj* successif(-ive)

successor [sək'sɛsə^r] *n* successeur *m*

succumb [sə'kʌm] *vi* succomber

such [sʌtʃ] *adj* tel (telle); (*of that kind*): **~ a book** un livre de ce genre or pareil, un tel livre; (*so much*): **~ courage** un tel courage ▷ *adv* si; **~ a long trip** un si long voyage; **~ a lot of** tellement or tant de; **~ as** (*like*) tel (telle) que, comme; **as ~** *adv* en tant que tel (telle), à proprement parler; **such-and-such** *adj* tel ou tel (telle ou telle)

suck [sʌk] *vt* sucer; (*breast, bottle*) téter

Sudan [su'dɑːn] *n* Soudan *m*

sudden ['sʌdn] *adj* soudain(e), subit(e); **all of a ~** soudain, tout à coup; **suddenly** *adv* brusquement, tout à coup, soudain

sudoku [su'dəʊkuː] *n* sudoku *m*

sue [suː] *vt* poursuivre en justice, intenter un procès à

suede [sweɪd] *n* daim *m*, cuir suédé

suffer ['sʌfə^r] *vt* souffrir, subir; (*bear*) tolérer, supporter, subir ▷ *vi* souffrir; **to ~ from** (*illness*) souffrir de, avoir; **suffering** *n* souffrance(s) *f(pl)*

suffice [sə'faɪs] *vi* suffire

sufficient [sə'fɪʃənt] *adj* suffisant(e)

suffocate ['sʌfəkeɪt] *vi* suffoquer; étouffer

sugar ['ʃʊgə^r] *n* sucre *m* ▷ *vt* sucrer

suggest [sə'dʒɛst] *vt* suggérer, proposer; (*indicate*) sembler indiquer; **suggestion** *n* suggestion *f*

suicide ['suɪsaɪd] *n* suicide *m*; **~ bombing** attentat *m* suicide; *see also* **commit**; **suicide bomber** *n* kamikaze *m/f*

suit [suːt] *n* (*man's*) costume *m*, complet *m*; (*woman's*) tailleur *m*, ensemble *m*; (*Cards*) couleur *f*; (*lawsuit*) procès *m* ▷ *vt* (*subj: clothes, hairstyle*) aller à; (*be convenient for*) convenir à; (*adapt*): **to ~ sth to** adapter or approprier qch à; **well ~ed** (*couple*) faits l'un pour l'autre, très bien assortis; **suitable** *adj* qui convient; approprié(e), adéquat(e); **suitcase** *n* valise *f*

suite [swiːt] *n* (*of rooms, also Mus*) suite *f*; (*furniture*): **bedroom/dining room ~** (*ensemble m de*) chambre *f* à coucher/salle *f* à manger; **a three-piece ~** un salon (canapé et deux fauteuils)

sulfur ['sʌlfə^r] (US) *n* = **sulphur**

sulk [sʌlk] *vi* bouder

sulphur, (US) **sulfur** ['sʌlfə^r] *n* soufre *m*

sultana [sʌl'tɑːnə] *n* (*fruit*) raisin (sec) de Smyrne

sum [sʌm] *n* somme *f*; (*Scol etc*) calcul *m*; **sum up** *vt* résumer ▷ *vi* résumer

summarize ['sʌməraɪz] *vt* résumer

summary ['sʌmərɪ] *n* résumé *m*

summer ['sʌmə^r] *n* été *m* ▷ *cpd* d'été, estival(e); **in (the) ~** en été, pendant l'été; **summer holidays** *npl* grandes vacances; **summertime** *n* (*season*) été *m*

summit ['sʌmɪt] *n* sommet *m*; (*also:* **~ conference**) (conférence *f* au) sommet *m*

summon ['sʌmən] *vt* appeler, convoquer; **to ~ a witness** citer or assigner un témoin

sun [sʌn] *n* soleil *m*

Sun. *abbr* (= *Sunday*) dim

sun: **sunbathe** *vi* prendre un bain de soleil; **sunbed** *n* lit pliant; (*with sun lamp*) lit à ultra-violets; **sunblock** *n* écran *m* total; **sunburn** *n* coup *m* de

S

soleil; **sunburned, sunburnt** *adj* bronzé(e), hâlé(e); *(painfully)* brûlé(e) par le soleil

Sunday [ˈsʌndɪ] *n* dimanche *m*

sunflower [ˈsʌnflaʊəʳ] *n* tournesol *m*

sung [sʌŋ] *pp of* **sing**

sunglasses [ˈsʌnɡlɑːsɪz] *npl* lunettes *fpl* de soleil

sunk [sʌŋk] *pp of* **sink**

sun: sunlight *n* (lumière *f* du) soleil *m*; **sun lounger** *n* chaise longue; **sunny** *adj* ensoleillé(e); **it is sunny** il fait (du) soleil, il y a du soleil; **sunrise** *n* lever *m* du soleil; **sun roof** *n* (Aut) toit ouvrant; **sunscreen** *n* crème *f* solaire; **sunset** *n* coucher *m* du soleil; **sunshade** *n* (over table) parasol *m*; **sunshine** *n* (lumière *f* du) soleil *m*; **sunstroke** *n* insolation *f*, coup *m* de soleil; **suntan** *n* bronzage *m*; **suntan lotion** *n* lotion *f* or lait *m* solaire; **suntan oil** *n* huile *f* solaire

super [ˈsuːpəʳ] *adj* (inf) formidable

superb [suːˈpəːb] *adj* superbe, magnifique

superficial [suːpəˈfɪʃəl] *adj* superficiel(le)

superintendent [suːpərɪnˈtɛndənt] *n* directeur(-trice); (Police) ≈ commissaire *m*

superior [suːˈpɪərɪəʳ] *adj* supérieur(e); (smug) condescendant(e), méprisant(e) ▷ *n* supérieur(e)

superlative [suːˈpəːlətɪv] *n* (Ling) superlatif *m*

supermarket [ˈsuːpəmɑːkɪt] *n* supermarché *m*

supernatural [suːpəˈnætʃərəl] *adj* surnaturel(le) ▷ *n*: **the ~** le surnaturel

superpower [ˈsuːpəpaʊəʳ] *n* (Pol) superpuissance *f*

superstition [suːpəˈstɪʃən] *n* superstition *f*

superstitious [suːpəˈstɪʃəs] *adj* superstitieux(-euse)

superstore [ˈsuːpəstɔːʳ] *n* (BRIT) hypermarché *m*, grande surface

supervise [ˈsuːpəvaɪz] *vt* (children etc) surveiller; (organization, work) diriger; **supervision** [suːpəˈvɪʒən] *n* surveillance *f*; (monitoring) contrôle *m*, (management) direction *f*; **supervisor** *n* surveillant(e); (in shop) chef *m* de rayon

supper [ˈsʌpəʳ] *n* dîner *m*; (late) souper *m*

supple [ˈsʌpl] *adj* souple

supplement *n* [ˈsʌplɪmənt] supplément *m* ▷ *vt* [sʌplɪˈmɛnt] ajouter à, compléter

supplier [səˈplaɪəʳ] *n* fournisseur *m*

supply [səˈplaɪ] *vt* (provide) fournir; (equip): **to ~ (with)** approvisionner or ravitailler (en); fournir (en) ▷ *n* provision *f*, réserve *f*; (supplying) approvisionnement *m*; **supplies** *npl* (food) vivres *mpl*; (Mil) subsistances *fpl*

support [səˈpɔːt] *n* (moral, financial etc) soutien *m*, appui *m*; (Tech) support *m*, soutien ▷ *vt* soutenir, supporter; (financially) subvenir aux besoins de; (uphold) être pour, être partisan de, appuyer; (Sport: team) être pour; **supporter** *n* (Pol etc) partisan(e); (Sport) supporter *m*

suppose [səˈpəʊz] *vt, vi* supposer; imaginer; **to be ~d to do/be** être censé(e) faire/être; **supposedly** [səˈpəʊzɪdlɪ] *adv* soi-disant; **supposing** *conj* si, à supposer que + sub

suppress [səˈprɛs] *vt* (revolt, feeling) réprimer; (information) faire disparaître; (scandal, yawn) étouffer

supreme [suːˈpriːm] *adj* suprême

surcharge [ˈsəːtʃɑːdʒ] *n* surcharge *f*

sure [ʃuəʳ] *adj* (gen) sûr(e); (definite, convinced) sûr, certain(e); **~!** (of course) bien sûr!; **~ enough** effectivement; **to make ~ of sth/that** s'assurer de qch/que, vérifier qch/que; **surely** *adv* sûrement; certainement

surf [səːf] *n* (waves) ressac *m* ▷ *vt*: **to ~ the Net** surfer sur Internet, surfer sur le Net

surface ['sə:fɪs] n surface f ▷ vt (road) poser un revêtement sur ▷ vi remonter à la surface; (fig) faire surface; **by ~ mail** par voie de terre; (by sea) par voie maritime

surfboard ['sə:fbɔ:d] n planche f de surf

surfer ['sə:fəʳ] n (in sea) surfeur(-euse); **web** or **Net ~** internaute m/f

surfing ['sə:fɪŋ] n (in sea) surf m

surge [sə:dʒ] n (of emotion) vague f ▷ vi déferler

surgeon ['sə:dʒən] n chirurgien m

surgery ['sə:dʒərɪ] n chirurgie f; (BRIT: room) cabinet m (de consultation); (also: **~ hours**) heures fpl de consultation

surname ['sə:neɪm] n nom m de famille

surpass [sə:'pɑ:s] vt surpasser, dépasser

surplus ['sə:pləs] n surplus m, excédent m ▷ adj en surplus, de trop; (Comm) excédentaire

surprise [sə'praɪz] n (gen) surprise f; (astonishment) étonnement m ▷ vt surprendre, étonner; **surprised** adj (look, smile) surpris(e), étonné(e); **to be surprised** être surpris; **surprising** adj surprenant(e), étonnant(e); **surprisingly** adv (easy, helpful) étonnamment, étrangement; **(somewhat) surprisingly, he agreed** curieusement, il a accepté

surrender [sə'rɛndəʳ] n reddition f, capitulation f ▷ vi se rendre, capituler

surround [sə'raund] vt entourer; (Mil etc) encercler; **surrounding** adj environnant(e); **surroundings** npl environs mpl, alentours mpl

surveillance [sə:'veɪləns] n surveillance f

survey n ['sə:veɪ] enquête f, étude f; (in house buying etc) inspection f, (rapport m d')expertise f; (of land) levé m ▷ vt [sə:'veɪ] (situation) passer en revue; (examine carefully) inspecter;

(building) expertiser; (land) faire le levé de; (look at) embrasser du regard; **surveyor** n (of building) expert m; (of land) (arpenteur m) géomètre m

survival [sə'vaɪvl] n survie f

survive [sə'vaɪv] vi survivre; (custom etc) subsister ▷ vt (accident etc) survivre à, réchapper de; (person) survivre à; **survivor** n survivant(e)

suspect adj, n ['sʌspɛkt] suspect(e) ▷ vt [səs'pɛkt] soupçonner, suspecter

suspend [səs'pɛnd] vt suspendre; **suspended sentence** n (Law) condamnation f avec sursis; **suspenders** npl (BRIT) jarretelles fpl; (US) bretelles fpl

suspense [səs'pɛns] n attente f, incertitude f; (in film etc) suspense m; **to keep sb in ~** tenir qn en suspens, laisser qn dans l'incertitude

suspension [səs'pɛnʃən] n (gen, Aut) suspension f; (of driving licence) retrait m provisoire; **suspension bridge** n pont suspendu

suspicion [səs'pɪʃən] n soupçon(s) m(pl); **suspicious** adj (suspecting) soupçonneux(-euse), méfiant(e); (causing suspicion) suspect(e)

sustain [səs'teɪn] vt soutenir; (subj: food) nourrir, donner des forces à; (damage) subir; (injury) recevoir

SUV n abbr (esp US: = sports utility vehicle) SUV m, véhicule m de loisirs

swallow ['swɔləu] n (bird) hirondelle f ▷ vt avaler; (fig: story) gober

swam [swæm] pt of **swim**

swamp [swɔmp] n marais m, marécage m ▷ vt submerger

swan [swɔn] n cygne m

swap [swɔp] n échange m, troc m ▷ vt: **to ~ (for)** échanger (contre), troquer (contre)

swarm [swɔ:m] n essaim m ▷ vi (bees) essaimer; (people) grouiller; **to be ~ing with** grouiller de

sway [sweɪ] vi se balancer, osciller ▷ vt (influence) influencer

S

swear [swɛəʳ] (pt **swore**, pp **sworn**) vt, vi jurer; **swear in** vt assermenter; **swearword** n gros mot, juron m

sweat [swɛt] n sueur f, transpiration f ▷ vi suer

sweater ['swɛtəʳ] n tricot m, pull m

sweatshirt ['swɛtʃəːt] n sweat-shirt m

sweaty ['swɛtɪ] adj en sueur, moite or mouillé(e) de sueur

Swede [swiːd] n Suédois(e)

swede [swiːd] n (BRIT) rutabaga m

Sweden ['swiːdn] n Suède f; **Swedish** ['swiːdɪʃ] adj suédois(e) ▷ n (Ling) suédois m

sweep [swiːp] (pt, pp **swept**) n (curve) grande courbe; (also: **chimney ~**) ramoneur m ▷ vt balayer; (subj: current) emporter

sweet [swiːt] n (BRIT: pudding) dessert m; (candy) bonbon m ▷ adj doux (douce); (not savoury) sucré(e); (kind) gentil(le); (baby) mignon(ne); **sweetcorn** n maïs doux; **sweetener** ['swiːtnəʳ] n (Culin) édulcorant m; **sweetheart** n amoureux(-euse); **sweetshop** n (BRIT) confiserie f

swell [swɛl] (pt **swelled**, pp **swollen** or **swelled**) n (of sea) houle f ▷ adj (US inf: excellent) chouette ▷ vt (increase) grossir, augmenter ▷ vi (increase) grossir, augmenter; (sound) s'enfler; (Med: also: **~ up**) enfler; **swelling** n (Med) enflure f (: lump) grosseur f

swept [swɛpt] pt, pp of **sweep**

swerve [swəːv] vi (to avoid obstacle) faire une embardée or un écart; (off the road) dévier

swift [swɪft] n (bird) martinet m ▷ adj rapide, prompt(e)

swim [swɪm] (pt **swam**, pp **swum**) n: **to go for a ~** aller nager or se baigner ▷ vi nager; (Sport) faire de la natation; (fig: head, room) tourner ▷ vt traverser (à la nage); **to ~ a length** nager une longueur; **swimmer** n nageur(-euse); **swimming** n nage f, natation f; **swimming costume** n

(BRIT) maillot m (de bain); **swimming pool** n piscine f; **swimming trunks** npl maillot m de bain; **swimsuit** n maillot m (de bain)

swine flu ['swaɪn-] n grippe f A

swing [swɪŋ] (pt, pp **swung**) n (in playground) balançoire f; (movement) balancement m, oscillations fpl; (change in opinion etc) revirement m ▷ vt balancer, faire osciller; (also: **~ round**) tourner, faire virer ▷ vi se balancer, osciller; (also: **~ round**) virer, tourner; **to be in full ~** battre son plein

swipe card ['swaɪp-] n carte f magnétique

swirl [swəːl] vi tourbillonner, tournoyer

Swiss [swɪs] adj suisse ▷ n (pl inv) Suisse(-esse)

switch [swɪtʃ] n (for light, radio etc) bouton m; (change) changement m, revirement m ▷ vt (change) changer; **switch off** vt éteindre; (engine, machine) arrêter; **could you ~ off the light?** pouvez-vous éteindre la lumière?; **switch on** vt allumer; (engine, machine) mettre en marche; **switchboard** n (Tel) standard m

Switzerland ['swɪtsələnd] n Suisse f

swivel ['swɪvl] vi (also: **~ round**) pivoter, tourner

swollen ['swəulən] pp of **swell**

swoop [swuːp] n (by police etc) rafle f, descente f ▷ vi (bird: also: **~ down**) descendre en piqué, piquer

swop [swɔp] n, vt = **swap**

sword [sɔːd] n épée f; **swordfish** n espadon m

swore [swɔːʳ] pt of **swear**

sworn [swɔːn] pp of **swear** ▷ adj (statement, evidence) donné(e) sous serment; (enemy) juré(e)

swum [swʌm] pp of **swim**

swung [swʌŋ] pt, pp of **swing**

syllable ['sɪləbl] n syllabe f

syllabus ['sɪləbəs] n programme m

symbol ['sɪmbl] *n* symbole *m*;
  symbolic(al) [sɪm'bɔlɪk(l)] *adj*
  symbolique
symmetrical [sɪ'mɛtrɪkl] *adj*
  symétrique
symmetry ['sɪmɪtrɪ] *n* symétrie *f*
sympathetic [sɪmpə'θɛtɪk] *adj*
  (*showing pity*) compatissant(e);
  (*understanding*) bienveillant(e),
  compréhensif(-ive); **~ towards** bien
  disposé(e) envers

  > Be careful not to translate
  > *sympathetic* by the French word
  > *sympathique*.

sympathize ['sɪmpəθaɪz] *vi*: **to
  ~ with sb** plaindre qn; (*in grief*)
  s'associer à la douleur de qn; **to ~
  with sth** comprendre qch
sympathy ['sɪmpəθɪ] *n* (*pity*)
  compassion *f*
symphony ['sɪmfənɪ] *n* symphonie *f*
symptom ['sɪmptəm] *n* symptôme
  m; indice *m*
synagogue ['sɪnəgɔg] *n* synagogue *f*
syndicate ['sɪndɪkɪt] *n* syndicat
  m, coopérative *f*; (*Press*) agence *f*
  de presse
syndrome ['sɪndrəum] *n*
  syndrome *m*
synonym ['sɪnənɪm] *n* synonyme *m*
synthetic [sɪn'θɛtɪk] *adj* synthétique
Syria ['sɪrɪə] *n* Syrie *f*
syringe [sɪ'rɪndʒ] *n* seringue *f*
syrup ['sɪrəp] *n* sirop *m*; (*BRIT: also:*
  golden ~) mélasse raffinée
system ['sɪstəm] *n* système *m*;
  (*Anat*) organisme *m*; **systematic**
  [sɪstə'mætɪk] *adj* systématique;
  méthodique; **systems analyst** *n*
  analyste-programmeur *m/f*

ta [tɑː] *excl* (*BRIT inf*) merci!
tab [tæb] *n* (*label*) étiquette *f*; (*on
  drinks can etc*) languette *f*; **to keep ~s
  on** (*fig*) surveiller
table ['teɪbl] *n* table *f* ⊳ *vt* (*BRIT:
  motion etc*) présenter; **to lay** *or*
  set the ~ mettre le couvert *or* la
  table; **tablecloth** *n* nappe *f*; **table
  d'hôte** [tɑːbl'dəut] *adj* (*meal*)
  à prix fixe; **table lamp** *n* lampe
  décorative *or* de table; **tablemat** *n*
  (*for plate*) napperon *m*, set *m*; (*for
  hot dish*) dessous-de-plat *m inv*;
  tablespoon *n* cuiller *f* de service;
  (*also:* **tablespoonful**: *as measurement*)
  cuillerée *f* à soupe
tablet ['tæblɪt] *n* (*Med*) comprimé *m*;
  (*Comput*) tablette *f* (tactile); (*of stone*)
  plaque *f*
table tennis *n* ping-pong *m*
tabloid ['tæblɔɪd] *n* (*newspaper*)
  quotidien *m* populaire
taboo [tə'buː] *adj*, *n* tabou (*m*)

t

tack [tæk] n (nail) petit clou; (fig) direction f ▷ vt (nail) clouer; (sew) bâtir ▷ vi (Naut) tirer un or des bord(s); **to ~ sth on to (the end of) sth** (of letter, book) rajouter qch à la fin de qch

tackle ['tækl] n matériel m, équipement m; (for lifting) appareil m de levage; (Football, Rugby) plaquage m ▷ vt (difficulty, animal, burglar) s'attaquer à; (person: challenge) s'expliquer avec; (Football, Rugby) plaquer

tacky ['tækɪ] adj collant(e); (paint) pas sec (sèche); (pej: poor-quality) minable; (: showing bad taste) ringard(e)

tact [tækt] n tact m; **tactful** adj plein(e) de tact

tactics ['tæktɪks] npl tactique f

tactless ['tæktlɪs] adj qui manque de tact

tadpole ['tædpəʊl] n têtard m

taffy ['tæfɪ] n (US) (bonbon m au) caramel m

tag [tæg] n étiquette f

tail [teɪl] n queue f; (of shirt) pan m ▷ vt (follow) suivre, filer; **tails** npl (suit) habit m; see also **head**

tailor ['teɪlər] n tailleur m (artisan)

Taiwan ['taɪ'wɑːn] n Taïwan (no article); **Taiwanese** [taɪwəˈniːz] adj taïwanais(e) ▷ n inv Taïwanais(e)

take [teɪk] (pt **took**, pp **taken**) vt prendre; (gain: prize) remporter; (require: effort, courage) demander; (tolerate) accepter, supporter; (hold: passengers etc) contenir; (accompany) emmener, accompagner; (bring, carry) apporter, emporter; (exam) passer, se présenter à; **to ~ sth from** (drawer etc) prendre qch dans; (person) prendre qch à; **I ~ it that** je suppose que; **to be ~n ill** tomber malade; **it won't ~ long** ça ne prendra pas longtemps; **I was quite ~n with her/it** elle/cela m'a beaucoup plu; **take after** vt fus ressembler à; **take apart** vt démonter; **take away** vt (carry off) emporter; (remove) enlever; (subtract) soustraire; **take back** vt (return) rendre, rapporter; (one's words) retirer; **take down** vt (building) démolir; (letter etc) prendre, écrire; **take in** vt (deceive) tromper, rouler; (understand) comprendre, saisir; (include) couvrir, inclure; (lodger) prendre; (dress, waistband) reprendre; **take off** vi (Aviat) décoller ▷ vt (remove) enlever; **take on** vt (work) accepter, se charger de; (employee) prendre, embaucher; (opponent) accepter de se battre contre; **take out** vt sortir; (remove) enlever; (invite) sortir avec; **to ~ sth out of** (out of drawer etc) prendre qch dans; **to ~ sb out to a restaurant** emmener qn au restaurant; **take over** vt (business) reprendre ▷ vi: **to ~ over from sb** prendre la relève de qn; **take up** vt (one's story) reprendre; (dress) raccourcir; (occupy: time, space) prendre, occuper; (engage in: hobby etc) se mettre à; (accept: offer, challenge) accepter; **takeaway** (BRIT) adj (food) à emporter ▷ n (shop, restaurant) ≈ magasin m qui vend des plats à emporter; **taken** pp of **take**; **takeoff** n (Aviat) décollage m; **takeout** adj, n (US) = **takeaway**; **takeover** n (Comm) rachat m; **takings** npl (Comm) recette f

talc [tælk] n (also: **~um powder**) talc m

tale [teɪl] n (story) conte m, histoire f; (account) récit m; **to tell ~s** (fig) rapporter

talent ['tælnt] n talent m, don m; **talented** adj doué(e), plein(e) de talent

talk [tɔːk] n (a speech) causerie f, exposé m; (conversation) discussion f; (interview) entretien m; (gossip) racontars mpl (pej) ▷ vi parler; (chatter) bavarder; **talks** npl (Pol etc) entretiens mpl; **to ~ about** parler de; **to ~ sb out of/into doing** persuader qn de ne pas faire/de faire; **to ~ shop** parler métier or affaires; **talk over** vt discuter (de); **talk show** n (TV, Radio) émission-débat f

tall [tɔːl] adj (person) grand(e); (building, tree) haut(e); **to be 6 feet ~** ≈ mesurer 1 mètre 80

tambourine [tæmbə'riːn] n tambourin m

tame [teɪm] adj apprivoisé(e); (fig: story, style) insipide

tamper ['tæmpə'] vi: **to ~ with** toucher à (en cachette ou sans permission)

tampon ['tæmpən] n tampon m hygiénique or périodique

tan [tæn] n (also: **sun~**) bronzage m ⊳ vt, vi bronzer, brunir ⊳ adj (colour) marron clair inv

tandem ['tændəm] n tandem m

tangerine [tændʒə'riːn] n mandarine f

tangle ['tæŋgl] n enchevêtrement m; **to get in(to) a ~** s'emmêler

tank [tæŋk] n réservoir m; (for fish) aquarium m; (Mil) char m d'assaut, tank m

tanker ['tæŋkə'] n (ship) pétrolier m, tanker m; (truck) camion-citerne m

tanned [tænd] adj bronzé(e)

tantrum ['tæntrəm] n accès m de colère

Tanzania [tænzə'nɪə] n Tanzanie f

tap [tæp] n (on sink etc) robinet m; (gentle blow) petite tape f ⊳ vt frapper or taper légèrement; (resources) exploiter, utiliser; (telephone) mettre sur écoute; **on ~** (fig: resources) disponible; **tap dancing** n claquettes fpl

tape [teɪp] n (for tying) ruban m; (also: **magnetic ~**) bande f (magnétique); (cassette) cassette f; (sticky) Scotch® m ⊳ vt (record) enregistrer (au magnétoscope or sur cassette); (stick) coller avec du Scotch®; **tape measure** n mètre m à ruban; **tape recorder** n magnétophone m

tapestry ['tæpɪstrɪ] n tapisserie f

tar [tɑː] n goudron m

target ['tɑːgɪt] n cible f; (fig: objective) objectif m

tariff ['tærɪf] n (Comm) tarif m; (taxes) tarif douanier

tarmac ['tɑːmæk] n (BRIT: on road) macadam m; (Aviat) aire f d'envol

tarpaulin [tɑː'pɔːlɪn] n bâche goudronnée

tarragon ['tærəgən] n estragon m

tart [tɑːt] n (Culin) tarte f; (BRIT inf: pej: prostitute) poule f ⊳ adj (flavour) âpre, aigrelet(te)

tartan ['tɑːtn] n tartan m ⊳ adj écossais(e)

tartar(e) sauce ['tɑːtə-] n sauce f tartare

task [tɑːsk] n tâche f; **to take to ~** prendre à partie

taste [teɪst] n goût m; (fig: glimpse, idea) idée f, aperçu m ⊳ vt goûter ⊳ vi: **to ~ of** (fish etc) avoir le or un goût de; **you can ~ the garlic (in it)** on sent bien l'ail; **to have a ~ of sth** goûter (à) qch; **can I have a ~?** je peux goûter?; **to be in good/bad** or **poor ~** être de bon/mauvais goût; **tasteful** adj de bon goût; **tasteless** adj (food) insipide; (remark) de mauvais goût; **tasty** adj savoureux(-euse), délicieux(-euse)

tatters ['tætəz] npl: **in ~** (also: **tattered**) en lambeaux

tattoo [tə'tuː] n tatouage m; (spectacle) parade f militaire ⊳ vt tatouer

taught [tɔːt] pt, pp of **teach**

taunt [tɔːnt] n raillerie f ⊳ vt railler

Taurus ['tɔːrəs] n le Taureau

taut [tɔːt] adj tendu(e)

tax [tæks] n (on goods etc) taxe f; (on income) impôts mpl, contributions fpl ⊳ vt taxer; imposer; (fig: patience etc) mettre à l'épreuve; **tax disc** n (BRIT Aut) vignette f (automobile); **tax-free** adj exempt(e) d'impôts

taxi ['tæksɪ] n taxi m ⊳ vi (Aviat) rouler (lentement) au sol; **taxi driver** n

t

chauffeur *m* de taxi; **taxi rank**, (US) **taxi stand** *n* station *f* de taxis

tax payer [-peɪə^r] *n* contribuable *m/f*

tax return *n* déclaration *f* d'impôts *or* de revenus

TB *n abbr* = **tuberculosis**

tbc *abbr* = **to be confirmed**

tea [tiː] *n* thé *m*; (BRIT: *snack: for children*) goûter *m*; **high ~** (BRIT) *collation combinant goûter et dîner*; **tea bag** *n* sachet *m* de thé; **tea break** *n* (BRIT) pause-thé *f*

teach (*pt, pp* **taught**) [tiːtʃ, tɔːt] *vt*: **to ~ sb sth, to ~ sth to sb** apprendre qch à qn; (*in school etc*) enseigner qch à qn ▷ *vi* enseigner; **teacher** *n* (*in secondary school*) professeur *m*; (*in primary school*) instituteur(-trice); **teaching** *n* enseignement *m*; **teaching assistant** *n* aide-éducateur(-trice)

tea: teacup *n* tasse *f* à thé; **tea leaves** *npl* feuilles *fpl* de thé

team [tiːm] *n* équipe *f*; (*of animals*) attelage *m*; **team up** *vi*: **to ~ up (with)** faire équipe (avec)

teapot [ˈtiːpɔt] *n* théière *f*

tear¹ [tɪə^r] *n* larme *f*; **in ~s** en larmes

tear² [tɛə^r] (*pt* **tore**, *pp* **torn**) *n* déchirure *f* ▷ *vt* déchirer ▷ *vi* se déchirer; **tear apart** *vt* (*also fig*) déchirer; **tear down** *vt* (*building, statue*) démolir; (*poster, flag*) arracher; **tear off** *vt* (*sheet of paper etc*) arracher; (*one's clothes*) enlever à toute vitesse; **tear up** *vt* (*sheet of paper etc*) déchirer, mettre en morceaux *or* pièces

tearful [ˈtɪəful] *adj* larmoyant(e)

tear gas [ˈtɪə-] *n* gaz *m* lacrymogène

tearoom [ˈtiːruːm] *n* salon *m* de thé

tease [tiːz] *vt* taquiner; (*unkindly*) tourmenter

tea: teaspoon *n* petite cuiller; (*also*: **teaspoonful**: *as measurement*) ≈ cuillerée *f* à café; **teatime** *n* l'heure *f* du thé; **tea towel** *n* (BRIT) torchon *m* (à vaisselle)

technical [ˈtɛknɪkl] *adj* technique

technician [tɛkˈnɪʃən] *n* technicien(ne)

technique [tɛkˈniːk] *n* technique *f*

technology [tɛkˈnɔlədʒɪ] *n* technologie *f*

teddy (bear) [ˈtɛdɪ-] *n* ours *m* (en peluche)

tedious [ˈtiːdɪəs] *adj* fastidieux(-euse)

tee [tiː] *n* (*Golf*) tee *m*

teen [tiːn] *adj* = **teenage** ▷ *n* (US) = **teenager**

teenage [ˈtiːneɪdʒ] *adj* (*fashions etc*) pour jeunes, pour adolescents; (*child*) qui est adolescent(e); **teenager** *n* adolescent(e)

teens [tiːnz] *npl*; **to be in one's ~** être adolescent(e)

teeth [tiːθ] *npl of* **tooth**

teetotal [ˈtiːˈtəutl] *adj* (*person*) qui ne boit jamais d'alcool

telecommunications [ˈtɛlɪkəmjuːnɪˈkeɪʃənz] *n* télécommunications *fpl*

telegram [ˈtɛlɪgræm] *n* télégramme *m*

telegraph pole [ˈtɛlɪgrɑː-f-] *n* poteau *m* télégraphique

telephone [ˈtɛlɪfəun] *n* téléphone *m* ▷ *vt* (*person*) téléphoner à; (*message*) téléphoner; **to be on the ~** (*be speaking*) être au téléphone; **telephone book** *n* = **telephone directory**; **telephone box**, (US) **telephone booth** *n* cabine *f* téléphonique; **telephone call** *n* appel *m* téléphonique; **telephone directory** *n* annuaire *m* (du téléphone); **telephone number** *n* numéro *m* de téléphone

telesales [ˈtɛlɪseɪlz] *npl* télévente *f*

telescope [ˈtɛlɪskəup] *n* télescope *m*

televise [ˈtɛlɪvaɪz] *vt* téléviser

television [ˈtɛlɪvɪʒən] *n* télévision *f*; **on ~** à la télévision; **television programme** *n* (BRIT) émission *f* de télévision

tell (*pt*, *pp* **told**) [tɛl, təʊld] *vt* dire; (*relate*: *story*) raconter; (*distinguish*): **to ~ sth from** distinguer qch de ▷ *vi* (*talk*): **to ~ of** parler de; (*have effect*) se faire sentir, se voir; **to ~ sb to do** dire à qn de faire; **to ~ the time** (*know how to*) savoir lire l'heure; **tell off** *vt* réprimander, gronder; **teller** *n* (*in bank*) caissier(-ière)

telly ['tɛlɪ] *n abbr* (BRIT inf: = *television*) télé *f*

temp [tɛmp] *n* (BRIT: = *temporary worker*) intérimaire *m/f* ▷ *vi* travailler comme intérimaire

temper ['tɛmpər] *n* (*nature*) caractère *m*; (*mood*) humeur *f*; (*fit of anger*) colère *f* ▷ *vt* (*moderate*) tempérer, adoucir; **to be in a ~** être en colère; **to lose one's ~** se mettre en colère

temperament ['tɛmprəmənt] *n* (*nature*) tempérament *m*; **temperamental** [tɛmprə'mɛntl] *adj* capricieux(-euse)

temperature ['tɛmprətʃər] *n* température *f*; **to have** *or* **run a ~** avoir de la fièvre

temple ['tɛmpl] *n* (*building*) temple *m*; (*Anat*) tempe *f*

temporary ['tɛmpərərɪ] *adj* temporaire, provisoire; (*job, worker*) temporaire

tempt [tɛmpt] *vt* tenter; **to ~ sb into doing** induire qn à faire; **temptation** *n* tentation *f*; **tempting** *adj* tentant(e); (*food*) appétissant(e)

ten [tɛn] *num* dix

tenant ['tɛnənt] *n* locataire *m/f*

tend [tɛnd] *vt* s'occuper de ▷ *vi*: **to ~ to do** avoir tendance à faire; **tendency** ['tɛndənsɪ] *n* tendance *f*

tender ['tɛndər] *adj* tendre; (*delicate*) délicat(e); (*sore*) sensible ▷ *n* (*Comm: offer*) soumission *f*; (*money*): **legal ~** cours légal ▷ *vt* offrir

tendon ['tɛndən] *n* tendon *m*

tenner ['tɛnər] *n* (BRIT inf) billet *m* de dix livres

tennis ['tɛnɪs] *n* tennis *m*; **tennis ball** *n* balle *f* de tennis; **tennis court** *n* (court *m* de) tennis *m*; **tennis match** *n* match *m* de tennis; **tennis player** *n* joueur(-euse) de tennis; **tennis racket** *n* raquette *f* de tennis

tenor ['tɛnər] *n* (*Mus*) ténor *m*

tenpin bowling ['tɛnpɪn-] *n* (BRIT) bowling *m* (à 10 quilles)

tense [tɛns] *adj* tendu(e) ▷ *n* (*Ling*) temps *m*

tension ['tɛnʃən] *n* tension *f*

tent [tɛnt] *n* tente *f*

tentative ['tɛntətɪv] *adj* timide, hésitant(e); (*conclusion*) provisoire

tenth [tɛnθ] *num* dixième

tent: tent peg *n* piquet *m* de tente; **tent pole** *n* montant *m* de tente

tepid ['tɛpɪd] *adj* tiède

term [tə:m] *n* terme *m*; (*Scol*) trimestre *m* ▷ *vt* appeler; **terms** *npl* (*conditions*) conditions *fpl*; (*Comm*) tarif *m*; **in the short/long ~** à court/long terme; **to come to ~s with** (*problem*) faire face à; **to be on good ~s with** bien s'entendre avec, être en bons termes avec

terminal ['tə:mɪnl] *adj* (*disease*) dans sa phase terminale; (*patient*) incurable ▷ *n* (*Elec*) borne *f*; (*for oil, ore etc: also Comput*) terminal *m*; (*also:* **air ~**) aérogare *f*; (BRIT: *also:* **coach ~**) gare routière

terminate ['tə:mɪneɪt] *vt* mettre fin à; (*pregnancy*) interrompre

termini ['tə:mɪnaɪ] *npl of* **terminus**

terminology [tə:mɪ'nɔlədʒɪ] *n* terminologie *f*

terminus (*pl* **termini**) ['tə:mɪnəs, 'tə:mɪnaɪ] *n* terminus *m inv*

terrace ['tɛrəs] *n* terrasse *f*; (BRIT: *row of houses*) rangée *f* de maisons (*attenantes les unes aux autres*); **the ~s** (BRIT Sport) les gradins *mpl*; **terraced** *adj* (*garden*) en terrasses; (*in a row: house*) attenant(e) aux maisons voisines

terrain [tɛ'reɪn] *n* terrain *m* (*sol*)

terrestrial [tɪˈrɛstrɪəl] *adj* terrestre
terrible [ˈtɛrɪbl] *adj* terrible, atroce;
(*weather, work*) affreux(-euse),
épouvantable; **terribly** *adv*
terriblement; (*very badly*)
affreusement mal
terrier [ˈtɛrɪəʳ] *n* terrier *m* (*chien*)
terrific [təˈrɪfɪk] *adj* (*very
great*) fantastique, incroyable,
terrible; (*wonderful*) formidable,
sensationnel(le)
terrified [ˈtɛrɪfaɪd] *adj* terrifié(e); **to
be ~ of sth** avoir très peur de qch
terrify [ˈtɛrɪfaɪ] *vt* terrifier; **terrifying**
adj terrifiant(e)
territorial [tɛrɪˈtɔːrɪəl] *adj*
territorial(e)
territory [ˈtɛrɪtərɪ] *n* territoire *m*
terror [ˈtɛrəʳ] *n* terreur *f*; **terrorism** *n*
terrorisme *m*; **terrorist** *n* terroriste
m/f; **terrorist attack** *n* attentat *m*
terroriste
test [tɛst] *n* (*trial, check*) essai *m*;
(*of courage etc*) épreuve *f*; (*Med*)
examen *m*; (*Chem*) analyse *f*; (*Scol*)
interrogation *f* de contrôle; (*also:
driving ~*) (examen du) permis *m*
de conduire ▷ *vt* essayer; mettre à
l'épreuve; examiner; analyser; faire
subir une interrogation à
testicle [ˈtɛstɪkl] *n* testicule *m*
testify [ˈtɛstɪfaɪ] *vi* (*Law*) témoigner,
déposer; **to ~ to sth** (*Law*) attester
qch
testimony [ˈtɛstɪmənɪ] *n* (*Law*)
témoignage *m*, déposition *f*
test: test match *n* (*Cricket, Rugby*)
match international; **test tube** *n*
éprouvette *f*
tetanus [ˈtɛtənəs] *n* tétanos *m*
text [tɛkst] *n* texte *m*; (*on mobile
phone*) SMS *m inv*, texto® *m* ▷ *vt*
(*inf*) envoyer un SMS or texto® à;
textbook *n* manuel *m*
textile [ˈtɛkstaɪl] *n* textile *m*
text message *n* SMS *m inv*, texto® *m*
text messaging [-ˈmɛsɪdʒɪŋ] *n*
messagerie textuelle

texture [ˈtɛkstʃəʳ] *n* texture *f*; (*of skin,
paper etc*) grain *m*
Thai [taɪ] *adj* thaïlandais(e) ▷ *n*
Thaïlandais(e)
Thailand [ˈtaɪlænd] *n* Thaïlande *f*
Thames [tɛmz] *n*: **the (River) ~**
la Tamise
than [ðæn, ðən] *conj* que; (*with
numerals*): **more ~ 10/once** plus de
10/d'une fois; **I have more/less ~
you** j'en ai plus/moins que toi; **she
has more apples ~ pears** elle a
plus de pommes que de poires; **it is
better to phone ~ to write** il vaut
mieux téléphoner (plutôt) qu'écrire;
she is older ~ you think elle est plus
âgée que tu le crois
thank [θæŋk] *vt* remercier, dire
merci à; **thanks** *npl* remerciements
mpl; **~s!** merci!; **~ you (very much)**
merci (beaucoup); **~ God** Dieu
merci; **~s to** *prep* grâce à; **thankfully**
adv (*fortunately*) heureusement;
Thanksgiving (Day) *n* jour *m*
d'action de grâce

● **THANKSGIVING (DAY)**
●
● *Thanksgiving (Day)* est un jour de
● congé aux États-Unis, le quatrième
● jeudi du mois de novembre,
● commémorant la bonne récolte
● que les Pèlerins venus de
● Grande-Bretagne ont eue en 1621;
● traditionnellement, c'était un jour
● où l'on remerciait Dieu et où l'on
● organisait un grand festin. Une
● fête semblable, mais qui n'a aucun
● rapport avec les Pères Pèlerins, a
● lieu au Canada le deuxième lundi
● d'octobre.

 KEYWORD

that [ðæt] *adj* (*demonstrative*) ce,
cet + *vowel or h mute*, cette *f*; **that
man/woman/book** cet homme/
cette femme/ce livre; (*not this*) cet

homme-là/cette femme-là/ce livre-là; **that one** celui-là (celle-là)
▶ *pron* **1** (*demonstrative*) ce; (: *not this one*) cela, ça; (: *that one*) celui (celle); **who's that?** qui est-ce?; **what's that?** qu'est-ce que c'est?; **is that you?** c'est toi?; **I prefer this to that** je préfère ceci à cela *or* ça; **that's what he said** c'est *or* voilà ce qu'il a dit; **will you eat all that?** tu vas manger tout ça?; **that is (to say)** c'est-à-dire, à savoir
2 (*relative*: *subject*) qui; (: *object*) que; (: *after prep*) lequel (laquelle), lesquels (lesquelles) *pl*; **the book that I read** le livre que j'ai lu; **the books that are in the library** les livres qui sont dans la bibliothèque; **all that I have** tout ce que j'ai; **the box that I put it in** la boîte dans laquelle je l'ai mis; **the people that I spoke to** les gens auxquels *or* à qui j'ai parlé
3 (*relative*, *of time*) où; **the day that he came** le jour où il est venu
▶ *conj* que; **he thought that I was ill** il pensait que j'étais malade
▶ *adv* (*demonstrative*): **I don't like it that much** ça ne me plaît pas tant que ça; **I didn't know it was that bad** je ne savais pas que c'était si *or* aussi mauvais; **it's about that high** c'est à peu près de cette hauteur

thatched [θætʃt] *adj* (*roof*) de chaume; **~ cottage** chaumière *f*
thaw [θɔː] *n* dégel *m* ▷ *vi* (*ice*) fondre; (*food*) dégeler ▷ *vt* (*food*) (faire) dégeler

KEYWORD

the [ðiː, ðə] *def art* **1** (*gen*) le, la *f*, l' + *vowel or h mute*, les *pl* (NB: à + le(s) = **au(x)**; de + le = **du**; de + les = **des**); **the boy/girl/ink** le garçon/la fille/l'encre; **the children** les enfants; **the history of the world** l'histoire du monde; **give it to the postman** donne-le au facteur; **to**

play the piano/flute jouer du piano/de la flûte
2 (+ *adj to form n*) le, la *f*, l' + *vowel or h mute*, les *pl*; **the rich and the poor** les riches et les pauvres; **to attempt the impossible** tenter l'impossible
3 (*in titles*): **Elizabeth the First** Elisabeth première; **Peter the Great** Pierre le Grand
4 (*in comparisons*): **the more he works, the more he earns** plus il travaille, plus il gagne de l'argent

theatre, (US) **theater** ['θɪətər] *n* théâtre *m*; (*Med: also*: **operating ~**) salle *f* d'opération
theft [θɛft] *n* vol *m* (*larcin*)
their [ðɛər] *adj* leur, leurs *pl*; *see also* **my**; **theirs** *pron* le (la) leur, les leurs; *see also* **mine**¹
them [ðɛm, ðəm] *pron* (*direct*) les; (*indirect*) leur; (*stressed*, *after prep*) eux (elles); **give me a few of ~** donnez m'en quelques uns (*or* quelques unes); *see also* **me**
theme [θiːm] *n* thème *m*; **theme park** *n* parc *m* à thème
themselves [ðəm'sɛlvz] *pl pron* (*reflexive*) se; (*emphatic*, *after prep*) eux-mêmes (elles-mêmes); **between ~** entre eux (elles); *see also* **oneself**
then [ðɛn] *adv* (*at that time*) alors, à ce moment-là; (*next*) puis, ensuite; (*and also*) et puis ▷ *conj* (*therefore*) alors, dans ce cas ▷ *adj*: **the ~ president** le président d'alors *or* de l'époque; **by ~** (*past*) à ce moment-là; (*future*) d'ici là; **from ~ on** dès lors; **until ~** jusqu'à ce moment-là, jusque-là
theology [θɪ'ɔlədʒɪ] *n* théologie *f*
theory ['θɪərɪ] *n* théorie *f*
therapist ['θɛrəpɪst] *n* thérapeute *m/f*
therapy ['θɛrəpɪ] *n* thérapie *f*

KEYWORD

there [ðɛər] *adv* **1**: **there is, there are** il y a; **there are 3 of them**

(*people, things*) il y en a 3; **there is no-one here/no bread left** il n'y a personne/il n'y a plus de pain; **there has been an accident** il y a eu un accident

2 (*referring to place*) là, là-bas; **it's there** c'est là(-bas); **in/on/up/down there** là-dedans/là-dessus/là-haut/en bas; **he went there on Friday** il y est allé vendredi; **I want that book there** je veux ce livre-là; **there he is!** le voilà!

3: **there, there!** (*esp to child*) allons, allons!

there: **thereabouts** *adv* (*place*) par là, près de là; (*amount*) environ, à peu près; **thereafter** *adv* par la suite; **thereby** *adv* ainsi; **therefore** *adv* donc, par conséquent

there's ['ðɛəz] = **there is; there has**

thermal ['θə:ml] *adj* thermique; **~ underwear** sous-vêtements *mpl* en Thermolactyl®

thermometer [θə'mɔmɪtə⁺] *n* thermomètre *m*

thermostat ['θə:məustæt] *n* thermostat *m*

these [ði:z] *pl pron* ceux-ci (celles-ci) ▷ *pl adj* ces; (*not those*): **~ books** ces livres-ci

thesis (*pl* **theses**) ['θi:sɪs, 'θi:si:z] *n* thèse *f*

they [ðeɪ] *pl pron* ils (elles); (*stressed*) eux (elles); **~ say that ...** (*it is said that*) on dit que ...; **they'd = they had; they would; they'll = they shall; they will; they're = they are; they've = they have**

thick [θɪk] *adj* épais(se); (*stupid*) bête, borné(e) ▷ *n*: **in the ~ of** au beau milieu de, en plein cœur de; **it's 20 cm ~** ça a 20 cm d'épaisseur; **thicken** *vi* s'épaissir ▷ *vt* (*sauce etc*) épaissir; **thickness** *n* épaisseur *f*

thief (*pl* **thieves**) [θi:f, θi:vz] *n* voleur(-euse)

thigh [θaɪ] *n* cuisse *f*

thin [θɪn] *adj* mince; (*skinny*) maigre; (*soup*) peu épais(se); (*hair, crowd*) clairsemé(e) ▷ *vt* (*also*: **~ down**: *sauce, paint*) délayer

thing [θɪŋ] *n* chose *f*; (*object*) objet *m*; (*contraption*) truc *m*; **things** *npl* (*belongings*) affaires *fpl*; **the ~ is ...** c'est que ...; **the best ~ would be to** le mieux serait de; **how are ~s?** comment ça va?; **to have a ~ about** (*be obsessed by*) être obsédé(e) par; (*hate*) détester; **poor ~!** le (*or* la) pauvre!

think (*pt, pp* **thought**) [θɪŋk, θɔ:t] *vi* penser, réfléchir ▷ *vt* penser, croire; (*imagine*) s'imaginer; **what did you ~ of them?** qu'avez-vous pensé d'eux?; **to ~ about sth/sb** penser à qch/qn; **I'll ~ about it** je vais y réfléchir; **to ~ of doing** avoir l'idée de faire; **I ~ so/ not** je crois *or* pense que oui/non; **to ~ well of** avoir une haute opinion de; **think over** *vt* bien réfléchir à; **think up** *vt* inventer, trouver

third [θə:d] *num* troisième ▷ *n* (*fraction*) tiers *m*; (*Aut*) troisième (vitesse) *f*; (*BRIT Scol: degree*) ≈ licence *f* avec mention passable; **thirdly** *adv* troisièmement; **third party insurance** *n* (*BRIT*) assurance *f* au tiers; **Third World** *n*: **the Third World** le Tiers-Monde

thirst [θə:st] *n* soif *f*; **thirsty** *adj* qui a soif, assoiffé(e); (*work*) qui donne soif; **to be thirsty** avoir soif

thirteen [θə:'ti:n] *num* treize; **thirteenth** [θə:'ti:nθ] *num* treizième

thirtieth ['θə:tɪɪθ] *num* trentième

thirty ['θə:tɪ] *num* trente

KEYWORD

this [ðɪs] *adj* (*demonstrative*) ce, cet + *vowel or h mute*, cette *f*; **this man/woman/book** cet homme/ cette femme/ce livre; (*not that*) cet homme-ci/cette femme-ci/ce livre-ci; **this one** celui-ci (celle-ci)

▶ *pron* (*demonstrative*) ce (: *not that one*) celui-ci (celle-ci), ceci; **who's this?** qui est-ce?; **what's this?** qu'est-ce que c'est?; **I prefer this to that** je préfère ceci à cela; **this is where I live** c'est ici que j'habite; **this is what he said** voici ce qu'il a dit; **this is Mr Brown** (*in introductions*) je vous présente Mr Brown; (*in photo*) c'est Mr Brown; (*on telephone*) ici Mr Brown
▶ *adv* (*demonstrative*): **it was about this big** c'était à peu près de cette grandeur *or* grand comme ça; **I didn't know it was this bad** je ne savais pas que c'était si *or* aussi mauvais

thistle ['θɪsl] *n* chardon *m*
thorn [θɔːn] *n* épine *f*
thorough ['θʌrə] *adj* (*search*) minutieux(-euse); (*knowledge, research*) approfondi(e); (*work, person*) consciencieux(-euse); (*cleaning*) à fond; **thoroughly** *adv* (*search*) minutieusement; (*study*) en profondeur; (*clean*) à fond; (*very*) tout à fait
those [ðəuz] *pl pron* ceux-là (celles-là) ▷ *pl adj* ces; (*not these*): **~ books** ces livres-là
though [ðəu] *conj* bien que + *sub*, quoique + *sub* ▷ *adv* pourtant
thought [θɔːt] *pt, pp of* **think** ▷ *n* pensée *f*; (*idea*) idée *f*; (*opinion*) avis *m*; **thoughtful** *adj* (*deep in thought*) pensif(-ive); (*serious*) réfléchi(e); (*considerate*) prévenant(e); **thoughtless** *adj* qui manque de considération
thousand ['θauzənd] *num* mille; **one ~** mille; **two ~** deux mille; **~s of** des milliers de; **thousandth** *num* millième
thrash [θræʃ] *vt* rouer de coups; (*inf: defeat*) donner une raclée à (*inf*)
thread [θrɛd] *n* fil *m*; (*of screw*) pas *m*, filetage *m* ▷ *vt* (*needle*) enfiler
threat [θrɛt] *n* menace *f*; **threaten** *vi* (*storm*) menacer ▷ *vt*: **to threaten**

sb with sth/to do menacer qn de qch/de faire; **threatening** *adj* menaçant(e)
three [θriː] *num* trois; **three-dimensional** *adj* à trois dimensions; **three-piece suite** *n* salon *m* (canapé et deux fauteuils); **three-quarters** *npl* trois-quarts *mpl*; **three-quarters full** aux trois-quarts plein
threshold ['θrɛʃhəuld] *n* seuil *m*
threw [θruː] *pt of* **throw**
thrill [θrɪl] *n* (*excitement*) émotion *f*, sensation forte; (*shudder*) frisson *m* ▷ *vt* (*audience*) électriser; **thrilled** *adj*: **thrilled (with)** ravi(e) de; **thriller** *n* film *m* (*or* roman *m or* pièce *f*) à suspense; **thrilling** *adj* (*book, play etc*) saisissant(e); (*news, discovery*) excitant(e)
thriving ['θraɪvɪŋ] *adj* (*business, community*) prospère
throat [θrəut] *n* gorge *f*; **to have a sore ~** avoir mal à la gorge
throb [θrɒb] *vi* (*heart*) palpiter; (*engine*) vibrer; **my head is ~bing** j'ai des élancements dans la tête
throne [θrəun] *n* trône *m*
through [θruː] *prep* à travers; (*time*) pendant, durant; (*by means of*) par, par l'intermédiaire de; (*owing to*) à cause de ▷ *adj* (*ticket, train, passage*) direct(e) ▷ *adv* à travers; **(from) Monday ~ Friday** (*us*) de lundi à vendredi; **to put sb ~ to sb** (*Tel*) passer qn à qn; **to be ~** (*BRIT Tel*) avoir la communication; (*esp us: have finished*) avoir fini; **"no ~ traffic"** (*US*) "passage interdit"; **"no ~ road"** (*BRIT*) "impasse"; **throughout** *prep* (*place*) partout dans; (*time*) durant tout(e) le ▷ *adv* partout
throw [θrəu] *n* jet *m*; (*Sport*) lancer *m* ▷ *vt* (*pt* **threw**, *pp* **thrown**) lancer, jeter; (*Sport*) lancer; (*rider*) désarçonner; (*fig*) déconcertancer; **to ~ a party** donner une réception; **throw away** *vt* jeter; (*money*) gaspiller; **throw in** *vt* (*Sport: ball*)

t

remettre en jeu; (include) ajouter; **throw off** vt se débarrasser de; **throw out** vt jeter; (reject) rejeter; (person) mettre à la porte; **throw up** vi vomir

thrown [θrəun] pp of **throw**

thru [θru:] (US) prep = **through**

thrush [θrʌʃ] n (Zool) grive f

thrust [θrʌst] vt (pt, pp **thrust**) pousser brusquement; (push in) enfoncer

thud [θʌd] n bruit sourd

thug [θʌg] n voyou m

thumb [θʌm] n (Anat) pouce m ▷ vt: **to ~ a lift** faire de l'auto-stop, arrêter une voiture; **thumbtack** n (US) punaise f (clou)

thump [θʌmp] n grand coup; (sound) bruit sourd ▷ vt cogner sur ▷ vi cogner, frapper

thunder ['θʌndə^r] n tonnerre m ▷ vi tonner; (train etc): **to ~ past** passer dans un grondement or un bruit de tonnerre; **thunderstorm** n orage m

Thursday ['θə:zdɪ] n jeudi m

thus [θʌs] adv ainsi

thwart [θwɔ:t] vt contrecarrer

thyme [taɪm] n thym m

Tibet [tɪ'bɛt] n Tibet m

tick [tɪk] n (sound: of clock) tic-tac m; (mark) coche f; (Zool) tique f ▷ vi faire tic-tac ▷ vt (item on list) cocher; **in a ~** (BRIT inf) dans un instant; **tick off** vt (item on list) cocher; (person) réprimander, attraper

ticket ['tɪkɪt] n billet m; (for bus, tube) ticket m; (in shop, on goods) étiquette f; (for library) carte f; (also: **parking ~**) contravention f, p.-v. m; **ticket barrier** n (BRIT Rail) portillon m automatique; **ticket collector** n contrôleur(-euse); **ticket inspector** n contrôleur(-euse); **ticket machine** n billetterie f automatique; **ticket office** n guichet m, bureau m de vente des billets

tickle ['tɪkl] vi chatouiller ▷ vt chatouiller; **ticklish** adj (person)

chatouilleux(-euse); (problem) épineux(-euse)

tide [taɪd] n marée f; (fig: of events) cours m

tidy ['taɪdɪ] adj (room) bien rangé(e); (dress, work) net (nette), soigné(e); (person) ordonné(e), qui a de l'ordre ▷ vt (also: **~ up**) ranger

tie [taɪ] n (string etc) cordon m; (BRIT: also: **neck~**) cravate f; (fig: link) lien m; (Sport: draw) égalité f de points match nul ▷ vt (parcel) attacher; (ribbon) nouer ▷ vi (Sport) faire match nul; finir à égalité de points; **to ~ sth in a bow** faire un nœud à or avec qch; **to ~ a knot in sth** faire un nœud à qch; **tie down** vt: **to ~ sb down to** (fig) contraindre qn à accepter; **to feel ~d down** (by relationship) se sentir coincé(e); **tie up** vt (parcel) ficeler; (dog, boat) attacher; (prisoner) ligoter; (arrangements) conclure; **to be ~d up** (busy) être pris(e) or occupé(e)

tier [tɪə^r] n gradin m; (of cake) étage m

tiger ['taɪgə^r] n tigre m

tight [taɪt] adj (rope) tendu(e), raide; (clothes) étroit(e), très juste; (budget, programme, bend) serré(e); (control) strict(e), sévère; (inf: drunk) ivre, rond(e) ▷ adv (squeeze) très fort; (shut) à bloc, hermétiquement; **hold ~!** accrochez-vous bien!; **tighten** vt (rope) tendre; (screw) resserrer; (control) renforcer ▷ vi se tendre; se resserrer; **tightly** adv (grasp) bien, très fort; **tights** npl (BRIT) collant m

tile [taɪl] n (on roof) tuile f; (on wall or floor) carreau m

till [tɪl] n caisse (enregistreuse) ▷ prep, conj = **until**

tilt [tɪlt] vt pencher, incliner ▷ vi pencher, être incliné(e)

timber ['tɪmbə^r] n (material) bois m de construction

time [taɪm] n temps m; (epoch: often pl) époque f, temps; (by clock) heure f; (moment) moment m; (occasion, also Math) fois f; (Mus) mesure f ▷ vt (*race*) chronométrer; (*visit*) minuter; (*programme*) fixer; (*remark etc*) choisir le moment de; **a long ~** un long moment, longtemps; **four at a ~** quatre à la fois; **for the ~ being** pour le moment; **from ~ to ~** de temps en temps; **at ~s** parfois; **in ~** (*soon enough*) à temps; (*after some time*) avec le temps, à la longue; (*Mus*) en mesure; **in a week's ~** dans une semaine; **in no ~** en un rien de temps; **any ~** n'importe quand; **on ~** à l'heure; **5 ~s 5** 5 fois 5; **what ~ is it?** quelle heure est-il?; **what ~ is the museum/shop open?** à quelle heure ouvre le musée/magasin?; **to have a good ~** bien s'amuser; **time limit** *n* limite *f* de temps, délai *m*; **timely** *adj* opportun(e); **timer** *n* (*in kitchen*) compte-minutes *m inv*; (*Tech*) minuteur *m*; **time-share** *n* maison *f*/appartement *m* en multipropriété; **timetable** *n* (*Rail*) (indicateur *m*) horaire *m*; (*Scol*) emploi *m* du temps; **time zone** *n* fuseau *m* horaire

timid ['timid] *adj* timide; (*easily scared*) peureux(-euse)

timing ['taimiŋ] *n* (*Sport*) chronométrage *m*; **the ~ of his resignation** le moment choisi pour sa démission

tin [tin] *n* étain *m*; (*also*: **~ plate**) fer-blanc *m*; (*BRIT: can*) boîte *f* (de conserve); (*for baking*) moule *m* (à gâteau); (*for storage*) boîte *f*; **tinfoil** *n* papier *m* d'étain *or* d'aluminium

tingle ['tiŋgl] *vi* picoter; (*person*) avoir des picotements

tinker ['tiŋkər]: **tinker with** *vt fus* bricoler, rafistoler

tinned [tind] *adj* (*BRIT: food*) en boîte, en conserve

tin opener [-'əupnər] *n* (*BRIT*) ouvre-boîte(s) *m*

tinsel ['tinsl] *n* guirlandes *fpl* de Noël (*argentées*)

tint [tint] *n* teinte *f*; (*for hair*) shampooing colorant; **tinted** *adj*

(*hair*) teint(e); (*spectacles, glass*) teinté(e)

tiny ['taini] *adj* minuscule

tip [tip] *n* (*end*) bout *m*; (*gratuity*) pourboire *m*; (*BRIT: for rubbish*) décharge *f*; (*advice*) tuyau *m* ▷ *vt* (*waiter*) donner un pourboire à; (*tilt*) incliner; (*overturn: also*: **~ over**) renverser; (*empty: also*: **~ out**) déverser; **how much should I ~?** combien de pourboire est-ce qu'il faut laisser?; **tip off** *vt* prévenir, avertir

tiptoe ['tiptəu] *n*: **on ~** sur la pointe des pieds

tire ['taiər] *n* (*US*) = **tyre** ▷ *vt* fatiguer ▷ *vi* se fatiguer; **tired** *adj* fatigué(e); **to be tired of** en avoir assez de, être las (lasse) de; **tire pressure** (*US*) *n* = **tyre pressure**; **tiring** *adj* fatigant(e)

tissue ['tiʃuː] *n* tissu *m*; (*paper handkerchief*) mouchoir *m* en papier, kleenex® *m*; **tissue paper** *n* papier *m* de soie

tit [tit] *n* (*bird*) mésange *f*; **to give ~ for tat** rendre coup pour coup

title ['taitl] *n* titre *m*

T-junction ['tiː'dʒʌŋkʃən] *n* croisement *m* en T

TM *n abbr* = **trademark**

KEYWORD

to [tuː, tə] *prep* (*with noun/pronoun*) **t**
1 (*direction*) à; (: *towards*) vers; envers; **to go to France/Portugal/London/school** aller en France/au Portugal/à Londres/à l'école; **to go to Claude's/the doctor's** aller chez Claude/le docteur; **the road to Edinburgh** la route d'Édimbourg
2 (*as far as*) (jusqu')à; **to count to 10** compter jusqu'à 10; **from 40 to 50 people** de 40 à 50 personnes
3 (*with expressions of time*): **a quarter to 5** 5 heures moins le quart; **it's twenty to 3** il est 3 heures moins vingt

4 (*for, of*) de; **the key to the front door** la clé de la porte d'entrée; **a letter to his wife** une lettre (adressée) à sa femme

5 (*expressing indirect object*) à; **to give sth to sb** donner qch à qn; **to talk to sb** parler à qn; **to be a danger to sb** être dangereux(-euse) pour qn

6 (*in relation to*) à; **3 goals to 2** 3 (buts) à 2; **30 miles to the gallon** ≈ 9,4 litres aux cent (km)

7 (*purpose, result*): **to come to sb's aid** venir au secours de qn, porter secours à qn; **to sentence sb to death** condamner qn à mort; **to my surprise** à ma grande surprise

▸ *prep* (*with vb*) **1** (*simple infinitive*): **to go/eat** aller/manger

2 (*following another vb*): **to want/try/start to do** vouloir/essayer de/commencer à faire

3 (*with vb omitted*): **I don't want to** je ne veux pas

4 (*purpose, result*) pour; **I did it to help you** je l'ai fait pour vous aider

5 (*equivalent to relative clause*): **I have things to do** j'ai des choses à faire; **the main thing is to try** l'important est d'essayer

6 (*after adjective etc*): **ready to go** prêt(e) à partir; **too old/young to …** trop vieux/jeune pour …

▸ *adv*: **push/pull the door to** tirez/poussez la porte

toad [təud] *n* crapaud *m*; **toadstool** *n* champignon (vénéneux)

toast [təust] *n* (*Culin*) pain grillé, toast *m*; (*drink, speech*) toast ▸ *vt* (*Culin*) faire griller; (*drink to*) porter un toast à; **toaster** *n* grille-pain *m inv*

tobacco [tə'bækəu] *n* tabac *m*

toboggan [tə'bɔgən] *n* toboggan *m*; (*child's*) luge *f*

today [tə'deɪ] *adv, n* (*also fig*) aujourd'hui (*m*)

toddler ['tɔdlə^r] *n* enfant *m/f* qui commence à marcher, bambin *m*

toe [təu] *n* doigt *m* de pied, orteil *m*; (*of shoe*) bout *m* ▸ *vt*: **to ~ the line** (*fig*) obéir, se conformer; **toenail** *n* ongle *m* de l'orteil

toffee ['tɔfɪ] *n* caramel *m*

together [tə'gɛðə^r] *adv* ensemble; (*at same time*) en même temps; **~ with** *prep* avec

toilet ['tɔɪlət] *n* (*BRIT: lavatory*) toilettes *fpl*, cabinets *mpl*; **to go to the ~** aller aux toilettes; **where's the ~?** où sont les toilettes?; **toilet bag** *n* (*BRIT*) nécessaire *m* de toilette; **toilet paper** *n* papier *m* hygiénique; **toiletries** *npl* articles *mpl* de toilette; **toilet roll** *n* rouleau *m* de papier hygiénique

token ['təukən] *n* (*sign*) marque *f*, témoignage *m*; (*metal disc*) jeton *m* ▸ *adj* (*fee, strike*) symbolique; **book/record ~** (*BRIT*) chèque-livre/-disque *m*

Tokyo ['təukjəu] *n* Tokyo

told [təuld] *pt, pp* of **tell**

tolerant ['tɔlərnt] *adj*: **~ (of)** tolérant(e) (à l'égard de)

tolerate ['tɔləreɪt] *vt* supporter

toll [təul] *n* (*tax, charge*) péage *m* ▸ *vi* (*bell*) sonner; **the accident ~ on the roads** le nombre des victimes de la route; **toll call** *n* (*US Tel*) appel *m* (à) longue distance; **toll-free** *adj* (*US*) gratuit(e) ▸ *adv* gratuitement

tomato [tə'mɑːtəu] (*pl* **tomatoes**) *n* tomate *f*; **tomato sauce** *n* sauce *f* tomate

tomb [tuːm] *n* tombe *f*; **tombstone** *n* pierre tombale

tomorrow [tə'mɔrəu] *adv, n* (*also fig*) demain (*m*); **the day after ~** après-demain; **a week ~** demain en huit; **~ morning** demain matin

ton [tʌn] *n* tonne *f* (*Brit*: = 1016 kg; *US* = 907 kg; *metric* = 1000 kg); **~s of** (*inf*) des tas de

tone [təun] *n* ton *m*; (*of radio, BRIT Tel*) tonalité *f* ▸ *vi* (*also*: **~ in**) s'harmoniser; **tone down** *vt* (*colour, criticism*) adoucir

tongs [tɔŋz] *npl* pinces *fpl*; (*for coal*) pincettes *fpl*; (*for hair*) fer *m* à friser

tongue [tʌŋ] *n* langue *f*; **~ in cheek** *adv* ironiquement

tonic ['tɔnɪk] *n* (*Med*) tonique *m*; (*also*: **~ water**) Schweppes® *m*

tonight [tə'naɪt] *adv, n* cette nuit; (*this evening*) ce soir

tonne [tʌn] *n* (BRIT: *metric ton*) tonne *f*

tonsil ['tɔnsl] *n* amygdale *f*; **tonsillitis** [tɔnsɪ'laɪtɪs] *n*: **to have tonsillitis** avoir une angine *or* une amygdalite

too [tu:] *adv* (*excessively*) trop; (*also*) aussi; **~ much** (*as adv*) trop; (*as adj*) trop de; **~ many** *adj* trop de

took [tuk] *pt of* **take**

tool [tu:l] *n* outil *m*; **tool box** *n* boîte *f* à outils; **tool kit** *n* trousse *f* à outils

tooth (*pl* **teeth**) [tu:θ, ti:θ] *n* (*Anat, Tech*) dent *f*; **to brush one's teeth** se laver les dents; **toothache** *n* mal *m* de dents; **to have toothache** avoir mal aux dents; **toothbrush** *n* brosse *f* à dents; **toothpaste** *n* (pâte *f*) dentifrice *m*; **toothpick** *n* cure-dent *m*

top [tɔp] *n* (*of mountain, head*) sommet *m*; (*of page, ladder*) haut *m*; (*of box, cupboard, table*) dessus *m*; (*lid: of box, jar*) couvercle *m*; (: *of bottle*) bouchon *m*; (*toy*) toupie *f*; (*Dress: blouse etc*) haut *m*; (: *of pyjamas*) veste *f* ▷ *adj* du haut; (*in rank*) premier(-ière); (*best*) meilleur(e) ▷ *vt* (*exceed*) dépasser; (*be first in*) être en tête de; **from ~ to bottom** de fond en comble; **on ~ of** sur; (*in addition to*) en plus de; **over the ~** (*inf*) (*behaviour etc*) qui dépasse les limites; **top up**, (US) **top off** *vt* (*bottle*) remplir; (*salary*) compléter; **to ~ up one's mobile (phone)** recharger son compte; **top floor** *n* dernier étage *m*; **top hat** *n* haut-de-forme *m*

topic ['tɔpɪk] *n* sujet *m*, thème *m*; **topical** *adj* d'actualité

topless ['tɔplɪs] *adj* (*bather etc*) aux seins nus

topping ['tɔpɪŋ] *n* (*Culin*) couche de crème, fromage etc qui recouvre un plat

topple ['tɔpl] *vt* renverser, faire tomber ▷ *vi* basculer; tomber

top-up ['tɔpʌp] *n* (*for mobile phone*) recharge *f*, minutes *fpl*; **top-up card** *n* (*for mobile phone*) recharge *f*

torch [tɔ:tʃ] *n* torche *f*; (BRIT: *electric*) lampe *f* de poche

tore [tɔ:ʳ] *pt of* **tear²**

torment *n* ['tɔ:mɛnt] tourment *m* ▷ *vt* [tɔ:'mɛnt] tourmenter; (*fig: annoy*) agacer

torn [tɔ:n] *pp of* **tear²**

tornado [tɔ:'neɪdəu] (*pl* **tornadoes**) *n* tornade *f*

torpedo [tɔ:'pi:dəu] (*pl* **torpedoes**) *n* torpille *f*

torrent ['tɔrnt] *n* torrent *m*; **torrential** [tɔ'rɛnʃl] *adj* torrentiel(le)

tortoise ['tɔ:təs] *n* tortue *f*

torture ['tɔ:tʃəʳ] *n* torture *f* ▷ *vt* torturer

Tory ['tɔ:rɪ] *adj, n* (BRIT *Pol*) tory *m/f*, conservateur(-trice)

toss [tɔs] *vt* lancer, jeter; (BRIT: *pancake*) faire sauter; (*head*) rejeter en arrière ▷ *vi*: **to ~ up for sth** (BRIT) jouer qch à pile ou face; **to ~ a coin** jouer à pile ou face; **to ~ and turn** (*in bed*) se tourner et se retourner

total ['təutl] *adj* total(e) ▷ *n* total *m* ▷ *vt* (*add up*) faire le total de, additionner; (*amount to*) s'élever à

totalitarian [təutælɪ'tɛərɪən] *adj* totalitaire

totally ['təutəlɪ] *adv* totalement

touch [tʌtʃ] *n* contact *m*, toucher *m*; (*sense, skill: of pianist etc*) toucher ▷ *vt* (*gen*) toucher; (*tamper with*) toucher à; **a ~ of** (*fig*) un petit peu de; une touche de; **to get in ~ with** prendre contact avec; **to lose ~** (*friends*) se perdre de vue; **touch down** *vi* (*Aviat*) atterrir; (*on sea*) amerrir; **touchdown** *n* (*Aviat*) atterrissage *m*; (*on sea*) amerrissage *m*; (US *Football*) essai *m*; **touched** *adj* (*moved*) touché(e); **touching**

adj touchant(e), attendrissant(e); **touchline** *n* (*Sport*) (ligne *f* de) touche *f*; **touch-sensitive** *adj* (*keypad*) à effleurement; (*screen*) tactile

tough [tʌf] *adj* dur(e); (*resistant*) résistant(e), solide; (*meat*) dur, coriace; (*firm*) inflexible; (*task, problem, situation*) difficile

tour ['tuə^r] *n* voyage *m*; (*also:* **package ~**) voyage organisé; (*of town, museum*) tour *m*, visite *f*; (*by band*) tournée *f* ▷ *vt* visiter; **tour guide** *n* (*person*) guide *m/f*

tourism ['tuərizm] *n* tourisme *m*

tourist ['tuərist] *n* touriste *m/f* ▷ *cpd* touristique; **tourist office** *n* syndicat *m* d'initiative

tournament ['tuənəmənt] *n* tournoi *m*

tour operator *n* (BRIT) organisateur *m* de voyages, tour-opérateur *m*

tow [təu] *vt* remorquer; (*caravan, trailer*) tracter; **"on ~"**, (US) **"in ~"** (*Aut*) "véhicule en remorque"; **tow away** *vt* (*subj: police*) emmener à la fourrière; (: *breakdown service*) remorquer

toward(s) [tə'wɔːd(z)] *prep* vers; (*of attitude*) envers, à l'égard de; (*of purpose*) pour

towel ['tauəl] *n* serviette *f* (de toilette); **towelling** *n* (*fabric*) tissu-éponge *m*

tower ['tauə^r] *n* tour *f*; **tower block** *n* (BRIT) tour *f* (d'habitation)

town [taun] *n* ville *f*; **to go to ~** aller en ville; (*fig*) y mettre le paquet; **town centre** *n* (BRIT) centre *m* de la ville, centre-ville *m*; **town hall** *n* ≈ mairie *f*

tow truck *n* (US) dépanneuse *f*

toxic ['tɔksik] *adj* toxique

toy [tɔɪ] *n* jouet *m*; **toy with** *vt fus* jouer avec; (*idea*) caresser; **toyshop** *n* magasin *m* de jouets

trace [treis] *n* trace *f* ▷ *vt* (*draw*) tracer, dessiner; (*follow*) suivre la trace de; (*locate*) retrouver

tracing paper ['treisiŋ-] *n* papier-calque *m*

track [træk] *n* (*mark*) trace *f*; (*path: gen*) chemin *m*, piste *f*; (: *of bullet etc*) trajectoire *f*; (: *of suspect, animal*) piste; (*Rail*) voie ferrée, rails *mpl*; (*Comput, Sport*) piste; (*on CD*) piste; (*on record*) plage *f* ▷ *vt* suivre la trace or la piste de; **to keep ~ of** suivre; **track down** *vt* (*prey*) trouver et capturer; (*sth lost*) finir par retrouver; **tracksuit** *n* survêtement *m*

tractor ['træktə^r] *n* tracteur *m*

trade [treid] *n* commerce *m*; (*skill, job*) métier *m* ▷ *vi* faire du commerce ▷ *vt* (*exchange*) **to ~ sth (for sth)** échanger qch (contre qch); **to ~ with/in** faire du commerce avec/ le commerce de; **trade in** *vt* (*old car etc*) faire reprendre; **trademark** *n* marque *f* de fabrique; **trader** *n* commerçant(e), négociant(e); **tradesman** (*irreg*) *n* (*shopkeeper*) commerçant *m*; **trade union** *n* syndicat *m*

trading ['treidiŋ] *n* affaires *fpl*, commerce *m*

tradition [trə'diʃən] *n* tradition *f*; **traditional** *adj* traditionnel(le)

traffic ['træfik] *n* trafic *m*; (*cars*) circulation *f* ▷ *vi*: **to ~ in** (*pej: liquor, drugs*) faire le trafic de; **traffic circle** *n* (US) rond-point *m*; **traffic island** *n* refuge *m* (pour piétons); **traffic jam** *n* embouteillage *m*; **traffic lights** *npl* feux *mpl* (de signalisation); **traffic warden** *n* contractuel(le)

tragedy ['trædʒədi] *n* tragédie *f*

tragic ['trædʒik] *adj* tragique

trail [treil] *n* (*tracks*) trace *f*, piste *f*; (*path*) chemin *m*, piste *f*; (*of smoke etc*) traînée *f* ▷ *vt* (*drag*) traîner, tirer; (*follow*) suivre ▷ *vi* traîner; (*in game, contest*) être en retard; **trailer** *n* (*Aut*) remorque *f*; (*US: caravan*) caravane *f*; (*Cine*) bande-annonce *f*

train [trein] *n* train *m*; (*in underground*) rame *f*; (*of dress*) traîne *f*; (BRIT: *series*):

~ **of events** série f d'événements
▷ vt (apprentice, doctor etc) former;
(Sport) entraîner; (dog) dresser;
(memory) exercer; (point: gun etc):
to ~ sth on braquer qch sur ▷ vi
recevoir sa formation; (Sport)
s'entraîner; **one's ~ of thought** le
fil de sa pensée; **what time does
the ~ from Paris get in?** à quelle
heure arrive le train de Paris?; **is this
the ~ for …?** c'est bien le train pour
…?; **trainee** [treɪˈniː] n stagiaire
m/f; (in trade) apprenti(e); **trainer** n
(Sport) entraîneur(-euse); (of dogs etc)
dresseur(-euse); **trainers** npl (shoes)
chaussures fpl de sport; **training** n
formation f; (Sport) entraînement m;
(of dog etc) dressage m; **in training**
(Sport) à l'entraînement; (fit) en
forme; **training course** n cours m de
formation professionnelle; **training
shoes** npl chaussures fpl de sport
trait [treɪt] n trait m (de caractère)
traitor [ˈtreɪtəʳ] n traître m
tram [træm] n (BRIT: also: ~**car**)
tram(way) m
tramp [træmp] n (person)
vagabond(e), clochard(e); (inf, pej:
woman): **to be a ~** être coureuse
trample [ˈtræmpl] vt: **to ~
(underfoot)** piétiner
trampoline [ˈtræmpəliːn] n
trampoline m
tranquil [ˈtræŋkwɪl] adj tranquille;
tranquillizer, (US) **tranquilizer** n
(Med) tranquillisant m
transaction [trænˈzækʃən] n
transaction f
transatlantic [ˈtrænzətˈlæntɪk] adj
transatlantique
transcript [ˈtrænskrɪpt] n
transcription f (texte)
transfer n [ˈtrænsfəʳ] (gen, also Sport)
transfert m; (Pol: of power) passation
f; (of money) virement m; (picture,
design) décalcomanie f (: stick-on)
autocollant m ▷ vt [trænsˈfəːʳ]
transférer; passer; virer; **to ~ the**

charges (BRIT Tel) téléphoner en
P.C.V.
transform [trænsˈfɔːm] vt
transformer; **transformation** n
transformation f
transfusion [trænsˈfjuːʒən] n
transfusion f
transit [ˈtrænzɪt] n: **in ~** en transit
transition [trænˈzɪʃən] n transition f
transitive [ˈtrænzɪtɪv] adj (Ling)
transitif(-ive)
translate [trænzˈleɪt] vt: **to ~
(from/into)** traduire (du/en); **can
you ~ this for me?** pouvez-vous
me traduire ceci?; **translation**
[trænzˈleɪʃən] n traduction f; (Scol: as
opposed to prose) version f; **translator**
n traducteur(-trice)
transmission [trænzˈmɪʃən] n
transmission f
transmit [trænzˈmɪt] vt
transmettre; (Radio, TV) émettre;
transmitter n émetteur m
transparent [trænsˈpærnt] adj
transparent(e)
transplant [ˈtrænsplɑːnt] n (Med)
transplantation f
transport n [ˈtrænspɔːt] transport
m ▷ vt [trænsˈpɔːt] transporter;
transportation [trænspɔːˈteɪʃən] n
(moyen m de) transport m
transvestite [trænzˈvɛstaɪt] n
travesti(e)
trap [træp] n (snare, trick) piège m;
(carriage) cabriolet m ▷ vt prendre au
piège; (confine) coincer
trash [træʃ] n (inf, pej: goods)
camelote f; (: nonsense) sottises fpl;
(US: rubbish) ordures fpl; **trash can** n
(US) poubelle f
trauma [ˈtrɔːmə] n traumatisme
m; **traumatic** [trɔːˈmætɪk] adj
traumatisant(e)
travel [ˈtrævl] n voyage(s) m(pl) ▷ vi
voyager; (news, sound) se propager ▷ vt
(distance) parcourir; **travel agency** n
agence f de voyages; **travel agent** n
agent m de voyages; **travel insurance**

t

n assurance-voyage *f*; **traveller**, (*us*) **traveler** *n* voyageur(-euse); **traveller's cheque**, (*us*) **traveler's check** *n* chèque *m* de voyage; **travelling**, (*us*) **traveling** *n* voyage(s) *m(pl)*; **travel-sick** *adj*: **to get travel-sick** avoir le mal de la route (*or* de mer *or* de l'air); **travel sickness** *n* mal *m* de la route (*or* de mer *or* de l'air)

tray [treɪ] *n* (*for carrying*) plateau *m*; (*on desk*) corbeille *f*

treacherous [ˈtrɛtʃərəs] *adj* traître(sse); (*ground, tide*) dont il faut se méfier

treacle [ˈtriːkl] *n* mélasse *f*

tread [trɛd] *n* (*step*) pas *m*; (*sound*) bruit *m* de pas; (*of tyre*) chape *f*, bande *f* de roulement ▷ *vi* (*pt* **trod**, *pp* **trodden**) marcher; **tread on** *vt fus* marcher sur

treasure [ˈtrɛʒəʳ] *n* trésor *m* ▷ *vt* (*value*) tenir beaucoup à; **treasurer** *n* trésorier(-ière)

treasury [ˈtrɛʒəri] *n*: **the T~**, (*us*) **the T~ Department** ≈ le ministère des Finances

treat [triːt] *n* petit cadeau, petite surprise ▷ *vt* traiter; **to ~ sb to sth** offrir qch à qn; **treatment** *n* traitement *m*

treaty [ˈtriːtɪ] *n* traité *m*

treble [ˈtrɛbl] *adj* triple ▷ *vt, vi* tripler

tree [triː] *n* arbre *m*

trek [trɛk] *n* (*long walk*) randonnée *f*; (*tiring walk*) longue marche, trotte *f*

tremble [ˈtrɛmbl] *vi* trembler

tremendous [trɪˈmɛndəs] *adj* (*enormous*) énorme; (*excellent*) formidable, fantastique

trench [trɛntʃ] *n* tranchée *f*

trend [trɛnd] *n* (*tendency*) tendance *f*; (*of events*) cours *m*; (*fashion*) mode *f*; **trendy** *adj* (*idea, person*) dans le vent; (*clothes*) dernier cri *inv*

trespass [ˈtrɛspəs] *vi*: **to ~ on** s'introduire sans permission dans; **"no ~ing"** "propriété privée", "défense d'entrer"

trial [ˈtraɪəl] *n* (*Law*) procès *m*, jugement *m*; (*test: of machine etc*) essai *m*; **trials** *npl* (*unpleasant experiences*) épreuves *fpl*; **trial period** *n* période *f* d'essai

triangle [ˈtraɪæŋgl] *n* (*Math, Mus*) triangle *m*

triangular [traɪˈæŋgjuləʳ] *adj* triangulaire

tribe [traɪb] *n* tribu *f*

tribunal [traɪˈbjuːnl] *n* tribunal *m*

tribute [ˈtrɪbjuːt] *n* tribut *m*, hommage *m*; **to pay ~ to** rendre hommage à

trick [trɪk] *n* (*magic*) tour *m*; (*joke, prank*) tour, farce *f*; (*skill, knack*) astuce *f*; (*Cards*) levée *f* ▷ *vt* attraper, rouler; **to play a ~ on sb** jouer un tour à qn; **that should do the ~** (*inf*) ça devrait faire l'affaire

trickle [ˈtrɪkl] *n* (*of water etc*) filet *m* ▷ *vi* couler en un filet *or* goutte à goutte

tricky [ˈtrɪkɪ] *adj* difficile, délicat(e)

tricycle [ˈtraɪsɪkl] *n* tricycle *m*

trifle [ˈtraɪfl] *n* bagatelle *f*; (*Culin*) ≈ diplomate *m* ▷ *adv*: **a ~ long** un peu long

trigger [ˈtrɪgəʳ] *n* (*of gun*) gâchette *f*

trim [trɪm] *adj* (*house, garden*) bien tenu(e); (*figure*) svelte ▷ *n* (*haircut etc*) légère coupe; (*on car*) garnitures *fpl* ▷ *vt* (*cut*) couper légèrement; (*Naut: a sail*) gréer; (*decorate*): **to ~ (with)** décorer (de)

trio [ˈtriːəu] *n* trio *m*

trip [trɪp] *n* voyage *m*; (*excursion*) excursion *f*; (*stumble*) faux pas ▷ *vi* faire un faux pas, trébucher; **trip up** *vi* trébucher ▷ *vt* faire un croc-en-jambe à

triple [ˈtrɪpl] *adj* triple

triplets [ˈtrɪplɪts] *npl* triplés(-ées)

tripod [ˈtraɪpɔd] *n* trépied *m*

triumph [ˈtraɪʌmf] *n* triomphe *m* ▷ *vi*: **to ~ (over)** triompher (de); **triumphant** [traɪˈʌmfənt] *adj* triomphant(e)

trivial ['trɪvɪəl] *adj* insignifiant(e); (*commonplace*) banal(e)

trod [trɔd] *pt of* **tread**

trodden ['trɔdn] *pp of* **tread**

troll [trɔl] *n* (*Comput*) troll *m*, trolleur(-euse) *m/f*

trolley ['trɔlɪ] *n* chariot *m*

trombone [trɔm'bəʊn] *n* trombone *m*

troop [truːp] *n* bande *f*, groupe *m*; **troops** *npl* (*Mil*) troupes *fpl* (: *men*) hommes *mpl*, soldats *mpl*

trophy ['trəʊfɪ] *n* trophée *m*

tropical ['trɔpɪkl] *adj* tropical(e)

trot [trɔt] *n* trot *m* ▷ *vi* trotter; **on the ~** (*BRIT fig*) d'affilée

trouble ['trʌbl] *n* difficulté(s) *f(pl)*, problème(s) *m(pl)*; (*worry*) ennuis *mpl*, soucis *mpl*; (*bother, effort*) peine *f*; (*Pol*) conflit(s) *m(pl)*, troubles *mpl*; (*Med*): **stomach** *etc* **~** troubles gastriques *etc* ▷ *vt* (*disturb*) déranger, gêner; (*worry*) inquiéter ▷ *vi*: **to ~ to do** prendre la peine de faire; **troubles** *npl* (*Pol etc*) troubles; (*personal*) ennuis, soucis; **to be in ~** avoir des ennuis; (*ship, climber etc*) être en difficulté; **to have ~ doing sth** avoir du mal à faire qch; **it's no ~!** je vous en prie!; **the ~ is ...** le problème, c'est que ...; **what's the ~?** qu'est-ce qui ne va pas?; **troubled** *adj* (*person*) inquiet(-ète); (*times, life*) agité(e); **troublemaker** *n* élément perturbateur, fauteur *m* de troubles; **troublesome** *adj* (*child*) fatigant(e), difficile; (*cough*) gênant(e)

trough [trɔf] *n* (*also*: **drinking ~**) abreuvoir *m*; (*also*: **feeding ~**) auge *f*; (*depression*) creux *m*

trousers ['traʊzəz] *npl* pantalon *m*; **short ~** (*BRIT*) culottes courtes

trout [traʊt] *n* (*pl inv*) truite *f*

truant ['truənt] *n*: **to play ~** (*BRIT*) faire l'école buissonnière

truce [truːs] *n* trêve *f*

truck [trʌk] *n* camion *m*; (*Rail*) wagon *m* à plate-forme; **truck driver** *n* camionneur *m*

true [truː] *adj* vrai(e); (*accurate*) exact(e); (*genuine*) vrai, véritable; (*faithful*) fidèle; **to come ~** se réaliser

truly ['truːlɪ] *adv* vraiment, réellement; (*truthfully*) sans mentir; **yours ~** (*in letter*) je vous prie d'agréer, Monsieur (*or* Madame *etc*), l'expression de mes sentiments respectueux

trumpet ['trʌmpɪt] *n* trompette *f*

trunk [trʌŋk] *n* (*of tree, person*) tronc *m*; (*of elephant*) trompe *f*; (*case*) malle *f*; (*US Aut*) coffre *m*; **trunks** *npl* (*also*: **swimming ~s**) maillot *m or* slip *m* de bain

trust [trʌst] *n* confiance *f*; (*responsibility*): **to place sth in sb's ~** confier la responsabilité de qch à qn; (*Law*) fidéicommis *m* ▷ *vt* (*rely on*) avoir confiance en; (*entrust*): **to ~ sth to sb** confier qch à qn; (*hope*): **to ~ (that)** espérer (que); **to take sth on ~** accepter qch les yeux fermés; **trusted** *adj* en qui l'on a confiance; **trustworthy** *adj* digne de confiance

truth [truːθ, truːðz] *n* vérité *f*; **truthful** *adj* (*person*) qui dit la vérité; (*answer*) sincère

try [traɪ] *n* essai *m*, tentative *f*; (*Rugby*) essai ▷ *vt* (*attempt*) essayer, tenter; (*test: sth new: also*: **~ out**) essayer, tester; (*Law: person*) juger; (*strain*) éprouver ▷ *vi* essayer; **to ~ to do** essayer de faire; (*seek*) chercher à faire; **try on** *vt* (*clothes*) essayer; **trying** *adj* pénible

T-shirt ['tiːʃəːt] *n* tee-shirt *m*

tub [tʌb] *n* cuve *f*; (*for washing clothes*) baquet *m*; (*bath*) baignoire *f*

tube [tjuːb] *n* tube *m*; (*BRIT: underground*) métro *m*; (*for tyre*) chambre f à air

tuberculosis [tjʊbəːkjuˈləʊsɪs] *n* tuberculose *f*

tube station *n* (*BRIT*) station *f* de métro

tuck [tʌk] *vt* (*put*) mettre; **tuck away** *vt* cacher, ranger; (*money*) mettre de côté; (building): **to be ~ed away** être caché(e); **tuck in** vt rentrer; (child) border ▷ vi (eat) manger de bon appétit; attaquer le repas

tucker ['tʌkəʳ] n (AUST, NZ inf) bouffe f (inf)

tuck shop n (BRIT Scol) boutique f à provisions

Tuesday ['tjuːzdɪ] n mardi m

tug [tʌg] n (ship) remorqueur m ▷ vt tirer (sur)

tuition [tjuːˈɪʃən] n (BRIT: lessons) leçons fpl; (: private) cours particuliers; (US: fees) frais mpl de scolarité

tulip ['tjuːlɪp] n tulipe f

tumble ['tʌmbl] n (fall) chute f, culbute f ▷ vi tomber, dégringoler; **to ~ to sth** (inf) réaliser qch; **tumble dryer** n (BRIT) séchoir m (à linge) à air chaud

tumbler ['tʌmbləʳ] n verre (droit), gobelet m

tummy ['tʌmɪ] n (inf) ventre m

tumour, (US) **tumor** ['tjuːməʳ] n tumeur f

tuna ['tjuːnə] n (pl inv: also: **~ fish**) thon m

tune [tjuːn] n (melody) air m ▷ vt (Mus) accorder; (Radio, TV, Aut) régler, mettre au point; **to be in/ out of ~** (instrument) être accordé/ désaccordé; (singer) chanter juste/ faux; **tune in** vi (Radio, TV): **to ~ in (to)** se mettre à l'écoute (de); **tune up** vi (musician) accorder son instrument

tunic ['tjuːnɪk] n tunique f

Tunis ['tjuːnɪs] n Tunis

Tunisia [tjuːˈnɪzɪə] n Tunisie f

Tunisian [tjuːˈnɪzɪən] adj tunisien(ne) ▷ n Tunisien(ne)

tunnel ['tʌnl] n tunnel m; (in mine) galerie f ▷ vi creuser un tunnel (or une galerie)

turbulence ['təːbjuləns] n (Aviat) turbulence f

turf [təːf] n gazon m; (clod) motte f (de gazon) ▷ vt gazonner

Turk [təːk] n Turc (Turque)

Turkey ['təːkɪ] n Turquie f

turkey ['təːkɪ] n dindon m, dinde f

Turkish ['təːkɪʃ] adj turc (turque) ▷ n (Ling) turc m

turmoil ['təːmɔɪl] n trouble m, bouleversement m

turn [təːn] n tour m; (in road) tournant m; (tendency: of mind, events) tournure f; (performance) numéro m; (Med) crise f, attaque f ▷ vt tourner; (collar, steak) retourner; (age) atteindre; (change): **to ~ sth into** changer qch en ▷ vi (object, wind, milk) tourner; (person: look back) se (re)tourner; (reverse direction) faire demi-tour; (become) devenir; **to ~ into** se changer en, se transformer en; **a good ~** un service; **it gave me quite a ~** ça m'a fait un coup; **"no left ~"** (Aut) "défense de tourner à gauche"; **~ left/right at the next junction** tournez à gauche/droite au prochain carrefour; **it's your ~** c'est (à) votre tour; **in ~** à son tour; à tour de rôle; **to take ~s** se relayer; **turn around** vi (person) se retourner ▷ vt (object) tourner; **turn away** vi se détourner, tourner la tête ▷ vt (reject: person) renvoyer; (: business) refuser; **turn back** vi revenir, faire demi-tour; **turn down** vt (refuse) rejeter, refuser; (reduce) baisser; (fold) rabattre; **turn in** vi (inf: go to bed) aller se coucher ▷ vt (fold) rentrer; **turn off** vi (from road) tourner ▷ vt (light, radio etc) éteindre; (tap) fermer; (engine) arrêter; **I can't ~ the heating off** je n'arrive pas à éteindre le chauffage; **turn on** vt (light, radio etc) allumer; (tap) ouvrir; (engine) mettre en marche; **I can't ~ the heating on** je n'arrive pas à allumer le chauffage; **turn out** vt (light, gas) éteindre; (produce) produire ▷ vi (voters, troops) se présenter; **to ~ out to be ...** s'avérer ..., se révéler ...; **turn over** vi (person) se retourner ▷ vt (object) retourner; (page) tourner; **turn round** vi faire demi-tour;

(rotate) tourner; **turn to** vt fus: **to ~ to sb** s'adresser à qn; **turn up** vi (person) arriver, se pointer (inf); (lost object) être retrouvé(e) ▷ vt (collar) remonter; (radio, heater) mettre plus fort; **turning** n (in road) tournant m; **turning point** n (fig) tournant m, moment décisif

turnip ['tə:nɪp] n navet m

turn: turnout n (of voters) taux m de participation; **turnover** n (Comm: amount of money) chiffre m d'affaires; (: of goods) roulement m; (of staff) renouvellement m, changement m; **turnstile** n tourniquet m (d'entrée); **turn-up** n (BRIT: on trousers) revers m

turquoise ['tə:kwɔɪz] n (stone) turquoise f ▷ adj turquoise inv

turtle ['tə:tl] n tortue marine; **turtleneck (sweater)** n pullover m à col montant

tusk [tʌsk] n défense f (d'éléphant)

tutor ['tju:tə'] n (BRIT Scol: in college) directeur(-trice) d'études; (private teacher) précepteur(-trice); **tutorial** [tju:'tɔ:rɪəl] n (Scol) (séance f de) travaux mpl pratiques

tuxedo [tʌk'si:dəu] n (US) smoking m

TV [ti:'vi:] n abbr (= television) télé f, TV f

tweed [twi:d] n tweed m

tweet [twi:t] (on Twitter) n tweet m ▷ vt, vi tweeter

tweezers ['twi:zəz] npl pince f à épiler

twelfth [twɛlfθ] num douzième

twelve [twɛlv] num douze; **at ~ (o'clock)** à midi; (midnight) à minuit

twentieth ['twɛntɪɪθ] num vingtième

twenty ['twɛntɪ] num vingt; **in ~ fourteen** en deux mille quatorze

twice [twaɪs] adv deux fois; **~ as much** deux fois plus

twig [twɪg] n brindille f ▷ vt, vi (inf) piger

twilight ['twaɪlaɪt] n crépuscule m

twin [twɪn] adj, n jumeau(-elle) ▷ vt jumeler; **twin-bedded room** n

= **twin room**; **twin beds** npl lits mpl jumeaux

twinkle ['twɪŋkl] vi scintiller; (eyes) pétiller

twin room n chambre f à deux lits

twist [twɪst] n torsion f, tour m; (in wire, flex) tortillon m; (bend: in road) tournant m; (in story) coup m de théâtre ▷ vt tordre; (weave) entortiller; (roll around) enrouler; (fig) déformer ▷ vi (road, river) serpenter; **to ~ one's ankle/wrist** (Med) se tordre la cheville/le poignet

twit [twɪt] n (inf) crétin(e)

twitch [twɪtʃ] n (pull) coup sec, saccade f; (nervous) tic m ▷ vi se convulser; avoir un tic

two [tu:] num deux; **to put ~ and ~ together** (fig) faire le rapprochement

type [taɪp] n (category) genre m, espèce f; (model) modèle m; (example) type m; (Typ) type, caractère m ▷ vt (letter etc) taper (à la machine); **typewriter** n machine f à écrire

typhoid ['taɪfɔɪd] n typhoïde f

typhoon [taɪ'fu:n] n typhon m

typical ['tɪpɪkl] adj typique, caractéristique; **typically** ['tɪpɪklɪ] adv (as usual) comme d'habitude; (characteristically) typiquement

typing ['taɪpɪŋ] n dactylo(graphie) f

typist ['taɪpɪst] n dactylo m/f

tyre, (US) **tire** [taɪə'] n pneu m; **tyre pressure** n (BRIT) pression f (de gonflage)

t

UFO [' juːfəu] *n abbr* (= *unidentified flying object*) ovni *m*
Uganda [juː'gændə] *n* Ouganda *m*
ugly ['ʌɡlɪ] *adj* laid(e), vilain(e); (*fig*) répugnant(e)
UHT *adj abbr* (= *ultra-heat treated*): **~ milk** lait *m* UHT *or* longue conservation
UK *n abbr* = **United Kingdom**
ulcer ['ʌlsəʳ] *n* ulcère *m*; **mouth ~** aphte *f*
ultimate ['ʌltɪmət] *adj* ultime, final(e); (*authority*) suprême; **ultimately** *adv* (*at last*) en fin de compte; (*fundamentally*) finalement; (*eventually*) par la suite
ultimatum (*pl* **ultimatums** *or* **ultimata**) [ˌʌltɪ'meɪtəm, -tə] *n* ultimatum *m*
ultrasound ['ʌltrəsaund] *n* (*Med*) ultrason *m*
ultraviolet ['ʌltrə'vaɪəlɪt] *adj* ultraviolet(te)

umbrella [ʌm'brɛlə] *n* parapluie *m*; (*for sun*) parasol *m*
umpire ['ʌmpaɪəʳ] *n* arbitre *m*; (*Tennis*) juge *m* de chaise
UN *n abbr* = **United Nations**
unable [ʌn'eɪbl] *adj*: **to be ~ to** ne (pas) pouvoir, être dans l'impossibilité de; (*not capable*) être incapable de
unacceptable [ʌnək'sɛptəbl] *adj* (*behaviour*) inadmissible; (*price, proposal*) inacceptable
unanimous [juː'nænɪməs] *adj* unanime
unarmed [ʌn'ɑːmd] *adj* (*person*) non armé(e); (*combat*) sans armes
unattended [ʌnə'tɛndɪd] *adj* (*car, child, luggage*) sans surveillance
unattractive [ʌnə'træktɪv] *adj* peu attrayant(e); (*character*) peu sympathique
unavailable [ʌnə'veɪləbl] *adj* (*article, room, book*) (qui n'est) pas disponible; (*person*) (qui n'est) pas libre
unavoidable [ʌnə'vɔɪdəbl] *adj* inévitable
unaware [ʌnə'wɛəʳ] *adj*: **to be ~ of** ignorer, ne pas savoir, être inconscient(e) de; **unawares** *adv* à l'improviste, au dépourvu
unbearable [ʌn'bɛərəbl] *adj* insupportable
unbeatable [ʌn'biːtəbl] *adj* imbattable
unbelievable [ʌnbɪ'liːvəbl] *adj* incroyable
unborn [ʌn'bɔːn] *adj* à naître
unbutton [ʌn'bʌtn] *vt* déboutonner
uncalled-for [ʌn'kɔːldfɔːʳ] *adj* déplacé(e), injustifié(e)
uncanny [ʌn'kænɪ] *adj* étrange, troublant(e)
uncertain [ʌn'səːtn] *adj* incertain(e); (*hesitant*) hésitant(e); **uncertainty** *n* incertitude *f*, doutes *mpl*
unchanged [ʌn'tʃeɪndʒd] *adj* inchangé(e)
uncle ['ʌŋkl] *n* oncle *m*

unclear [ʌnˈklɪəʳ] *adj* (qui n'est) pas clair(e) *or* évident(e); **I'm still ~ about what I'm supposed to do** je ne sais pas encore exactement ce que je dois faire

uncomfortable [ʌnˈkʌmfətəbl] *adj* inconfortable, peu confortable; *(uneasy)* mal à l'aise, gêné(e); *(situation)* désagréable

uncommon [ʌnˈkɔmən] *adj* rare, singulier(-ière), peu commun(e)

unconditional [ʌnkənˈdɪʃənl] *adj* sans conditions

unconscious [ʌnˈkɔnʃəs] *adj* sans connaissance, évanoui(e); *(unaware)*: **~ (of)** inconscient(e) (de) ▷ *n*: **the ~** l'inconscient *m*

uncontrollable [ʌnkənˈtrəʊləbl] *adj* *(child, dog)* indiscipliné(e); *(temper, laughter)* irrépressible

unconventional [ʌnkənˈvɛnʃənl] *adj* peu conventionnel(le)

uncover [ʌnˈkʌvəʳ] *vt* découvrir

undecided [ʌndɪˈsaɪdɪd] *adj* indécis(e), irrésolu(e)

undeniable [ʌndɪˈnaɪəbl] *adj* indéniable, incontestable

under [ˈʌndəʳ] *prep* sous; *(less than)* (de) moins de; au-dessous de; *(according to)* selon, en vertu de ▷ *adv* au-dessous; en dessous; **~ there** là-dessous; **~ the circumstances** étant donné les circonstances; **~ repair** en (cours de) réparation; **undercover** *adj* secret(-ète), clandestin(e); **underdone** *adj* *(Culin)* saignant(e); *(: pej)* pas assez cuit(e); **underestimate** *vt* sous-estimer, mésestimer; **undergo** *vt* *(irreg: like* **go***)* subir; *(treatment)* suivre; **undergraduate** *n* étudiant(e) (qui prépare la licence); **underground** *adj* souterrain(e); *(fig)* clandestin(e) ▷ *n* *(BRIT: railway)* métro *m*; *(Pol)* clandestinité *f*; **undergrowth** *n* broussailles *fpl*, sous-bois *m*; **underline** *vt* souligner; **undermine** *vt* saper, miner; **underneath**

[ʌndəˈniːθ] *adv* (en) dessous ▷ *prep* sous, au-dessous de; **underpants** *npl* caleçon *m*, slip *m*; **underpass** *n* *(BRIT: for pedestrians)* passage souterrain; *(: for cars)* passage inférieur; **underprivileged** *adj* défavorisé(e); **underscore** *vt* souligner; **undershirt** *n* *(US)* tricot *m* de corps; **underskirt** *n* *(BRIT)* jupon *m*

understand [ʌndəˈstænd] *vt, vi (irreg: like* **stand***)* comprendre; **I don't ~** je ne comprends pas; **understandable** *adj* compréhensible; **understanding** *adj* compréhensif(-ive) ▷ *n* compréhension *f*; *(agreement)* accord *m*

understatement [ˈʌndəsteɪtmənt] *n*: **that's an ~** c'est (bien) peu dire, le terme est faible

understood [ʌndəˈstud] *pt, pp of* **understand** ▷ *adj* entendu(e); *(implied)* sous-entendu(e)

undertake [ʌndəˈteɪk] *vt (irreg: like* **take***)* *(job, task)* entreprendre; *(duty)* se charger de; **to ~ to do sth** s'engager à faire qch

undertaker [ˈʌndəteɪkəʳ] *n* *(BRIT)* entrepreneur *m* des pompes funèbres, croque-mort *m*

undertaking [ˈʌndəteɪkɪŋ] *n* entreprise *f*; *(promise)* promesse *f*

under: underwater *adv* sous l'eau ▷ *adj* sous-marin(e); **underway** *adj*: **to be underway** *(meeting, investigation)* être en cours; **underwear** *n* sous-vêtements *mpl*; *(women's only)* dessous *mpl*; **underwent** *pt of* **undergo**; **underworld** *n* *(of crime)* milieu *m*, pègre *f*

undesirable [ʌndɪˈzaɪərəbl] *adj* peu souhaitable; *(person, effect)* indésirable

undisputed [ˈʌndɪsˈpjuːtɪd] *adj* incontesté(e)

undo [ʌnˈduː] *vt (irreg: like* **do***)* défaire

undone [ʌnˈdʌn] *pp of* **undo** ▷ *adj*: **to
come ~** se défaire
undoubtedly [ʌnˈdaʊtɪdlɪ] *adv* sans
aucun doute
undress [ʌnˈdrɛs] *vi* se déshabiller
unearth [ʌnˈɜːθ] *vt* déterrer; *(fig)*
dénicher
uneasy [ʌnˈiːzɪ] *adj* mal à l'aise,
gêné(e); *(worried)* inquiet(-ète); *(feeling)*
désagréable; *(peace, truce)* fragile
unemployed [ʌnɪmˈplɔɪd] *adj* sans
travail, au chômage ▷ *n*: **the ~** les
chômeurs *mpl*
unemployment [ʌnɪmˈplɔɪmənt]
n chômage *m*; **unemployment
benefit**, *(us)* **unemployment
compensation** *n* allocation *f* de
chômage
unequal [ʌnˈiːkwəl] *adj* inégal(e)
uneven [ʌnˈiːvn] *adj* inégal(e);
(quality, work) irrégulier(-ière)
unexpected [ʌnɪkˈspɛktɪd]
adj inattendu(e), imprévu(e);
unexpectedly *adv (succeed)* contre
toute attente; *(arrive)* à l'improviste
unfair [ʌnˈfɛəʳ] *adj*: **~ (to)** injuste
(envers)
unfaithful [ʌnˈfeɪθful] *adj* infidèle
unfamiliar [ʌnfəˈmɪlɪəʳ] *adj* étrange,
inconnu(e); **to be ~ with sth** mal
connaître qch
unfashionable [ʌnˈfæʃnəbl] *adj*
(clothes) démodé(e); *(place)* peu
chic *inv*
unfasten [ʌnˈfɑːsn] *vt* défaire; *(belt,
necklace)* détacher; *(open)* ouvrir
unfavourable, *(us)* **unfavorable**
[ʌnˈfeɪvrəbl] *adj* défavorable
unfinished [ʌnˈfɪnɪʃt] *adj*
inachevé(e)
unfit [ʌnˈfɪt] *adj (physically: ill)* en
mauvaise santé; *(: out of condition)*
pas en forme; *(incompetent)*: **~ (for)**
impropre (à); *(work, service)* inapte (à)
unfold [ʌnˈfəʊld] *vt* déplier ▷ *vi* se
dérouler
unforgettable [ʌnfəˈɡɛtəbl] *adj*
inoubliable

unfortunate [ʌnˈfɔːtʃnət] *adj*
malheureux(-euse); *(event,
remark)* malencontreux(-euse);
unfortunately *adv* malheureusement
unfriend [ʌnˈfrɛnd] *vt (Internet)*
supprimer de sa liste d'amis
unfriendly [ʌnˈfrɛndlɪ] *adj* peu
aimable, froid(e)
unfurnished [ʌnˈfɜːnɪʃt] *adj* non
meublé(e)
unhappiness [ʌnˈhæpɪnɪs] *n*
tristesse *f*, peine *f*
unhappy [ʌnˈhæpɪ] *adj* triste,
malheureux(-euse); *(unfortunate:
remark etc)* malheureux(-euse); *(not
pleased)*: **~ with** mécontent(e) de, peu
satisfait(e) de
unhealthy [ʌnˈhɛlθɪ] *adj (gen)*
malsain(e); *(person)* maladif(-ive)
unheard-of [ʌnˈhɜːdɒv] *adj* inouï(e),
sans précédent
unhelpful [ʌnˈhɛlpful] *adj (person)*
peu serviable; *(advice)* peu utile
unhurt [ʌnˈhɜːt] *adj* indemne, sain(e)
et sauf
unidentified [ʌnaɪˈdɛntɪfaɪd] *adj*
non identifié(e); *see also* **UFO**
uniform [ˈjuːnɪfɔːm] *n* uniforme *m*
▷ *adj* uniforme
unify [ˈjuːnɪfaɪ] *vt* unifier
unimportant [ʌnɪmˈpɔːtənt] *adj*
sans importance
uninhabited [ʌnɪnˈhæbɪtɪd] *adj*
inhabité(e)
unintentional [ʌnɪnˈtɛnʃənəl] *adj*
involontaire
union [ˈjuːnjən] *n* union *f*; *(also:
trade ~)* syndicat *m* ▷ *cpd* du
syndicat, syndical(e); **Union Jack** *n*
drapeau du Royaume-Uni
unique [juːˈniːk] *adj* unique
unisex [ˈjuːnɪsɛks] *adj* unisexe
unit [ˈjuːnɪt] *n* unité *f*; *(section: of
furniture etc)* élément *m*, bloc *m*; *(team,
squad)* groupe *m*, service *m*; **kitchen ~**
élément de cuisine
unite [juːˈnaɪt] *vt* unir ▷ *vi* s'unir;
united *adj* uni(e); *(country, party)*

unifié(e); (*efforts*) conjugué(e);
United Kingdom n Royaume-Uni
m; **United Nations (Organization)**
n (Organisation f des) Nations unies;
United States (of America) n
États-Unis mpl
unity ['ju:nɪtɪ] n unité f
universal [ju:nɪ'və:sl] adj
universel(le)
universe ['ju:nɪvə:s] n univers m
university [ju:nɪ'və:sɪtɪ] n
université f ▷ cpd (*student, professor*)
d'université; (*education, year, degree*)
universitaire
unjust [ʌn'dʒʌst] adj injuste
unkind [ʌn'kaɪnd] adj peu gentil(le),
méchant(e)
unknown [ʌn'nəun] adj inconnu(e)
unlawful [ʌn'lɔ:ful] adj illégal(e)
unleaded [ʌn'lɛdɪd] n (*also: ~ petrol*)
essence f sans plomb
unleash [ʌn'li:ʃ] vt (*fig*) déchaîner,
déclencher
unless [ʌn'lɛs] conj: **~ he leaves** à
moins qu'il (ne) parte; **~ otherwise
stated** sauf indication contraire
unlike [ʌn'laɪk] adj dissemblable,
différent(e) ▷ prep à la différence de,
contrairement à
unlikely [ʌn'laɪklɪ] adj (*result,
event*) improbable; (*explanation*)
invraisemblable
unlimited [ʌn'lɪmɪtɪd] adj illimité(e)
unlisted ['ʌn'lɪstɪd] adj (*US Tel*) sur
la liste rouge
unload [ʌn'ləud] vt décharger
unlock [ʌn'lɔk] vt ouvrir
unlucky [ʌn'lʌkɪ] adj (*person*)
malchanceux(-euse); (*object, number*)
qui porte malheur; **to be ~** (*person*) ne
pas avoir de chance
unmarried [ʌn'mærɪd] adj
célibataire
unmistak(e)able [ʌnmɪs'teɪkəbl]
adj indubitable; qu'on ne peut pas ne
pas reconnaître
unnatural [ʌn'nætʃrəl] adj non
naturel(le); (*perversion*) contre nature

unnecessary [ʌn'nɛsəsərɪ] adj
inutile, superflu(e)
UNO ['ju:nəu] n abbr = **United
Nations Organization**
unofficial [ʌnə'fɪʃl] adj (*news*)
officieux(-euse), non officiel(le);
(*strike*) ≈ sauvage
unpack [ʌn'pæk] vi défaire sa valise
▷ vt (*suitcase*) défaire; (*belongings*)
déballer
unpaid [ʌn'peɪd] adj (*bill*) impayé(e);
(*holiday*) non-payé(e), sans salaire;
(*work*) non rétribué(e)
unpleasant [ʌn'plɛznt] adj
déplaisant(e), désagréable
unplug [ʌn'plʌg] vt débrancher
unpopular [ʌn'pɔpjulər] adj
impopulaire
unprecedented [ʌn'prɛsɪdɛntɪd]
adj sans précédent
unpredictable [ʌnprɪ'dɪktəbl] adj
imprévisible
unprotected ['ʌnprə'tɛktɪd] adj
(*sex*) non protégé(e)
unqualified [ʌn'kwɔlɪfaɪd] adj
(*teacher*) non diplômé(e), sans titres;
(*success*) sans réserve, total(e);
(*disaster*) total(e)
unravel [ʌn'rævl] vt démêler
unreal [ʌn'rɪəl] adj irréel(le);
(*extraordinary*) incroyable
unrealistic ['ʌnrɪə'lɪstɪk] adj (*idea*)
irréaliste; (*estimate*) peu réaliste
unreasonable [ʌn'ri:znəbl] adj qui
n'est pas raisonnable
unrelated [ʌnrɪ'leɪtɪd] adj sans
rapport; (*people*) sans lien de parenté
unreliable [ʌnrɪ'laɪəbl] adj sur qui
(*or quoi*) on ne peut pas compter,
peu fiable
unrest [ʌn'rɛst] n agitation f,
troubles mpl
unroll [ʌn'rəul] vt dérouler
unruly [ʌn'ru:lɪ] adj indiscipliné(e)
unsafe [ʌn'seɪf] adj (*in danger*) en
danger; (*journey, car*) dangereux(-euse)
unsatisfactory ['ʌnsætɪs'fæktərɪ]
adj peu satisfaisant(e)

u

unscrew [ʌn'skruː] vt dévisser
unsettled [ʌn'sɛtld] adj (restless) perturbé(e); (unpredictable) instable; incertain(e); (not finalized) non résolu(e)
unsettling [ʌn'sɛtlɪŋ] adj qui a un effet perturbateur
unsightly [ʌn'saɪtlɪ] adj disgracieux(-euse), laid(e)
unskilled [ʌn'skɪld] adj: ~ **worker** manœuvre m
unspoiled ['ʌn'spɔɪld], **unspoilt** ['ʌn'spɔɪlt] adj (place) non dégradé(e)
unstable [ʌn'steɪbl] adj instable
unsteady [ʌn'stɛdɪ] adj mal assuré(e), chancelant(e), instable
unsuccessful [ʌnsək'sɛsful] adj (attempt) infructueux(-euse); (writer, proposal) qui n'a pas de succès; **to be ~** (in attempting sth) ne pas réussir; ne pas avoir de succès; (application) ne pas être retenu(e)
unsuitable [ʌn'suːtəbl] adj qui ne convient pas, peu approprié(e); (time) inopportun(e)
unsure [ʌn'ʃuər] adj pas sûr(e); **to be ~ of o.s.** ne pas être sûr de soi, manquer de confiance en soi
untidy [ʌn'taɪdɪ] adj (room) en désordre; (appearance, person) débraillé(e); (person: in character) sans ordre, désordonné(e); (work) peu soigné(e)
untie [ʌn'taɪ] vt (knot, parcel) défaire; (prisoner, dog) détacher
until [ən'tɪl] prep jusqu'à; (after negative) avant ▷ conj jusqu'à ce que + sub; (in past, after negative) avant que + sub; **~ now** jusqu'à présent, jusqu'ici; **~ then** jusque-là
untrue [ʌn'truː] adj (statement) faux (fausse)
unused¹ [ʌn'juːzd] adj (new) neuf (neuve)
unused² [ʌn'juːst] adj: **to be ~ to sth/to doing sth** ne pas avoir l'habitude de qch/de faire qch

unusual [ʌn'juːʒuəl] adj insolite, exceptionnel(le), rare; **unusually** adv exceptionnellement, particulièrement
unveil [ʌn'veɪl] vt dévoiler
unwanted [ʌn'wɒntɪd] adj (child, pregnancy) non désiré(e); (clothes etc) à donner
unwell [ʌn'wɛl] adj souffrant(e); **to feel ~** ne pas se sentir bien
unwilling [ʌn'wɪlɪŋ] adj: **to be ~ to do** ne pas vouloir faire
unwind [ʌn'waɪnd] vt (irreg: like wind²) dérouler ▷ vi (relax) se détendre
unwise [ʌn'waɪz] adj imprudent(e), peu judicieux(-euse)
unwittingly [ʌn'wɪtɪŋlɪ] adv involontairement
unwrap [ʌn'ræp] vt défaire; ouvrir
unzip [ʌn'zɪp] vt ouvrir (la fermeture éclair de); (Comput) dézipper

KEYWORD

up [ʌp] prep: **he went up the stairs/ the hill** il a monté l'escalier/la colline; **the cat was up a tree** le chat était dans un arbre; **they live further up the street** ils habitent plus haut dans la rue; **go up that road and turn left** remontez la rue et tournez à gauche
▶ adv 1 en haut; en l'air; (upwards, higher): **up in the sky/the mountains** (là-haut) dans le ciel/les montagnes; **put it a bit higher up** mettez-le un peu plus haut; **to stand up** (get up) se lever, se mettre debout; (be standing) être debout; **up there** là-haut; **up above** au-dessus
2: **to be up** (out of bed) être levé(e); (prices) avoir augmenté or monté; (finished): **when the year was up** à la fin de l'année
3: **up to** (as far as) jusqu'à; **up to now** jusqu'à présent
4: **to be up to** (depending on): **it's up**

to you c'est à vous de décider; (*equal to*): **he's not up to it** (*job, task etc*) il n'en est pas capable; (*inf: be doing*): **what is he up to?** qu'est-ce qu'il peut bien faire?
▶ *n*: **ups and downs** hauts et bas *mpl*

up-and-coming [ʌpənd'kʌmɪŋ] *adj* plein(e) d'avenir *or* de promesses
upbringing ['ʌpbrɪŋɪŋ] *n* éducation *f*
update [ʌp'deɪt] *vt* mettre à jour
upfront [ʌp'frʌnt] *adj* (*open*) franc (franche) ▷ *adv* (*pay*) d'avance; **to be ~ about sth** ne rien cacher de qch
upgrade [ʌp'greɪd] *vt* (*person*) promouvoir; (*job*) revaloriser; (*property, equipment*) moderniser
upheaval [ʌp'hi:vl] *n* bouleversement *m*; (*in room*) branle-bas *m*; (*event*) crise *f*
uphill [ʌp'hɪl] *adj* qui monte; (*fig: task*) difficile, pénible ▷ *adv* (*face, look*) en amont, vers l'amont; **to go ~** monter
upholstery [ʌp'həulstərɪ] *n* rembourrage *m*; (*cover*) tissu *m* d'ameublement; (*of car*) garniture *f*
upload [ʌp'ləud] *vt* (*Comput*) télécharger
upmarket [ʌp'mɑ:kɪt] *adj* (*product*) haut de gamme *inv*; (*area*) chic *inv*
upon [ə'pɔn] *prep* sur
upper ['ʌpə*r*] *adj* supérieur(e); du dessus ▷ *n* (*of shoe*) empeigne *f*; **upper-class** *adj* de la haute société, aristocratique; (*district*) élégant(e), huppé(e); (*accent, attitude*) caractéristique des classes supérieures
upright ['ʌpraɪt] *adj* droit(e); (*fig*) droit, honnête
uprising ['ʌpraɪzɪŋ] *n* soulèvement *m*, insurrection *f*
uproar ['ʌprɔ:*r*] *n* tumulte *m*, vacarme *m*; (*protests*) protestations *fpl*
upset *n* ['ʌpset] dérangement *m* ▷ *vt* [ʌp'set] (*irreg: like* **set**) (*glass etc*) renverser; (*plan*) déranger;

(*person: offend*) contrarier; (: *grieve*) faire de la peine à; bouleverser ▷ *adj* [ʌp'set] contrarié(e); peiné(e); **to have a stomach ~** (*BRIT*) avoir une indigestion
upside down ['ʌpsaɪd-] *adv* à l'envers; **to turn sth ~** (*fig: place*) mettre sens dessus dessous
upstairs [ʌp'stɛəz] *adv* en haut ▷ *adj* (*room*) du dessus, d'en haut ▷ *n*: **the ~** l'étage *m*
up-to-date ['ʌptə'deɪt] *adj* moderne; (*information*) très récent(e)
upward ['ʌpwəd] *adj* ascendant(e); vers le haut ▷ *adv* = **upwards**
upwards *adv* vers le haut; (*more than*): **~ of** plus de
uranium [juə'reɪnɪəm] *n* uranium *m*
Uranus [juə'reɪnəs] *n* Uranus *f*
urban ['ə:bən] *adj* urbain(e)
urge [ə:dʒ] *n* besoin (impératif), envie (pressante) ▷ *vt* (*person*): **to ~ sb to do** exhorter qn à faire, pousser qn à faire, recommander vivement à qn de faire
urgency ['ə:dʒənsɪ] *n* urgence *f*; (*of tone*) insistance *f*
urgent ['ə:dʒənt] *adj* urgent(e); (*plea, tone*) pressant(e)
urinal ['juərɪnl] *n* (*BRIT: place*) urinoir *m*
urinate ['juərɪneɪt] *vi* uriner
urine ['juərɪn] *n* urine *f*
URL *abbr* (= *uniform resource locator*) URL *f*
US *n abbr* = **United States**
us [ʌs] *pron* nous; *see also* **me**
USA *n abbr* = **United States of America**
USB stick *n* clé *f* USB
use *n* [ju:s] emploi *m*, utilisation *f*; (*usefulness*) utilité *f* ▷ *vt* [ju:z] se servir de, utiliser, employer; **in ~** en usage; **out of ~** hors d'usage; **to be of ~** servir, être utile; **it's no ~** ça ne sert à rien; **to have the ~ of** avoir l'usage de; **she ~d to do it** elle le faisait (autrefois), elle avait

u

coutume de le faire; **to be ~d to** avoir l'habitude de, être habitué(e) à; **use up** vt finir, épuiser; (*food*) consommer; **used** [juːzd] *adj* (*car*) d'occasion; **useful** *adj* utile; **useless** *adj* inutile; (*inf: person*) nul(le); **user** *n* utilisateur(-trice), usager *m*; **user-friendly** *adj* convivial(e), facile d'emploi ; **username** *n* (*Comput*) nom *m* d'utilisateur

usual ['juːʒuəl] *adj* habituel(le); **as ~** comme d'habitude; **usually** *adv* d'habitude, d'ordinaire

ute [juːt] *n* (AUST, NZ) pick-up *m inv*

utensil [juː'tɛnsl] *n* ustensile *m*; **kitchen ~s** batterie *f* de cuisine

utility [juː'tɪlɪtɪ] *n* utilité *f*; (*also:* **public ~**) service public

utilize ['juːtɪlaɪz] *vt* utiliser; (*make good use of*) exploiter

utmost ['ʌtməust] *adj* extrême, le plus grand(e) ▷ *n*: **to do one's ~** faire tout son possible

utter ['ʌtə*r*] *adj* total(e), complet(-ète) ▷ *vt* prononcer, proférer; (*sounds*) émettre; **utterly** *adv* complètement, totalement

U-turn ['juː'təːn] *n* demi-tour *m*; (*fig*) volte-face *f inv*

V

v. *abbr* = **verse**; (= *vide*) v.; (= *versus*) vs; (= *volt*) V

vacancy ['veɪkənsɪ] *n* (*job*) poste vacant; (*room*) chambre *f* disponible; **"no vacancies"** "complet"

vacant ['veɪkənt] *adj* (*post*) vacant(e); (*seat etc*) libre, disponible; (*expression*) distrait(e)

vacate [və'keɪt] *vt* quitter

vacation [və'keɪʃən] *n* (*esp US*) vacances *fpl*; **on ~** en vacances; **vacationer, vacationist** (*US*) *n* vacancier(-ière)

vaccination [væksɪ'neɪʃən] *n* vaccination *f*

vaccine ['væksiːn] *n* vaccin *m*

vacuum ['vækjum] *n* vide *m*; **vacuum cleaner** *n* aspirateur *m*

vagina [və'dʒaɪnə] *n* vagin *m*

vague [veɪg] *adj* vague, imprécis(e); (*blurred: photo, memory*) flou(e)

vain [veɪn] *adj* (*useless*) vain(e); (*conceited*) vaniteux(-euse); **in ~** en vain

Valentine's Day ['væləntaɪnz-] n
Saint-Valentin f

valid ['vælɪd] adj (document) valide,
valable; (excuse) valable

valley ['vælɪ] n vallée f

valuable ['væljuəbl] adj (jewel)
de grande valeur; (time, help)
précieux(-euse); **valuables** npl objets
mpl de valeur

value ['væljuː] n valeur f ▷ vt (fix
price) évaluer, expertiser; (appreciate)
apprécier; **values** npl (principles)
valeurs fpl

valve [vælv] n (in machine) soupape f;
(on tyre) valve f; (Med) valve, valvule f

vampire ['væmpaɪəʳ] n vampire m

van [væn] n (Aut) camionnette f

vandal ['vændl] n vandale m/f;
vandalism n vandalisme m;
vandalize vt saccager

vanilla [və'nɪlə] n vanille f

vanish ['vænɪʃ] vi disparaître

vanity ['vænɪtɪ] n vanité f

vapour, (US) **vapor** ['veɪpəʳ] n
vapeur f; (on window) buée f

variable ['vɛərɪəbl] adj variable;
(mood) changeant(e)

variant ['vɛərɪənt] n variante f

variation [vɛərɪ'eɪʃən] n variation f;
(in opinion) changement m

varied ['vɛərɪd] adj varié(e), divers(e)

variety [və'raɪətɪ] n variété f;
(quantity) nombre m, quantité f

various ['vɛərɪəs] adj divers(e),
différent(e); (several) divers, plusieurs

varnish ['vɑːnɪʃ] n vernis m ▷ vt vernir

vary ['vɛərɪ] vt, vi varier, changer

vase [vɑːz] n vase m

Vaseline® ['væsɪliːn] n vaseline f

vast [vɑːst] adj vaste, immense;
(amount, success) énorme

VAT [væt] n abbr (BRIT: = value added
tax) TVA f

vault [vɔːlt] n (of roof) voûte f; (tomb)
caveau m; (in bank) salle f des coffres;
chambre forte ▷ vt (also: **~ over**)
sauter (d'un bond)

VCR n abbr = **video cassette recorder**

VDU n abbr = **visual display unit**

veal [viːl] n veau m

veer [vɪəʳ] vi tourner; (car, ship) virer

vegan ['viːgən] n végétalien(ne)

vegetable ['vɛdʒtəbl] n légume m
▷ adj végétal(e)

vegetarian [vɛdʒɪ'tɛərɪən] adj,
n végétarien(ne); **do you have
any ~ dishes?** avez-vous des plats
végétariens?

vegetation [vɛdʒɪ'teɪʃən] n
végétation f

vehicle ['viːɪkl] n véhicule m

veil [veɪl] n voile m

vein [veɪn] n veine f; (on leaf) nervure f

Velcro® ['vɛlkrəu] n velcro® m

velvet ['vɛlvɪt] n velours m

vending machine ['vɛndɪŋ-] n
distributeur m automatique

vendor ['vɛndəʳ] n vendeur(-euse);
street ~ marchand ambulant

Venetian blind [vɪ'niːʃən-] n store
vénitien

vengeance ['vɛndʒəns] n
vengeance f; **with a ~** (fig) vraiment,
pour de bon

venison ['vɛnɪsn] n venaison f

venom ['vɛnəm] n venin m

vent [vɛnt] n conduit m d'aération;
(in dress, jacket) fente f ▷ vt (fig: one's
feelings) donner libre cours à

ventilation [vɛntɪ'leɪʃən] n
ventilation f, aération f

venture ['vɛntʃəʳ] n entreprise f ▷ vt
risquer, hasarder ▷ vi s'aventurer, se
risquer; **a business ~** une entreprise
commerciale

venue ['vɛnjuː] n lieu m

Venus ['viːnəs] n (planet) Vénus f

verb [vəːb] n verbe m; **verbal** adj
verbal(e)

verdict ['vəːdɪkt] n verdict m

verge [vəːdʒ] n bord m; **"soft ~s"**
(BRIT) "accotements non stabilisés";
on the ~ of doing sur le point de faire

verify ['vɛrɪfaɪ] vt vérifier

versatile ['vəːsətaɪl] adj
polyvalent(e)

V

verse [vəːs] n vers mpl; (stanza) strophe f; (in Bible) verset m

version ['vəːʃən] n version f

versus ['vəːsəs] prep contre

vertical ['vəːtɪkl] adj vertical(e)

very ['vɛrɪ] adv très ▷ adj: **the ~ book which** le livre même que; **the ~ last** le tout dernier; **at the ~ least** au moins; **~ much** beaucoup

vessel ['vɛsl] n (Anat, Naut) vaisseau m; (container) récipient m; see also **blood vessel**

vest [vɛst] n (BRIT: underwear) tricot m de corps; (US: waistcoat) gilet m

vet [vɛt] n abbr (BRIT: = veterinary surgeon) vétérinaire m/f; (US: = veteran) ancien(ne) combattant(e) ▷ vt examiner minutieusement

veteran ['vɛtərn] n vétéran m; (also: **war ~**) ancien combattant

veterinary surgeon ['vɛtrɪnərɪ-] (BRIT) n vétérinaire m/f

veto ['viːtəu] n (pl **vetoes**) veto m ▷ vt opposer son veto à

via ['vaɪə] prep par, via

viable ['vaɪəbl] adj viable

vibrate [vaɪ'breɪt] vi: **to ~ (with)** vibrer (de)

vibration [vaɪ'breɪʃən] n vibration f

vicar ['vɪkər] n pasteur m (de l'Église anglicane)

vice [vaɪs] n (evil) vice m; (Tech) étau m; **vice-chairman** (irreg) n vice-président e

vice versa ['vaɪsɪ'vəːsə] adv vice versa

vicinity [vɪ'sɪnɪtɪ] n environs mpl, alentours mpl

vicious ['vɪʃəs] adj (remark) cruel(le), méchant(e); (blow) brutal(e); (dog) méchant(e), dangereux(-euse); **a ~ circle** un cercle vicieux

victim ['vɪktɪm] n victime f

victor ['vɪktər] n vainqueur m

Victorian [vɪk'tɔːrɪən] adj victorien(ne)

victorious [vɪk'tɔːrɪəs] adj victorieux(-euse)

victory ['vɪktərɪ] n victoire f

video ['vɪdɪəu] n (video film) vidéo f; (also: **~ cassette**) vidéocassette f; (also: **~ cassette recorder**) magnétoscope m ▷ vt (with recorder) enregistrer; (with camera) filmer; **video camera** n caméra f vidéo inv; **video game** n jeu m vidéo inv; **videophone** n vidéophone m; **video recorder** n magnétoscope m; **video shop** n vidéoclub m; **video tape** n bande f vidéo inv; (cassette) vidéocassette f

vie [vaɪ] vi: **to ~ with** lutter avec, rivaliser avec

Vienna [vɪ'ɛnə] n Vienne

Vietnam, Viet Nam ['vjɛt'næm] n Viêt-nam or Vietnam m; **Vietnamese** [vjɛtnə'miːz] adj vietnamien(ne) ▷ n (pl inv) Vietnamien(ne)

view [vjuː] n vue f; (opinion) avis m, vue ▷ vt voir, regarder; (situation) considérer; (house) visiter; **on ~** (in museum etc) exposé(e); **in full ~ of sb** sous les yeux de qn; **in my ~** à mon avis; **in ~ of the fact that** étant donné que; **viewer** n (TV) téléspectateur(-trice); **viewpoint** n point m de vue

vigilant ['vɪdʒɪlənt] adj vigilant(e)

vigorous ['vɪgərəs] adj vigoureux(-euse)

vile [vaɪl] adj (action) vil(e); (smell, food) abominable; (temper) massacrant(e)

villa ['vɪlə] n villa f

village ['vɪlɪdʒ] n village m; **villager** n villageois(e)

villain ['vɪlən] n (scoundrel) scélérat m; (BRIT: criminal) bandit m; (in novel etc) traître m

vinaigrette [vɪneɪ'grɛt] n vinaigrette f

vine [vaɪn] n vigne f

vinegar ['vɪnɪgər] n vinaigre m

vineyard ['vɪnjɑːd] n vignoble m

vintage ['vɪntɪdʒ] n (year) année f, millésime m ▷ cpd (car) d'époque; (wine) de grand cru

vinyl ['vaɪnl] n vinyle m
viola [vɪ'əʊlə] n alto m
violate ['vaɪəleɪt] vt violer
violation [vaɪə'leɪʃən] n violation f;
in ~ of (rule, law) en infraction à, en
violation de
violence ['vaɪələns] n violence f
violent ['vaɪələnt] adj violent(e)
violet ['vaɪələt] adj (colour) violet(te)
▷ n (plant) violette f
violin [vaɪə'lɪn] n violon m
VIP n abbr (= very important person)
VIP m
viral ['vaɪərəl] adj (also Comput)
viral(e)
virgin ['vɜːdʒɪn] n vierge f
Virgo ['vɜːgəʊ] n la Vierge
virtual ['vɜːtjuəl] adj (Comput,
Physics) virtuel(le); (in effect): **it's a
~ impossibility** c'est quasiment
impossible; **virtually** adv (almost)
pratiquement; **virtual reality** n
(Comput) réalité virtuelle
virtue ['vɜːtjuː] n vertu f; (advantage)
mérite m, avantage m; **by ~ of** en
vertu or raison de
virus ['vaɪərəs] n virus m
visa ['viːzə] n visa m
vise [vaɪs] n (us Tech) = **vice**
visibility [vɪzɪ'bɪlɪtɪ] n visibilité f
visible ['vɪzəbl] adj visible
vision ['vɪʒən] n (sight) vue f, vision f;
(foresight, in dream) vision
visit ['vɪzɪt] n visite f; (stay) séjour m
▷ vt (person: us: also: **~ with**) rendre
visite à; (place) visiter; **visiting
hours** npl heures fpl de visite; **visitor**
n visiteur(-euse); (to one's house)
invité(e); **visitor centre**, (us) **visitor
center** n hall m or centre m d'accueil
visual ['vɪzjuəl] adj visuel(le);
visualize vt se représenter
vital ['vaɪtl] adj vital(e); **of ~
importance (to sb/sth)** d'une
importance capitale (pour qn/qch)
vitality [vaɪ'tælɪtɪ] n vitalité f
vitamin ['vɪtəmɪn] n vitamine f

vivid ['vɪvɪd] adj (account) frappant(e),
vivant(e); (light, imagination) vif (vive)
V-neck ['viːnɛk] n décolleté m en V
vocabulary [vəu'kæbjulərɪ] n
vocabulaire m
vocal ['vəukl] adj vocal(e); (articulate)
qui n'hésite pas à s'exprimer, qui sait
faire entendre ses opinions
vocational [vəu'keɪʃənl] adj
professionnel(le)
vodka ['vɔdkə] n vodka f
vogue [vəug] n: **to be in ~** être en
vogue or à la mode
voice [vɔɪs] n voix f ▷ vt (opinion)
exprimer, formuler; **voice mail** n
(system) messagerie f vocale, boîte f
vocale; (device) répondeur m
void [vɔɪd] n vide m ▷ adj (invalid)
nul(le); (empty): **~ of** vide de,
dépourvu(e) de
volatile ['vɔlətaɪl] adj volatil(e);
(fig: person) versatile; (: situation)
explosif(-ive)
volcano [vɔl'keɪnəu] (pl **volcanoes**)
n volcan m
volleyball ['vɔlibɔːl] n volley(-ball) m
volt [vəult] n volt m; **voltage** n
tension f, voltage m
volume ['vɔljuːm] n volume m; (of
tank) capacité f
voluntarily ['vɔləntrɪlɪ] adv
volontairement
voluntary ['vɔləntərɪ] adj
volontaire; (unpaid) bénévole
volunteer [vɔlən'tɪəʳ] n volontaire
m/f ▷ vt (information) donner
spontanément ▷ vi (Mil) s'engager
comme volontaire; **to ~ to do** se
proposer pour faire
vomit ['vɔmɪt] n vomissure f ▷ vt,
vi vomir
vote [vəut] n vote m, suffrage m;
(votes cast) voix f, vote; (franchise)
droit m de vote ▷ vt (chairman) élire;
(propose): **to ~ that** proposer que +
sub ▷ vi voter; **~ of thanks**
discours m de remerciement;

V

voter *n* électeur(-trice); **voting** *n*
scrutin *m*, vote *m*
voucher ['vautʃə^r] *n (for meal, petrol,
gift)* bon *m*
vow [vau] *n* vœu *m*, serment *m*
▷ *vi* jurer
vowel ['vauəl] *n* voyelle *f*
voyage ['vɔɪɪdʒ] *n* voyage *m* par mer,
traversée *f*
vulgar ['vʌlgə^r] *adj* vulgaire
vulnerable ['vʌlnərəbl] *adj*
vulnérable
vulture ['vʌltʃə^r] *n* vautour *m*

waddle ['wɔdl] *vi* se dandiner
wade [weɪd] *vi*: **to ~ through**
marcher dans, patauger dans; *(fig:
book)* venir à bout de
wafer ['weɪfə^r] *n (Culin)* gaufrette *f*
waffle ['wɔfl] *n (Culin)* gaufre *f* ▷ *vi*
parler pour ne rien dire; faire du
remplissage
wag [wæg] *vt* agiter, remuer ▷ *vi*
remuer
wage [weɪdʒ] *n (also: ~s)* salaire *m*,
paye *f* ▷ *vt*: **to ~ war** faire la guerre
wag(g)on ['wægən] *n (horse-drawn)*
chariot *m*; *(BRIT Rail)* wagon *m* (de
marchandises)
wail [weɪl] *n* gémissement *m*; *(of siren)*
hurlement *m* ▷ *vi* gémir; *(siren)* hurler
waist [weɪst] *n* taille *f*, ceinture *f*;
waistcoat *n (BRIT)* gilet *m*
wait [weɪt] *n* attente *f* ▷ *vi* attendre;
to ~ for sb/sth attendre qn/qch; **to
keep sb ~ing** faire attendre qn; **~ for
me, please** attendez-moi, s'il vous

plaît; **I can't ~ to ...** (*fig*) je meurs d'envie de ...; **to lie in ~ for** guetter; **wait on** *vt fus* servir; **waiter** *n* garçon *m* (de café), serveur *m*; **waiting list** *n* liste *f* d'attente; **waiting room** *n* salle *f* d'attente; **waitress** ['weɪtrɪs] *n* serveuse *f*

waive [weɪv] *vt* renoncer à, abandonner

wake [weɪk] (*pt* **woke** *or* **waked**, *pp* **woken** *or* **waked**) *vt* (*also*: **~ up**) réveiller ▷ *vi* (*also*: **~ up**) se réveiller ▷ *n* (*for dead person*) veillée *f* mortuaire; (*Naut*) sillage *m*

Wales [weɪlz] *n* pays *m* de Galles; **the Prince of ~** le prince de Galles

walk [wɔːk] *n* promenade *f*; (*short*) petit tour; (*gait*) démarche *f*; (*path*) chemin *m*; (*in park etc*) allée *f* ▷ *vi* marcher; (*for pleasure, exercise*) se promener ▷ *vt* (*distance*) faire à pied; (*dog*) promener; **10 minutes' ~ from** à 10 minutes de marche de; **to go for a ~** se promener; faire un tour; **from all ~s of life** de toutes conditions sociales; **walk out** *vi* (*go out*) sortir; (*as protest*) partir (en signe de protestation); (*strike*) se mettre en grève; **to ~ out on sb** quitter qn; **walker** *n* (*person*) marcheur(-euse); **walkie-talkie** ['wɔːkɪ'tɔːkɪ] *n* talkie-walkie *m*; **walking** *n* marche *f* à pied; **walking shoes** *npl* chaussures *fpl* de marche; **walking stick** *n* canne *f*; **Walkman®** *n* Walkman® *m*; **walkway** *n* promenade *f*, cheminement piéton

wall [wɔːl] *n* mur *m*; (*of tunnel, cave*) paroi *f*

wallet ['wɔlɪt] *n* portefeuille *m*; **I can't find my ~** je ne retrouve plus mon portefeuille

wallpaper ['wɔːlpeɪpəʳ] *n* papier peint *m* ▷ *vt* tapisser

walnut ['wɔːlnʌt] *n* noix *f*; (*tree, wood*) noyer *m*

walrus ['wɔːlrəs] (*pl* **walrus** *or* **walruses**) *n* morse *m*

waltz [wɔːlts] *n* valse *f* ▷ *vi* valser

wand [wɔnd] *n* (*also*: **magic ~**) baguette *f* (magique)

wander ['wɔndəʳ] *vi* (*person*) errer, aller sans but; (*thoughts*) vagabonder ▷ *vt* errer dans

want [wɔnt] *vt* vouloir; (*need*) avoir besoin de ▷ *n*: **for ~ of** par manque de, faute de; **to ~ to do** vouloir faire; **to ~ sb to do** vouloir que qn fasse; **wanted** *adj* (*criminal*) recherché(e) par la police

war [wɔːʳ] *n* guerre *f*; **to make ~ (on)** faire la guerre (à)

ward [wɔːd] *n* (*in hospital*) salle *f*; (*Pol*) section électorale; (*Law: child: also*: **~ of court**) pupille *m/f*

warden ['wɔːdn] *n* (BRIT: *of institution*) directeur(-trice); (*of park, game reserve*) gardien(ne); (BRIT: *also*: **traffic ~**) contractuel(le)

wardrobe ['wɔːdrəub] *n* (*cupboard*) armoire *f*; (*clothes*) garde-robe *f*

warehouse ['wɛəhaus] *n* entrepôt *m*

warfare ['wɔːfɛəʳ] *n* guerre *f*

warhead ['wɔːhɛd] *n* (*Mil*) ogive *f*

warm [wɔːm] *adj* chaud(e); (*person, thanks, welcome, applause*) chaleureux(-euse); **it's ~** il fait chaud; **I'm ~** j'ai chaud; **warm up** *vi* (*person, room*) se réchauffer; (*athlete, discussion*) s'échauffer ▷ *vt* (*food*) (faire) réchauffer; (*water*) (faire) chauffer; (*engine*) faire chauffer; **warmly** *adv* (*dress*) chaudement; (*thank, welcome*) chaleureusement; **warmth** *n* chaleur *f*

warn [wɔːn] *vt* avertir, prévenir; **to ~ sb (not) to do** conseiller à qn de (ne pas) faire; **warning** *n* avertissement *m*; (*notice*) avis *m*; **warning light** *n* avertisseur lumineux

warrant ['wɔrnt] *n* (*guarantee*) garantie *f*; (*Law: to arrest*) mandat *m* d'arrêt; (: *to search*) mandat de perquisition ▷ *vt* (*justify, merit*) justifier

warranty ['wɔrəntɪ] *n* garantie *f*

W

warrior ['wɒrɪəʳ] n guerrier(-ière)

Warsaw ['wɔːsɔː] n Varsovie

warship ['wɔːʃɪp] n navire m de guerre

wart [wɔːt] n verrue f

wartime ['wɔːtaɪm] n: **in ~** en temps de guerre

wary ['wɛərɪ] adj prudent(e)

was [wɒz] pt of **be**

wash [wɒʃ] vt laver ▷ vi se laver; (sea): **to ~ over/against sth** inonder/ baigner qch ▷ n (clothes) lessive f; (washing programme) lavage m; (of ship) sillage m; **to have a ~** se laver, faire sa toilette; **wash up** vi (BRIT) faire la vaisselle; (US: have a wash) se débarbouiller; **washbasin** n lavabo m; **washer** n (Tech) rondelle f, joint m; **washing** n (BRIT: linen etc: dirty) linge m; (: clean) lessive f; **washing line** n (BRIT) corde f à linge; **washing machine** n machine f à laver; **washing powder** n (BRIT) lessive f (en poudre)

Washington ['wɒʃɪŋtən] n Washington m

wash: washing-up n (BRIT) vaisselle f; **washing-up liquid** n (BRIT) produit m pour la vaisselle; **washroom** n (US) toilettes fpl

wasn't ['wɒznt] = **was not**

wasp [wɒsp] n guêpe f

waste [weɪst] n gaspillage m; (of time) perte f; (rubbish) déchets mpl; (also: **household ~**) ordures fpl ▷ adj (land, ground: in city) à l'abandon; (leftover): **~ material** déchets ▷ vt gaspiller; (time, opportunity) perdre; **waste ground** n (BRIT) terrain m vague; **wastepaper basket** n corbeille f à papier

watch [wɒtʃ] n montre f; (act of watching) surveillance f; (guard: Mil) sentinelle f; (: Naut) homme m de quart; (Naut: spell of duty) quart m ▷ vt (look at) observer; (: match, programme) regarder; (spy on, guard) surveiller; (be careful of) faire attention à ▷ vi regarder; (keep guard) monter la garde; **to keep ~** faire le guet; **watch out** vi faire attention; **watchdog** n chien m de garde; (fig) gardien(ne); **watch strap** n bracelet m de montre

water ['wɔːtəʳ] n eau f ▷ vt (plant, garden) arroser ▷ vi (eyes) larmoyer; **in British ~s** dans les eaux territoriales Britanniques; **to make sb's mouth ~** mettre l'eau à la bouche de qn; **water down** vt (milk etc) couper avec de l'eau; (fig: story) édulcorer; **watercolour**, (US) **watercolor** n aquarelle f; **watercress** n cresson m (de fontaine); **waterfall** n chute f d'eau; **watering can** n arrosoir m; **watermelon** n pastèque f; **waterproof** adj imperméable; **water-skiing** n ski m nautique

watt [wɒt] n watt m

wave [weɪv] n vague f; (of hand) geste m, signe m; (Radio) onde f; (in hair) ondulation f; (fig) vague ▷ vi faire signe de la main; (flag) flotter au vent; (grass) ondoyer ▷ vt (handkerchief) agiter; (stick) brandir; **wavelength** n longueur f d'ondes

waver ['weɪvəʳ] vi vaciller; (voice) trembler; (person) hésiter

wavy ['weɪvɪ] adj (hair, surface) ondulé(e); (line) onduleux(-euse)

wax [wæks] n cire f; (for skis) fart m ▷ vt cirer; (car) lustrer; (skis) farter ▷ vi (moon) croître

way [weɪ] n chemin m, voie f; (distance) distance f; (direction) chemin, direction f; (manner) façon f, manière f; (habit) habitude f, façon; **which ~? — this ~/that ~** par où or de quel côté? — par ici/par là; **to lose one's ~** perdre son chemin; **on the ~ (to)** en route (pour); **to be on one's ~** être en route; **to be in the ~** bloquer le passage; (fig) gêner; **it's a long ~ away** c'est loin d'ici; **to go out of one's ~ to do** (fig) se donner beaucoup de mal pour faire; **to be under ~** (work, project) être en cours; **in a ~** dans un sens; **by the ~** à propos; **"~ in"** (BRIT) "entrée"; **"~ out"** (BRIT) "sortie"; **the ~ back** le chemin du retour; **"give ~"** (BRIT Aut) "cédez la priorité"; **no ~!** (inf) pas question!

W.C. n abbr (BRIT: = water closet) w.-c. mpl, waters mpl

we [wiː] pl pron nous

weak [wiːk] adj faible; (health) fragile; (beam etc) peu solide; (tea, coffee) léger(-ère); **weaken** vi faiblir ▷ vt affaiblir; **weakness** n faiblesse f; (fault) point m faible

wealth [wɛlθ] n (money, resources) richesse(s) f(pl); (of details) profusion f; **wealthy** adj riche

weapon ['wɛpən] n arme f; **~s of mass destruction** armes fpl de destruction massive

wear [wɛəʳ] (pt **wore**, pp **worn**) n (use) usage m; (deterioration through use) usure f ▷ vt (clothes) porter; (put on) mettre; (damage: through use) user ▷ vi (last) faire de l'usage; (rub etc through) s'user; **sports/baby~** vêtements mpl de sport/pour bébés; **evening ~** tenue f de soirée; **wear off** vi disparaître; **wear out** vt user; (person, strength) épuiser

weary ['wɪərɪ] adj (tired) épuisé(e); (dispirited) las (lasse); abattu(e) ▷ vi: **to ~ of** se lasser de

weasel ['wiːzl] n (Zool) belette f

weather ['wɛðəʳ] n temps m ▷ vt (storm: lit, fig) essuyer; (crisis) survivre à; **under the ~** (fig: ill) mal fichu(e); **weather forecast** n prévisions fpl météorologiques, météo f

weave (pt **wove**, pp **woven**) [wiːv, wəuv, 'wəuvn] vt (cloth) tisser; (basket) tresser

web [wɛb] n (of spider) toile f; (on duck's foot) palmure f; (fig) tissu m; (Comput): **the (World-Wide) W~** le Web; **web address** n adresse f Web; **webcam** n webcam f; **webinar** ['wɛbɪnɑːʳ] n (Comput) séminaire m en ligne; **web page** n (Comput) page f Web; **website** n (Comput) site m Web

wed [wɛd] (pt, pp **wedded**) vt épouser ▷ vi se marier

we'd [wiːd] = **we had; we would**

wedding ['wɛdɪŋ] n mariage m; **wedding anniversary** n anniversaire m de mariage; **silver/golden wedding anniversary** noces fpl d'argent/d'or; **wedding day** n jour m du mariage; **wedding dress** n robe f de mariée; **wedding ring** n alliance f

wedge [wɛdʒ] n (of wood etc) coin m; (under door etc) cale f; (of cake) part f ▷ vt (fix) caler; (push) enfoncer, coincer

Wednesday ['wɛdnzdɪ] n mercredi m

wee [wiː] adj (SCOTTISH) petit(e); tout(e) petit(e)

weed [wiːd] n mauvaise herbe ▷ vt désherber; **weedkiller** n désherbant m

week [wiːk] n semaine f; **a ~ today/on Tuesday** aujourd'hui/mardi en huit; **weekday** n jour m de semaine; (Comm) jour ouvrable; **weekend** n week-end m; **weekly** adv une fois par semaine, chaque semaine ▷ adj, n hebdomadaire (m)

weep [wiːp] (pt, pp **wept**) vi (person) pleurer

weigh [weɪ] vt, vi peser; **to ~ anchor** lever l'ancre; **weigh up** vt examiner

weight [weɪt] n poids m; **to put on/lose ~** grossir/maigrir; **weightlifting** n haltérophilie f

weir [wɪəʳ] n barrage m

weird [wɪəd] adj bizarre; (eerie) surnaturel(le)

welcome ['wɛlkəm] adj bienvenu(e) ▷ n accueil m ▷ vt accueillir; (also: **bid ~**) souhaiter la bienvenue à; (be glad of) se réjouir de; **you're ~!** (after thanks) de rien, il n'y a pas de quoi

weld [wɛld] vt souder

welfare ['wɛlfɛəʳ] n (wellbeing) bien-être m; (social aid) assistance sociale; **welfare state** n État-providence m

well [wɛl] n puits m ▷ adv bien ▷ adj: **to be ~** aller bien ▷ excl eh bien!; (relief also) bon!; (resignation) enfin!; **~ done!** bravo!; **get ~ soon!** remets-toi

W

vite!; **to do ~** bien réussir; (business)
prospérer; **as ~** (in addition) aussi,
également; **as ~ as** aussi bien que or
de; en plus de
we'll [wi:l] = **we will; we shall**
well: well-behaved adj sage,
obéissant(e); **well-built** adj
(person) bien bâti(e); **well-dressed**
adj bien habillé(e), bien vêtu(e);
well-groomed ['-'gru:md] adj très
soigné(e)
wellies ['welɪz] npl (BRIT inf)
= **wellingtons**
wellingtons ['welɪŋtənz] npl (also:
wellington boots) bottes fpl en
caoutchouc
well: well-known adj (person) bien
connu(e); **well-off** adj aisé(e), assez
riche; **well-paid** [wel'peɪd] adj bien
payé(e)
Welsh [welʃ] adj gallois(e) ▷ n (Ling)
gallois m; **the Welsh** npl (people) les
Gallois; **Welshman** (irreg) n Gallois m;
Welshwoman (irreg) n Galloise f
went [went] pt of **go**
wept [wept] pt, pp of **weep**
were [wəːʳ] pt of **be**
we're [wɪəʳ] = **we are**
weren't [wəːnt] = **were not**
west [west] n ouest m ▷ adj (wind)
d'ouest; (side) ouest inv ▷ adv à or vers
l'ouest; **the W~** l'Occident m, l'Ouest;
westbound ['westbaʊnd] adj en
direction de l'ouest; (carriageway)
ouest inv; **western** adj occidental(e),
de or à l'ouest ▷ n (Cine) western
m; **West Indian** adj antillais(e) ▷ n
Antillais(e); **West Indies** ['-'ɪndɪz] npl
Antilles fpl
wet [wet] adj mouillé(e); (damp)
humide; (soaked: also: **~ through**)
trempé(e); (rainy) pluvieux(-euse);
to get ~ se mouiller; **"~ paint"**
"attention peinture fraîche"; **wetsuit**
n combinaison f de plongée
we've [wi:v] = **we have**
whack [wæk] vt donner un grand
coup à

whale [weɪl] n (Zool) baleine f
wharf (pl **wharves**) [wɔːf, wɔːvz]
n quai m

 KEYWORD

what [wɔt] adj 1 (in questions)
quel(le); **what size is he?** quelle
taille fait-il?; **what colour is it?**
de quelle couleur est-ce?; **what
books do you need?** quels livres
vous faut-il?
2 (in exclamations): **what a mess!**
quel désordre!; **what a fool I am!**
que je suis bête!
▷ pron 1 (interrogative) que; de/à/
en etc quoi; **what are you doing?**
que faites-vous?, qu'est-ce que vous
faites?; **what is happening?** qu'est-
ce qui se passe?, que se passe-t-il?;
what are you talking about? de
quoi parlez-vous?; **what are you
thinking about?** à quoi pensez-
vous?; **what is it called?** comment
est-ce que ça s'appelle?; **what about
me?** et moi?; **what about doing …?**
et si on faisait …?
2 (relative: subject) ce qui; (: direct
object) ce que; (: indirect object) ce à
quoi, ce dont; **I saw what you did/
was on the table** j'ai vu ce que vous
avez fait/ce qui était sur la table; **tell
me what you remember** dites-moi
ce dont vous vous souvenez; **what I
want is a cup of tea** ce que je veux,
c'est une tasse de thé
▷ excl (disbelieving) quoi!, comment!

whatever [wɔt'evəʳ] adj: **take ~
book you prefer** prenez le livre que
vous préférez, peu importe lequel;
~ book you take quel que soit le
livre que vous preniez ▷ pron: **do ~
is necessary** faites (tout) ce qui est
nécessaire; **~ happens** quoi qu'il
arrive; **no reason ~** or **whatsoever**
pas la moindre raison; **nothing ~** or
whatsoever rien du tout

whatsoever [wɔtsəʊ'evər] adj see
whatever
wheat [wiːt] n blé m, froment m
wheel [wiːl] n roue f; (Aut: also:
steering ~) volant m; (Naut)
gouvernail m ▷ vt (pram etc) pousser,
rouler ▷ vi (birds) tournoyer; (also:
~ round: person) se retourner, faire
volte-face; **wheelbarrow** n brouette f;
wheelchair n fauteuil roulant; **wheel**
clamp n (Aut) sabot m (de Denver)
wheeze [wiːz] vi respirer
bruyamment

when [wen] adv quand; **when did he**
go? quand est-ce qu'il est parti?
▷ conj **1** (at, during, after the time that)
quand, lorsque; **she was reading**
when I came in elle lisait quand or
lorsque je suis entré
2 (on, at which): **on the day when I**
met him le jour où je l'ai rencontré
3 (whereas) alors que; **I thought I**
was wrong when in fact I was right
j'ai cru que j'avais tort alors qu'en fait
j'avais raison

whenever [wɛn'evər] adv quand
donc ▷ conj quand; (every time that)
chaque fois que
where [wɛər] adv, conj où; **this is**
~ c'est là que; **whereabouts** adv
où donc ▷ n: **nobody knows his**
whereabouts personne ne sait où
il se trouve; **whereas** conj alors que;
whereby adv (formal) par lequel (or
laquelle etc); **wherever** adv où donc
▷ conj où que + sub; **sit wherever**
you like asseyez-vous (là) où vous
voulez
whether ['wɛðər] conj si; **I don't**
know ~ to accept or not je ne sais
pas si je dois accepter ou non; **it's**
doubtful ~ il est peu probable que
+ sub; **~ you go or not** que vous y
alliez ou non

which [wɪtʃ] adj **1** (interrogative, direct,
indirect) quel(le); **which picture**
do you want? quel tableau voulez-
vous?; **which one?** lequel (laquelle)?
2: **in which case** auquel cas; **we**
got there at 8pm, by which time
the cinema was full quand nous
sommes arrivés à 20h, le cinéma
était complet
▷ pron **1** (interrogative) lequel
(laquelle), lesquels (lesquelles) pl;
I don't mind which peu importe
lequel; **which (of these) are yours?**
lesquels sont à vous?; **tell me which**
you want dites-moi lesquels or ceux
que vous voulez
2 (relative: subject) qui; (: object) que;
sur/vers etc lequel (laquelle) (NB: à +
lequel = **auquel**; de + lequel = **duquel**);
the apple which you ate/which
is on the table la pomme que vous
avez mangée/qui est sur la table; **the**
chair on which you are sitting la
chaise sur laquelle vous êtes assis;
the book of which you spoke le
livre dont vous avez parlé; **he said he**
knew, which is true/I was afraid
of il a dit qu'il le savait, ce qui est vrai/
ce que je craignais; **after which**
après quoi

whichever [wɪtʃ'evər] adj: **take ~**
book you prefer prenez le livre que
vous préférez, peu importe lequel; **~**
book you take quel que soit le livre
que vous preniez
while [waɪl] n moment m ▷ conj
pendant que; (as long as) tant que;
(as, whereas) alors que; (though) bien
que + sub, quoique + sub; **for a ~**
pendant quelque temps; **in a ~** dans
un moment
whilst [waɪlst] conj = **while**
whim [wɪm] n caprice m
whine [waɪn] n gémissement m; (of
engine, siren) plainte stridente ▷ vi

gémir, geindre, pleurnicher; (*dog, engine, siren*) gémir

whip [wɪp] *n* fouet *m*; (*for riding*) cravache *f*; (*Pol: person*) chef *m* de file (*assurant la discipline dans son groupe parlementaire*) ▷ *vt* fouetter; (*snatch*) enlever (*or sortir*) brusquement; **whipped cream** *n* crème fouettée

whirl [wəːl] *vi* tourbillonner; (*dancers*) tournoyer ▷ *vt* faire tourbillonner; faire tournoyer

whisk [wɪsk] *n* (Culin) fouet *m* ▷ *vt* (*eggs*) fouetter, battre; **to ~ sb away** *or* **off** emmener qn rapidement

whiskers ['wɪskəz] *npl* (*of animal*) moustaches *fpl*; (*of man*) favoris *mpl*

whisky, (IRISH, US) **whiskey** ['wɪskɪ] *n* whisky *m*

whisper ['wɪspəʳ] *n* chuchotement *m* ▷ *vt, vi* chuchoter

whistle ['wɪsl] *n* (*sound*) sifflement *m*; (*object*) sifflet *m* ▷ *vi* siffler ▷ *vt* siffler, siffloter

white [waɪt] *adj* blanc (blanche); (*with fear*) blême ▷ *n* blanc *m*; (*person*) blanc (blanche); **White House** *n* (US): **the White House** la Maison-Blanche; **whitewash** *n* (*paint*) lait *m* de chaux ▷ *vt* blanchir à la chaux; (*fig*) blanchir

whiting ['waɪtɪŋ] *n* (*pl inv: fish*) merlan *m*

Whitsun ['wɪtsn] *n* la Pentecôte

whittle ['wɪtl] *vt*: **to ~ away, to ~ down** (*costs*) réduire, rogner

whizz [wɪz] *vi* aller (*or* passer) à toute vitesse

who [huː] *pron* qui

whoever [huːˈɛvəʳ] *pron*: **~ finds it** celui (celle) qui le trouve (, qui que ce soit), quiconque le trouve; **ask ~ you like** demandez à qui vous voulez; **~ he marries** qui que ce soit *or* quelle que soit la personne qu'il épouse; **~ told you that?** qui a bien pu vous dire ça?, qui donc vous a dit ça?

whole [həul] *adj* (*complete*) entier(-ière), tout(e); (*not broken*) intact(e), complet(-ète) ▷ *n* (*entire unit*) tout

m; (*all*): **the ~ of** la totalité de, tout(e) le; **the ~ of the town** la ville tout entière; **on the ~, as a ~** dans l'ensemble; **wholefood(s)** *n(pl)* aliments complets; **wholeheartedly** [həul'hɑːtɪdlɪ] *adv* sans réserve; **to agree wholeheartedly** être entièrement d'accord; **wholemeal** *adj* (BRIT: *flour, bread*) complet(-ète); **wholesale** *n* (vente *f* en) gros *m* ▷ *adj* (*price*) de gros; (*destruction*) systématique; **wholewheat** *adj* = **wholemeal**; **wholly** *adv* entièrement, tout à fait

KEYWORD

whom [huːm] *pron* **1** (*interrogative*) qui; **whom did you see?** qui avez-vous vu?; **to whom did you give it?** à qui l'avez-vous donné?
2 (*relative*) que à *qui etc* qui; **the man whom I saw/to whom I spoke** l'homme que j'ai vu/à qui j'ai parlé

whore [hɔːʳ] *n* (*inf: pej*) putain *f*

KEYWORD

whose [huːz] *adj* **1** (*possessive, interrogative*): **whose book is this?, whose is this book?** à qui est ce livre?; **whose pencil have you taken?** à qui est le crayon que vous avez pris?, c'est le crayon de qui que vous avez pris?; **whose daughter are you?** de qui êtes-vous la fille?
2 (*possessive, relative*): **the man whose son you rescued** l'homme dont *or* de qui vous avez sauvé le fils; **the girl whose sister you were speaking to** la fille à la sœur de qui *or* de laquelle vous parliez; **the woman whose car was stolen** la femme dont la voiture a été volée
▷ *pron* à qui; **whose is this?** à qui est ceci?; **I know whose it is** je sais à qui c'est

why [waɪ] adv pourquoi; **why not?** pourquoi pas?
▶ conj: **I wonder why he said that** je me demande pourquoi il a dit ça; **that's not why I'm here** ce n'est pas pour ça que je suis là; **the reason why** la raison pour laquelle
▶ excl eh bien!, tiens!; **why, it's you!** tiens, c'est vous!; **why, that's impossible!** voyons, c'est impossible!

wicked ['wɪkɪd] adj méchant(e); (mischievous: grin, look) espiègle, malicieux(-euse); (crime) pervers(e); (inf: very good) génial(e) (inf)

wicket ['wɪkɪt] n (Cricket: stumps) guichet m; (: grass area) espace compris entre les deux guichets

wide [waɪd] adj large; (area, knowledge) vaste, très étendu(e); (choice) grand(e) ▷ adv: **to open ~** ouvrir tout grand; **to shoot ~** tirer à côté; **it is 3 metres ~** cela fait 3 mètres de large; **widely** adv (different) radicalement; (spaced) sur une grande étendue; (believed) généralement; (travel) beaucoup; **widen** vt élargir ▷ vi s'élargir; **wide open** adj grand(e) ouvert(e); **widespread** adj (belief etc) très répandu(e)

widow ['wɪdəu] n veuve f; **widower** n veuf m

width [wɪdθ] n largeur f

wield [wiːld] vt (sword) manier; (power) exercer

wife (pl **wives**) [waɪf, waɪvz] n femme f, épouse f

Wi-Fi ['waɪfaɪ] n wifi m

wig [wɪg] n perruque f

wild [waɪld] adj sauvage; (sea) déchaîné(e); (idea, life) fou (folle); (behaviour) déchaîné(e), extravagant(e); (inf: angry) hors de soi, furieux(-euse) ▷ n: **the ~** la nature; **wilderness** ['wɪldənɪs] n désert m, région f sauvage; **wildlife** n faune f (et flore f); **wildly** adv (behave) de manière déchaînée; (applaud) frénétiquement; (hit, guess) au hasard; (happy) follement

will [wɪl] aux vb **1** (forming future tense): **I will finish it tomorrow** je le finirai demain; **I will have finished it by tomorrow** je l'aurai fini d'ici demain; **will you do it? — yes I will/ no I won't** le ferez-vous? — oui/non
2 (in conjectures, predictions): **he will** or **he'll be there by now** il doit être arrivé à l'heure qu'il est; **that will be the postman** ça doit être le facteur
3 (in commands, requests, offers): **will you be quiet!** voulez-vous bien vous taire!; **will you help me?** est-ce que vous pouvez m'aider?; **will you have a cup of tea?** voulez-vous une tasse de thé?; **I won't put up with it!** je ne le tolérerai pas!
▶ vt (pt, pp **willed**): **to will sb to do** souhaiter ardemment que qn fasse; **he willed himself to go on** par un suprême effort de volonté, il continua
▶ n **1** volonté f; **against one's will** à contre-cœur
2 (document) testament m

willing ['wɪlɪŋ] adj de bonne volonté, serviable; **he's ~ to do it** il est disposé à le faire, il veut bien le faire; **willingly** adv volontiers

willow ['wɪləu] n saule m

willpower ['wɪl'pauər] n volonté f

wilt [wɪlt] vi dépérir

win [wɪn] (pt, pp **won**) n (in sports etc) victoire f ▷ vt (battle, money) gagner; (prize, contract) remporter; (popularity) acquérir ▷ vi gagner; **win over** vt convaincre

wince [wɪns] vi tressaillir

wind¹ [wɪnd] n (also Med) vent m; (breath) souffle m ▷ vt (take breath

away) couper le souffle à; **the ~(s)**
(*Mus*) les instruments *mpl* à vent
wind² (*pt, pp* **wound**) [waɪnd,
waʊnd] *vt* enrouler; (*wrap*)
envelopper; (*clock, toy*) remonter ▷ *vi*
(*road, river*) serpenter; **wind down** *vt*
(*car window*) baisser; (*fig: production,
business*) réduire progressivement;
wind up *vt* (*clock*) remonter; (*debate*)
terminer, clôturer

windfall ['wɪndfɔːl] *n* coup *m* de
chance

wind farm *n* ferme *f* éolienne

winding ['waɪndɪŋ] *adj* (*road*)
sinueux(-euse); (*staircase*)
tournant(e)

windmill ['wɪndmɪl] *n* moulin *m*
à vent

window ['wɪndəʊ] *n* fenêtre *f*; (*in car,
train: also:* **~pane**) vitre *f*; (*in shop etc*)
vitrine *f*; **window box** *n* jardinière *f*;
window cleaner *n* (*person*) laveur(-
euse) de vitres; **window pane** *n*
vitre *f*, carreau *m*; **window seat** *n* (*on
plane*) place *f* côté hublot; **windowsill**
n (*inside*) appui *m* de la fenêtre;
(*outside*) rebord *m* de la fenêtre

windscreen ['wɪndskriːn] *n* pare-
brise *m inv*; **windscreen wiper** *n*
essuie-glace *m inv*

windshield ['wɪndʃiːld] (*us*) *n*
= **windscreen**

windsurfing ['wɪndsəːfɪŋ] *n*
planche *f* à voile

wind turbine [-təːbaɪn] *n* éolienne *f*

windy ['wɪndɪ] *adj* (*day*) de vent,
venteux(-euse); (*place, weather*)
venteux; **it's ~** il y a du vent

wine [waɪn] *n* vin *m*; **wine bar** *n* bar
m à vin; **wine glass** *n* verre *m* à vin;
wine list *n* carte *f* des vins; **wine
tasting** *n* dégustation *f* (de vins)

wing [wɪŋ] *n* aile *f*; **wings** *npl* (*Theat*)
coulisses *fpl*; **wing mirror** *n* (*BRIT*)
rétroviseur latéral

wink [wɪŋk] *n* clin *m* d'œil ▷ *vi* faire un
clin d'œil; (*blink*) cligner des yeux

winner ['wɪnəʳ] *n* gagnant(e)

winning ['wɪnɪŋ] *adj* (*team*)
gagnant(e); (*goal*) décisif(-ive);
(*charming*) charmeur(-euse)

winter ['wɪntəʳ] *n* hiver *m* ▷ *vi*
hiverner; **in ~** en hiver; **winter
sports** *npl* sports *mpl* d'hiver;
wintertime *n* hiver *m*

wipe [waɪp] *n*: **to give sth a ~**
donner un coup de torchon/de
chiffon/d'éponge à qch ▷ *vt* essuyer;
(*erase: tape*) effacer; **to ~ one's
nose** se moucher; **wipe out** *vt*
(*debt*) éteindre, amortir; (*memory*)
effacer; (*destroy*) anéantir; **wipe up**
vt essuyer

wire ['waɪəʳ] *n* fil *m* (de fer); (*Elec*)
fil électrique; (*Tel*) télégramme
m ▷ *vt* (*house*) faire l'installation
électrique de; (*also:* **~ up**)
brancher; (*person: send telegram to*)
télégraphier à

wireless ['waɪəlɪs] *adj* sans fil;
wireless technology *n* technologie
f sans fil

wiring ['waɪərɪŋ] *n* (*Elec*) installation
f électrique

wisdom ['wɪzdəm] *n* sagesse *f*; (*of
action*) prudence *f*; **wisdom tooth** *n*
dent *f* de sagesse

wise [waɪz] *adj* sage, prudent(e);
(*remark*) judicieux(-euse)

wish [wɪʃ] *n* (*desire*) désir *m*; (*specific
desire*) souhait *m*, vœu *m* ▷ *vt*
souhaiter, désirer, vouloir; **best ~es**
(*on birthday etc*) meilleurs vœux; **with
best ~es** (*in letter*) bien amicalement;
to ~ sb goodbye dire au revoir à qn;
he ~ed me well il m'a souhaité bonne
chance; **to ~ to do/sb to do** désirer
or vouloir faire/que qn fasse; **to ~ for**
souhaiter

wistful ['wɪstful] *adj* mélancolique

wit [wɪt] *n* (*also:* **~s**: *intelligence*)
intelligence *f*, esprit *m*; (*presence of
mind*) présence *f* d'esprit; (*wittiness*)
esprit; (*person*) homme/femme
d'esprit

witch [wɪtʃ] *n* sorcière *f*

KEYWORD

with [wɪð, wɪθ] prep **1** (in the company of) avec; (: at the home of) chez; **we stayed with friends** nous avons logé chez des amis; **I'll be with you in a minute** je suis à vous dans un instant **2** (descriptive): **a room with a view** une chambre avec vue; **the man with the grey hat/blue eyes** l'homme au chapeau gris/aux yeux bleus **3** (indicating manner, means, cause): **with tears in her eyes** les larmes aux yeux; **to walk with a stick** marcher avec une canne; **red with anger** rouge de colère; **to shake with fear** trembler de peur; **to fill sth with water** remplir qch d'eau **4** (in phrases): **I'm with you** (I understand) je vous suis; **to be with it** (inf: up-to-date) être dans le vent

withdraw [wɪθ'drɔː] vt (irreg: like **draw**) retirer ▷ vi se retirer; **withdrawal** n retrait m; (Med) état m de manque; **withdrawn** pp of **withdraw** ▷ adj (person) renfermé(e)
withdrew [wɪθ'druː] pt of **withdraw**
wither ['wɪðər] vi se faner
withhold [wɪθ'həuld] vt (irreg: like **hold**) (money) retenir; (decision) remettre; **to ~ (from)** (permission) refuser (à); (information) cacher (à)
within [wɪð'ɪn] prep à l'intérieur de ▷ adv à l'intérieur; **~ his reach** à sa portée; **~ sight of** en vue de; **~ a mile of** à moins d'un mille de; **~ the week** avant la fin de la semaine
without [wɪð'aut] prep sans; **~ a coat** sans manteau; **~ speaking** sans parler; **to go** or **do ~ sth** se passer de qch
withstand [wɪθ'stænd] vt (irreg: like **stand**) résister à
witness ['wɪtnɪs] n (person) témoin m ▷ vt (event) être témoin de; (document)

attester l'authenticité de; **to bear ~ to sth** témoigner de qch
witty ['wɪtɪ] adj spirituel(le), plein(e) d'esprit
wives [waɪvz] npl of **wife**
wizard ['wɪzəd] n magicien m
wk abbr = **week**
wobble ['wɔbl] vi trembler; (chair) branler
woe [wəu] n malheur m
woke [wəuk] pt of **wake**
woken ['wəukn] pp of **wake**
wolf (pl **wolves**) [wulf, wulvz] n loup m
woman (pl **women**) ['wumən, 'wɪmɪn] n femme f ▷ cpd: **~ doctor** femme f médecin; **~ teacher** professeur m femme
womb [wuːm] n (Anat) utérus m
women ['wɪmɪn] npl of **woman**
won [wʌn] pt, pp of **win**
wonder ['wʌndər] n merveille f, miracle m; (feeling) émerveillement m ▷ vi: **to ~ whether/why** se demander si/pourquoi; **to ~ at** (surprise) s'étonner de; (admiration) s'émerveiller de; **to ~ about** songer à; **it's no ~ that** il n'est pas étonnant que + sub; **wonderful** adj merveilleux(-euse)
won't [wəunt] = **will not**
wood [wud] n (timber, forest) bois m; **wooden** adj en bois; (fig: actor) raide; (: performance) qui manque de naturel; **woodwind** n: **the woodwind** les bois mpl; **woodwork** n menuiserie f
wool [wul] n laine f; **to pull the ~ over sb's eyes** (fig) en faire accroire à qn; **woollen**, (US) **woolen** adj de or en laine; **woolly**, (US) **wooly** adj laineux(-euse); (fig: ideas) confus(e)
word [wəːd] n mot m; (spoken) mot, parole f; (promise) parole; (news) nouvelles fpl ▷ vt rédiger, formuler; **in other ~s** en d'autres termes; **to have a ~ with sb** toucher un mot à qn; **to break/keep one's ~** manquer à sa parole/tenir (sa) parole;

w

wording n termes mpl, langage m; (of document) libellé m; **word processing** n traitement m de texte; **word processor** n machine f de traitement de texte

wore [wɔːʳ] pt of **wear**

work [wəːk] n travail m; (Art, Literature) œuvre f ▷ vi travailler; (mechanism) marcher, fonctionner; (plan etc) marcher; (medicine) agir ▷ vt (clay, wood etc) travailler; (mine etc) exploiter; (machine) faire marcher or fonctionner; (miracles etc) faire; **works** n (BRIT: factory) usine f; **how does this ~?** comment est-ce que ça marche?; **the TV isn't ~ing** la télévision est en panne or ne marche pas; **to be out of ~** être au chômage or sans emploi; **to ~ loose** se défaire, se desserrer; **work out** vi (plans etc) marcher; (Sport) s'entraîner ▷ vt (problem) résoudre; (plan) élaborer; **it ~s out at £100** ça fait 100 livres; **worker** n travailleur(-euse), ouvrier(-ière); **work experience** n stage m; **workforce** n main-d'œuvre f; **working class** n classe ouvrière ▷ adj: **working-class** ouvrier(-ière), de la classe ouvrière; **working week** n semaine f de travail; **workman** (irreg) n ouvrier m; **work of art** n œuvre f d'art; **workout** n (Sport) séance f d'entraînement; **work permit** n permis m de travail; **workplace** n lieu m de travail; **worksheet** n (Scol) feuille f d'exercices; **workshop** n atelier m; **work station** n poste m de travail; **work surface** n plan m de travail; **worktop** n plan m de travail

world [wəːld] n monde m ▷ cpd (champion) du monde; (power, war) mondial(e); **to think the ~ of sb** (fig) ne jurer que par qn; **World Cup** n: **the World Cup** (Football) la Coupe du monde; **world-wide** adj universel(le); **World-Wide Web** n: **the World-Wide Web** le Web

worm [wəːm] n (also: **earth~**) ver m

worn [wɔːn] pp of **wear** ▷ adj usé(e); **worn-out** adj (object) complètement usé(e); (person) épuisé(e)

worried ['wʌrɪd] adj inquiet(-ète); **to be ~ about sth** être inquiet au sujet de qch

worry ['wʌrɪ] n souci m ▷ vt inquiéter ▷ vi s'inquiéter, se faire du souci; **worrying** adj inquiétant(e)

worse [wəːs] adj pire, plus mauvais(e) ▷ adv plus mal ▷ n pire m; **to get ~** (condition, situation) empirer, se dégrader; **a change for the ~** une détérioration; **worsen** vt, vi empirer; **worse off** adj moins à l'aise financièrement; (fig): **you'll be worse off this way** ça ira moins bien de cette façon

worship ['wəːʃɪp] n culte m ▷ vt (God) rendre un culte à; (person) adorer

worst [wəːst] adj le (la) pire, le (la) plus mauvais(e) ▷ adv le plus mal ▷ n pire m; **at ~** au pis aller

worth [wəːθ] n valeur f ▷ adj: **to be ~** valoir; **it's ~ it** cela en vaut la peine, ça vaut la peine; **it is ~ one's while (to do)** ça vaut le coup (inf) (de faire); **worthless** adj qui ne vaut rien; **worthwhile** adj (activity) qui en vaut la peine; (cause) louable

worthy ['wəːðɪ] adj (person) digne; (motive) louable; **~ of** digne de

 KEYWORD

would [wʊd] aux vb **1** (conditional tense): **if you asked him he would do it** si vous le lui demandiez, il le ferait; **if you had asked him he would have done it** si vous le lui aviez demandé, il l'aurait fait
2 (in offers, invitations, requests): **would you like a biscuit?** voulez-vous un biscuit?; **would you close the door please?** voulez-vous fermer la porte, s'il vous plaît?
3 (in indirect speech): **I said I would do**

it j'ai dit que je le ferais
4 (emphatic): **it would have to snow today!** naturellement il neige aujourd'hui!, il fallait qu'il neige aujourd'hui!
5 (insistence): **she wouldn't do it** elle n'a pas voulu or elle a refusé de le faire
6 (conjecture): **it would have been midnight** il devait être minuit; **it would seem so** on dirait bien
7 (indicating habit): **he would go there on Mondays** il y allait le lundi

wouldn't ['wudnt] = **would not**
wound¹ [wu:nd] n blessure f ⊳ vt blesser
wound² [waund] pt, pp of **wind²**
wove [wəuv] pt of **weave**
woven ['wəuvn] pp of **weave**
wrap [ræp] vt (also: **~ up**) envelopper; (parcel) emballer; (wind) enrouler; **wrapper** n (on chocolate etc) papier m; (BRIT: of book) couverture f; **wrapping** n (of sweet, chocolate) papier m; (of parcel) emballage m; **wrapping paper** n papier m d'emballage; (for gift) papier cadeau
wreath [ri:θ] n couronne f
wreck [rɛk] n (sea disaster) naufrage m; (ship) épave f; (vehicle) véhicule accidentée; (pej: person) loque (humaine) ⊳ vt démolir; (fig) briser, ruiner; **wreckage** n débris mpl; (of building) décombres mpl; (of ship) naufrage m
wren [rɛn] n (Zool) troglodyte m
wrench [rɛntʃ] n (Tech) clé f (à écrous); (tug) violent mouvement de torsion; (fig) déchirement m ⊳ vt tirer violemment sur, tordre; **to ~ sth from** arracher qch (violemment) à or de
wrestle ['rɛsl] vi: **to ~ (with sb)** lutter (avec qn); **wrestler** n lutteur(-euse); **wrestling** n lutte f; (BRIT: also: **all-in wrestling**) catch m
wretched ['rɛtʃɪd] adj misérable
wriggle ['rɪgl] vi (also: **~ about**) se tortiller

wring (pt, pp **wrung**) [rɪŋ, rʌŋ] vt tordre; (wet clothes) essorer; (fig): **to ~ sth out of** arracher qch à
wrinkle ['rɪŋkl] n (on skin) ride f; (on paper etc) pli m ⊳ vt rider, plisser ⊳ vi se plisser
wrist [rɪst] n poignet m
write (pt **wrote**, pp **written**) [raɪt, rəut, 'rɪtn] vt, vi écrire; (prescription) rédiger; **write down** vt noter; (put in writing) mettre par écrit; **write off** vt (debt) passer aux profits et pertes; (project) mettre une croix sur; (smash up: car etc) démolir complètement; **write out** vt écrire; (copy) recopier; **write-off** n perte totale; **the car is a write-off** la voiture est bonne pour la casse; **writer** n auteur m, écrivain m
writing ['raɪtɪŋ] n écriture f; (of author) œuvres fpl; **in ~** par écrit; **writing paper** n papier m à lettres
written ['rɪtn] pp of **write**
wrong [rɔŋ] adj (incorrect) faux (fausse); (incorrectly chosen: number, road etc) mauvais(e); (not suitable) qui ne convient pas; (wicked) mal; (unfair) injuste ⊳ adv mal ⊳ n tort m ⊳ vt faire du tort à, léser; **you are ~ to do it** tu as tort de le faire; **you are ~ about that, you've got it ~** tu te trompes; **what's ~?** qu'est-ce qui ne va pas?; **what's ~ with the car?** qu'est-ce qu'elle a, la voiture?; **to go ~** (person) se tromper; (plan) mal tourner; (machine) se détraquer; **I took a ~ turning** je me suis trompé de route; **wrongly** adv à tort; (answer, do, count) mal, incorrectement; **wrong number** n (Tel): **you have the wrong number** vous vous êtes trompé de numéro
wrote [rəut] pt of **write**
wrung [rʌŋ] pt, pp of **wring**
WWW n abbr = **World-Wide Web**

W

XL *abbr* (= *extra large*) XL
Xmas ['ɛksməs] *n abbr* = **Christmas**
X-ray ['ɛksreɪ] *n* (*ray*) rayon *m* X;
(*photograph*) radio(graphie) *f* ▷ *vt*
radiographier
xylophone ['zaɪləfəun] *n*
xylophone *m*

yacht [jɔt] *n* voilier *m*; (*motor, luxury
yacht*) yacht *m*; **yachting** *n* yachting
m, navigation *f* de plaisance
yard [jɑːd] *n* (*of house etc*) cour *f*; (*US:
garden*) jardin *m*; (*measure*) yard *m*
(= 914 *mm*; 3 *feet*); **yard sale** *n* (*US*)
brocante *f* (dans son propre jardin)
yarn [jɑːn] *n* fil *m*; (*tale*) longue
histoire
yawn [jɔːn] *n* bâillement *m* ▷ *vi* bâiller
yd. *abbr* = **yard; yards**
yeah [jɛə] *adv* (*inf*) ouais
year [jɪəʳ] *n* an *m*, année *f*; (*Scol etc*)
année; **to be 8 ~s old** avoir 8 ans;
an eight-~-old child un enfant de
huit ans; **yearly** *adj* annuel(le) ▷ *adv*
annuellement; **twice yearly** deux
fois par an
yearn [jəːn] *vi*: **to ~ for sth/to do**
aspirer à qch/à faire
yeast [jiːst] *n* levure *f*
yell [jɛl] *n* hurlement *m*, cri *m* ▷ *vi*
hurler

yellow ['jɛləu] *adj, n* jaune (*m*); **Yellow Pages®** *npl* (Tel) pages *fpl* jaunes

yes [jɛs] *adv* oui; (*answering negative question*) si ▷ *n* oui *m*; **to say ~ (to)** dire oui (à)

yesterday ['jɛstədɪ] *adv, n* hier (*m*); **~ morning/evening** hier matin/soir; **all day ~** toute la journée d'hier

yet [jɛt] *adv* encore; (*in questions*) déjà ▷ *conj* pourtant, néanmoins; **it is not finished ~** ce n'est pas encore fini or toujours pas fini; **have you eaten ~?** vous avez déjà mangé?; **the best ~** le meilleur jusqu'ici or jusque-là; **as ~** jusqu'ici, encore

yew [ju:] *n* if *m*

Yiddish ['jɪdɪʃ] *n* yiddish *m*

yield [ji:ld] *n* production *f*, rendement *m*; (Finance) rapport *m* ▷ *vt* produire, rendre, rapporter; (*surrender*) céder ▷ *vi* céder; (us Aut) céder la priorité

yob(bo) ['jɔb(əu)] *n* (BRIT *inf*) loubar(d) *m*

yoga ['jəugə] *n* yoga *m*

yog(h)urt ['jɔgət] *n* yaourt *m*

yolk [jəuk] *n* jaune *m* (d'œuf)

 KEYWORD

you [ju:] *pron* **1** (*subject*) tu; (: *polite form*) vous; (: *plural*) vous; **you are very kind** vous êtes très gentil; **you French enjoy your food** vous autres Français, vous aimez bien manger; **you and I will go** toi et moi or vous et moi, nous irons; **there you are!** vous voilà!

2 (*object: direct, indirect*) te, t' + *vowel*; vous; **I know you** je te or vous connais; **I gave it to you** je te l'ai donné, je vous l'ai donné

3 (*stressed*) toi; vous; **I told you to do it** c'est à toi or vous que j'ai dit de le faire

4 (*after prep, in comparisons*) toi; vous; **it's for you** c'est pour toi or vous; **she's younger than you** elle est plus jeune que toi or vous

5 (*impersonal: one*) on; **fresh air does you good** l'air frais fait du bien; **you never know** on ne sait jamais; **you can't do that!** ça ne se fait pas!

you'd [ju:d] = **you had; you would**

you'll [ju:l] = **you will; you shall**

young [jʌŋ] *adj* jeune ▷ *npl* (*of animal*) petits *mpl*; **the ~** (*people*) les jeunes, la jeunesse; **my ~er brother** mon frère cadet; **youngster** *n* jeune *m/f*; (*child*) enfant *m/f*

your [jɔːʳ] *adj* ton (ta), tes *pl*; (*polite form, pl*) votre, vos *pl*; see also **my**

you're [juəʳ] = **you are**

yours [jɔːz] *pron* le (la) tien(ne), les tiens (tiennes); (*polite form, pl*) le (la) vôtre, les vôtres; **is it ~?** c'est à toi (or à vous)?; **a friend of ~** un(e) de tes (or de vos) amis; see also **faithfully; mine¹; sincerely**

yourself [jɔːˈsɛlf] *pron* (*reflexive*) te; (: *polite form*) vous; (*after prep*) toi; vous; (*emphatic*) toi-même; vous-même; see also **oneself**; **yourselves** *pl pron* vous; (*emphatic*) vous-mêmes; see also **oneself**

youth [ju:θ] *n* jeunesse *f*; (*young man*) jeune homme *m*; **youth club** *n* centre *m* de jeunes; **youthful** *adj* jeune; (*enthusiasm etc*) juvénile; **youth hostel** *n* auberge *f* de jeunesse

you've [ju:v] = **you have**

Yugoslav ['ju:gəuslɑːv] *adj* (Hist) yougoslave ▷ *n* Yougoslave *m/f*

Yugoslavia [ju:gəuˈslɑːvɪə] *n* (Hist) Yougoslavie *f*

y

zoology [zuːˈɒlədʒɪ] n zoologie f
zoom [zuːm] vi: **to ~ past** passer en
trombe; **zoom lens** n zoom m
zucchini [zuːˈkiːnɪ] n (US) courgette f

Z

zeal [ziːl] n (revolutionary etc) ferveur f;
(keenness) ardeur f, zèle m
zebra [ˈziːbrə] n zèbre m; **zebra
crossing** n (BRIT) passage clouté or
pour piétons
zero [ˈzɪərəu] n zéro m
zest [zɛst] n entrain m, élan m; (of
lemon etc) zeste m
zigzag [ˈzɪgzæg] n zigzag m ▷ vi
zigzaguer, faire des zigzags
Zimbabwe [zɪmˈbɑːbwɪ] n
Zimbabwe m
zinc [zɪŋk] n zinc m
zip [zɪp] n (also: **~ fastener**) fermeture
f éclair® or à glissière ▷ vt (file)
zipper; (also: **~ up**) fermer (avec une
fermeture éclair®); **zip code** n (US)
code postal; **zip file** n (Comput) fichier
m zip inv; **zipper** n (US) = **zip**
zit [zɪt] (inf) n bouton m
zodiac [ˈzəudɪæk] n zodiaque m
zone [zəun] n zone f
zoo [zuː] n zoo m

VERB TABLES

Introduction

The **Verb Tables** in the following section contain 29 tables of French verbs (some regular and some irregular) in alphabetical order. Each table shows you the following forms: **Present**, **Perfect**, **Future**, **Subjunctive**, **Imperfect**, **Conditional**, **Imperative** and the **Present** and **Past Participles**.

In order to help you use the verbs shown in Verb Tables correctly, there are also a number of example phrases at the bottom of each page to show the verb as it is used in context.

In French there are both **regular** verbs (their forms follow the normal rules) and **irregular** verbs (their forms do not follow the normal rules). The regular verbs in these tables are:

donner (regular -**er** verb, Verb Table 11)
finir (regular -**ir** verb, Verb Table 16)
attendre (regular -**re** verb, Verb Table 3)

The irregular verbs are shown in full.

For a further list of French irregular verb forms see pages xiv–xvi.

▶ **aller** (to go)

PRESENT

je	vais
tu	vas
il/elle/on	va
nous	allons
vous	allez
ils/elles	vont

PRESENT SUBJUNCTIVE

j'	aille
tu	ailles
il/elle/on	aille
nous	allions
vous	alliez
ils/elles	aillent

PERFECT

je	suis allé(e)
tu	es allé(e)
il/elle/on	est allé(e)
nous	sommes allé(e)s
vous	êtes allé(e)(s)
ils/elles	sont allé(e)s

IMPERFECT

j'	allais
tu	allais
il/elle/on	allait
nous	allions
vous	alliez
ils/elles	allaient

FUTURE

j'	irai
tu	iras
il/elle/on	ira
nous	irons
vous	irez
ils/elles	iront

CONDITIONAL

j'	irais
tu	irais
il/elle/on	irait
nous	irions
vous	iriez
ils/elles	iraient

IMPERATIVE

va / allons / allez

PAST PARTICIPLE

allé

PRESENT PARTICIPLE

allant

EXAMPLE PHRASES

*Vous **allez** au cinéma?* Are you going to the cinema?
*Je **suis allé** à Londres.* I went to London.
*Est-ce que tu **es** déjà **allé** en Allemagne?* Have you ever been to Germany?

---

je/j' = I **tu** = you **il** = he/it **elle** = she/it **on** = we/one **nous** = we **vous** = you **ils/elles** = they

▶ **attendre** (to wait)

PRESENT

j'	attends
tu	attends
il/elle/on	attend
nous	attendons
vous	attendez
ils/elles	attendent

PRESENT SUBJUNCTIVE

j'	attende
tu	attendes
il/elle/on	attende
nous	attendions
vous	attendiez
ils/elles	attendent

PERFECT

j'	ai attendu
tu	as attendu
il/elle/on	a attendu
nous	avons attendu
vous	avez attendu
ils/elles	ont attendu

IMPERFECT

j'	attendais
tu	attendais
il/elle/on	attendait
nous	attendions
vous	attendiez
ils/elles	attendaient

FUTURE

j'	attendrai
tu	attendras
il/elle/on	attendra
nous	attendrons
vous	attendrez
ils/elles	attendront

CONDITIONAL

j'	attendrais
tu	attendrais
il/elle/on	attendrait
nous	attendrions
vous	attendriez
ils/elles	attendraient

IMPERATIVE

attends / attendons / attendez

PAST PARTICIPLE

attendu

PRESENT PARTICIPLE

attendant

EXAMPLE PHRASES

***Attends**-moi!* Wait for me!
*Tu **attends** depuis longtemps?* Have you been waiting long?
*Je l'**ai attendu** à la poste.* I waited for him at the post office.
*Je **m'attends** à ce qu'il soit en retard.* I expect he'll be late.

je/j' = I **tu** = you **il** = he/it **elle** = she/it **on** = we/one **nous** = we **vous** = you **ils/elles** = they

▶ **avoir** (to have)

PRESENT

j'	ai
tu	as
il/elle/on	a
nous	avons
vous	avez
ils/elles	ont

PRESENT SUBJUNCTIVE

j'	aie
tu	aies
il/elle/on	ait
nous	ayons
vous	ayez
ils/elles	aient

PERFECT

j'	ai eu
tu	as eu
il/elle/on	a eu
nous	avons eu
vous	avez eu
ils/elles	ont eu

IMPERFECT

j'	avais
tu	avais
il/elle/on	avait
nous	avions
vous	aviez
ils/elles	avaient

FUTURE

j'	aurai
tu	auras
il/elle/on	aura
nous	aurons
vous	aurez
ils/elles	auront

CONDITIONAL

j'	aurais
tu	aurais
il/elle/on	aurait
nous	aurions
vous	auriez
ils/elles	auraient

IMPERATIVE

aie / ayons / ayez

PAST PARTICIPLE

eu

PRESENT PARTICIPLE

ayant

EXAMPLE PHRASES

*Il **a** les yeux bleus.* He's got blue eyes.
*Quel âge **as**-tu?* How old are you?
*Il **a eu** un accident.* He's had an accident.
*J'**avais** faim.* I was hungry.
*Il y **a** beaucoup de monde.* There are lots of people.

je/j' = I **tu** = you **il** = he/it **elle** = she/it **on** = we/one **nous** = we **vous** = you **ils/elles** = they

▶ **boire** (to drink)

PRESENT

je	bois
tu	bois
il/elle/on	boit
nous	buvons
vous	buvez
ils/elles	boivent

PRESENT SUBJUNCTIVE

je	boive
tu	boives
il/elle/on	boive
nous	buvions
vous	buviez
ils/elles	boivent

PERFECT

j'	ai bu
tu	as bu
il/elle/on	a bu
nous	avons bu
vous	avez bu
ils/elles	ont bu

IMPERFECT

je	buvais
tu	buvais
il/elle/on	buvait
nous	buvions
vous	buviez
ils/elles	buvaient

FUTURE

je	boirai
tu	boiras
il/elle/on	boira
nous	boirons
vous	boirez
ils/elles	boiront

CONDITIONAL

je	boirais
tu	boirais
il/elle/on	boirait
nous	boirions
vous	boiriez
ils/elles	boiraient

IMPERATIVE

bois / buvons / buvez

PAST PARTICIPLE

bu

PRESENT PARTICIPLE

buvant

EXAMPLE PHRASES

Qu'est-ce que tu veux boire? What would you like to drink?
Il ne boit jamais d'alcool. He never drinks alcohol.
J'ai bu un litre d'eau. I drank a litre of water.

---

je/j' = I **tu** = you **il** = he/it **elle** = she/it **on** = we/one **nous** = we **vous** = you **ils/elles** = they

▶ **connaître** (to know)

PRESENT

je	connais
tu	connais
il/elle/on	connaît
nous	connaissons
vous	connaissez
ils/elles	connaissent

PRESENT SUBJUNCTIVE

je	connaisse
tu	connaisses
il/elle/on	connaisse
nous	connaissions
vous	connaissiez
ils/elles	connaissent

PERFECT

j'	ai connu
tu	as connu
il/elle/on	a connu
nous	avons connu
vous	avez connu
ils/elles	ont connu

IMPERFECT

je	connaissais
tu	connaissais
il/elle/on	connaissait
nous	connaissions
vous	connaissiez
ils/elles	connaissaient

FUTURE

je	connaîtrai
tu	connaîtras
il/elle/on	connaîtra
nous	connaîtrons
vous	connaîtrez
ils/elles	connaîtront

CONDITIONAL

je	connaîtrais
tu	connaîtrais
il/elle/on	connaîtrait
nous	connaîtrions
vous	connaîtriez
ils/elles	connaîtraient

IMPERATIVE

connais / connaissons / connaissez

PAST PARTICIPLE

connu

PRESENT PARTICIPLE

connaissant

EXAMPLE PHRASES

*Je ne **connais** pas du tout cette région.* I don't know the area at all.
*Vous **connaissez** M. Amiot?* Do you know Mr Amiot?
*Il n'a pas **connu** son grand-père.* He never knew his granddad.
*Ils **se sont connus** à Rouen.* They first met in Rouen.

je/j' = I **tu** = you **il** = he/it **elle** = she/it **on** = we/one **nous** = we **vous** = you **ils/elles** = they

▶ **courir** (to run)

PRESENT

je	cours
tu	cours
il/elle/on	court
nous	courons
vous	courez
ils/elles	courent

PRESENT SUBJUNCTIVE

je	coure
tu	coures
il/elle/on	coure
nous	courions
vous	couriez
ils/elles	courent

PERFECT

j'	ai couru
tu	as couru
il/elle/on	a couru
nous	avons couru
vous	avez couru
ils/elles	ont couru

IMPERFECT

je	courais
tu	courais
il/elle/on	courait
nous	courions
vous	couriez
ils/elles	couraient

FUTURE

je	courrai
tu	courras
il/elle/on	courra
nous	courrons
vous	courrez
ils/elles	courront

CONDITIONAL

je	courrais
tu	courrais
il/elle/on	courrait
nous	courrions
vous	courriez
ils/elles	courraient

IMPERATIVE

cours / courons / courez

PAST PARTICIPLE

couru

PRESENT PARTICIPLE

courant

EXAMPLE PHRASES

*Je ne **cours** pas très vite.* I can't run very fast.
*Elle est sortie en **courant**.* She ran out.
*Ne **courez** pas dans le couloir.* Don't run in the corridor.
*J'**ai couru** jusqu'à l'école.* I ran all the way to school.

je/j' = I **tu** = you **il** = he/it **elle** = she/it **on** = we/one **nous** = we **vous** = you **ils/elles** = they

▶ **croire** (to believe)

PRESENT

je	crois
tu	crois
il/elle/on	croit
nous	croyons
vous	croyez
ils/elles	croient

PRESENT SUBJUNCTIVE

je	croie
tu	croies
il/elle/on	croie
nous	croyions
vous	croyiez
ils/elles	croient

PERFECT

j'	ai cru
tu	as cru
il/elle/on	a cru
nous	avons cru
vous	avez cru
ils/elles	ont cru

IMPERFECT

je	croyais
tu	croyais
il/elle/on	croyait
nous	croyions
vous	croyiez
ils/elles	croyaient

FUTURE

je	croirai
tu	croiras
il/elle/on	croira
nous	croirons
vous	croirez
ils/elles	croiront

CONDITIONAL

je	croirais
tu	croirais
il/elle/on	croirait
nous	croirions
vous	croiriez
ils/elles	croiraient

IMPERATIVE

crois / croyons / croyez

PAST PARTICIPLE

cru

PRESENT PARTICIPLE

croyant

EXAMPLE PHRASES

*Je ne te **crois** pas.* I don't believe you.
*J'**ai cru** que tu n'allais pas venir.* I thought you weren't going to come.
*Elle **croyait** encore au père Noël.* She still believed in Santa.

---

je/j' = I **tu** = you **il** = he/it **elle** = she/it **on** = we/one **nous** = we **vous** = you **ils/elles** = they

▶ **devoir** (to have to; to owe)

PRESENT

je	dois
tu	dois
il/elle/on	doit
nous	devons
vous	devez
ils/elles	doivent

PRESENT SUBJUNCTIVE

je	doive
tu	doives
il/elle/on	doive
nous	devions
vous	deviez
ils/elles	doivent

PERFECT

j'	ai dû
tu	as dû
il/elle/on	a dû
nous	avons dû
vous	avez dû
ils/elles	ont dû

IMPERFECT

je	devais
tu	devais
il/elle/on	devait
nous	devions
vous	deviez
ils/elles	devaient

FUTURE

je	devrai
tu	devras
il/elle/on	devra
nous	devrons
vous	devrez
ils/elles	devront

CONDITIONAL

je	devrais
tu	devrais
il/elle/on	devrait
nous	devrions
vous	devriez
ils/elles	devraient

IMPERATIVE

dois / devons / devez

PAST PARTICIPLE

dû (*NB*: due, dus, dues)

PRESENT PARTICIPLE

devant

EXAMPLE PHRASES

Je **dois** aller faire les courses ce matin. I have to do the shopping this morning.
À quelle heure est-ce que tu **dois** partir? What time do you have to leave?
Il **a dû** faire ses devoirs hier soir. He had to do his homework last night.
Il **devait** prendre le train pour aller travailler. He had to go to work by train.

je/j' = I **tu** = you **il** = he/it **elle** = she/it **on** = we/one **nous** = we **vous** = you **ils/elles** = they

▶ **dire** (to say)

PRESENT

je	dis
tu	dis
il/elle/on	dit
nous	disons
vous	dites
ils/elles	disent

PRESENT SUBJUNCTIVE

je	dise
tu	dises
il/elle/on	dise
nous	disions
vous	disiez
ils/elles	disent

PERFECT

j'	ai dit
tu	as dit
il/elle/on	a dit
nous	avons dit
vous	avez dit
ils/elles	ont dit

IMPERFECT

je	disais
tu	disais
il/elle/on	disait
nous	disions
vous	disiez
ils/elles	disaient

FUTURE

je	dirai
tu	diras
il/elle/on	dira
nous	dirons
vous	direz
ils/elles	diront

CONDITIONAL

je	dirais
tu	dirais
il/elle/on	dirait
nous	dirions
vous	diriez
ils/elles	diraient

IMPERATIVE

dis / disons / dites

PAST PARTICIPLE

dit

PRESENT PARTICIPLE

disant

EXAMPLE PHRASES

*Qu'est-ce qu'elle **dit**?* What is she saying?
*"Bonjour!", **a**-t-il **dit**.* "Hello!" he said.
*Ils m'**ont dit** que le film était nul.* They told me that the film was rubbish.
*Comment ça **se dit** en anglais?* How do you say that in English?

---

je/j' = I **tu** = you **il** = he/it **elle** = she/it **on** = we/one **nous** = we **vous** = you **ils/elles** = they

▶ **donner** (to give)

PRESENT

je	donne
tu	donnes
il/elle/on	donne
nous	donnons
vous	donnez
ils/elles	donnent

PRESENT SUBJUNCTIVE

je	donne
tu	donnes
il/elle/on	donne
nous	donnions
vous	donniez
ils/elles	donnent

PERFECT

j'	ai donné
tu	as donné
il/elle/on	a donné
nous	avons donné
vous	avez donné
ils/elles	ont donné

IMPERFECT

je	donnais
tu	donnais
il/elle/on	donnait
nous	donnions
vous	donniez
ils/elles	donnaient

FUTURE

je	donnerai
tu	donneras
il/elle/on	donnera
nous	donnerons
vous	donnerez
ils/elles	donneront

CONDITIONAL

je	donnerais
tu	donnerais
il/elle/on	donnerait
nous	donnerions
vous	donneriez
ils/elles	donneraient

IMPERATIVE

donne / donnons / donnez

PAST PARTICIPLE

donné

PRESENT PARTICIPLE

donnant

EXAMPLE PHRASES

Donne-moi la main. Give me your hand.
Est-ce que je t'**ai donné** mon adresse? Did I give you my address?
L'appartement **donne** sur la place. The flat overlooks the square.

je/j' = I **tu** = you **il** = he/it **elle** = she/it **on** = we/one **nous** = we **vous** = you **ils/elles** = they

▶ écrire (to write)

PRESENT

j'	écris
tu	écris
il/elle/on	écrit
nous	écrivons
vous	écrivez
ils/elles	écrivent

PRESENT SUBJUNCTIVE

j'	écrive
tu	écrives
il/elle/on	écrive
nous	écrivions
vous	écriviez
ils/elles	écrivent

PERFECT

j'	ai écrit
tu	as écrit
il/elle/on	a écrit
nous	avons écrit
vous	avez écrit
ils/elles	ont écrit

IMPERFECT

j'	écrivais
tu	écrivais
il/elle/on	écrivait
nous	écrivions
vous	écriviez
ils/elles	écrivaient

FUTURE

j'	écrirai
tu	écriras
il/elle/on	écrira
nous	écrirons
vous	écrirez
ils/elles	écriront

CONDITIONAL

j'	écrirais
tu	écrirais
il/elle/on	écrirait
nous	écririons
vous	écririez
ils/elles	écriraient

IMPERATIVE

écris / écrivons / écrivez

PAST PARTICIPLE

écrit

PRESENT PARTICIPLE

écrivant

EXAMPLE PHRASES

Tu **as écrit** à ta correspondante récemment? Have you written to your penfriend lately?
Elle **écrit** des romans. She writes novels.
Comment ça **s'écrit**, "brouillard"? How do you spell "brouillard"?

je/j' = I **tu** = you **il** = he/it **elle** = she/it **on** = we/one **nous** = we **vous** = you **ils/elles** = they

▶ **être** (to be)

PRESENT

je	suis
tu	es
il/elle/on	est
nous	sommes
vous	êtes
ils/elles	sont

PRESENT SUBJUNCTIVE

je	sois
tu	sois
il/elle/on	soit
nous	soyons
vous	soyez
ils/elles	soient

PERFECT

j'	ai été
tu	as été
il/elle/on	a été
nous	avons été
vous	avez été
ils/elles	ont été

IMPERFECT

j'	étais
tu	étais
il/elle/on	était
nous	étions
vous	étiez
ils/elles	étaient

FUTURE

je	serai
tu	seras
il/elle/on	sera
nous	serons
vous	serez
ils/elles	seront

CONDITIONAL

je	serais
tu	serais
il/elle/on	serait
nous	serions
vous	seriez
ils/elles	seraient

IMPERATIVE

sois / soyons / soyez

PAST PARTICIPLE

été

PRESENT PARTICIPLE

étant

EXAMPLE PHRASES

*Mon père **est** professeur.* My father's a teacher.
*Quelle heure **est**-il? – Il **est** dix heures.* What time is it? – It's 10 o'clock.
*Ils ne **sont** pas encore arrivés.* They haven't arrived yet.

je/j' = I **tu** = you **il** = he/it **elle** = she/it **on** = we/one **nous** = we **vous** = you **ils/elles** = they

▶ **faire** (to do; to make)

PRESENT

je	fais
tu	fais
il/elle/on	fait
nous	faisons
vous	faites
ils/elles	font

PRESENT SUBJUNCTIVE

je	fasse
tu	fasses
il/elle/on	fasse
nous	fassions
vous	fassiez
ils/elles	fassent

PERFECT

j'	ai fait
tu	as fait
il/elle/on	a fait
nous	avons fait
vous	avez fait
ils/elles	ont fait

IMPERFECT

je	faisais
tu	faisais
il/elle/on	faisait
nous	faisions
vous	faisiez
ils/elles	faisaient

FUTURE

je	ferai
tu	feras
il/elle/on	fera
nous	ferons
vous	ferez
ils/elles	feront

CONDITIONAL

je	ferais
tu	ferais
il/elle/on	ferait
nous	ferions
vous	feriez
ils/elles	feraient

IMPERATIVE

fais / faisons / faites

PAST PARTICIPLE

fait

PRESENT PARTICIPLE

faisant

EXAMPLE PHRASES

*Qu'est-ce que tu **fais**?* What are you doing?
*Qu'est-ce qu'il **a fait**?* What has he done? *or* What did he do?
*J'**ai fait** un gâteau.* I've made a cake *or* I made a cake.
*Il **s'est fait** couper les cheveux.* He's had his hair cut.

je/j' = I **tu** = you **il** = he/it **elle** = she/it **on** = we/one **nous** = we **vous** = you **ils/elles** = they

▶ **falloir** (to be necessary)

PRESENT

il faut

PRESENT SUBJUNCTIVE

il faille

PERFECT

il a fallu

IMPERFECT

il fallait

FUTURE

il faudra

CONDITIONAL

il faudrait

IMPERATIVE

not used

PAST PARTICIPLE

fallu

PRESENT PARTICIPLE

not used

EXAMPLE PHRASES

Il **faut** se dépêcher! We have to hurry up!
Il me **fallait** de l'argent. I needed money.
Il **faudra** que tu sois là à 8 heures. You'll have to be there at 8.

je/j' = I **tu** = you **il** = he/it **elle** = she/it **on** = we/one **nous** = we **vous** = you **ils/elles** = they

▶ **finir** (to finish)

PRESENT

je	finis
tu	finis
il/elle/on	finit
nous	finissons
vous	finissez
ils/elles	finissent

PRESENT SUBJUNCTIVE

je	finisse
tu	finisses
il/elle/on	finisse
nous	finissions
vous	finissiez
ils/elles	finissent

PERFECT

j'	ai fini
tu	as fini
il/elle/on	a fini
nous	avons fini
vous	avez fini
ils/elles	ont fini

IMPERFECT

je	finissais
tu	finissais
il/elle/on	finissait
nous	finissions
vous	finissiez
ils/elles	finissaient

FUTURE

je	finirai
tu	finiras
il/elle/on	finira
nous	finirons
vous	finirez
ils/elles	finiront

CONDITIONAL

je	finirais
tu	finirais
il/elle/on	finirait
nous	finirions
vous	finiriez
ils/elles	finiraient

IMPERATIVE

finis / finissons / finissez

PAST PARTICIPLE

fini

PRESENT PARTICIPLE

finissant

EXAMPLE PHRASES

Finis ta soupe! Finish your soup!
J'ai fini! I've finished!
Je finirai mes devoirs demain. I'll finish my homework tomorrow.

je/j' = I **tu** = you **il** = he/it **elle** = she/it **on** = we/one **nous** = we **vous** = you **ils/elles** = they

▶ **se laver** (to wash oneself)

PRESENT

je	me lave
tu	te laves
il/elle/on	se lave
nous	nous lavons
vous	vous lavez
ils/elles	se lavent

PRESENT SUBJUNCTIVE

je	me lave
tu	te laves
il/elle/on	se lave
nous	nous lavions
vous	vous laviez
ils/elles	se lavent

PERFECT

je	me suis lavé(e)
tu	t'es lavé(e)
il/elle/on	s'est lavé(e)
nous	nous sommes lavé(e)s
vous	vous êtes lavé(e)(s)
ils/elles	se sont lavé(e)s

IMPERFECT

je	me lavais
tu	te lavais
il/elle/on	se lavait
nous	nous lavions
vous	vous laviez
ils/elles	se lavaient

FUTURE

je	me laverai
tu	te laveras
il/elle/on	se lavera
nous	nous laverons
vous	vous laverez
ils/elles	se laveront

CONDITIONAL

je	me laverais
tu	te laverais
il/elle/on	se laverait
nous	nous laverions
vous	vous laveriez
ils/elles	se laveraient

IMPERATIVE

lave-toi / lavons-nous / lavez-vous

PAST PARTICIPLE

lavé(e)

PRESENT PARTICIPLE

se lavant

EXAMPLE PHRASES

Lave-toi vite, tu vas être en retard. Have a quick wash, you're going to be late.
Lavez-vous les mains avant de vous mettre à table. Wash your hands before you sit at the table.
Nous nous sommes lavés les dents puis nous sommes allés nous coucher. We cleaned our teeth and went to bed.

je/j' = I **tu** = you **il** = he/it **elle** = she/it **on** = we/one **nous** = we **vous** = you **ils/elles** = they

▶ **mettre** (to put)

PRESENT

je	mets
tu	mets
il/elle/on	met
nous	mettons
vous	mettez
ils/elles	mettent

PRESENT SUBJUNCTIVE

je	mette
tu	mettes
il/elle/on	mette
nous	mettions
vous	mettiez
ils/elles	mettent

PERFECT

j'	ai mis
tu	as mis
il/elle/on	a mis
nous	avons mis
vous	avez mis
ils/elles	ont mis

IMPERFECT

je	mettais
tu	mettais
il/elle/on	mettait
nous	mettions
vous	mettiez
ils/elles	mettaient

FUTURE

je	mettrai
tu	mettras
il/elle/on	mettra
nous	mettrons
vous	mettrez
ils/elles	mettront

CONDITIONAL

je	mettrais
tu	mettrais
il/elle/on	mettrait
nous	mettrions
vous	mettriez
ils/elles	mettraient

IMPERATIVE

mets / mettons / mettez

PAST PARTICIPLE

mis

PRESENT PARTICIPLE

mettant

EXAMPLE PHRASES

Mets ton manteau! Put your coat on!
Où est-ce que tu as mis les clés? Where have you put the keys?
J'ai mis le livre sur la table. I put the book on the table.
Elle s'est mise à pleurer. She started crying.

▶ **mourir** (to die)

PRESENT

je	meurs
tu	meurs
il/elle/on	meurt
nous	mourons
vous	mourez
ils/elles	meurent

PRESENT SUBJUNCTIVE

je	meure
tu	meures
il/elle/on	meure
nous	mourions
vous	mouriez
ils/elles	meurent

PERFECT

je	suis mort(e)
tu	es mort(e)
il/elle/on	est mort(e)
nous	sommes mort(e)s
vous	êtes mort(e)(s)
ils/elles	sont mort(e)s

IMPERFECT

je	mourais
tu	mourais
il/elle/on	mourait
nous	mourions
vous	mouriez
ils/elles	mouraient

FUTURE

je	mourrai
tu	mourras
il/elle/on	mourra
nous	mourrons
vous	mourrez
ils/elles	mourront

CONDITIONAL

je	mourrais
tu	mourrais
il/elle/on	mourrait
nous	mourrions
vous	mourriez
ils/elles	mourraient

IMPERATIVE

meurs / mourons / mourez

PAST PARTICIPLE

mort

PRESENT PARTICIPLE

mourant

EXAMPLE PHRASES

*Elle **est morte** en 1998.* She died in 1998.
*Ils **sont morts**.* They're dead.
*On **meurt** de froid ici!* We're freezing to death in here!

je/j' = I **tu** = you **il** = he/it **elle** = she/it **on** = we/one **nous** = we **vous** = you **ils/elles** = they

▶ naître (to be born)

PRESENT

je	nais
tu	nais
il/elle/on	naît
nous	naissons
vous	naissez
ils/elles	naissent

PRESENT SUBJUNCTIVE

je	naisse
tu	naisses
il/elle/on	naisse
nous	naissions
vous	naissiez
ils/elles	naissent

PERFECT

je	suis né(e)
tu	es né(e)
il/elle/on	est né(e)
nous	sommes né(e)s
vous	êtes né(e)(s)
ils/elles	sont né(e)s

IMPERFECT

je	naissais
tu	naissais
il/elle/on	naissait
nous	naissions
vous	naissiez
ils/elles	naissaient

FUTURE

je	naîtrai
tu	naîtras
il/elle/on	naîtra
nous	naîtrons
vous	naîtrez
ils/elles	naîtront

CONDITIONAL

je	naîtrais
tu	naîtrais
il/elle/on	naîtrait
nous	naîtrions
vous	naîtriez
ils/elles	naîtraient

IMPERATIVE

nais / naissons / naissez

PAST PARTICIPLE

né

PRESENT PARTICIPLE

naissant

EXAMPLE PHRASES

*Je **suis née** le 12 février.* I was born on 12 February.
*Le bébé de Delphine **naîtra** en mars.* Delphine is going to have a baby in March.
*Quand est-ce que tu **es né**?* When were you born?

▶ **ouvrir** (to open)

PRESENT

j'	ouvre
tu	ouvres
il/elle/on	ouvre
nous	ouvrons
vous	ouvrez
ils/elles	ouvrent

PRESENT SUBJUNCTIVE

j'	ouvre
tu	ouvres
il/elle/on	ouvre
nous	ouvrions
vous	ouvriez
ils/elles	ouvrent

PERFECT

j'	ai ouvert
tu	as ouvert
il/elle/on	a ouvert
nous	avons ouvert
vous	avez ouvert
ils/elles	ont ouvert

IMPERFECT

j'	ouvrais
tu	ouvrais
il/elle/on	ouvrait
nous	ouvrions
vous	ouvriez
ils/elles	ouvraient

FUTURE

j'	ouvrirai
tu	ouvriras
il/elle/on	ouvrira
nous	ouvrirons
vous	ouvrirez
ils/elles	ouvriront

CONDITIONAL

j'	ouvrirais
tu	ouvrirais
il/elle/on	ouvrirait
nous	ouvririons
vous	ouvririez
ils/elles	ouvriraient

IMPERATIVE

ouvre / ouvrons / ouvrez

PAST PARTICIPLE

ouvert

PRESENT PARTICIPLE

ouvrant

EXAMPLE PHRASES

*Elle **a ouvert** la porte.* She opened the door.
*Est-ce que tu pourrais **ouvrir** la fenêtre?* Could you open the window?
*Je me suis coupé en **ouvrant** une boîte de conserve.* I cut myself opening a tin.
*La porte **s'est ouverte**.* The door opened.

je/j' = I **tu** = you **il** = he/it **elle** = she/it **on** = we/one **nous** = we **vous** = you **ils/elles** = they

▶ **pouvoir** (to be able)

PRESENT		**PRESENT SUBJUNCTIVE**	
je	peux	je	puisse
tu	peux	tu	puisses
il/elle/on	peut	il/elle/on	puisse
nous	pouvons	nous	puissions
vous	pouvez	vous	puissiez
ils/elles	peuvent	ils/elles	puissent

PERFECT		**IMPERFECT**	
j'	ai pu	je	pouvais
tu	as pu	tu	pouvais
il/elle/on	a pu	il/elle/on	pouvait
nous	avons pu	nous	pouvions
vous	avez pu	vous	pouviez
ils/elles	ont pu	ils/elles	pouvaient

FUTURE		**CONDITIONAL**	
je	pourrai	je	pourrais
tu	pourras	tu	pourrais
il/elle/on	pourra	il/elle/on	pourrait
nous	pourrons	nous	pourrions
vous	pourrez	vous	pourriez
ils/elles	pourront	ils/elles	pourraient

IMPERATIVE

not used

PAST PARTICIPLE

pu

PRESENT PARTICIPLE

pouvant

EXAMPLE PHRASES

*Je **peux** t'aider, si tu veux.* I can help you if you like.
*J'ai fait tout ce que j'**ai pu**.* I did all I could.
*Je ne **pourrai** pas venir samedi.* I won't be able to come on Saturday.

▶ **prendre** (to take)

PRESENT

je	prends
tu	prends
il/elle/on	prend
nous	prenons
vous	prenez
ils/elles	prennent

PRESENT SUBJUNCTIVE

je	prenne
tu	prennes
il/elle/on	prenne
nous	prenions
vous	preniez
ils/elles	prennent

PERFECT

j'	ai pris
tu	as pris
il/elle/on	a pris
nous	avons pris
vous	avez pris
ils/elles	ont pris

IMPERFECT

je	prenais
tu	prenais
il/elle/on	prenait
nous	prenions
vous	preniez
ils/elles	prenaient

FUTURE

je	prendrai
tu	prendras
il/elle/on	prendra
nous	prendrons
vous	prendrez
ils/elles	prendront

CONDITIONAL

je	prendrais
tu	prendrais
il/elle/on	prendrait
nous	prendrions
vous	prendriez
ils/elles	prendraient

IMPERATIVE

prends / prenons / prenez

PAST PARTICIPLE

pris

PRESENT PARTICIPLE

prenant

EXAMPLE PHRASES

*J'**ai pris** plein de photos.* I took lots of pictures.
*N'oublie pas de **prendre** ton passeport.* Don't forget to take your passport.
*Il **prendra** le train de 8h20.* He'll take the 8.20 train.
*Pour qui est-ce qu'il **se prend**?* Who does he think he is?

je/j' = I **tu** = you **il** = he/it **elle** = she/it **on** = we/one **nous** = we **vous** = you **ils/elles** = they

▶ **savoir** (to know)

PRESENT

je	sais
tu	sais
il/elle/on	sait
nous	savons
vous	savez
ils/elles	savent

PRESENT SUBJUNCTIVE

je	sache
tu	saches
il/elle/on	sache
nous	sachions
vous	sachiez
ils/elles	sachent

PERFECT

j'	ai su
tu	as su
il/elle/on	a su
nous	avons su
vous	avez su
ils/elles	ont su

IMPERFECT

je	savais
tu	savais
il/elle/on	savait
nous	savions
vous	saviez
ils/elles	savaient

FUTURE

je	saurai
tu	sauras
il/elle/on	saura
nous	saurons
vous	saurez
ils/elles	sauront

CONDITIONAL

je	saurais
tu	saurais
il/elle/on	saurait
nous	saurions
vous	sauriez
ils/elles	sauraient

IMPERATIVE

sache / sachons / sachez

PAST PARTICIPLE

su

PRESENT PARTICIPLE

sachant

EXAMPLE PHRASES

*Tu **sais** ce que tu vas faire l'année prochaine?* Do you know what you're doing next year?
*Je ne **sais** pas.* I don't know.
*Elle ne **sait** pas nager.* She can't swim.
*Tu **savais** que son père était pakistanais?* Did you know her father was Pakistani?

je/j' = I **tu** = you **il** = he/it **elle** = she/it **on** = we/one **nous** = we **vous** = you **ils/elles** = they

▶ **sortir** (to go out)

PRESENT

je	sors
tu	sors
il/elle/on	sort
nous	sortons
vous	sortez
ils/elles	sortent

PRESENT SUBJUNCTIVE

je	sorte
tu	sortes
il/elle/on	sorte
nous	sortions
vous	sortiez
ils/elles	sortent

PERFECT

je	suis sorti(e)
tu	es sorti(e)
il/elle/on	est sorti(e)
nous	sommes sorti(e)s
vous	êtes sorti(e)(s)
ils/elles	sont sorti(e)s

IMPERFECT

je	sortais
tu	sortais
il/elle/on	sortait
nous	sortions
vous	sortiez
ils/elles	sortaient

FUTURE

je	sortirai
tu	sortiras
il/elle/on	sortira
nous	sortirons
vous	sortirez
ils/elles	sortiront

CONDITIONAL

je	sortirais
tu	sortirais
il/elle/on	sortirait
nous	sortirions
vous	sortiriez
ils/elles	sortiraient

IMPERATIVE

sors / sortons / sortez

PAST PARTICIPLE

sorti

PRESENT PARTICIPLE

sortant

EXAMPLE PHRASES

*Je ne **suis** pas **sortie** ce week-end.* I didn't go out this weekend.
*Aurélie **sort** avec Bruno.* Aurélie is going out with Bruno.
*Elle **est sortie** de l'hôpital hier.* She came out of hospital yesterday.
*Je n'**ai** pas **sorti** le chien parce qu'il pleuvait.* I didn't take the dog out for a walk because it was raining.

ⓘ Note that **sortir** takes **avoir** in the perfect tense when it is used with a noun.

je/j' = I **tu** = you **il** = he/it **elle** = she/it **on** = we/one **nous** = we **vous** = you **ils/elles** = they

▶ **tenir** (to hold)

PRESENT

je	tiens
tu	tiens
il/elle/on	tient
nous	tenons
vous	tenez
ils/elles	tiennent

PRESENT SUBJUNCTIVE

je	tienne
tu	tiennes
il/elle/on	tienne
nous	tenions
vous	teniez
ils/elles	tiennent

PERFECT

j'	ai tenu
tu	as tenu
il/elle/on	a tenu
nous	avons tenu
vous	avez tenu
ils/elles	ont tenu

IMPERFECT

je	tenais
tu	tenais
il/elle/on	tenait
nous	tenions
vous	teniez
ils/elles	tenaient

FUTURE

je	tiendrai
tu	tiendras
il/elle/on	tiendra
nous	tiendrons
vous	tiendrez
ils/elles	tiendront

CONDITIONAL

je	tiendrais
tu	tiendrais
il/elle/on	tiendrait
nous	tiendrions
vous	tiendriez
ils/elles	tiendraient

IMPERATIVE

tiens / tenons / tenez

PAST PARTICIPLE

tenu

PRESENT PARTICIPLE

tenant

EXAMPLE PHRASES

Tiens-moi la main. Hold my hand.
Elle **tenait** beaucoup à son chat. She was really attached to her cat.
Tiens, prends mon stylo. Here, have my pen.
Tiens-toi droit! Sit up straight!

---

je/j' = I **tu** = you **il** = he/it **elle** = she/it **on** = we/one **nous** = we **vous** = you **ils/elles** = they

▶ **venir** (to come)

PRESENT

je	viens
tu	viens
il/elle/on	vient
nous	venons
vous	venez
ils/elles	viennent

PRESENT SUBJUNCTIVE

je	vienne
tu	viennes
il/elle/on	vienne
nous	venions
vous	veniez
ils/elles	viennent

PERFECT

je	suis venu(e)
tu	es venu(e)
il/elle/on	est venu(e)
nous	sommes venu(e)s
vous	êtes venu(e)(s)
ils/elles	sont venu(e)s

IMPERFECT

je	venais
tu	venais
il/elle/on	venait
nous	venions
vous	veniez
ils/elles	venaient

FUTURE

je	viendrai
tu	viendras
il/elle/on	viendra
nous	viendrons
vous	viendrez
ils/elles	viendront

CONDITIONAL

je	viendrais
tu	viendrais
il/elle/on	viendrait
nous	viendrions
vous	viendriez
ils/elles	viendraient

IMPERATIVE

viens / venons / venez

PAST PARTICIPLE

venu

PRESENT PARTICIPLE

venant

EXAMPLE PHRASES

*Elle ne **viendra** pas cette année.* She won't be coming this year.
*Fatou et Malik **viennent** du Sénégal.* Fatou and Malik come from Senegal.
*Je **viens** de manger.* I've just eaten.

---

je/j' = I **tu** = you **il** = he/it **elle** = she/it **on** = we/one **nous** = we **vous** = you **ils/elles** = they

▶ **vivre** (to live)

PRESENT

je	vis
tu	vis
il/elle/on	vit
nous	vivons
vous	vivez
ils/elles	vivent

PRESENT SUBJUNCTIVE

je	vive
tu	vives
il/elle/on	vive
nous	vivions
vous	viviez
ils/elles	vivent

PERFECT

j'	ai vécu
tu	as vécu
il/elle/on	a vécu
nous	avons vécu
vous	avez vécu
ils/elles	ont vécu

IMPERFECT

je	vivais
tu	vivais
il/elle/on	vivait
nous	vivions
vous	viviez
ils/elles	vivaient

FUTURE

je	vivrai
tu	vivras
il/elle/on	vivra
nous	vivrons
vous	vivrez
ils/elles	vivront

CONDITIONAL

je	vivrais
tu	vivrais
il/elle/on	vivrait
nous	vivrions
vous	vivriez
ils/elles	vivraient

IMPERATIVE

vis / vivons / vivez

PAST PARTICIPLE

vécu

PRESENT PARTICIPLE

vivant

EXAMPLE PHRASES

*Ma sœur **vit** en Espagne.* My sister lives in Spain.
*Il **a vécu** dix ans à Lyon.* He lived in Lyons for 10 years.
*Les gorilles **vivent** surtout dans la forêt.* Gorillas mostly live in the forest.

---

je/j' = I **tu** = you **il** = he/it **elle** = she/it **on** = we/one **nous** = we **vous** = you **ils/elles** = they

▶ **voir** (to see)

PRESENT

je	vois
tu	vois
il/elle/on	voit
nous	voyons
vous	voyez
ils/elles	voient

PRESENT SUBJUNCTIVE

je	voie
tu	voies
il/elle/on	voie
nous	voyions
vous	voyiez
ils/elles	voient

PERFECT

j'	ai vu
tu	as vu
il/elle/on	a vu
nous	avons vu
vous	avez vu
ils/elles	ont vu

IMPERFECT

je	voyais
tu	voyais
il/elle/on	voyait
nous	voyions
vous	voyiez
ils/elles	voyaient

FUTURE

je	verrai
tu	verras
il/elle/on	verra
nous	verrons
vous	verrez
ils/elles	verront

CONDITIONAL

je	verrais
tu	verrais
il/elle/on	verrait
nous	verrions
vous	verriez
ils/elles	verraient

IMPERATIVE

vois / voyons / voyez

PAST PARTICIPLE

vu

PRESENT PARTICIPLE

voyant

EXAMPLE PHRASES

*Venez me **voir** quand vous serez à Paris.* Come and see me when you're in Paris.
*Je ne **vois** rien sans mes lunettes.* I can't see anything without my glasses.
*Est-ce que tu l'**as vu**?* Did you see him? or Have you seen him?
*Est-ce que cette tache **se voit**?* Does that stain show?

▶ **vouloir** (to want)

PRESENT

je	veux
tu	veux
il/elle/on	veut
nous	voulons
vous	voulez
ils/elles	veulent

PRESENT SUBJUNCTIVE

je	veuille
tu	veuilles
il/elle/on	veuille
nous	voulions
vous	vouliez
ils/elles	veuillent

PERFECT

j'	ai voulu
tu	as voulu
il/elle/on	a voulu
nous	avons voulu
vous	avez voulu
ils/elles	ont voulu

IMPERFECT

je	voulais
tu	voulais
il/elle/on	voulait
nous	voulions
vous	vouliez
ils/elles	voulaient

FUTURE

je	voudrai
tu	voudras
il/elle/on	voudra
nous	voudrons
vous	voudrez
ils/elles	voudront

CONDITIONAL

je	voudrais
tu	voudrais
il/elle/on	voudrait
nous	voudrions
vous	voudriez
ils/elles	voudraient

IMPERATIVE

veuille / veuillons / veuillez

PAST PARTICIPLE

voulu

PRESENT PARTICIPLE

voulant

EXAMPLE PHRASES

Elle **veut** un vélo pour Noël. She wants a bike for Christmas.
Ils **voulaient** aller au cinéma. They wanted to go to the cinema.
Tu **voudrais** une tasse de thé? Would you like a cup of tea?

---

je/j' = I **tu** = you **il** = he/it **elle** = she/it **on** = we/one **nous** = we **vous** = you **ils/elles** = they

Collins

easy learning French

Easy Learning French Dictionary 978-0-00-753096-0	£9.99
Easy Learning French Conversation 978-0-00-811198-4	£7.99
Easy Learning French Grammar 978-0-00-814199-8	£7.99
Easy Learning French Verbs 978-0-00-815841-5	£7.99
Easy Learning French Vocabulary 978-0-00-748391-4	£9.99
Easy Learning French Idioms 978-0-00-733735-4	£6.99
Easy Learning Complete French Grammar, Verbs and Vocabulary (3 books in 1) 978-0-00-814172-1	£14.99
Easy Learning French Grammar & Practice 978-0-00-814163-9	£9.99
Easy Learning French Verbs & Practice 978-0-00-814208-7	£10.99

Available to buy from all good booksellers and online.
Many titles are also available as ebooks.
www.collins.co.uk/languagesupport

 facebook.com/collinsdictionary

 @collinsdict

Collins

easy learning Spanish

Easy Learning Spanish Dictionary
978-0-00-753094-6   £9.99

Easy Learning Spanish Conversation
978-0-00-811197-7   £7.99

Easy Learning Spanish Grammar
978-0-00-814201-8   £7.99

Easy Learning Spanish Verbs
978-0-00-815843-9   £7.99

Easy Learning Spanish Vocabulary
978-0-00-748393-8   £9.99

Easy Learning Spanish Idioms
978-0-00-733736-1   £9.99

Easy Learning Complete Spanish Grammar, Verbs and Vocabulary
(3 books in 1) 978-0-00-814173-8   £14.99

Easy Learning Spanish Grammar & Practice
978-0-00-814164-6   £9.99

Easy Learning Spanish Verbs & Practice
978-0-00-814209-4   £10.99

Available to buy from all good booksellers and online.
Many titles are also available as ebooks.
www.collins.co.uk/languagesupport

 facebook.com/collinsdictionary

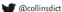 @collinsdict